The
ABERDEEN
Football Companion

Aberdeen, one of Scotland's leading teams in the 'eighties. Here the players and manager Alex Ferguson, celebrate winning the 1980 Premier League Championship.

The
ABERDEEN
Football Companion

A Factual History, 1946-86

CLIVE LEATHERDALE

PUBLISHED BY JOHN DONALD PUBLISHERS LTD
IN ASSOCIATION WITH
ABERDEEN FOOTBALL CLUB

ISBN 0 85976 182 7

By the same author
So you want to teach English to foreigners
   (Abacus Press, 1980)
Britain and Saudi Arabia 1925-1939: The Imperial Oasis
   (Frank Cass, 1983)

England's Quest for the World Cup – A complete Record
   (Methuen, 1984)
Dracula: The Novel and the Legend
   A study of Bram Stoker's Gothic Masterpiece
     (Aquarian Press, 1985)

Scotland's Quest for the World Cup
   (John Donald, 1986)

The publishers would like to thank D.C. Thomson &
Co. Ltd., Dundee, for kindly supplying many of the
illustrations used in this book.
Also Scotpix, Aberdeen.

Phototypeset by Newtext Composition Ltd., Glasgow.
Printed in Great Britain by Bell & Bain Ltd., Glasgow.

Preface

Aberdeen are the Scottish team of the 1980s. During this decade, under Alex Ferguson's stewardship, the club have already been Scottish champions three times, Scottish Cup winners four times, Skol League Cup winners once. Crowning these achievements was Aberdeen's triumph in the European Cup-Winners Cup Final in 1983. For good measure the team won the European Super Cup before that year was out.

But Aberdeen have not always been so successful. They have known lean times as well as rich ones. This the match-by-match history of Aberdeen Football Club since 1946. Each official fixture – in League, League Cup, Scottish Cup and European competition – is recorded in detail.

Team-sheets, goal-scorers and times of goals are provided for every match, together with appearance and goal-scoring lists for each season. There is also a match summary for every fixture. Referees and attendance figures are shown if these appeared in the Aberdeen *Press and Journal* or Aberdeen *Evening Express*.

In all, this book offers the perfect companion to the changing fortunes of Aberdeen FC.

Clive Leatherdale

Contents

The Aberdeen line-up at the start of the season 1986-87. Back row: J. Miller, McQueen, Angus, Grant, Gray, I. Robertson, D. Robertson. Centre row: McIntyre, Weir, Stark, Irvine, Leighton, Gunn, McLeish, Falconer, Mitchell, Bett. Front row: Wright, Porteous, Hewitt, McKimmie, W. Miller, Simpson, McDougall and McMaster

Introduction

Way back in 1881 the new sport of Association Rules Football made its first appearance in Britain's northernmost city. In those bygone years soccer was very different to what it is today. The essence of the sport was the art of 'dribbling'. When a player received the ball he would try to weave his way towards goal, obstructed and pursued by a pack of opponents. When he finally lost possession the same process would commence in reverse. And so on. Nobody thought of passing the ball. That was evading your responsibilities.

By the turn of the century the city of Aberdeen could boast three different football clubs. They competed in the Northern League. One of them was called 'Aberdeen', and they played on a dung hill near the beach. The place was referred to locally as Pittodrie – a Celtic derivative of 'place of manure'.

Rather than persist with fragmenting the city's resources among rival clubs, amalgamation took place in 1903. Aberdeen, Victoria United, and Orion joined together to establish the new Aberdeen Football Club, a limited liability company with the express aim 'to promote the practice and play of football, cricket, lacrosse, lawn tennis, hockey, bowling, cycle-riding, running, jumping and the physical training and development of the human frame'. The club appointed local man Jimmy Phelp to take charge.

A year later Aberdeen were admitted to membership of the Scottish League Second Division. Not the First, as they had hoped. To announce their arrival in the national league the club discarded their traditional white strip in favour of black and gold stripes. The Wasps – as they were known – did not exactly sting the rest of the Division into submission. Aberdeen finished 7th out of 12. But at the end of the 1904-5 season it was proposed to enlarge the First Division from 14 to 16 clubs. Anyone could apply for the vacant places. Aberdeen did, and were lucky. Clyde, who were Second Division Champions, were not. So, from 1905-6 Aberdeen enjoyed exalted status among the élite of Scottish football, a status they have never lost to this day – and an honour shared only with Rangers and Celtic.

The Big Time can be said to have arrived at the open-plan Pittodrie Stadium on 21 March 1908. A crowd in excess of 20,000 turned up to witness a Scottish Cup Semi-Final with mighty Celtic. It was a nasty, unsporting match, won by Celtic by the only goal. The crowd chastised the referee, who halted play and strode over to lecture them for their bad manners. Three years later Aberdeen reached the same stage, against the same opponents, and lost by the same score – this time at Parkhead.

Aberdeen's most famous player of this era was full-back Donald Colman, who represented his country four times and captained them against the Irish in Dublin in 1913.

The First World War was hardly conducive to the continuation of professional football. Many of the players belonged to the Territorials, and could be called away at short notice. The Scottish Cup was suspended for the duration of the conflict. In 1917 Aberdeen finished bottom of the League, and, along with Dundee and Raith, withdrew from the competition for the following two seasons. When peacetime soccer was re-introduced the War was found to have taken a heavy toll at Pittodrie. Of the club's 33 players and officials who had served with the armed forces, eight had perished.

Jimmy Phelp's first post-war signing was Jock Hutton, of medium height but monumental breadth – later to play for Scotland ten times. When Donald Colman departed the stage at the venerable age of 42 (he would later become club coach) it was left to Hutton to assume the mantle of Aberdeen's chief 'personality'.

By this time the game was becoming increasingly competitive and commercial. Promotion and relegation arrived in 1921. Two years later Aberdeen crushed Peterhead 13-0 in the Scottish Cup, after eight of the Highland League team had been dropped for insisting on a share of the hand-out Aberdeen had offered in order that the match be switched to Pittodrie.

Manager Jimmy Phelp finally quit in 1924, after a reign of 21 years which had seen Aberdeen reach four Scottish Cup Semi-Finals but bring no silverware back north. He was succeeded by Paddy Travers, the club coach. Travers almost faced a catastrophic inauguration. Aberdeen flirted with relegation throughout his first season and only fended off that fate by winning their final match. Nor could the new manager avoid the unpopularity incurred by selling the teenage prodigy winger Alec Jackson to Huddersfield.

Fortunately a new idol was not long in arriving. Benny Yorston was raised in the Granite City. Despite his squat frame he could outjump most defenders. Between 1929-31 he bagged over a hundred goals – a record 46 in League and Cup in 1929-30 alone. His time at Pittodrie was short, leaving the club along with several other players, under a cloud of innuendo.

Other heroes kept the conveyor belt of great players in motion. Young Willie Mills – he of the filmstar looks and twinkling footwork – made his debut in 1932. In time he was joined by dashing centre forward Matt Armstrong to complete one of the most exciting of all Pittodrie's attacking partnerships.

Both were part of the Aberdeen team which became the first to reach a Scottish Cup Final. The attendance on that spring afternoon in 1937 was a staggering 146,433. Johnny Crum gave Celtic an early lead – a lead cancelled out by Armstrong connecting with a cross as it dropped on his instep. But the joy was short-lived. Buchan netted the winner for Celtic.

All too soon Paddy Travers was on his way to Clyde, guiding them to the Scottish Cup success that had eluded him at Pittodrie. His replacement – a former Dundee forward, David Halliday – barely had time to change Aberdeen's strip from black and gold to red than war once again sent Europe into flames. In the 35 years since the club was admitted to the Scottish League Aberdeen were still waiting for their first championship and their first Scottish Cup. Before they could try again they would have to wait until Hitler was defeated.

With the War's end those players who had been scattered to the cause of victory regrouped under the welcoming embrace of Pittodrie. Among them was manager David Halliday, who assembled around him a gaggle of familiar faces from 1939 – Archie Baird, Willie Cooper, Andy Cowie, Frank Dunlop, George Hamilton, George Johnstone, George Taylor, Willie Waddell and Stanley Williams. Indeed, three of the reassembled Dons – Johnstone, Cooper and Dunlop – had featured in Aberdeen's Cup Final appearance at Hampden in 1937. The players at Halliday's disposal provided him with instant camaraderie, but he was now supervising an ageing – very ageing – team.

There wasn't time, following the cessation of World War II, to re-establish official competition for the 1945-46 season. (The conflict with Japan continued till August 1945). Nevertheless, two Divisions were hastily set up in an attempt to restore peacetime normality. In the first months of 1946 a makeshift League Cup competition was inaugurated. Not all those clubs eligible to compete were able to take part, and it took Aberdeen only two rounds – beating Ayr and then Airdrie (after a replay) – to reach the Final. Awaiting them at Hampden were Glasgow Rangers.

League Cup Final at Hampden May 11 1946
RANGERS (0) 2   ABERDEEN (2) 3
   Duncanson (49),   Baird (1), Williams (19),
   Thornton (70)   Taylor (90)
RANGERS: John Shaw; Gray, Jock Shaw; Watkins, Young, Symon; Waddell, Thornton, Arnison, Duncanson, Caskie
ABERDEEN: Johnstone; Cooper, McKenna; Cowie, Dunlop, Taylor; Kiddie, Hamilton, Williams, Baird, McCall
Attendance: 115,000. *Referee:* W. Webb

Jock 'Tiger' Shaw, Rangers' captain, won the toss and allowed Stan Williams to kick off into the breeze. Within seconds Williams nodded on Cowie's throw and there was Archie Baird to nod Aberdeen in front. The Dons' young amateur, Alec Kiddie, gave Shaw a roasting, and it was his dispossession of the full-back which brought Aberdeen's second goal – by Stan Williams. Rangers nearly hit back. The ball struck Dons' post and rebounded across the goalmouth. After half-time Duncanson headed home in a scramble to reduce the deficit. The Dons continued to perform handsomely: Kiddie's cross bounced off the Rangers' bar and Cowie's effort was deflected on to a post. When Thornton broke away to equalise the Dons must have feared the worst. But then, with 15 seconds remaining, Kiddie crossed, Taylor shot from the edge of the box, and Aberdeen had won. The match had been played in sweltering heat and the victorious Dons barely had the energy to climb the steps to collect the trophy. It was too bad that Aberdeen's first-ever national prize should not appear in the official records. But they had enjoyed the taste of glory and would soon be back for more.

An Aberdeen team at the outset of the Second World War, 1939-40. Back row: Laing, Scott, Graham, Johnstone, Cooper, Taylor. Front Row: Smith, Baird, Patillo, Ferguson, Williams.

Season 1946-47

Aberdeen bounced back into 'official' competition with a bang, setting a standard for succeeding seasons that would prove difficult to sustain. They got off to a flyer in the League and headed the table after eight matches. By December, however, Rangers had hauled themselves in front and stayed out of reach till the season's end. Aberdeen had to settle for the bronze medal behind 'Gers and Hibs. But for an infuriating inconsistency Aberdeen would surely have presented a stiffer challenge for the title. For example their three New Year results were 0-4, 5-1, 0-4 – and away from home Aberdeen were either bursting the net or failing to score altogether. Their final 11 away fixtures produced 17 goals, but 15 of them came in just three games.

It was in the two cup competitions that Aberdeen really came into their own. In the League Cup they headed their qualifying section; disposed of Dundee home and away; crushed Hearts in the semis; and earned themselves a re-run of the 1946 League Cup Final. This time the tables were turned, Rangers winning 4-0. But Aberdeen had only fourteen days to wait for a second appointment at Hampden – this time in the Scottish Cup Final. Partick, Ayr, Morton, Dundee and Arbroath had been pushed aside in earlier rounds. Against Hibs in the final Aberdeen hit back from a goal conceded within thirty seconds of the kick-off to take the trophy 2-1 and put the seal on a season to remember.

League: Third
League Cup: Runners-up
Scottish Cup: Winners

SCOTTISH LEAGUE DIVISION A

No 1 Saturday, 10 August
THIRD LANARK (0) 0   ABERDEEN (0) 3
                        Hamilton (74), Taylor
                        (84 pen), Harris (89)

THIRD LANARK: Petrie, Balunas, Kelly, Bolt, Black, Sinclair, Henderson, Mason, McCulloch, Venters, Kinnear

ABERDEEN: Johnstone, Cowie, McKenna, Dunlop, Waddell, Taylor, Kiddie, Hamilton, Harris, Baird, McCall

P	W	D	L	F	A	Pts
1	1	0	0	3	0	2

Attendance: 12,000
Referee: J. Calder

The Dons, wearing blue shirts, make an immediate return to Hampden, scene of their League Cup triumph.

No 2 Wednesday, 14 August
ABERDEEN (0) 1   KILMARNOCK (0) 0
Baird (69)

ABERDEEN: Johnstone, Cowie, McKenna, Dunlop, Waddell, Taylor, Kiddie, Hamilton, Harris, Baird, McCall

KILMARNOCK: Downie, Hood, Landsborough, Turnbull, McClure, Davie, Sinclair, Reid, Walsh, Devlin, McAvoy

P	W	D	L	F	A	Pts
2	2	0	0	4	0	4

Attendance: 18,000
Referee: J. Martin

Aberdeen struggle against Killie. Taylor misses a penalty and near the end Reid heads against the Dons' crossbar.

No 3 Saturday, 17 August
ABERDEEN (3) 6   CELTIC (2) 2
Harris (10), Hamilton   Kiernan 2 (16, 19)
(13), Williams (14),
Kiddie (55),
Baird 2 (70, 88)

ABERDEEN: Johnston, Cowie, McKenna, Dunlop, Waddell, McCall, Kiddie, Hamilton, Harris, Baird, Williams

CELTIC: Miller, Hogg, Milne, Gallacher, Corbett, McAuley, Sirrell, Kiernan, Cantwell, Bogan, Shields

Leading positions

	P	W	D	L	F	A	Pts
1 Hibernian	3	3	0	0	12	2	6
2 ABERDEEN	3	3	0	0	10	2	6
3 Partick	3	3	0	0	12	5	6
4 Clyde	3	2	1	0	9	3	5

Attendance: 30,000   *Referee:* D. Alexander

30,000 spectators turned out on a sunny afternoon for the visit of Celtic, who had made a poor start to the season, taking just one point from two games. The match had the crowd on its toes with five goals inside the first 19 minutes. Harris paved the way when Celtic's international goalkeeper, Miller, failed to hold Kiddie's low cross. Hamilton drove home a second and Williams hooked a third to leave Celtic stunned. Two lightning strikes by Kiernan then brought the visitors back into contention. Early in the second half Kiddie cut in and sent a soft shot under Miller's body. When Archie Baird headed home a corner all five Dons forwards had found the net. Baird then outstripped the Celtic defence to register No 6.

No 4 Wednesday, 21 August
MOTHERWELL (0) 2   ABERDEEN (2) 2
Humphries (61),   Kiddie (3), Williams (5)
Barclay (85)

MOTHERWELL: Johnston, Kilmarnock, Shaw, McLeod, Paton, Russell, Gibson, Humphries, Brown, Bremner, Barclay

ABERDEEN: Johnstone, Cowie, McKenna, Dunlop, Waddell, Taylor, Kiddie, Hamilton, Williams, Baird, McCall

P	W	D	L	F	A	Pts
4	3	1	0	12	4	7

Referee: C. Dale

Aberdeen fail to hang on after a whirlwind start. Motherwell twice hit the woodwork before scoring the goals which saved the match. Williams missed a great chance at the end.

No 5 Saturday, 24 August
ST MIRREN (3) 4   ABERDEEN (1) 2
Aikman (1), Deakin   Baird 2 (23, 73 pen)
2 (36, 48), Crowe (41)

ST MIRREN: Newlands, Telfer, Lindsay, Stenhouse, Drinkwater, Scott, Crowe, Telford, Aikman, Deakin, McLaren

ABERDEEN: Johnstone, Cowie, McKenna, Taylor, Dunlop, McCall, Kiddie, Hume, Harris, Baird, Williams

P	W	D	L	F	A	Pts
5	3	1	1	14	8	7

Attendance: 13,000   *Referee:* T. Shirley

Aberdeen are without George Hamilton who is playing for Scotland against England at Manchester in a representative match to aid the Bolton disaster fund.

No 6 Wednesday, 28 August
ABERDEEN (1) 2   HIBERNIAN (0) 1
Harris (29), Howie   Cuthbertson (49)
o.g. (80)

ABERDEEN: Johnstone, Cowie, McKenna, Dunlop, Waddell, Taylor, Kiddie, Hamilton, Harris, Baird, Williams

HIBERNIAN: Kerr, Howie, Shaw, Fraser, Aird, McCabe, Smith, Buchanan, Weir, Cuthbertson, Aitkenhead

P	W	D	L	F	A	Pts
6	4	1	1	16	9	9

Attendance: 29,000   *Referee:* J. R. Boyd

Aberdeen are fortunate to end Hibs' 100% record. After just eight minutes international winger Gordon Smith is taken off with ligament damage. The Dons take the lead when Hamilton backheels Dunlop's throw and Harris beats Shaw. Cuthbertson equalises when heading home Aitkenhead's cross. 10-man Hibs desperately try to hang on but are finally beaten when the ball spins off Howie's boot past his own 'keeper.

No 7 Saturday, 31 August
CLYDE (0) 0   ABERDEEN (1) 2
          Harris 2 (29, 46)

CLYDE: Sweeney, Gibson, Galbraith, Campbell, McCormack, Long, Buchanan, Hepburn, Johnstone, Dixon, Galletly

ABERDEEN: Johnstone, Cowie, McKenna, Dunlop, Waddell, Taylor, Kiddie, Hamilton, Harris, McCall, Williams

P	W	D	L	F	A	Pts
7	5	1	1	18	9	11

Attendance: 17,000
Referee: A. M. Campbell

Aberdeen lay their Shawfield bogey, winning for the first time since ex-Aberdeen manager Pat Travers took charge at Clyde in 1938.

No 8 Wednesday, 4 September
ABERDEEN (1) 1   RANGERS (0) 0
Taylor (40)

ABERDEEN: Johnstone, Cowie, McKenna, Dunlop, Waddell, Taylor, McCall, Hamilton, Harris, Baird, Williams

RANGERS: Brown, Gray, Shaw, Cox, Young, Symon, Watkins, Gillick, Arnison, Duncanson, Caskie

Leading positions

	P	W	D	L	F	A	Pts
1 ABERDEEN	8	6	1	1	19	9	13
2 Hibernian	8	6	0	2	24	8	12
3 Morton	8	5	2	1	25	15	12
4 Partick	7	5	1	1	20	9	11
5 Rangers	7	5	0	2	23	8	10

Attendance: 35,000   *Referee:* D. Alexander

Aberdeen entertain Rangers for the first time since the epic League Cup Final in May. Rangers are without international forwards Thornton and Waddell, and their reshaped attack rarely threatens the Aberdeen rearguard. In a tough game played on a heavy pitch George Taylor shoots the only goal through a crowd of players. The two points take the Dons to the top of the league.

No 9 Saturday, 7 September
FALKIRK (0) 2   ABERDEEN (0) 0
  Fitzsimmons (79 pen),
  Brooks (83)
FALKIRK: Dawson, Stewart, McPhee, Rice,
R. Henderson, Telfer, J. Henderson, Brooks, Wardlaw,
Allison, Fitzsimmons
ABERDEEN: Johnstone, Cowie, McKenna, Dunlop,
Waddell, Taylor, McCall, Hamilton, Harris, Baird,
Williams

P	W	D	L	F	A	Pts	
9	6	1	2	19	11	13	

Attendance: 10,000
Referee: J. Calder
The Dons hold out on a clinging pitch until Waddell
fouls Wardlaw inside the box.

No 10 Saturday, 14 September
ABERDEEN (2) 2   PARTICK THISTLE (1) 2
  McCall (12), Harris (21)   Smith (35), Glover (77)
ABERDEEN: Johnstone, Cowie, McKenna, Dunlop,
Waddell, Taylor, Kiddie, McCall, Harris, Williams,
Millar
PARTICK: Steadward, McGowan, Curran, Brown,
Parker, Husband, Glover, Gourlay, Sharp, O'Donnell,
Smith

P	W	D	L	F	A	Pts
10	6	2	2	21	13	14

Attendance: 25,000
Referee: J. Godfrey
New signing Willie Millar turns out for the Dons
against his old club. High-flying Thistle snatch a second
equaliser with Waddell off the pitch receiving attention.
The league is now suspended for six weeks to
accommodate the group rounds of the League Cup.

No 11 Saturday, 2 November
ABERDEEN (0) 0   QUEEN OF THE
                        SOUTH   (0) 0
ABERDEEN: Johnstone, Cooper, McKenna, Cowie,
Dunlop, McLaughlin, Jamieson, Hamilton, Williams,
McCall, Millar.
QUEEN OF THE SOUTH: Henderson, Savage,
Dryburgh, Fitzsimmons, Denmark, Gilmour, Oakes,
Armstrong, Houliston, Law, Johnstone

P	W	D	L	F	A	Pts
11	6	3	2	21	13	15

Attendance: 18,000
Referee: R. Duthie
A repeat of the miserable recent League Cup encounter
between the sides. Injury-hit Aberdeen bring in young
Jamieson on the right wing.

No 12 Saturday, 9 November
MORTON (0) 0   ABERDEEN (0) 0
MORTON: McFeat, Maley, Fyfe, Campbell, Aird,
White, McGowan, Jones, Gibson, Divers, McInnes
ABERDEEN: Johnstone, Cooper, McKenna,
McLaughlin, Dunlop, Taylor, Harris, Hume,
Hamilton, McCall, Millar

P	W	D	L	F	A	Pts
12	6	4	2	21	13	16

Attendance: 8,000
Referee: F. Scott

A scrappy game despite the fine weather. Morton come
nearest to a goal when Johstone touches Gibson's shot
onto the bar.

No 13 Saturday, 16 November
ABERDEEN (2) 3   QUEENS PARK (0) 1
  McCall (15),   Aitken (65)
  Millar 2 (34, 79)
ABERDEEN: Johnstone, Cooper, McKenna,
McLaughlin, Dunlop, Taylor, Harris, Hamilton,
Williams, McCall, Millar
QUEENS PARK: Hamilton, Mitchell, Johnstone,
Letham, Whigham, Harnett, MacAulay, Miller,
Aitken, McPhail, Irvine
Leading positions

	P	W	D	L	F	A	Pts
1 Rangers	13	10	0	3	44	16	20
2 ABERDEEN	13	7	4	2	24	14	18
3 Hearts	13	7	4	2	25	19	18
4 Hibernian	13	8	1	4	33	16	17
5 Partick	13	7	2	4	31	22	16

Attendance: 15,000
Referee: J. Calder
Both teams wear black armbands in memory of Alec
Jackson, Aberdeen and Scotland player of the 1920s,
who was killed in a car crash in Cairo.

No 14 Saturday, 23 November
ABERDEEN (0) 2   HEARTS (0) 1
  Waldron (65),   Conn (84)
  Hamilton (72)
ABERDEEN: Johnstone, Cooper, McKenna,
McLaughlin, Dunlop, Taylor, Harris, Hamilton,
Waldron, McCall, Williams
HEARTS: Brown, McSpadyen, McKenzie, Whitehead,
Baxter, Laing, Sloan, Martin, Conn, McCrae, Walker
McCrae, Walker

P	W	D	L	F	A	Pts
14	8	4	2	26	15	20

Attendance: 14,000
Referee: C. Dale
Miserable weather reduced the attendance for the clash
between two sides separated only by goal average. There
was much interest in the debut at centre forward of
Ernie Waldron, signed from Crystal Palace. A goalless
first half was followed by a hectic second period. Stan
Williams thumped the ball against the junction of post
and bar before Waldron put his new club ahead. Sloan
missed a sitter for Hearts before Hamilton put the game
out of their reach. Conn's effort came too late to affect
the outcome. The following Wednesday George
Hamilton won his first cap for Scotland in the goalless
draw with Northern Ireland at Hampden.

No 15 Saturday, 30 November
HAMILTON   ABERDEEN (1) 5
  ACADEMICALS (2) 2   Hamilton 3 (43, 80 pen,
  Bremner (31),   86), Harris (73),
  Dunlop o.g. (40)   Williams (85)
HAMILTON: Campbell, McGurk, Johnstone, Daly,
Rothera, Crainie, Paterson, Bremner, Steel, Lindsay,
Gillan

ABERDEEN: Johnstone, Cooper, McKenna, McLaughlin, Dunlop, Taylor, Harris, Hamilton, Waldron, McCall, Williams.

P W D L F A Pts
15 9 4 2 31 17 22   *Referee:* J. Calder

Aberdeen, wearing blue, recover from losing two soft goals to overwhelm the bottom-placed club.

No 16 Saturday, 7 December
ABERDEEN (0) 1   THIRD LANARK (0) 0
Hamilton (75)

ABERDEEN: Johnstone, Cooper, McKenna, McLaughlin, Dunlop, Taylor, Harris, Hamilton, Waldron, McCall, Williams

THIRD LANARK: Fraser, Balunas, Kelly, Bolt, Palmer, Mooney, Bogan, Mason, Nelson, Ayton, Mitchell

Leading positions

	P	W	D	L	F	A	Pts
1 Rangers	16	13	0	3	51	18	26
2 ABERDEEN	16	10	4	2	32	17	24
3 Hibernian	16	11	1	4	42	18	23
4 Partick	16	9	2	5	39	29	20

Attendance: 12,000   *Referee:* G. Mitchell

Aberdeen survive a hailstorm, allowing the best player afield – Hamilton – to score the only goal.

No 17 Saturday, 14 December
KILMARNOCK (1) 2   ABERDEEN (0) 1
Stevenson 2 (35, 48)   Hamilton (46)

KILMARNOCK: Downie, Dornan, Lansborough, Turnbull, Thyne, Davie, Stevenson, Devlin, Walsh, Henry, McAvoy.

ABERDEEN: Johnstone, Cooper, McKenna, McLaughlin, Dunlop, Taylor, Harris, Hamilton, Waldron, McCall, Williams

P W D L F A Pts
17 10 4 3 33 19 24   *Referee:* M. C. Dale

Bottom-but-one Killie obtains a rare win, resisting the Dons' second-half onslaught.

No 18 Saturday, 21 December
ABERDEEN (1) 3   MOTHERWELL (0) 1
Hume (40),   Johnston (75)
Waldron 2 (60, 61)

ABERDEEN: Johnstone, Cooper, McKenna, McLaughlin, Dunlop, Taylor, Harris, Hamilton, Waldron, Hume, McCall

MOTHERWELL: Johnston, Kilmarnock, Shaw, McLeod, Paton, Redpath, Humphries, Watson, Reid, Bremner, Joe Johnston

P W D L F A Pts
18 11 4 3 36 20 26   *Attendance:* 15,000
   Referee: J. M. Martin

Aberdeen avenge home defeat by Motherwell in the League Cup.

No 19 Saturday, 28 December
HIBERNIAN (1) 1   ABERDEEN (0) 1
Turnbull (4)   Harris (87)

HIBERNIAN: Kerr, Howie, Shaw, Finnegan, Aird, Kean, Smith, Turnbull, Weir, Peat, Ormond

ABERDEEN: Johnstone, Cooper, McKenna, McLaughlin, Dunlop, Harris, Hamilton, Waldron, Williams, McCall

P W D L F A Pts   *Attendance:* 30,000
19 11 5 3 37 21 27   *Referee:* D. Alexander

Aberdeen embark on a 4-match 8-day sequence, beginning at Easter Road. The Dons are outplayed in the first half, falling behind to Turnbull's low angled shot. A second Hibs 'goal' is chalked off for offside. The Dons' fortunes revive after the interval, but it takes a stunning individual effort from Harris to earn a point. With only three minutes left to play, and with the injured McKenna hobbling on the touchline, Harris wriggles past three defenders to beat Kerr from 15 yards.

No 20 Wednesday, 1 January
ABERDEEN (0) 0   FALKIRK (1) 4
   Fiddes (42), Dawson
   (46), Johnstone o.g. (58),
   Inglis (83)

ABERDEEN: Johnstone, Cooper, Cowie, McLaughlin, Dunlop, Taylor, Harris, Hamilton, Waldron, Baird, McCall

FALKIRK: J. Dawson, Whyte, McPhee, Rice, Henderson, Sinclair, Fiddes, Bain, Inglis, Allison, K. Dawson

P W D L F A Pts   *Attendance:* 20,000
20 11 5 4 37 25 27   *Referee:* R. Duthie

Appalling defensive blunders enable lowly Falkirk to achieve the double over the Dons. Aberdeen record their heaviest home defeat in many years, despite having most of the game. McLaughlin hits the Falkirk crossbar and veteran goalkeeper Dawson makes repeated saves before the visitors go in front – former Don Willie Bain sending Fiddes clear. Goal No 2 comes when Cooper loses possession; No 3 when Johnstone drops a corner over his own-goal line; and No 4 when Dunlop miskicks. All four of Aberdeen's league defeats have now been registered by teams from the nether region of the league table.

No 21 Thursday, 2 January
CELTIC (0) 1   ABERDEEN (1) 5
   Hazlett (85)   Hamilton 4 (39, 48, 59,
      71), Harris (47)

CELTIC: Miller, Hogg, Mallan, Lynch, McMillan, Milne, Evans, McAloon, Airlie, Gallacher, Hazlett

ABERDEEN: Watson, Cooper, Cowie, McLaughlin, Dunlop, Taylor, Kiddie, Hamilton, Harris, Williams, McCall

P W D L F A Pts   *Attendance:* 25,000
21 12 5 4 42 26 29   *Referee:* R. Calder

Brushing aside their humiliation 24 hours earlier, Aberdeen complete a crushing double over Celtic, amassing 11 goals in the process. Man-of-the-match George Hamilton was Celtic's principal destroyer with four goals. The match would have provided the perfect debut for Frank Watson in the Dons' goal – but for Hazlett's late consolation for the homesters.

No 22 Saturday, 4 January
PARTICK THISTLE (0) 4 ABERDEEN (0) 0
   O'Donnell 2 (50, 75),
   Mathie 2 (57, 59)
PARTICK: Steadward, McGowan, Curran, Hewitt, Husband, Brown, Campbell, O'Donnell, Mathie, Sharp, Chisholm
ABERDEEN: Watson, Cooper, Cowie, McLaughlin, Dunlop, Taylor, Kiddie, Hamilton, Harris, Williams, McCall
P W D L F A Pts
22 12 5 5 42 30 29   *Referee:* R. G. Benzie
Partick adapted to the quagmire better than Aberdeen, who played in Thistle's borrowed reserve strip – blue shirts with white sleeves. The following Saturday Aberdeen were leading St Mirren 2-0 at Pittodrie when the match was abandoned.

No 23 Saturday, 18 January
RANGERS (1) 1   ABERDEEN (0) 0
   Waddell (28)
RANGERS: Brown, Young, Shaw, McColl, Woodburn, Rae, Rutherford, Gillick, Thornton, Parlane, Waddell
ABERDEEN: Johnstone, Cooper, McKenna, McLaughlin, Dunlop, Taylor, Kiddie, Hamilton, Harris, Williams, McCall
Leading positions

	P	W	D	L	F	A	Pts
1 Rangers	24	17	3	4	63	23	37
2 Hibernian	24	14	6	4	58	29	34
3 Partick	24	14	2	8	62	43	30
4 ABERDEEN	23	12	5	6	42	31	29

Attendance: 57,000   *Referee:* T. Shirley
Aberdeen's title hopes depend on their restricting Rangers' lead at the top of the table. Although the Dons enjoy an equal share of the ball, it is Rangers who present all the danger. Waddell scores the only goal, but Thornton twice hits the Dons' woodwork. Aberdeen are now eight points adrift.

No 24 Saturday, 1 February
ABERDEEN (1) 2   CLYDE (0) 1
   Hamilton (37),   Gourlay (50)
   Williams (68)
ABERDEEN: Johnstone, Cowie, McKenna, McLaughlin, Dunlop, Taylor, Botha, Hamilton, Williams, Harris, McCall
CLYDE: Sweeney, Duffy, Galbraith, Campbell, McCormack, Long, Hepburn, Gourlay, Johnstone, McGill, Dixon
P W D L F A Pts   *Attendance:* 10,000
24 13 5 6 44 32 31   *Referee:* W. Brown

Postponements and commitments in the League Cup and Scottish Cup meant that Aberdeen would not resume their league engagements for nearly three months. In that time Aberdeen played ten successive cup-ties.

No 25 Saturday, 26 April
QUEENS PARK (0) 0   ABERDEEN (0) 0
QUEENS PARK: Simpson, McColl, Mitchell, Harnett, Whigham, Hardie, Farquhar, Gallagher, Liddell, Aitken, Alexander
ABERDEEN: Johnstone, Preston, Taylor, McLaughlin, Dunlop, Waddell, Harris, Colman, Williams, Baird, McCall
P W D L F A Pts
25 13 6 6 44 32 32   *Referee:* W. S. Smillie
Aberdeen's return to league commitments results in a forgettable match, though the point gained secures Queens from relegation.

No 26 Monday, 28 April
QUEEN OF THE   ABERDEEN (2) 5
   SOUTH (0) 1   Hamilton (8), McCall
   Armstrong (61 pen)   2 (30, 75), Harris (80),
                        Williams (85)
QUEEN OF THE SOUTH: Wilson, Savage, James, Fulton, Denmark, Collier, Armstrong, Law, Baker, Dempsey, Johnstone
ABERDEEN: Johnstone, Preston, Robson, McLaughlin, Dunlop, Taylor, Harris, Hamilton, Williams, Hume, McCall
P W D L F A Pts
26 14 6 6 49 33 34
Aberdeen continue to introduce fresh faces into the first team – in this instance Robson and Hume.

No 27 Saturday, 3 May
ABERDEEN (2) 4   ST MIRREN (1) 2
   Kiddie 3 (18, 71, 72), Milne (45), Stenhouse
   McCall (37)   (88)
ABERDEEN: Johnstone, McKenna, McDonald, McLaughlin, Dunlop, Taylor, Kiddie, Harris, Williams, Baird, McCall
ST MIRREN: Newlands, Smith, Lindsay, Hunter, Telfer, Martin, Stenhouse, Crowe, Milne, Cunningham, Deakins
P W D L F A Pts
27 15 6 6 53 35 36   *Referee:* J. Calder
Alex Kiddie scores a fine hat-trick on his return to the side. Saints miss relegation by one point.

No 28 Monday, 5 May
ABERDEEN (2) 2   MORTON (2) 2
   Hamilton (31), Taylor   Orr (24), Gillies (35 pen)
   (39 pen)
ABERDEEN: Johnstone, Cowie, McKenna, McLaughlin, McKenzie, Taylor, Harris, Hamilton, Williams, Baird, McCall

MORTON: McFeat, Maley, Fyfe, Kilpatrick, Samuels, Reynolds, Cupples, Orr, Henderson, McGarrity, Gillies

P	W	D	L	F	A	Pts	*Attendance:* 12,000
28	15	7	6	55	37	37	*Referee:* J. R. Boyd

Dunlop misses his first league game of the season.

No 29 Wednesday, 14 May
ABERDEEN (1) 3   HAMILTON
  Hamilton 2 (37, 62),   ACADEMICALS (0) 0
  Baird (84)
ABERDEEN: Watson, Cowie, McKenna, McLaughlin, Waddell, Taylor, Millar, Harris, Hamilton, Baird, McCall
HAMILTON: Campbell, McGurk, Devine, Daly, Rothera, McFarlane, McGuigan, Stewart, Smith, Johnstone, McVinish

P	W	D	L	F	A	Pts	
29	16	7	6	58	37	39	*Referee:* R. Duthie

'Hamilton sinks Hamilton'. George Hamilton switches to centre forward against doomed Academicals.

No 30 Saturday, 17 May
HEARTS (2) 4   ABERDEEN (0) 0
  Conn (2), Kelly 2 (45, 59),
  McCrae (48)   *Referee:* R. E. Carruthers
HEARTS: Brown, McSpadyen, McKenzie, Cox, Pithie, Laing, Sloan, Conn, Kelly, McCrae, Urquhart
ABERDEEN: Watson, Cowie, McKenna, Waddell, McKenzie, Taylor, Kiddie, Harris, Hamilton, Baird, McCall

Aberdeen hit rock bottom. Two months previously they had hit Hearts for six in the League Cup.

Aberdeen's complete home and away record:

HOME						AWAY						
P	W	D	L	F	A		W	D	L	F	A	Pts
30	11	3	1	32	17		5	4	6	26	24	39

Scottish League Division A 1946-47

		P	W	D	L	F	A	Pts
1	Rangers	30	21	4	5	76	26	46
2	Hibernian	30	19	6	5	69	33	44
3	ABERDEEN	30	16	7	7	58	41	39
4	Hearts	30	16	6	8	52	43	38
5	Partick Thistle	30	16	3	11	74	59	35
6	Morton	30	12	10	8	58	45	34
7	Celtic	30	13	6	11	53	55	32
8	Motherwell	30	12	5	13	58	54	29
9	Third Lanark	30	11	6	13	56	64	28
10	Clyde	30	9	9	12	55	65	27
11	Falkirk	30	8	10	12	62	61	26
12	Queen of the South	30	9	8	13	44	69	26
13	Queens Park	30	8	6	16	47	60	22
14	St Mirren	30	9	4	17	47	65	22
15	Kilmarnock	30	6	9	15	44	66	21
16	Hamilton	30	2	7	21	38	85	11

LEAGUE CUP

Saturday, 21 September
ABERDEEN (4) 4   FALKIRK (1) 3
  Hamilton 4 (12, 20 pen,   Wardlaw (36),
  34, 39)   Fitzsimmons 2 (80, 85)
ABERDEEN: Johnstone, Cowie, McKenna, Dunlop, Waddell, McCall, Kiddie, Hamilton, Harris, Williams, Millar
FALKIRK: Dawson, Stewart, McPhee, Rice, R. Henderson, Telfer, J. Henderson, Brooks, Wardlaw, Alison, Fitzpatrick

Attendance: 25,000   *Referee:* W. Davidson

Falkirk field the same team as recently defeated Aberdeen in the league, Hamilton bangs four goals past them before they retaliate. Fitzsimmons misses a penalty, but Falkirk still nearly save the game.

Saturday, 28 September
QUEEN OF THE   ABERDEEN (4) 5
  SOUTH (0) 2   Kiddie (1), Hamilton
  Dempsey (61), Oakes (78) (12 pen), Harris (16),
                            Millar 2 (26, 89)
QUEEN OF THE SOUTH: Henderson, Savage, Dryburgh, Fitzsimmons, Denmark, Holt, Oakes, Dempsey, Armstrong, Law, Johnstone
ABERDEEN: Johnstone, Cooper, McKenna, Cowie, Dunlop, Waddell, Kiddie, Hamilton, Harris, McCall, Millar

Attendance: 17,000   *Referee:* W. Brown

The visit of Aberdeen establishes a new ground record at Dumfries, overtaking by 3,000 that set up against Rangers the previous season.

Saturday, 5 October
ABERDEEN (1) 2   MOTHERWELL (1) 3
  McCall 2 (12, 83)   Brown (23), Robertson
                             2 (53, 73)
ABERDEEN: Johnstone, Cooper, McKenna, Cowie, Waddell, Taylor, Kiddie, Hamilton, Harris, McCall, Williams
MOTHERWELL: Johnston, Kilmarnock, Shaw, McLeod, Paton, Russell, Humphries, Watson, Brown, Robertson, Barclay

Attendance: 25,000   *Referee:* G. Bruce

Aberdeen called the tune until Brown equalised for Motherwell. Thereafter the Dons were always second best. Hamilton's late 'goal' for Aberdeen was cancelled out for offside.

Saturday, 12 October
FALKIRK (0) 0   ABERDEEN (1) 1
                            Hamilton (43)
FALKIRK: Dawson, Stewart, McPhee, Doig, R. Henderson, Sinclair, J. Henderson, Campbell, Wardlaw, Allison, Fitzsimmons
ABERDEEN: Johnstone, Cooper, McKenna, Cowie, Dunlop, McLaughlin, Harris, Hamilton, Williams, McCall, Millar

Attendance: 17,000   *Referee:* W. Brown

Joe McLaughlin makes his debut after signing from Hamilton. The Dons hold out despite relentless second-half Falkirk pressure.

Saturday, 19 October
ABERDEEN (1) 1   QUEEN OF THE
  McCall (5)   SOUTH (0) 0

ABERDEEN: Johnstone, Cooper, McKenna, Cowie, Dunlop, Taylor, Kiddie, Williams, Harris, McLaughlin, McCall

QUEEN OF THE SOUTH: Henderson, Savage, Dryburgh, Fitzsimmons, Denmark, Holt, Armstrong, McInally, Houliston, Law, Oakes

Attendance: 22,000   *Referee:* G. Mitchell

Queens protest that McCall's header is offside. They 'score' a split second after the final whistle. Aberdeen qualify from Section D with a match to spare.

Saturday, 26 October
MOTHERWELL (1) 3   ABERDEEN (0) 0
  Brown 2 (9, 47),
  Kilmarnock (71 pen)

MOTHERWELL: Johnston, Kilmarnock, Shaw, McLeod, Paton, Russell, Humphries, Watson, Brown, Bremner, Barclay

ABERDEEN: Johnstone, Cooper, McKenna, Cowie, Dunlop, McLaughlin, Millar, Hamilton, Harris, McCall, Williams

Attendance: 8,000   *Referee:* W. M. Crawford

Meaningless match. The result might have been otherwise had not Harris fluffed an open goal in the first minutes.

Section D

	P	W	D	L	F	A	Pts
ABERDEEN	6	4	0	2	13	11	8
Motherwell	6	3	1	2	15	11	7
Falkirk	6	2	1	3	11	12	5
Queen of the South	6	2	0	4	8	13	4

Quarter Final 1st Leg Saturday, 1 March
DUNDEE (0) 0   ABERDEEN (0) 1
                      Millar (51)

DUNDEE: Bennett, Fallon, Ancell, McKenzie, Gray, Smith, Gunn, Pattillo, Turnbull, Ewen, Joyner

ABERDEEN: Johnstone, Cooper, McKenna, McLaughlin, Dunlop, Waddell, Miller, Hamilton, Williams, Harris, McCall

Attendance: 28,300   *Referee:* R. G. Benzie

Dundee top Division B. They include two ex-Dons – Bobby Ancell and Johnny Pattillo. On an icy, snow-covered pitch, Aberdeen seized a welcome first-leg lead.

Quarter Final 2nd Leg Wednesday, 5 March
ABERDEEN (2) 3   DUNDEE (1) 2
  Hamilton 2 (30, 64),   Juliussen 2 (35, 88)
  McCall (89)

ABERDEEN: Johnstone, Cooper, McKenna, McLaughlin, Dunlop, Waddell, Miller, Hamilton, Williams, Harris, McCall

DUNDEE: Bennett, Fallon, Ancell, McKenzie, Gray, Smith, Turnbull, Ewen, Juliussen, Pattillo, Gunn

Attendance: 18,000   *Referee:* R. G. Benzie

Despite Dundee's remodelled attack, Aberdeen are always in control, save when Albert Juliussen is on the ball.

Semi Final (Easter Road) Saturday, 22 March
HEARTS (2) 2   ABERDEEN (2) 6
  Kelly (21), Urquhart (34)   Baird (12), Hamilton
                     3 (48, 71 pen, 80), Wood
                     o.g. (37), McCall (76)

ABERDEEN: Johnstone, Cooper, McKenna, McLaughlin, Dunlop, Waddell, Harris, Hamilton, Williams, Baird, McCall

HEARTS: Brown, McSpadyen, McKenzie, Wood, Baxter, Miller, McFarlane, Currie, Kelly, Urquhart, Dewar

Attendance: 36,200   *Referee:* R. Calder

The Dons change their strip – wearing blue shirts with white sleeves. Hearts are stronger in the first half, deserving an interval lead denied them by Wood's own goal. Thereafter Aberdeen – and Hamilton – go on the rampage.

League Cup Final (Hampden) Saturday, 5 April
RANGERS (3) 4   ABERDEEN (0) 0
  Gillick (25), Williamson
  (34), Duncanson 2 (41, 55)

RANGERS: Brown, Young, Shaw, McColl, Woodburn, Rae, Rutherford, Gillick, Williamson, Thornton, Duncanson

ABERDEEN: Johnstone, Cooper, McKenna, McLaughlin, Dunlop, Taylor, Harris, Hamilton, Williams, Baird, McCall

Attendance: 82,000   *Referee:* R. Calder

The only difference between the 1947 League Cup Final and its predecessor was that one was official, the other was not. The teams were the same. Aberdeen were thus bidding to beat the same opponents in order to enter the official records for the first time. Once again the Dons warmed up at Largs for a few days beforehand. But there the similarity ended. Aberdeen won the toss and – suicidally – elected to play into a hurricane wind and driving rain. Clearly they hoped to be 0-0 at the change-round. Instead they were three goals down. Rangers didn't even miss the absent Waddell, injured in the semi-final tie with Hibs. A four-nil defeat hardly reflected the balance of the play or the roll of the dice. Hamilton was crocked in the second half, and two stout penalty claims by the Dons for handball were brushed aside. The defeat was heavy, but Aberdeen would shortly be back – in the Scottish Cup Final.

SCOTTISH CUP

1st Round Saturday, 25 January
ABERDEEN (1) 2   PARTICK THISTLE (0) 1
  McCall (30), Cooper (85)   Mathie (66)
ABERDEEN: Johnstone, Cooper, McKenna,
McLaughlin, Dunlop, Taylor, Botha, Hamilton,
Harris, McCall, Williams
PARTICK: Steadward, Pirrie, Curran, Hewitt,
Husband, Brown, Wilson, O'Donnell, Mathie, Sharp,
Chisholm
Attendance: 34,000   *Referee:* R. G. Benzie
Aberdeen faced a tough first-round tie against Partick
Thistle, who had taken three points off the Dons in the
league. The game provided a debut for South African
Ray Botha. McCall's first-half goal for the Dons was
neutralised by Mathie in the second, at the moment
when Dunlop was lying on the ground. On balance,
Thistle would have deserved a replay, but they were
denied it by a moment of Pittodrie folklore. With five
minutes left, 36-year-old Willie Cooper advanced to
meet a Partick clearance and belt the ball from 30 yards
which dipped suddenly behind an astonished
Steadward.

2nd Round Saturday, 8 February
ABERDEEN (1) 8   AYR UNITED (0) 0
  Hamilton 3 (44, 55, 89),
  Harris 3 (46, 62, 73),
  Williams (50), Botha (64)
ABERDEEN: Johnstone, Cooper, McKenna,
McLaughlin, Dunlop, Taylor, Botha, Hamilton,
Williams, Harris, McCall
AYR: Barbour, McNeil, Kelly, Stewart, Smith, Nesbit,
McGuigan, Ouchterlonie, Tyson, Wallace, Beattie
Attendance: 15,500   *Referee:* R. Calder
Poor Ayr United from the lower reaches of Division B
were struck by a second-half blitz, having held out for
44 minutes.

3rd Round Saturday, 22 February
ABERDEEN (1) 1   MORTON (0) 1
  Millar (25)   McKillop (56)
ABERDEEN: Johnstone, Cooper, McKenna,
McLaughlin, Dunlop, Taylor, Millar, Hamilton,
Williams, Harris, McCall
MORTON: McFeat, Maley, Fyfe, Divers, Aird, White,
McKillop, Steel, Henderson, McGarrity, McInnes
Attendance: 30,000   *Referee:* J. M. Martin
Aberdeen face a difficult replay after failing to protect
Miller's first-half goal.

3rd Round Replay Saturday, 8 March
MORTON (0) 1   ABERDEEN (2) 2
  McKillop (61)   McCall (16),
              Hamilton (34)
MORTON: McFeat, Maley, Fyfe, Divers, Aird, White,
McKillop, Steel, Henderson, McGarrity, McInnes

ABERDEEN: Johnstone, Cooper, McKenna,
McLaughlin, Dunlop,Waddell, Millar, Hamilton,
Williams, Harris, McCall
Attendance: 18,500   *Referee:* J. M. Martin
An all-ticket crowd watched breathlessly as Morton
powered forward in a death or glory surge to wipe out
the Dons opening goals.

Quarter Final Saturday, 29 March
DUNDEE (1) 1 *1*   ABERDEEN (0) 1 *2*
  Ewen (40)   Williams 2 (60, 129)
              (after extra time)
DUNDEE: Lynch, Fallon, Ancell, McKenzie, Gray,
Boyd, Gunn, Pattillo, Juliussen, Ewen, Smith
ABERDEEN: Johnstone, Cooper, McKenna,
McLaughlin, Dunlop, Taylor, Harris, Hamilton,
Williams, Baird, McCall
Attendance: 35,000   *Referee:* W. Brown
Having beaten Dundee home and away in the League
Cup, Aberdeen were now invited to dispose of them in
the Scottish Cup at Dens Park. The B Division leaders
had bagged 98 goals from 23 matches, including ten
goals twice in recent games. The cup-tie was reported as
one of the hardest, grimmest and most fiercely
contested that had been seen for many a long day.
Dundee deserved their interval lead, secured by Ewen's
powerful drive which went in off the post. Williams
equalised, and only a wonder save by Lynch off Harris
in the closing minutes pushed the match into extra time
– which was to be played to the finish. Fixture
congestion ruled out the normal provision for a replay.
Stan Williams' decisive volley arrived after 129 minutes
play following which all twenty-two players were almost
too exhausted to traipse off the pitch.

Semi Final (Dens Park) Saturday, 12 April
ARBROATH (0) 0   ABERDEEN (1) 2
              Williams 2 (42, 69)
ARBROATH: Bonnar, English, Evans, Fraser, Hynd,
McGinley, Timmins, McMullen, Carrie, Hill, Smith
ABERDEEN: Johnstone, Cooper, McKenna,
McLaughlin, Dunlop, Taylor, Harris, Hamilton,
Williams, Baird, McCall
              Referee: M. C. Dale
The semi final draw was kind to the Dons, sending
them back to Dens Park to meet B Division stragglers
Arbroath. The Red Lichties, making a nonsense of their
league form, had overcome Hearts at Gayfield in the
quarter final. They were not so fortunate against
Aberdeen, but it needed another two-goal burst by Stan
Williams to earn the Dons' passage to Hampden. Sadly
Willie Cooper, whose unforgettable goal against Partick
had made possible Aberdeen's later triumph, had pulled
a leg muscle and would miss the final.

Scottish Cup Final (Hampden) Saturday, 19 April
HIBERNIAN (1) 1   ABERDEEN (2) 2
  Cuthbertson (1)   Hamilton (36), Williams
              (42)

HIBERNIAN: Kerr, Govan, Shaw, Howie, Aird, Kean, Smith, Finnegan, Cuthbertson, Turnbull, Ormond

ABERDEEN: Johnstone, McKenna, Taylor, McLaughlin, Dunlop, Waddell, Harris, Hamilton, Williams, Baird, McCall

Attendance: 82,100   *Referee:* R. Calder

Cooper's absence meant a reshaped Aberdeen defence at Hampden. Perhaps they were still getting used to one another, for they were a goal behind after thirty seconds. George Johnstone had played in the Dons' only previous Scottish Cup Final, ten years earlier. Now he allowed a straightforward backpass from George Taylor to squeeze through his arms and legs. Cuthbertson could hardly believe his luck as he gleefully put Hibs in front. After 36 minutes Aberdeen were all square, Hamilton's head converting Williams' centre. Six minutes later Williams chased a Harris through ball, kept it in play, and bore in towards Kerr along the goalline. Williams chose to shoot towards the near post rather than pull the ball back, and it flew into the net from the tightest of angles. After the turnaround Williams was floored by Kerr, but the goalkeeper redeemed himself by repelling Hamilton's penalty. In the end it didn't matter. Aberdeen had won the Scottish Cup for the first time in their history. Later Rangers would pip Hibs in the race for the League championship to complete a frustrating season for the Edinburgh club.

1946-47

APPEARANCES	League	League Cup	Scottish Cup
McCall	29	10	7
Harris	28	10	7
Taylor	28	3	6
Dunlop	27	9	7
Hamilton	26	9	7
Johnstone	26	10	7
McKenna	25	10	7
Williams	23	9	7
McLaughlin	19	7	7
Cowie	18	6	
Baird	14	2	3
Cooper	13	9	6
Kiddie	13	4	
Waddell	12	6	2
Waldron	7		
Millar	5	6	2
Hume	4		
Watson	4		
McKenzie	2		
Preston	2		
Botha	1		2
Colman	1		
Jamieson	1		
McDonald	1		
Robson	1		
25 players			

GOALS	Total	League	League Cup	Scottish Cup
Hamilton	33	17	11	5
Harris	14	10	1	3
McCall	12	5	5	2
Williams	11	5		6
Baird	7	6	1	
Kiddie	6	5	1	
Millar	6	2	3	1
Taylor	3	3		
Waldron	3	3		
Botha	1			1
Hume	1	1		
Cooper	1			1
own-goals	2	1	1	
Total	100	58	23	19

The successful Dons' side that won the Scottish Cup for the first time in 1947. Frank Dunlop (captain) is carried by (left to right) Taylor, McCall, McKenna, Hamilton, McLaughlin, Williams, Harris, Waddell. Looking on is the Chairman, Mr. W. Mitchell.

Season 1947-48

After such an encouraging return to peacetime football the events of season 1947-48 were a source of grave disappointment to the Dons. Far from heralding a further assault on all three Scottish trophies, the successes of the previous season served merely to underline how far the team was to fall in the course of the next twelve months.

There were reports of dissent among the playing staff, not helped by the sudden reversal of the club's fortunes. The first-team squad was accused of being too old, with too many over-thirties dominating the team. By mid-season key players had departed and the transfer tills were ringing.

Aberdeen's league position became dire. After eight matches they were three from bottom. They were denied a place in their third successive League Cup Final by East Fife from Division B. Aberdeen's interest in the Scottish Cup was terminated by Hibs, leaving the Dons to face a barren spring with only the fight against relegation to occupy their minds. On St Valentine's Day only a couple of points separated Aberdeen from the bottom two, but a point a game thereafter gradually hauled them to safety.

The Dons' main problem all season was their weakness in attack. Only three sides scored fewer league goals, and Aberdeen managed to net more than once in only twelve of their thirty league matches.

League:	Tenth
League Cup:	Semi Finalists
Scottish Cup:	Third Round

SCOTTISH LEAGUE DIVISION A

No 1 Wednesday, 13 August
ABERDEEN (0) 0   HIBERNIAN (0) 2
                                    Turnbull (67), Smith (88)
ABERDEEN: Bruce, Cowie, McKenna, McLaughlin, Dunlop, Taylor, Harris, Hamilton, Waldron, Baird, McCall
HIBERNIAN: Kerr, Govan, Howie, Buchanan, Aird, Finnegan, Smith, Combe, Linwood, Turnbull, Ormond

P	W	D	L	F	A	Pts		
1	0	0	1	0	2	0		

Attendance: 40,000
Referee: J. M. Martin

Aberdeen commenced their league programme by giving Hibs an early opportunity to avenge their Scottish Cup Final defeat. A vast crowd spilled over onto the cinder track, and some 200 fans perched themselves on the roof of the King St. stand. The gate of 40,000 was a record for a midweek match. The previous year Gordon Smith had been carried off near the start. Now he inspired every Hibs attack. Aberdeen's best chance came when Kerr brushed a Harris effort onto a post. But in the second half Turnbull collected a throw-in to fire a low shot past stand-in keeper Bruce. As Aberdeen besieged the Hibernian goal the visitors broke away for Smith to settle the outcome.

No 2 Tuesday, 26 August
ST MIRREN (2) 3   ABERDEEN (0) 0
Jack 3 (13, 39, 77)
ST MIRREN: Rennie, Drinkwater, Smith, Hunter, Telfer, Martin, Burrell, Guthrie, Jack, Lesz, Milne
ABERDEEN: Johnstone, Cowie, McKenna, McLaughlin, Waddell, Taylor, Kiddie, Hamilton, Harris, Baird, Millar

P	W	D	L	F	A	Pts		
2	0	0	2	0	5	0		

Attendance: 13,000
Referee: A. Mowatt

Aberdeen are never in the hunt at Paisley. They are still without a point and without a goal.

No 3 Saturday, 20 September
ABERDEEN (0) 3   DUNDEE (1) 2
  Williams (60), Baird (71),   Juliussen 2 (17, 82)
  Hamilton (84)
ABERDEEN: Johnstone, Cowie, McKenna, Waddell, Dunlop, Taylor, McCall, Hamilton, Williams, Baird, Millar
DUNDEE: Lynch, Fallon, Ancell, Cowie, Boyd, Smith, Pattillo, Ewen, Turnbull, Gallagher, Juliussen

P	W	D	L	F	A	Pts		
3	1	0	2	3	7	2		

Referee: J. Calder

Promoted Dundee – and Albert Juliussen in particular – stretch the Dons to the limit. Only in the last half-hour do Aberdeen exert their superiority.

No 4 Saturday, 4 October
ABERDEEN (1) 2   CELTIC (0) 0
    Kiddie (19), Baird (77)
ABERDEEN: Johnstone, Cowie, McKenna, McLaughlin, Waddell, Taylor, Kiddie, Baird, Williams, Harris, Millar
CELTIC: Ugolini, Ferguson, Mallan, Quinn, Corbett, McAuley, Hazlett, Bogan, Rae, Evans, Paton

P	W	D	L	F	A	Pts	
4	2	0	2	5	7	4	*Attendance:* 25,000

Referee: R. G. Benzie

Celtic come to Pittodrie struggling in the league. They have the edge until Kiddie rifles a first-timer past Ugolini. Not until Baird scores a late second is the Celtic challenge finally stilled.

No 5 Saturday, 18 October
ABERDEEN (0) 1   FALKIRK (1) 2
    Millar (47)   Aikman 2 (13, 78)
ABERDEEN: Johnstone, Cowie, McKenna, McVean, Waddell, Taylor, Kiddie, Williams, Harris, Baird, Millar
FALKIRK: J. Dawson, Whyte, McPhee, Bolt, R. Henderson, Gallacher, Fiddes, Allison, Aikman, J. Henderson, K. Dawson

P	W	D	L	F	A	Pts	
5	2	0	3	6	9	4	*Attendance:* 17,000

Referee: R. E. Carruthers

Last season Falkirk were the only side to gain a league double over the Dons. Now they are on their way again.

No 6 Saturday, 25 October
PARTICK THISTLE (2) 2   ABERDEEN (0) 1
    McKennan (9),   Kiddie (88)
    Mathie (11)
PARTICK: Henderson, McGowan, Curran, Brown, Forsyth, Husband, Wright, McKennan, Mathie, Sharp, Glover
ABERDEEN: Johnstone, Cowie, McKenna, McVean, Waddell, Taylor, Kiddie, Harris, Williams, Baird, Millar

P	W	D	L	F	A	Pts	
6	2	0	4	7	11	4	*Attendance:* 25,000

Referee: W. Brown

The league pace-setters take an early grip against Aberdeen, who now have only Queens Park below them.

No 7 Saturday, 1 November
ABERDEEN (0) 2   QUEEN OF THE
    Taylor (52 pen),   SOUTH (1) 2
    Harris (78)   Aird (17 pen),
                            Jenkins (59)
ABERDEEN: Johnstone, Cowie, McKenna, McVean, Waddell, Taylor, Kiddie, Harris, Williams, Baird, Millar

QUEEN OF THE SOUTH: Henderson, Fulton, James, Scott, Aird, Sharp, Nutley, Brown, Houliston, Jenkins, Johnstone

P	W	D	L	F	A	Pts
7	2	1	4	9	13	5

The previous month Aberdeen had hit nine goals past a Queens side down to nine men. This time it is the Dons who play most of the match a man short, when Baird retires. Johnstone was a lonely figure in the last ten minutes as the Dons urgently sought the winner.

No 8 Saturday, 8 November
AIRDRIEONIANS (1) 2   ABERDEEN (0) 1
    G. Watson 2 (13, 72)   McCall (56)
AIRDRIE: Downie, Peters, Cunningham, McKenzie, Kelly, Duncan, McCulloch, Picken, Flavell, Elliott, G. Watson
ABERDEEN: Johnstone, Cowie, McKenna, McVean, Waddell, Taylor, Kiddie, Harris, Williams, McCall, Millar

Bottom Positions	P	W	D	L	F	A	Pts
12 Celtic	9	3	0	6	13	18	6
13 Airdrie	9	3	0	6	12	36	6
14 ABERDEEN	8	2	1	5	10	15	5
15 Morton	10	1	3	6	15	21	5
16 Queens Park	9	1	0	8	13	28	2

Attendance: 5,000   *Referee:* M. C. Dale

Fellow strugglers Airdrie dump Aberdeen deeper into the mire. In heavy rain Watson causes their downfall to capitalise on two errors by Johnstone.

No 9 Saturday, 15 November
ABERDEEN (0) 1   HEARTS (0) 1
    Kiddie (61)   Sloan (88)
ABERDEEN: Johnstone, Cowie, McKenna, Waddell, Dunlop, Taylor, Kiddie, Harris, Williams, McCall, Millar
HEARTS: Brown, Mathieson, McKenzie, Cox, Parker, Laing, Sloan, Urquhart, Currie, Dixon, Kelly

P	W	D	L	F	A	Pts	
9	2	2	5	11	16	6	*Attendance:* 10,000

Referee: W. J. Livingstone

Another precious point slips away in the final seconds when hoop-shirted Hearts snatch a leveller.

No 10 Saturday, 22 November
ABERDEEN (4) 6   QUEENS PARK (0) 0
    Williams 2 (11, 67), Millar
    (17), Harris 2 (35, 60),
    Taylor (43 pen)
ABERDEEN: Johnstone, Cowie, McKenna, Waddell, Dunlop, Taylor, Millar, Hamilton, Williams, Harris, McCall
QUEENS PARK: Simpson, McColl, Johnstone, McBain, Letham, Harnett, Alexander, Aitken, Farquhar, Hardie, Brown

P	W	D	L	F	A	Pts	
10	3	2	5	17	16	8	*Attendance:* 15,000

Referee: R. J. Smith

Aberdeen crush basement team Queens Park, for whom Harnett broke a leg in the closing stages.

No 11 Saturday, 29 November
MORTON (0) 0   ABERDEEN (0) 1
                      Hamilton (75)
MORTON: Cowan, Mitchell, Fyfe, Campbell, Millar, Whyte, Henderson, Orr, Liddell, Divers, Gillies
ABERDEEN: Johnstone, Cowie, McKenna, Waddell, Dunlop, Taylor, Millar, Hamilton, Williams, Harris, McCall

P	W	D	L	F	A	Pts
11	4	2	5	18	16	10

Attendance: 10,000
Referee: A. B. Gebbie

Never mind the performance: it's the result that matters. Hamilton scored the vital goal, but then Gillies fluffed a penalty for Morton.

No 12 Saturday, 6 December
ABERDEEN (2) 3   CLYDE (1) 1
  McCall (4), Gullan o.g.   McPhail (26)
  (24), Williams (51)
ABERDEEN: Johnstone, Cowie, McKenna, Waddell, Dunlop, Taylor, Millar, Hamilton, Williams, Harris, McCall
CLYDE: Gullan, Gibson, Deans, Campbell, McCormack, Long, Galletly, Hepburn, Johnstone, McPhail, Fitzsimmons

P	W	D	L	F	A	Pts
12	5	2	5	21	17	12

Attendance: 10,000
Referee: J. M. Martin

Aberdeen's third win in a row against relegation-haunted sides thrusts them into the top half of the table.

No 13 Saturday, 13 December
RANGERS (2) 4   ABERDEEN (0) 0
  Rutherford (20), Gillick
  2 (29, 51), Thornton (87)
RANGERS: Brown, Cox, Shaw, McColl, Woodburn, Rae, Rutherford, Gillick, Thornton, Duncanson, Caskie
ABERDEEN: Johnstone, Cowie, McKenna, Waddell, Dunlop, Taylor, Millar, Hamilton, Williams, Harris, McCall

P	W	D	L	F	A	Pts
13	5	2	6	21	21	12

Attendance: 25,000
Referee: J. Calder

Rangers have lost only once so far this season, and have no inclination to permit Aberdeen to add to that figure Minus Young and Waddell, Rangers still manage to repeat the 4-0 scoreline from the League Cup Final. Gillick is the man who masterminded Aberdeen's downfall and who takes Rangers to the top of the league.

No 14 Saturday, 20 December
HIBERNIAN (3) 4   ABERDEEN (0) 0
  Dunlop o.g. (5),
  Linwood (21),
  Ormond 2 (37 pen, 48)
HIBERNIAN: Kerr, Govan, Shaw, Finnegan, Aird, Buchanan, Smith, Combe, Linwood, Turnbull, Ormond

ABERDEEN: Johnstone, Cowie, McKenna, Waddell, Dunlop, Taylor, Kiddie, Hamilton, Harris, McCall, Millar

P	W	D	L	F	A	Pts
14	5	2	7	21	25	12

Referee: J. B. Smillie

Hibernian are second to Rangers only on goal average. They set about the Dons as if determined to rectify that arithmetical inferiority. Hibs looked strong at Pittodrie on the league's opening day. Now they look even stronger, encouraged by Dunlop glancing Smith's wayward shot into his own net after just five minutes. Before long Hamilton had to be carried off with a thigh injury and later Waddell's dislocated elbow forced his withdrawal. If 11 Dons couldn't stop Hibs, 9 certainly couldn't. A few days later George Hamilton signed for Hearts, Aberdeen obtaining Archie Kelly in return, plus a sum of around £7,000.

No 15 Thursday, 25 December
THIRD LANARK (2) 3   ABERDEEN (1) 2
  Bogan 2 (40, 83),   Yorston (23),
  McCulloch (43)   Taylor (64 pen)
THIRD LANARK: Fraser, Balunas, Kelly, Young, Barclay, Mooney, Bogan, Mason, McCulloch, Baillie, McGeachie
ABERDEEN: Johnstone, Cooper, McKenna, Cowie, Dunlop, Taylor, Kiddie, Yorston, Kelly, Harris, McCall

P	W	D	L	F	A	Pts
15	5	2	8	23	28	12

Referee: A. Young

Christmas Day produces Aberdeen's third straight defeat, this time against bottom-placed Third Lanark. It marks Third's first win in ten games and the debuts for Archie Kelly and Harry Yorston.

No 16 Saturday, 27 December
ABERDEEN (1) 5   ST MIRREN (0) 0
  Kelly (24), McCall (49),
  Kiddie (60), Yorston
  2 (61, 84)
ABERDEEN: Johnstone, Cooper, McKenna, Cowie, Dunlop, Taylor, Kiddie, Yorston, Kelly, Harris, McCall
ST MIRREN: Rennie, Smith, Lindsay, Reid, Telfer, Martin, Burrell, Telford, Milne, Deakin, Lesz

P	W	D	L	F	A	Pts
16	6	2	8	28	28	14

Attendance: 10,000
Referee: J. R. Boyd

The Kelly-Yorston combination inspires the Dons to a mighty win over the Saints, and sweet revenge for a heavy defeat at Paisley.

No 17 Thursday, 1 January
DUNDEE (0) 0   ABERDEEN (0) 0
DUNDEE: Lynch, Follon, Ancell, Irvine, Gray, Boyd, Gunn, Gallagher, Juliussen, Smith, Hill
ABERDEEN: Johnstone, Cooper, McKenna, Cowie, Dunlop, Taylor, Kiddie, Yorston, Kelly, Harris, McCall

P W D L F A Pts
17 6 3 8 28 28 15

In recent months Aberdeen have seen off Dundee in the league, League Cup and Scottish Cup. Now Dundee are awarded a late penalty when Dunlop impedes Juliussen. Fallon sends the spot kick against a post.

No 18 Saturday, 3 January
ABERDEEN (1) 2   MOTHERWELL (1) 1
  Yorston (9), Kelly (64)   Watson (35)
ABERDEEN: Johnstone, Cooper, McKenna, Cowie, Dunlop, Taylor, Kiddie, Yorston, Kelly, Harris, McCall
MOTHERWELL: Johnston, Kilmarnock, Sinclair, McLeod, Paton, Redpath, Watters, Watson, Humphries, Bremner, Barclay
P W D L F A Pts   *Attendance:* 25,000
18 7 3 8 30 29 17   *Referee:* G. Macdonald
High flying Motherwell are brought to earth by a spirited second-half performance which carried the Dons into 7th position. After the match Willie McCall was transferred to Newcastle United. At one time it appeared that future England international Roy Bentley would come to Pittodrie in part exchange. He declined the offer.

No 19 Saturday, 10 January
CELTIC (0) 1   ABERDEEN (0) 0
  Corbett (54 pen)
CELTIC: Miller, Ferguson, Milne, McPhail, Corbett, McAuley, Paton, McDonald, Gormley, Gallacher, Kapler
ABERDEEN: Johnstone, Cooper, McKenna, Cowie, Dunlop, Taylor, Kiddie, McLaughlin, Kelly, Harris, Millar
P W D L F A Pts   *Referee:* R. J. Smith
19 7 3 9 30 30 17
Handicapped by a first-minute injury to Frank Dunlop, the Dons were always disadvantaged. The points were decided when McLaughlin pulled Gallacher down inside the box.

No 20 Saturday, 17 January
ABERDEEN (0) 2   THIRD LANARK (2) 2
  Yorston 2 (80, 84)   Mason (14), Mitchell (41)
ABERDEEN: Johnstone, Cooper, McKenna, Cowie, McLaughlin, Taylor, Kiddie, Yorston, Kelly, Harris, Millar
THIRD LANARK: Petrie, Balunas, Kelly, Young, Barclay, Mooney, Staroscik, Mason, Scott, Orr, Mitchell
P W D L F A Pts   *Attendance:* 14,000
20 7 4 9 32 32 18   *Referee:* R. Duthie
Jimmy Mason was the architect of Third Lanark's first-half superiority, as the Dons slipped and slithered on the frosty surface. A late rally by Harry Yorston saved a point.

No 21 Saturday, 31 January
FALKIRK (2) 3   ABERDEEN (0) 1
  Aikman 2 (19, 38),   Kelly (82)
  Inglis (53)
FALKIRK: J. Dawson, McPhee, Gallacher, Bolt, R. Henderson, Whitelaw, Fiddes, Aikman, Inglis, Aitken, Allison
ABERDEEN: Johnstone, Cooper, McKenna, Cowie, Waddell, Taylor, Harris, Baird, Williams, Owens, Kelly
P W D L F A Pts   *Attendance:* 8,000
21 7 4 10 33 35 18   *Referee:* J. Calder
Four wins out of four is Falkirk's league record against Aberdeen, who never got to grips with their opponents on the mud.

No 22 Saturday, 14 February
ABERDEEN (0) 0   PARTICK THISTLE (0) 1
                          Walker (65)
ABERDEEN: Johnstone, Cowie, McKenna, Waddell, Dunlop, Taylor, Harris, Stenhouse, Kelly, Williams, Pearson
PARTICK: Henderson, McGowan, Husband, Candlin, Forsyth, Hewitt, Wright, McInnes, O'Donnell, McCallum, Walker

Bottom positions	P	W	D	L	F	A	Pts
11 ABERDEEN	22	7	4	11	33	36	18
12 Celtic	23	7	4	12	30	42	18
13 Queen of the South	23	7	4	12	39	59	18
14 Airdrie	23	6	5	12	28	64	17
15 Hearts	22	6	4	12	25	37	16
16 Queens Park	23	6	1	16	37	63	13

Attendance: 25,000   *Referee:* F. Scott
Not even the inclusion of Tommy Pearson from Newcastle can deflate third-placed Thistle, who were outplayed for much of the ninety minutes but who scored the vital goal out of the blue. The Dons are now in deep trouble.

No 23 Saturday, 28 February
ABERDEEN (0) 3   AIRDRIE (0) 0
  Pearson (47), Baird
  (85 pen), Harris (87)
ABERDEEN: Johnstone, Cowie, McKenna, Waddell, Roy, Taylor, Harris, Williams, Kelly, Baird, Pearson
AIRDRIE: Downie, Peters, Cunningham, Stevenson, Kelly, Black, H. Watson, Brown, Anderson, Duncan, G. Watson
P W D L F A Pts   *Attendance:* 18,000
23 8 4 11 36 36 20   *Referee:* G. Mitchell
With only the escape from relegation to occupy their minds – following their elimination from the Scottish Cup – Aberdeen reap the benefit from this four pointer against fellow-strugglers Airdrie. But it took a goal from polished Pearson to break the deadlock.

No 24 Saturday, 6 March

HEARTS (0) 1	ABERDEEN (0) 1
Dixon (90 pen)	Kelly (54)

HEARTS: Brown, McSpadyen, McKenzie, Laing, Parker, Dougan, Sloan, Hamilton, Flavell, Dixon, Williams

ABERDEEN: Johnstone, Cowie, McKenna, Waddell, Roy, Taylor, Williams, Harris, Kelly, Baird, Pearson

P	W	D	L	F	A	Pts	
24	8	5	11	37	37	21	*Referee:* W. Webb

As they had done at Pittodrie, Hearts snatched a dramatic late equaliser against Aberdeen to ease their fears of relegation. Cowie fouled Flavell, Dixon took the kick and the final whistle went immediately.

No 25 Saturday, 13 March

QUEENS PARK (1) 3	ABERDEEN (0) 1
Alexander (35), Gunn	Williams (64)
(50), Cunningham (72)	

QUEENS PARK: Curran, McColl, Carmichael, McBain, Ross, Letham, Cunningham, Farquhar, Burgess, Gunn, Alexander

ABERDEEN: Scott, Cowie, McKenna, Waddell, Roy, Taylor, Williams, Yorston, Kelly, Harris, Pearson

P	W	D	L	F	A	Pts	*Attendance:* 15,000
28	8	5	12	38	40	21	*Referee:* R. Duthie

Queens Park may be adrift at the foot of the table, but the Dons still granted them their first triumph of 1948.

No 26 Saturday, 20 March

ABERDEEN (2) 2	MORTON (1) 1
Kelly (19), Williams (36)	Murphy (8)

ABERDEEN: Johnstone, Cowie, McKenna, Waddell, Roy, Taylor, Kelly, Harris, Williams, Hume, Pearson

MORTON: Cowan, Mitchell, Whigham, Campbell, Miller, White, Hepburn, Crichton, Cupples, Murphy, Liddell

P	W	D	L	F	A	Pts	*Attendance:* 18,000
26	9	5	12	40	41	23	*Referee:* T. Shirley

Morton need the points even more than Aberdeen, but couldn't capitalise on Murphy's strike which Johnstone let slip through his hands.

No 27 Friday, 26 March

CLYDE (1) 1	ABERDEEN (3) 3
Davis (1)	Kelly 3 (6, 7, 31)

CLYDE: Gullan, Gibson, Deans, McCormack, Milligan, Campbell, Davies, Garth, Johnstone, Long, Galletly

ABERDEEN: Johnstone, Cowie, McKenna, McLaughlin, Roy, Waddell, Kiddie, Harris, Kelly, Baird, Pearson

P	W	D	L	F	A	Pts
27	10	5	12	43	42	25

Aberdeen retrieve the points after Davis' first-minute goal with a Kelly hat-trick – the first of the season by an Aberdeen player in the league. With this result fears of relegation are at last banished.

No 28 Saturday, 3 April

ABERDEEN (0) 1	RANGERS (0) 1
Kelly (57)	Duncanson (69)

ABERDEEN: Johnstone, McLaughlin, McKenna, Waddell, Roy, Taylor, Kiddie, Harris, Kelly, Baird, Pearson

RANGERS: Brown, Young, Shaw, McColl, Woodburn, Cox, Waddell, Gillick, Thornton, Duncanson, Rutherford

P	W	D	L	F	A	Pts	*Attendance:* 43,800
28	10	6	12	44	43	26	*Referee:* A. Watt

With the Dons free of relegation worries and Rangers desperate for points in their pursuit of Hibs for the championship, this match had all the ingredients for being a cracker. The Pittodrie gates were closed before kick-off with 43,800 people inside the ground, a new record in this, the Dons' last home fixture of the season. The game itself was dour and unremitting. Midway through the first half a Harris header came back off the bar. The Dons went ahead when Kelly cleared Woodburn to score past Brown, only for Duncanson to level when Johnstone punched out a Young free kick to his feet.

No 29 Friday, 9 April

QUEEN OF THE	ABERDEEN (0) 0
SOUTH (0) 0	

QUEEN OF THE SOUTH: Henderson, Sharp, James, Fitzsimmons, Aird, Hamilton, Stephens, Jenkins, Houliston, Law, Johnstone

ABERDEEN: Johnstone, McLaughlin, McKenna, Waddell, Roy, Taylor, Stenhouse, Harris, Kelly, Hume, Pearson

P	W	D	L	F	A	Pts	*Attendance:* 12,000
29	10	7	12	44	43	27	*Referee:* P. Fitzpatrick

Queen of the South desperately wanted two points in their fight against relegation, but could not break through in an uninspiring contest.

No 30 Saturday, 17 April

MOTHERWELL (1) 2	ABERDEEN (1) 1
Watters (29),	Kelly (31)
Kilmarnock (68 pen)	

MOTHERWELL: Johnston, Kilmarnock, Shaw, McLeod, Paton, Redpath, Watters, Humphries, Mathie, Bremner, Johnston

ABERDEEN: Johnstone, McLaughlin, McKenna, Waddell, Roy, Taylor, Kiddie, Stenhouse, Kelly, Baird, Pearson

Referee: J. Kerr

Aberdeen said farewell to a disappointing season. An inconsequential match was settled by a penalty when McLaughlin was adjudged to have fouled Mathie.

Aberdeen's complete home and away record:

HOME						AWAY						
P	W	D	L	F	A		W	D	L	F	A	Pts
30	8	4	3	33	16		2	3	10	12	29	27

Scottish League Division A 1947-48

	P	W	D	L	F	A	Pts
1 Hibernian	30	22	4	4	86	27	48
2 Rangers	30	21	4	5	64	28	46
3 Partick Thistle	30	16	4	10	61	42	36
4 Dundee	30	15	3	12	67	51	33
5 St Mirren	30	13	5	12	54	58	31
6 Clyde	30	12	7	11	52	57	31
7 Falkirk	30	10	10	10	55	48	30
8 Motherwell	30	13	3	14	45	47	29
9 Hearts	30	10	8	12	37	42	28
10 ABERDEEN	30	10	7	13	45	45	27
11 Third Lanark	30	10	6	14	56	73	26
12 Celtic	30	10	5	15	41	56	25
13 Queen of the South	30	10	5	15	49	74	25
14 Morton	30	9	6	15	47	43	24
15 Airdrie	30	7	7	16	39	78	21
16 Queens Park	30	9	2	19	45	75	20

LEAGUE CUP

Saturday, 9 August
ST MIRREN (0) 0   ABERDEEN (1) 1
                                    Williams (20)
ST MIRREN: Newlands, Telfer, Smith, Hunter,
Lindsay, Cunningham, Stenhouse, Telford, Milne,
Reid, Deakin
ABERDEEN: Johnstone, Cowie, McKenna,
McLaughlin, Dunlop, Taylor, Harris, Hamilton,
Williams, Baird, McCall
Attendance: 8,000   *Referee:* J. R. Boyd
The inclusion of full-back Andy Cowie is the only
change to the Dons' line-up in the new season.

Saturday, 16 August
ABERDEEN (1) 2   MOTHERWELL (0) 0
Millar (16), Kiddie (47)
ABERDEEN: Johnstone, Cowie, McKenna,
McLaughlin, Waddell, Taylor, Kiddie, Hume, Harris,
McCall, Millar
MOTHERWELL: Johnston, Kilmarnock, Shaw,
McLeod, Paton, Redpath, Watters, Watson,
Humphries, Bremner, Barclay
Attendance: 20,000   *Referee:* J. Jackson
Aberdeen, forced to reshape their attack due to injuries,
gain revenge for the double that Motherwell inflicted on
them in the League Cup last season.

Saturday, 23 August
QUEEN OF THE   ABERDEEN (1) 2
    SOUTH (0) 1   Baird 2 (35, 84)
Baker (60)
QUEEN OF THE SOUTH: Wilson, Savage, James,
Scott, Aird, Sharp, Law, Brown, Houliston, Jenkins,
Baker
ABERDEEN: Johnstone, Cowie, McKenna,
McLaughlin, Dunlop, Taylor, Kiddie, Hamilton,
Harris, Baird, McCall
Attendance: 14,000   *Referee:* R. J. Smith

For the second successive season, Aberdeen win 'at
Dumfries in the League Cup – only this time time they
leave it late.

Saturday, 30 August
ABERDEEN (2) 2   ST MIRREN (0) 0
    Hamilton 2 (23, 34)
ABERDEEN: Johnstone, Cowie, McKenna, Waddell,
Dunlop, Taylor, Harris, Baird, Hamilton, McCall,
Millar
ST MIRREN: Rennie, Drinkwater, Smith, Hunter,
Telfer, Martin, Burrell, Guthrie, Telford, Lesz, Milne
Attendance: 20,000   *Referee:* W. Brown
Despite losing to the Saints in the league in midweek,
Aberdeen record a comfortable double in the League
Cup.

Saturday, 6 September
MOTHERWELL (1) 2   ABERDEEN (0) 0
    Kilmarnock (26 pen),
    Bremner (70)
MOTHERWELL: Johnston, Kilmarnock, Shaw,
McLeod, Paton, Redpath, Watters, Watson,
Humphries, Bremner, Barclay
ABERDEEN: Johnstone, Cowie, McKenna, Waddell,
Dunlop, Taylor, Harris, Baird, Hamilton, McCall,
Millar
Attendance: 21,000   *Referee:* A. Watt
Aberdeen need a point to qualify at the expense of
Motherwell, who now have a better goal average.

Saturday, 13 September
ABERDEEN (1) 9   QUEEN OF THE
    Hamilton 4 (22, 57, 80,   SOUTH (0) 0
    84), Williams 3 (55, 69,
    73), Baird (63), Millar (71)
ABERDEEN: Johnstone, Cowie, McKenna, Waddell,
Dunlop, Taylor, McCall, Hamilton, Williams, Baird,
Millar
QUEEN OF THE SOUTH: Wilson, Savage, James,
Scott, Aird, Sharp, Nutley, Brown, Houliston,
Dempsey, Hope
Attendance: 25,000   *Referee:* W. Davidson
A freak result earned almost entirely by injuries to
Queen of the South. Resuming after the interval with
only ten men they immediately lost goalkeeper Wilson
with a shattered finger. Down to 9 players and a stand-
in 'keeper they were unable to prevent Aberdeen
scoring 8 more goals. They were all needed, for they
enabled Aberdeen to qualify from Section A on goal
average ahead of Motherwell. Had Queens replied just
once it would have been enough to send Motherwell
through.

Section A	P	W	D	L	F	A	Pts
ABERDEEN	6	5	0	1	16	3	10
Motherwell	6	5	0	1	13	6	10
St Mirren	6	1	0	5	9	18	2
Queen of the South	6	1	0	5	10	24	2

Quarter Final Saturday, 27 September
ABERDEEN (5) 8   LEITH ATHLETIC (1) 2
  Baird (17),   Roberts (4),
  Millar 3 (20, 22, 57)   Bradley (87)
  Williams 3 (25, 43, 48)
  Hamilton (54)
ABERDEEN: Johnstone, Cowie, McKenna,
McLaughlin, Waddell, Taylor, Harris, Hamilton,
Williams, Baird, Millar
LEITH: King, Paterson, Peat, Skinner, Johnstone,
McCall, Robertson, Love, Bradley, Landells, Roberts
Attendance: 17,000   *Referee:* G. MacDonald
Tiny Leith rock Aberdeen with a fourth-minute goal,
but are soon made to pay for their effrontery.

Semi Final (Dens Park) Saturday, 11 October
EAST FIFE (0) 1   ABERDEEN (0) 0
  Morris (81)
EAST FIFE: Niven, Laird, Stewart, Philp, Finlay,
Aitken, Adams, T. Davidson, Morris, J. Davidson,
Duncan
ABERDEEN: Johnstone, Cowie, McKenna,
McLaughlin, Waddell, Taylor, Kiddie, Harris,
Williams, Baird, Millar
Attendance: 30,000   *Referee:* W. Webb
All that stands between Aberdeen and their third
consecutive League Cup Final is little East Fife of
Division B. But complacency is out of order. It is only
nine years since the Methil club won a Scottish Cup 3rd
round replay at Pittodrie en route to lifting the trophy.
The present East Fife team reached the semis by
defeating Hearts at Tynecastle and are still unbeaten in
their league engagements. Their attack is led by Henry
Morris, shortly to be capped by his country. And it is
Morris who does the damage. Duncan's shot rebounds
from Johnstone's shoulder to Morris, who takes the ball
past McKenna before ballooning the net. Aberdeen,
handicapped by McLaughlin's broken wrist, rued their
missed chances – and the size of the goal! Three times
before Morris scored Williams had hit the woodwork,
and afterwards there was still time for Baird to head the
ball squarely against the crossbar.

SCOTTISH CUP

1st Round Bye

2nd Round Saturday, 7 February
NITHSDALE   ABERDEEN (0) 5
  WANDERERS (0) 0   Kelly 2 (55, 56), Harris
                           (62), Stenhouse 2 (63, 76)
NITHSDALE: Anderson, Phillips, Maxwell, Fleming,
Lorraine, Saddington, McGourty, Milligan, Keggans,
Coupland, Chisholm
ABERDEEN: Johnstone, Cowie, McKenna,
McLaughlin, Waddell, Taylor, Harris, Stenhouse,
Kelly, Baird, Williams
Attendance: 2,600   *Referee:* W. Livingstone

In defence of the Scottish Cup Aberdeen are awarded a
first-round bye and a second-round trip to Sanquhar in
Dumfriesshhire. Nithsdale don't play in any league, and
play only friendlies – aside from the Scottish Cup.
Boosted by new recruit Jimmy Stenhouse from St
Mirren, Aberdeen still find themselves embarrassed
during a first half in which they could have easily fallen
behind. All's well that ends well, however, and
Stenhouse scored twice on his debut to help raise the
final tally to five.

3rd Round Saturday, 21 February
HIBERNIAN (2) 4   ABERDEEN (1) 2
  Cuthbertson (1), Smith   Pearson (23), Harris (85)
  2 (40, 83), Linwood (56)
HIBERNIAN: Kerr, Govan, Shaw, Kean, Howie,
Buchanan, Smith, Combe, Linwood, Cuthbertson,
Ormond
ABERDEEN: Johnstone, McKenna, Taylor, Cowie,
Dunlop, Waddell, Harris, Stenhouse, Williams, Baird,
Pearson
Attendance: 37,000   *Referee:* P. Fitzpatrick
The Dons could never feel truly confident about
repeating their 1947 Scottish Cup win over Hibernian.
In the current season the Edinburgh club had twice
comprehensively disposed of Aberdeen in the league,
and with home advantage were strong favourites to
progress to the quarter finals. Not even the loss of
Eddie Turnbull could dampen Hibs' optimism. It was
his replacement, Cuthbertson, who put Hibs in front
inside 20 seconds – shades of the Scottish Cup Final –
despite Dons' protests that the ball had not crossed the
line when crashing down from the crossbar. Aberdeen
hit back through a Pearson header, but when Ormond
had to be carried off Hibs simply rolled up their sleeves.
Man-of-the-match Gordon Smith retrieved their lead
when Hibs were down to nine men, when goalkeeper
Kerr went off for temporary repairs. He returned for
the second half, but even against ten men Aberdeen
were transparently second best. More bad news
followed the final whistle. The exodus of unsettled
players from Aberdeen threatened to turn into a
stampede. Now it was 'keeper George Johnstone's turn
to request a transfer.

1947-48
APPEARANCES

	League	League Cup	Scottish Cup
McKenna	30	8	2
Taylor	29	8	2
Harris	28	7	2
Johnstone	28	8	2
Cowie	27	8	2
Waddell	23	6	2
Williams	17	4	2
Kiddie	17	3	
Kelly	16		1
Millar	15	6	
Dunlop	14	5	1
Baird	13	7	2
McCall	13	6	
McLaughlin	9	5	1
Pearson	9		1
Hamilton	8	6	
Roy	8		
Cooper	7		
Yorston	6		
McVean	4		
Stenhouse	3		2
Hume	2	1	
Bruce	1		
Owens	1		
Scott	1		
Waldron	1		
26 players			

GOALS

	Total	League	League Cup	Scottish Cup
Williams	13	6	7	
Kelly	12	10		2
Hamilton	9	2	7	
Baird	7	3	4	
Millar	7	2	5	
Yorston	6	6		
Harris	6	4		2
Kiddie	5	4	1	
McCall	3	3		
Taylor	3	3		
Pearson	2	1		1
Stenhouse	2			2
own-goals	1	1		
Total	76	45	24	7

This picture from the forties shows several players who were to make a lasting impression on the supporters. Back row: Stenhouse, Dunlop, Anderson, Foss, Robson, Preston. Front row: Harris, Hamilton, Williams, Baird, Pearson.

Season 1948-49

If 1947-48 was disappointing, 1948-49 was close to a disaster. The dispiriting spiral from the heights of 1947 seemed bottomless. The first six league fixtures left Aberdeen precariously placed as they embarked on the round-robin section of the League Cup. There they threw away a promising position and failed to qualify – on goal average – for the match-play rounds. When the league recommenced they were stuck in the fatal 15th position week after week. Third Lanark sent them spinning out of the Scottish Cup at the first hurdle, and by mid-February Aberdeen looked cast-iron certainties for relegation. Eleven matches remained for them to rescue their dire predicament, but all but three of those matches were away from home. When the Dons won 2-1 at Falkirk on 19 February it was their first away success of the season and their first win in any competition for three months.

Remarkably, Aberdeen lost only one of those eleven games, and went the last eight unbeaten. East Fife – traditionally a bogey-team for the Dons – provided what few happy memories Aberdeen could take from a wretched season. Their last win of 1948 was against the Fifers – then topping the league. With two points needed from their last two matches to survive the drop, the Dons won emphatically 4-1 at Methil to finally banish the relegation miseries.

The principal cause of Aberdeen's malaise was self-evident. They couldn't score goals. Their meagre tally of 39 was exceeded only by bottom-placed Albion Rovers.

League: Thirteenth
League Cup: Second in qualifying group
Scottish Cup: First Round

SCOTTISH LEAGUE DIVISION A

No 1 Saturday, 14 August
THIRD LANARK (0) 1   ABERDEEN (0) 0
Ayton (60)
THIRD LANARK: Petrie, Balunas, Kelly, Orr, Barclay, Harrower, Staroscik, Mason, Stirling, Ayton, Mitchell
ABERDEEN: Johnstone, Emery, McKenna, McLaughlin, Roy, Waddell, Kiddie, Hamilton, Williams, Baird, Pearson

P	W	D	L	F	A	Pts		*Attendance:* 20,000
1	0	0	1	0	1	0		*Referee:* J. Jaffrey

Despite the return of George Hamilton from Hearts and the inclusion of Don Emery from Swindon, Aberdeen turn in a lacklustre performance.

No 2 Wednesday, 18 August
ABERDEEN (0) 1   CELTIC (0) 0
Williams (55)
ABERDEEN: Johnstone, McLaughlin, McKenna, Stenhouse, Roy, Waddell, Harris, Hamilton, Williams, Baird, Pearson

CELTIC: Miller, Milne, Mallan, Evans, Boden, McAuley, Weir, McPhail, Lavery, Tully, Paton

P	W	D	L	F	A	Pts		*Attendance:* 35,000
2	1	0	1	1	1	2		*Referee:* A. Watt

Both teams are still looking for their first goal of the season. Afterwards Celtic are still looking for it. The match was memorable more for the ruthlessness of its tackling than for any inspiration. Aberdeen might have won by a bigger margin had not the referee cancelled Baird's 'goal' and awarded the Dons a penalty instead. Hamilton shot wide from the spot.

No 3 Saturday, 21 August
DUNDEE (3) 3   ABERDEEN (0) 0
Stott (11), Gunn (28),
Ewen (40)
DUNDEE: Lynch, Fallon, Ancell, Gallacher, Gray, Boyd, Gunn, Pattillo, Stott, Ewen, Andrews
ABERDEEN: Johnstone, McLaughlin, McKenna, Stenhouse, Roy, Waddell, Harris, Hamilton, Williams, Baird, Pearson

P	W	D	L	F	A	Pts		*Attendance:* 30,000
3	1	0	2	1	4	2		*Referee:* W. G. Livingstone

Exhilarating Dundee put Aberdeen to the sword, with Johnstone performing heroics to keep the score down.

No 4 Saturday, 28 August
ABERDEEN (0) 2   MOTHERWELL (0) 0
  Kelly (69), Hamilton (75)
ABERDEEN: Johnstone, McLaughlin, McKenna, Stenhouse, Waddell, Baird, Harris, Hamilton, Kelly, Williams, Pearson
MOTHERWELL: Johnston, Kilmarnock, Shaw, McLeod, Paton, Redpath, Humphries, Watson, Mathie, Bremner, Barclay

P	W	D	L	F	A	Pts	
4	2	0	2	3	4	4	*Attendance:* 35,000
							Referee: W. Webb

The Dons handed 'Well their first defeat of the season, for whom Kilmarnock wasted a late penalty.

No 5 Tuesday, 31 August
ST MIRREN (2) 3   ABERDEEN (0) 1
  Willie Reid (27), Walter   Kelly (76)
  Reid (35), Burrell (60)
ST MIRREN: Miller, Smith, Drinkwater, Walter Reid, Telfer, Martin, Burrell, Stewart, Milne, Willie Reid, Telford
ABERDEEN: Johnstone, McLaughlin, McKenna, Stenhouse, Waddell, Baird, Harris, Hamilton, Kelly, Williams, Pearson

P	W	D	L	F	A	Pts	
5	2	0	3	4	7	4	*Attendance:* 15,000
							Referee: A. B. Gebbie

High-flying Saints crush the Dons with ruthless ease. The result might have been different had not Williams hit the bar and then prodded the rebound against a post when Aberdeen were only two goals down.

No 6 Saturday, 4 September
ABERDEEN (0) 1   HIBERNIAN (1) 2
  Baird (82 pen)   Cuthbertson 2 (18, 60)
ABERDEEN: Johnstone, Preston, McKenna, Stenhouse, Waddell, McLaughlin, Williams, Hamilton, Kelly, Baird, Pearson
HIBERNIAN: Kerr, Howie, Shaw, Finnegan, Aird, Buchanan, Smith, Combe, Linwood, Cuthbertson, Reilly

Bottom positions

	P	W	D	L	F	A	Pts
12 Clyde	6	1	2	3	13	16	4
13 Albion R	6	1	2	3	11	17	4
14 ABERDEEN	6	2	0	4	5	9	4
15 Morton	5	1	2	2	7	11	2
16 Hearts	6	1	0	5	7	15	2

Attendance: 35,000   *Referee:* M. A. Mann

Pittodrie welcomes the unbeaten league leaders, who also top the league's goalscoring charts. Once again it is Cuthbertson who wields the axe against the Dons, scoring twice after earlier heading wide of a yawning goal. Aberdeen are left in the bottom three as the league is adjourned for six weeks to accommodate the League Cup rounds.

No 7 Saturday, 23 October
ABERDEEN (3) 4   CLYDE (3) 4
  Kiddie (4), Hamilton   Wright (1),
  (12), Pearson (27 pen),   Ackerman 2 (22, 25),
  Williams (62)   Davies (67)
ABERDEEN: Curran, Massie, McKenna, McLaughlin, Thomson, Kelly, Kiddie, Hamilton, Williams, Harris, Pearson
CLYDE: Gullan, Gibson, Deans, Dunn, McCormack, Campbell, Davies, Wright, Johnstone, Garth, Ackerman

P	W	D	L	F	A	Pts	
7	2	1	4	9	13	5	*Attendance:* 20,000
							Referee: R. G. Benzie

Both sides went potty, sharing six goals inside 27 minutes. Williams restored to centre-forward, puts Aberdeen back in the lead – a lead soon cancelled out by Davies.

No 8 Saturday, 6 November
ABERDEEN (1) 1   FALKIRK (0) 4
  Pearson (28 pen)   Logan 2 (47, 75),
                           Aikman (52),
                           K. Dawson (86)
ABERDEEN: Johnstone, Massie, Emery, McVean, Waddell, McLaughlin, Harris, Hamilton, Williams, Baird, Pearson
FALKIRK: Carrie, Whyte, McPhee, Fiddes, R. Henderson, Telfer, Allison, Aikman, Inglis, Logan, K. Dawson

P	W	D	L	F	A	Pts	
8	2	1	5	10	17	5	*Attendance:* 15,000
							Referee: J. Gaffney

Falkirk have become an insufferable bogey-team for Aberdeen. This is their fifth straight league win over the Dons, and the second time they have scored four at Pittodrie since the War. To make matters worse Aberdeen were leading 1-0 at the break. Falkirk's second goal, by Aikman, produced frantic Aberdeen appeals for offside – to no avail.

No 9 Saturday, 13 November
PARTICK THISTLE (0) 0   ABERDEEN (0) 0
PARTICK: Henderson, McGowan, Pirrie, Haddow, Forsyth, Davidson, MacKenzie, Kinnell, O'Donnell, McCallum, Walker
ABERDEEN: Johnstone, Massie, Emery, McVean, Waddell, McLaughlin, Millar, Hamilton, Williams, Harris, Pearson

P	W	D	L	F	A	Pts	
9	2	2	5	10	17	6	*Attendance:* 15,000
							Referee: J. R. Boyd

Two teams haunted by fear are determined to prevent a goal at all costs.

No 10 Saturday, 20 November
ABERDEEN (1) 3   EAST FIFE (0) 1
  Kelly 3 (43, 70, 85)   Black (52)
ABERDEEN: Johnstone, Massie, Emery, McVean, Waddell, McLaughlin, Millar, Hamilton, Kelly, Harris, Williams

EAST FIFE: Clark, Proudfoot, Stewart, Philp, Finlay, Aitken, Black, Fleming, Morris, Brown, Duncan

P	W	D	L	F	A	Pts	*Attendance:* 20,000
10	3	2	5	13	18	8	*Referee:* D. McKerchar

Scott Symon's new table-toppers come to Aberdeen as the sensation of the season, having won both the B Division championship and League Cup six months earlier. They are unbeaten in Division A since the opening week of the season. Charlie Fleming and Henry Morris are Scotland's leading scorers, sharing 29 league and League Cup goals. Yet shrugging off the absence of Pearson, Aberdeen notched their first win in two months. Dons' hero was Archie Kelly, back at No 9, who bagged a scorching hat-trick. Nevertheless, the result might have been very different when Emery clattered his cross bar at 0-0.

No 11 Saturday, 4 December

ABERDEEN (0) 2   HEARTS (0) 2
Hamilton (50),   Wardhaugh (64),
Harris (70)   Bauld (76)

ABERDEEN: Johnstone, Massie, McKenna, McVean, Waddell, McLaughlin, Millar, Hamilton, Kelly, Harris, Williams
HEARTS: Brown, Mathieson, McKenzie, Parker, Dougan, Laing, Sloan, Conn, Bauld, Wardhaugh, Flavell

P	W	D	L	F	A	Pts	*Attendance:* 20,000
11	3	3	5	15	20	9	*Referee:* D. Alexander

Aberdeen are unable to put two good performances together. The first half is consigned to oblivion, and when Aberdeen do find the net struggling Hearts are twice able to equalise.

No 12 Saturday, 11 December

ABERDEEN (1) 1   QUEEN OF SOUTH (0) 2
Kelly (36)   Houliston (55),
                          Jenkins (85)

ABERDEEN: Johnstone, Massie, McKenna, Stenhouse, Waddell, McLaughlin, Millar, Hamilton, Kelly, Harris, Williams
QUEEN OF THE SOUTH: Henderson, McColl, James, McBain, Aird, Hamilton, McCulloch, Brown, Houliston, Jenkins, Johnstone

Bottom positions

	P	W	D	L	F	A	Pts
13 Morton	13	4	3	6	20	27	11
14 Clyde	14	3	4	7	26	39	10
15 ABERDEEN	12	3	3	6	16	22	9
16 Albion R	11	2	2	7	15	32	6

Attendance: 15,000   *Referee:* D. McKerchar

Desperation-time for the Dons following Jenkins' late winner. Headers from Hamilton and Kelly almost save a point, but eight of Aberdeen's twelve league games have been at Pittodrie, and they have won only three.

No 13 Saturday, 18 December

MORTON (0) 1   ABERDEEN (1) 1
Mochan (9)   Hamilton (40)

MORTON: Clark, Mitchell, Fyfe, Campbell, Miller, White, Alexander, Farquhar, Mochan, Murphy, Liddell
ABERDEEN: Johnstone, Massie, McKenna, Stenhouse, Waddell, McLaughlin, Rice, Hamilton, Kelly, Harris, Pearson

P	W	D	L	F	A	Pts	*Referee:* J. Lynch
13	3	4	6	17	23	10	

Aberdeen introduce Peter Rice, a £5,000 buy from Hibs, in this relegation battle with Morton. The match is fearsomely contested. After 35 minutes Hamilton equalises Mochan's early score, only for the linesman to intervene after the referee had confirmed the goal. The effort was annulled, but five minutes later Hamilton swept Stenhouse's free kick past Clark from a seeming offside position. Johnstone's goal was under siege in the final minutes.

No 14 Saturday, 25 December

CELTIC (3) 3   ABERDEEN (0) 0
McPhail (15), Paton (19),
Johnstone (22)

CELTIC: Miller, Milne, Mallan, Evans, Boden, McAuley, Weir, Johnstone, McPhail, Tully, Paton
ABERDEEN: Curran, Massie, McKenna, Stenhouse, Waddell, McLaughlin, Rice, Hamilton, Kelly, Harris, Williams

P	W	D	L	F	A	Pts	*Attendance:* 40,000
14	3	4	7	17	26	10	*Referee:* R. J. Smith

Celtic win only their second home game in eleven months – since the 1-0 victory over the Dons in January 1948. Christmas Day brings no presents to the Dons who had lost irretrievably mid-way through the first half.

No 15 Saturday, 1 January

ABERDEEN (0) 1   DUNDEE (2) 3
Rice (57)   Pattillo (15), Stott (28),
                          Watson o.g. (85)

ABERDEEN: Watson, McLaughlin, Emery, Anderson, Waddell, McVean, Rice, Stenhouse, Kelly, Hamilton, Hather
DUNDEE: Lynch, Fallon, Irvine, Gallagher, Cowie, Boyd, Gunn, Pattillo, Stott, Ewen, Hill

Bottom positions

	P	W	D	L	F	A	Pts
13 Morton	16	4	4	8	22	33	12
14 Clyde	17	4	4	9	29	44	12
15 ABERDEEN	15	3	4	8	18	29	10
16 Albion R	14	2	2	10	19	43	6

Attendance: 26,000   *Referee:* J. A. Mowat

Numerous team changes are made for the visit of Dundee, riding high in the league, including debuts for Chris Anderson and Jackie Hather. In the event Aberdeen lost but performed with great gusto. Dundee were on the rack in the second half. Kelly was denied an equaliser by a goalpost, and it took Watson's own goal to seal Aberdeen's fate.

No 16 Saturday, 8 January

ABERDEEN (2) 2   THIRD LANARK (1) 2
Rice (5), Hamilton   McCulloch (40), Mitchell
(21 pen)   (65)

ABERDEEN: Johnstone, Ancell, McKenna, Anderson, Waddell, Stenhouse, Rice, Hamilton, Kelly, Harris, Hather

THIRD LANARK: Fraser, Balunas, Harrower, Orr, Barclay, Mooney, Henderson, Mason, McCulloch, Staroscik, Mitchell

P	W	D	L	F	A	Pts	*Attendance:* 20,000
16	3	5	8	20	31	11	*Referee:* G. MacDonald

Aberdeen, handicapped by a knee injury to Kelly, throw away a two-goal lead. Harris' late header is net-bound until headed off the line by Balunas.

No 17 Saturday, 15 January

HIBERNIAN (0) 4   ABERDEEN (0) 1
Plumb (59), Cairns   Hamilton (85)
(60 pen), Smith (63),
Ormond (89)

HIBERNIAN: Kerr, Govan, Cairns, Kean, Paterson, Buchanan, Smith, Combe, Plumb, Turnbull, Ormond

ABERDEEN: Johnstone, McKenna, Ancell, Anderson, Waddell, McLaughlin, Rice, Harris, Hamilton, Pearson, Hather

P	W	D	L	F	A	Pts	*Attendance:* 15,000
17	3	5	9	21	35	11	*Referee:* J. Kerr

Hibs' championship bid is being hampered by a suspect defence, but it is their prolific attack which lets them down in the first half. Aberdeen are burdened by an injury to Waddell, but on the hour the floodgates are opened. Plumb's accurate header is immediately followed by a penalty awarded against McLaughlin for handball, at which the Dons' player showed furious dissent.

No 18 Saturday, 29 Janaury

ABERDEEN (0) 0   ST MIRREN (1) 2
    Lesz 2 (7, 86)

ABERDEEN: Johnstone, McKenna, Ancell, Anderson, Thomson, Harris, Rice, Stenhouse, Gibson, Williams, Hather

ST MIRREN: Kirk, Lapsley, Martin, Drinkwater, Telfer, Willie Reid, Burrell, Stewart, Jack, Davie, Lesz

P	W	D	L	F	A	Pts	*Attendance:* 18,000
18	3	5	10	21	37	11	*Referee:* W. Davidson

Alfons Lesz, Polish left-winger, punishes inept Aberdeen performance as Dons show Cup-hangover.

No 19 Saturday, 12 February

ABERDEEN (0) 0   RANGERS (1) 2
    Thornton (1), Paton (72)

ABERDEEN: Curran, Ancell, McKenna, Anderson, Thomson, Harris, Rice, Williams, Emery, Smith, Hather

RANGERS: Brown, Young, Shaw, McColl, Woodburn, Cox, Waddell, Paton, Thornton, Duncanson, Rutherford

Bottom positions

	P	W	D	L	F	A	Pts
13 Clyde	22	6	4	12	37	54	16
14 Morton	20	4	5	11	24	39	13
15 ABERDEEN	19	3	5	11	21	39	11
16 Albion R	19	2	2	15	22	62	6

Attendance: 42,000   *Referee:* A. Watt

It took Willie Thornton just 45 seconds to pierce Aberdeen's brittle defence. With Don Emery operating as an experimental centre-forward in the absence of Kelly and Hamilton, Aberdeen had an untried forward five who rarely looked like scoring. The Dons look strong favourites for relegation.

No 20 Saturday, 19 February

FALKIRK (0) 1   ABERDEEN (1) 2
K. Dawson (81)   Williams (16), Emery
    (65 pen)

FALKIRK: J. Dawson, Whyte, McPhee, Fiddes, Henderson, Whitelaw, Allison, Silcock, Aikman, McLaughlin, K. Dawson

ABERDEEN: Curran, Ancell, McKenna, McLaughlin, Roy, Harris, Rice, Williams, Emery, Glen, Hather

P	W	D	L	F	A	Pts	*Attendance:* 10,000
20	4	5	11	23	40	13	*Referee:* P. Fitzpatrick

Aberdeen achieve their most remarkable result of the season against bogey team Falkirk lying fifth. It provided their first points against Falkirk since the War, their first away win of the season, and their first of any description since 20 November. It also marked Archie Glen's debut.

No 21 Saturday, 26 February

ABERDEEN (3) 4   PARTICK THISTLE (1) 2
Williams (20), Emery   Davidson (7), Thomson
2 (25, 77), Hather (32)   (49)

ABERDEEN: Curran, Ancell, McKenna, McLaughlin, Roy, Harris, Rice, Williams, Emery, Glen, Hather

PARTICK: Ledgerwood, McGowan, Gibb, Thomson, Forsyth, Davidson, McKenzie, Wright, O'Donnell, Sharp, Walker

P	W	D	L	F	A	Pts	*Attendance:* 17,000
21	5	5	11	27	42	15	*Referee:* J. R. Boyd

Another vital win, obtained despite Davidson's cruel goal, deflected past Curran in the seventh minute.

No 22 Saturday, 5 March

ALBION ROVERS (0) 2   ABERDEEN (1) 1
McKinnon (82), Kerr (84)   Glen (6)

ALBION: McGregor, Paterson, Kerr, Hunter, English, Imrie, McKinnon, Martin, McLean, P. Smith, McLeod

ABERDEEN: Curran, Ancell, McKenna, Anderson, Roy, Waddell, Rice, Williams, Emery, Glen, Hather

P	W	D	L	F	A	Pts	
22	5	5	12	28	44	15	*Attendance:* 750
							Referee: P. Fitzpatrick

A chance for two more points against Albion, already doomed to Division B, seven points adrift. But Aberdeen fritter away Glen's opening goal. In sleet and rain only 750 spectators watch Albion's fight back, and their first win since October.

No 23 Saturday, 12 March
ABERDEEN (2) 4   ALBION ROVERS (0) 0
  Emery 2 (30, 37), Hather
  (72), Williams (81)

ABERDEEN: Curran, Ancell, McKenna, Anderson, Waddell, Harris, Rice, Williams, Emery, Glen, Hather
ALBION: McGregor, Paterson, Kerr, Hunter, English, Imrie, McKinnon, Martin, McLean, P. Smith, McLeod

P	W	D	L	F	A	Pts	
23	6	5	12	32	44	17	*Attendance:* 15,000
							Referee: M. A. Mann

The return against Albion within a week. Aberdeen win so comfortably that the loss of both points at Cliftonville appears inexcusable. Once McGregor had handed Emery a gift goal the result is never in doubt.

No 24 Saturday, 19 March
HEARTS (1) 1   ABERDEEN (0) 1
  Bauld (10)   Hather (85)

HEARTS: Brown, Mathieson, McKenzie, Whitehead, Dougan, Laing, McFarlane, Conn, Bauld, Wardhaugh, Flavell
ABERDEEN: Curran, Ancell, McKenna, McLaughlin, Roy, Waddell, Rice, Williams, Emery, Harris, Hather

P	W	D	L	F	A	Pts	
24	6	6	12	33	45	18	*Attendance:* 20,000
							Referee: R. G. Benzie

Hearts have already fought their way clear of the drop. Goalkeeper Curran keeps the Dons in the hunt. Hather's priceless late equaliser produces the fourth straight draw between the clubs.

No 25 Saturday, 26 March
QUEEN OF THE   ABERDEEN (0) 0
  SOUTH (0) 0

QUEEN OF THE SOUTH: Henderson, McColl, James, McBain, Aird, Hamilton, McCulloch, J. Brown, Houliston, Jenkins, Johnston
ABERDEEN: Curran, Ancell, McKenna, Stenhouse, Roy, Waddell, Rice, Williams, Harris, Pearson, Hather

P	W	D	L	F	A	Pts	
25	6	7	12	33	45	19	*Referee:* C. E. Faultless

Backs-to-the-wall Aberdeen earn another hard-earned point.

No 26 Saturday, 2 April
ABERDEEN (0) 0   MORTON (0) 0

ABERDEEN: Curran, Ancell, McKenna, Stenhouse, Roy, Waddell, Rice, Williams, Emery, Harris, Hather

MORTON: Cowan, Mitchell, Westwater, Wardlaw, Whigham, Gibson, Farquhar, Orr, Mochan, McGarrity, Liddell

Bottom positions

	P	W	D	L	F	A	Pts
12 Motherwell	25	8	4	13	36	40	20
13 ABERDEEN	26	6	8	12	33	45	20
14 Clyde	26	8	4	14	45	62	20
15 Morton	25	6	6	13	32	45	18
16 Albion R	25	3	2	20	26	88	8

Attendance: 20,000   *Referee:* W. Webb

A vital four-pointer in this, Aberdeen's final home fixture. There were no frills, no goals, and precious few chances for all Aberdeen's pressure.

No 27 Saturday, 9 April
CLYDE (0) 0   ABERDEEN (0) 0

CLYDE: Gullan, Gibson, Mennie, Campbell, Milligan, Long, Davies, Wright, Linwood, Galletly, Bootland
ABERDEEN: Curran, Ancell, McKenna, Stenhouse, Roy, Waddell, Rice, Williams, Hamilton, Harris, Hather

P	W	D	L	F	A	Pts	
27	6	9	12	33	45	21	*Referee:* R. G. Benzie

Another four-pointer and Aberdeen's third consecutive goalless draw. The match is a woeful spectacle. Aberdeen wanted both points in view of the coming trip to Ibrox.

No 28 Saturday, 16 April
RANGERS (0) 1   ABERDEEN (1) 1
  Duncanson (62)   Hather (17)

RANGERS: Brown, Young, Shaw, McColl, Woodburn, Cox, Waddell, Paton, Thornton, Duncanson, Rutherford
ABERDEEN: Curran, Ancell, McKenna, Stenhouse, Roy, Waddell, Pearson, Williams, Emery, Harris, Hather

Bottom positions

	P	W	D	L	F	A	Pts
13 Motherwell	27	9	4	14	41	46	22
14 Morton	28	7	8	13	39	49	22
15 ABERDEEN	28	6	10	12	34	46	22
16 Albion R	27	3	2	22	27	93	8

Attendance: 35,000   *Referee:* G. Mitchell

Both teams need the points for different reasons. Rangers are being closely pursued by Dundee at the top of the table. Aberdeen sensationally take the lead on the break. Williams' shot cannons back off the crossbar and Jackie Hather drives back the loose ball. Now it is over to young Curran in the Dons' goal. He makes a blinding save from Thornton. In the second half Roy's backpass is tragically short and Duncanson nips in to score. It was Roy's only mistake of the game. Waddell then cleared off the Dons' line and Curran saved from Paton to earn Aberdeen that precious point. Even so, with two games to play the Dons are still in the fatal 15th position.

No 29 Wednesday, 20 April
EAST FIFE (1) 1   ABERDEEN (2) 4
  Stewart (45)   Hamilton 3 (21, 42, 89),
                              Williams (76)

EAST FIFE: Niven, Laird, Stewart, Philp, Finlay, Hudson, Black, Fleming, Morris, Davidson, Brown
ABERDEEN: Curran, Ancell, McKenna, Stenhouse, Roy, Waddell, Hamilton, Williams, Emery, Harris, Pearson

P W D L F A Pts
29 7 10 12 38 47 24   *Referee:* A. Watt

East Fife, who wrecked Aberdeen's League Cup hopes last season, now virtually guarantee their survival in Division A. George Hamilton is the hero with a timely hat-trick to boost the Dons' goal average. Unless they lose by four goals to Motherwell, Aberdeen's safety is assured, at the expense of Clyde, who have finished their programme.

No 30 Saturday, 30 April
MOTHERWELL (1) 1   ABERDEEN (1) 1
  Watson (36)   Hamilton (28)

MOTHERWELL: Johnston, Kilmarnock, Sinclair, Russell, Paton, Redpath, Humphries, Watson, Mathie, Robertson, McCall
ABERDEEN: Curran, Ancell, McKenna, Stenhouse, Roy, Waddell, Rice, Williams, Emery, Hamilton, Pearson

Attendance: 8,000   *Referee:* J. A. Mowat

By the time of Aberdeen's last match, both they and Motherwell were mathematically safe, and Morton's fate was sealed. Consequently, the match had a holiday touch to it.

Aberdeen's complete home and away record:

HOME						AWAY						
P	W	D	L	F	A	W	D	L	F	A		Pts
30	5	4	6	26	26	2	7	6	13	22		25

Scottish League Division A 1948-49

	P	W	D	L	F	A	Pts
1 Rangers	30	20	6	4	63	32	46
2 Dundee	30	20	5	5	71	48	45
3 Hibernian	30	17	5	8	75	52	39
4 East Fife	30	16	3	11	64	46	35
5 Falkirk	30	12	8	10	70	54	32
6 Celtic	30	12	7	11	48	40	31
7 Third Lanark	30	13	5	12	56	52	31
8 Hearts	30	12	6	12	64	54	30
9 St Mirren	30	13	4	13	51	47	30
10 Queen of the South	30	11	8	11	47	53	30
11 Partick Thistle	30	9	9	12	50	63	27
12 Motherwell	30	10	5	15	44	49	25
13 ABERDEEN	30	7	11	12	39	48	25
14 Clyde	30	9	6	15	50	67	24
15 Morton	30	7	8	15	39	51	22
16 Albion Rovers	30	3	2	25	30	105	8

LEAGUE CUP

Saturday, 11 September
ABERDEEN (3) 3   ST MIRREN (0) 1
  Morris (15), Hamilton   Milne (49)
  2 (23, 43)

ABERDEEN: Johnstone, Massie, McKenna, McLaughlin, Thomson, Waddell, Williams, Stenhouse, Harris, Hamilton, Pearson
ST MIRREN: Miller, Smith, Drinkwater, Walter Reid, Telfer, Martin, Burrell, Stewart, Milne, William Reid, Telford

Attendance: 25,000   *Referee:* P. Fitzpatrick

Aberdeen introduce youngsters Massie and Thomson, who assist the Dons in handsomely avenging a recent league defeat.

Saturday, 18 September
THIRD LANARK (0) 1   ABERDEEN (0) 1
  McCulloch (72)   Williams (83)

THIRD LANARK: Petrie, Balunas, Kelly, Mooney, Harrower, Christie, Staroscik, Orr, McCulloch, Mason, Mitchell
ABERDEEN: Johnstone, McKenna, Emery, Waddell, Thomson, McLaughlin, Williams, Stenhouse, Harris, Hamilton, Pearson

Attendance: 17,000   *Referee:* G. MacDonald

Until the last seven minutes it looked like Aberdeen would suffer a replica scoreline to that on the opening day of the new season. The Dons twice hit the bar. The second time Williams swept home the rebound.

Saturday, 25 September
ABERDEEN (2) 3   MORTON (0) 1
  Hamilton 2 (11, 78),   Mochan (49)
  Stenhouse (16)

ABERDEEN: Johnstone, McKenna, Emery, Waddell, Thomson, McLaughlin, Williams, Stenhouse, Harris, Hamilton, Pearson
MORTON: Cowan, Mitchell, Fyfe, Campbell, Whigham, White, Alexander, Farquhar, Liddell, Orr, Mochan

Attendance: 20,000   *Referee:* G. Mitchell

Early Aberdeen frolics are replaced by second-half tension as Morton threaten to get back on terms.

Saturday, 2 October
ST MIRREN (0) 1   ABERDEEN (0) 1
  Drinkwater (88)   Harris (54)

ST MIRREN: Kirk, Smith, Drinkwater, Lapsley, Telfer, Martin, Burrell, Stewart, Milne, William Reid, Lesz
ABERDEEN: Johnstone, Massie, McKenna, Stenhouse, Thomson, Waddell, Millar, Hamilton, Harris, Kelly, Pearson

Attendance: 17,000   *Referee:* J. Jackson

Aberdeen fall back to protect Harris' second-half goal, despite having the wind in their favour. The lost point makes all the difference between qualifying and not qualifying.

Saturday, 9 October

ABERDEEN (1) 2   THIRD LANARK (1) 4
Pearson (11 pen), Harris   Ayton (8), Scott
(65)   2 (47, 62), Mitchell (52)

ABERDEEN: Johnstone, McKenna, Emery, Stenhouse, Thomson, Waddell, Williams, Hamilton, Harris, Smith, Pearson

THIRD LANARK: Petrie, Balunas, Kelly, Orr, Harrower, Mooney, Downs, Mason, Scott, Ayton, Mitchell

Attendance: 12,000   *Referee:* D. McKerchar

Skating over the slushy surface, slick Third Lanark are complete masters, crushing the Dons immediately after half-time.

Saturday, 16 October

MORTON (1) 3   ABERDEEN (1) 1
Mochan 2 (39, 47),   Harris (18)
Liddell (63)

MORTON: Cowan, Mitchell, Whigham, Campbell, Batton, Gibson, McKillop, Orr, Mochan, McGarrity, Liddell

ABERDEEN: Johnstone, Massie, McKenna, Stenhouse, Thomson, Waddell, Botha, Hamilton, Kelly, Harris, Pearson

Attendance: 15,000   *Referee:* J. A. Kerr

Aberdeen can only qualify if they gain a better result than St Mirren. Although the Saints lost at Cathkin, and the Dons take a priceless lead at Cappielow, Morton found a soft equaliser and thereafter Aberdeen 'fumbled footered and fiddled their way to defeat'.

Section D

	P	W	D	L	F	A	Pts
St Mirren	6	2	2	2	12	9	6
ABERDEEN	6	2	2	2	11	11	6
Third Lanark	6	2	2	2	12	13	6
Morton	6	2	2	2	9	11	6

SCOTTISH CUP

1st Round Saturday, 22 January

THIRD LANARK (1) 2   ABERDEEN (1) 1
McCulloch (43),   Hamilton (37)
Staroscik (80)

THIRD LANARK: Fraser, Balunas, Harrower, Orr, Barclay, Mooney, Henderson, Mason, McCulloch, Staroscik, Mitchell

ABERDEEN: Johnstone, McKenna, Ancell, Anderson, Thomson, Harris, Rice, Hamilton, Williams, Pearson, Hather

Attendance: 26,000   *Referee:* G. MacDonald

This is the fifth meeting of the sides this season, Aberdeen having lost two and drawn two in the league and League Cup. Understandably the Dons started out as underdogs. In depressing drizzle Hamilton gave the Dons a merited lead. Johnstone almost prevented McCulloch's equalising header, but the ball trickled over the line. Hather was floored within the penalty area without gaining a penalty before Staroscik clinched matters with a fierce half-volley.

1948-49

APPEARANCES	League	League Cup	Scottish Cup
McKenna	26	6	1
Williams	26	4	1
Harris	25	6	1
Waddell	25	6	
Hamilton	20	6	1
McLaughlin	19	3	
Stenhouse	17	6	
Rice	16		1
Pearson	15	6	1
Johnstone	15	6	1
Emery	15	3	
Ancell	15		1
Hather	14		1
Curran	14		
Roy	13		
Kelly	11	2	
Massie	8	3	
Anderson	7		1
Baird	7		
McVean	5		
Millar	4	1	
Glen	4		
Thomson	3	6	1
Kiddie	2		
Smith	1	1	
Gibson	1		
Preston	1		
Watson	1		
Botha		1	
29 players			

GOALS	Total	League	League Cup	Scottish Cup
Hamilton	15	10	4	1
Williams	7	6	1	
Kelly	6	6		
Emery	5	5		
Harris	5	1	4	
Hather	4	4		
Pearson	3	2	1	
Rice	2	2		
Glen	1	1		
Baird	1	1		
Kiddie	1	1		
Stenhouse	1		1	
Total	51	39	11	1

Season 1949-50

1949-50 was the season that till January looked to be heading nowhere; then looked to be heading for the stars – and finally ended up nowhere. Seldom can Aberden fans have suffered such conflicting hopes and fears. No blame could be heaped upon the players for failing to qualify from their League Cup group – which included Rangers, Celtic and St Mirren. But the league programme commenced with three home fixtures. When none were won it was evident that this was to be another barren season.

Come the New Year Aberdeen were still losing regularly, but then came a 4-0 crushing of high-flying Celtic and for the next two months Aberdeen carried all before them. In that time only one point was dropped in the league – away to champions-elect Rangers – and Aberdeen embarked on a glorious run in the Scottish Cup that saw them sweep past St Mirren, Hearts and Celtic – all well above them in the league. The Dons' season died in the quarter finals when, despite two bites at the cherry, they could not overcome a Queen of the South side on its way into Division B.

But for Queen of the South and Stirling Albion conveniently being adrift in the league, Aberdeen might well have suffered acute relegation blues. It was their goals-against column which was chiefly to blame for their problems. It had increased with each of the four post-war seasons, and was now not far short of two per game. Aberdeen misleadingly squeezed into the top half of the league, despite losing four matches more than they won.

> League: Eighth
> League Cup: Third in qualifying group
> Scottish Cup: Quarter Final

SCOTTISH LEAGUE DIVISION A

No 1 Saturday, 10 September

ABERDEEN (1) 2	ST MIRREN (2) 3
Emery (1 pen),	Lapsley (10 pen), Crowe
Kelly (68)	(30), Martin (88)

ABERDEEN: Curran, Emery, McKenna, Anderson, Roy, Harris, Kiddie, Yorston, Kelly, Smith, Pearson

ST MIRREN: Miller, Lapsley, Martin, Drinkwater, Telfer, Reid, Blyth, Deakin, Crowe, Davie, Lesz

P	W	D	L	F	A	Pts	
1	0	0	1	2	3	0	Referee: H. P. Anderson

Aberdeen had been fortunate to overcome Saints in the League Cup – and couldn't repeat the feat in the league, despite the assistance of a first-minute penalty. Full-back Martin, who conceded the award, made amends with his late strike deflected past Curran.

No 2 Saturday, 17 September

ABERDEEN (0) 1	CLYDE (1) 1
Stenhouse (53)	Davies (14)

ABERDEEN: Curran, Ashe, McKenna, Anderson, Roy, J. Chalmers, Millar, Stenhouse, Kelly, Harris, Pearson

CLYDE: Hewkins, Gibson, Deans, Campbell, Milligan, Long, Davies, Galletly, Linwood, Baird, Bootland

P	W	D	L	F	A	Pts	
2	0	1	1	3	4	1	Attendance: 18,000
							Referee: H. P. Anderson

The Dons gain their first point when Hewkins almost saves Stenhouse's shot – but not quite.

No 3 Saturday, 24 September

ABERDEEN (0) 2	DUNDEE (1) 2
Kelly 2 (75, 80)	Fraser (5), Rattray (83)

ABERDEEN: Curran, Emery, McKenna, Anderson, Roy, Harris, Millar, Stenhouse, Kelly, Hamilton, Pearson

DUNDEE: Lynch, Follon, Cowan, Gallagher, Cowie, Boyd, Gunn, Rattray, Fraser, Gerrie, Andrews

P	W	D	L	F	A	Pts	
3	0	2	1	5	6	2	Referee: W. Webb

Three home games: no wins – this record confirms the sort of season Aberdeen are about to experience. Aberdeen are handicapped by Curran's concussion and deprived of a victory by Rattray near the finish to preserve Dundee's unbeaten record.

No 4 Saturday, 1 October
HIBERNIAN (2) 2   ABERDEEN (0) 0
   Ormond (53),
   Turnbull (65)
HIBERNIAN: Younger, Shaw, Cairns, Gallagher, McNeil, Buchanan, McDonald, Johnstone, Turnbull, Combe, Ormond
ABERDEEN: Curran, Emery, McKenna, Anderson, Thomson, Harris, Millar, Hamilton, Kelly, Stenhouse, Pearson
Bottom positions

	P	W	D	L	F	A	Pts
14 Partick	3	1	0	2	5	7	2
15 ABERDEEN	4	0	2	2	5	8	2
16 Queen of the South	4	1	0	3	5	10	2

Attendance: 25,000   *Referee:* W. Davidson

Hibs are without Reilly and Govan – on duty for Scotland in Belfast; and Smith – unfit. Even so, Aberdeen are no better than a team of shreds and patches, and can have no complaints.

No 5 Saturday, 8 October
ABERDEEN (0) 2   THIRD LANARK (1) 1
   Yorston 2 (52, 61)   Cuthbertson (4)
ABERDEEN: Curran, Emery, McKenna, Anderson, Waddell, Harris, Rice, Hamilton, Kelly, Yorston, Hather
THIRD LANARK: Petrie, Balunas, Harrower, Orr, Christie, Mooney, Henderson, Mason, Baker, Cuthbertson, Staroscik

P	W	D	L	F	A	Pts
5	1	2	2	7	9	4

Attendance: 18,000   *Referee:* M. A. Mann

Aberdeen were put through the mill in the first half, especially by their ex-Hibs tormentor Johnny Cuthbertson. Harry Yorston gave the Dons the scent of their first league victory but it took Curran's brave save when Mason was clean through to secure it.

No 6 Saturday, 15 October
CELTIC (1) 4   ABERDEEN (1) 2
   Waddell o.g. (36),   Kelly (6), Rice (85)
   McPhail 2 (78, 90),
   Haughney (81)
CELTIC: Miller, Boden, Milne, Evans, McGrory, McAuley, Collins, McPhail, Haughney, Taylor, Tully
ABERDEEN: Curran, Emery, McKenna, Anderson, Waddell, Harris, Rice, Hamilton, Kelly, Yorston, Hather

P	W	D	L	F	A	Pts
6	1	2	3	9	13	4

Attendance: 30,000   *Referee:* J. Gaffney

Aberdeen had won praiseworthily at Parkhead in the League Cup. But now Celtic sit on top of the league and they are determined to remain there. They do so, but require three 'iffish' goals to do so. Kelly's quick opener for the Dons was cancelled by Waddell turning Collins' cross into his own goal. Twelve minutes from time McPhail put Celtic in front with a flick-shot that barely made contact, and Haughney was surely offside when

contributing the third home goal. Rice restored hope to Aberdeen, only for McPhail to emphatically seal the points when bulleting home Tully's lob.

No 7 Saturday, 22 October
CLYDE (0) 0   ABERDEEN (0) 1
                        Kelly (62)
CLYDE: Thomson, Gibson, Dunn, Campbell, Milligan, Haddock, Buchanan, Ackerman, Linwood, Long, McPhail
ABERDEEN: Curran, Emery, McKenna, Anderson, Waddell, Harris, Rice, Hamilton, Kelly, Yorston, Hather

P	W	D	L	F	A	Pts
7	2	2	3	10	13	6

Attendance: 15,000   *Referee:* W. Bowman

Third-placed Clyde are shocked when Kelly's shot hits a defender to deviate past Thomson.

No 8 Saturday, 29 October
ABERDEEN (0) 1   RANGERS (2) 3
   Hamilton (81)   McKenna o.g. (12),
                           Thornton (44),
                           Rutherford (60)
ABERDEEN: Curran, Emery, McKenna, Anderson, Waddell, Harris, Rice, Hamilton, Kelly, Yorston, Hather
RANGERS: Brown, Young, Shaw, McColl, Woodburn, Cox, Gillick, Findlay, Thornton, Williamson, Rutherford

P	W	D	L	F	A	Pts
8	2	2	4	11	16	6

Attendance: 40,000   *Referee:* J. R. Boyd

Rangers, with games in hand over the leaders, come to Pittodrie with a 100% league record. No points dropped: no goals conceded. The Rangers machine ground on relentlessly, abetted by an absurd goal after twelve minutes. Findlay crossed, Curran moved out to cover, and McKenna headed into his own, vacant, goal. McKenna soon compensated, heading another effort off the goalline – while lying on the ground. The game was safe for Rangers by the hour, but Hamilton smacked home a loose ball after three Dons' shots had been blocked to breach the 'Gers defence for the first time this season.

No 9 Saturday, 5 November
FALKIRK (1) 1   ABERDEEN (0) 0
   Kinloch (42)
FALKIRK: Nicol, Whyte, McPhee, Fiddes, Henderson, Kinloch, Brown, Reid, Inglis, Allison, McCue
ABERDEEN: Curran, Emery, McKenna, Anderson, Waddell, Harris, Hamilton, Yorston, Kelly, Baird, Hather

P	W	D	L	F	A	Pts
9	2	2	5	11	17	6

Attendance: 10,000   *Referee:* R. J. Smith

Aberdeen had the chances: Falkirk took the goal. The match was Archie Kelly's last for the Dons before being transferred to Motherwell.

No 10 Saturday, 12 November
ABERDEEN (2) 3   PARTICK THISTLE (1) 1
  Baird (10), Yorston   Davidson (33)
  2 (37, 69)
ABERDEEN: Curran, Emery, McKenna, Anderson,
Waddell, Harris, Pearson, Yorston, Hamilton, Baird,
Hather
PARTICK: Ledgerwood, McGowan, Gibb, Davidson,
Kinnell, Haddow, Thomson, Brown, Stott, Howitt,
Walker

P	W	D	L	F	A	Pts	
10	3	2	5	14	18	8	*Attendance:* 8,000
							Referee: C. Doig

Partick are bottom of the league and their performance
is as sodden as the pitch, they made the Dons look
good.

No 11 Saturday, 19 November
STIRLING ALBION (0) 0   ABERDEEN (1) 1
                         Hamilton (35)
STIRLING: Gerhard, Muir, McKeown, Bain,
Whiteford, Wilson, Dick, Keith, Jones, Martin, Szpula
ABERDEEN: Watson, Emery, McKenna, Anderson,
Waddell, Harris, Pearson, Yorston, Hamilton, Baird,
Hather

P	W	D	L	F	A	Pts	
11	4	2	5	15	18	10	*Attendance:* 15,000
							Referee: J. Oakes

Stirling are having a good start to the season, though
they will eventually finish bottom. Hamilton breaks
their hearts when prodding home the ball after Gerhard
had lost it. Whiteford threw away a point for Stirling,
hitting a post with a penalty.

No 12 Saturday, 26 November
ABERDEEN (2) 3   RAITH ROVERS (0) 0
  Hamilton 2 (9, 83),
  Hather (29)
ABERDEEN: Watson, Emery, McKenna, Anderson,
Waddell, Harris, Pearson, Yorston, Hamilton, Baird,
Hather
RAITH: McGregor, Kelly, McNaught, Till,
Woodcock, Brown, Goldie, Maule, Colville, Collins,
Penman

P	W	D	L	F	A	Pts	
12	5	2	5	18	18	12	*Attendance:* 16,000
							Referee: F. Scott

Raith have only one win to boast all season, and fail to
halt the Dons' revival. They are now 7th in the league
table.

No 13 Saturday, 3 December
HEARTS (2) 4   ABERDEEN (1) 1
  Conn 2 (41, 68),   Hather (32)
  Wardhaugh 2 (42, 87)
HEARTS: Brown, Parker, McKenzie, Cox, Dougan,
Laing, Sloan, Conn, Bauld, Wardhaugh, Flavell
ABERDEEN: Watson, Emery, McKenna, Anderson,
Waddell, Harris, Pearson, Yorston, Hamilton, Baird,
Hather

P	W	D	L	F	A	Pts	
13	5	2	6	19	22	12	*Attendance:* 23,000
							Referee: T. Shirley

Hearts are the League's highest scoring team, as
Aberdeen find out to their cost, once Hather had put
them in front. Hearts score four and miss countless
others.

No 14 Saturday, 10 December
QUEEN OF THE   ABERDEEN (0) 0
  SOUTH (0) 1
  Johnstone (70)
QUEEN OF THE SOUTH: Henderson, W. Brown,
James, McBain, Waldie, Hamilton, MacKinnon, Sharp,
Houliston, Neilson, Johnstone
ABERDEEN: Watson, Emery, McKenna, Anderson,
Waddell, Harris, Kiddie, Yorston, Hamilton, Baird,
Hather

P	W	D	L	F	A	Pts	
14	5	2	7	19	23	12	*Referee:* P. Fitzpatrick

Queen of the South languish in 15th position with only
twelve goals to show all season. Johnstone scored a
super thirteenth against a Dons' eleven who thought
they could win at a canter.

No 15 Saturday, 17 December
ABERDEEN (4) 5   MOTHERWELL (0) 0
  Yorston 2 (15, 38),
  Kiddie (23), Harris (34),
  Baird (73)
ABERDEEN: Watson, Emery, McKenna, Anderson,
Waddell, Baikie, Kiddie, Yorston, Harris, Baird,
Hather
MOTHERWELL: Hamilton, Kilmarnock, Higgins,
McLeod, Paton, Redpath, McCall, Watson, Kelly,
Bremner, Aitkenhead

P	W	D	L	F	A	Pts	
15	6	2	7	24	23	14	*Attendance:* 15,000
							Referee: D. McIntosh

Ex-Dons Willie McCall and Archie Kelly return to their
old stomping ground, only to find their new club swept
aside. Last week Motherwell crushed mighty Rangers
4-0. Today they are overwhelmed by shoot-on-sight
Dons.

No 16 Saturday, 24 December
ST MIRREN (1) 4   ABERDEEN (0) 0
  Henderson (40), Stewart
  (49), Burrell (72), Lapsley
  (74 pen)
ST MIRREN: Kirk, Lapsley, Martin, Gardiner, Telfer,
Reid, Burrell, Stewart, Henderson, Neilson, Lesz
ABERDEEN: Watson, Emery, McKenna, Anderson,
Thomson, Baikie, Kiddie, Yorston, Harris, Baird,
Hather

P	W	D	L	F	A	Pts	
16	6	2	8	24	27	14	*Referee:* D. McKerchar

Inconsistent as ever, Aberdeen fall apart in the second
half, to give Saints a happy Christmas.

No 17 Saturday, 31 December
ABERDEEN (1) 1   EAST FIFE (0) 2
  Yorston (4)   Duncan (72 pen),
                            Morris (78)
ABERDEEN: Watson, Emery, McKenna, Anderson,
Roy, Harris, Kiddie, Yorston, Hamilton, Baird, Hather
EAST FIFE: Niven, Laird, Stewart, Philip, Weir,
Aitken, Mackay, Aikman, Morris, Brown, Duncan

P W D L F A Pts   *Attendance:* 17,000
17 6 2 9 25 29 14   *Referee:* A. Watt

Last season four points off East Fife kept Aberdeen in
Division A. This time Aberdeen started off like
thoroughbreds and ended up like journeymen.

No 18 Monday, 2 January
DUNDEE (1) 1   ABERDEEN (1) 1
  Gerrie (21)   Pearson (36)
DUNDEE: Lynch, Massie, Ancell, Cowie, Pattillo,
Boyd, Gunn, Toner, Stewart, Gerrie, Hill
ABERDEEN: Watson, Emery, McKenna, Harris,
Anderson, Robb, Rice, Yorston, Hamilton, Baird,
Pearson

P W D L F A Pts
18 6 3 9 26 30 15   *Referee:* J. R. Boyd

Dundee are going well, take the moral honours from the
first half, but are stonewalled by the Dons in the
second.

No 19 Tuesday, 3 January
ABERDEEN (0) 0   HIBERNIAN (0) 3
                         Ormond (49), Smith
                         2 (80, 85)
ABERDEEN: Watson, Emery, McKenna, Harris,
Anderson, Robb, Rice, Yorston, Hamilton, McIntyre,
Pearson
HIBERNIAN: Younger, Shaw, Cairns, Combe,
Paterson, Buchanan, Smith, Johnstone, Reilly,
Turnbull, Ormond

P W D L F A Pts
19 6 3 10 26 33 15

Hibs retain their two-point lead at the top of the table.
Aberdeen more than hold their own during a goalless
first half. But when Ormond swept past McKenna, cut in
and scored a cool goal Hibs were always likely winners.
Smith and Ormond constantly had the beating of
McKenna and Emery. Although the season is only half
completed, David Halliday has now called upon 27
players in the search for an effective blend.

No 20 Saturday, 7 January
THIRD LANARK (1) 3   ABERDEEN (1) 1
  Cuthbertson 2 (12, 56),   Emery (28)
  Henderson (46 pen)
THIRD LANARK: McKellar, Balunas, Crawford,
Mooney, Christie, Harrower, Henderson, Mason,
Cuthbertson, Orr, McLeod
ABERDEEN: Watson, McKeown, McKenna, Harris,
Anderson, Robb, Yorston, Hamilton, Emery,
McIntyre, Pearson

P W D L F A Pts   *Attendance:* 12,000
20 6 3 11 27 36 15   *Referee:* J. A. Mowat

From the top to the bottom. Third Lanark are staring
up at the rest of the division but they still manage a
comprehensive win over disjointed Aberdeen. Only
three points separate the teams after the match.

No 21 Saturday, 14 January
ABERDEEN (2) 4   CELTIC (0) 0
  Baird (7), Pearson (12),
  Hather (55), Emery
  (90 pen)
ABERDEEN: Watson, Emery, McKenna, Anderson,
McKenzie, Harris, Hather, Yorston, Hamilton, Baird,
Pearson
CELTIC: Bonner, Boden, Mallan, Evans, McGrory,
Baillie, Collins, Taylor, Weir, McAuley, Tully

P W D L F A Pts   *Attendance:* 25,000
21 7 3 11 31 36 17   *Referee:* H. P. Anderson

Celtic have slipped down to fifth and are beaten out of
sight by an Aberdeen side so unpredictable as to be
infuriating.

No 22 Saturday, 4 February
RANGERS (2) 2   ABERDEEN (1) 2
  Young 2 (34 pen, 45 pen)   Hamilton (5),
                             Yorston (74)
RANGERS: Brown, Young, Shaw, McColl, Woodburn,
Cox, McCulloch, Findlay, Williamson, Johnston, Paton
ABERDEEN: Watson, Emery, McKenna, Anderson,
McKenzie, Harris, Stenhouse, Yorston, Hamilton,
Baird, Pearson

P W D L F A Pts   *Attendance:* 50,000
22 7 4 11 33 38 18   *Referee:* W. Davidson

A game of three penalties with Rangers, who are locked
in a titanic struggle with Hibs for the championship.
They have already taken five points from the Dons in
league and League Cup, but Hamilton's fifth-minute
piece of opportunism sparks a frantic Rangers
fightback. They level from a penalty when McKenna
was adjudged to have felled McKenzie, although
Watson got his hands to Young's spot kick. On the
stroke of half-time Harris unnecessarily handled and
Young despatched his second penalty. After the
resumption Woodburn presented Aberdeen with a
penalty of their own – only for Emery to direct the kick
straight at Brown. Emery's pain was alleviated within a
minute thanks to Yorston's equaliser; and Brown's
breathtaking save from Yorston earned Rangers their
point.

No 23 Saturday, 18 February
PARTICK THISTLE (0) 0   ABERDEEN (1) 2
                         Yorston (1),
                         Hamilton (87)
PARTICK: Henderson, Husband, Gibb, Thomson,
Kinnell, Hewitt, McCallum, Howitt, Stott, Sharp,
Walker

ABERDEEN: Watson, Emery, McKenna, Anderson, McKenzie, Harris, Stenhouse, Yorston, Hamilton, Baird, Pearson

P W D L F A Pts   *Attendance:* 25,000
23 8 4 11 35 38 20   *Referee:* J. B. Smillie

Aberdeen do the double over Partick. In addition to their two goals the Dons hit the Partick woodwork three times, Emery almost snapping the crossbar with a free kick.

No 24 Saturday, 4 March
RAITH ROVERS (1) 1   ABERDEEN (2) 2
   Emery o.g. (21)   Baird (1), Hamilton (26)
RAITH: Johnstone, McSpadyen, Young, Till, Colville, Leigh, Smith, Maule, McLaughlin, Collins, Penman
ABERDEEN: Watson, Emery, McKenna, Anderson, McKenzie, Harris, Stenhouse, Yorston, Hamilton, Baird, Pearson

P W D L F A Pts   *Attendance:* 10,000
24 9 4 11 37 39 22   *Referee:* F. Scott

Dons perform at half throttle to defeat struggling Raith, who are down to ten men for most of the game. In the dying minutes Raith hit the woodwork and Watson saved ex-Don McLaughlin's penalty.

No 25 Saturday, 18 March
ABERDEEN (0) 2   QUEEN OF SOUTH (0) 0
   Hamilton (64),
   Baird (77)
McKenzie, Harris, Stenhouse, Yorston, Hamilton, Baird, Pearson
QUEEN OF THE SOUTH: Henderson, Sharp, James, McBain, Waldie, Hamilton, Houliston, J. Brown, C. Brown, McAvoy, Johnston

P W D L F A Pts .   *Attendance:* 12,000
25 10 4 11 39 39 24   *Referee:* J. R. Boyd

Such is the unpredictability of football. Three days after losing a Scottish Cup replay at home to Queen of the South, Aberdeen turn the tables.

No 26 Saturday, 25 March
MOTHERWELL (1) 5   ABERDEEN (0) 1
   Watters (26), Kelly   Emery (78 pen)
   4 (46, 59, 63, 74)
MOTHERWELL: Hamilton, Kilmarnock, Shaw, McLeod, Paton, Redpath, Watters, Forrest, Kelly, Bremner, Aitkenhead
ABERDEEN: Watson, Emery, McKenna, Anderson, McKenzie, Harris, Stenhouse, Yorston, Hamilton, Baird, Pearson

P W D L F A Pts   *Attendance:* 7,000
26 10 4 12 40 44 24   *Referee:* J. Kerr

Aberdeen have nothing to play for – and it shows, despite their sending out an unchanged team for the tenth consecutive time. Ex-Don Kelly bags four.

No 27 Saturday, 1 April
ABERDEEN (0) 1   FALKIRK (1) 2
   Pearson (52)   Anderson (14), Brown
                    (89)
ABERDEEN: Watson, Emery, McKenna, Anderson, McKenzie, Robb, Stenhouse, Yorston, Hamilton, Baird, Pearson
FALKIRK: Nicol, Fiddes, Whitelaw, Gallacher, Henderson, McCabe, Souness, Wright, Plumb, Anderson, Brown

P W D L F A Pts   *Attendance:* 12,000
27 10 4 13 41 46 24   *Referee:* J. Kerr

Falkirk extend their winning sequence at Pittodrie to four – though it takes a last-minute strike to maintain that distinction.

No 28 Saturday, 8 April
ABERDEEN (0) 0   HEARTS (1) 5
                   Wardhaugh (33), Bauld
                   3 (49, 56, 63), Flavell
                   (73)
ABERDEEN: Watson, Emery, McKenna, Anderson, McKenzie, Harris, Hather, I. Rodger, Hamilton, Yorston, Pearson
HEARTS: Watters, Parker, McKenzie, Cox, Dougan, Laing, Sloan, Flavell, Bauld, Wardhaugh, Liddell

P W D L F A Pts   *Attendance:* 16,000
28 10 4 14 41 51 24   *Referee:* R. J. Smith

Hearts gain handsome revenge for the cup defeat at Pittodrie, despite Aberdeen's first-half dominance.

No 29 Friday, 14 April
EAST FIFE (0) 3   ABERDEEN (0) 1
   Fleming (51), Morris   Hather (82)
   (64), Martin o.g. (90)
EAST FIFE: Niven, Laird, Stewart, Philip, Finlay, Aitken, Black, Fleming, Morris, Brown, Duncan
ABERDEEN: Martin, McKeown, Emery, Bruce, McKenzie, Harris, Kiddie, I. Rodger, Hamilton, Glen, Hather

P W D L F A Pts
29 10 4 15 42 54 24   *Referee:* A. B. Geddie

A fine debut in goal for Fred Martin – until the last minute, when he catches a lob then drops it over the line.

No 30 Saturday, 22 April
ABERDEEN (4) 6   STIRLING ALBION (0) 2
   Hather 2 (12, 40),   Laird (78),
   Emery (16 pen),   Henderson (79)
   Yorston (37), Hamilton
   (65), Baird (74)
ABERDEEN: Martin, Bruce, Emery, Anderson, McKenzie, Harris, Rice, Yorston, Hamilton, Baird, Hather
STIRLING: Newman, Muir, Rodgers, Bain, Marshall, Guy, Millar, Martin, Laird, Keith, Henderson

Aberdeen round off the season with a party, but not for ex-Don Willie Millar, now with doomed Stirling.

Referee: J. Jackson

Aberdeen's complete home and away record:

HOME						AWAY					
P	W	D	L	F	A	W	D	L	F	A	Pts
30	7	2	6	33	25	4	2	9	15	31	26

Scottish League Division A 1949-50

		P	W	D	L	F	A	Pts
1	Rangers	30	22	6	2	58	26	50
2	Hibs	30	22	5	3	86	34	49
3	Hearts	30	20	3	7	86	40	43
4	East Fife	30	15	7	8	58	43	37
5	Celtic	30	14	7	9	51	50	35
6	Dundee	30	12	7	11	49	46	31
7	Partick	30	13	3	14	55	45	29
8	ABERDEEN	30	11	4	15	48	56	26
9	Raith Rovers	30	9	8	13	45	54	26
10	Motherwell	30	10	5	15	53	58	25
11	St Mirren	30	8	9	13	42	49	25
12	Third Lanark	30	11	3	16	43	62	25
13	Clyde	30	10	4	16	56	73	24
14	Falkirk	30	7	10	13	48	72	24
15	Queen of the South	30	5	6	19	31	63	16
16	Stirling Albion	30	6	3	21	38	77	15

LEAGUE CUP

Saturday, 13 August

ST MIRREN (2) 3   ABERDEEN (1) 1
 Lesz (30), Deakin (44),   Kelly (38)
 Burrell (84)

ST MIRREN: Kirk, Lapsley, Martin, Drinkwater, Telfer, Reid, Burrell, Davie, Crowe, Deakin, Lesz

ABERDEEN: Curran, Emery, McKenna, Anderson, McKenzie, Harris, Rice, Hamilton, Kelly, Glen, Pearson

Referee: A. Watt

Aberdeen line up without George Johnstone, Frank Dunlop and Stan Williams, all departed from Pittodrie for the new season. For an hour against St Mirren the Dons are reduced to nine men – Hamilton's leg injury and Glen's concussion taking them from the field.

Wednesday, 17 August

ABERDEEN (2) 4   CELTIC (3) 5
 Emery (1), Yorston (6),   Haughney 3 (3, 10, 16),
 Kelly (50), Harris (76)   Cousins (64), McPhail
                           (85)

ABERDEEN: Curran, Emery, McKenna, Anderson, McKenzie, Waddell, Rice, Yorston, Kelly, Harris, Pearson

CELTIC: Miller, McGuire, Baillie, Evans, Boden, McAuley, Collins, McPhail, Johnstone, Tully, Haughney

Attendance: 40,000   *Referee:* D. McKerchar

A match to savour – except for the result. After sixteen minutes' exhilarating play Celtic lead 3-2. It is 4-4 with only five minutes remaining when John McPhail scores

from a debatably offside position. With two League Cup matches played Aberdeen are almost out of contention.

Saturday, 20 August

RANGERS (2) 4   ABERDEEN (2) 2
 Findlay 2 (12, 62),   Harris (2), Emery (45)
 Duncanson 2 (23, 60),

RANGERS: Brown, Young, Shaw, McColl, Woodburn, Cox, Waddell, Findlay, Thornton, Duncanson, Rutherford

ABERDEEN: Curran, Emery, McKenna, Anderson, McKenzie, Waddell, Rice, Yorston, Kelly, Harris, Pearson

Attendance: 50,000   *Referee:* W. Davidson

Aberdeen's first-minute goal against Celtic is followed by a second-minute goal against Rangers. Again the Dons can't capitalise on their lead. Two home goals on the hour finally break Aberdeen's resistance.

Saturday, 27 August

ABERDEEN (1) 1   ST MIRREN (0) 0
 Yorston (22)

ABERDEEN: Curran, Emery, McKenna, Anderson, Roy, Harris, Kiddie, Yorston, Kelly, Glen, Pearson

ST MIRREN: Miller, Lapsley, Martin, Cowie, Telfer, Reid, Drinkwater, Stewart, Milne, Deakin, Lesz

Attendance: 22,000   *Referee:* P. Fitzpatrick

Yorston claimed the goal, but then it was all St Mirren – especially in the nervous closing minutes.

Wednesday, 31 August

CELTIC (1) 1   ABERDEEN (3) 3
 Haughney (5)   Pearson (10), Kelly (15),
                       Yorston (34)

CELTIC: Miller, Mallan, Baillie, Evans, Boden, McAuley, Collins, McPhail, Haughney, Peacock, Tully

ABERDEEN: Curran, Emery, McKenna, Anderson, Roy, Harris, Kiddie, Yorston, Kelly, Smith, Pearson

Against Celtic the Dons showed everything they lacked against St Mirren – punch, pep and personality.

Saturday, 3 September

ABERDEEN (0) 1   RANGERS (0) 1
 Emery (55)   Findlay (75)

ABERDEEN: Curran, Emery, McKenna, Anderson, Roy, Harris, Kiddie, Yorston, Kelly, Smith, Pearson

RANGERS: Brown, Young, Shaw, McColl, Woodburn, Cox, Waddell, Findlay, Williamson, Gillick, Duncanson

Attendance: 43,000   *Referee:* G. Mitchell

Rangers were already sure of qualifying, so that the game had no real significance. Nevertheless, 43,000 rolled up to witness a game that became a minor classic. Emery's explosive free kick opened the way. Waddell struck the Dons' bar before Findlay ran on unchallenged for the equaliser.

Section A

	P	W	D	L	F	A	Pts
Rangers	6	3	2	1	15	8	8
Celtic	6	3	0	3	13	13	6
ABERDEEN	6	2	1	3	12	14	5
St Mirren	6	2	1	3	7	12	5

SCOTTISH CUP

1st Round Saturday, 28 January
ST MIRREN (0) 1   ABERDEEN (1) 2
  Stewart (49)   Yorston 2 (1, 50)
ST MIRREN: Kirk, Lapsley, Martin, Drinkwater,
Telfer, Reid, Burrell, Stewart, Henderson, Blyth, Lesz
ABERDEEN: Watson, Emery, McKenna, Anderson,
McKenzie, Harris, Stenhouse, Yorston, Hamilton,
Baird, Pearson

Attendance: 20,000   *Referee: J. S. Cox*

This is the fifth meeting between the clubs; league and
League Cup clashes resulting in two wins apiece. On a
hard pitch Aberdeen turn out in rubber soles and are on
their way to victory from the moment Yorston gives
them an instant lead.

2nd Round Saturday, 11 February
ABERDEEN (2) 3   HEARTS (0) 1
  Emery (8 pen), Pearson   McKenna o.g. (7)
  (21), Hamilton (58)
ABERDEEN: Watson, Emery, McKenna, Anderson,
McKenzie, Harris, Stenhouse, Yorston, Hamilton,
Baird, Pearson
HEARTS: Brown, Parker, McKenzie, Curran,
Dougan, Laing, Sloan, Conn, Bauld, Wardhaugh,
Flavell

Attendance: 42,000   *Referee: W. Davidson*

In a stunning opening McKenna misconnects in trying
to clear Wardhaugh's centre and loops the ball over
Watson's head. In an instant Pearson's cross to the back
post comes back off the wood and McKenzie sticks out
his hand. Don Emery takes his third penalty in recent
games and blasts the ball beyond Brown. A Pearson
screamer then puts Aberdeen in front. A Flavell
'equaliser' is annulled for offside, and Hamilton takes
the Dons into the third round when Baird's header flies
back off a post to his feet. An all-ticket crowd left the
stadium in high spirits.

3rd Round Saturday, 25 February
CELTIC (0) 0   ABERDEEN (1) 1
       Anderson (35)
CELTIC: Bonner, Boden, McAuley, Evans, McGrory,
Baillie, Collins, McPhail, Weir, Tully, Rennet
ABERDEEN: Watson, Emery, McKenna, Anderson,
McKenzie, Harris, Stenhouse, Yorston, Hamilton,
Baird, Pearson

Attendance: 65,000   *Referee: J. R. Boyd*

Two wins each from their league and League Cup
engagements make the outcome of this third-round cup-
tie difficult to predict. Celtic are the first to settle.

McPhail scores but is given offside. Collins' inswinging
corner then bounces off the face of the Dons' bar. On a
counter-attack Aberdeen take the lead with Anderson's
shot on the turn from twenty yards. In the second half
it is the turn of full-back Boden to strike the Dons'
crossbar. Aberdeen hang on bravely to the finish.

Quarter Final Saturday, 11 March
QUEEN OF THE   ABERDEEN (3) 3
  SOUTH (1) 3   Yorston 2 (4, 13),
  McAvoy 2 (31, 82),   Pearson (16)
  McBain (80)
QUEEN OF THE SOUTH: Henderson, Sharp, James,
McBain, Waldie, Hamilton, Houliston, J. Brown,
C. Brown, McAvoy, Johnstone
ABERDEEN: Watson, Emery, McKenna, Anderson,
McKenzie, Harris, Stenhouse, Yorston, Hamilton,
Baird, Pearson

Referee: W. Davidson

After three cup-ties against the division's leading lights
Aberdeen are now drawn away to doomed Queen of the
South. The Dons are being widely tipped to lift the
trophy — even though they lost on their league trip to
Dumfries. After sixteen minutes everything seemed to
be wrapped up. Aberdeen led 3-0 and the game was
theirs for the taking. With ten minutes to play they still
led 3-1 yet conspicuously lost their concentration.
McBain and McAvoy made them pay for their
complacency, and dulled Aberdeen's achievement of
eight league and cup games without defeat.

Quarter Final Replay Wednesday, 15 March
ABERDEEN (1) 1   QUEEN OF SOUTH (0) 2
  Hamilton (27)   Houliston (80),
       Johnstone (82)
ABERDEEN: Watson, Emery, McKenna, Anderson,
McKenzie, Harris, Stenhouse, Yorston, Hamilton,
Baird, Pearson
QUEEN OF THE SOUTH: Henderson, Sharp, James,
McBain, Waldie, Hamilton, Houliston, J. Brown,
C. Brown, McAvoy, Johnstone

Attendance: 32,000   *Referee: W. Davidson*

'Never say die', announced the fighters from Queen of
the South. Two unchanged sides resumed their battle.
As at Dumfries, Aberdeen are well in control. Baird
nods on Emery's free kick for Hamilton to put the Dons
in front. And so it stays until the fateful 80th minute.
Aberdeen, tense at the memory of Saturday's
turnaround, promptly offered a repeat performance.
What St Mirren, Hearts and Celtic couldn't do, Queen
of the South could. It would be no consolation when
three days later Queens returned to Pittodrie desperate
for league points. This time Aberdeen won 2-0.

1949-50

APPEARANCES	League	League Cup	Scottish Cup
Anderson	29	6	5
Emery	29	6	5
Harris	29	6	5
McKenna	28	6	5
Yorston	26	5	5
Hamilton	26	1	5
Pearson	19	6	5
Baird	18		5
Watson	18		5
Hather	17		
Waddell	11	2	
McKenzie	10	3	5
Curran	10	6	
Kelly	9	6	
Stenhouse	9		5
Rice	7	3	
Kiddie	6	3	
Roy	4	3	
Robb	4		
Millar	3		
Baikie	2		
Bruce	2		
Martin	2		
McKeown	2		
McIntyre	2		

1949-50

APPEARANCES	League	League Cup	Scottish Cup
Rodger	2		
Thomson	2		
Glen	1	2	
Smith	1	2	
Ashe	1		
Chalmers	1		
31 players			

GOALS	Total	League	League Cup	Scottish Cup
Yorston	17	10	3	4
Hamilton	11	9		2
Emery	9	5	3	1
Kelly	8	5	3	
Baird	6	6		
Pearson	6	3	1	2
Hather	5	5		
Harris	3	1	2	
Kiddie	1	1		
Rice	1	1		
Stenhouse	1	1		
Anderson	1			1
own-goals	1	1		
Total	69	48	12	10

A team group from the early fifties.
Back row: Harris, Baird, Young, Martin, Anderson, Emery. Front row: Hather, Hamilton, D. Shaw, Yorston, Boyd.

Season 1950-51

1950-51 was Aberdeen's most profitable season since 1946-47. In the league they were up with the leaders all season, and in the space of a frenetic 24 hours in the New Year programme saw off leaders Dundee at Pittodrie, only to receive a 6-2 thumping by champions-elect Hibs the following day. Later in January Aberdeen briefly touched top-spot before being swept aside by an Easter Road outfit which went on to take the title by a clear ten points. Disappointingly, Celtic put paid to Aberdeen's Scottish Cup hopes, and the season ended in anti-climax as the Dons slipped down to fifth place in the league.

Nevertheless, 1950-51 is remembered for several notable matches. Principally they concerned Rangers and Hibernian. Before the season was ten weeks old the 'Gers had been beaten three times in succession – twice at Ibrox – by the spirited Dons. The League Cup encounters with Hibs still rank amongst the most stirring of post-war memories. At the end of 210 minutes of relentless endeavour in the quarter final the aggregate scores were locked together at 5-5. A reply at Ibrox failed to break the deadlock. A second replay was necessary, at Hampden, before Hibs finally crushed the Dons' resistance.

Once again it was Aberdeen's porous defence which hampered their bid for honours. Fifty league goals were conceded, a far higher number than any other championship contender. All but three of the fifteen league visitors to Pittodrie found the net at least once. Encouragingly, the Dons' 61 league goals were their highest tally since the War – and their away record also surpassed anything since 1945.

League: Fifth
League Cup: Quarter Final
Scottish Cup: Quarter Final

SCOTTISH LEAGUE DIVISION A

No 1 Saturday, 9 September
AIRDRIEONIANS (0) 2   ABERDEEN (4) 5
  McMillan (47 pen),   Hamilton (6), Yorston
  Kelly (90)   3 (9, 26, 41), Hather (79)
AIRDRIE: McArthur, Hinshelwood, Kelly, Docherty, Dingwall, Knox, Duncan, McMillan, Bannan, Cairns, Seawright
ABERDEEN: Martin, Emery, Shaw, Anderson, Young, Harris, Boyd, Yorston, Hamilton, Baird, Hather

P W D L F A Pts   Attendance: 8,000
1 1 0 0 5 2 2   Referee: J. R. Boyd

Aberdeen continue their impressive League Cup form by overrunning Airdrie.

No 2 Saturday, 23 September
DUNDEE (0) 2   ABERDEEN (0) 0
  Steel (72), Toner (84)
DUNDEE: Brown, Follon, Cowan, Gallacher, Cowie, Boyd, Gunn, Toner, Williams, Steel, Andrews
ABERDEEN: Martin, McKenna, Shaw, Bruce, Thomson, Baikie, Boyd, Yorston, Hamilton, Baird, Hather

P W D L F A Pts   Attendance: 30,000
2 1 0 1 5 4 2   Referee: W. G. Livingstone

Dundee parade their new signing, £23,000 worth of Billy Steel from Derby County, and his acquisition pushes the gate up to 30,000. Two unbeaten teams give their all, but Steel scores on his debut to deflate the Dons.

No 3 Saturday, 30 September
ABERDEEN (1) 2   HIBERNIAN (1) 1
  Pearson (27),   Turnbull (1)
  Hamilton (55)
ABERDEEN: Martin, Emery, Shaw, Anderson, Young, Glen, Boyd, Yorston, Hamilton, Baird, Pearson
HIBERNIAN: Younger, Govan, Ogilvie, Howie, Paterson, Combe, Smith, Johnstone, Reilly, Turnbull, Ormond

P W D L F A Pts   Attendance: 15,000
3 2 0 1 7 5 4   Referee: J. F. Fox

With a League Cup quarter-final replay looming on Monday Aberdeen gain the ideal confidence booster, shrugging off Turnbull's first-minute strike.

No 4 Saturday, 7 October
ST MIRREN (0) 4   ABERDEEN (1) 2
  Drinkwater (60), Reid   Hather (20), Boyd (51)
  (68), Rennie (77), Blyth
  (84)
ST MIRREN: Kirk, Lapsley, Drinkwater, Reid, Telfer, Johnston, Blyth, Neilson, Rennie, Stewart, Ritchie
ABERDEEN: Martin, Emery, Shaw, Harris, Thomson, Glen, Boyd, Yorston, Hamilton, Baird, Hather

P	W	D	L	F	A	Pts	
4	2	0	2	9	9	4	*Attendance:* 10,000
							Referee: A. B. Gebbie

Aberdeen are still crestfallen after losing their marathon League Cup quarter-final with Hibs. Despite being 2-0 ahead they fell apart in the final stages.

No 5 Saturday, 14 October
ABERDEEN (0) 2   CELTIC (0) 1
  Hamilton 2 (75, 84)   McPhail (89)
ABERDEEN: Martin, Emery, Shaw, Anderson, Young, Glen, Boyd, Yorston, Hamilton, Baird, Hather
CELTIC: Bonner, Fallon, Milne, Evans, Mallan, Baillie, Collins, D. Weir, McPhail, Peacock, Tully

P	W	D	L	F	A	Pts	
5	3	0	2	11	10	6	*Attendance:* 30,000
							Referee: G. Mitchell

Celtic look like leaving with a fortuitous draw until Hamilton glanced a Yorston shot into the net to send the Dons on their way – Hather had earlier hit a post.

No 6 Saturday, 21 October
ABERDEEN (3) 5   CLYDE (2) 3
  Boyd (18), Baird (32),   Buchanan 2 (10, 33),
  Yorston 2 (44, 52),   Ring (63)
  Hather (74)
ABERDEEN: Martin, Emery, Shaw, Anderson, Young, Glen, Boyd, Yorston, Hamilton, Baird, Hather
CLYDE: Allan, Lindsay, Mennie, Campbell, Milligan, Long, Davies, Bolton, Buchanan, McPhail, Ring

P	W	D	L	F	A	Pts	
6	4	0	2	16	13	8	*Attendance:* 15,000
							Referee: R. J. Smith

When Clyde visited Pittodrie in the League Cup the Dons won 4-3. Aberdeen go one better in a thriller packed with fluctuating fortunes. Martin saved a second-half Campbell penalty with the score at 4-2.

No 7 Saturday, 28 October
RANGERS (0) 1   ABERDEEN (1) 2
  Thornton (47)   Boyd (12), Yorston (83)
RANGERS: Brown, Young, Shaw, McColl, Woodburn, Rae, Waddell, Paton, Simpson, Thornton, Rutherford
ABERDEEN: Martin, Emery, Shaw, Anderson, Young, Glen, Boyd, Yorsten, Hamilton, Baird, Hather
Leading positions

	P	W	D	L	F	A	Pts	
1 Dundee	8	5	2	1	12	6	12	
2 Hearts	8	5	1	2	17	10	11	
3 Morton	8	5	1	2	19	13	11	
4 ABERDEEN	7	5	0	2	18	14	10	

Attendance: 50,000   *Referee:* H. Phillips

Who would have believed it? Aberdeen's third victory of the season over the champions establishes a Dons' record. Boyd's screaming first-timer set them on their way, and when Martin saved his second penalty in consecutive weeks – this one from Waddell – there was no holding the Dons. On the resumption Thornton's header just eluded the desperate lunges of Martin and Young. But Aberdeen had the last laugh. Hather drove against the post, and seven minutes from time Yorston headed the winner from close range. At the death Thornton's 'equalising' header was ruled offside, much to Rangers' chagrin.

No 8 Saturday, 4 November
ABERDEEN (1) 1   THIRD LANARK (0) 2
  Hamilton (36)   Goddall (58),
                              Staroscik (80)
ABERDEEN: Martin, Emery, Shaw, Anderson, Young, Glen, Boyd, Yorston, Hamilton, Baird, Hather
THIRD LANARK: Simpson, Balunas, Harrower, Adams, Samuels, Orr, Goodall, Mason, Mitchell, Dick, Staroscik

P	W	D	L	F	A	Pts	
8	5	0	3	19	16	10	*Attendance:* 17,000
							Referee: H. Anderson

What a let-down. At half-time Aberdeen looked set for two more points. But they played the second period minus the injured Glen and Third Lanark stole two goals.

No 9 Saturday, 11 November
PARTICK THISTLE (1) 1   ABERDEEN (3) 4
  Stott (41)   Gibb o.g. (3), Anderson
                              (37), Yorston 2 (40, 75)
PARTICK: Ledgerwood, McGowan, Gibb, Davidson, Kinnel, Sharp, McKenzie, McCallum, Stott, O'Donnell, Walker
ABERDEEN: Martin, Emery, Shaw, Anderson, Young, Harris, Boyd, Yorston, Hamilton, Baird, Pearson

P	W	D	L	F	A	Pts	
9	6	0	3	23	17	12	*Attendance:* 10,000
							Referee: H. Phillips

Partick's Gibb, trying to hook the ball for a corner, scores a gem of an own goal, and Aberdeen don't look back. A few days later Aberdeen sign the veteran Jimmy Delaney from Manchester United, recent visitors to Pittodrie in a friendly.

No 10 Saturday, 18 November
ABERDEEN (2) 5   FALKIRK (0) 1
  Baird (3), Hamilton   Johnson (72)
  4 (44, 52, 59, 64)
ABERDEEN: Martin, Emery, McKenna, Anderson, Young, Harris, Delaney, Yorston, Hamilton, Baird, Pearson

FALKIRK: Barrie, Fiddes, Wilson, Gallacher, Henderson, Whitelaw, Morrison, Wright, Johnson, Lennon, Brown

Leading positions

	P	W	D	L	F	A	Pts
1 Dundee	11	6	3	2	13	8	15
2 ABERDEEN	10	7	0	3	28	18	14
3 Hearts	11	6	2	3	26	19	14
4 Morton	11	6	2	3	24	18	14

Attendance: 20,000   *Referee:* J. Jackson

At last! At the fifth attempt Aberdeen manage to avoid defeat at home by bogey-team Falkirk. Jimmy Delaney has a useful debut, manufacturing two goals and George Hamilton helps himself to four.

No 11 Saturday, 25 November
RAITH ROVERS (1) 1   ABERDEEN (0) 0
   Collins (24)

RAITH: Johnstone, McClure, McNaught, McLaughlin, Colville, Leigh, McIlhatton, Maule, Young, Collins, Brander

ABERDEEN: Martin, Emery, McKenna, Anderson, Young, Harris, Delaney, Yorston, Hamilton, Baird, Pearson

P	W	D	L	F	A	Pts	
11	7	0	4	28	19	14	*Attendance:* 15,000

Referee: W. Davidson

Lacklustre Dons get off lightly. Colville wastes a penalty when Emery blocks Young, and Collins likewise hits a post.

No 12 Saturday, 2 December
ABERDEEN (1) 2   HEARTS (0) 0
   Yorston 2 (23, 58)

ABERDEEN: Martin, Emery, McKenna, Anderson, Young, Harris, Delaney, Yorston, Hamilton, Baird, Pearson

HEARTS: Brown, Parker, McKenzie, Cox, Dougan, Laing, Sloan, Conn, Bauld, Wardhaugh, Williams

P	W	D	L	F	A	Pts	
12	8	0	4	30	19	16	*Attendance:* 20,000

Referee: W. Livingstone

4th place Aberdeen versus 2nd place Hearts, and it's the Dons who come out on top. In treacherous conditions Aberdeen benefit from Hearts' first-half squandermania. Yorston then decides to give some shooting lessons.

No 13 Saturday, 9 December
ABERDEEN (3) 4   MOTHERWELL (1) 2
   Hamilton (4), Baird (15),   Aitkenhead (44 pen),
   Emery (17 pen), Yorston   Kelly (68)
   (75)

ABERDEEN: Martin, Emery, McKenna, Anderson, Young, Glen, Delaney, Yorston, Hamilton, Baird, Hather

MOTHERWELL: Johnston, Kilmarnock, Shaw, McLeod, Paton, Redpath, Watters, Forrest, Kelly, Watson, Aitkenhead

P	W	D	L	F	A	Pts	
13	9	0	4	34	21	18	*Attendance:* 20,000

Referee: D. McKerchar

Aberdeen are already the league's leading scorers, and on this performance it is easy to see why.

No 14 Saturday, 16 December
MORTON (0) 1   ABERDEEN (2) 2
   McGarrity (49)   Emery (1 pen), Baird (7)

MORTON: Cowan, Mitchell, Whigham, Boyd, Thom, Whyte, McGarrity, Gourlay, Mochan, Orr, McVinish

ABERDEEN: Martin, Emery, McKenna, Anderson, Young, Harris, Delaney, Yorston, Hamilton, Baird, Pearson

P	W	D	L	F	A	Pts	
14	10	0	4	36	22	20	*Referee:* J. Jackson

The pitch was more suitable for curling, but Aberdeen notch up their fifth win in six games, helped by a soft penalty award in the first minute.

No 15 Saturday, 23 December
ABERDEEN (1) 1   AIRDRIEONIANS (1) 1
   Hamilton (21)   McCulloch (32)

ABERDEEN: Martin, Emery, McKenna, Anderson, Young, Harris, Delaney, Yorston, Hamilton, Baird, Pearson

AIRDRIE: Fraser, Cosh, Elliott, Cairns, Kelly, Shankland, Picken, Docherty, McGurn, Welsh, McCulloch

P	W	D	L	F	A	Pts	
15	10	1	4	37	23	21	*Attendance:* 15,000

Referee: D. McIntosh

The Dons' toss away a priceless point to last-placed Airdrie. Once McCulloch had equalised Airdrie hung on gallantly, Baird hammers the ball on to a post, Hamilton lashes at the rebound and Fraser pushes the ball back on to the post.

No 16 Saturday, 30 December
EAST FIFE (0) 0   ABERDEEN (0) 0

EAST FIFE: Easson, Proudfoot, Stewart, Philp, Finlay, McLennan, Black, Fleming, Morris, Bonthrone, Duncan

ABERDEEN: Martin, Shaw, McKenna, Anderson, Young, Harris, Delaney, Yorston, Hamilton, Baird, Hather

P	W	D	L	F	A	Pts	
16	10	2	4	37	23	22	*Attendance:* 10,000

Referee: J. Brown

Neither side can settle on the ice-bound pitch, and Aberdeen once again forfeit a point to a struggling side.

No 17 Monday, 1 January
ABERDEEN (0) 1   DUNDEE (0) 0
   Hamilton (88)

ABERDEEN: Curran, Shaw, McKenna, Anderson, Young, Harris, Delaney, Yorston, Hamilton, Baird, Hather

DUNDEE: Lynch, Follon, Cowan, Irvine, Cowie, Boyd, Hill, Pattillo, Williams, Steel, Christie

Leading positions

	P	W	D	L	F	A	Pts
1 Dundee	18	10	4	4	27	13	24
2 ABERDEEN	17	11	2	4	38	23	24
3 Hearts	18	9	4	5	36	29	22
4 Hibs	14	10	1	3	37	12	21

Attendance: 30,000   *Referee:* R. J. Smith

Dundee lead the Dons by two points as they come north for what promises to be one of the matches of the season. Fred Martin couldn't keep goal, injuring his wrist at Methil. Aberdeen had the edge – against the wind – in the first half: Dundee were equally impressive after half-time. Dundee deserved a draw, but were denied it by Hamilton's conversion of Delaney's corner kick. Now only goal average separates the sides, but Aberdeen have a game in hand. Unfortunately Hibs have four.

No 18 Saturday, 2 January

HIBERNIAN (2) 6   ABERDEEN (2) 2
  Johnstone 2 (12, 62),   Hamilton (6), Pearson
  Reilly 2 (35, 47), Smith   (20)
  (55), Wood (57)

HIBERNIAN: Younger, Howie, Ogilvie, Buchanan, Paterson, Combe, Smith, Johnstone, Reilly, Wood, Ormond

ABERDEEN: Curran, Shaw, McKenna, Anderson, Thomson, Harris, Delaney, Yorston, Hamilton, Baird, Pearson

P	W	D	L	F	A	Pts
18	11	2	5	40	29	24

Attendance: 35,000   *Referee:* D. McKerchar

Hibs are coming up strongly on the rails. This is the sixth meeting of the sides, the tally standing at two wins and a draw apiece. But the match is anything but close. Hibs repeat the thrashing handed out at Hampden in the League Cup. Twice Aberdeen took the lead before half-time, and twice Hibs responded. It took the Easter Road club only 17 minutes of the second half to bang in another four and put Aberdeen to the sword.

No 19 Saturday, 6 January

ABERDEEN (1) 1   ST MIRREN (1) 1
  McNeill (20)   Stewart (36)

ABERDEEN: Curran, Emery, Shaw, Anderson, Young, Harris, Delaney, Yorston, Hamilton, McNeill, McMillan

ST MIRREN: Kirk, Lapsley, Cunningham, Neilson, Telfer, Johnston, Kiernan, Stewart, Graham, Duncanson, Ritchie

P	W	D	L	F	A	Pts
19	11	3	5	41	30	25

Attendance: 15,000   *Referee:* R. M. Main

Shell-shocked Aberdeen can't even fend off relegation-haunted St Mirren. This proves to be Curran's last match for the Dons before he is transferred to East Fife in February.

No 20 Saturday, 13 January

CELTIC (2) 3   ABERDEEN (1) 4
  Collins (12 pen),   Yorston (24), Tully o.g.
  Anderson o.g. (16),   (61), Mallan o.g. (67),
  Tully (80)   Emery (79 pen)

CELTIC: Bonner, Fallon, Rollo, Evans, Mallan, Baillie, Weir, Collins, McAlinden, Peacock, Tully

ABERDEEN: Watson, Emery, Shaw, Anderson, Young, Harris, Delaney, Yorston, Hamilton, Baird, Pearson

P	W	D	L	F	A	Pts
20	12	3	5	45	33	27

Attendance: 45,000   *Referee:* A. B. Gebbie

Celtic are on the fringe of the championship race, though they will fade away by the season's end. With this win Aberdeen make it four wins out of four against the Old Firm in league and League Cup. Goals are cheap at Parkhead. Three were deflected and another arrived from a penalty. Celtic got off to a rattling start. Harris conceded a penalty from which Collins scored, and Anderson put through his own net. Yorston required no help with his goal, but both Emery and Delaney did. Emery's free kick was stabbed into goal off a post by Tully, and Delaney's shot was deflected by Mallan. These goals came when Celtic were reduced to ten men by an injury to McAlinden. When Hamilton was pulled down, Emery's penalty gave the Dons their fourth, but Tully immediately put Celtic back into contention to leave Aberdeen hanging on nervously for the final ten minutes.

No 21 Saturday, 20 January

CLYDE (0) 0   ABERDEEN (2) 2
          Hamilton (11), Yorston
          (26)

CLYDE: Millar, Lindsay, Mennie, Campbell, Somerville, Long, Davies, McPhail, Linwood, Robertson, Ring

ABERDEEN: Watson, Emery, McKenna, Stenhouse, Young, Harris, Delaney, Yorston, Hamilton, Baird, Pearson

Leading positions

	P	W	D	L	F	A	Pts
1 ABERDEEN	21	13	3	5	47	33	29
2 Hibs	18	13	2	3	50	17	28
3 Dundee	21	12	4	5	33	17	28

Attendance: 10,000   *Referee:* J. R. Boyd

Aberdeen avenge a League Cup defeat at Shawfield to go top of the league for the first time this season. But look out for Hibs. Long missed a penalty for Clyde at 1-0.

No 22 Saturday, 3 February

ABERDEEN (1) 2   RANGERS (2) 4
  Pearson (18),   Paton (3), Thornton
  Yorston (53)   2 (23, 83), Simpson (62)

ABERDEEN: Watson, Emery, Shaw, Anderson, Young, Harris, Delaney, Yorston, Hamilton, Baird, Pearson

RANGERS: Brown, Young, Shaw, Cox, Woodburn, Rae, Waddell, Findlay, Simpson, Thornton, Paton

P	W	D	L	F	A	Pts
22	13	3	6	49	37	29

Attendance: 42,000   *Referee:* R. Yacamini

At last Rangers get their own back – at the fourth attempt. Twice Rangers went in front, and twice the Dons levelled. On pressure Aberdeen deserved to be in front, but Simpson and Thornton finally put the game beyond their reach. Hibs leapfrog over Aberdeen at the top of the league, and it is clear where the Dons' problems lie. Despite their league position they have conceded more goals than all but four other teams.

No 23 Saturday, 17 February
ABERDEEN (3) 4   PARTICK THISTLE (1) 1
  Yorston 2 (11, 23),   Walker (34)
  Delaney (27), Hamilton
  (83)
ABERDEEN: Martin, Emery, Shaw, O'Neil, Young, Harris, Delaney, Yorston, Hamilton, McNeill, Pearson
PARTICK: Ledgerwood, Brown, Gibb, Thomson, Forsyth, Davidson, McKenzie, Crawford, Walker, Sharp, McCready

P W D L F A Pts   *Attendance:* 16,000
23 14 3 6 53 38 31   *Referee:* H. Anderson

The Dons gain their second 4-1 thrashing of Partick. Despite the score it is a patchy game.

No 24 Saturday, 24 February
FALKIRK (1) 1   ABERDEEN (0) 1
  Whitelaw (28)   Emery (58)
FALKIRK: Scott, Fiddes, McPhie, Young, Henderson, James Gallagher, Plumb, Wright, Jack Gallacher, Johnson, Whitelaw
ABERDEEN: Martin, Emery, Shaw, Stenhouse, Young, Harris, Delaney, Yorston, Hamilton, McKenna, Pearson

P W D L F A Pts   *Attendance:* 10,000
24 14 4 6 54 39 32   *Referee:* R.J. Smith

Falkirk might be bottom, but they can still hold Aberdeen. Thirty seconds from time Delaney bags Aberdeen's 'winner'. The referee gives a goal but Falkirk protest about it being offside. The linesman agrees with them.

No 25 Saturday, 3 March
ABERDEEN (0) 1   RAITH ROVERS (1) 2
  Delaney (75)   Penman 2 (27, 66)
ABERDEEN: Martin; McKenna, Shaw, Anderson, Thomson, Harris, Delaney, Yorston, Rodger, Baird, Pearson
RAITH: Johnstone, McLure, McNaught, McLaughlin, Colville, Leigh, Maule, Young, Penman, Murray, Brander

P W D L F A Pts   *Attendance:* 15,000
25 14 4 7 55 41 32   *Referee:* J. Jackson

Disaster for the Dons. Raith do the double as Aberdeen's title chase fades. Baird misses a penalty for Aberdeen at 0-0. Still, Hibs lose too!

No 26 Saturday, 17 March
MOTHERWELL (1) 1   ABERDEEN (1) 1
  Redpath (27)   Yorston (36)
MOTHERWELL: Johnston, Kilmarnock, Shaw, McLeod, Paton, Redpath, Watters, Forrest, Kelly, Watson, Joe Johnson
ABERDEEN: Martin, Emery, Shaw, Lowrie, Young, Harris, Delaney, Yorston, Bogan, Baird, Pearson

P W D L F A Pts   *Attendance:* 10,000
26 14 5 7 56 42 33   *Referee:* J. R. Boyd

Raith and Celtic on successive Saturdays have ruined Aberdeen's season. The Dons could not afford to drop another point.

No 27 Saturday, 24 March
ABERDEEN (0) 3   MORTON (0) 0
  Delaney (57), Hamilton
  (69), Yorston (81)
ABERDEEN: Martin, Emery, Shaw, Lowrie, Young, Harris, Delaney, Yorston, Hamilton, Baird, Pearson
MORTON: Cowan, J. Mitchell, Westwater, G. Mitchell, Whigham, Whyte, Cupples, Boyd, Mochan, McGarrity, Alexander

Leading positions
                      P   W   D   L   F   A Pts
1 Hibernian   24 18   2   4 62 22 38
2 ABERDEEN   27 15   5   7 59 42 35
3 Dundee   26 14   5   7 41 26 33
4 Rangers   25 14   4   7 53 28 32
5 Hearts   25 13   4   8 60 38 30

Attendance: 15,000   *Referee:* J. L. Weir

Morton are by no means clear of the drop. They hold on for nearly an hour before Aberdeen contrive three super goals.

No 28 Saturday, 7 April
ABERDEEN (1) 1   EAST FIFE (1) 2
  Hamilton (8)   Fleming 2 (36, 60)
ABERDEEN: Martin, Emery, Shaw, Lowrie, Young, Harris, Delaney, Yorston, Hamilton, Baird, Pearson
EAST FIFE: Curran, Findlay, Stewart, Christie, Aird, McLennan, Stewart, Fleming, Gardiner, Black, Duncan

P W D L F A Pts   *Attendance:* 7,000
28 15 5 8 60 44 35   *Referee:* W. Davidson

Filthy rain accompanies Aberdeen's last home match of the season. Ex-Don Curran helps his new team to the points which save them from relegation.

No 29 Wednesday, 18 April
HEARTS (1) 4   ABERDEEN (0) 1
  Bauld 2 (39, 79),   Baird (66)
  Conn 2 (58, 68)
HEARTS: Brown, Parker, McKenzie, Whitehead, Dougan, Laing, Sloan, Conn, Bauld, Wardhaugh, Cumming
ABERDEEN: Martin, Emery, Shaw, Lowrie, Young, Harris, Delaney, Yorston, Hamilton, Baird, Pearson

P W D L F A Pts   *Attendance:* 20,000
29 15 5 9 61 48 35   *Referee:* P. Fitzpatrick

The score in no way flatters Hearts. Aberdeen are falling away as the season ends.

No 30 Saturday, 28 April
THIRD LANARK (1) 2   ABERDEEN (0) 0
 Henderson (28),
 Cuthbertson (66)

THIRD LANARK: Petrie, Balunas, Harrower, Mooney, Samuel, Aitken, Henderson, Dick, Goodall, Cuthbertson, Bradley
ABERDEEN: Martin, Shaw, Emery, Lowrie, Young, Harris, Boyd, Hamilton, Delaney, Baird, Pearson

Attendance: 13,000   *Referee:* A. B. Gebbie

Third Lanark had to win to avoid the drop, and do so to complete a league double over Aberdeen, who lost their last three games, to slip to fifth position. Yorston was unfit, denying him the honour of being the Dons' only ever-present.

Aberdeen's complete home and away record:

HOME						AWAY						
P	W	D	L	F	A	W	D	L	F	A		Pts
30	9	2	4	35	21	6	3	6	26	29		35

Scottish League Division A 1950-51

	P	W	D	L	F	A	Pts
1 Hibernian	30	22	4	4	78	26	48
2 Rangers	30	17	4	9	64	37	38
3 Dundee	30	15	8	7	47	30	38
4 Hearts	30	16	5	9	72	45	37
5 ABERDEEN	30	15	5	10	61	50	35
6 Partick Thistle	30	13	7	10	57	48	33
7 Celtic	30	12	5	13	48	46	29
8 Raith Rovers	30	13	2	15	52	52	28
9 Motherwell	30	11	6	13	58	65	28
10 East Fife	30	10	8	12	48	66	28
11 St Mirren	30	9	7	14	35	51	25
12 Morton	30	10	4	16	47	59	24
13 Third Lanark	30	11	2	17	40	51	24
14 Airdrieonians	30	10	4	16	52	67	24
15 Clyde	30	8	7	15	37	57	23
16 Falkirk	30	7	4	19	35	81	18

LEAGUE CUP

Saturday, 12 August
ABERDEEN (2) 4   CLYDE (1) 3
 Anderson (4), Hamilton   Galletly (27), Linwood
 2 (36, 80), Emery (47)   (68), McPhail (75)

ABERDEEN: Martin, Emery, Shaw, Anderson, McKenzie, Harris, Boyd, Yorston, Hamilton, Baird, Hather
CLYDE: Millar, Lindsay, S. Dunn, J. Dunn, Milligan, Haddock, Galletly, Davis, Linwood, McPhail, Barclay

Attendance: 28,000   *Referee:* D. McKerchar

Among the Dons' new signings are Alan Boyd from Queens Park and Dave Shaw from Hibs. Three times Clyde pegged back Aberdeen's lead, but not the fourth time.

Wednesday, 16 August
RANGERS (1) 1   ABERDEEN (0) 2
 Findlay (11)   Hamilton 2 (50, 86)

RANGERS: Brown, Young, Shaw, McColl, Woodburn, Cox, Waddell, Findlay, Thornton, Paton, Rutherford
ABERDEEN: Martin, Emery, Shaw, Anderson, Young, Harris, Boyd, Yorston, Hamilton, Baird, Hather

Attendance: 40,000   *Referee:* H. Phillips

Aberdeen's super-charged second-half performance gives them a great chance of heading Section D. Once again the Dons have to thank Hamilton for their late winner.

Saturday, 19 August
MORTON (0) 0   ABERDEEN (1) 2
      Yorston (26), Boyd (87)

MORTON: Cowan, Connell, Westwater, G. Mitchell, Whigham, Hunter, Farquhar, Orr, Mochan, Garth, Alexander
ABERDEEN: Martin, Emery, Shaw, Anderson, Young, Harris, Boyd, Yorston, Hamilton, Baird, Hather

     Referee: W. N. Graham

An anti-climactic match, which only turned in Aberdeen's favour once Yorston had put them in front.

Saturday, 26 August
CLYDE (3) 4   ABERDEEN (1) 1
 Galletly 2 (1, 44),   Hamilton (4)
 McPhail 2 (9, 75)

CLYDE: Miller, Lindsay, Mennie, Murphy, Campbell, Long, Ring, Galletly, Linwood, McPhail, Barclay
ABERDEEN: Martin, Emery, Shaw, Anderson, Young, Harris, Boyd, Yorston, Hamilton, Baird, Hather

     Referee: H. P. Anderson

Everything is back in the melting pot. Aberdeen's defence disintegrates and Rangers head the table on goal average.

Wednesday, 30 August
ABERDEEN (0) 2   RANGERS (0) 0
 Hather (54), Baird (60)

ABERDEEN: Martin, Emery, Shaw, Anderson, Young, Harris, Boyd, Yorston, Hamilton, Baird, Hunter
RANGERS: Brown, Lindsay, Shaw, McColl, Young, Cox, Waddell, Findlay, Thornton, Paton, Rutherford

Attendance: 42,000   *Referee:* J. McLean

Very rarely do Rangers suffer defeat by the same team twice in a fortnight. Aberdeen, playing commendably as a unit, fully justified the result. Baird, on his comeback, played with a broken nose. Aberdeen scored when Hather gained, lost, and regained possession to let fly from 25 yards. Brown seemed to have the ball covered – but he didn't. Shortly afterwards a Baird header was repulsed by Young, and Baird dived forward to meet the rebound. Now the Dons need only a point from Morton to qualify.

Saturday, 2 September
ABERDEEN (4) 6   MORTON (1) 1
 Baird (8), Yorston   Orr (23)
 2 (15, 57), Boyd (16),
 Hamilton 2 (36, 69)

ABERDEEN: Martin, Emery, Shaw, Anderson,
Young, Harris, Boyd, Yorston, Hamilton, Baird,
Hather
MORTON: Cowan, Westwater, Whigham, J. Mitchell,
Batten, Mochan, Aird, Orr, Cantwell, McGarrity,
Alexander

Morton are devastated by injuries and devastated by
Aberdeen's ruthless finishing.

Section D

	P	W	D	L	F	A	Pts
ABERDEEN	6	5	0	1	17	9	10
Rangers	6	4	0	2	18	7	8
Clyde	6	1	2	3	15	21	4
Morton	6	0	2	4	10	23	2

Quarter Final 1st Leg Saturday, 16 September
ABERDEEN (0) 4   HIBERNIAN (1) 1
 Hather (51), Emery   Johnstone (22)
 (53 pen), Yorston (72),
 Hamilton (80)

ABERDEEN: Martin, Emery, Shaw, Anderson,
Young, Harris, Boyd, Yorston, Hamilton, Baird,
Hather

HIBERNIAN: Younger, Govan, Cairns, Howie,
Paterson, Combe, Souness, Johnstone, Reilly,
Turnbull, Ormond
Attendance: 42,000   *Referee:* J. Jackson
A thriller to set before the King. Hibs journey north
with thirty goals under their belts already. Johnstone
takes advantage of the Dons' under-populated defence
in the first half. The referee came out late for the
second, with everybody hanging around waiting for
him. In the space of two minutes Hather and Emery
turn the game around. In a fever pitch of excitement
Yorston and Hamilton add the goals which give
Aberdeen a comfortable cushion for the second leg.

Quarter Final 2nd Leg Wednesday, 20 September
HIBERNIAN (1) 3 *4*   ABERDEEN (0) 0 *1*
 Anderson o.g. (3),   (after extra time)
 Johnstone (61), Ormond   Yorston (120)
 (65), Reilly (92)

HIBERNIAN: Younger, Govan, Ogilvie, Howie,
Paterson, Combe, Smith, Johnstone, Reilly, Turnbull,
Ormond
ABERDEEN: Martin, Emery, Shaw, Anderson,
Young, Baikie, Boyd, Yorston, Hamilton, Baird, Hather
Attendance: 35,000   *Referee:* J. Jackson
Aberdeen desperately needed to avoid losing an early
goal, but Anderson obliged, lobbing into his own net.
But with an hour played the Dons still retained a two-
goal advantage. Two softish goals took the tie into extra

time and immediately Reilly seized on Smith's overhead
kick to power Hibs in front. Now it was Aberdeen's
turn to surge forward. Thirty seconds from the end of
the extra period a frantic scrimmage developed in which
Yorston popped in the vital goal.

Quarter Final Replay (Ibrox) Monday, 2 October
HIBERNIAN (1) 1 *1*   ABERDEEN (0) 1 *1*
 Turnbull (23)   (after extra time)
                          Baird (62)

HIBERNIAN: Younger, Govan, Ogilvie, Buchanan,
Paterson, Combe, Smith, Johnstone, Reilly, Turnbull,
Ormond
ABERDEEN: Martin, Emery, Shaw, Anderson,
Young, Glen, Boyd, Yorston, Hamilton, Baird, Pearson
Attendance: 52,000   *Referee:* J. Jackson
A magnificent match fails to separate the sides after
extra time. Gordon Smith is credited with the miss of
the match, lofting over the Dons' crossbar at the end of
the scheduled ninety minutes.

Quarter Final 2nd Replay (Hampden) Tuesday,
3 October
HIBERNIAN (3) 5   ABERDEEN (1) 1
 Johnstone 2 (14, 23),   Baird (25)
 Turnbull (18), Smith (56),
 Reilly (79)

HIBERNIAN: Younger, Govan, Ogilvie, Buchanan,
Paterson, Combe, Smith, Johnstone, Reilly, Turnbull,
Ormond
ABERDEEN: Martin, Emery, Shaw, Anderson,
Young, Harris, Boyd, Yorston, Hamilton, Baird,
Hather
Attendance: 50,000   *Referee:* J. Jackson
This is the fifth meeting of the sides in 17 days in the
league and League Cup. They know everything there is
to know about each other, but Hibs put that knowledge
to better use. The match was settled midway through
the first half when Hibs led 3-0. Baird pulled one back,
and had Boyd scored when striking the crossbar early in
the second half the outcome might have been other than
it was.

SCOTTISH CUP

1st Round Saturday, 27 January
ABERDEEN (2) 6   INVERNESS
 Yorston 3 (2, 70, 87),   CALEDONIAN (1) 1
 Baird (34), Delaney (53), Jamieson (16)
 Hamilton (89)

ABERDEEN: Watson, Emery, McKenna, Anderson,
Young, Harris, Delaney, Yorston, Hamilton, Baird,
Pearson
INVERNESS CALEY: Bruce, McGillivray,
Mrowonski, Bolt, MacKinnon, Mackintosh, MacBeath,
Jamieson, Mitchell, MacKenzie, Fraser
Attendance: 22,000   *Referee:* W. N. Graham
Only in the second half does Aberdeen's greater
strength and fitness see off Caley.

2nd Round, Saturday, 10 February
ABERDEEN (1) 4   THIRD LANARK (0) 0
  Hamilton 3 (42, 50, 81),
  Emery (69 pen)
ABERDEEN: Martin, Emery, Shaw, Anderson,
Young, Harris, Delaney, Yorston, Hamilton, Baird,
Pearson
THIRD LANARK: Simpson, Balunas, Harrower,
Adams, Samuels, Aitken, Goodall, Mason,
Cuthbertson, Dick, Staroscik
Attendance: 28,000   *Referee:* W. Brown

Aberdeen lost at home to lowly Third Lanark in the
league. In the Cup it is a different story. Hamilton's
hat-trick makes him the hero of Pittodrie.

3rd Round (Bye)

Quarter Final Saturday, 10 March
CELTIC (2) 3   ABERDEEN (0) 0
  McPhail 2 (14, 80),
  Tully (42)
CELTIC: Hunter, Fallon, Rollo, Evans, Boden, Baillie,
Weir, Collins, McPhail, Peacock, Tully
ABERDEEN: Martin, McKenna, Shaw, Anderson,
Young, Harris, Delaney, Yorston, Bogan, Baird,
Pearson
Attendance: 75,000   *Referee:* J. A. Mowat

Aberdeen's season, when they are chasing a league and
cup double, comes to a sticky end. Raith scuttled their
championship hopes last week. Now Celtic dump them
out of the Scottish Cup after Aberdeen had beaten the
Parkhead side home and away in the league. Celtic took
a grip when McPhail bundled both McKenna and the
ball over the line. Tully sank the Dons before the
interval. Throughout, Hunter in the Celtic goal was
little occupied.

1950-51 APPEARANCES	League	League Cup	Scottish Cup
Yorston	29	10	3
Hamilton	28	10	2
Baird	27	10	3
Young	26	9	3
Emery	25	10	2
Martin	24	10	2
Shaw	23	10	2
Harris	23	8	3
Delaney	21		3
Anderson	20	10	3
Pearson	19	2	3
McKenna	13		2
Boyd	10	10	
Hather	10	8	
Glen	7	1	
Lowrie	5		
Thomson	4		
Watson	3		1
Curran	3		
McNeill	2		
Stenhouse	2		
Bakie	1	1	
McMillan	1		
Bruce	1		
O'Neil	1		
Rodger	1		
Bogan	1		1
McKenzie		1	
28 players			

GOALS	Total	League	League Cup	Scottish Cup
Hamilton	29	17	8	4
Yorston	26	18	5	3
Baird	10	5	4	1
Emery	7	4	2	1
Hather	5	3	2	
Boyd	5	3	2	
Delaney	4	3		1
Pearson	3	3		
Anderson	2	1	1	
McNeill	1	1		
own-goals	3	3		
Total	95	61	24	10

Stan Williams beats Hibs goalkeeper Kerr,
and the Scottish Cup of 1947 is on its way to
Aberdeen.

Two views from the mid fifties.
Top picture: Jimmy Mitchell leads Aberdeen out at Pittodrie followed by Fred Martin, Archie Glen and Paddy Buckley.

Bottom picture. Back row: Hamilton, Paterson, Smith, O'Neil, Martin, Allister, Young, Glen. Front row: Leggatt, Yorston, Mitchell, Buckley, Wishart, Hather.

Season 1951-52

After the hopes raised in 1950-51, 1951-52 was a season of sighs and groans. Aberdeen never looked like qualifying from their League Cup section, which opened the season, and in fact finished bottom. There was a brief flurry at the start of the league programme. Five points from the opening three matches saw Aberdeen perch briefly on top of the pile. This opening burst included a dramatic 4-4 draw with Hibs at Easter Road which revived memories of recent stirring battles between the clubs. But from then on the results began to go against Aberdeen. The last fixture of 1951 saw them beaten 4-3 at Pittodrie by an undistinguished Celtic eleven. Two of the Celts' goals came from penalties, another was an own-goal, and these misfortunes somehow seemed to sum up the Dons' season. As Winter turned to Spring one or two anxious glances were being cast in the direction of the relegation dog-fight at the bottom of the table.

Nor was there any solace in the Scottish Cup. Division B outfits Kilmarnock and Dundee United were bypassed only with difficulty. A Quarter Final trip back to Tayside to meet Dundee ended with a 0-4 thumping.

The blame for Aberdeen's mediocre season could not be laid with the forwards. Both at home and away more goals were scored than in any previous post-war season. Only three times in thirty league matches did Aberdeen fail to find the net. The problems lay at the other end, where a new post-1945 goals-against column was established. Looking back through the season's fixtures, there were very few epic battles to reflect upon.

League: Eleventh
League Cup: Bottom of qualifying group
Scottish Cup: Quarter Final

SCOTTISH LEAGUE DIVISION A

No 1 Saturday, 8 September

ABERDEEN (2) 3   ST MIRREN (0) 0
Yorston 2 (19, 27),
Delaney (85)

ABERDEEN: Martin, Emery, McKenna, Anderson, Young, Lowrie, Bogan, Yorston, Delaney, Harris, Hather

ST MIRREN: Crabtree, Drinkwater, Ashe, Neilson, Telfer, Reid, Burrell, Rice, Crowe, Goldthorpe, Martin

P	W	D	L	F	A	Pts
1	1	0	0	3	0	2

Attendance: 18,000
Referee: H. Phillip

Twelve minutes from time McKenna and Burrell come to blows and are ordered off. Saints finish the match with seven fit men and later McKenna is suspended for 21 days.

No 2 Saturday, 15 September

HIBERNIAN (4) 4   ABERDEEN (1) 4
Johnstone 2 (1, 42),   Harris (28), Yorston (55),
Reilly 2 (5, 25)   Bogan (83), Lowrie (89)

HIBERNIAN: Kerr, Govan, Howie, Ward, Paterson, Combe, Smith, Johnstone, Reilly, Turnbull, Ormond

ABERDEEN: Martin, Emery, McKenna, Anderson, Young, Lowrie, Bogan, Yorston, Delaney, Harris, Hather

P	W	D	L	F	A	Pts
2	1	1	0	7	4	3

Attendance: 30,000
Referee: G. Mitchell

An astonishing game. Johnstone lashes home Young's clearance for Hibs' first; Reilly's header makes it two. Reilly then follows up when Martin saves from Johnstone and Aberdeen are facing a disaster. It is 4-1 at half-time, immediately after which Aberdeen are reduced to ten men when Young is carried off. Yorston bagged a second in a breakaway, then handed Bogan the opportunity to make it 4-3. Delaney heads just wide before taking a last-minute corner which is finished off by Lowrie to bring Aberdeen back from the dead.

No 3 Saturday, 22 September

ABERDEEN (3) 3   DUNDEE (1) 1
Yorston (7), Hamilton Irvine (33)
2 (25, 30)

46

ABERDEEN: Martin, Emery, McKenna, Anderson, Young, Lowrie, Delaney, Yorston, Hamilton, Harris, Hather

DUNDEE: Brown, Follon, Frew, Irvine, Cowie, Boyd, Flavell, Williams, Zeising, Steel, Christie

Leading positions

	P	W	D	L	F	A	Pts
1 ABERDEEN	3	2	1	0	10	5	5
2 Morton	3	2	0	1	6	3	4
3 East Fife	3	2	0	1	8	5	4
4 Hibernian	3	1	2	0	7	5	4
5 Queen of the South	3	1	2	0	4	3	4

Attendance: 25,000   *Referee:* H. P. Anderson

Hamilton celebrates his return with two goals as Aberdeen perch proudly on top of the league.

No 4 Saturday, 29 September
EAST FIFE (1) 2   ABERDEEN (1) 1
  Gardiner 2 (8, 82)   Yorston (36)

EAST FIFE: Curran, Finlay, S. Stewart, Christie, Laird, McLellan, J. Stewart, Fleming, Gardiner, Bonthrone, Duncan

ABERDEEN: Martin, Emery, McKenna, Anderson, Young, Lowrie, Boyd, Yorston, Hamilton, Harris, Hather

P W D L F A Pts   *Attendance:* 10,000
4 2 1 1 11 7 5   *Referee:* C. E. Faultless

East Fife's third win over the Dons in the opening month of the season ends their unbeaten league record.

No 5 Saturday, 6 October
ABERDEEN (0) 1   AIRDRIEONIANS (1) 4
  Yorston (88)   Emery o.g. (45), Lennox
                       (52), McCulloch
                       2 (60, 78)

ABERDEEN: Martin, Emery, A. Rodger, Anderson, Young, Lowrie, Delaney, Yorston, I. Rodger, Baird, Hather

AIRDRIE: Fraser, Pryde, T. Brown, Cairns, Rodger, Shankland, McGurn, Quinn, Lennox, McMillan, McCulloch

P W D L F A Pts
5 2 1 2 12 11 5

Dreadful Aberdeen stumble to defeat once Emery slices McGurn's cross into his own net.

No 6 Saturday, 13 October
QUEEN OF THE   ABERDEEN (1) 2
  SOUTH (0) 1   Hamilton (31), Delaney
  Inglis (68)   (75)

QUEEN OF THE SOUTH: Henderson, Sharpe, Binning, Rothera, Aird, McBain, Oakes, Paterson, Inglis, J. Brown, Johnstone

ABERDEEN: Martin, Emery, Shaw, Harris, Young, Lowrie, Delaney, Yorston, Hamilton, Baird, Pearson

P W D L F A Pts   *Attendance:* 10,000
6 3 1 2 14 12 7   *Referee:* W. Brown

Aberdeen bring back Harris and Shaw, and remodel their forward line in an effort to stop the rot.

No 7 Saturday, 20 October
THIRD LANARK (1) 2   ABERDEEN (0) 0
  Dick 2 (43, 65)

THIRD LANARK: Petrie, Archibald, Harrower, Mooney, Samuel, Aitken, Smellie, Dick, Cuthbertson, Henderson, McLeod

ABERDEEN: Martin, Emery, Shaw, Harris, Young, Lowrie, Delaney, Yorston, Hamilton, Baird, Pearson

P W D L F A Pts   *Attendance:* 4,000
7 3 1 3 14 14 7   *Referee:* W. J. Brown

It is cold and wet and miserable, especially for the Dons. The score in no way flattered the Warriors.

No 8 Saturday, 3 November
ABERDEEN (1) 1   QUEEN OF SOUTH (1) 1
  Shaw (8)   Paterson (22)

ABERDEEN: Martin, Emery, Shaw, Samuel, Thomson, Harris, Newlands, Yorston, Hamilton, Lowrie, Pearson

QUEEN OF THE SOUTH: Henderson, Sharpe, Binning, McBain, Aird, McNight, Inglis, J. Brown, Paterson, Neilson, Oakes

P W D L F A Pts   *Attendance:* 12,000
8 3 2 3 15 15 8   *Referee:* T. S. Edwards

An appalling spectacle for the fans, who are drifting away in their thousands long before the end.

No 9 Saturday, 10 November
ABERDEEN (3) 4   PARTICK THISTLE (0) 2
  Hamilton (17), Yorston   Stott 2 (79, 82)
  (25), Baird (32), Delaney
  (65)

ABERDEEN: Martin, McKenna, A. Rodger, Lowrie, Thomson, Harris, Delaney, Yorston, Hamilton, Baird, Pearson

PARTICK: Ledgerwood, McGowan, Gibb, Thomson, Davidson, Mathers, McKenzie, Anderson, Stott, Sharp, Walker

P W D L F A Pts   *Attendance:* 6,000
9 4 2 3 19 17 10   *Referee:* R. J. Smith

After a sequence of drab matches Aberdeen hit form, then relax to live nervously through the last minutes. Partick 'scored' a third but it was disallowed.

No 10 Saturday, 17 November
STIRLING ALBION (0) 0   ABERDEEN (1) 4
                            Baird (10), Yorston
                            (50), Delaney (69),
                            Hamilton (83)

STIRLING: Jenkins, J. Henderson, Hadden, Mitchell, Paton, Wilson, McFarlane, Bain, G. Henderson, Brown, Anderson

ABERDEEN: Martin, McKenna, Shaw, Lowrie, Thomson, Harris, Delaney, Yorston, Hamilton, Baird, Pearson

Leading positions

	P	W	D	L	F	A	Pts
1 East Fife	12	8	2	2	31	20	18
2 Hibernian	11	6	4	1	29	14	16
3 ABERDEEN	10	5	2	3	23	17	12
4 Hearts	11	5	2	4	22	17	12

Attendance: 9,000   *Referee:* W. Brittle

Stirling look a dreadful side. Aberdeen could have had a dozen. Despite their patchy form they are now third.

No 11 Saturday, 24 November

ABERDEEN (2) 2	RAITH ROVERS (0) 2
Yorston (6), Hamilton (40)	Young (48 pen), Wood (64)

ABERDEEN: Martin, McKenna, Shaw, Lowrie, Thomson, Harris, Delaney, Yorston, Hamilton, Baird, Pearson

RAITH: Johnstone, Wilkie, McNaught, Young, Colville, Leigh, Wood, McEwan, Copland, Maule, Brander

P W D L F A Pts   *Attendance:* 15,000
11 5 3 3 25 19 13   *Referee:* S. Hilton

Aberdeen's bright opening was followed by Raith's bright close. The Dons might have been 3-0 ahead when Yorston hit the bar. But McKenna handled to give away a penalty and Wood's equaliser came as no surprise.

No 12 Saturday, 1 December

HEARTS (2) 2	ABERDEEN (1) 2
Bauld (16), Whittle (39)	Yorston 2 (6, 52)

HEARTS: Brown, Parker, McKenzie, Glidden, Milne, Laing, Rutherford, Conn, Bauld, Whittle, Cumming
ABERDEEN: Martin, McKenna, Emery, Lowrie, Thomson, Harris, Delaney, Yorston, Hamilton, Baird, Pearson

P W D L F A Pts   *Attendance:* 20,000
12 5 4 3 27 21 14   *Referee:* J. R. Boyd

A cracking game to warm the cockles. Yorston opened the way with a shot deflected by Laing. Bauld equalised when Martin pushed his shot onto the underside of the bar. McKenna whacked clear off the goal-line but the referee decided the ball had already crossed it. Whittle powered Hearts in front. After the change-around Pearson's cross dropped sweetly for Yorston to level. Aberdeen clung on to a point when Emery cleared off the line from Whittle. The Dons' full-back had earlier made himself unpopular with the Tynecastle crowd, who had their own strongman Bobby Parker, equally uncompromising. The match was Delaney's last for Aberdeen before being transferred to Falkirk.

No 13 Saturday, 8 December

MOTHERWELL (1) 3	ABERDEEN (3) 3
Humphries (41), Kelly 2 (79, 89)	Baird (4), Hamilton (20), Yorston (25)

MOTHERWELL: Hamilton, Kilmarnock, Shaw, McLeod, Paton, Redpath, Humphries, Robinson, Kelly, Aitken, Aitkenhead
ABERDEEN: Martin, Young, Emery, Lowrie, Thomson, Harris, Bogan, Yorston, Hamilton, Baird, Pearson

P W D L F A Pts   *Attendance:* 7,000
13 5 5 3 30 24 15   *Referee:* W. G. Livingstone

An ill-tempered match snatched from Aberdeen's grasp by ex-Don Archie Kelly in the last seconds. His header is saved on the goal-line by Martin, but the ref blew for a goal. This was Bogan's final game for the Dons: he was soon transferred to Southampton.

No 14 Saturday, 15 December

ABERDEEN (0) 3	MORTON (0) 1
Yorston 2 (62, 64), Boyd (89)	Orr (71)

ABERDEEN: Martin, Young, Emery, Lowrie, Thomson, Harris, Boyd, Yorston, Hamilton, Baird, Pearson
MORTON: Cowan, Mitchell, Westwater, Little, Batten, Hunter, Cupples, Orr, Linwood, McGarrity, Alexander

Leading positions

	P	W	D	L	F	A	Pts
1 East Fife	16	11	3	2	42	26	25
2 Hibernian	16	10	4	1	44	15	24
3 Hearts	15	8	3	4	36	22	19
4 ABERDEEN	14	6	5	3	33	25	17
5 Rangers	12	6	4	2	23	10	16

Attendance: 17,000   *Referee:* J. A. Mowat

In the last few minutes a white ball was used for the first time in an Aberdeen match. The linesmen entered into the spirit by using luminous flags and armbands.

No 15 Saturday, 22 December

ST MIRREN (1) 3	ABERDEEN (1) 1
Crowe 2 (37, 55), Lesz (57)	Hamilton (27)

ST MIRREN: Lynch, Lapsley, Cunningham, Neilson, Telfer, Martin, McEwan, Blyth, Crowe, Gemmell, Lesz
ABERDEEN: Watson, Young, McKenna, Lowrie, Thomson, Harris, Boyd, Yorston, Hamilton, Baird, Pearson

P W D L F A Pts
15 6 5 4 34 28 17   *Referee:* W. Bowman

A nondescript match. Saints hit back from Hamilton's effort to score three and dent the crossbar.

No 16 Saturday, 29 December

ABERDEEN (1) 3	CELTIC (3) 4
Baird (4), Emery (82 pen), Yorston (89)	Collins 2 (1 pen, 24 pen), McKenna o.g. (26), Walsh (65)

ABERDEEN: Watson, Emery, McKenna, Lowrie, Thomson, Harris, Boyd, Yorston, Hamilton, Baird, Pearson

CELTIC: Bell, Fallon, Jack, Evans, Stein, Baillie, Collins, Walsh, J. Weir, Peacock, Tully

P	W	D	L	F	A	Pts	*Attendance:* 22,000
16	6	5	5	37	32	17	*Referee:* D. McKerchar

Celtic come to Aberdeen in the lower half of the league to provide a golden spectacle filled with incident. Emery's handball gave Collins a first-minute penalty in off the post. After Baird had nodded an equaliser Emery used his hands again, and again Collins despatched the spot kick. Before Aberdeen could draw breath McKenna diverted Peacock's centre into his own net. Walsh was totally unattended for No. 4. In a furious climax Emery scored a penalty for himself, Tully hit the Dons' bar, and Yorston finished off an Aberdeen free kick.

No 17 Tuesday, 1 January
DUNDEE (2) 3   ABERDEEN (1) 2
  Pattillo (33), Hill (45),   Harris (40), Emery
  Flavell (73)   (80 pen)
DUNDEE: Brown, Follon, Cowan, Gallacher, Merchant, Boyd, Hill, Pattillo, Flavell, Steel, Christie
ABERDEEN: Watson, Young, Emery, Lowrie, Thomson, Harris, Boyd, Yorston, Hamilton, Baird, Pearson

P	W	D	L	F	A	Pts	
17	6	5	6	39	35	17	*Referee:* J. Jackson

The Dons are wrecked by injury during the match. Their walking wounded are on the receiving end throughout though they hang on grimly. Dundee might have had four when at the close Emery brought down Hill but Christie blazed the penalty wide.

No 18 Wednesday, 2 January
ABERDEEN (1) 2   EAST FIFE (0) 1
  Boyd (18), Hamilton (87)   Aitken (65)
ABERDEEN: Watson, Smith, Shaw, Lowrie, Young, Anderson, Boyd, Yorston, Hamilton, Baird, Pearson
EAST FIFE: Curran, Weir, Stewart, Frame, Finlay, Hudson, J. Stewart, Aitken, Gardiner, McLellan, Duncan

P	W	D	L	F	A	Pts	*Attendance:* 20,000
18	7	5	6	41	36	19	*Referee:* H. Phillips

After three straight defeats Aberdeen return to form against the league's No 3 team. Hamilton's late winner arrived after he had taken the ball from his own half to beat Curran.

No 19 Saturday, 5 January
AIRDRIEONIANS (2) 3   ABERDEEN (0) 0
  Lennox 2 (14, 89), Welsh
  (39)
AIRDRIE: Fraser, Cosh, Brown, Cairns, Murray, Shankland, Quinn, McMillan, Lennox, Welsh, McCulloch
ABERDEEN: Watson, Smith, Shaw, Lowrie, Young, Anderson, Boyd, Yorston, I. Rodger, Baird, Pearson

P	W	D	L	F	A	Pts	*Attendance:* 10,000
19	7	5	7	41	39	19	*Referee:* P. Fitzpatrick

Lowly Airdrie complete an embarrassingly easy double over a Dons side missing the injured Hamilton.

No 20 Saturday, 12 January
ABERDEEN (0) 1   HIBERNIAN (0) 2
  Yorston (89)   Johnstone (63), Smith
                         (88)
ABERDEEN: Watson, Young, Shaw, Lowrie, Thomson, Harris, Boyd, Yorston, Smith, Baird, Pearson
HIBERNIAN: Younger, Govan, Howie, Buchanan, Paterson, Gallacher, Smith, Johnstone, Reilly, Turnbull, Combe

P	W	D	L	F	A	Pts	*Attendance:* 20,000
20	7	5	8	42	41	19	*Referee:* C. E. Faultless

Aberdeen appear to be on the slide: their visitors are table-topping Hibs. There was to be no repeat of the 4-4 thriller at Easter Road. Hibs were never really in danger, and their win sends Aberdeen below the halfway line in Division A.

No 21 Saturday, 19 January
ABERDEEN (1) 2   THIRD LANARK (2) 3
  Yorston (6), Hamilton   Henderson (11),
  (78)   Docherty (34), McLeod
                         (60)
ABERDEEN: Martin, Young, Shaw, Lowrie, Thomson, Harris, Newlands, Yorston, Hamilton, Baird, Hather
THIRD LANARK: Robertson, Balunas, Cairns, Mooney, Forsyth, Harrower, Henderson, Docherty, Cuthbertson, Dick, McLeod

P	W	D	L	F	A	Pts	*Attendance:* 17,000
21	7	5	9	44	44	19	*Referee:* D. McIntosh

Thirds are fighting against the drop and clock up their fifth consecutive league victory against the Dons.

No 22 Saturday, 26 January
ABERDEEN (1) 3   HEARTS (0) 0
  Rodger 2 (42, 80), Boyd
  (86)
ABERDEEN: Martin, Shaw, Emery, Anderson, Thomson, Harris, Boyd, Yorston, I. Rodger, Baird, Pearson
HEARTS: Brown, Parker, McKenzie, Glidden, Milne, Laing, Rutherford, Conn, Bauld, Wardhaugh, Urquhart

P	W	D	L	F	A	Pts	*Attendance:* 16,000
22	8	5	9	47	44	21	*Referee:* D. McKerchar

Aberdeen halt their bad run with an exciting win over second-placed Hearts, for whom this is their first setback in thirteen matches. The snowbound pitch helps neither team.

No 23 Saturday, 2 February
RANGERS (1) 3   ABERDEEN (1) 2
  Thornton (37), Paton   Prentice o.g. (31),
  (67), Young (77 pen)   Baird (48)
RANGERS: Brown, Young, Little, McColl,
Woodburn, Prentice, McCulloch, Finlay, Thornton,
Paton, Liddell
ABERDEEN: Martin, Shaw, Emery, Anderson,
Thomson, Harris, Boyd, Yorston, I. Rodger, Baird,
Pearson

P W D L F A Pts   *Attendance:* 25,000
23 8 5 10 49 47 21   *Referee:* R. J. Smith

Rangers are stalking Hibs and Hearts. They gain two
more points on a virtually unplayable pitch covered in
part by snow, in part by puddles. Prentice toed the ball
into his own goal off a post to put Aberdeen ahead.
Thornton's bullet header levelled matters until Baird's
twenty yarder restored the Dons advantage. Findlay
headed on for Paton to equalise and Rangers took both
points following a soft penalty awarded against
Thomson for an innocuous tackle on Liddell.

No 24 Saturday, 16 February
PARTICK THISTLE (1) 1   ABERDEEN (1) 4
  Sharp (44)   Yorston 2 (26, 75),
                           Rodger (52), Boyd (54)
PARTICK: Ledgerwood, Brown, McCreadie, Hewitt,
Davidson, Mathers, McKenzie, Harvey, Stott, Sharpe,
Walker
ABERDEEN: Martin, Shaw, Emery, Anderson,
Thomson, Harris, Boyd, Yorston, I. Rodger, Baird,
Pearson

P W D L F A Pts   *Attendance:* 15,000
24 9 5 10 53 48 23   *Referee:* G. Mitchell

Partick must hate the sight of Aberdeen. This is the
Dons' seventh straight win over Thistle, who have not
come within a goal of Aberdeen in that time.

No 25 Saturday, 1 March
RAITH ROVERS (0) 2   ABERDEEN (1) 1
  McIntyre (46), Copland   Rodger (27)
  (90)
RAITH: Johnstone, McLure, Condie, Young, Colville,
Williamson, McEwan, Maule, Copland, Kelly,
McIntyre
ABERDEEN: Watson, McKenna, Emery, Anderson,
Young, Lowrie, Boyd, Yorston, I. Rodger, Baird,
Hather

P W D L F A Pts   *Attendance:* 7,000
25 9 5 11 54 50 23   *Referee:* S. Hilton

Copland's last-gasp goal deprives Aberdeen of a point
they scarcely deserved on the run of play.

No 26 Wednesday, 12 March
ABERDEEN (3) 6   STIRLING ALBION (0) 0
  Hamilton 2 (5, 63),
  Pearson (21), Rodger
  2 (36, 76), Emery (85 pen)

ABERDEEN: Martin, McKenna, Emery, Lowrie,
Thomson, Harris, Boyd, Hamilton, I. Rodger, Hay,
Pearson
STIRLING: Jenkins, Gibson, MacCabe, Rutherford,
Paton, Mitchell, Bertolini, MacFarlane, Silcock, Dick,
Anderson

P W D L F A Pts   *Referee:* W. J. Brown
26 10 5 11 60 50 25

Stirling are speeding into Division B and enable the
Dons to take their aggregate tally to ten.

No 27 Saturday, 15 March
ABERDEEN (1) 2   MOTHERWELL (0) 2
  Rodger (9), Hamilton (67) Sloan (49), Kelly (66)
ABERDEEN: Martin, Young, Emery, Lowrie,
Thomson, Harris, Boyd, Hamilton, I. Rodger, Hay,
Pearson
MOTHERWELL: Johnstone, Kilmarnock, Shaw, Cox,
Paton, Redpath, Sloan, Humphries, Kelly, Watson,
Aitkenhead

P W D L F A Pts   *Attendance:* 15,000
27 10 6 11 62 52 26   *Referee:* J. R. Boyd

When Hamilton instantly cancelled out Motherwell's
second goal it gave Aberdeen the point they needed to
finally banish those faint relegation clouds.

No 28 Saturday, 22 March
MORTON (2) 3   ABERDEEN (2) 2
  Cupples (6), Garth (30),   Boyd (31), Samuel (40)
  Linwood (89)
MORTON: Cowan, Mitchell, Whigham, Little, Thom,
Whitelaw, Garth, Cupples, Linwood, McGarrity,
McVinish
ABERDEEN: Martin, Young, Emery, Samuel,
Thomson, Harris, Boyd, Hamilton, I. Rodger, Baird,
Hather

P W D L F A Pts   *Attendance:* 10,000
28 10 6 12 64 55 26   *Referee:* W. Brittle

Desperate Morton celebrate Linwood's fairytale winner,
but it won't save them from the drop.

No 29 Saturday, 29 March
CELTIC (2) 2   ABERDEEN (0) 0
  Weir (3), McPhail (4)
CELTIC: Bonner, Fallon, Baillie, Fernie, Boden,
Milsopp, Weir, Collins, McPhail, Walsh, Tully
ABERDEEN: Martin, Young, Shaw, Samuel,
Thomson, Harris, Boyd, Yorston, I. Rodger, Baird,
Hather

P W D L F A Pts   *Referee:* J. R. Boyd
29 10 6 13 64 57 26

A few weeks ago Celtic were in the bottom two. They
are safe now, thanks to a quick one-two in the opening
minutes.

No 30 Saturday, 19 April
ABERDEEN (0) 1   RANGERS (1) 1
  Rodger (47)   Liddell (35)

ABERDEEN: Martin, Smith, Shaw, Samuel, Thomson, Harris, Newlands, Yorston, Rodger, Baird, Hather

RANGERS: Niven, Young, Shaw, McColl, Woodburn, Cox, Waddell, Niellands, Gardiner, Prentice, Liddell

Referee: D. McIntosh

Aberdeen have to wait three weeks for their final league match against a Rangers side who have conceded the league title to Hibs. The match was one of the poorest ever played between Aberdeen and Rangers.

Aberdeen's complete home and away record:

HOME						AWAY						
P	W	D	L	F	A	W	D	L	F	A		Pts
30	7	4	4	37	24	3	3	9	28	34		27

Scottish League Division A 1951-52

	P	W	D	L	F	A	Pts
1 Hibernian	30	20	5	5	92	36	45
2 Rangers	30	16	9	5	61	31	41
3 East Fife	30	17	3	10	71	49	37
4 Hearts	30	14	7	9	69	53	35
5 Raith Rovers	30	14	5	11	43	42	33
6 Partick Thistle	30	12	7	11	48	51	31
7 Motherwell	30	12	7	11	51	57	31
8 Dundee	30	11	6	13	53	52	28
9 Celtic	30	10	8	12	52	55	28
10 Queen of the South	30	10	8	12	50	60	28
11 ABERDEEN	30	10	7	13	65	58	27
12 Airdrieonians	30	11	4	15	54	69	26
13 Third Lanark	30	9	8	13	51	62	26
14 St Mirren	30	10	5	15	43	58	25
15 Morton	30	9	6	15	49	56	24
16 Stirling Albion	30	5	5	20	36	99	15

LEAGUE CUP

Saturday, 11 August
ABERDEEN (3) 5   QUEEN OF THE SOUTH
Hay (2), Hamilton (8),   (0) 4
Emery (17), Pearson (50),   Inglis (52), Paterson (70),
Delaney (56)   Johnstone (71),
    McKeown (85)

ABERDEEN: Martin, Emery, Shaw, Harris, Thomson, Lowrie, Delaney, Yorston, Hamilton, Hay, Pearson

QUEEN OF THE SOUTH: Henderson, Sharpe, Binning, McBain, Aird, Waldie, Oakes, Paterson, Inglis, McKeown, Johnstone

Attendance: 17,000   *Referee:* R. Yacamini

Aberdeen start the new season straight from their 3-2 defeat by Celtic in the final of the St Mungo Cup to celebrate the Festival of Britain. Against Queen of the South Hugh Hay scores within 2 minutes on his debut to send the Dons on their way. After scoring five times in an hour Aberdeen nearly throw away a point.

Wednesday, 15 August
RANGERS (0) 2   ABERDEEN (1) 1
Rutherford (63), Paton   Yorston (37)
(75)

RANGERS: Brown, Young, Little, McColl, Woodburn, Cox, Waddell, Findlay, Simpson, Paton, Rutherford

ABERDEEN: Martin, Emery, Shaw, Harris, Thomson, Lowrie, Delaney, Yorston, Hamilton, Hay, Pearson

Attendance: 60,000

The Dons fall back to protect their lead and hand Rangers the initiative.

Saturday, 18 August
EAST FIFE (1) 3   ABERDEEN (0) 0
Fleming (24), Gardiner
2 (49, 64)

EAST FIFE: Curran, Finlay, S. Stewart, Christie, Aird, McLellan, J. Stewart, Fleming, Gardiner, Bonthrone, Matthews

ABERDEEN: Martin, Emery, Shaw, Harris, Thomson, Lowrie, Delaney, Yorston, Hamilton, Bogan, Pearson

Attendance: 10,000   *Referee:* R. Fitzpatrick

Aberdeen are outplayed from start to finish by the losing finalists of the Scottish Cup. Once Fleming's cannonball opener puts the hosts in front Aberdeen are on a hiding.

Saturday, 25 August
QUEEN OF THE   ABERDEEN (0) 0
SOUTH (0) 2
Pearson (48), Oakes (75)

QUEEN OF THE SOUTH: Henderson, Sharpe, Binning, Rothera, Aird, Greenock, Inglis, Paterson, Houliston, McKeown, Oakes

ABERDEEN: Martin, Emery, A. Rodger, Harris, Thomson, Shaw, Bogan, Yorston, Hamilton, Lowrie, Pearson

Referee: R. J. Smith

In the first half Aberdeen played against driving wind and rain yet held out. With the elements in their favour they fall behind and lose all hope of qualifying.

Wednesday, 29 August
ABERDEEN (2) 2   RANGERS (1) 1
Delaney (33), Hay (77)   Simpson (5)

ABERDEEN: Martin, Emery, A. Rodger, Lowrie, Thomson, Harris, Bogan, Yorston, Delaney, Hay, Hather

RANGERS: Brown, Young, Little, McColl, Woodburn, Cox, Waddell, Findlay, Simpson, Thornton, Rutherford

Attendance: 28,000   *Referee:* J. R. Boyd

Rangers have already qualified from Section D. Delaney deputises at centre forward for the absent Hamilton and is a considerable success. On the same day manager David Halliday signed the youngster Bobby Wishart from an Edinburgh juvenile club.

Saturday, 1 September
ABERDEEN (1) 2   EAST FIFE (3) 3
Yorston 2 (6, 52)   Fleming 2 (9, 41),
    Gardiner (26)

ABERDEEN: Martin, Emery, A. Rodger, Lowrie, Thomson, Harris, Bogan, Yorston, Delaney, Hay, Hather

EAST FIFE: Curran, Smith, S. Stewart, Christie, Aird, McLellan, J. Stewart, Fleming, Gardiner, Bonthrone, Matthews

Attendance: 18,000   *Referee:* W. G. Livingstone

Aberdeen cannot capitalise on Yorston's early goal and East Fife are in command by the interval.

Section D

	P	W	D	L	F	A	Pts
Rangers	6	4	1	1	15	6	9
East Fife	6	3	1	2	10	9	7
Queen of the South	6	2	0	4	11	16	4
ABERDEEN	6	2	0	4	10	15	4

SCOTTISH CUP

1st Round (Bye)

2nd Round Saturday, 9 February
ABERDEEN (1) 2   KILMARNOCK (1) 1
  Rodger (10), Boyd (88)   Harvey (37)

ABERDEEN: Martin, Shaw, Emery, Anderson, Thomson, Harris, Boyd, Yorston, I. Rodger, Baird, Pearson

KILMARNOCK: Niven, Collins, Hood, Russell, Thyne, Middlemas, Anderson, Harvey, Jack, Cowan, Donaldson

Attendance: 19,000   *Referee:* R. J. Smith

Before the match a military band played a salute to the late King George. The game itself, played on a blanket of snow, went within 2 minutes of a replay as the B Division side played above themselves. In a desperate final offensive Baird beat two men to set up Boyd for Aberdeen's winner.

3rd Round Saturday, 23 February
DUNDEE UNITED (1) 2   ABERDEEN (1) 2
  Cruickshank (8), McKay   Yorston (31), Baird (61)
  (80)

DUNDEE UNITED: Wyllie, Swan, Berrie, Downie, Ross, Mitchell, Quinn, Grant, McKay, Dunsmore, Cruickshank

ABERDEEN: Martin, Shaw, Emery, Anderson, Thomson, Harris, Boyd, Yorston, Rodger, Baird, Pearson

Attendance: 26,000   *Referee:* G. Mitchell

Dundee United, chasing promotion from Division B, fought a grim and exciting tussle with the Dons. As they piled forward in search of an equaliser in the final third of the match the Aberdeen goal had some narrow escapes. Dunsmore missed a penalty shortly before McKay earned the Tannadice club a merited second chance. The attendance, 26,000, set a new record for the ground.

3rd Round Replay Wednesday, 27 February
ABERDEEN (2) 3   DUNDEE UNITED (0) 2
  Yorston 2 (1, 51),   Dunsmore (77),
  Rodger (34)   Grant (86 pen)

ABERDEEN: Martin, Shaw, Emery, Anderson, Thomson, Harris, Boyd, Yorston, Rodger, Baird, Pearson

DUNDEE UNITED: Wyllie, Swan, Berrie, Downie, Ross, Mitchell, Quinn, Grant, McKay, Dunsmore, Cruickshank

Attendance: 30,000   *Referee:* G. Mitchell

Forget the scoreline. United were overwhelmed. Aberdeen created chance after chance, led by three goals shortly after half-time, and only when Emery conceded a rash penalty in the closing minutes did Dundee United sniff a possible second replay.

Quarter Final Saturday, 8 March
DUNDEE (1) 4   ABERDEEN (0) 0
  Zeising (31), Steel
  2 (51, 82), Boyd (60 pen)

DUNDEE: Henderson, Follon, Cowan, Gallacher, Cowie, Boyd, Burrell, Pattillo, Zeising, Steel, Christie

ABERDEEN: Martin, Shaw, Emery, Anderson, Thomson, Harris, Boyd, Yorston, Rodger, Baird, Pearson

Attendance: 40,000   *Referee:* J. A. Mowat

Ten thousand Dons fans journeyed to Dens Park to see their team sunk without trace by a Dundee team inspired by Billy Steel. Emery gave away yet another penalty. Aberdeen's only moment of hope came at 0-1 when Pearson's lob came back off the face of the bar.

Yorston, prominent for Aberdeen in the fifties.

1951-52 APPEARANCES	League	League Cup	Scottish Cup
Yorston	27	6	4
Harris	26	6	4
Lowrie	24	6	
Martin	23	6	4
Baird	23		4
Emery	20	6	4
Thomson	20	6	4
Pearson	20	4	4
Hamilton	19	4	
Young	19		
Boyd	16		4
Shaw	14	4	4
McKenna	12		
Anderson	11		4
I. Rodger	11		4
Delaney	10	5	
Hather	10	2	
Watson	7		
Samuel	4		
Smith	4		
Bogan	3	4	
Newlands	3		
Hay	2	4	
A. Rodger	2	3	
24 players			

GOALS	Total	League	League Cup	Scottish Cup
Yorston	25	19	3	3
Hamilton	14	13	1	
I. Rodger	10	8		2
Baird	6	5		1
Boyd	6	5		1
Delaney	6	4	2	
Emery	4	3	1	
Harris	2	2		
Pearson	2	1	1	
Hay	2		2	
Bogan	1	1		
Lowrie	1	1		
Shaw	1	1		
Samuel	1	1		
own-goals	1	1		
Total	82	65	10	7

A look at the past. The Aberdeen team in season 1933-34. Back row: Mr Travers (Manager), O'Riley, Cooper, Smith, McGill, Fraser, Thomson, Coleman (trainer). Front row: Beynon, Beattie, Armstrong, Mills, Gall.

Season 1952-53

1952-53 was one of those seasons that defies swift summary. From one month to the next nobody could foresee which way the Pittodrie pendulum would tilt. For two months disaster loomed. Aberdeen failed to win any of their six League Cup matches or opening five league games. Then, having waited twelve long games for the taste of victory, the Dons barnstormed their way up the table. 33 goals in seven matches hoisted them to fifth with the leaders only three points ahead. Septembers' fears were replaced by November's soaring hopes.

Alas, Aberdeen had flattered to deceive. They were soon on the downward slide. By early March the relegation clouds hovered, and did not finally disperse till Aberdeen harvested both points from Parkhead. Even so, the final margin of safety was a bare two points.

Both Aberdeen's rise and their fall were easy to explain. The 45 league goals they scored at Pittodrie were easily their highest total since the War. But those same forwards were less prolific on their travels, only twice finding the net more than once. The side's defensive failings, however, were almost calamitous. The debit column had been increasing relentlessly year by year since 1945, and now stood at 68 – well over two per match.

What gave 1952-53 its final twist was Aberdeen's sensational run in the Scottish Cup. The team that found league victories so hard to come by in the second half of the season was simultaneously marauding past St Mirren, Motherwell, Hibs and Third Lanark (the last three requiring replays) to earn a place at Hampden for the first time in six years. There Rangers (in Aberdeen's fourth Cup replay) finally shattered Aberdeen's dreams.

League:	Eleventh
League Cup:	Bottom of qualifying group
Scottish Cup:	Runners up

SCOTTISH LEAGUE DIVISION A

No 1 Saturday, 6 September
PARTICK THISTLE (1) 1   ABERDEEN (1) 1
. Stott (40)   Rodger (8)
PARTICK: Ledgerwood, McGowan, McCreadie, McNab, Kerr, Mathers, Howitt, Crawford, Stott, Sharp, Walker
ABERDEEN: Martin, Mitchell, Smith, Anderson, Young, Wallace, Buckley, Rodger, Dunbar, Yorston, Hather

P	W	D	L	F	A	Pts		
1	0	1	0	1	1	1	*Attendance:* 15,000
							Referee: H. Phillips

A drab game sees Partick stop the rot after seven straight Dons' wins.

No 2 Saturday, 13 September
ABERDEEN (1) 1   AIRDRIEONIANS (1) 2
  Yorston (37)   Welsh (24), Quinn (82)
ABERDEEN: Martin, Mitchell, Smith, Anderson, Young, Wallace, Buckley, Rodger, Dunbar, Yorston, Hather

AIRDRIE: Fraser, Pryde, T. Brown, Cairns, Rodger, Shankland, Seawright, McMillan, Quinn, Welsh, McCulloch

P	W	D	L	F	A	Pts		
2	0	1	1	2	3	1	*Attendance:* 15,000
							Referee: R. J. Smith

Aberdeen just cannot seem to beat Airdrie at Pittodrie. The crowd have to pay increased admission prices to watch the Dons' fourth home defeat of the season.

No 3 Saturday, 20 September
DUNDEE (1) 3   ABERDEEN (1) 1
  Flavell (25), Burrell (47),   Hay (63)
  Harris o.g. (84)
DUNDEE: R. Henderson, Follon, Cowan, Zeising, Boyd, Cowie, Toner, A. Henderson, Flavell, Steel, Burrell
ABERDEEN: Martin, Mitchell, Smith, Anderson, Young, Harris, Boyd, Yorston, Hamilton, Hay, Pearson

P	W	D	L	F	A	Pts		
3	0	1	2	3	6	1	*Attendance:* 20,000
							Referee: C. E. Faultless

At times the Aberdeen defence is reduced to panic. Only goal average keeps the Dons off the bottom.

No 4 Saturday, 27 September
ABERDEEN (2) 2   CELTIC (1) 2
  Boyd (3), Hamilton (21)   Peacock (39), Fallon (66)
ABERDEEN: Martin, Mitchell, Smith, Harris, Young, Wallace, Boyd, Yorston, Hamilton, Hay, Hather
CELTIC: Bonner, Boden, Meechan, Evans, Stein, Baillie, Rollo, Walsh, Fallon, Tully, Peacock

P W D L F A Pts
4 0 2 2 5 8   2   *Referee:* R. Yacimini

Celtic haven't yet lost, Aberdeen haven't yet won, and both records remain intact. Aberdeen couldn't hang on to a two-goal lead and Fallon finally equalised after Rollo's header had rattle the Dons' crossbar.

No 5 Saturday, 4 October
ST MIRREN (2) 2   ABERDEEN (1) 1
  McGill 2 (12, 20)   Hather (33)
ST MIRREN: Park, Lapsley, Ashe, Neilson, Telfer, Johnstone, Rice, McGill, Stewart, Gemmell, Blyth
ABERDEEN: Martin, Mitchell, Smith, Harris, Young, Wallace, Boyd, I. Rodger, Hamilton, Hay, Hather
Bottom positions

	P	W	D	L	F	A	Pts
13 Third Lanark	4	1	1	2	9	8	3
14 ABERDEEN	5	0	2	3	6	10	2
15 Falkirk	4	0	1	3	4	11	1
16 Raith Rovers	4	0	1	3	2	7	1

Attendance: 12,000   *Referee:* W. Bowman

Aberdeen lose to second-place Saints and their plight is now serious. They have gone eleven league and League Cup games without a win.

No 6 Saturday, 11 October
ABERDEEN (3) 4   THIRD LANARK (0) 3
  Hamilton 2 (19, 28),   Dick 2 (66, 67),
  Hather 2 (25, 55)   Cuthbertson (88)
ABERDEEN: Martin, Mitchell, Smith, Harris, Young, Allister, Boyd, Hamilton, Buckley, Hay, Hather
THIRD LANARK: Robertson, Balunas, Harrower, Mooney, Samuel, Duncan, Brown, Docherty, Cuthbertson, Dick, McLeod

P W D L F A Pts
6 1 2 3 10 13 4   *Attendance:* 17,000
                           Referee: J. P. Barclay

Aberdeen's first win of the season coincides with the signing of Jack Allister from Chelsea. Thirds have won their last five games against Aberdeen and nearly save this one after being 4-0 down.

No 7 Saturday, 18 October
AIRDRIEONIANS (2) 4   ABERDEEN (2) 7
  McGurn (23), McCulloch Hather 2 (20, 56),
  (34), McMillan (58 pen), Hamilton 2 (22, 49 pen),
  Welsh (65)   Buckley 2 (71, 87), Hay
                        (80)

AIRDRIE: Walker, Pryde, Cross, Cairns, Rodger, Quinn, Seawright, McMillan, McGurn, Welsh, McCulloch
ABERDEEN: Martin, Mitchell, Smith, Harris, Young, Allister, Boyd, Hamilton, Buckley, Hay, Hather

P W D L F A Pts   *Attendance:* 7,000
7 2 2 3 17 17 6   *Referee:* G. Mitchell

Who would believe it? With twenty minutes to play of a bizarre match it is already 4-4. The Dons go on to establish their highest league tally since the war.

No 8 Saturday, 25 October
ABERDEEN (4) 6   EAST FIFE (2) 3
  Boyd 3 (6, 24, 46),   Bonthrone (1), Fleming
  Buckley (19), Hamilton (20), Gardiner (53)
  2 (34 pen, 79)
ABERDEEN: Martin, Mitchell, Smith, Harris, Young, Allister, Boyd, Hamilton, Buckley, Hay, Hather
EAST FIFE: Curran, Emery, S. Stewart, Whyte, Finlay, Christie, J. Stewart, Fleming, Gardiner, Bonthrone, Duncan

P W D L F A Pts   *Attendance:* 20,000
8 3 2 3 23 20 8   *Referee:* J. S. Aitken

East Fife sit proudly on top of the league, having dropped only one point. With ex-Dons Curran and Emery in their ranks the score almost defies belief. A minute after a Hamilton penalty puts Aberdeen 4-2 up, Young flattened Gardiner but Duncan stroked the penalty wide to boost Aberdeen's hopes.

No 9 Saturday, 1 November
ABERDEEN (2) 5   MOTHERWELL (0) 1
  Hay 2 (41, 57), Buckley Humphries (59)
  (44), Hamilton 2 (48, 80)
ABERDEEN: Martin, Mitchell, Smith, Harris, Young, Allister, Boyd, Hamilton, Buckley, Hay, Hather
MOTHERWELL: Johnston, Kilmarnock, Shaw, Cox, Paton, Redpath, Sloan, Humphries, Kelly, Dawson, Aitkenhead

P W D L F A Pts   *Attendance:* 20,000
9 4 2 3 28 21 10   *Referee:* J. Bisset

This is going beyond the bounds of fantasy. 22 goals in four games and the Dons are now fifth.

No 10 Saturday, 8 November
RAITH ROVERS (1) 2   ABERDEEN (0) 1
  McIntyre (5), Copland   Buckley (63)
  (57)
RAITH: Johnstone, McLure, McNaught, Young, Clunie, Leigh, Maule, McIntyre, Copland, Kelly, Penman
ABERDEEN: Martin, Mitchell, Smith, Harris, Young, Allister, Boyd, Hamilton, Buckley, Hay, Hather

P W D L F A Pts   *Attendance:* 5,000
10 4 2 4 29 23 10   *Referee:* D. Graham

Aberdeen play in black armbands following the death from polio of goalkeeper Frank Watson. The Dons' goalscoring feats are forgotten and they hand bottom-placed Raith their first victory of the season.

No 11 Saturday, 15 November
ABERDEEN (2) 3　　　　HEARTS (0) 0
　Hather 2 (10, 65),
　Hamilton (35)
ABERDEEN: Martin, Mitchell, Smith, Harris, Young, Allister, Boyd, Hamilton, Buckley, Hay, Hather
HEARTS: Watters, Parker, MacKenzie, Dougan, Milne, Laing, Kilgannon, Bauld, Whittle, Urquhart, Blackwood

P	W	D	L	F	A	Pts	
11	5	2	4	32	23	12	*Attendance:* 15,000 *Referee:* W. Brittle

Hearts have not started the season brightly. Aberdeen are now the division's top scorers.

No 12 Saturday, 22 November
ABERDEEN (2) 7　　　　FALKIRK (2) 2
　Boyd (3), Hay 2 (43,72),　Delaney (6), Plumb (20)
　Buckley 2 (51, 67),
　Hather 2 (54, 82)
ABERDEEN: Morrison, Mitchell, Smith, Harris, Young, Allister, Boyd, Hamilton, Buckley, Hay, Hather
FALKIRK: Scott, McDonald, Wilson, Gallagher, McKenzie, Hunter, Delaney, Dunlop, Plumb, Morrison, Rae

Leading positions

	P	W	D	L	F	A	Pts
1 East Fife	12	8	1	3	33	24	17
2 Hibernian	10	8	0	2	31	18	16
3 St Mirren	12	6	4	2	21	12	16
4 Celtic	12	6	4	2	23	18	16
5 ABERDEEN	12	6	2	4	39	25	14

Attendance: 17,000　　　*Referee:* S. Hilton

Here we go, here we go! Aberdeen take their total to 33 goals from seven matches. Falkirk take a 2-1 lead and are then made to suffer! Reggie Morrison makes his debut in goal as Martin has damaged a finger.

No 13 Saturday, 29 November
QUEEN OF THE　　　　ABERDEEN (0) 0
　SOUTH (2) 4
　Johnstone (19), Black (28),
　Patterson 2 (67, 88)
QUEEN OF THE SOUTH: Henderson, Sharpe, Hall, McBain, Smith, Binning, Oakes, Black, Patterson, Greenock, Johnstone
ABERDEEN: Martin, Mitchell, Smith, Harris, Young, Allister, Boyd, Hamilton, Buckley, Hay, Hather

P	W	D	L	F	A	Pts
13	6	2	5	39	29	14

On an icy pitch Aberdeen come a cropper against lowly Queen of the South. But Buckley, Hather, Hamilton and Hay all leave their mark on the Dumfries crossbar.

No 14 Saturday, 6 December
RANGERS (2) 4　　　　ABERDEEN (0) 0
　McCulloch 2 (12, 79),
　Simpson (36), Young
　(68 pen)
RANGERS: Niven, Young, Little, McColl, Woodburn, Cox, McCulloch, Grierson, Simpson, Prentice, Hubbard
ABERDEEN: Martin, Mitchell, Smith, Harris, Young, Allister, Boyd, Rodger, Buckley, Hay, Hather

P	W	D	L	F	A	Pts	
14	6	2	6	39	33	14	*Attendance:* 35,000 *Referee:* R. H. Davidson

Rangers have games in hand over the leaders. In a match played with a novel white ball the Dons had no excuses, as they had at Dumfries. Towards the end of the match Ibrox's new floodlighting system was switched on.

No 15 Saturday, 13 December
ABERDEEN (1) 3　　　　CLYDE (1) 2
　Hather (14), Allister (46),　McPhail (28), Buchanan
　Buckley (72)　　　　　(84)
ABERDEEN: Martin, Mitchell, Smith, Harris, Anderson, Allister, McNeill, Yorston, Buckley, Hay, Hather
CLYDE: Wilson, Lindsay, Haddock, Anderson, Campbell, Long, Buchanan, Baird, McPhail, Robertson, Ring

P	W	D	L	F	A	Pts	
15	7	2	6	42	35	16	*Attendance:* 15,000 *Referee:* D. McKerchar

This match brings together Division A's two highest-scoring sides, and Aberdeen return to their winning ways.

No 16 Saturday, 20 December
ABERDEEN (0) 4　　　　PARTICK THISTLE (1) 2
　Hamilton 3 (46, 54, 90),　Howitt (40), McInnes
　Buckley (52)　　　　　(59)
ABERDEEN: Martin, Mitchell, Shaw, Harris, Smith, Allister, McNeill, Hamilton, Buckley, Hay, Hather
PARTICK: Ledgerwood, McGowan, McNab, Harvey, Davidson, Kerr, McInnes, Howitt, Stott, Sharp, Walker

P	W	D	L	F	A	Pts	
16	8	2	6	46	37	18	*Attendance:* 18,000 *Referee:* D. MacIntosh

The Dons climb back to fifth position with a 5-star second-half performance. Hamilton grabs a hat-trick on his return from injury. Aberdeen will win only three more league matches all season.

No 17 Saturday, 27 December
HIBERNIAN (1) 3　　　　ABERDEEN (0) 0
　Smith (38), Reilly (83),
　Ormond (84)
HIBERNIAN: Younger, Clark, Cowie, Buchanan, Paterson, Combe, Smith, Johnstone, Reilly, Turnbull, Ormond

ABERDEEN: Martin, Mitchell, Shaw, Harris, Smith, Allister, McNeill, Yorston, Buckley, Baird, Hather

P W D L F A Pts   *Attendance:* 20,000
17 8 2 7 46 40 18   *Referee:* W. Brittle

Hibs are going strong for their third championship in a row. The Dons try to defend but are beaten by Gordon Smith's 300th goal in first-class matches.

No 18 Thursday 1 January
ABERDEEN (0) 2   DUNDEE (1) 2
   Rodger (64), Yorston (73)   Flavell 2 (15, 62)

ABERDEEN: Martin, Mitchell, Shaw, Harris, Smith, Allister, Rodger, Yorston, Buckley, Hay, Hather
DUNDEE: R. Henderson, Follon, Cowan, Cowie, Bob Henderson, Boyd, Christie, Gallacher, Flavell, Steel, Burrell

P W D L F A Pts
18 8 3 7 48 42 19   *Referee:* J. Jackson

Over-robust tackling sours this eagerly awaited derby. Two goals by Bobby Flavell looked to have sealed the points for Dundee. Rodger gave Aberdeen hope, but Yorston's equaliser produced a raised flag by a linesman which was ignored by the referee – much to Dundee's disgust.

No 19 Saturday, 10 January
ABERDEEN (0) 1   ST MIRREN (1) 2
   Hay (67)   McGill (13), Anderson
                 (52)

ABERDEEN: Martin, Mitchell, Shaw, Harris, Smith, Allister, Rodger, Yorston, Buckley, Hay, Hather
ST MIRREN: Park, Lapsley, Reid, Neilson, Telfer, Johnston, Rice, McGill, Stewart, Gemmell, Anderson

P W D L F A Pts
19 8 3 8 49 44 19   *Referee:* J. Jackson

A second defeat by high-flying Saints. As against Dundee, Aberdeen are two goals down before they get going.

No 20 Saturday, 17 January
THIRD LANARK (0) 0   ABERDEEN (0)1
                            Hather (47)

THIRD LANARK: Robertson, Balunas, Phillips, Simpson, Forsyth, Moonie, Wilson, Henderson, Cuthbertson, Dick, McLeod
ABERDEEN: Martin, Mitchell, Shaw, Harris, Smith, Allister, Rodger, Yorston, Buckley, Baird, Hather

P W D L F A Pts
20 9 3 8 50 44 21   *Referee:* C. E. Faultless

In view of Third Lanark's curse over Aberdeen in recent years it is a pleasure to record a Dons double over the Warriors. Third Lanark are now bottom.

No 21 Saturday, 24 January
CLYDE (2) 3   ABERDEEN (0) 0
   McPhail 2 (30, 62),
   Robertson (44)

CLYDE: Wilson, Murphy, Haddock, Anderson, Campbell, Long, Buchanan, Baird, McPhail, Robertson, Ring
ABERDEEN: Martin, Mitchell, Shaw, Harris, Smith, Allister, Rodger, Yorston, Buckley, Glen, Hather

P W D L F A Pts   *Attendance:* 12,000
21 9 3 9 50 47 21   *Referee:* G. Mitchell

Aberdeen have no complaints. Clyde are now the undisputed leading scorers of Division A.

No 22 Saturday, 14 February
EAST FIFE (3) 4   ABERDEEN (0) 1
   Fleming (19), Matthew   Yorston (70)
   2 (20, 22), Gardiner (50)

EAST FIFE: Curran, Emery, S. Stewart, Christie, Finlay, McLennan, J. Stewart, Fleming, Bonthrone, Gardiner, Matthew
ABERDEEN: Martin, Mitchell, Shaw, Harris, Young, Allister, Rodger, Hamilton, Buckley, Yorston, Hather

P W D L F A Pts   *Attendance:* 6,000
22 9 3 10 51 51 21   *Referee:* J. Bisset

A 4-0 defeat by Rangers has allowed Hibs to overtake East Fife, who now avenge their earlier humiliation at Pittodrie. Three goals in three minutes put the game out of Aberdeen's reach.

No 23 Saturday, 28 February
ABERDEEN (0) 0   RAITH ROVERS (2) 2
                      Young (9), Copland (19)

ABERDEEN: Martin, Mitchell, Shaw, Harris, Young, Allister, Rodger, Yorston, Buckley, Glen, Hather
RAITH: Johnstone, McLure, McNaught, Leigh, Colville, Williamson, Wood, McEwan, Copland, Young, Penman

P W D L F A Pts   *Attendance:* 20,000
23 9 3 11 52 53 21   *Referee:* S. Hilton

Aberdeen return to league duties after two stirring cup clashes with Motherwell. They have now taken only one point from their last six meetings with Raith, who snatched two quick goals and then refused to surrender.

No 24 Saturday, 7 March
HEARTS (1) 3   ABERDEEN (0) 1
   Wardhaugh 2 (21, 50),   Hay (82)
   Blackwood (84)

HEARTS: Watter, Parker, MacKenzie, Laing, Dougan, Armstrong, Blackwood, Conn, Bauld, Wardhaugh, Urquhart
ABERDEEN: Martin, Smith, Shaw, Harris, Young, Allister, Rodger, Yorston, Buckley, Hay, Pearson

Bottom positions

	P	W	D	L	F	A	Pts
11 ABERDEEN	24	9	3	12	52	56	21
12 Airdrie	24	8	5	11	40	57	21
13 Queen of the South	23	8	5	10	34	49	21
14 Motherwell	25	8	5	12	48	68	21
15 Third Lanark	25	8	3	14	47	56	19
16 Falkirk	25	7	4	14	39	56	18

C

Attendance: 20,000   *Referee:* J. A. Mowat

The Dons' fourth straight defeat. Aberdeen's red army has nothing to do with the death of Stalin far away in Moscow, but their team are now only two points clear of a relegation spot, and are in dire straits.

No 25 Saturday, 21 March

ABERDEEN (1) 4	QUEEN OF THE SOUTH
Yorston (12), Rodger	(0) 0
2 (49, 82), Allister (77 pen)	

ABERDEEN: Martin, Mitchell, Shaw, Ewen, Young, Allister, Rodger, Yorston, Buckley, Hamilton, Hather

QUEEN OF THE SOUTH: Henderson, Sharpe, Binning, Sweeney, Smith, Greenock, Black, Rothera, Patterson, J. Brown, Oakes

P W D L F A Pts   *Attendance:* 16,000
25 10 3   12 56 56 23   *Referee:* J. S. Aitken

With a huge sigh of relief Aberdeen secure two priceless points. They are helped by Brown hobbling for the last hour.

No 26 Saturday, 28 March

ABERDEEN (1) 2	RANGERS (1) 2
Yorston (21), Rodger (60)	Grierson (20), Gardiner (87)

ABERDEEN: Martin, Mitchell, Shaw, Glen, Young, Allister, Rodger, Yorston, Buckley, Smith, Hather

RANGERS: Niven, Young, Little, McColl, Woodburn, Rae, McCulloch, Grierson, Gardiner, Prentice, Hubbard

P W D L F A Pts   *Attendance:* 28,000
26 10 4   12 58 58 24   *Referee:* R. Yacamini

Before the match there is a one-minute silence for the death of Queen Mary. Rangers went in front when Grierson's shot passed through Martin's legs. Yorston silenced the Ibrox contingent with a blistering 30-yarder, and Hather then struck a post. As Rangers piled forward in search of a second point Rodger smashed a vicious shot past Niven. Aberdeen looked to be stronger at the finish and were not prepared for Gardiner's later equaliser.

No 27 Saturday, 11 April

ABERDEEN (1) 1	HIBERNIAN (1) 1
Hather (2)	Reilly (9)

ABERDEEN: Martin, Mitchell, Smith, Harris, Young, Allister, Rodger, Yorston, Buckley, Hamilton, Hather

HIBERNIAN: Younger, Govan, Howie, Buchanan, Paterson, Ward, Smith, Johnstone, Reilly, Turnbull, Combe

P W D L F A Pts   *Attendance:* 20,000
27 10 5   12 59 59 25   *Referee:* J. S. Cox

Hibs come searching for revenge for their cup K.O. and to gather the two points in their quest for the championship. After an opening flourish the game swung from end to end with neither side able to land the decisive goal. The Dons came nearest. In the last minute Hamilton's header bounced onto the bar and over.

No 28 Wednesday, 15 April

CELTIC (0) 1	ABERDEEN (2) 3
McPhail (49)	Hamilton 2 (40, 42)
	Yorston (86)

CELTIC: Bonner, Haughney, Meechan, Evans, Stein, McGrory, Collins, Walsh, Fallon, McPhail, Peacock

ABERDEEN: Martin, Mitchell, Smith, Harris, Young, Allister, Rodger, Yorston, Buckley, Hamilton, Hather

P W D L F A Pts
28 11 5   12 62 60 27

With this win Aberdeen recorded their eighth game without defeat in league and Scottish Cup, and ensured their continuing membership of Division A. But until Hamilton put them in front the Dons looked like a side resigned to the drop.

No 29 Saturday, 18 April

MOTHERWELL (3) 4	ABERDEEN (0) 1
Shaw o.g (22), Kelly	Hather (48)
2 (28, 42), Redpath	
(85 pen)	

MOTHERWELL: Johnston, Kilmarnock, Shaw, Cox, Paton, Redpath, Sloan, Humphries, Kelly, Forrest, Williams

ABERDEEN: Martin, Mitchell, Shaw, Glen, Young, Allister, Rodger, Yorston, Buckley, Hamilton, Hather

P W D L F A Pts
29 11 5   13 63 64 27   *Referee:* G. Jackson

Motherwell have everything to play for; Aberdeen nothing. In the circumstances the result was hardly surprising as Motherwell avenged their cup defeat.

No 30 Monday, 20 April

FALKIRK (1) 4	ABERDEEN (1) 1
Delaney 2 (32, 80),	Hather (35)
Campbell (52), Brown (65)	

FALKIRK: McFeat, McDonald, Rae, Gallacher, McKenzie, Hunter, Delaney, Campbell, Plumb, McCrae, J. Brown

ABERDEEN: Morrison, Mitchell, Shaw, Glen, Young, Allister, Rodger, Yorston, Buckley, Hamilton, Hather

Aberdeen helped out Motherwell on the Saturday and extend the same charity to Falkirk on the Monday.

Aberdeen's complete home and away record:

HOME						AWAY						
P	W	D	L	F	A		W	D	L	F	A	Pts
30	8	4	3	45	26		3	1	11	19	42	27

Scottish League Division A 1952-53

	P	W	D	L	F	A	Pts
1 Rangers	30	18	7	5	80	39	43
2 Hibernian	30	19	5	6	93	51	43
3 East Fife	30	16	7	7	72	48	39
4 Hearts	30	12	6	12	59	50	30
5 Clyde	30	13	4	13	78	78	30
6 St Mirren	30	11	8	11	52	58	30
7 Dundee	30	9	11	10	44	37	29
8 Celtic	30	11	7	12	51	54	29
9 Partick Thistle	30	10	9	11	55	63	29
10 Queen of the South	30	10	8	12	43	61	28
11 ABERDEEN	30	11	5	14	64	68	27
12 Raith Rovers	30	9	8	13	47	53	26
13 Falkirk	30	11	4	15	53	63	26
14 Airdrieonians	30	10	6	14	53	75	26
15 Motherwell	30	10	5	15	57	80	25
16 Third Lanark	30	8	4	18	52	75	20

LEAGUE CUP

Saturday, 9 August
MOTHERWELL (2) 5   ABERDEEN (1) 2
Kelly (5), Humphries   Buckley (18), Yorston
2 (28, 85), Kilmarnock   (57)
(60), Aitkenhead (71)

MOTHERWELL: Johhnston, Kilmarnock, Shaw, Cox, Paton, Redpath, Sloan, Humphries, Kelly, Forrest, Aitkenhead

ABERDEEN: Watson, Mitchell, Shaw, Anderson, Thomson, Harris, Rodger, Yorston, Buckley, Baird, Hather

Referee: J. A. Mowat
The Dons display new signing Jimmy Mitchell from Morton. For an hour they hold their own. Then Kilmarnock scored with a free kick from 50 yards as all the Aberdeen defenders left it to each other.

Wednesday, 13 August
ABERDEEN (0) 2   HEARTS (4) 4
Ewen (57 pen), Yorston   Bauld 2 (12, 20), Parker
(65)   (22 pen), Rutherford (31)

ABERDEEN: Martin, Mitchell, Smith, Samuel, Thomson, Harris, Rodger, Yorston, Buckley, Ewen, Hather

HEARTS: Watters, Parker, Mackenzie, Glidden, Milne, Laing, Rutherford, Conn, Bauld, Wardhaugh, Urquhart

Attendance: 33,000   *Referee:* D. McKerchar
The Dons suffer a first-half mauling from a Hearts side superior in every department, and already have no further interest in the competition.

Saturday, 16 August
RANGERS (2) 3   ABERDEEN (0) 1
Grierson 2 (15, 31),   Buckley (50)
Thornton (89)

RANGERS: Niven, Young, Little, McColl, Woodburn, Cox, Waddell, Grierson, Thornton, Prentice, Liddell

ABERDEEN: Martin, Mitchell, Shaw, Smith, Thomson, Harris, Rodger, Yorston, Buckley, Baird, Hather

Aberdeen take the field without Hamilton, who did not feel up to playing. Their defeat means they have conceded 12 goals in three games. A few days later Emery is transferred to East Fife and Lowrie to Oldham. The Dons Board later suspend Hamilton for a month.

Referee: J. Jackson
Saturday, 23 August
ABERDEEN (0) 0   MOTHERWELL (0) 1
Aitkenhead (82)

ABERDEEN: Martin, Pattillo, Shaw, Harris, Thomson, Wallace, Boyd, McNeill, Buckley, Baird, Hather

MOTHERWELL: Johnston, Kilmarnock, Shaw, Cox, Paton, Redpath, Sloan, Humphries, Kelly, Forrest, Aitkenhead

Attendance: 25,000   *Referee:* P. Fitzpatrick
Both teams wear black armbands in memory of former Dons skipper and trainer Bob McDermid. His replacement, Jock Pattillo, has to turn out as full-back.

Wednesday, 27 August
HEARTS (0) 1   ABERDEEN (1) 1
Bauld (46)   Hather (8)

HEARTS: Watters, Parker, Mackenzie, Dougan, Milne, Laing, Adie, Cumming, Bauld, Wardhaugh, Urquhart

ABERDEEN: Martin, Mitchell, Smith, Anderson, Thomson, Harris, Boyd, Rodger, Dunbar, Baird, Hather

Attendance: 22,000
Aberdeen do irreparable harm to Hearts' hopes of qualifying from Section C.

Saturday, 30 August
ABERDEEN (1) 1   RANGERS (0) 2
Yorston (1)   Waddell (73), Thornton
(86)

ABERDEEN: Martin, Mitchell, Smith, Anderson, Thomson, Wallace, Boyd, Rodger, Dunbar, Yorston, Hather

RANGERS: Niven, Young, Little, McColl, Woodburn, Cox, Waddell, Paton, Thornton, Prentice, Liddell

Attendance: 35,000   *Referee:* G. Mitchell
Rangers come looking for two points, and get them when Thornton collides with Thomson and the ball rolls over the line. This is Kenny Thomson's last match before his transfer to Stoke.

Section C

	P	W	D	L	F	A	Pts
Rangers	6	4	1	1	12	10	9
Hearts	6	3	1	2	12	7	7
Motherwell	6	3	1	2	11	9	7
ABERDEEN	6	0	1	5	7	16	1

SCOTTISH CUP

1st Round (Bye)

2nd Round Saturday, 7 February
ABERDEEN (2) 2   ST MIRREN (0) 0
  Hather 2 (7, 9)
ABERDEEN: Martin, Mitchell, Shaw, Harris, Young, Allister, Rodger, Hamilton, Buckley, Yorston, Hather
ST MIRREN: Park, Lapsley, Johnston, Neilson, Telfer, Reid, Rice, McGill, Stewart, Blyth, Anderson
Attendance: 22,000   *Referee:* W. Brittle
St Mirren have already taken four points off Aberdeen in the league so have every reason for confidence. Their hopes lasted just nine minutes – courtesy of Jackie Hather. When Saints lost Neilson with a broken leg later in the opening half their hopes of salvaging a replay disappeared.

3rd Round Saturday, 21 February
ABERDEEN (4) 5   MOTHERWELL (2) 5
  Buckley 2 (16, 27),   Kelly (9), Aitkenhead
  Yorston (20)   (30 pen), Humphries (73),
  Allister 2 (40 pen, 76 pen) Shaw (84), Cox (89)
ABERDEEN: Martin, Mitchell, Shaw, Harris, Young, Allister, Rodger, Hamilton, Buckley, Yorston, Hather
MOTHERWELL: Johnston, Kilmarnock, Shaw, Forrest, Brown, Cox, Sloan, Humphries, Kelly, Robinson, Aitkenhead
Attendance: 28,000   *Referee:* J. A. Mowat
Motherwell are the defending holders of the Scottish Cup, and feature in one of Pittodrie's never-to-be-forgotten encounters. On the eve of the match Dave Shaw is appointed Dons' player/trainer. Although Motherwell scored first, Aberdeen took control. At 3-1 Shaw handled on the goalline to present Aitkenhead with a penalty which Martin nearly saved. Allister then converted two spot kicks for Aberdeen, first when Brown handled and then when Rodger appeared to be fouled outside the box. With the score at 5-3 in Aberdeen's favour Rodger proceeded to shoot wide of a gaping goal. But Motherwell were determined to cling on to their prize. Shaw fired past Martin from 30 yards and Cox equalised with only seconds left.

3rd Round Replay Wednesday, 25 February
MOTHERWELL (1) 1   ABERDEEN (4) 6
  Aitkenhead (17)   Rodger (7), Yorston
                           3 (22, 55, 75), Buckley
                           (27), Hather (35)
MOTHERWELL: Johnston, Kilmarnock, Shaw, Forrest, Brown, Cox, Sloan, Humphries, Kelly, Robinson, Aitkenhead
ABERDEEN: Martin, Mitchell, Shaw, Harris, Young, Allister, Rodger, Yorston, Buckley, Hay, Hather
Attendance: 20,000   *Referee:* J. A. Mowat
Yet another astonishing result for the unpredictable Dons. Again they score four by half-time, but this time

there is no way back for Motherwell. Hibs' players and officials watch their quarter-final opponents from the stand.

Quarter Final Saturday, 14 March
HIBERNIAN (0) 1   ABERDEEN (1) 1
  Buchanan (82)   Rodger (10)
HIBERNIAN: Younger, Clark, Howie, Buchanan, Paterson, Combe, Smith, Johnstone, Reilly, Turnbull, Ormond
ABERDEEN: Martin, Mitchell, Shaw, Harris, Young, Allister, Rodger, Yorston, Buckley, Hay, Hather
Attendance: 47,500   *Referee:* W. Brittle
Hibs may top the league and have their sights set on a famous double but Aberdeen are no respecter of reputations. This was a game to savour: 7,000 Dons fans roared their approval when Rodger's header from Buckley's cross bounced down and up beyond Younger. Rodger had a gorgeous chance of a second when Buckley again set him up, only this time he fired wide. In the closing minutes, with Hibs piling men forward, Smith took a free kick and Buchanan's header was straight and true.

Quarter Final Replay Wednesday, 18 March
ABERDEEN (1) 2   HIBERNIAN (0) 0
  Hamilton 2 (12, 49)
ABERDEEN: Martin, Mitchell, Shaw, Harris, Young, Allister, Rodger, Yorston, Buckley, Hamilton, Hather
HIBERNIAN: Younger, Govan, Clark, Buchanan, Paterson, Gallacher, Combe, Johnstone, Reilly, Turnbull, Ormond
Attendance: 42,000   *Referee:* W. Brittle
Pittodrie was jammed to capacity. Both sides went in search of goals and Aberdeen found one. Rodger's chipped centre was flashed home by Hamilton's head. Hammy's second goal, after the interval, put paid to Hibs' hopes. Once again the Hibernian team that could do no wrong in the league could not make a sustained bid for the Scottish Cup.

Semi Final (Ibrox) Saturday, 4 April
THIRD LANARK (0) 1   ABERDEEN (0) 1
  Cuthbertson (77)   Buckley (59)
THIRD LANARK: Robertson, Balunas, Harrower, Mooney, Forsyth, Duncan, Dobbie, Henderson, Cuthbertson, Dick, Barclay
ABERDEEN: Martin, Mitchell, Shaw, Harris, Young, Allister, Rodger, Yorston, Buckley, Hay, Hather
Attendance: 20,000   *Referee:* C. E. Faultless
Aberdeen are not displeased to be paired with Third Lanark in the semi final. Their opponents are destined for Division B, and have already lost to the Dons in the league 3-4 and 0-1. Like many semi finals the game was unenterprising and tense. Its only moments of excitement arrived once Buckley had put the Dons in front. Forsyth made a hash of a backpass and Buckley shot into goal off Robertson's body. Yorston then drove

inches too high. But eventually Cuthbertson got the vital touch in a scrimmage and followed up by prompting a wonder save from Martin which kept the Dons alive.

Semi Final Replay (Ibrox) Wednesday, 8 April
THIRD LANARK (0) 1   ABERDEEN (1) 2
Dick (30)   Yorston 2 (32, 71)

THIRD LANARK: Robertson, Balunas, Harrower, Mooney, Forsyth, Duncan, Dobbie, Henderson, Cuthbertson, Dick, Barclay

ABERDEEN: Martin, Mitchell, Smith, Harris, Young, Allister, Rodger, Yorston, Buckley, Hamilton, Hather

Attendance: 25,000   *Referee:* C. E. Faultless

The replay was no classic either. This time it was Third Lanark who took advantage of a suicidal backpass, Dick thanking Allister for his error. Within two minutes Yorston scored an equally soft goal, accidentally directing Rodger's shot past Robertson. The second half was a continuous yawn, relieved only when Hamilton sent the ball ahead for Yorston to score off a post.

Scottish Cup Final (Hampden) Saturday, 25 April
RANGERS (1) 1   ABERDEEN (0) 1
Prentice (8)   Yorston (80)

RANGERS: Niven, Young, Little, McColl, Stanners, Pryde, Waddell, Grierson, Paton, Prentice, Hubbard

ABERDEEN: Martin, Mitchell, Shaw, Harris, Young, Allister, Rodger, Yorston, Buckley, Hamilton, Hather

Attendance: 134,000   *Referee:* J. A. Mowat

Three Dons players turn out for their second Scottish Cup Final – George Hamilton and Tony Harris from the 1947 Dons side, and Dave Shaw who had worn a Hibs shirt on that occasion. Prentice's angular drive put the 'Gers in front. Midway through the first half Buckley drove the ball hard against Niven who was carried off on a stretcher. Until the keeper returned for the second period George Young borrowed Rangers' keeper's jersey. Aberdeen looked strangely punchless considering the battling qualities they had demonstrated in reaching Hampden. But with ten minutes remaining Yorston swept the ball out to Hather and then dashed forward to connect with the winger's cross to square the score. Alive at last, Aberdeen were on the ascendant during the minutes that remained but could do no better than when Buckley brought a fine save from Niven.

Scottish Cup Final Replay (Hampden) Wednesday, 29 April
RANGERS (1) 1   ABERDEEN (0) 0
Simpson (42)

RANGERS: Niven, Young, Little, McColl, Woodburn, Pryde, Waddell, Grierson, Simpson, Paton, Hubbard

ABERDEEN: Martin, Mitchell, Shaw, Harris, Young, Allister, Rodger, Yorston, Buckley, Hamilton, Hather

Attendance: 113,700   *Referee:* J. A. Mowat

You very rarely get a second chance against Rangers, and so it proved. Man for man Aberdeen performed better in the replay than on the Saturday, but Simpson's firm drive in the closing stages of the first half – against the general run of play – gave Rangers a lead they were determined not to squander in the second half. Rangers duly went on to take the league title from Hibs – on goal average.

1952-53

APPEARANCES	League	League Cup	Scottish Cup
Mitchell	29	5	9
Hather	28	6	9
Martin	28	5	9
Buckley	27	4	9
Allister	25		9
W. Smith	25	4	1
Harris	24	5	9
Young	23		9
Yorston	19	4	9
Hamilton	18		6
Rodger	17	5	9
Hay	17		3
Shaw	13	3	8
Boyd	12	3	
Glen	5		
Anderson	4	3	
Wallace	4	2	
McNeill	3	1	
Baird	2	4	
Dunbar	2	2	
Morrison	2		
Pearson	2		
Ewen	1	1	
Thomson		6	
Samuel		1	
Watson		1	
Pattillo		1	
27 players			

GOALS	Total	League	League Cup	Scottish Cup
Hather	18	14	1	3
Hamilton	17	15		2
Yorston	16	6	3	7
Buckley	15	9	2	4
Hay	8	8		
Rodger	7	5		2
Boyd	5	5		
Allister	4	2		2
Ewen	1		1	
Total	91	64	7	20

Season 1953-54

Season 1953-54 was the year in which north-east Scotland began to be charged with expectancy. It had a drab opening but a massive climax, which took the Dons to Hampden for a second successive year.

The season began encouragingly with an away win over Celtic in the League Cup. Aberdeen then shipped eight goals to Airdrie and East Fife and the chance to qualify for the quarter finals had passed.

The start of the league season suggested that the Dons would be presented with yet another fight for survival. Only one point was collected from the opening four matches. But then, repeating the experience of the previous season, Aberdeen got the bit between their teeth. They surged up the table, reaching second place by mid-November, and maintained their challenge for the title until the last few matches when they slipped dramatically down the league.

Aberdeen's league resurgence was due to their conceding fewer home goals and scoring more away than in any season since the War. Away from home, however, Aberdeen's defence couldn't record a single clean sheet.

As with the previous season, 1953-54 was to be remembered chiefly for Aberdeen's assault on the Scottish Cup. In 1953 they had fought their way groggily past every opponent to reach Hampden. In 1954 they knocked everyone contemptuously aside. Aberdeen dealt a double blow to Edinburgh. Having disposed of Hibs, they set about league-leaders Hearts in a match which still provides Pittodrie with its record attendance. Next it was the turn of the Old Firm. Rangers were crushed 6-0 in the semi to leave only Celtic – captained by Jock Stein to the league title – standing in their way. Again it was to be disappointment for the Dons, but their was no doubting that the future held more promise than the past. As a bonus, Fred Martin played for Scotland in the 1954 World Cup Finals in Switzerland.

League:	Ninth
League Cup:	Second in qualifying group
Scottish Cup:	Runners up

SCOTTISH LEAGUE DIVISION A

No 1 Saturday, 5 September

ABERDEEN (0) 0   ST MIRREN (1) 3
Lapsley (39), Stewart 2 (48, 78)

ABERDEEN: Morrison, Mitchell, Caldwell, Harris, Smith, Allister, Dunbar, Yorston, Buckley, Hamilton, Hather

ST MIRREN: Park, Lapsley, Cunningham, Neilson, Telfer, Johnston, Rice, McGill, Stewart, Gemmell, Blyth

P	W	D	L	F	A	Pts	
1	0	0	1	0	3	0	*Attendance:* 15,000
							Referee: J. P. Barclay

St Mirren win in a canter despite having Rice hobbling for 85 minutes. The stadium is drained long before the end.

No 2 Saturday, 12 September

STIRLING ALBION (1) 1   ABERDEEN (0) 0
Anderson (25)

STIRLING: Jenkins, Ferguson, Forsyth, Bain, Milligan, Whitehead, Chalmers, McFarlane, Williamson, Smith, Anderson

ABERDEEN: Morrison, Mitchell, Caldwell, Harris, Young, Allister, Leggat, Yorston, Buckley, Hamilton, Hather

P	W	D	L	F	A	Pts	
2	0	0	2	0	4	0	*Attendance:* 10,000
							Referee: D. J. Murphy

62

Graham Leggat makes his debut in another grim Aberdeen performance.

No 3 Saturday, 19 September
ABERDEEN (0) 1   DUNDEE (0) 1
  Yorston (73)   Flavell (75)
ABERDEEN: Martin, Mitchell, Caldwell, Allister, Young, Glen, Leggat, Hamilton, Buckley, Yorston, Hather
DUNDEE: R. Henderson, Frew, Cowan, Ziesing, Malloy, Cowie, Turnbull, Gallacher, Flavell, Steel, Hill

P	W	D	L	F	A	Pts
3	0	1	2	1	5	1

Attendance: 18,000
Referee: J. A. Mowat

Much chopping and changing of the Aberdeen team brings them their first point. Flavell hit the Dons' bar before Yorston's goal, but equalises immediately afterwards.

No 4 Saturday, 26 September
CELTIC (2) 3   ABERDEEN (0) 0
  Collins 3 (18 pen, 44 pen,
  65 pen)
CELTIC: Bell, Haughney, Fallon, Evans, Stein, Peacock, Collins, Walsh, Duncan, Tully, Mochan
ABERDEEN: Martin, Mitchell, Caldwell, Allister, Young, Glen, Leggat, Smith, Buckley, Hay, Hather

Bottom positions

	P	W	D	L	F	A	Pts
12 Partick	3	1	0	2	5	5	2
13 Hamilton	4	1	0	3	5	8	2
14 Clyde	4	1	0	3	4	8	2
15 Hibernian	3	1	0	2	4	9	2
16 ABERDEEN	4	0	1	3	1	8	1

Attendance: 35,000
Referee: A. McEwan

Aberdeen already have two League Cup wins over Celtic under their belts. This time Celtic are victorious by three penalties all conceded by Jimmy Mitchell and all scored by Bobby Collins. All three awards were doubtful: first when Mitchell brought down Walsh; second after a brush with Collins; third when he swung at the ball and missed.

No 5 Saturday, 3 October
ABERDEEN (1) 2   PARTICK THISTLE (1) 1
  Allister (7), Leggat (68)   Mitchell o.g. (37)
ABERDEEN: Martin, Mitchell, Caldwell, Allister, Young, Glen, Leggat, Smith, Buckley, Yorston, Hather
PARTICK: Ledgerwood, McGowan, Gibb, Crawford, Davidson, McNab, McKenzie, Howitt, Wright, Sharp, Walker

P	W	D	L	F	A	Pts
5	1	1	3	3	9	3

Referee: D. Graham

Mitchell continues his tales of woe. After giving three penalties to Celtic he heads a splendid own goal for Partick. Leggat's first senior goal for Aberdeen brings them their first win of the season.

No 6 Saturday, 10 October
ABERDEEN (0) 5   HAMILTON
  Hay (64), Buckley   ACADEMICALS (0) 1
  3 (66, 71, 81), Hather   Cunning (61)
  (74)
ABERDEEN: Martin, Paterson, Caldwell, Allister, Young, Glen, Leggat, Yorston, Buckley, Hay, Hather
HAMILTON: Houston, Ferguson, Johnstone, Wilson, G. Scott, Lindsay, McKirdy, Brown, J. Scott, Shearer, Cunning

P	W	D	L	F	A	Pts
6	2	1	3	8	10	5

Attendance: 12,000
Referee: P. Fitzpatrick

Hay makes hay in the 64th minute, equalising Cunning's breakaway goal, then goes off injured.

No 7 Saturday, 17 October
ABERDEEN (2) 5   AIRDRIEONIANS (0) 0
  Leggat (10), Buckley
  2 (44, 84), Yorston (63),
  Young (79)
ABERDEEN: Martin, Paterson, Caldwell, Allister, Young, Glen, Leggat, Yorston, Buckley, Smith, Hather
AIRDRIE: Fraser, Shanks, T. Brown, Cairns, Rodger, Henderson, McMillan, Thomson, Baird, Welsh, McCulloch

P	W	D	L	F	A	Pts
7	3	1	3	13	10	7

Attendance: 15,000
Referee: C. E. Faultless

The League Cup encounter at Pittodrie was a drab affair. This time the Dons go nap for the second week in succession.

No 8 Saturday, 31 October
CLYDE (1) 2   ABERDEEN (3) 4
  Hill (24), Ring (52)   Buckley (5), Leggat (22),
                           Hather 2 (31, 78)
CLYDE: Wilson, Murphy, Haddock, Robertson, Campbell, Baird, Hill, Divers, Buchanan, McPhail, Ring
ABERDEEN: Martin, Mitchell, Aitken, Allister, Smith, Glen, Leggat, Yorston, Buckley, Hay, Hather

P	W	D	L	F	A	Pts
8	4	1	3	17	12	9

Attendance: 10,000
Referee: G. Mitchell

After taking one point from their first four matches Aberdeen take all eight from their next four in a puzzling re-enactment of their frenzied variation in form of last year. Clyde have 80% of the game but Aberdeen show the way to goal.

No 9 Saturday, 7 November
ABERDEEN (0) 1   RANGERS (1) 1
  Allister (70 pen)   Simpson (43)
ABERDEEN: Martin, Mitchell, Smith, Allister, Young, Glen, Boyd, Yorston, Buckley, Kelly, Hather
RANGERS: Niven, Young, Little, McColl, Stanners, Cox, Waddell, Paton, Simpson, Thornton, Hubbard

P	W	D	L	F	A	Pts
9	4	2	3	18	13	10

Attendance: 25,000
Referee: J. Jackson

Rangers, would you believe, travel to Pittodrie in the bottom three to meet a Dons outfit seeking a fifth successive win. The match was fast and frantic with little cohesion. Aberdeen took a point when Buckley, clean through, was baulked by Niven. The referee only awarded a penalty after consulting a linesman and Allister did the rest.

No 10 Saturday, 14 November
ABERDEEN (1) 2   QUEEN OF THE SOUTH
  Hather (42), Yorston (82)   (0) 0
ABERDEEN: Martin, Mitchell, Caldwell, Allister, Young, Glen, Leggat, Yorston, Buckley, Smith, Hather
QUEEN OF THE SOUTH: Henderson, Sharpe, Binning, McBain, Smith, Greenock, Black, McGill, Brown, Rothera, Oakes
Leading positions

	P	W	D	L	F	A	Pts
1 Queen of the South	11	8	1	2	31	14	17
2 ABERDEEN	10	5	2	3	20	13	12
3 Hearts	11	5	2	4	24	16	12
4 Dundee	11	4	4	3	15	14	12
5 St Mirren	10	5	2	3	17	16	12

Attendance: 27,000   *Referee:* H. J. Gallacher
These are strange times in Division A. Queen of the South have opened a six-point gap as they journey north with 31 goals in their ten matches. A Jackie Hather thunderbolt sets them on their heels. Aberdeen are now second, and were bottom only six matches ago.

No 11 Saturday, 21 November
FALKIRK (0) 2   ABERDEEN (1) 2
  McCrae (50), Sinclair (88)   Yorston (30), Leggat (82)
FALKIRK: McFeat, McDonald, Rae, Black, McKenzie, Hunter, Sinclair, Parker, Campbell, McCrae, Kelly
ABERDEEN: Martin, Mitchell, Caldwell, Allister, Young, Glen, Leggat, Yorston, Buckley, Hay, Hather

P	W	D	L	F	A	Pts
11	5	3	3	22	15	13

Attendance: 10,000   *Referee:* J. S. Aitken
Aberdeen slip to fourth as a result of Sinclair's late leveller when Mitchell was off the field receiving attention.

No 12 Saturday, 28 November
HEARTS (2) 3   ABERDEEN (1) 2
  Rutherford (17),   Yorston (43), Hay (47)
  Wardhaugh (31), Conn
  (63)
HEARTS: Watters, Parker, Adie, Armstrong, Glidden, Cumming, Rutherford, Conn, Bauld, Wardhaugh, Urquhart
ABERDEEN: Martin, Mitchell, Caldwell, Allister, Young, Glen, Leggat, Yorston, Buckley, Hay, Hather

P	W	D	L	F	A	Pts
12	5	3	4	24	18	13

Attendance: 28,000   *Referee:* A. McClintock
The Dons' seven-match unbeaten run comes to an end at second-placed Hearts. Aberdeen defenders stand

around to gift Rutherford Hearts' opener. They are also deprived of Hather for the final twenty minutes.

No 13 Saturday, 5 December
ABERDEEN (1) 2   RAITH ROVERS (0) 0
  Leggat (36), Buckley (77)
ABERDEEN: Martin, Mitchell, Caldwell, Allister, Young, Glen, Leggat, Yorston, Buckley, Hay, Wishart
RAITH: Johnston, Kirk, McNaught, Williamson, Clunie, Colville, McEwan, Young, Copland, Kelly, Penman

P	W	D	L	F	A	Pts
13	6	3	2	26	18	15

Attendance: 14,000
Referee: J. S. Cox
All this game had to offer was the sight of Raith keeper Johnston fumbling Leggat's header inside a post, and of Buckley netting from the acutest of angles.

No 14 Saturday, 12 December
HAMILTON   ABERDEEN (1) 2
  ACADEMICALS (1) 3   Leggat (15), Yorston (87)
  J. Scott 2 (28, 80), Brown
  (68)
HAMILTON: Houston, Ferguson, Johnston, Wilson, Devlin, G. Scott, Young, Shearer, J. Scott, Brown, Cunning
ABERDEEN: Martin, Mitchell, Caldwell, Allister, Young, Glen, Leggat, Yorston, Buckley, Hamilton, Hather

P	W	D	L	F	A	Pts
14	6	3	5	28	21	15

Referee: J. A. Mowat
Hamilton are four points adrift of the rest of Division A but they still fight back from Leggat's scoring header to fully merit their win.

No 15 Saturday, 19 December
ST MIRREN (0) 1   ABERDEEN (0) 4
  Gemmell (56)   Hay (53), Hather (55),
                         Buckley 2 (83, 88)
ST MIRREN: Park, Lapsley, McDonald, Neilson, Telfer, Johnston, Stewart, McGill, Henry, Gemmell, McGuigan
ABERDEEN: Martin, Mitchell, Caldwell, Allister, Young, Glen, Leggat, Hamilton, Buckley, Hay, Hather

P	W	D	L	F	A	Pts
15	7	3	5	32	22	17

Attendance: 7,000
Referee: R. H. Davidson
On the opening day of the season 10-man Saints won 3-0 at Pittodrie. It's a different story at Paisley as Aberdeen open the vaults in the second half.

No 16 Saturday, 26 December
ABERDEEN (4) 8   STIRLING ALBION (0) 0
  Hay (24), Buckley
  3 (27, 50, 68), Leggat
  2 (40, 74), Hather
  2 (44, 52)
ABERDEEN: Martin, Mitchell, Caldwell, Allister, Young, Glen, Leggat, Hamilton, Buckley, Hay, Hather

STIRLING: Jenkins, Ferguson, Whitehead, Bain, Milligan, Smith, Chalmers, Williamson, Kelly, Swanson, Allan

Leading positions

	P	W	D	L	F	A	Pts
1 Queen of the South	17	11	2	4	46	25	24
2 Dundee	16	8	5	3	22	17	21
3 Hearts	17	8	4	5	39	26	20
4 Celtic	15	8	3	4	33	17	19
5 ABERDEEN	16	8	3	5	40	22	19

Attendance: 15,000
Referee: P. Fitzpatrick

It's certainly a Boxing Day for Stirling. Aberdeen hit their highest league score since the War against a side fresh from victory over several leading sides. Hamilton is the only Aberdeen forward to miss out.

No 17 Friday, 1 January
DUNDEE (2) 4   ABERDEEN (2) 2
  Toner 2 (5, 60), Steel   Allister (8 pen), Hay (18)
  (33), Malloy (79 pen)
DUNDEE: Brown, Frew, Cowan, Gallacher, Malloy, Cowie, Hill, Toner, Henderson, Steel, Christie
ABERDEEN: Martin, Mitchell, Caldwell, Allister, Young, Glen, Leggat, Hamilton, Buckley, Hay, Hather

P	W	D	L	F	A	Pts	
17	8	3	6	42	26	19	*Attendance:* 25,000

A top-of-the-table North-East derby swung in Dundee's favour through the mercurial skills of Billy Steel. Aberdeen led 2-1 at one stage, but an inquiry to Allister partly explained Aberdeen's fade-out.

No 18 Saturday, 2 January
ABERDEEN (1) 2   CELTIC (0) 0
  Buckley 2 (8, 46)
ABERDEEN: Morrison, Mitchell, Caldwell, O'Neil, Young, Glen, Leggat, Hamilton, Buckley, Hay, Hather
CELTIC: Bonner, Haughney, Meechan, Evans, Stein, Peacock, Collins, Fernie, Hemple, Walsh, Mochan

P	W	D	L	F	A	Pts	
18	9	3	6	44	26	21	*Attendance:* 28,000
							Referee: J. A. S. Bisset

Youngsters Morrison and O'Neil are drafted into the firing line and feature strongly in Aberdeen's win. The Dons were always likely winners from the moment Buckley beat Bonner in a one-to-one situation. After Buckley's second goal Morrison stopped Collins' penalty awarded when Young brought Fernie crashing.

No 19 Saturday, 9 January
PARTICK THISTLE (3) 6   ABERDEEN (2) 3
  Harvey (15), McInnes   Hay (13), Leggat
  (23), Crawford 2 (35, 55),   2 (19, 71)
  Howitt 2 (49, 82)
PARTICK: Ledgerwood, McGowan, Gibb, Harvey, Davidson, Mathers, McKenzie, Howitt, Sharp, Crawford, McInnes
ABERDEEN: Morrison, Mitchell, Caldwell, O'Neil, Young, Glen, Leggat, Hamilton, Buckley, Hay, Hather

P	W	D	L	F	A	Pts	
19	9	3	7	47	32	21	*Attendance:* 18,000
							Referee: D. McKerchar

A pulsating match. There were five goals in a twenty-minute spell. By the end Aberdeen had conceded six goals for only the second time since the War.

No 20 Saturday, 16 January
ABERDEEN (1) 1   HIBERNIAN (1) 3
  Yorston (36)   Combe (7), Reilly (70),
                           Johnstone (87)
ABERDEEN: Morrison, Mitchell, Caldwell, O'Neil, Young, Glen, Leggat, Hamilton, Buckley, Yorston, Hather
HIBERNIAN: Hamilton, Boyle, Paterson, Gallacher, Ward, Brown, McDonald, Johnstone, Reilly, Combe, Ormond

P	W	D	L	F	A	Pts	
20	9	3	8	48	35	21	*Attendance:* 18,000
							Referee: R. Yacamini

Hibs are surprisingly in the bottom six. The match was finally balanced at half-time but Hather was a passenger throughout the second half.

No 21 Saturday, 23 January
AIRDRIEONIANS (0) 1   ABERDEEN (2) 3
  McCulloch (87)   Buckley (13), O'Neil
                           (37), Wishart (82)
AIRDRIE: Walker, Pryde, T. Brown, Cairns, Gordon, Shankland, Welsh, McMillan, Baird, Slingsby, McCulloch
ABERDEEN: Martin, Mitchell, Aitken, Harris, Young, Glen, Leggat, John Brown, Buckley, O'Neil, Wishart

P	W	D	L	F	A	Pts	
21	10	3	8	51	36	23	*Referee:* C. E. Faultless

Airdrie are on their way to Division B. Aberdeen, with five reserves, win as they please.

No 22 Saturday, 6 February
ABERDEEN (0) 1   EAST FIFE (0) 0
  Allister (50)
ABERDEEN: Martin, Mitchell, Caldwell, Harris, Young, Glen, Leggat, Allister, Buckley, O'Neil, Wishart
EAST FIFE: Curran, Emery, S. Stewart, Christie, Finlay, McLennan, J. Stewart, Fleming, Gardiner, Bonthrone, Matthew

P	W	D	L	F	A	Pts	
22	11	3	8	52	36	25	*Referee:* W. Brittle

Hard graft and few thrills marked this match, settled by Allister's header from Wishart's cross.

No 23 Saturday 20 February
ABERDEEN (1) 5   CLYDE (1) 3
  Leggat 3 (27, 46, 49),   Devine (31), Keogh (82),
  O'Neil 2 (65, 70),   Ring (88)
ABERDEEN: Martin, Mitchell, Caldwell, Allister, Young, Glen, Leggat, Hamilton, Buckley, O'Neil, Wishart

CLYDE: Wilson, A. Murphy, Haddock, Robertson, E. Murphy, Keogh, Galletly, Divers, Buchanan, Devine, Ring

Leading positions

	P	W	D	L	F	A	Pts
1 Hearts	25	14	6	5	63	38	34
2 Celtic	22	12	3	7	45	26	27
3 ABERDEEN	23	12	3	8	57	39	27
4 Queen of the South	23	12	3	8	58	42	27

Attendance: 15,000   *Referee:* W. Bowman

19-year old Graham Leggat announces his arrival in the bigtime. His hat–trick and O'Neil's pair make this match an exciting guide to the future. Hearts' lead at the top of the table looks unassailable. But it isn't.

No 24 Saturday, 6 March

QUEEN OF THE SOUTH (1) 2   ABERDEEN (1) 4
Brown (20), Rothera (87 pen)   Boyd (24), O'Neil 2 (50, 76), Buckley (68)

QUEEN OF THE SOUTH: Henderson, Sharp, Binning, McBain, Hollywood, Greenock, Black, McGill, Patterson, Rothera, Brown

ABERDEEN: Martin, Mitchell, Caldwell, Allister, Young, Glen, Boyd, Wishart, Buckley, O'Neil, Hather

P	W	D	L	F	A	Pts
24	13	3	8	61	41	29

Attendance: 7,000   *Referee:* H. Phillips

Both sides needed to win if they are to sustain their title challenge. Once seven inches of snow had been cleared the Dons powered through the rain to win with ease – if not in comfort.

No 25 Wednesday, 17 March

ABERDEEN (0) 0   FALKIRK (1) 1
                        Aikman (17)

ABERDEEN: Martin, Mitchell, Caldwell, Allister, Young, Harris, Leggat, Wishart, Dunbar, O'Neil, Hather

FALKIRK: McFeat, Ralston, Sievwright, Gallacher, McKenzie, Campbell, Sinclair, Morrison, Aikman, Dunlop, Kelly

P	W	D	L	F	A	Pts
25	13	3	9	61	42	29

Attendance: 5,000   *Referee:* J. B. Barclay

Glen and Buckley are absent, playing in an Inter-League match in Dublin. Falkirk are back to their old points-snatching ways. Aberdeen hit the woodwork four times and O'Neil suffers a fractured skull.

No 26 Saturday, 20 March

ABERDEEN (1) 1   HEARTS (0) 0
Leggat (6)

ABERDEEN: Martin, Mitchell, Caldwell, Allister, Young, Glen, Leggat, Hamilton, Buckley, Yorston, Wishart

HEARTS: Watters, Adie, Mackenzie, Laing, Glidden, Mackay, Souness, Cochrane, Bauld, Cumming, Urquhart

Leading positions

	P	W	D	L	F	A	Pts
1 Hearts	28	15	6	7	68	43	36
2 Celtic	25	15	3	7	58	28	33
3 ABERDEEN	26	14	3	9	62	42	31

Attendance: 17,000   *Referee:* J. Jackson

Aberdeen's second home victory over Hearts on successive Saturdays threatens to wreck the Tynecastle club's season. The game was decided by Leggat's header which flashed between Mackenzie and the post. But all four remaining fixtures are away and the Dons' title hopes look forlorn.

No 27 Saturday, 27 March

RAITH ROVERS (1) 3   ABERDEEN (1) 1
Duncan (36 pen), McEwan 2 (75, 85)   Wishart (13)

RAITH: Drummond, McClure, McNaught, McNeil, Colville, McIntyre, McEwan, Rice, Copland, Kelly, Duncan

ABERDEEN: Martin, Mitchell, Caldwell, Allister, Young, Glen, Leggat, Hamilton, Buckley, Wishart, Hather

P	W	D	L	F	A	Pts
27	14	3	10	63	45	31

Referee: D. J. Murphy

With their minds on the Cup Aberdeen don't have the resolve to hang onto Wishart's lead. The turning point was Mitchell's foul on Copland which brought about the penalty.

No 28 Wednesday, 14 April

EAST FIFE (2) 2   ABERDEEN (0) 0
Fleming 2 (15, 38)

EAST FIFE: Curran, Emery, Stewart, Christie, Finlay, McLennan, Stewart, Fleming, Gardiner, Bonthrone, Matthew

ABERDEEN: Martin, Mitchell, Caldwell, Allister, Young, Glen, Boyd, Hamilton, Buckley, O'Neil, Hather

P	W	D	L	F	A	Pts
28	14	3	11	63	47	31

Charlie Fleming bags his 30th and 31st goals of the season.

No 29 Saturday, 17 April

RANGERS (1) 1   ABERDEEN (1) 3
Paton (22)   Leggat (40), Buckley (52), Allister (80 pen)

RANGERS: Brown, Caldow, Cox, McColl, Woodburn, Rae, Waddell, Paton, Simpson, Grierson, Hubbard

ABERDEEN: Martin, W. Smith, Caldwell, Allister, Young, Glen, Leggat, Hamilton, Buckley, O'Neil, Hather

P	W	D	L	F	A	Pts
29	15	3	11	66	48	33

Referee: G. Mitchell

This was a tame affair compared to Aberdeen's 6-0 crushing of those same opponents at Hampden in the

Cup. Tragically for Aberdeen O'Neil wrenches his ankle and will miss the Scottish Cup Final.

No 30 Monday, 19 April

HIBERNIAN (2) 3   ABERDEEN (0) 0
Thomson (30), Ormond 2 (31, 82)

HIBERNIAN: Miller, MacFarlane, Patterson, Campbell, Ward, Combe, Johnstone, Preston, Thomson, Turnbull, Ormond

ABERDEEN: Martin, W. Smith, Caldwell, Allister, Clunie, Glen, Leggat, Yorston, Buckley, I. Smith, Hather

Referee: D. J. Murphy

Hibs gain hollow revenge for their cup defeat at Easter Road. Aberdeen lose Yorston from the Final when he is injured. Had Aberdeen won they would have finished third; they didn't and dropped to ninth.

Aberdeen's complete home and away record:

HOME						AWAY					
P	W	D	L	F	A	W	D	L	F	A	Pts
30	10	2	3	36	14	5	1	9	30	37	33

Scottish League Division A 1953-54

	P	W	D	L	F	A	Pts
1 Celtic	30	20	3	7	72	29	43
2 Hearts	30	16	6	8	70	45	38
3 Partick Thistle	30	17	1	12	76	54	35
4 Rangers	30	13	8	9	56	35	34
5 Hibernian	30	15	4	11	72	51	34
6 East Fife	30	13	8	9	55	45	34
7 Dundee	30	14	6	10	46	47	34
8 Clyde	30	15	4	11	64	67	34
9 ABERDEEN	30	15	3	12	66	51	33
10 Queen of the South	30	14	4	12	72	58	32
11 St Mirren	30	12	4	14	44	54	28
12 Raith Rovers	30	10	6	14	56	60	26
13 Falkirk	30	9	7	14	47	61	25
14 Stirling Albion	30	10	4	16	39	62	24
15 Airdrieonians	30	5	5	20	41	92	15
16 Hamilton Acas	30	4	3	23	29	94	11

LEAGUE CUP

Saturday, 8 August

CELTIC (0) 0   ABERDEEN (0) 1
Brown (64)

CELTIC: Bonner, Haughney, Rollo, Evans, Stein, McPhail, Tully, Walsh, Mochan, Peacock, Fernie

ABERDEEN: Martin, Mitchell, Smith, Harris, Young, Allister, James Brown, Yorston, Buckley, Hamilton, Hather

Attendance: 50,000   *Referee:* G. Mitchell

Celtic overrun Aberdeen for all but the last twenty-five minutes, when Dons' new winger from Falkirk, Jimmy Brown, scores the only goal.

Wednesday, 12 August

ABERDEEN (2) 2   AIRDRIEONIANS (0) 0
Hather (12), Henderson o.g. (18)

ABERDEEN: Martin, Mitchell, Smith, Harris, Young, Allister, James Brown, Yorston, Buckley, Hamilton, Hather

AIRDRIE: Fraser, Pryde, Cross, Henderson, Rodger, Shankland, Quigley, Brown, Baird, Quinn, McCulloch

Attendance: 28,000   *Referee:* D. McKerchar

Despite the result, the game is so tedious that the Dons are treated to a slow handclap.

Saturday, 15 August

EAST FIFE (0) 2   ABERDEEN (0) 0
Fleming (53), Matthew (73)

EAST FIFE: Curran, Emery, S. Stewart, Christie, Finlay, McLennan, J. Stewart, Fleming, Bonthrone, Gardiner, Matthew

ABERDEEN: Martin, Mitchell, Smith, Harris, Young, Allister, James Brown, Yorston, Dunbar, Hamilton, Hather

Attendance: 8,000   *Referee:* H. Phillips

In the second half Smith takes over in goal for Martin, who has damaged a finger. East Fife score their second goal when Young is off injured.

Saturday, 22 August

ABERDEEN (2) 5   CELTIC (1) 2
Yorston 2 (12, 43),   Walsh (27), Mochan (89)
Buckley 2 (64, 87),
Hather (74)

ABERDEEN: Morrison, Mitchell, Caldwell, Harris, Smith, Allister, Dunbar, Yorston, Buckley, Hamilton, Hather

CELTIC: Hunter, Haughney, Rollo, Evans, Stein, McPhail, Walsh, Fernie, White, Peacock, Mochan

Attendance: 30,000   *Referee:* J. A. S. Bisset

An emphatic win over Celtic. Once Yorston restores Aberdeen's lead just before half-time Celtic are swept aside.

Wednesday, 26 August

AIRDRIEONIANS (3) 4   ABERDEEN (2) 3
McMillan 2 (4 pen, 83),   Yorston 2 (8, 80),
Baird (11), Quigley (17)   Hather (24)

AIRDRIE: Fraser, Pryde, Cross, Cairns, Rodger, Quinn, Quigley, McMillan, Baird, Docherty, McCulloch

ABERDEEN: Morrison, Mitchell, Caldwell, Harris, Young, Allister, Dunbar, Yorston, Smith, Hamilton, Hather

Referee: J. S. Cox

Morrison saves a McMillan penalty at 3-2 to keep Aberdeen alive. Yorston duly equalises only for McMillan to make up for his penalty miss.

Saturday, 29 August
ABERDEEN (1) 3   EAST FIFE (2) 4
  Hamilton (45), Buckley   Fleming 2 (27, 80),
  (71), Allister (89)   Bonthrone (35), Stewart
                             (83)
ABERDEEN: Morrison, Mitchell, Caldwell, Harris, Smith, Allister, Dunbar, Yorston, Buckley, Hamilton, Hather
EAST FIFE: Curran, Emery, S. Stewart, Christie, Finlay, McLennan, J. Stewart, Fleming, Bonthrone, Gardiner, Matthew

Attendance: 30,000   *Referee:* J. S. Aitken

Aberdeen must beat East Fife to qualify, but after 35 minutes the visitors are two goals up. The Dons fight back to 2-2 but are floored by Charlie Fleming. East Fife go on to lift the League Cup for the third time in seven years.

Section B

	P	W	D	L	F	A	Pts
East Fife	6	4	1	1	14	9	9
ABERDEEN	6	3	0	3	14	12	6
Airdrieonians	6	3	0	3	11	14	6
Celtic	6	1	1	4	6	10	3

SCOTTISH CUP

1st Round (Bye)

2nd Round Saturday, 13 February
DUNS (0) 0   ABERDEEN (4) 8
                     Buckley 4 (10, 17, 45,
                     75), Leggat 2 (22, 63),
                     Hamilton 2 (49, 85)
DUNS: Smith, Bremner, Muir, Sharp, Holt, Paton, Burns, Reid, Duff, Walters, Bootland
ABERDEEN: Martin, Mitchell, Caldwell, Allister, Young, Glen, Leggat, Hamilton, Buckley, O'Neil, Wishart

Attendance: 700   *Referee:* J. A. S. Bisset

This is no contest in the mud and slush at Duns. Farcical conditions did not stop Buckley helping himself to a hat-trick before half-time.

3rd Round Saturday, 27 February
HIBERNIAN (0) 1   ABERDEEN (2) 3
  Johnstone (62)   Hather 2 (4, 7), Buckley
                           (46)
HIBERNIAN: Hamilton, Govan, Paterson, Gallagher, Ward, Combe, McDonald, Johnstone, Reilly, Turnbull, Ormond
ABERDEEN: Martin, Mitchell, Caldwell, Allister, Young, Glen, Leggat, Hamilton, Buckley, O'Neil, Hather

Attendance: 47,700   *Referee:* J. A. Mowat

Hibs are missing their long-standing absentees, Smith and Buchanan. For Aberdeen Hather, too, was thought to be unfit, and Hibs only discovered he was playing minutes before the kick-off. Inside seven minutes he had put Aberdeen two goals up. Buckley later made it three. When Johnstone at last put some hope into the home side Martin distinguished himself with several fine saves.

Quarter Final Saturday, 13 March
ABERDEEN (1) 3   HEARTS (0) 0
  O'Neil (44), Leggat (57),
  Hamilton (67)
ABERDEEN: Martin, Mitchell, Caldwell, Allister, Young, Glen, Leggat, Hamilton, Buckley, O'Neil, Hather
HEARTS: Watters, Parker, Adie, Laing, Glidden, Cumming, Souness, Conn, Bauld, Wardhaugh, Urquhart

Attendance: 45,061   *Referee:* H. Phillips

The visit of the league leaders attracts an all-time record attendance to Pittodrie for this Quarter Final tie. Hearts' nerves are showing, however, and their confidence is not helped by losing four goals at Raith the previous week. On a beautiful spring day the game takes decisive shape just before half-time. Bauld's header for Hearts flew wide with Martin nowhere, and then O'Neil drove the ball past Watters from 25 yards. When Leggat slipped the ball home from a tight angle and Hamilton converted the young winger's corner Aberdeen were home and dry.

Semi Final (Hampden) Saturday, 10 April
RANGERS (0) 0   ABERDEEN (2) 6
                        O'Neil 3 (13, 34, 80),
                        Leggat (70), Allister
                        (86 pen), Buckley (89)
RANGERS: Brown, Caldow, Little, McColl, Woodburn, Cox, Waddell, Grierson, Simpson, Prentice, Hubbard
ABERDEEN: Martin, Mitchell, Caldwell, Allister, Young, Glen, Leggat, Hamilton, Buckley, O'Neil, Hather

Attendance: 111,000   *Referee:* J. A. Mowat

This is certainly the right time for any side to be meeting Rangers. They are still floundering in mid-table. They let Falkirk score four against them in their last league match and have yet to meet an A Division side in defence of their Scottish Cup. Indeed, they took three attempts to overcome Third Lanark. In this re-run of the 1953 Final the Dons' hero is O'Neil, who makes a miraculous return to the side three weeks after suffering a depressed fracture of the skull. It is who scores the first two goals, the second with his head. Rangers' attempted resurrection is finally stilled in the final 20 minutes when the Dons smash four more goals. One of them belongs to O'Neil, and it is he who is brought down to give Allister a penalty. At the end of the day nobody could complain about Aberdeen's first-ever victory over Rangers in the Scottish Cup.

Scottish Cup Final (Hampden) Saturday, 24 April

CELTIC (0) 2   ABERDEEN (0) 1
Young o.g. (50), Fallon   Buckley (51)
  (64)

CELTIC: Bonner, Haughney, Meechan, Evans, Stein, Peacock, Higgins, Fernie, Fallon, Tully, Mochan

ABERDEEN: Martin, Mitchell, Caldwell, Allister, Young, Glen, Leggat, Hamilton, Buckley, Clunie, Hather

Referee: C. E. Faultless

Celtic have just won the league following a surging late season run that carried them past flagging Hearts. In four matches against Aberdeen this season the score stands three to one for Aberdeen. Now, however, the Dons are deprived of the services of Yorston and O'Neil as they attempt to replay the 1937 final when they lost 2-1. Jim Clunie deputises for O'Neil at inside left although he has never performed in that position in his life. Sadly for Aberdeen the result is a replica of that in 1937, even down to the order of scoring. Celtic were the moral victors of a goal-less first half, but go in front early in the second only when Young flicks Mochan's shot beyond Martin. The goalkeeper had had the shot covered. Within a minute Buckley took the ball round Stein, drew Bonner, and slotted home the equaliser. Now it was the Dons who had the edge. But it was Celtic who scored the goal – Fernie pulling the ball back from the bye-line for Fallon to secure Parkhead's league and Cup double.

1953-54

APPEARANCES	League	League Cup	Scottish Cup
Buckley	29	4	5
Young	27	4	5
Caldwell	27	3	5
Glen	27		5
Mitchell	26	6	5
Allister	26	6	5
Leggat	26		5
Hather	25	6	4
Martin	25	3	5
Yorston	16	6	
Hamilton	15	6	5
Hay	11		
O'Neil	10		4
W. Smith	9	6	
Wishart	8		1
Harris	5	6	
Morrison	5	3	
Boyd	3		
Dunbar	2	4	
Aitken	2		
Paterson	2		
Clunie	1		1
John Brown	1		
Kelly	1		
I. Smith	1		
James Brown		3	
26 players			

GOALS	Total	League	League Cup	Scottish Cup
Buckley	27	17	3	7
Leggat	19	15		4
Hather	12	7	3	2
Yorston	11	7	4	
O'Neil	9	5		4
Allister	7	5	1	1
Hay	6	6		
Hamilton	4		1	3
Wishart	2	2		
Young	1	1		
Boyd	1	1		
James Brown	1		1	
own-goals	1		1	
Total	101	66	14	21

Billy Graham joins the Dons in 1963. Welcoming him is Davie Shaw.

Season 1954-55

1954-55 was 'The Year'. Although Aberdeen failed to distinguish themselves in the group rounds of the League Cup, from the moment the league's starting gun had fired they were off into the rarefied heights of immortality. Traditionally poor starters, Aberdeen clocked up four quick wins before Celtic stole the precious points from Pittodrie to knock the Dons off the top for the first and only time. Far from denting Aberdeen's confidence they marched ever onwards, opening up a six-point gap over their rivals by the New Year. Would their nerve hold? To their credit it did. As Celtic inched closer it looked as if everything would hinge on the clash at Parkhead on 16 April. But Aberdeen sensibly – to the despair of Celtic supporters worldwide – sewed matters up the previous week, becoming uncatchable following Archie Glen's penalty goal at Clyde.

Clyde it was who, five days earlier, had spoiled Aberdeen's dreams of a league and Cup double, when winning at Easter Road in a semi final replay.

Aberdeen's statistics for 1954-55 make impressive reading. Their 49 points were ten more than they had ever managed since the War, and were bettered only by Rangers' winning tally in 1949-50. The Dons' 24 wins from 30 starts were a post-War record. The won 14 at home and 10 away. Although their 73 league goals were also a Dons' post-War record, it was their goals-against column which was probably decisive. Since the resumption of peacetime football it had been their defensive frailty which had caused the Dons their greatest headaches. The tally of 1953-54 was slashed by half: the miserly total of 26 equalling the all-time lowest figure for a 30-match season. This defensive resilience was the hallmark of Aberdeen's counter-attacking style at this time. Meanwhile, in attack, the 73 goals were shared around unselfishly; and only 19 players were called upon throughout the season. Manager Halliday's favoured eleven each made more than 20 league appearances.

League:	Champions
League Cup:	2nd in qualifying group
Scottish Cup:	Semi Final

SCOTTISH LEAGUE DIVISION A

No 1 Saturday, 11 September

ABERDEEN (2) 5   STIRLING ALBION (0) 0
O'Neil 2 (11, 52),
Buckley (23), Wallace
(50), Yorston (60)

ABERDEEN: Martin, Mitchell, Smith, Wallace, Young, Glen, Leggat, Yorston, Buckley, O'Neil, Hather

STIRLING: Jenkins, Gibson, M. Nicol, Bain, Milligan, Whitehead, Chalmers, Smith, Rattray, Paterson, Joyner

P	W	D	L	F	A	Pts	Attendance: 17,000
1	1	0	0	5	0	2	Referee: W. Brittle

Aberdeen are used to slaughtering Stirling at Pittodrie. It was 8-0 last season and 6-0 the time before that.

No 2 Saturday, 18 September

DUNDEE (0) 0   ABERDEEN (0) 2
                      Glen (54 pen), O'Neil
                      (85)

DUNDEE: R. Henderson, Follon, Irvine, Gallacher, Malloy, Craig, Christie, Easson, A. Henderson, Roy, Hill

ABERDEEN: Martin, Mitchell, Smith, Wallace, Young, Glen, Leggat, Yorston, Buckley, O'Neil, Hather

P	W	D	L	F	A	Pts	Attendance: 27,000
2	2	0	0	7	0	4	Referee: W. Harvie

The Dons have the edge throughout but might never have found the net had not Gallacher foolishly handled.

No 3 Saturday, 25 September
ABERDEEN (1) 3   HIBERNIAN (1) 1
  Yorston 2 (5, 79),   Johnstone (28 pen)
  O' Neil (68)

ABERDEEN: Martin, Mitchell, Smith, Wallace, Young, Glen, Leggat, Yorston, Buckley, O'Neil, Hather

HIBERNIAN: Younger, Higgins, McFarlane, Buchanan, Paterson, Combe, Smith, Johnstone, Preston, Turnbull, Ormond

P	W	D	L	F	A	Pts
3	3	0	0	10	1	6

Attendance: 25,000
Referee: R. H. Davidson

Hibs took 3 points off Aberdeen in the League Cup. As before, they equalise an early Aberdeen goal with a penalty. Mitchell was the transgressor. On half-time Hibs' Buchanan broke a leg in a collision with Hather, and they succumb in the second half.

No 4 Saturday, 2 October
MOTHERWELL (1) 1   ABERDEEN (2) 3
  Bain (10)   Yorston (2), Leggat (45),
                            Hather (80)

MOTHERWELL: Weir, Kilmarnock, Shaw, Cox, Paton, Redpath, Hunter, Aitken, Bain, Humphries, Williams

ABERDEEN: Martin, Mitchell, Smith, Wallace, Young, Glen, Leggat, Yorston, Buckley, O'Neil, Hather

Leading Positions

	P	W	D	L	F	A	Pts
1 ABERDEEN	4	4	0	0	13	2	8
2 Celtic	4	3	1	0	13	6	7
3 Clyde	4	2	2	0	14	9	6
4 Falkirk	4	2	2	0	6	3	6
5 St Mirren	3	2	1	0	13	6	5

Attendance: 12,000
Referee: A. McClintock

Motherwell suffer their first defeat. The Dons are now clear leaders of Division A.

No 5 Saturday, 9 October
ABERDEEN (0) 0   CELTIC (0) 2
                    Mochan (52), Haughney
                    (71 pen)

ABERDEEN: Martin, Mitchell, Smith, Wallace, Young, Glen, Leggat, Yorston, Buckley, O'Neil, Hather

CELTIC: Bonner, Haughney, Fallon, Evans, Stein, Peacock, Higgins, Tully, Walsh, Fernie, Mochan

P	W	D	L	F	A	Pts
5	4	0	1	13	4	8

Attendance: 38,000
Referee: J. P. Barclay

A repeat of the Scottish Cup Final between the leading two. Celtic have the edge in the first half and Tully struck the bar. Yorston resumed after the break with three stitches in a head wound. Celtic deservedly scored when Mochan drove home Walsh's corner, and again when Haughney was grassed by Young. In the closing minutes Stein ripped off Buckley's shorts. With the final whistle Celtic topple Aberdeen from the top spot for the first and only time.

No 6 Saturday, 16 October
ST MIRREN (0) 0   ABERDEEN (2) 4
                    Glen (35 pen), Wishart 2
                    (45, 52), Hamilton (77)

ST MIRREN: Lornie, Cunningham, Johnstone, Neilson, Hamilton, Holmes, McMaster, Laird, McGrory, Gemmell, Callan

ABERDEEN: Morrison, Mitchell, Smith, Allister, Young, Glen, Leggat, Wishart, Hamilton, O'Neil, Hather

P	W	D	L	F	A	Pts
6	5	0	1	17	4	10

Attendance: 15,000
Referee: R. Morris

Aberdeen are without Martin who has flu and Yorston and Buckley who are playing for Scotland against Wales in Cardiff. (Buckley scores the only goal.) With Celtic being held by Queen of the South, Aberdeen return to th top on goal average.

No 7 Saturday, 23 October
ABERDEEN (2) 4   EAST FIFE (1) 1
  Christie o.g. (6),   Bonthrone (30)
  Allister (15), Buckley
  (60), Yorston (80)

ABERDEEN: Martin, Mitchell, Smith, Allister, Young, Glen, Leggat, Yorston, Buckley, O'Neil, Hather

EAST FIFE: Curran, Emery, S. Stewart, Christie, Finlay, Liddell, J. Stewart, Fleming, Cousins, Bonthrone, Matthew

P	W	D	L	F	A	Pts
7	6	0	1	21	5	12

Attendance: 14,000
Referee: D. J. Murphy

Aberdeen beat East Fife 5-1 in the League Cup when it didn't matter, and now 4-1 when it did. By the end three East Fifers had been booked.

No 8 Saturday, 30 October
PARTICK THISTLE (1) 1   ABERDEEN (0) 0
  Davidson (9 pen)

PARTICK: Ledgerwood, McGowan, Gibb, Harvey, Davidson, Thomson, Mackenzie, Howitt, Sharp, Wright, McParland

ABERDEEN: Martin, Mitchell, Smith, Allister, Young, Glen, Brown, Yorston, Buckley, O'Neil, Hather

Leading Positions

	P	W	D	L	F	A	Pts
1 ABERDEEN	8	6	0	2	21	6	12
2 Celtic	7	5	2	0	19	8	12
3 Clyde	8	5	2	1	25	14	12
4 Rangers	7	4	1	2	23	10	9
5 St Mirren	7	4	1	2	16	15	9

Attendance: 20,000
Referee: R. Yacamini

On a gluepot pitch Aberdeen surrender their 100% away record. Thistle scored the only goal when Mitchell handléd on the goal-line with Martin beaten. Injuries whittled Partick down to nine men but Aberdeen rarely threatened an equaliser.

    The following Wednesday Buckley is capped against Northern Ireland at Hampden.

No 9 Saturday, 6 November
ABERDEEN (1) 2   QUEEN OF THE
  Buckley (26), Glen   SOUTH (0) 0
  (84 pen)
ABERDEEN: Martin, Mitchell, Smith, Allister, Young, Glen, Leggat, Yorston, Buckley, Wishart, Hather

QUEEN OF THE SOUTH: Henderson, Sharpe, Binning, McBain, Smith, Greenock, Black, McGill, Paterson, Rothera, Oakes

P	W	D	L	F	A	Pts		*Attendance:* 15,000
9	7	0	2	236	14			*Referee:* J. Lackie

Not the best of matches. Glen missed with one penalty but scored with the next. Rothera hit Martin's crossbar at 1-0.

No 10 Saturday, 13 November
RAITH ROVERS (0) 1   ABERDEEN (2) 2
  Kelly (75)   Allister (32), Yorston (40)
RAITH: Drummond, McClure, McNaught, Archibald, Colville, Leigh, Kirk, Kelly, Young, Buchan, Duncan
ABERDEEN: Martin, Mitchell, Smith, Allister, Young, Glen, Leggat, Yorston, Buckley, Wishart, Hather

P	W	D	L	F	A	Pts	
10	8	0	2	257	16		*Referee:* F. S. Crossley

Aberdeen have lost at Raith on all their last four visits, but Allister and Yorston lay the Stark's Park bogey.

No 11 Saturday, 20 November
ABERDEEN (1) 1   HEARTS (0) 0
  Yorston (21)
ABERDEEN: Martin, Mitchell, Smith, Allister, Young, Glen, Leggat, Yorston, Buckley, Wishart, Hather
HEARTS: Duff, Parker, McKenzie, Mackay, Glidden, Cumming, Souness, Conn, Bauld, Wardhaugh, Urquhart

P	W	D	L	F	A	Pts		*Attendance:* 28,000
11	9	0	2	267	18			*Referee:* H. Phillips

Hearts have four games in hand over Aberdeen and are determined to keep them in their sight. Blue-shirted Hearts have a chance to equalise Yorston's tap-in when Mitchell concedes his third penalty of the season, but Martin saves Parker's penalty. Near the end Parker cleared off the line from Buckley.

No 12 Saturday, 27 November
ABERDEEN (1) 1   FALKIRK (0) 0
  Hather (6)
ABERDEEN: Martin, Mitchell, Smith, Allister, Young, Glen, Leggat, Yorston, Buckley, Wishart, Hather
FALKIRK: Slater, Parker, Rae, Black, McKenzie, Campbell, Taylor, Morrison, Davidson, McCrae, Kelly

Leading positions

	P	W	D	L	F	A	Pts
1 ABERDEEN	12	10	0	2	27	7	20
2 Rangers	11	7	2	2	34	11	16
3 Celtic	11	6	4	1	31	15	16
4 Clyde	12	6	4	2	31	18	16
5 St Mirren	11	7	2	2	28	19	16

Attendance: 17,000   *Referee:* C. E. Faultless
This is the sort of match Aberdeen have a habit of losing. Hather's early goal should have opened the floodgates. But his team-mates missed chance after chance and the had to live through an anxious last ten minutes. With the final whistle Aberdeen stood four points clear.

No 13 Saturday, 4 December
KILMARNOCK (0) 0   ABERDEEN (2) 4
              Buckley 2 (7, 59),
              Leggat 2 (42, 66)
KILMARNOCK: Brown, Hood, Rollo, Curlett, Thyne, Middlemass, Murray, Beattie, Toner, Jack, Henaughen
ABERDEEN: Martin, Mitchell, Smith, Allister, Young, Glen, Leggat, Yorston, Buckley, Wishart, Hather

P	W	D	L	F	A	Pts		*Attendance:* 12,000
13	11	0	2	317	22			*Referee:* P. Fitzpatrick

Feeble Kilmarnock have no answer to the Dons in a one-sided match. On the following Wednesday Martin was capped against Hungary at Hampden.

No 14 Saturday, 11 December
RANGERS (2) 3   ABERDEEN (0) 1
  Simpson 2 (38, 72),   Buckley (83)
  Grierson (41)
RANGERS: Brown, Little, Cox, McColl, Young, Rae, Waddell, Paton, Simpson, Grierson, Hubbard
ABERDEEN: Martin, Mitchell, Smith, Allister, Young, Glen, Leggat, Yorston, Buckley, Wishart, Hather

P	W	D	L	F	A	Pts	*Attendance:* 50,000
14	11	0	3	32	10	22	*Referee:* J. Jackson

Rangers are Aberdeen's closest challengers, and are eager to obliterate the memory of their 6-0 crushing by the Dons in last season's Scottish Cup. This time Aberdeen are never in the hunt and never look like potential champions.

No 15 Saturday, 18 December
ABERDEEN (1) 3   CLYDE (0) 0
  Wishart (14), Allister
  (82 pen), Yorston (88)
ABERDEEN: Martin, Mitchell, Smith, Allister, Young, Glen, Leggat, Yorston, Buckley, Wishart, Hather
CLYDE: Wilson, Murphy, Haddock, Gallacher, Anderson, Laing, Hill, Robertson, Buchanan, Carmichael, Ring

P W D L F A Pts   *Attendance:* 17,000
15 12 0 3 35 10 24   *Referee:* I. C. Inglis

Clyde have slipped out of the championship race. Glen misses his second penalty of recent weeks, before Wishart puts the Dons in front. A second spot kick is taken by Allister later in the match.

No 16 Saturday, 25 December
STIRLING ALBION (2) 3   ABERDEEN (1) 4
Paterson (22),   Leggat (34), Yorston
  McGill 2 (30, 89)   (49), Hather (68),
                              Wishart (72)

STIRLING: Nicol, Almond, McNichol, McKechnie, Williamson, Swanson, Chalmers, Rattray, Laird, McGill, Paterson

ABERDEEN: Martin, Mitchell, Smith, Allister, Young, Glen, Leggat, Yorston, Buckley, Wishart, Hather

P W D L F A Pts   *Attendance:* 3,000
16 13 0 3 39 13 26   *Referee:* R. J. Smith

Two draws are all Stirling have to show so far this season. But the Christmas spirit extends to Aberdeen who grant Stirling a two-goal lead before pulling themselves together. They are assisted by an injury to Albion's Williamson.

No 17 Saturday, 1 January
ABERDEEN (0) 1   DUNDEE (0) 0
  Wishart (61)

ABERDEEN: Martin, Mitchell, Smith, Allister, Young, Glen, Leggat, Yorston, Buckley, Wishart, Hather

DUNDEE: Brown, Follon, Irvine, Gallacher, Malloy, Cowie, Carmichael, Henderson, Merchant, Roy, Christie

P W D L F A Pts
17 14 0 3 40 13 28

A single goal settled this hard-fought duel. Brown was hurt diving at Buckley's feet; the ball ran clear to Wishart, who steered it through three flailing defenders.

No 18 Monday, 3 January
HIBERNIAN (0) 0   ABERDEEN (0) 1
                    Buckley (48)

HIBERNIAN: Younger, Ward, Paterson, Grant, Plenderleith, Preston, Smith, Johnstone, Reilly, Combe, Ormond

ABERDEEN: Martin, Mitchell, Smith, Allister, Young, Glen, Leggat, Yorston, Buckley, Wishart, Hather

Leading Positions

	P	W	D	L	F	A	Pts
1 ABERDEEN	18	15	0	3	41	13	30
2 Rangers	17	11	2	4	48	21	24
3 Celtic	17	9	6	2	49	25	24
4 St Mirren	17	10	4	3	40	27	24
5 Hearts	15	10	2	3	50	25	22

Attendance: 30,000   *Referee:* H. J. Gallacher

Buckley scored the only goal, then watched his defenders earn their wages. On the one occasion Martin was beaten Glen headed off the line. Aberdeen's lead is now six points.

No 19 Saturday, 8 January
ABERDEEN (2) 4   MOTHERWELL (1) 1
  Buckley 2 (22, 28),   McSeveney (44)
  Leggat 2 (69, 86)

ABERDEEN: Martin, Mitchell, Smith, Allister, Young, Glen, Leggat, Yorston, Buckley, Wishart, Hather

MOTHERWELL: McIntyre, Kilmarnock, Shaw, Cox, Mason, Redpath, Sloan, Aitken, McSeveney, Humphries, Williams

P W D L F A Pts   *Attendance:* 22,000
19 16 0 3 45 14 32   *Referee:* G. Bowman

Leggat's 69th minute goal came not a moment too soon, for Motherwell were surging back into contention. The Dons' line-up was unchanged for the eleventh match in succession. They were now due to visit Celtic, but Arctic weather causes its postponement.

No 20 Saturday, 22 January
ABERDEEN (2) 2   ST MIRREN (0) 1
  Hather (36, Brown (42)   McMaster (48)

ABERDEEN: Martin, Mitchell, Smith, Allister, Young, Glen, Brown, Yorston, Buckley, Wishart, Hather

ST MIRREN: Lornie, Lapsley, Johnston, Neilson, Telfer, Holmes, McMaster, Moore, McGrory, Gemmell, Callan

P W D L F A Pts   *Attendance:* 18,000
20 17 0 3 47 15 34   *Referee:* D. McKerchar

St Mirren are in the pack pursuing Aberdeen. Hather and Brown – Leggat's deputy – gave Aberdeen a comfortable interval advantage. But it is quickly halved and thereafter the Dons were never secure.

No 21 Saturday, 29 January
EAST FIFE (1) 1   ABERDEEN (1) 1
  Maclennan (4)   Leggat (2)

EAST FIFE: Curran, Emery, S. Stewart, Cousins, Finlay, Maclennan, J. Stewart, Gardiner, Matthew

ABERDEEN: Martin, Mitchell, Smith, Allister, Young, Glen, Leggat, Yorston, Buckley, Wishart, Hather

P W D L F A Pts   *Attendance:* 9,000
21 17 1 3 48 16 35   *Referee:* C. E. Faultless

All the excitement comes in the first four minutes. Thereafter East Fife fully deserve their draw – Aberdeen's first of the season.

No 22 Saturday, 12 February
ABERDEEN (1) 4   PARTICK THISTLE (0) 0
  Hather 2 (42, 74), Buckley
  (71), Allister (80)

ABERDEEN: Martin, Mitchell, Smith, Allister, Young, Glen, Brown, Yorston, Buckley, Wishart, Hather

PARTICK: Ledgerwood, Brown, Kerr, Harvey, Davidson, McNab, McKenzie, Howitt, Crowe, Wright, McParland

P	W	D	L	F	A	Pts	
22	18	1	3	52	16	37	*Attendance:* 14,000
							Referee: W. Harvie

Aberdeen avenge their narrow defeat at Partick on a pitch caked in snow. It was so cold that both linesmen wore trousers – as did the idle Martin.

No 23 Saturday, 26 February

QUEEN OF THE SOUTH (2) 2   ABERDEEN (2) 6

Oakes (5), Greenock (26)   Hather (17), Buckley 2 (24, 73), Yorston 2 (64, 89), Hamilton (69)

QUEEN OF THE SOUTH: Henderson, Sharpe, Binning, McBain, Smith, Greenock, Black, McGill, Brown, Rothera, Oakes

ABERDEEN: Martin, Mitchell, Smith, Allister, Young, Glen, Hamilton, Yorston, Buckley, Wishart, Hather

Leading positions

	P	W	D	L	F	A	Pts
1 ABERDEEN	23	19	1	3	58	18	39
2 Celtic	22	13	7	2	61	29	33
3 Clyde	23	10	8	5	53	39	28
4 St Mirren	22	11	6	5	47	37	28
5 Rangers	21	12	3	6	52	25	27
6 Hearts	19	12	3	4	57	30	27

Attendance: 9,000   *Referee:* C. E. Faultless

It was rat-a-tat stuff at Dumfries, the score standing at 2-2 midway through the opening half. In the second period Aberdeen stepped on the throttle. As the league enters the home straight only Celtic – and perhaps Hearts – have a realistic chance of catching Aberdeen.

No 24 Saturday, 12 March

HEARTS (2) 2   ABERDEEN (0) 0

Bauld 2 (18, 40)

HEARTS: Duff, Parker, Mackenzie, Mackay, Glidden, Cumming, Souness, Conn, Bauld, Wardhaugh, Urquhart

ABERDEEN: Martin, Mitchell, Smith, Allister, Young, Glen, Leggat, Yorston, Buckley, Wishart, Hather

P	W	D	L	F	A	Pts	
24	19	1	4	58	20	39	*Attendance:* 28,000
							Referee: W. Brittle

The third meeting inside eight days. Thanks to Aberdeen, Hearts now have only the league to aim for. The Dons play in blue and are unrecognisable in every way. Martin was injured as Bauld scored his first goal and Smith was deputising when Bauld claimed his second.

No 25 Saturday, 19 March

FALKIRK (1) 1   ABERDEEN (1) 2

McCrae (8)   Wishart (3), Hather (50)

FALKIRK: Slater, Parker, Ralston, Black, McKenzie, Campbell, Sinclair, Grant, Davidson, McCrae, Forrest

ABERDEEN: Martin, Mitchell, Smith, O'Neil, Young, Glen, Leggat, Hamilton, Buckley, Wishart, Hather

P	W	D	L	F	A	Pts	
25	20	1	4	60	21	41	*Attendance:* 17,000
							Referee: P. Fitzpatrick

This was a nervy Aberdeen, showing the strain of going for a league and Cup double. Hather was possibly offside when scoring from a tight angle. Falkirk nearly levelled when Sinclair's header came back off Martin's bar.

No 26 Wednesday, 30 March

ABERDEEN (3) 4   KILMARNOCK (0) 1

Leggat 2 (14, 26),   McKay (64)
Yorston (17), Wishart (55)

ABERDEEN: Morrison, Mitchell, Caldwell, Allister, Young, Glen, Leggat, Yorston, Buckley, Wishart, Hather

KILMARNOCK: Brown, Watson, Rollo, Curlett, Dougan, McKay, Murray, Toner, Flavell, Beattie, Henaughan

Leading positions

	P	W	D	L	F	A	Pts
1 ABERDEEN	26	21	1	4	64	22	43
2 Celtic	26	16	8	2	69	34	40
3 Rangers	26	16	3	7	60	27	35
4 Hearts	22	14	4	4	62	31	32

Attendance: 17,000   *Referee:* G. Mitchell

Aberdeen dare not slip up now. While Celtic are winning 4-3 at East Fife, Aberdeen cruise to victory. They need five more points from four matches for the title, with games against Rangers and Celtic still to come.

No 27 Saturday, 2 April

ABERDEEN (1) 4   RANGERS (0) 0

Buckley 3 (20, 49, 76), Leggat (88)

ABERDEEN: Morrison, Mitchell, Caldwell, Allister, Young, Glen, Leggat, Yorston, Buckley, Wishart, Hather

RANGERS: Niven, Caldow, McKenzie, McColl, Young, Prentice, Scott, Paton, Gardiner, Rae, Waddell

P	W	D	L	F	A	Pts	
27	22	1	4	68	22	45	*Attendance:* 32,000
							Referee: F. S. Crossley

Rangers have nothing to play for except to assist Celtic to snatch the title. Aberdeen power to victory; then hear wonderful news from Parkhead. Celtic have lost at home to Hibs. Martin is missing, playing for Scotland at Wembley, and picking the ball out of the net seven times.

No 28 Saturday, 9 April

CLYDE (0) 0   ABERDEEN (1) 1

Glen (13 pen)

CLYDE: Hewkins, Murphy, Haddock, Granville, Anderson, Laing, Divers, Robertson, Hill, Brown, Ring

ABERDEEN: Martin, Mitchell, Caldwell, O'Neil,
Young, Glen, Leggat, Yorston, Hamilton, Wishart,
Hather

P	W	D	L	F	A	Pts	
28	23	1	4	69	22	47	*Attendance:* 15,000

Referee: J. A. S. Bisset

Five days earlier Clyde had denied Aberdeen a place in
the Scottish Cup Final. At Shawfield Aberdeen could
secure the championship. Should they fail they will have
to live through the fires of Parkhead next week. The
game is scrappy, but Murphy handled Wishart's shot.
Glen has missed penalties this season, but this one
screams high to Hewkins' left. Hail the Dons! –
Scottish Champions.

No 29 Saturday, 16 April
CELTIC (1) 2   ABERDEEN (1) 1
Tully (21), McPhail (61)   Leggat (86)
CELTIC: Bonner, Haughney, Meechan, Evans, Stein,
Peacock, Collins Reid, McPhail, Mochan, Tully
ABERDEEN: Martin, Paterson, Caldwell, O'Neil,
Young, Glen, Leggat, Yorston, Buckley, Wishart,
Hather

P	W	D	L	F	A	Pts	
29	23	1	5	70	24	47	*Attendance:* 35,000

Referee: R. H. Davidson

Who knows what this match might have produced had
the title depended upon it. Instead the deposed
champions issue a final gesture of defiance in
completing a comfortable double over the Dons.

No 30 Saturday, 23 April
ABERDEEN (3) 3   RAITH ROVERS (1) 2
Buckley 2 (11, 32),   Copland 2 (43, 84)
Hather (44)
ABERDEEN: Martin, Mitchell, Caldwell, O'Neil,
Young, Glen, Leggat, Yorston, Buckley, Wishart,
Hather
RAITH: Stewart, Weir, McClure, Bain, McNaught,
Leigh, McEwan, Young, Copland, Kelly, Duncan
Attendance: 10,000   *Referee:* J. A. S. Bisset

The curtain comes down on Aberdeen's greatest season
so far. But Raith are desperate for points. Only 10,000
arrive to acknowledge the champions. Copland's second
goal, with Glen deputising in goal for the wrist-damaged
Martin, was a joke. It spoiled Aberdeen's hopes of
establishing a new defensive record for a thirty-match
season.

Aberdeen's complete home and away record:

HOME						AWAY						
P	W	D	L	F	A		W	D	L	F	A	Pts
30	14	0	1	41	9		10	1	4	32	17	49

Scottish League Division A 1954-55

	P	W	D	L	F	A	Pts
1 ABERDEEN	30	24	1	5	73	26	49
2 Celtic	30	19	8	3	76	37	46
3 Rangers	30	19	3	8	67	33	41
4 Hearts	30	16	7	7	74	45	39
5 Hibernian	30	15	4	11	64	54	34
6 St Mirren	30	12	8	10	55	54	32
7 Clyde	30	11	9	10	59	50	31
8 Dundee	30	13	4	13	48	48	30
9 Partick Thistle	30	11	7	12	49	61	29
10 Kilmarnock	30	10	6	14	46	58	26
11 East Fife	30	9	6	15	51	62	24
12 Falkirk	30	8	8	14	42	54	24
13 Queen of the South	30	9	6	15	38	56	24
14 Raith Rovers	30	10	3	17	49	57	23
15 Motherwell	30	9	4	17	42	62	22
16 Stirling Albion	30	2	2	16	29	105	6

LEAGUE CUP

Saturday, 14 August
ABERDEEN (1) 4   QUEEN OF THE SOUTH
Leggat 2 (42, 66),   (0) 0
Hather (71), Buckley (75)
ABERDEEN: Martin, Mitchell, Smith, Allister,
Young, Glen, Leggat, Hamilton, Buckley, O'Neil,
Hather
QUEEN OF THE SOUTH: Henderson, Sharp,
Binning, McBain, Smith, Greenock, Black, McGill,
Patterson, Cruickshank, Oakes
Attendance: 18,000   *Referee:* P. Fitzpatrick
Once Aberdeen settle down the forwards score
regularly. But the big danger in this section are
defending League Cup holders East Fife.

Wednesday, 18 August
HIBERNIAN (2) 2   ABERDEEN (0) 0
Preston 2 (16, 39)
HIBERNIAN: Younger, Higgins, Paterson, Buchanan,
Ward, Combe, Smith, Johnstone, Preston, Turnbull,
Ormond
ABERDEEN: Martin, Mitchell, Smith, Allister,
Young, Glen, Brown, Hamilton, Buckley, O'Neil,
Hather
Attendance: 23,000   *Referee:* D. McKerchar
Hibs did not miss Lawrie Reilly's absence. Tommy
Preston stepped in to sink Aberdeen.

Saturday, 21 August
EAST FIFE (0) 0   ABERDEEN (2) 3
     Buckley (22), O'Neil
     (34), Hather (63)
EAST FIFE: Curran, Emery, S. Stewart, Christie,
Finlay, McLennan, J. Stewart, Fleming, Gardiner,
Bonthrone, Matthew
ABERDEEN: Martin, Mitchell, Smith, Allister,
Young, Glen, Leggat, Hamilton, Buckley, O'Neil,
Hather

Referee: J. Jackson

Playing against the wind in the first half, Aberdeen take control against the group favourites.

Saturday, 28 August

QUEEN OF THE   ABERDEEN (0) 0
SOUTH (0) 3
Adams (52), Patterson
(82), Oakes (87)

QUEEN OF THE SOUTH: Henderson, Sharpe, Binning, McBain, Hollywood, Greenock, Black, Patterson, Brown, Adams, Oakes

ABERDEEN: Martin, Mitchell, Smith, Allister, Young, Glen, Leggat, Hamilton, Buckley, O'Neil, Hather

Attendance: 10,000   *Referee:* R. J. Smith

Queens have lost their first three League Cup ties but Aberdeen have no answer to their second-half enthusiasm.

Wednesday, 1 September

ABERDEEN (1) 1   HIBERNIAN (0) 1
Hamilton (11)   Ormond (80 pen)

ABERDEEN: Martin, Mitchell, Smith, Allister, Clunie, Glen, Leggat, Hamilton, Buckley, Yorston, Hather

HIBERNIAN: Younger, Higgins, McFarlane, Buchan, Paterson, Combe, Smith, Johnstone, Preston, Turnbull, Ormond

Attendance: 30,000   *Referee:* J. A. Mowat

Aberdeen can still qualify if they beat both Hibs and East Fife at Pittodrie. But Hibs piled forward in the second half and won a penalty when Clunie held off Johnstone.

Saturday, 4 September

ABERDEEN (4) 5   EAST FIFE (1) 1
Hather (3), Buckley 4   Emery (12 pen)
(21, 31, 42, 52)

ABERDEEN: Martin, Mitchell, Smith, Wallace, Clunie, Glen, Leggat, Hamilton, Buckley, Yorston, Hather

EAST FIFE: Curran, Emery, S. Stewart, Christie, Finlay, Whyte, J. Stewart, Fleming, Gardiner, Bonthrone, Matthew

Attendance: 15,000   *Referee:* C. E. Faultless

East Fife are three points ahead of Aberdeen, so the match is meaningless, except to Buckley, who helps himself to four goals.

Section B

	P	W	D	L	F	A	Pts
East Fife	6	4	0	2	13	11	8
ABERDEEN	6	3	1	2	13	7	7
Hibernian	6	3	1	2	13	10	7
Queen of the South	6	1	0	5	8	19	2

SCOTTISH CUP

5th Round Saturday, 5 February

STIRLING ALBION (0) 0   ABERDEEN (5) 6
    Yorston 2 (2, 44),
    Hather 2 (7, 43),
    Buckley 2 (25, 70)

STIRLING: Mitchell, Almond, McNichol, McKechnie, Milligan, Swanson, Laird, Smith, Brander, McGill, Paterson

ABERDEEN: Martin, Mitchell, Smith, Allister, Young, Glen, Leggat, Yorston, Buckley, Wishart, Hather

Attendance: 7,500   *Referee:* R. J. Smith

When Aberdeen visited Annfield in the league they scraped through 4-3. It was rather easier in the Cup.

6th Round Saturday, 19 February

ABERDEEN (1) 2   RANGERS (1) 1
Hather (7), Wishart (51)   Neillands (11)

ABERDEEN: Martin, Mitchell, Smith, Allister, Young, Glen, Hamilton, Yorston, Buckley, Wishart, Hather

RANGERS: Niven, Little, Cox, McColl, Young, Rae, McCulloch, Paton, Miller, Neillands, Hubbard

Attendance: 44,647   *Referee:* J. A. Mowat

Rangers still harbour bitter memories of their extraordinary semi final whitewash last year. On a treacherous surface George Hamilton, now on the fringes of the team, comes in at outside right. His cross engineers Wishart's second-half goal that takes Aberdeen through.

Quarter Final Saturday, 5 March

HEARTS (0) 1   ABERDEEN (1) 1
Bauld (59)   Allister (3)

HEARTS: Duff, Parker, Mackenzie, Mackay, Glidden, Cumming, Souness, Conn, Bauld, Wardhaugh, Urquhart

ABERDEEN: Martin, Mitchell, Smith, Allister, Young, Glen, Leggat, Yorston, Buckley, Wishart, Hather

Attendance: 49,000   *Referee:* H. Phillips

Last season defeats by Aberdeen in league and Cup in quick succession shattered Hearts' season. When Allister headed home a weak clearance Hearts must have feared the worst. But at last Bauld hooked an equaliser and then forced Smith to head off the line. Aberdeen were grateful for the replay.

Quarter-Final Replay Wednesday, 9 March

ABERDEEN (0) 2   HEARTS (0) 0
Buckley (48), Yorston
(60)

ABERDEEN: Martin, Mitchell, Smith, Allister, Young, Glen, Leggat, Yorston, Buckley, Wishart, Hather

HEARTS: Duff, Parker, Mackenzie, Mackay, Glidden, Cumming, Souness, Conn, Bauld, Wardhaugh, Urquhart

Attendance: 41,000   *Referee:* H. Phillips

Hearts' forwards rarely gained a glimpse of goal. Neither did Aberdeen's until Buckley seized on Wishart's pass. Hearts seemed sunk before Yorston's raking drive put them out of their misery.

Semi Final (Easter Road) Saturday, 26 March
CLYDE (1) 2   ABERDEEN (2) 2
  Ring 2 (9, 89)   Buckley 2 (37, 40)

CLYDE: Hewkins, Murphy, Haddock, Gallacher, Anderson, Laing, Divers, Robertson, McPhail, Brown, Ring

ABERDEEN: Martin, Smith, Caldwell, Allister, Young, Glen, Leggat, Yorston, Buckley, Wishart, Hather

Attendance: 33,000   *Referee:* R. H. Davidson

Only Clyde stand between Aberdeen and their third successive Scottish Cup Final. Skipper Jimmy Mitchell stands down with flu. Ring scores for Clyde after Martin drops a corner, but Buckley is on hand to finish off two free kicks laid into his path. Just before half-time Billy Smith breaks a leg and Aberdeen have to grit their teeth throughout the second period. Clyde are given a penalty when Ring is sandwiched, but Robertson's aim is awry. In injury time a goalmouth scramble leads to Ring keeping Clyde afloat.

Semi Final Replay (Easter Road) Monday, 4 April
CLYDE (1) 1   ABERDEEN (0) 0
  Robertson (28 pen)

CLYDE: Hewkins, Murphy, Haddock, Granville, Anderson, Laing, Divers, Robertson, McPhail, Brown, Ring

ABERDEEN: Martin, Mitchell, Caldwell, Allister, Young, Glen, Leggat, Yorston, Buckley, Wishart, Hather

Attendance: 28,000   *Referee:* R. H. Davidson

The double for Aberdeen seems increasingly probable. But their form deserts them at the critical moment. Young handles while lying on the ground to give Robertson the chance to atone for his penalty miss in the first match. Buckley did manage to hit a post, but, that apart, there was no denying Clyde were the better team.

1954-55 APPEARANCES	League	League Cup	Scottish Cup
Glen	30	6	6
Hather	30	6	6
Young	30	4	6
Mitchell	29	6	5
Buckley	28	6	6
Yorston	28	2	6
Martin	27	6	6
Leggat	26	5	5
W. Smith	25	6	5
Wishart	23		6
Allister	21	5	6
O'Neil	12	4	
Wallace	5	1	
Caldwell	5		2
Hamilton	4	6	1
Brown	3	1	
Morrison	3		
Paterson	1		
Clunie		2	
19 players			

GOALS	Total	League	League Cup	Scottish Cup
Buckley	28	17	6	5
Yorston	15	12		3
Hather	15	9	3	3
Leggat	13	11	2	
Wishart	8	7		1
Allister	5	4		1
O'Neil	5	4	1	
Glen	4	4		
Hamilton	3	2	1	
Brown	1	1		
Wallace	1	1		
own-goals	1	1		
Total	99	73	13	13

Mulhall, to star for Aberdeen in the late fifties and early sixties.

Season 1955-56

Unrest set in following Aberdeen's championship triumph. The players were unhappy at the lack of financial reward from the club, while the manager – David Halliday – was lured south by Leicester City. Dave Shaw was promoted from trainer to the hot seat. There were no major comings and goings, but George Hamilton had played his last game.

David Shaw had high standards to maintain, yet he was determined to encourage Aberdeen to play brighter soccer than the style which took them to the title. The first three months of the season were highly successful. After fifteen league and League Cup games Aberdeen had proudly claimed the League Cup from St Mirren to give them a clean sweep of domestic trophies since the War. They also appeared to be marching irresistibly towards retaining their league crown.

The Hampden triumph seemed to unsettle the Dons, giving them a trophy too early in the season. They then went eight matches without a win, a spell that was to cost them their crown. When eventually they pulled themselves together – on Christmas Eve – they surged back up the table during an unbeaten league run of fifteen games. But they could never quite get back on terms with Rangers, who K.O.'d Aberdeen from the Scottish Cup at the first hurdle and went on to take the league title by a clear six points. Aberdeen had to struggle to finish second, having been burdened throughout the season with a chaotic injury problem.

Even taking into account the extra four fixtures entailed by expanding the league from sixteen to eighteen clubs, it was easy to see why Aberdeen had been dethroned (injuries aside). Their goals-against column doubled. At Pittodrie 29 goals were lost, the highest number since the War.

By rights Aberdeen should have been Scotland's representatives in the first European Cup competition. But in its inaugural year participation was by invitation rather than possession of the domestic championship and at the SFA's request Hibs filled Scotland's berth.

League:	Runners Up
League Cup:	Winners
Scottish Cup:	Fifth Round

SCOTTISH LEAGUE DIVISION A

No 1 Saturday, 10 September
ABERDEEN (4) 6   HIBERNIAN (1) 2
  Leggat 2 (5, 38),   Reilly (22), Turnbull (76)
  Buckley 3 (12, 36, 60),
  Yorston (78)

ABERDEEN: Martin, Mitchell, Caldwell, Wilson, Clunie, Glen, Leggat, Yorston, Buckley, Wishart, Hather
HIBERNIAN: Younger, Paterson, Muir, Thomson, Plenderleith, Preston, Smith, Turnbull, Reilly, Fox, Ormond

P	W	D	L	F	A	Pts
1	1	0	0	6	2	2

Attendance: 17,000
Referee: W. Brittle

Aberdeen have already beaten Hibs twice in the League Cup, but could hardly have expected such a margin of victory. Buckley has now scored eight goals already, but injury will wreck his season and he will score only three more by its end.

No 2 Saturday, 24 September
ABERDEEN (0) 2   DUNDEE (0) 0
  Hather (75), Glen (80 pen)

ABERDEEN: Martin, Paterson, Mitchell, Wilson, Clunie, Glen, Leggat, Yorston, Buckley, Wishart, Hather
DUNDEE: Brown, Reid, Irvine, Black, Malloy, Cowie, Chalmers, Roy, Easson, Henderson, Christie

P	W	D	L	F	A	Pts
2	2	0	0	8	2	4

Attendance: 20,000
Referee: G. Bowman

After the fire and fury of the performance against Hibs and Hearts this was more mundane fare.

No 3 Saturday, 8 October

ABERDEEN (1) 3	QUEEN OF THE SOUTH (1) 2
Clunie (21 pen), Hather (52), Buckley (73)	Patterson (3), Mitchell o.g. (80)

ABERDEEN: Martin, Mitchell, Caldwell, Wilson, Clunie, Paterson, Boyd, Kelly, Buckley, Wishart, Hather

QUEEN OF THE SOUTH: Henderson, Sharp, Binning, Sweeney, Smith, Gibson, Black, McGill, Patterson, Rothera, Macguire

P	W	D	L	F	A	Pts		
3	3	0	0	11	4	6	*Attendance:* 17,000 *Referee:* H. J. Gallacher	

Aberdeen are without Archie Glen, who is playing for Scotland in Belfast. Nevertheless they continue their winning ways against high-flying Queens. The match turns on a Queens penalty late in the first half. Martin saves brilliantly from Patterson. In addition to his goal, Jackie Hather also becomes the father of a son.

No 4 Saturday, 15 October

ST MIRREN (0) 0	ABERDEEN (1) 3
	Wishart (5), Davidson 2 (54, 81)

ST MIRREN: Lornie, Lapsley, Mallan, Neilson, Telfer, Holmes, Rodger, Laird, Brown, Wilson, Callan

ABERDEEN: Martin, Mitchell, Macfarlane, Wilson, Clunie, Glen, Mulhall, Yorston, Davidson, Wishart, Hather

Leading positions

	P	W	D	L	F	A	Pts
1 ABERDEEN	4	4	0	0	14	4	8
2 Queen of the South	6	4	0	2	16	8	8
3 Raith	6	3	1	2	12	10	7
4 Hibernian	5	3	1	1	9	8	7
5 Dunfermline	6	3	1	2	7	8	7

Attendance: 15,000   *Referee:* R. Morris

St Mirren are awaiting Aberdeen in the League Cup Final next week. But they still cannot win in the league and hand the Dons a major morale booster, even though they are short of the services of Caldwell, Buckley and Leggat. Norman Davidson scores twice on his debut.

No 5 Saturday, 29 October

EAST FIFE (1) 1	ABERDEEN (1) 1
Kirkwood (43)	Ingram (27)

EAST FIFE: Curran, Adie, Stewart, Christie, Finlay, McLennan, Wright, Kirkwood, Plumb, Bonthrone, Matthew

ABERDEEN: Martin, Mitchell, Caldwell, Wilson, Clunie, Glen, Ingram, Yorston, Davidson, Wishart, Hather

P	W	D	L	F	A	Pts		
5	4	1	0	15	5	9	*Attendance:* 10,000 *Referee:* G. Mitchell	

Aberdeen drop their first point and could have dropped two. They slip to fifth place with games in hand. Jimmy Ingram scores the Dons' goal on his debut. Afterwards Jack Allister's transfer request is turned down.

No 6 Saturday, 5 November

ABERDEEN (1) 1	CLYDE (4) 4
Davidson (30)	Ring (10), Lennox 2 (19, 22), Divers (38)

ABERDEEN: Martin, Mitchell, Caldwell, Wilson, Clunie, Glen, Ingram, Yorston, Davidson, Wishart, Hather

CLYDE: Wilson, Murphy, Haddock, Gallacher, Anderson, Laing, Divers, Robertson, Lennox, Carmichael, Ring

P	W	D	L	F	A	Pts		
6	4	1	1	16	9	9	*Attendance:* 15,000 *Referee:* R. Yacamini	

Clyde seem to feature in all Aberdeen's milestones of late. Now it is they who inflict Aberdeens' first defeat in any competition in their sixteenth match. The only thing Pittodrie has to be thankful about is the fog, which shrouded the view of Clyde's goals.

No 7 Saturday, 12 November

DUNFERMLINE ATHLETIC (0) 2	ABERDEEN (0) 2
Dickson (66), Miller (89)	Hather (67), Yorston (75)

DUNFERMLINE: Mackin, Laird, Williamson, Samuel, Duthie, Bakie, Peebles, Mailer, Dickson, Reilly, Anderson

ABERDEEN: Martin, Mitchell, Macfarlane, Wilson, Clunie, Glen, Davidson, Yorston, Wishart, Hay, Hather

P	W	D	L	F	A	Pts		
7	4	2	1	18	11	10	*Attendance:* 10,000 *Referee:* A. McLintock	

Newcomers Dunfermline are going well as Aberdeen discovered in the League Cup. Without their goalkeeper for the last hour they still snatch a draw at the close.

No 8 Saturday, 19 November

ABERDEEN (0) 1	MOTHERWELL (0) 1
Wilson (66)	McSeveney (64)

ABERDEEN: Martin, Mitchell, Macfarlane, Wilson, Clunie, Glen, Davidson, Yorston, Buckley, Wishart, Hather

MOTHERWELL: Weir, Kilmarnock, Shaw, Humphries, Paton, McFadyen, Sloan, Aitken, McSeveney, Gardiner, Aitkenhead

P	W	D	L	F	A	Pts		
8	4	3	1	19	12	11	*Attendance:* 20,000 *Referee:* W. D. Liston	

Aberdeen are still out of sorts. Motherwell hang on to repel the Dons' final surge.

No 9 Saturday, 26 November

RAITH ROVERS (0) 1	ABERDEEN (1) 1
McEwan (73)	Buckley (6)

RAITH: Drummond, Polland, Weir, McMillan, McNaught, Leigh, McEwan, Murney, Young, Thomson, Scott

ABERDEEN: Martin, Mitchell, Macfarlane, Wilson, Clunie, Glen, McNeill, Yorston, Buckley, Hay, Hather

P W D L F A Pts   *Attendance:* 12,000
9 4 4 1 20 13 12   *Referee:* T. S. Edwards

Aberdeen flatter to deceive after Buckley capitalised on McNaught's weak backpass. It's Buckley's last match for twenty games.

No 10 Saturday, 3 December
HEARTS (1) 3   ABERDEEN (0) 0
  Young 2 (42, 64),
  Bauld (81)
HEARTS: Duff, Parker, Kirk, Mackay, Glidden, Cumming, Hamilton, Young, Bauld, Wardhaugh, Urquhart
ABERDEEN: Martin, Mitchell, Macfarlane, Allister, Clunie, Glen, McNeill, Yorston, Davidson, Hay, Hather

P W D L F A Pts   *Attendance:* 30,000
10 4 4 2 20 16 12   *Referee:* J. A. Mowat

Aberdeen didn't win a match in November. On this form they won't win another in 1955 either. Nineteen-year old Alex Young sunk the Dons with two goals. Wearing blue shirts, Aberdeen are nothing like the side which won 4-2 at Tynecastle in the League Cup.

No 11 Saturday, 10 December
ABERDEEN (0) 0   RANGERS (0) 0
ABERDEEN: Morrison, Mitchell, Macfarlane, Allister, Clunie, Glen, Boyd, Wishart, Davidson, Hay, Hather
RANGERS: Niven, Caldow, Little, McColl, Young, Rae, Scott, Simpson, Kichenbrand, Baird, Hubbard

P W D L F A Pts   *Attendance:* 20,000
11 4 5 2 20 16 13   *Referee:* H. Phillips

Aberdeen have three games in hand over most of the other clubs and find themselves in the bottom half of the table. Rangers labour under a massive inferiority complex from the past two seasons' results. In the circumstances Rangers are pleased with their goalless draw – though Aberdeen played the second half with Mitchell a passenger on the wing.

No 12 Saturday, 17 December
KILMARNOCK (0) 1   ABERDEEN (0) 0
  Curlett (68)
KILMARNOCK: Brown, Watson, Rollo, Taggart, Toner, McKay, Mays, Lawlor, Curlett, Beattie, Fletcher
ABERDEEN: Martin, Macfarlane, Caldwell, Allister, Clunie, Glen, Boyd, Wishart, Davidson, Hay, Hather

P W D L F A Pts   *Attendance:* 15,000
12 4 5 3 20 17 13   *Referee:* R. H. Davidson

Since lifting the League Cup Aberdeen have gone eight games without the scent of victory. This barren two-month spell will cost them their championship. Killie's margin of victory could have been greater. Mays fired a first half penalty straight at Martin.

No 13 Saturday, 24 December
ABERDEEN (2) 7   AIRDRIEONIANS (0) 2
  Wishart (8), Glen (42),   Baird (65), McCulloch
  Hather 2 (50, 72),   (80)
  Yorston (61), Allan (82),
  Leggat (89)
ABERDEEN: Martin, Macfarlane, Caldwell, Allister, Clunie, Glen, Leggat, Yorston, Allan, Wishart, Hather
AIRDRIE: Walker, Miller, McNeil, Quinn, Quigley, Price, Rankin, McMillan, Baird, Welsh, McCulloch

P W D L F A Pts   *Attendance:* 18,000
13 5 5 3 27 19 15   *Referee:* D. Weir

Somebody had to pay for the Dons' loss of form. But Aberdeen pay a heavy price in Jim Clunie's broken leg.

No 14 Saturday, 31 December
FALKIRK (2) 3   ABERDEEN (2) 6
  Sinclair 3 (12, 34, 80)   Hather (21), Allan
                3 (25, 54,76), Leggat
                2 (56, 85)
FALKIRK: Slater, Parker, Rae, Campbell, Colville, McIntosh, Sinclair, Wright, Ormond, McCrae, O'Hara
ABERDEEN: Martin, Macfarlane, Caldwell, Allister, Young, Glen, Leggat, Yorston, Allan, Wishart, Hather

P W D L F A Pts   *Attendance:* 15,000
14 6 5 3 33 22 17   *Referee:* W. Harvie

As if at the flick of a switch Aberdeen are back on song. Fifth-placed Falkirk suffer a second-half battering. Johnny Allan seems to have made all the difference to Aberdeen's front line.

No 15 Monday, 2 January
DUNDEE (1) 2   ABERDEEN (1) 4
  Christie (40), Merchant   Glen (25 pen), Leggat
  (77)   (67), Yorston (82),
                Hather (84)
DUNDEE: Brown, Reid, Irvine, Gallacher, Black, Cowie, Stables, Henderson, Merchant, Smith, Christie
ABERDEEN: Martin, Macfarlane, Caldwell, Allister, Young, Glen, Leggat, Yorston, Allan, Wishart, Hather

P W D L F A Pts
15 7 5 3 37 24 19   *Referee:* W. Davidson

Dundee are the next to feel Aberdeen's wrath. But this time the Dons leave it late.

No 16 Tuesday, 3 January
ABERDEEN (4) 7   STIRLING ALBION (0) 0
  Leggat (6), Allan
  4 (16, 29, 54, 89), Hather
  (17), Allister (86)
ABERDEEN: Martin, Macfarlane, Caldwell, Allister, Young, Glen, Leggat, Yorston, Allan, Wishart, Hather
STIRLING: Houston, Gibson, Erskine, John Smith, McNichol, Rankin, Vandermotten, Timmins, Kerr, Swanson, Rowan

P W D L F A Pts   *Attendance:* 25,000
16 8 5 3 44 24 21   *Referee:* R. Yacamini

Twenty-four goals in four games is Aberdeen's reply to their critics. Poor Stirling have now lost 8-0, 6-0, 5-0 and 7-0 on their last four visits to Pittodrie.

No 17 Saturday, 7 January
ABERDEEN (1) 1   CELTIC (0) 0
  Leggat (42)
ABERDEEN: Martin, Macfarlane, Caldwell, Allister, Young, Glen, Leggat, Yorston, Allan, Wishart, Hather
CELTIC: Beattie, Haughney, Fallon, Evans, Stein, Peacock, Smith, Fernie, Sharkey, Collins, Mochan
Leading positions

	P	W	D	L	F	A	Pts
1 Rangers	17	10	6	1	42	16	26
2 Hearts	18	11	3	4	56	24	25
3 Celtic	19	11	3	5	37	20	25
4 Hibernian	18	11	3	4	47	30	25
5 ABERDEEN	17	9	5	3	45	24	23

Attendance: 38,000   *Referee:* J. Lackie

Aberdeen owe Celtic a defeat. Aberdeen topple the league leaders after a no-holds-barred encounter in which one goal was always likely to settle the outcome. It came when Allan laid the ball into the path of the onrushing Leggat. With this win Aberdeen are back in the frame.

No 18 Saturday, 14 January
HIBERNIAN (1) 1   ABERDEEN (1) 3
  Reilly (38)   Boyd (12), Wishart
                                   2 (65, 73)
HIBERNIAN: Younger, Macfarlane, McClelland, Thomson, Plenderleith, Grant, Smith, Preston, Reilly, Turnbull, Frye
ABERDEEN: Martin, Macfarlane, Caldwell, Allister, Young, Glen, Boyd, Yorston, Allan, Wishart, Hather
P W D L F A Pts
18 10 5 3 48 25 25   *Referee:* G. Mitchell

Aberdeen climb into third spot after this fine win against another of the title contenders. On a skating rink surface Aberdeen win their fourth match of the season against Hibs.

No 19 Saturday, 28 January
QUEEN OF THE   ABERDEEN (1) 2
SOUTH (1) 2   Yorston (40),
  Patterson (28),   Glen (48 pen)
  Rothera (69)
QUEEN OF THE SOUTH: Henderson, Sharpe, Binning, Sweeney, Smith, Whitehead, Black, McGill, Patterson, Rothera, Oakes
ABERDEEN: Martin, Macfarlane, Caldwell, Allister, Glen, Brownlee, Leggat, Yorston, Allan, Wishart, Hather
P W D L F A Pts
19 10 6 3 50 27 26   *Attendance:* 10,000
                              Referee: G. Bowman

Queens are still going well and halt Aberdeen's sequence of six wins. In the final seconds Aberdeen's Caldwell heads off the line from Sweeney.

No 20 Saturday, 11 February
ABERDEEN (2) 4   ST MIRREN (0) 1
  Allan (23), Mulhall (44),   McLeod (67)
  Leggat 2 (60, 84)
ABERDEEN: Martin, Macfarlane, Caldwell, Allister, Glen, Brownlee, Leggat, Wishart, Allan, Hay, Mulhall
ST MIRREN: Lornie, Lapsley, Mallan, Neilson, Telfer, Johnston, McGill, Henry, Holmes, Gemmell, McLeod
P W D L F A Pts   *Attendance:* 15,000
20 11 6 3 54 28 28   *Referee:* H. J. Gallacher

Aberdeen shrugged off the disappointment of their Cup K.O. by Rangers to sweep aside the challenge of St. Mirren.

No 21 Saturday, 18 February
ABERDEEN (1) 2   FALKIRK (0) 2
  Wishart (14), Yorston   McCrae (52), Ormond
  (55)   (87)
ABERDEEN: Martin, Mitchell, Caldwell, Allister, Glen, Brownlee, Leggat, Yorston, Allan, Wishart, Mulhall
FALKIRK: Slater, Parker, Rae, Wright, McKenzie, Fletcher, Sinclair, Ormond, McCrae, Morrison, O'Hara
Leading positions

	P	W	D	L	F	A	Pts
1 Rangers	20	13	6	1	50	16	32
2 Hearts	22	13	5	4	65	28	31
3 ABERDEEN	21	11	7	3	56	30	29
4 Hibernian	22	13	3	6	56	35	29
5 Celtic	22	11	6	5	41	24	28

Attendance: 16,000   *Referee:* R. Yacamini

This is the only Division A fixture of the day – Falkirk had beaten Hibs last week and now snatch a late equaliser following a bad clearance by Caldwell. It is an expensive point for Aberdeen to drop.

No 22 Saturday, 25 February
STIRLING ALBION (0) 0   ABERDEEN (1) 2
                               Boyd (21), Yorston (82)
STIRLING: Robertson, Gibson, McNicol, Smith, Stanners, Swanson, Rowan, Pierson, Kerr, McKenzie, Pattison
ABERDEEN: Martin, Mitchell, Caldwell, Allister, Scott, Brownlee, Boyd, Yorston, Allan, Wishart, Hather
P W D L F A Pts   *Attendance:* 5,000
22 12 7 3 58 30 31   *Referee:* F. S. Crossley

Oh so casual were Aberdeen. They thought they could win as they pleased and nearly came unstuck.

No 23 Saturday, 3 March
ABERDEEN (3) 7   EAST FIFE (1) 3
  Wishart (7), Yorston   Bonthrone 3 (6, 68, 70)
  (11), Hather 2 (21, 58),
  Allan (60), Leggat
  2 (73, 86)

ABERDEEN: Martin, Mitchell, Caldwell, Allister, Glen, Brownlee, Leggat, Yorston, Allan, Wishart, Hather

EAST FIFE: Steedman, Adie, S. Stewart, Fox, Finlay, McLenna, J. Stewart, Leishman, Plumb, Bonthrone, Matthew

P	W	D	L	F	A	Pts		
23	13	7	3	65	33	33		

Attendance: 15,000

Referee: J. A. Bisset

East Fife have taken some hammer at Pittodrie in league and League Cup in recent seasons, but nothing as bad as this. All five forwards share the goals.

No 24 Saturday, 10 March

CLYDE (0) 0	ABERDEEN (1) 5
	Leggat 2 (12, 86),
	Yorston (55), Allan (70),
	Wishart (85)

CLYDE: Watson, Gallacher, Haddock, Laing, Keoch, Innes, Hill, Robertson, McPhail, Ring, Kemp

ABERDEEN: Martin, Mitchell, Caldwell, Allister, Glen, Brownlee, Leggat, Yorston, Allan, Wishart, Hather

Leading positions

	P	W	D	L	F	A	Pts
1 Rangers	23	16	6	1	63	16	38
2 Hearts	25	16	5	4	75	30	37
3 ABERDEEN	24	14	7	3	70	33	35

Attendance: 15,000

Referee: H. Phillips

Clyde pay heavily for inflicting upon the Dons their first defeat of the season. On this performance it is easy to see why they are heading for relegation

No 25 Saturday, 17 March

ABERDEEN (1) 1	DUNFERMLINE
Leggat (23)	ATHLETIC (0) 0

ABERDEEN: Martin, Macfarlane, Caldwell, Allister, Glen, Brownlee, Leggat, Yorston, Allan, Wishart, Hather

DUNFERMLINE: Mackin, Laird, Duthie, Samuel, Colville, Mailer, McKinlay, O'Brien, Dickson, Reilly, Anderson

P	W	D	L	F	A	Pts		
25	15	7	3	71	33	37		

Attendance: 17,000

Referee: J. Lackie

All eyes are on Tynecastle where Rangers drew 1-1 with Hearts. Aberdeen almost forget that they had a job on their hands, and are grateful for Leggat's deflected shot.

No 26 Saturday, 24 March

MOTHERWELL (0) 1	ABERDEEN (0) 1
Quinn (79 pen)	Wishart (76)

MOTHERWELL: Weir, Kilmarnock, McSeveney, Mason, Paton, Forrest, Kerr, Quinn, Gardiner, S. Brown, Rea

ABERDEEN: Martin, Mitchell, Caldwell, Allister, Glen, Brownlee, Leggat, Yorston, Allan, Wishart, Hather

P	W	D	L	F	A	Pts		
26	15	8	3	72	34	38		

Attendance: 10,000

Referee: J. Fulton

A black day for Dave Caldwell who concedes the penalty and for Jackie Hather who breaks an arm.

No 27 Saturday, 31 March

ABERDEEN (2) 3	RAITH ROVERS (3) 5
Leggat (20), Boyd (30),	Copland 4 (5, 42, 49, 88),
Young o.g. (89)	McEwan (39)

ABERDEEN: Martin, Mitchell, Caldwell, Wilson, Young, Glen, Leggat, Yorston, Allan, Wishart, Boyd

RAITH: Stewart, Polland, Bain, Young, McNaught, Leigh, Carr, McEwan, Copland, Kelly, McMillan

Leading positions

	P	W	D	L	F	A	Pts
1 Rangers	27	19	7	1	73	21	45
2 Hearts	27	17	6	4	81	31	40
3 ABERDEEN	27	15	8	4	75	39	38

Attendance: 18,000

Referee: T. S. Edwards

Disaster for Aberdeen. Their first league defeat since 17 December, fifteen games ago. Copland is their principal tormentor. The title is now surely beyond Aberdeen. The result spoiled Glen's and Leggat's news that they will play against England in a fortnight.

No 28 Saturday, 7 April

ABERDEEN (3) 4	HEARTS (0) 1
Leggat 3 (1, 40, 80),	Crawford (67)
Boyd (6)	

ABERDEEN: Martin, Mitchell, Caldwell, Wilson, Young, Glen, Leggat, Yorston, Allan, Wishart, Boyd

HEARTS: Duff, Kirk, Mackenzie, Mackay, Glidden, Cumming, Young, Murray, Whittle, Conn, Crawford

P	W	D	L	F	A	Pts		
28	16	8	4	79	40	40		

Attendance: 20,000

Referee: D. McTaggart

Hearts also seem to know it's Rangers' title, and are a beaten side after 22 seconds.

No 29 Tuesday, 10 April

CELTIC (0) 1	ABERDEEN (0) 1
McAlinden (46)	Yorston (68)

CELTIC: Beattie, Haughney, Fallon, Goldie, Evans, Peacock, McAlinden, Craig, Mochan, Fernie, Tully

ABERDEEN: Martin, Mitchell, Caldwell, Wilson, Young, Glen, Leggat, Yorston, Allan, Wishart, Boyd

P	W	D	L	F	A	Pts		
29	16	9	4	80	41	41		

Attendance: 14,000

Referee: H. Phillips

A sparse crowd endured end of season fare. Rangers now need only two points for the title. On Saturday 14 April Glen and Leggat won caps at Hampden against England. Leggat scored in the 1-1 draw.

No 30 Wednesday, 18 April

RANGERS (0) 1	ABERDEEN (0) 0
Scott (62)	

RANGERS: Niven, Shearer, Little, McColl, Young, Rae, Scott, Simpson, Murray, Baird, Hubbard

ABERDEEN: Morrison, Mitchell, Caldwell, Wilson, Young, Allister, Leggat, Yorston, Buckley, Wishart, Boyd

P W D L F A Pts
30 16 9 5 80 42 41   *Referee:* G. Mitchell

Rangers hammer in the final nail to Aberdeen's dethronement. The result flattered the Dons who were outplayed throughout. The golden goal arrived when Martin punched Hubbard's cross high in the air. It dropped for Scott to head home.

No 31 Saturday, 21 April
ABERDEEN (1) 3   KILMARNOCK (1) 2
Buckley (1), Yorston   Beattie (25), Flavell (82)
(69), Mulhall (89)

ABERDEEN: Martin, Mitchell, Caldwell, Allister, Young, Paterson, Boyd, Yorston, Buckley, Wishart, Mulhall
KILMARNOCK: Brown, Collins, Watson, Stewart, Toner, Mackay, Mays, Fletcher, Curlett, Beattie, Flavell
P W D L F A Pts   *Attendance:* 11,000
31 17 9 5 83 44 43   *Referee:* R. Yacamini

Lucky Aberdeen win with a last-gasp goal from Mulhall, even though they were ahead in 28 seconds. The season cannot end quickly enough for them.

No 32 Wednesday, 25 April
AIRDRIEONIANS (0) 2   ABERDEEN (0) 2
Welsh (52), Baird (88)   Yorston (49), Mulhall
                          (75)

AIRDRIE: Goldie, Miller, McNeill, Price, Quigley, Davidson, Welsh, Rankin, Baird, McMillan, McCulloch
ABERDEEN: Martin, Mitchell, Caldwell, Allister, Young, Paterson, Boyd, Yorston, Buckley, Wishart, Mulhall
P W D L F A Pts
32 17 10 5 85 46 44   *Referee:* T. Wharton

Aberdeen would have won but for Hugh **Baird's** spectacular cannonball header.

No 33 Saturday, 28 April
ABERDEEN (0) 0   PARTICK THISTLE (2) 4
                        McKenzie (17), Mathers
                        (32), Ewing (84), Wright
                        (89)

ABERDEEN: Martin, Mitchell, Caldwell, Allister, Young, Paterson, Boyd, Yorston, Buckley, Wishart, Mulhall
PARTICK: Smith, Kerr, Gibb, Harvey, Davidson, Mathers, McKenzie, Wright, Sharp, Crawford, Ewing
P W D L F A Pts   *Attendance:* 16,000
33 17 10 6 85 50 44   *Referee:* W. Davidson

The Dons required two points from their two meetings with Partick to secure runners-up spot. Following this debacle they now need two points from one meeting with Partick.

No 34 Monday, 30 April
PARTICK THISTLE (0) 0   ABERDEEN (0) 2
                        Davidson 2 (72, 74)

PARTICK: W. Smith, Kerr, Gibb, Harvey, Davidson, Mathers, G. Smith, Wright, Sharp, Crawford, Ewing
ABERDEEN: Martin, Mitchell, Caldwell, Allister, Clunie, Brownlee, Boyd, Yorston, Davidson, Wishart, Mulhall
                    Referee: W. Liston

Should Aberdeen have drawn or lost they would finish fourth. If they won they would be second. Davidson's half-hit shot put them on their way.

Aberdeen's complete home and away record:
		HOME					AWAY					
P	W	D	L	F	A		W	D	L	F	A	Pts
34	11	3	3	52	29		7	7	3	35	21	46

Scottish League Division A 1955-56

	P	W	D	L	F	A	Pts
1 Rangers	34	22	8	4	85	27	52
2 ABERDEEN	34	18	10	6	87	50	46
3 Hearts	34	19	7	8	99	47	45
4 Hibernian	34	19	7	8	86	50	45
5 Celtic	34	16	9	9	55	39	41
6 Queen of the South	34	16	5	13	69	73	37
7 Airdrieonians	34	14	8	12	85	96	36
8 Kilmarnock	34	12	10	12	52	45	34
9 Partick Thistle	34	13	7	14	62	60	33
10 Motherwell	34	11	11	12	53	59	33
11 Raith Rovers	34	12	9	13	58	75	33
12 East Fife	34	13	5	16	61	69	31
13 Dundee	34	12	6	16	56	65	30
14 Falkirk	34	11	6	17	58	75	28
15 St Mirren	34	10	7	17	57	70	27
16 Dunfermline Athletic	34	10	6	18	42	82	26
17 Clyde	34	8	6	20	50	74	22
18 Stirling Albion	34	4	5	25	23	82	13

LEAGUE CUP

Saturday, 13 August
HIBERNIAN (0) 0   ABERDEEN (0) 1
                        Buckley (68)

HIBERNIAN: Younger, Higgins, Paterson, Thomson, Plenderleith, Preston, Smith, Turnbull, Reilly, Combe, Ormond
ABERDEEN: Martin, Mitchell, Caldwell, Allister, Young, Glen, Leggat, Yorston, Buckley, Wishart, Mulhall
Attendance: 30,000   *Referee:* R. J. Smith

Dave Shaw's new regime starts off as David Halliday's left off. Aberdeen hit the woodwork twice before Buckley's raging goal. Shortly afterwards Turnbull blazed wide from the penalty spot after Young had handled.

Wednesday, 17 August
ABERDEEN (1) 3   DUNFERMLINE
Mulhall (20), Leggat (65),   ATHLETIC (2) 2
Yorston (69)   Reilly (2), Millar (32)

ABERDEEN: Martin, Mitchell, Caldwell, Allister, Young, Glen, Leggat, Yorston, Buckley, Wishart, Mulhall

DUNFERMLINE: Mackin, Laird, Mackie, Samuel, Duthie, Chalmers, McKinlay, Millar, Dickson, Reilly, Anderson

Attendance: 24,000   *Referee:* D. McKerchar

Aberdeen had to come from behind twice against newly promoted Dunfermline.

Saturday, 20 August
ABERDEEN (1) 3   CLYDE (1) 2
  Wishart (8), Glen   Currie (44), Ring (89)
  (54 pen), Buckley (72)

ABERDEEN: Martin, Mitchell, Caldwell, O'Neil, Young, Glen, Leggat, Yorston, Buckley, Wishart, Mulhall

CLYDE: Hewkins, Murphy, Haddock, Granville, Anderson, Laing, W. Currie, Robertson, D. Currie, Divers, Ring

Attendance: 24,000   *Referee:* R. Yacamini

Aberdeen have bitter-sweet memories of Clyde from last season. Young is hurt and taken to hospital.

Saturday, 27 August
ABERDEEN (0) 2   HIBERNIAN (1) 1
  Buckley (65), O'Neil (88)   Reilly (44)

ABERDEEN: Martin, Mitchell, Caldwell, O'Neil, Clunie, Glen, Leggat, Yorston, Buckley, Wishart, Mulhall

HIBERNIAN: Younger, Higgins, Paterson, Thomson, Plenderleith, Preston, Smith, Turnbull, Reilly, Combe, Ormond

Attendance: 30,000   *Referee:* R. H. Davidson

Joe O'Neil's bullet, out of nothing, takes Aberdeen through to the knock-out stages with two matches to spare.

Wednesday, 31 August
DUNFERMLINE   ABERDEEN (1) 2
  ATHLETIC (1) 2   Buckley 2 (20, 71)
  Millar 2 (7, 64)

DUNFERMLINE: Mackin, Laird, Mackie, Samuel, Duthie, Chalmers, Peebles, Millar, Bryans, Reilly, Anderson

ABERDEEN: Martin, Mitchell, Caldwell, O'Neil, Clunie, Glen, Leggat, McNeill, Buckley, Wishart, Mulhall

                        Referee: W. Syme

Harry Yorston is dropped and demands a transfer. It is refused.

Saturday, 3 September
CLYDE (0) 1   ABERDEEN (0) 2
  McHard (66)   Leggat 2 (46, 83)

CLYDE: Hewkins, Murphy, Haddock, Granville, Anderson, Laing, McHard, D. Currie, McPhail, Brown, Ring

ABERDEEN: Martin, Mitchell, Caldwell, Wilson, Clunie, Glen, Leggat, McNeill, Buckley, Wishart, Hather

Attendance: 8,000   *Referee:* J. A. S. Bisset

Clyde had most of the play: Aberdeen scored most of the goals.

Section 3

	P	W	D	L	F	A	Pts
ABERDEEN	6	5	1	0	13	8	11
Hibernian	6	3	1	2	11	8	7
Dunfermline	6	1	1	4	12	16	3
Clyde	6	1	1	4	11	15	3

Quarter Final 1st Leg Wednesday, 14 September
ABERDEEN (3) 5   HEARTS (2) 3
  Leggat 3 (21, 35, 64),   Young 2 (36, 51),
  Buckley 2 (15, 55)   Urquhart (43)

ABERDEEN: Martin, Mitchell, Caldwell, Wilson, Clunie, Glen, Leggat, Yorston, Buckley, Wishart, Hather

HEARTS: Brown, Parker, Kirk, Bowman, Glidden, Cumming, Blackwood, Conn, Young, Wardhaugh, Urquhart

Attendance: 30,000   *Referee:* W. Brittle

Four days after hammering six goals past Hibs in the league, Aberdeen served up another tasty dish before Pittodrie. Hearts looked to be dead and buried at one stage, but fought back to 3-3. During the course of the second half Hearts were reduced to only eight fit men and Aberdeen opened up a two-goal first-leg lead.

Quarter Final 2nd Leg Saturday, 17 September
HEARTS (1) 2   ABERDEEN (1) 4
  Urquhart (42), Conn (77)   Yorston (34), Leggat
                             (55), Hather 2 (70, 83)

HEARTS: Brown, Parker, Kirk, Mackay, Glidden, Cumming, Blackwood, Conn, Young, Campbell, Urquhart

ABERDEEN: Martin, Mitchell, Caldwell, Wilson, Clunie, Glen, Leggat, Yorston, Buckley, Wishart, Hather

Attendance: 35,000   *Referee:* W. Brittle

Hearts pummel the Dons' defence but it is Yorston who effectively puts the tie beyond them, netting after Leggat's shot came back off the post. Urquhart's equaliser was only allowed to stand once the referee had consulted his linesman. There was no way back for Hearts once Leggat had restored Aberdeen's advantage.

Semi Final (Hampden) Saturday, 1 October
RANGERS (0) 1   ABERDEEN (2) 2
  Hubbard (50)   Leggat (4), Wishart (39)

RANGERS: Niven, Caldow, Little, McColl, Young, Rae, Scott, Arnison, Miller, Baird, Hubbard

ABERDEEN: Martin, Paterson, Mitchell, Wilson, Clunie, Glen, Leggat, Yorston, Buckley, Wishart, Hather

Attendance: 80,000   *Referee:* R. H. Davidson

It seems that the name of Glasgow Rangers will be drawn every time Aberdeen embark on cup competition. The game was, as they say, one of two halves. Lightning first-half raids brought Aberdeen goals by Leggat and Wishart – the latter a beauty from 22 yards. But after the interval Hubbard reduced the arrears, Leggat was rushed to hospital with a shoulder injury, and Aberdeen were put through the mill. McColl hit the Dons' bar; Miller the post.

League Cup Final (Hampden) Saturday, 22 October
ST MIRREN (0) 1   ABERDEEN (0) 2
  Holmes (58)   Mallan o.g. (47), Leggat
                    (80)

ST MIRREN: Lornie, Lapsley, Mallan, Neilson, Telfer, Holmes, Rodger, Laird, Brown, Gemmell, Callan
ABERDEEN: Martin, Mitchell, Caldwell, Wilson, Clunie, Glen, Leggat, Yorston, Buckley, Wishart, Hather

Attendance: 44,100   *Referee:* H. Phillips

Aberdeen won the Scottish Cup in 1947, the league in 1955, but – excluding the unofficial tournament in 1946 – never the League Cup, which is a different trophy to that claimed by the Dons on that occasion. They go into the Final against St Mirren as the only unbeaten club in Britain, having played thirteen league and League Cup fixtures, won twelve and drawn one. St Mirren, in contrast, have scratched and picked their way to the Final, and have yet to win in the league. Being such overwhelming favourites is frequently a handicap, and the contest was much closer than predicted. A sunny day could not encourage many fans to venture out. Those who stayed at home missed a goal-less first half. In the second Mallan breasted Hather's cross into his own net. Saints equalised when Holmes got his head to Lapsley's free kick. There were no signs of either side finding the winning goal when Leggat released a harmless shot from the right which confused Lornie. Aberdeen had won their second major trophy in six months. They had no medals to show for it, however, none being issued by the Scottish League.

SCOTTISH CUP

5th Round Saturday, 4 February
RANGERS (1) 2   ABERDEEN (0) 1
  Scott (20), Kichenbrand   Leggat (80)
  (75)

RANGERS: Niven, Shearer, Little, McColl, Young, Rae, Scott, Simpson, Kichenbrand, Baird, Hubbard.
ABERDEEN: Martin, Macfarlane, Caldwell, Allister, Glen, Brownlee, Leggat, Yorston, Allan, Wishart, Hather

Attendance: 50,000   *Referee:* J. Bisset

Aberdeen's meetings with Rangers in cup competition are becoming indecently frequent. This is the fourth Scottish Cup clash in successive seasons, not to mention the League Cup encounter in October. This time the weather was atrocious, threatening the spectacle, and forcing a white ball to be used. Rangers merited their victory. Kichenbrand all but splintered the Dons' crossbar in the opening minuts. Martin had vacated his goalmouth when Scott did put Rangers in front. Hubbard then hit the Dons' bar again. Rangers appeared to settle the outcome when Martin pushed out Scott's cross straight to Kichenbrand. Then Aberdeen woke up. Allen had a goal disallowed; Leggat had a goal that was allowed; and Niven followed up to make a thrilling save from Leggat's header in the closing minute.

1955-56

APPEARANCES	League	League Cup	Scottish Cup
Martin	32	10	1
Wishart	32	10	1
Yorston	30	8	1
Glen	27	10	1
Caldwell	27	9	1
Mitchell	24	10	
Hather	24	5	1
Allister	22	2	1
Leggat	18	10	1
Allan	17		1
Macfarlane	16		1
Clunie	14	7	
Wilson	13	5	
Boyd	13		
Young	12	3	
Buckley	9	10	
Brownlee	9		1
Davidson	9		
Mulhall	7	5	
Hay	6		
Paterson	5	1	
McNeill	2	2	
Ingram	2		
Morrison	2		
Kelly	1		
Scott	1		
O'Neil		3	
27 players			

GOALS	Total	League	League Cup	Scottish Cup
Leggat	29	19	9	1
Yorston	14	12	2	
Buckley	13	6	7	
Hather	12	10	2	
Allan	11	11		
Wishart	10	8	2	
Davidson	5	5		
Glen	5	4	1	
Boyd	4	4		
Mulhall	4	3	1	
Clunie	1	1		
Ingram	1	1		
Allister	1	1		
Wilson	1	1		
O'Neil	1		¯1	
own-goals	2	1	1	
Total	114	87	26	1

Season 1956-57

A quick look at the final league table for 1956-57 will show that Aberdeen finished in a respectable sixth positions. But like many another bald fact this one conceals the deepening malaise at Pittodrie. After all, the two previous seasons had seen Aberdeen as champions and runners-up, so there was much to live up to. In particular, Aberdeen ventured on a disastrous League Cup programme in August and early September, losing all but one of their six group matches.

It was also the season in which the Old Firm rediscovered its dual domination over Aberdeen. Both Rangers and Celtic faced Aberdeen four times in league and League Cup. Both won four out of four, leaving Aberdeen to suffer the indignity of eight straight defeats spanning August through to April.

In the Scottish Cup Aberdeen survived one thrilling encounter with Hibs – in what was probably the Dons' only truly memorable match of the whole season – only to succumb to modest Falkirk in the next round.

So the quest for self-respect had to be realised in the bread and butter environment of league competition. First the good news: away from Pittodrie Aberdeen scored 43 goals in 17 league matches, easily surpassing the previous post-War record established one year earlier. In fact, not until late April did Aberdeen fail to find the net at least once, home or away, in any competition.

Now the bad news: the defensive record was worrying in itself – especially on opponents' grounds. But there was one special feature of 1956-57 which to many Dons' fans must have been symptomatic of what appeared to be a team with no backbone. By mid-November Aberdeen had lost a total of ten matches in the league and League Cup. In seven of those matches Aberdeen had been leading at one stage. They threw away a three-goal lead at East Fife and on several occasions could not protect a two-goal advantage. In other words, teams found it easy to come back at Aberdeen: the Dons, when they were behind, found it less easy to redeem themselves.

Overall, it was clear that the championship-winning squad was breaking up, and – for sure – matters would get worse before they got better.

League: 6th
League Cup: 3rd in qualifying group
Scottish Cup: 6th Round

SCOTTISH LEAGUE DIVISION ONE

No 1 Saturday, 8 September
ST MIRREN (0) 0   ABERDEEN (1) 2
                         Hather (16), Buckley (61)
ST MIRREN: Lornie, Lapsley, Moore, Neilson, Dallas, Holmes, Rodger, Humphries, Telfer, Gemmell, Cameron
ABERDEEN: Morrison, Smith, Caldwell, Allister, Young, Glen, Boyd, Yorston, Buckley, Wishart, Hather

P	W	D	L	F	A	Pts
1	1	0	0	2	0	2

Attendance: 15,000
Referee: J. Mackie

Aberdeen try to put out of their minds their League Cup failings. They ought to have been behind when Hather put them in front, but thereafter they gained in confidence.

No 2 Saturday, 15 September
ABERDEEN (0) 2   QUEENS PARK (0) 1
  Hather (65), Buckley   Devine (80)
  (72)

ABERDEEN: Martin, Smith, Caldwell, Allister, Young, Glen, Leggat, Yorston, Buckley, Wishart, Hather

QUEENS PARK: Crampsey, Harnett, Hastie, Cromar, Valentine, Glen, Herd, Robb, McEwan, Devine, Ormond

P	W	D	L	F	A	Pts		*Attendance:* 12,000
2	2	0	0	4	1	4		*Referee:* D. Weir

If points are all that matter, then Aberdeen can be satisfied. If quality of play is important, then they can't. The two captains are brothers: Archie Glen for Aberdeen, Alec Glen for Queens.

No 3 Saturday, 22 September
DUNDEE (2) 4   ABERDEEN (1) 2
O'Hara (34), Chalmers 2   Yorston (30), Buckley
(42, 80), Christie (54)   (86)

DUNDEE: Brown, Reid, Irvine, Henderson, McKenzie, Cowie, Chalmers, Black, Birse, O'Hara, Christie

ABERDEEN: Martin, Smith, Caldwell, Allister, Young, Glen, Allan, Yorston, Buckley, Wishart, Hather

P	W	D	L	F	A	Pts		*Attendance:* 20,000
3	2	0	1	6	5	4		*Referee:* J. A. Mowat

Even with the advantage of Yorston's goal, Aberdeen's defence is penetrated with worrying ease.

No 4 Saturday, 29 September
ABERDEEN (1) 3   HIBERNIAN (0) 1
Glen 2 (21, 47 pen),   Turnbull (61 pen)
Buckley (74)

ABERDEEN: Martin, Smith, Caldwell, Wallace, Clunie, Glen, Leggat, Yorston, Buckley, Brownlee, Hather

HIBERNIAN: Leslie, Grant, Muir, Higgins, Plenderleith, Combe, J. Buchanan, Turnbull, Reilly, A. Buchanan, Ormond

P	W	D	L	F	A	Pts		*Attendance:* 18,000
4	3	0	1	9	6	6		*Referee:* J. P. Barclay

Hibs are no longer the great team of the past few seasons. Even so, this was a better Dons' performance than of late. Jim Clunie's inclusion has stiffened the Dons' defence.

No 5 Saturday, 6 October
EAST FIFE (0) 4   ABERDEEN (1) 3
Wallace o.g. (56),   Hather (27), Davidson
Leishman (57), Plumb   (46), Wishart (48)
(65), Matthew (80)

EAST FIFE: McCluskey, Adie, S. Stewart, Cox, Christie, McLennan, J. Stewart, Leishman, Plumb, Bonthrone, Matthew

ABERDEEN: Martin, Smith, Caldwell, Wallace, Clunie, Glen, Leggat, Yorston, Davidson, Wishart, Hather

P	W	D	L	F	A	Pts		*Attendance:* 7,000
5	3	0	2	12	10	6		*Referee:* D. McTaggart

Oh dear! Oh dear! After 48 minutes Aberdeen led 3-0. After 90 they had lost 4-3. They would have been second in the table had they held on, but from the moment Wallace headed Jackie Stewart's cross into his own goal East Fife saw the victory lights ahead. Aberdeen's defence simply crumbles under pressure.

No 6 Saturday, 13 October
ABERDEEN (0) 2   AIRDRIEONIANS (1) 3
Leggat (46), Davidson   Baird 3 (34, 74, 75)
(79)

ABERDEEN: Martin, Smith, Caldwell, Wallace, Clunie, Glen, Leggat, Yorston, Davidson, Wishart, Hather

AIRDRIE: Walker, Miller, Quigley, Price, Baillie, Quinn, Duncan, J. Welsh, Baird, McMillan, McCulloch

P	W	D	L	F	A	Pts		*Attendance:* 17,000
6	3	0	3	14	13	6		*Referee:* W. M. Syme

Aberdeen couldn't finish: Hugh Baird could – and did.

No 7 Saturday, 20 October
AYR UNITED (0) 1   ABERDEEN (4) 6
Paton (59)   Mulhall (1), Hay (15),
                         Yorston (25), Allan 3 (27,
                         54, 70)

AYR: Travers, Paterson, Thomson, Traynor, Gallacher, Haugh, Japp, McMillan, Paton, Stevenson, Murray

ABERDEEN: Martin, Mitchell, Caldwell, Wallace, Clunie, Glen, Boyd, Yorston, Allan, Hay, Mulhall

P	W	D	L	F	A	Pts		*Attendance:* 8,000
7	4	0	3	20	14	8		*Referee:* P. Fitzpatrick

Ayr look out of their depth in the top flight and will shortly leave it. Leggat missed the party. He was playing for Scotland against Wales at Cardiff.

No 8 Saturday, 3 November
RAITH ROVERS (1) 3   ABERDEEN (2) 2
Copland (26), Williamson Wishart (6), Allan (9)
2 (55, 78)

RAITH: Drummond, Polland, McLure, Young, McNaught, Leigh, McEwan, Kelly, Copland, Williamson, Urquhart

ABERDEEN: Martin, Mitchell, Caldwell, Wallace, Clunie, Glen, Boyd, Yorston, Allan, Wishart, Hather

P	W	D	L	F	A	Pts		*Attendance:* 7,000
8	4	0	4	22	17	8		*Referee:* G. Bowman

Raith are surprisingly lying third. For the umpteenth time this season Aberdeen strike first (and second), but are then overtaken and end the match in total confusion.

No 9 Saturday, 10 November
ABERDEEN (1) 1   KILMARNOCK (0) 3
Boyd (26)   Mays (53), Beattie (65),
                         Fletcher (85)

ABERDEEN: Martin, Mitchell, Caldwell, Wallace, Clunie, Glen, Boyd, Yorston, Allan, Wishart, Hather

KILMARNOCK: Brown, Collins, Watson, Falls, Toner, Campbell, Muir, Harvey, Mays, Beattie, Fletcher

P	W	D	L	F	A	Pts	
9	4	0	5	23	20	8	

Attendance: 11,000
Referee: W. Davidson

Things go from bad to worse. Yet again Aberdeen score first: yet again they were run ragged by the close.

No 10 Saturday, 17 November

ABERDEEN (2) 3	DUNFERMLINE
Hay 2 (4, 77), Boyd (44)	ATHLETIC (1) 2, Miller (15), McWilliam (86)

ABERDEEN: Martin, Smith, Caldwell, Allister, Young, Glen, Boyd, Yorston, Buckley, Hay, Hather
DUNFERMLINE: Mackin, Laird, Duthie, Samuel, Colville, Mailer, Peebles, Miller, McWilliam, Reilly, Anderson

P	W	D	L	F	A	Pts	
10	5	0	5	26	22	10	

Attendance: 13,000
Referee: G. Mitchell

In view of their recent habits Aberdeen must have feared the worst when Hay put them in front. Sure enough, Dunfermline equalised, and finished strongly after Boyd and Hay had brought Aberdeen further goals. In the last few minutes McWilliam made it 3-2, and the same player then planted an equalising header in the Dons' net. The crowd were both surprised and relieved to see it chalked off for offside.

No 11 Saturday, 24 November

RANGERS (2) 3	ABERDEEN (0) 1
Simpson (2), Hubbard (30 pen), Murray (80)	Yorston (46)

RANGERS: Niven, Shearer, Caldow, McColl, Davis, Logie, Scott, Simpson, Murray, Baird, Hubbard
ABERDEEN: Martin, Mitchell, Caldwell, Allister, Young, Glen, Boyd, Yorston, Buckley, Hay, Hather

P	W	D	L	F	A	Pts	
11	5	0	6	27	25	10	

Attendance: 30,000
Referee: R. H. Davidson

Rangers gain their third victory over Aberdeen, and clock up thirteen goals in the process. They are not handicapped by the absence of George Young. Aberdeen have already conceded the league title and have only the Scottish Cup to aim for.

No 12 Saturday, 1 December

ABERDEEN (3) 5	QUEEN OF SOUTH (0) 1
Buckley (24), Yorston (33), Leggat 2 (36, 68), Wishart (67)	Black (65)

ABERDEEN: Martin, Mitchell, Caldwell, Allister, Young, Glen, Leggat, Yorston, Buckley, Wishart, Hather
QUEEN OF THE SOUTH: Selkirk, Sharpe, Binning, Gibson, Smith, Greenock, Oakes, McGill, Black, Rankin, McGuire

P	W	D	L	F	A	Pts	
12	6	0	6	32	26	12	

Attendance: 12,000
Referee: J. Lackie

Aberdeen's 'old guard' enjoy a welcome respite from the hail of criticism flying in their direction.

No 13 Saturday, 8 December

QUEENS PARK (0) 0	ABERDEEN (2) 2
	Buckley (25), Wishart (28)

QUEEN'S PARK: Crampsey, Harnett, Hastie, Cromar, Valentine, Glen, Herd, Robb, McEwan, Dalziel, Omand
ABERDEEN: Martin, Mitchell, Caldwell, Allister, Young, Glen, Leggat, Yorston, Buckley, Wishart, Hather

P	W	D	L	F	A	Pts	
13	7	0	6	34	26	14	

Attendance: 12,000
Referee: R. Morris

In front of Hampden's open spaces, Archie Glen's Dons complete the double over Alec Glen's Queens Park.

No 14 Saturday, 15 December

FALKIRK (1) 2	ABERDEEN (4) 5
Ormond (6), Prentice (52)	Yorston 2 (7, 50), Hather (10), Buckley (22), Leggat (29)

FALKIRK: Brown, Parker, Rae, Prentice, Ralston, McIntosh, Morrison, Murray, Ormond, Dudman, O'Hara
ABERDEEN: Martin, Mitchell, Caldwell, Allister, Young, Glen, Leggat, Yorston, Buckley, Wishart, Hather

P	W	D	L	F	A	Pts	
14	8	0	6	39	28	16	

Attendance: 6,000
Referee: T. S. Edwards

Three wins in a row and things are looking up. The pitch was unplayable but didn't prevent Aberdeen rattling in 5 goals. Conditions were so bad that both teams changed their strip at half-time. Otherwise friend would have been indistinguishable from foe.

No 15 Saturday, 22 December

ABERDEEN (1) 2	MOTHERWELL (3) 3
Yorston (4), Wishart (65)	Hunter (28), Gardiner 2 (29, 43)

ABERDEEN: Martin, Mitchell, Caldwell, Allister, Young, Glen, Leggat, Yorston, Buckley, Wishart, Hather
MOTHERWELL: Weir, McSeveney, Holton, Aitken, Paton, Forrest, Hunter, Reid, Gardiner, Quinn, McCann

P	W	D	L	F	A	Pts	
15	8	0	7	41	31	16	

Attendance: 13,000
Referee: J. P. Barclay

Motherwell arrive at Pittodrie in second place. Fog threatened to postpone the game – and in retrospect Aberdeen must have wished it had. Mitchell was taken to hospital with a shoulder injury half an hour before the end, but the Dons were 3-1 down at that stage.

No 16 Saturday, 29 December

ABERDEEN (2) 2	HEARTS (2) 3
Wishart (20), Buckley (24),	Young 2 (3, 86), Murray (15)

ABERDEEN: Martin, Caldwell, Hogg, Wilson, Young, Glen, Leggat, Brown, Buckley, Wishart, Hather

HEARTS: Brown, Parker, Kirk, Mackay, Glidden, Cumming, Hamilton, Murray, Bauld, Young, Crawford

P W D L F A Pts   *Attendance:* 20,000
16 8 0 8 43 34 16   *Referee:* H. J. Gallacher

Hearts are top of the league, but at least Aberdeen stretch them. Their problem all season has been being caught when in front. But this time they nearly turn the tables. Hearts were off to a flier, capitalising on two Martin blunders. But Aberdeen fought back to 2-2. Near the end Martin palmed out Murray's effort and Young netted the winner.

No 17 Tuesday, 1 January
ABERDEEN (0) 2   DUNDEE (1) 1
Brown (66), Buckley (71)   Chalmers (27)
ABERDEEN: Morrison, Mitchell, Caldwell, Wilson, Young, Glen, Boyd, Brown, Buckley, Wishart, Hather
DUNDEE: Brown, Reid, Cox, Henderson, McKenzie, Cowie, Chalmers, Black, Birse, O'Hara, Christie

P W D L F A Pts
17 9 0 8 45 35 18   *Referee:* J. A. S. Bisset

Dundee were worth a point. But the rarity of seeing Aberdeen come from behind was more significant than the points. Buckley scored one but missed half a dozen more.

No 18 Wednesday, 2 January
PARTICK THISTLE (0) 1   ABERDEEN (2) 2
G. Smith (77)   Wright o.g. (37), Hather (44)
PARTICK: W. Smith, Kerr, Baird, Wright, McNab, Mathers, McKenzie, G. Smith, Crowe, McParland, Ewing
Young, Glen, Boyd, Brown, Davidson, Wishart, Hather

P W D L F A Pts   *Attendance:* 10,000
18 10 0 8 47 36 20   *Referee:* F. S. Crossley

Aberdeen's appalling injury problems continue. This time Boyd has cartilege problems and won't play again this season.

No 19 Saturday, 5 January
ABERDEEN (1) 4   ST MIRREN (0) 0
Davidson (24), Hay 2
(55, 83), Glen (60)
ABERDEEN: Morrison, Mitchell, Caldwell, Wilson, Young, Glen, Buckley, Brown, Davidson, Hay, Hather
ST MIRREN: Forsyth, McTurk, Johnston, Dallas, Telfer, Holmes, Duncan, Gemmell, Humphries, Wilson, McGill

Leading Positions
	P	W	D	L	F	A	Pts
1 Hearts	20	15	2	3	53	34	32
2 Motherwell	19	12	4	3	49	30	28
3 Raith	20	10	6	4	54	33	26
4 Rangers	17	12	1	4	49	27	25
5 Kilmarnock	20	9	6	5	39	26	24
6 ABERDEEN	19	11	0	8	51	36	22

Attendance: 13,000   *Referee:* R. Yacamini

The Dons continue their 100% record for 1957. With this win they peep inside the top six.

No 20 Saturday, 12 January
HIBERNIAN (0) 4   ABERDEEN (0) 1
Fraser (48), Reilly   Leggat (79)
(54), Ormond 2 (60, 85)
HIBERNIAN: Leslie, Grant, Paterson, Nicol, Plenderleith, Hughes, Fraser, Turnbull, Reilly, Gibson, Ormond
ABERDEEN: Morrison, Mitchell, Caldwell, Glen, Young, Wishart, Leggat, Brown, Davidson, Hay, Hather

P W D L F A Pts   *Attendance:* 18,000
20 11 0 9 52 40 22   *Referee:* H. Phillips

Aberdeen will return to Easter Road in three weeks in the Scottish Cup. Their prospects cannot be encouraging after their second-half pummelling by Hibs.

No 21 Saturday, 19 January
ABERDEEN (1) 1   EAST FIFE (0) 0
Davidson (23)
ABERDEEN: Morrison, Mitchell, Smith, Wilson, Young, Glen, Leggat, Yorston, Davidson, Wishart, Hather
EAST FIFE: McCluskey, Cox, S. Stewart, Bowie, Christie, McLennan, J. Stewart, Wilson, Plumb, Leishman, Matthew

P W D L F A Pts   *Attendance:* 14,000
21 12 0 9 53 40 24   *Referee:* W. Davidson

This was a near-farcical contest. East Fife were obsessed with the offside trap. Three Dons goals were disallowed for offside and yet the Davidson goal which was allowed to stand was itself yards offside.

No 22 Saturday, 26 January
AIRDRIEONIANS (0) 1   ABERDEEN (2) 5
McMillan (78)   Leggat 3 (3, 66, 85), Yorston (35), Davidson (64)
AIRDRIE: Walker, Kilmarnock, Shanks, Price, Quigley, Slingsby, Rankine, McMillan, Baird, McNeil, Kearney
ABERDEEN: Morrison, Mitchell, Caldwell, Wilson, Clunie, Glen, Leggat, Yorston, Davidson, Wishart, Hather

P W D L F A Pts   *Attendance:* 5,000
22 13 0 9 58 41 26   *Referee:* J. A. Mowat

Aberdeen's minds are on next week's Scottish Cup-tie at Hibs and Leggat's hat-trick puts them in good heart.

No 23 Saturday, 9 February
ABERDEEN (2) 2   AYR UNITED (2) 2
Wishart (2), Davidson   Price (37), Paton
(33),   (44)

ABERDEEN: Morrison, Mitchell, Caldwell, Wilson, Clunie, Glen, Leggat, Yorston, Davidson, Wishart, Hather

AYR: Travers, Paterson, Thomson, Traynor, Brice, Haugh, Murray, Paton, Price, Whittle, McMillan

P W D L F A Pts   *Attendance:* 12,000
23 13 1 9 60 43 27   *Referee:* T. Wharton

Two-goal leads are no protection for a defence as porous as Aberdeen's. This is the Don's first draw of the season, and during it Yorston dislocates his elbow.

No 24 Saturday, 23 February
CELTIC (2) 2   ABERDEEN (1) 1
  McPhail (20), Mochan   Allister (37)
  (36)

CELTIC: Beattie, Haughney, Fallon, Evans, Jack, Peacock, Tully, Fernie, McPhail, Mochan, Collins

ABERDEEN: Martin, Mitchell, Caldwell, Allister, Young, Glen, Leggat, Brownlee, Davidson, Wishart, Mulhall

P W D L F A Pts   *Attendance:* 10,000
24 13 1 10 61 45 27   *Referee:* W. D. Liston

Aberdeen's Cup defeat by Falkirk has effectively ended their season. Now they are asked to play in a blizzard.

No 25 Wednesday, 6 March
ABERDEEN (1) 1   RAITH ROVERS (0) 0
  Leggat (5)

ABERDEEN: Martin, Mitchell, Caldwell, Allister, Young, Glen, Leggat, Brownlee, Clunie, Wishart, Hather

RAITH: Stewart, Polland, Bain, Young, McNaught, Leigh, McEwan, Kelly, Copland, Williamson, Urquhart

P W D L F A Pts   *Attendance:* 5,000
25 14 1 10 62 45 29   *Referee:* W. Brittle

This time last year Raith won 5-3 at Pittodrie to shatter Aberdeen's title hopes. Now Raith themselves are in second place. A small, disillusioned crowd were left talking about the experiment of playing centre-half Jim Clunie at centre-forward.

No 26 Saturday, 9 March
KILMARNOCK (2) 2   ABERDEEN (0) 1
  Curlett (24), Mays (32)   Hather (65)

KILMARNOCK: Brown, Collins, J. Stewart, R. Stewart, Toner, Mackay, Muir, Curlett, Mays, Black, Burns

ABERDEEN: Martin, Mitchell, Caldwell, Allister, Young, Glen, Leggat, Brownlee, Clunie, Wishart, Hather

P W D L F A Pts   *Attendance:* 11,000
26 14 1 11 63 47 29   *Referee:* R. Morris

Aberdeen were restricted by Glen being reduced to a passenger. They had their chances but wasted them.

No 27 Saturday, 16 March
DUNFERMLINE   ABERDEEN (1) 3
  ATHLETIC (0) 1   Leggat (13), Wishart
McWilliam (56)   (69), Allister (75 pen)

DUNFERMLINE: Mackin, Laird, Duthie, Melrose, Colville, Mailer, Peebles, Miller, McWilliam, Reilly, Anderson

ABERDEEN: Martin, Mitchell, Caldwell, Allister, Young, Brownlee, Leggat, Yorston, Davidson, Wishart, Hather

Leading Positions
	P	W	D	L	F	A	Pts
1 Hearts	28	19	5	4	69	45	43
2 Rangers	25	17	3	5	67	37	37
3 Raith	28	14	7	7	74	45	35
4 Kilmarnock	28	13	9	6	50	32	35
5 Motherwell	26	15	4	7	64	43	34
6 ABERDEEN	27	15	1	11	66	48	31

Referee: G. Bowman

Dunfermline are heading for the drop. The two points they handed to Aberdeen would have enabled them to survive. Out-manoeuvred from the start, Aberdeen gained a highly improbable victory – and owe a debt to Fred Martin.

No 28 Saturday, 23 March
ABERDEEN (0) 1   RANGERS (0) 2
  Davidson (64)   Hubbard (66), Simpson
                           (70)

ABERDEEN: Martin, Caldwell, Hogg, Allister, Young, Glen, Leggat, Yorston, Davidson, Wishart, Hather

RANGERS: Niven, Shearer, Caldow, McColl, Young, Davis, Scott, Simpson, Murray, Baird, Hubbard

P W D L F A Pts   *Attendance:* 28,000
28 15 1 12 67 50 31   *Referee:* G. Mitchell

Rangers are poised to overtake Hearts for the title. It's the old, old, story for Aberdeen, going in front and then losing. Within a couple of minutes of Davidson's shot-cum-lob Alec Young fluffed a pass-back to Martin. Hubbard nipped in. Before long a Simpson shot passed under Martin's body. This turns out to be Harry Yorston's last game for Aberdeen before he quit at the age of 28.

No 29 Saturday, 30 March
QUEEN OF THE   ABERDEEN (1) 2
  SOUTH (0) 2,   Leggat (5), Wishart
Oakes (74),   (77)
Black (76)

QUEEN OF THE SOUTH: Henderson, Sharpe, Binning, Rae, Smith, Greenock, Black, McGill, Patterson, McMillan, Oakes

ABERDEEN: Martin, Caldwell, Hogg, Allister, Young, Glen, Leggat, Ward, Davidson, Wishart, Hather

P W D L F A Pts
29 15 2 12 69 52 32   *Referee:* R. H. Davidson

It was almost to be expected. Aberdeen were in front and were now losing. What was not expected was that the ball would then rebound off a Queen's defender and Wishart would lash it home.

No 30 Saturday, 13 April
ABERDEEN (1) 3   FALKIRK (0) 1
  Allister 3 (14 pen,   Merchant (70)
  72, 82 pen)
ABERDEEN: Martin, Caldwell, Hogg, Allister,
Young, Brownlee, Leggat, Ward, Davidson, Wishart,
Hather
FALKIRK: Slater, McIntosh, Rae, McCormack,
Ralston, Prentice, Murray, Grierson, Merchant, Moran,
O'Hara

P W D L F A Pts   *Attendance:* 10,000
30 16 2 12 72 53 34   *Referee:* D. Weir

This win cannot compensate Aberdeen for their
crushing Cup K.O. by the same opponents, but it
heralded Falkirk's first defeat in 13 games. McIntosh
conceded two penalties, both converted by Allister.

No 31 Saturday, 20 April
MOTHERWELL (1) 2   ABERDEEN (4) 5
  Hunter (33), Forrest   Leggat (4), Hather
  (80)   (34), Davidson 2
                             (38, 63), Allister (41)
MOTHERWELL: Weir, Holton, McSeveney, Forrest,
Paton, Aitken, Hunter, Quinn, Gardiner, S. Brown,
McCann
ABERDEEN: Martin, Caldwell, Hogg, Allister,
Young, Brownlee, Leggat, Ward, Davidson, Wishart,
Hather

P W D L F A Pts
31 17 2 12 77 55 36   *Referee:* J. A. S. Bisset

Motherwell's championship bid is consigned to
memory, for they have gone seven games without a win.
It's all too easy for Aberdeen.

No 32 Monday, 22 April
ABERDEEN (0) 0   CELTIC (0) 1
                             Higgins (83)
ABERDEEN: Martin, Caldwell, Hogg, Allister,
Young, Brownlee, Leggat, Ward, Davidson, Wishart,
Hather
CELTIC: McCreadie, Haughney, Fallon, Evans, Jack,
Mochan, Higgins, Fernie, Ryan, Collins, Tully

P W D L F A Pts   *Attendance:* 15,000
32 17 2 13 77 56 36   *Referee:* G. Mitchell

Celtic's fourth win of the season over Aberdeen. The
only noteworthy aspect of the scoreline is that it is the
first occasion Aberdeen have failed to score in any
competition this season. Celtic won with a soft goal.
Martin blocked Higgin's shot but the ball trickled over
the line as Caldwell miskicked.

No 33 Wednesday, 24 April
ABERDEEN (1) 2   PARTICK THISTLE (0) 0
  Glen (44), Davidson (56)
ABERDEEN: Martin, Caldwell, Hogg, Allister,
Young, Glen, Leggat, Ward, Davidson, Wishart,
Hather

PARTICK: Ledgerwood, Kerr, Donlevy, Harvey,
Davidson, Mathers, McKenzie, Smith, Gilmour,
Wright, Ewing

P W D L F A Pts   *Attendance:* 7,000
33 18 2 13 79 56 38   *Referee:* T. S. Edwards

This time it is Glen who is carried off injured. He had
earlier put Aberdeen on the winning trail.

No 34 Saturday, 27 April
HEARTS (1) 3   ABERDEEN (0) 0
  Wardhaugh 2 (34, 85),
  Mackay (55)
HEARTS: Marshall, Kirk, McKenzie, Mackay, Milne,
Thomson, Hamilton, Conn, Young, Wardhaugh,
Crawford
ABERDEEN: Martin, Caldwell, Hogg, Allister,
Young, Brownlee, Leggat, Ward, Davidson, Wishart,
Hather

Attendance: 15,000   *Referee:* W. Harvie

Hearts can still win the championship if Rangers lose at
Dumfries. Rangers win – and so do Hearts – with the
greatest of ease. Aberdeen put up no serious resistance.
Had they prevented Wardhaugh's second goal Aberdeen
would have finished 5th instead of 6th.

Aberdeen's complete home and away record:

HOME						AWAY					
P	W	D	L	F	A	W	D	L	F	A	Pts
34	10	1	6	36	24	8	1	8	43	35	38

Scottish League Division One 1956-57

	P	W	D	L	F	A	Pts
1 Rangers	34	26	3	5	96	48	55
2 Hearts	34	24	5	5	81	48	53
3 Kilmarnock	34	16	10	8	57	39	42
4 Raith Rovers	34	16	7	11	84	58	39
5 Celtic	34	15	8	11	58	43	38
6 ABERDEEN	34	18	2	14	79	59	38
7 Motherwell	34	16	5	13	72	66	37
8 Partick Thistle	34	13	8	13	53	51	34
9 Hibernian	34	12	9	13	69	56	33
10 Dundee	34	13	6	15	55	61	32
11 Airdrieonians	34	13	4	17	77	89	30
12 St Mirren	34	12	6	16	58	72	30
13 Queens Park	34	11	7	16	55	59	29
14 Falkirk	34	10	8	16	51	70	28
15 East Fife	34	10	6	18	59	82	26
16 Queen of the South	34	10	5	19	54	96	25
17 Dunfermline	34	9	6	19	54	74	24
18 Ayr United	34	7	5	22	48	89	19

LEAGUE CUP

Saturday, 11 August
ABERDEEN (0) 1   CELTIC (1) 2
  Yorston (84)   Fernie (34), Higgins (63)
ABERDEEN: Morrison, Mitchell, Caldwell, Wilson,
Young, Glen, Leggat, Yorston, Buckley, Wishart,
Hather

CELTIC: Beattie, Haughney, Fallon, Evans, Jack, Peacock, Higgins, Collins, McPhail, Fernie, Tully

Referee: R. Yacamini

Heavy rain tried to dampen spirits but it was Celtic who drowned Aberdeen, who were pitiful. During the pre-match warm-up Reggie Morrison knocked a finger out of joint, delaying the kick-off while it was fixed.

Wednesday, 15 August

EAST FIFE (2) 2   ABERDEEN (0) 1
  Bonthrone 2 (10, 42)   Hather (81)

EAST FIFE: Watters, Adie, S. Stewart, Cox, Christie, McLennan, J. Stewart, Bonthrone, Plumb, Leishman, Matthew

ABERDEEN: Morrison, Mitchell, Caldwell, Wilson, Young, Glen, Leggat, Yorston, Buckley, Wishart, Hather

Referee: R. Morris

The score fails to reflect East Fife's superiority, and the visit to Pittodrie of Rangers is now viewed with some trepidation.

Saturday, 18 August

ABERDEEN (0) 2   RANGERS (1) 6
  Wishart (46), Yorston   Murray 2 (8, 64), Shearer
  (54)   (55), Simpson 2 (59, 60),
                             Hubbard (67)

ABERDEEN: Morrison, Mitchell, Hogg, Allister, Young, Glen, Boyd, Yorston, Davidson, Wishart, Hather

RANGERS: Niven, Caldow, Little, McColl, Young, Shearer, Scott, Simpson, Murray, Baird, Hubbard

Attendance: 35,000   *Referee:* W. Davidson

Alarm bells are ringing at Pittodrie. Aberdeen looked well set when leading 2-1 but all of a sudden Rangers turned on the power. And look what happened!

Saturday, 25 August

CELTIC (1) 3   ABERDEEN (1) 2
  Collins (15), Tully (77),   Leggat (7), Davidson (57)
  Fernie (85)

CELTIC: Beattie, Haughney, Fallon, Evans, Jack, Peacock, Smith, Collins, McPhail, Fernie, Tully

ABERDEEN: Morrison, Mitchell, Hogg, Allister, Glen, Brownlee, Leggat, Yorston, Davidson, Hay, Hather

Attendance: 25,000   *Referee:* A. McLintock

Four games, four defeats, is Aberdeen's worrying record. As against Rangers, Aberdeen were ahead after half-time, but Dons' reshaped line-up still cannot protect their lead.

Wednesday, 29 August

ABERDEEN (1) 4   EAST FIFE (0) 1
  Hay (27), Leggat 2 (67,   Hogg o.g. (72)
  85), Hather (86)

ABERDEEN: Martin, Mitchell, Hogg, Allister, Glen, Brownlee, Leggat, Yorston, Davidson, Hay, Hather

EAST FIFE: McCluskie, Adie, S. Stewart, Christie, Davis, McLennan, J. Stewart, Leishman, Plumb, Cox, Matthew

Attendance: 17,000   *Referee:* W. Brittle

Aberdeen played better against Celtic – and lost – than they did against East Fife, when they won. Two late goals distorted the even nature of the match.

Saturday, 1 September

RANGERS (1) 4   ABERDEEN (1) 1
  Simpson 2 (37, 77),   Davidson (14)
  Hubbard (62 pen),
  Scott (74)

RANGERS: Niven, Caldow, Little, McColl, Young, Shearer, Scott, Paton, Murray, Simpson, Hubbard

ABERDEEN: Martin, Mitchell, Hogg, Allister, Young, Glen, Leggat, Yorston, Davidson, Hay, Hather

Attendance: 35,000   *Referee:* W. Harvie

Rangers romped to victory, overcoming an early defensive mix-up from which Davidson scored. Three times in their group matches Aberdeen were leading but then lost.

Section 2

	P	W	D	L	F	A	Pts
Celtic	6	5	1	0	10	5	11
Rangers	6	4	1	1	18	6	9
ABERDEEN	6	1	0	5	11	18	2
East Fife	6	1	0	5	5	15	2

SCOTTISH CUP

5th Round Saturday, 2 February

HIBERNIAN (0) 3   ABERDEEN (4) 4
  Smith (47), Nicol (70),   Leggat (3), Wishart 2
  Reilly (75)   (15, 35), Yorston (30)

HIBERNIAN: Wren, Grant, Paterson, Nicol, Plenderleith, Hughes, Smith, Turnbull, Reilly, Combe, Ormond

ABERDEEN: Morrison, Mitchell, Caldwell, Wilson, Clunie, Glen, Leggat, Yorston, Davidson, Wishart, Hather

Attendance: 27,300   *Referee:* J. A. Mowat

Hibs go into this vital cup-tie after two league defeats; Aberdeen after two wins. The Dons capitalise on their greater confidence in the first half of an unforgettable match. Before everyone is in the ground Leggat is on hand to punish Wren, who can only palm out Davidson's shot. Then Wishart hammers in a free kick from 22 yards. Headers by Yorston and Wishart make the interval scoreline an unbelievable 4-0 in Aberdeen's favour. The tie should have been dead. But it wasn't. From the turnaround Smith scored off the bar. Aberdeen held out till twenty minutes from time. Then Nicol's low drive sped past the unsighted Martin, and Reilly's flashing shot from the edge of the box brought Easter Road to fever pitch. In a pulsating finish Ormond's shot crashed against a post. It bounced out, not in, and Aberdeen were through.

6th Round Saturday, 16 February
FALKIRK (3) 3   ABERDEEN (1) 1
  Grierson (16), Merchant 2   Davidson (20)
  (26, 34)

FALKIRK: Slater, Parker, McIntosh, Wright, Irvine, Prentice, Murray, Grierson, Merchant, Moran, O'Hara

ABERDEEN: Morrison, Mitchell, Caldwell, Wilson, Clunie, Glen, Leggat, Hay, Davidson, Wishart, Hather

Attendance: 16,600   *Referee:* G. Bowman

The facts are these: Falkirk are next to bottom. They have won only five matches all season. In December Aberdeen travelled to Brockville in the league and won 5-2. The pitch is almost as unplayable now as it was then. But then Aberdeen prospered: now they drowned. After nine minutes Mitchell brought down Moran from behind, but Martin saved Merchant's penalty. Seven minutes later Falkirk did go in front though Grierson, who looked offside. Davidson hurtled forward to equalise, and then sent another header against the bar. Two rapid breakouts by Falkirk brought two goals for ex-Don George Merchant and Aberdeen were out of the Cup.

1956-57

APPEARANCES	League	League Cup	Scottish Cup
Caldwell	33	2	2
Hather	32	6	2
Glen	29	6	2
Wishart	29	3	2
Young	26	4	
Martin	26	2	
Leggat	24	5	2
Yorston	20	6	1
Allister	20	4	
Mitchell	19	6	2

APPEARANCES	League	League Cup	Scottish Cup
Davidson	17	4	2
Buckley	13	2	
Clunie	10		2
Brownlee	9	2	
Morrison	8	4	2
Hogg	8	4	
Boyd	8	1	
W. Smith	8		
Wilson	7	2	2
Wallace	6		
Ward	6		
Hay	5	3	1
Allan	4		
John Brown	4		
Mulhall	2		
25 players			

Goals	Total	League	League Cup	Scottish Cup
Leggat	16	12	3	1
Davidson	13	10	2	1
Wishart	12	9	1	2
Yorston	11	8	2	1
Buckley	9	9		
Hather	9	7	2	
Allister	6	6		
Hay	6	5	1	
Allan	4	4		
Glen	4	4		
Boyd	2	2		
John Brown	1	1		
Mulhall	1	1		
own-goals	1	1		
Totals	95	79	11	5

This team picture was taken in 1959. Back row: Cadenhead, Hogg, McBride, Burns, Clunie, Glen. Front row: Ewen, Little, Baird, Wishart and Mulhall.

Season 1957-58

For the new season Aberdeen had to do without their established strike-force of Buckley and Yorston, so important to the Dons' championship-winning side. And as for Graham Leggat, he only re-signed as the season commenced. There were high hopes for the months ahead when Aberdeen won six out of six in the League Cup qualifying rounds. These hopes were dashed when losing home and away to Clyde in the Quarter Finals.

In the league Aberdeen were anonymously placed in mid-table throughout the first half of the season. But come New Year they turned over a new leaf, took nine points from five January fixtures, and squeezed into the top six. There was no possibility of challenging for the championship – Hearts had it sewn up already – but every hope of improving on the previous season's sixth place. Unfortunately Aberdeen were not in the mood. They won only three of the last thirteen and slumped down to twelfth.

Hopes of salvation in the Scottish Cup were shattered by Motherwell in the Quarter Final. In all, it was a thoroughly unrewarding season, as shown by the spiralling attendances at Pittodrie. True, injuries had taken their toll, none worse than when Leggat had to miss four months of the season with a broken leg. He managed seven league goals by the season's end – five of them coming in an extraordinary match at Airdrie.

In view of Aberdeen's terrible defensive record in 1957-58 perhaps they escaped lightly. 76 league goals were lost, far and away the worst figure since the War. What was even more disappointing for the paying Pittodrie customers was that of 17 home league matches nine were lost. This made it the first season since 1945 that Aberdeen had lost more than they won at Pittodrie.

Graham Leggat played for Scotland in the 1958 World Cup Finals in Sweden.

League: Twelfth
League Cup: Quarter-Final
Scottish Cup: Quarter-Final

SCOTTISH LEAGUE DIVISION ONE

No 1 Saturday, 7 September
ABERDEEN (0) 0   HIBERNIAN (1) 1
                        Turnbull (5)
ABERDEEN: Martin, Caldwell, Hogg, Allister, Young, Glen, Leggat, Burns, Davidson, Wishart, Hather
HIBERNIAN: Leslie, Muir, Boyle, Hughes, Plenderleith, Baxter, Smith, Turnbull, Harrower, Preston, Ormond

P	W	D	L	F	A	Pts		*Attendance:* 18,000
1	0	0	1	0	1	0		*Referee:* J. Stewart

After Aberdeen's rampaging form in the League Cup, the performance against Hibs was a grave setback. Turnbull's close-range goal settled the points – and Hibs were well worth them.

No 2 Saturday, 21 September
ABERDEEN (2) 3   DUNDEE (0) 0
  Davidson 2 (22, 43),
  Wishart (75)
ABERDEEN: Martin, Caldwell, Mitchell, Glen, Clunie, Brownlee, Little, Boyd, Davidson, Wishart, Hather
DUNDEE: Brown, Reid, Cox, Henderson, McKenzie, Cowie, Wallace, Reilly, Cousin, O'Hara, Robertson

P	W	D	L	F	A	Pts		*Attendance:* 10,000
2	1	0	1	3	1	2		*Referee:* J. A. Mowat

Aberdeen shake off the disappointment of League Cup elimination by Clyde with this comprehensive win.

No 3 Saturday, 28 September
ST MIRREN (2) 3   ABERDEEN (1) 1
  McKay 2 (8, 55), McGill   Boyd (20)
  (45)

ST MIRREN: Lornie, Lapsley, Higgins, Neilson, Telfer, Buchanan, Murray, Gemmell, McKay, McGill, McCulloch

ABERDEEN: Martin, Mitchell, Caldwell, Glen, Clunie, Brownlee, Leggat, Boyd, Davidson, Wishart, Hather

P	W	D	L	F	A	Pts	*Attendance: 9,000*
3	1	0	2	4	4	2	*Referee:* W. M. Syme

Not only are Aberdeen soundly beaten, but the team-spirit which carried them through their League Cup group seems to have deserted them.

No 4 Saturday, 5 October

ABERDEEN (1) 5	AIRDRIEONIANS (0) 1
Hay 3 (42, 48, 87),	Price (80 pen)
Davidson 2 (53, 66)	

ABERDEEN: Morrison, Caldwell, Hogg, Glen, Wallace, Brownlee, Boyd, Burns, Davidson, Hay, Hather

AIRDRIE: Goldie, Millar, Shanks, I. Reid, Quigley, Price, J. Reid, Welsh, Baillie, McMillan, Caven

P	W	D	L	F	A	Pts	*Attendance: 10,000*
4	2	0	2	9	5	4	*Referee:* R. Morris

Transfer-listed Hugh Hay leads the way in this reshaped Dons' line-up. Leggat is playing for Scotland in Belfast and scores in the 1-1 draw.

No 5 Saturday, 12 October

AIRDRIEONIANS (1) 2	ABERDEEN (2) 6
Duncan (32), McMillan	Leggat 5 (19, 40, 50 pen,
(58)	76, 78), Little (89)

AIRDRIE: Walker, Kilmarnock, Shanks, Price, Baillie, Quigley, Rankine, McMillan, Caven, Duncan, McLean

ABERDEEN: Martin, Walker, Caldwell, Glen, Wallace, Brownlee, Leggat, Burns, Little, Hay, Hather

P	W	D	L	F	A	Pts	
5	3	0	2	15	7	6	*Referee:* P. Fitzpatrick

Fresh from his goal against Northern Ireland, Leggat smashes five goals past Airdrie to send them to the bottom of the league.

No 6 Saturday, 19 October

HEARTS (2) 4	ABERDEEN (0) 0
Murray 2 (26, 42),	
Young (77), Blackwood	
(85)	

HEARTS: Brown, Kirk, Thomson, Mackay, Glidden, Higgins, Young, Murray, Bauld, Wardhaugh, Blackwood

ABERDEEN: Martin, Caldwell, Hogg, Glen, Wallace, Brownlee, Leggat, Davidson, Little, Hay, Mulhall

P	W	D	L	F	A	Pts	*Attendance: 30,000*
6	3	0	3	15	11	6	*Referee:* H. Phillips

Unbeaten Hearts welcome 'man-in-the-news' Leggat, shackle him from the outset, and then take Aberdeen apart.

No 7 Saturday, 26 October

ABERDEEN (1) 1	PARTICK THISTLE (2) 3
Little (34)	Mallon (1), McParland
	(16), Davidson (70 pen)

ABERDEEN: Morrison, Caldwell, Hogg, Ward, Wallace, Glen, Leggat, Burns, Little, Hay, Hather

PARTICK: Thomson, Kerr, Baird, Wright, Davidson, Mathers, McKenzie, McIntosh, Mallon, McParland, Ewing

P	W	D	L	F	A	Pts	*Attendance: 12,000*
7	3	0	4	16	14	6	*Referee:* T. S. Edwards

John Ward is drafted in to pep-up the Dons. He witnesses a tale of woe. Mallon was quickest to the ball in the first minute to put Thistle ahead, and then Leggat broke his leg in a tackle with Baird. He will not play again till February.

No 8 Saturday, 2 November

FALKIRK (2) 4	ABERDEEN (3) 4
White 2 (21, 77),	Wishart (35), Ewen (39),
O'Hara 2 (41, 55)	Glen (42), Hather (80)

FALKIRK: Slater, Parker, McIntosh, Wright, Irvine, Prentice, Murray, Grierson, White, Moran, O'Hara

ABERDEEN: Morrison, Caldwell, Hogg, Ward, Young, Glen, Ewen, Boyd, Davidson, Wishart, Hather

P	W	D	L	F	A	Pts	*Attendance: 12,000*
8	3	1	4	20	18	7	*Referee:* H. J. Gallacher

A fast and furious match – a delight to the fans if not the managers. Wishart equalises White's header with a shot which was deflected on to Slater's shoulder and into the net. Dick Ewen, deputising for Leggat, put the Dons ahead. Goals at both ends brought the tally to 4-4 and Grierson drove a Falkirk penalty against the bar.

No 9 Saturday, 9 November

ABERDEEN (4) 5	QUEENS PARK (0) 2
Davidson 3 (2, 7,80),	McEwan (75), Church
Ewen (17), Wishart (43)	(85)

ABERDEEN: Morrison, Caldwell, Hogg, Ward, Young, Allister, Ewen, Boyd, Davidson, Wishart, Hather

QUEENS PARK: Crampsey, Harnett, Hastie, Cromar, Ferguson, Chalmers, Scobie, Omand, McEwan, Devine, Church

P	W	D	L	F	A	Pts	*Attendance: 10,000*
9	4	1	4	25	20	9	*Referee:* J. A. S. Bisset

An RAF band entertained the crowd before the start, whereupon Aberdeen's forwards entertained them.

No 10 Saturday, 16 November

THIRD LANARK (1) 3	ABERDEEN (1) 1
Welsh (1), Craig (78),	Davidson (2)
Brown (86)	

THIRD LANARK: Robertson, Smith, Brown, Kelly, Lewis, Slingsby, McInnes, Craig, Allan, Welsh, Callan

ABERDEEN: Morrison, Caldwell, Hogg, Ward, Young, Glen, Ewen, Boyd, Davidson, Wishart, Hather

P W D L F A Pts
10 4 1 5 26 23 9   *Referee:* R. H. Davidson

After two minutes the score stood at 1-1, but Aberdeen couldn't maintain the tempo and by the end were sightless in the fog.

No 11 Saturday, 23 November
ABERDEEN (1) 1   KILMARNOCK (0) 2
Wishart (20)   Curlett 2 (50, 67)

ABERDEEN: Martin, Caldwell, J. Hogg, Brownlee, Clunie, Glen, Ewen, W. Hogg, Davidson, Wishart, Hather
KILMARNOCK: Brown, Collins, J. Stewart, R. Stewart, Toner, Kennedy, Muir, Curlett, Mays, Henaughen, Black

P W D L F A Pts   *Attendance:* 11,000
11 4 1 6 27 25 9   *Referee:* D. McTaggart

More team changes by Aberdeen. Willie Hogg makes his debut and helps Aberdeen to shine in the first half, though they sink in the second.

No 12 Saturday, 30 November
RAITH ROVERS (0) 0   ABERDEEN (1) 1
                  Brownlee (4)

RAITH: Drummond, Polland, Williamson, Young, McNaught, Leigh, McEwen, Kerray, Copland, Kelly, Urquhart
ABERDEEN: Martin, Caldwell, J. Hogg, Brownlee, Clunie, Glen, Ewen, W. Hogg, Davidson, Wishart, Hather

P W D L F A Pts   *Attendance:* 7,000
12 5 1 6 28 25 11   *Referee:* A. McClintock

A cloud of despondency hung over Aberdeen as they travelled to Raith, second in the table and beaten only once all season. Their win was all the more remarkable for the manner of its achievement. Raith's Kelly blazed a first half penalty high and wide and for most of the second period Norman Davidson deputised in goal for Martin.

No 13 Saturday, 7 December
ABERDEEN (1) 2   CLYDE (0) 1
Davidson (19), Hather   Keogh (80)
(70)

ABERDEEN: Morrison, Caldwell, J. Hogg, Brownlee, Clunie, Glen, Ewen, W. Hogg, Davidson, Wishart, Hather
CLYDE: McCulloch, Murphy, Haddock, Walters, Finlay, Clinton, Herd, Currie, Keogh, Robertson, Ring

P W D L F A Pts   *Attendance:* 11,000
13 6 1 6 30 26 13   *Referee:* W. D. Massie

Aberdeen avenge their League Cup quarter final defeat. Keogh's late goal gave the 'Bully Wee' hopes of salvaging a point.

No 14 Saturday, 14 December
MOTHERWELL (2) 4   ABERDEEN (0) 1
Quinn 2 (20, 56),   Hather (88)
Gardiner (23), Baker (89)

MOTHERWELL: Wylie, Holton, McFadyen, Forrest, Shaw, Aitken, Hunter, Quinn, McSeveney, Gardiner, Baker
ABERDEEN: Morrison, Caldwell, J. Hogg, Brownlee, Clunie, Glen, Ewen, W. Hogg, Little, Wishart, Hather

P W D L F A Pts   *Referee:* R. J. Smith
14 6 1 7 31 30 13

Aberdeen's mini-revival comes to a sticky end. They have nothing to laugh about after this.

No 15 Saturday, 21 December
QUEEN OF THE   ABERDEEN (1) 2
  SOUTH (0) 1   Davidson (5), Binning
Oakes (50)   o.g. (72)

QUEEN OF THE SOUTH: W. Smith, Sharpe, Binning, Whitehead, A. Smith, Greenock, Black, McGill, Patterson, Tasker, Oakes
ABERDEEN: Morrison, Caldwell, J. Hogg, Brownlee, Clunie, Glen, Ewen, W. Hogg, Davidson, Wishart, Hather

P W D L F A Pts   *Attendance:* 4,000
15 7 1 7 33 31 15   *Referee:* P. Fitzpatrick

Aberdeen had all the play yet the score stood at 1-1 after an hour. In the end they needed an own goal to give them both points.

No 16 Saturday, 28 December
ABERDEEN (1) 1   RANGERS (1) 2
W. Hogg (19)   Brand (22), Scott (74)

ABERDEEN: Morrison, Caldwell, J. Hogg, Brownlee, Clunie, Glen, Ewen, W. Hogg, Davidson, Wishart, Hather
RANGERS: Ritchie, Shearer, Caldow, McColl, Telfer, Baird, Scott, Miller, Murray, Brand, Wilson

P W D L F A Pts   *Attendance:* 21,000
16 7 1 8 34 33 15   *Referee:* J. P. Barclay

This is the Dons' first encounter with the Old Firm this season. It lived up to expectations, and Willie Hogg gave the Dons heart when scoring past a heavy-footed Ritchie. Rangers soon levelled and their winner came when McColl's long ball eluded Clunie and broke free as Morrison challenged Murray. Scott was unmarked to slot home.

No 17 Wednesday, 1 January
DUNDEE (0) 1   ABERDEEN (0) 2
Sneddon (66)   W. Hogg (72), Ewen (79)

DUNDEE: Ferguson, Hamilton, Cox, Black, McKenzie, Cowie, McIvor, Cousin, O'Hara, Sneddon, Robertson
ABERDEEN: Morrison, Caldwell, J. Hogg, Brownlee, Clunie, Glen, Ewen, W. Hogg, Davidson, Wishart, Hather

P W D L F A Pts
17 8 1 8 36 34 17   *Referee:* J. A. Mowat

Dundee fans leave Dens Park shaking their heads in disbelief. How could their team have lost after having all the play? The match kicked off with Caldwell in the dressing room changing his boots. Dundee thereafter took command, but were stunned at Willie Hogg's equaliser and shattered when Ewen's curving shot went in off the far post.

No 18 Thursday, 2 January
ABERDEEN (2) 6   EAST FIFE (2) 2
  Wishart (2), Hather   Duchart (8), Bonthrone
  3 (32, 47, 73), Davidson   (25)
  (67), W. Hogg (74)
ABERDEEN: Morrison, Caldwell, J. Hogg, Brownlee, Clunie, Glen, Ewen, W. Hogg, Davidson, Wishart, Hather
EAST FIFE: Allan, Wilkie, Cox, Christie, Bowie, Mochan, Ingram, Leishman, Duchart, Bonthrone, Matthew

P	W	D	L	F	A	Pts	
18	9	1	8	42	36	19	*Referee:* W. D. Massie

Just the tonic for keeping the fans warm. It's pretty even until half-time – one-way traffic afterwards.

No 19 Saturday, 4 January
HIBERNIAN (0) 0   ABERDEEN (0) 1
       Ewen (51)
HIBERNIAN: Leslie, Grant, Muir, Turnbull, Paterson, Baxter, Smith, Frye, Baker, Thomson, McLeod
ABERDEEN: Morrison, Caldwell, J. Hogg, Brownlee, Clunie, Glen, Ewen, W. Hogg, Davidson, Wishart, Hather

P	W	D	L	F	A	Pts	*Attendance:* 14,000
19	10	1	8	43	36	21	*Referee:* J. Stewart

Hibs are third but have lost their last three games – now their last four. Aberdeen continue their sequence of smash and grab victories on opponents' soil. Hibs turned the screw throughout but had nothing to show for their pressure. Ewen's goal came from a speculative lob, and it brought Aberdeen their sixth league point in four days.

No 20 Saturday, 11 January
ABERDEEN (2) 3   ST MIRREN (1) 1
  Hather (6), W. Hogg   Caldwell o.g. (9)
  (19), Glen (69)
ABERDEEN: Morrison, Caldwell, J. Hogg, Brownlee, Clunie, Glen, Ewen, W. Hogg, Davidson, Wishart, Hather
ST MIRREN: Forsyth, Higgins, Wilson, Neilson, Buchanan, Johnstone, Devine, Gemmell, McKay, McGill, McCulloch

P	W	D	L	F	A	Pts	*Attendance:* 11,000
20	11	1	8	46	37	23	*Referee:* G. Bowman

1958 continues to be a bountiful year for the Dons. They win again, once they overcome the shock of seeing Caldwell pass back wide of his goalkeeper.

No 21 Saturday, 18 January
CELTIC (1) 1   ABERDEEN (0) 1
  Collins (27)   Ewen (84)

CELTIC: Beattie, Donnelly, Fallon, Smith, Evans, Peacock, Collins, Ryan, Byrne, Wilson, Auld
ABERDEEN: Morrison, Caldwell, J. Hogg, Brownlee, Clunie, Allister, Ewen, W. Hogg, Davidson, Wishart, Hather

Leading positions

	P	W	D	L	F	A	Pts
1 Hearts	22	19	2	1	89	15	40
2 Rangers	18	12	3	3	49	28	27
3 Clyde	20	13	1	6	53	35	27
4 Celtic	19	10	5	4	40	22	25
5 Raith	21	10	5	6	42	26	25
6 ABERDEEN	21	11	2	8	47	38	24

Attendance: 20,000   *Referee:* G. Mitchell

The league race has long been academic. The only race left is for runners-up spot and Aberdeen seem to have as much chance as anybody. On a snow-covered pitch Morrison allowed the ball to squirm from his hands for Collins to score. Jimmy Hogg then handled but Ryan's spot-kick sailed wide, and against the tide of play Ewen snatched an equaliser.

No 22 Saturday, 1 February
PARTICK THISTLE (0) 1   ABERDEEN (0) 0
  Ewing (72)
PARTICK: Thomson, Brodie, Baird, Mathers, Davidson, Donlevy, Smith, Harvey, Kerr, McParland, Ewing
ABERDEEN: Morrison, Walker, Caldwell, Brownlee, Clunie, Glen, Ewen, Hogg, Davidson, Wishart, Hather

P	W	D	L	F	A	Pts	*Attendance:* 10,000
22	11	2	9	47	39	24	*Referee:* J. A. S. Bisset

January was a golden month for Aberdeen. February looks less promising after this uninspiring showing.

No 23 Saturday, 22 February
ABERDEEN (0) 1   FALKIRK (2) 2
  Hather (64)   McCole (1), Moran (38)
ABERDEEN: Morrison, Caldwell, J. Hogg, Ward, Clunie, Glen, Leggat, W. Hogg, Davidson, Boyd, Hather
FALKIRK: Slater, Parker, McIntosh, McMillan, Irvine, Prentice, Murray, McCole, Merchant, Moran, O'Hara

P	W	D	L	F	A	Pts	*Attendance:* 12,000
23	11	2	10	48	41	24	*Referee:* W. M. Syme

Thirty seconds was all it took for McCole to seize on a loose ball and put Aberdeen behind. And there they stayed.

No 24 Wednesday, 5 March
QUEENS PARK (1) 2   ABERDEEN (3) 5
  Cromar (42 pen),   Ewen (20), Wishart (24),
  Stevenson (62)   Little (31), Leggat
                2 (50, 75)
QUEENS PARK: Pinkerton, Harnett, Holt, Cromar, McKinven, Robb, Stevenson, Omand, McEwan, Darroch, Church
ABERDEEN: Morrison, Caldwell, J. Hogg, Brownlee, Clunie, Glen, Ewen, Little, Leggat, Wishart, Hather

P W D L F A Pts
24 12 2 10 53 43 26   *Referee:* W. Harvie

Newcastle are anxious to sign Bobby Wishart. But after the game Aberdeen refuse to sell him.

No 25 Saturday, 8 March
ABERDEEN (2) 2   THIRD LANARK (2) 4
  Wallace (21), Ewen (35)   R. Craig (11), Hogg o.g.
                              (28), Gray (74), W. Craig
                              (83)

ABERDEEN: Morrison, Caldwell, J. Hogg, Brownlee, Clunie, Wallace, Ewen, Burns, Leggat, Wishart, Mulhall

THIRD LANARK: Robertson, Smith, Brown, Higgins, Lewis, Slingsby, W. Craig, R. Craig, Allan, Gray, McInnes

P W D L F A Pts   *Attendance:* 10,000
25 12 2 11 55 47 26   *Referee:* R. Morris

Aberdeen's defence give an imitation of a seive. All four Thirds' goals were engineered by ex-Don Johnny Allen.

No 26 Wednesday, 19 March
KILMARNOCK (1) 2   ABERDEEN (0) 0
  Black 2 (4, 51)

KILMARNOCK: Brown, Watson, Stewart, Falls, Toner, Kennedy, Henaughen, McBride, Chalmers, Black, Burns

ABERDEEN: Morrison, Walker, Caldwell, Brownlee, Clunie, Glen, Leggat, Burns, Davidson, Wishart, Hather

P W D L F A Pts
26 12 2 12 55 49 26

Aberdeen show all the signs of a cup hangover following their defeat by Motherwell. Killie keeper Brown did not have a worthwhile shot to save in the whole game.

No 27 Saturday, 22 March
ABERDEEN (1) 3   RAITH ROVERS (1) 2
  Mulhall (25), Davidson   Kerray (40), McEwan
  (74), Hay (79)   (78)

ABERDEEN: Morrison, Walker, Clydesdale, Brownlee, Clunie, Glen, Leggat, Wishart, Davidson, Hay, Mulhall

RAITH: Drummond, Polland, Lockerbie, Young, McNaught, Leigh, McEwan, Kerray, Williamson, Kelly, Urquhart

P W D L F A Pts   *Attendance:* 7,000
27 13 2 12 58 51 28   *Referee:* J. Holburn

Aberdeen's smallest crowd of the season. A flurry of goals late in the game woke them up.

No 28 Saturday, 29 March
CLYDE (2) 5   ABERDEEN (0) 1
  Robertson 2 (38, 85),   Davidson (62)
  Currie (45), Coyle (50),
  Ring (67)

CLYDE: McCulloch, Murphy, Haddock, Walters, Finlay, Clinton, Herd, Currie, Coyle, Robertson, Ring

ABERDEEN: Morrison, Walker, Clydesdale, Brownlee, Clunie, Burns, Ewen, Wishart, Davidson, Hay, Mulhall

P W D L F A Pts
28 13 2 13 59 56 28   *Referee:* J. Stewart

David Shaw rings the changes. Only two of the side which began the season are included – but Aberdeen are promptly given a hiding.

No 29 Saturday, 5 April
ABERDEEN (0) 0   CELTIC (0) 1
                            Byrne (77)

ABERDEEN: Morrison, Walker, Hogg, Burns, Clunie, Glen, Leggat, Brownlee, Davidson, Wishart, Hather

CELTIC: Beattie, Meechan, Mochan, Smith, Evans, Peacock, Collins, McVittie, Byrne, Wilson, Fernie

P W D L F A Pts
29 13 2 14 59 57 28   *Referee:* R. Rodger

A game that neither side would remember with favour. Both teams wore black armbands and there was a minute's silence in memory of Celtic's Willie Maley. Aberdeen's offside trap had successfully stifled Celtic until Byrne outpaced Clunie.

No 30 Wednesday, 9 April
ABERDEEN (4) 4   MOTHERWELL (1) 3
  Davidson 3 (2, 37, 41),   St John 2 (33, 83),
  Little (7)   Gardiner (60)

ABERDEEN: Martin, Walker, Hogg, Burns, Clunie, Glen, Ewen, Little, Davidson, Brownlee, Hather

MOTHERWELL: Wyllie, McSeveney, Holton, Aitken, Martis, McCann, J. Hunter, Gardiner, St John, Forrest, W. Hunter

P W D L F A Pts
30 14 2 14 63 60 30   *Referee:* J. P. Barclay

What consolation is this? Motherwell won when it mattered, in the Cup. Davidson's hat-trick would have been useful in that earlier contest.

No 31 Saturday, 12 April
ABERDEEN (0) 3   QUEEN OF THE
  Ward (49), Burns (78),   SOUTH (1) 4
  Hather (83)   Patterson 3 (32, 63, 70),
                              Ewing (56)

ABERDEEN: Martin, Walker, Hogg, Burns, Young, Brownlee, Ewen, Little, Leggat, Ward, Hather

QUEEN OF THE SOUTH: Smith, Sharp, Binning, Whitehead, Elliot, Greenock, Black, Crosbie, Patterson, Ewing, Oakes

P W D L F A Pts   *Attendance:* 8,000
31 14 2 15 66 64 30   *Referee:* G. Mitchell

Pittodrie has witnessed 14 goals in four days, but the crowd are not in the mood to become excited. Their team appears to be falling apart.

No 32 Wednesday, 16 April
ABERDEEN (0) 0   HEARTS (1) 4
                            Crawford (14),
                            Wardhaugh (74), Young
                            (85), Bowman (88)

ABERDEEN: Morrison, Walker, Hogg, Burns, Clunie, Brownlee, Ewen, Leggat, Davidson, Wishart, Hather

HEARTS: Marshall, Kirk, Thomson, Cumming, Milne, Bowman, Blackwood, Conn, Young, Wardhaugh, Crawford

P W D L F A Pts   *Attendance:* 12,000
32 14 2 16 66 68 30   *Referee:* T. Wharton

Hearts secured the Scottish championship for the first time in 61 years – some time ago. They have already scored 125 league goals at an average of 4 per match, and have lost just once. Strangely the game was more evenly contested than the score suggests and only in the last phase of the game did Hearts pull away.

No 33 Monday, 21 April
EAST FIFE (0) 3   ABERDEEN (2) 2
Duchart (49), Mochan (75),   Wishart (31), Davidson
  Reilly (80)   (35)
EAST FIFE: McCluskey, Stirrat, Cox, Christie, Bowie, Mochan, Gillon, Ford, Duchart, Reilly, Matthew
ABERDEEN: Morrison, Walker, Hogg, Burns, Clunie, Brownlee, Ewen, Leggat, Davidson, Wishart, Hather

P W D L F A Pts
33 14 2 17 68 71 30   *Referee:* W. Brittle

Last season at Methil East Fife won 4-3 after being three goals down. Now they win 3-2 after being two goals behind.

No 34 Saturday, 26 April
RANGERS (3) 5   ABERDEEN (0) 0
  Murray 3 (32, 35, 69),
  Brand 2 (43, 52)
RANGERS: Ritchie, Shearer, Caldow, McColl, Telfer, Baird, Scott, Millar, Murray, Brand, Hubbard
ABERDEEN: Morrison, Walker, Hogg, Burns, Clunie, Brownlee, Ewen, Leggat, Davidson, Wishart, Hather

Attendance: 10,000   *Referee:* J. A. S. Bisset

Aberdeen end the season with a fourth successive defeat, and are simply crumpled underfoot at Ibrox.

Aberdeen's complete home and away record:
HOME						AWAY						
P	W	D	L	F	A		W	D	L	F	A	Pts
34	8	0	9	40	35		6	2	9	28	41	30

Clunie, with Aberdeen in the late fifties.

Scottish League Division One 1957-58

		P	W	D	L	F	A	Pts
1	Hearts	34	29	4	1	132	29	62
2	Rangers	34	22	5	7	89	49	49
3	Celtic	34	19	8	7	84	47	46
4	Clyde	34	18	6	10	84	61	42
5	Kilmarnock	34	14	9	11	60	55	37
6	Partick	34	17	3	14	69	71	37
7	Raith	34	14	7	13	66	56	35
8	Motherwell	34	12	8	14	68	67	32
9	Hibernian	34	13	5	16	59	60	31
10	Falkirk	34	11	9	14	64	82	31
11	Dundee	34	13	5	16	49	65	31
12	ABERDEEN	34	14	2	18	68	76	30
13	St Mirren	34	11	8	15	59	66	30
14	Third Lanark	34	13	4	17	69	88	30
15	Queen of the South	34	12	5	17	61	72	29
16	Airdrieonians	34	13	2	19	71	92	28
17	East Fife	34	10	3	21	45	88	23
18	Queens Park	34	4	1	29	41	114	9

LEAGUE CUP

Saturday, 10 August
ABERDEEN (3) 5   QUEEN OF SOUTH (1) 1
  Leggat 2 (2, 4), Wishart   Patterson (44)
  (20), Davidson (62),
  Hather (80)
ABERDEEN: Martin, Caldwell, Hogg, Allister, Young, Glen, Leggat, Burns, Davidson, Wishart, Hather
QUEEN OF THE SOUTH: Henderson, Sharpe, Binning, Rae, Smith, Greenock, Black, McGill, Patterson, King, Oakes

Attendance: 22,000   *Referee:* J. Davidson

Graham Leggat spent all summer refusing to resign for the Dons. At last he does sign and scores Aberdeen's first goals of the season.

Wednesday, 14 August
FALKIRK (1) 3   ABERDEEN (1) 4
  Moran (7), Prentice   Leggat (33), Davidson
  (47 pen), Grierson (63)   (77), Burns 2 (82, 85)
FALKIRK: Brown, Thomson, Rae, Wright, Irvine, Prentice, Murray, Grierson, Merchant, Moran, O'Hara
ABERDEEN: Martin, Caldwell, Hogg, Allister, Young, Brownlee, Leggat, Burns, Davidson, Wishart, Hather

                         Referee: R. J. Smith

Aberdeen were 3-1 down with fifteen minutes to play – yet still won. What a contrast to the lack of fighting qualities displayed last season.

Saturday, '7 August
MOTHERWELL (1) 2   ABERDEEN (2) 3
  Gardiner (32), Quinn   Davidson 3 (13, 20, 61)
  (70 pen)
MOTHERWELL: Weir, Gilchrist, Holton, Aitken, Cowie, Forrest, Baker, Quinn, Gardiner, McPhee, McCann

ABERDEEN: Martin, Caldwell, Hogg, Allister, Young, Glen, Leggat, Burns, Davidson, Wishart, Hather

Attendance: 6,000   *Referee:* W. Brittle

In the last moments Forrest had a great chance to equalise for Motherwell, but he shot into the side net.

Saturday, 24 August
QUEEN OF SOUTH (1) 2   ABERDEEN (3) 3
  McGill (6),   Davidson 2 (9, 11),
  Smith (70 pen)   Leggat (27)

QUEEN OF THE SOUTH: Henderson, Sharpe, Binning, Rae, Smith, Greenock, Black, McGill, Crosbie, King, Oakes

ABERDEEN: Martin, Caldwell, Hogg, Allister, Young, Glen, Leggat, Burns, Davidson, Wishart, Hather

Attendance: 5,000   *Referee:* T. Wharton

Queens scored first and last. In between Aberdeen taught them a lesson.

Wednesday, 28 August
ABERDEEN (0) 2   FALKIRK (1) 1
  Davidson (48), Allister   O'Hara (9)
  (77 pen)

ABERDEEN: Martin, Caldwell, Hogg, Allister, Young, Glen, Leggat, Burns, Davidson, Wishart, Hather

FALKIRK: Brown, Nicol, Rae, Wright, Irvine, Prentice, Murray, Grierson, Merchant, Moran, O'Hara

Referee: W. D. Massie

Only Falkirk can stop Aberdeen qualifying. Ex-Rangers and Scotland goalkeeper Bobby Brown did his best to do so, but he couldn't prevent Norman Davidson's eighth goal in five games.

Saturday, 31 August
ABERDEEN (1) 5   MOTHERWELL (1) 3
  Burns 2 (18, 80), Leggat   Hogg o.g. (4), McPhee
  3 (52, 63, 83)   (70), Forrest (82)

ABERDEEN: Martin, Caldwell, Hogg, Allister, Young, Brownlee, Leggat, Burns, Davidson, Wishart, Hather

MOTHERWELL: Weir, Gilchrist, Holton, Aitken, Cowie, Forrest, J. Hunter, McCann, Gardiner, McPhee, S. Reid

Attendance: 18,000   *Referee:* H. J. Gallacher

Aberdeen march into the quarter finals with a 100% group record, all the goals stemming from the Dons' right-wing combination of Burns and Leggat.

Section 1

	P	W	D	L	F	A	Pts
ABERDEEN	6	6	0	0	23	12	12
Falkirk	6	2	1	3	13	11	5
Motherwell	6	2	0	4	11	15	4
Queen of the South	6	1	1	4	8	14	3

Quarter Final 1st Leg Wednesday, 11 September
ABERDEEN (0) 1   CLYDE (2) 2
  Boyd (82)   Currie (13), Robertson
                         (31)

ABERDEEN: Martin, Caldwell, Hogg, Allister, Clunie, Glen, Boyd, Burns, Davidson, Wishart, Hather

CLYDE: Watson, Murphy, Haddock, Walters, Finlay, Clinton, Herd, Currie, Keogh, Robertson, Ring

Referee: J. P. Barclay

Clyde's Albert Murphy twice saved his team with goal-line clearances; then was responsible for the backpass which led to Aberdeen's scarcely deserved goal. But at least they now have a chance at Shawfield.

Quarter Final 2nd Leg Saturday, 14 September
CLYDE (3) 4   ABERDEEN (1) 2
  Keogh 2 (6, 13), Clunie   Boyd (1), Davidson (81)
  o.g. (8), Robertson (78)

CLYDE: Watson, Murphy, Haddock, Walters, Finlay, Clinton, Herd, Currie, Keogh, Robertson, Ring

ABERDEEN: Martin, Caldwell, Mitchell, Allister, Clunie, Glen, Little, Boyd, Davidson, Wishart, Mulhall

Attendance: 15,000   *Referee:* J. P. Barclay

Needing to win to take the tie into extra-time Aberdeen find the perfect start when Boyd scores off a post. But after 13 minutes they are 1-3 down (2-5 on aggregate) and that was the end of Aberdeen.

SCOTTISH CUP

1st Round (Bye)

2nd Round Saturday, 15 February
MORTON (0) 0   ABERDEEN (1) 1
                         Wishart (7)

MORTON: Kay, Wylie, Stirling, Orr, Gourlay, Hinshelwood, Nelson, Frizzell, Beaton, Fleming, Shaw

ABERDEEN: Morrison, Caldwell, J. Hogg, Brownlee, Clunie, Glen, Leggat, W. Hogg, Davidson, Wishart, Hather

Attendance: 10,000   *Referee:* R. Davidson

So far the draw in the Scottish Cup has been kind to Aberdeen. A bye in the first round has been followed by a trip to Morton – in the lower reaches of Division II – in the second. Wishart's cracking goal from eighteen yards brought the Dons the start they needed, but they needed all their resources to hold out afterwards. Graham Leggat made a quiet return after breaking his leg in October.

3rd Round Saturday, 1 March
DUNDEE (0) 1   ABERDEEN (1) 3
  Robertson (65)   Wishart 2 (6, 77), Leggat
                         (52)

DUNDEE: Brown, Hamilton, Cox, Henderson, McKenzie, Cowie, Chalmers, Cousin, O'Hara, Sneddon, Robertson

ABERDEEN: Morrison, Caldwell, Hogg, Brownlee, Clunie, Glen, Ewen, Little, Leggat, Wishart, Hather

Attendance: 24,000   *Referee:* W. Syme

Aberdeen won flukily at Dens Park in the league on New Year's Day. Once again they have to withstand intense pressure. The turning point came when, at 0-1, Morrison made a flying save from Cousin. He cleared downfield, where Brownlee set up Leggat to score a gem.

Quarter Final Saturday, 15 March
MOTHERWELL (1) 2   ABERDEEN (0) 1
  Glen o.g. (34), St John   Davidson (49)
  (61)

MOTHERWELL: H. Weir, Holton, McFadyen, Aitken, Martis, McCann, St John, Quinn, McSeveney, Forrest, A Weir

ABERDEEN: Morrison, Walker, Caldwell, Brownlee, Clunie, Glen, Leggat, Ewen, Davidson, Wishart, Hather

Attendance: 19,000   *Referee:* W. Brittle

Motherwell have two tasks: to stay in Division I and to do well in the Cup. Glen takes the credit for 'Well's first goal, turning McSeveney's shot wide of Morrison. The scores were level when Hather's shot was blocked by the keeper but the ball rebounded to Davidson. With McFadyen carried off, Aberdeen had only ten opponents to contend with for the final 36 minutes. But Caldwell's weak clearance was the prelude to Ian St John's winning goal.

1957-58

APPEARANCES	League	League Cup	Scottish Cup
Hather	30	7	3
Davidson	28	8	2
Brownlee	28	2	3
Wishart	27	8	3
J. Hogg	27	7	2
Caldwell	26	8	3
Glen	26	6	3
Clunie	25	2	3

APPEARANCES	League	League Cup	Scottish Cup
Morrison	25		3
Ewen	23		2
Leggat	15	6	3
Burns	13	7	
W. Hogg	13		1
Walker	11		1
Martin	9	8	
Little	8	1	1
Boyd	7	2	
Hay	6		
Ward	6		
Young	5	6	
Wallace	5		
Mulhall	4	1	
Allister	3	8	
Mitchell	2	1	
Clydesdale	2		
25 players			

GOALS	Total	League	League Cup	Scottish Cup
Davidson	27	17	9	1
Leggat	15	7	7	1
Wishart	11	7	1	3
Hather	10	9	1	
Ewen	7	7		
Burns	5	1	4	
Little	4	4		
Hay	4	4		
W. Hogg	4	4		
Boyd	3	1	2	
Allister	2	2		
Brownlee	1	1		
Mulhall	1	1		
Wallace	1	1		
Ward	1	1		
Allister	1		1	
own-goals	1	1		
Total	98	68	25	5

A team group from 1961. Back row: David Shaw (trainer), Ian Burns, George Kinnell, Hugh Baird, John Ogsten, Jimmy Hogg, David Bennett, Tommy Pearson (Manager). Front row: Dick Ewen, Charles Cooke, William Little, Ken Brownlee and George Mulhall.

Season 1958-59

There were no major comings and goings in the close season – but Graham Leggat finally signed for Fulham as competition got under way. Aberdeen made a quick exit from the League Cup, but then survived two opening defeats in the league to mount an early assault on the leadership. By early November Aberdeen were still in third position.

But then the rot set in. A depressing run of only four wins from twenty-two games plunged Aberdeen down into the relegation mire. The only light in their tunnel was steady progress through the rounds of the Scottish Cup. Three Second Division opponents were pushed aside – not without considerable difficulty. Kilmarnock were next to fall to Aberdeen, followed by Third Lanark in the Semi Final after a replay. This provided Aberdeen with a Cup Final appointment with St Mirren.

In essence Aberdeen's entire season was compressed into two consecutive Saturdays at the end of April. Needing to take a point off championship-seeking Rangers at Ibrox, to ensure survival, Aberdeen came from behind to win, when even the most optimistic Dons' supporter must have feared the worst. Seven days later Aberdeen stepped out at Hampden for their third Scottish Cup Final in seven years – and their third defeat. In a re-run of the **1956 League Cup Final Aberdeen battled for the trophy against St Mirren, but this time came off comprehensively beaten.**

League:	Thirteenth
League Cup:	Third in qualifying group
Scottish Cup:	Runners Up

SCOTTISH LEAGUE DIVISION ONE

No 1 Wednesday, 20 August
ABERDEEN (0) 0   AIRDRIEONIANS (1) 1
                  Rankine (7 pen)
ABERDEEN: Morrison, Caldwell, Hogg, Burns, Clunie, Glen, Little, Logie, Davidson, Wishart, Hather
AIRDRIE: Wallace, Miller, Shanks, Rankine, Baillie, Johnstone, Blair, McGill, Sharkey, Storrie, Ormond

P	W	D	L	F	A	Pts	*Attendance:* 15,000
1	0	0	1	0	1	0	*Referee:* W. D. Massie

Aberdeen's league campaign gets off to the worst possible start. The slow handclap resounds around the stadium. The penalty resulted from Clunie clipping the heels of Shanks who was in the clear.

No 2 Saturday, 6 September
DUNDEE (2) 2   ABERDEEN (0) 1
  Robertson (22),   Little (77)
  McGeachie (39)
DUNDEE: Brown, Hamilton, Cox, Henderson, Gabriel, Cowie, McGeachie, Cousin, Hill, Sneddon, Robertson
ABERDEEN: Morrison, Clydesdale, Hogg, Burns, Clunie, Glen, Ewen, Little, Kelly, Wishart, Hather

P	W	D	L	F	A	Pts	*Attendance:* 10,000
2	0	0	2	1	3	0	*Referee:* W. Brittle

Aberdeen were murdered 2-1, the score doing no credit to Dundee's massive control. Some of Dundee's misses would be candidates for the miss of the season competition.

No 3 Saturday, 13 September
ABERDEEN (2) 4   DUNFERMLINE
  Little (2),   ATHLETIC (0) 0
  2 (42, 74), Ewen (49)
ABERDEEN: Morrison, Clydesdale, Hogg, Burns, Clunie, Glen, Ewen, Little, Davidson, Wishart, Hather
DUNFERMLINE: Beaton, Duthie, Sweeney, Bain, Colville, Burns, Peebles, Napier, Dickson, Watson, Melrose

P	W	D	L	F	A	Pts	*Attendance:* 7,000
3	1	0	2	5	3	2	*Referee:* T. Alexander

The Dons desperately needed this win. But it should be seen in context. It was Dunfermline's second league game. In their first they conceded six.

No 4 Saturday, 20 September
THIRD LANARK (0) 0   ABERDEEN (0) 2
                      Clydesdale (55), Little
                      (69)

THIRD LANARK: Ramage, Smith, Brown, Cunningham, Lewis, Robb, Hilley, R. Craig, Dick, Grant, McInnes

ABERDEEN: Morrison, Clydesdale, Hogg, Burns, Clunie, Glen, Ewen, Little, Mulhall, Wishart, Hather

P	W	D	L	F	A	Pts	
4	2	0	2	7	3	4	*Attendance:* 8,000

Referee: J. P. Barclay

This was Third Lanark's first defeat. Clydesdale scored with a lob from forty yards which Ramage lost in the sun. McInnes was sent off for successive fouls on Clydesdale and Clunie. Morrison stopped a Robb penalty after Clunie had fouled Dick.

No 5 Saturday, 27 September
ABERDEEN (2) 3   CELTIC (0) 1
  Glen (8), Little (11),   Peacock (82)
  Mulhall (55)

ABERDEEN: Morrison, Clydesdale, Hogg, Burns, Clunie, Glen, Ewen, Little, Davidson, Wishart, Mulhall

CELTIC: Beattie, McKay, Mochan, Smith, McNeill, Peacock, Tully, Fernie, Colrain, Wilson, Auld

P	W	D	L	F	A	Pts	
5	3	0	2	10	4	6	*Attendance:* 20,000

Referee: G. Mitchell

Much better Aberdeen. In a bad-tempered game Aberdeen took all the credit – apart from Willie Fernie who struck a post and later set up Peacock for a thirty-yard consolation.

No 6 Saturday, 4 October
PARTICK THISTLE (1) 2   ABERDEEN (1) 3
  Smith 2 (6, 79)   Hather 2 (16, 50),
                          Ewen (72)

PARTICK: Renucci, Hogan, Baird, Mathers, Crawford, Donlevy, McKenzie, Wright, Kerr, Smith, McParland

ABERDEEN: Morrison, Clydesdale, Hogg, Burns, Clunie, Glen, Ewen, Little, Mulhall, Wishart, Hather

Leading positions

	P	W	D	L	F	A	Pts
1 Hearts	6	5	1	0	25	10	11
2 Dundee	6	4	1	1	12	9	9
3 ABERDEEN	6	4	0	2	13	6	8
4 Motherwell	6	3	2	1	17	10	8
5 Airdrie	6	4	0	2	15	9	8

Referee: R. Morris

Four straight wins for Aberdeen. Mulhall started off leading the attack, then switched with Hather, whereupon Aberdeen prospered.

No 7 Saturday, 11 October
STIRLING ALBION (2) 3   ABERDEEN (1) 2
  Spence (14 pen), Gilmour   Glen 2 (22 pen, 67 pen)
  (40), Benvie (53)

STIRLING: Smith, Gibson, Pettigrew, McKechie, Menzies, Pierson, Ryce, Benvie, Gilmour, Spence, Callan

ABERDEEN: Morrison, Clydesdale, Hogg, Burns, Clunie, Glen, Ewen, Little, Baird, Wishart, Mulhall

P	W	D	L	F	A	Pts	
7	4	0	3	15	9	8	*Referee:* J. A. Mowat

Hugh Baird, Aberdeen's £11,000 signing from Leeds, wore the No 9 shirt. It was a game of three penalties on a swamp, and it ended Aberdeen's winning run.

No 8 Saturday, 18 October
ABERDEEN (1) 4   HIBERNIAN (0) 0
  Glen (25 pen), Little
  3 (52, 75, 83)

ABERDEEN: Morrison, Clydesdale, Hogg, Burns, Clunie, Glen, Ewen, Little, Baird, Wishart, Hather

HIBERNIAN: Leslie, Paterson, Nicol, Turnbull, Plenderleith, Higgins, McLeod, Allison, Baker, Preston, Ormond

P	W	D	L	F	A	Pts	
8	5	0	3	19	9	10	*Attendance:* 20,000

Referee: A. McClintock

Hibs beat Aberdeen twice in the League Cup – but not now. There has been a buzz about Aberdeen for some weeks which suggests better things ahead. Glen's third penalty in two games sent the Dons on their merry way.

No 9 Saturday, 25 October
ABERDEEN (4) 5   FALKIRK (0) 0
  Baird 4 (8, 27, 29, 70),
  Ewen (31)

ABERDEEN: Morrison, Clydesdale, Hogg, Burns, Clunie, Glen, Ewen, Little, Baird, Wishart, Hather

FALKIRK: Slater, Richmond, Hunter, Wright, Prentice, Price, McCulloch, White, Grierson, Moran, Lachlan

P	W	D	L	F	A	Pts	
9	6	0	3	24	9	12	*Attendance:* 17,000

Referee: T. Wharton

Aberdeen scored five against Falkirk at Pittodrie in the League Cup – and repeat the punishment to a much-changed Falkirk side. Baird scored four times. When it was 1-0 Morrison saved a Prentice penalty.

No 10 Saturday, 1 November
KILMARNOCK (2) 2   ABERDEEN (0) 0
  McBride (10), Black (16)

KILMARNOCK: Brown, Collins, Watson, Beattie, Dougan, McKay, Chalmers, Stewart, McBride, Black, Muir

ABERDEEN: Morrison, Clydesdale, Hogg, Burns, Clunie, Glen, Ewen, Little, Baird, Wishart, Hather

P	W	D	L	F	A	Pts	
10	6	0	4	24	11	12	*Attendance:* 6,000

Referee: D. McTaggart

Aberdeen lost the toss, were asked to face driving wind and rain, and sixteen minutes later were out of contention.

No 11 Saturday, 8 November
ST MIRREN (0) 1   ABERDEEN (1) 5
  Lapsley (89 pen)   Ewen (25), Little
                          2 (66, 69), Baird
                          2 (80, 84)

ST MIRREN: Forsyth, Lapsley, McTurk, Neilson, McGugan, Gregal, Flynn, Ryan, Wilson, Bryceland, Campbell

ABERDEEN: Morrison, Clydesdale, Hogg, Burns, Clunie, Glen, Ewen, Little, Baird, Wishart, Hather

Leading positions

	P	W	D	L	F	A	Pts
1 Hearts	11	8	2	1	40	15	18
2 Motherwell	11	6	4	1	32	15	16
3 ABERDEEN	11	7	0	4	29	12	14
4 Dundee	11	5	4	2	23	18	14
5 Rangers	11	5	4	2	34	21	14
6 Airdrie	11	7	0	4	24	21	14

Referee: G. Bowman

A remarkable scoreline. Baird was again the Dons' architect of victory, sending them back to third position.

No 12 Saturday, 15 November
ABERDEEN (1) 2   RAITH ROVERS (0) 2
  Hather (39), Little (48)   Urquhart (49),
                            Dobbie (51)

ABERDEEN: Morrison, Clydesdale, Hogg, Burns, Clunie, Glen, Ewen, Little, Baird, Wishart, Hather
RAITH: Drummond, Polland, McFarlane, Leigh, McNaught, Baxter, McEwen, Young, Dobbie, Urquhart, McMillan

P	W	D	L	F	A	Pts	
12	7	1	4	31	14	15	*Attendance:* 17,000
							Referee: E. T. Cowan

Anarchy broke out in the second half. Ewen was stretchered off. Three goals after half time set the game alright. Jim Baxter was always prominent in Raith's revival.

No 13 Saturday, 22 November
CLYDE (3) 4   ABERDEEN (0) 0
  Coyle 2 (18, 25),
  Ring (24), Currie (52)

CLYDE: McCulloch, Murphy, Haddock, Walters, Finlay, Clinton, Herd, Currie, Coyle, Robertson, Ring
ABERDEEN: Morrison, Clydesdale, Hogg, Burns, Logie, Glen, McInnes, Little, Baird, Wishart, Paterson

P	W	D	L	F	A	Pts	
13	7	1	5	31	18	15	*Attendance:* 7,000
							Referee: R. Rodger

An inglorious day for Aberdeen. Clyde were next to bottom and played an hour without winger Herd, yet they still steam-rollered over Aberdeen.

No 14 Saturday, 29 November
ABERDEEN (2) 5   QUEEN OF THE
  Wishart (7), Little   SOUTH (0) 0
  2 (16, 80), Glen (67 pen),
  Baird (81)

ABERDEEN: Morrison, Clydesdale, Hogg, Brownlee, Clunie, Glen, Ewen, Little, Baird, Wishart, Hather
QUEEN OF THE SOUTH: Gebbie, Sharpe, Binning, Greenock, Smith, Ewing, Black, Patterson, McGill, King, Robertson

P	W	D	L	F	A	Pts	
14	8	1	5	36	18	17	*Attendance:* 10,000
							Referee: A. Crossman

Queen of the South chalk up their ninth successive defeat, which is why they are adrift at the foot of the table.

No 15 Saturday, 6 December
HEARTS (3) 5   ABERDEEN (0) 1
  Murray 2 (34, 53),   Wishart (80)
  Bauld 3 (38, 45, 50)

HEARTS: Marshall, Kirk, Thomson, Mackay, Milne, Cumming, Young, Murray, Bauld, Wardhaugh, Crawford
ABERDEEN: Morrison, Clydesdale, Hogg, Brownlee, Clunie, Glen, Ewen, Little, Baird, Wishart, Hather

P	W	D	L	F	A	Pts	
15	8	1	6	37	23	17	*Attendance:* 20,000
							Referee: P. Fitzpatrick

Last season Hearts thrashed Aberdeen 4-0 home and away. Now the league leaders dish out some more hammer. Before the match Aberdeen could boast the best defensive record in the division, but they gifted Hearts three goals, and tried to repel them with an offside trap. Afterwards Hearts' Dave Mackay learned that he had broken a bone in his foot.

No 16 Saturday, 13 December
ABERDEEN (0) 0   MOTHERWELL (2) 4
                        St John 2 (6, 23), Reid
                        (53), Weir (89)

ABERDEEN: Morrison, Clydesdale, Hogg, Brownlee, Clunie, Glen, Ewen, Little, Baird, Wishart, Hather
MOTHERWELL: Wylie, McSeveney, Holton, Aitken, Martis, McCann, Weir, S. Reid, St John, Quinn, Hunter

P	W	D	L	F	A	Pts	
16	8	1	7	37	27	17	*Attendance:* 14,000
							Referee: J. A. S. Bisset

Bobby Ancell's Motherwell have lost only one league match all season and have no intention of letting Aberdeen spoil that record. Ian St John masterminds Aberdeen's third mountainous defeat of recent weeks.

No 17 Saturday, 20 December
ABERDEEN (0) 1   RANGERS (1) 3
  Baird (77)   Murray (41), Brand (47),
                        Scott (82)

ABERDEEN: Ogston, Clydesdale, Hogg, Burns, Clunie, Glen, Cooper, Little, Baird, Davidson, Hather
RANGERS: Niven, Shearer, Caldow, Davis, Telfer, Stevenson, Scott, McMillan, Murray, Brand, Matthew

P	W	D	L	F	A	Pts	
17	8	1	8	38	30	17	*Attendance:* 18,000
							Referee: R. H. Davidson

Aberdeen had spirit but nothing else. Baird was left to carry the Dons threat single handed. Soon after Murray put Rangers in front a Baird equaliser was kept out by a goalpost. This win carries Rangers to the top of the league.

No 18 Saturday, 27 December
AIRDRIEONIANS (1) 2   ABERDEEN (0) 1
  McGill 2 (12, 54)   Ewen (56)
AIRDRIE: Wallace, Neil, Miller, Quinn, Baillie,
Johnston, Black, McGill, Sharkey, Rankin, Ormond
ABERDEEN: Ogston, Clydesdale, Hogg, Burns,
Clunie, Glen, Ewen, Davidson, Baird, Wishart, Hather

P W D L F A Pts   *Attendance:* 7,000
18 8 1 9 39 32 17   *Referee:* F. S. Crossley

After this latest setback Aberdeen have found
themselves outplayed by all the top four in consecutive
games. Hugh Baird captained Aberdeen against his old
club.

No 19 Thursday, 1 January
ABERDEEN (1) 1   DUNDEE (1) 1
  Wishart (43)   Curlett (38)
ABERDEEN: Morrison, Clydesdale, Hogg, Patience,
Clunie, Glen, Little, Davidson, Baird, Wishart, Hather
DUNDEE: Brown, Reid, Cox, Henderson, Gabriel,
Cowie, Curlett, Bonthrone, Cousin, Sneddon,
Robertson

P W D L F A Pts   *Attendance:* 12,000
19 8 2 9 40 33 18   *Referee:* G. Mitchell

A greasy pitch hampered the play of both sides.
Dundee's international keeper Brown required stitches
behind an ear after a collision with Davidson. Cousin
wore Brown's jersey for the last eleven minutes.

No 20 Saturday, 3 January
DUNFERMLINE   ABERDEEN (1) 1
  ATHLETIC (1) 1   Hather (31)
  Morrison o.g. (26)
DUNFERMLINE: Connachan, Duthie, Sweeney,
Bain, Colville, Mailer, Peebles, Smith, McWilliam,
Watson, Melrose
ABERDEEN: Morrison, Clydesdale, Hogg, Patience,
Clunie, Glen, Little, Davidson, Baird, Wishart, Hather

P W D L F A Pts
20 8 3 9 41 34 19   *Referee:* D. Weir

Dunfermline scored a goal which would not be allowed
according to modern interpretation of the laws.
Morrison clutched a cross and was charged into the net
by Smith. The goal was allowed to stand despite the
Dons protests.

No 21 Saturday, 24 January
ABERDEEN (2) 3   PARTICK THISTLE (1) 4
  Baird (16), Hather   Hogg o.g. (29), Kerr
  2 (24, 52)   (78), Fleming (85),
                          Anderson (88)
ABERDEEN: Morrison, Clydesdale, Hogg, Logie,
Clunie, Glen, Ewen, Little, Baird, Wishart, Hather
PARTICK: Freebairn, Hogan, Baird, Mathers, Harvey,
Donlevy, Anderson, Wilson, Kerr, McParland,
Fleming

P W D L F A Pts   *Attendance:* 10,000
21 8 3 10 44 38 19   *Referee:* W. D. Massie

Aberdeen provide a glimpse of the past, wearing gold
shirts and black shorts. This result is Aberdeen's
seventh without a win. It was suicide for the Dons after
they had led 2-0 and 3-1. Hogg sent the ball flying into
his own net for Partick's first, and two Partick goals in
the last five minutes saw them take the lead for the first
time in the match.

No 22 Saturday, 7 February
ABERDEEN (3) 4   STIRLING ALBION (0) 1
  Davidson 2 (20, 27),   Gilmour (53)
  Wishart (37), Little (79)
ABERDEEN: Martin, Walker, Clydesdale, Logie,
Clunie, Glen, Little, Davidson, Baird, Wishart, Hather
STIRLING: Stewart, Hailstones, Pettigrew, McKechie,
Sinclair, Pierson, Callan, Spence, Gilmour, Kilgannon,
McPhee

P W D L F A Pts   *Attendance:* 6,000
22 9 3 10 48 39 21   *Referee:* J. Stewart

This is Aberdeen's first win since November. The
margin would have been greater had Glen not
squandered a penalty.

No 23 Wednesday, 18 February
HIBERNIAN (0) 1   ABERDEEN (0) 0
  Gibson (75)
HIBERNIAN: Leslie, Grant, McClelland, Turnbull,
Paterson, Baxter, Smith, Fox, Preston, Gibson, Aitken
ABERDEEN: Martin, Clydesdale, Hogg, Logie,
Gibson, Glen, Ewen, Davidson, Baird, Wishart, Hather

P W D L F A Pts   *Attendance:* 14,000
23 9 3 11 48 40 21   *Referee:* W. D. Massie

Minus Joe Baker Hibs do not pack their usual punch,
but 36-year old Eddie Turnbull still steered his side to
victory.

No 24 Saturday, 21 February
FALKIRK (4) 5   ABERDEEN (1) 1
  Moran (13), Grierson   Baird (29)
  (16), Oliver (24), Murray
  (33), White (59 pen)
FALKIRK: Slater, McCormack, Hunter, Wright,
Richmond, Prentice, Murray, Grierson, White, Moran,
Oliver
ABERDEEN: Martin, Clydesdale, Hogg, Brownlee,
Clunie, Glen, Ewen, Davidson, Baird, Wishart, Hather

Bottom positions

	P	W	D	L	F	A	Pts
15 ABERDEEN	24	9	3	12	49	45	21
16 Clyde	25	8	3	14	45	49	19
17 Raith Rovers	26	6	7	13	46	62	19
18 Queen of the South	26	4	5	17	30	83	13

Referee: J. A. Mowat

Every Brockville forward found the net against an
Aberdeen side who have sunk from 3rd to 15th and are
now in real trouble.

No 25 Wednesday, 4 March
ABERDEEN (1) 2   KILMARNOCK (2) 2
  Hather (19), Glen (70)   Burns (8), Black (36)
ABERDEEN: Martin, Walker, Hogg, Burns, Gibson, Glen, Ewen, Baird, Davidson, Wishart, Hather
KILMARNOCK: Brown, Watson, McKay, Beattie, Dougan, Stewart, Muir, Henaughen, Wentzel, Black, Burns

P W D L F A Pts   *Attendance:* 5,000
25 9 4 12 51 47 22   *Referee:* J. Holborn

This tousy tussle led to a number of cuts and bruises. Both sides had an eye on gaining a psychological advantage for the coming Scottish Cup clash.

No 26 Saturday, 7 March
ABERDEEN (1) 2   ST MIRREN (0) 1
  Ewen (11), Davidson (87)   Kerrigan (60)
ABERDEEN: Morrison, J. Walker, Hogg, Burns, Clunie, A. Walker, Ewen, Little, Davidson, Wishart, Hather
ST MIRREN: Walker, Lapsley, Wilson, Neilson, McGugan, Leishman, Riddell, Laird, Baker, Gemmell, Kerrigan

P W D L F A Pts   *Attendance:* 10,000
26 10 4 12 53 48 24   *Referee:* J. P. Barclay

For Aberdeen the points were priceless. It was bustling Norman Davidson who did the trick, forcing the ball home after acting-captain Clunie swung over a free-kick.

No 27 Wednesday, 11 March
ABERDEEN (0) 3   THIRD LANARK (1) 3
  Ewen (48), Glen (75 pen),   McInnes (3), Gray (57),
  Wishart (84)   Dick (65)
ABERDEEN: Morrison, J. Walker, Hogg, Burns, Glen, A. Walker, Ewen, Little, Davidson, Wishart, Hather
THIRD LANARK: Ramage, Caldwell, Brown, Kelly, McCallum, Robb, Hilley, Craig, Dick, Gray, McInnes

P W D L F A Pts   *Attendance:* 4,000
27 10 5 12 56 51 25

Aberdeen were handed two gift goals and a soft penalty to rob Third Lanark of a point. They now have five away fixtures out of seven to come.

No 28 Wednesday, 18 March
RAITH ROVERS (0) 0   ABERDEEN (0) 1
                    Baird (50)
RAITH: Drummond, Polland, McFarlane, Young, McNaught, Leigh, McEwan, Conn, Kerray, Gardiner, Urquhart
ABERDEEN: Morrison, Walker, Hogg, Caldwell, Gibson, Glen, Little, Davidson, Baird, Wishart, Hather

P W D L F A Pts
28 11 5 12 57 51 27   *Referee:* A. Crossman

The Dons come straight from a memorable Scottish Cup win over Kilmarnock. But it is an insipid match, with both teams struggling for survival and looking the part.

No 29 Saturday, 21 March
ABERDEEN (1) 1   CLYDE (2) 2
  Baird (44)   Ring (10), Coyle (12)
ABERDEEN: Morrison, Walker, Hogg, Caldwell, Clunie, Glen, Little, Davidson, Baird, Wishart, Ewen
CLYDE: McCulloch, Murphy, Haddock, Walters, Finlay, Clinton, Herd, Currie, Coyle, Robertson, Ring

P W D L F A Pts   *Attendance:* 10,000
29 11 5 13 58 53 27   *Referee:* J. A. Bisset

Clyde are even worse than Aberdeen – and thoroughly earned their win. Morrison seemed to have Ring's opener covered, but the ball squirmed out of his hands over the line.

No 30 Wednesday, 25 March
CELTIC (1) 4   ABERDEEN (0) 0
  Lochhead (28), Mochan
  (55 pen), Colrain (67),
  McVittie (79)
CELTIC: Haffey, Mackay, Mochan, McNeil, Evans, Peacock, McVittie, Colrain, Lochhead, Divers, Auld
ABERDEEN: Ogston, Walker, Hogg, Caldwell, Gibson, Glen, Ewen, Little, Baird, Wishart, Paterson

P W D L F A Pts   *Attendance:* 5,000
30 11 5 14 58 57 27   *Referee:* R. Rodger

Lifeless Dons had no bite. Celtic were not too hot either, which made the scoreline all the more painful.

No 31 Saturday, 28 March
QUEEN OF THE   ABERDEEN (1) 1
  SOUTH (2) 2   Wishart (36)
  Ewing 2 (12, 15)
QUEEN OF THE SOUTH: Gebbie, Sharpe, Hindmarsh, Patterson, Smith, Whitehead, Black, Knox, Garrett, Ewing, Oakes
ABERDEEN: Martin, Clydesdale, Caldwell, Burns, Clunie, Glen, Little, Baird, Davidson, Wishart, Hather

P W D L F A Pts
31 11 5 15 59 59 27   *Referee:* G. Bowman

The Dons' third defeat in eight days. Doomed Queen of the South sunk Aberdeen even deeper into the mire. Aberdeen never looked like saving the game once Ewing had put them two goals behind.

No 32 Saturday, 11 April
MOTHERWELL (0) 2   ABERDEEN (0) 0
  Reid (76), Hunter (84)
MOTHERWELL: H. Weir, McSeveney, Forrest, Aitken, Martis, McCann, Hunter, Reid, St John, Quinn, A. Weir
ABERDEEN: Martin, Caldwell, Hogg, Burns, Clunie, Glen, Ewen, Little, Davidson, Baird, Hather

Bottom positions

	P	W	D	L	F	A	Pts
15 ABERDEEN	32	11	5	16	59	61	27
16 Falkirk	33	10	6	17	56	77	26
17 Dunfermline	32	9	7	16	56	84	25
18 Queen of the South	33	6	6	21	38	96	18

Attendance: 5,000   *Referee:* W. M. Syme

Aberdeen can't ask for a more arduous climax to the season. Their final three matches are against the top three. Poor finishing by Motherwell's forwards and fine goalkeeping by Martin kept the score respectable.

No 33 Wednesday, 15 April
ABERDEEN (1) 2   HEARTS (3) 4
 Ewen (44), Clunie (87)   Rankin 3 (3, 14, 69),
                            Blackwood (23)
ABERDEEN: Martin, Caldwell, Hogg, Burns, Clunie, Glen, Ewen, Little, Davidson, Wishart, Hather
HEARTS: Marshall, Kirk, Lough, Thomson, Milne, Cumming, Blackwood, Murray, Young, Rankin, Hamilton

Bottom positions

	P	W	D	L	F	A	Pts
15 ABERDEEN	33	11	5	17	61	65	27
16 Falkirk	33	10	6	17	56	77	26
17 Dunfermline	33	9	8	16	58	86	26
18 Queen of the South	33	6	6	21	38	96	18

Attendance: 18,000   *Referee:* W. M. Syme

The Dons can expect no favours from Hearts who are involved in a desperate tussle with Rangers for the championship. Rankin shatters Aberdeen with his hat-trick, which takes his total up to eight in four matches since his transfer from Queen of the South. Aberdeen have two cup finals to come – against Rangers in the league and St Mirren in the Cup.

No 34 Saturday, 18 April
RANGERS (1) 1   ABERDEEN (1) 2
 Brand (24)   Davidson 2 (42, 50)
RANGERS: Niven, Shearer, Caldow, Davis, Telfer, Stevenson, Scott, McMillan, Murray, Brand, Matthew
ABERDEEN: Martin, Caldwell, Hogg, Brownlee, Clunie, Glen, Ewen, Davidson, Baird, Wishart, Hather
Attendance: 40,000   *Referee:* A. Crossman

Rangers need a point for the championship: Aberdeen need a point for survival. After taking the lead Rangers were eventually booed off the pitch at Ibrox. But then news filtered through that Celtic had beaten Hearts at Parkhead, despite Hearts leading 1-0. Celtic, in other words, had handed Rangers the championship. Aberdeen were safe, and now for St Mirren in the Scottish Cup Final.

Aberdeen's complete home and away record:
HOME   AWAY
P W D L F A   W D L F A   Pts
34 7 4 6 42 29   5 1 11 21 37 37

Scottish League Division One 1958-59

	P	W	D	L	F	A	Pts
1 Rangers	34	21	8	5	92	51	50
2 Hearts	34	21	6	7	92	51	48
3 Motherwell	34	18	8	8	83	50	44
4 Dundee	34	16	9	9	61	51	41
5 Airdrie	34	15	7	12	64	62	37
6 Celtic	34	14	8	12	70	53	36
7 St Mirren	34	14	7	13	71	74	35
8 Kilmarnock	34	13	8	13	58	51	34
9 Partick Thistle	34	14	6	14	59	66	34
10 Hibernian	34	13	6	15	68	70	32
11 Third Lanark	34	11	10	13	74	83	32
12 Stirling Albion	34	11	8	15	54	64	30
13 ABERDEEN	34	12	5	17	63	66	29
14 Raith Rovers	34	10	9	15	60	70	29
15 Clyde	34	12	4	18	62	66	28
16 Dunfermline	34	10	8	16	68	87	28
17 Falkirk	34	10	7	17	58	79	27
18 Queen of the South	34	6	6	22	38	101	18

LEAGUE CUP

Saturday, 9 August
KILMARNOCK (0) 1   ABERDEEN (1) 2
 Kennedy (52)   Davidson (13), Wishart
                       (71)
KILMARNOCK: J. Brown, Collins, Watson, Kennedy, Toner, McKay, H. Brown, McBride, Chalmers, Black, Burns
ABERDEEN: Morrison, Walker, Hogg, Burns, Clunie, Glen, Ewen, Little, Davidson, Wishart, Hather
Attendance: 6,000   *Referee:* J. A. Mowat

Admission prices of Scottish grounds have risen to 2s 6d for the new season. Graham Leggat is about to sign for Fulham.

Wednesday, 13 August
ABERDEEN (1) 1   HIBERNIAN (2) 2
 Wishart (41)   Aitken (4), Baker (21)
ABERDEEN: Morrison, Walker, Hogg, Burns, Clunie, Glen, Ewen, Little, Davidson, Wishart, Hather
HIBERNIAN: Leslie, Grant, McClelland, Turnbull, Nicol, Baxter, Frye, Aitken, Baker, Preston, Ormond
Attendance: 15,000   *Referee:* R. H. Davidson

Aitken didn't strike the ball cleanly when he scored the opening goal. In the second half a mighty shot by Wishart hit the Hibs' crossbar.

Saturday, 16 August
ABERDEEN (2) 5   FALKIRK (0) 1
 Hather 2 (3, 15), Wishart Grierson (50)
 (56), Mulhall 2 (85, 89)
ABERDEEN: Morrison, Caldwell, Hogg, Burns, Clunie, Glen, Mulhall, Little, Davidson, Wishart, Hather
FALKIRK: Ferguson, McCarry, Lachlan, Wright, Richmond, Moran, White, Grierson, Merchant, Sinclair, Murray

Attendance: 12,000　　　*Referee:* P. Fitzpatrick

Bobby Wishart was Aberdeen's jewel in this comfy, comfy win.

Saturday, 23 August

ABERDEEN (0) 0　　　KILMARNOCK (2) 2
　　　　　　　　　　　McBride 2 (39, 44)

ABERDEEN: Morrison, Caldwell, Hogg, Burns, Clunie, Glen, Ewen, Little, Davidson, Wishart, Hather

KILMARNOCK: J. Brown, Collins, Watson, R. Stewart, Toner, McKay, H. Brown, Henaughen, McBride, Black, Burns

Attendance: 14,000　　　*Referee:* W. M. Syme

Kilmarnock destroyed Aberdeen's League Cup hopes. A puerile performance leads to the Dons' third home defeat of the season.

Wednesday, 27 August

HIBERNIAN (1) 4　　　ABERDEEN (1) 2
　Preston (54), Baker　　Little (28), Kelly (53)
　3 (12, 63, 77)

HIBERNIAN: Leslie, Grant, McClelland, Turnbull, Paterson, Baxter, McLeod, Aitken, Baker, Preston, Ormond

ABERDEEN: Morrison, Clydesdale, Hogg, Burns, Clunie, Glen, Ewen, Little, Kelly, Wishart, Hather

　　　　　　　　　Referee: G. Bowman

Aberdeen gave as good as they got – but they didn't have Joe Baker.

Saturday, 30 August

FALKIRK (1) 1　　　ABERDEEN (1) 1
　Haughey (33)　　　Wishart (43)

FALKIRK: Slater, Richmond, Lachlan, Wright, Thomson, Moran, Murray, Grierson, McCole, Haughey, Sinclair

ABERDEEN: Morrison, Clydesdale, Hogg, Burns, Glen, Brownlee, Ewen, Little, Kelly, Wishart, Hather

Attendance: 6,000　　　*Referee:* J. Stewart

A dreadful match. It was end of season stuff – in August.

Section 4

	P	W	D	L	F	A	Pts
Kilmarnock	6	4	0	2	12	6	8
Hibernian	6	4	0	2	14	10	8
ABERDEEN	6	2	1	3	11	11	5
Falkirk	6	1	1	4	7	17	3

SCOTTISH CUP

1st Round Saturday, 31 January

ABERDEEN (0) 2　　　EAST FIFE (1) 1
　Davidson (62), Little (86)　McIvor (42)

ABERDEEN: Martin, Walker, Clydesdale, Logie, Clunie, Glen, Little, Davidson, Baird, Wishart, Hather

EAST FIFE: McCluskey, Stirrat, Stewart, Adam, Christie, Bryce, Boyd, Ross, Duchart, Reilly, McIvor

Attendance: 14,000　　　*Referee:* G. Mitchell

East Fife were relegated last season and are in mid-table this. They still gave Aberdeen a desperate run for their money, leading at half-time. Sammy Stewart had a fine game at 39 years of age. Little missed countless chances before securing a late winner off a post.

2nd Round Saturday, 14 February

ABERDEEN (1) 3　　　ARBROATH (0) 0
　Davidson (15), Baird
　(51), Hather (73)

ABERDEEN: Martin, Clydesdale, Hogg, Logie, Clunie, Glen, Ewen, Davidson, Baird, Wishart, Hather

ARBROATH: Williamson, McLevy, Sinclair, Brown, Young, McLean, McIntosh, Anderson, Easson, Stephen, Quinn

Attendance: 15,600　　　*Referee:* G. Bowman

Arbroath are fighting for promotion from Division Two. Aberdeen might have found matters more difficult had not Arbroath's Easson missed his first penalty of the season, after he had been fouled by Clydesdale. His spot-kick hit a post. McIntosh also headed against the Dons' bar at 1-0.

3rd Round Saturday, 28 February

ST JOHNSTONE (0) 1　　　ABERDEEN (0) 2
　Carr (60)　　　　　　Davidson (75),
　　　　　　　　　　　Wishart (82)

ST JOHNSTONE: Taylor, Reid, Hawthorne, Brown, Valentine, Docherty, Liddell, Walker, McInnes, Anderson, Carr

ABERDEEN: Martin, Walker, Hogg, Davidson, Clunie, Glen, Ewen, Little, Baird, Wishart, Hather

Attendance: 14,000　　　*Referee:* G. Mitchell

Aberdeen's third Cup opponents from the Second Division. Carr's spectacular diving header for St Johnstone looked to be sending Aberdeen out of the Cup. But no sooner had Davidson switched to centre forward than he put the finishing touch to Wishart's shot to keep Aberdeen afloat. They would have been sunk again had Anderson's shot gone in instead of rebounding from a post. But the last word belonged to Wishart. Denied being credited with the first goal, he powered in a second which required no help from anybody.

Quarter Final Saturday 14 March

ABERDEEN (2) 3　　　KILMARNOCK (1) 1
　Little (19), Davidson (22),　Mays (29)
　Hather (87)

ABERDEEN: Morrison, Walker, Hogg, Burns, Clunie, Glen, Little, Davidson, Baird, Wishart, Hather

KILMARNOCK: Brown, Watson, McKay, Beattie, Dougan, Stewart, Mays, McBride, Wentzel, Black, Burns

Attendance: 19,000　　　*Referee:* J. A. Mowat

Ten days earlier the two teams had fought out a hectic 2-2 league draw at Pittodrie. In the Cup all the action was concentrated in a ten-minute first-half spell. Little's fine header put Aberdeen in front. After Davidson had added a second, Clunie was harshly adjudged to have fouled McBride. Mays' penalty hit the top of the bar, but a few minutes later the same player did score despite a linesman's raised flag. An Aberdeen supporter had to be removed from the pitch. At the finish Watson miskicked to allow Hather to dribble round Brown.

Semi Final (Hampden) Saturday, 4 April
THIRD LANARK (1) 1   ABERDEEN (1) 1
  Dick (2)   Davidson (15)
THIRD LANARK: Ramage, Caldwell, Brown, Kelly, McCallum, Robb, Hilley, Craig, Dick, Gray, Christie
ABERDEEN: Martin, Clydesdale, Hogg, Caldwell, Clunie, Glen, Ewen, Burns, Davidson, Wishart, Hather
Attendance: 25,000   *Referee:* W. Brittle
Caldwell made a gift of a goal to Dick inside ninety seconds. After a cross came back off a post the Dons' player turned the ball right into the path of the Third's leader. Fortunately a rocket left-foot equaliser by Davidson calmed the Dons' nerves. After the turnaround Kelly's 25-yard drive cracked against Aberdeen's bar, and thereafter a firm rearguard action kept them alive.

Semi Final Replay (Ibrox) Wednesday, 8 April
THIRD LANARK (0) 0   ABERDEEN (1) 1
                            Davidson (35)
THIRD LANARK: Ramage, Caldwell, Brown, Kelly, McCallum, Robb, Hilley, Goodfellow, Dick, Craig, McInnes
ABERDEEN: Martin, Caldwell, Hogg, Burns, Clunie, Glen, Ewen, Little, Davidson, Wishart, Hather
Attendance: 17,500   *Referee:* W. Brittle
Third Lanark skipper Jock Brown won the toss and elected to play against the wind and rain. Davidson controlled Little's pass and swept the ball past Ramage. Fifteen minutes from time Hather side-footed the ball over a gaping goal when he could have settled Aberdeen's nerves. The Dons, second fiddle for much of the first match, were indubitably worthy winners of the second.

Scottish Cup Final (Hampden) Saturday, 25 April
ST MIRREN (1) 3   ABERDEEN (0) 1
  Bryceland (43), Miller   Baird (89)
  (65), Baker (76)
ST MIRREN: Walker, Lapsley, Wilson, Neilson, McGugan, Leishman, Rodger, Bryceland, Baker, Gemmell, Miller
ABERDEEN: Martin, Caldwell, Hogg, Brownlee, Clunie, Glen, Ewen, Davidson, Baird, Wishart, Hather
Attendance: 108,591   *Referee:* J. A. Mowat
St Mirren are the only team beaten twice by Aberdeen in the league. But the Saints have been transformed since the arrival of Gerry Baker from Motherwell. An exhibition of cycle-racing preceded the match. Just before half-time Bryceland was unmarked to head

Gemmell's cross past Martin. Caldwell had already been reduced to hobbling on the wing, forcing Hather's withdrawal into defence. Aberden posed little threat to St Mirren's goal. The Cup was won when Bryceland's shot was parried by Martin but rolled across goal for Miller to net. Baker produced number three and Baird scored a late consolation for Aberdeen.

1958-59

APPEARANCES	League	League Cup	Scottish Cup
Glen	33	6	7
Wishart	32	6	7
Hogg	32	6	6
Hather	29	6	7
Little	29	6	4
Clunie	28	5	7
Ewen	26	5	5
Baird	25		5
Clydesdale	24	2	3
Morrison	23	6	1
Burns	21	6	3
Davidson	19	4	7
Martin	8		6
Caldwell	8	2	3
J. Walker	7	2	3
Logie	5		2
Brownlee	5	1	1
Gibson	4		
Mulhall	4	1	
Ogston	3		
Paterson	2		
Patience	2		
A. Walker	2		
Kelly	1	2	
McInnes	1		
Cooper	1		
26 players			

GOALS	Total	League	League Cup	Scottish Cup
Little	16	13	1	2
Baird	14	12		2
Wishart	13	8	4	1
Davidson	12	5	1	6
Hather	11	7	2	2
Ewen	8	8		
Glen	7	7		
Mulhall	3	1	2	
Clydesdale	1	1		
Clunie	1	1		
Kelly	1		1	
Total	87	63	11	13

Season 1959-60

1959-60 was, without doubt, Aberdeen's most miserable season since the War. Before the season was three months old Davie Shaw had stepped down as manager, to be replaced by Tommy Pearson who had played for Aberdeen not so long before. If two managers in one season suggested that all was not well, the use of seven goalkeepers by the time of Pearson's appointment could only indicate a chronic instability in defence. There were also strong rumours of disaffection among the playing staff.

The season had, ironically, so much for the Pittodrie support to look forward to. In October, during a friendly match with Luton Town, the stadium's floodlights were switched on for the first time. But the months that followed provided nothing except a relentless grind against relegation. The previous season that fate had been staved off by winning at Ibrox in the final game. Now Aberdeen were once again inside the bottom two with just four games to play. But who would have believed it? All four were won and Aberdeen were spared again.

Even so, Aberdeen's league position had deteriorated year by year since becoming champions in 1955. They dropped to 2nd in 1956; 6th in 1957; 12th in 1958; 13th in 1959 . . . and were now 15th. Aberdeen's standing had never been lower at any other time since the War. Their forwards scored the club's fewest number of goals in ten years: their defenders conceded more than in any season since the War bar one (1957-58).

Nor was there any respite in the two cup competitions. There were home defeats by Hearts and Kilmarnock in the League Cup; while in the Scottish Cup Aberdeen had the devil of a job to see off tiny Brechin City. Having done so they were beaten at home by Clyde.

League: Fifteenth
League Cup: Second in qualifying group
Scottish Cup: Second Round

SCOTTISH LEAGUE DIVISION ONE

No 1 Wednesday, 19 August
HIBERNIAN (0) 2   ABERDEEN (0) 1
  Baker 2 (49, 88)   Mulhall (73)
HIBERNIAN: Wilson, Grant, Young, Preston, Plenderleith, Baxter, Scott, Fox, Baker, Aitken, Ormond
ABERDEEN: Ogston, Caldwell, Hogg, Brownlee, Clunie, Glen, McCall, Little, Baird, Wishart, Mulhall

P W D L F A Pts
1 0 0 1 1 2 0   *Referee:* P. Fitzpatrick

Billy Little limped on the wing for the last 25 minutes. Mulhall scored and also hit a post, but that was all Aberdeen had to offer in a disappointing opening fixture.

No 2 Saturday, 5 September
ABERDEEN (0) 0   DUNDEE (1) 3
                           Cousin (10), Waddell
                           (50), Hill (85)
ABERDEEN: Martin, Clydesdale, Hogg, Brownlee, Clunie, Glen, Ewen, Burns, Baird, Wishart, Mulhall
DUNDEE: Liney, Hamilton, Cox, Henderson, McMillan, Cowie, Hill, Cousin, Waddell, McGeachie, Robertson

P W D L F A Pts
2 0 0 2 1 5 0   *Referee:* A. Crossman

Aberdeen's injury crisis worsens, and the season is not yet a month old. In the twelfth minute Fred Martin broke his jaw in a collision with Waddell. Hugh Baird went in goal and saved a Cowie penalty.

No 3 Saturday, 12 September
DUNFERMLINE   ABERDEEN (1) 3
  ATHLETIC (1) 1   Glen (11), Little (57),
  Dickson (21)   Mulhall (59)
DUNFERMLINE: McAulay, Thomson, Sweeney, Bain, Colville, Mailer, Peebles, Williamson, Dickson, Smith, Melrose
ABERDEEN: McBride, Cadenhead, Hogg, Burns, Clunie, Glen, Ewen, Little, Baird, Wishart, Mulhall

P	W	D	L	F	A	Pts
3	1	0	2	4	6	2

Referee: G. Mitchell

The Dons' first league points arrive, courtesy of outstanding showings by Glen and Mulhall.

No 4 Saturday, 19 September
ABERDEEN (2) 5   PARTICK THISTLE (2) 2
  Baird 2 (10, 37), Little   Smith (33), Fleming (40)
  (52), Clunie 2 (73, 77)
ABERDEEN: McBride, Cadenhead, Hogg, Burns, Clunie, Glen, Ewen, Little, Baird, Wishart, Mulhall
PARTICK: Freebairn, Hogan, Baird, Harvey, Davidson, Donlevy, Smith, McParland, Thomson, Brown, Fleming

P	W	D	L	F	A	Pts
4	2	0	2	9	8	4

Referee: R. Morris

Partick come to Aberdeen having conceded only one goal in their opening three games. Aberdeen's hero is Jim Clunie, who was taken off injured in the first half – but who returned to score twice in the second.

No 5 Saturday, 26 September
AIRDRIEONIANS (1) 1   ABERDEEN (0) 0
  Duncan (10)
AIRDRIE: Wallace, Watson, Miller, Quinn, Baillie, Johnston, Duncan, Rankine, Sharkey, Storrie, G. Ormond
ABERDEEN: Ogston, Cadenhead, Hogg, Burns, Glen, Wishart, Ewen, Little, Baird, Kelly, Mulhall

P	W	D	L	F	A	Pts
5	2	0	3	9	9	4

Referee: T. Alexander

Airdrie had only one point from four matches. Aberdeen experimented with Bernie Kelly – ex-Nottingham Forest – but he was short of match practice.

No 6 Saturday, 3 October
ABERDEEN (1) 3   ST MIRREN (0) 1
  Wishart 2 (15, 50), Baird Riddell (83 pen)
  (62)
ABERDEEN: Ogston, Cadenhead, Hogg, Burns, Clunie, Glen, Ewen, Little, Baird, Wishart, Hather
ST MIRREN: Forsyth, Wilson, Riddell, Leishman, McGugan, Gragal, Rodger, Gemmell, Baker, Laird, Miller

P	W	D	L	F	A	Pts
6	3	0	3	12	10	6

Referee: W. L. Fyfe

Mulhall was absent, playing and scoring for Scotland against Northern Ireland in Belfast. Without him,

Aberdeen still gain emphatic revenge for their Cup Final defeat, though St Mirren lost Laird with a broken leg. Glen missed a penalty for Aberdeen.

No 7 Saturday, 10 October
CELTIC (1) 1   ABERDEEN (0) 1
  Conway (24)   Baird (80)
CELTIC: Fallon, Curran, Mochan, Smith, Evans, Clark, Chalmers, Jackson, Conway, Peacock, Auld
ABERDEEN: Ogston, Cadenhead, Hogg, Burns, Clunie, Glen, Ewen, Little, Baird, Wishart, Mulhall

P	W	D	L	F	A	Pts	
7	3	1	3	13	11	7	*Attendance:* 25,000

Referee: F. S. Crossley

Conway controlled the ball with his arm before scoring – which the referee did not see. Baird diverted Little's cross for an unexpected equaliser.

No 8 Saturday, 17 October
KILMARNOCK (1) 2   ABERDEEN (0) 0
  Black 2 (30, 68 pen)
KILMARNOCK: J. Brown, Watson, McKay, Beattie, Toner, O'Connor, H. Brown, Henaughen, McBride, Black, Horne
ABERDEEN: Ogston, Cadenhead, Hogg, Brownlee, McConnachie, Glen, Ewen, Davidson, Baird, Wishart, Mulhall

P	W	D	L	F	A	Pts
8	3	1	4	13	13	7

Referee: J. A. Mowat

In a heavy downpour Glen and Toner collide after 15 seconds. Glen is taken to hospital with a leg injury and will never be the same player again. Aberdeen have now called upon 23 players this season.

No 9 Saturday, 24 October
ABERDEEN (0) 0   RANGERS (1) 5
          Brand (20), Millar (49),
          Scott 2 (50, 85),
          McMillan (70)
ABERDEEN: Russell, Cadenhead, Hogg, Baird, McConnachie, Brownlee, Ewen, Little, Davidson, Wishart, Mulhall
RANGERS: Niven, Shearer, Caldow, Davis, Paterson, Stevenson, Scott, McMillan, Millar, Brand, Matthew

P	W	D	L	F	A	Pts	
9	3	1	5	13	18	7	*Attendance:* 20,000

Referee: W. L. Fyfe

Rangers lie second. A white ball was used and a white flag raised by Aberdeen. This time it is George Mulhall's turn to be stretchered off.

No 10 Saturday, 31 October
CLYDE (2) 7   ABERDEEN (1) 2
  Haddock (24 pen), White Kelly (22 pen), Little
  (34), Boyd (53),   (55)
  A. Wilson (58), Coyle (70),
  Currie (79), Herd (82)
CLYDE: Thomson, Haddock, T. Wilson, White, Sim, McPhail, A. Wilson, Herd, Coyle, Currie, Boyd
ABERDEEN: Yule, Caldwell, Hogg, Burns, Clunie, Brownlee, Baird, Kelly, Little, Wishart, Hather

Bottom positions

	P	W	D	L	F	A	Pts
14 Dunfermline	10	3	2	5	29	28	8
15 ABERDEEN	10	3	1	6	15	25	7
16 Stirling Albion	10	2	2	6	13	20	6
17 Airdrie	10	2	1	7	13	33	5
18 Arbroath	10	1	1	8	8	37	3

Referee: J. A. S. Bissett

The future looks black for the Dons after this second-half capitulation at Shawfield. Twelve goals have been lost in two games. Only four Clyde players failed to score – and all this after Aberdeen had drawn first blood.

No 11 Saturday, 7 November

MOTHERWELL (1) 3   ABERDEEN (0) 1
    St John (3), Quinn (66),   Baird (46)
    McCann (68)

MOTHERWELL: Mackin, McSeveney, Forrest, Aitken, Martis, McCann, Strachan, Quinn, St John, Hunter, Weir

ABERDEEN: Harker, Caldwell, Hogg, Burns, Clunie, Kinnell, Ewen, Little, Baird, Wishart, Sim

P W D L F A Pts
11 3 1 7 16 28 7   *Referee:* T. Wharton

Rumours of unrest among the players are sweeping Pittodrie. Chris Harker makes his debut in goal after signing from Newcastle. He is the seventh goalkeeper Aberdeen have used so far this season. George Kinnell and Gordon Sim also make their debuts. But Ian St John still sinks Aberdeen.

No 12 Saturday, 14 November

ABERDEEN (1) 3   THIRD LANARK (1) 1
    Clunie 2 (35 pen, 89 pen),   Fraser (27)
    Davidson (49)

ABERDEEN: Harker, Caldwell, Hogg, Baird, Clunie, Kinnell, Little, Kelly, Davidson, Wishart, Hather

THIRD LANARK: Robertson, Smith, Brown, Reilly, Cosker, Cunningham, Harley, Goodfellow, Boyle, Gray, Fraser

P W D L F A Pts   *Attendance:* 8,000
12 4 1 7 19 29 9   *Referee:* T. Alexander

Both Aberdeen and Third Lanark had lost their last four games. Third Lanark have now lost their last five. A few days later David Shaw reverts to being club trainer and Tommy Pearson is appointed team manager.

No 13 Saturday, 21 November

ABERDEEN (1) 1   HEARTS (1) 3
    Davidson (17)   Hamilton (11), Crawford
                (60), Young (81)

ABERDEEN: Harker, Sang, Hogg, Baird, Clunie, Burns, Little, McKenzie, Davidson, Wishart, Hather

HEARTS: Marshall, Kirk, Thomson, Bowman, Cumming, Higgins, Crawford, Murray, Young, Blackwood, Hamilton

P W D L F A Pts
13 4 1 8 20 32 9   *Referee:* G. Bowman

Leaders Hearts have dropped only two points from 12 games. They looked a well-oiled team – their only damage being self-inflicted when Marshall dropped the ball at Davidson's feet.

No 14 Saturday, 28 November

RAITH ROVERS (1) 5   ABERDEEN (0) 1
    Urquhart (19), Wallace   Wishart (89)
    (67), Spence (69), Conn
    2 (74, 76)

RAITH: Drummond, Polland, Mochan, Young, McNaught, Baxter, Wallace, Conn, Kerray, Spence, Urquhart

ABERDEEN: Ogston, Sang, Hogg, Baird, Clunie, Burns, McKenzie, Wishart, Little, Kelly, Hather

Bottom positions

	P	W	D	L	F	A	Pts
15 Dunfermline	14	4	2	8	37	39	10
16 ABERDEEN	14	4	1	9	21	37	9
17 Stirling Albion	14	2	4	8	18	28	8
18 Arbroath	14	2	1	11	11	49	5

Referee: E. F. Cowan

This is Raith's sixth straight win. Inspired by Jim Baxter they slaughter Aberdeen and stay on Hearts' shoulder at the top of the league.

No 15 Saturday, 5 December

ABERDEEN (0) 3   STIRLING ALBION (1) 1
    Little (50), Clunie   Colquhoun (4)
    (60 pen), Ewen (89)

ABERDEEN: Ogston, Hogg, Sim, Baird, Clunie, Kinnell, Ewen, Wishart, Davidson, Little, Mulhall

STIRLING: Morrison, McKechie, Pettigrew, Bell, Little, Pierson, Colquhoun, Sinclair, Gilmour, Glancy, McPhee

P W D L F A Pts   *Attendance:* 6,000
15 5 1 9 24 38 11   *Referee:* W. M. Syme

Stirling Albion's train breaks down and there is a near-riot at Pittodrie when admission money is not returned. To placate the crowd Aberdeen stage a 5-a-side match including an Indian player by the name of Mascarenhas. Finally Stirling arrive, the game kicks off at 4.10 and the visitors lead by a Colquhoun goal for half the match.

No 16 Saturday, 12 December

ABERDEEN (0) 0   ARBROATH (0) 0

ABERDEEN: Ogston, Hogg, Sim, Baird, Clunie, Kinnell, Ewen, Wishart, Davidson, Little, Mulhall

ARBROATH: Williamson, McLevy, Young, Brown, Fraser, Wright, Shirreffs, Dunn, Easson, Grierson, Quinn

P W D L F A Pts   *Attendance:* 6,000
16 5 2 9 24 38 12   *Referee:* R. H. Davidson

Having taken two points off Stirling, Aberdeen want two more off basement-club Arbroath. But not even the sending off of Wright 17 minutes from time could lift Aberdeen out of their trough.

No 17 Saturday, 19 December
AYR UNITED (1) 2   ABERDEEN (0) 1
   Price (34), Paton (58)   Davidson (56)
AYR: Hamilton, Burn, Paterson, McIntyre, McLean,
Telfer, Fulton, McMillan, Price, Paton, McGhee
ABERDEEN: Ogston, Hogg, Sim, Baird, Clunie,
Kinnell, Brownlee, Little, Davidson, Wishart, Mulhall
P W D L F A Pts
17 5 2 10 25 40 12   *Referee:* D. McTaggart
Ayr – a man short from the 53rd minute – find that no
handicap in beating the Dons.

No 18 Saturday, 26 December
ABERDEEN (3) 6   HIBERNIAN (2) 4
   Davidson 2 (32, 65),   Ormond (3), Preston (6),
   Mulhall (34), Clunie   Johnstone 2 (73, 85 pen)
   (42 pen), Hather (60),
   Brownlee (82)
ABERDEEN: Ogston, Hogg, Sim, Baird, Clunie,
Kinnell, Brownlee, Little, Davidson, Hather, Mulhall
HIBERNIAN: Wren, Grant, McClelland, Young,
Plenderleith, Baxter, McLeod, Johnstone, Baker,
Preston, Ormond
P W D L F A Pts   *Attendance:* 15,000
18 6 2 10 31 44 14   *Referee:* D. Weir

Hibs were third and provide a Boxing Day feast for
Aberdeen, which is totally inexplicable on their recent
wretched form. Hibs led 2-0 after six minutes and
thereafter were hit for six. The match was a personal
success for Jackie Hather, playing at inside forward
instead of the 'rested' Wishart.

No 19 Friday, 1 January
DUNDEE (1) 4   ABERDEEN (1) 1
Henderson 2 (18, 54),   Davidson (12)
   Robertson (57), Penman
   (70)
DUNDEE: Liney, Hamilton, Cox, Gabriel, Smith,
Cowie, Penman, McGeachie, Cousin, Henderson,
Robertson
ABERDEEN: Ogston, Hogg, Sim, Baird, Clunie,
Kinnell, Brownlee, Little, Davidson, Hather, Mulhall
P W D L F A Pts
19 6 2 11 32 48 14   *Referee:* J. Stewart
Aberdeen folded up in the latter stages. Cowie missed
his second penalty against Aberdeen this season.

No 20 Saturday, 2 January
ABERDEEN (0) 1   DUNFERMLINE
   Davidson (50)   ATHLETIC (1) 1
                          Dickson (18)
ABERDEEN: Ogston, Hogg, Sim, Baird, Clunie,
Kinnell, Brownlee, Hosie, Davidson, Hather, Mulhall
DUNFERMLINE: Connachan, Fraser, Miller,
Rattray, Williamson, Mailer, Peebles, Benvie, Dickson,
Smith, Melrose
P W D L F A Pts
20 6 3 11 33 49 15   *Referee:* J. Holburn

Dunfermline are two points worse off than Aberdeen.
The Dons' equaliser came out of nothing. Brownlee –
well offside – had a shot blocked. So did Hosie with his
follow-up effort. But Davidson finally forced the ball
over the line past flailing defenders.

No 21 Saturday, 9 January
PARTICK THISTLE (1) 1   ABERDEEN (0) 0
   Nimmo (40)
PARTICK: Freebairn, Brown, Baird, Wright, Harvey,
Donlevy, Fleming, Smith, Nimmo, McParland, Devine
ABERDEEN: Ogston, Caldwell, Hogg, Baird, Clunie,
Kinnell, Little, Hosie, Davidson, Brownlee, Mulhall
Bottom positions
                     P W D L F A Pts
14 Third Lanark   21 7 1 13 42 53 15
15 ABERDEEN   21 6 3 12 33 50 15
16 Dunfermline   21 4 6 11 49 57 14
17 Stirling Albion   21 3 6 12 27 39 12
18 Arbroath   21 4 3 14 25 64 11
                     Referee: R. D. Minto
Norman Davidson twice hit the Thistle bar in the
second half, first with a header, then with a shot.
Aberdeen are relieved to learn that Stirling and
Arbroath also lost.

No 22 Saturday, 16 January
ABERDEEN (1) 2   AIRDRIEONIANS (2) 2
   Hather (34), Clunie   Baillie 2 (12, 24)
   (75 pen)
ABERDEEN: Martin, Caldwell, Hogg, Baird, Clunie,
Kinnell, Little, Burns, Davidson, Mulhall, Hather
AIRDRIE: Thomson, Miller, Shanks, Quinn, Stewart,
Quigley, Sharkey, McGill, Baillie, Rankin, Duncan
P W D L F A Pts   *Attendance:* 8,000
22 6 4 12 35 52 16   *Referee:* W. D. Massie
2-0 down at one stage – both goals gifted by Martin on
his return – then suggests a barren afternoon for
Aberdeen. But Thomson then lets the ball slip through
his legs to Hather – 2-1. Stewart then needlessly
bundled Davidson off the ball when Thomson had
gathered it. Penalty!

No 23 Saturday, 23 January
ST MIRREN (1) 3   ABERDEEN (0) 0
   Gemmell (11), Miller (51),
   McTurk (67 pen)
ST MIRREN: Walker, McTurk, Wilson, McGugan,
Tierney, Riddell, Rodger, Kerrigan, Baker, Gemmell,
Miller
ABERDEEN: Ogston, Sang, Hogg, Baird, Clunie,
Kinnell, Mulhall, Little, Davidson, Wishart, Hather
P W D L F A Pts
23 6 4 13 35 55 16   *Referee:* R. Rodger
St Mirren aren't safe either. Aberdeen's offside tactics
irritate the Paisley crowd. Near the end Clunie had a
penalty saved, but Aberdeen were dead long before
then.

No 24 Saturday, 6 February
ABERDEEN (1) 3   CELTIC (1) 2
  Kinnell (35), Davidson   Mochan 2 (31 pen,
  (53), Brownlee (88)   71 pen)
ABERDEEN: Ogston, Cadenhead, Hogg, Burns, Clunie, Kinnell, Brownlee, Little, Davidson, Wishart, Mulhall
CELTIC: Haffey, McKay, Kennedy, Crerand, Evans, Peacock, Carroll, O'Hara, Byrne, Mochan, Divers

P	W	D	L	F	A	Pts	
24	7	4	13	38	57	18	*Attendance:* 14,000

Referee: J. P. Barclay

Drama at Pittodrie: Kinnell clattered Mochan who scored from the penalty. Kinnell equalised with a shot touched by Haffey. Davidson's thumping header put Aberdeen in front, only for Mochan to be pulled down by Burns – seemingly outside the box – for Mochan to score his second spot kick. Wishart's header then crashes down off the bar. "No goal" said the referee. At the death Brownlee seized on misplaced back-pass.

No 25 Tuesday, 1 March
RANGERS (2) 2   ABERDEEN (1) 2
  Caldow (30 pen),   Wishart (42), Davidson
  McMillan (32)   (48)
RANGERS: Niven, Caldow, Little, Davis, Paterson, Stevenson, Scott, McMillan, Millar, Wilson, Hughes
ABERDEEN: Harker, Kinnell, Hogg, Baird, Clunie, Burns, Cummings, Little, Davidson, Wishart, Mulhall

P	W	D	L	F	A	Pts	
25	7	5	13	40	59	19	*Referee:* W. L. Fyfe

Last season Aberdeen secured their First Division survival by coming from behind at Ibrox in the last match of the season. It looks more difficult this time as Clunie concedes a foolish penalty, grabbing Millar by the leg. McMillan adds a second Rangers goal before Wishart breathes new life into Aberdeen. Davidson's leveller came when his header was blocked by Paterson – but came back to him to drive past Niven.

No 26 Tuesday, 8 March
ABERDEEN (0) 0   CLYDE (0) 2
                        Robertson (59), White
                        (61)
ABERDEEN: Ogston, Kinnell, Hogg, Baird, Coutts, Burns, Little, Cummings, Davidson, Wishart, Mulhall
CLYDE: McCulloch, Walters, Haddock, White, Finlay, Clinton, Wilson, Herd, Coyle, Robertson, Boyd

P	W	D	L	F	A	Pts	
26	7	5	14	40	61	19	*Referee:* T. Alexander

Clyde repeat the score inflicted on Aberdeen in the Scottish Cup last month – even the two goalscorers are the same.

No 27 Saturday, 12 March
ABERDEEN (2) 2   MOTHERWELL (2) 2
  Cummings (9), Little   McPhee (20), St John
  (26)   (25)
ABERDEEN: Harker, Kinnell, Hogg, Baird, Clunie, Burns, Little, Cummings, Davidson, Wishart, Mulhall
MOTHERWELL: H. Weir, Strachan, Reid, Aitken, Martis, McCann, Hunter, Quinn, St John, McPhee, A. Weir

Bottom positions

	P	W	D	L	F	A	Pts
14 St Mirren	25	9	2	14	57	64	20
15 Third Lanark	26	9	2	15	53	65	20
16 ABERDEEN	27	7	6	14	42	63	20
17 Dunfermline	28	4	9	15	58	76	17
18 Arbroath	28	4	6	18	33	81	14

Referee: A. Crossman

All the action was packed into the first quarter of the match. Ian St John continued his unwelcome habit of finding the Dons' net. His header was arguably offside, but Little unleashed a twenty-yarder to cancel it out.

No 28 Saturday, 19 March
THIRD LANARK (1) 2   ABERDEEN (0) 1
  Gray (27), McInnes (65)   Cummings (72)
THIRD LANARK: Robertson, Lewis, Caldwell, Reilly, Robb, Cunningham, Goodfellow, Hilley, Harley, Gray, McInnes
ABERDEEN: Harker, Kinnell, Hogg, Burns, Clunie, Glen, Little, Cummings, Davidson, Wishart, Mulhall

P	W	D	L	F	A	Pts	
28	7	6	15	43	65	20	*Referee:* W. Harvey

Shot-shy Aberdeen don't trouble Thirds. Every time there is a chance to shoot the Dons' forwards release the ball to someone else. Not even the return of Archie Glen after a lengthy lay-off can inject life into his colleagues.

No 29 Tuesday, 22 March
ABERDEEN (0) 0   KILMARNOCK (0) 1
                        Black (86)
ABERDEEN: Harker, Kinnell, Hogg, Burns, Clunie, Glen, Little, Davidson, Baird, Cummings, Mulhall
KILMARNOCK: Brown, Richmond, Watson, Beattie, Toner, Kennedy, Stewart, McInally, Kerr, Black, Wentzel

Bottom positions

	P	W	D	L	F	A	Pts
15 Stirling Albion	29	7	7	15	50	58	21
16 ABERDEEN	29	7	6	16	43	66	20
17 Dunfermline	29	5	9	15	61	78	19
18 Arbroath	29	4	7	18	34	82	15

Attendance: 13,000

Kilmarnock are on an astonishing run, winning seventeen and drawing one of their last eighteen games. Black's goal brought despair to Aberdeen. Clunie intercepted Stewart's cross but the ball broke away to Bertie Black.

No 30 Saturday, 26 March
HEARTS (1) 3   ABERDEEN (0) 0
  McFadzean (22), Bauld
  (83), Crawford (85)

HEARTS: Marshall, Kirk, Thomson, Cumming, Milne, Higgins, Smith, Murray, Bauld, McFadzean, Crawford

ABERDEEN: Harker, Kinnell, Hogg, Burns, Clunie, Glen, Hather, Davidson, Brownlee, Cummings, Mulhall

Bottom positions

	P	W	D	L	F	A	Pts
15 Stirling	30	7	8	15	51	59	22
16 Dunfermline	30	6	9	15	63	78	21
17 ABERDEEN	30	7	6	17	43	69	20
18 Arbroath	30	4	7	19	36	85	15

Referee: J. Blair

League leaders Hearts offer no crumb of comfort to demoralised Aberdeen. The Dons' experiment of using Brownlee as a deep-lying centre-forward never looked like paying off. Aberdeen are now inside the bottom two with just four matches to go.

No 31 Saturday, 2 April
ABERDEEN (2) 4   RAITH ROVERS (1) 2
Little 2 (6, 89), Brownlee   Kinnell o.g. (13), (32), Glen (87)   Wallace (66 pen)
ABERDEEN: Harker, Kinnell, Hogg, Burns, Coutts, Glen, Brownlee, Little, Davidson, Hather, Mulhall
RAITH: Thorburn, Stevenson, Mochan, Young, McGregor, Duffy, Wallace, French, Lawson, Spence, Urquhart

P W D L F A Pts   *Attendance:* 5,000
31 8 6 17 47 71 22   *Referee:* D. McTaggart

Tragedy for George Kinnell when his diving header put Raith level at 1-1 – and for Archie Glen who felled Spence, paving the way for Wallace to net Raith's second equaliser. But all was forgiven when Glen raced on to Little's pass to bag the winner.

No 32 Saturday, 16 April
STIRLING ALBION (0) 0   ABERDEEN (1) 2
    Mulhall 2 (7, 50)
STIRLING: Morrison, McKechie, Pettigrew, Pierson, Little, Johnstone, Rowan, Bonthrone, Hill, Glancy, Colquhoun
ABERDEEN: Harker, Kinnell, Hogg, Burns, Couts, Glen, Brownlee, Little, Baird, Hather, Mulhall

Bottom positions

	P	W	D	L	F	A	Pts
15 Dunfermline	32	8	9	15	65	78	25
16 ABERDEEN	32	9	6	17	49	71	24
17 Stirling Albion	32	7	8	17	53	64	22
18 Arbroath	32	4	7	21	37	97	15

Referee: J. Mackie

This is a match the Dons dare not lose. Archie Glen won the toss and elected to play down the slope. A corner was not properly cleared and Mulhall fired in Aberdeen's first goal. His second, was followed by a spell of frantic Stirling assaults, but Aberdeen's defence stood firm.

No 33 Saturday, 23 April
ARBROATH (1) 1   ABERDEEN (1) 3
  Shirreffs (41 pen)   Davidson 2 (20, 89),   Little (82)
ARBROATH: Williamson, McLevy, Young, Crawford, Fraser, Wright, Souter, Dunn, Easson, Grierson, Shirreffs
ABERDEEN: Harker, Kinnell, Hogg, Burns, Coutes, Glen, Brownlee, Little, Davidson, Hather, Mulhall
P W D L F A Pts
33 10 6 17 52 72 26   *Referee:* E. F. Cowan

More important to the Dons than this grimly-fought win, secured only in the dying minutes, was Stirling's defeat at Dundee. Aberdeen are now safe.

No 34 Saturday, 30 April
ABERDEEN (1) 2   AYR UNITED (0) 0
  Little (24),
  Brownlee (89)
ABERDEEN: Harker, Cadenhead, Hogg, Burns, Coutts, Wishart, Brownlee, Little, Fraser, Davidson, Hather
AYR: Hamilton, Burn, Thomson, Elliot, Paterson, Telfer, McIntyre, McMillan, Price, Fulton, McGhee
Attendance: 8,000   *Referee:* H. McClintock

How odd: Aberdeen end the season with eight points from four games. But this was a spring stroll. And Ayr couldn't care less.

Aberdeen's complete home and away record:

HOME						AWAY						
P	W	D	L	F	A		W	D	L	F	A	Pts
34	8	4	5	35	32		3	2	12	19	40	28

Scottish League Division One 1959-60

	P	W	D	L	F	A	Pts
1 Hearts	34	23	8	3	102	51	54
2 Kilmarnock	34	24	2	8	67	45	50
3 Rangers	34	17	8	9	72	38	42
4 Dundee	34	16	10	8	70	49	42
5 Motherwell	34	16	8	10	71	61	40
6 Clyde	34	15	9	10	77	69	39
7 Hibernian	34	14	7	13	106	85	35
8 Ayr United	34	14	6	14	65	73	34
9 Celtic	34	12	9	13	73	59	33
10 Partick Thistle	34	14	4	16	54	78	32
11 Raith Rovers	34	14	3	17	64	62	31
12 Third Lanark	34	13	4	17	75	83	30
13 Dunfermline	34	10	9	15	72	80	29
14 St Mirren	34	11	6	17	78	86	28
15 ABERDEEN	34	11	6	17	54	72	28
16 Airdrieonians	34	11	6	17	56	80	28
17 Stirling Albion	34	7	8	19	55	72	22
18 Arbroath	34	4	7	23	38	106	15

LEAGUE CUP
Saturday, 8 August
ABERDEEN (1) 3   STIRLING ALBION (0) 1
  Brownlee (4), Ewen (52),   Gilmour (86)
  Mulhall (53)

ABERDEEN: Martin, Caldwell, Hogg, Brownlee, Clunie, Glen, Ewen, Little, Baird, Wishart, Mulhall
STIRLING: Smith, Hailstones, Pettigrew, McKechie, Sinclair, Pierson, Colquhoun, Grant, Gilmour, Benvie, McPhee

Attendance: 18,000   *Referee:* W. Brittle

David Shaw brings in Little and Mulhall for the new season, omitted from the Scottish Cup Final.

Wednesday, 12 August
HEARTS (1) 2   ABERDEEN (2) 2
Wardhaugh (35), Crawford   Wishart (2), Baird (12)
(52)

HEARTS: Marshall, Kirk, Thomson, Fraser, Milne, Cumming, Hamilton, Blackwood, Bauld, Wardhaugh, Crawford
ABERDEEN: Ogston, Caldwell, Hogg, Burns, Clunie, Brownlee, Ewen, Little, Baird, Wishart, Mulhall

Attendance: 25,000   *Referee:* H. Phillips

Hearts are the League Cup holders. Fast open football, with a draw the proper result.

Saturday, 15 August
KILMARNOCK (2) 2   ABERDEEN (1) 3
McInally (21), Wentzel   Mulhall (19), Wishart
(35)   (48), Ewen (82)

KILMARNOCK: Brown, Watson, Cook, R. Stewart, Dougan, Kennedy, Copeland, McInally, Wentzel, Black, McPike
ABERDEEN: Ogston, Caldwell, Hogg, Brownlee, Clunie, Glen, Ewen, Little, Baird, Wishart, Mulhall

Referee: W. M. Syme

It is good to see Aberdeen fighting back. They lost a lead, but then impressively reclaimed it.

Saturday, 22 August
STIRLING ALBION (0) 2   ABERDEEN (3) 5
Sinclair (83 pen),   McKenzie (8), Glen (11),
Simpson (90)   Ewen 2 (17, 89),
                           Davidson (88)

STIRLING: McCallum, Hailstones, Pettigrew, Pierson, Sinclair, Johnstone, Grant, Benvie, Simpson, Spence, McPhee
ABERDEEN: Martin, Caldwell, Hogg, Brownlee, Clunie, Glen, Ewen, McKenzie, Davidson, Wishart, Mulhall

Referee: J. Blair

Aberdeen were cruising when the game exploded into life with four goals in the final seven minutes. The Dons are now ready for their showdown with Hearts.

Wednesday, 26 August
ABERDEEN (0) 1   HEARTS (2) 4
Glen (80 pen)   Bauld 2 (2, 12),
                          Blackwood (55),
                          Smith (60)

ABERDEEN: Ogston, Caldwell, Hogg, Brownlee, Clunie, Glen, Ewen, Baird, Davidson, Wishart, Mulhall

HEARTS: Marshall, Kirk, Thomson, Bowman, Milne, Cumming, Smith, Murray, Bauld, Blackwood, Hamilton

Attendance: 31,000   *Referee:* T. Wharton

What a let down: Aberdeen were clinically dissected. Hugh Baird is taking most of the brickbats for Aberdeens' poor form.

Saturday, 29 August
ABERDEEN (0) 2   KILMARNOCK (2) 4
Ewen (72), Watson o.g.   McBride (19),
(87)   Henaughan (40), Burns
                           (46), McInally (70)

ABERDEEN: Low, Caldwell, Hogg, Burns, McConnachie, Glen, Ewen, McKenzie, Baird, Wishart, Mulhall
KILMARNOCK: Brown, Watson, Cook, Stewart, Dougan, O'Connor, Copeland, McInally, McBride, Henaughen, Burns

Referee: W. D. Massie

Buckie Thistle goalkeeper John Low kept goal for Aberdeen, and he alone is blameless for this further humiliating defeat.

Section 3

	P	W	D	L	F	A	Pts
Hearts	6	4	2	0	16	6	10
ABERDEEN	6	3	1	2	16	15	7
Kilmarnock	6	2	1	3	13	13	5
Stirling Albion	6	0	2	4	8	19	2

SCOTTISH CUP

1st Round Saturday, 30 January
ABERDEEN (0) 0   BRECHIN CITY (0) 0

ABERDEEN: Harker, Clydesdale, Hogg, Burns, Clunie, Kinnell, Baird, Little, Davidson, Wishart, Mulhall
BRECHIN: Edmiston, Simpson, Hodge, Stewart, Bowie, Smith, Russell, Thoms, McIntosh, Donachie, McGuire

Attendance: 12,000   *Referee:* G. Bowman

Brechin lie midway inside the Second Division, but obtain an insultingly easy draw. In the closing stages Brechin's part-time players were pressing strongly for the winner. Aberdeen's best chance came when Edmiston turned Davidson's header against a post.

1st Round Replay Wednesday, 3 February
BRECHIN CITY (2) 3 3   ABERDEEN (1) 3 6 (after
McGuire (17), McIntosh   extra time)
(33), Russell (62)   Davidson 5 (10, 55, 79,
                         98, 100), Brownlee (94)

BRECHIN: Edmiston, Simpson, Hodge, Stewart, Bowie, Smith, Russell, Thoms, McIntosh, Warrender, McGuire
ABERDEEN: Harker, Cadenhead, Hogg, Burns, Clunie, Kinnell, Brownlee, Little, Davidson, Baird, Mulhall

Attendance: 4,300   *Referee:* G. Bowman

It was only in extra time that Aberdeen's extra strength began to tell. Without the massive contribution of Davidson – who scored five times – Aberdeen may have fallen by the wayside. When Russell put Brechin 3-2 up with less than half an hour left the omens looked dark, but Baird placed a free kick onto Davidson's head to take the tie into extra time.

2nd Round Saturday, 13 February
ABERDEEN (0) 0   CLYDE (1) 2
                        White (2), Robertson (51)
ABERDEEN: Ogston, Cadenhead, Hogg, Baird, Clunie, Kinnell, Hather, Little, Davidson, Wishart, Mulhall
CLYDE: McCulloch, Walters, Haddock, White, Finlay, Clinton, Wilson, Herd, McLaughlin, Robertson, Boyd
Attendance: 15,000   *Referee:* G. Mitchell
On a white pitch Clyde stun Pittodrie within two minutes. McLaughlin's shot came back to White who drove into the far corner past a rooted Ogston. Aberdeen pressed heartily, but were sunk by Robertson's goal after the break.

1959-60
APPEARANCES

	League	League Cup	Scottish Cup
Hogg	34	6	3
Little	30	3	3
Baird	28	5	3
Mulhall	27	6	3
Clunie	26	5	3
Wishart	24	6	2
Davidson	23	2	3
Burns	22	2	2
Kinnell	21		3
Brownlee	16	5	1
Ogston	16	3	1
Hather	15		1
Glen	14	5	
Harker	12		2

1959-60
APPEARANCES

	League	League Cup	Scottish Cup
Ewen	11	6	
Cadenhead	9		2
Sim	7		
Caldwell	6	6	
Cummings	6		
Coutts	5		
Kelly	4		
Sang	3		
McKenzie	2	2	
Martin	2	2	
McConnachie	2	1	
Hosie	2		
McBride	2		
Clydesdale	1		1
McCall	1		
Russell	1		
Yule	1		
Fraser	1		
Low		1	
33 players			

GOALS

	Total	League	League Cup	Scottish Cup
Davidson	17	11	1	5
Little	9	9		
Clunie	7	7		
Mulhall	7	5	2	
Baird	6	5	1	
Brownlee	6	4	1	1
Wishart	6	4	2	
Ewen	6	1	5	
Glen	4	2	2	
Cummings	2	2		
Hather	2	2		
Kelly	1	1		
Kinnell	1	1		
McKenzie	1		1	
own goals	1		1	
Total	76	54	16	6

Season 1962-63. Back row: McMillan, Coutts, Bennett, Law, Allan, Smith. Front row: Callaghan, Donald, Cadenhead, Wilson and Turnbull.

Season 1960-61

1960-61 was the year Aberdeen rung the changes. New manager Tommy Pearson heralded the end of the old guard – Clunie, Glen and Hather – and the introduction of teenage replacements, most notably Charlie Cooke. There was no joy for Aberdeen in the League Cup, but there was a distinct improvement in league performances. Following a defeat in their opening league fixture Aberdeen went the next eleven games unbeaten, becoming the draw specialists of Scottish football. By the New Year Aberdeen were in second position, seven points behind Rangers.

But the Dons' season effectively ended on 25 February. Jock Stein's Dunfermline crushed Aberdeen 6-3 at Pittodrie in the Scottish Cup. That setback was the prelude to six successive league defeats. Against the odds Aberdeen then walloped champions-elect Rangers 6-1 to bring a happier note to the season's end.

Aberdeen had an unlikely hero in 1960-61. Utility player Ken Brownlee bagged 23 goals in all competitions. Aberdeen needed him. His defenders were shipping goals alarmingly – especially at Pittodrie where only St Mirren, in the final game of the season, failed to score. In total, only three sides scored more league goals than Aberdeen in 1960-61; only four sides conceded more.

League:	Sixth
League Cup:	Second in qualifying group
Scottish Cup:	Third Round

SCOTTISH LEAGUE DIVISION ONE

No 1 Wednesday, 24 August
ABERDEEN (0) 1   DUNFERMLINE
Davidson (56)   ATHLETIC (1) 4
                                   McDonald (23), Melrose
                                   (46), Smith (65), Peebles
                                   (79)
ABERDEEN: Harker, Bennett, Kinnell, Burns, Coutts, Wishart, Herron, Little, Davidson, Cooke, Mulhall
DUNFERMLINE: Connachan, Fraser, Sweeney, Mailer, Stevenson, Miller, McDonald, Smith, Dickson, Melrose, Peebles

P	W	D	L	F	A	Pts
1	0	0	1	1	4	0

Referee: W. L. Fyfe

This result followed two 4-1 defeats in the League Cup. The Dons' lack of experience in defence is the cause of the trouble.

No 2 Saturday, 10 September
DUNDEE (1) 3   ABERDEEN (1) 3
Gilzean 3 (41, 50, 60) Burns (44), Hamilton
                                   o.g. (78), Little (81)
DUNDEE: Liney, Hamilton, Cox, Seith, Smith, Ure, Penman, McGeachie, Cousin, Gilzean, Robertson

ABERDEEN: Ogston, Bennett, Hogg, Burns, Kinnell, Fraser, Cooke, Davidson, Little, Brownlee, Mulhall

P	W	D	L	F	A	Pts
2	0	1	1	4	7	1

Referee: R. H. Davidson

Last Saturday on the same ground Aberdeen lost 6-0 in the League Cup. They owe a debt of thanks to Hamilton's second own goal for the Dons this season. A hat-trick for Alan Gilzean. That's eight in three games.

No 3 Saturday, 17 September
ABERDEEN (2) 4   ST JOHNSTONE (2) 2
Mulhall (10), Hogg (40), McVittie (11), Innes
Davidson (64), Brownlee (16)
(74)
ABERDEEN: Ogston, Bennett, Hogg, Baird, Kinnell, Fraser, Cooke, Davidson, Little, Brownlee, Mulhall
ST JOHNSTONE: Taylor, McFadyean, Lachan, Walker, Little, Docherty, Newlands, Innes, Gardiner, Ferguson, McVittie

P	W	D	L	F	A	Pts
3	1	1	1	8	9	3

Referee: W. M. Syme

Aberdeen needed to come from behind. Brownlee had a penalty saved at 2-2.

No 4 Saturday, 24 September
CELTIC (0) 0   ABERDEEN (0) 0

CELTIC: Fallon, McKay, Kennedy, Crerand, McNeill, Peacock, Conway, Gallacher, Carroll, Divers, Auld

ABERDEEN: Ogston, Bennett, Hogg, Brownlee, Kinnell, Fraser, Ewen, Davidson, Little, Cooke, Mulhall

P W D L F A Pts   *Attendance:* 18,000
4 1 2 1 8 9 4   *Referee:* W. Elliot

Celtic have only one point to show from their first three matches, so this was hardly a memorable result for Aberdeen. In the second half Parkhead treated both sides to the slow handclap.

No 5 Saturday, 1 October
AYR UNITED (1) 1   ABERDEEN (1) 1
Price (18)   Mulhall (8)

AYR: Hamilton, Burn, Paterson, W. McIntyre, McLean, Walker, A. McIntyre, McMillan, Price, Fulton, McGhee

ABERDEEN: Ogston, Bennett, Cadenhead, Burns, Coutts, Fraser, Ewen, Davidson, Little, Brownlee, Mulhall

P W D L F A Pts   *Attendance:* 7,000
5 1 3 1 9 10 5   *Referee:* H. Phillips

A carbon copy of the League Cup-tie at Somerset Park. Mulhall puts Aberdeen in front. Price answers for Ayr. The only difference was the time of the kick-off. The late arrival of Aberdeen's train caused it to be delayed.

No 6 Saturday, 8 October
ABERDEEN (2) 5   THIRD LANARK (0) 3
Cooke (5), Kinnell (15),   Gray (56), Hilley (71),
Little (50), Davidson   Goodfellow (85)
2 (62, 80)

ABERDEEN: Harker, Bennett, Hogg, Burns, Kinnell, Fraser, Ewen, Davidson, Little, Cooke, Mulhall

THIRD LANARK: Robertson, McGillivray, Lewis, Reilly, McCormack, Cunningham, Goodfellow, Hilley, Harley, Gray, McInnes

P W D L F A Pts   *Attendance:* 11,000
6 2 3 1 14 13 7   *Referee:* H. B. Sturgeon

Exciting stuff. Charlie Cooke scores his first goal for Aberdeen. The Dons wore blue and a white ball was used so it was altogether an unusual spectacle. Third's missed a penalty at 4-2.

No 7 Saturday, 15 October
CLYDE (0) 1   ABERDEEN (1) 1
Robertson (72)   Cooke (21)

CLYDE: McCulloch, Cameron, Haddock, Steel, Finlay, Clinton, Wilson, Herd, McLaughlin, Robertson, Boyd

ABERDEEN: Ogston, Bennett, Hogg, Burns, Kinnell, Fraser, Ewen, Davidson, Little, Cooke, Mulhall

P W D L F A Pts   *Attendance:* 10,000
7 2 4 1 15 14 8   *Referee:* D. R. Minto

Aberdeen stretch their sequence of away draws to four. But for Robertson's bullet header Aberdeen might have won.

No 8 Saturday, 22 October
RAITH ROVERS (0) 0   ABERDEEN (1) 3
     Mulhall (33), Cooke (55),
     Little (87)

RAITH: Thorburn, Wilson, Mochan, Stein, Polland, Leigh, Wallace, Kelly, French, Matthew, Urquhart

ABERDEEN: Ogston, Bennett, Hogg, Burns, Kinnell, Fraser, Ewen, Davidson, Little, Cooke, Mulhall

P W D L F A Pts   *Attendance:* 5,000
8 3 4 1 18 14 10   *Referee:* G. Bowman

Before Aberdeen took a grip Stein's shot thudded against Ogston's upright. The points were destined for Pittodrie from the moment Cooke blasted in No. 2.

No 9 Saturday, 29 October
ABERDEEN (1) 1   AIRDRIEONIANS (0) 1
Cooke (21)   Storrie (73)

ABERDEEN: Ogston, Bennett, Hogg, Burns, Kinnell, Fraser, Ewen, Davidson, Little, Cooke, Mulhall

AIRDRIE: Leslie, Shanks, Keenan, Stewart, Johnston, McNeil, Sharkey, Storrie, Caven, Rankin, Duncan

Leading positions

	P	W	D	L	F	A	Pts
1 Rangers	8	7	0	1	29	11	14
2 Dundee United	9	5	1	3	14	8	11
3 ABERDEEN	9	3	5	1	19	15	11
4 Dundee	9	5	1	3	17	15	11
5 Airdrie	9	4	3	2	19	19	11

Attendance: 13,000   *Referee:* A. Cook

Airdrie are going well. Like Aberdeen they are in the pack pursuing Rangers. It was a welcome point for Airdrie who lost Rankin after 16 minutes with a broken nose – courtesy of Ian Burns. Cooke scored for the fourth game in a row. Jim Storrie, under the eyes of watching spies, snatched the equaliser.

No 10 Saturday, 5 November
HEARTS (0) 3   ABERDEEN (2) 4
Cumming (75), Young   Cooke (25), Mulhall (29),
(77), Crawford (86)   Davidson (59), Little (90)

HEARTS: Marshall, Kirk, Thomson, Cumming, Milne, Higgins, Hamilton, Blackwood, Young, McFadzean, Crawford

ABERDEEN: Ogston, Bennett, Hogg, Burns, Kinnell, Fraser, Brownlee, Davidson, Little, Cooke, Mulhall

P W D L F A Pts   *Attendance:* 20,000
10 4 5 1 23 18 13   *Referee:* E. F. Cowan

Here was a game to remember. Hearts are in the bottom half of the table – not a pleasant situation for the defending champions. Cooke's goal for the fifth successive match set Aberdeen on the way to a 3-0 lead. Hearts fought back: 3-1, 3-2. Then they equalised when Ogston palmed away a corner and Crawford scrambled the ball in. With the last kick Little drove Brownlee's pass beyond Marshall to register Aberdeen's first win at Tynecastle since 1945.

No 11 Saturday, 12 November
ABERDEEN (3) 3   MOTHERWELL (2) 3
  Davidson 2 (9, 29),   McSeveney (28 pen),
  Little (23)   Weir (37), Hogg o.g. (47)
ABERDEEN: Ogston, Bennett, Hogg, Burns, Kinnell, Fraser, Brownlee, Davidson, Little, Cooke, Mulhall
MOTHERWELL: H. Weir, McSeveney, I. Weir, Reid, Martis, McPhee, Young, A. Weir, Roberts, Hunter, Lindsay

P W D L F A Pts   *Attendance:* 11,000
11 4 6 1 26 21 14   *Referee:* T. Wharton

Goals-a-plenty at Pittodrie, though Aberdeen drop a point after leading 3-1. Burns 'nudged' Hunter for 'Well's penalty. Hogg then got in the way of Weir's shot.

No 12 Saturday, 19 November
HIBERNIAN (1) 2   ABERDEEN (1) 2
  Kinloch 2 (42, 83)   Brownlee 2 (38, 56)
HIBERNIAN: Simpson, Fraser, McClelland, Hughes, Easton, Baird, Buchanan, Kinloch, Baker, Preston, MacLeod
ABERDEEN: Ogston, Bennett, Sim, Burns, Kinnell, Fraser, Brownlee, Davidson, Little, Cooke, Mulhall

P W D L F A Pts
12 4 7 1 28 23 15   *Referee:* J. Blair

Drama as Aberdeen extend their unbeaten run to eleven games. Once again Aberdeen cannot protect their lead – even against next-to-bottom Hibs. Acting skipper Burns is sent off near the end, the first Aberdeen player to be ordered off since Pat McKenna in September 1951.

No 13 Saturday, 26 November
ABERDEEN (1) 1   DUNDEE UNITED (2) 3
  Kinnell (43 pen)   Mochan (19), Briggs
                        (22 pen), Gillespie (70)
ABERDEEN: Ogston, Bennett, Sim, Wishart, Kinnell, Fraser, Brownlee, Davidson, Little, Cooke, Mulhall
DUNDEE UNITED: Ugolini, Graham, Briggs, Neilson, Yeats, Fraser, Carlyle, Gillespie, Mochan, Howieson, Ormond

P W D L F A Pts   *Attendance:* 13,000
13 4 7 2 29 26 15   *Referee:* W. J. Mullen

Newly-promoted Dundee United inflict Aberdeen's first defeat since the opening league game of the season. In the absence of Hogg and Burns, George Kinnell assumes the captaincy. He conceded the penalty, then scored one himself. Little hit the United crossbar at 0-0.

No 14 Saturday, 3 December
RANGERS (2) 4   ABERDEEN (0) 0
  Wilson (10), Brand (41),
  McMillan 2 (68, 70)
RANGERS: Niven, Shearer, Caldow, Davis, Paterson, Baxter, Scott, McMillan, Millar, Brand, Wilson
ABERDEEN: Ogston, Bennett, Sim, Fraser, Kinnell, Wishart, Brownlee, Davidson, Little, Cooke, Mulhall

P W D L F A Pts   *Attendance:* 25,000
14 4 7 3 29 30 15   *Referee:* T. Alexander

It's December and at last Aberdeen are defeated away from home. On the previous Wednesday Rangers scored eight past Borussia Moenchengladbach in the European Cup-Winners Cup – so the Dons escaped lightly! It proved to be the last match for Aberdeen for Bobby Wishart and Norman Davidson – who were later transferred to Dundee and Hearts respectively.

No 15 Saturday, 10 December
ABERDEEN (2) 3   KILMARNOCK (1) 2
  Brownlee 2 (37, 42),   McInally (12), Kerr (75)
  Little (78)
ABERDEEN: Ogston, Bennett, Sim, Fraser, Coutts, Kinnell, Ewen, Brownlee, Little, Cooke, Mulhall
KILMARNOCK: McLaughlin, Richmond, Watson, Davidson, Toner, Kennedy, Black, Brown, Kerr, McInally, Muir

P W D L F A Pts   *Attendance:* 13,000
15 5 7 3 32 32 17   *Referee:* J. P. Barclay

Kilmarnock are second behind Rangers. This is only their second defeat of the season. The crowd roared from first to last at this epic battle. McInally was upset when his equaliser for Killie at 2-1 was disallowed because a team-mate was offside.

No 16 Saturday, 17 December
ABERDEEN (1) 2   PARTICK THISTLE (1) 1
  Donlevy o.g. (28),   McBride (38)
  Cooke (77)
ABERDEEN: Ogston, Bennett, Sim, Fraser, Coutts, Kinnell, Ewen, Brownlee, Little, Cooke, Mulhall
PARTICK: Freebairn, Muir, Brown, Wright, Harvey, Donlevy, Ewing, Closs, McBride, Duffy, McParland

P W D L F A Pts   *Attendance:* 13,000
16 6 7 3 34 33 19   *Referee:* W. D. Massie

Partick are third, so Aberdeen have faced the top three in successive games. Thistle look a lively side but never recover from Donlevy's own goal.

No 17 Saturday, 24 December
ST MIRREN (1) 1   ABERDEEN (1) 3
  Bryceland (11)   Mulhall 2 (35, 87),
                        Cooke (60)
ST MIRREN: Brown, Campbell, Wilson, McTavish, Clunie, Thomson, Rodger, Frye, Bryceland, Hume, Miller
ABERDEEN: Ogston, Bennett, Sim, Burns, Coutts, Kinnell, Ewen, Brownlee, Little, Cooke, Mulhall

P W D L F A Pts
17 7 7 3 37 34 21   *Referee:* H. B. Sturgeon

Ex-Don Jim Clunie turns out for next-to-bottom St Mirren. Acting captain Burns urges the Dons to victory upon his return to the side.

No 18 Saturday, 31 December
DUNFERMLINE   ABERDEEN (3) 6
  ATHLETIC (1) 2   Brownlee 4 (35, 42, 45,
  Melrose (9),   54), Cooke (49),
  McDonald (85)   Kinnell (62 pen)

DUNFERMLINE: Herriot, Fraser, Williamson, Mailer, Clark, Millar, McDonald, Smith, Dickson, Peebles, Melrose

ABERDEEN: Ogston, Bennett, Sim, Burns, Coutts, Kinnell, Ewen, Brownlee, Hosie, Cooke, Mulhall

P W D L F A Pts
18 8 7 3 43 36 23   *Referee:* F. S. Crossley

Aberdeen see out 1960 with a cracker, avenging their defeat on the opening day of the league season. There are four goals for the Dons' utility player Ken Brownlee.

No 19 Monday, 2 January
ABERDEEN (1) 2   DUNDEE (0) 1
  Brownlee (9), Mulhall   Gilzean (53)
  (69)

ABERDEEN: Ogston, Bennett, Sim, Burns, Coutts, Kinnell, Ewen, Brownlee, Hosie, Cooke, Mulhall

DUNDEE: Liney, Reid, Cox, Seith, Ure, Cowie, Crichton, Henderson, Adamson, Gilzean, Robertson

Leading positions

	P	W	D	L	F	A	Pts
1 Rangers	19	16	0	3	59	20	32
2 ABERDEEN	19	9	7	3	45	37	25
3 Kilmarnock	19	9	6	4	39	31	24
4 Motherwell	19	9	4	6	40	29	22

Attendance: 23,000

Pittodrie's highest attendance of the season witnesses Alan Gilzean's ninth goal in four matches against Aberdeen. But he can't prevent Aberdeen's fifth win on the trot, which carries them to second place. Two wonder saves by Ogston prevented a late Dundee equaliser. After the match Bobby Wishart – who was not playing – was transferred to Dundee.

No 20 Saturday, 7 January
ST JOHNSTONE (1) 2   ABERDEEN (1) 1
  Walker (12), Burns (54)   Brownlee (33)

ST JOHNSTONE: Taylor, McFadyen, Lachlan, Walker, Little, Rattray, McVittie, Docherty, Thomson, Innes, Burns

ABERDEEN: Ogston, Bennett, Sim, Burns, Coutts, Kinnell, Ewen, Brownlee, Hosie, Cooke, Mulhall

P W D L F A Pts   *Attendance:* 11,000
20 9 7 4 46 39 25   *Referee:* W. Brittle

All good things come to an end. Aberdeen's winning run is halted by lowly St Johnstone. Conditions were better suited to ice-skating than football. In the closing minutes Taylor grabbed Ewen's ankles but no penalty resulted.

No 21 Saturday, 14 January
ABERDEEN (0) 1   CELTIC (2) 3
  Brownlee (66)   Gallacher (37), Chalmers
                           (41), Divers (83)

ABERDEEN: Ogston, Bennett, Sim, Burns, Coutts, Kinnell, Ewen, Brownlee, Little, Cooke, Mulhall

CELTIC: Haffey, McKay, Kennedy, Crerand, McNeill, Peacock, Gallacher, Divers, Hughes, Chalmers, Auld

P W D L F A Pts   *Attendance:* 20,000
21 9 7 5 47 42 25   *Referee:* J. Holburn

Celtic did leaders Rangers a hefty favour with this win. Pittodrie had to acknowledge that Celtic were the better side. Young Billy McNeill and his defenders held firm.

No 22 Saturday, 21 January
ABERDEEN (1) 3   AYR UNITED (1) 1
  Curlett o.g. (10), Little   McMillan (6)
  (69), Brownlee (89)

ABERDEEN: Ogston, Bennett, Hogg, Burns, Kinnell, Baird, Ewen, Cooke, Little, Brownlee, Mulhall

AYR: Gallacher, Burn, G. McIntyre, Walker, McLean, W. McIntyre, A. McIntyre, McMillan, McGuinness, Curlett, McGhee

P W D L F A Pts   *Attendance:* 9,000
22 10 7 5 50 43 27   *Referee:* J. R. P. Gordon

Ayr are bottom and take the field with three McIntyres. But what might have happened had Curlett not deflected a Bennett free kick into his own goal?

No 23 Saturday, 4 February
THIRD LANARK (2) 5   ABERDEEN (0) 1
  McGillivray 2 (3 pen,   Brownlee (65)
  59 pen), Harley 2 (44, 70),
  Gray (76)

THIRD LANARK: Robertson, McGillivray, Caldwell, Reilly, McCormack, Cunningham, Goodfellow, Hilley, Harley, Gray, McInnes

ABERDEEN: Ogston, Bennett, Sim, Burns, Coutts, Kinnell, Ewen, Cooke, Little, Brownlee, Mulhall

P W D L F A Pts
23 10 7 6 51 48 27   *Referee:* G. Mitchell

Here's a turn-up for the book. This defeat is a bad omen for next Saturday's Scottish Cup-tie. It was a game of two penalties and two bookings for Aberdeen – those of Coutts and Sims.

No 24 Saturday, 18 February
ABERDEEN (3) 4   CLYDE (2) 2
  Little 2 (30, 35),   McLean (6),
  Brownlee (31),   Haddock (34 pen)
  Mulhall (79)

ABERDEEN: Ogston, Bennett, Sim, Fraser, Coutts, Kinnell, Ewen, Cooke, Little, Brownlee, Mulhall

CLYDE: Thomson, Cameron, Haddock, Colrain, Finlay, Clinton, McLean, Herd, McLaughlin, Robertson, Steele

Leading positions

	P	W	D	L	F	A	Pts
1 Rangers	25	18	3	4	68	29	39
2 Kilmarnock	24	13	6	5	55	38	32
3 Motherwell	24	12	5	7	51	37	29
4 ABERDEEN	24	11	7	6	55	50	29

Attendance: 12,000   *Referee:* W. J. Mullen

E

Clyde are on their way down, largely due to their fragile defence, after Scotland's top-scoring winger Jim McLean gave them a perfect start.

No 25 Wednesday, 1 March
ABERDEEN (0) 0   RAITH ROVERS (1) 1
                                      Fox (9 pen)
ABERDEEN: Harker, Bennett, Sim, Burns, Coutts, Fraser, Robertson, Cooke, Little, Brownlee, Mulhall
RAITH: Thorburn, McDonald, McNaught, Stein, Polland, Leigh, Wallace, Fox, Buchanan, Benvie, Urquhart
P W D L F A Pts
25 11 7 7 55 51 29
Aberdeen have just been knocked out of the Cup by Dunfermline. Without goalkeeper John Ogston – playing for Scotland's Under-23 side against England at Middlesbrough – Aberdeen collapse to defeat by Raith, who had lost their previous five games.

No 26 Saturday, 4 March
AIRDRIEONIANS (3) 3   ABERDEEN (1) 1
   Caven 2 (15, 40),   Little (42)
   Duncan (30)
AIRDRIE: Leslie, Shanks, Keenan, Stewart, Johnstone, McNeill, Hume, Rankin, Sharkey, Caven, Duncan
ABERDEEN: Ogston, Bennett, Sim, Burns, Coutts, Fraser, Robertson, Cooke, Little, Brownlee, Tait
P W D L F A Pts   *Attendance:* 5,000
26 11 7 8 56 54 29   *Referee:* E. F. Cowan
The Dons cannot shake off their Cup hangover. They were three goals down before they woke up.

No 27 Saturday, 11 March
KILMARNOCK (1) 4   ABERDEEN (0) 1
   McInally 2 (21, 70),   Mulhall (80)
   Cadenhead o.g. (71),
   Kerr (76)
KILMARNOCK: McLaughlin, Richmond, Cook, Beattie, Toner, Kennedy, Brown, Davidson, Kerr, McInally, Muir
ABERDEEN: Ogston, Bennett, Cadenhead, Burns, Coutts, Kinnell, Ewen, Cooke, Little, Brownlee, Mulhall
P W D L F A Pts   *Attendance:* 8,000
27 11 7 9 57 58 29   *Referee:* J. Mackie
Kilmarnock are still Rangers' closest pursuers. Aberdeen's performance was again airy-fairy. Again their solitary reply arrived after all the damage had been done.

No 28 Tuesday, 14 March
ABERDEEN (0) 0   HEARTS (0) 2
                                      Cumming (56 pen),
                                      Murray (72)
ABERDEEN: Harker, Bennett, Cadenhead, Burns, Coutts, Kinnell, Ewen, Brownlee, Cummings, Cooke, Mulhall

HEARTS: Marshall, Kirk, Ferguson, Higgins, Milne, Cumming, Smith, Murray, Davidson, Docherty, Hamilton
P W D L F A Pts   *Attendance:* 8,000
28 11 7 10 57 60 29
Hearts are in relegation trouble though they will fight their way to mid-table, helped by ex-Don Norman Davidson. Ten minutes from time Kinnell missed for the first time from the penalty spot for Aberdeen, Marshall saving with his legs.

No 29 Saturday, 18 March
MOTHERWELL (0) 1   ABERDEEN (0) 0
   Quinn (52)
MOTHERWELL: Wylie, Delaney, Strachan, Aitken, Martis, McCann, Hunter, Quinn, St John, Stevenson, Roberts
ABERDEEN: Harker, Bennett, Cadenhead, Baird, Coutts, Kinnell, Fraser, Hosie, Cummings, Brownlee, Mulhall
P W D L F A Pts   *Attendance:* 8,000
29 11 7 11 57 61 29   *Referee:* A. J. T. Cook
Motherwell are third, and collect both points through Quinn's soft shot in an otherwise forgettable game.

No 30 Saturday, 25 March
ABERDEEN (0) 1   HIBERNIAN (4) 4
   Coutts (57)   Baker 2 (17, 28), Scott
                                 (41), McLeod (43)
ABERDEEN: Harker, Bennett, Cadenhead, Baird, Coutts, Kinnell, Fraser, Brownlee, Little, Cooke, Tait
HIBERNIAN: Simpson, Davin, McClelland, Baxter, Easton, Baird, Scott, Preston, Baker, Stevenson, McLeod
P W D L F A Pts   *Attendance:* 6,000
30 11 7 12 58 65 29   *Referee:* D. Weir
Hibs – like Hearts – are at the wrong end of the table. It was 4-0 at half time and Aberdeen's humiliating slide continues. This was their seventh consecutive defeat. Only 6,000 fans bothered to turn up. Afterward Manager Tommy Pearson defended his youth policy at an annual Shareholders' Meeting.

No 31 Saturday, 1 April
DUNDEE UNITED (2) 3 ABERDEEN (1) 3
   Briggs (12), Gillespie   Cummings 2 (15, 78),
   (25), Boner (61)   Brownlee (59)
DUNDEE UNITED: Brown, Cairns, Gordon, Neilson, Yeats, Fraser, Boner, Gillespie, Mochan, Briggs, Ormond
ABERDEEN: Harker, Bennett, Hogg, Baird, Kinnell, Fraser, Cummings, Brownlee, Little, Cooke, Mulhall
P W D L F A Pts
31 11 8 12 61 68 30   *Referee:* J. P. Barclay
Three times Aberdeen were behind, three times they struck back. They move off the 29-point mark for the first time since 18 February.

No 32 Saturday, 8 April
ABERDEEN (3) 6   RANGERS (1) 1
  Cummings 3 (14, 20, 49),   Scott (29)
  Little (19), Brownlee (58),
  Cooke (68)
ABERDEEN: Harker, Cadenhead, Hogg, Baird,
Kinnell, Fraser, Cummings, Brownlee, Little, Cooke,
Mulhall
RANGERS: Ritchie, Shearer, Caldow, Davis, Baillie,
Stevenson, Scott, Brand, McLean, Penman, Wilson
P W D L F A Pts   *Attendance:* 20,000
32 12 8 12 67 69 32   *Referee:* W. D. Massie

With Kilmarnock breathing down their necks this was a
dreadful result for Rangers, the worst possible time to
allow Aberdeen to rediscover their winning ways.
Aberdeen's first three goals came in a six-minute spell
when Caldow was off the field receiving attention.
Cummings takes his total to five from two games.

No 33 Saturday, 22 April
PARTICK THISTLE (1) 3   ABERDEEN (2) 4
  McBride 2 (5, 84 pen),   Cooke (13), Cummings
  McParland (64)   (43), Mulhall (50),
                           Brownlee (67)
PARTICK: Freebairn, Hogan, Brown, Harvey,
McKinnon, Donlevy, Ewing, Closs, McBride, Duffy,
McParland
ABERDEEN: Ogston, Cadenhead, Hogg, Baird,
Kinnell, Fraser, Cummings, Brownlee, Little, Cooke,
Mulhall
P W D L F A Pts
33 13 8 12 71 72 34   *Referee:* F. S. Crossley

A goal behind in five minutes on a quagmire pitch,
Aberdeen rolled up their sleeves. After Cooke had
equalised McBride's early goal Hogg flattened Ewing
but Ogston kept out Brown's penalty. Within seconds
Hogan helped home Cummings' shot to put Aberdeen
in front.

No 34 Saturday, 29 April
ABERDEEN (1) 1   ST MIRREN (0) 0
  Little (35)
ABERDEEN: Ogston, Cadenhead, Hogg, Baird,
Kinnell, Fraser, Cummings, Brownlee, Little, Cooke,
Mulhall
ST MIRREN: Brown, Campbell, Wilson, Henderson,
Clunie, Riddell, Rodger, Stewart, Kerrigan,
McFadzean, Miller
Attendance: 8,000   *Referee:* W. L. Frye

Such is the frailty of Aberdeen's defence that St Mirren
become the first side not to score at Pittodrie all season.

Aberdeen's complete home and away record:
HOME   AWAY
P W D L F A   W D L F A   Pts
34 9 2 6 38 34   5 5 6 34 38   36

Scottish League Division One 1960-61

		P	W	D	L	F	A	Pts
1	Rangers	34	23	5	8	88	46	51
2	Kilmarnock	34	21	8	5	77	45	50
3	Third Lanark	34	20	2	12	100	80	42
4	Celtic	34	15	9	10	64	46	39
5	Motherwell	34	15	8	11	70	57	38
6	ABERDEEN	34	14	8	12	72	72	36
7	Hearts	34	13	8	13	51	53	34
8	Hibernian	34	15	4	15	66	69	34
9	Dundee United	34	13	7	14	60	58	33
10	Dundee	34	13	6	15	61	53	32
11	Partick Thistle	34	13	6	15	59	69	32
12	Dunfermline	34	12	7	15	65	81	31
13	Airdrieonians	34	10	10	14	61	71	30
14	St Mirren	34	11	7	16	53	58	29
15	St Johnstone	34	10	9	15	47	63	29
16	Raith Rovers	34	10	7	17	46	67	27
17	Clyde	34	6	11	17	55	77	23
18	Ayr United	34	5	12	17	51	81	22

LEAGUE CUP

Saturday, 13 August
ABERDEEN (0) 4   AYR UNITED (1) 3
  McIntyre o.g. (52),   McMillan (43), Price
  Herron (67), Brownlee   (50), Paton (74)
  (68 pen), Davidson (80)
ABERDEEN: Harker, Kinnell, Hogg, Burns, Coutts,
Brownlee, Herron, Little, Davidson, Cooke, Mulhall
AYR: Hamilton, Burn, Thomson, W. McIntyre,
McLean, Walker, Fulton, McMillan, Price, Paton,
McGhee
Attendance: 14,000   *Referee:* W. J. Mullen

A new-look Dons. Jimmy Hogg succeeded Archie Glen
as captain. Three 17-18 year olds took the field – Cooke,
Herron and Coutts. Pittodrie is treated to a rousing
second half.

Wednesday, 17 August
RAITH ROVERS (1) 4   ABERDEEN (0) 1
  Urquhart (44),   Little (89)
  Brownlee o.g. (60),
  Spence (76), Wallace (85)
RAITH: Thorburn, Stevenson, Mochan, Polland,
McGregor, Duffy, Wallace, Wood, Easson, Spence,
Urquhart
ABERDEEN: Harker, Kinnell, Hogg, Burns, Coutts,
Brownlee, Herron, Little, Davidson, Robertson,
Mulhall

As against Airdrie, Aberdeen fall behind just on half-
time – but there the comparison ended.

Saturday, 20 August
ABERDEEN (0) 1   DUNDEE (2) 4
  Hamilton o.g. (73)   Gilzean 2 (2, 40), Cousin
                        (47), Penman (78)

ABERDEEN: Harker, Kinnell, Hogg, Burns, Coutts, Baird, Herron, Little, Cummings, Cooke, Mulhall

DUNDEE: Liney, Hamilton, Cox, Seith, Smith, Ure, Penman, McGeachie, Gilzean, Cousin, Robertson

Attendance: 18,000   *Referee:* J. P. Barclay

The name to note is Alan Gilzean. It took him two minutes to score his first goal against Aberdeen. He would come to make a habit of it.

Saturday, 27 August
AYR UNITED (0) 1   ABERDEEN (1) 1
  Price (65)   Mulhall (41)

AYR: Hamilton, Burn, Thomson, W. McIntyre, McLean, Walker, A. McIntyre, McMillan, Price, Fulton, McGhee

ABERDEEN: Ogston, Bennett, Sim, Burns, Kinnell, Brownlee, Herron, Cooke, Davidson, Wishart, Mulhall

                 Referee: A. McKenzie

Dundee have already qualified so Aberdeen have two more meaningless matches to complete. Bobby Wishart kept a parental eye on Aberdeen's 'babes'.

Wednesday, 31 August
ABERDEEN (2) 3   RAITH ROVERS (0) 0
  Davidson 2 (16, 57),
  Mulhall (18)

ABERDEEN: Ogston, Bennett, Sim, Burns, Kinnell, Brownlee, Herron, Cooke, Davidson, Wishart, Mulhall

RAITH: Thorburn, McGregor, Mochan, Wilson, Polland, Leigh, Malcolm, Spence, Peebles, Kelly, Urquhart

Playing without any pressure Aberdeen keep a clean sheet for the first time this season.

Saturday, 3 September
DUNDEE (2) 6   ABERDEEN (0) 0
  Gilzean 3 (20 pen, 86, 89),
  McGeachie 2 (42, 70),
  Waddell (56)

DUNDEE: Liney, Hamilton, Cox, Seith, Smith, Ure, Penman, McGeachie, Waddell, Gilzean, Robertson

ABERDEEN: Ogston, Bennett, Sim, Burns, Kinnell, Brownlee, Herron, Cooke, Davidson, Wishart, Mulhall

                 Referee: A. Crossman

The less said about this debacle the better. Three more goals for Alan Gilzean, taking him to five in two matches against Aberdeen.

Section 4

	P	W	D	L	F	A	Pts
Dundee	6	6	0	0	23	2	12
ABERDEEN	6	2	1	3	10	18	5
Raith Rovers	6	2	1	3	7	14	5
Ayr United	6	0	2	4	7	13	2

SCOTTISH CUP
1st Round (Bye)

2nd Round Saturday, 11 February
ABERDEEN (2) 4   DEVERONVALE (1) 2
  Brownlee 2 (2, 86), Ewen   Beattie (21), Murray (57)
  (38), Hosie (70)

ABERDEEN: Ogston, Bennett, Sim, Burns, Coutts, Kinnell, Ewen, Cooke, Hosie, Brownlee, Mulhall

DEVERONVALE: Morrison, Gordon, Cormack, Allister, W. Smith, V. Smith, Beattie, Reid, Murray, Hay, Christie

Attendance: 14,200   *Referee:* W. J. Allan

Highland-league club Deveronvale gave the Dons a desperate run for their money, inspired by ex-Don Billy Smith. At 2-2 it was Deveronvale who looked more likely to snatch the winner. Cooke master-minded Aberdeen's first three goals.

3rd Round Saturday, 25 February
ABERDEEN (1) 3   DUNFERMLINE
  Brownlee 2 (1, 59),   ATHLETIC (2) 6
  Coutts (89)   Smith (21), Dickson (32),
                            McDonald (49), Melrose
                            (60), Fraser o.g. (82),
                            Miller (90)

ABERDEEN: Ogston, Bennett, Sim, Burns, Coutts, Fraser, Ewen, Cooke, Little, Brownlee, Mulhall

DUNFERMLINE: Herriot, Cunningham, Sweeney, Mailer, Williamson, Miller, McDonald, Smith, Dickson, Peebles, Melrose

                 Referee: G. Mitchell

On the opening day of the league season Dunfermline won 4-1 at Pittodrie. On New Year's Eve Aberdeen won 6-2 in the return fixture. Who, then, could believe the turn of events of this pulsating cup-tie. In mud-bath conditions Brownlee's header put Aberdeen in front inside forty seconds. A problem for Jock Stein's famed tactical know-how. But at regular intervals Dunfermline breached the Aberdeen defence. With eight minutes remaining Fraser could only deflect Peebles' shot past Ogston. This put Dunfermline 5-2 ahead and there was no way back for Aberdeen. Dunfermline went on to win the Scottish Cup.

1960-61
APPEARANCES

	League	League Cup	Scottish Cup
Mulhall	32	6	2
Cooke	32	5	2
Kinnell	31	6	1
Bennett	31	3	2
Brownlee	29	5	2
Little	29	3	1
Ogston	26	3	2
Fraser	24		1
Burns	21	6	2

1960-61 APPEARANCES	League	League Cup	Scottish Cup
Ewen	18		2
Coutts	17	3	2
Davidson	14	5	
Sim	14	3	2
Hogg	14	3	
Harker	8	3	
Baird	8	1	
Cadenhead	8		
Cummings	6	1	
Hosie	4		1
Wishart	3	3	
Robertson	2	1	
Tait	2		
Herron	1	6	
23 players			

GOALS	Total	League	League Cup	Scottish Cup
Brownlee	23	18	1	4
Little	13	12	1	
Mulhall	12	10	2	
Cooke	10	10		
Davidson	10	7	3	
Cummings	6	6		
Kinnell	3	3		
Coutts	2	1		1
Burns	1	1		
Hogg	1	1		
Herron	1		1	
Ewen	1			1
Hosie	1			1
own-goals	5	3	2	
Total	89	72	10	7

The Aberdeen team picture for season 1964-65. Back row: Burns, Bennett, Shewan, Ogston, Cooke, Coutts, Smith. Front row: Kerrigan, Morrison, Kerr, Winchester and McIntosh.

Season 1961-62

An anti-climactic season in every sense. There was a feeling of expectancy after the changing of the guard in 1960-61 and the brighter league performances which occasionally illuminated that season. But now it all went wrong again. There was the usual – of late – half-hearted challenge in the group rounds of the League Cup. There followed a poor start to the league which left Aberdeen separated from the bottom club only by goal average after seven games. A recovery temporarily lifted the Dons, but they were once again looking over their shoulder from January through to March. All that Aberdeen could remember with favour was a league double over deposed champions Rangers.

And even that sweet taste was rendered sour in the Scottish Cup. Aberdeen thrashed ten goals past Second Division Clyde in a second-round replay to earn the right to meet Rangers. An all-ticket Pittodrie crowd saw Aberdeen snatch a late equaliser to force a replay, where the Dons were blown away without trace.

Aberdeen were indebted to Billy Little's 26 goals in 1961-62, but the statistics also told their own story. Aberdeen could score only 33 league goals at Pittodrie – the lowest number since 1949. On their travels the Dons' defence was punctured 46 times – the highest number since the War.

League:	Twelfth
League Cup:	Third in qualifying group
Scottish Cup:	Third Round

SCOTTISH LEAGUE DIVISION ONE

No 1 Wednesday, 23 August
ABERDEEN (2) 7   STIRLING ALBION (0) 0
  Cummings 2 (14, 62),
  Little 3 (39, 58, 87),
  Baird 2 (59, 65)
ABERDEEN: Ogston, Cadenhead, Hogg, Burns, Coutts, Fraser, Cummings, Little, Baird, Cooke, Mulhall
STIRLING: Wren, Pettigrew, McGuinness, Rowan, Johnstone, Spence, Addison, Maxwell, Gilmour, Dyson, Colquhoun

P	W	D	L	F	A	Pts
1	1	0	0	7	0	2

Poor Stirling continue their woeful losing sequence at Pittodrie, and sent Aberdeen off to a flier.

No 2 Saturday, 9 September
ST JOHNSTONE (2) 4   ABERDEEN (0) 1
  Gardiner (7), Wright   Little (73)
  (12), Bell 2 (68, 85)
ST JOHNSTONE: Taylor, McFadyen, Lachlan, Little, J. Ferguson, McKinven, McVittie, Wright, Gardiner, Bell, Henderson
ABERDEEN: Ogston, Cadenhead, Hogg, Burns, Coutts, Kinnell, Brownlee, Little, Fraser, Cooke, Mulhall

P	W	D	L	F	A	Pts
2	1	0	1	8	4	2

Attendance: 10,500
Referee: R. H. Davidson

Tommy Pearson keeps juggling with his front line. Aberdeen were beaten from the seventh minute when they hesitated, hoping for offside against Gardiner.

No 3 Saturday, 16 September
ABERDEEN (2) 3   DUNDEE (0) 1
  Kinnell (23 pen),   Gilzean (66)
  Brownlee (44), Little (51)
ABERDEEN: Ogston, Cadenhead, Hogg, Burns, Kinnell, Fraser, Baird, Brownlee, Little, Cooke, Thom
DUNDEE: Liney, Hamilton, Cox, Seith, Ure, Stuart, Smith, Penman, Gilzean, Cousin, Robertson

P	W	D	L	F	A	Pts
3	2	0	1	11	5	4

Attendance: 12,000
Referee: A. Crossman

A beautiful autumn day. 17-year old Lewis Thom makes his debut on the wing. Aberdeen were beneficiaries of a dreadful mistake by a linesman flagging for handball when Hamilton headed off his goal-line. Kinnell despatched the penalty. Gilzean later scored his customary goal for Dundee.

No 4 Saturday, 23 September
AIRDRIEONIANS (2) 7   ABERDEEN (0) 1
  Storrie 3 (20, 59, 84),   Mulhall (58)
  Caven 2 (23, 62), Duncan
  (48), Cooper (75)
AIRDRIE: Dempster, Shanks, Keenan, Hosie,
Johnstone, McNeil, Cooper, Storrie, Caven, Rankin,
Duncan
ABERDEEN: Ogston, Cadenhead, Hogg, Burns,
Kinnell, Fraser, Cummings, Brownlee, Little, Cooke,
Mulhall

P W D L F A Pts   *Attendance:* 3,000
4 2 0 2 12 12 4   *Referee:* J. Stewart

Airdrie's first win or points of the season. Where do
Aberdeen go from here?

No 5 Saturday, 30 September
ABERDEEN (1) 1   PARTICK THISTLE (1) 3
  Ewen (22)   McBride 2 (20, 82),
                      McParland (72)
ABERDEEN: Harker, Cadenhead, Hogg, Burns,
Kinnell, Fraser, Ewen, Hosie, Brownlee, Cooke,
Mulhall
PARTICK: Gray, Hogan, Brown, Cunningham,
Harvey, Donlevy, Ewing, McBride, Smith, Duffy,
McParland

P W D L F A Pts   *Attendance:* 6,000
5 2 0 3 13 15 4   *Referee:* A. J. P. Cook

These are dark days for Aberdeen. If only they had a
finisher as clinical as McBride of Partick.

No 6 Saturday, 7 October
ST MIRREN (3) 3   ABERDEEN (1) 2
  Henderson (17), Kerrigan Cooke (34), Herron (87)
  2 (33, 42)
ST MIRREN: Brown, Wilson, Riddell, Stewart, Clark,
McTavish, Rodger, Henderson, Kerrigan, Gemmell,
Miller
ABERDEEN: Harker, Bennett, Cadenhead, Burns,
Kinnell, Brownlee, Callaghan, Hosie, Herron, Cooke,
Mulhall

P W D L F A Pts
6 2 0 4 15 18 4   *Referee:* A. MacKenzie

Newcomer Willie Callaghan from East Stirling does his
best to get Aberdeen moving.

No 7 Saturday, 14 October
ABERDEEN (0) 0   HEARTS (1) 2
                      Stenhouse (11), Hamilton
                      (48)
ABERDEEN: Harker, Bennett, Cadenhead, Burns,
Kinnell, Brownlee, Callaghan, Hosie, Herron, Cooke,
Mulhall
HEARTS: Marshall, Kirk, Holt, Cumming, Polland,
Higgins, Ferguson, Stenhouse, Wallace, Ross,
Hamilton

Bottom positions

		P	W	D	L	F	A	Pts
15	Airdrie	7	2	1	4	15	17	5
16	ABERDEEN	7	2	0	5	15	20	4
17	Raith Rovers	7	1	2	4	11	18	4
18	Stirling	7	2	0	5	8	22	4

Attendance: 10,000   *Referee:* J. Mackie

Aberdeen's fourth successive defeat leaves them
separated from the bottom only by goal average. Hearts
chose to play with only four forwards, but still won the
tactical battle with ease. Aberdeen played like a team
without heart or conviction. One of the spectators was a
home-town lad, Denis Law, on a break from Torino.

No 8 Saturday, 21 October
FALKIRK (0) 0   ABERDEEN (0) 1
                      Little (67)
FALKIRK: Whigham, Rae, Hunter, Pierson,
Thomson, McIntosh, Oliver, Murray, Duchart, Reid,
Ormond
ABERDEEN: Ogston, Bennett, Cadenhead, Brownlee,
Kinnell, Fraser, Callaghan, Cooke, Little, Cummings,
Mulhall

P W D L F A Pts
8 3 0 5 16 20 6   *Referee:* T. Wharton

Falkirk had gone three matches without defeat:
Aberdeen had lost four on the trot, so it was high time
for both sequences to come to an end. Little scored the
goal, but all the activity was taking place around
Ogston.

No 9 Saturday, 28 October
ABERDEEN (2) 3   MOTHERWELL (0) 0
  Little 2 (17, 23), Callaghan
  (83)
ABERDEEN: Ogston, Bennett, Cadenhead, Brownlee,
Kinnell, Fraser, Callaghan, Cooke, Little, Allan,
Mulhall
MOTHERWELL: H. Weir, McSeveney, Thomson,
Aitken, McCallum, McCann, McPhee, Quinn, Roberts,
Hunter, A. Weir

P W D L F A Pts   *Attendance:* 7,000
9 4 0 5 19 20 8   *Referee:* E. F. Cowan

Aberdeen had their League Cup defeats to avenge – and
did so handsomely.

No 10 Saturday, 4 November
HIBERNIAN (1) 1   ABERDEEN (1) 1
  McLeod (4)   Callaghan (19)
HIBERNIAN: Simpson, Davin, McClelland, Baxter,
Easton, Hughes, Stevenson, Baird, Fraser, Preston,
McLeod
ABERDEEN: Ogston, Bennett, Cadenhead, Brownlee,
Kinnell, Fraser, Callaghan, Cooke, Little, Allan,
Mulhall

P W D L F A Pts   *Attendance:* 5,000
10 4 1 5 20 21 9   *Referee:* D. Weir

Hibs are once again right at the bottom end of the table, and on Wednesday suffered a 4-0 defeat in Belgrade in the Fairs Cup. The game was all about blunders, apart from Callaghan's out of the blue 25-yarder for Aberdeen.

No 11 Saturday, 11 November
ABERDEEN (1) 2   THIRD LANARK (1) 1
Callaghan 2 (17, 81)   Harley (38)
ABERDEEN: Ogston, Bennett, Cadenhead, Brownlee, Kinnell, Fraser, Callaghan, Cooke, Little, Allan, Mulhall
THIRD LANARK: Robertson, McGillivray, Robb, Reilly, McCormack, Cunningham, Goodfellow, Hilley, Harley, Gray, Fletcher

P	W	D	L	F	A	Pts	*Attendance:* 8,000
11	5	1	5	22	22	11	*Referee:* W. J. Allan

Two more goals for wee Willie Callaghan lit up an indifferent match.

No 12 Saturday, 18 November
DUNFERMLINE   ABERDEEN (0) 0
ATHLETIC (2) 4
Miller 2 (10, 44), Melrose
(56), Sinclair (89)
DUNFERMLINE: Connachan, Fraser, Cunningham, Thomson, Williamson, Miller, Sinclair, Smith, Dickson, Peebles, Melrose
ABERDEEN: Ogston, Bennett, Cadenhead, Brownlee, Kinnell, Fraser, Callaghan, Cooke, Little, Allan, Mulhall

P	W	D	L	F	A	Pts	
12	5	1	6	22	26	11	*Referee:* G. Mitchell

In the League Cup Aberdeen won 2-1 at Dunfermline. Not this time. Their powder-puff forwards carry no threat.

No 13 Saturday, 25 November
ABERDEEN (0) 0   CELTIC (0) 0
ABERDEEN: Ogston, Bennett, Cadenhead, Burns, Kinnell, Fraser, Callaghan, Brownlee, Little, Baird, Mulhall
CELTIC: Haffey, McKay, Kennedy, Crerand, McNeill, Price, Chalmers, Jackson, Hughes, Divers, Carroll

P	W	D	L	F	A	Pts	*Attendance:* 15,000
13	5	2	6	22	26	12	*Referee:* W. D. Massie

Many goal-less games are drab. This one is an exception. Both teams went hell for leather from the start. Burns' header hit the Celtic bar and passed over.

No 14 Saturday, 2 December
KILMARNOCK (3) 4   ABERDEEN (1) 2
Yard (23), Sneddon (24),   Baird (20), Little (55)
Kerr (42), Muir (59 pen)
KILMARNOCK: McLaughlin, Richmond, Watson, Beattie, Toner, Davidson, Black, Yard, Kerr, Sneddon, Muir

ABERDEEN: Ogston, Bennett, Cadenhead, Burns, Kinnell, Fraser, Callaghan, Brownlee, Little, Baird, Mulhall

P	W	D	L	F	A	Pts	
14	5	2	7	24	30	12	*Referee:* G. Bowman

Killie are once again up among the leaders. But they secured the points only with a debatable Muir penalty, when the ball had been driven hard against Fraser's hand.

No 15 Saturday, 16 December
ABERDEEN (0) 1   DUNDEE UNITED (2) 3
Baird (83)   Mochan 2 (6, 57),
                       Carlyle (38)
ABERDEEN: Ogston, Bennett, Cadenhead, Burns, Kinnell, Fraser, Callaghan, Baird, Little, Cooke, Mulhall
DUNDEE UNITED: Brown, Gordon, Briggs, Neilson, Smith, Fraser, Carlyle, Brodie, Mochan, Gillespie, Ormond

P	W	D	L	F	A	Pts	*Attendance:* 7,000
15	5	2	8	25	33	12	*Referee:* W. M. Syme

Veteran Neil Mochan scored his fifth goal against Aberdeen this season. The Dons have no complaint about this latest defeat.

No 16 Saturday, 23 December
RANGERS (1) 2   ABERDEEN (2) 4
Brand (30), Greig (77)   Brownlee (1), Mulhall
                       (43), Cooke (55), Kinnell
                       (58 pen)
RANGERS: Ritchie, Shearer, Caldow, Davis, Baillie, Baxter, Henderson, Greig, Scott, Brand, Hume
ABERDEEN: Ogston, Bennett, Hogg, Burns, Kinnell, Fraser, Callaghan, Brownlee, Little, Cooke, Mulhall

P	W	D	L	F	A	Pts	*Attendance:* 28,000
16	6	2	8	29	35	14	*Referee:* W. J. Mullen

A good look at the league tables beforehand would not have forecast this result. Defending champions Rangers were behind after twenty seconds, when the ball skidded off Baxter's head to Brownlee. Aberdeen's fourth goal, a penalty by Kinnell on his 24th birthday, was awarded after Cooke's header had been punched away by Caldow. All the New Year's fixtures were then snowed off.

No 17 Saturday, 6 January
STIRLING ALBION (0) 3   ABERDEEN (0) 0
Park 3 (62, 74, 76)
STIRLING: J. Brown, D. Brown, McGuinness, Rowan, Weir, Johnstone, Kilgannon, Sinclair, Park, Maxwell, Spence
ABERDEEN: Ogston, Bennett, Hogg, Burns, Kinnell, Fraser, Callaghan, Brownlee, Little, Cooke, Mulhall

P	W	D	L	F	A	Pts	
17	6	2	9	29	38	14	*Referee:* H. Phillips

Farcical conditions. Players on both sides protested about the match going ahead. It did – and Stirling avenged their 7-0 thrashing at Pittodrie.

No 18 Wednesday, 10 January
ABERDEEN (0) 1   ST JOHNSTONE (1) 1
  Little (76)   Bell (23)
ABERDEEN: Ogston, Bennett, Cadenhead, Burns, Kinnell, Smith, Callaghan, Brownlee, Little, Cooke, Mulhall
ST JOHNSTONE: Taylor, McFadyen, Lachlan, McKinven, Little, Donlevy, Rankin, Walker, Thomson, Bell, Kemp

P W D L F A Pts   *Attendance:* 4,500
18 6 3 9 30 39 15

St Johnstone score their first goal in 563 minutes of football.

No 19 Saturday, 13 January
ABERDEEN (0) 1   AIRDRIEONIANS (0) 1
  Little (84)   Newlands (74)
ABERDEEN: Ogston, Bennett, Cadenhead, Burns, Kinnell, Smith, Callaghan, Brownlee, Little, Cooke, Mulhall
AIRDRIE: Dempster, Shanks, Keenan, Reid, Hannah, Stewart, Cooper, Newlands, Caven, McNeil, Duncan

P W D L F A Pts   *Attendance:* 4,200
19 6 4 9 31 40 16   *Referee:* W. D. Massie

In front of one of Pittodrie's lowest-ever attendances it took Aberdeen 52 minutes to produce their first shot at goal. Ex-Don Doug Newlands netted for Airdrie.

No 20 Wednesday, 17 January
DUNDEE (1) 2   ABERDEEN (0) 1
  Cousin (37),   Mulhall (57)
  Penman (79 pen)
DUNDEE: Liney, Hamilton, Cox, Seith, Ure, Wishart, Smith, Penman, Cousin, Gilzean, Robertson
ABERDEEN: Ogston, Bennett, Cadenhead, Burns, Kinnell, Fraser, Hosie, Callaghan, Little, Pearson, Mulhall

P W D L F A Pts   *Attendance:* 13,000
20 6 4 10 32 42 16   *Referee:* A. Crossman

Under Bob Shankley's management Dundee are the division's runaway leaders. They think of themselves highly: although there is no need for a change of strip Dundee turn out in Real Madrid's all-white kit. The decisive goal was a giveaway by Bennett, handling the ball as he fell on it after charging it down.

No 21 Saturday, 20 January
PARTICK THISTLE (0) 4   ABERDEEN (0) 2
  McBride 2 (54, 86),   Pearson (64), Little
  Harvey (76), Duffy (81)   (66)
PARTICK: Gray, Hogan, Brown, Harvey, McKinnon, Cunningham, Ewing, McBride, Smith, Duffy, McParland
ABERDEEN: Ogston, Bennett, Cadenhead, Burns, Kinnell, Fraser, Callaghan, Little, Coutts, Pearson, Mulhall

Bottom positions

	P	W	D	L	F	A	Pts
13 ABERDEEN	21	6	4	11	34	46	16
14 Raith Rovers	21	5	4	12	30	47	14
15 St Johnstone	22	4	6	12	17	37	14
16 Stirling Albion	21	5	3	14	25	54	13
17 Airdrie	22	4	4	14	36	56	12
18 Falkirk	21	4	3	14	20	42	11

Attendance: 10,000   *Referee:* J. W. Paterson

A thrill-a-minute contest in which the Dons played their part, overturning McBride's opening goal to take a 2-1 lead, and then being put to the sword in the final 15 minutes. For the first half Aberdeen experimented with centre-half Coutts at centre-forward. Bennett played throughout the second half with concussion.

No 22 Tuesday, 23 January
ABERDEEN (1) 3   RAITH ROVERS (3) 3
  Callaghan (27), Cooke   Fox 2 (7, 42), Watson
  (55), Mulhall (84)   (40)
ABERDEEN: Ogston, Cadenhead, Hogg, Burns, Kinnell, Fraser, Callaghan, Cooke, Little, Pearson, Mulhall
RAITH: Thorburn, Wilson, Mochan, Stein, Forsyth, Clinton, Adamson, Fox, White, Price, Watson

P W D L F A Pts   *Attendance:*
22 6 5 11 37 49 17   *Referee:* R. Rodger

Leeds manager Don Revie sat in the stand, casting his eye over Cooke. He watched a spirited Aberdeen fight-back – including a goal from Cooke.

No 23 Saturday, 3 February
ABERDEEN (3) 3   ST MIRREN (0) 1
  Little 2 (5, 37), Cooke (8)   McLean (84)
ABERDEEN: Ogston, Bennett, Hogg, Burns, Kinnell, Fraser, Ewen, Little, Cummings, Cooke, Mulhall
ST MIRREN: Brown, Doonan, Wilson, Stewart, Clunie, McTavish, Henderson, McLean, Beck, Fernie, Miller

P W D L F A Pts   *Attendance:* 8,000
23 7 5 11 40 50 19   *Referee:* W. J. Mullen

Pepped up by their 10 goals against Clyde in the Scottish Cup, Aberdeen record their first home league win since 11 November. They did the damage in the first half and went to sleep in the second.

No 24 Saturday, 10 February
HEARTS (0) 1   ABERDEEN (1) 1
  Davidson (77)   Little (41)
HEARTS: Cruickshank, Kirk, Holt, Ferguson, Cumming, Higgins, Rodger, Davidson, Bauld, Gordon, Hamilton
ABERDEEN: Ogston, Bennett, Hogg, Brownlee, Kinnell, Fraser, Callaghan, Little, Cummings, Cooke, Mulhall

P W D L F A Pts   *Attendance:* 14,000
24 7 6 11 41 51 20   *Referee:* R. H. Davidson

Last season Davidson scored with a header for Aberdeen at Hearts. Now he does the same to his old club. It cancelled out Little's peculiar goal scored from near the corner flag which eluded Cruickshank's outstretched arms.

No 25 Saturday, 24 February
MOTHERWELL (1) 1   ABERDEEN (0) 3
  Weir (24)   Little 2 (61, 80),
                               Mulhall (86)
MOTHERWELL: Wylie, Delaney, McCallum, Aitken, Martis, McCann, Young, Quinn, Weir, Hunter, McPhee
ABERDEEN: Ogston, Bennett, Hogg, Brownlee, Coutts, Kinnell, Callaghan, Little, Cummings, Cooke, Mulhall

P W D L F A Pts
25 8 6 11 44 52 22   *Referee:* E. F. Cowan

Aberdeen tried to forget their 5-1 hiding by Rangers in the Cup. For they were teased and tormented by Motherwell. But then Little seized on a massive clearance from his own half.
  The following Wednesday, 28 February, Ogston played in the Scottish Under-23 side against England.

No 26 Saturday, 3 March
ABERDEEN (1) 1   HIBERNIAN (1) 2
  Callaghan (25)   Baker (4), Fraser (48)
ABERDEEN: Ogston, Bennett, Hogg, Burns, Coutts, Kinnell, Callaghan, Little, Cummings, Cooke, Mulhall
HIBERNIAN: Simpson, Grant, McClelland, Preston, Easton, Baxter, Stevenson, Baker, Fraser, Falconer, McLeod

P W D L F A Pts   *Attendance:* 6,000
26 8 6 12 45 54 22   *Referee:* W. J. Allan

A white pitch, a small crowd and Burns hobbling on the wing with his leg strapped up. The crowd would be smaller next time after this shambles.

No 27 Saturday, 17 March
ABERDEEN (0) 1   DUNFERMLINE
  Kinnell (53 pen)   ATHLETIC (1) 4
                        Paton (35), Peebles (59),
                        Dickson (71),
                        Melrose (72)
ABERDEEN: Ogston, Cadenhead, Hogg, Kinnell, Coutts, Fraser, Callaghan, Little, Cummings, Brownlee, Mulhall
DUNFERMLINE: Connachan, Fraser, Cunningham, Thomson, Williamson, Miller, McDonald, Paton, Dickson, Melrose, Peebles

Bottom positions
	P	W	D	L	F	A	Pts
13 ABERDEEN	27	8	6	13	46	58	22
14 Airdrie	28	7	5	16	49	71	19
15 St Johnstone	29	6	7	16	29	52	19
16 Raith Rovers	29	6	6	17	43	70	18
17 Falkirk	28	7	3	18	32	58	17
18 Stirling Albion	29	6	4	19	28	66	16

Attendance: 5,000   *Referee:* J. Blair

Looking back, Aberdeen would have welcomed a repeat of the tedious goal-less draw in the League Cup. Fourth-placed Dunfermline's centre forward, Dickson, hobbled on the wing for the last seventy minutes – but still scored. Aberdeen's play was jeered by the sparse crowd.

No 28 Tuesday, 20 March
THIRD LANARK (1) 3   ABERDEEN (2) 5
  Kinnell o.g. (34), Harley   Brownlee 2 (10, 49),
  (83), Hilley (87)   Cummings (35),
                              Callaghan (66),
                              Allan (69)
THIRD LANARK: McKinlay, McGillivray, Caldwell, Reilly, McCormack, Cunningham, Goodfellow, Hilley, Harley, Gray, Bryce
ABERDEEN: Ogston, Shewan, Hogg, Brownlee, Kinnell, Fraser, Cummings, Allan, Callaghan, Cooke, Mulhall

P W D L F A Pts
28 9 6 13 51 61 24   *Referee:* W. Elliot

Shock team changes bring about this unexpected – and timely – win, which should keep Aberdeen safe. The high score was more of a reflection on two panicky defences than alert forwards.

No 29 Saturday, 24 March
CELTIC (1) 2   ABERDEEN (0) 0
  Brogan 2 (41, 58)
CELTIC: Haffey, McKay, O'Neil, Crerand, McNeill, Clark, Brogan, Chalmers, Hughes, Divers, Byrne
ABERDEEN: Ogston, Shewan, Hogg, Brownlee, Kinnell, Fraser, Cummings, Little, Callaghan, Cooke, Thom

P W D L F A Pts   *Attendance:* 21,000
29 9 6 14 51 63 24   *Referee:* G. Mitchell

Aberdeen had once tried to sign Frank Brogan – and he reminds them why. Aberdeen had their chances before Brogan got in on the act – but then faded away.

No 30 Wednesday, 28 March
ABERDEEN (1) 2   FALKIRK (0) 2
  Little (2), Mulhall (87)   Duchart (59), Thomson
                             (68 pen)
ABERDEEN: Ogston, Shewan, Hogg, Brownlee, Kinnell, Fraser, Cummings, Allan, Little, Cooke, Mulhall
FALKIRK: Whigham, Thomson, Rae, Pierson, Harra, McIntosh, Reid, Harrower, Duchart, Innes, Oliver

P W D L F A Pts   *Attendance:* 3,000
30 9 7 14 53 65 25   *Referee:* A. J. Cook

Aberdeen's lowest crowd in memory. Mulhall spared Aberdeen's blushes with three minutes left.

No 31 Saturday, 31 March
ABERDEEN (2) 3   KILMARNOCK (1) 3
  Cummings 2 (17, 76),   Kerr 2 (11, 54),
  Mulhall (31)   McInally (70)
ABERDEEN: Ogston, Shewan, Cadenhead, Brownlee,
Kinnell, Fraser, Ewen, Little, Cummings, Cooke,
Mulhall
KILMARNOCK: McLaughlan, King, Watson,
Richmond, Toner, Beattie, Brown, McInally, Kerr,
Sneddon, Muir
P W D L F A Pts   *Attendance:* 3,000
31 9 8 14 56 68 26   *Referee:* W. M. Syme
A see-saw match in front of empty terraces. Wee Alickie
said 'If we'd invaded the pitch naebody wid hae
noticed'.

No 32 Saturday, 7 April
DUNDEE UNITED (2) 2 ABERDEEN (1) 2
  Gillespie (6), Carlyle (25)   Mulhall (43), Ewen (62)
DUNDEE UNITED: Ugolini, Gordon, Briggs,
Neilson, Smith, Fraser, Carlyle, Miller, Gillespie,
Irvine, Mochan
ABERDEEN: Ogston, Shewan, Hogg, Brownlee,
Coutts, Fraser, Ewen, Little, Cummings, Cooke,
Mulhall
P W D L F A Pts
32 9 9 14 58 70 27   *Referee:* W. L. Fyfe
This is Dundee United's seventh unbeaten game, and
still Aberdeen can't get the better of them. In the days
that followed there were contractual problems with
several Aberdeen players.

No 33 Wednesday, 25 April
ABERDEEN (0) 1   RANGERS (0) 0
  Cummings (49)
ABERDEEN: Ogston, Shewan, Hogg, Brownlee,
Kinnell, Fraser, Cummings, Little, Winchester, Cooke,
Mulhall
RANGERS: Ritchie, Shearer, Caldow, Davis,
McKinnon, Baxter, Henderson, McMillan, Millar,
Brand, Wilson
P W D L F A Pts   *Attendance:* 22,000
33 10 9 14 59 70 29   *Referee:* G. Mitchell
Bobby Cummings keeps his Indian Sign over Rangers –
and destroys their championship hopes. A memorable
double for Aberdeen – though Rangers knocked
Aberdeen out of the Cup. 17-year old Ernie Winchester
has a fine debut. The goal itself was a comic affair, after
Caldow's clearance hit Ritchie and spun high in the air.

No 34 Saturday, 28 April
RAITH ROVERS (2) 3   ABERDEEN (0) 1
  Urquhart (4),   Mulhall (49)
  Kerr 2 (11, 81)
RAITH: Thorburn, Stevenson, Mochan, Stein,
Forsyth, Leigh, Adamson, Kerr, Gilfillan, McFadzean,
Urquhart

ABERDEEN: Ogston, Bennett, Shewan, Brownlee,
Kinnell, Fraser, Cummings, Little, Winchester, Cooke,
Mulhall
                         Referee: J. R. P. Gordon
This match meant nothing to Aberdeen, everything to
Raith who could have been relegated had they lost.

Aberdeen's complete home and away record:
  HOME   AWAY
P W D L F A   W D L F A   Pts
34 6 6 5 33 27   4 3 10 27 46   29

Scottish League Division One 1961-62
                        P   W   D   L   F   A Pts
1 Dundee   34 25 4   5   80 46 54
2 Rangers   34 22 7   5   84 31 51
3 Celtic   34 19 8   7   81 37 46
4 Dunfermline Athletic 34 19 5   10 77 46 43
5 Kilmarnock   34 16 10 8   74 58 42
6 Hearts   34 16 6   12 54 49 38
7 Partick Thistle   34 16 3   15 60 55 35
8 Hibernian   34 14 5   15 58 72 33
9 Motherwell   34 13 6   15 65 62 32
10 Dundee United   34 13 6   15 70 71 32
11 Third Lanark   34 13 5   16 59 60 31
12 ABERDEEN   34 10 9   15 60 73 29
13 Raith Rovers   34 10 7   17 51 73 27
14 Falkirk   34 11 4   19 45 68 26
15 Airdrie   34 9   7   18 57 78 25
16 St Mirren   34 10 5   19 52 80 25
17 St Johnstone   34 9   7   18 35 61 25
18 Stirling Albion   34 6   6   22 34 76 18

LEAGUE CUP

Saturday, 12 August
DUNFERMLINE   ABERDEEN (1) 2
  ATHLETIC (0) 1   Little (13), Brownlee (48)
  Fraser (49)
DUNFERMLINE: Connachan, Fraser, Cunningham,
Mailer, Williamson, Miller, McDonald, Smith,
Dickson, Peebles, Melrose
ABERDEEN: Ogston, Cadenhead, Hogg, Baird,
Kinnell, Fraser, Cummings, Brownlee, Little, Cooke,
Mulhall
Attendance: 12,000   *Referee:* C. Bowman
Aberdeen won the hard way against the Scottish Cup
holders, almost throwing away a two-goal lead.

Wednesday, 16 August
ABERDEEN (2) 3   MOTHERWELL (3) 4
  Brownlee (16), Little   Quinn 2 (9 pen, 72)
  (30), Kinnell (78 pen) Roberts (23), Hunter (37)
ABERDEEN: Ogston, Cadenhead, Hogg, Baird,
Kinnell, Fraser, Cummings, Brownlee, Little, Cooke,
Mulhall
MOTHERWELL: Wylie, Delaney, Strachan, Aitken,
Martis, McCann, Lindsay, Quinn, Roberts, Stevenson,
Hunter
Attendance: 18,000

A home defeat to open the season is not to be recommended. Baird gave away an early penalty for obstruction.

Saturday, 19 August
DUNDEE UNITED (2) 5   ABERDEEN (1) 3
   Irvine (17), Ormond (23),   Cooke (44), Cummings
   Mochan 2 (70, 78), Hogg   2 (52, 83)
   o.g. (71)
DUNDEE UNITED: Brown, Gordon, Briggs, Neilson, Smith, Fraser, Boner, Gillespie, Mochan, Irvine, Ormond
ABERDEEN: Ogston, Cadenhead, Hogg, Baird, Kinnell, Fraser, Cummings, Brownlee, Little, Cooke, Mulhall

                Referee: A. J. Paterson
Reconstruction of Tannadice meant that the teams had to change at a sports field two miles away and take their half-time break in a nearby works canteen. Aberdeen then lost their ninth goal in four days.

Saturday, 26 August
ABERDEEN (0) 0   DUNFERMLINE
                    ATHLETIC (0) 0
ABERDEEN: Ogston, Cadenhead, Kinnell, Burns, Coutts, Fraser, Cummings, Little, Baird, Cooke, Mulhall
DUNFERMLINE: Connachan, Fraser, Cunningham, Mailer, Williamson, Miller, McDonald, Peebles, Dickson, Melrose, Matthew
Attendance: 10,000   *Referee:* W. D. Massie
No goals, no thrills, no nothing – except a slow handclap and plenty of niggling fouls.

Wednesday, 30 August
MOTHERWELL (1) 2   ABERDEEN (0) 1
   Quinn (23 pen), Strachan   Little (63)
   (65)
MOTHERWELL: H. Weir, McSeveney, Thomson, Roberts, Martis, McPhee, Lindsay, Quinn, Strachan, Hunter, A. Weir
ABERDEEN: Ogston, Cadenhead, Hogg, Burns, Kinnell, Fraser, Cummings, Brownlee, Baird, Little, Mulhall

                  Referee: D. Weir
Charlie Cooke was dropped. Quinn's penalty came after Ogston had fouled Hunter seemingly outside the box.

Saturday, 2 September
ABERDEEN (2) 2   DUNDEE UNITED (1) 2
   Baird (2), Cooke (20)   Mochan (40), Gillespie
                    (83)
ABERDEEN: Ogston, Cadenhead, Hogg, Burns, Kinnell, Fraser, Cummings, Brownlee, Baird, Cooke, Mulhall
DUNDEE UNITED: Ugolini, Graham, Briggs, Neilson, Smith, Fraser, Boner, Gillespie, Carlyle, Irvine, Mochan
Attendance: 7,000   *Referee:* J. Holburn

Gillespie's late equaliser prevents Aberdeen's first win over United since they were promoted.

Section 2

	P	W	D	L	F	A	Pts
Motherwell	6	4	1	1	14	10	9
Dunfermline	6	2	3	1	7	3	7
ABERDEEN	6	1	2	3	11	14	4
Dundee United	6	1	2	3	10	15	4

SCOTTISH CUP

1st Round Saturday, 9 December
ABERDEEN (2) 5   AIRDRIEONIANS (1) 2
   Kinnell (39 pen),   Storrie (45), McNeil
   Callaghan 3 (41, 60, 87),   (73 pen)
   Little (85)
ABERDEEN: Ogston, Bennett, Cadenhead, Burns, Kinnell, Fraser, Callaghan, Brownlee, Little, Cooke, Thom
AIRDRIE: Dempster, Shanks, Keenan, Hosie, Johnston, McNeil, Cooper, Storrie, Caven, Reid, Newlands
Attendance: 8,800   *Referee:* J. R. P. Gordon
In September Aberdeen lost 7-1 at Broomfield in the league. The score tells of a Willie Callaghan hat trick and a comfortable turning of the tables. It doesn't say that when Airdrie pulled back from 3-0 to 3-2 the Dons looked worried.

2nd Round Saturday, 27 January
CLYDE (0) 2   ABERDEEN (2) 2
   McLaughlin (48),   Cummings (5), Little (21)
   Steel (73)
CLYDE: T. McCulloch, Walters, Haddock, White, Finlay, Newlands, W. McCulloch, Currie, McLaughlin, Steel, Colrain
ABERDEEN: Ogston, Bennett, Hogg, Burns, Kinnell, Fraser, Ewen, Little, Cummings, Cooke, Mulhall
Attendance: 10,000   *Referee:* A. Crossman
Clyde are heading for the Second Division championship. Aberdeen collapsed without warning in the second half and lived on their nerves till the end. Clyde might have equalised sooner than they did but Colrain's penalty was palmed away by Ogston.

2nd Round Replay Wednesday, 31 January
ABERDEEN (4) 10   CLYDE (1) 3
   Little 2 (10, 25),   McLaughlin (40), Currie
   Cummings 5 (28, 37, 58,   (47), Steel (89)
   75, 82), Mulhall 2 (55, 87),
   Fraser (77)
ABERDEEN: Ogston, Bennett, Hogg, Burns, Kinnell, Fraser, Ewen, Little, Cummings, Cooke, Mulhall
CLYDE: T. McCulloch, Walters, Haddock, White, Finlay, Newlands, W. McCulloch, Currie, McLaughlin, Steel, Divers
Attendance: 16,400   *Referee:* A. Crossman

Not since 1923 when Aberdeen beat Peterhead 13-0 had Pittodrie witnessed 13 goals in the Cup. It is their highest score since the War.

3rd Round Saturday, 17 February
ABERDEEN (1) 2   RANGERS (1) 2
  Kinnell (23 pen), Little   Caldow (37 pen), Brand
  (85)   (77)
ABERDEEN: Ogston, Bennett, Hogg, Burns, Kinnell, Fraser, Ewen, Little, Cummings, Cooke, Mulhall
RANGERS: Ritchie, Shearer, Caldow, Davis, Baillie, Baxter, Henderson, Greig, Millar, Brand, Wilson
Attendance: 41,139   *Referee:* T. Wharton

This was Aberdeen's first all ticket match for several years. There was unrest beforehand when both Brownlee and Callaghan requested transfers. It was a game of three penalties. Baxter charged Little for Aberdeen's, despite furious Rangers' protests. Then Bennett impeded Brand for Rangers to level. When the same participants were involved again in the second half, Ogston saved from Caldow.

3rd Round Replay Wednesday, 21 February
RANGERS (3) 5   ABERDEEN (1) 1
  McMillan (15), Millar   Cummings (11)
  2 (17, 76), Wilson (24),
  Brand (70)
RANGERS: Ritchie, Shearer, Caldow, Davis, Baillie, Baxter, Henderson, McMillan, Millar, Brand, Wilson
ABERDEEN: Ogston, Bennett, Hogg, Brownlee, Kinnell, Fraser, Ewen, Little, Cummings, Cooke, Mulhall
Attendance: 57,600   *Referee:* T. Wharton

Bobby Cummings had never previously been on the losing side against Rangers. His early goal sought to maintain that distinction. But then Aberdeen were blown away as if so much fluff.

1961-62 APPEARANCES	League	League Cup	Scottish Cup
Kinnell	32	6	5
Mulhall	32	6	4
Ogston	31	6	5
Little	30	5	5
Cooke	29	5	5
Fraser	28	6	5
Brownlee	27	5	2
Callaghan	24		1
Cadenhead	22	6	1
Bennett	20		5
Burns	19	3	4
Hogg	18	5	4
Cummings	15	6	4
Coutts	7	1	
Shewan	7		
Allan	6		
Baird	5	6	
Ewen	4		4
Hosie	4		
Pearson	3		
Harker	3		
Thom	2		1
Herron	2		
Smith	2		
Winchester	2		
25 players			

GOALS	Total	League	League Cup	Scottish Cup
Little	26	18	3	5
Cummings	15	6	2	7
Mulhall	11	9		2
Callaghan	10	7		3
Brownlee	6	4	2	
Cooke	6	4	2	
Kinnell	6	3	1	2
Baird	5	4	1	
Ewen	2	2		
Herron	1	1		
Allan	1	1		
Pearson	1	1		
Fraser	1			1
Total	91	60	11	20

A training session at Pittodrie in 1965.

Season 1962-63

This was a season of marked improvement, but also one in which Aberdeen squandered a promising position in each of the three main competitions. In the League Cup Aberdeen won their first three qualifying fixtures and seemed poised to progress to the Quarter Finals. But then came thumping defeats by Partick and Motherwell, and it was goodbye to the League Cup.

The league campaign opened with a powerful sprint from the starting pistol. Aberdeen harvested nine points from the first five games – and that one dropped point was all due to Alan Gilzean's injury-time equaliser at Dens Park. Aberdeen continued to jostle among the leaders. They were 4th on 1st December and a New Year's Day victory over champions Dundee took them to 3rd. Rangers were always well out of reach at the top, but consolidation behind them was a realistic Aberdeen objective.

The worst winter in memory then wrecked the season's schedule. But on the morning of Saturday, 30 March Aberdeen stood 4th in the league with an afternoon appointment with Raith Rovers in the Quarter Final of the Scottish Cup. Raith were bottom of the league and hadn't won at home all season. Aberdeen had crushed them 10-0 at Pittodrie. But, as they say, 'there is nothing predictable in the Cup'. Raith won 2-1. Aberdeen's season was in tatters and four successive league defeats followed. They eventually finished sixth, just failing to qualify for the Fairs Cup.

The Dons' comparatively prosperous season was due almost entirely to the stiffening of their defence, which conceded fewer goals than at any time since their championship-winning year, 1954-55.

League: Sixth
League Cup: Second in qualifying group
Scottish Cup: Quarter Final

SCOTTISH LEAGUE DIVISION ONE

No 1 Wednesday, 22 August
ABERDEEN (0) 2   AIRDRIEONIANS (1) 1
Callaghan (56),   McNeil (40)
Winchester (72)
ABERDEEN: Ogston, Shewan, Hogg, Brownlee, Kinnell, Fraser, Callaghan, Little, Winchester, Cooke, Mulhall
AIRDRIE: Samson, Shanks, Keenan, Reid, Hannah, Thomson, Murray, Newlands, Tees, McNeil, Duncan

P W D L F A Pts   *Attendance:* 12,000
1 1 0 0 2 1 2   *Referee:* J. Kelly

Former Don, Doug Newlands, is a constant menace to Aberdeen in the first half. Incessant second-half pressure brought its reward for Aberdeen.

No 2 Saturday, 8 September
DUNDEE (1) 2   ABERDEEN (2) 2
Penman (40), Gilzean   Cooke (11), Winchester
(90)   (42)
DUNDEE: Slater, Hamilton, Cox, Seith, Ure, Wishart, Smith, Penman, Cousin, Gilzean, Robertson
ABERDEEN: Ogston, Bennett, Hogg, Kinnell, Coutts, Smith, Cummings, Allan, Winchester, Cooke, Mulhall

P W D L F A Pts   *Attendance:* 12,000
2 1 1 0 4 3 3   *Referee:* J. P. Barclay

Dundee had whacked Cologne 8-1 in the European Cup on Wednesday. Cooke's goal against the champions – an exquisite lob – was a goal in a thousand. The bane of Aberdeen – Alan Gilzean – rescued Dundee in injury time. This is George Mulhall's last match for Aberdeen before his transfer to Sunderland.

No 3 Saturday, 15 September
ABERDEEN (1) 4 DUNFERMLINE
Cooke 2 (37, 46), ATHLETIC (0) 0
Winchester 2 (56, 65)

ABERDEEN: Ogston, Bennett, Hogg, Kinnell, Coutts, Smith, Cummings, Allan, Winchester, Cooke, Thom
DUNFERMLINE: Herriot, Fraser, Cunningham, Thomson, Williamson, Miller, Edwards, Smith, Dickson, Melrose, Peebles

P W D L F A Pts   *Attendance:* 10,000
3 2 1 0 8 3 5   *Referee:* A. J. T. Cook

Dunfermline's record as they travelled north was – played 2, won 2, scored 10. They are then dumped firmly on their backsides, chiefly by the magic of Charlie Cooke.

No 4 Saturday, 22 September
CELTIC (0) 1 ABERDEEN (2) 2
Hughes (48) Cooke (10),
 Cummings (18)

CELTIC: Haffey, McKay, Kennedy, Crerand, McNeill, Price, Chalmers, Divers, Hughes, Murdoch, Carroll
ABERDEEN: Ogston, Bennett, Hogg, Kinnell, Coutts, Smith, Cummings, Allan, Winchester, Cooke, Thom

P W D L F A Pts   *Attendance:* 29,000
4 3 1 0 10 4 7   *Referee:* W. L. Fyfe

The Dons had to struggle once Hughes brought Celtic back into the game. Once again all eyes are on Charlie Cooke.

No 5 Saturday, 29 September
ABERDEEN (2) 4 THIRD LANARK (1) 1
Thom 2 (25, 34), Grant (9)
Cummings (60),
Winchester (80)

ABERDEEN: Ogston, Bennett, Hogg, Kinnell, Coutts, Smith, Cummings, Allan, Winchester, Cooke, Thom
THIRD LANARK: McKinlay, McGillivray, Cunningham, Robb, McCormack, Hewlett, Bryce, Reilly, Grant, Gray, Buckley

Leading Positions

	P	W	D	L	F	A	Pts
1 Hearts	5	5	0	0	20	5	10
2 Rangers	5	4	1	0	12	3	9
3 ABERDEEN	5	4	1	0	14	5	9
4 Dunfermline	5	4	0	1	13	5	8

Attendance: 14,000   *Referee:* H. Phillips

18-year old Lewis Thom, having to fill the gap left by the departure of George Mulhall warms to the cheers of the crowd as he plots Third Lanark's downfall. After five matches only Alan Gilzean's late goal stands as a blemish on the Dons' record.

No 6 Saturday, 6 October
ST MIRREN (1) 2 ABERDEEN (0) 1
White 2 (30, 75) Little (55)

ST MIRREN: Williamson, Murray, Wilson, R. Campbell, Clunie, McTavish, B. Campbell, McLean, White, Queen, Provan

ABERDEEN: Ogston, Bennett, Hogg, Kinnell, Coutts, Smith, Cummings, Allan, Winchester, Cooke, Little

P W D L F A Pts
6 4 1 1 15 7 9   *Referee:* R. Rodger

Ex-Don, Jim Clunie, took a penalty at 1-1 when Ogston grabbed White's ankles. He missed. It's a happy day for Saints' Tommy White who scores twice on his debut.

No 7 Saturday, 13 October
ABERDEEN (4) 10 RAITH ROVERS (0) 0
Winchester 3 (1, 73, 80),
Cooke (8), Cummings 4
(30, 44, 57, 63), Little
(61), Kinnell (82 pen)

ABERDEEN: Ogston, Bennett, Hogg, Kinnell, Coutts, Smith, Cummings, Allan, Winchester, Cooke, Little
RAITH: Thorburn, Wilson, McGuire, Stein, Burrows, Leigh, Adamson, Aitken, Lourie, McFadzean, McNamee

P W D L F A Pts   *Attendance:* 9,000
7 5 1 1 25 7 11   *Referee:* W. Elliott

Raith are bottom, not surprisingly, and provide Aberdeen with their biggest league win since the War. Aberdeen are on their way from the first minute.

No 8 Saturday, 20 October
QUEEN OF THE ABERDEEN (1) 1
SOUTH (1) 2 Cummings (31)
Murphy (40 pen),
Anderson (89)

QUEEN OF THE SOUTH: Farm, Morrison, Kerr, Irving, Rugg, Murphy, Hannigan, Martin, McGhee, Anderson, Shields
ABERDEEN: Ogston, Bennett, Hogg, Kinnell, Coutts, Smith, Cummings, Allan, Winchester, Cooke, Little

P W D L F A Pts
8 5 1 2 26 9 11   *Referee:* W. Elliott

This is a painful setback for Aberdeen. Anderson's winning goal was hit from way out on the touchline. It swerved and was helped into goal by John Ogston.

No 9 Saturday, 27 October
ABERDEEN (1) 2 RANGERS (2) 3
Cummings 2 (17, 53) Millar (3), Wilson (5),
 Greig (81)

ABERDEEN: Ogston, Bennett, Hogg, Kinnell, Coutts, Smith, Cummings, Allan, Winchester, Cooke, Little
RANGERS: Ritchie, Shearer, Caldow, Davis, McKinnon, Baxter, Henderson, Greig, Millar, Brand, Wilson

P W D L F A Pts   *Attendance:* 36,000
9 5 1 3 28 12 11   *Referee:* A. McKenzie

Here was a case of swings and roundabouts, set before an all-ticket crowd. Table-topping Rangers' whirlwind start ought to have sunk Aberdeen. The tide turned when Cooke chipped the ball into the middle for Cummings to jab home. When Cummings then equalised off the post, Aberdeen had their tails up. But they hadn't reckoned with Rangers' final surge or Greig's classic winner. He clipped the ball over transfer-seeking Kinnell's head and hammered it past Ogston.

No 10 Saturday, 3 November
HEARTS (0) 1   ABERDEEN (0) 1
Paton (65)   Cooke (60)
HEARTS: Marshall, Polland, Holt, Ferguson, Barry, Higgins, Rodger, Paton, Wallace, Docherty, J. Hamilton
ABERDEEN: Ogston, Bennett, Hogg, Kinnell, Coutts, Smith, Cummings, Allan, Winchester, Cooke, Thom

P	W	D	L	F	A	Pts
10	5	2	3	29	13	12

Referee: J. M. Kelly

Hearts are second to Rangers, but don't rise above the ordinary against Aberdeen. The Dons drew first blood when Cooke's shot was helped into goal by a defender. They deserved to be leading but five minutes later they weren't. Ogston and Coutts stood and watched as Paton headed an equaliser.

No 11 Saturday, 10 November
ABERDEEN (0) 3   HIBERNIAN (0) 0
Cummings 2 (47, 63),
Smith (75)
ABERDEEN: Ogston, Bennett, Hogg, Fraser, Kinnell, Smith, Cummings, Allan, Winchester, Cooke, Thom
HIBERNIAN: Simpson, Fraser, McClelland, Grant, Easton, McLeod, Scott, Baker, McCreadie, M. Stevenson, Byrne

P	W	D	L	F	A	Pts
11	6	2	3	32	13	14

Attendance: 11,000
Referee: W. J. Allan

Three points from five matches had plummeted Aberdeen down the league table. But now they restore faith with their supporters with a second-half onslaught.

No 12 Wednesday, 21 November
MOTHERWELL (0) 0   ABERDEEN (1) 2
                    Cummings 2 (38, 61)
MOTHERWELL: Wylie, Delaney, McCallum, Aitken, Martis, Roberts, Ramsay, Lindsay, McBride, I. Thomson, Weir
ABERDEEN: Ogston, Bennett, Hogg, Kinnell, Coutts, Smith, Cummings, Allan, Winchester, Cooke, Thom

P	W	D	L	F	A	Pts
12	7	2	3	34	13	16

Attendance: 3,000
Referee: W. Syme

This match was rescheduled from the previous Saturday. Bobby Cummings has run into a purple patch. He has now scored 11 times in his last six matches. Motherwell have not won since 8 September.

No 13 Saturday, 24 November
ABERDEEN (1) 1   FALKIRK (0) 0
Smith (14)
ABERDEEN: Ogston, Bennett, Hogg, Kinnell, Coutts, Smith, Cummings, Allan, Winchester, Cooke, Thom
FALKIRK: Whigham, Rae, Hunter, Pierson, Thomson, McCarry, Hamilton, Fulton, Bain, Reid, McIntosh

P	W	D	L	F	A	Pts
13	8	2	3	35	13	18

Attendance: 9,000
Referee: R. A. S. Crockett

One goal was poor reward for Aberdeen's intense pressure. But in the end they were grateful to Hogg for clearing off the line from McIntosh.

No 14 Saturday, 1 December
CLYDE (1) 1   ABERDEEN (1) 3
Hood (8)   Brownlee (20),
                    Winchester (40),
                    Smith (89)
CLYDE: McCulloch, McDonald, Finnegan, White, Malloy, McHugh, Steel, Hood, Grant, Colrain, Muir
ABERDEEN: Ogston, Bennett, Hogg, Kinnell, Coutts, Smith, Cummings, Allan, Winchester, Brownlee, Thom

Leading Positions

	P	W	D	L	F	A	Pts
1 Rangers	14	10	3	1	38	13	23
2 Partick	14	11	1	2	31	13	23
3 Hearts	14	9	4	1	38	15	22
4 ABERDEEN	14	9	2	3	38	14	20
5 Kilmarnock	14	7	5	2	42	16	19
6 Celtic	14	7	3	4	27	11	17

Referee: A. F. J. Webster

Hapless Clyde are destined for Division Two. Hood's accurate header raised their spirits, but Aberdeen took control without ever playing really well. They are now only three points behind the leaders.

No 15 Saturday, 8 December
DUNDEE UNITED (1) 3 ABERDEEN (2) 3
Carlyle (42), Mitchell   Cummings (8), Thom
(53) Mochan (87)   (44), Winchester (56)
DUNDEE UNITED: Davie, Millar, Briggs, Neilson, Smith, Fraser, Carlyle, Gillespie, Mochan, Irvine, Mitchell
ABERDEEN: Ogston, Bennett, Hogg, Kinnell, Coutts, Smith, Cummings, Allan, Winchester, Cooke, Thom

P	W	D	L	F	A	Pts
15	9	3	3	41	17	21

Referee: J. Barclay

The Dons haven't beaten Dundee United in seven attempts. They might have done so had not Ogston permitted them to equalise near the final whistle. He watched a speculative forward pass from Briggs bounce on the six-yard line where Mochan darted in unchallenged to score.

No 16 Saturday, 15 December
ABERDEEN (0) 1   PARTICK THISTLE (0) 1
Kinnell (71 pen)   Cowan (64)
ABERDEEN: Ogston, Bennett, Hogg, Kinnell, Coutts, Smith, Cummings, Allan, Winchester, Cooke, Thom
PARTICK: Niven, Hogan, Brown, McParland, Harvey, Cunningham, Cowan, Whitelaw, Hainey, Duffy, Smith

P	W	D	L	F	A	Pts
16	9	4	3	42	18	22

Attendance: 15,000
Referee: W. J. Mullen

Second-placed Partick are unbeaten in eleven games. Kinnell rescued Aberdeen from the spot after Cooke had been brought down.

No 17 Saturday, 22 December
ABERDEEN (0) 1   KILMARNOCK (0) 0
   Winchester (71)
ABERDEEN: Ogston, Bennett, Hogg, Kinnell, Coutts, Smith, Cummings, Allan, Winchester, Cooke, Thom
KILMARNOCK: McLaughlin, Richmond, Watson, Murray, McGrory, Beattie, Brown, Mason, Kerr, Black, McIlroy

P	W	D	L	F	A	Pts	
17	10	4	3	43	18	24	*Attendance:* 13,000

Referee: A. Kidd

Kilmarnock are among the leading lights. Winchester's all-important goal came when heading Thom's cross down and away from McLaughlin.

No 18 Tuesday, 1 January
ABERDEEN (1) 1   DUNDEE (0) 0
   Winchester (37)
ABERDEEN: Ogston, Bennett, Hogg, Kinnell, Coutts, Smith, Cummings, Allan, Winchester, Cooke, Thom.
DUNDEE: Slater, Hamilton, Cox, Ryden, Ure, Wishart, Smith, Penman, Cousin, Gilzean, Houston.

Leading positions

	P	W	D	L	F	A	Pts
1 Rangers	18	14	3	1	54	16	31
2 Partick	18	14	2	2	39	17	30
3 ABERDEEN	18	11	4	3	44	18	26
4 Hearts	16	9	6	1	42	19	24
5 Kilmarnock	19	9	5	5	50	28	23
6 Celtic	19	9	4	6	33	21	22

Referee: J. P. Barclay

Aberdeen had two holiday fixtures postponed due to the weather. Now they welcome champions Dundee, including former Don, Bobby Wishart, to Pittodrie. Dundee had as much of the game and created as many chances as Aberdeen. But again Ernie Winchester came to the rescue. In the second half Kinnell failed with a penalty for the first time after Wishart had whispered to Slater which way the ball would go. Gilzean for once, failed to score, and was booked instead. So was Cooke. Aberdeen are now unbeaten since 27 October.

No 19 Saturday, 5 January
ABERDEEN (0) 1   CELTIC (4) 5
   Winchester (66)   Hughes 3 (13, 33, 82),
                             Craig 2 (19, 29)
ABERDEEN: Ogston, Bennett, Hogg, Kinnell, Coutts, Smith, Cummings, Allan, Winchester, Cooke, Thom
CELTIC: Haffey, Young, Gemmell, McNamee, McNeill, Price, Gallacher, Craig, Hughes, Divers, Chalmers

P	W	D	L	F	A	Pts	
19	11	4	4	45	23	26	*Attendance:* 15,000

Referee: A. J. T. Cook

Celtic are not handicapped by the absence of Crerand. Yogi Hughes is Aberdeen's prime tormentor. Winchester managed his customary goal, but this time it

was to no avail. Because of the appalling winter it was six weeks before Aberdeen could play again.

No 20 Saturday, 16 February
ABERDEEN (0) 0   ST MIRREN (1) 1
                            White (8)
ABERDEEN: Ogston, Bennett, Hogg, Kinnell, Coutts, Smith, Cummings, Allan, Winchester, Cooke, Thom
ST. MIRREN: Beattie, Murray, Riddell, Campbell, Clunie, McTavish, Carroll, Kerrigan, White, Beck, Robertson

P	W	D	L	F	A	Pts	
20	11	4	5	45	24	26	*Attendance:* 8,000

Referee: A. J. Webster

This is the only match which could go ahead in Division One, and afterwards Aberdeen must have wished for its postponement. Tommy White brought about their downfall, as he had on his debut at Paisley.

No 21 Saturday, 9 March
ABERDEEN (1) 2   HEARTS (1) 1
   Winchester 2 (25, 81)   Hamilton (8)
ABERDEEN: Ogston, Bennett, Hogg, Kinnell, Coutts, Smith, Cummings, Allan, Winchester, Cooke, Thom.
HEARTS: Marshall, Polland, Holt, Ferguson, Cumming, Higgins, Paton, Wallace, Davidson, Gordon, J. Hamilton.

P	W	D	L	F	A	Pts	
21	12	4	5	47	25	28	*Attendance:* 11,000

Referee: T. Wharton

To herald the spring Aberdeen sported their new outfit – red, white and blue stripes. The kick-off was delayed while everyone waited for the train carrying referee Tiny Wharton. Again Pittodrie acclaimed the feats of Ernie Winchester rescuing Aberdeen after Ogston had allowed the ball to slip through his hands for Hamilton to score.

HIBERNIAN (1) 2   ABERDEEN (3) 3
   O'Rourke (19),   Cooke (21),
   Baker (54)   Cummings (35),
                            Coutts (41)
HIBERNIAN: Wilson, Grant, McClelland, Leishman, Hughes, Baxter, Scott, M. Stevenson, Baker, O'Rourke, McLeod
ABERDEEN: Ogston, Bennett, Hogg, Kinnell, Coutts, Smith, Cummings, Allan, Little, Cooke, Thom

P	W	D	L	F	A	Pts	
22	13	4	5	50	27	30	*Referee:* W. M. Syme

This is Aberdeen's first away game since 8 December. Hibs are next to bottom. Before a goal had been scored Coutts injured a leg and hobbled through the match on the wing. He still managed to score Aberdeen's third goal – from close in.

No 23 Saturday, 23 March
ABERDEEN (0) 1   MOTHERWELL (1) 1
   Winchester (81)   McBride (10)
ABERDEEN: Ogston, Shewan, Hogg, Kinnell, Coutts, Smith, Cummings, Cooke, Winchester, Little, Thom

MOTHERWELL: Wylie, Thomson, McCallum, Aitken, Martis, Roberts, Lindsay, McBride, Russell, McCann, Weir

P	W	D	L	F	A	Pts
23	13	5	5	51	28	31

Attendance: 10,000
Referee: W. M. Syme

Motherwell hold on to Joe McBride's goal for 71 minutes, forcing Aberdeen to abandon their 4-2-4 formation in the search for the equaliser.

No 24 Saturday, 26 March
ABERDEEN (0) 4   QUEEEN OF THE
  Cummings 2 (56, 75),   SOUTH (1) 1
  Thom (56), Cooke (89)   Martin (6)

ABERDEEN: Ogston, Shewan, Hogg, Kinnell, Coutts, Smith, Cummings, Allan, Winchester, Cooke, Thom
QUEEN OF THE SOUTH: Hamilton, Morrison, McTurk, Irvine, Rugg, Anderson, Hannigan, Frye, Martin, Sansom, Murray

Leading positions

	P	W	D	L	F	A	Pts
1 Rangers	22	18	3	1	68	17	39
2 Kilmarnock	26	16	5	5	76	33	37
3 Partick	23	16	3	4	48	23	35
4 ABERDEEN	24	14	5	5	55	29	33
5 Celtic	26	14	5	7	55	35	33
6 Hearts	22	12	6	4	58	29	30

Attendance: 9,000   *Referee:* W. Brittle

Aberdeen continued their recent habit of coming from behind. Before they had found their bearings, Martin had netted for Queens. Ogston made a breathtaking save from Frye, and the same forward's header was whacked off the line by Hogg.

No 25 Wednesday, 3 April
FALKIRK (2) 2   ABERDEEN (0) 1
  Maxwell 2 (28, 41)   Winchester (48)

FALKIRK: Whigham, Rae, Hunter, Pierson, Thomson, Fulton, Henderson, Harrower, Bain, Maxwell, Redpath
ABERDEEN: Ogston, Bennett, Hogg, Kinnell, Coutts, Smith, Little, Allan, Winchester, Cooke, Thom

P	W	D	L	F	A	Pts
25	14	5	6	56	31	33

Referee: J. M. Kelly

Aberdeen are still looking for a possible Fairs Cup place, now that they are out of the Scottish Cup. Their cause was impeded by Hugh Maxwell's first-half brace.

No 26 Saturday, 6 April
ABERDEEN (0) 0   CLYDE (1) 2
                             McLean (13),
                             White (70 pen)

ABERDEEN: Ogston, Shewan, Hogg, Kinnell, Coutts, Smith, Little, Allan, Cummings, Cooke, Ring
CLYDE: McCulloch, White, Blain, McHugh, Fraser, Currie, McLean, Reid, Ferguson, Hood, Blair

P	W	D	L	F	A	Pts
26	14	5	7	56	33	33

Attendance: 4,000
Referee: W. J. Allan

Pittodrie's sparsely populated terraces were an indication of Aberdeen's recent form. This result won't save Clyde from the drop.

No 27 Wednesday, 10 April
AIRDRIEONIANS (2) 2   ABERDEEN (0) 0
  Murray (17), Newlands (38)

AIRDRIE: Sansom, Jonquin, Keenan, Rowan, Hannah, Thomson, McCall, Newlands, Tees, Murray, Duncan
ABERDEEN: Ogston, Shewan, Hogg, Kinnell, Coutts, Smith, Cummings, Allan, Winchester, Brownlee, Ring

P	W	D	L	F	A	Pts
27	14	5	8	56	35	33

Referee: G. Bowman

Aberdeen play with ten men for most of the game after Smith takes a heavy knock. Aberdeen continue to plunge down the table.

No 28 Wednesday, 17 April
DUNFERMLINE   ABERDEEN (0) 0
ATHLETIC (1) 3
  Paton (25), Kinnell
  o.g. (80), Melrose (83)

DUNFERMLINE: Connachan, Thomson, Lunn, Smith, McLean, Miller, Peebles, Melrose, Kerray, Paton, Callaghan
ABERDEEN: Ogston, Shewan, Hogg, Kinnell, Coutts, Fraser, Cummings, Allan, Little, Cooke, Thom

P	W	D	L	F	A	Pts
28	14	5	9	56	38	33

Five defeats on the trot, and Jock Stein's Dunfermline take some compensation for their Cup elimination at Pittodrie.

No 29 Saturday, 20 April
PARTICK THISTLE (2) 2 ABERDEEN (2) 3
  Smith (34), Duffy (43)   Kinnell 3 (7, 14, 56)

PARTICK: Niven, Muir, Brown, Closs, Harvey, Cunningham, Cowan, Fleming, Smith, Duffy, McParland
ABERDEEN: Ogston, Shewan, Hogg, Brownlee, Coutts, Smith, Fraser, Kinnell, Little, Wilson, Thom

P	W	D	L	F	A	Pts
29	15	5	9	59	40	35

Referee: W. Elliott

George Kinnell plays at inside forward for only the second time in his career – and bags a hat trick – as Charlie Cooke is dropped. Leeds Manager Don Revie offers Billy Bremner and a cash adjustment in return for Cooke.

No 30 Wednesday, 24 April
THIRD LANARK (0) 1   ABERDEEN (0) 2
  Cunningham (88)   Kinnell (55), Wilson (79)

THIRD LANARK: Robertson, McGillivray, Davies, Reilly, Lewis, Baird, Goodfellow, Spence, Cunningham, McMorran, McInnes
ABERDEEN: Ogston, Shewan, Hogg, Brownlee, Coutts, Smith, Fraser, Kinnell, Little, Wilson, Thom

P W D L F A Pts   *Attendance:* 2,100
30 16 5 9 61 41 37

Kinnell sticks to his scoring ways in front of one of the smallest ever crowds at a First Division match.

No 31 Saturday, 27 April
KILMARNOCK (1) 2   ABERDEEN (1) 2
  Yard 2 (15, 59)   Little (38), Cummings
                                (61)
KILMARNOCK: Forsyth, Richmond, Watson, O'Connor, McGrory, Beattie, Brown, Black, Yard, Sneddon, McIlroy
ABERDEEN: Ogston, Shewan, Hogg, Brownlee, Anderson, Fraser, Cummings, Kinnell, Little, Wilson, Thom
P W D L F A Pts
31 16 6 9 63 43 38   *Referee:* T. Wharton
Kilmarnock aim to consolidate second place – Rangers have the title sewn up. Aberdeen twice peg the Killies back.

No 32 Saturday, 4 May
RAITH ROVERS (0) 0   ABERDEEN (2) 4
                                Kinnell 2 (22, 73 pen),
                                Little 2 (37, 83)
RAITH: Thorburn, Stevenson, Haig, Wilson, Bolton, Burrows, McDonald, Stein, Gilfillan, Menzies, McGrogan
ABERDEEN: Ogston, Shewan, Hogg, Brownlee, Coutts, Fraser, Cummings, Kinnell, Little, Wilson, Smith
P W D L F A Pts   *Attendance:* 1,000
32 17 6 9 67 43 40   *Referee:* J. R. P. Gordon
Aberdeen's little burst has now brought them seven points from four away games – during which George Kinnell has scored six times. This result was poor reward for the Cup defeat at Raith the previous month. Raith haven't won a home league match all season.

No 33 Tuesday, 7 May
ABERDEEN (1) 1   DUNDEE UNITED (0) 2
  Kinnell (12 pen)   Gillespie (55),
                                Smith o.g. (88)
ABERDEEN: Ogston, Shewan, Hogg, Brownlee, Coutts, Fraser, Cummings, Kinnell, Little, Wilson, Smith
DUNDEE UNITED: Davie, Millar, Gordon, Fraser, Smith, Briggs, Carlyle, Gillespie, Mochan, Irvine, Mitchell
P W D L F A Pts   *Attendance:* 5,000
33 17 6 10 68 45 40   *Referee:* A. Mackenzie
This is the eighth time Aberdeen have tired – and failed – to beat Dundee United, who have a happy knack of scoring late goals to save themselves. This one was a farce. Ogston's clearance struck Smith and flew back into the net.

No 34 Monday, 27 May
RANGERS (1) 2   ABERDEEN (2) 2
  Wilson 2 (18, 90)   Kinnell (8), Little (26)
RANGERS: Ritchie, Shearer, Provan, Greig, McKinnon, Baxter, Watson, Willoughby, Millar, Brand, Wilson
ABERDEEN: Ogston, Shewan, Hogg, Brownlee, Coutts, Fraser, Cummings, Kinnell, Little, Cooke, Smith
Attendance: 14,000   *Referee:* J. W. Paterson
A three-week delay due to Rangers' Cup commitments. Kinnell's eighth goal in six games at inside right threatened Rangers' unbeaten home record. Wilson equalised, but Little put Aberdeen back in front. Then Rangers turned the screw. In a hectic finish Brand shot against Ogston's post. Then Baxter's drive was blocked on the penalty spot, and Wilson reached it first to save Rangers' embarrassment.

Aberdeen's complete home and away record:

	HOME					AWAY					
P	W	D	L	F	A	W	D	L	F	A	Pts
34	10	2	5	38	19	7	5	5	32	28	41

Scottish League Division One 1962-63

		P	W	D	L	F	A	Pts
1	Rangers	34	25	7	2	94	28	57
2	Kilmarnock	34	20	8	6	92	40	48
3	Partick Thistle	34	20	6	8	66	44	46
4	Celtic	34	19	6	9	76	44	44
5	Hearts	34	17	9	8	85	59	43
6	ABERDEEN	34	17	7	10	70	47	41
7	Dundee United	34	15	11	8	67	52	41
8	Dunfermline Athletic	34	13	8	13	50	47	34
9	Dundee	34	12	9	13	60	49	33
10	Motherwell	34	10	11	13	60	63	31
11	Airdrie	34	14	2	18	52	76	30
12	St Mirren	34	10	8	16	52	72	28
13	Falkirk	34	12	3	19	54	69	27
14	Third Lanark	34	9	8	17	56	68	26
15	Queen of the South	34	10	6	18	36	75	26
16	Hibernian	34	8	9	17	47	67	25
17	Clyde	34	9	5	20	49	83	23
18	Raith Rovers	34	2	5	27	35	118	9

LEAGUE CUP

Saturday, 11 August
PARTICK THISTLE (0) 1   ABERDEEN (0) 2
  Duffy (89)   Mulhall (68),
                                Brownlee (87)
PARTICK: Niven, Hogan, Brown, Closs, McKinnon, Cunningham, Smith, Duffy, McBride, Whitelaw, McParland.
ABERDEEN: Ogston, Shewan, Hogg, Brownlee, Kinnell, Fraser, Cummings, Little, Winchester, Cooke, Mulhall.

Referee: J. P. Barclay
Thistle lost centre-half McKinnon with concussion in

the first half, and were then down to nine men when Mulhall put Aberdeen in front

Wednesday, 15 August
ABERDEEN (1) 4   MOTHERWELL (0) 0
  Mulhall (40), Little (75),
  Winchester (83),
  Cummings (86)
ABERDEEN: Ogston, Shewan, Hogg, Brownlee, Kinnell, Fraser, Cummings, Little, Winchester, Cooke, Mulhall
MOTHERWELL: Wylie, Delaney, McCallum, Aitken, Martis, Roberts, Lindsay, Quinn, Russell, Ramsay, Weir
Attendance: 12,000   *Referee:* J. R. P. Gordon
Atrocious conditions can't stop Aberdeen. Nor can Motherwell, as English spies gaze down upon the Dons – especially George Mulhall.

Saturday, 18 August
ABERDEEN (0) 3   FALKIRK (0) 0
  Mulhall (56), Rae o.g.
  (58), Little (71)
ABERDEEN: Ogston, Shewan, Hogg, Brownlee, Kinnell, Fraser, Cummings, Little, Winchester, Cooke, Mulhall
FALKIRK: Whigham, Rae, McIntosh, Pierson, Lowry, McCarry, Blues, Reid, Cunningham, Fulton, Adam
Attendance: 12,500   *Referee:* R. A. S. Crockett
Aberdeen took a long time to get going – but now look good bets to qualify.

Saturday, 25 August
ABERDEEN (0) 0   PARTICK THISTLE (2) 3
                   Williamson (12),
                   McParland (20),
                   Whitelaw (81)
ABERDEEN: Ogston, Shewan, Hogg, Brownlee, Kinnell, Fraser, Callaghan, Little, Winchester, Cooke, Mulhall
PARTICK: Niven, Hogan, Brown, Ferguson, Harvey, Cunningham, Williamson, Whitelaw, Hainey, Duffy, McParland.
Attendance: 14,500   *Referee:* W. J. Allan
The most prominent personality at Pittodrie was the referee. Three Dons were booked in the closing minutes and there were ugly crowd scenes at the finish.

Wednesday, 29 August
MOTHERWELL (1) 4   ABERDEEN (0) 1
  Roberts 2 (10, 80),   Brownlee (88)
  Hunter (49), Delaney (60)
MOTHERWELL: Wylie, McSeveney, McCallum, Aitken, Martis, McCann, Lindsay, Quinn, Delaney, Hunter, Roberts
ABERDEEN: Ogston, Shewan, Hogg, Brownlee, Kinnell, Fraser, Cummings, Allan, Winchester, Cooke, Mulhall

Referee: T. Wharton
Aberdeen have tossed away their chances of qualifying. Of Motherwell one Don said, 'It seemed as if they had 40 players on the field'.

Saturday, 1 September
FALKIRK (0) 1   ABERDEEN (1) 2
  Hamilton (82)   Winchester (44), Peacock
                     o.g. (63)
FALKIRK: Whigham, Rae, Hunter, Peacock, Lowry, Pierson, Hamilton, Reid, Davidson, Redpath, Henderson
ABERDEEN: Ogston, Shewan, Hogg, Bennett, Coutts, Smith, Little, Allan, Winchester, Cooke, Mulhall
Referee: W. J. Mullen
Falkirk have now lost six out of six but it doesn't help Aberdeen who experiment with a 4-2-4 formation. The only way Aberdeen could have qualified was if they had won 6-0 while Motherwell and Partick drew.

Section 3

	P	W	D	L	F	A	Pts
Partick Thistle	6	4	1	1	12	5	9
ABERDEEN	6	4	0	2	12	9	8
Motherwell	6	3	1	2	15	8	7
Falkirk	6	0	0	6	4	21	0

SCOTTISH CUP

1st Round (Bye)

2nd Round Wednesday, 13 March
ST JOHNSTONE (1) 1   ABERDEEN (1) 2
  A. Ferguson (8)   Cummings (31),
                    Winchester (52)
ST JOHNSTONE: Taylor, McFadyen, Lachlan, Booth, J. Ferguson, McKinven, McIntyre, Townsend, Young, A. Ferguson, Kemp
ABERDEEN: Ogston, Bennett, Hogg, Kinnell, Coutts, Smith, Cummings, Allan, Winchester, Cooke, Thom
Attendance: 9,000   *Referee:* T. Wharton
St. Johnstone are chasing promotion to the First Division. Ernie Winchester missed a hatful but netted the one that mattered to take Aberdeen into Round 3. Once Cummings had levelled Ferguson's shock opener, the Dons were rarely in difficulty.

3rd Round Wednesday, 20 March
ABERDEEN (2) 4   DUNFERMLINE
  Cummings 2 (26, 42),   ATHLETIC (0) 0
  Kinnell 2 (62 pen,
  67 pen)
ABERDEEN: Ogston, Bennett, Hogg, Kinnell, Coutts, Smith, Cummings, Allan, Winchester, Cooke, Thom
DUNFERMLINE: Herriot, Callaghan, Cunningham, Thomson, McLean, Miller, McLinden, Smith, Dickson, Melrose, Peebles
Attendance: 20,000   *Referee:* R. H. Davidson
Two years earlier Jock Stein's side won 6-3 in the Cup at Pittodrie. The referee was the most controversial

figure in this bruising battle, as Aberdeen put the record straight. Dunfermline keeper Herriot went off after just ten minutes with a dislocated thumb. Miller took over in goal. In the second half McLinden clashed with Cooke, and McLinden was sent off while Cooke was not. Aberdeen were then awarded two penalties. Kinnell scored with the first but hit the second over the top. To Dunfermline's fury Kinnell was instructed to try again, and he did.

Quarter Final Saturday, 30 March
RAITH ROVERS (1) 2   ABERDEEN (1) 1
  Gilfillan 2 (15, 80)   Cummings (27)
RAITH: Thorburn, Stevenson, Haig, Wilson, Bolton, Burrows, Lourie, McDonald, Gilfillan, Smith, Adamson
ABERDEEN: Ogston, Bennett, Hogg, Kinnell, Coutts, Smith, Cummings, Allan, Winchester, Cooke, Thom
Attendance: *Referee:* H. Phillips
Raith were beaten 10-0 at Pittodrie earlier in the season. They would be beaten 4-0 by Aberdeen at Raith later on. Raith haven't won a home league game all season. Yet somehow Aberdeen make a hash of beating them in the Cup. Bennett was responsible for Gilfillan's first goal, making a mess of a backpass and poking the ball straight into the path of the Raith forward. Cummings equalised with a shot which hit Thorburn yet rolled into goal despite a desperate lunge by Haig. After the break Smith hit the Raith crossbar. Then a tackle by Hogg on Lourie gave Raith a penalty, which Ogston saved by flinging himself to his right to thwart Wilson. But then came Lourie's fateful cross. Gilfillan latched onto it and rifled the winner.

1962-63

APPEARANCES	League	League Cup	Scottish Cup
Hogg	34	6	3
Ogston	34	6	3
Kinnell	34	5	3
Coutts	31	1	3
D. Smith	31	1	3
Cummings	30	4	3
Cooke	27	6	3
Allan	26	2	3
Winchester	25	6	3
Thom	23		3
Bennett	22	1	3
Little	16	5	
Shewan	12	6	
Brownlee	9	5	
Fraser	9	5	
Wilson	5		
Mulhall	2	6	
Ring	2		
Callaghan	1	1	
Anderson	1		
20 players			

GOALS	Total	League	League Cup	Scottish Cup
Cummings	23	18	1	4
Winchester	20	17	2	1
Kinnell	12	10		2
Cooke	8	8		
Little	8	6	2	
Thom	4	4		
D. Smith	3	3		
Brownlee	3	1	2	
Mulhall	3		3	
Callaghan	1	1		
Coutts	1	1		
Wilson	1	1		
own-goals	2		2	
Total	89	70	12	7

Season 1964-65. Aberdeen's signings from Denmark meet their new team mates. From left: Lief Mortensen, Jorgen Ravn and Jens Petersen.

Season 1963-64

In the post-War history of Aberdeen F.C., Saturday 15 February 1964 stands out. For years beforehand the fortunes of north-east Scotland's premier club had been on the wane. Attendances were never lower; enthusiasm among the public at large was never so little in evidence. On 15 February Aberdeen entertained Ayr United in the third round of the Scottish Cup. In the second round Aberdeen had needed two attempts, extra time, and a wicked deflection to squeeze past the amateurs from Queens Park. Now litte Ayr, sunk near the bottom of the Second Division, came from behind to snatch victory at Pittodrie. From that moment Tommy Pearson's job as manager was always on borrowed time.

There were many heads on the chopping block that day, as Aberdeen grabbed the headlines for all the wrong reasons. The season had gone woefully wrong from the start. In the League Cup group rounds Aberdeen had looked forward to a home decider with Hibs for the right of access to the quarter finals. Aberdeen lost 2-0. In the league the Dons collected just a single point from their four opening games and by mid-October were only a point off the bottom. Then came the almost traditional, false-bottomed, revival. A 4-1 win at Dens Park on New Year's Day saw Aberdeen comfortably placed in mid-table – in an ideal position from which to concert their energies for the Scottish Cup. Their season died at the moment the final whistle sounded against Ayr – though they still contrived to hand doomed East Stirling their first league win in fourteen games, as if seeking to sink to further depths.

Aberdeen's main problem was their inability to win at home. In 23 league, League Cup and Scottish Cup matches played at Pittodrie the Dons won only seven. Their home league record was the worst since the War. Aberdeen always looked more comfortable on their travels – perhaps hinting that the 'support' from the Pittodrie terraces was not all it might be.

League:	Ninth
League Cup:	Second in qualifying group
Scottish Cup:	Third Round

SCOTTISH LEAGUE DIVISION ONE

No 1 Wednesday, 21 August
PARTICK THISTLE (0) 1   ABERDEEN (1) 1
  Duffy (77)   Hume (19)

PARTICK: Niven, Hogan, Brown, Ferguson, McKinnon, Staite, Smith, Cunningham, Hainey, Duffy, McParland

ABERDEEN: Ogston, Shewan, Hogg, Kinnell, Coutts, Fraser, Cummings, Little, Winchester, Cooke, Hume

P	W	D	L	F	A	Pts		*Attendance:* 9,000
1	0	1	0	1	1	1		*Referee:* J. Stewart

Hume scores a beauty from 25 yards, in off the bar. But then Ogston dropped a long Smith cross and Duffy pounced. For almost all the second half Aberdeen played without Coutts, who had damaged his back.

No 2 Saturday, 7 September
ABERDEEN (1) 2   DUNDEE (2) 4
  Cummings (19),   Gilzean 2 (3, 41),
  Fraser (70)   Cameron (63), Penman
                           (66)

ABERDEEN: Ogston, Shewan, Hogg, Fraser, Kinnell, Smith, Cummings, Allan, Little, Cooke, Hume.

DUNDEE: Slater, Hamilton, Cox, Seith, Ryden, Houston, Penman, Cousin, Cameron, Gilzean, Robertson

P	W	D	L	F	A	Pts		
2	0	1	1	3	5	1		*Referee:* D. Weir

Opportunist Alan Gilzean is up to his old tricks. His two first-half goals against the run of play showed Aberdeen how they should be taken. All the Dons' outfield dominance came to nothing.

142

No 3 Saturday, 14 September
ST JOHNSTONE (1) 3   ABERDEEN (0) 1
  McIntyre 2 (38, 58),   Kinnell (50 pen)
  Harrower (85)
ST JOHNSTONE: Taylor, Roe, Lachlan, Townsend, McKinven, McGarry, Flanagan, Harrower, McIntyre, Bell, Kemp
ABERDEEN: Ogston, Shewan, Hogg, Fraser, Kinnell, Smith, Cummings, Allan, Little, Cooke, Hume

P	W	D	L	F	A	Pts
3	0	1	2	4	8	1

Attendance: 8,700
Referee: W. Elliott

St Johnstone repeatedly won possession of the ball. Harrower's screaming goal direct from a free kick ended Aberdeen's hopes. This is Doug Fraser's last match for Aberdeen before his transfer to West Bromwich Albion.

No 4 Saturday, 21 September
ABERDEEN (0) 0   ST MIRREN (1) 2
                          Carroll (14),
                          Kerrigan (59)
ABERDEEN: Ogston, Bennett, Shewan, Burns, Coutts, Smith, Allan, Kinnell, Cummings, Cooke, Hume
ST MIRREN: Dempster, Murray, Wilson, Campbell, Clunie, McTavish, Kerrigan, Carroll, White, Beck, Robertson
Bottom positions

	P	W	D	L	F	A	Pts
16 ABERDEEN	4	0	1	3	4	10	1
17 Partick	4	0	1	3	4	11	1
18 Airdrie	4	0	0	4	5	13	0

Attendance: 8,000   *Referee: J. N. Wallace*

Part of the Pittodrie crowd chanted 'We want Pearson' – a reference to the manager turning back the clock to his playing heyday. Aberdeen looked to be playing a 3-3-4 formation – which failed dismally.

No 5 Saturday, 28 September
AIRDRIE (0) 1   ABERDEEN (3) 7
  Bennett o.g. (72)   Graham 2 (25, 43), Cooke
                              (39), Hume (60), Thom
                              (73), Kinnell 2 (83 pen,
                              89 pen)
AIRDRIE: McKenzie, Caldwell, Keenan, Rowan, Hannah, Duddy, Ferguson, Whitelaw, Boyd, Murray, Newlands
ABERDEEN: Ogston, Bennett, Shewan, Burns, Coutts, Kinnell, Hume, Cooke, Graham, Smith, Thom

P	W	D	L	F	A	Pts
5	1	1	3	11	13	3

Attendance:
Referee: W. Small

New signing Billy Graham from Gateshead scores a comic first goal on his debut. Trying to control a centre, he hits the ball with the sole of his boot and it bobbles past McKenzie. Despite the remarkable score it is Airdrie who did most of the attacking.

No 6 Saturday, 5 October
ABERDEEN (0) 1   THIRD LANARK (0) 1
  Graham (67)   Murray (49)
ABERDEEN: Ogston, Bennett, Hogg, Burns, Coutts, Kinnell, Hume, Cooke, Graham, Smith, Thom
THIRD LANARK: Paul, McGillivray, Davis, Dickson, McCormick, MacLeod, Bryce, Anderson, Murray, Brownlee, Buckley

P	W	D	L	F	A	Pts
6	1	2	3	12	12	4

Referee: A. McKenzie

Lucky Aberdeen. MacLeod missed a penalty in the opening minutes after Burns handled. The Dons never looked like scoring and only did so when Paul fumbled the ball for Graham to follow up. Incidentally, Aberdeen's 7 goals against Airdrie last week were put into perspective. Today Dundee United hit 9 past them.

No 7 Saturday, 12 October
CELTIC (1) 3   ABERDEEN (0) 0
  McKay (18 pen),
  Chalmers, 2 (63, 68)
CELTIC: Haffey, Young, Gemmell, McKay, Cushley, Kennedy, Johnstone, Murdoch, Chalmers, Divers, Hughes
ABERDEEN: Ogston, Bennett, Hogg, Kinnell, Coutts, Smith, Cummings, Morrison, Little, Wilson, Thom

P	W	D	L	F	A	Pts
7	1	2	4	12	15	4

Attendance: 15,000
Referee: A. Crossman

Billy Graham is dropped to make way for Tommy Morrison from the reserves. McKay netted from the spot after Bennett had challenged Chalmers, though the referee was forty yards away from the incident. A further foul on Chalmers brought a second penalty for Celtic, but this time McKay's aim was shaky. Having earned two penalties, Chalmers then scored two second-half goals himself.

No 8 Saturday, 19 October
KILMARNOCK (1) 2   ABERDEEN (0) 0
  McIlroy (26),
  Murray (64)
KILMARNOCK: Forsyth, King, Watson, O'Connor, McGrory, Beattie, Brown, McInally, Murray, Sneddon, McIlroy
ABERDEEN: Ogston, Shewan, Hogg, Kinnell, Coutts, Smith, Lister, Cooke, Graham, Morrison, Hume
Bottom positions

	P	W	D	L	F	A	Pts
14 ABERDEEN	8	1	2	5	12	17	4
15 East Stirling	8	2	0	6	8	15	4
16 Third Lanark	8	1	2	5	9	20	4
17 Hibernian	8	1	1	6	10	24	3
18 Airdrie	8	1	1	6	11	32	3

Referee: W. M. Syme

An all-change Aberdeen front line can't inflict any damage on second-placed Killie.

No 9 Saturday, 26 October
ABERDEEN (3) 3   FALKIRK (0) 0
  Winchester 2 (17, 35),
  Kerrigan (19)

ABERDEEN: Ogston, Shewan, Hogg, Kinnell, Coutts, Smith, Kerrigan, Cooke, Graham, Winchester, Hume
FALKIRK: Whigham, Lambie, Stewart, Pierson, Rae, Fulton, O'Donnell, Redpath, Wilson, Maxwell, Gourlay

P	W	D	L	F	A	Pts	
9	2	2	5	15	17	6	*Attendance:* 8,000

Referee: W. J. Allan

It's the transfer merry-go-round. Cummings has gone to Newcastle for £5,000, and Allan to St Mirren in part-exchange for Don Kerrigan, who has already scored twice against Aberdeen this season. Ogston and Kinnell are the only Dons ever-presents after just nine games. The new-look team helps bring about Aberdeen's first home league win of the season.

No 10 Saturday, 2 November
HEARTS (0) 0   ABERDEEN (0) 0
HEARTS: Cruickshank, Shevlane, Holt, Polland, Barry, Higgins, Hamilton, Murphy, Ferguson, Wallace, Cumming
ABERDEEN: Ogston, Shewan, Hogg, Kinnell, Coutts, Smith, Kerrigan, Cooke, Graham, Winchester, Hume

P	W	D	L	F	A	Pts	
10	2	3	5	15	17	7	*Attendance:* 8,000

What an appalling waste of money for those who turned up to this non-event.

No 11 Saturday, 9 November
RANGERS (0) 0   ABERDEEN (0) 0
RANGERS: Ritchie, Shearer, Provan, Greig, McKinnon, Millar, Henderson, Willoughby, Brand, Forrest, Watson
ABERDEEN: Ogston, Shewan, Hogg, Kinnell, Coutts, Smith, Kerrigan, Cooke, Graham, Winchester, Hume

P	W	D	L	F	A	Pts	
11	2	4	5	15	17	8	*Referee:* J. Hamilton

Leaders Rangers are unbeaten and have lost only three goals all season. It seems a home banker, but for the third season in a row the 'Gers fail to beat the Dons at Ibrox.

No 12 Saturday, 16 November
ABERDEEN (3) 6   MOTHERWELL (0) 2
  Winchester 3 (15, 31,   Carlyle (73), Weir (76)
  65), Kerrigan 2 (23, 83),
  Smith (48)
ABERDEEN: Ogston, Shewan, Hogg, Burns, Coutts, Smith, Kerrigan, Cooke, Graham, Winchester, Hume
MOTHERWELL: Wylie, Thomson, McCallum, Delaney, Martis, McCann, Lindsay, Robertson, Carlyle, McBride, Weir.

P	W	D	L	F	A	Pts	
12	3	4	5	21	19	10	*Attendance:* 8,000

Referee: J. R. P. Gordon

Dons' skipper George Kinnell has been transferred to Stoke City. Tommy Pearson celebrates four complete seasons in charge at Pittodrie, and Ernie Winchester celebrates a hat-trick.

No 13 Saturday, 23 November
QUEEN OF THE   ABERDEEN (2) 3
  SOUTH (1) 2   Graham (7), Kerrigan
  Coates (38), Kerr (78)   (27), Winchester (87)
QUEEN OF THE SOUTH: Farm, Morrison, Kerr, Irving, Rugg, McChesney, Hannigan, Pirie, Coates, Gardiner, Muir
ABERDEEN: Ogston, Shewan, Hogg, Burns, Coutts, Smith, Kerrigan, Cooke, Graham, Winchester, Hume

P	W	D	L	F	A	Pts	
13	4	4	5	24	21	12	*Referee:* G. Bowman

In pouring rain Aberdeen stretch their unbeaten run, following the signing of Kerrigan, to five. Queens are renowned for fighting back once they are two goals down, and live up to their reputation. Ernie Winchester put paid to their rally.

No 14 Saturday, 30 November
HIBERNIAN (1) 2   ABERDEEN (0) 0
  Baxter (6),
  Stevenson (50 pen)
HIBERNIAN: R. Simpson, W. Simpson, Grant, Leishman, Easton, Baxter, Scott, Quinn, Baker, Martin, E. Stevenson
ABERDEEN: Ogston, Shewan, Hogg, Burns, Coutts, Smith, Kerrigan, Cooke, Graham, Winchester, Hume

P	W	D	L	F	A	Pts	
14	4	4	6	24	23	12	*Attendance:*

Referee: W. Elliott

Desperate for points, Hibs halt Aberdeen's winning ways. In the first half Hibs keeper Ronnie Simpson kept the Dons' forwards at bay.

No 15 Saturday, 7 December
ABERDEEN (1) 4   EAST STIRLING (0) 1
  Frickleton o.g. (30),   Kilgannon (80)
  Graham (61), Winchester
  (62), Kerrigan (77)
ABERDEEN: Ogston, Shewan, Hogg, Burns, Coutts, Smith, Kerrigan, Cooke, Graham, Winchester, Hume
EAST STIRLING: Swan, McNab, McQueen, Collumbine, Craig, Frickleton, Hamill, Sanderman, Kemp, Kilgannon, McIntosh

P	W	D	L	F	A	Pts	
15	5	4	6	28	24	14	*Attendance:* 7,000

Referee: T. Wharton

This is East Stirling's first league visit to Pittodrie for 31 years, and they are heading straight back where they came from.

No 16 Saturday, 14 December
DUNDEE UNITED (1) 1   ABERDEEN (1) 2
  Burns o.g. (30)   Hume (1), Kerrigan (77)
DUNDEE UNITED: Davie, Millar, Briggs, Neilson, Smith, Fraser, Irvine, Howieson, Davidson, Gillespie, Mitchell
ABERDEEN: Ogston, Shewan, Hogg, Burns, Coutts, Smith, Kerrigan, Cooke, Graham, Winchester, Hume

P	W	D	L	F	A	Pts	
16	6	4	6	30	25	16	*Referee:* A. Kidd

Aberdeen win at Tannadice for the first time in six visits since United were promoted in 1961. This was John Ogston's 100th consecutive game in the Dons' goal.

No 17 Saturday, 28 December
ABERDEEN (0) 0   PARTICK THISTLE (3) 5
                       Hainey 2 (44, 57), Staite
                       2 (26, 45), Duffy (75)
ABERDEEN: Ogston, Shewan, Hogg, Stewart, Burns, Smith, Kerrigan, Cooke, Graham, Winchester, Hume
PARTICK: Niven, Hogan, Tinney, Closs, Harvey, Cunningham, Cowan, Hainey, Staite, Duffy, McParland
P W D L F A Pts
17 6 4 7 30 30 16   *Referee:* W. L. Frye
Without the sidelined Doug Coutts, Aberdeen's defence crumbled. Partick sauntered to their first away win of the season to provide Aberdeen with a torrid end to 1963. It was in the last seconds of the first half that Thistle scored two goals to end Aberdeen's interest in the match.

No 18 Wednesday, 1 January
DUNDEE (1) 1   ABERDEEN (2) 4
  Gilzean (55)   Winchester 2 (24, 27),
                         Cooke (60), Graham (83)
DUNDEE: Slater, Hamilton, Cox, Seith, Stuart, Wishart, Smith, Waddell, Cousin, Gilzean, Penman
ABERDEEN: Ogston, Shewan, Hogg, Burns, Anderson, Smith, Kerrigan, Cooke, Graham, Winchester, Hume
P W D L F A Pts   *Attendance:* 15,000
18 7 4 7 34 31 18   *Referee:* W. Elliot·
Aberdeen had power, precision and punch, and were completely unrecognisable from the team which folded against Partick. Alan Gilzean is up to his old tricks again, but fortunately Aberdeen have the rest of the magic.

No 19 Thursday, 2 January
ABERDEEN (0) 0   ST JOHNSTONE (1) 1
                         Flanagan (11)
ABERDEEN: Ogston, Shewan, Hogg, Burns, Anderson, Smith, Kerrigan, Cooke, Graham, Winchester, Hume
ST JOHNSTONE: Fallon, McFadyen, Richmond, Townsend, McKinven, McCarry, Flanagan, Jackson, McIntyre, Harrower, Kemp
P W D L F A Pts   *Attendance:* 10,000
19 7 4 8 34 32 18   *Referee:* R. A. S. Crockett
Who can possibly predict Aberdeen's result from one game to another? Flanagan scored the all-important goal when he intercepted Hogg's square pass across the penalty area to shoot home off a post.

No 20 Saturday, 4 January
ST MIRREN (2) 3   ABERDEEN (0) 1
  J. Robertson (4),   Winchester (58)
  T. Robertson (43), Queen
  (55)
ST MIRREN: Beattie, Murray, Wilson, Clark, Clunie, Ross, T. Robertson, Beck, Queen, Allan, J. Robertson
ABERDEEN: Ogston, Shewan, Hogg, Burns, Anderson, Smith, Kerrigan, Cooke, Little, Winchester, Thom
P W D L F A Pts   *Attendance:* 5,000
20 7 4 9 35 35 18   *Referee:* J. Callaghan
St Mirren could do with the points, as they complete their first double of the season. This is a terrible preparation as Aberdeen get ready for their Scottish Cup campaign.

No 21 Saturday, 18 January
ABERDEEN (1) 2   AIRDRIEONIANS (1) 2
  Winchester (3),   Murray 2 (19, 70)
  Kerrigan (77)
ABERDEEN: Ogston, Shewan, Hogg, Burns, Coutts, Smith, Kerrigan, Cooke, Little, Winchester, Hume
AIRDRIE: Samson, Jonquin, Keena, Duddy, Hannah, Thomson, Ferguson, Hastings, Rowan, Murray, Newlands
P W D L F A Pts   *Attendance:* 7,000
21 7 5 9 37 37 19   *Referee:* W. M. Syme
Airdrie are next to bottom, and recover from their 7-1 home defeat by Aberdeen. The only excitement arrived after Murray put Airdrie ahead. Only then did Aberdeen wake up.

No 22 Saturday, 1 February
THIRD LANARK (1) 1   ABERDEEN (1) 2
  Graham (27)   Hume (5), Cooke (80)
THIRD LANARK: Paul, Lewis, Davis, Cunningham, McCormack, Geddes, Graham, McMorran, Murray, Brownlee, Buckley
ABERDEEN: Ogston, Shewan, Hogg, Burns, Coutts, Smith, Kerrigan, Cooke, Little, Winchester, Hume
P W D L F A Pts
22 8 5 9 39 38 21   *Referee:* J. M. Kelly
Third Lanark are deep in relegation trouble, and were not helped by having to play the last half hour – when Aberdeen found the winner – without the injured Cunningham.

No 23 Saturday, 8 February
ABERDEEN (0) 0   CELTIC (1) 3
                         Smith o.g. (16), Brogan
                         (61), Divers (74)
ABERDEEN: Ogston, Shewan, Hogg, Burns, Coutts, Smith,·Kerrigan, Cooke, Little, Winchester, Hume
CELTIC: Fallon, Young, Gemmell, Clark, McNeill, Kennedy, Johnstone, Murdoch, Chalmers, Divers, Brogan

P W D L F A Pts   *Attendance:* 15,000
23 8 5 10 39 41 21   *Referee:* W. J. Mullen

Fourth-placed Celtic inflict Aberdeen's first defeat in six league and Cup games. Celtic were streets ahead. The Dons continually switched positions but succeeded only in confusing themselves. Chalmers' first-half header was going wide when Dave Smith lashed it behind Ogston to send Celtic on their way. In the first nine minutes of the game Coutts committed three harsh fouls to remind Celtic that Aberdeen would not stand on ceremony.

No 24 Wednesday, 19 February
ABERDEEN (0) 0   KILMARNOCK (0) 0
ABERDEEN: Ogston, Shewan, Hogg, Burns, Coutts, Smith, Lister, Morrison, Kerrigan, Winchester, Thom
KILMARNOCK: Forsyth, King, Watson, O'Connor, McGrory, Beattie, Brown, McFadzean, Murray, Sneddon, McIlroy

P W D L F A Pts   *Attendance:* 6,000
24 8 6 10 39 41 22   *Referee:* A. Mackenzie

With their tails firmly between their legs following the debacle against Ayr, the Dons battle for their lives against title-chasing Killie. Their confidence is not helped by Dave Smith asking for a transfer beforehand.

No 25 Saturday, 22 February
FALKIRK (1) 2   ABERDEEN (1) 3
Redpath (38), Maxwell   Winchester 2 (7, 61)
(74),   Morrison (57)
FALKIRK: Whigham, Lambie, Hunter, Pierson, Rae, Stewart, Blues, Fulton, Redpath, Maxwell, O'Donnell
ABERDEEN: Ogston, Shewan, Hogg, Burns, Coutts, Smith, Lister, Morrison, Kerrigan, Winchester, Donaldson

P W D L F A Pts
25 9 6 10 42 43 24   *Referee:* J. R. P. Gordon

All the players lost their footing, but at least Aberdeen didn't lose any points. The Dons conceded 15 corners in the last ten minutes.

No 26 Saturday, 29 February
ABERDEEN (1) 1   HEARTS (1) 2
Winchester (23)   White 2 (32, 81)
ABERDEEN: Ogston, Shewan, Hogg, Burns, Coutts, Smith, Lister, Morrison, Kerrigan, Winchester, Donaldson
HEARTS: Cruickshank, Shevlane, Holt, Polland, Barry, Higgins, Hamilton, Wallace, White, Gordon, Traynor

P W D L F A Pts   *Attendance:* 10,000
26 9 6 11 43 45 24   *Referee:* G. Bowman

Hearts have hopes of the title, hopes which are strengthened by this win. The Dons' babes fought their ground, though, and Tommy White's second goal was scored when Coutts was limping aimlessly among the Aberdeen forwards.

No 27 Wednesday, 11 March
ABERDEEN (1) 1   RANGERS (0) 1
Winchester (37)   Baxter (50 pen)
ABERDEEN: Ogston, Shewan, Hogg, Burns, Coutts, Smith, Lister, Morrison, Kerrigan, Winchester, Thom
RANGERS: Ritchie, Shearer, Provan, Greig, Baillie, Baxter, Henderson, McMillan, Forrest, Brand, Wilson

P W D L F A Pts   *Attendance:* 22,000
27 9 7 11 44 46 25   *Referee:* H. Phillips

Aberdeen's largest gate of the season turns out for the visit of the defending champions and the champions-elect. The Dons flex their muscles. In the first half Willie Henderson is taken off with damaged ankle ligaments. In the second Jim Forrest is rendered a virtual passenger. Aberdeen have now played the league's top three sides in successive home games, and only two points have been gathered. They might have beaten Rangers had not Hogg conceded the penalty which Baxter converted off the bar.

No 28 Saturday, 14 March
MOTHERWELL (0) 0   ABERDEEN (0) 1
   Morrison (67)
MOTHERWELL: Wylie, Delaney, McCallum, Murray, Martis, Moore, Carlyle, Lindsay, McBride, Robertson, Weir
ABERDEEN: Ogston, Shewan, Hogg, Burns, Coutts, Smith, Lister, Morrison, Kerrigan, Winchester, Thom

P W D L F A Pts
28 10 7 11 45 46 27   *Referee:* A. F. J. Webster

Filthy weather. A scrappy game saw Aberdeen scrap for the points, secured with a save by Ogston from a McBride penalty.

No 29 Saturday, 21 March
ABERDEEN (0) 3   QUEEN OF THE
Kerrigan 3 (59 pen,   SOUTH (0) 0
75, 77)
ABERDEEN: Ogston, Shewan, Hogg, Burns, Coutts, Smith, Lister, Morrison, Kerrigan, Winchester, Thom
QUEEN OF THE SOUTH: Ball, Rugg, Kerr, Morrison, Plenderleith, Murphy, Hannigan, Franks, Coates, Byrne, Law

P W D L F A Pts   *Attendance:* 3,400
29 11 7 11 48 46 29   *Referee:* J. Dearie

Aberdeen's lowest attendance of the season, and their first home win since 7 December.

No 30 Saturday, 28 March
ABERDEEN (0) 3   HIBERNIAN (0) 1
Lister (53), Winchester   Martin (59)
(79), Kerrigan (85)
ABERDEEN: Ogston, Bennett, Shewan, Burns, Coutts, Smith, Lister, Morrison, Kerrigan, Winchester, Thom
HIBERNIAN: Simpson, Fraser, Baxter, Cormack, Stanton, Preston, Vincent, Hamilton, Scott, Martin, Grant

Action from the match played at Pittodrie on 8th February, 1964. Aberdeen lost this match by 3 goals to nil.

This match against Hearts was played at Pittodrie in February, 1964.

P W D L F A Pts   *Attendance:* 5,000
30 12 7 11 51 47 31   *Referee:* R. A. S. Crockett

Aberdeen's post-Ayr revival continues. Lister scored his first league goal, and Kerrigan ended the contest with one of his typical free kicks which flashed past the defending wall.

No 31 Saturday, 4 April
EAST STIRLING (0) 2   ABERDEEN (0) 1
  McIntosh (60), Hamill   Smith (78)
  (67)

EAST STIRLING: Arrol, Stobo, McQueen, Collumbine, Craig, McPhee, Hamill, Davidson, Coburn, Frickleton, McIntosh

ABERDEEN: Ogston, Shewan, Hogg, Burns, Coutts, Smith, Lister, Winchester, Kerrigan, Wilson, Thom

P W D L F A Pts   *Attendance:* 1,000
31 12 7 12 52 49 31   *Referee:* D.Small

East Stirling had not won for 14 games. Aberdeen expected a formality in obtaining their fourth double of the season.

No 32 Wednesday, 8 April
ABERDEEN (0) 0   DUNFERMLINE
                         ATHLETIC (0) 1
                         Sinclair (78)

ABERDEEN: Ogston, Shewan, Hogg, Burns, Coutts, Smith, Lister, Kerrigan, Winchester, Wilson, Hume

DUNFERMLINE: Herriot, W. Callaghan, Lunn, Smith, Fraser, Miller, Edwards, Peebles, Dickson, T. Callaghan, Sinclair

P W D L F A Pts
32 12 7 13 52 50 31   *Referee:* A. Webster

Dunfermline have slipped out of the championship race. They might have sewn up their victory earlier, but Peebles' penalty was well stopped by Ogston.

No 33 Saturday, 18 April
ABERDEEN (0) 0   DUNDEE UNITED (0) 0

ABERDEEN: Ogston, Shewan, Hogg, Burns, Coutts, Smith, Lister, Little, Winchester, Wilson, Kerrigan

DUNDEE UNITED: Davie, Millar, Gordon, Fraser, D. Smith, Briggs, Young, Rooney, Gillespie, Irvine, G. Smith

P W D L F A Pts   *Attendance:* 3,500
33 12 8 13 52 50 32   *Referee:* D. Weir

Aberdeen's first home league game brought defeat by Dundee: their last a struggling draw with Dundee United. United's captain is Doug Smith, brother of Aberdeen's Dave.

No 34 Friday, 24 April
DUNFERMLINE   ABERDEEN (0) 1
  ATHLETIC (2) 3   Kerrigan (71)
  Peebles (10), Kerray
  (44), Sinclair (50)

DUNFERMLINE: Herriot, Callaghan, Lunn, Smith, McLean, Miller, Peebles, Kerray, Dickson, Melrose, Sinclair

ABERDEEN: Ogston, Shewan, Hogg, Burns, Coutts, Smith, Kerrigan, Lister, Kerr, Winchester, Hume

Andy Kerr, Aberdeen's new signing from Sunderland, shot against an upright. Ogston saved yet another penalty.

Aberdeen's complete home and away record:

	HOME						AWAY						
	P	W	D	L	F	A		W	D	L	F	A	Pts
	34	5	5	7	26	26		7	3	7	27	27	32

Scottish League Division One 1963-64

		P	W	D	L	F	A	Pts
1	Rangers	34	25	5	4	85	31	55
2	Kilmarnock	34	22	5	7	77	40	49
3	Celtic	34	19	9	6	89	34	47
4	Hearts	34	19	9	6	74	40	47
5	Dunfermline	34	18	9	7	64	33	45
6	Dundee	34	20	5	9	94	50	45
7	Partick Thistle	34	15	5	14	55	54	35
8	Dundee United	34	13	8	13	65	49	34
9	ABERDEEN	34	12	8	14	53	53	32
10	Hibernian	34	12	6	16	59	66	30
11	Motherwell	34	9	11	14	51	62	29
12	St Mirren	34	12	5	17	44	74	29
13	St Johnstone	34	11	6	17	54	70	28
14	Falkirk	34	11	6	17	54	84	28
15	Airdrieonians	34	11	4	19	52	97	26
16	Third Lanark	34	9	7	18	47	74	25
17	Queen of the South	34	5	6	23	40	92	16
18	East Stirling	34	5	2	27	37	91	12

LEAGUE CUP

Saturday, 10 August
DUNDEE UNITED (0) 1 ABERDEEN (1) 1
  Mitchell (46)   Cummings (15)

DUNDEE UNITED: Davie, Millar, Gordon, Neilson, Smith, Fraser, Carlyle, Gillespie, Rooney, Irvine, Mitchell

ABERDEEN: Ogston, Shewan, Hogg, Fraser, Coutts, Smith, Cummings, Allan, Little, Kinnell, Hume

Attendance: *Referee:* W. Brittle

Cooke is missing, serving a suspension, as Aberdeen earn their fourth successive draw at Tannadice. New winger Bobby Hume took the eye, while Coutts was forced to limp out the second half on the wing.

Wednesday, 14 August
ABERDEEN (1) 2   ST MIRREN (1) 2
  Hume 2 (2, 56)   Carroll (42),
                         Kerrigan (64)

ABERDEEN: Ogston, Shewan, Hogg, Fraser, Coutts, Smith, Cummings, Allan, Little, Kinnell, Hume

ST MIRREN: Beattie, Murray, Riddell, Campbell, Clunie, Ross, Robertson, Carroll, White, Beck, Kerrigan

Attendance: 11,000   *Referee:* R. A. S. Crockett

Aberdeen deployed Little as a deep-lying centre forward at rain-sodden Pittodrie. Ex-Don Jim Clunie was Saints' strong-man in defence.

Saturday, 17 August
HIBERNIAN (1) 2   ABERDEEN (0) 2
  O'Rourke (36),   Hume (70), Little (87)
  Stevenson (59)
HIBERNIAN: Simpson, Grant, McClelland, Preston, Easton, Baxter, Scott, O'Rourke, Fraser, Martin, Stevenson
ABERDEEN: Ogston, Shewan, Hogg, Fraser, Anderson, Smith, Cummings, Kinnell, Little, Cooke, Hume
Attendance: 10,000   *Referee:* J. Callaghan
A phantom whistler in the crowd helped Hume reduce Hibs' lead. Martin stopped in his tracks, declined to challenge, and stood back as Hume put the ball in the net. Little's thunderous drive from Cooke's short free kick brought about the Dons' third draw.

Saturday, 24 August
ABERDEEN (0) 2   DUNDEE UNITED (0) 0
  Cummings (47),
  Hume (88)
ABERDEEN: Ogston, Shewan, Hogg, Fraser, Kinnell, Smith, Cummings, Little, Winchester, Cooke, Hume
DUNDEE UNITED: Davie, Millar, Briggs, Neilson, Smith, Fraser, Carlyle, Gillespie, Rooney, Mitchell, McManus
Attendance: *Referee:* W. J. Mullen
Dundee United have a happy knack of scoring late goals against Aberdeen. They very nearly did so again. With four minutes to play Kinnell fouled Rooney, but Ogston saved Mitchell's penalty. Two minutes later Bobby Hume settled the matter.

Wednesday, 28 August
ST MIRREN (0) 0   ABERDEEN (1) 3
                           Winchester 2 (37, 60),
                           Hume (88)
ST MIRREN: Beattie, Murray, Wilson, Campbell, Clunie, Gray, Quinn, Kerrigan, White, Queen, Robertson
ABERDEEN: Ogston, Shewan, Hogg, Fraser, Kinnell, Smith, Cummings, Little, Winchester, Cooke, Hume
Attendance: 7,000   *Referee:* H. Phillips
Winchester set things moving after a Little shot was blocked. Hume continued his knack of scoring a goal a game. Thus everything is set up for a cracker with Hibs.

Saturday, 31 August
ABERDEEN (0) 0   HIBERNIAN (1) 2
                           Martin (13), Baker (48)
ABERDEEN: Ogston, Shewan, Hogg, Fraser, Kinnell, Smith, Cummings, Little, Winchester, Cooke, Hume

HIBERNIAN: Simpson, Fraser, McClelland, Grant, Easton, Preston, Scott, Martin, Baker, Byrne, Stevenson
                        Referee: J. B. Barclay
Aberdeen had to win to qualify from Section 2. Anything else and Hibs would be through. The Dons had their chances but were given a lesson in taking them by Neil Martin and Joe Baker.

Section 2

	P	W	D	L	F	A	Pts
Hibernian	6	4	2	0	15	7	10
ABERDEEN	6	2	3	1	10	7	7
Dundee United	6	2	1	3	11	14	5
St Mirren	6	0	2	4	7	15	2

SCOTTISH CUP

1st Round Saturday, 11 January
ABERDEEN (3) 5   HIBERNIAN (0) 2
  Winchester 2 (11, 78),   Hamilton (67),
  Kerrigan 2 (23, 33),   O'Rourke (69)
  Hume (52)
ABERDEEN: Ogston, Shewan, Hogg, Burns, Coutts, Smith, Kerrigan, Cooke, Little, Winchester, Hume
HIBERNIAN: Simpson, Fraser, McClelland, Leishman, Grant, Baxter, Scott, Hamilton, Martin, Quinn, O'Rourke
Attendance: 15,500   *Referee:* H. Phillips
Teenager Ernie Winchester, so often barracked by the crowd, found himself being roared on today. Hibs had won at Pittodrie in the League Cup. On a fog-shrouded pitch the Dons found themselves hanging on after Hibs had pulled back from 4-0 to 4-2. It was then that a Kerrigan cross was powered into the net by Winchester to take Aberdeen into the second round.

2nd Round Saturday, 25 January
ABERDEEN (1) 1   QUEENS PARK (1) 1
  Winchester (21)   Hopper (5)
ABERDEEN: Ogston, Shewan, Hogg, Burns, Coutts, Smith, Kerrigan, Cooke, Little, Winchester, Hume
QUEENS PARK: Clark, Polatschek, Neil, Stewart, Cole, Grant, Hopper, Miller, Buchanan, Ingram, Kilpatrick
Attendance: 13,300   *Referee:* J. P. Barclay
The cynics said that the nearest Aberdeen would ever get to Hampden would be to force a replay with Queens Park, languishing in the anonymity of the Second Division. And it came to pass. The amateurs deserved to win, never mind draw. In the old days it was a Queens Park tradition never to congratulate a goalscorer. When Hopper put them in front early on he was mobbed.

2nd Round Replay Wednesday, 29 January
QUEENS PARK (1) 1 *1*   ABERDEEN (1) 1 *2*
  Buchanan (34)   (after extra time)
                          Hume (45), Smith (96)

QUEENS PARK: Clark, Polatschek, Neil, Stewart, Cole, Grant, Hopper, Miller, Buchanan, Ingram, Kilpatrick

ABERDEEN: Ogston, Shewan, Hogg, Burns, Coutts, Smith, Kerrigan, Cooke, Little, Winchester, Hume

Attendance: 6,100   *Referee:* J. P. Barclay

This was a hollow victory for Aberdeen, a moral one for the amateurs. In a frantic period of extra time Kerrigan twice hit the bar for Aberdeen, while Ingram walloped the base of the Dons post for Queens. Aberdeen scored a freak winner. Smith's 25-yarder was going straight towards young goalkeeper Bobby Clark when it struck Stewart and was deflected wide of the helpless goalie. Clark stood and held his head in his hands, but he had made his name and would soon be heading north.

3rd Round Saturday, 15 February

ABERDEEN (0) 1	AYR UNITED (0) 2
Graham (55)	Cunningham (77),
	Kilgannon (86)

ABERDEEN: Ogston, Shewan, Hogg, Burns, Coutts, Smith, Kerrigan, Cooke, Graham, Winchester, Hume

AYR: Gallacher, Murphy, Maxwell, Frew, Toner, Lindsay, Hubbard, McMillan, Kilgannon, Grant, Cunningham

Attendance: 10,300   *Referee:* W. Elliot

This was probably the blackest day in Aberdeen's history. 'Years of frustration for North-East football enthusiasts reached a climax this afternoon', pronounced the *Evening Express*. Ayr United were just off the bottom of Division Two. All seemed well when Graham – playing in his first Scottish Cup-tie – scored off a post to give Aberdeen the lead. But then Ayr abandoned their defensive formation. Ogston dropped a high ball to permit Cunningham on equaliser – and Kilgannon lobbed an insulting winner for the Ayrshire side. The reverberations of this defeat resounded around Pittodrie for months to come.

1963-64

APPEARANCES	League	League Cup	Scottish Cup
Ogston	34	6	4
Shewan	33	6	4
D. Smith	33	6	4
Hogg	31	6	4
Coutts	28	2	4
Winchester	27	3	4
Burns	26		4
Kerrigan	26		4
Hume	23	6	4
Cooke	22	4	4
Graham	14		1
Lister	12		
Kinnell	11	6	
Thom	10		
Little	9	6	3
Morrison	9		
Cummings	5	6	
Bennett	4		
Wilson	4		
Fraser	3	6	
Allan	3	2	
Anderson	3	1	
Donaldson	2		
Kerr	1		
Stewart	1		
25 players			

GOALS	Total	League	League Cup	Scottish Cup
Winchester	21	16	2	3
Kerrigan	14	12		2
Hume	11	4	5	2
Graham	7	6		1
Kinnell	3	3		
Cooke	3	3		
D. Smith	3	2		1
Cummings	3	1	2	
Morrison	2	2		
Fraser	1	1		
Lister	1	1		
Thom	1	1		
Little	1		1	
own-goal	1	1		
Totals	72	53	10	9

Fred Martin, Aberdeen goalkeeper of the fifties. Fred was Scotland's first World Cup keeper in 1954.

Season 1964-65

Uncannily, 1964-65 turned out to be an almost identical season to the one before. Both league records read: Played 34, Won 12, Drew 8, Lost 14, Points 32. Both seasons turned on ignominious cup exits at the hands of Second Division opponents. Tommy Pearson's job lasted exactly a year following the debacle against Ayr. This time it was East Fife who put the skids under Aberdeen, who couldn't find the net once in 180 minutes of frantic endeavour. Tommy Pearson had to go. And did. Some weeks later Eddie Turnbull assumed the reins.

1964-65 was also the season in which Aberdeen first paraded three Danes at the same time – Pearson's farewell gesture towards bringing livelier soccer to the north-east, having recently sold Charlie Cooke to Dundee. The Danes must have wondered whether it was worth coming at all. They were part of the Dons eleven hammered 8-0 by Celtic – Aberdeen's heaviest defeat of modern times. They were part of the team that was outmanoeuvred by little East Fife a week later in the Scottish Cup.

In 1964-65 it was Aberdeen's fear of travel that was their undoing. They shipped 48 league goals in 17 away games, overtaking their previous worst defensive record on opponents' grounds established three years earlier. Without ever-present John Ogston in goal they might have conceded even more.

Now, however, all minds were on the future. Turnbull's first match in charge brought about a 2-0 home win over Rangers, who became the first league visitors to fail to score at Pittodrie all season. Some stiffening of the Dons' leaky defence was desperately needed, for their goals-against column was exceeded only by the three bottom clubs in the league. Perhaps next year might be better.

League:	Twelfth
League Cup:	Third in qualifying group
Scottish Cup:	First Round

SCOTTISH LEAGUE DIVISION ONE

No 1 Wednesday, 19 August

ABERDEEN (0) 2	ST MIRREN (1) 1
Winchester 2 (69, 80)	Beck (16)

ABERDEEN: Ogston, Bennett, Shewan, Burns, Coutts, Smith, Lister, Cooke, Hume, Winchester, McIntosh

ST MIRREN: Liney, Murray, Wilson, Clark, Clunie, Gray, Ross, Carroll, McIntyre, Beck, Robertson

P	W	D	L	F	A	Pts
1	1	0	0	2	1	2

Referee: W. J. Mullen

Ogston's 200th first team match for Aberdeen. He ended it in hospital having a finger X-rayed. It threatens his unbroken run of 135 games. Winchester demanded that he be credited with the first goal, although he was sitting on the ground as the ball went in, and not defender Clunie.

No 2 Saturday, 5 September

DUNDEE (1) 3	ABERDEEN (0) 1
Penman 2 (15 pen, 85)	Winchester (89)
Stuart (53)	

DUNDEE: Donaldson, Hamilton, Totten, Seith, Ryden, Stuart, Penman, Scott, Waddell, Cousin, Robertson

ABERDEEN: Ogston, Bennett, Shewan, Burns, Coutts, Smith, Fraser, Cooke, Winchester, Little, Hume

P	W	D	L	F	A	Pts
2	1	0	1	3	4	2

Attendance: 8,000

Referee: J. M. Wallace

Rain has drenched Dens Park. It all went wrong for Aberdeen from the moment Coutts fouled 16-year old John Scott in the box.

No 3 Saturday, 12 September

ABERDEEN (4) 5	ST JOHNSTONE (2) 5
Little (2), Kerr 2	Kerray (10), Hawkshaw
(18, 35), Coutts (40),	(33), McLindon 2 (64,
McKinven o.g. (54)	(66), Richmond (89)

ABERDEEN: Ogston, Shewan, Hogg, Burns, Bennett, Smith, Coutts, Cooke, Kerr, Little, Hume

ST JOHNSTONE: Fallon, McFadyen, Coburn, Richmond, McKinven, Renton, Hawkshaw, Harrower, Kerray, McLindon, Kemp

P	W	D	L	F	A	Pts	*Attendance:* 5,000
3	1	1	1	8	9	3	*Referee:* A. Crossman

Well, well, well. This match also had two goals disallowed. As it was, Aberdeen led 5-2 after an hour. Coutts, playing experimentally on the wing, had his goal allowed although he clearly palmed the ball over the line. Richmond finally levelled the scores after Shewan had headed one Saints' effort off the line.

No 4 Saturday, 19 September

HIBERNIAN (4) 4	ABERDEEN (0) 2
Scott 3 (1, 30, 31 pen)	Kerr 2 (59, 64)
Hamilton (35)	

HIBERNIAN: Wilson, Fraser, Parke, Stanton, McNamee, J. Stevenson, Cormack, Martin, Scott, Hamilton, E. Stevenson

ABERDEEN: Ogston, Shewan, Hogg, Cooke, Coutts, Winchester, Hume, Kerrigan, Kerr, Little, McIntosh

P	W	D	L	F	A	Pts	
4	1	1	2	10	13	3	*Referee:* A. F. Webster

The contest was over at half-time, the consquence of a Scott hat-trick, which was completed when Hogg flattened Cormack in the box. Kerr reduced Aberdeen's blushes after the interval, but Aberdeen were never going to save the game. This takes the number of goals conceded in the last two matches up to nine.

No 5 Saturday, 26 September

ABERDEEN (3) 5	PARTICK THISTLE (0) 1
Little (3), Kerrigan (20),	Hainey (81)
Kerr 2 (27, 89),	
McIntosh (60)	

ABERDEEN: Ogston, Shewan, Hogg, Cooke, Coutts, Smith, Hume, Kerrigan, Kerr, Little, McIntosh

PARTICK: Niven, Hogan, Tinney, Davis, McKinnon, Cunningham, Ewing, Hainey, Staite, Fleming, McParland

P	W	D	L	F	A	Pts	
5	2	1	2	15	14	5	*Attendance:* 5,000

It seems a long time since Aberdeen actually won – seven games, in fact. But the goals continue to fly in: this time Aberdeen capitalised on an early goal, not frittering it away.

No 6 Saturday, 3 October

THIRD LANARK (2) 4	ABERDEEN (0) 1
Murray (18), Jackson (42),	Little (78)
Evans (63), Baillie (87)	

THIRD LANARK: Mitchell, Connell, Davis, Little, McCormick, Evans, Todd, Jackson, Baillie, Black, Murray

ABERDEEN: Ogston, Shewan, Hogg, Cooke, Coutts, Smith, Hume, Kerrigan, Kerr, Little, McIntosh

P	W	D	L	F	A	Pts	*Attendance:* 3,000
6	2	1	3	16	18	5	*Referee:* R. Stonehouse

Thirds' first win of the season – and how!

No 7 Saturday, 10 October

ABERDEEN (1) 1	CELTIC (1) 3
Kerrigan (12 pen)	Hughes (33), Murdoch
	67, Chalmers (78)

ABERDEEN: Ogston, Shewan, Hogg, Cooke, Coutts, Smith, Hume, Kerrigan, Kerr, Little, McIntosh

CELTIC: Fallon, Young, Gemmell, Clark, Cushley, Kennedy, Johnstone, Murdoch, Chalmers, Divers, Hughes

P	W	D	L	F	A	Pts	*Attendance:* 13,000
7	2	1	4	17	21	5	*Referee:* R. D. Henderson

'Sell the lot' suggested Pittodrie to manager Pearson after Celtic had recovered from an early penalty to stroll to victory and send Aberdeen into the bottom six. The Dons' penalty was the reward for Kennedy's foul on Hume, although McIntosh had already stuck the ball away as the referee blew. The game had drifted well beyond Aberdeen by the end.

No 8 Saturday, 17 October

ABERDEEN (0)	MOTHERWELL (1) 1
	McBride (40)

ABERDEEN: Ogston, Shewan, Hogg, Cooke, McCormick, Smith, Lister, Little, Kerr, Winchester, McIntosh

MOTHERWELL: Wylie, Thomson, McCallum, McCann, Delaney, Murray, Coakley, Weir, McBride, Robertson, Hunter

P	W	D	L	F	A	Pts	*Attendance:* 5,000
8	2	1	5	17	22	5	*Referee:* J. P. Barclay

Newcomer John McCormick must have wondered what he'd let himself into. A fortnight earlier he had helped Third Lanark to an easy, easy win over Aberdeen. Now McBride does them no favours either. His shot is blocked by Ogston but flies into the net off the forward's body.

No 9 Saturday, 24 October

DUNFERMLINE	ABERDEEN (0) 0
ATHLETIC (1) 2	
McLaughlin (24),	
Hogg o.g. (60)	

DUNFERMLINE: Herriot, Callaghan, Lunn, Thomson, Miller, Sinclair, Smith, McLaughlin, Ferguson, Melrose

ABERDEEN: Ogston, Shewan, Hogg, Cooke, McCormick, Burns, Coutts, Little, Morrison, Smith, Hume

Bottom positions

	P	W	D	L	F	A	Pts
14 ABERDEEN	9	2	1	6	17	24	5
15 Third Lanark	9	2	1	6	12	22	5
16 St Johnstone	9	1	2	6	14	22	4
17 St Mirren	8	1	2	5	4	15	4
18 Airdrie	9	0	2	7	14	37	2

Referee: D. Weir

McCormick's short backpass fell to McLaughlin who gratefully accepted Aberdeen's first gift. Hogg's headed own-goal was their second.

No 10 Saturday, 31 October

ABERDEEN (2) 2   FALKIRK (0) 1
  Morrison (8),   Houston (69)
  Kerrigan (19)

ABERDEEN: Ogston, Bennett, Shewan, Burns, Coutts, Smith, Lister, Cooke, Morrison, Kerrigan, Hume

FALKIRK: Whigham, Lambie, Hunter, Fulton, Markie, Scott, Houston, Allan, Wilson, Maxwell, Gourlay

P	W	D	L	F	A	Pts	
10	3	1	6	19	25	7	*Attendance:* 4,000
							Referee: W. J. Mullen

Pearson makes eight team changes. The Witches of Hallowe'en are on Aberdeen's side. They looked to be cruising, but a second-half Falkirk revival kept them on their toes.

No 11 Saturday, 7 November

RANGERS (0) 2   ABERDEEN (0) 2
  Baxter (64), Forrest (75)   Kerrigan (54),
                               Morrison (71)

RANGERS: Ritchie, Provan, Caldow, Greig, McKinnon, Wood, Brand, Millar, Forrest, Baxter, Johnston

ABERDEEN: Ogston, Bennett, Shewan, Burns, McCormick, Smith, Lister, Cooke, Morrison, Kerrigan, Kerr

P	W	D	L	F	A	Pts	
11	3	2	6	21	27	8	*Referee:* J. M. McConville

Mid-table Rangers are not firing on all cylinders, and are held by a resolute performance from Aberdeen. Bennett was stretchered off just after the interval but Aberdeen still managed to take the lead twice in a fog-shrouded Ibrox during a no-quarter-asked second half. At 2-1 Kerrigan headed a cross onto Ritchie's bar. Rangers escaped and in their next attack Baxter manufactured Forrest's equaliser. And to think that in the League Cup Rangers had thrashed Aberdeen 4-0 at Ibrox.

No 12 Saturday, 14 November

ABERDEEN (0) 2   MORTON (0) 1
  Kerr (53), Morrison (57)   Sorensen (67 pen)

ABERDEEN: Ogston, Shewan, Hogg, Burns, McCormick, Smith, Lister, Cooke, Morrison, Kerrigan, Kerr

MORTON: Miller, Boyd, Johansen, Ferguson, Kiernan, Strachan, Adamson, Stevenson, Bertelsen, Sorensen, McBeth

P	W	D	L	F	A	Pts	
12	4	2	6	23	28	10	*Attendance:* 5,000
							Referee: R. H. Davidson

Newly promoted Morton slump to a fifth consecutive defeat. In a blustery Pittodrie they sported three Danish imports, one of whom scored from a penalty.

No 13 Saturday, 21 November

ABERDEEN (1) 1   KILMARNOCK (0) 1
  Morrison (34)   McInally (90)

ABERDEEN: Ogston, Shewan, Hogg, Burns, McCormick, Smith, Lister, Cooke, Morrison, Kerrigan, Kerr

KILMARNOCK: Forsyth, King, Watson, Murray, McGrory, Beattie, McLean, McInally, Hamilton, McFadzean, Sneddon

P	W	D	L	F	A	Pts	
13	4	3	6	24	29	11	*Attendance:* 10,000
							Referee: J. Callaghan

Title-chasing Killie are unbeaten in the league this season. That record would have fallen had not Jackie McInally rewarded relentless Kilmarnock pressure by shooting an equaliser off a post in the last seconds.

No 14 Saturday, 28 November

DUNDEE UNITED (0) 0 ABERDEEN (2) 3
                     Kerrigan (15), Morrison
                     (26), Lister (87)

DUNDEE UNITED: Mackay, Millar, Briggs, Gordon, Smith, Fraser, Graham, Neilson, Dick, Gillespie, Mitchell

ABERDEEN: Ogston, Shewan, Hogg, Burns, Coutts, Smith, Lister, Cooke, Morrison, Kerrigan, Kerr

P	W	D	L	F	A	Pts	
14	5	3	6	27	29	13	*Attendance:* 6,000

This takes Aberdeen's points tally to eight from the last five games, and lowly United's to two from the same number. Morrison has scored for Aberdeen in all those five outings. Despite the score, Ogston was the busier keeper.

No 15 Saturday, 12 December

HEARTS (5) 6   ABERDEEN (1) 3
  White (5),   Kerrigan 2 (37, 86)
  Hamilton 2 (8 pen, 49),   Cooke (65)
  Gordon 3 (27, 31, 43)

HEARTS: Cruickshank, Shevlane, Holt, Polland, Anderson, Higgins, Wallace, Traynor, White, Gordon, Hamilton

ABERDEEN: Ogston, Shewan, Hogg, Burns, Coutts, Smith, Lister, Cooke, Morrison, Kerrigan, Kerr

P	W	D	L	F	A	Pts	
15	5	3	7	30	35	13	*Referee:* T. Wharton

Hearts are unbeaten and sit on top of the league. After this performance it's easy to see why. Before Aberdeen had a chance to draw breath they were two goals down. When the second half was only four minutes old Hearts

F

led 6-1. Aberdeen must have feared double figures, but the Jam Tarts became too casual and it was Aberdeen who scored face-saving goals. It turns out to be the last time Charlie Cooke scored for the Dons.

No 16 Saturday, 19 December
ABERDEEN (0) 0   CLYDE (0) 3
                        Knox 2 (53, 86), McLean
                        (60)
ABERDEEN: Ogston, Shewan, Hogg, Stewart, McCormick, Smith, Lister, Ronaldson, Morrison, Winchester, Kerr
CLYDE: McCulloch, Glasgow, Mulherron, McHugh, Fraser, White, Reid, Gilroy, Knox, McLean, Hastings

P   W D L   F A Pts   *Attendance:* 3,000
16 5 3 8 30 38 13   *Referee:* R. A. S. Crockett

Yesterday Aberdeen sold Charlie Cooke to Dundee. Without him they are shorn of any real talent. When Clyde scored their second goal, manager Pearson appeared on the touchline and was booed.

No 17 Saturday, 26 December
ST MIRREN (0) 4   ABERDEEN (0) 0
  Carroll 2 (48, 67), Quinn
  (65), McCormick o.g. (80)
ST MIRREN: Liney, Murray, Riddell, Gray, Clunie, Wilson, Robertson, Quinn, Carroll, Ross, Queen
ABERDEEN: Ogston, Shewan, Hogg, Burns, McCormick, Wilson, Morrison, Kerrigan, Little, Smith, Hume

P   W D L   F A Pts
17 5 3 9 30 42 13   *Referee:* J. W. Paterson

Tommy Pearson and members of the Board were away hunting players – which was probably just as well, for Aberdeen were 'boxed' good and proper.

No 18 Friday, 1 January
ABERDEEN (1) 1   DUNDEE (1) 1
  Winchester (28)   Penman (20)
ABERDEEN: Ogston, Shewan, Hogg, Burns, McCormick, Smith, Lister, Winchester, Morrison, Kerrigan, Kerr
DUNDEE: Donaldson, Hamilton, Reid, Cousin, Easton, Stuart, Murray, Penman, Harley, Cooke, Robertson

P   W D L   F A Pts   *Attendance:* 8,000
18 5 4 9 31 43 14

Dundee are (thankfully) without Alan Gilzean – gone to Spurs – but they include Charlie Cooke. Fortunately for Aberdeen he missed several straightforward chances on his old patch. Dundee's goal was the result of Smith dallying and allowing Penman to boot the ball off his toes. Winchester levelled the score by rifling home Morrison's lob.

No 19 Saturday, 9 January
ABERDEEN (1) 1   HIBERNIAN (1) 1
  Kerrigan (8)   Hamilton (5)

ABERDEEN: Ogston, Bennett, Shewan, Burns, McCormick, Smith, Fraser, Winchester, Morrison, Kerrigan, Wilson
HIBERNIAN: Wilson, Fraser, Davis, Stanton, McNamee, Baxter, Cormack, Quinn, Vincent, Hamilton, Martin

P   W D L   F A Pts   *Attendance:* 8,000
19 5 5 9 32 44 15   *Referee:* A. J. Crawley

A burst of activity at either end in the opening minutes promised a game above the ordinary. Hibs needed both points to sustain their title claim. When Burns appeared to handle in the box it looked as though they might get them, but the referee was not interested in giving penalties.

No 20 Saturday, 16 January
PARTICK THISTLE (1) 2   ABERDEEN (1) 1
  Hainey (16), Ewing (85)   Fraser (32)
PARTICK: Gray, Campbell, Muir, Davis, Harvey, McParland, Cowan, Hainey, McLindon, Ewing, Kilpatrick
ABERDEEN: Ogston, Bennett, Shewan, Burns, McCormick, Smith, Fraser, Winchester, Morrison, Kerrigan, McIntosh

Bottom positions

	P	W	D	L	F	A	Pts
14 ABERDEEN	20	5	5	10	33	46	15
15 Dundee United	20	5	4	11	27	36	14
16 Falkirk	21	4	6	11	22	46	14
17 Airdrie	21	3	2	16	24	66	8
18 Third Lanark	20	3	1	16	16	56	7

                              Referee: A. McKenzie

It looked like Aberdeen's third straight draw until Ewing's late header that hit Burns on the way into goal.

No 21 Wednesday, 27 January
ABERDEEN (0) 3   THIRD LANARK (1) 1
  Ravn (47), Kerrigan (74),   Kilgannon (7)
  Fraser (80)
ABERDEEN: Ogston, Bennett, Shewan, Petersen, McCormick, Smith, Fraser, Winchester, Ravn, Kerrigan, Mortensen
THIRD LANARK: Williams, Connell, May, Little, Baillie, Geddes, McKay, Kilgannon, Murray, Jackson, Kirk

P   W D L   F A Pts   *Attendance:* 9,000
21 6 5 10 36 47 17   *Referee:* R. D. Henderson

This match had to be postponed on the previous Saturday. An unusually healthy attendance turned out to take in Aberdeen's three Danish imports, who hadn't played a competitive match since November. This is all part of the recent Scandinavian invasion of Scottish football.

No 22 Saturday, 30 January
CELTIC (3) 8   ABERDEEN (0) 0
  Hughes 5 (27, 35, 61, 81, 87),
  Auld (41 pen), Murdoch (71),
  Lennox (76)

CELTIC: Fallon, Young, Gemmell, Clark, McNeill, Brogan, Chalmers, Murdoch, Hughes, Lennox, Auld
ABERDEEN: Ogston, Bennett, Shewan, Petersen, McCormick, Smith, Fraser, Winchester, Ravn, Kerrigan, Mortensen

P W D L F A Pts
22 6 5 11 36 55 17   *Referee:* J. P. Barclay

This was Celtic's first win of 1965 – and what a way to achieve it. John Hughes mastered the conditions with soft-soled shoes and mastered the Dons with five goals. Aberdeen's three Danes must have been bemused as they contributed to Aberdeen's worst humiliation of modern times – since 1931-32 to be precise. Simultaneously with Celtic's demolition of Aberdeen came Jock Stein's announcement that he will leave Hibs to take over at Parkhead.

No 23 Wednesday, 17 February
ST JOHNSTONE (1) 2   ABERDEEN (2) 4
  Duffy (16), Whitelaw   Winchester (6), Ravn 2
  (62),   (18, 66), Kerrigan (73)
ST JOHNSTONE: McVittie, McFadyen, Coburn, McCarry, McKinven, Renton, Kerray, Harrower, Whitelaw, Duffy, McGrogan
ABERDEEN: Ogston, Bennett, Shewan, Burns, McCormick, Smith, Little, Winchester, Ravn, Kerrigan, Mortensen

P W D L F A Pts   *Attendance:* 6,500
23 7 5 11 40 57 19

Aberdeen are managerless following Tommy Pearson's resignation – the consequence of cup defeat at East Fife. Ten of that side do their best to restore their pride. Jorgen Ravn scored his second goal after dislocating a shoulder and having it put back.

No 24 Saturday, 27 February
ABERDEEN (1) 2   DUNFERMLINE (1) 2
  Ravn (38), Mortensen (90)   Kilgannon (22), Fleming
                                      (60)
ABERDEEN: Ogston, Bennett, Shewan, Burns, McCormick, Smith, Little, Winchester, Ravn, Kerrigan, Mortensen
DUNFERMLINE: Herriot, W. Callaghan, Lunn, Smith, McLean, T. Callaghan, Fleming, Peebles, McLaughlin, Kilgannon, Melrose

P W D L F A Pts   *Attendance:* 7,000
24 7 6 11 42 59 20   *Referee:* W. Brittle

Dunfermline are making desperate efforts to overtake Hearts at the top. They were deprived of a second point by Leif Mortensen's breathtaking equaliser with the last kick. Dunfermline left out striker Alex Ferguson before the kick-off.

No 25 Saturday, 6 March
FALKIRK (0) 0   ABERDEEN (1) 1
                              Cummings (37)
FALKIRK: Whigham, Lambie, Brown, Stewart, Baillie, Scott, Graham, Allan, Wilson, Duncan, McKinney

ABERDEEN: Ogston, Bennett, Shewan, Burns, McCormick, Smith, Little, Winchester, Cummings, Kerrigan, Mortensen

P W D L F A Pts
25 8 6 11 43 59 22   *Referee:* D. Small

The only good thing about this stale match was John Cummings' goal on his promotion from the reserves.

No 26 Saturday, 13 March
ABERDEEN (2) 2   RANGERS (0) 0
  Winchester (3),
  Kerrigan (28)
ABERDEEN: Ogston, Bennett, Shewan, Burns, McCormick, Smith, Little, Winchester, Ravn, Kerrigan, Mortensen
RANGERS: Ritchie, Provan, Caldow, Greig, McKinnon, Hynd, Henderson, Wood, McLean, Baxter, Johnston

P W D L F A Pts   *Attendance:* 25,000
26 9 6 11 45 59 24   *Referee:* A. McKenzie

A wonderful first result for new manager Eddie Turnbull. Naughty Jim Baxter committed numerous petty fouls but wasn't spoken to by the referee. Fifth-placed Rangers were never likely to rescue the game. What a start by Ernie Winchester. Hynd made a hash of a backpass and Winchester thundered the ball into goal off a post. Kerrigan then brought Pittodrie to its feet, selling Greig a dummy and driving the ball wide of Ritchie. Rangers, of all people, became the first team to fail to score at Pittodrie this season.

No 27 Saturday, 20 March
MORTON (0) 1   ABERDEEN (0) 1
  Stevenson (53)   Kerrigan (59)
MORTON: Millar, Johansen, Mallon, Smith, Strachan, Neilsen, Bertelsen, Sorensen, Stevenson, McGraw, Wilson
ABERDEEN: Ogston, Bennett, Shewan, Stewart, McCormick, Smith, Little, Winchester, Ravn, Kerrigan, Mortensen

P W D L F A Pts
27 9 7 11 46 60 25   *Referee:* D. Weir

Greenock must have seemed like Copenhagen. There were six Danes on the field.

No 28 Wednesday, 24 March
ABERDEEN (4) 5   AIRDRIEONIANS (1) 2
  Winchester 3 (22, 35, 40)   Murray (15), Newlands
  Ravn (25), Kerrigan   (53)
  (59 pen)
ABERDEEN: Ogston, Bennett, Shewan, Stewart, McCormick, Smith, Little, Winchester, Ravn, Kerrigan, Mortensen
AIRDRIE: Samson, Black, Keenan, Rowan, Hannah, Reid, Moonie, McMillan, Marshall, Murray, Newlands

P W D L F A Pts   *Attendance:* 4,000
28 10 7 11 51 62 27   *Referee:* N. Watson

Aberdeen's revival continues. This makes ten points from six games. Airdrie have the nerve to score first, and then provoke Ernie Winchester into a first-half hat-trick.

No 29 Saturday, 27 March
KILMARNOCK (2) 2   ABERDEEN (0) 1
   Murray (10), Black (40)   Kerrigan (49)
KILMARNOCK: Ferguson, King, McFadzean, Murray, McGrory, Beattie, McLean, Mason, Black, Hamilton, McIlroy
ABERDEEN: Ogston, Bennett, Shewan, Stewart, McCormick, Smith, Little, Winchester, Ravn, Kerrigan, Mortensen
P W D L F A Pts   *Referee:* W. M. Syme
29 10 7 12 52 64 27
Aberdeen lose their first match in seven, since the cataclysmic defeat by East Fife. Dons' skipper Ally Shewan was booed every time he touched the ball following a booking when he crunched Tommy McLean. Mortensen shot over near the end when well placed. Had it gone in it would have denied Killie the title that would soon be theirs.

No 30 Saturday, 3 April
ABERDEEN (1) 1   DUNDEE UNITED (0) 0
   Winchester (16)
ABERDEEN: Ogston, Bennett, Shewan, Stewart, McCormick, Smith, Kerrigan, Little, Ravn, Winchester, Mortensen
DUNDEE UNITED: Mackay, Millar, Briggs, Gordon, Smith, Wing, Persson, Gillespie, Dossing, Berg, Mitchell
P W D L F A Pts   *Attendance:* 11,000
30 11 7 12 53 64 29   *Referee:* R. K. Wilson
Another match with six Scandinavians afield, plus two brothers on opposing sides – Doug and Dave Smith.

No 31 Saturday, 10 April
AIRDRIEONIANS (2) 2   ABERDEEN (2) 4
   Murray (18), Newlands   Ravn (5), Winchester 2
   (36)   (21, 78), Fraser (79)
AIRDRIE: Samson, McCall, Keenan, Reid, Hannah, Kerr, Ferguson, McMillan, Marshall, Murray, Newlands
ABERDEEN: Ogston, Bennett, Shewan, Stewart, McCormick, Smith, Fraser, Little, Ravn, Winchester, Mortensen
P W D L F A Pts   *Referee:* J. Hamilton
31 12 7 12 57 66 31
Two hefty wins over doomed Airdrie inside three weeks. But Aberdeen needed two goals inside a minute to complete their third double of the season.

No 32 Wednesday, 14 April
MOTHERWELL (1) 2   ABERDEEN (2) 2
   McBride 2 (8, 68)   Winchester (29), Fraser
                                       (35)

MOTHERWELL: Wylie, Delaney, R. McCallum, Aitken, Martis, W. McCallum, Coakley, Donnachie, McBride, Weir, Hume
ABERDEEN: Ogston, Bennett, Shewan, Stewart, McCormick, Smith, Fraser, Little, Ravn, Winchester, Mortensen
P W D L F A Pts
32 12 8 12 59 68 32
Aberdeen managed only two shots at goal throughout the first half but still took an interval lead. Near the end of the match Fraser 'armed' the ball into the net. The referee did not see it; the linesman did, and waved his flag furiously.

No 33 Saturday, 17 April
ABERDEEN (0) 0   HEARTS (1) 3
                                 Hamilton (8), Barry (70),
                                 Wallace (71)
ABERDEEN: Ogston, Bennett, Hogg, Stewart, Shewan, Smith, Fraser, Little, Kerrigan, Winchester, Mortensen
HEARTS: Cruickshank, Ferguson, Holt, Polland, Anderson, Higgins, Jensen, Barry, Wallace, Gordon, Hamilton
P W D L F A Pts   *Attendance:* 15,000
33 12 8 13 59 71 32   *Referee:* R. H. Davidson
This is pace-setting Hearts' penultimate match. They defended once Hamilton's early penalty had punished Shewan's careless tackle on Jensen, who was running harmlessly across the penalty area. As Aberdeen pushed forward in the second half the Hearts' players could be seen arguing among themselves, a sure sign of their tension. Then came a quick one-two to secure the points. Kilmarnock won by an identical score at home to Morton, and everything depends on their final match with Hearts.

No 34 Saturday, 24 April
CLYDE (2) 4   ABERDEEN (0) 0
   Hastings (25), Bruce
   (33), Knox (63), Gilroy (71)
CLYDE: McCulloch, Glasgow, Soutar, McHugh, Fraser, White, Bryce, Gilroy, Knox, McLean, Hastings
ABERDEEN: Ogston, Bennett, Shewan, Petersen, McCormick, Smith, Fraser, Little, Ravn, Kerrigan, Mortensen
                                       Referee: S. Stewart
Aberdeen are sunk in the Clyde. Manager Turnbull now has the summer to sort out his massive squad of players. He inherited 42 of them. But all ears were on Tynecastle where Kilmarnock won 2-0 to take their first championship.

Aberdeen's complete home and away record:

	HOME					AWAY					
P	W	D	L	F	A	W	D	L	F	A	Pts
34	8	5	4	33	27	4	3	10	26	48	32

Scottish League Division One

	P	W	D	L	F	A	Pts
1 Kilmarnock	34	22	6	6	62	33	50
2 Hearts	34	22	6	6	90	49	50
3 Dunfermline	34	22	5	7	83	36	49
4 Hibernian	34	21	4	9	75	47	46
5 Rangers	34	18	8	8	78	35	44
6 Dundee	34	15	10	9	86	63	40
7 Clyde	34	17	6	11	64	58	40
8 Celtic	34	16	5	13	76	57	37
9 Dundee United	34	15	6	13	59	51	36
10 Morton	34	13	7	14	54	54	33
11 Partick Thistle	34	11	10	13	57	58	32
12 ABERDEEN	34	12	8	14	59	75	32
13 St Johnstone	34	9	11	14	57	62	29
14 Motherwell	34	10	8	16	45	54	28
15 St Mirren	34	9	6	19	38	70	24
16 Falkirk	34	7	7	20	43	85	21
17 Airdrieonians	34	5	4	25	48	110	14
18 Third Lanark	34	3	1	30	22	99	7

LEAGUE CUP

Saturday, 8 August
RANGERS (2) 4   ABERDEEN (0) 0
  Forrest (28), McLean 2
  (35, 52), Wilson (79)
RANGERS: Ritchie, Shearer, Provan, Greig,
McKinnon, Baxter, Henderson, McLean, Forrest,
Brand, Wilson
ABERDEEN: Ogston, Bennett, Shewan, Cooke,
Coutts, Smith, Kerrigan, Ronaldson, Kerr, Winchester,
McIntosh
Attendance: 30,000   *Referee:* A. McKenzie
Aberdeen came out late for the second half. Perhaps
they didn't want to come out at all. Errors by Ogston
had already cost them the game.

Wednesday, 12 August
ABERDEEN (0) 2   ST JOHNSTONE (0) 1
  Kerrigan (56),   Flanagan (68)
  Winchester (61)
ABERDEEN: Ogston, Bennett, Shewan, Cooke,
Coutts, Smith, Kerrigan, Ronaldson, Hume,
Winchester, McIntosh
ST JOHNSTONE: Fallon, McFadyen, Coburn,
McCarry, Richmond, Dickson, Flanagan, McLindon,
Whitelaw, Kerray, Kemp
          Referee: R. K. Wilson
St Johnstone came to defend, but Flanagan almost
found a late equaliser, foiled thrillingly by Ogston.
McCarry had earlier hit a post for St Johnstone.

Saturday, 15 August
ST MIRREN (2) 3   ABERDEEN (2) 3
  Robertson 3 (34, 42, 83   Hume (6), Cooke (43),
  pen)   Smith (57)
ST MIRREN: Liney, Murray, Wilson, Clark, Clunie,
Gray, Quinn, Carroll, Hughes, Beck, Robertson

ABERDEEN: Ogston, Bennett, Shewan, Burns,
Coutts, Smith, Kerrigan, Cooke, Hume, Winchester,
McIntosh
Attendance: 5,000   *Referee:* H. Callaghan
Aberdeen had to do without the services of Coutts who
was dazed for most of the game and who had to wander
harmlessly out on the wing. St Mirren's late equaliser
came when the ball was driven hard against Burns' arm
from close range.

Saturday, 22 August
ABERDEEN (2) 3   RANGERS (2) 4
  McIntosh (14), Kerr   Forrest 3 (25, 28, 85)
  (24), Smith (87)   Brand (70)
ABERDEEN: Ogston, Bennett, Shewan, Burns, Coutts,
Smith, Lister, Cooke, Kerr, Winchester, McIntosh
RANGERS: Ritchie, Hynd, Provan, Watson,
McKinnon, Baxter, Henderson, McLean, Forrest,
Brand, Wilson
Attendance: 30,000   *Referee:* R. A. S. Crockett
There's many a sip twixt the cup and the lip. Aberdeen
were two goals up inside 24 minutes. Four minutes later
it is all square. Aside from his hat-trick Forrest also hit
a post.

Wednesday, 26 August
ST JOHNSTONE (1) 1   ABERDEEN (0) 1
  McLindon (16)   Smith (59)
ST JOHNSTONE: Fallon, Richmond, Coburn,
McCarry, McKinven, Renton, Flanagan, Kerray,
McLindon, Harrower, Kemp
ABERDEEN: Ogston, Bennett, Shewan, Burns,
Coutts, Smith, Kerrigan, Cooke, Hume, Winchester,
McIntosh
          Referee: J. R. P. Gordon
This game produced many unsavoury incidents, with
three players booked. Aberdeen fell behind as
McLindon latched onto the ball after Kerray had lobbed
Coutts. The equaliser arrived only once Winchester and
Smith had changed positions.

Saturday, 29 August
ABERDEEN (1) 2   ST MIRREN (0) 2
  Winchester (25),   Robertson (65),
  Smith (57)   Winchester o.g. (80)
ABERDEEN: Ogston, Bennett, Shewan, Burns,
Coutts, Smith, Kerrigan, Cooke, Fraser, Winchester,
McIntosh
ST MIRREN: Liney, Murray, Wilson, Clark, Clunie,
Gray, McIntyre, Carroll, Queen, Beck, Robertson
Attendance: 7,000   *Referee:* W. M. Syme
Aberdeen resume their habit of tossing away games that
appear to be won. Here, Robertson was allowed to score
with a twenty-yard free kick, and then Winchester
steered a shot past Ogston.

Section 1

	P	W	D	L	F	A	Pts
Rangers	6	5	1	0	26	7	11
St Mirren	6	2	3	1	11	12	7
ABERDEEN	6	1	3	2	11	15	5
St Johnstone	6	0	1	5	5	19	1

SCOTTISH CUP

1st Round Saturday, 6 February
ABERDEEN (0) 0   EAST FIFE (0) 0
ABERDEEN: Ogston, Bennett, Shewan, Petersen, McCormick, Smith, Fraser, Winchester, Ravn, Kerrigan, Mortensen
EAST FIFE: Hamilton, Davidson, Smith, Aitken, Walker, Donnelly, Rodger, Dewar, Young, Stewart, Waddell
Attendance: 10,100   *Referee:* W. J. Mullen

East Fife are in mid-table in Division 2. Aberdeen had nobody with the ideas to break down the Fifers' defence, whose No 9 played as a second orthodox No 5.

1st Round Replay Wednesday, 10 February
EAST FIFE (1) 1   ABERDEEN (0) 0
Dewar (26)
EAST FIFE: Hamilton, Stirrat, Smith, Aitken, Walker, Donnelly, Ross, Dewar, Young, Stewart, Rodger
ABERDEEN: Ogston, Bennett, Shewan, Burns, Coutts, McCormick, Winchester, Kerrigan, Ravn, Smith, Mortensen
                              Referee: W. J. Mullen

Catastrophe for Aberdeen. This is their third defeat in the Scottish Cup in successive years by rank outsiders – Raith, Ayr and now East Fife. Manager Pearson made numerous changes from Saturday's eleven. This included playing battling Ernie Winchester on the wing for the first half. Dewar's critical header was the most expensive goal Pearson had ever watched his team lose. Afterwards he resigned.

1964-65

APPEARANCES	League	League Cup	Scottish Cup
Ogston	34	6	2
Shewan	34	6	2
D. Smith	33	6	2
Kerrigan	26	5	2
McCormick	23		2
Bennett	21	6	2
Winchester	21	6	2
Little	21		
Burns	18	4	1
Cooke	15	6	
Hogg	15	1	
Mortensen	14		2
Kerr	13	1	
Ravn	12		2
Morrison	12		
Coutts	11	6	1
Hume	10	3	
Lister	10	1	
Fraser	9	1	1
Stewart	8		
McIntosh	7	6	
Petersen	3		1
Wilson	2		
Ronaldson	1	2	
Cummings	1		
25 players			

GOALS	Total	League	League Cup	Scottish Cup
Kerrigan	15	14	1	
Winchester	15	13	2	
Kerr	8	7	1	
Ravn	6	6		
Morrison	5	5		
Fraser	4	4		
D. Smith	4		4	
Little	3	3		
Cooke	2	1	1	
McIntosh	2	1	1	
Coutts	1	1		
Lister	1	1		
Mortensen	1	1		
Cummings	1	1		
Hume	1		1	
own-goal	1	1		
Totals	70	59	11	

Still to come in the eighties are the heading skills of Eric Black.

Season 1965-66

Eddie Turnbull's first full season at the helm started with high hopes and ended in anti-climax. In the League Cup a home win over Rangers looked to be sending Aberdeen into the last eight, but successive defeats at Tynecastle and Ibrox ended that aspiration. The league campaign began dismally. Aberdeen were next to bottom after four matches, having been massacred at Parkhead for the second season in a row. But then came the almost predictable recovery. Ten unbeaten games carried Aberdeen into the top six by early December.

But what goes up must come down. And so did Aberdeen. They slipped back into anonymity and remained in mid-table till the season's end.

Their objective for the second half of the season was to reach Hampden for the Scottish Cup Final. Straightforward wins over Hamilton, Dundee United and Dumbarton set up the Dons for a semi-final encounter with Rangers. The first match was a colourless goal-less draw; the second a colourless 2-1 defeat for Aberdeen.

1965-66 will, however, be remembered for bringing two of Aberdeen's all-time greats to the surface. Turnbull had brought the promising young goalkeeper Bobby Clark in his wake from Queens Park. Before the season was a few weeks old the ever-reliable John Ogston had lost his place. At the season's end, as soon as Aberdeen's interest in the Scottish Cup was terminated, Turnbull also gave a run to a prodigiously gifted midfielder – Jim Smith.

Regular Pittodrie-goers did not have much to cheer from one month to the next. For the third season on the trot Aberdeen won less than half of their home games.

League:	Eighth
League Cup:	Third in qualifying group
Scottish Cup:	Semi Final

SCOTTISH LEAGUE DIVISION ONE

No 1 Wednesday, 25 August

ABERDEEN (2) 2   STIRLING ALBION (1) 2
Little (11),   Fleming (41), Hall (46)
Winchester (25)

ABERDEEN: Ogston, Bennett, Shewan, Burns, McMillan, Smith, Little, Winchester, Ravn, Scott, Wilson

STIRLING: Taylor, McGuinness, Murray, Thomson, Robb, Anderson, Westwater, McKinnon, Fleming, Dickson, Hall

P W D L F A Pts   *Attendance:* 7,000
1 0 1 0 2 2 1   *Referee:* R. D. Davidson

Aberdeen let a two-goal lead slip away against a team who since the War have come to regard Pittodrie as a graveyard. The Dons look to be suffering from a superiority complex.

No 2 Saturday, 11 September

ST JOHNSTONE (1) 2   ABERDEEN (1) 2
Kerray 2 (1, 48)   Shewan (13), Ravn (81)

ST JOHNSTONE: McVittie, McFadyen, Coburn, McCarry, McKinven, Renton, Carlyle, Kerray, Whitelaw, Duffy, Kemp

ABERDEEN: Clark, Bennett, Shewan, Whyte, McMillan, Smith, Little, Millar, T. White, Ravn, Wilson

P W D L F A Pts   *Attendance:* 6,000
2 0 2 0 4 4 2   *Referee:* I. M. D. Foote

Jim Kerray looked suspiciously offside when collecting a through-ball to put Saints back in front at the start of the second half.

No 3 Saturday, 18 September

ABERDEEN (2) 2   DUNDEE (0) 3
Little (25), Wilson (37)   Cooke (65), Penman (80),
                                Bertelsen (87)

ABERDEEN: Clark, Bennett, Shewan, Stewart, McMillan, Smith, Little, Millar, White, Ravn, Wilson

DUNDEE: Donaldson, Hamilton, Cox, Cooke, Easton, Houston, Murray, Penman, Bertelsen, McLean, Scott

P W D L F A Pts   *Attendance:* 8,000
3 0 2 1 6 7 2   *Referee:* W. J. Mullen

159

Charlie Cooke makes a telling return to Pittodrie, sparking off Dundee's resurgence. With time running out it looks like a third successive 2-2 draw in the league, but then the Danish centre-forward Bertelsen blasted the ball beyond poor Clark.

No 4 Saturday, 25 September

CELTIC (4) 7   ABERDEEN (0) 1
  Lennox 2 (3, 15),   Winchester (61)
  Johnstone 2 (13, 55),
  Hughes (43), Auld (71),
  McBride (72)

CELTIC: Simpson, Young, Gemmell, Murdoch, McNeill, Clark, Johnstone, Auld, McBride, Lennox, Hughes

ABERDEEN: Clark, Bennett, Shewan, Burns, McCormick, Smith, Wilson, Little, Ravn, Winchester, Mortensen

Bottom positions

	P	W	D	L	F	A	Pts
14 Clyde	4	1	0	3	6	8	2
15 St Mirren	4	1	0	3	5	8	2
16 Partick	4	0	2	2	4	7	2
17 ABERDEEN	4	0	2	2	7	14	2
18 Hamilton	4	0	0	4	4	12	0

Attendance: 20,000   *Referee:* J. R. P. Gordon

Last season Celtic thrashed Aberdeen 8-0. Now, Jock Stein's influence seems to be particularly bad news for Aberdeen who crumble under the pressure. The season has barely begun and already Aberdeen look in big trouble. The critical first goal arrived following a partially cleared Celtic corner. McNeill headed on to Lennox and Clark was helpless.

No 5 Saturday, 2 October

ABERDEEN (2) 4   ST MIRREN (0) 1
  White (15), Shewan (41),   Kiernan (78)
  Riddell o.g. (46),
  Finnie (84)

ABERDEEN: Clark, Bennett, Shewan, Whyte, McCormick, Smith, Little, Winchester, White, Finnie, Wilson

ST MIRREN: Liney, McLardie, Riddell, Clark, Murray, Kiernan, Robertson, McCallum, Queen, Faulds, Adamson

P	W	D	L	F	A	Pts	
5	1	2	2	11	15	4	*Attendance:* 5,000

Referee: A. J. Crawley

This meeting between two of the division's early stragglers produced a handsome score for the Dons – but all that could really be said was that St Mirren were worse than Aberdeen.

No 6 Saturday, 9 October

HAMILTON   ABERDEEN (2) 4
  ACADEMICALS (0) 0   Little (3), Wilson (15),
                       White (46), Finnie (60)

HAMILTON: Lamont, Bowman, Holton, Anderson, Small, McCann, McClure, Horne, Alexander, Gilmour, Frye

ABERDEEN: Clark, Bennett, Shewan, Whyte, McMIllan, Smith, Little, Melrose, White, Finnie, Wilson

P	W	D	L	F	A	Pts
6	2	2	2	15	15	6

Referee: W. M. Syme

Before the champagne corks start to pop it should be realised that Hamilton have now lost all six league matches so far. The Dons' overnight signing from Dunfermline, Harry Melrose, would have scored had not Holton punched out his shot. The referee for some reason awarded a corner.

No 7 Saturday, 16 October

ABERDEEN (1) 2   DUNFERMLINE
  Winchester (20),   ATHLETIC (1) 2
  Whyte (61)   T. Callaghan 2 (8, 63)

ABERDEEN: Clark, Bennett, Shewan, Whyte, McMillan, Smith, Little, Finnie, Winchester, Melrose, Wilson

DUNFERMLINE: Martin, W. Callaghan, Lunn, Smith, McLean, Thomson, Edwards, Paton, Hunter, T. Callaghan, Robertson

P	W	D	L	F	A	Pts	
7	2	3	2	17	17	7	*Attendance:* 7,000

Referee: R. A. S. Crockett

Harry Melrose quickly renews his acquaintance with his old pals. They won the battle, not he. Tommy Callaghan tried hard for his hat-trick. He did, however, make it into the referee's book a third time when cautioned for an assault on Clark.

No 8 Saturday, 23 October

CLYDE (1) 2   ABERDEEN (0) 2
  Bryce (44), Staite (60)   Scott (79),
                        Winchester (89)

CLYDE: Wright, Glasgow, Mulherron, McHugh, Fraser, White, McFarlane, Gilroy, Staite, Bryce, Hastings

ABERDEEN: Clark, Bennett, Shewan, Whyte, McMcMillan, Smith, Little, Scott, Winchester, Melrose, Wilson

P	W	D	L	F	A	Pts	
8	2	4	2	19	19	8	*Attendance:* 1,500

Referee: J. Hamilton

2-2 draws are all the rage for Aberdeen at the moment. This is their fourth. The Dons beat Clyde twice in the League Cup but this time rely on two stolen goals in the last eleven minutes. Good old Ernie Winchester saves the day at the death.

No 9 Saturday, 30 October

HEARTS (0) 1   ABERDEEN (1) 1
  Ferguson (76)   Whyte (26)

HEARTS: Cruickshank, Shevlane, Holt, Ferguson, Anderson, Polland, Ford, Kerrigan, Wallace, Traynor, Hamilton

ABERDEEN: Clark, Whyte, Shewan, Petersen, McMillan, Smith, Little, Melrose, White, Winchester, Wilson

P	W	D	L	F	A	Pts
9	2	5	2	20	20	9

Referee: R. Rodger

No angels on either side – but only one devil. Aberdeen's Jimmy Wilson was ordered off with 15 minutes to go. Ex-Don Kerrigan, playing for Hearts, looked better than ex-Heart Tommy White, playing for Aberdeen. The Dons took the lead when Cruickshank in attempting to clear sent the ball straight to Jim Whyte. Ferguson equalised for Hearts within a minute of Wilson's dismissal.

No 10 Saturday, 6 November
ABERDEEN (0) 1   KILMARNOCK (0) 0
  Melrose (68)

ABERDEEN: Clark, Whyte, Shewan, Petersen, McMillan, Smith, Little, Melrose, White, Winchester, Wilson

KILMARNOCK: Ferguson, King, Watson, Murray, McGrory, Beattie, McLean, Black, Hamilton, Sneddon, McIlroy

P W D L F A Pts
10 3 5 2 21 20 11   *Referee:* E. Thomson

Killie come to Pittodrie as defending league champions, but they have no answer to Aberdeen's lucky striker – Harry Melrose. He had yet to be in a losing Aberdeen side, but had yet to score – until now. Up in the stand the spies from Real Madrid gazed down on their future opponents in the European Cup. They saw Melrose score with a daisy-cutting 20-yarder.

No 11 Saturday, 13 November
PARTICK THISTLE (0) 0   ABERDEEN (2) 3
                         Little 2 (32, 64),
                         Winchester (38)

PARTICK: Gray, Campbell, Muir, Cunningham, Harvey, Gibb, McLindon, Hainey, Roxburgh, McParland, Gallagher

ABERDEEN: Clark, White, Shewan, Petersen, McMillan, Smith, Little, Melrose, Whyte, Winchester, Wilson

P W D L F A Pts   *Attendance:* 4,000
11 4 5 2 24 20 13   *Referee:* R. H. Davidson

Partick have won only once all season. Little's goal, after a Melrose effort had been charged down, extends Aberdeen's run to seven games without defeat.

No 12 Saturday, 20 November
ABERDEEN (1) 2   FALKIRK (0) 0
  Winchester (9),
  Wilson (76)

ABERDEEN: Clark, White, Shewan, Petersen, McMillan, Smith, Little, Melrose, Whyte, Winchester, Wilson

FALKIRK: Whigham, Markie, Hunter, Rowan, Baillie, Fulton, McManus, McKinney, Moran, Graham, Scott

P W D L F A Pts   *Attendance:* 4,000
12 5 5 2 26 20 15   *Referee:* D. Weir

Harry Melrose earned himself the distinction of being the second Don sent off in three weeks, following a clash with Rowan – who was booked.

No 13 Saturday, 27 November
MORTON (1) 1   ABERDEEN (1) 3
  Stevenson (28)   Winchester (29), White
                         (62), Wilson (70)

MORTON: Sorensen, Laughlan, Kennedy, Strachan, Madsen, Stevenson, Watson, Arentoft, Harper, McGraw, Graham

ABERDEEN: Clark, White, Shewan, Petersen, McMillan, Smith, Little, Melrose, Whyte, Winchester, Wilson

Leading positions

	P	W	D	L	F	A	Pts
1 Rangers	13	11	2	0	43	8	24
2 Celtic	12	10	1	1	43	14	21
3 Dunfermline	13	8	4	1	40	20	20
4 Dundee United	13	9	1	3	41	19	19
5 Hibs	13	7	3	3	43	20	17
6 ABERDEEN	13	6	5	2	29	21	17

Referee: W. Anderson

Morton still haven't won at home this season – though they scored first on a snow-sprinkled pitch. Near the end Bobby Clark pulled off a spectacular save from McGraw's penalty. Aberdeen have climbed eleven places in the league in two months.

No 14 Saturday, 11 December
ABERDEEN (0) 0   DUNDEE UNITED (0) 0

ABERDEEN: Clark, Whyte, Shewan, Petersen, McMillan, Smith, Little, Melrose, White, Winchester, Wilson

DUNDEE UNITED: Mackay, Millar, Briggs, Neilson, Smith, Wing, Seemann, Munro, Dossing, Gillespie, Persson

P W D L F A Pts
14 6 6 2 29 21 18   *Referee:* R. K. Wilson

On a rock-hard pitch Bobby Clark sharpened his spurs to earn Aberdeen their tenth league game without defeat.

No 15 Saturday, 18 December
MOTHERWELL (0) 1   ABERDEEN (0) 0
  McCallum (89 pen)

MOTHERWELL: McCloy, M. Thomson, McCallum, Aitken, Martis, Murray, Lindsay, Campbell, Delaney, I. Thomson, Hunter

ABERDEEN: Clark, Whyte, Shewan, Petersen, McMillan, Smith, Little, Melrose, White, Winchester, Wilson

P W D L F A Pts
15 6 6 3 29 22 18   *Referee:* I. M. D. Foote

Damn! Lowly Motherwell shatter the Dons' confidence-building sequence. The ball is driven hard against Smith's hand in the last minute for a highly contentious penalty.

No 16 Saturday, 25 December
ABERDEEN (1) 1   HIBERNIAN (0) 3
  White (34)   McNamee (46), Scott
                         (50), Cormack (51)

ABERDEEN: Clark, Whyte, Shewan, Petersen, McMillan, Smith, Little, Melrose, White, Winchester, Wilson

HIBERNIAN: Wilson, Simpson, Davis, Stanton, McNamee, Baxter, Hogg, Cousin, Scott, O'Rourke, Cormack

P	W	D	L	F	A	Pts	
16	6	6	4	30	25	18	*Attendance:* 9,000
							Referee: J. P. Barclay

This was a miserable Christmas present for the Dons. Hibs hit them with a sucker punch at the start of the second half. Winchester's header onto the bar was the nearest Aberdeen came to salvaging something from a match which slipped from their grasp. Still, Turnbull's terriers have added an average of 1,100 extra fans to home league gates.

No 17 Monday, 3 January
ABERDEEN (2) 2   ST JOHNSTONE (0) 3
  Wilson (10), Little (45)   Coburn (55), Kemp (68),
                                        Anderson (71)

ABERDEEN: Clark, Whyte, Shewan, Petersen, McMillan, Smith, Little, Melrose, White, Fraser, Wilson

ST JOHNSTONE: McVittie, Michie, Coburn, McCarry, McKinven, Renton, Cowan, Kerray, Anderson, Duffy, Kemp

P	W	D	L	F	A	Pts	
17	6	6	5	32	27	18	*Attendance:* 6,000
							Referee: W. Elliott

Oh dear. A game that seemed to be won was somehow lost. Coburn's speculative shot from 25 yards crept through Clark's hands, and all of a sudden the skids were under Aberdeen.

No 18 Saturday, 8 January
STIRLING ALBION (0) 2   ABERDEEN (1) 1
  Hall 2 (47, 87)   Little (5)

STIRLING: Murray, Dickson, McGuinness, Reid, Rogerson, Thomson, Bowie, Anderson, Fleming, Gardner, Hall

ABERDEEN: Clark, Whyte, Shewan, Petersen, McMillan, Smith, Little, Melrose, White, Winchester, Wilson

P	W	D	L	F	A	Pts	
18	6	6	6	33	30	18	*Referee:* D. Small

Ten unbeaten games are followed by four defeats on the trot. For the third time running Aberdeen gain the ideal start. But then came Whyte's inattentive backpass, eagerly snapped up by Hall. His late winner was the result of Clark and McMillan finding themselves in a tangle.

No 19 Saturday, 15 January
ABERDEEN (2) 3   CELTIC (1) 1
  Ravn (24), Winchester   McBride (6)
  (34), Little (71)

ABERDEEN: Clark, Shewan, McCormick, Petersen, McMillan, Smith, Little, Melrose, Winchester, Ravn, Wilson

CELTIC: Simpson, Craig, Gemmell, Murdoch, Cushley, Clark, Johnstone, Gallagher, McBride, Chalmers, Hughes

P	W	D	L	F	A	Pts	
19	7	6	6	36	31	20	*Attendance:* 18,000
							Referee: J. R. P. Gordon

What are we to make of this Dons' side? They had lost their last two matches at Celtic 8-0 and 7-1. The table-topping Celts come to Pittodrie with a run of 24 unbeaten games behind them. This is only their second league defeat of the season. Joe McBride gave them a dream start on a white pitch after Clark appeared to lose possession. Celtic were forced to concede defeat once Wilson's cross eluded Winchester and Cushley and fell for Little to put the Dons 3-1 ahead.

No 20 Saturday, 22 January
ST MIRREN (1) 1   ABERDEEN (0) 0
  Hamilton (19)

ST MIRREN: Liney, Murray, Clark, Pinkerton, Kiernan, Gemmell, Aird, Redpath, Hamilton, Adamson, Robertson

ABERDEEN: Clark, Shewan, McCormick, Petersen, McMillan, Smith, Little, Millar, Winchester, Ravn, Wilson

P	W	D	L	F	A	Pts	
20	7	6	7	36	32	20	*Referee:* R. A. S. Crockett

St Mirren need points more than gold. Yesterday Ronnie Hamilton signed for them from Kilmarnock – and look what happened.

No 21 Saturday, 29 January
ABERDEEN (1) 5   HAMILTON
  Winchester 3 (39, 57, 88), ACADEMICALS (0) 2
  Ravn (67), Wilson (75)   Anderson (83), Gilmour
                                         (86)

ABERDEEN: Clark, Shewan, McCormick, Petersen, McMillan, Smith, Little, Melrose, Winchester, Ravn, Wilson

HAMILTON: Brown, Forrest, Halpin, Hinshelwood, Gaughan, King, McClare, Currie, Anderson, Gilmour, Holton

P	W	D	L	F	A	Pts	
21	8	6	7	41	34	22	*Referee:* R. D. Henderson

Hamilton have now played 20 league games this term. They have managed a solitary win and a solitary draw as they prepare for the Cup-tie with Aberdeen next week.

No 22 Saturday, 26 February
ABERDEEN (0) 0   HEARTS (1) 1
                                       Shewan o.g. (5)

ABERDEEN: Clark, Whyte, Shewan, Petersen, McMillan, Smith, Little, Melrose, Winchester, Ravn, Wilson

HEARTS: Cruickshank, Polland, Holt, Higgins, Anderson, Miller, Hamilton, Cumming, Wallace, Kerrigan, Traynor

P	W	D	L	F	A	Pts	
22	8	6	−8	41	35	22	*Attendance:* 12,000
							Referee: A. F. J. Webster

Dumbarton manager, Willie Toner, sits in the stand to watch his team's opponents in the Third Round of the Scottish Cup. He sees Wallace's cross elude Clark and turned into his own net by Ally Shewan.

No 23 Wednesday, 2 March
ABERDEEN (1) 2   CLYDE (0) 0
  Winchester 2 (30, 80)
ABERDEEN: Clark, Whyte, Shewan, Petersen, McMillan, Smith, Little, Melrose, Winchester, Ravn, Wilson
CLYDE: Wright, Glasgow, Mulherron, McHugh, Fraser, Soutar, Reid, Gilroy, Murray, Bryce, Hastings

P	W	D	L	F	A	Pts	*Attendance:* 6,000
23	9	6	8	43	35	24	*Referee:* J. Hamilton

This takes Aberdeen's record against Clyde in four league and League Cup matches to three wins and a draw. The tannoy announced that the No 9 shirt would be worn by Ravn – but its wearer looked suspiciously like Ernie Winchester. The crowd booed him until he silenced them in the best possible way.

No 24 Wednesday, 9 March
KILMARNOCK (0) 1   ABERDEEN (0) 3
  McLean (60 pen)   Beattie o.g. (49), Melrose
                                 (56), Smith (58)
KILMARNOCK: Ferguson, King, McFadzean, Murray, McGrory, Beattie, McLean, McInally, Bertelsen, Queen, Black
ABERDEEN: Clark, Whyte, Shewan, Petersen, McMillan, Smith, Little, Melrose, Winchester, Ravn, Wilson

P	W	D	L	F	A	Pts
24	10	6	8	46	36	26

Defending champions Kilmarnock are in third position and can't afford to drop points. But an own-goal sends Aberdeen on their way. For the last half-hour the Dons played possession football which did not please Rugby Park.

No 25 Saturday, 12 March
ABERDEEN (2) 2   PARTICK THISTLE (0) 1
  Little (12), Winchester   McLindon (85)
  (26)
ABERDEEN: Clark, Whyte, Shewan, Petersen, McMillan, Smith, Little, Melrose, Winchester, Ravn, Wilson
PARTICK: Niven, Campbell, Muir, Cunningham, McKinnon, Gibb, McLindon, Flanagan, Hainey, McParland, Duncan

P	W	D	L	F	A	Pts
25	11	6	8	48	37	28	*Referee:* R. A. S. Crockett

The Tottenham manager sat in the stand casting his eye over Dave Smith – due to play for the Scottish League at Newcastle next Wednesday. But Smith chooses to have one of his least distinguished games for months.

No 26 Saturday, 19 March
FALKIRK (1) 3   ABERDEEN (0) 0
  McManus (33), Fulton
  (80), Graham (85)
FALKIRK: Whigham, Markie, Hunter, Rowan, Baillie, Fulton, McKinney, Lambie, Moran, Graham, McManus
ABERDEEN: Clark, Whyte, Shewan, Petersen, McMillan, Smith, Little, Melrose, Winchester, Ravn, Wilson

P	W	D	L	F	A	Pts
26	11	6	9	48	40	28	*Referee:* J. M. Kelly

Naturally enough, the excuse for this shoddy display was that the Dons were saving themselves for their Scottish Cup semi-final with Rangers next week.

No 27 Monday, 21 March
DUNFERMLINE   ABERDEEN (0) 3
  ATHLETIC (1) 2   Wilson (59), Lunn o.g.
  Ferguson 2 (26, 80)   (60), Winchester (73)
DUNFERMLINE: Martin, W. Callaghan, Lunn, Smith, McLean, Thomson, Peebles, Ferguson, Fleming, T. Callaghan, Robertson
ABERDEEN: Clark, Whyte, Shewan, Petersen, McMillan, Smith, Little, Melrose, Winchester, Ravn, Wilson

P	W	D	L	F	A	Pts
27	12	6	9	51	42	30	*Referee:* R. K. Wilson

Aberdeen are five days away from their mighty Cup clash with Rangers. While the 'Gers were losing at Tannadice Aberdeen registered this notable victory over 4th-placed Dunfermline. But Bobby Clark has suddenly become vulnerable with crosses, as Dunfermline's Alex Ferguson found out to his delight.

No 28 Monday, 4 April
ABERDEEN (3) 5   MORTON (0) 3
  Melrose (14), Winchester   Arentoft (60), Neilson
  (38), D. Smith (44),   (67), McGraw (89)
  Little (78), Wilson (81)
ABERDEEN: Clark, Whyte, Shewan, Petersen, McMillan, D. Smith, Little, Melrose, Winchester, J. Smith, Wilson
MORTON: Devlin, Boyd, Kennedy, Strachan, Madsen, Gray, Arentoft, Neilson, Campbell, McGraw, Watson

P	W	D	L	F	A	Pts	*Attendance:* 3,500
28	13	6	9	56	45	32	

A promising debut for Jim Smith, 19, deputising for Ravn. Morton's team watched both Hampden games to figure out how to take points from the Dons that might safeguard them from relegation. But how did Aberdeen lose three second-half goals to a 10-man Morton in the second half once Strachan had been taken off with a head injury?

No 29 Saturday, 9 April
RANGERS (0) 1   ABERDEEN (0) 0
  Greig (79)

RANGERS: Ritchie, Johansen, Provan, Greig, McKinnon, Millar, Henderson, Willoughby, Forrest, Johnston, Wilson
ABERDEEN: Clark, Whyte, Shewan, Petersen, McMillan, D. Smith, Little, Melrose, Winchester, J. Smith, Wilson

P W D L F A Pts
29 13 6 10 56 46 32   *Referee:* A. McKenzie

Rangers see the title slipping away from them to Parkhead. Another disappointing game with Aberdeen to follow the two recent Cup encounters. The only goal came when several Aberdeen headed clearances had failed to ease the pressure around Clark. Greig finally unleashed a long-range grounder to whizz past the keeper.

No 30 Wednesday, 13 April
ABERDEEN (1) 1   RANGERS (1) 2
  Melrose (25)   Johnston (34),
                         Willoughby (56)
ABERDEEN: Clark, Whyte, Shewan, Petersen, McMillan, D. Smith, Little, Melrose, Winchester, J. Smith, Wilson
RANGERS: Ritchie, Johansen, Provan, Greig, McKinnon, Millar, Henderson, Willoughby, Forrest, Johnston, Wilson

P W D L F A Pts   *Attendance:* 16,000
30 13 6 11 57 48 32   *Referee:* A. F. J. Webster

This is the fourth meeting between the sides in 18 days. Aberdeen have yet to win, but Rangers stole this result. Aberdeen peppered Ritchie's goal throughout. On one occasion the ball hit pivot McKinnon on the back of the head and crashed onto the Rangers' post.

No 31 Saturday, 16 April
DUNDEE UNITED (1) 3 ABERDEEN (0) 0
  Hainey (37), Dossing (55),
  Mitchell (59)
DUNDEE UNITED: Mackay, Millar, Briggs, Neilson, Smith, Wing, Hainey, Gillespie, Dossing, Mitchell, Persson
ABERDEEN: Clark, Whyte, Shewan, Millar, McMillan, D. Smith, Little, Melrose, Winchester, J. Smith, Wilson

P W D L F A Pts
31 13 6 12 57 51 32   *Referee:* R. K. Wilson

The pitch was more suitable to mud-fights than football. When Jimmy Smith shot high over the bar from close in late in the game it was as near as Aberdeen came to scoring.

No 32 Wednesday, 20 April
DUNDEE (0) 1   ABERDEEN (1) 2
  Murray (87)   J. Smith (33),
                        D. Smith (50)
DUNDEE: Donaldson, R. Wilson, Hamilton, Murray, Easton, Stuart, Penman, Scott, S. Wilson, McLean, Cameron

ABERDEEN: Clark, Bennett, Shewan, Millar, McMillan, D. Smith, Little, Melrose, Winchester, J. Smith, Wilson

P W D L F A Pts
32 14 6 12 59 52 34   *Referee:* N. Watson

Two trips to the Jute City for Aberdeen within four days. Ex-Don Charlie Cooke has rocked Dens Park with a transfer request, and he was omitted from the side. Jim Smith scored his first senior goal for Aberdeen.

No 33 Saturday, 23 April
ABERDEEN (0) 1   MOTHERWELL (1) 2
  Melrose (43)   Cairney 2 (15, 89)
ABERDEEN: Clark, Bennett, Shewan, Millar, McMillan, D. Smith, Little, Melrose, Winchester, J. Smith, Wilson
MOTHERWELL: McCloy, Thomson, R. McCallum, W. McCallum, Martin, Murray, Lindsay, Hunter, Delaney, Cairney, Campbell

P W D L F A Pts   *Attendance:* 4,000
33 14 6 13 60 54 34   *Referee:* A. D. Fleming

A sad end to Aberdeen's home fixtures. Cairney's last-minute winner was a header straight at Clark, who fumbled it into the net.

No 34 Saturday, 30 April
HIBERNIAN (0) 0   ABERDEEN (0) 1
                        Wilson (81)
HIBERNIAN: Simpson, Davis, Stanton, McNamee, J. Stevenson, Cormack, Stein, Scott, Cousin, E. Stevenson
ABERDEEN: Clark, Bennett, Shewan, Petersen, McMillan, D. Smith, Little, Melrose, Winchester, J. Smith, Wilson

                        Referee: W. M. Syme

Tiny Jimmy Wilson headed the perfect goal to crown a match played as if Aberdeen had their pride at stake.

Aberdeen's complete home and away record:
HOME						AWAY					
P	W	D	L	F	A	W	D	L	F	A	Pts
34	8	3	6	35	26	7	3	7	26	28	36

Scottish League Division One

	P	W	D	L	F	A	Pts
1 Celtic	34	27	3	4	106	30	57
2 Rangers	34	25	5	4	91	29	55
3 Kilmarnock	34	20	5	9	73	46	45
4 Dunfermline	34	19	6	9	94	55	44
5 Dundee United	34	19	5	10	79	51	43
6 Hibernian	34	16	6	12	81	55	38
7 Hearts	34	13	12	9	56	48	38
8 ABERDEEN	34	15	6	13	61	54	36
9 Dundee	34	14	6	14	61	61	34
10 Falkirk	34	15	1	18	48	72	31
11 Clyde	34	13	4	17	62	64	30
12 Partick	34	10	10	14	55	64	30
13 Motherwell	34	12	4	18	52	69	28
14 St Johnstone	34	9	8	17	58	81	26
15 Stirling Albion	34	9	8	17	40	68	26
16 St Mirren	34	9	4	21	44	82	22
17 Morton	34	8	5	21	42	84	21
18 Hamilton	34	3	2	29	27	117	8

LEAGUE CUP

Saturday, 14 August
CLYDE (0) 1   ABERDEEN (1) 2
Knox (67)   Scott (13), White (76)
CLYDE: McCulloch, Glasgow, Mulherron, McHugh, Fraser, White, Bryce, Gilroy, Knox, McLean, Hastings
ABERDEEN: Ogston, Bennett, Shewan, Burns, McCormick, Smith, Scott, Little, White, Winchester, Wilson

Referee: A. McKenzie

Aberdeen's first match of the new season is against the same team who beat them 4-0 in the final fixture of last season. Now the two Pittodrie newcomers, George Scott and Tommy White, net the goals in a 2-1 win. Ogston's place in goal after 180 consecutive first-team games is under threat from young Bobby Clark, signed by Eddie Turnbull from Queens Park.

Wednesday, 18 August
ABERDEEN (0) 1   HEARTS (0) 1
Wilson (72)   Wallace (56)
ABERDEEN: Ogston, Bennett, Shewan, Burns, McCormick, Smith, Scott, Winchester, Fraser, Little, Wilson
HEARTS: Cruickshank, Ferguson, Holt, Barry, Anderson, Higgins, Jensen, Gordon, Wallace, Traynor, Hamilton

Attendance: 18,000   Referee: J. Callaghan

After six minutes Hearts lost Higgins with a knee injury, so a draw was a moral victory for the ten survivors. Both goals went in off the post.

Saturday, 21 August
ABERDEEN (0) 2   RANGERS (0) 0
Little (87), Ravn (90)
ABERDEEN: Ogston, Bennett, Shewan, Burns, McMillan, Smith, Scott, Winchester, Ravn, Little, Wilson

RANGERS: Martin, Johansen, Provan, Watson, McKinnon, Greig, Wilson, Wood, Forrest, Willoughby, Johnston
Attendance: 24,000   *Referee:* N. Watson

Rangers' Jim Forrest came to Pittodrie looking for his 200th senior goal. 20-year-old Dons centre-half Tommy McMillan prevented it. With 25 minutes left 'Gers keeper Martin was carried off with concussion. Davie Wilson took his place and almost kept a clean sheet.

Saturday, 28 August
ABERDEEN (1) 2   CLYDE (0) 0
Winchester (22), Wilson (56)
ABERDEEN: Clark, Bennett, Shewan, Burns, McMillan, Smith, Little, Winchester, White, Scott, Wilson
CLYDE: McCulloch, Glasgow, Blain, McHugh, Staite, White, Bryce, Stewart, Knox, McLean, Hastings.
Attendance: 12,000   *Referee:* J. P. Barclay

With Ogston injured, Bobby Clark gets his chance in goal. Aberdeen are still getting the pace in Section 2 and now require two points from their last two matches to progress.

Wednesday, 1 September
HEARTS (0) 2   ABERDEEN (0) 0
Hamilton (51 pen), Barry (76)
HEARTS: Cruickshank, Ferguson, Shevlane, Polland, Anderson, Cumming, Ford, Barry, Wallace, Traynor, Hamilton
ABERDEEN: Clark, Bennett, Shewan, Burns, McMillan, Smith, Little, Winchester, White, Scott, Wilson
Referee: T. Wharton

Victory at Tynecastle, or Ibrox, will take Aberdeen through to the match-play stage of the League Cup for the first time since 1957. But Shewan's illegal challenge on Wallace after the break means that everything will hinge on the visit to Ibrox.

Saturday, 4 September
RANGERS (1) 4   ABERDEEN (0) 0
Forrest (3), McLean 3 (62, 85, 89)
RANGERS: Ritchie, Johansen, Provan, Watson, McKinnon, Greig, Henderson, Willoughby, Forrest, McLean, Johnston
ABERDEEN: Ogston, Bennett, Shewan, Burns, McMillan, Petersen, Little, Millar, White, Smith, Wilson
Attendance: 45,000   *Referee:* R. H. Davidson

Results elsewhere meant that Aberdeen needed only to draw with Rangers to survive. Their hopes lasted only as long as it took Rangers to feed the ball to Willie Henderson. From the bye-line it was pulled back to

Forrest whose shot hit Bennett and ended up in the net. A second-half Tommy McLean hat-trick put Aberdeen firmly in their place.

Section 2

	P	W	D	L	F	A	Pts
Rangers	6	4	0	2	13	7	8
Hearts	6	3	1	2	10	7	7
ABERDEEN	6	3	1	2	7	8	7
Clyde	6	1	0	5	5	13	2

SCOTTISH CUP

1st Round Saturday, 5 February
HAMILTON   ABERDEEN (1) 3
  ACADEMICALS (0) 1   Melrose (15), Ravn (75),
  Anderson (82)   Winchester (76)
HAMILTON: Brown, Forrest, Holton, Hinshelwood, Gaughan, King, McClare, Currie, Anderson, Gilmour, McCann
ABERDEEN: Clark, Whyte, Shewan, Petersen, McMillan, Smith, Wilson, Melrose, Winchester, Ravn, Mortensen
Attendance: 2,600   *Referee:* R. K. Wilson
This season the Dons have beaten Hamilton 4-0 away and 5-2 at home. Fortunately there are no slip-ups in the Cup, but there were some anxious moments nevertheless.

2nd Round Wednesday, 23 February
ABERDEEN (4) 5   DUNDEE UNITED (0) 0
  Whyte (25), Ravn (32),
  Winchester 2 (34, 89),
  Petersen (43)
ABERDEEN: Clark, Whyte, Shewan, Petersen, McMillan, Smith, Little, Melrose, Winchester, Ravn, Wilson
DUNDEE UNITED: Mackay, Millar, Briggs, Neilson, Smith, Fraser, Rooney, Gillespie, Dossing, Mitchell, Pearson
Attendance: 14,000   *Referee:* R. K. Davidson
What a difference two months makes. In December Dundee United deserved more than a 0-0 draw at Pittodrie. Now they are trodden underfoot, and at long last it seems that the bogey myth of the Tannadice Terrors has been laid. Jim Whyte lofted the first goal from forty yards which Donald Mackay dropped over his head.

Quarter Final Saturday, 5 March
DUMBARTON (0) 0   ABERDEEN (1) 3
                                Wilson (29), Little (70),
                                Winchester (77)
DUMBARTON: Crayford, Govan, Jardine, Johnstone, Curran, Harris, McCall, Nelson, Lynas, Miller, Muir
ABERDEEN: Clark, Whyte, Shewan, Petersen, McMillan, Smith, Little, Melrose, Winchester, Ravn, Wilson
Attendance: 10,000   *Referee:* W. J. Mullen

Dumbarton are seventh in Division Two. As with Hamilton, it takes Aberdeen a long time to find that second goal to calm their nerves. This win puts Aberdeen in the Scottish Cup semi-finals for the first time since 1959.

Semi Final (Hampden) Saturday, 26 March
RANGERS (0) 0   ABERDEEN (0) 0
RANGERS: Ritchie, Johansen, Provan, Greig, McKinnon, Mathieson, Henderson, Millar, McLean, Sorensen, Johnston
ABERDEEN: Clark, Whyte, Shewan, Petersen, McMillan, Smith, Little, Melrose, Winchester, Ravn, Wilson
Attendance: 49,350   *Referee:* J. W. Paterson
Bobby Clark returned to his 'home' with Queen's Park and shone in an otherwise forgettable semi-final. Twelve years earlier at a similar stage Aberdeen had taken Rangers apart 6-0, but there were no signs of a repeat mayhem this time around.

Semi Final Replay (Hampden) Tuesday, 29 March
RANGERS (1) 2   ABERDEEN (1) 1
  Forrest (8), McLean (80)   Melrose (38)
RANGERS: Ritchie, Johansen, Provan, Greig, McKinnon, Millar, Henderson, Willoughby, Forrest, McLean, Johnston
ABERDEEN: Clark, Whyte, Shewan, Petersen, McMillan, Smith, Little, Melrose, Winchester, Ravn, Wilson
Attendance: 40,850   *Referee:* J. W. Paterson
Aberdeen at least have a settled side. Their team-sheet is unchanged for the tenth successive match. Even though hopes were raised once Melrose equalised, the Dons never really looked like they believed they could win. McLean's feeble prod which produced the winner brought looks of dismay in the direction of Bobby Clark. He was not to blame for Rangers' first – when Smith laid the ball into the path of Forrest who blasted it into the net.

1965-66
APPEARANCES

	League	League Cup	Scottish Cup
Shewan	34	6	5
D. Smith	34	6	5
J. Wilson	34	6	5
Little	34	6	4
Clark	33	2	5
McMillan	32	4	5
Winchester	30	5	5
Melrose	28		5
J. Whyte	25		5
Petersen	23	1	5
T. White	14	4	
Ravn	13	1	5
Bennett	11	6	
J. Smith	7		

1965-66 APPEARANCES	League	League Cup	Scottish Cup
D. Millar	6	1	
McCormick	5	2	
Finnie	3		
Burns	2	6	
Scott	2	5	
Ogston	1	4	
Fraser	1	1	
Mortensen	1		1
Stewart	1		
23 players			

GOALS	Total	League	League Cup	Scottish Cup
Winchester	21	16	1	4
Little	12	10	1	1
J. Wilson	12	9	2	1
Melrose	7	5		2
Ravn	6	3	1	2
T. White	5	4	1	
D. Smith	3	3		
J. Whyte	3	2		1
Shewan	2	2		
Finnie	2	2		
Scott	1	1	1	
J. Smith	1	1		
Petersen	3			1
own-goals		3		
Total	80	61	7	12

The Aberdeen squad preparing for the Scottish Cup Final against Celtic in April 1967. The Dons lost 2-0. Back row: W. Watt, P. Wilson, I. Taylor, M. Buchan. Centre row: J. Hermiston, F. Munro, T. McMillan, R. Clark, A. Shewan, J. Petersen, J. Whyte. Front row: J. Storrie, J. Smith, D. Johnston, E. Turnbull (Manager), H. Melrose, J. Wilson, D. Shaw (trainer).

Season 1966-67

A stimulating season by any standards. The best for a decade. In each competition they entered Aberdeen made a spirited challenge. In the end no silverware came their way, but that could not detract from a season which brought passion and cheers back to Pittodrie.

It all started in the League Cup. Aberdeen strolled through the qualifying rounds, bagging a twelve-point maximum and twenty goals into the bargain. An epic two-leg quarter final with Morton pitched them into a semi-final with Rangers. A replay was necessary before Aberdeen were forced to concede defeat.

In the league, Aberdeen quickly chalked up eight straight wins to sit on Celtics' and Rangers' shoulder in the league table. By the New Year Aberdeen were second. There followed a few hiccups as progress in the Scottish Cup took priority, but Aberdeen still finished fourth – good enough to qualify for Europe – and their highest league placing since 1956.

It was in the Scottish Cup, however, that Aberdeen really showed their mettle. Dundee were hit by five scorching Aberdeen goals. So were St Johnstone. A late Dons equaliser at Easter Road allowed Hibs the opportunity to be destroyed amid chants of 'Easy Easy' during the Pittodrie replay. In the semis Dundee United could find no way through Aberdeen's massed defensive ranks. This left a Hampden appointment with Jock Stein's Celtic, on the brink of clearing up every domestic and European competition they had entered. Celtic proved too strong for Aberdeen that day, but the fact that an identical Celtic eleven would within weeks lift the European Cup served to put Aberdeen's unavailing challenge into better perspective.

The number of league goals scored and conceded were the best an Aberdeen team could boast for ten years. Less praiseworthy was the number of bookings that came Aberdeen's way. The Dons were nothing if not 'hard' – critics might say 'dirty'.

League:	Fourth
League Cup:	Semi Final
Scottish Cup:	Runners Up

SCOTTISH LEAGUE DIVISION ONE

No 1 Saturday, 10 September

DUNDEE (1) 2 ABERDEEN (0) 1
Cameron (44), J. Wilson (86 pen)
Penman (73)

DUNDEE: Donaldson, Wilson, Cox, Selway, Easton, Stuart, McKay, Penman, Cameron, Murray, Campbell

ABERDEEN: Clark, Whyte, Shewan, Millar, McMillan, Petersen, Little, Melrose, Winchester, P. Wilson, J. Wilson

P W D L F A Pts   *Attendance:* 10,000
1 0 0 1 1 2 0   *Referee:* N. Watson

After beating both Dundee clubs twice in the League Cup, Aberdeen lose to one as soon as the league gets under way. Billy Little missed a penalty for the Dons at 0-0 and both full backs, Whyte and Shewan, were booked.

No 2 Saturday, 17 September

ABERDEEN (1) 3 ST JOHNSTONE (2) 2
Winchester 2 (28, 71), Kemp (25), McPhee (41)
Smith (52)

ABERDEEN: Clark, Whyte, Shewan, Millar, McMillan, Petersen, Little, Melrose, Winchester, Smith, J. Wilson

ST JOHNSTONE: McVittie, McCarry, Coburn, Whitelaw, Ryden, McPhee, O'Donnell, Townsend, Kilgannon, Duffy, Kemp

P W D L F A Pts   *Attendance:* 7,000
2 1 0 1 4 4 2   *Referee:* C. H. Hutton

Aberdeen seem to be meeting all their League Cup opponents early in the league. This is their third straight win over St Johnstone. This time they had to do it the hard way and come from behind – twice.

No 3 Saturday, 24 September
RANGERS (0) 3   ABERDEEN (0) 0
Henderson (50), Johnston
(59), McLean (63)
RANGERS: Ritchie, Johansen, Provan, Millar, McKinnon, D. Smith, Henderson, Greig, McLean, A. Smith, Johnston
ABERDEEN: Clark, Whyte, Shewan, Millar, McMillan, Petersen, Smith, Melrose, Winchester, Watt, J. Wilson

P W D L F A Pts
3 1 0 2 4 7 2   *Referee:* J. Stewart

This dress rehearsal for the League Cup semi final went dreadfully wrong for Aberdeen. Centre half Tommy McMillan protested furiously about McLean's goal and was booked.

No 4 Saturday, 1 October
ABERDEEN (1) 1   CLYDE (0) 1
Winchester (37)   Stewart (85 pen)
ABERDEEN: Clark, Whyte, Shewan, Millar, McMillan, Petersen, Little, Melrose, Winchester, Smith, J. Wilson
CLYDE: Wright, Glasgow, Mulherron, McHugh, Fraser (Staite), Anderson, McFarlane, Soutar, Gilroy, Stewart, Hastings

P W D L F A Pts   *Attendance:* 5,000
4 1 1 2 5 8 3   *Referee:* R. A. S. Crockett

Aberdeen's 100% home record in league and League Cup was spoiled by a late penalty converted by former Banks o' Dee player Ian Stewart, after Millar used his hands to stop Glasgow's header.

No 5 Saturday, 8 October
DUNFERMLINE   ABERDEEN (0) 1
ATHLETIC (0) 1   Shewan (89)
Barry (73)
DUNFERMLINE: Martin, W. Callaghan, Lunn, Thomson, Delaney, T. Callaghan, Edwards, Barry, Hunter (Fleming), Ferguson, Robertson
ABERDEEN: Clark, Whyte, Shewan, Petersen, McMillan, Buchan, P. Wilson, Melrose, Winchester, Smith, J. Wilson

P W D L F A Pts
5 1 2 2 6 9 4   *Referee:* J. M. Kelly

Plenty of talking points at East End Park. 17-year-old Martin Buchan makes his senior debut for Aberdeen; Harry Melrose is ordered off; and Ally Shewan heads a last-gasp equaliser.

No 6 Saturday, 15 October
ABERDEEN (0) 2   AYR UNITED (0) 0
Smith (60), Winchester
(74)

ABERDEEN: Clark, Hermiston, Shewan, Millar, McMillan, Munro, P. Wilson, Melrose, Winchester, Smith, J. Wilson
AYR: Miller, Malone, Murphy, Quinn, Monan, Mitchell, Grant, McMillan, Black, Ingram, Hawkshaw

P W D L F A Pts
6 2 2 2 8 9 6   *Referee:* R. K. Wilson

More young players are drafted into the Dons side. This time it's the turn of Francis Munro and Jim Hermiston.

No 7 Saturday, 22 October
AIRDRIEONIANS (1) 1   ABERDEEN (1) 2
Keenan (42 pen)   Taylor (12), J. Wilson
(89 pen)
AIRDRIE: McKenzie, Jonquin, Keenan, Goodwin, Black, Ramsey, Ferguson, McPheat, Marshall, Murray, Irvine
ABERDEEN: Clark, Hermiston, Shewan, Millar, McMillan, Munro, P. Wilson, Winchester, Taylor, Smith, J. Wilson

P W D L F A Pts
7 3 2 2 10 10 8   *Referee:* A. G. Crawley

Airdrie are already downcast over losing a League Cup semi final to Celtic in midweek. They are not made any happier by the sight of Ian Taylor's dream debut for Aberdeen, sending a 25-yarder flashing past McKenzie.

No 8 Saturday, 29 October
ABERDEEN (0) 2   HIBERNIAN (0) 1
Winchester (64), Watt   Cormack (55)
(79)
ABERDEEN: Clark, Whyte, Shewan, Munro, McMillan, Petersen (Winchester), J. Wilson, Melrose, Taylor, Smith, Watt
HIBERNIAN: Wilson, Duncan, Davis, Stanton, Cousin, O'Rourke, Cormack, Stein, Scott, McGraw, Stevenson

Leading positions

	P	W	D	L	F	A	Pts
1 Celtic	7	7	0	0	26	6	14
2 Kilmarnock	7	5	1	1	12	7	11
3 ABERDEEN	8	4	2	2	12	11	10
4 Rangers	6	4	1	1	18	6	9
5 Hibernian	8	4	1	3	25	13	9

Attendance: 10,000   *Referee:* R. Davidson

Aberdeen shrug off the disappointment of their League Cup exit at the hands of Rangers to move into third position in the league. Winchester replaced Petersen for the second half and it was he who managed to land the decisive touch in a goalmouth scramble. A rip-roaring second half had more than its fair share of incidents – and free kicks.

No 9 Saturday, 5 November
ABERDEEN (0) 3   HEARTS (0) 1
Taylor (80), Watt   Murphy (67)
2 (84, 87)

ABERDEEN: Clark, Whyte, Shewan, Munro, McMillan, Millar, Little, Melrose, Taylor, Smith, Watt

HEARTS: Cruickshank, Polland, Pedan, Cumming, Anderson, Gordon, Hamilton, Davidson, Wallace, Murphy, Traynor

P	W	D	L	F	A	Pts
9	5	2	2	15	12	12

Attendance: 10,000

Referee: T. Wharton

Having seen off Hibs the previous match, Aberdeen set about Hearts the same way, and gain a famous Guy Fawkes Day victory. Once again the Dons found themselves trailing in the second half to defensively minded opponents. They left their reply late – but that only added to the thrills for the crowd. There is plenty of needle in all Aberdeen's matches this season, and Harry Melrose, Jimmy Whyte and Jim Smith are all about to start suspensions.

No 10 Saturday, 12 November
ST MIRREN (1) 1   ABERDEEN (0) 3
  Treacy (40)   Watt 2 (51, 72),
                            Winchester (75)

ST MIRREN: Connachan, Murray, Gemmell, Clark, Kiernan, Pinkerton, Hutton, Taylor (McLardy), Adamson, McLaughlin, Treacy

ABERDEEN: Clark, Hermiston, Shewan, Millar (Winchester), McMillan, Petersen, J. Wilson, Munro, Taylor, Little, Watt

P	W	D	L	F	A	Pts
10	6	2	2	18	13	14

Referee: D. Small

Five league wins in a row for the dandy Dons. Once again they save their best efforts for when they are behind, and this result leaves St Mirren propping up the rest of the table. Five goals in three games for Willie Watt makes him the man of the moment. Again the appearance of substitute Ernie Winchester at half-time puts the pep into the Dons.

No 11 Saturday, 19 November
ABERDEEN (2) 5   PARTICK THISTLE (1) 2
  Petersen (36), Whyte   Whyte o.g. (44), Rae (88)
  (41), Wilson 2 (68 pen,
  80), Winchester (71)

ABERDEEN: Clark, Whyte, Shewan, Munro, McMillan, Petersen, Little, Winchester, Taylor, Smith, J. Wilson

PARTICK: Niven, Tinney, Muir, Gibb, McKinnon, O'Neill, McLindon, Rae, Divers, Cunningham, Duncan

P	W	D	L	F	A	Pts
11	7	2	2	23	15	16

Referee: J. R. P. Gordon

It's a relief to know that Aberdeen can still score goals without injured marksman Willie Watt. In the first half it's the Dons' defenders who show the route to goal.

No 12 Saturday, 26 November
DUNDEE UNITED (1) 1   ABERDEEN (1) 3
  Wing (38 pen)   Winchester (3), Briggs
                               o.g. (52), Wilson (84)

DUNDEE UNITED: Davie, Millar, Briggs, Neilson, Smith, Wing, Berg, Hainey, Mitchell, Gillespie, Persson (Dossing)

ABERDEEN: Clark, Whyte, Shewan, Munro, McMillan, Petersen, Little, Winchester, Taylor, Smith, J. Wilson

P	W	D	L	F	A	Pts
12	8	2	2	26	16	18

Referee: E. Thomson

It is now seven wins out of seven for the rampant Dons – and still there is no let-up in their physical commitment. Both Munro and McMillan were booked – Munro for protesting about the penalty. This was Aberdeen's third win so far over Dundee United, and United captain Briggs' second own-goal for Aberdeen.

No 13 Saturday, 3 December
ABERDEEN (0) 2   MOTHERWELL (0) 1
  J. Wilson 2 (50, 75 pen)   Hunter (54)

ABERDEEN: Clark, Whyte, Shewan, Munro, McMillan, Petersen, Little, Smith, Taylor, Winchester, J. Wilson

MOTHERWELL: McCloy, Whiteford, R. McCallum, W. McCallum, Martis, Campbell, Lindsay, Cairney, Deans, Murray, Hunter

Leading positions

	P	W	D	L	F	A	Pts
1 Celtic	13	11	2	0	45	14	24
2 Rangers	13	9	2	2	41	13	20
3 ABERDEEN	13	9	2	2	28	17	20
4 Kilmarnock	13	7	4	2	19	12	18
5 Dundee	13	7	3	3	25	15	17

Attendance: 8,000   *Referee:* J. Stewart

Now it's eight wins on the trot. Jimmy Wilson's second goal was a hotly disputed penalty after Willie McCallum handled.

No 14 Saturday, 10 December
FALKIRK (0) 1   ABERDEEN (0) 0
  Graham (62)

FALKIRK: Connachan, Lambie, Hunter, Fulton, Markie (Moran), Baxter, Cowan, Rowan, Vincent, Graham, McKinney

ABERDEEN: Clark, Whyte, Shewan, Munro, McMillan, Petersen, Melrose, Smith, Taylor, Winchester, J. Wilson

P	W	D	L	F	A	Pts
14	9	2	3	28	18	20

Referee: D. Small

It had to happen. After eight successive wins Aberdeen are sent crashing by struggling Falkirk, who happen to find their first win in eight games. It is a fine start for the Bairns' new manager John Prentice.

No 15 Saturday, 17 December
STIRLING ALBION (1) 2   ABERDEEN (3) 6
  Symington (1); Caldow   Whyte (15), J. Wilson
  (85)   3 (17, 27, 87 pen),
                                 Johnston (51), Taylor
                                 (73)

STIRLING: Murray, Dickson, Caldow, Thomson, Rodgerson, Laing, Peebles, McKinnon, Grant, Kerray, Symington

ABERDEEN: Clark, Whyte, Shewan, Munro, McMillan, Petersen, J. Wilson, Smith, Johnston, Melrose, Taylor

P	W	D	L	F	A	Pts	
15	10	2	3	34	20	22	*Referee:* N. Watson

Filthy weather and a first-minute deficit can't stop Aberdeen roaring to their biggest win of the season. Dave Johnston – from Nairn County – scores for Aberdeen on his debut. Now bring on the Celts.

No 16 Saturday, 24 December
ABERDEEN (1) 1   CELTIC (1) 1
  Melrose (30)   Lennox (23)

ABERDEEN: Clark, Whyte, Shewan, Munro, McMillan, Petersen, J. Wilson, Melrose, Johnston, Smith, Taylor

CELTIC: Simpson, Gemmell, O'Neil, Murdoch, McNeill, Clark, Chalmers, Auld, McBride, Wallace, Lennox

P	W	D	L	F	A	Pts	
16	10	3	3	35	21	23	*Attendance:* 28,000
							Referee: C. H. Hutton

In rock-hard conditions Bobby Clark sports track-suit trousers and jacket. He is helpless as the unbeaten league leaders score first through Lennox, after McMillan had failed to control the ball. But Aberdeen grit their teeth and Shewan's cross produces a back-header from Munro and a firm header by Melrose. Simpson got a touch but couldn't save.

No 17 Saturday, 31 December
ABERDEEN (0) 4   KILMARNOCK (0) 0
  Melrose (55), Smith (76),
  Little (87), Munro (89)

ABERDEEN: Clark, Whyte, Shewan, Munro, McMillan, Petersen, Little, Smith, Johnston, Melrose, J. Wilson

KILMARNOCK: Ferguson, King, McFadzean, O'Connor, McGrory, Beattie, McLean, McInally, Bertelsen, Queen, McIlroy

P	W	D	L	F	A	Pts	
17	11	3	3	39	21	25	*Attendance:* 14,000
							Referee: R. Gordon

Killie have slipped out of the championship contenders – but their Scottish international keeper, Bobby Ferguson, keeps them in the game throughout the first half.

No 18 Monday, 2 January
ABERDEEN (3) 5   DUNDEE (0) 2
  Melrose (13), Smith (15),   Cameron 2 (60, 69)
  Wilson (35 pen), Munro
  2 (59, 88)

ABERDEEN: Clark, Whyte, Shewan, Munro, McMillan, Petersen, Little, Smith, Johnston, Melrose, J. Wilson

DUNDEE: Arrol, Hamilton, Cox, Murray, Easton, Stuart, Bryce, Kinninmonth, Cameron, McLean, Scott

P	W	D	L	F	A	Pts	
18	12	3	3	44	23	27	*Attendance:* 17,000
							Referee: J. W. Paterson

Nine goals from two holiday games, and there is an undeniable air of expectancy about Aberdeen. The Dons are now second, behind Celtic, and there seems every chance that they will qualify for Europe for the first time.

No 19 Tuesday, 3 January
ST JOHNSTONE (1) 1   ABERDEEN (0) 0
  Whitelaw (37)

ST JOHNSTONE: Donaldson, McCarry, Coburn, Townsend, Rooney, McPhee, Clark, Whitelaw, Kilgannon, McDonald, Johnston

ABERDEEN: Clark, Whyte, Shewan, Munro, McMillan, Petersen, Little, Smith, Johnston, Melrose (Winchester), J. Wilson

P	W	D	L	F	A	Pts	
19	12	3	4	44	24	27	*Attendance:* 8,200
							Referee: R. A. S. Crockett

Jim Smith, back from a seven-day suspension, is booked again. So is Tommy McMillan – after the game – for an incident in the tunnel. Next Saturday's fixture with Rangers is then postponed.

No 20 Saturday, 14 January
CLYDE (0) 0   ABERDEEN (0) 0

CLYDE: McCulloch, Glasgow, Mulherron, Anderson, Statie, McHugh, McFarland, Hood, Gilroy, Stewart, Hastings

ABERDEEN: Clark, Whyte, Shewan, Munro, McMillan, Petersen, J. Wilson, Smith, Johnston, Melrose, Taylor

P	W	D	L	F	A	Pts	
20	12	4	4	44	24	28	*Referee:* B. Padden

Aberdeen still haven't won at Shawfield since Clyde returned to the First Division in 1964.

No 21 Wednesday, 18 January
ABERDEEN (1) 1   RANGERS (0) 2
  Johnston (27)   McLean 2 (48, 81)

ABERDEEN: Clark, Whyte, Shewan, Munro, McMillan, Petersen, J. Wilson, Smith, Winchester, Melrose, Johnston

RANGERS: Martin, Johansen, Provan, Greig, McKinnon, D. Smith, Henderson, A. Smith, McLean, Forrest, Johnston

P	W	D	L	F	A	Pts	
21	12	4	5	45	26	28	*Attendance:* 31,000
							Referee: J. R. P. Gordon

This is the Dons' first home defeat of the season. To make matters worse, bookings for Winchester and Shewan take the Aberdeen total to 14 so far. As for the match, Aberdeen started well: Rangers finished well. It was as simple as that. None the less, their winner came from nothing. Rangers' keeper Martin dropped a ball from a corner. Provan rescued him by belting the ball downfield and McLean ran on to take Johnston's return pass. This result means that Rangers have completed the league double over Aberdeen as well as knocking them out of the League Cup.

No 22 Saturday, 21 January
ABERDEEN (1) 1   DUNFERMLINE
  Winchester (17)   ATHLETIC (1) 2
                           Robertson (32), Ferguson
                           (60)
ABERDEEN: Clark, Whyte, Shewan, Munro,
McMillan, Petersen, J. Wilson (Taylor), Smith,
Winchester, Melrose, Johnston
DUNFERMLINE: Martin, Totten, Lunn, Thomson,
Fraser, Barry, Edwards, Paton, Delaney, A. Ferguson,
Robertson
Leading positions

	P	W	D	L	F	A	Pts
1 Celtic	21	17	3	1	74	24	37
2 Rangers	20	14	4	2	57	18	32
3 ABERDEEN	22	12	4	6	46	28	28
4 Hibernian	22	12	2	8	53	30	26
5 Kilmarnock	22	10	6	6	36	31	26

Referee: J. Callaghan

Aberdeen are going through a sticky patch: only one
point from four games. Dunfermline's winner was
scored by a gentleman named Alex Ferguson, who had
earlier been caught repeatedly offside.

No 23 Saturday, 4 February
AYR UNITED (2) 2   ABERDEEN (3) 5
  Rutherford (23 pen),   Smith 2 (8, 21), Robb
  Murphy (39)   (15), Johnston (48),
                            Whyte (70)
AYR: Millar, Malone (Monan), Murphy, Oliphant,
Quinn, Thomson, Rutherford, McMillan, Ingram,
Mitchell, Paterson
ABERDEEN: Clark, Whyte, Shewan, Munro, McCabe
(Watt), Petersen, Robb, Smith, Johnston, Melrose,
J. Wilson

P	W	D	L	F	A	Pts
23	13	4	6	51	30	30

Referee: W. Elliot

Ayr are bottom and still looking for their first win of
the season. Newcomer Robb is the latest Aberdeen
player to be booked. Clark saved Rutherford's last-
minute penalty.

No 24 Saturday, 11 February
ABERDEEN (4) 7   AIRDRIEONIANS (0) 0
  Munro (3), Johnston
  3 (4, 43, 77), Smith (36),
  J. Wilson 2 (52, 83)
ABERDEEN: Clark, Whyte, Shewan, Munro,
McMillan, Petersen, Little, Smith, Johnston, Melrose,
J. Wilson
AIRDRIE: McKenzie, Jonquin, Keenan, Goodwin,
Black, Ramsay, Ferguson, Murray, Menzies, Fyfe,
Phillips

P	W	D	L	F	A	Pts	
24	14	4	6	58	30	32	*Attendance:* 8,000

Referee: W. J. Mullen

What's this? Aberdeen are unstoppable, and local boy
Dave Johnston is the toast of Pittodrie. Next week the
Cup.

No 25 Saturday, 25 February
HIBERNIAN (0) 1   ABERDEEN (0) 0
  Cormack (60)
HIBERNIAN: Allan, Duncan, Davis, Stanton,
Madsen, Cousin, Quinn, O'Rourke, Scott, Cormack,
Stevenson
ABERDEEN: Clark, Whyte, Shewan, Munro,
McMillan, Petersen, Buchan, Smith, Johnston,
Melrose, Wilson

P	W	D	L	F	A	Pts	
25	14	4	7	58	31	32	*Attendance:* 18,500

Referee: W. M. Syme

These two sides will soon meet again in the Third
Round of the Scottish Cup. Martin Buchan wore the No
7 shirt but played in defence. Cormack followed up to
score when Clark failed to hold Scott's attempt.

No 26 Saturday, 4 March
HEARTS (0) 0   ABERDEEN (1) 3
                           Johnston 2 (13, 82),
                           Smith (64)
HEARTS: Cruickshank, Polland, Shevlane, Ferguson,
Thomson, Aitchison, Kemp, Kerrigan, Milne, Gordon,
Hamilton
ABERDEEN: Clark, Whyte, Shewan, Munro,
McMillan, Petersen, Storrie (Robb), Smith, Johnston,
Melrose, J. Wilson

P	W	D	L	F	A	Pts
26	15	4	7	61	31	34

Referee: T. Kellock

Aberdeen parade new signing Jim Storrie from Leeds,
who wanders across the forward line at will. This win
provides a welcome double over Hearts.

No 27 Saturday, 18 March
PARTICK THISTLE (1) 1   ABERDEEN (1) 1
  McLindon (76)   Storrie (44)
PARTICK: Niven, Campbell, Muir, McLindon,
McKinnon, Gibb, Rae (Gallagher), Cunningham,
Flanagan, O'Neill, Duncan
ABERDEEN: Clark, Whyte, Shewan, Munro,
McMillan, Buchan, Robb, Storrie, Johnston, Melrose,
J. Wilson

P	W	D	L	F	A	Pts
27	15	5	7	62	32	35

Referee: W. Anderson

Jim Storrie, unmarked, scores his first goal for
Aberdeen. Another late "goal" for Aberdeen was
allowed by the referee, then disallowed after he
consulted the linesman.

No 28 Saturday, 25 March
ABERDEEN (0) 0   DUNDEE UNITED (1) 1
                           Graham (39)
ABERDEEN: Clark, Whyte, Shewan, Munro,
McMillan, Petersen, J. Wilson, Winchester, Storrie,
Melrose, Johnston
DUNDEE UNITED: Davie, Millar, Briggs, Neilson,
Smith, Wing, Hainey, Graham, Dossing, Mitchell,
Persson

P W D L F A Pts   *Attendance:* 13,000
28 15 5 8   62 33 35   *Referee:* R. Gordon

Aberdeen drop to 6th after this shock home defeat by their future Scottish Cup Semi-Final opponents, having scored thirteen goals past them in three earlier matches. Jimmy Wilson misses a second-half penalty.

No 29 Monday, 27 March
ABERDEEN (0) 0   ST MIRREN (0) 0
ABERDEEN: Clark, Whyte, Shewan, Munro, McMillan, Petersen, Little, Smith, Johnston, Melrose, J. Wilson
ST MIRREN: Connachan, Murray, Clark, Kiernan, Heaps, Renton, Aird, Pinkerton, Kane, Gemmell, Hutton

P W D L F A Pts   *Attendance:* 10,000
29 15 6 8   62 33 36

A barren two games at Aberdeen. No goals and only one point. The chance of a Fairs Cup place seems to be slipping away.

No 30 Tuesday, 4 April
MOTHERWELL (1) 3   ABERDEEN (0) 2
Deans (26), Campbell   Winchester (60), Smith
(53), Hunter (89)   (82)
MOTHERWELL: McCloy, Whiteford, M. Thomson, I. Thomson, Martis, W. McCallum, Moffat, Hunter, Deans, Campbell (Murray), Weir
ABERDEEN: Clark, Hermiston, Shewan, Millar, Munro, Petersen, Little, Smith, Winchester, Buchan, Johnston

P W D L F A Pts
30 15 6 9   64 36 36   *Referee:* J. R. P. Gordon

Francis Munro captains the side in the absence of Harry Melrose. He spoils his copy book with a slack lob back to Clark in the last minute which fell short leaving Hunter to score.

No 31 Saturday, 8 April
ABERDEEN (4) 6   FALKIRK (0) 1
Johnston 2 (7, 37 pen),   Cowan (66)
Smith (15), Munro
2 (41, 86), Melrose (72)
ABERDEEN: Clark, Whyte, Shewan, Munro, McMillan, Petersen, J. Wilson, Smith, Storrie, Melrose, Johnston
FALKIRK: Connachan, Lambie, Hunter, Markie, Gibson, Moran, McManus, Smith, Fulton, Graham, Cowan

Leading positions

	P	W	D	L	F	A	Pts
1 Celtic	30	25	4	1	105	28	54
2 Rangers	31	24	4	3	88	27	52
3 ABERDEEN	31	16	6	9	70	37	38
4 Hibernian	31	17	4	10	66	46	38
5 Kilmarnock	30	15	7	8	55	42	37
6 Clyde	29	16	5	8	51	44	37

Attendance: 7,000   *Referee:* I. M. D. Foote

Aberdeen climb back into third position with this enormous win. A number of sides are involved in a ding-dong struggle for entry to the European Fairs Cup.

No 32 Saturday, 15 April
ABERDEEN (0) 1   STIRLING ALBION (0) 0
Melrose (58)
ABERDEEN: Clark, Whyte, Shewan, Munro, McMillan, Petersen, J. Wilson, Smith, Storrie, Melrose, Johnston
STIRLING: Murray, Caldow, McGuinness, Reid, Rogerson, Thomson, Peebles, Smith, Grant, Kerray, Hall

P W D L F A Pts   *Attendance:* 7,500
32 17 6 9   71 37 40   *Referee:* E. Thomson

Aberdeen made dreadfully hard work of this. Murray, out of his goal, pushed Melrose's 30-yard shot up, over his head, and into the net.

No 33 Wednesday, 19 April
CELTIC (0) 0   ABERDEEN (0) 0
CELTIC: Simpson, Craig, Gemmell, Murdoch, McNeill, Clark, Johnstone, Wallace, Chalmers, Auld, Lennox
ABERDEEN: Clark, Whyte, Shewan, Munro, McMillan, Petersen, J. Wilson, Smith, Storrie, Melrose, Johnston

P W D L F A Pts   *Attendance:* 33,000
33 17 7 9   71 37 41   *Referee:* R. H. Davidson

Celtic still haven't got the league championship title sewn up. Rangers could still overtake them if Aberdeen win this rehearsal for the Scottish Cup Final. In the event, Aberdeen become the first side to hold Celtic to two league draws this season. Even the 100-up Celtic forward line cannot find a way through Aberdeen's well-drilled defence.

No 34 Monday, 1 May
KILMARNOCK (0) 1   ABERDEEN (0) 1
McLean (78 pen)   McGrory o.g. (51)
KILMARNOCK: Ferguson, King, McFadzean, Murray, McGrory, O'Connor, McLean, McInally, Bertelsen, Queen, Watson
ABERDEEN: Clark, Whyte, Shewan, Munro, McMillan, Petersen, P. Wilson, Smith, Johnston, Storrie, Taylor

Attendance: 5,500   *Referee:* J. Callaghan

Aberdeen can guarantee at least a place in the Fairs Cup if they win at Kilmarnock. Aberdeen's was a bizarre goal. McFadzean handled on the ground; Johnston's penalty was blocked by Ferguson; but McGrory could only slash the ball back into the net. Near the end Munro handled and McLean equalised.

Aberdeen's complete home and away record:

HOME						AWAY					
P	W	D	L	F	A	W	D	L	F	A	Pts
34	11	3	3	44	17	6	5	6	28	21	42

Scottish League Division One

		P	W	D	L	F	A	Pts
1	Celtic	34	26	6	2	111	33	58
2	Rangers	34	24	7	3	92	31	55
3	Clyde	34	20	6	8	64	48	46
4	ABERDEEN	34	17	8	9	72	38	42
5	Hibernian	34	19	4	11	72	49	42
6	Dundee	34	16	9	9	74	51	41
7	Kilmarnock	34	16	8	10	59	46	40
8	Dunfermline	34	14	10	10	72	52	38
9	Dundee United	34	14	9	11	68	62	37
10	Motherwell	34	10	11	13	59	60	31
11	Hearts	34	11	8	15	39	48	30
12	Partick Thistle	34	9	12	13	49	68	30
13	Airdrieonians	34	11	6	17	41	53	28
14	Falkirk	34	11	4	19	33	70	26
15	St Johnstone	34	10	5	19	53	73	25
16	Stirling Albion	34	5	9	20	31	85	19
17	St Mirren	34	4	7	23	25	81	15
18	Ayr United	34	1	7	26	20	86	9

LEAGUE CUP

Saturday, 13 August

ABERDEEN (0) 3   ST JOHNSTONE (0) 0
J. Smith 2 (56, 83), Little
(87 pen)

ABERDEEN: Clark, Whyte, Shewan, Petersen, McMillan, Millar, Little, Melrose, Winchester, Smith, Wilson

ST JOHNSTONE: Donaldson, Mitchie, Coburn, McCarry, Ryden, McPhee, Clark, Townsend, Littlejohn, Duffy, Kemp

Attendance: 5,000   *Referee:* R. D. Henderson

Dave Smith's eve of season transfer to Rangers deadens interest in the match. His namesake, Jim, fills the gap nicely – scoring twice.

Wednesday, 17 August

DUNDEE (1) 3   ABERDEEN (1) 4
Scott (30), McLean   Wilson 2 (4, 71),
2 (70, 82)   Winchester 2 (52, 80)

DUNDEE: Donaldson, Hamilton, Cox, Selway, Easton, Stuart, Penman, Murray, McLean, Scott, Cameron

ABERDEEN: Clark, Whyte, Shewan, Millar, McMillan, Paterson, Little, Melrose, Winchester, Smith, J. Wilson

Referee: J. R. P. Gordon

A seven-goal thriller sets Aberdeen up for a place in the last eight. There was a blunder from Clark who allowed John Scott's equalising shot from thirty yards to pass over his head. A cracking climax produced four goals in the last twenty minutes. More please.

Saturday, 20 August

ABERDEEN (2) 4   DUNDEE UNITED (1) 1
Winchester (25), Briggs   Millar o.g. (10)
o.g. (45), Smith (49),
Melrose (84)

ABERDEEN: Clark, Whyte, Shewan, Millar, McMillan, Petersen, Little, Melrose, Winchester, Smith, Wilson

DUNDEE UNITED: Mackay, Dick, Briggs, Neilson, Smith, Fraser, Seemann, Munro, Dossing, Hainey, Persson

Attendance: 11,000   *Referee:* I. M. D. Foote

A game of two headed own-goals. Briggs, for Aberdeen, just on the half-time whistle, gave the Dons the upper hand they exploited after the break.

Saturday, 27 August

ST JOHNSTONE (0) 0   ABERDEEN (1) 3
          Wilson (16), Little (59),
          Winchester (69)

ST JOHNSTONE: Donaldson, McCarry, Coburn, Townsend, Ryden, McPhee, Clark, Kilgannon, Rooney, Duffy, Kemp

ABERDEEN: Clark, Whyte, Shewan, Millar, McMillan, Petersen, Little, Melrose, Winchester, Smith, J. Wilson

Attendance: 5,000   *Referee:* R. Gordon

Surely the Dons won't blow it now. One point from their last two matches will be enough.

Wednesday, 31 August

ABERDEEN (0) 2   DUNDEE (0) 0
Smith (72), Melrose (88)

ABERDEEN: Clark, Whyte, Shewan, Millar, McMillan, Petersen, Little, Melrose, Winchester, Smith, J. Wilson

DUNDEE: Donaldson, Wilson, Selway, Houston, Easton, Stuart, Kinninmonth, Murray, McLean, Scott, McKay

Attendance: 12,000   *Referee:* J. P. Barclay

This is the 67th match between the clubs in all competitions since 1945. Beforehand the tally was 27 wins each. Dundee's ultra-defensive methods looked like keeping things that way until Jim Smith found a way through.

Saturday, 3 September

DUNDEE UNITED (2) 3   ABERDEEN (3) 4
Seemann (10 pen),   Wilson (4), Little (13),
Mitchell 2 (16, 69)   Whyte 2 (25, 65)

DUNDEE UNITED: Mackay, Millar, Dick, Neilson, Smith, Fraser (Carroll), Seemann, Hainey, Dossing, Mitchell, Persson

ABERDEEN: Clark, Whyte, Shewan, Millar, McMillan, Petersen, Little, Melrose, Winchester, Smith, J. Wilson

Attendance: 5,000   *Referee:* A. D. Fleming

A meaningless match for both sides turns into a party. But Aberdeen make sure they win the party.

Section 1

	P	W	D	L	F	A	Pts
ABERDEEN	6	6	0	0	20	7	12
Dundee United	6	2	2	2	12	12	6
Dundee	6	1	2	3	8	11	4
St Johnstone	6	0	2	4	5	15	2

Quarter Final 1st Leg Wednesday, 14 September
MORTON (2) 3   ABERDEEN (1) 1
  Mason 2 (27, 78), Gray   Smith (21)
  (35)

MORTON: Sorensen, Boyd, Kennedy, Madsen
(Davin), Strachan, Gray, Harper, Arentoft, Mason,
Bolton, Stevenson

ABERDEEN: Clark, Whyte, Shewan, Millar,
McMillan, Petersen, Little, Melrose, Winchester,
Smith, J. Wilson

                  Referee: A. J. F. Webster
Aberdeen scored first and then tried to mix it with the
no-holds-barred Second Division pacemakers. Two
Dons were booked in the second half and the referee left
the ground hugely unpopular with the Aberdeen
players. Mason's second goal for Morton makes it an
uphill struggle for Aberdeen in the second leg.

Quarter Final 2nd Leg Wednesday, 21 September
ABERDEEN (0) 3   MORTON (0) 0
  Winchester (46), Smith
  (85), Petersen (89)

ABERDEEN: Clark, Whyte, Shewan, Millar,
McMillan, Petersen, Little, Melrose, Winchester,
Smith, J. Wilson

MORTON: Sorensen, Boyd, Kennedy, Madsen,
Strachan, Gray, Harper, Arentoft, Mason, Bolton,
Stevenson

Attendance: 19,000   *Referee:* A. J. F. Webster
Bobby Clark stood and watched the game in distant
parts as Aberdeen tried to bludgeon their way past
Morton's packed defence. With five minutes to play,
Aberdeen were out. Smith then looked to have taken
the game into extra time, but then came Petersen's
winner which lifted the lid off Pittodrie. He breasted
down Little's lob and hammered in an unstoppable shot
from 15 yards. Afterwards Aberdeen counted their
bruises: Shewan had a gashed chin; Millar a cut eye.

Semi Final (Hampden) Wednesday, 19 October
RANGERS (2) 2   ABERDEEN (1) 2
  Henderson 2 (12, 26)   J. Wilson (24),
                            Shewan (71)

RANGERS: Ritchie, Johansen, Provan, Greig,
McKinnon, D. Smith, Henderson, A. Smith, Millar
(Wilson), McLean, Johnston

ABERDEEN: Clark, Whyte, Shewan, Millar,
McMillan, Petersen, Little (P. Wilson), Melrose,
Winchester, Smith, J. Wilson

Attendance: 38,600   *Referee:* R. H. Davidson
Aberdeen are determined to avenge last season's
Scottish Cup semi-final defeat by Rangers. In doing so

Jim Smith is booked for the third time this season. Both
clubs are criticised for using substitutes in extra time,
when the ruling which introduced them was designed to
replace incapacitated players, not to seek to gain a
tactical advantage. In the 87th minute Aberdeen's
defence had an extraordinary escape when McLean
burrowed through to plant his shot against Clark's
crossbar.

Semi Final Replay (Hampden) Monday, 24 October
RANGERS (2) 2   ABERDEEN (0) 0
  Johnston (4), A. Smith
  (39)

RANGERS: Martin, Johansen, Provan, Greig,
McKinnon, D. Smith, Wilson, Watson, McLean,
A. Smith, Johnston

ABERDEEN: Clark, Whyte, Shewan, Millar,
McMillan, Petersen, Little, Melrose, Winchester,
Smith, J. Wilson

Attendance: 38,000   *Referee:* R. H. Davidson
Deputy Rangers keeper Norrie Martin didn't have a
single shot to save, such was Aberdeen's inability to
make a match of it. Rangers won through despite their
preferred forward line being wrecked by injury.
Aberdeen never recovered from Willie Johnston's early
goal, and full-back Jimmy Whyte was cautioned for the
third time this season, this time for crunching McLean.

SCOTTISH CUP

1st Round Saturday, 28 January
DUNDEE (0) 0   ABERDEEN (1) 5
                Smith 2 (15, 86), Wilson
                (49), Johnston 2 (62, 77)

DUNDEE: Arrol, Hamilton, Stuart, Murray, Easton,
Houston, Scott (Penman), Kinninmonth, Cameron,
McLean, Bryce

ABERDEEN: Clark, Whyte, Shewan, Munro,
McMillan, Petersen, Robb, Smith, Johnston, Melrose,
J. Wilson

Attendance: 23,000   *Referee:* J. W. Paterson
Dave Robb makes his debut on the wing in this thrilling
Aberdeen performance. Poor demoralised Dundee can
only stand and watch as their side melt away in the
second half and leave the stage to Jim Smith. Pick of the
Dons' goals was Dave Johnston's second. Smith rolled
the ball into his path for the inrushing centre forward to
fire past Arrol.

2nd Round Saturday, 18 February
ABERDEEN (0) 5   ST JOHNSTONE (0) 0
  Wilson (47), Smith (60),
  Johnston 2 (65, 88),
  Melrose (89)

ABERDEEN: Clark, Whyte, Shewan, Munro,
McMillan, Petersen, Little, Smith, Johnston, Melrose,
J. Wilson

ST JOHNSTONE: Donaldson, McGarry, Coburn,
Townsend, Rooney, McPhee, Clark, Whitelaw,
Kilgannon, Weir, Johnston

Attendance: 22,800   *Referee:* T. Wharton

The good times are back at Pittodrie. Aberdeen are thrown up against the same opponents in League Cup and Scottish Cup. Bobby Clark saved a Coburn penalty at 3-0 on a day in which nothing went right for St Johnstone. Who's next for the chopping block?

Quarter Final Saturday, 11 March
HIBERNIAN (1) 1   ABERDEEN (0) 1
  Stevenson (15)   Smith (86)
HIBERNIAN: Allan, Duncan, Davin, Stanton, Madsen, Cousin, Quinn, O'Rourke, Scott, Cormack, Stevenson
ABERDEEN: Clark, Whyte, Shewan, Munro, McMillan, Petersen, Storrie, Smith, Johnston, Melrose, J. Wilson
Attendance: 37,200   *Referee:* T. Wharton
For much of this match it looked like Hibs would repeat their 1-0 league victory over Aberdeen at Easter Road. Blustery conditions spoiled the spectacle for the fans; Wilson and McMillan were booked in the second half; and then up popped Jimmy Smith to head in the equaliser from a corner.

Quarter Final Replay Wednesday, 22 March
ABERDEEN (2) 3   HIBERNIAN (0) 0
  Winchester 2 (3, 56),
  Storrie (15)
ABERDEEN: Clark, Whyte, Shewan, Munro, McMillan, Petersen, J. Wilson, Storrie, Winchester, Melrose, Johnstone
HIBERNIAN: Allan, Duncan, Davis, Stanton, Madsen, Cousin, Quinn, Stein, Scott, Cormack (O'Rourke), Stevenson
Attendance: 44,000   *Referee:* T. Wharton
A record midweek crowd witnesses transfer-seeking Ernie Winchester shoot Aberdeen into a third-minute lead, prodding the ball home after it had rebounded off Duncan. Then Allan failed to hold Petersen's rocket and Storrie tapped in the loose ball. The second half provided chants of 'Easy Easy' from the terraces for the first time in years.

Semi Final (Dens Park) Saturday, 1 April
DUNDEE UNITED (0) 0 ABERDEEN (1) 1
                      Millar o.g. (4)
DUNDEE UNITED: Davie, Millar, Briggs, Neilson, Smith, Wing, Gillespie, Graham, Dossing, Mitchell, Persson
ABERDEEN: Clark, Whyte, Shewan, Munro, McMillan, Petersen, Storrie, Smith, Johnston, Melrose, J. Wilson
                      Referee: T. Wharton
The last time Aberdeen played a Scottish Cup semi-final at Dens Park was in 1947 on their way to take the Cup. This season, too, Aberdeen won 5-0 in the same stadium against Dundee in the first round. So the omens are set fair. The game was only four minutes old

when United full-back Tommy Miller turned the ball past Davie. Jim Storrie then sent a penalty wide of the United post. The game wasn't pretty to watch and Aberdeen players spent much of the last minutes booting the ball out of the ground.

Scottish Cup Final (Hampden) Saturday, 29 April
CELTIC (1) 2   ABERDEEN (0) 0
  Wallace 2 (42, 49)
CELTIC: Simpson, Craig, Gemmell, Murdoch, McNeill, Clark, Johnstone, Wallace, Chalmers, Auld, Lennox
ABERDEEN: Clark, Whyte, Shewan, Munro, McMillan, Petersen, J. Wilson, Smith, Storrie, Melrose, Johnston
Attendance: 126,100   *Referee:* W. M. Syme
Celtic are not yet Scottish league champions, so Aberdeen's place in Europe – in whatever competition – is not yet secure. Manager Eddie Turnbull is taken unwell and is unable to appear at Hampden with his players. It is a ragged match, turned in Celtic's direction by two strikes by ex-Hearts poacher Willie Wallace either side of the interval. Jim Smith received his fourth caution of the season. Perhaps Turnbull's absence and a mishap to the players' coach on its way to Hampden, causing them to arrive late, unsettled the Dons.

Exactly the same Celtic eleven would, the following month, lift the European Cup. Not even that could settle Aberdeen's European place, for Rangers had still to play in the European Cup-Winners Cup Final. When everything had been sorted out, Aberdeen would appear in next season's Cup-Winners Cup competition as losing finalists to Celtic in the Cup Final.

1966-67

APPEARANCES	League	League Cup	Scottish Cup
Clark	34	10	6
Shewan	34	10	6
McMillan	32	10	6
J. Wilson	31	10	6
Petersen	30	10	6
Whyte	30	10	6
J. Smith	30	10	5
Munro	29		6
Melrose	27	10	6
Johnston	20		6
Winchester	15(+3)	10	1
Little	14	10	1
Taylor	12(+1)		
D. Millar	9	10	
Storrie	7		4
P. Wilson	5	−(+1)	
Watt	4(+1)		
Buchan	4		
Hermiston	4		
Robb	2(+1)		1
McCabe	1		
21 players			

GOALS	Total	League	League Cup	Scottish Cup
J. Wilson	20	13	5	2
J. Smith	20	10	6	4
Winchester	17	10	5	2
Johnston	14	10		4
Melrose	8	5	2	1
Munro	6	6		
Watt	5	5		
Whyte	5	3	2	
Little	4	1	3	
Taylor	3	3		
Shewan	2	1	1	
Storrie	2	1		1
Petersen	2	1	1	
Robb	1	1		
own-goals	4	2	1	1
Total	113	72	26	15

A team group taken in 1969. Back row: Whyte, Boel, Petersen, McGarr, A. Smith, Buchan, Hermiston. Front row: J. Smith, Willoughby, Forrest, Robb and Hamilton.

Season 1967-68

1967-68 saw Aberdeen's first taste of European soccer. Eligible for the Cup-Winners Cup – owing to Celtic forfeiting that right in preference for the European Cup – Aberdeen promptly belted 14 goals past the Icelanders of Kevlavik to suggest they could go far in the tournament. In the event they got only as far as the next round, where the experienced Standard Liège did all the necessary damage in the first leg.

In each of the three domestic competitions Aberdeen fared badly in comparison with the standards set the previous year. Linked with Celtic and Rangers in their League Cup group, Aberdeen failed to win a single game. When the Scottish Cup came around, Aberdeen took two bites at the Raith cherry before successfully swallowing it – and then proceeded to choke at Dunfermline.

In the league, expectations were high following Aberdeen's fourth position in 1967. They finished only one place lower in 1968, but that was a misleading comparison. Aberdeen had been lodged in mid-table from the Autumn through to the Spring. They had been unable to win away from home until the New Year. Only by winning their final four games were they able to stake fifth position and make themselves available for the following season's Fairs Cup.

Aberdeen's last match of 1967-68 was at Ibrox. Rangers were within sixty seconds of going the whole league season unbeaten when Ian Taylor popped in a shock goal and handed the title to Celtic.

League:	Fifth
League Cup:	Bottom of qualifying group
Scottish Cup:	Second Round
European Cup Winners Cup:	Second Round

SCOTTISH LEAGUE DIVISION ONE

No 1 Saturday, 9 September
ABERDEEN (3) 4   DUNDEE (0) 2
Storrie (7), Munro (22),   Campbell (48),
Taylor 2 (44, 59)   Stuart (78)

ABERDEEN: Clark, Whyte, Shewan, Petersen, McMillan, Buchan, J. Wilson, Munro, Storrie, Smith, Taylor
DUNDEE: Arrol, R. Wilson, Cox, Murray, Stewart, Stuart, Campbell, J. McLean, S. Wilson, G. McLean, Scott

P	W	D	L	F	A	Pts	
1	1	0	0	4	2	2	*Attendance:* 15,000
							Referee: J. W. Paterson

Dundee's first defeat in 25 games is inflicted in impressive style. Both Jimmy Smith and Martin Buchan take the eye.

No 2 Saturday, 16 September
ST JOHNSTONE (0) 1   ABERDEEN (0) 1
Whitelaw (50)   J. Wilson (72)

ST JOHNSTONE: Donaldson, McGillivray, Coburn, Miller, Rooney, McPhee, Aird, Whitelaw, McCarry, McDonald, Wilson
ABERDEEN: Clark, Whyte, Shewan, Petersen, McMillan, Buchan, J. Wilson, Munro, Storrie, Smith, Taylor

P	W	D	L	F	A	Pts	
2	1	1	0	5	3	3	*Attendance:* 6,400
							Referee: R. G. Greenlees

It seems to be the case that when Jim Smith plays well Aberdeen play well. At Perth he didn't: neither did they.

No 3 Saturday, 23 September
ABERDEEN (1) 1   CLYDE (1) 2
Watt (17)   Hood (25), Gilroy (85)

ABERDEEN: Clark, Whyte, Shewan, Munro, McMillan, Buchan, J. Wilson, Smith, Storrie, Watt, Taylor

CLYDE: Wright, Glasgow, Soutar, McFarlane, Fraser, Staite, Knox, Hood, Gilroy, Stewart, Hastings

P	W	D	L	F	A	Pts		
3	1	1	1	6	5	3	*Attendance:* 12,000
							Referee: R. D. Crawford

Not much entertainment here. Not many smiles either – unless you were a Clyde fan. Three minutes before Gilroy's winner Munro blazed a penalty against the bar.

No 4 Saturday, 30 September
MORTON (0) 3   ABERDEEN (0) 3
  Mason (51), Allan (61)   Shewan (78), Watt (89)
  Sweeney (84)   Whyte (90)

MORTON: Russell, Loughlan, Kennedy, Arentoft, Strachan, Gray, Jensen, Allan, Mason, Stevenson, Sweeney

ABERDEEN: Clark, Whyte, Shewan, Millar, McMillan, Munro, J. Wilson, Smith, Taylor, Watt, Johnston

P	W	D	L	F	A	Pts	
4	1	2	1	9	8	4	*Referee:* R. K. Wilson

Top scorer Jim Storrie is mysteriously omitted from the Dons' travelling party. He missed a Roy of the Rovers fightback by Aberdeen – sparked by Watt's 20-yard free kick and Whyte's savage low cross turned into goal by a defender. Earlier, poor Morton had done enough to win half a dozen matches.

No 5 Saturday, 7 October
ABERDEEN (0) 0   DUNFERMLINE
                  ATHLETIC (1) 1,
                  Gardner (30)

ABERDEEN: Clark, Whyte, Shewan, Munro, McMillan, Petersen, J. Wilson, Smith, Storrie, Millar, Johnston

DUNFERMLINE: Martin, W. Callaghan, Lunn, Delaney, Barry, Thomson, Hunter, T. Callaghan, Gardner, Paton, Robertson

P	W	D	L	F	A	Pts	
5	1	2	2	9	9	4	*Referee:* R. K. Wilson

Aberdeen's disciplinary record, bad last season, is now becoming embarrassing. In this match Shewan was booked in the second half and Jimmy Wilson ordered off. Now it is clear why Aberdeen wear shirts numbered on the front and back: it is to prevent the need for the referee to turn the player round.

No 6 Saturday, 14 October
ABERDEEN (2) 6   DUNDEE UNITED (0) 0
  Taylor (12), Munro (38),
  Johnston 2 (48, 66 pen),
  Smith (62), Robb (88)

ABERDEEN: Clark, Hermiston, Shewan, Munro, McMillan, Petersen, Johnston, Smith, Robb, Melrose, Taylor

DUNDEE UNITED: Davie, T. Miller, Briggs, Wood, Smith, Gillespie, Seemann, Dossing, J. Millar, Rowland, Mitchell

P	W	D	L	F	A	Pts		
6	2	2	2	15	9	6	*Attendance:* 9,000
							Referee: J. H. KcKee

A new-look forward line creates countless chances and gains handsome revenge for the 5-0 crushing at Tannadice in the League Cup.

No 7 Saturday, 21 October
HEARTS (1) 2   ABERDEEN (0) 1
  Jensen (9), Ford (85)   Storrie (62)

HEARTS: Garland, Sneddon, Holt, Macdonald, Thomson, Miller, Jensen, Townsend, Ford, Irvine, Traynor (Fleming)

ABERDEEN: McGarr, Hermiston, Shewan, Munro, McMillan, Petersen, Johnston, Storrie, Robb, Melrose, Taylor

P	W	D	L	F	A	Pts		
7	2	2	3	16	11	6	*Attendance:* 11,000
							Referee: D. Small

Jim Storrie was both the hero and the villain at Tynecastle. His magnificent diving header to make it 1-1 was followed by a frivolous blaze over the bar before Ford restored Hearts' lead. Up in the stand Bill Shankly and Wolves' scouts sat sizing up Jim Smith and Francis Munro. They watched Aberdeen's Ernie McGarr have a faultless debut in goal.

No 8 Saturday, 4 November
PARTICK THISTLE (1) 2   ABERDEEN (2) 2
  McParland (3), Rae (71)   Smith (8), Little (42)

PARTICK: Niven, Campbell, Muir, O'Neil, McKinven, Gibb, Rae, McParland, Coulston, Flanagan, Duncan

ABERDEEN: Clark, Hermiston, Shewan, Buchan, McMillan, Petersen, Little, Smith, Johnston, Melrose, J. Wilson

P	W	D	L	F	A	Pts	
8	2	3	3	18	13	7	*Referee:* A. McKenzie

Bobby Clark is watched by a member of the Scottish Selection Committee – but he permits Rae's half-hit shot to deprive Aberdeen of a point.

No 9 Saturday, 11 November
ABERDEEN (1) 6   RAITH ROVERS (1) 2
  Johnston (42 pen),   Wallace 2 (30, 86)
  Little (58), Petersen
  2 (69 pen, 82), Mackle
  o.g. (72), Wilson (88)

ABERDEEN: Clark, Hermiston, Shewan, Buchan, McMillan, Petersen, Little, Smith, Johnston, Melrose, J. Wilson

RAITH: Reid, Bolton, Gray, Kinloch, Davidson, Porterfield, Wallace, Stein, Cunningham, Sneddon, Mackle

P	W	D	L	F	A	Pts		
9	3	3	3	24	15	9	*Attendance:* 8,000
							Referee: W. Anderson

For a long time this result looked beyond the bounds of plausibility. The turning point was Johnston's equalising penalty which he miscued past Reid.

No 10 Saturday, 18 November
HIBERNIAN (0) 1　　　ABERDEEN (0) 0
　Cormack (56)
HIBERNIAN: Allan, Duncan, Davis, Stanton, Madsen, McGraw, Scott, Quinn, Stein, Cormack, O'Rourke
ABERDEEN: Clark, Hermiston, Shewan, Buchan, McMillan, Petersen, Little, Smith, Robb (Munro), Melrose, Wilson

P　W　D　L　F　A　Pts　　　*Attendance:* 11,000
10　3　3　4　24　16　9

Hibs alone seem able to challenge the Old Firm at the head of the table. Aberdeen lost Robb early on with a cut eye, and later a hooked goal to Cormack after a corner wasn't properly cleared.

No 11 Saturday, 25 November
ABERDEEN (1) 2　　　MOTHERWELL (0) 1
　Wilson (37), Melrose (67)　　Murray (79)
ABERDEEN: Clark, Hermiston, Shewan, Buchan (Little), Munro, Petersen, Johnston, Smith, Robb, Melrose, J. Wilson
MOTHERWELL: McCloy, Whiteford, Mackay, Forsyth, Martis, Murray, Lindsay, McCall, Deans, Campbell, Moffat (W. McCallum)

P　W　D　L　F　A　Pts　　　*Attendance:* 9,000
11　4　3　4　26　17　11　　　*Referee:* A. J. Crawley

Motherwell are entrenched in the bottom two, no thanks to Aberdeen who are now in the right mood to travel to Standard Liège in the Cup-Winners Cup.

No 12 Saturday, 2 December
FALKIRK (0) 2　　　ABERDEEN (2) 2
　Markie (47), Watson (60)　　Melrose (43), Smith (44)
FALKIRK: Devlin, Lambie, Hunter, Markie, Baillie, Gibson, Marshall, Smith, Graham, McLaughlin, Watson
ABERDEEN: Clark, Whyte, Shewan, Munro, McMillan, Petersen, Johnston, Smith, Robb, Melrose, J. Wilson

P　W　D　L　F　A　Pts
12　4　4　4　28　19　12　　　*Referee:* A. F. McDonald

Bang! Bang! Aberdeen score twice as the interval beckons. Then Markie's shot is deflected in by Buchan and eventually Aberdeen are denied their first away league win.

No 13 Saturday, 9 December
KILMARNOCK (1) 3　　　ABERDEEN (0) 0
　Queen (20),
　Morrison 2 (51, 75)
KILMARNOCK: McLaughlin, Arthur, McFadzean, Murray, McGrory, Beattie, McLean, Queen, Morrison, Sinclair, Cameron

ABERDEEN: Clark, Whyte, Shewan, Munro, McMillan, Petersen, Little, Smith, Robb, Melrose, Taylor (Murray)

P　W　D　L　F　A　Pts
13　4　4　5　28　22　12　　　*Referee:* J. Callaghan

Aberdeen have to forget their Cup-Winners Cup elimination by Standard Liège. Shewan and Munro were cautioned in the second half.

No 14 Saturday, 16 December
ABERDEEN (0) 1　　　STIRLING ALBION (0) 0
　Shewan (72)
ABERDEEN: Clark, Whyte, Shewan, Munro, McMillan, Petersen, Little, Smith, Storrie, Murray, Craig
STIRLING: Murray, Cunningham, McGuinness, Grant, Corrigan, Thomson, Hall, Peebles, Hughes, Laing, Symington

P　W　D　L　F　A　Pts　　　*Attendance:* 6,000
14　5　4　5　29　22　14　　　*Referee:* A. F. MacDonald

Ally Shewan's run of more than 230 consecutive first-team games is crowned with a goal to break the tedium. Another Pittodrie babe has his baptism – Tommy Craig.

No 15 Saturday, 23 December
AIRDRIEONIANS (0) 1　　　ABERDEEN (0) 0
　Marshall (72)
AIRDRIE: McKenzie, Jonquin, Caldwell, Goodwin, Black, Whiteford, Wilson, Ramsay, Marshall, Fyfe, Train
ABERDEEN: Clark, Whyte, Shewan, Munro, McMillan, Petersen, Little (Buchanan), Smith, Johnston, Murray, Craig

P　W　D　L　F　A　Pts
15　5　4　6　29　23　14　　　*Referee:* R. K. Wilson

The race for the most bookings is hotting up. Francis Munro goes into the little black book for the fourth time this season.

No 16 Saturday, 30 December
ABERDEEN (0) 1　　　RANGERS (1) 4
　Smith (71)　　　Penman (12), Watson
　　　　　　　　　(55), Johnston (77),
　　　　　　　　　Willoughby (83)
ABERDEEN: Clark, Whyte, Shewan, Petersen, McMillan, Munro, Little, Buchanan, Johnston, Smith, Craig
RANGERS: Sorensen, Johansen, Greig, Watson, McKinnon, D. Smith, Penman, Willoughby, A. Smith, Johnston, Persson

P　W　D　L　F　A　Pts
16　5　4　7　30　27　14　　　*Referee:* J. W. Paterson

Unbeaten Rangers were rarely in difficulty at Pittodrie. Ex-Don Dave Smith swept up majestically at the back. The Dons' version – Jim – spread hope throughout Pittodrie with twenty minutes to go, but Willie Johnston clamped down on any possible resurgence.

No 17 Monday, 1 January
DUNDEE (0) 0   ABERDEEN (2) 2
                 Johnston (1), Easton o.g.
                 (20)

DUNDEE: Donaldson, R. Wilson, Houston, Murray, Easton, Stuart, Scott, J. McLean, S. Wilson, G. McLean, Campbell

ABERDEEN: Clark, Whyte, Shewan, Petersen, McMillan, Buchan, Little, Buchanan, Johnston, Smith, Craig

P W D L F A Pts
17 6 4 7 32 27 16   *Referee:* E. H. Pringle

This is Aberdeen's first away win in Scotland since beating Hearts at Tynecastle last March. The conditions made for a farcical match. Johnston scored the first goal of 1968, 40 seconds after the kick off, and later Eddie Buchanan harassed Jim Easton into scoring an own-goal.

No 18 Saturday, 20 January
DUNFERMLINE   ABERDEEN (1) 2
  ATHLETIC (1) 4   Johnston (36), Buchanan
  Robertson 2 (28, 68 pen),   (85)
  Paton (48), Fraser (71)

DUNFERMLINE: Martin, W. Callaghan, Lunn, Fraser, Barry, Thomson, Edwards, Paton, Gardner, T. Callaghan, Robertson

ABERDEEN: Clark, Whyte, Shewan, Petersen, McMillan, Murray, Robb, Buchanan, Johnston, Smith, Craig

P W D L F A Pts
18 6 4 8 34 31 16   *Referee:* W. M. Syme

Dunfermline had taken 13 points from the last seven games. Now it's 15 from eight. The turning point was Robertson's penalty after Murray had grassed Edwards.

No 19 Saturday, 3 February
DUNDEE UNITED (0) 2 ABERDEEN (2) 3
  Seemann (48), Mitchell   Murray (12), Smith (37),
  (87)   Johnston (79)

DUNDEE UNITED: Mackay, Millar, Cameron, Neilson, Smith, Gillespie, Seemann, Rolland, Scott (Wood), Mitchell, Wilson

ABERDEEN: Clark, Whyte, Shewan, Murray, McMillan, Petersen, Johnston, Smith, Robb, Buchan, Craig

P W D L F A Pts   *Attendance:* 6,500
19 7 4 8 37 33 18   *Referee:* W. Elliott

There are no frills about this Dons side, who took the points when Johnston beat Mackay in a one-to-one situation. This gives Aberdeen the double over both Dundee teams.

No 20 Saturday, 10 February
ABERDEEN (1) 2   HEARTS (0) 0
  Craig (24), Johnston (66)

ABERDEEN: Clark, Whyte, Shewan, Murray, McMillan, Petersen, Johnston, Smith, Robb, Buchan, Craig

HEARTS: Garland, Sneddon, Mann, E. Thomson, A. Thomson, Miller, Ford, Townsend, Moller (Fleming), Irvine, Traynor

P W D L F A Pts   *Attendance:* 12,000
20 8 4 8 39 33 20

Dave Robb is the new choice for the Pittodrie barrackers. Craig scored his first senior goal for Aberdeen, and then Hearts' keeper Garland offered a helping hand for the Dons' second. Craig's corner was not properly cleared and Johnston was on hand to jab the ball over the line.

No 21 Monday, 12 February
ABERDEEN (0) 1   MORTON (0) 0
  Robb (82)

ABERDEEN: Clark, Whyte, Shewan, Murray, McMillan, Petersen, Johnston, Smith, Robb, Buchan, Craig

MORTON: Russell, Loughlan, Kennedy, Rankine, Strachan, Gray, Sweeney, Arentoft, Mason, Allan, Taylor

P W D L F A Pts   *Attendance:* 10,000
21 9 4 8 40 33 22   *Referee:* A. McKenzie

Boo-boy Robb scores the one and only goal which sustains Aberdeen's revival, after Buchan had nodded on a Craig corner. Soon after, Clark's one-handed save from Taylor's powerful header denied Morton a point.

No 22 Saturday, 2 March
ABERDEEN (0) 0   PARTICK THISTLE (0) 1
                    Gibb (46)

ABERDEEN: Clark, Whyte, Shewan, Petersen, McMillan, Murray, Johnston, Smith, Robb (Watt), Buchan, Craig

PARTICK: Niven, Campbell, Muir, O'Neil, Hansen, Gibb, Rae, McParland, Coulston, Flanagan, Duncan (Gallagher)

P W D L F A Pts   *Attendance:* 7,000
22 9 4 9 40 34 22   *Referee:* R. H. Davidson

Partick's goal was in keeping with the improverished state of the match as a whole. Gibb's feeble shot was mishandled over the line by Clark.

No 23 Wednesday, 6 March
CELTIC (4) 4   ABERDEEN (0) 1
  Lennox 3 (3, 31, 35),   Johnston (70)
  McNeill (7)

CELTIC: Simpson, Gemmell, O'Neil, Murdoch, McNeill, Brogan, Johnstone, Lennox, Wallace, Gallagher (Hay), Hughes

ABERDEEN: Clark, Whyte, Shewan, Petersen, McMillan, Murray, Johnston, Smith, Watt, Buchan, Craig

P W D L F A Pts   *Attendance:* 28,000
23 9 4 10 41 38 22   *Referee:* W. J. Mullen

Aberdeen were simply brushed aside, as if so much fluff. Celtic are now four points behind unbeaten Rangers with only one game in hand. Lennox's delicate header, followed by McNeill's thumping variety, gave Celtic the whip-hand after just seven minutes.

No 24 Saturday, 9 March
RAITH ROVERS (2) 3   ABERDEEN (1) 1
  Wallace 2 (36, 45),   Taylor (1)
  Gillespie (63)
RAITH: Reid, Hislop, Gray, Stein, Polland, Millar, Wilson, Falconer, Wallace, Judge, Gillespie
ABERDEEN: Clark, Whyte, Shewan, Petersen, McMillan, Murray (Robb), Johnston, Smith, Taylor, Buchan, Craig

P W D L F A Pts
24 9 4 11 42 41 22   *Referee:* R. S. Crawford

Gordon Wallace's two goals make him the division's top scorer. Celtic have apparently bid £50,000 for Jim Smith. In recent weeks Aberdeen have transferred Jim Storrie to Rotherham, Francis Munro to Wolves, Jimmy Wilson to Hearts and both Dave Millar and Pat Wilson to Raith. Both line up against the Dons.

No 25 Saturday, 16 March
ABERDEEN (2) 5   HIBERNIAN (0) 0
  Johnston 2 (9, 23), Smith
  (22), Taylor (85),
  Buchan (87)
ABERDEEN: Clark, Whyte, Shewan, Petersen, McMillan, Buchan, Johnston, Cumming, Taylor, Smith, Watt
HIBERNIAN: Allan, Simpson, Davis, Cousin, Madsen, McGraw, Scott, Quinn, Stein, O'Rourke, Stevenson

P W D L F A Pts   *Attendance:* 7,000
25 10 4 11 47 41 24   *Referee:* R. C. Greenlees

You would never believe that Hibs were third, so bad are they. Skipper Joe Davis even fluffed a penalty. Ian Cumming had an unobtrusive debut for Aberdeen. Johnston may have been offside when scoring his first; he was practically on his knees when heading his second.

No 26 Saturday, 23 March
MOTHERWELL (0) 0   ABERDEEN (0) 3
                          Watt (65), Cumming
                          (76), Smith (87 pen)
MOTHERWELL: McCloy, Whiteford, McKay, Campbell, Martis, W. McCallum, Beaton, McInally, Deans (Forsyth), Goldthorpe, Wilson
ABERDEEN: Clark, Whyte, Shewan, Petersen, McMillan, Buchan, Johnston, Cumming, Taylor, Smith, Watt

P W D L F A Pts   *Attendance:* 2,360
26 11 4 11 50 41 26   *Referee:* A. J. Crawley

Motherwell couldn't afford to lose this game if they are to stay up. The pitch had to be sanded before the referee would let the game start. Ally Shewan was handed the captaincy to mark his 250th consecutive first-team appearance.

No 27 Wednesday, 27 March
CLYDE (0) 1   ABERDEEN (0) 0
  Knox (52)
CLYDE: Wright, Glasgow, Soutar, McHugh, Fraser, Staite, Knox, Anderson, Hood, Stewart, Hastings
ABERDEEN: Clark, Whyte, Shewan, Petersen, McMillan, Buchan, Johnston, Cumming, Taylor, Smith, Watt

P W D L F A Pts
27 11 4 12 50 42 26   *Referee:* R. C. Greenlees

Lively Clyde complete the double. Cumming hit a post for Aberdeen in the first half.

No 28 Saturday, 30 March
ABERDEEN (1) 2   FALKIRK (0) 0
  Shewan (43), Johnston (69)
ABERDEEN: Clark, Whyte, Shewan, Petersen, McMillan, Buchan, Johnston, Cumming, Taylor, Smith, Watt
FALKIRK: Devlin, Lambie, Hunter, Markie, Baillie, Gibson, McManus, Smith, Graham, McLaughlin, Watson

P W D L F A Pts   *Attendance:* 5,000
28 12 4 12 52 42 28   *Referee:* W. Balfour

Aberdeen are still in with a hope of a Fairs Cup place, though nobody yet knows how many places will be available. Falkirk had little interest in attacking.

No 29 Saturday, 6 April
ABERDEEN (1) 1   KILMARNOCK (1) 1
  Johnston (4)   Morrison (6)
ABERDEEN: Clark, Whyte, Shewan, Petersen, McMillan, Buchan, Johnston, Cumming, Taylor, (Little), Smith, Watt
KILMARNOCK: McLaughlin, Arthur, King, Murray, McGrory, Beattie, McLean, Queen, Morrison, McFadzean, McIlroy

P W D L F A Pts   *Attendance:* 6,000
29 12 5 12 53 43 29   *Referee:* E. Thomson

Kilmarnock wanted to attack in the first half; defend in the second. Calamity when Killie equalised. Clark emerged to gather the ball: McMillan poked it past him; and Morrison was presented with an empty net.

No 30 Wednesday, 10 April
ABERDEEN (0) 0   CELTIC (0) 1
                        Lennox (60)
ABERDEEN: Clark, Whyte, Shewan, Petersen, McMillan, Buchan, Little, Smith, Johnston, Robb, Watt
CELTIC: Simpson, Craig, Gemmell, Murdoch, McNeill, Brogan, Johnstone, Lennox, Wallace, Gallagher, Hughes

P W D L F A Pts   *Attendance:* 22,000
30 12 5 13 53 44 29   *Referee:* E. Thomson

In view of Celtic's tightrope finish with Rangers, Bobby Lennox's goal is without price. Overall Celtic were hardly worth their win. Aberdeen looked the more likely to score throughout. Simpson's goal was enduring siege conditions when Shewan miskicked at a Johnstone cross to leave Lennox unattended. Two Dons were booked – Jim Smith and Tommy McMillan.

No 31 Saturday, 13 April
STIRLING ALBION (0) 0   ABERDEEN (1) 3
Petersen (7), Robb (50), Smith (60)

STIRLING: Murray, Reid, Corrigan, Grant, Rogerson, Henderson, Laurie, Thomson, Lynn, Hughes, Hall
ABERDEEN: Clark, Whyte, Shewan, Petersen, McMillan, Buchan, Little, Smith, Johnston, Robb, Watt

P W D L F A Pts   *Attendance:* 1,600
31 13 5   13 56 44 31   *Referee:* T. Marshall

Scotland team manager Bobby Brown cast his critical eye over Bobby Clark and Jim Smith. This win takes Aberdeen to fifth, and Stirling's goals-against column to 101.

No 32 Wednesday, 17 April
ABERDEEN (0) 1   ST JOHNSTONE (0) 0
Buchan (80)

ABERDEEN: Clark, Whyte, Shewan, Petersen, McMillan, Buchan, Little, Smith, Johnston, Robb, Craig
ST JOHNSTONE: Robertson, McGillivray, Coburn, Miller, Rooney, McPhee, Aird, Gordon, McDonald, McCarry, Aitken (Whitelaw)

P W D L F A Pts
32 14 5   13 57 44 33

Relegation-haunted St Johnstone hold out till Buchan's head meets Craig's corner. There was still time for McCarry's header to rebound from Clark's post and come out.

No 33 Saturday, 20 April
ABERDEEN (2) 3   AIRDRIEONIANS (0) 2
Little (21), Robb (37)   Goodwin (60), Marshall
Smith (73 pen)   (65)

ABERDEEN: Clark, Whyte, Shewan, Petersen, McMillan, Buchan, Little, Smith, Johnston, Robb, Taylor (Craig)
AIRDRIE: McKenzie, Jonquin, Keenan, Goodwin, Black, Whiteford, Madden (McPheat), Jarvie, Marshall, Irvine, Phillips

P W D L F A Pts   *Attendance:* 8,000
33 15 5   13 60 46 35   *Referee:* S. Anderson

Panic for Aberdeen after they appeared to be coasting. Both sides made substitutes at 2-1. For Airdrie young Drew Jarvie caught the eye with some neat footwork. Smith nets a late penalty, though it looks as though Black fouled Robb outside the box.

No 34 Saturday, 27 April
RANGERS (1) 2   ABERDEEN (1) 3
D. Smith (17),   Johnston 2 (29, 58),
Ferguson (56)   Taylor (89)

RANGERS: Sorensen, Johansen, Mathieson, Greig, McKinnon, Smith, Henderson, Willoughby, Ferguson, Johnston, Persson
ABERDEEN: Clark, Whyte, Shewan, Petersen, McMillan, Buchan, Little, Smith, Johnston, Robb, Craig (Taylor)

Attendance: 40,000   *Referee:* T. Kellock

This extraordinary result – Rangers' first and only league defeat of the season – hands the championship to Celtic. On the same day Dunfermline beat Celtic in the Scottish Cup Final, guaranteeing Aberdeen a place in next season's Fairs Cup. When Alex Ferguson was put in the clear to restore Rangers' lead it looked like the end for Aberdeen. But Little immediately sent Johnstone away for the equaliser, and then substitute Ian Taylor was unmarked for a last-gasp winner.

Aberdeen's complete home and away record:

HOME						AWAY						
P	W	D	L	F	A		W	D	L	F	A	Pts
34	11	1	5	36	17		5	4	8	27	31	37

Scottish League Division One

	P	W	D	L	F	A	Pts
1 Celtic	34	30	3	1	106	24	63
2 Rangers	34	28	5	1	93	34	61
3 Hibernian	34	20	5	9	67	49	45
4 Dunfermline	34	17	5	12	64	41	39
5 ABERDEEN	34	16	5	13	63	48	37
6 Morton	34	15	6	13	57	53	36
7 Kilmarnock	34	13	8	13	59	57	34
8 Clyde	34	15	4	15	55	55	34
9 Dundee	34	13	7	14	62	59	33
10 Partick Thistle	34	12	7	15	51	67	31
11 Dundee United	34	10	11	13	53	72	31
12 Hearts	34	13	4	17	56	61	30
13 Airdrieonians	34	10	9	15	45	58	29
14 St. Johnstone	34	10	7	17	43	52	27
15 Falkirk	34	7	12	15	36	50	26
16 Raith Rovers	34	9	7	18	58	86	25
17 Motherwell	34	6	7	21	40	66	19
18 Stirling Albion	34	4	4	26	29	105	12

LEAGUE CUP

Saturday, 12 August
ABERDEEN (0) 1   RANGERS (1) 1
Storrie (82)   Persson (25)

ABERDEEN: Clark, Whyte, Shewan, Munro, McMillan, Petersen, P. Wilson, Storrie, Johnston, Buchan, J. Wilson
RANGERS: Sorensen, Johansen, Provan, Jardine, McKinnon, Greig, Henderson, Penman, Ferguson, D. Smith, Persson

Attendance: 36,000

A huge turn-out reflects high hopes for the new season. Beforehand Aberdeen hadn't beaten Rangers in nine matches. Now it's ten. Alex Ferguson makes his first appearance at Pittodrie in a Rangers shirt. Aberdeen's shirts have the player's number on the front, as well as on the back.

Wednesday, 16 August
DUNDEE UNITED (0) 5   ABERDEEN (0) 0
  Hainey (57), Wilson (69),
  Seemann 2 (72, 86),
  Gillespie (89)
DUNDEE UNITED: Mackay, T. Miller, Briggs, J. Millar, Smith, Wood, Seemann, Berg, Hainey, Gillespie, Wilson
ABERDEEN: Clark, Whyte, Shewan, Munro, McMillan, Petersen, P. Wilson, Storrie, Johnston, Buchan, J. Wilson

Referee: W. J. Mullen

It's not often that Turnbull's Dons suffer a scoreline like this. The second-half torrent began with Bill Hainey's overhead kick.

Saturday, 19 August
CELTIC (0) 3   ABERDEEN (0) 1
  Gemmell (48 pen),   Storrie (77)
  Lennox (78), Auld (89)
CELTIC: Simpson, Craig, Gemmell, Murdoch, McNeill, Clark, Johnstone, Wallace, Chalmers, Auld, Lennox
ABERDEEN: Clark, Whyte, Shewan, Munro, McMillan, Petersen, P. Wilson, Storrie, Robb, Buchan, Johnston
Attendance: 50,000   *Referee:* J. M. Kelly

The game – Aberdeen's first meeting with the new European champions – turned on a questionable penalty when Lennox seemed to stumble when attended to by Whyte and Shewan. Storrie gave Aberdeen hope after Petersen's free kick had almost snapped Simpson's crossbar.

Saturday, 26 August
RANGERS (2) 3   ABERDEEN (0) 0
  Jardine (23),
  Penman 2 (30, 80)
RANGERS: Sorensen, Johansen, Provan, Jardine, McKinnon, Greig, Henderson, Penman, Ferguson, D. Smith, Persson
ABERDEEN: Clark, Whyte, Shewan, Munro, McMillan, Petersen, Storrie, Smith, Johnston, Melrose, Taylor
Attendance: 50,000   *Referee:* T. Kellock

Turnbull has now called upon nine different forwards in four matches. Two more Dons were booked – Melrose for fouling Alex Ferguson, and Munro for toppling ex-Don Dave Smith. Both Rangers' first two goals came from piledrivers from outside the box.

Wednesday, 30 August
ABERDEEN (1) 2   DUNDEE UNITED (0) 2
  Storrie (23), Munro (55)   Hainey (49), Smith (78)
ABERDEEN: Clark, Whyte, Shewan, Petersen, McMillan, Buchan, J. Wilson, Munro, Storrie, Smith, Taylor
DUNDEE UNITED: Mackay, T. Miller, Briggs, J. Millar, Smith, Gillespie, Berg, Dossing, Hainey, Mitchell, Wilson (Graham)
Attendance: 10,000   *Referee:* R. Gordon

Aberdeen have nearly all the game but have to settle for half the goals – dropping a point when United pivot Doug Smith shot home off Bobby Clark's head.

Saturday, 2 September
ABERDEEN (1) 1   CELTIC (2) 5
  Smith (7)   Gemmell (16 pen),
                        McMahon (32),
                        Johnstone (63), Auld
                        (87), Craig, (90)
ABERDEEN: Clark, Whyte, Shewan, Petersen, McMillan, Buchan, J. Wilson, Munro, Storrie (Robb), Smith, Taylor
CELTIC: Simpson, Craig, Gemmell (Auld), Clark, McNeill, O'Neil, Johnstone, Wallace, Murdoch, McMahon, Lennox
Attendance: 23,000   Referee: J. R. P. Gordon

A game remembered for the on-field assault on the referee by a man and a dog. The tension was sparked by a 16th-minute penalty awarded to Celtic after Clark had saved bravely at Lennox's feet. Two Dons were booked for protesting. Then Clark saved Gemmell's spot-kick, only for the referee to instruct that it be retaken. Thereafter the Dons fell apart and Jimmy Jonnston turned on a one-man show.

Section 2

	P	W	D	L	F	A	Pts
Celtic	6	5	1	0	14	4	11
Rangers	6	3	2	1	10	5	8
Dundee United	6	1	1	4	7	8	3
ABERDEEN	6	0	2	4	5	19	2

SCOTTISH CUP

1st Round Saturday, 27 January
ABERDEEN (1) 1   RAITH ROVERS (1) 1
  Robb (25)   Mackle (20)
ABERDEEN: Clark, Whyte, Shewan, Buchan, McMillan, Murray, Robb, Buchanan (Little), Johnston, Smith, Craig
RAITH: Reid, Selfridge, Hislop, Bolton, Davidson, Gray, Stein, Wallace, Cunningham, Sneddon, Mackle
Attendance: 10,700   *Referee:* A. McKenzie

It's only a few years since Raith sent Aberdeen scuttling out of the Cup. Now they threaten to do so again. In the league Raith have only won two out of twenty, not that there was any conspicuous difference between the teams on the field. Aberdeen were grateful that Sneddon's penalty at 1-1 should hit the junction of post and bar and come out. Long before the end the slow handclap reverberated around Pittodrie.

1st Round Replay Wednesday, 31 January
RAITH ROVERS (0) 0   ABERDEEN (0) 1
                          Petersen (68)
RAITH: Reid, Selfridge, Hislop, Bolton, Davidson, Gray, Stein, Wallace, Cunningham, Sneddon, Mackle
ABERDEEN: Clark, Whyte, Shewan, Murray, McMillan, Petersen, Johnston, Smith, Robb, Buchan, Craig
              Referee: A. McKenzie
Lucky Aberdeen. In a match played in an Arctic gale they survive because of a freak goal. Petersen floated over a free kick which Reid pushed into the air and then punched into his own net.

2nd Round Monday, 19 February
DUNFERMLINE   ABERDEEN (1) 1
  ATHLETIC (0) 2   Smith (39)
  Robertson (55),
  Edwards (84)
DUNFERMLINE: Martin, W. Callaghan, Lunn (Gordon), Thomson, Barry, T. Callaghan, Edwards, Paton, Gardner, Totten, Robertson
ABERDEEN: Clark, Whyte, Shewan, Murray, McMillan, Petersen, Johnston, Smith, Robb, Buchan, Craig
Attendance: 14,700   *Referee:* T. Wharton
Fourth-placed Dunfermline squeeze past Aberdeen into the Third Round. Jim Smith was the man of the first half. He was booked in the 27th minute and scored twelve minutes later after Martin had failed to gather Shewan's effort. After the break Dunfermline scored twice. Aberdeen would still have forced a replay had not Dunfermline keeper Martin been equal to Robb's flying header.

EUROPEAN CUP-WINNERS CUP

1st Round, 1st Leg Wednesday, 6 September
ABERDEEN (4) 10   K. R. KEVLAVIK
  Munro 3 (19, 53, 62),   (Iceland) (0) 0
  Storrie 2 (21, 56), Smith
  2 (32, 78), McMillan (44),
  Taylor (49), Petersen (72)
ABERDEEN: Clark, Whyte, Shewan, Petersen, McMillan, Buchan, J. Wilson, Munro, Storrie, Smith, Taylor
KEVLAVIK: Petursson, K. Jonsson, B. Felixson, P. Jonsson, Schram, Kjartansson, Markan, G. Felixson, Baldvinsson, Hafsteinsson, Jacobsson
Attendance: 14,000   *Referee:* A. Aalbrecht
                    (Holland)
Aberdeen are in the Cup-Winners cup as losing finalists to Celtic, who are in the European Cup. 14,000 turned out to see what continental football is all about, and

watched Aberdeen inflict unnecessary suffering on the Icelandic amateurs. Bobby Clark did not have a single shot to save till the closing minutes.

1st Round, 2nd Leg Wednesday, 13 September
K. R. KEVLAVIK (0) 1   ABERDEEN (2) 4
  Hafsteinsson (74)   Storrie 2 (42, 59)
                   Buchan (45), Munro (52)
KEVLAVIK: Petursson, K. Jonsson, B. Felixson, Gudmundsson, Schram, Kjartansson, G. Felixson, T. Jonsson, Baldvinsson, Hafsteinsson, Lalusson
ABERDEEN: Clark, Whyte, Shewan, Munro, McMillan, Kirkland, J. Wilson, Smith, Storrie, Buchan, Taylor
Aberdeen win 14-1 on aggregate
Attendance: 1,500   *Referee:* I. Hornstein
                    (Norway)
The little stadium was in uproar when Hafsteinsson burst the net to reduce the deficit to 14-1.

2nd Round, 1st Leg Wednesday, 29 November
STANDARD LIÈGE   ABERDEEN (0) 0
  (Belgium) (2) 3,
  Claesson (7), Cajou (11),
  Pilot (64)
STANDARD: Nivolay, Onclin, Jeck, Pilot, Beurlet, Dewalquye, Naumovic, Semmeling, Claesson, Galic, Cajou
ABERDEEN: Clark, Whyte, Shewan, Munro, McMillan, Petersen, Johnston, Smith, Robb, Melrose, J. Wilson
Attendance: 30,000   *Referee:* S. Ellonaro
                    (Portugal)
Standard Liège have in the past reached the semi-finals of all three European competitions. Aberdeen's hopes of survival in the Sclessin Stadium were severely dented in the first eleven minutes. International striker Claessen crashed a corner past Clark, and it was from another corner that Cajou whipped the ball into the net.

2nd Round, 2nd Leg Wednesday, 6 December
ABERDEEN (1) 2   STANDARD LIÈGE (0) 0
  Munro (20), Melrose (65)
ABERDEEN: Clark, Whyte, Shewan, Munro, McMillan, Petersen, Little, Smith, Robb, Melrose, J. Wilson
STANDARD: Nicolay, Beurlet, Jeck, Pilot, Thissen, Dewalque, Naumovic, Semmeling, Claessen, Galic, Cajou
Standard win 3-2 on aggregate
Attendance: 13,000   *Referee:* M. Petursson
                    (Iceland)
The match kicked off in a snowstorm. Munro's raging volley pulled a goal back for Aberdeen. Then Jim Whyte blazed wide with the goal at his mercy. Aberdeen had to wait till midway through the second half before finding a second goal, but the third wouldn't come.

1967-68 APPEARANCES	League	League Cup	Scottish Cup	Cup Winners Cup
Shewan	34	6	3	4
Clark	33	6	3	4
McMillan	33	6	3	4
J. Smith	33	3	3	4
Petersen	32	6	2	3
Whyte	28	6	3	4
Johnston	28	4	3	1
Buchan	24	5	3	2
Robb	16(+1)	1(+1)	3	2
Taylor	14(+1)	3		2
Munro	13(+1)	6		4
Craig	13(+1)		3	
Little	13(+2)		−(+1)	1
J. Wilson	10	4		4
Watt	10(+1)			
Murray	9(+1)		3	
Melrose	8	1		2
Storrie	6	6		2
Hermiston	6			
Cumming	5			
Buchanan	3(+1)		1	
D. Millar	2			
McGarr	1			
P. Wilson			3	
Kirkland				1
25 players				

GOALS	Total	League	League Cup	Scottish Cup	Cup Winners Cup
Johnston	14	14			
J. Smith	13	9	1	1	2
Storrie	9	2	3		4
Munro	8	2	1		5
Taylor	7	6			1
Robb	5	4	1		
Petersen	5	3		1	1
Shewan	3	3			
J. Wilson	3	3			
Watt	3	3			
Little	3	3			
Buchan	3	2			1
Melrose	3	2			1
Whyte	1	1			
Murray	1	1			
Craig	1	1			
Buchanan	1	1			
Cumming	1	1			
McMillan	1				1
own-goals	2	2			
Totals	87	63	5	3	16

Fire at Pittodrie. The Grandstand blazes on 5th February, 1971.

Season 1968-69

There was no indication in Eddie Turnbull's earlier years with Aberdeen that 1968-69 would see his side struggle so badly. With hindsight, the warning was there in the Dons' first League Cup match of the season, when they failed 4-1 at Clyde – who went on to beat Aberdeen at Pittodrie and to qualify for the next stage.

In the league Aberdeen struggled from the start. A sequence of one-goal reverses in September and October was succeeded by two thumping defeats by Dunfermline and Hibs which led to Bobby Clark being dropped from goal – for a year. Aberdeen's league form never did improve, but they were saved from relegation only because Arbroath and Falkirk proved to be even worse than themselves. Even so, Aberdeen recorded their lowest points total and fewest league wins for 20 years, and scored their lowest number of league goals for 19.

Aberdeen's second European adventure ended at the same stage as their first – an own-goal by Tommy McMillan giving Real Zaragoza a first-leg pick-me-up which they exploited in the second leg.

Had it not been for Aberdeen's challenge for the Scottish Cup, the 1968-69 season would have gone down as one with hardly any redeeming moments. But the Dons, after being held at home by Dunfermline, then by Kilmarnock, triumphed against the odds in the replays to set up a semi-final with Rangers. Aberdeen had won at Ibrox on their two most recent league visits, but at 'neutral' Parkhead, Rangers swamped Aberdeen with six goals. That crushing disappointment was to be followed by two more: both Tommy Craig and Jim Smith left the club at the end of the season.

League:	Fifteenth
League Cup:	Third in qualifying group
Scottish Cup:	Semi Final
European Fairs Cup:	Second Round

SCOTTISH LEAGUE DIVISION ONE

No 1 Saturday, 7 September

DUNDEE (1) 4   ABERDEEN (2) 4
Scott (38), Campbell   Taylor (19), Robb 2
(48), Wilson (54),   (28, 83), Shewan (87)
Duncan (56)

DUNDEE: Donaldson, Wilson, Houston, Murray, Easton, Stewart, Campbell, McLean, Duncan, Scott, Georgeson

ABERDEEN: Clark, Hermiston, Shewan, Petersen, McMillan, Craig, Rae, Robb, Forrest, Smith, Taylor

P	W	D	L	F	A	Pts	
1	0	1	0	4	4	1	*Attendance:* 10,000
							Referee: W. Anderson

This is not the sort of score commonly associated with Eddie Turnbull's teams. Aberdeen's two-goal lead was transformed into a 4-2 deficit before their late rally. Robb came so close to snatching the winning goal – and his hat-trick – in the last minute.

No 2 Saturday, 14 September

ABERDEEN (0) 2   ST JOHNSTONE (0) 0
Smith (49),
Craig (68 pen)

ABERDEEN: Clark, Hermiston, Shewan, Petersen, McMillan, Craig, Rae, Robb, Forrest, Smith, Taylor

ST JOHNSTONE: Robertson, McGillivray, Miller, Gordon, Rooney, McPhee, Aird, Whitelaw, McCarry, MacDonald, Aitken

P	W	D	L	F	A	Pts	
2	1	1	0	6	4	3	*Referee:* R. K. Wilson

Saints' stuffy defence holds out capably until pierced by Smith's header from Rae's corner. But minds are concentrated on Europe.

No 3 Saturday, 21 September
ABERDEEN (0) 0   DUNDEE UNITED (1) 1
                                            K. Cameron (8)

ABERDEEN: Clark, Hermiston, Shewan, Petersen, McMillan, Craig, Rae, Smith, Forrest, Robb, Taylor
DUNDEE UNITED: Mackay, Rolland, J. Cameron, Gillespie, Smith, Wood, Hogg, Reid, K. Cameron (Scott), Mitchell, Wilson

P W D L F A Pts   *Attendance:* 13,000
3 1 1 1 6 5 3   *Referee:* T. Wharton

Aberdeen are perked by their 0-0 draw in Sofia, so this was an anti-climax. Cameron's mis-hit shot did not deserve to beat Aberdeen.

No 4 Saturday, 28 September
CELTIC (1) 2   ABERDEEN (1) 1
  Connelly (2),   Rae (19)
  Lennox (75)

CELTIC: Simpson, Craig, Gemmell, Murdoch, McNeill, Brogan, Johnstone, Lennox, Wallace, Connelly, Hughes
ABERDEEN: Clark, Hermiston, Shewan, Petersen, McMillan, Craig, Rae, Robb, Forrest, Smith, Taylor

P W D L F A Pts   *Attendance:* 35,000
4 1 1 2 7 7 3   *Referee:* B. Padden

Aberdeen did not welcome the circumstances which led to Celtic's winning goal. Lennox punched the ball out of Clark's hands to score. Uproar followed, as Clark and his team-mates besieged the referee and linesman. Earlier George Connelly's bullet 20-yarder was cancelled out by Tommy Rae's first goal for Aberdeen after gliding past three Celtic defenders.

No 5 Saturday, 5 October
ABERDEEN (0) 1   HEARTS (1) 2
  Robb (34)   Fleming (5), Hamilton
                                           (48)

ABERDEEN: Clark, Hermiston, Shewan, Petersen, McMillan, Buchan, Rae (Johnston), Robb, Hamilton, Smith, Taylor
HEARTS: Cruickshank, Holt, Mann, Townsend, E. Thomson, McDonald, Ford, Hamilton, J. Fleming (Miller), Moller, G. Fleming

P W D L F A Pts   *Attendance:* 12,000
5 1 1 3 8 9 3   *Referee:* J. M. Kelly

A rough-house contest saw Aberdeen – wearing all white – come off worse, handicapped by the absence of Craig and Forrest. A corner brought Heart's first goal after Clark had parried Fleming's first attempt. Robb levelled from an acute angle, and when Willie Hamilton fired Hearts back in front Hearts decided to shut up shop.

No 6 Saturday, 12 October
PARTICK THISTLE (0) 1   ABERDEEN (0) 0
  Bone (51)

PARTICK: Ritchie, Cumming, McLindon, McParland, McKinnon, O'Neil, Flanagan, Stewart, Coulston, Bone, Duncan

ABERDEEN: Clark, Hermiston, Shewan, Petersen, McMillan, Craig, Rae, Robb, Johnston, Smith, Taylor

P W D L F A Pts
6 1 1 4 8 10 3   *Referee:* A. F. J. Webster

Four league defeats in a row, all by a single goal. Jim Bone's header sent the Partick fans home happy.

No 7 Saturday, 19 October
ABERDEEN (0) 0   CLYDE (0) 1
                                           Buchan o.g. (20)

ABERDEEN: Clark, Hermiston, Shewan, Petersen, McMillan, Buchan (Johnston), Hamilton, Smith, Forrest, Craig, Taylor
CLYDE: Wright, Glasgow, Mulherron, Anderson, Fraser, McHugh, Soutar, McFarlane, Hood, Burns, Hastings

Bottom positions

	P	W	D	L	F	A	Pts
14 St Johnstone	7	2	1	4	8	13	5
15 Airdrie	7	2	1	4	9	15	5
16 ABERDEEN	7	1	1	5	8	11	3
17 Falkirk	7	1	0	6	6	14	2
18 Arbroath	7	0	1	6	7	19	1

Attendance: 8,000   *Referee:* R. D. Henderson

Clyde's third win of the season over Aberdeen comes when Buchan tries to intercept a Hood through-pass. The Dons then hit the woodwork twice, and so are not in the best of spirits for the visit of Real Zaragoza.

No 8 Saturday, 26 October
RANGERS (0) 2   ABERDEEN (2) 3
  Ferguson (83),   Johnston (3), Forrest 2
  Henderson (85)   (13, 76)

RANGERS: Martin, Jackson, Mathieson, Greig, Hynd, D. Smith, Henderson, Penman, Jardine (Ferguson), Johnston, Persson
ABERDEEN: Clark, Whyte, Shewan, Petersen, McMillan, Craig, Johnston, Smith, Forrest, Buchan, Taylor

P W D L F A Pts   *Attendance:* 40,000
8 2 1 5 11 13 5

Aberdeen win at Ibrox for the second year running. This time they are totally in control – except for the last seven minutes. Rangers' Greig missed a first-half penalty. Later the crowd chant 'Bring on Fergie' and substitute Alex Ferguson immediately cut Aberdeen's lead.

No 9 Saturday, 2 November
ABERDEEN (1) 2   RAITH ROVERS (1) 1
  Forrest (23),   Wallace (24)
  Craig (60 pen)

ABERDEEN: Clark, Hermiston, Shewan, Petersen, McMillan, Craig, Johnston, Smith (Buchan), Forrest, Robb, Taylor
RAITH; Reid, Hislop, Gray, Millar, McDonald, Bolton, Wilson, Falconer, Wallace, Judge, Gillespie

P W D L F A Pts   *Attendance:* 8,000
9 3 1 5 13 14 7   *Referee:* A. J. Crawley

Teams are frequently at their most vulnerable right after they have scored – as Wallace confirms. Fortunately, for Aberdeen, Reid then took hold of Taylor's legs to provide the Dons with a penalty.

No 10 Saturday, 9 November
MORTON (0) 1   ABERDEEN (0) 0
  Harper (54)

MORTON: Crawford, Thorup, Sweeney, Arentoft, Gray, Strachan, Coakley, Harper, Mason, Allan, McNeill

ABERDEEN: Clark, Hermiston, Shewan, Petersen, McMillan, Craig, Johnston, Robb, Forrest, Smith, Taylor

P	W	D	L	F	A	Pts
10	3	1	6	13	15	7

Referee: W. M. Syme

Tiny Joseph Harper threatened the Aberdeen goal several times before breaking away to project a shot-cum-cross that escaped Clark and McNeill and which went in off the post.

No 11 Saturday, 16 November
ABERDEEN (0) 2   ARBROATH (0) 2
  Riddle o.g. (55),   Jack (50), Bruce (59)
  Forrest (88)

ABERDEEN: Clark, Hermiston, Shewan, Petersen (Buchan), McMillan, Craig, Johnston, Robb, Forrest, Smith, Watt

ARBROATH: Williamson, Booth, Riddle, Cargill, Stirling, Finnie (Pierson), Cant, Jack, Reid, Bruce, Wilkie

P	W	D	L	F	A	Pts	
11	3	2	6	15	17	8	

Attendance: 8,000
Referee: A. McKenzie

Arbroath come to Pittodrie with only one point from ten league outings. They were in front twice and were denied both points only by an own-goal and a late face-saver by Forrest.

No 12 Saturday, 23 November
ABERDEEN (1) 2   ST MIRREN (0) 0
  Forrest 2 (32, 53)

ABERDEEN: Clark, Hermiston, Shewan, Petersen, Murray, Craig, Johnston, Smith, Forrest, Buchan, Taylor

ST MIRREN: Connachan, C. Murray, Connell, Fulton, McFadden, E. Murray, Adamson, Hainey, Kane, Pinkerton, Gilshan

P	W	D	L	F	A	Pts
12	4	2	6	17	17	10

Attendance: 12,000
Referee: T. Marshall

St Mirren were undefeated, but have no complaints as the Dons' Jekyll and Hyde season continues.

No 13 Saturday, 30 November
DUNFERMLINE   ABERDEEN (1) 1
  ATHLETIC (2) 5   Craig (35)
  Edwards (5), Paton (6),
  Gardner 3 (74, 78, 87)

DUNFERMLINE: Martin, W. Callaghan, Lunn, Fraser, Barry, Renton, Robertson, Paton, Edwards, Gardner, Mitchell (Totten)

ABERDEEN: Clark, Hermiston, Shewan, Petersen, Murray, Craig, Johnston (Robb), Smith, Forrest, Buchan, Rae

P	W	D	L	F	A	Pts
13	4	2	7	18	22	10

Referee: J. Callaghan

Dunfermline don't appear at all fatigued by their midweek encounter in Greece with Olympiakos Piraeus. Two home goals within thirty seconds of one another rocked the Aberdeen boat. Craig steadied things, but then Gardner holed her irreparably.

No 14 Saturday, 7 December
ABERDEEN (1) 2   HIBERNIAN (5) 6
  Buchan (14), Forrest (49)   Cormack 3 (9, 27, 29),
                              Davis (33 pen), Scott
                              (36), McBride (83)

ABERDEEN: Clark, Whyte, Shewan, Buchan, Murray, Petersen, Little, Smith, Forrest, Craig, Taylor

HIBERNIAN: Allen, Shevlane, Davis, Cousin, Madsen, Stanton, Scott, Quinn, McBride, Cormack, Stevenson

P	W	D	L	F	A	Pts
14	4	2	8	20	28	10

Referee: A. E. Currie

Eleven goals lost in two games shows the extent of Aberdeen's problems. Peter Cormack destroyed Aberdeen virtually single-handed. He began with a fierce half-volley, followed up with a downward header away from Clark, and finished by imperiously sweeping Scott's centre into goal.

No 15 Saturday, 14 December
AIRDRIEONIANS (0) 2   ABERDEEN (0) 0
  Wilson (49),
  Goodwin (81 pen)

AIRDRIE: McKenzie, Jonquin, Keenan, Goodwin, Black, Whiteford, Wilson, Fyfe, Marshall, McPheat, Jarvie

ABERDEEN: McGarr, Whyte, Shewan, Buchan, McMillan, Petersen, Hamilton, Smith (Cumming), Forrest, Craig, Johnston

Bottom positions

	P	W	D	L	F	A	Pts
15 Raith	15	4	2	9	23	28	10
16 ABERDEEN	15	4	2	9	20	30	10
17 Falkirk	15	2	2	11	13	30	6
18 Arbroath	15	0	4	11	18	46	4

Attendance: 3,500
Referee: W. J. Mullen

Bobby Clark – and others – had been dropped after Aberdeen's defence sprung a severe leak. The flood becomes a trickle. Drew Jarvie was felled near the end and won a penalty for Airdrie.

No 16 Saturday, 21 December
ABERDEEN (2) 2   FALKIRK (0) 0
  Forrest (2),
  Johnston (43)

ABERDEEN: McGarr, Whyte, Shewan, Petersen, McMillan, Murray, Johnston, Smith, Forrest, Buchan, Craig

FALKIRK: Rennie, Lambie, J. Hunter, Smith, Markie, Miller, Marshall, McLaughlan, Young, Gibson, Watson (Hunter)

P W D L F A Pts　　　*Attendance:* 7,000
16 5 2 9 22 30 12　　*Referee:* E. H. Pringle

Play began earlier than scheduled and many spectators were still outside the ground when Forrest capitalised on Markie's slip inside ninety seconds.

No 17 Saturday, 28 December
KILMARNOCK (1) 2　　　ABERDEEN (0) 1
　McIlroy (10),　　　　　Johnston (53)
　Morrison (51)

KILMARNOCK: McLaughlan, King, Dickson, Gilmour, McGrory, Beattie, T. McLean, Queen, Morrison, J. McLean, McIlroy

ABERDEEN: McGarr, Whyte, Shewan, Petersen, McMillan, Murray, Johnston, Smith, Forrest, Buchan, Craig

P W D L F A Pts
17 5 2 10 23 32 12　　*Referee:* R. K. Wilson

Third-placed Killie are stretched in a tempestuous match. Their second goal came when McGarr was challenged by Morrison as he tried to clear. The ball flew onto a post and Morrison poked it in. Later the same forward was ordered off after a clash with McGarr.

No 18 Wednesday, 1 January
ABERDEEN (0) 0　　　　DUNDEE (0) 0

ABERDEEN: McGarr, Whyte, Shewan, Petersen, McMillan, Murray, Johnston, Smith, Forrest, Buchan, Craig

DUNDEE: Donaldson, Wilson, Swan, Murray, Stuart, Houston, Campbell, Gilroy, Kinninmonth, Bryce, Scott

P W D L F A Pts　　*Attendance:* 12,000
18 5 3 10 23 32 13

Dundee keeper Alistair Donaldson was the sole reason his team left with a point.

No 19 Thursday, 2 January
ST JOHNSTONE (2) 3　　ABERDEEN (1) 1
　Aitken (6),　　　　　　Buchan (12)
　Hall 2 (36, 61)

ST JOHNSTONE: Robertson, Miller, Coburn, Gordon, Rooney, McPhee, Hall, McCarry, Whitelaw, Rennie, Aitken

ABERDEEN: McGarr, Whyte, Shewan, Petersen, McMillan, Murray, Johnston, Smith, Forrest, Buchan (Robb), Craig

Bottom positions

	P	W	D	L	F	A	Pts
13 St Johnstone	18	5	3	10	30	36	13
14 ABERDEEN	19	5	3	11	24	35	13
15 Partick	18	4	5	9	19	30	13
16 Raith	18	4	2	12	24	36	10
17 Falkirk	18	3	3	12	18	34	9
18 Arbroath	17	0	4	13	21	51	4

Referee: W. Anderson

Aberdeen should have handed St Johnstone a first-half pasting, but suffered an attack of squandermania. Worst miss of all was Forrest's, who dribbled round Robertson and then shot wide.

No 20 Saturday, 4 January
DUNDEE UNITED (0) 1　ABERDEEN (2) 4
　K. Cameron (70)　　　Shewan (25), Robb (30),
　　　　　　　　　　　Craig (61), Forrest (79)

DUNDEE UNITED: Mackay, Miller, J. Cameron, Markland, Smith, Wood, Hogg (Wilson), Reid, K. Cameron, Mitchell, Rolland

ABERDEEN: McGarr, Whyte, Shewan, Petersen, Boel, Murray, Johnston, Smith, Forrest, Robb, Craig

P W D L F A Pts　　*Attendance:* 15,000
20 6 3 11 28 36 15　　*Referee:* R. Gordon

Only Celtic's superior goal average is keeping United off the top. Aberdeen's breakthrough comes when Shewan's header from Craig's corner slipped through Mackay's butter-fingers. At 2-0 Kenny Cameron squandered a penalty for United. Aberdeen's Henning Boel, another Dane, makes his first senior appearance.

No 21 Saturday, 11 January
ABERDEEN (0) 1　　　CELTIC (2) 3
　Forrest (79)　　　　Hughes (3), Wallace
　　　　　　　　　　　(27), Boel o.g. (53)

ABERDEEN: McGarr, Whyte, Shewan, Petersen, Boel, Murray, Johnston, Smith, Forrest, Robb, Craig

CELTIC: Simpson, Craig, Gemmell, Murdoch, McNeill, Brogan, Johnstone, Callaghan, Wallace, Lennox, Hughes

P W D L F A Pts　　*Attendance:* 31,000
21 6 3 12 29 39 15　　*Referee:* W. Balfour

Celtic have had the breaks against Aberdeen in recent matches. This time there were no complaints: they oozed class and were in control from the moment of Hughes' raging goal from outside the box.

No 22 Saturday, 18 January
HEARTS (1) 3　　　　ABERDEEN (1) 2
　Ford 2 (19, 86),　　Robb (29), Johnston (46)
　Anderson (52)

HEARTS: Cruickshank, Holt, McAlpine, Anderson, E. Thomson, A. Thomson, J. Fleming, Hamilton, Ford, G. Fleming, Jensen (Brown)

ABERDEEN: McGarr, Whyte, Shewan, Petersen, Boel, Buchan, Rae, Smith, Johnston, Robb, Craig

P W D L F A Pts　　*Attendance:* 8,000
22 6 3 13 31 42 15　　*Referee:* R. D. Henderson

Aberdeen deserved a point, and looked set for two when Hearts blundered to let Johnston through straight after the restart. Even after Anderson equalised for Hearts, Robb sent a shot crashing against a Tynecastle goalpost.

No 23 Saturday, 1 February
ABERDEEN (1) 1   PARTICK THISTLE (1) 1
  Craig (13)   Duncan (30)
ABERDEEN: McGarr, Whyte, Shewan, Buchan (Paul), Boel, Petersen, Johnston, Smith, Forrest, Robb, Craig
PARTICK: Ritchie, Campbell, Gray, Hansen, McKinnon, O'Neil, McLindon, McParland, Flanagan, Bone, Duncan

P W D L F A Pts   *Attendance:* 8,000
23 6 4 13 32 43 16   *Referee:* J. H. McKee

Partick have just lost to Celtic 8-1 in the Cup. Pittodrie is almost totally under water by the time the game ends, having earlier drowned all possibility of further goals.

No 24 Saturday, 8 March
ARBROATH (1) 2   ABERDEEN (1) 1
  Bruce (14), Sellars (52) Forrest (9)
ARBROATH: Hodge, Booth, Hughes, Cargill, Stirling, Reid (Kennedy), Sellars, Cant, Jack, Bruce, Wilkie
ABERDEEN: McGarr, Whyte, Shewan, Petersen, Boel, Buchan, Hamilton, Smith, Forrest, Robb, Craig
Bottom positions

	P	W	D	L	F	A	Pts
15 ABERDEEN	24	6	4	14	33	45	16
16 Raith	26	5	4	17	31	50	14
17 Falkirk	25	4	5	16	23	47	13
18 Arbroath	25	3	4	18	30	67	10

Attendance: 4,700   *Referee:* T. Kellock

Inclement weather and cup duties mean this is Aberdeen's first league match for five weeks. They follow up their memorable Cup triumphs at Dunfermline and Kilmarnock with this abject defeat. Arbroath's winner was disputed. McGarr clutched a high cross and was bundled over the line by Sellars.

No 25 Saturday, 15 March
ST MIRREN (0) 1   ABERDEEN (1) 2
  Kane (66)   Robb (4),
                          Connell o.g. (80)
ST MIRREN: Thorburn, Young, Connell, Fulton, McFadden, E. Murray, Adamson (Duffy), Urquhart, McLaughlan, Kane, Gilshan
ABERDEEN: McGarr, Whyte, Shewan, Petersen, Boel, Buchan, Johnston, Smith, Forrest, Robb, Taylor (Craig)

P W D L F A Pts
25 7 4 14 35 46 18   *Referee:* R. C. Greenlees

Aberdeen haven't had too many breaks this season, but they get one when Connell dives full length to head into his own goal two minutes after Gilshan had headed against the Dons' post.

No 26 Wednesday, 19 March
RAITH ROVERS (1) 3   ABERDEEN (1) 2
  Wallace (4), Millar   Johnston (5),
  (61), Sneddon (77)   Forrest (53)
RAITH: Reid, McDonald, Gray, D. Millar, Polland, Bolton, A. Miller, Falconer (Judge), Wallace, Sneddon, Wilson
ABERDEEN: McGarr, Whyte, Shewan, Petersen, Boel, Buchan, Johnston (Murray), Craig, Forrest, Robb, Hamilton

P W D L F A Pts
26 7 4 15 37 49 18   *Referee:* B. Padden

Ernie McGarr has an unhappy match, allowing Millar's so-so shot from 25 yards to squirm into the net. Not the best preparation for the Cup semi-final with Rangers.

No 27 Monday, 24 March
ABERDEEN (1) 2   DUNFERMLINE
  Robb (44),   ATHLETIC (2) 2
  Craig (50 pen)   McLean (32),
                          Callaghan (37)
ABERDEEN: McGarr, Whyte, Shewan, Petersen, Boel, M. Buchan, G. Buchan (Hamilton), Smith, Forrest, Robb, Craig
DUNFERMLINE: Duff, Callaghan, Lunn, Fraser, Barry, Renton, Robertson, McKimmie (Baillie), Edwards, McLean, Mitchell

P W D L F A Pts
27 7 5 15 39 51 19   *Referee:* A. J. Crawley

Out of the Cup, Aberdeen must now concentrate on league survival. Before there is any scoring the game is held up for eight minutes by an intruding alsation. After half-time Aberdeen equalised when George Buchan (Martin's younger brother) on his debut was hurt when Duff took away his legs. The youngster was stretchered off leaving Craig to convert the penalty.

No 28 Saturday, 29 March
HIBERNIAN (0) 1   ABERDEEN (0) 1
  Davis (58 pen)   Forrest (60)
HIBERNIAN: Allan, Shevlane, Davis, Blackley, Madsen, Stanton, Marinello, O'Rourke, Grant (McGraw), Cormack, Stevenson
ABERDEEN: McGarr, Whyte, Shewan, Petersen, Boel, M. Buchan, Johnston, Smith, Forrest, Robb, Hamilton (Taylor)

P W D L F A Pts   *Attendance:* 6,321
28 7 6 15 40 52 20   *Referee:* J. M. Kelly

The Grand National on television accounts for the poor attendance. Those who came did not miss much, except two goals and Johnston hitting a Hibs' post late on. Boel had earlier handled to give away the penalty.

No 29 Wednesday, 2 April
ABERDEEN (2) 6   MORTON (2) 3
  Petersen (9), Craig   Mason (4), Coakley
  (23), Forrest (50),   (25), Harper (58)
  Johnston 2 (52, 65),
  Whyte (88)

ABERDEEN: McGarr, Whyte, Shewan, Petersen, Boel, M. Buchan, Johnston, Smith, Forrest, Robb, Craig

MORTON: Neilsen, Ferguson, Laughton, Rankine, Gray, Sweeney, Coakley, Allan, Mason, Harper, Bartram

P	W	D	L	F	A	Pts	*Attendance:* 10,000
29	8	6	15	46	55	22	*Referee:* R. H. Davidson

Aberdeen virtually banish the relegation clouds with this second-half fiesta. Falkirk are now seven points behind. Aberdeen are keen to sign Morton's Joe Harper.

No 30 Saturday, 5 April
ABERDEEN (3) 3   AIRDRIEONIANS (0) 1
  Forrest (7), Johnston   Wilson (48)
  (14), Robb (33)

ABERDEEN: McGarr, Whyte, Shewan, Petersen, Boel, M. Buchan, Johnston, Smith, Forrest, Robb, Craig

AIRDRIE: McKenzie, Jonquin, Caldwell, Goodwin, Black, Whiteford, Bird, Fyfe, Marshall, McFeat (Menzies), Wilson

P	W	D	L	F	A	Pts	*Attendance:* 11,000
30	9	6	15	49	56	24	*Referee:* R. Gordon

Aberdeen are now formally safe. The other good news is the healthy gate of 11,000.

No 31 Wednesday, 9 April
ABERDEEN (0) 0   RANGERS (0) 0

ABERDEEN: McGarr, Whyte, Shewan, Petersen, Boel, M. Buchan, Johnston, Smith, Forrest, Robb (G. Buchan), Craig

RANGERS: Martin, Johansen, Mathieson, Greig, McKinnon, D. Smith, Henderson, Jardine (Conn), Ferguson, W. Johnston, Persson

P	W	D	L	F	A	Pts	*Attendance:* 23,000
31	9	7	15	49	56	25	*Referee:* W. J. Paterson

Aberdeen took three points off Rangers in the league but were hammered 6-1 in the Cup. Rangers can now say goodbye to the league title.

No 32 Saturday, 12 April
FALKIRK (0) 1   ABERDEEN (0) 0
  Young (52)

FALKIRK: Rennie, Lambie, J. Hunter, Gibson, Markie, Miller, Marshall, Smith (Young), I. Hunter, McLaughlan, Watson

ABERDEEN: McGarr, Shewan, M. Buchan, Petersen, Boel, Craig, Johnston, Smith, Forrest, Robb, G. Buchan

P	W	D	L	F	A	Pts	*Attendance:* 2,500
32	9	7	16	49	57	25	*Referee:* W. M. Syme

This desperate yawn needed a goal – any goal.

No 33 Saturday, 19 April
ABERDEEN (0) 0   KILMARNOCK (1) 1
                                   Cook (38)

ABERDEEN: McGarr, Hermiston, Shewan, Petersen, Boel, M. Buchan, Johnston, Smith, Forrest, Robb, Craig

KILMARNOCK: McLaughlan, King, Dickson, Queen, McGrory, Beattie, Cook, J. McLean, Morrison, Evans, McIlroy

P	W	D	L	F	A	Pts	*Attendance:* 8,000
33	9	7	17	49	58	25	*Referee:* T. Marshall

This was wretchedly dull stuff. The match proves to be the last in a red shirt for 18-year old Tommy Craig, set to sign for Sheffield Wednesday.

No 34 Wednesday, 23 April
CLYDE (1) 1   ABERDEEN (0) 1
  Quinn (15)   Forrest (89)

CLYDE: Wright, Glasgow, McGregor, Staite, McVie, McHugh, McFarlane, Anderson, Quinn, Burns, Hastings

ABERDEEN: McGarr, Hermiston, Shewan, Petersen, Boel, M. Buchan, Johnston, Smith, Forrest, Robb, G. Buchan

Attendance: 987	*Referee:* E. Thomson

Jim Forrest's 25-yard blockbuster rescued a point for Aberdeen. Ally Shewan made his 350th appearance and 313th consecutive appearance in an Aberdeen strip. Jim Smith made his last.

Aberdeen's complete home and away record:

HOME						AWAY						
P	W	D	L	F	A		W	D	L	F	A	Pts
34	6	5	6	26	24		3	3	11	24	35	26

Scottish League Division One

	P	W	D	L	F	A	Pts
1 Celtic	34	23	8	3	89	32	54
2 Rangers	34	21	7	6	81	32	49
3 Dunfermline	34	19	7	8	63	45	45
4 Kilmarnock	34	15	14	5	50	32	44
5 Dundee United	34	17	9	8	61	49	43
6 St. Johnstone	34	16	5	13	66	59	37
7 Airdrieonians	34	13	11	10	46	44	37
8 Hearts	34	14	8	12	52	54	36
9 Dundee	34	10	12	12	47	48	32
10 Morton	34	12	8	14	58	68	32
11 St Mirren	34	11	10	13	40	54	32
12 Hibernian	34	12	7	15	60	59	31
13 Clyde	34	9	13	12	35	50	31
14 Partick Thistle	34	9	10	15	39	53	28
15 ABERDEEN	34	9	8	17	50	59	26
16 Raith Rovers	34	8	5	21	45	67	21
17 Falkirk	34	5	8	21	33	69	18
18 Arbroath	34	5	6	23	41	82	16

LEAGUE CUP

Saturday, 10 August
CLYDE (2) 4   ABERDEEN (1) 1
  Anderson 2 (38, 42),   Robb (18)
  Hood (47), Burns (61)

CLYDE: McCulloch, Glasgow, Mulherron, McHugh, Fraser, Anderson, McFarlane, Hood, Staite, Burns, Hastings

ABERDEEN: Clark, Whyte, Shewan, Buchan, McMillan, Petersen, Rae, Robb, Forrest, Craig, Johnston

Referee: E. H. Pringle

Jim Smith must miss the first four matches of the season through suspension. Three of Clyde's goals stem from corner kicks.

Wednesday, 14 August
ABERDEEN (0) 1   DUNFERMLINE
  Forrest (75)   ATHLETIC (0) 0

ABERDEEN: Clark, Whyte, Shewan, Buchan, McMillan, Petersen, Rae, Robb, Forrest, Craig, Taylor

DUNFERMLINE: Martin, W. Callaghan, Lunn, Thomson, McGarty, T. Callaghan, Lister, Paton, Gardner, Robertson, Edwards

Attendance: 18,000

£25,000 Jim Forrest from Preston – once of Rangers – opens his account from the edge of the box.

Saturday, 17 August
ABERDEEN (1) 4   DUNDEE UNITED (0) 1
  Buchan (5), Craig   Mitchell (79)
  (50 pen), Forrest 2
  (60, 65)

ABERDEEN: Clark, Whyte, Shewan, Buchan, McMillan, Petersen, Rae, Robb, Forrest, Craig, Taylor

DUNDEE UNITED: Mackay, Rolland, J. Cameron, Gillespie, Smith, Wood, Hogg, Reid, K. Cameron, Dunne, Mitchell

Attendance: 16,000   *Referee:* J. W. Paterson

Martin Buchan's thunderous volley shows he can score goals as well as make them and prevent them.

Saturday, 24 August
ABERDEEN (0) 0   CLYDE (2) 2
                         McFarlane (30),
                         Staite (37)

ABERDEEN: Clark, Whyte, Shewan, Buchan, McMillan, Petersen, Rae, Johnston, Forrest, Craig, Taylor

CLYDE: McCulloch, Glasgow, Mulherron, Anderson, Fraser, McHugh, McFarlane, Hood, Staite, Burns, McGregor

Attendance: 19,000   *Referee:* R. D. Crawford

Part-timers Clyde inflict a second defeat on the Dons with consummate ease. They now look favourites to qualify.

Wednesday, 28 August
DUNFERMLINE   ABERDEEN (1) 2
  ATHLETIC (0) 1   Smith (25),
  Lister (73)   Taylor (68)

DUNFERMLINE: Martin, W. Callaghan, Lunn, Thomson, McGarty, T. Callaghan (Mitchell), Lister, Paton, Gardner, Renton, Edwards

ABERDEEN: Clark, Whyte, Shewan, Petersen, McMillan, Buchan, Rae, Robb, Forrest, Smith, Craig (Taylor)

Referee: R. Gordon

What's this? Clyde have lost 4-0 at home to Dundee United. Everything now depends on the final round of matches. Jim Smith cannot be kept out of the news. He returns after his suspension; sees Martin punch his shot into goal; and is then booked for upending Edwards.

Saturday, 31 August
DUNDEE UNITED (0) 1 ABERDEEN (0) 0
  Smith o.g. (61)

DUNDEE UNITED: Mackay, Rolland, J. Cameron, Gillespie, Smith, Wood, Hogg (Scott), Reid, K. Cameron, Mitchell, Wilson

ABERDEEN: Clark, Whyte, Shewan, Petersen, McMillan, Buchan, Rae, Robb, Forrest, Smith, Craig (Taylor)

Attendance: 12,000   Referee: E. Thomson

Jimmy Smith is in the news again. This time it's because of his wayward backpass.

Section 3

	P	W	D	L	F	A	Pts
Clyde	6	4	0	2	13	9	8
Dundee United	6	3	0	3	12	11	6
ABERDEEN	6	3	0	3	8	9	6
Dunfermline	6	2	0	4	7	11	4

SCOTTISH CUP

1st Round Saturday, 25 January
ABERDEEN (1) 3   BERWICK RANGERS (0) 0
  Forrest 2 (36, 82),
  Robb (73)

ABERDEEN: McGarr, Whyte, Shewan, Petersen, Boel, Buchan, Forrest (Taylor), Smith, Johnston, Robb, Craig

BERWICK: Wallace, Petterson, Haig, Smith, Coutts, Gilchrist, Tait, Craig, Bowron, Jones, Dowds

Attendance: 13,600   *Referee:* R. D. Henderson

It was as easy as pie for Aberdeen – though until Jock Wallace picked the ball out of his net a second time there was always the risk of an upset. Jim Forrest had been in the Rangers side beaten at Berwick in the Cup two years earlier, and gained belated revenge with two goals. Ex-Don Doug Coutts captained his new side against his old.

2nd Round Tuesday, 25 February
ABERDEEN (1) 2   DUNFERMLINE
  Johnston (31),   ATHLETIC (0) 2
  Hamilton (47)   Fraser (56), Renton (88)

ABERDEEN: McGarr, Whyte, Shewan, Petersen, Boel, Buchan, Johnston, Smith, Forrest, Robb, Taylor (Hamilton)

DUNFERMLINE: Duff, Callaghan, Thomson, Fraser, Barry, Renton, Robertson (Baillie), Paton, Edwards, Gardner, Mitchell

Attendance: 14,685   *Referee:* W. M. Syme

Dunfermline are the defending Scottish Cup holders; semi-finalists in the Cup-Winners Cup; and on the heels of the Old Firm in the league. Yet only a desperately late goal gives them a second chance against Aberdeen, whose substitute, Hamilton, put the Dons two up with his first touch of the ball – a searing diving header.

2nd Round Replay Wednesday, 26 February
DUNFERMLINE   ABERDEEN (1) 2
   ATHLETIC (0) 0   Robb 2 (10, 76)
DUNFERMLINE: Duff, Callaghan, Thomson, Fraser, Barry, Renton, Robertson, Paton, Edwards, Gardner, Mitchell
ABERDEEN: McGarr, Whyte, Shewan, Petersen, Boel, Buchan, Johnston, Smith, Forrest, Robb, Hamilton

Referee: W. M. Syme

This cup replay takes place just 24 hours after the first match. Aberdeen eliminate the Cup holders with two goals from Dave Robb. His first came when Fraser slashed the ball at Duffy and it fell to Robb's feet. Thereafter Aberdeen fought a feverish rearguard action.

Quarter Final Saturday, 1 March
ABERDEEN (0) 0   KILMARNOCK (0) 0
ABERDEEN: McGarr, Whyte, Shewan, Petersen, Boel, Buchan, Johnston, Smith, Forrest, Robb, Hamilton (Craig)
KILMARNOCK: McLaughlan, King, Dickson, Gilmour, McGrory, Beattie, T. McLean, Evans, Morrison, J. McLean, McIlroy

Attendance: 24,000

The immovable object comes up against the irresistible force. The result is a stalemate with neither side creating a chance worthy of the name – apart from when McLaughlan turned Johnston's shot on to the inside of a post.

Quarter Final Replay Wednesday, 5 March
KILMARNOCK (0) 0   ABERDEEN (1) 3
                         Robb (43), Craig (67),
                         Hamilton (85)
KILMARNOCK: McLaughlan, King, Dickson, Gilmour, McGrory, McFadzean, T. McLean, Queen, Morrison, J. McLean, McIlroy
ABERDEEN: McGarr, Whyte, Shewan, Petersen, Boel, Buchan, Johnston (Craig), Smith, Forrest, Robb, Hamilton

Attendance: 17,183   *Referee:* T. Wharton

Kilmarnock, like Dunfermline, are hot on Celtic's heels in the league. This is Aberdeen's fourth cup-tie in nine days on heavy pitches. Again it is Dave Robb with the eye for goal. Pick of Aberdeen's three was Craig's blistering shot from Forrest's pull-back.

Semi Final (Celtic Park) Saturday, 22 March
RANGERS (2) 6   ABERDEEN (1) 1
   Penman 2 (14, 51),   Forrest (45)
   Henderson (39), Johnston
   3 (47, 72, 84)
RANGERS: Martin, Johansen, Mathieson, Greig, McKinnon, D. Smith, Henderson, Penman, Stein, Johnston, Persson
ABERDEEN: McGarr, Whyte, Shewan, Petersen, Boel, Buchan, Johnston, Smith, Forrest, Robb, Craig

Referee: W. J. Mullen

Winning the Scottish Cup is Aberdeen's only route back into Europe. They were still in the hunt at half-time, but immediately afterwards Jimmy Smith – under the eye of numerous scouts – lost the ball to Persson. It was despatched into the middle for the lurking Willie Johnston to put Rangers 3-1 ahead. Aberdeen had beaten Rangers twice at Ibrox in the league within the last year, but have no answer to them now – or to Willie Johnston in particular.

EUROPEAN FAIRS CUP

1st Round, 1st Leg Tuesday, 17 September
SLAVIA SOFIA   ABERDEEN (0) 0
   (Bulgaria) (0) 0
SOFIA: Simeonov, Alexiev, Petrov, Jonov, Davidov, Kristev, Haralampiev, Dimitrov, Grigorov, Tassev, Lukach
ABERDEEN: Clark, Hermiston, Shewan, Petersen, McMillan, Craig, Rae, Robb, Forrest, Smith, Buchan

Attendance: 13,000   *Referee:* S. Petri (Hungary)

After the Soviet invasion of Czechoslovakia the draw from the European Cup and Cup-Winners Cup was re-made to segregate eastern and western countries. The Fairs Cup draw was allowed to stand despite an Aberdeen protest that it be nullified. For their first-ever trip behind the Iron Curtain Aberdeen adopted a defensive 5-2-3 formation which neither the Bulgarian forwards nor the 85° temperatures could break down.

1st Round, 2nd Leg Wednesday, 2 October
ABERDEEN (2) 2   SLAVIA SOFIA (0) 0
   Robb (7), Taylor (39)
ABERDEEN: Clark, Hermiston, Shewan, Petersen, McMillan, Craig (Buchan), Rae, Robb, Forrest, Smith, Taylor
SOFIA: Simeonov, Petrov, Charliev, Jonov, Davidov, Kristev, Haralampiev, Vassilov, Grigorov, Tassev, Letchov
Aberdeen won 2-0 on aggregate

Attendance: 29,000   *Referee:* C. Liedberg
                              (Sweden)

All-action Aberdeen power their way past Sofia. Dave Robb side-flicked Forrest's pass beyond Simeonov. Before half-time Petrov slipped while trying to cut out Shewan's lateral pass, allowing Taylor an unstoppable, unforgettable shot.

2nd Round, 1st Leg Wednesday, 23 October
ABERDEEN (1) 2   **REAL ZARAGOZA**
   Forrest (32),   (Spain) (0) 1
   Smith (64)   McMillan o.g. (73)
ABERDEEN: Clark, Hermiston, Shewan, Petersen,
McMillan, Craig, Johnston, Smith, Forrest, Buchan,
Taylor
ZARAGOZA: Nieves, Rico, Reija, Violeta, Gonzales,
Borras, Oliveros, Pais (Planas), Marcelino, Tejedor,
Lapetra
Attendance: 25,000   *Referee:* R. Schaut
                              (Belgium)

Real Zaragoza won this competition in 1964 and reached
the final again two years later. This season, however,
they are near the bottom of the Spanish League. Forrest
controlled Buchan's chip on his chest to smash the ball
past Nieves. After Jim Smith had converted Taylor's
cross for No 2, tragedy struck Aberdeen. McMillan
slashed a Lapetra cross past Clark for a priceless away
goal for the Spanish team.

2nd Round, 2nd Leg Wednesday, 30 October
REAL ZARAGOZA (2) 3   **ABERDEEN** (0) 0
   Marcelino (35)
   Tejedor (43), Villa (78)
ZARAGOZA: Nieves, Rico (Bustillo), Reija (Planas),
Violeta, Gonzales, Borras, Tejedor, Santos, Marcelino,
Villa, Lapetra
ABERDEEN: Clark, Hermiston, Shewan, Petersen,
McMillan, Craig, Robb, Smith, Forrest, Buchan,
Taylor
Real Zaragoza won 4-2 on aggregate
Attendance: 30,000   *Referee:* J. Rodriguez
                              (Portugal)

The Romareda Stadium is awash with noise as Zaragoza
maintain their record of never having lost to a British
team in Europe – though they will be beaten by the
eventual winners, Newcastle United, in the next round.
Hermiston had a chance at 0-0 but shot wide. But then
Marcelino headed in Lapetra's corner and the home
team were ahead by virtue of their away goal.

1968-69

APPEARANCES	League	League Cup	Scottish Cup	Fairs Cup
Petersen	34	6	6	4
Shewan	34	6	6	4
J. Smith	33	2	6	4
Forrest	31	6	6	4
Craig	30(+1)	6	2(+2)	4
Johnston	25(+2)	2	6	1
M. Buchan	24(+2)	6	6	3(+1)
Robb	24(+2)	5	6	3
McGarr	20		6	
Whyte	19	6	6	
McMillan	16	6		4
Boel	15		6	
Clark	14	6		4
Hermiston	14			4
Taylor	13(+1)	3(+2)	1(+1)	3
G. Murray	9(+1)			
Rae	8	6		2
Hamilton	6(+1)		3(+1)	
G. Buchan	3(+1)			
Little	1			
Watt	1			
Cumming	−(+1)			
Paul	−(+1)			
23 players				

GOALS	Total	League	League Cup	Scottish Cup	Fairs Cup
Forrest	23	16	3	3	1
Robb	14	8	1	4	1
Johnston	9	8		1	
Craig	9	7	1	1	
M. Buchan	3	2	1		
J. Smith	3	1	1		1
Taylor	3	1	1		1
Shewan	2	2			
Hamilton	2			2	
Rae	1	1			
Whyte	1	1			
Petersen	1	1			
own-goals	2	2			
Total	73	50	8	11	4

Kennedy of Rangers is beaten and it is a goal
for Aberdeen. This match took place in
December, 1974.

Season 1969-70

Aberdeen entered the 1970s with a bang – a glorious Scottish Cup Final win over Celtic. It was their first trophy since lifting the League Cup in 1955-56, and it produced its legendary hero. Derek McKay, who came from nowhere and later disappeared back to nowhere, scored four priceless goals for Aberdeen in their Cup-winning campaign.

At the start of the season talk of trophies seemed like a pipedream. Jim Smith and Tommy Craig had gone south for English gold. A car crash forced Martin Buchan to miss the first third of the season. Who could forecast that the Dons' Cup Final team would include such names for the future as Joe Harper and Arthur Graham?

Aberdeen managed to head their qualifying group in the League Cup, but were then beaten by Celtic over two legs in the quarter finals. The league campaign offered nothing to excite Aberdeen's success-starved supporters. The team were glued in mid-table from the season's start till its end. As in the previous year, the Dons found it devilishly hard to win matches at home, but on their travels it was necessary to go back to their championship-winning season, 1954-55, to find them winning more games.

But it was the Scottish Cup for which 1969-70 is remembered. Aberdeen had reached the semi-finals four times in five years, but at last – for the first time since 1947 – had gone all the way. Now, would Aberdeen be good enough to challenge Celtic for the league championship in 1970-71?

League: Eighth
League Cup: Quarter Final
Scottish Cup: Winners

SCOTTISH LEAGUE DIVISION ONE

No 1 Saturday, 30 August
ABERDEEN (1) 6   CLYDE (0) 0
  Robb 3 (14, 46, 66,)
  Forrest 2 (48, 62),
  Petersen (61)

ABERDEEN: McGarr, Boel, Hermiston, G. Murray (Rae), McMillan, Petersen, Willoughby, Robb, Forrest, Wilson, Hamilton

CLYDE: Wright, Glasgow, Mulherron, Burns, McVie, McHugh, McFarlane, Hay (Hastings), Staite, Hulston, McLean

P	W	D	L	F	A	Pts
1	1	0	0	6	0	2

Attendance: 13,000
Referee: R. D. Henderson

Some of these goals were for the connoisseur: Forrest's left-foot volley, for example, or Petersen's ballistic drive into the roof of the net. This is the third meeting between the sides this season and still Clyde haven't scored.

No 2 Wednesday, 3 September
RANGERS (0) 2   ABERDEEN (0) 0
  Provan (75 pen),
  Stein (88)

RANGERS: Neef, Johansen, Provan, Greig, McKinnon, Baxter, MacDonald, Jardine, Stein, Penman, Johnston

ABERDEEN: McGarr, Boel, Hermiston, Murray, McMillan, Petersen, Willoughby, Robb, Forrest (Clark), Wilson, Hamilton

P	W	D	L	F	A	Pts
2	1	0	1	6	2	2

Attendance: 40,000
Referee: T. Kellock

What's this? Aberdeen's displaced goalkeeper, Bobby Clark, comes on as an outfield substitute as soon as Rangers go ahead from a penalty. Boel had handled as he fell on the ball. Aberdeen were already down to ten men when McMillan was sent off after 20 minutes for retaliating against Colin Stein. Under the watchful eye of Scotland manager Bobby Brown, Ernie McGarr performed wonders in the Aberdeen goal. Perhaps Bobby Clark was less impressed.

No 3 Saturday, 6 September
AIRDRIEONIANS (1) 3   ABERDEEN (1) 4
  J. Whiteford (35),   Robb 2 (44, 68),
  Marshall (49),   Forrest (54), Rae (63)
  McPheat (78)

AIRDRIE: McKenzie, Jonquin, Caldwell, Goodwin, Delaney, D. Whiteford, Bird (McPheat), Jarvie, Marshall, J. Whiteford, Stewart

ABERDEEN: McGarr, Boel, Hermiston, Murray, McMillan, Petersen, Rae, Robb, Forrest, Wilson, Hamilton

P	W	D	L	F	A	Pts	
3	2	0	1	10	5	4	*Referee:* R. K. Wilson

Broomfield has not been a favourite haunt of Aberdeen of late. Three minutes from time Hermiston's swallow dive saved a certain equaliser but gave Airdrie a penalty. McGarr parried Goodwin's spot-kick and his follow-up. Now for Celtic in the League Cup.

No 4 Saturday, 13 September
ABERDEEN (2) 2   MORTON (1) 2
  Hamilton (1),   Laughton (7),
  Wilson (24)   Allan (52)

ABERDEEN: McGarr, Boel, Hermiston, Murray, McMillan, Petersen, Rae, Robb, Forrest, Wilson, Hamilton

MORTON: Neilsen, Ferguson, Laughton, Sweeney, Gray, Rankine, Harper, Collins, Ferry, Allan (Jensen), Gallagher

P	W	D	L	F	A	Pts	
							Attendance: 14,000
4	2	1	1	12	7	5	*Referee:* A. McKenzie

Aberdeen were interested in Morton's Joe Harper last season after the wee man scored against them twice. Now they are even more interested as his two free kicks produce two goals.

No 5 Saturday, 20 September
ST JOHNSTONE (2) 3   ABERDEEN (0) 1
  McCarry (26), Hall (36),   Forrest (49)
  Connolly (57)

ST JOHNSTONE: Donaldson, Lambie, Coburn, Gordon, Rooney, Rennie (Whitelaw), Aird, Hall, McCarry, Connolly, Aitken

ABERDEEN: McGarr, Boel, Hermiston (Rae), Petersen, McMillan, Clark, Robb, Murray, Forrest, Wilson, Hamilton

P	W	D	L	F	A	Pts	
							Attendance: 9,400
5	2	1	2	13	10	5	*Referee:* I. M. D. Foote

Wonders will never cease. This time displaced goalkeeper Bobby Clark is on from the start in defence. He has been described as the best header of a ball at Pittodrie. The following day Ernie McGarr won his first cap in the 1-1 draw with the Irish Republic in Dublin. He was taken off injured after 25 minutes.

No 6 Saturday, 27 September
ABERDEEN (1) 1   DUNDEE (0) 1
  Hermiston (32 pen)   Wilson (83)

ABERDEEN: McGarr, Boel, Hermiston, Murray, McMillan, Petersen, Adams, Robb, Forrest, Wilson, Taylor (Hamilton)

DUNDEE: Donaldson, Wilson, Swan, Selway, Stewart, Houston (Kinninmonth), Murray, Scott, Gilroy, Bryce, Wallace

P	W	D	L	F	A	Pts	
							Attendance: 12,000
6	2	2	2	14	11	6	*Referee:* S. Anderson

Aberdeen are despondent about their League Cup defeat by Celtic. They scored against Dundee when Forrest's shot was 'saved' by full-back Wilson with his hands.

No 7 Saturday, 4 October
AYR UNITED (0) 1   ABERDEEN (0) 2
  Malone (49 pen)   Robb 2 (48, 61)

AYR: Stewart, Malone, Murphy, Fleming, Quinn, Mitchell, Young, Ferguson (Hood), Ingram, McCulloch, Rough

ABERDEEN: McGarr, Boel, Hermiston, Murray, McMillan, (McKay), Petersen, Harper, Robb, Forrest, Wilson, Hamilton

P	W	D	L	F	A	Pts	
							Attendance: n.a.
7	3	2	2	16	12	8	*Referee:* J. M. Kelly

At last, Aberdeen have taken the plunge and spent £40,000 on Morton's Joe Harper. The Aberdeen *Evening Express* remarked: 'He had a serviceable start for the Dons and looked as if he will fit in.'

No 8 Saturday, 11 October
ABERDEEN (1) 2   PARTICK THISTLE (0) 1
  Hamilton (24),   Coulston (74)
  Harper (85 pen)

ABERDEEN: McGarr, Boel, Hermiston, Murray, McMillan, Petersen, Harper, Robb, Forrest, Wilson (McKay), Hamilton

PARTICK: Dick, Reid, Gray (Coulston), McLindon, McKinnon, Rowan, Flanagan, Smith, Bone, Hansen, Duncan

P	W	D	L	F	A	Pts	
							Attendance: 12,500
8	4	2	2	18	13	10	*Referee:* E. H. Pringle

Partick are bottom and could have done with the points denied them by Joe Harper's first goal for Aberdeen. Pittodrie likes the look of him.

No 9 Wednesday, 29 October
ABERDEEN (1) 2   CELTIC (1) 3
  Fallon o.g. (34),   Murdoch (5), Johnstone
  Robb (55)   (78), Brogan (83)

ABERDEEN: McGarr, Boel, Kirkland, Hermiston, McMillan, Murray, Harper (Petersen), Robb, Forrest, Willoughby, McIlroy

CELTIC: Fallon, Craig, Hay, Murdoch, McNeill, Clark, Johnstone, Callaghan, Hughes, Hood (Brogan), Auld

P	W	D	L	F	A	Pts	
							Attendance: 25,000
9	4	2	3	20	16	10	*Referee:* R. H. Davidson

Celtic have already eliminated Aberdeen from the League Cup. Now they emerge triumphant after a 90 minute thriller. Aberdeen levelled Murdoch's thunderous 25-yard goal when Fallon dropped the ball over the line under pressure from McIlroy. Robb's header put the Dons in front, but when the inspirational Harper was forced to withdraw, Aberdeen were left hanging on. Pittodrie couldn't bear to watch as Celtic's storming finish turned defeat into victory.

No 10 Saturday, 1 November
DUNFERMLINE   ABERDEEN (0) 1
  ATHLETIC (1) 2   Forrest (63)
  Edwards 2 (20 pen, 90)
DUNFERMLINE: Martin, Callaghan, Lunn, McGarty, Baillie, Robertson, Mitchell, McKimmie, Edwards, Gardner, McLean
ABERDEEN: McGarr, Hermiston, Kirkland, Petersen (Hamilton), McMillan, Murray, Harper, Robb, Forrest, Willoughby, McIlroy

P	W	D	L	F	A	Pts		*Attendance:* 7,000
10	4	2	4	21	18	10		*Referee:* A. J. Crawley

A farcical penalty is awarded to pace-setting Dunfermline when Gardner's shot strikes Kirkland on the upper arm. Alex Edwards scored his side's second goal in injury time.

No 11 Wednesday, 5 November
ST MIRREN (0) 2   ABERDEEN (0) 0
  Gilshan (50), Blair (75)
ST MIRREN: Connachan, Murray, Connell, Cumming, McFadden, Kane, Gilshan, Lister, McLaughlin (Urquhart), Blair, Pinkerton
ABERDEEN: Clark, Sutherland, Kirkland, Hermiston, Robb, Murray, Willoughby, Harper, Forrest, Wilson (A. Smith), McIlroy

P	W	D	L	F	A	Pts	
11	4	2	5	21	20	10	*Referee:* A. F. McDonald

With all Aberdeen's central defenders unfit it was the turn of Dave Robb to wear the No 5 shirt. Bobby Clark is temporarily back in goal because Ernie McGarr is playing for Scotland in Austria.

No 12 Saturday, 8 November
ABERDEEN (0) 0   DUNDEE UNITED (0) 0
ABERDEEN: McGarr, Sutherland, Kirkland, Hermiston, McMillan, Murray, Harper, Robb, Forrest, Willoughby, McIlroy
DUNDEE UNITED: Mackay, Rolland, Cameron, Gillespie, Smith, Henry, Hogg, Reid, Gordon, Mitchell, Scott (Wilson)

P	W	D	L	F	A	Pts		*Attendance:* 10,000
12	4	3	5	21	20	11		*Referee:* T. Wharton

League leaders United, unbeaten all season, couldn't master a swirling wind any more than could Aberdeen. In the last minute McGarr saved splendidly from Rolland.

No 13 Saturday, 15 November
HEARTS (1) 2   ABERDEEN (1) 2
  Moller (43), Ford (81)   Robb (3), Forrest (52)
HEARTS: Cruickshank, Clunie, Oliver, Macdonald, Anderson, Thomson, Jensen, Moller, Ford, Brown, Murray (Fleming)

ABERDEEN: McGarr, Hermiston, Kirkland (Fleming), Murray, McMillan, M. Buchan, Harper, Robb, Forrest, Willoughby, McIlroy

P	W	D	L	F	A	Pts		*Attendance:* 11,500
13	4	4	5	23	22	12		*Referee:* A. E. Currie

Both teams persisted with the offside trap, producing much whistle. Five players were booked. There is a welcome to Martin Buchan playing his first game of the season after a road accident.

No 14 Saturday, 22 November
ABERDEEN (1) 4   MOTHERWELL (1) 1
  Robb (11), Hermiston   Muir (27)
  (75), Buchan (76),
  Forrest (89)
ABERDEEN: McGarr, Hermiston, Kirkland, Murray, McMillan, M. Buchan, Harper, Robb, Forrest, Willoughby, McIlroy
MOTHERWELL: McCloy, Campbell, Wark, Donnelly, Forsyth, Goldthorpe, Murphy, McInally (McCrae), Deans, Wilson, Muir

P	W	D	L	F	A	Pts		*Attendance:* 7,000
14	5	4	5	27	23	14		*Referee:* R. D. Crawford

This was Aberdeen's first win in six games. Jim Hermiston's 25-yarder put them in front for the second and decisive time to cheer up the crowd on a miserable day.

No 15 Saturday, 29 November
KILMARNOCK (0) 0   ABERDEEN (0) 2
                          Forrest (62), Harper (66)
KILMARNOCK: McLaughlan, King, Dickson, Gilmour, McGrory, Beattie, T. McLean, Morrison, Mathie, Strachan, Cook
ABERDEEN: McGarr, Hermiston, Kirkland, Murray, McMillan, Petersen, Harper, Robb, Forrest, Willoughby, Hamilton

P	W	D	L	F	A	Pts		*Attendance:* 3,000
15	6	4	5	29	23	16		*Referee:* T. Kellock

Kilmarnock have just returned from a Fairs Cup trip to Bulgaria, and tire towards the end of the match.

No 16 Saturday, 13 December
CLYDE (0) 2   ABERDEEN (1) 1
  Mulherron (52),   Harper (45 pen)
  Staite (57)
CLYDE: McCulloch, Anderson, Mulherron, Beattie, McHugh, Burns, Glasgow, Hulston, Staite, Stewart, Hastings
ABERDEEN: McGarr, Hermiston, Kirkland, Murray, Boel, Petersen, Harper, Robb, Forrest, Willoughby (McIlroy), Hamilton

P	W	D	L	F	A	Pts	
16	6	4	6	30	25	16	*Referee:* R. C. Greenlees

Clyde are in relegation difficulties and are pleased to score their first goals against Aberdeen in four attempts this season. Beattie had earlier pulled down Hamilton to give Aberdeen a penalty.

No 17 Saturday, 20 December
ABERDEEN (2) 2   RANGERS (2) 3
  Robb 2 (3, 28)   Stein 2 (10, 41),
                        Johnston (54)

ABERDEEN: McGarr, Hermiston, Kirkland, Murray, Boel, Petersen, Harper, Robb, Forrest, M. Buchan, Hamilton
RANGERS: Neef, Johansen, Mathieson, Smith, McKinnon, Greig, Henderson, Baxter, Stein, Setterington (Penman), Johnston

P W D L F A Pts   *Attendance:* 22,000
17 6 4 7 32 28 16   *Referee:* E. H. Pringle

Once again it appears to be Celtic versus Rangers for the title. What a start for Aberdeen: the Rangers' defence is transfixed as Harper glides the ball across for Robb to score unmolested. But Rangers finally took both points thanks to Johnston's wheeling shot on the turn.

No 18 Saturday, 27 December
RAITH ROVERS (0) 0   ABERDEEN (1) 1
                        Hamilton (5)

RAITH: Reid, McDonald, Lindsay, D. Millar, Buchanan, Bolton, Hislop, Judge, Sneddon, Sinclair, A. Miller (Polland)
ABERDEEN: McGarr, Hermiston, Kirkland, Murray (Petersen), Boel, Buchan, Harper, Robb, Hamilton, Willoughby, Forrest

P W D L F A Pts   *Attendance:* 4,000
18 7 4 7 33 28 18   *Referee:* W. J. Mullen

Raith are in danger of the drop and fight desperately for some reward. The Dons were punch-drunk by the close, hanging on to Hamilton's early mis-hit.

No 19 Thursday, 1 January
DUNDEE (2) 2   ABERDEEN (0) 0
  Steele (8), Bryce (15)

DUNDEE: Donaldson, Wilson, Houston, Murray, Easton, Selway, Steele, Kinninmonth, Wallace, Scott, Bryce
ABERDEEN: McGarr, Sutherland, Hermiston, Buchan, Boel, Murray (Petersen), Harper, Robb, Forrest, Willoughby, Hamilton

P W D L F A Pts
19 7 4 8 33 30 18   *Referee:* R. Gordon

The first match of the 1970s. Aberdeen's front line cried out for a taker of chances – Harper was being used as a winger.

No 20 Saturday, 10 January
ABERDEEN (2) 5   RAITH ROVERS (1) 1
  Murray (30), Harper   Lindsay (10)
  3 (32 pen, 79, 81),·
  Robb (64)

ABERDEEN: McGarr, Sutherland, Kirkland, Hermiston, Boel, M. Buchan, Willoughby, Robb, Forrest, Murray, Harper
RAITH: Reid, Hislop, Lindsay, Cooper, Polland, Buchanan, Brand, Miller, Judge, Bolton, Vincent

P W D L F A Pts   *Attendance:* 8,000
20 8 4 8 38 31 20   *Referee:* E. Thomson

McGarr makes a hash of Lindsay's cross-cum-shot. Bobby Clark is on the brink of signing for Rangers. Joe Harper doubles his goal tally since arriving at Pittodrie. This is Aberdeen's first double of the season.

No 21 Saturday, 17 January
MORTON (1) 3   ABERDEEN (2) 2
  Osborne (42 pen),   Neilsen o.g. (20),
  Ferguson (61),   Robb (35)
  Coakley (69)

MORTON: Neilsen, Ferguson, Laughton, Sweeney, Gray, Rankin, Coakley, Collins, Osborne, O'Neill, Allan
ABERDEEN: McGarr, Sutherland, Kirkland, Hermiston (T. Wilson), Boel, M. Buchan, Willoughby, Robb, Forrest, Murray, Harper

P W D L F A Pts
21 8 4 9 40 34 20   *Referee:* H. Dempsey

This was a game to ponder. There was an own-goal by Morton keeper Nielsen in gathering a harmless pass back; a mysterious Morton penalty; a disallowed Harper equaliser in the last minute; and a bad ankle injury to Jim Hermiston.

No 22 Saturday, 31 January
ABERDEEN (0) 0   AIRDRIEONIANS (0) 1
                        Jarvie (58)

ABERDEEN: McGarr, Boel, Kirkland, Petersen (Willoughby), McMillan, M. Buchan, Hamilton, Robb, Forrest, Murray, Harper
AIRDRIE: McKenzie, Jonquin, Caldwell, Menzies, Delaney, Whiteford, Wilson, Jarvie, Marshall, Goodwin, Cowan

P W D L F A Pts   *Attendance:* 9,000
22 8 4 10 40 35 20   *Referee:* A. McKenzie

Aberdeen's worst display of the season. Jarvie's header earned the points and Pittodrie jeered its own players. It was the end of the road for Ernie McGarr in goal.

No 23 Wednesday, 25 February
ABERDEEN (0) 1   AYR UNITED (0) 0
  Buchan (90)

ABERDEEN: Clark, Boel, Murray, Petersen (T. Wilson), McMillan, M. Buchan, McKay, Robb, Forrest, Hamilton, Harper
AYR: Stewart, Malone, Murphy, McAnespie, Fleming, Mitchell, Young, Reynolds, Hood (McGregor), McCulloh, McColl

P W D L F A Pts   *Attendance:* 8,000
23 9 4 10 41 35 22   *Referee:* R. K. Wilson

A night of exasperation and frustration for Aberdeen until Buchan fires in Boel's back-header.

No 24 Saturday, 28 February
PARTICK THISTLE (0) 0 ABERDEEN (2) 3
                        Petersen (11),
                        Forrest 2 (40, 68)

PARTICK: Ritchie, Reid, Holt, Clark, Gray, Johnston, Rae, Smith (Hansen), Flanagan, Bone, Lawrie
ABERDEEN: Clark, Boel, Murray, Petersen, McMillan, M. Buchan, McKay, Robb, Forrest, Hamilton, G. Buchan

P	W	D	L	F	A	Pts	
24	10	4	10	44	35	24	*Attendance:* 6,000
							Referee: B. Padden

Partick are staring relegation in the face; the more so after this result – their fourth straight defeat. Aberdeen played without any league worries and casually took the chances that came their way.

No 25 Monday, 2 March
ABERDEEN (0) 0   ST JOHNSTONE (0) 0
ABERDEEN: Clark, Boel, Murray, Petersen, McMillan, M. Buchan, McKay, Robb, Forrest, Hamilton, G. Buchan
ST JOHNSTONE: Robertson, Millar, Coburn, Gordon, Rooney, McPhee, Aird, Hall, McCarry, Whitelaw, Aitken

P	W	D	L	F	A	Pts	
25	10	5	10	44	35	25	*Attendance:* 7,000
							Referee: T. Marshall

The white pitch and strange yellow ball evidently disconcerted Aberdeen, who did everything but score. Buchan almost repeated his late winner against Ayr but his shot lifted too high.

No 26 Monday, 29 March
ABERDEEN (0) 0   HIBERNIAN (2) 2
                               McBride (28 pen),
                               Cormack (32)
ABERDEEN: Clark, Boel, Murray, Petersen, McMillan, M. Buchan, McKay, Robb, Forrest, Hamilton, Harper
HIBERNIAN: Marshall, Shevlane, McEwan, Blackley, Black, Stanton, Graham, Hamilton, McBride, Cormack, Stevenson

P	W	D	L	F	A	Pts	
26	10	5	11	44	37	25	*Attendance:* 11,000
							Referee: W. Anderson

This was not the result Aberdeen wanted on the eve of a Scottish Cup semi-final. Hibs, third in the league, enjoyed their first win in five games. It was a physical contest: a dubious penalty against McMillan brought the first goal; a misplaced pass by Buchan gave Cormack – Hibs' captain – the second.

No 27 Wednesday, 18 March
ABERDEEN (1) 1   ST MIRREN (1) 1
   Robb (37)   McMillan o.g. (24)
ABERDEEN: Clark, Boel, G. Murray, S. Murray, McMillan, M. Buchan, McKay, Robb, Forrest, Hamilton, Harper
ST MIRREN: McGann, Murray, Connell, Fulton, McFadden, Palmer, Gilshan, Lister, Hamilton, Blair, Pinkerton

P	W	D	L	F	A	Pts	
27	10	6	11	45	38	26	*Referee:* R. Gordon

A game of three Murrays. Aberdeen have two of them, now that they have picked up midfielder Steve from Dundee for a Dons record fee of £50,000. He is ineligible for the Scottish Cup Final with Celtic.

No 28 Saturday, 21 March
ABERDEEN (1) 2   DUNFERMLINE
   Forrest 2 (44, 63)   ATHLETIC (0) 0
ABERDEEN: Clark, Boel, G. Murray, S. Murray, McMillan, M. Buchan, McKay (Graham), Robb, Forrest, Hamilton, Harper
DUNFERMLINE: Arrol, Callaghan, Lunn, Fraser, McNicoll, Renton, Mitchell, McLaren (Gardner), Edwards, McLean, Gillespie

P	W	D	L	F	A	Pts	
28	11	6	11	47	38	28	*Attendance:* 10,000
							Referee: T. Kellock

More stars of the future come along. This time it's 17-year old Arthur Graham who makes his first appearance as a second-half substitute. After Forrest's second goal Dunfermline's Alex Edwards was ordered off for protesting to the referee.

No 29 Wednesday, 25 March
CELTIC (0) 1   ABERDEEN (0) 2
   Gemmell (87)   G. Murray (49),
                           Graham (65)
CELTIC: Williams, Craig, Gemmell, Murdoch, McNeill, Brogan, Johnstone, Connelly, Wallace, Lennox, Auld
ABERDEEN: Clark, Boel, G. Murray, S. Murray, McMillan, M. Buchan, McKay, Hermiston, Robb, Willoughby, Graham

P	W	D	L	F	A	Pts	
29	12	6	11	49	39	30	*Attendance:* 33,000
							Referee: J. W. Paterson

Celtic need two points for the championship in this dress rehearsal for the Scottish Cup Final. What a shock they received, and what an experience for young Arthur Graham who tee'd the ball up for George Murray for the first goal, and then had the temerity to head the second. This was the first time Aberdeen had beaten Celtic in thirteen matches, since January 1966. Aberdeen's last win at Parkhead was during the 1962-63 season. What omens are these for the Cup Final?

No 30 Saturday, 28 March
DUNDEE UNITED (0) 2   ABERDEEN (0) 0
   Mitchell (49),
   K. Cameron (75)
DUNDEE UNITED: Mackay, Rolland, J. Cameron, Gillespie, Smith, Henry (Markland), Wilson, Stevenson, K. Cameron, Mitchell, Dunne
ABERDEEN: Clark, Boel, G. Murray, S. Murray, McMillan, M. Buchan, Harper, Hermiston (McKay), Robb, Willoughby, Forrest

P	W	D	L	F	A	Pts	
30	12	6	12	49	41	30	*Attendance:* 7,000
							Referee: R. D. Crawford

It's asking too much for two inspired Dons performances in a row. A boring first half is followed by

Aberdeen have won the 1970 Scottish Cup Final, defeating Celtic 3-1 at Hampden Park. The Dons' fans welcome the team in Union Street.

United taking control and having the nerve to indulge in some exhibition stuff by the end.

No 31 Saturday, 4 March
ABERDEEN (0) 0   HEARTS (1) 1
                             Moller (34)
ABERDEEN: Clark, Boel, G. Murray, S. Murray, McMillan, M. Buchan, McKay, Robb, Forrest, Willoughby, Graham
HEARTS: Cruickshank, Clunie, Oliver, Veitch, Anderson, Thomson, Traynor, Winchester, Irvine, Townsend (Ford), Moller

P W D L F A Pts   *Attendance:* 9,500
31 12 6 13 49 42 30   *Referee:* R. Davidson

Aberdeen's minds are somewhere else – Hampden perhaps? The only goal of this untidy match belonged to Hearts' Rene Moller, whose free kick was politely left to one another by Aberdeen's defenders. Harper has been in the reserves for weeks. Should he be recalled?

No 32 Monday, 6 April
ABERDEEN (0) 2   KILMARNOCK (0) 2
  G. Buchan (66),   Mathie (23),
  Graham (84)   Morrison (61)
ABERDEEN: Clark, Whyte, G. Murray, Hermiston, Boel, S. Murray, G. Buchan, Harper, Robb, Willoughby (Hamilton), Graham
KILMARNOCK: McLaughlan, King, Dickson, Gilmour, Rodman, McGrory, T. McLean, Morrison, Mathie, McDonald, Cook

P W D L F A Pts
32 12 7 13 51 44 31   *Referee:* S. Anderson

Arthur Graham to the rescue. His shot (cross?) from the wing leaves McLaughlan flapping in mid-air to give Aberdeen a late draw. Harper celebrated his return to the first team with a confident display that confirms his inclusion at Hampden. Willoughby's injury will keep him out of the Final.

No 33 Monday, 13 April
HIBERNIAN (1) 1   ABERDEEN (1) 2
  Stevenson (41)   Robb (37), Forrest (76)
HIBERNIAN: Allan, Duncan, Jones, Blackley, Black, McBride, Graham, Hamilton, O'Rourke, Stevenson, Cropley
ABERDEEN: Clark, Whyte, G. Murray, Hermiston, Boel, M. Buchan, McKay, S. Murray, Robb, Harper, G. Buchan (Forrest)

P W D L F A Pts
33 13 7 13 53 45 33   *Referee:* G. Anderson

Hibs' players line up to applaud the Cup-winning Dons out at Easter Road. Aberdeen thank them in the best possible way – by beating them.

No 34 Saturday, 18 April
MOTHERWELL (0) 0   ABERDEEN (0) 2
                             Forrest 2 (47, 69)

MOTHERWELL: McCrae, Whiteford, Wark, Forsyth, McCallum, Watson, Wilson, Muir, Deans, McInally, Heron
ABERDEEN: McGarr, Whyte, G. Murray, Hermiston, Boel, M. Buchan, McKay, Robb, Forrest, Harper, Graham

Attendance: 6,100   *Referee:* J. R. Grant

At the final whistle Henning Boel and Motherwell's John Deans had a bust-up in the players' tunnel, and both were retrospectively 'ordered off'.

Aberdeen's complete home and away record:
      HOME   AWAY
P W D L F A   W D L F A   Pts
34 6 6 5 30 19   8 1 8 25 26   35

Scottish League Division One

	P	W	D	L	F	A	Pts
1 Celtic	34	27	3	4	96	33	57
2 Rangers	34	19	7	8	67	40	45
3 Hibernian	34	19	6	9	65	40	44
4 Hearts	34	13	12	9	50	36	38
5 Dundee United	34	16	6	12	62	64	38
6 Dundee	34	15	6	13	49	44	36
7 Kilmarnock	34	13	10	11	62	57	36
8 ABERDEEN	34	14	7	13	55	45	35
9 Dunfermline	34	15	5	14	45	45	35
10 Morton	34	13	9	12	52	52	35
11 Motherwell	34	11	10	13	49	51	32
12 Airdrieonians	34	12	8	14	59	64	32
13 St Johnstone	34	11	9	14	50	62	31
14 Ayr United	34	12	6	16	37	52	30
15 St Mirren	34	8	9	17	39	54	25
16 Clyde	34	9	7	18	34	56	25
17 Raith Rovers	34	5	11	18	32	67	21
18 Partick Thistle	34	5	7	22	41	82	17

LEAGUE CUP

Saturday, 9 August
ABERDEEN (1) 2   DUNFERMLINE
  Forrest (37),   ATHLETIC (0) 2
  A. Smith (87)   Mitchell (50),
                             Peterson o.g. (73)
ABERDEEN: McGarr, Whyte (Hamilton), Hermiston, A. Smith, McMillan, Petersen, Willoughby, Robb, Forrest, Wilson, G. Buchan
DUNFERMLINE: Martin, Callaghan, Lunn, Fraser (Thomson), Barry, Renton, Mitchell, Paton, Edwards, McLaren, McLean

Attendance: 16,000   *Referee:* R. Gordon

Aberdeen try to make up the loss of Tommy Craig and Jim Smith by signing the Rangers pair Alex Willoughby and Alex Smith. Meanwhile Martin Buchan has broken his ankle in a car crash. Against Dunfermline there was more pain and anguish. Aberdeen's Jim Whyte was carried off with a ruptured Achilles tendon, while Dunfermline's Jim Fraser broke a leg in a collision with Petersen.

Wednesday, 13 August
CLYDE (0) 0   ABERDEEN (0) 0

CLYDE: Wright, Glasgow, McGregor, Anderson, McVie, Burns, McFarlane, Hay, Hulston, McLean, Hastings

ABERDEEN: McGarr, Boel, Hamilton, A. Smith, McMillan, Petersen, Willoughby, Robb, Forrest, T. Wilson, G. Buchan

Referee: R. D. Crawford

Both sets of forwards weren't allowed to breathe – let alone score.

Saturday, 16 August
ABERDEEN (1) 2   HIBERNIAN (1) 2
  Hermiston (35 pen),   McBride (43), Grant (63)
  Hamilton (62)

ABERDEEN: McGarr, Boel, Hermiston, A. Smith, McMillan, Petersen, Willoughby, Robb, Forrest, Wilson, Hamilton

HIBERNIAN: Marshall, Shevlane, Davis, Wilkinson, Black, Stanton, Marinello (Hamilton), Grant, McBride, O'Rourke, Stevenson

Attendance: 16,000   *Referee:* T. Marshall

Aberdeen were twice in front. They might have stayed that way too. But Robb's flick which crashed off the Hibs' post to nestle in Marshall's arms eventually cost them dear.

Wednesday, 20 August
ABERDEEN (1) 3   CLYDE (0) 0
  Wilson 3 (35, 61, 68)

ABERDEEN: McGarr, Boel, Hermiston, Murray, McMillan, Petersen, Willoughby, Robb, Forrest, Wilson, Hamilton

CLYDE: Wright, Glasgow, Mulherron, Anderson, McVie, McHugh, McFarlane, Hay, Hulston, Burns, Hastings

Attendance: 13,500   *Referee:* E. Thomson

A memorable hat-trick for 18-year old Tommy Wilson, who hails from Sandyhills Youth Club. His second goal was a pile-driver from 22 yards.

Saturday, 23 August
DUNFERMLINE   ABERDEEN (1) 1
  ATHLETIC (0) 0   Willoughby (15)

DUNFERMLINE: Duff, Callaghan, Lunn, McGarty, Barry, Renton, Mitchell, Paton, Edwards, Gardner (McLaren), McLean

ABERDEEN: McGarr, Boel, Hermiston, Murray, McMillan, Petersen, Willoughby, Robb, Forrest, Wilson, Hamilton

Referee: R. H. Davidson

Willoughby's header from Hamilton's corner sets up an eagerly awaited last match with Hibs.

Wednesday, 27 August
HIBERNIAN (0) 0   ABERDEEN (0) 0

HIBERNIAN: Marshall, Shevlane, Davis, Wilkinson, Black, Stanton, Marinello, O'Rourke, McBride, Cormack, Stevenson

ABERDEEN: McGarr, Boel, Hermiston, Murray, McMillan, Petersen, Willoughby, Robb, Forrest, Wilson, Hamilton

Attendance: 18,300   *Referee:* J. W. Paterson

Goal difference has replaced goal average this season. So Aberdeen can afford to lose by one goal and still go through to the quarter finals. Jock Stein – manager of quarter-final opponents Celtic – sent three players to send back reports. They noted another resolute defensive display and the third shut-out in three away games.

Section 2

	P	W	D	L	F	A	Pts
ABERDEEN	6	2	4	0	8	4	8
Hibernian	6	2	2	2	10	9	6
Dunfermline	6	1	3	2	5	6	5
Clyde	6	1	3	2	4	8	5

Quarter Final 1st Leg Wednesday, 10 September
ABERDEEN (0) 0   CELTIC (0) 0

ABERDEEN: McGarr, Boel, Hermiston, Murray, McMillan, Petersen, Rae, Robb, Forrest, Wilson, Hamilton

CELTIC: Fallon, Hay, Gemmell, Murdoch, McNeill, Clark, Hood (Brogan), Chalmers, Wallace, Callaghan, Lennox

Attendance: 33,000   *Referee:* W. J. Mullen

Aberdeen wanted a lead to take to Parkhead. Hamilton hit the bar in the first half; Celtic came out of their shell in the second.

Quarter Final 2nd Leg Wednesday, 24 September
CELTIC (0) 2   ABERDEEN (0) 1
  Lennox (52), Wallace (55)   Forrest (31)

CELTIC: Fallon, Hay, Gemmell, Brogan, McNeill, Clark, Wallace, Chalmers, Johnstone, Hood, Lennox

ABERDEEN: McGarr, Boel, Hermiston, Murray, McMillan, Petersen, Adams, Robb, Forrest, Wilson, Hamilton

Attendance: 47,000   *Referee:* W. Mullen

What a shock for Celtic as Jim Forrest ran on to Wilson's pass to bang Aberdeen in front. At half-time Jimmy Johnstone was switched to centre forward. It was he who manufactured Celtic's equaliser for Lennox, and within minutes Wallace outwitted an ill-conceived Aberdeen offside plan to fire the winner past McGarr.

SCOTTISH CUP

1st Round Saturday, 24 January
ABERDEEN (3) 4   CLYDE (0) 0
  Harper 2 (6, 36),
  Robb 2 (20, 51)

ABERDEEN: McGarr, Boel, Kirkland, Petersen, McMillan, M. Buchan, Hamilton, Robb, Forrest, Murray, Harper

CLYDE: McCulloch, Anderson, Soutar, Beattie, McHugh, Burns, Glasgow, Hulston, Staite (McFarlane), Stewart, Hastings

Attendance: 12,200   *Referee:* n.a.

Poor Clyde are never in with a shout once Harper and Robb had given Aberdeen a picture-book start. This follows home wins over Clyde by 3-0 in the League Cup and 6-0 in the league.

2nd Round Wednesday, 11 February
ABERDEEN (2) 2   CLYDEBANK (1) 1
  Forrest (5), Robb (32)   McGhee (11)
ABERDEEN: Clark, Boel, Kirkland, Murray, McMillan, M. Buchan, Willoughby, Robb, Forrest, Hamilton, Harper
CLYDEBANK: McDonnell, Mitchell, Gray, Ruddy, Fallon, Hay, Caskie, Love, Munro, McGhee (McMillan), O'Brien
Attendance: 13,100

This match had had to be postponed from the Saturday because of snow. It was a shambles for Aberdeen. The crowd cheered Second Division Clydebank's spirited efforts to equalise. Perhaps they did not recognise their own players, kitted out in unfamiliar striped shirts.

Quarter Final Saturday, 21 February
FALKIRK (0) 0   ABERDEEN (0) 1
                              McKay (66)
FALKIRK: Rennie, Abel, Miller, Ford, Markie, Gibson, Hoggan, Roxburgh (Scott), Young, Ferguson, Watson
ABERDEEN: Clark, Boel, Murray, Petersen, McMillan, M. Buchan, McKay, Hermiston, Forrest, Hamilton, Harper
Attendance: 13,500   *Referee:* J. W. Paterson

What a difference the inclusion of livewire Derek McKay makes. The free transfer from Dundee was the man-of-the-match against the Second Division title-chasers. He provided the decisive touch after a bout of head tennis in the Falkirk goalmouth. This takes Aberdeen to the Scottish Cup semi-finals for the fourth time in five seasons.

Semi Final (Perth) Saturday, 14 March
KILMARNOCK (0) 0   ABERDEEN (1) 1
                              McKay (21)
KILMARNOCK: McLaughlan, King, Dickson, Gilmour, McGrory, McDonald, T. McLean, Morrison, Mathie, J. McLean, Cook
ABERDEEN: Clark, Boel, Murray, Hermiston (G. Buchan), McMillan, M. Buchan, McKay, Robb, Forrest, Hamilton, Harper

For the second successive season Kilmarnock block Aberdeen's path in the Scottish Cup. And for the second time the obstacle is cleared. Like most semi-finals, this was no classic. But Derek McKay's knack of scoring golden goals is maintained. By the end there were plenty of chewed finger nails, and a good number of cuts and bruises in the crowd as hooligans let fly with bottles and cans.

Scottish Cup Final (Hampden) Saturday, 11 April
CELTIC (0) 1   ABERDEEN (1) 3
  Lennox (89)   Harper (27 pen),
                            McKay 2 (83, 90)
CELTIC: Williams, Hay, Gemmell, Murdoch, McNeill, Brogan, Johnstone, Wallace, Connelly, Lennox, Hughes (Auld)
ABERDEEN: Clark, Boel, G. Murray, Hermiston, McMillan, M. Buchan, McKay, Robb, Forrest, Harper, Graham
Attendance: 108,464   *Referee:* R. H. Davidson

Champions Celtic have won 1-0 at Leeds in the first leg of the European Cup semi-final with the second leg just four days away. This is Aberdeen's seventh Cup final, and they have won it only once before, in 1947 – losing in 1937, 1953, 1954, 1959 and 1967. The bookies made Celtic 4-11 on: with Aberdeen 5-1 against.

Aberdeen performed the impossible, inflicting on Celtic only their third defeat at Hampden in their 26 appearances in the national stadium under Jock Stein. Midway through the first half McKay's cross struck Murdoch's arm. 'Penalty' said the referee. Tommy Gemmell flung the ball at him and was booked. Harper coolly scored from the spot. Three minutes later a Celtic 'goal' was disallowed for an infringement by Lennox on Clark. Near the end of the match Williams could only parry Forrest's drive and Derek McKay pounced. Lennox did pull a goal back, but McKay then promptly controlled the ball with his left foot and scored with his right. 21-year old skipper Martin Buchan held aloft the Cup. 50,000 welcomed him, it, and his team-mates back to Aberdeen on Eddie Turnbull's 48th birthday.

Jock Stein warmly congratulates Aberdeen's manager, Eddie Turnbull in winning the 1974 Scottish Cup.

1969-70 APPEARANCES	League	League Cup	Scottish Cup
Robb	34	8	4
G. Murray	34	5	5
Forrest	31(+1)	8	5
Boel	28	7	5
Hermiston	26	8	3
McMillan	24	8	5
Harper	24		5
McGarr	22	8	1
Hamilton	19(+3)	6(+1)	4
M. Buchan	19		5
Willoughby	18(+1)	6	1
Petersen	17(+3)	8	2
Clark	13(+1)		4
Kirkland	13		2
McKay	10(+3)		3
T. Wilson	9(+2)	8	
S. Murray	7		
McIlroy	6(+1)		
Sutherland	5		
Graham	4(+1)		1
G. Buchan	4	2	−(+1)
Whyte	3	1	
Rae	2(+2)	1	
Adams	1	1	

1969-70 APPEARANCES	League	League Cup	Scottish Cup
Taylor	1		
A. Smith	−(+1)	3	
Fleming	−(+1)		
27 players			

GOALS	Total	League	League Cup	Scottish
Robb	19	16		3
Forrest	18	15	2	1
Harper	9	6		3
Hamilton	4	3	1	
T. Wilson	4	1	3	
McKay	4			4
Hermiston	3	2	1	
G. Murray	2	2		
Petersen	2	2		
M. Buchan	2	2		
Graham	2	2		
Rae	1	1		
G. Buchan	1	1		
Willoughby	1		1	
A. Smith	1		1	
own-goals	2	2		
Total	75	55	9	11

An Aberdeen line-up from 1972. Back row: J. Forrest, S. Murray, J. Murray, G. Marshall, W. Young, M. Buchan, J. Hermiston. Front row: B. Miller, D. Robb, J. Harper, A. Willoughby, A. Graham

Season 1970-71

That unforgettable Scottish Cup victory over Celtic was just the spur Aberdeen needed to 'have a go' at their Glasgow rivals the following season. Having snatched one trophy from them, there seemed no reason why the Dons couldn't snatch another – the league championship itself. Such hopes seemed to have slender foundations when Aberdeen threw away their chance of qualifying from their League Cup section – shipping seven goals to Airdrie and Hibs. Their first, crucial, league matches were none too heart-warming either, as first Airdrie, then St Johnstone, left Pittodrie with a point.

Then came disaster in the 1st Round of the European Cup-Winners Cup. A 3-1 first-leg victory at home over the Hungarians of Honved was followed by a defeat by the same score in Budapest. Extra time failed to break the deadlock. In previous seasons a coin would have been spun: but now UEFA had introduced sudden-death penalties. With the score 2-2 Jim Forrest's kick smacked against the bar; the Hungarians netted all theirs; and Aberdeen were out.

The demoralised Dons returned home and promptly lost to Morton. Then something remarkable happened. Aberdeen won their next fifteen league games – twelve of them without conceding a goal. By mid-January 1971 all they needed was to keep cool and the title was theirs. Then came defeat at Hibs; then at Dunfermline on the day that part of the main stand at Pittodrie burned down. Rangers knocked Aberdeen out of the Cup and more league points went astray. Aberdeen found themselves needing to beat Celtic at Pittodrie on 17 April to regain the initiative. But the game was drawn and Celtic went on to take their sixth successive championship.

Nevertheless, there were several outstanding features of the Dons' league performances in 1970-71. They amassed 54 points equalling their highest ever tally. They lost only four games – their fewest since the War. They conceded a miserly 18 goals in 34 league matches – their lowest figure ever. They went the whole season unbeaten at home in league, League Cup, Scottish Cup and European games – the only time they had achieved this feat since the War. Eddie Turnbull could also pick a settled side: ten players each made 28 or more league appearances. As a bonus, opponents often came to Aberdeen's aid, providing no less than six precious own-goals.

Why, then, did the title slip away? Perhaps the Pittodrie fire cast a spell on Joe Harper. He scored 19 league goals up to that point. None afterwards.

League:	Second
League Cup:	Second in qualifying group
Scottish Cup:	Quarter Final
European Cup-Winners Cup:	First Round

SCOTTISH LEAGUE DIVISION ONE

No 1 Saturday, 29 August
ABERDEEN (1) 1   AIRDRIEONIANS (0) 1
Harper (26)   Busby (86)

ABERDEEN: Clark, Boel, G. Murray, Hermiston (Hamilton), McMillan, M. Buchan, Forrest, S. Murray, Robb, Harper, Graham

AIRDRIE: McKenzie, Jonquin, Caldwell, Menzies, Delaney, D. Whiteford, Wilson, Jarvie, Busby, McPheat, Cowan (Bird)

P	W	D	L	F	A	Pts	
1	0	1	0	1	1	1	*Attendance:* 9,000
							Referee: R. Henderson

It's only seven days since Aberdeen beat Airdrie 7-3 in the League Cup. Airdrie equalised when Aberdeen failed to clear a free kick.

No 2 Saturday, 5 September
DUNDEE (0) 1   ABERDEEN (2) 2
  Duncan (75)   Harper (33),
                   Hamilton (45)

DUNDEE: Donaldson, R. Wilson, Johnston, Selway, Stewart, Houston, Kinninmonth, Bryce, Duncan, Scott, J. Wilson

ABERDEEN: Clark, Boel, G. Murray, S. Murray, Young, M. Buchan, McKay, Robb, Hamilton, Harper, G. Buchan

P	W	D	L	F	A	Pts	
2	1	1	0	3	2	3	*Attendance:* 8,000
							Referee: A. F. J. Webster

Aberdeen introduce their new 18-year old centre-half, Willie Young. Both he and Jim Hermiston were booked. Donaldson got his hands to Harper's header but couldn't stop it.

No 3 Saturday, 12 September
ABERDEEN (0) 0   ST JOHNSTONE (0) 0

ABERDEEN: Clark, Boel, G. Murray, S. Murray, Young, M. Buchan, McKay, Robb, Hamilton (Forrest), Harper, G. Buchan

ST JOHNSTONE: Donaldson, McManus, Argue, Rooney, Gordon, Rennie, Leslie (Lambie), Hall, Connolly, McPhee, Muir

P	W	D	L	F	A	Pts	
3	1	2	0	3	2	4	*Attendance:* 10,000
							Referee: R. H. Davidson

Aberdeen exerted a lot of huff and puff, yet achieved very little. They have now let slip two home points which will be very expensive by the season's end. Two more Dons were booked.

No 4 Saturday, 19 September
KILMARNOCK (0) 0   ABERDEEN (4) 4
                     Arthur o.g. (16),
                     Hamilton (34), Harper
                     (35), Boel (39)

KILMARNOCK: Hunter, Dickson, Swan, Maxwell, McGrory, Arthur, McLean, Morrison, Mathie, McSherry, Cook (McCulloch)

ABERDEEN: Clark, Boel, Hermiston, S. Murray, Young, M. Buchan, G. Buchan, Hamilton, Harper, Robb, Graham

P	W	D	L	F	A	Pts	
4	2	2	0	7	2	6	*Attendance:* 6,000
							Referee: R. Gordon

Kilmarnock were barracked by their own crowd throughout the second half as Aberdeen cruised to a comfortable win, helped by Arthur running the ball into his own net.

No 5 Saturday, 26 September
ABERDEEN (1) 3   HIBERNIAN (0) 0
  Forrest (43), Robb (58),
  Harper (85 pen)

ABERDEEN: Clark, Boel, Hermiston, S. Murray, Young, M. Buchan, G. Buchan, Robb, Forrest, Harper, Willoughby

HIBERNIAN: Marshall, Shevlane, Schaedler, Blackley, Black, Stanton, Hamilton (Blair), Graham, McBride, McEwan, Cropley

Leading positions

	P	W	D	L	F	A	Pts
1 Celtic	5	4	0	1	12	2	8
2 ABERDEEN	5	3	2	0	10	2	8
3 St. Johnstone	5	3	2	0	9	3	8
4 Rangers	5	3	1	1	9	2	7

Attendance: 13,000   *Referee:* J. W. Paterson

Aberdeen gain revenge for their humiliating elimination from the League Cup. Three Hibs' players are booked in the process. Harper's penalty was the result of Willoughby being sandwiched between two green-shirted defenders. This result sets up Aberdeen nicely for their Cup-Winners Cup trip to Hungary.

No 6 Saturday, 3 October
MORTON (1) 2   ABERDEEN (0) 0
  Mason 2 (31, 78)

MORTON: Nielsen, Murray, McDerment, Sweeney, Gray, O'Neill, Hannigan, Collins, Osborne (Jordan), Mason, Anderson

ABERDEEN: Clark, Boel, Hermiston, S. Murray, Young, M. Buchan, Willoughby, Robb (G. Murray), Forrest, Harper, Graham

P	W	D	L	F	A	Pts	
6	3	2	1	10	4	8	*Attendance:* 7,000
							Referee: H. Dempsey

Nothing went right for Aberdeen who are still suffering the after-effects of Forrest's penalty miss in Budapest. Dave Robb was injured early in the game and Joe Harper sent off after Morton's second goal. This is Aberdeen's third successive defeat at Greenock.

No 7 Saturday, 10 October
ABERDEEN (2) 3   DUNFERMLINE
  M. Buchan (20),   ATHLETIC (1) 2
  Graham 2 (29, 66)   Mitchell (25), Fraser (75)

ABERDEEN: Clark, Boel, Hermiston, S. Murray, Young, M. Buchan, G. Buchan (Willoughby), Hamilton, Forrest, Harper, Graham

DUNFERMLINE: Arrol, Callaghan, Lunn, Fraser, Cushley, J. Thomson, Gardner, Robertson, Mitchell, Walsh, McKimmie (Scott)

P	W	D	L	F	A	Pts	
7	4	2	1	13	6	10	*Attendance:* 10,000
							Referee: R. K. Wilson

Dunfermline are bottom without a win. But they took advantage of Joe Harper's penalty miss to pressurise the home defence for the last few minutes.

No 8 Saturday, 17 October
RANGERS (0) 0   ABERDEEN (1) 2
                         Jackson o.g. (44),
                         Harper (58)
RANGERS: McCloy, Jardine, Miller, Greig,
McKinnon, Jackson, Henderson, Frye, Stein, A.
MacDonald (Smith), Johnston
ABERDEEN: Clark, Boel, Hermiston, S. Murray,
McMillan, M. Buchan, Taylor, Harper, Forrest, Robb,
Graham

P W D L F   A Pts   *Attendance:* 32,000
8 5 2 1 15 6 12   *Referee:* A. McKenzie

Aberdonian Colin Jackson, the Rangers' pivot, slices the
ball over McCloy's head to put the Dons ahead. It was a
piece of fortune they deserved, for Aberdeen were
clearly the better side.

No 9 Saturday, 24 October
ST MIRREN (0) 1   ABERDEEN (1) 3
  Hamilton (79)   Robb (19), Murray (55),
                           Forrest (73)
ST MIRREN: McCann, McFadden, Brown, Fulton,
C. Murray, Munro, McKean, Gilshan, Knox,
Hamilton, Lister
ABERDEEN: Clark, Boel, Hermiston, S. Murray,
McMillan, M. Buchan, Taylor, Harper, Forrest, Robb,
Graham

P W D L F   A Pts   *Attendance:* 3,000
9 6 2 1 18 7 14   *Referee:* J. Callaghan

When Hamilton scored by taking the ball round Clark
in the 79th minute it turned out to be the last goal
Aberdeen would concede till 16 January.

No 10 Saturday, 31 October
ABERDEEN (1) 4   DUNDEE UNITED (0) 0
  Robb (44), S. Murray (62),
  Harper 2 (80, 89)
ABERDEEN: Clark, Boel, Hermiston, S. Murray,
McMillan, M. Buchan, Taylor, Robb, Forrest, Harper,
Graham
DUNDEE UNITED: McAlpine, Markland,
J. Cameron, Stevenson, Smith, Henry, Wilson,
A. Reid, K. Cameron, Gordon (Gillespie), Traynor

Leading positions
                  P   W   D   L   F   A Pts
1 Celtic   10 9   0   1   26 5   18
2 ABERDEEN   10 7   2   1   22 7   16
3 Rangers   9   6   1   2   18 5   13
4 St Johnstone   9   5   3   1   18 8   13

Attendance: 10,000   *Referee:* A. F. McDonald

What a strange sight, Aberdeen playing in royal blue
shirts and shorts and white socks – imitating Chelsea?
With United playing in all-tangerine there were some
vivid colours for the eye to behold. Alas, the filthy
weather turned the strip of both sides into an insipid
grey. United's Hamish McAlpine in goal was a busy
man.

No 11 Saturday, 7 November
ABERDEEN (1) 3   CLYDE (0) 0
  Harper 2 (15, 52),
  Hermiston (55)
ABERDEEN: Clark, Boel, Hermiston, S. Murray,
McMillan, M. Buchan, Taylor (Willoughby), Robb,
Forrest, Harper, Graham
CLYDE: Wallace, Burns, Mulherron (McColligan),
Beattie, McGoldrick, McHugh, Sullivan, Hay, Hulston,
Flanagan, Hastings

P   W D L F   A Pts   *Attendance:* 13,000
11 8 2 1 25 7 18   *Referee:* E. H. Pringle

Such was Aberdeen's early dominance that the crowd
expected a feast of goals. They got a morsel in the first
half and enjoyed two more in the second.

No 12 Saturday, 14 November
AYR UNITED (0) 0   ABERDEEN (1) 1
                           Harper (44)
AYR: Stewart, Filippi, Murphy, McAnespie, Fleming,
Mitchell, Young, McFadzean, McLean, Whitehead
(Reynolds), McGovern
ABERDEEN: Clark, Boel, Hermiston, S. Murray,
McMillan, M. Buchan, Willoughby, Robb, Forrest,
Harper, Graham

P   W D L F   A Pts   *Attendance:* 11,500
12 9 2 1 26 7 20   *Referee:* P. Hunter

Aberdeen took only one of the chances that came their
way against struggling Ayr. Three players were booked,
including Robb and McMillan of Aberdeen.

No 13 Saturday, 21 November
ABERDEEN (0) 1   HEARTS (0) 0
  Harper (60 pen)
ABERDEEN: Clark, Boel, Hermiston, S. Murray,
McMillan, M. Buchan, Willoughby, Robb, Forrest,
Harper, Graham
HEARTS: Cruickshank, Clunie, Oliver, Thomson,
Anderson, Brown (Young), Winchester, Townsend,
Ford, Wood, Fleming

P   W   D L F   A Pts   *Attendance:* 13,500
13 10 2 1 27 7 22   *Referee:* J. McRoberts

Hearts are at the wrong end of the table, but they still
stretch Aberdeen all the way. When Harper was pulled
down from behind in the box he needed attention before
agreeing to take the penalty himself to give Aberdeen
their seventh successive win. With Celtic drawing at
Falkirk, the Dons are now only one point behind.

No 14 Saturday, 28 November
MOTHERWELL (0) 0   ABERDEEN (0) 2
                           Boel (48), Taylor (77)
MOTHERWELL: McCrae, Whiteford, Wark, Forsyth,
McCallum, Donnelly, Campbell, Watson, Deans, Muir,
Heron
ABERDEEN: Clark, Boel, Hermiston, S. Murray,
McMillan, M. Buchan, Taylor, Robb, Forrest, Harper,
Graham

P W D L F A Pts   *Attendance:* 10,000
14 11 2 1 29 7 24   *Referee:* I. M. D. Foote

Aberdeen took 45 minutes to become accustomed to the opposition and to the mud. When they had done so, they were always likely winners.

No 15 Saturday, 5 December
ABERDEEN (3) 7   COWDENBEATH (0) 0
  Kinnell 2 o.g.'s (26, 83),
  Graham (28), Harper
  3 (34, 79, 89), Murray (60)
ABERDEEN: Clark, Boel, Hermiston, S. Murray, McMillan, M. Buchan, Taylor, Robb, Forrest, Harper, Graham
COWDENBEATH: Wyllie, McLaughlin, Bostock, Taylor, Kinnell, Moore, McCullie, Dickson, Thomson, Kennedy (Laing), Ross

Leading positions

	P	W	D	L	F	A	Pts
1 Celtic	15	13	1	1	37	6	27
2 ABERDEEN	15	12	2	1	36	7	26
3 Rangers	15	8	3	4	29	12	19

Attendance: 14,000   *Referee:* A. J. Crawley

Doomed Cowdenbeath make an unhappy first league visit to Aberdeen for 30 years. It's all too much for their centre half Andy Kinnell who scores twice for Aberdeen. Next Saturday's clash with Celtic can hardly come quickly enough. It's already a two-horse race for the championship.

No 16 Saturday, 12 December
CELTIC (0) 0   ABERDEEN (0) 1
                             Harper (53)
CELTIC: Fallon, Craig, Gemmell, Murdoch, McNeill, Brogan, Johnstone, Connelly (Hood), Macari, Hay, Hughes
ABERDEEN: Clark, Boel, Hermiston, S. Murray, McMillan, M. Buchan, Taylor, Robb, Forrest (Willoughby), Harper, Graham

P W D L F A Pts   *Attendance:* 63,000
16 13 2 1 37 7 28   *Referee:* A. F. Webster

Aberdeen surge past Celtic to the top of the league as a result of this momentous win – their tenth in succession. Bobby Clark's goal was under siege after Harper's impertinent goal. Robb back-headed and Harper sprang forward to beat Fallon with his header.

No 17 Saturday, 19 December
ABERDEEN (1) 1   FALKIRK (0) 0
  Harper (19 pen)
ABERDEEN: Clark, Boel, Hermiston, S. Murray, McMillan, M. Buchan, Taylor, Robb, Forrest, Harper, Graham
FALKIRK: Rennie, Abel, McLaughlin, Markie, Miller, Gibson, Hoggan, Roxburgh, Ferguson, Shirra, Setterington

P W D L F A Pts   *Attendance:* 19,000
17 14 2 1 38 7 30   *Referee:* R. H. Davidson

Falkirk are having a good season. In fact their last defeat was in late September. George Miller, their captain was booked for protesting about the penalty, awarded when the ball struck Markie's arm. Alex Ferguson was often in trouble with the referee.

No 18 Saturday, 26 December
AIRDRIEONIANS (0) 0   ABERDEEN (1) 4
                           Taylor (35), Murray (57),
                           Harper 2 (65, 80)
AIRDRIE: McKenzie, Jonquin, McKay, Menzies, Goodwin, Whiteford, Wilson, McKinlay, Busby (Bird), Jarvie, Cowan
ABERDEEN: Clark, Boel, Hermiston, S. Murray, McMillan, M. Buchan, Taylor (Willoughby), Robb, Forrest, Harper, Graham

P W D L F A Pts   *Attendance:* 8,000
18 15 2 1 42 7 32   *Referee:* J. W. Paterson

It wasn't that Airdrie were bad. It was simply that Aberdeen were better – much better. When will this run end? How many goals is Joe Harper going to end up with?

No 19 Friday, 1 January
ABERDEEN (2) 3   DUNDEE (0) 0
  McMillan (11), S. Murray
  (27), Graham (89)
ABERDEEN: Clark, Boel, Hermiston, S. Murray, McMillan, M. Buchan, Willoughby, Robb, Forrest, Harper, Graham
DUNDEE: Donaldson, R. Wilson, Soutar, Selway, Phillip, Houston, Gilroy, Kinninmonth, Wallace, Scott, Johnston (Falconer)

P W D L F A Pts   *Attendance:* 24,000
19 16 2 1 45 7 34   *Referee:* R. Gordon

A standing ovation from Pittodrie for this scintillating performance – summed up by Arthur Graham's last-minute goal. He veered 25 yards infield from the wing to beat Donaldson from a similar distance.

No 20 Saturday, 2 January
ST JOHNSTONE (0) 0   ABERDEEN (0) 1
                            Forrest (76)
ST JOHNSTONE: Donaldson, Lambie, Argue, Rooney, Gordon, Rennie, Aird, Hall, Connelly, McPhee, McCarry
ABERDEEN: Clark, Boel, Hermiston, S. Murray, McMillan, M. Buchan, Willoughby, Robb, Forrest, Harper, Graham

P W D L F A Pts   *Attendance:* 21,500
20 17 2 1 46 7 36   *Referee:* B. Padden

St Johnstone were in third position – ten points behind the Dons. Now the gap is twelve points. Joe Harper didn't score, but he did the next best thing, flashing the ball across the goal for Jim Forrest to net. Thereafter there were 21 players in Aberdeen's half.

No 21 Saturday, 9 January
ABERDEEN (1) 3   KILMARNOCK (0) 0
  Robb (25), Forrest (64),
  Willoughby (71)
ABERDEEN: Clark, Boel, Hermiston, S. Murray, McMillan, M. Buchan, Willoughby, Robb, Forrest, Harper, Graham
KILMARNOCK: Hunter, Whyte, Dickson, Gilmour, McGrory, McDonald (Morrison), McLean, Graham, Mathie, Cairns, Cook
Leading positions

	P	W	D	L	F	A	Pts
1 ABERDEEN	21	18	2	1	49	7	38
2 Celtic	20	16	2	2	45	10	34
3 Rangers	20	10	4	6	37	20	24

Attendance: 18,000   *Referee:* E. Thomson

The facts are astonishing. This was Aberdeen's 15th straight win and their twelfth game without losing a goal. The last player to score against them was Hamilton of St Mirren on 24 October. There was a minute's silence before the kick-off out of respect for the victims of the Ibrox tragedy. Jim Whyte didn't do much against his old club.

No 22 Saturday, 16 January
HIBERNIAN (0) 2   ABERDEEN (0) 1
  Stanton (64), Baker (68)   Robb (84)
HIBERNIAN: Baines, Brownlie, Jones, Blackley, Black, Stanton, Duncan, O'Rourke, Baker, Hamilton, Davidson (Blair)
ABERDEEN: Clark, Boel, G. Murray, S. Murray, McMillan, M. Buchan, Willoughby, Robb, Forrest, Harper, Graham

P	W	D	L	F	A	Pts
22	18	2	2	50	9	38

Attendance: 23,400   *Referee:* J. H. McKee

Hibs have got it in for Aberdeen this season, as Aberdeen return to the ground where they lost 4-0 in the League Cup. Stanton's raging cross-shot puts an end to Aberdeen's defensive record. Four minutes later Joe Baker – captain for the day on his return to the club – is unmarked as his header beats Clark to send Easter Road into raptures.

No 23 Saturday, 30 January
ABERDEEN (3) 3   MORTON (1) 1
  Harper (30), Taylor   Bartram (14)
  2 (35, 40)
ABERDEEN: Clark, Boel, Hermiston, S. Murray, McMillan, M. Buchan, Taylor, Robb, Forrest, Harper, Graham
MORTON: Sorensen, Murray, Laughton, Sweeney, Gray, Rankin, Hannigan, O'Neill, Bartram, Masch, Thomson

P	W	D	L	F	A	Pts
23	19	2	2	53	10	40

Attendance: 18,000   *Referee:* T. Marshall

This otherwise insignificant result means that Aberdeen have now beaten every one of their opponents in the league this season. The following Wednesday Jim

Forrest came on as a substitute for Scotland against Belgium in Liège.

No 24 Saturday, 6 February
DUNFERMLINE   ABERDEEN (0) 0
  ATHLETIC (1) 1
  Robertson (42)
DUNFERMLINE: McGarr, Thomson, Lunn, Fraser, Cushley, McNicoll, Edwards, Mitchell, McBride, Gardner, Robertson
ABERDEEN: Clark, Boel, Hermiston, S. Murray, McMillan, M. Buchan, Taylor (Willoughby), Robb, Forrest, Harper, Graham

P	W	D	L	F	A	Pts
24	19	2	3	53	11	40

Attendance: 9,000   *Referee:* A. J. Crawley

Dunfermline are next to bottom. Their goalkeeper is former Don Ernie McGarr. He isn't overworked. Fortunately Celtic lost at St Johnstone. Unfortunately, fire engulfed the main stand at Pittodrie while the players were away.

No 25 Saturday, 20 February
ABERDEEN (0) 0   RANGERS (0) 0
ABERDEEN: Clark, Boel, Hermiston, S. Murray, McMillan, M. Buchan, Taylor, Robb, Forrest, Hamilton (Willoughby), Graham
RANGERS: McCloy, Jardine, Mathieson, Greig, McKinnon, Jackson, Henderson, McDonald, Johnstone (Conn), Smith, Johnston
Leading positions

	P	W	D	L	F	A	Pts
1 ABERDEEN	25	19	3	3	53	11	41
2 Celtic	24	19	2	3	60	15	40
3 St Johnstone	25	14	4	7	45	36	32
4 Rangers	24	12	6	6	41	22	30

Attendance: 36,000   *Referee:* A. McKenzie

This is a vital point dropped, for Celtic now have the advantage with their game in hand. It was a game contested entirely in midfield. Neither goalkeeper was extended, and neither side was able to derive a psychological advantage for their future meetings in the Scottish Cup. Dave Robb and Colin Jackson were booked.

No 26 Saturday, 27 February
ABERDEEN (0) 1   ST MIRREN (1) 1
  Forrest (63)   Munro (20)
ABERDEEN: Clark, Boel, Hermiston, S. Murray, McMillan, M. Buchan, Taylor (Willoughby), Robb, Forrest, Harper, Graham
ST MIRREN: Connaghan, Connell, McLaughlin, Murray, McQueen, Fulton, McKean, Blair, Knox, Munro, Lawson

P	W	D	L	F	A	Pts
26	19	4	3	54	12	42

Attendance: 15,000   *Referee:* S. Anderson

Aberdeen are wobbling. Struggling Saints snatch a first-half lead and then defend it by fair means or foul. But it could have been worse: Celtic could only draw at

Hearts. Eddie Turnbull has now been Aberdeen manager for six years.

No 27 Wednesday, 10 March
DUNDEE UNITED (0) 0   ABERDEEN (1) 2
                      M. Buchan (22),
                      Forrest (64)
DUNDEE UNITED: McAlpine, Rolland, J. Cameron, W. Smith, D. Smith, Stevenson, Wilson, A. Reid, Copland, Gordon, Traynor (Henry)
ABERDEEN: Clark, Boel, Hermiston, M. Buchan, McMillan, Young, Forrest (Willoughby), S. Murray, G. Buchan, Taylor, Graham

P	W	D	L	F	A	Pts
27	20	4	3	56	12	44

Attendance: 7,000
Referee: E. H. Pringle

Aberdeen, minus Harper and Robb, are simply too strong for United. Martin Buchan abandons his sweeper's role and turns goal-scorer.

No 28 Saturday, 13 March
CLYDE (1) 1   ABERDEEN (2) 2
  Flanagan (33)   McGoldrick o.g. (4),
                          Forrest (7)
CLYDE: McCulloch, Anderson, Mulherron, Beattie, McGoldrick, McHugh, Sullivan, Hay, Flanagan, Burns, Hastings
ABERDEEN: Clark, Boel, Hermiston, M. Buchan, McMillan, Young, G. Buchan (Taylor), S. Murray, Forrest, Robb, Graham

P	W	D	L	F	A	Pts
28	21	4	3	58	12	46

Attendance: 4,500
Referee: J. R. Grant

Robb's shot is wickedly deflected by McGoldrick and Aberdeen are on their way. Within minutes Forrest dribbles round McCulloch to put the Dons two up. Then they fall back on an unpopular offside trap which produced the slow handclap at Shawfield.

No 29 Wednesday, 24 March
ABERDEEN (1) 4   AYR UNITED (0) 1
  Robb (43), Graham (52),   Ingram (65)
  Forrest (55), Murray (86)
ABERDEEN: Clark, Boel, Hermiston, S. Murray, McMillan, M. Buchan, Forrest, Robb, Harper, Graham, G. Buchan
AYR: Stewart, Filippi, Murphy, Fleming, Quinn, Mitchell, Young, McGovern, Ingram, McCulloch (Doyle), Rough

P	W	D	L	F	A	Pts
29	22	4	3	62	13	48

Attendance: 18,000
Referee: W. J. Mullen

Jim Forrest scores his 200th goal in senior football in Scotland. By then the Dons are coasting.

No 30 Saturday, 27 March
HEARTS (1) 1   ABERDEEN (0) 3
  Ford (8)   Robb 3 (46, 60, 85)
HEARTS: Cruickshank, Clunie, Kay, Thomson, **Anderson, Brown, Carruthers** (Veitch), Fleming, Ford, **Wood, Lynch**

ABERDEEN: Clark, Boel, Hermiston, S. Murray, Young, M. Buchan, Forrest, Robb, Harper, Graham, G. Buchan

	P	W	D	L	F	A	Pts
1 ABERDEEN	30	23	4	3	65	14	50
2 Celtic	28	22	3	3	74	18	47

Attendance: 13,500
Referee: R. Henderson

The finishing post is in sight. Aberdeen must not only win all their games: they must hope that Celtic drop a point or two. The match at Tynecastle was blood and thunder. Ford dispossessed Martin Buchan to put Hearts in front. There followed a famous hat-trick for Dave Robb and less-than-famous bookings for Boel and Hermiston. What might have happened had Fleming's penalty been more accurate when Hearts led 1-0?

No 31 Saturday, 3 April
ABERDEEN (0) 0   MOTHERWELL (0) 0
ABERDEEN: Clark, Boel, Hermiston, S. Murray (Taylor), McMillan, M. Buchan, Forrest, Robb, Harper, Graham, G. Buchan
MOTHERWELL: MacRae, Whiteford, Wark, Forsyth, McCallum, Goldthorp, Martin, Watson, Lawson, Muir, Heron

Leading positions

	P	W	D	L	F	A	Pts
1 ABERDEEN	31	23	5	3	65	14	51
2 Celtic	28	22	3	3	74	18	47

Attendance: 13,000
Referee: J. Callaghan

This could be the result that deprives Aberdeen of the championship. They couldn't come to grips with a swirling wind or the fact that Bobby Brown was watching them. The nearest they came was a late header by George Buchan that hit the bar.

No 32 Saturday, 10 April
COWDENBEATH (1) 1   ABERDEEN (1) 2
  Boel o.g. (11)   Bostock o.g. (4),
                          G. Buchan (76)
COWDENBEATH: McArthur, McLaughlan, Bostock, Taylor, Kinnell, Moore, McCullie (Judge), Dickson, Laing, Kennedy, Thomson
ABERDEEN: Clark, Williamson, Hermiston, M. Buchan, Boel, McMillan, Forrest, Robb, G. Buchan, Harper (Willoughby), Graham

Leading positions

	P	W	D	L	F	A	Pts
1 ABERDEEN	32	24	5	3	67	15	53
2 Celtic	29	22	4	3	75	19	48

Attendance: 4,000
Referee: P. Hunter

Aberdeen make hard work of beating bottom-placed Cowdenbeath – but Celtic drop a home point to Dundee United. George Buchan's late header could yet be decisive.

No 33 Saturday, 17 April
ABERDEEN (1) 1   CELTIC (1) 1
  Willoughby (38)   Hood (3)
ABERDEEN: Clark, Boel, Hermiston, S. Murray, McMillan, M. Buchan, Forrest, Willoughby, Robb, Graham, G. Buchan (Harper)

CELTIC: Williams, Craig, Brogan, Connelly, McNeill, Hay, Johnstone, Lennox, Wallace, Callaghan, Hood (Quinn)

Leading positions

	P	W	D	L	F	A	Pts
1 ABERDEEN	33	24	6	3	68	16	54
2 Celtic	31	23	5	3	79	20	51

Attendance: 35,000   *Referee:* W. Anderson

An all-ticket match. Aberdeen desperately needed both points which could have sewn up the title. But near the start Harry Hood – Scotland's leading marksman – hooked home Johnstone's corner. A corner also brought Aberdeen's equaliser. In the second half Arthur Graham took the ball round Williams but shot against McNeill who had raced back onto the goal-line. The title is now Celtic's for the taking. On Wednesday, 21 April Clark and Robb were in the Scotland team beaten 2-0 by Portugal in Lisbon.

No 34 Saturday, 24 April

FALKIRK (1) 1   ABERDEEN (0) 0
Miller (22 pen)

FALKIRK: Rennie, Abel, McLaughlan, Markie, Miller, Gibson, Hoggan, Ferguson, McLeod, Shirra, Setterington

ABERDEEN: Clark, Boel, Hermiston, S. Murray, McMillan, M. Buchan, Forrest, Robb, Harper, Graham, Willoughby

Attendance: 8,000   *Referee:* J. C. B. McRoberts

Aberdeen had to win to exert maximum pressure on Celtic. But Robb handled Miller's free kick – and that was that.

Aberdeen's complete home and away record:

HOME						AWAY						
P	W	D	L	F	A	W	D	L	F	A		Pts
34	11	6	0	38	7	13	0	4	30	11		54

Scottish League Division One

	P	W	D	L	F	A	Pts
1 Celtic	34	25	6	3	89	23	56
2 ABERDEEN	34	24	6	4	68	18	54
3 St Johnstone	34	19	6	9	59	44	44
4 Rangers	34	16	9	9	58	34	41
5 Dundee	34	14	10	10	53	45	38
6 Dundee United	34	14	8	12	53	54	36
7 Falkirk	34	13	9	12	46	53	35
8 Morton	34	13	8	13	44	44	34
9 Motherwell	34	13	8	13	43	47	34
10 Airdrieonians	34	13	8	13	60	65	34
11 Hearts	34	13	7	14	41	40	33
12 Hibernian	34	10	10	14	47	53	30
13 Kilmarnock	34	10	8	16	43	67	28
14 Ayr United	34	9	8	17	37	54	26
15 Clyde	34	8	10	16	33	59	26
16 Dunfermline	34	6	11	17	44	56	23
17 St Mirren	34	7	9	18	38	56	23
18 Cowdenbeath	34	7	3	24	33	77	17

LEAGUE CUP

Saturday, 8 August

AIRDRIEONIANS (0) 1   ABERDEEN (1) 1
Menzies (78)   S. Murray (44)

AIRDRIE: McKenzie, Jonquin, Caldwell, Goodwin, Delaney, Whiteford, Wilson, Jarvie, Marshall (Menzies), McPheat, Cowan

ABERDEEN: Clark, Whyte, G. Murray, Hermiston, McMillan, M. Buchan, Forrest, S. Murray, Robb, Harper, Graham

Referee: E. H. Pringle

Murray scored after Hermiston's shot was blocked. Airdrie's sub equalised.

Wednesday, 12 August

ABERDEEN (1) 2   ST JOHNSTONE (0) 1
Harper (17), Robb (58)   Hall (68)

ABERDEEN: Clark, Boel, G. Murray, Hermiston, McMillan, M. Buchan, Forrest, S. Murray, Robb, Harper (G. Buchan), Graham

ST JOHNSTONE: Donaldson, McManus, Argue, Gordon, Rooney, Rennie (McPhee), Aird, Hall, Whitelaw, Connolly, Leslie

Attendance: 13,500   *Referee:* J. R. P. Gordon

Aberdeen are so much on top that it's an hour before Clark has a shot to save. Jim Donaldson at the other end performs wonders.

Saturday, 15 August

ABERDEEN (0) 1   HIBERNIAN (1) 1
Robb (46)   Duncan (41)

ABERDEEN: Clark, Boel, G. Murray, Hermiston, McMillan, M. Buchan, Forrest, S. Murray, Robb, Harper, Graham

HIBERNIAN: Marshall, Brownlie, Schaedler, Blackley, Black, Stanton, Stevenson, Graham, McBride, Hamilton, Duncan

Attendance: 16,000   *Referee:* T. Marshall

Scotland manager Bobby Brown watched this hard-fought affair. Robb equalised with a deft back-header. This result leaves Hibs as favourites to qualify.

Wednesday, 19 August

ST JOHNSTONE (0) 0   ABERDEEN (1) 1
                                     Forrest (44)

ST JOHNSTONE: Donaldson, McManus, Argue, Rooney, Gordon, Rennie, Muir, Hall, Connolly, McPhee, Aitken

ABERDEEN: Clark, Boel, G. Murray, Hermiston, McMillan, M. Buchan, Forrest, S. Murray (Hamilton), Robb, Willoughby, G. Buchan

Attendance: 3,300   *Referee:* R. C. Greenlees

Willoughby's inspired pass opens St Johnstone's defence for Forrest to score. The home team had to contend with Aberdeen's offside trap which four times required Clark to clear outside his box in the second half.

Saturday, 22 August
ABERDEEN (5) 7   AIRDRIEONIANS (1) 3
  Harper 4 (18, 20, 36 pen,   Jarvie (23), Cowan (63),
  89), Robb (25), Boel (35),   Busby (71)
  Jonquin o.g. (86)
ABERDEEN: Clark, Boel, G. Murray, Hermiston,
McMillan, M. Buchan, Forrest, Hamilton, Robb,
Harper, Graham
AIRDRIE: McKenzie, Jonquin, Caldwell, Goodwin,
Delaney, D. Whiteford, Wilson, Jarvie, Busby,
McPheat, Cowan
Attendance: 12,000   *Referee:* A. F. McDonald
For the first 45 minutes Aberdeen were irresistible. For
the second they fell apart as if by the turn of a switch.
But two more goals in the last four minutes mean that
they have overtaken Hibs on goal difference.

Wednesday, 26 August
HIBERNIAN (4) 4   ABERDEEN (0) 0
  Stanton (7), Graham (24),
  Duncan (31),
  McBride (40)
HIBERNIAN: Marshall, Brownlie, Schaedler,
Blackley, Black, Stanton, Stevenson, Graham, McBride
McEwan, Duncan
ABERDEEN: Clark, Boel, G. Murray, Hermiston,
McMillan, M. Buchan, Forrest, S. Murray, Robb,
Harper, Graham
Attendance: 24,900   *Referee:* J. Callaghan
Aberdeen wanted only a draw to book a quarter-final
appearance with Rangers. They held on for only seven
minutes, whereupon McBride drove a free kick across
the box and Stanton hooked the ball into the net off a
post. Thereafter the match turned into a nightmare for
the Dons' defence.

Section 4

	P	W	D	L	F	A	Pts
Hibernian	6	4	2	0	16	7	10
ABERDEEN	6	3	2	1	12	10	8
Airdrieonians	6	2	1	3	10	15	5
St Johnstone	6	0	1	5	3	9	1

SCOTTISH CUP

1st Round Monday, 25 January
ABERDEEN (2) 5   ELGIN CITY (0) 0
  Taylor (30),
  Forrest 2 (35, 84),
  Harper 2 (72, 89)
ABERDEEN: Clark, Boel, Hermiston, S. Murray,
McMillan, M. Buchan, Taylor (Willoughby), Robb,
Forrest, Harper, Graham
ELGIN: Lawtie, Gerrard, Cowie, Soutar, Grant,
Shewan, Duncan, Douglas, McArthur, Graham,
Macdonald (Thom)
Attendance: 24,136   *Referee:* J. R. P. Gordon
This match was postponed from the Saturday because of
torrential rain. An eagerly awaited all-North East clash

could have gone Elgin's way had Soutar done better
than shoot straight into Clark's arms when in the clear.
It was then 0-0. Pittodrie welcomed back former
stalwart Ally Shewan, sold to Elgin for £3,000.

2nd Round Saturday, 13 February
DUNDEE UNITED (1) 1 ABERDEEN (0) 1
  D. Smith (40 pen)   Forrest (75)
DUNDEE UNITED: McAlpine, Rolland, J. Cameron,
W. Smith, D. Smith, Stevenson, Wilson, A. Reid,
Gordon, Henry, Traynor
ABERDEEN: Clark, Boel, Hermiston, S. Murray,
McMillan, M. Buchan, Willoughby (Taylor), Robb,
Forrest, Harper, Graham
                              Referee: R. H. Davidson
An all-ticket match. Aberdeen lost a penalty when Boel
rugby-tackled Alan Gordon. After Forrest had
equalised, Harper took the ball round McAlpine but
Walter Smith got back to clear off the line. Both teams
wore black armbands out of respect for Aberdeen
director Douglas Philip, who died the previous evening.

2nd Round Replay Wednesday, 17 February
ABERDEEN (0) 2   DUNDEE UNITED (0) 0
  Boel (67), Robb (88)
ABERDEEN: Clark, Boel, Hermiston, S. Murray,
McMillan, M. Buchan, Taylor, Robb, Forrest, Harper
(Willoughby), Graham
DUNDEE UNITED: McAlpine, Rolland, Cameron,
W. Smith, D. Smith, Stevenson, Wilson, Reid (Scott),
Gordon, Henry, Traynor
Attendance: 29,000   *Referee:* R. H. Davidson
Aberdeen's biggest gate of the season crams inside the
fire-damaged stadium. Harper collides with Hamish
McAlpine at the start of the second half and goes off to
have eight stitches in a shin gash. United held the Dons
at bay until Boel swooped on to Robb's header to score
off a post.

Quarter Final Saturday, 6 March
RANGERS (0) 1   ABERDEEN (0) 0
  Jackson (67)
RANGERS: McCloy, Jardine, Mathieson, Greig,
McKinnon, Jackson, Henderson, Conn (MacDonald),
Stein, Smith, Johnston
ABERDEEN: Clark, Boel, Hermiston, S. Murray,
McMillan, M. Buchan, Taylor (Willoughby), Robb,
Forrest, Harper, Graham
Attendance: 65,000   *Referee:* W. J. Mullen
A scrappy game, but Rangers were undeniably the
better side. It was Dons' captain Martin Buchan's 22nd
birthday, but his team were beaten by Aberdonian Colin
Jackson's goal after Greig's effort had come back off the
bar. Jackson must have felt relieved: it was his own-goal
which had set the Dons on the victory road at Ibrox in
the league. The Dons have now relinquished their hold
on the Scottish Cup.

EUROPEAN CUP-WINNERS CUP

1st Round, 1st Leg Wednesday, 16 September
ABERDEEN (2) 3   HONVED (Hungary) (1) 1
    Graham (14), Harper   Pusztai (9)
    (34), S. Murray (83)

ABERDEEN: Clark, Hermiston, G. Murray
(Hamilton), S. Murray, Boel, M. Buchan, McKay
(G. Buchan), Robb, Forrest, Harper, Graham

HONVED: Bicskei, Molnar, Ruzsinszky, Pusztai
(Pinter), Vari, Vagi, Tajfi, Toth, Kocsis, Komora,
Szurgent

Attendance: 21,500   *Referee:* A. Bucheli
                                        (Switzerland)

A night to remember. The white-clad Hungarians take a
surprise lead when Pusztai is on hand after Clark turned
Kocsis' 25-yarder onto a post. Aberdeen retaliated in
the best possible way, leading 2-1 at half-time. Honved
were pushed back but were forced to concede a third
goal when Steve Murray held off two challenges before
scoring. Afterwards, the Hungarian manager
complained that Harper's goal had been offside.

1st Round, 2nd Leg Wednesday, 30 September
HONVED (1) 3   ABERDEEN (0) 1
    Kocsis 2 (17, 67),   S. Murray (77)
    Kosma (59)

HONVED: Bicskei, Tajfi, Ruzsinszky, Marosi, Vari
(Toth), Vagi, Pusztai, Kocsis, Pinter, Kosma, Karakas
(Tichy)

ABERDEEN: Clark, Boel, Hermiston, G. Murray,
Young (Willoughby), M. Buchan, Robb, Harper,
Forrest, S. Murray, Graham

Aggregate score 4-4. Honved won 5-4 on penalties

                    Referee: C. Lo Bello (Italy)

Agony for Aberdeen – and for Jim Forrest. Honved
halved Aberdeen's lead with a linesman flagging
furiously for offside. Kosma, unmarked, later chipped
the ball over Clark to put Honved ahead on the away
goals rule. Kocsis blasted a third from a twice-taken free
kick. At last Steve Murray scored off a defender to level
the scores and take the tie into extra time – and to
penalties. It was 2 penalties each when Jim Forrest's hit
the bar. Honved's winning penalty was taken by their
keeper.

1970-71

APPEARANCES	League	League Cup	Scottish Cup	Cup Winners Cup
M. Buchan	34	6	4	2
Clark	34	6	4	2
Boel	34	5	4	2
S. Murray	33	5	4	2
Robb	32	6	4	2
Harper	30(+1)	5	4	2
Forrest	31(+1)	6	4	2
Graham	31	5	4	2
Hermiston	31	6	4	2
McMillan	27	6	4	
Taylor	14(+2)		3(+1)	
G. Buchan	12	1(+1)		−(+1)
Willoughby	10(+9)	1	1(+3)	−(+1)
Young	9			1
Hamilton	5(+1)	1(+1)		
G. Murray	4(+1)	6		2
McKay	2			1
Williamson	1			
Whyte		1		
19 players				

GOALS	Total	League	League Cup	Scottish Cup	Cup Winners Cup
Harper	27	19	5	2	1
Robb	13	9	3	1	
Forrest	12	8	1	3	
S. Murray	9	6	1		2
Graham	6	5			1
Taylor	5	4		1	
Boel	4	2	1	1	
M. Buchan	2	2			
Willoughby	2	2			
Hamilton	2	2			
G. Buchan	1	1			
Hermiston	1	1			
McMillan	1	1			
own-goals	7	6	1		
Total	92	68	12	8	4

Season 1971-72

A quick look at the league table tells that in 1971-72 Aberdeen finished second to Celtic – as they had done a year earlier. But that bald fact does not tell of the drama behind the scenes. The season had yet to begin when manager Eddie Turnbull announced he was leaving Pittodrie for Hibernian, the club with which he had grown to fame in the 1940s and '50s. Aberdeen duly promoted coach Jimmy Bonthrone to the hot seat.

The new boss was not to find instant success. Aberdeen looked to be heading for the quarter finals of the League Cup, but successive 3-1 defeats at Dundee and Falkirk cost them their continuing involvement in that competition.

In the league, however, it was a different story. The Dons even surpassed the start they had made the previous season. On the morning of Saturday, 27 November 1971 Aberdeen had won ten and drawn two of their opening twelve league fixtures. That month had already been a notable one in the club's history. Not only had Pittodrie staged a full international for the first time – against Belgium – but it had also had its turf blessed by the glittering talents of Juventus in the UEFA Cup. Aberdeen went out, but there was no need for tears or shame.

But when Donald Ford scored twice for Hearts in the last four minutes on that Saturday in November it brought about Aberdeen's first home defeat since March 1970 – again inflicted by Hearts. Celtic leapfrogged over Aberdeen to the head of the league and steadily widened the gap to ten points by the season's end.

All hope of Aberdeen sustaining their title challenge effectively ended in February when club captain Martin Buchan was transferred to Manchester United for £125,000. Rarely have Aberdeen supporters been so pained by the transfer of one of their young heroes. A pall of gloom hung over Aberdeen FC for months to come, made worse when Hibs booted a Buchan-less Dons team out of the Scottish Cup.

As with 1970-71, the league season was just too long for Aberdeen. They garnered 30 points from their first 17 games: only 20 from the last 17. As Winter turned into Spring Aberdeen forgot the knack of scoring on opponents' grounds.

But if there was one jewel in Aberdeen's ultimately frustrating season, it came in the shape of Joe Harper. His 33 league goals were a post-War record for the club. English hawks were poised to swoop . . .

> League: Second
> League Cup: Third in qualifying group
> Scottish Cup: Quarter Final
> UEFA Cup: Second Round

SCOTTISH LEAGUE DIVISION ONE

No 1 Saturday, 4 September
ABERDEEN (0) 3   DUNDEE (0)
  Willoughby (59),
  Robb (68), Harper (69)

ABERDEEN: Clark, Boel, Hermiston, S. Murray (Taylor), Young, M. Buchan, Forrest, Robb, Harper, Willoughby, Graham

DUNDEE: Hewitt, Wilson, Johnston, Steele, Phillip, Houston, Duncan, (Bryce), Kinninmonth, Wallace, Scott, Lambie

P W D L F A Pts   *Attendance:* 15,000
1 1 0 0 3 0 2   *Referee:* E. H. Pringle

The third meeting of the clubs this season and Aberdeen's first win. They struggled early on, but Willoughby's header just beat Hewitt's effort to save. Harper's goal was a jewel, beating two men on the left before cutting in.

No 2 Saturday, 11 September
ST JOHNSTONE (1) 1   ABERDEEN (1) 1
  Hall (10)   Robb (30)
ST JOHNSTONE: Donaldson, Lambie, Coburn, Rennie, Gordon, Rooney, Aird, Hall, Pearson, Connolly, Aitken
ABERDEEN: Clark, Boel, Hermiston, S. Murray, Young, M. Buchan, Forrest, Robb, Harper, Taylor, Graham

P W D L F A Pts   *Attendance:* 8,000
2 1 1 0 4 1 3   *Referee:* R. Gordon

Dave Robb entered the referee's book twice; once for his goal – once for a naughty foul. Aberdeen deserved both points for their second-half offensive, but Forrest's aim was wanting and Harper was thwarted by a post.

No 3 Saturday, 18 September
ABERDEEN (2) 5   AIRDRIEONIANS (0) 0
  Harper 2 (12, 15)
  Graham (71),
  Robb 2 (72, 78)
ABERDEEN: Geoghegan, Boel, Hermiston, S. Murray, Young, M. Buchan, Forrest, Robb, Harper (Taylor), Willoughby, Graham
AIRDRIE: Gourlay, Jonquin, McKay, Delaney, Goodwin, Whiteford, Wilson, Menzies, Busby, Jarvie, Cowan

P W D L F A Pts   *Attendance:* 15,000
3 2 1 0 9 1 5   *Referee:* J. P. Gordon

Aberdeen follow up their good result in Spain in the UEFA Cup with another at home. An injury to Clark gives Geoghegan his first taste of the Big Time. Harper scores twice before being substituted in the second half.

No 4 Saturday, 25 September
RANGERS (0) 0   ABERDEEN (1) 2
            S. Murray (37),
            Harper (78)
RANGERS: McCloy, Jardine, Mathieson, Greig, Jackson, Smith, Penman, Conn, Stein, MacDonald (McLean), Johnston
ABERDEEN: Geoghegan, Boel, Hermiston, S. Murray, Young, M. Buchan, Forrest, Robb, Harper, Willoughby (Taylor), Miller
Leading positions

	P	W	D	L	F	A	Pts
1 Celtic	4	4	0	0	20	4	8
2 Hibernian	4	4	0	0	9	2	8
3 ABERDEEN	4	3	1	0	11	1	7

Attendance: 38,000   *Referee:* A. McKenzie

This is Rangers' third defeat in four league matches. It was also the fourth time Aberdeen have won at Ibrox in the league in the past five seasons. Rangers didn't take kindly to it – they forced umpteen corners.

No 5 Saturday, 2 October
ABERDEEN (1) 2   DUNFERMLINE
  Harper (23 pen)   ATHLETIC (0) 0
  S. Murray (81)
ABERDEEN: Geoghegan, Boel, G. Murray, S. Murray, Young, M. Buchan, Forrest, Robb, Harper, Willoughby, Miller
DUNFERMLINE: McGarr, Callaghan, Mercer, Fraser, Cushley, McNicoll, Scott, Mitchell, Edwards, O'Neill, Gillespie (McBride)

P W D L F A Pts   *Attendance:* 16,000
5 4 1 0 13 1 9   *Referee:* J. Callaghan

Harper sends Ernie McGarr the wrong way with a spot-kick: Steve Murray left him equally helpless after he set up the chance. Bertie Miller was involved in both goals. With Celtic losing and Hibs drawing, Aberdeen go top. top.

No 6 Saturday, 9 October
KILMARNOCK (0) 0   ABERDEEN (0) 3
            Harper (62), S. Murray
            (75), Forrest (86)
KILMARNOCK: Hunter, Whyte, Cairns, Maxwell, Rodman, McGrory, Morrison, Gilmour, McCulloch, McSherry, Cook
ABERDEEN: Clark, G. Murray, Hermiston, S. Murray, Young, M. Buchan, Forrest, Robb, Harper, Willoughby, Miller

P W D L F A Pts   *Attendance:* 8,500
6 5 1 0 16 1 11   *Referee:* R. H. Davidson

A Juventus spy sitting in the stand at Rugby Park must have left impressed with Aberdeen. So was Bobby Brown. The following Wednesday Martin Buchan won his first full cap as a substitute in the 2-1 Hampden win over Portugal.

No 7 Saturday, 16 October
ABERDEEN (0) 2   HIBERNIAN (1) 1
  Harper (57),   Duncan (39)
  Young (65)
ABERDEEN: Clark, G. Murray, Hermiston, S. Murray, Young, M. Buchan, Forrest, Robb, Harper, Willoughby, Miller
HIBERNIAN: Herriot, Brownlie, Schaedler, Stanton, Black, Blackley, Duncan, Hamilton, Baker, Gordon, Cropley

P W D L F A Pts   *Attendance:* 25,000
7 6 1 0 18 2 13   *Referee:* J. W. Paterson

A grudge match: Eddie Turnbull's new team versus his old. His new'uns take the first round: his old'uns the second – and third.

No 8 Saturday, 23 October
MORTON (0) 0   ABERDEEN (1) 1
                  S. Murray (1)

MORTON: Sorensen, Hayes, Laughton, Lumsden, McDerment, Clark, Chalmers, Mason, Osborne, Murphy, Smith

ABERDEEN: Clark, G. Murray, Hermiston, S. Murray, Young, M. Buchan, Forrest, Robb, Harper, Willoughby, Graham

P W D L F A Pts   *Attendance:* 6,000
8 7 1 0 19 2 15   *Referee:* W. Anderson

Steve Murray's instant goal puts Aberdeen three points clear of Celtic. It's as well Aberdeen scored when they did. They didn't look likely to afterwards.

No 9 Saturday, 30 October
ABERDEEN (3) 7   PARTICK THISTLE (1) 2
  Forrest (4),   Young o.g. (40),
  Robb (25),   Bone (64)
  Harper 3 (29, 89, 90),
  Willoughby 2 (53, 80)

ABERDEEN: Clark, G. Murray, Hermiston, S. Murray, Young, M. Buchan, Forrest, Robb, Harper, Willoughby, Graham

PARTICK: Rough, Hansen, Forsyth, Clark, Campbell, Strachan (Gibson), McQuade, Coulston, Bone, A. Rae, Lawrie

P W D L F A Pts   *Attendance:* 20,000
9 8 1 0 26 4 17   *Referee:* n.a.

Partick Thistle are the new holders of the League Cup – but it got them nowhere. Allan Rough bungled Forrest's shot, letting it slip under his body. Best goal of them all was Willie Young's bullet header – into his own goal.

No 10 Saturday, 6 November
CELTIC (0) 1   ABERDEEN (0) 1
  Hood (60)   McNeill o.g. (78)

CELTIC: Connaghan, Craig, Brogan, Hay, McNeill, Connelly, Johnstone, Hood, Dalglish, Macari, Callaghan

ABERDEEN: Clark, G. Murray, Hermiston, S. Murray, Young, M. Buchan, Forrest, Robb, Harper, Willoughby, Graham

Leading Positions
	P	W	D	L	F	A	Pts
1 ABERDEEN	10	8	2	0	27	5	18
2 Celtic	10	8	1	1	28	8	17
3 Hibernian	10	6	1	3	20	8	13
4 Rangers	10	6	0	4	27	13	12

Attendance: 64,000   *Referee:* J. McRoberts

That's the way to do it. Aberdeen took an absolute battering from Celtic, and capitulated when Johnston's cross was controlled then fired past Clark by Harry Hood. That goal would have taken Celtic to the top of the league but for the assistance of Billy McNeill who, with no danger threatening moved in front of Connaghan to net into his own goal. At the death young Kenny Dalglish forced an agile save from Clark.

On Wednesday, 10 November Bobby Clark, Martin Buchan and Steve Murray were capped at Pittodrie against Belgium.

No 11 Saturday, 13 November
ABERDEEN (1) 5   EAST FIFE (0) 0
  Young (21), Robb
  (50), Harper (56),
  Taylor (75),
  Hermiston (84)

ABERDEEN: Clark, G. Murray, Hermiston, Taylor, Young, M. Buchan, Forrest, Robb, Harper, Willoughby (Miller), Graham

EAST FIFE: Gorman, Duncan, McQuade, Cairns, Martis, Clarke, Honeyman, Hamilton, Borthwick, Hughes, Dailey (Bernard)

P W D L F A Pts   *Attendance:* 14,000
11 9 2 0 32 5 20   *Referee:* R. B. Valentine

This wasn't fair. It was top versus bottom – and top won. Aberdeen hardly bothered to raise a sweat – which was just as well. Juventus are the visitors on Wednesday.

No 12 Saturday, 20 November
MOTHERWELL (0) 0   ABERDEEN (2) 4
                      S. Murray 2 (5, 89),
                      Forrest (33),
                      Harper (80)

MOTHERWELL: MacCrae, Gillespie, Main, Forsyth, John Muir, McInally, Campbell, Wark, Jim Muir, Goldthorpe, Heron (Lawson)

ABERDEEN: Clark, G. Murray, Hermiston, S. Murray, McMillan, M. Buchan, Forrest, Robb, Harper, Willoughby (Miller), Graham

P W D L F A Pts   *Attendance:* 6,250
12 10 2 0 36 5 22   *Referee:* R. D. Crawford

Aberdeen show no ill-effects after the experience of Juventus. Joe Harper had one shot kicked off the line; was booked for kicking the ball away – and then scored.

No 13 Saturday, 27 November
ABERDEEN (0) 2   HEARTS (0) 3
  Harper (69),   Ford 3 (54, 86, 87)
  Robb (73)

ABERDEEN: Clark, G. Murray, Hermiston, S. Murray, McMillan, M. Buchan, Forrest, Robb, Harper, Willoughby, Graham (Miller)

HEARTS: Cruickshank, Sneddon, Kay, Brown, Anderson, Thomson, Townsend, Benton, Ford, Winchester, T. Murray

Leading positions
	P	W	D	L	F	A	Pts
1 Celtic	13	11	1	1	40	10	23
2 ABERDEEN	13	10	2	1	38	8	22
3 Hearts	13	7	4	2	26	17	18

Attendance: 21,000   *Referee:* T. Marshall

Disaster for Aberdeen as they lose their first home league match for two seasons. The man who does the damage is Donald Ford, who began by putting Hearts ahead with an angled drive. Back came the Dons. Harper equalised; then Robb scored, leading to Heart's pivot Townsend being sent off for protesting. Ford replied with two late headers for 10-man Hearts.

No 14 Saturday, 4 December

AYR UNITED (0) 1	ABERDEEN (2) 5
Graham (88 pen)	Miller (14), Robb
	(23), S. Murray (47),
	Harper 2 (67, 78),

AYR: Stewart, Filippi, Murphy, Fleming, Campbell, Reynolds, Doyle, Graham, Ingram, McGovern, Stevenson

ABERDEEN: Clark, G. Murray, Hermiston, S. Murray, McMillan, M. Buchan, Forrest, Robb, Harper, Willoughby, Miller

P	W	D	L	F	A	Pts	*Attendance:* 8,000
14	11	2	1	43	9	24	*Referee:* J. R. Grant

Ayr had only two draws to show for their past seven games. They start off with high hopes but then Bertie Miller scores for Aberdeen direct from a corner. Robb was booked for the second successive week.

No 15 Saturday, 11 December

ABERDEEN (3) 4	CLYDE (1) 1
Willoughby (29),	McBride (17)
Harper (30),	
G. Murray (39),	
M. Buchan (75)	

ABERDEEN: Clark, G. Murray, Hermiston (Graham), S. Murray, McMillan, M. Buchan, Forrest, Robb, Harper, Willoughby, Miller

CLYDE: Cairney, Anderson, Swan, Burns, McHugh, Glasgow, Sullivan, McGrain, McBride, Hay, Ahern, (Hastings)

P	W	D	L	F	A	Pts	*Attendance:* 14,000
15	12	2	1	47	10	26	*Referee:* E. Thomson

Struggling Clyde have the nerve to go in front – and are taught a painful lesson. Bertie Miller was involved in three of Aberdeen's goals.

No 16 Saturday, 18 December

ABERDEEN (1) 3	DUNDEE UNITED (0) 0
S. Murray (24)	
Willoughby (67),	
Harper (89 pen)	

ABERDEEN: Clark, G. Murray, Hermiston (Graham), S. Murray, McMillan, M. Buchan, Forrest, Robb, Harper, Willoughby, Miller

DUNDEE UNITED: McAlpine, J. White, Cameron, Markland (Reid), D. Smith, Henry, Traynor, W. Smith, Copland, Rolland, A. White

P	W	D	L	F	A	Pts	*Attendance:* 14,000
16	13	2	1	50	10	28	*Referee:* A. J. Crawley

Walter Smith, wearing No 8, tried to mark Joe Harper out of the game. Hamish McAlpine is becoming a bit of a nuisance at Pittodrie, but his defenders are less resilient than he is.

No 17 Saturday, 25 December

FALKIRK (0) 0	ABERDEEN (0) 3
	Harper 2 (51, 89),
	Miller (80)

FALKIRK: Rennie, Gibson, Jones, Markie, Miller, Shirra, Hoggan, Young, Somner, Ferguson, Setterington

ABERDEEN: Clark, G. Murray, Hermiston, S. Murray, McMillan, M. Buchan, Miller, Robb, Harper, Willoughby, Graham

P	W	D	L	F	A	Pts	*Attendance:* 7,000
17	14	2	1	53	10	30	*Referee:* J. W. Patterson

Aberdeen are due a victory over Falkirk. They lost at Brockville in the last game of last season, and in the League Cup in September. Joe Harper is making a habit out of scoring in the last minute. It was a perfect Christmas for Aberdeen.

No 18 Saturday, 1 January

DUNDEE (1) 1	ABERDEEN (0) 1
Duncan (26)	Harper (65 pen)

DUNDEE: Hewitt, R. Wilson, Johnston, Stewart, Phillip Ford (Kinninmonth), Duncan, Lambie, Wallace, J. Scott, T. Wilson

ABERDEEN: Clark, G. Murray, Hermiston, S. Murray, McMillan, M. Buchan, Miller, Robb, Harper, Willoughby, Graham

P	W	D	L	F	A	Pts	*Attendance:* 19,000
18	14	3	1	54	11	31	

Aberdeen were on top when Duncan broke away to score for Dundee. They deservedly equalised from the spot after Miller had his legs taken from under him.

No 19 Monday, 3 January

ABERDEEN (3) 4	ST JOHNSTONE (1) 2
Harper (5),	Aitken (20)
Graham 2 (15, 54),	
S. Murray (19)	

ABERDEEN: Clark, G. Murray, Hermiston, S. Murray, McMillan, M. Buchan, Forrest (G. Buchan), Robb, Harper, Willoughby, Graham

ST JOHNSTONE: Robertson, Coburn, Argue, Rennie, Gordon, Rooney, Aird, Mercer, Connolly, Hall, Aitken

P	W	D	L	F	A	Pts	*Attendance:* 23,000
19	15	3	1	58	13	33	*Referee:* J. R. P. Gordon

A holiday crowd enjoy a Pittodrie goal spree. Best of Aberdeen's goals was the first, scored by Harper from a near-impossible angle.

No 20 Saturday, 8 January

AIRDRIEONIANS (0) 1	ABERDEEN (1) 2
Wilson (65)	Robb (1),
	Willoughby (59)

AIRDRIE: McKenzie, Jonquin, Clark, Menzies, McKinlay, D. Whiteford, Cowan, Walker, J. Whiteford (Busby), Jarvie, Wilson

ABERDEEN: Clark, G. Murray, Hermiston, Taylor, Young, M. Buchan, Miller, Robb, Harper, Willoughby, Graham

P W D L F A Pts   *Attendance:* 5,500
20 16 3 1 60 14 35   *Referee:* S. Anderson

This was Aberdeen's first double of the season. They opened with a flourish, but by the end were hanging on by their finger nails. Willie Young made his comeback after injury against Juventus. Harper's crosses produced both goals, and they sent Airdrie to the bottom of the league.

No 21 Saturday, 15 January
ABERDEEN (0) 0   RANGERS (0) 0
ABERDEEN: Geoghegan, G. Murray, Hermiston, S. Murray, Young, M. Buchan, Miller, Robb, Harper, Willoughby, Graham
RANGERS: McCloy, Jardine, Mathieson, Greig, D. Johnstone, Smith, McLean, A. McDonald, Stein (Jackson), W. Johnston, I. McDonald

Leading positions

	P	W	D	L	F	A	Pts
1 Celtic	21	18	2	1	67	17	38
2 ABERDEEN	21	16	4	1	60	14	36
3 Rangers	21	14	1	6	46	22	29

Attendance: 36,000   *Referee:* E. H. Pringle

As had happened last year, this particular fixture ends goal-less. A miserable day and a miserable afternoon for Dave Robb, booked for the fourth time this season. Rangers become the first side to prevent Aberdeen from scoring this season.

No 22 Saturday, 22 January
DUNFERMLINE   ABERDEEN (0) 0
 ATHLETIC (1) 1
 Gillespie (40)
DUNFERMLINE: Arrol, Callaghan, Mercer, Fraser, McNicoll, O'Neil, Paterson, Scott, Millar, Mitchell, Gillespie
ABERDEEN: Geoghegan, G. Murray, Hermiston, S. Murray, Young, M. Buchan, Miller, Robb, Harper, Willoughby (Taylor), Graham

P W D L F A Pts   *Attendance:* 6,500
22 16 4 2 60 15 36   *Referee:* R. Gordon

Aberdeen can say goodbye to the championship. Last season Dunfermline's 1-0 home win over the Dons entitled them to avoid relegation on goal difference. This result brings about the Fifers' first win in 13 games, and is achieved when Steve Murray's back pass stops short in the mud.

No 23 Saturday, 29 January
ABERDEEN (2) 4   KILMARNOCK (1) 2
 Harper 2 (18, 30)   Fleming (35), Cook (64)
 Graham (57),
 S. Murray (76)
ABERDEEN: Marshall, G. Murray, Hermiston, S. Murray, Young, M. Buchan, Miller, Robb, Harper, Willoughby, Graham
KILMARNOCK: Hunter, Whyte, Dickson, Maxwell, Rodman, McGrory, McSherry, Gilmour, Mathie, Fleming, Cook

P W D L F A Pts   *Attendance:* 14,000
23 17 4 2 64 17 38   *Referee:* A. McKenzie

A welcome back to Pittodrie for former-Don, Jim Whyte. Fortunately he doesn't overdo the welcome. Harper scores his first when McSherry passes back to his goalkeeper without looking.

No 24 Saturday, 12 February
HIBERNIAN (1) 2   ABERDEEN (1) 2
 O'Rourke (30),   Harper 2 (39, 71)
 Duncan (62)
HIBERNIAN: Herriot, McEwan, Schaedler, Stanton, Black, Blackley, Hamilton, O'Rourke, Gordon, Cropley, Duncan
ABERDEEN: Marshall, G. Murray, Hermiston, S. Murray, Young, M. Buchan, Miller, Robb, Harper, Willoughby, Graham

P W D L F A Pts   *Attendance:* 21,300
24 17 5 2 66 19 39   *Referee:* R. H. Davidson

New Scotland boss Tommy Docherty takes in a pulsating match. Harper takes his tally to six in three league and cup games. O'Rourke scored for Hibs round a defensive wall, and later hit the Aberdeen crossbar.

No 25 Saturday, 19 February
ABERDEEN (1) 1   MORTON (0) 0
 Willoughby (5)
ABERDEEN: Marshall, G. Murray, Hermiston, S. Murray, Young, M. Buchan, Miller, Robb, Harper, Willoughby, Graham (Forrest)
MORTON: Sorensen, Thorup, Shevlane, Clark, Anderson, Rankin, Booth, Lumsden, Gillies, Mason, Murphy

Leading positions

	P	W	D	L	F	A	Pts
1 Celtic	24	21	2	1	73	18	44
2 ABERDEEN	25	18	5	2	67	19	41
3 Rangers	25	17	1	7	54	24	35
4 Hibernian	25	13	5	7	43	25	31

Attendance: 15,000   *Referee:* A. F. J. Webster

These two sides will meet again next Saturday in the Scottish Cup. It had better be more entertaining than this. Anderson kept Joe Harper in his pocket throughout.

No 26 Saturday, 4 March
PARTICK THISTLE (2) 2   ABERDEEN (0) 0
 Forsyth (11 pen),
 Glavin (31)
PARTICK: Rough, Hansen, Forsyth, Smith, Clark, Strachan, McQuade (Gibson), Glavin, Coulston, A. Rae, Lawrie
ABERDEEN: Marshall, Boel, Hermiston, S. Murray, Young, G. Murray, Miller (Taylor), Robb, Harper, Willoughby, Graham

P W D L F A Pts   *Attendance:* 10,000
26 18 5 3 67 21 41   *Referee:* B. Padden

Buchan-less Aberdeen are sunk at Firhill. Everything went wrong. Thistle's penalty was a farce; Willoughby

The Aberdeen Football Companion

headed against the bar; and Rough made saves beyond the call of duty. This result takes the edge off next weeks much anticipated clash with Celtic.

No 27 Saturday, 11 March
ABERDEEN (0) 1   CELTIC (0) 1
  Harper (82)   Lennox (73)
ABERDEEN: Marshall, Boel, Hermiston, S. Murray, Young, G. Murray, Forrest, Robb, Harper, Willoughby, Graham
CELTIC: Williams, McGrain, Brogan, Murdoch, McNeill, Connelly, Hood, Hay, Dalglish (Callaghan), Macari, Lennox
Leading positions

	P	W	D	L	F	A	Pts
1 Celtic	26	22	3	1	76	19	47
2 ABERDEEN	27	18	6	3	68	22	42
3 Rangers	27	19	1	7	58	25	39

Attendance: 33,000   *Referee:* J. R. P. Gordon

Even if Aberdeen win, the title will surely stay at Parkhead. The Dons have a fine recent record against Celtic – this is their eighth game without defeat, but Celtic were powering forward in the second half when Connelly made a goal for Lennox. Joe Harper saved a point; and the recent record; but not the championship. This was only the second point Celtic had dropped in 17 games.

No 28 Tuesday, 21 March
EAST FIFE (0) 0   ABERDEEN (0) 1
                          Harper (49)
EAST FIFE: Gorman, Duncan, McQuade, McLaren, Martis, Clarke, Bernard, Borthwick, Hughes, Love (Walker), McPhee.
ABERDEEN: Marshall, Boel, Hermiston, S. Murray, Young, Wilson, Miller, Robb, Harper, Taylor, Graham

P	W	D	L	F	A	Pts
28	19	6	3	69	22	44

Attendance: 4,850   *Referee:* A. Patterson

Out of the Cup and resigned to conceding the championship, it is going to be a long run-in for Aberdeen.

No 29 Saturday, 25 March
ABERDEEN (1) 4   MOTHERWELL (1) 1
  Forrest (20), Harper 2   McInally (37)
  (53 pen, 87), Robb (79)
ABERDEEN: Marshall, Boel, Hermiston, S. Murray, Young, Wilson, Forrest (Willoughby), Robb, Harper, Taylor, Graham
MOTHERWELL: Fallon, Muir, Whiteford, Forsyth, McCallum, Watson, Campbell, McInally, McCabe, Lawson, Heron (Main)

P	W	D	L	F	A	Pts
29	20	6	3	73	23	46

Attendance: 10,000   *Referee:* R. B. Valentine

Referee Bob Valentine refuses two blatant penalty awards for Aberdeen; sends Jim Hermiston off; and provokes some unpleasant crowd demonstrations.

No 30 Saturday, 1 April
HEARTS (0) 1   ABERDEEN (0) 0
  Renton (52)
HEARTS: Garland, Clunie, Jefferies, Thomson, Anderson, Wood, T. Murray, Brown, Ford, Carruthers, Renton
ABERDEEN: Clark, Boel, Hermiston, S. Murray, Young, Wilson, Miller, Robb, Harper, Taylor, Graham (Willoughby)
Leading positions

	P	W	D	L	F	A	Pts
1 Celtic	28	24	3	1	80	20	51
2 ABERDEEN	30	20	6	4	73	24	46

Attendance: 8,500   *Referee:* T. Kellock

The city of Edinburgh is becoming a graveyard for Aberdeen this season. Knocked out of the Cup at Easter Road, they now find themselves beaten a second time in the league by Hearts. Behind the scenes Aberdeen have signed up 16 year old winger John McMaster.

No 31 Saturday, 8 April
ABERDEEN (2) 7   AYR UNITED (0) 0
  Harper 4 (27, 38, 61,
  83), Miller (55), Taylor
  (64), Young (68)
ABERDEEN: Clark, Boel, Hermiston, S. Murray, Young, Wilson, Miller, Robb, Harper, Taylor, Graham
AYR: Stewart, McFadzean, Murphy, Fleming, Quinn, Filippi, Graham, McLean, Ingram, McGregor (Stevenson), Doyle

P	W	D	L	F	A	Pts
31	21	6	4	80	24	48

Attendance: 8,500   *Referee:* J. W. Paterson

'Joey for Scotland', sing the Pittodrie faithful, as the wee man confirms his place as the country's leading marksman. The players are now off for a short holiday in Greece.

No 32 Saturday, 15 April
CLYDE (0) 0   ABERDEEN (0) 0
CLYDE: McCulloch, Anderson, McHugh, Beattie, McVie, Burns, McGrain, Millar, Flanagan, Hulston, Ahern (Sullivan)
ABERDEEN: Clark, Boel, Hermiston, S. Murray, Young, Wilson, Miller (Purdie), Robb, Harper, Taylor, Graham

P	W	D	L	F	A	Pts
32	21	7	4	80	24	49

Attendance: 1,000   *Referee:* R. Anderson

As a result of this result Celtic have clinched the championship at the expense of Aberdeen – who have clinched runners-up spot at the expense of Rangers.

No 33 Saturday, 22 April
DUNDEE UNITED (2) 2   ABERDEEN (0) 0
  Mitchell (25),
  D. Smith (32 pen)
DUNDEE UNITED: McAlpine, Rolland, J. Cameron, Copland, D. Smith, Gray, Fleming, Kopel, Gardner, Mitchell, K. Cameron

ABERDEEN: Clark, Boel, Hermiston, S. Murray, Young, Wilson, Forrest, Robb, Harper, Taylor, Graham (Willoughby)

P	W	D	L	F	A	Pts	*Attendance:* 5,000
33	21	7	5	80	26	49	*Referee:* I. M. D. Foote

You would never believe that Aberdeen won 4-0 on the same ground in February in the Scottish Cup. No wonder Dons' officials are off hunting players.

No 34 Saturday, 29 April
ABERDEEN (0) 0   FALKIRK (0) 0

ABERDEEN: Clark, Boel, Hermiston, S. Murray, Young, Wilson, Forrest, Robb, Harper, Taylor, Graham
FALKIRK: Donaldson, S. Kennedy, Shirra, Cattanach, Markie, J. Kennedy, Hoggan, Harley, Jack, Ferguson, Somner
Attendance: 9,000   *Referee:* G. Smith

Pittodrie is not amused at this apology of a football match. The high hopes of the season's beginning are replaced by a lack of heart and spirit. The crowd are actually booing and slow-handclapping.

Aberdeen's complete home and away record:

HOME						AWAY						
P	W	D	L	F	A		W	D	L	F	A	Pts
34	13	3	1	54	13		8	5	4	26	13	50

Scottish League Division One

	P	W	D	L	F	A	Pts
1 Celtic	34	28	4	2	96	28	60
2 ABERDEEN	34	21	8	5	80	26	50
3 Rangers	34	21	2	11	71	38	44
4 Hibernian	34	19	6	9	62	34	44
5 Dundee	34	14	13	7	59	38	41
6 Hearts	34	13	13	8	53	49	39
7 Partick Thistle	34	12	10	12	53	54	34
8 St Johnstone	34	12	8	14	52	58	32
9 Dundee United	34	12	7	15	55	70	31
10 Motherwell	34	11	7	16	49	69	29
11 Kilmarnock	34	11	6	17	49	64	28
12 Ayr United	34	9	10	15	40	58	28
13 Morton	34	10	7	17	46	52	27
14 Falkirk	34	10	7	17	44	60	27
15 Airdrieonians	34	7	12	15	44	76	26
16 East Fife	34	5	15	14	34	61	25
17 Clyde	34	7	10	17	33	66	24
18 Dunfermline	34	7	9	18	31	50	23

LEAGUE CUP

Saturday, 14 August
ABERDEEN (0) 1   DUNDEE (1) 1
Robb (57)   Duncan (17)

ABERDEEN: Clark, Williamson, G. Murray, S. Murray, McMillan, M. Buchan, G. Buchan, Robb, Harper, Willoughby, Graham
DUNDEE: Hewitt, Wilson, Johnston, Steele, Phillip, Houston, Duncan, I. Scott, Wallace, J. Scott, Lambie (Bryce)

Attendance: 20,000   *Referee:* E. H. Thomson

George Buchan holds his head in despair as he shoots against the post and watches the ball fly across the goalmouth and behind the line for a goal-kick.

Wednesday, 18 August
CLYDE (0) 0   ABERDEEN (2) 2
                            Harper 2 (18, 33)

CLYDE: McCulloch, Glasgow, Swan, Burns, McVie, McHugh, McGrain, Thomson, Hulston, Ahern, McColligan (Flanagan)
ABERDEEN: Clark, Boel, G. Murray, S. Murray, McMillan, M. Buchan, G. Buchan (Williamson), Robb, Harper, Willoughby, Graham

Attendance: 4,000   *Referee:* W. J. Mullen

Aberdeen did the business in the first half – and were then relieved that Hulston missed the chances that came Clyde's way.

Saturday, 21 August
ABERDEEN (0) 1   FALKIRK(0) 0
Harper (78)

ABERDEEN: Clark, Boel, Hermiston, G. Murray (Williamson), McMillan, M. Buchan, S. Murray, Robb, Harper, Willoughby, Graham
FALKIRK: Rennie, Jones, McLaughlan, Markie, Miller, Gibson, Hoggan, Young, Jack, Ferguson, Shirra

Attendance: 14,000   *Referee:* I. M. D. Foote

Aberdeen tried to beat Falkirk with the heavy artillery, but had to rely on a moment of Harper magic.

Wednesday, 25 August
ABERDEEN (0) 5   CLYDE (0) 0
Graham 3 (56, 64,
83), Harper (62),
Willoughby (79)

ABERDEEN: Clark, Boel, Hermiston, S. Murray, McMillan, Buchan, Forrest, Robb, Harper, Willoughby, Graham
CLYDE: McCulloch, Anderson, Swan, Burns, McVie, Beattie, Sullivan, McDonald, Thomson (McHugh), McGrain, McColligan

Attendance: 15,000   *Referee:* J. R. Grant

The Dons spent nearly an hour knocking at the door. Then it caved in. Arthur Graham's volley did the trick.

Saturday, 28 August
DUNDEE (1) 3   ABERDEEN (1) 1
Wallace 2 (26, 48),   Willoughby (38)
Houston (55)

DUNDEE: Hewitt, R. Wilson, Johnston, Steele, Phillip, Houston, Duncan, Kimminmonth, Wallace, Scott, J. Wilson
ABERDEEN: Clark, Boel, Hermiston, S. Murray, McMillan (G. Buchan), M. Buchan, Forrest, Robb, Harper, Willoughby, Graham

Attendance: 13,000   *Referee:* J. McRoberts

As a result of this defeat Falkirk and Dundee are breathing down Aberdeen's necks. Willoughby gave away Dundee's first goal, then headed an equalizer.

Wednesday, 1 September
FALKIRK (0) 3   ABERDEEN (1) 1
  McLaughlin (46),   Forrest (19)
  Ferguson 2 (60, 65)
FALKIRK: Rennie, Jones, McLaughlin, Markie, Miller, Shirra, Hoggan, Jack (Gibson), Young, Ferguson, Setterington
ABERDEEN: Clark, Boel, Hermiston, S. Murray, Young, M. Buchan, Forrest, Robb, Harper, Willoughby, Graham
Attendance: 20,000   *Referee:* T. Marshall

Aberdeen need a draw to qualify for a quarter-final with Eddie Turnbull's Hibs. But they are sunk by the pace and power of Alex Ferguson.

Section 2

	P	W	D	L	F	A	Pts
Falkirk	6	4	1	1	12	6	9
Dundee	6	3	2	1	10	5	8
ABERDEEN	6	3	1	2	11	6	7
Clyde	6	0	0	6	2	17	0

SCOTTISH CUP

1st Round Saturday, 5 February
DUNDEE UNITED (0) 0 ABERDEEN (1) 4
                      Miller (7), Harper 2
                      (64 pen, 67),
                      Young (90)
DUNDEE UNITED: McAlpine, Rolland, J. Cameron, Markland, D. Smith, W. Smith, K. Cameron, Knox, Copland (Traynor), Gardner, Mitchell
ABERDEEN: Clark, G. Murray, Hermiston, S. Murray, Young, M. Buchan, Miller, Robb, Harper, Willoughby, Graham
Attendance: 13,500   *Referee:* A. McKenzie

A repeat of last season's cup-draw. The end result made it look easier than it was. Bobby Clark saved a Kenny Cameron penalty at 1-0 after Buchan had handled.

2nd Round Saturday, 26 February
ABERDEEN (1) 1   MORTON (0) 0
  Willoughby (42)
ABERDEEN: Marshall, G. Murray, Hermiston, S. Murray, Young, M. Buchan, Forrest, Robb, Harper, Willoughby, Miller (Graham)
MORTON: Sorensen, Thorup, Shevlane, Clark, Anderson, Rankin, Chalmers, Lumsden, Gillies (Osborne), Mason, Murphy
Attendance: 18,300   *Referee:* R. H. Davidson

A carbon copy of last week's league match. Both times Alec Willoughby notches the one and only goal. Morton substitute Osborne was sent off two minutes after he came on following a difference of opinion with Willie Young. Martin Buchan plays his last match for Aberdeen before being transferred to Manchester

United. The crowd show their appreciation – in the hope that he will stay.

Quarter Final Saturday, 18 March
HIBERNIAN (1) 2   ABERDEEN (0) 0
  O'Rourke (1), Baker (49)
HIBERNIAN: Herriot, Brownlie, Schaedler, Stanton, Black, Blackley, Hamilton, O'Rourke, Baker, Gordon, Duncan
ABERDEEN: Marshall, Boel, Hermiston, S. Murray (Wilson), Young, G. Murray, Forrest, Taylor, Harper, Willoughby, Graham
                Referee: W. Mullen

Hibs are becoming the Dons' bogey team of the 1970s. It took Jim O'Rourke just 17 seconds to snap up Gordon's pass and fire left-footed past Marshall. Aberdeen didn't manage a shot at goal in the first half, and as soon as the second was under way Baker scored at the second attempt – after the first had been blocked by Marshall. Fifteen minutes from the end new Dons' skipper Steve Murray was substituted – and didn't like it. Before the end Joe Harper was stretchered off.

UEFA CUP

1st Round, 1st Leg Wednesday, 15 September
CELTA VIGO   ABERDEEN (0) 2
  (Spain) (0) 0   Harper (51), Forrest (73)
VIGO: Gost, Pedrito, Dominguez, Hidalgo, Manolo, Rivera, Lezcano, Juan, Rodilla, Almagro (Rivas), Jiminez
ABERDEEN: Clark, Boel, Hermiston (G Murray), S. Murray, Young, M. Buchan, Forrest, Robb, Harper, Willoughby, Graham
                Referee: R. Ellis (France)

The Fairs Cup has been renamed the UEFA Cup. The Spanish club were unbeaten at home throughout all last season. Aberdeen adopted offside tactics which were not wise, because the two linesmen assisting the French referee were Spanish. Having drawn the home team's fire, Aberdeen did a spot of poaching. Harper lobbed the first goal before Forrest scored direct from a corner.

1st Round, 2nd Leg Wednesday, 29 September
ABERDEEN (0) 1   CELTA VIGO (0) 0
  Harper (89)
ABERDEEN: Geoghegan, Boel, G. Murray, S. Murray, Young, M. Buchan, Forrest, Robb, Harper, Willoughby, G. Buchan
VIGO: Alarcia, Pedrito, Navarro, Manolo, Dominguez, Rivas, Lezcano, Juan, Rodilla, Almagro (Rivera), Suco (Jiminez)
Aberdeen won 3-0 on aggregate
Attendance: 20,000   *Referee:* K. Wahlen
                          (Norway)

Aberdeen already had it won in Spain. They knew it: and so did their opponents. This was Harper's 100th match for Aberdeen. He proceeded to waste a penalty before crashing the ball home from 25 yards.

2nd Round, 1st Leg, Wednesday, 27 October
JUVENTUS (Italy) (1) 2   ABERDEEN (0) 0
  Anastasi (5),
  Capello (55)
JUVENTUS: Carmignani, Spinosi, Marchetti, Morini (Roveta), Salvadore, Furino, Haller, Savoldi, Anastasi, Capello, Bettega
ABERDEEN: Clark, G. Murray, Hermiston, S. Murray, Young (Taylor), M. Buchan, Forrest, Robb, Harper, Willoughby, Graham
Attendance: 35,000   *Referee:* P. Nicolov
                                             (Bulgaria)

This is a great occasion for Aberdeen – a trip to the Communale Stadium in Turin. Fortunately for them, the talented Franco Causio will not line up against them, being sent off in the first round against Malta. Juventus start out as overwhelming favourites. They reached the final of last season's Fairs Cup with Leeds. Now, with Aberdeen feeling their way, the world's most expensive player – Pietro Anastasi – races towards Clark from the centre circle and finishes with a mighty, low shot. In the second half Capello's free kick is deflected past Clark and manager Bonthrone hauls off Willie Young – before he is sent off!

2nd Round, 2nd Leg Wednesday, 17 November
ABERDEEN (0) 1   JUVENTUS (0) 1
  Harper (77)   Anastasi (50)
ABERDEEN: Clark, G. Murray, Hermiston (G. Buchan), S. Murray, Young (Taylor), M. Buchan, Forrest, Robb, Harper, Willoughby, Graham
JUVENTUS: Carmignani, Spinosi, Marchetti, Furino, Morini, Salvadore, Haller, Causio, Anastasi, Capello, Bettega
Juventus won 3-1 on aggregate
Attendance: 29,500   *Referee:* T. Boosten
                                            (Holland)

Last week Pittodrie staged a full international with Belgium: now it hosts the might of Juventus, top of the Italian League. Aberdeen had all the spirit, Juventus all the class on a pitch sprinkled with snow. Just after half-time Juventus made sure of their place in the next round when Anastasi beat Buchan and hammered his shot inside Clark's near post. Aberdeen now needed four goals to survive. They managed one, through Harper's glorious header.

1971-72

APPEARANCES	League	League Cup	Scottish Cup	UEFA Cup
Harper	34	6	3	4
Robb	34	6	2	4
Hermiston	33	4	3	3
S. Murray	32	6	3	4
Graham	27(+2)	6	2(+1)	3
Willoughby	26(+3)	6	3	4
Young	26	1	3	4
M. Buchan	25	6	2	4
G. Murray	23	3	3	3(+1)
Clark	22	6	1	3
Forrest	21(+1)	3	2	4
R. Miller	20(+3)		2	
Boel	14	5	1	2
Taylor	10(+5)		1	–(+2)
McMillan	8	5		
Marshall	7		2	
Wilson	7		–(+1)	
Geoghegan	5			1
G. Buchan	–(+1)	2(+1)		1(+1)
Purdie	–(+1)			
Williamson		1(+2)		
21 players				

GOALS	Total	League	League Cup	Scottish Cup	UEFA Cup
Harper	42	33	4	2	3
Robb	11	10	1		
S. Murray	10	10			
Willoughby	10	7	2	1	
Graham	7	4	3		
Forrest	6	4	1		1
R. Miller	4	3		1	
Young	4	3		1	
Taylor	2	2			
M. Buchan	1	1			
Hermiston	1	1			
G. Murray	1	1			
own-goals	1	1			
Totals	100	80	11	5	4

Gordon Strachan, always popular with the fans.

Season 1972-73

Season 1972-73 was not about trophies won or points gathered. It was about two players: one who left, one who came. The one who departed was Pittodrie idol Joe Harper. He said goodbye in December, bound for Everton, just ten months after Martin Buchan had also packed his bags for the lure of industrial Lancashire. The sense of despondency hanging over Pittodrie was tangible. Many life-long supporters vowed never to set foot inside the stadium again. Their threats were happily short-lived, but perhaps only because of a will-of-the-wisp Hungarian international footballer by the name of Zoltan Varga, who paraded his talents for the Dons' cause from October 1972 to April 1973. Those six months were enough to convince many fans – some with long memories – that they were witnessing the most magical player ever to pull on an Aberdeen shirt.

As for the season's prizes, Aberdeen came close – but not close enough. They were fifteen minutes from a place in the League Cup Final, but had that place rudely snatched from them by Celtic. In the Scottish Cup it was Celtic once again who were the source of the Dons' downfall, surviving a Quarter Final replay at Pittodrie through a late Billy McNeill header. Aberdeen finished fourth in the league, a distant 14 points behind the champions from Parkhead, but good enough to secure the last remaining UEFA Cup place on goal difference from Dundee. The Dons' involvement in this season's UEFA Cup trail had been terminated at the first hurdle, when they finished 1-1 down on aggregate to the dazzling talents of Borussia Moenchengladbach.

The season offered a little cameo as a postscript. Half an hour from the end of the final league match – at Cappielow – Jimmy Bonthrone threw on a young substitute. His name was Willie Miller. For those brief, fleeting thirty minutes, the future Aberdeen captain humbly shared the stage with arguably the most gifted Don of them all – Zoltan Varga.

League:	Fourth
League Cup:	Semi Final
Scottish Cup:	Quarter Final
UEFA Cup:	First Round

SCOTTISH LEAGUE DIVISION ONE

No 1 Saturday, 2 September
ABERDEEN (0) 1   HIBERNIAN (0) 0
Harper (48)

ABERDEEN: Clark, G. Murray, Hermiston, S. Murray (G. Buchan), Boel, Young, Willoughby, Robb, Harper, Jarvie, Taylor

HIBERNIAN: Herriot, Brownlie, Schaedler, Stanton, Black, Blackley, Edwards, Hazel, Gordon, Cropley, Duncan

P	W	D	L	F	A	Pts
1	1	0	0	1	0	2

Attendance: 21,000
Referee: A. McKenzie

Harper, having put himself in the hedlines with a midweek hat-trick against Queens Park in the League Cup, now accepts Taylor's pass to send Eddie Turnbull's boys home pointless.

No 2 Saturday, 9 September
DUNDEE (0) 0   ABERDEEN (0) 0

DUNDEE: Hewitt, R. Wilson, Houston, Robinson, Phillip, Stewart, J. Wilson, Duncan, Wallace, J. Scott, I. Scott (Ford)

ABERDEEN: Geoghegan, Willoughby, Hermiston, S. Murray, Boel, Young, Forrest, Robb, Harper, Jarvie (Graham), Taylor

P W D L F A Pts
2 1 1 0 1 0 3

Attendance: 12,000
Referee: R. H. Davidson

This game had its moments. But there were not many of them. Geoghegan made two splendid saves from Duncan – one in each half.

No 3 Saturday, 16 September
ABERDEEN (0) 0   ST JOHNSTONE (0) 0
ABERDEEN: Clark, Willoughby, Hermiston, G. Murray, Boel, Young, G. Buchan (Graham), Robb, Harper, Jarvie, Taylor
ST JOHNSTONE: Donaldson, Lambie, Argue, Kinnell, Rennie, Rooney, Hall, Muir, Pearson, McPhee, Aitken

P W D L F A Pts
3 1 2 0 1 0 4

Attendance: 10,000
Referee: J. W. Paterson

Aberdeen have still to concede a league goal. Trouble is they don't look like scoring any either. George Buchan needed to be stretchered off.

No 4 Saturday, 23 September
DUMBARTON (1) 1   ABERDEEN (0) 2
  D. Wilson (32)   Jarvie (49), Harper (52)
DUMBARTON: Williams, Menzies, Wilkinson, Cushley, Bolton, Graham, Coleman (Paterson), Jenkins, McCormick, K. Wilson, D. Wilson
ABERDEEN: Clark, Willoughby, Hermiston, S. Murray, Boel, Young, G. Buchan, Robb, Harper, Jarvie, Graham (Miller)

P W D L F A Pts
4 2 2 0 3 1 6

Attendance: 6,000

Willie Young gives away countless free-kicks as Aberdeen back-peddle in the closing stages. Harpers' winner is a delightful left-footed shot-on-the-turn.

No 5 Saturday, 30 September
ABERDEEN (5) 7   MOTHERWELL (1) 2
  Robb (2), Harper 3   McClymont (44 pen),
  (12, 18 pen, 79)   Gray (55)
  Whiteford o.g. (20),
  Jarvie (21),
  S. Murray (86)
ABERDEEN: Clark, Willoughby, Hermiston, S. Murray, G. Murray, Young, Graham (Miller), Robb, Harper, Jarvie, Taylor
MOTHERWELL: MacRae, Whiteford, Wark, Forsyth, McCallum, Muir, Gray, Murray (Goldthorp), Lawson, McClymont, Martin

Leading positions

	P	W	D	L	F	A	Pts
1 Celtic	5	4	0	1	12	5	8
2 ABERDEEN	5	3	2	0	10	3	8
3 Hibernian	5	4	0	1	9	4	8
4 Dundee United	5	4	0	1	10	6	8

Attendance: 10,000   *Referee:* I. M. D. Foote

This is Motherwell's first defeat of the season. They don't take kindly to it. Their principal tormentor was Dave Robb. He was treated unkindly, especially by

Goldthorp who was sent off near the end. Earlier, Dons fans had looked forward to a cricket score. It was 5-0 after just 21 minutes. Aberdeen are making a habit of compensating for European elimination by burying their next opponents.

No 6 Saturday, 7 October
HEARTS (1) 2   ABERDEEN (0) 1
  Carruthers (35),   Harper (79)
  Ford (51)
HEARTS: Garland, Clunie, Oliver, Kay, Anderson, Wood, Murray, Brown, Ford, Carruthers, Lynch
ABERDEEN: Clark, Willoughby, Hermiston, S. Murray, G. Murray, Young, Forrest, Robb, Harper, Jarvie, Graham (Miller)

P W D L F A Pts
6 3 2 1 11 5 8

Attendance: 14,000
Referee: R. Gordon

Hearts continue to be a thorn in Aberdeen's side in recent seasons. Carruthers missed a hatful before opening the scoring. Harper's counter came too late – pity he had hit the post earlier.

No 7 Saturday, 14 October
ABERDEEN (1) 2   FALKIRK (2) 2
  Taylor 2 (40, 81)   Scott (16),
                         Willoughby o.g. (45)
ABERDEEN: Clark, Willoughby, Hermiston, S. Murray, Young, Taylor, Varga, Robb, Harper, Jarvie, Miller (Graham)
FALKIRK: Donaldson, S. Kennedy, Shirra, Markie, McMillan, McLeod, Setterington, Harley, Scott, Young, Jack

P W D L F A Pts
7 3 3 1 13 7 9

Attendance: 15,000
Referee: R. Marshall

The game came alive just before half time. Taylor equalised for Aberdeen; then Donaldson saved Harper's penalty after Jarvie had been pulled down by Shirra; then Willoughby turned Harley's cross into his own goal. This match marked the debut of Zoltan Varga. The following Wednesday Clark and Harper (sub) were capped in Denmark. Harper scored.

No 8 Saturday, 21 October
AYR UNITED (1) 2   ABERDEEN (3) 3
  McLean (23),   Jarvie (8),
  Fleming (88)   Harper 2 (18, 40)
AYR: Stewart, Filippi, Murphy, Fleming, McAnespie, McCulloch, Doyle, Graham, Ingram, McLean, Stevenson (McGovern)
ABERDEEN: Clark, Willoughby, Hermiston, S. Murray, Young, Taylor, Varga, Robb, Harper, Jarvie, Mitchell

P W D L F A Pts
8 4 3 1 16 9 11

Attendance: 7,500
Referee: T. R. Kyle

Zoltan Varga must wonder what kind of football Scottish fans like. Harper and Ayr's Graham were sent off after a touchline tussle which the linesman brought to the referee's attention. Several of the players were booked in an altogether unpleasant match.

No 9 Saturday, 28 October
ABERDEEN (1) 2   CELTIC (2) 3
Varga 2 (25, 83)   Deans (13), Macari
                        (16), Dalglish (67)
ABERDEEN: Clark, Willoughby, Hermiston,
S. Murray, Young (Graham), Taylor, Varga, Robb,
Harper, Jarvie, Mitchell
CELTIC: Williams, McGrain, McCluskey, Hay,
McNeill, Connelly, Dalglish, Macari, Deans, Callaghan,
Lennox
Leading positions

	P	W	D	L	F	A	Pts
1 Celtic	9	7	1	1	23	8	15
2 Dundee United	9	7	0	2	19	11	14
3 Hibernian	9	6	1	2	19	10	13
4 ABERDEEN	9	4	3	2	18	12	11

Attendance: 36,000   *Referee:* E. H. Pringle
This is the stage Zoltan Varga needed. His first goal was
a swerving 20 yarder; his second an exquisite lob. Too
bad they weren't enough to protect Aberdeen from their
first defeat by Celtic for several seasons. Bobby Clark
wants a transfer.

No 10 Saturday, 4 November
PARTICK THISTLE (0) 0 ABERDEEN (1) 2
                        Harper (29), Miller (80)
PARTICK: Rough, Forsyth, Ralston, Glavin, Clark,
Strachan, Gibson, Coulston, Craig, A. Rae, McQuade
(Chalmers)
ABERDEEN: Clark, G. Murray, Hermiston,
S. Murray, Mitchell, Taylor, Varga, Robb, Harper,
Jarvie, Miller

P	W	D	L	F	A	Pts
10	5	3	2	20	12	13

Attendance: 7,000   *Referee:* J. R. P. Gordon
Partick belied their lowly position to play their part in a
cracking match that was once again illuminated by the
extravagant skills of Zoltan Varga. Aberdeen were never
secure until Miller's late header went in off a post.

No 11 Saturday, 11 November
ABERDEEN (0) 4   EAST FIFE (2) 3
Jarvie (48), Willoughby McPhee (21), Honeyman
(60), McQuade o.g. (68) (32), Hegarty (85)
Robb (70 pen)
ABERDEEN: Clark, Willoughby, Hermiston,
S. Murray, Mitchell, Taylor, Varga, Robb, Forrest,
Jarvie, Miller
EAST FIFE: McGarr, Duncan, McQuade, Borthwick,
Martis, Clarke, Hegarty, Hamilton, Honeyman,
McPhee, Bernard

P	W	D	L	F	A	Pts
11	6	3	2	24	15	15

Attendance: 11,000   *Referee:* A. F. McDonald
This is the stuff to have the fans roaring. Two down at
the break, Aberdeen besiege East Fife's goal thereafter.
East Fife went potty at Willoughby's equaliser, claiming
that Robb impeded McGarr. The suspended Harper
was hardly missed. But the wee man played for Scotland
the following Wednesday against Denmark and scored.

No 12 Saturday, 18 November
ABERDEEN (1) 3   KILMARNOCK (0) 0
Taylor (28), Harper
(50), Jarvie (54)
ABERDEEN: Clark, Willoughby, Hermiston,
S. Murray, G. Murray, Taylor, Varga, Robb,
Harper, Jarvie, Miller
KILMARNOCK: Hunter, Whyte, Robertson,
Maxwell, Rodman, Lee, McSherry, Dickson,
Morrison, Smith, Cook (Cairns)

P	W	D	L	F	A	Pts
12	7	3	2	27	15	17

Attendance: 11,000   *Referee:* G. B. Smith
Harper scored one; hit the post twice. Of Scotland's two
international keepers on view, Alistair Hunter was
much the busier.

No 13 Saturday, 25 November
DUNDEE UNITED (1) 3 ABERDEEN (0) 2
Gardner 2 (29, 70),   Varga (58),
Copland (48)   S. Murray (86)
DUNDEE UNITED: McAlpine, Rolland, Markland,
Copland, D. Smith, Henry, Kopel, Fleming, Mitchell,
Gardner, White
ABERDEEN: Clark, Willoughby, Hermiston,
S. Murray, G. Murray, Taylor, Varga, Robb,
Harper, Jarvie, Miller

P	W	D	L	F	A	Pts
13	7	3	3	29	18	17

Attendance: 8,500   *Referee:* W. J. Mullen
Aberdeen look jittery in defence and are a well-beaten
side by the close. When Copland made it 2-0, Clark had
come for a cross and was left stranded, holding his head
in his hands.

No 14 Saturday, 2 December
AIRDRIEONIANS (0) 1   ABERDEEN (0) 1
Wilson (77)   S. Murray (54)
AIRDRIE: McKenzie, Jonquin, Clark, Menzies,
Fraser, Whiteford, Wilson, Walker, Busby, McRoberts
(Thomson), Cowan
ABERDEEN: Clark, Willoughby, Hermiston,
S. Murray, Young, Taylor, Varga, Robb, Harper,
Jarvie, Miller

P	W	D	L	F	A	Pts
14	7	4	3	30	19	18

Attendance: 4,000   *Referee:* J. R. Grant
Airdrie have won only once all season. After Wilson's
headed equaliser they threatened to make it twice. This
is Joe Harper's last match before his transfer to
Everton.

No 15 Saturday, 9 December
ABERDEEN (0) 0   ARBROATH (0) 0
ABERDEEN: Clark, Willoughby, Hermiston,
S. Murray, Young, Taylor, Varga, Robb, Forrest,
Jarvie, Miller (G Buchan)
ARBROATH: Marshall, Milne, Rylance, Cargill,
Waddell, Winchester, Sellars, Cant, Pirie, Stanton,
Payne

Leading positions

	P	W	D	L	F	A	Pts
1 Celtic	14	12	1	1	44	14	25
2 Hibernian	14	10	1	3	33	15	21
3 Rangers	15	9	2	4	27	16	20
4 Hearts	15	9	2	4	24	14	20
5 ABERDEEN	15	7	5	3	30	19	19

Attendance: 9,000   *Referee:* D. F. Syme

Just hours before kick-off Joe Harper was transferred to Everton for £180,000. The crowd learn of his departure only as they reach the ground and are not happy. Harper didn't think Aberdeen could win any trophies this year. They boo and jeer throughout the match. Alec Willoughby later describes them as 'diabolical'.

No 16 Saturday, 16 December
RANGERS (0)   ABERDEEN (0) 0
RANGERS: McCloy, Jardine, Mathieson, MacDonald, Johnstone, Smith, McLean, Conn (Fyfe), Parlane, Mason, Young
ABERDEEN: Clark, Willoughby, Hermiston, S. Murray, Young, Wilson, Varga, J. Smith, Mitchell, Jarvie, Miller

P	W	D	L	F	A	Pts
16	7	6	3	30	19	20

Attendance: 30,000   *Referee:* E. Thomson

One star goes: another is born. Following the departure of Joe Harper another Joe - Joe Smith, brother of ex-Don Jim Smith – makes his debut. Aberdeen took some punishment in the first half; handed some out in the second.

No 17 Saturday, 23 December
ABERDEEN (3) 3   MORTON (0) 0
Varga 2 (10, 12)
Mitchell (36)
ABERDEEN: Clark, Willoughby, Hermiston, S. Murray, Young, Wilson, Varga, J. Smith, Mitchell, Jarvie, Miller
MORTON: Baines, Shevlane, Laughton, Reid, Anderson, Clark, Christensen, Townsend, Gillies, Murphy, Rankin (Lavelle)

P	W	D	L	F	A	Pts
17	8	6	3	33	19	22

Attendance: 8,000   *Referee:* R. D. Henderson

These would be dark days for Aberdeen were they not illuminated by Zoltan Varga. In ten minutes he swept past Gillies to score an unstoppable goal from 30 yards. Two minutes later he scores with his head – and the crowd love him.

No 18 Saturday, 30 December
HIBERNIAN (1) 3   ABERDEEN (1) 2
Stanton (24), O'Rourke   Jarvie (35), Miller (75)
(50), Gordon (60)
HIBERNIAN: Herriot, Brownlie, Schaedler, Stanton, Black, Blackley, Edwards, O'Rourke, Gordon, Cropley, Duncan
ABERDEEN: Clark, Willoughby (G Buchan), Hermiston, Graham, Young, Wilson, Varga, J. Smith, Mitchell, Jarvie, Miller

P	W	D	L	F	A	Pts
18	8	6	4	35	22	22

Attendance: 22,000   *Referee:* J. W. Paterson

Aberdeen now slip to sixth after this absorbing, enthralling contest. In the absence of Steve Murray. Willie Young is temporary team-captain. Best goal of the match was Hibs' third – a searing diving header by Gordon.

No 19 Monday, 1 January
ABERDEEN (1) 3   DUNDEE (0) 1
Hermiston (28), Varga   J. Scott (60)
(52), Jarvie (76)
ABERDEEN: Clark, Willoughby, Hermiston, Graham, Young, Wilson, Varga, J. Smith (G. Buchan), Mitchell, Jarvie, Miller
DUNDEE: Allan, R. Wilson, Johnston, Houston, Stewart, Pringle, I. Scott, Wallace, Duncan, J. Scott, Lambie

P	W	D	L	F	A	Pts
19	9	6	4	38	23	24

Attendance: 13,000   *Referee:* R. Gordon

Pittodrie was the place to be for New Year drama. It was a party for Zoltan Varga and not just to celebrate his 28th birthday. Hermiston blasted the first goal off the bar, and then everybody sat back and watched as Varga went through his repertoire. Near the end Dundee's Pringle was sent packing.

No 20 Saturday, 27 January
ABERDEEN (2) 3   HEARTS (1) 1
Jarvie 2 (17, 24),   Renton (15)
Varga (71)
ABERDEEN: Clark, Willoughby, Hermiston, S. Murray, Young, Wilson, Varga, Graham, Mitchell, Jarvie, Miller
HEARTS: Garland, Clunie, Jefferies, Thomson, Anderson, Kay, Park (Carruthers), Renton, Ford, Brown, T. Murray

Leading positions

	P	W	D	L	F	A	Pts
1 Rangers	23	16	3	4	46	21	34
2 Celtic	20	15	2	3	54	22	32
3 Hibernian	21	14	3	4	54	21	31
4 Dundee United	22	13	1	8	41	36	27
5 ABERDEEN	20	10	6	4	41	24	26

Attendance: 14,000   *Referee:* J. Callaghan

Bad weather has ruined three successive Saturdays. The crowd turn up in their thousands – word of mouth has spread the news about Zoltan Varga. He shines like a beacon light, scoring a superlative goal to crown a memorable match.

No 21 Wednesday, 7 February
MOTHERWELL (0) 2   ABERDEEN (0) 0
Lawson (47),
Campbell (49)
MOTHERWELL: MacRae, Whiteford, Wark, Watson, McCallum, Goodwin, Campbell, McCabe, Goldthorp (Martin), Lawson, Millar

ABERDEEN: Clark, Willoughby, Hermiston, S. Murray, Young, Wilson, Varga (J. Smith), Graham, Mitchell, Jarvie, Miller

P	W	D	L	F	A	Pts	
21	10	6	5	41	26	26	

Attendance: 4,000
Referee: A. J. F. Webster

Aberdeen come to Fir Park with four straight wins under their belt. But they lose Varga after 15 minutes with a pulled hamstring. As Motherwell then found out, Aberdeen are not the same side without him.

No 22 Saturday, 10 February
FALKIRK (0) 0   ABERDEEN (0) 0

FALKIRK: Donaldson, S. Kennedy, Young, McMillan, Markie, J. Kennedy, Hoggan, Eadie, Somner, Ferguson, Setterington

ABERDEEN: Clark, Willoughby, Hermiston, S. Murray, Young, Wilson, G. Buchan, Graham, Mitchell, Jarvie, Taylor

P	W	D	L	F	A	Pts	
22	10	7	5	41	26	27	

Attendance: 5,500
Referee: A. McCririck

If the Scottish Cup Fourth Round tie between these two is as shoddy as this rehearsal – no-one will bother to turn up. Aberdeen's Ian Taylor was sent off for a stupid foul on Somner. Falkirk player-coach Alex Ferguson was booked for speaking out of turn to the referee. On 14 February Clark kept goal for Scotland in the 5-0 hammering by England at Hampden.

No 23 Saturday, 17 February
ABERDEEN (0) 1   AYR UNITED (0) 0
Jarvie (89)

ABERDEEN: Clark, Williamson, Hermiston, S. Murray, Young, Wilson, Varga, Graham, Mitchell, Jarvie, G. Buchan

AYR: Stewart, Wells, Murphy, McAnespie, Fleming, Filippi, Doyle, Graham, Ingram, McGregor, McCulloch

P	W	D	L	F	A	Pts	
23	11	7	5	42	26	29	

Attendance: 9,500
Referee: A. F. McDonald

Jim Hermiston missed a penalty, leaving it to Jarvie to bag the last-gasp winner. Ayr manager Ally McLeod jumped to his feet pointing to his watch. Time was up, he said.

No 24 Tuesday, 20 February
ABERDEEN (2) 6   DUMBARTON (0) 0
Purdie 2 (8, 65)
Forrest (35), Jenkins o.g.
(67), Varga (79),
Jarvie (88)

ABERDEEN: Clark, Williamson, Hermiston, S. Murray, Young, Wilson, Varga, Graham (Willoughby), Forrest, Jarvie, Purdie

DUMBARTON: Livingstone, Jenkins, McKay, Cushley, Bolton (Wilson), Graham, Coleman, Kidd, Mathie, Wallace, Heron

P	W	D	L	F	A	Pts	
24	12	7	5	48	26	31	

Attendance: 8,000
Referee: R. C. Greenlees

This is Dumbarton's first visit to Pittodrie since the War. They probably never want to come back again.

No 25 Saturday, 3 March
CELTIC (0) 2   ABERDEEN (0) 0
Lennox (60 pen),
Dalglish (83)

CELTIC: Hunter, McGrain, Quinn, Murdoch (McCluskey), McNeill, Connelly, Johnstone, Dalglish, Deans, Hood, Lennox

ABERDEEN: Clark, Williamson, Hermiston, S. Murray, Young, Willoughby, Varga, Graham, Forrest, Jarvie, Purdie

Leading positions

	P	W	D	L	F	A	Pts
1 Rangers	26	19	3	4	55	23	41
2 Celtic	25	18	4	3	67	25	40
3 Hibernian	24	17	3	4	66	22	37
4 Dundee	26	13	7	6	49	30	33
5 ABERDEEN	25	12	7	6	48	28	31

Attendance: 38,000
Referee: A. McKenzie

Aberdeen produced only one save from Alistair Hunter throughout the match. They were concerned only to protect their goal. This they did until Willie Young handled on the hour. By then Purdie had been booked for three tough fouls on McGrain in quick succession.

No 26 Wednesday, 7 March
ST JOHNSTONE (0) 1   ABERDEEN (0) 0
Muir (54)

ST JOHNSTONE: Donaldson, McManus, Argue, Kinnell, Macdonald, Rennie, Hall, Hotson, Muir, Rooney, Aitken

ABERDEEN: Clark, Williamson, Hermiston, J. Smith, Young, Taylor, Varga, Graham, Forrest, Jarvie, Purdie (Willoughby)

P	W	D	L	F	A	Pts	
26	12	7	7	48	29	31	

Attendance: 4,500
Referee: C. H. Hutton

This is St Johnstone's first win in nine games since the New Year, and they fully deserved it.

No 27 Saturday, 10 March
ABERDEEN (0) 0   PARTICK THISTLE (0) 0

ABERDEEN: Clark, Williamson, Hermiston, S. Murray, Young, J. Smith, Varga, Graham, Forrest, Jarvie (Street), Taylor

PARTICK: Rough, Hansen, Gray, Glavin, Campbell, Strachan, Gibson, Coulston, Craig (Lawrie), A. Rae, Chalmers

P	W	D	L	F	A	Pts	
27	12	8	7	48	29	32	

Attendance: 10,000
Referee: J. R. P. Gordon

Aberdeen have forgotten how to score. They are forced to concede defeat to Alan Rough – who plays for Scotland in Wales next week. Will Aberdeen remember how to score against Celtic in the Cup!

No 28 Saturday, 24 March
KILMARNOCK (0) 0   ABERDEEN (0) 2
Robb (70), Young (88)

KILMARNOCK: Stewart, Whyte, Robertson, Dickson, Rodman, Maxwell, McSherry, Morrison, Fleming, Smith, Cook

ABERDEEN: Clark, Williamson, Hermiston, Thomson, Young, J. Smith, S. Murray, Robb, Forrest, Jarvie, Graham

P W D L F A Pts   *Attendance:* 4,000
28 13 8 7 50 29 34   *Referee:* R. Marshall

Out of the Scottish Cup, Aberdeen have only a UEFA Cup place to aim for. When Dave Robb netted it was Aberdeen's first goal in six league and cup games. Ex-Hearts skipper Eddie Thomson makes his debut for the Dons.

No 29 Tuesday, 27 March
EAST FIFE (0) 0   ABERDEEN (1) 1
                              Varga (19)

EAST FIFE: McGarr, Duncan, Printy, Hamilton, Martis, Clarke, Hegarty, Love, Dailey, McPhee, Bernard

ABERDEEN: Clark, Williamson, Hermiston, Thomson (Jarvie), Young, J. Smith, S. Murray, Robb, Forrest, Varga, Graham

P W D L F A Pts   *Attendance:* 4,500
29 14 8 7 51 29 36   *Referee:* E. Thomson

These two points lift Aberdeen from sixth to fourth, thanks to Varga's side-footed goal from close range.

No 30 Saturday, 31 March
ABERDEEN (0) 0   DUNDEE UNITED (0) 0

ABERDEEN: Clark, Williamson, Hermiston, Thomson, Young, J. Smith, S. Murray (Willoughby), Robb, Jarvie, Varga, Graham

DUNDEE UNITED: Davie, Kopel, J. Cameron, Copland, D. Smith, W. Smith, K. Cameron, Fleming, Gardner, Mitchell, Traynor

P W D L F A Pts   *Attendance:* 9,500
30 14 9 7 51 29 37   *Referee:* I. M. D. Foote

Both teams – seeking a European place – have to battle against each other and a blustery wind. The wind wins.

No 31 Saturday, 7 April
ABERDEEN (2) 5   AIRDRIEONIANS (1) 1
  Jarvie 3 (22, 30, 62)   McKinley (13)
  Robb (79), Murray (87)

ABERDEEN: Clark, Williamson, Hermiston, Thomson, Young, J. Smith, S. Murray, Robb, Jarvie, Varga, Graham (Willoughby)

AIRDRIE; McKenzie, Jonquin, Caldwell, Fraser, McKinley, Whiteford, Wilson, McRoberts, Busby, Walker, Cowan

P W D L F A Pts   *Attendance:* 6,500
31 15 9 7 56 30 39   *Referee:* R. C. Greenlees

Before today Aberdeen have scored just three goals in eight league and cup games. Bottom-placed Airdrie, saying goodbye to the First Division, allow the Dons' marksmen some practice – after Airdrie had gone in front. How the visitors must miss Drew Jarvie!

No 32 Saturday, 14 April
ARBROATH (1) 1   ABERDEEN (1) 1
  Sellars (33)   Varga (12)

ARBROATH: Marshall, Milne, Rylance, Cargill, Waddell, Winchester, Sellars, Penman, Pirie, Fletcher, Payne

ABERDEEN: Clark, Williamson, Boel, Thomson, Young, J. Smith, S. Murray, Street, Jarvie, Varga, Forrest (Miller)

P W D L F A Pts   *Attendance:* 4,000
32 15 10 7 57 31 40   *Referee:* G. B. Smith

Bertie Miller wanted to come on as substitute – but he had forgotten his shorts. At the time Aberdeen were winning 1-0 through a delicately curled free kick by Varga, who was later booked.

No 33 Saturday, 21 April
ABERDEEN (0) 2   RANGERS (1) 2
  Hermiston (67 pen)   McLean (22) Conn (87)
  Taylor (85)

ABERDEEN: Clark, Williamson, Hermiston, Thomson, Young, J. Smith (Boel), S. Murray, Taylor, Jarvie, Varga, Graham

RANGERS: McCloy, Jardine, Mathieson, Greig, Johnstone, Smith, McLean, Forsyth, Parlane, MacDonald, Conn

P W D L F A Pts   *Attendance:* 32,000
33 15 11 7 59 33 41   *Referee:* J. W. Paterson

Rangers simply have to win if they want to deprive Celtic of the title. Calamity for them when Derek Johnstone hauls down Taylor in the box – and again when Taylor slips the ball past McCloy with time running out. But then Conn exchanges passes with Parlane for a clever equaliser.

No 34 Saturday, 28 April
MORTON (1) 1   ABERDEEN (0) 2
  Anderson (35)   Young (61),
                           Jarvie (62)

MORTON: Baines, Hayes, Ritchie, Rankin, Anderson, Clark, Brown (Hepburn), Lavelle, Murray, McNab, Armstrong

ABERDEEN: Clark, Williamson, Hermiston, Thomson, Young, Boel, J. Smith, Taylor, Jarvie, Varga, Graham (W. Miller)

Attendance: 3,000   *Referee:* R. W. Henderson

Aberdeen complete their fifth league double. With 37 minutes of the season remaining, Bonthrone gave young Willie Miller his first taste of league football.

Aberdeen's complete home and away record:

HOME						AWAY					
P	W	D	L	F	A	W	D	L	F	A	Pts
34	10	6	1	42	15	6	5	6	19	19	43

Scottish League Division One

		P	W	D	L	F	A	Pts
1	Celtic	34	26	5	3	93	28	57
2	Rangers	34	26	4	4	74	30	56
3	Hibernian	34	19	7	8	74	33	45
4	ABERDEEN	34	16	11	7	61	34	43
5	Dundee	34	17	9	8	68	43	43
6	Ayr United	34	16	8	10	50	51	40
7	Dundee United	34	17	5	12	56	51	39
8	Motherwell	34	11	9	14	38	48	31
9	East Fife	34	11	8	15	46	54	30
10	Hearts	34	12	6	16	39	50	30
11	St Johnstone	34	10	9	15	52	67	29
12	Morton	34	10	8	16	47	53	28
13	Partick Thistle	34	10	8	16	40	53	28
14	Falkirk	34	7	12	15	38	56	26
15	Arbroath	34	9	8	17	39	63	26
16	Dumbarton	34	6	11	17	43	72	23
17	Kilmarnock	34	7	8	19	40	71	22
18	Airdrieonians	34	4	8	22	34	75	16

LEAGUE CUP

Saturday, 12 August

QUEEN OF THE SOUTH (0) 0   ABERDEEN (1) 4
                            G. Buchan (39), Jarvie
                            (50), Hermiston (80),
                            Robb (88)

QUEEN OF THE SOUTH: Ball, Totten, Connell, Easton, Boyd, Dickson, Dempster, Hamilton, Malcolmson, Hannigan (Donald), Bryce

ABERDEEN: Clark, Willoughby, Hermiston, S. Murray, Boel, Young, G. Buchan, Robb, Harper, Jarvie, Taylor

Attendance: 5,000   *Referee:* J. Callaghan

New signing Drew Jarvie from Airdrie does not take long to bag his first goal. Robb and Harper set up the chance.

Wednesday, 16 August

ABERDEEN (3) 4   HIBERNIAN (0) 1
Jarvie 2 (28, 41),   Edwards (54)
Harper 2 (39, 62)

ABERDEEN: Clark, G. Murray, Hermiston, S. Murray, Boel, Young, G. Buchan, Robb, Harper, Jarvie, Taylor

HIBERNIAN: Herriot, Brownlie, Schaedler, Stanton, Black, Blackley, Hamilton, Edwards, Higgins, Cropley, Duncan

Attendance: 21,000   *Referee:* J. C. B. McRoberts

Eddie Turnbull didn't like this. Strangely, Hibs looked the better side until Aberdeen hit them with a triple blow. Most spectacular was the Don's fourth, by Harper, who lobbed a stranded Herriot from out near the touchline.

Saturday, 19 August

ABERDEEN (0) 5   QUEENS PARK (0) 1
Young 2 (40, 50),   Scott (54)
Harper 2 (78, 88),
Jarvie (81)

ABERDEEN: Clark, Willoughby, Hermiston, S. Murray, G. Murray, Young, G. Buchan (R. Miller), Robb, Harper, Jarvie, Taylor

QUEENS PARK: Purvis, Barr, Thomson, Robertson, Hunter, Whyte, Morrison, Campbell (Malloy), Scott, Mackay, Borland

Attendance: 12,500   *Referee:* E. Thomson

Thirteen goals in three games – four of them to Drew Jarvie. The temporary drought was ended by two Taylor corners: two flashing Young headers.

Wednesday, 23 August

HIBERNIAN (1) 2   ABERDEEN (0) 1
Duncan (28),   Jarvie (80)
O'Rourke (66)

HIBERNIAN: Herriot, Brownlie, Schaedler, Stanton, Black, Blackley, Edwards, O'Rourke, Gordon, Cropley (Hamilton), Duncan

ABERDEEN: Clark, G. Murray, Hermiston, S. Murray, Boel, Young, G. Buchan (R. Miller), Robb, Harper, Jarvie, Taylor

Attendance: 18,000   *Referee:* T. Marshall

Seven players were booked as Hibs exact revenge for their Pittodrie setback. With two teams to qualify it has not dampened Aberdeen's prospects.

Saturday, 26 August

ABERDEEN (1) 2   QUEEN OF SOUTH (0) 1
Taylor (13), Purdie (85)   Dickson (68)

ABERDEEN: Clark, Willoughby, Hermiston, S. Murray, G. Murray, Young, Purdie, Robb, Harper, Jarvie, Taylor

QUEEN OF THE SOUTH: Ball, Totten, Thorburn, Connell, Easton, Boyd, Dempster, Dickson, Malcolmson, McChesney, Donald

Attendance: 10,000   Referee: R. C. Greenlees

Just before Dickson equalised for Queens, Harper's penalty was saved by Ball – his second miss from the spot this season. He was mighty grateful for Purdie's winner.

Wednesday, 30 August

QUEENS PARK (0) 0   ABERDEEN (1) 3
                            Harper 3 (11, 53, 60)

QUEENS PARK: Taylor, Barr, Thomson, Hastie, Hunter, Robertson, Mackay, Gibson, Scott, Whyte, Colgan

ABERDEEN: Clark, Willoughby, Hermiston, S. Murray, G. Murray, Young, Purdie, Robb, Harper, Jarvie, Taylor

Attendance: 1,500   *Referee:* E. H. Pringle

Aberdeen won as they pleased at an eerily empty Hampden Park.

Section 2

	P	W	D	L	F	A	Pts
ABERDEEN	6	5	0	1	19	5	10
Hibernian	6	5	0	1	14	8	10
Queen of the South	6	2	0	4	5	13	4
Queens Park	6	0	0	6	4	16	0

2nd Round, 1st Leg Wednesday, 20 September
ABERDEEN (0) 8   FALKIRK (0) 0
   Forrest (50),
   Jarvie 2 (53, 74),
   Harper 3 (63, 77 pen, 86),
   Graham (87), Robb (88)
ABERDEEN: Clark, Willoughby, Hermiston, S. Murray, Boel, Young, Graham, Robb, Harper, Jarvie, Taylor (Forrest)
FALKIRK: Donaldson, S. Kennedy, Shirra (Setterington), Markie, McMillan, Cattenach, Hoggan, Harley, Young, J. Kennedy, McLeod
Attendance: 10,000   *Referee:* E. Thomson

When was the last time Aberdeen scored eight goals in 38 minutes? It was all sparked off by Forrest who came on as a second-half substitute.

2nd Round, 2nd Leg Wednesday, 4 October
FALKIRK (0) 3   ABERDEEN (2) 2
   Harley (49), Hoggan   Harper 2 (30, 40)
   (63), Young (79)
FALKIRK: Donaldson, S. Kennedy, Shirra, Markie, McMillan, J. Kennedy (Eadie), Hoggan, Harley, Scott, Young, McLeod
ABERDEEN: Clark, Willoughby, Hermiston, S. Murray, G. Murray, Young, Forrest, Taylor, Harper, Jarvie, R. Miller
        Referee: E. Thomson

At half-time Falkirk were 10-0 down on aggregate. That's a difficult margin to make up. But they did their best.

Quarter Final 1st Leg Wednesday, 11 October
ABERDEEN (1) 3   EAST FIFE (0) 0
   Taylor (24), Jarvie (38),
   Harper (75)
ABERDEEN: Clark, Willoughby, Hermiston, S. Murray, Young, Taylor (Graham), Forrest, Robb, Harper, Jarvie, R. Miller
EAST FIFE: Gorman, Duncan, McQuade, McIvor, Martis, Clarke, Honeyman, Hegarty, Dailey (Green), Borthwick, McPhee
Attendance: 14,000   *Referee:* A. F. Webster

No doubt about the hero of this match – East Fife goalkeeper David Gorman. Without him East Fife would doubtless have gone the same way as Falkirk.

Quarter Final 2nd Leg Wednesday, 1 November
EAST FIFE (0) 1   ABERDEEN (2) 4
   Hegarty (80)   Harper (22), Jarvie 2
                (32, 55), Clarke o.g. (57)

EAST FIFE: Gorman, Printy, McQuade, McIvor, Martis, Clarke, Hegarty, Hamilton, Honeyman, McPhee, Bernard
ABERDEEN: Clark, Willoughby (Forrest), Hermiston, S. Murray, Mitchell, Taylor, Varga, Robb, Harper, Jarvie, R. Miller
Attendance: 4,500   *Referee:* A. J. F. Webster

East Fife did their best, but it wasn't good enough. Harper's head-flick ended the match as a contest.

Semi Final (Hampden) Monday, 27 November
CELTIC (1) 3   ABERDEEN (1) 2
   Hood (33 pen), Johnstone   Harper (30), Robb (74)
   (75), Callaghan (80)
CELTIC: Williams, McGrain, Brogan, McCluskey, Connelly, Hay, Johnstone, Deans, Dalglish, Hood, Callaghan
ABERDEEN: Clark, Willoughby, Hermiston, S. Murray, Young, Taylor, Varga, Robb, Harper, Jarvie, R. Miller
Attendance: 39,682   *Referee:* J. W. Paterson

What a cracker. Driving rain couldn't spoil this contest as a spectacle. Twice Aberdeen took the lead and twice Celtic quickly drew level. When Robb headed the Dons 2-1 in front from Varga's corner Aberdeen must have thought they'd done it. But Johnstone – looking offside – beat Clark from close range and Callaghan volleyed the winner. In the final moments Taylor's effort was parried by Williams.

SCOTTISH CUP

3rd Round, Saturday, 4 February
BRECHIN CITY (0) 2   ABERDEEN (3) 4
   Coutts (73),   Mitchell 2 (16, 44),
   Clark (87 pen)   Jarvie (33),
                Milne o.g. (64)
BRECHIN: McEwan, Kidd, Gillespie, Donnelly, Milne, Clark, Miller (Britton), Coutts, Reid, Cunningham, Dow
ABERDEEN: Clark, Willoughby, Hermiston, J. Smith, Young, Wilson, Varga, Graham, Mitchell, Jarvie, R. Miller
Attendance: 8,100   *Referee:* J. Gordon

There was a hint of crowd bother before the match – and more than a hint of bother for Brechin, who were effectively buried by half-time. But they never stopped fighting – literally.

4th Round Wednesday, 28 February
ABERDEEN (1) 3   FALKIRK (0) 1
   Forrest (44), Purdie   Harley (68)
   (47), Murray (75)
ABERDEEN: Clark, Williamson, Hermiston, S. Murray, Young, Wilson, Varga, Graham, Forrest, Jarvie, Purdie
FALKIRK: Donaldson, S. Kennedy, J. Kennedy, McMillan, Markie, McLeod, Hoggan, Harley, Somner, Ferguson, Setterington

Attendance: 17,700   *Referee:* J. R. P. Gordon

Falkirk must be dreading the thought of a repeat 8-0 drubbing handed out to them in the League Cup. Seconds after Jim Forrest put the Dons in front Falkirk player-coach Alex Ferguson was involved in a skirmish with Willie Young and was ordered off.

Quarter Final Saturday, 17 March

CELTIC (0) 0   ABERDEEN (0) 0

CELTIC: Hunter, McGrain, Brogan, Murdoch, McNeill, Connelly, Johnstone, Dalglish, Deans, Hay, Lennox

ABERDEEN: Clark, Williamson, Hermiston, S. Murray, Young, J. Smith, Varga (Jarvie), Robb, Forrest, Graham, Taylor

Referee: R. H. Davidson

In a recent league match at Parkhead, Aberdeen held out for an hour. This time they grit their teeth for the extra thirty minutes in the face of pulsating Celtic attacks. Well over twenty corners were conceded by a desperate back-peddling Dons' defence. Celtic's cause was not helped by having Jimmy Johnstone sent off after being a bad boy with Jim Hermiston. Aberdeen were no saints, either, having three players booked.

Quarter Final Replay Wednesday, 21 March

ABERDEEN (0) 0   CELTIC (0) 1

                     McNeill (86)

ABERDEEN: Clark, Williamson, Hermiston, S. Murray, Young, J. Smith, Forrest, Robb, (G. Buchan), Jarvie, Graham, R. Miller

CELTIC: Hunter, McGrain, Brogan, Murdoch, McNeill, Connelly, Johnstone (Davidson), Hood, Deans, Hay, Lennox

Attendance: 33,465   *Referee:* R. H. Davidson

When Billy McNeill headed home Hood's corner four minutes from time it heralded Aberdeen's first home defeat in the Scottish Cup since 1964. It was a pity that either side had to lose an epic battle. But Celtic had more of the pressure, forcing 14 corners to Aberdeen's six.

UEFA CUP

1st Round, 1st Leg Wednesday, 13 September

ABERDEEN (0) 2   BORUSSIA

   Harper (55),   MOENCHEN-GLADBACH

   Jarvie (67)   (W Germany) (2) 3

                  Kulik (20),

                  Heynckes (38),

                  Jensen (76)

ABERDEEN: Geoghegan, Willoughby, Hermiston, Taylor, Boel, Young, Forrest, Robb, Harper, Jarvie, Graham (R. Miller)

BORUSSIA: Kleff, Michalik, Rosenthal, Kulik (Bleidik), Vogts, Bonhof, Rupp, Wimmer, Heynckes, Netzer (Danner), Jensen

Attendance: 21,000   *Referee:* R. Machin

                       (France)

Gunther Netzer, Josef Heynckes, Bertie Vogts, Reiner

Bonhof: these are just some of the illustrious names to enthall Pittodrie. Netzer strode imperiously around the pitch throughout the first half, producing the slide-rule pass from which Heynckes put the German side two up. Netzer's thigh injury prompted his substitution at half-time and Aberdeen hit back bravely. Pandemonium when Jarvie headed the equaliser. But Borussia broke upfield to snatch a cruel third goal.

1st Round, 2nd Leg Wednesday, 27 September

BORUSSIA   ABERDEEN (3) 3

   MOENCHEN-   Jarvie (23),

   GLADBACH (2) 6,   Willoughby (26),

   Rupp (3), Heynckes 3   S. Murray (45)

   (40 pen, 74, 88), Vogts

   (70), Danner (83 pen)

BORUSSIA: Kleff, Michalik, Bonhof, Rosenthal, Vogts, Danner, Kulik, Rupp (Fuhrmann), Wimmer, Heynckes, Jensen

ABERDEEN: Clark, Willoughby, Hermiston, S. Murray, Boel (G. Murray), Young, Taylor, Robb, Harper, Jarvie, Graham

Borussia won 9-5 on aggregate

Attendance: 19,000   *Referee:* F. Rion (Belgium)

This was not as bad as it sounds. Aberdeen shrugged off the loss of an early goal at Nuremburg, and the loss of Henning Boel on a stretcher, to launch a first-half blitzkrieg that saw them square the aggregate scores at 5-5 by the interval. It took a surging run and shot by Vogts to break Aberdeen's resistance – and their hearts.

1972-73

APPEARANCES	League	League Cup	Scottish Cup	UEFA Cup
Jarvie	33(+1)	11	3(+1)	2
Clark	33	11	4	1
Hermiston	33	11	4	2
Young	30	10	4	2
S. Murray	29	11	3	1
Varga	26	2	3	
Willoughby	22(+4)	9	1	2
Graham	19(+4)	1(+1)	4	2
Robb	19	10	2	2
Taylor	18	11	1	2
R. Miller	13(+5)	4(+2)	2	–(+1)
Joe Smith	13(+1)		3	
Harper	13	11		2
Mitchell	12	1	1	
Williamson	12		3	
Forrest	11	2(+2)	3	1
Wilson	9		2	
G. Murray	7	6		–(+1)
Thomson	7			
Boel	6(+1)	4		2
G. Buchan	4(+4)	4	–(+1)	
Purdie	3	2	1	
Street	1(+1)			
Geoghegan	1			1
W. Miller	–(+1)			

25 players

GOALS	Total	League	League Cup	Scottish Cup	UEFA Cup	GOALS	Total	League	League Cup	Scottish Cup	UEFA Cup
Jarvie	28	15	10	1	2	Forrest	3	1	1	1	
Harper	26	10	15		1	Mitchell	3	1		2	
Varga	10	10				R. Miller	2	2			
Robb	8	5	3			Willoughby	2	1			1
Taylor	6	4	2			G. Buchan	1		1		
S. Murray	6	4		1	1	Graham	1		1		
Purdie	4	2	1	1		own-goals	4	2	1	1	
Young	4	2	2			Totals	111	61	38	7	5
Hermiston	3	2	1								

An Aberdeen squad of 1973. Back row: Hermiston, Williamson, Joe Smith, Clark, Boel, Geoghegan, Thomson, Mitchell, Graham. Front row: Bertie Miller, Purdie, Jarvie, Young, Taylor, Willoughby and Varga.

Season 1973-74

1973-74 was the season Aberdeen became universally popular in the world of Pools punters. They took on the role of Scotland's draw specialists, tieing more of their matches than in any other season since the War.

Aberdeen were less popular with their fans. Without Zoltan Varga (later to replace Johan Cruyff at Ajax) and Steve Murray (bound for Parkhead), the Dons' engine room lacked polish. Up front, the supply of goals without Joe Harper to score them dried up alarmingly. It was necessary to go back 25 years to find an Aberdeen team which hit the net less frequently. Fortunately, a stalwart defence – now marshalled by Willie Young and Willie Miller – ensured that the Dons kept a tight rein on the goals-against column.

In the League Cup Aberdeen were squeezed out of their group section on goal difference. In the second round Stirling Albion failed to provide sterling opposition, but in the quarter finals Celtic duly dumped Aberdeen by the wayside. Some weeks earlier, inthe UEFA Cup, Aberdeen had faced an English club for the first time in official competition. Tottenham Hotspur were old hands at European warfare, as they showed both at Pittodrie and White Hart Lane.

In the league Jock Stein's Celtic were once again streaking away from all pretenders to their crown, leaving Aberdeen to toil unsuccessfully for the right of entry into next year's UEFA Cup. As for the Scottish Cup, Aberdeen's participation was short, and anything but sweet. Dundee came north and won crisply and deservedly.

League:	Fourth
League Cup:	Quarter Final
Scottish Cup:	Third Round
UEFA Cup:	Second Round

SCOTTISH LEAGUE DIVISION ONE

No 1 Saturday, 1 September
MOTHERWELL (0) 0   ABERDEEN (0) 0
MOTHERWELL: MacRae, John Muir, Wark, Watson, Jim Muir, Goodwin (Goldthorp), Campbell, Millar, Lawson (Martin), McCabe, McClymont
ABERDEEN: Clark, Hair, Willoughby, Thomson, Young, W. Miller, J. Smith, Graham, Taylor, Jarvie, R. Miller (Purdie)

P	W	D	L	F	A	Pts	
1	0	1	0	0	0	1	*Attendance:* 6,100
							Referee: R. Gordon

Aberdeen have yet to concede a goal in four league and League Cup games on opponents' grounds.

No 2 Saturday, 8 September
ABERDEEN (0) 0   DUNDEE (0) 0
ABERDEEN: Clark, Hair, Hermiston, Thomson, Young, W. Miller, J. Smith, Graham, Taylor, Jarvie, Purdie (R. Miller)

DUNDEE: Allan, Ford, Johnston, Robinson, Stewart (Pringle), Gemmell, Anderson (Wilson), Duncan, Wallace, Scott, Lambie

P	W	D	L	F	A	Pts	
2	0	2	0	0	0	2	*Attendance:* 10,000
							Referee: A. McKenzie

It seems ages since Aberdeen have been involved in a goal – at either end.

No 3 Saturday, 15 September
ST JOHNSTONE (0) 1   ABERDEEN (2) 2
  Smith (71)   R. Miller (17), Hair (42)
ST JOHNSTONE: Donaldson, Lambie, Argue, Rennie, Macdonald, Rooney (Ritchie), Hall, Smith, Pearson, Muir (McGregor), Aitken
ABERDEEN: Clark, Hair, Hermiston, Thomson, Young, W. Miller, Willoughby, Graham (Craig), Taylor, Jarvie, R. Miller

P	W	D	L	F	A	Pts	
3	1	2	0	2	1	4	*Attendance:* 3,000
							Referee: J. W. Paterson

St Johnstone wiped the smile off Bobby Clark's face: he lost his first goal in six games. But Aberdeen had the last laugh.

No 4 Saturday, 29 September
CLYDE (0) 1   ABERDEEN (2) 3
  McVie (54)   Robb 2 (20, 89),
                                 Jarvie (40)
CLYDE: Cairney, McHugh, Swan, Beattie, McVie, Ahern, Sullivan, Burns, Miller, McGrain, Boyle
ABERDEEN: Clark, Hair, Hermiston, Thomson, Young, W. Miller, Willoughby, Robb, Taylor, Jarvie, Purdie

P	W	D	L	F	A	Pts
4	2	2	0	5	2	6

Attendance: 3,000
Referee: W. Anderson

Clyde made the mistake of unfurling the Second Division championship flag before the match. They had little to celebrate during it, having Burns ordered off for crocking Taylor.

No 5 Saturday, 6 October
ABERDEEN (1) 1   HIBERNIAN (1) 1
  Jarvie (29)   Gordon (8)
ABERDEEN: Clark, Hair, Hermiston, Thomson, Young, W. Miller, Graham, Robb, Taylor, Jarvie, R. Miller
HIBERNIAN: McKenzie, Bremner, Schaedler, Stanton, Black, Blackley, Edwards, O'Rourke (Higgins), Gordon, Cropley, Duncan

P	W	D	L	F	A	Pts
5	2	3	0	6	3	7

Attendance: 15,000
Referee: R. B. Valentine

Young Willie Miller commits a howler. He passes back to a goalkeeper who wasn't there . . . His game collapsed afterwards. Jarvie's equaliser eases his torment.

No 6 Saturday, 13 October
DUMBARTON (0) 0   ABERDEEN (0) 1
                                 Jarvie (61)
DUMBARTON: Williams, McKay, Wilkinson, Menzies, Cushley, Ruddy, Coleman (Graham), Wallace, McCormack, Paterson, McAdam (Jenkins)
ABERDEEN: Clark, Hair, Hermiston, Thomson (Graham), Young, W. Miller, Willoughby, Robb, Taylor, Jarvie, R. Miller

P	W	D	L	F	A	Pts
6	3	3	0	7	3	9

Attendance: 5,500
Referee: T. Muirhead

A bread and butter match with a bread and butter goal. Willie Miller's cross eluded Williams, came back off the far post and was tucked in by Jarvie.

No 7 Saturday, 20 October
ABERDEEN (0) 0   DUNFERMLINE
                                 ATHLETIC (0) 0
ABERDEEN: Clark, Hair, Hermiston, Thomson, Young, W. Miller, Willoughby (R. Miller), Robb, Taylor (Craig), Jarvie, Graham

DUNFERMLINE: Arrol, Leishman, Wallace, Thomson, McNicoll (Nelson), Kinninmonth, Campbell, Scott, Mackie, Shaw, Gillespie

P	W	D	L	F	A	Pts
7	3	4	0	7	3	10

Attendance: 7,000
Referee: A. F. McDonald

As Dunfermline edged nearer their objective, 30-yard pass-backs to their goalkeeper became more frequent.

No 8 Saturday, 27 October
ABERDEEN (1) 3   DUNDEE UNITED (0) 1
  Graham (33), Robb (65),   Gray (54)
  Jarvie (76)
ABERDEEN: Clark, Hair, Hermiston, Thomson, Young, W. Miller, Graham, Robb, Jarvie, J. Smith, Taylor.
DUNDEE UNITED: McAlpine, Rolland, Kopel, Copland, D. Smith, W. Smith, Henry (Gray), Knox (K. Cameron), Gardner, Fleming, Traynor
Leading positions

	P	W	D	L	F	A	Pts
1 Celtic	8	6	1	1	17	6	13
2 Hearts	9	5	3	1	20	10	13
3 Ayr	9	5	2	2	17	11	12
4 ABERDEEN	8	4	4	0	10	4	12
5 Dundee United	8	5	0	3	13	11	10

Attendance: 8,000
Referee: E. Thomson

Goals at last. This is Aberdeen's first home league win. They are the last unbeaten side in Scotland, and have the best defensive record. For a while Andy Gray threatened Aberdeen's winning prospects.

No 9 Saturday, 3 November
MORTON (0) 2   ABERDEEN (0) 0
  Thomas (46),
  Osborne (89)
MORTON: Baines, Hayes, Ritchie, Townsend, Anderson, Nelson, Osborne, Reid, McIlmoyle, McCallion, Thomas
ABERDEEN: Clark, Hair, Hermiston, Thomson, Young, Mitchell, Graham, Robb, Jarvie, Willoughby, R. Miller (Taylor)

P	W	D	L	F	A	Pts
9	4	4	1	10	6	12

Attendance: 4,000
Referee: R. R. McGinlay

Morton's second win of the season and their first at Cappielow. Aberdeen left their concentration in the dressing room at half-time.

No 10 Saturday, 10 November
FALKIRK (0) 1   ABERDEEN (1) 3
  Fowler (64)   Robb 2 (11, 52),
                                 Jarvie (84)
FALKIRK: Donaldson, D. Whiteford, Cameron, Markie, Gibson, McLeod, Thomas, Fowler, Lawson, Shirra, Mitchell (Young)
ABERDEEN: Clark, Hair, Hermiston, Thomson, Young, W. Miller, Willoughby, Robb, Jarvie, J. Smith, Graham (J. Miller)

P W D L F A Pts   *Attendance:* 3,000
10 5 4 1 13 7 14   *Referee:* R. Gordon

Falkirk are still looking for their first win. All these Millers are becoming confusing. Aberdeen have one of them on from the start – Willie – and two more on the bench – Jimmy and Bertie. It's Jimmy who takes over from Arthur Graham.

No 11 Saturday, 17 November
ABERDEEN (1) 3   HEARTS (1) 1
   Anderson o.g. (21),   Ford (27)
   W. Miller (75), Jarvie (89)

ABERDEEN: Clark, Hair, Hermiston, Thomson, Young, W. Miller, J. Miller, Robb, Jarvie, J. Smith (Craig), Graham
HEARTS: Garland, Kay, Clunie, Cant, Anderson, Jefferies, Park, Ford, Busby, Stevenson, Prentice

P W D L F A Pts   *Attendance:* 10,800
11 6 4 1 16 8 16   *Referee:* T. Kellock

More of the same please. Both sides looked good: Aberdeen better. A minute after Craig came on as a sub his cross was knocked out to Willie Miller who hit a screamer from 20 yards past Garland.

No 12 Saturday, 24 November
EAST FIFE (1) 2   ABERDEEN (0) 2
   Borthwick (9),   Hermiston (63 pen),
   Hegarty (64)   Robb (67)

EAST FIFE: McGarr, Duncan, Printy, Hamilton (McIvor), Martis, Clarke, Love, Hegarty, Borthwick, McPhee, Ritchie
ABERDEEN: Clark, Boel, Hermiston, Thomson, Young, W. Miller, J. Miller, Robb, Jarvie, Craig, Graham

P W D L F A Pts   *Attendance:* 2,600
12 6 5 1 18 10 17   *Referee:* D. Ramsay

Dave Robb is the saint and the sinner. His suicidal, inattentive back-pass was gobbled up by Hegarty to restore the Fifers' lead. Minutes later he was on the receiving end of Willie Miller's through ball to level the scores. Robb, to cap it all, had earlier been booked.

No 13 Saturday, 22 December
ARBROATH (0) 1   ABERDEEN (0) 3
   Sellars (72)   Taylor 3 (55, 73, 77)

ARBROATH: Marshall, Milne, Rylance, Cargill, Waddell, Murray (Walker), Sellars, Cant, Pirie, Penman, Fletcher
ABERDEEN: Clark, Boel, Hermiston, Thomson, Young, W. Miller, J. Miller (Willoughby), Taylor, Jarvie, Craig, Graham

P W D L F A Pts   *Attendance:* 2,600
13 7 5 1 21 11 19   *Referee:* I. Muirhead

Ian Taylor only scored three goals throughout the 1973-74 league season. They all came at Gayfield Park.

No 14 Saturday, 29 December
ABERDEEN (0) 0   MOTHERWELL (0) 0

ABERDEEN: Clark, Boel, Hermiston, Thomson, Young, W. Miller, J. Miller (Willoughby), Taylor, Jarvie, Craig, Graham
MOTHERWELL: Rennie, John Muir, Wark, R. Watson, Jim Muir, McCabe, Campbell, Graham, Goldthorp, Martin, McClymont

P W D L F A Pts   *Attendance:* 8,000
14 7 6 1 21 11 20   *Referee:* J. R. P. Gordon

Tedium reigns. This is Aberdeen and Motherwell's third goal-less draw of the season – but McCabe struck Clark's upright near the end.

No 15 Tuesday, 1 January
DUNDEE (1) 1   ABERDEEN (1) 1
   J. Wilson (26)   Graham (44)

DUNDEE: Allan, R. Wilson, Johnston, Ford, Gemmell, Phillip, J. Wilson, Robinson, Duncan, J. Scott, Lambie
ABERDEEN: Clark, Boel, Hermiston, Thomson, Young, W. Miller, Willoughby, Williamson, Jarvie (Purdie), Craig (J. Smith), Graham

P W D L F A Pts   *Attendance:* 9,450
15 7 7 1 22 12 21   *Referee:* G. B. Smith

Graham's beauty, switching the ball from right foot to left and bending his shot inside the far post, brought a smile to Jimmy Bonthrone. Jimmy Wilson's crunching collision with John Craig which broke the Aberdeen player's leg wiped it off again.

No 16 Saturday, 5 January
ABERDEEN (0) 0   ST JOHNSTONE (0) 1
                             Hall (74)

ABERDEEN: Clark, Boel, Hermiston, Thomson, Young, W. Miller, Graham (Willoughby), Taylor, McCall, J. Smith, Purdie
ST JOHNSTONE: Donaldson, Ritchie, Argue, Rennie, Macdonald, Cramond, Muir, Smith, Pearson, Hall, Hotson

P W D L F A Pts   *Attendance:* 5,000
16 7 7 2 22 13 21   *Referee:* D. F. T. Syme

If he'd played his cards right Henry Hall would have been an Aberdeen player. Instead Pittodrie casts its critical eye on debutant Walker McCall. They are soon chanting 'We want Joey Harper', who is to be freed by Everton.

No 17 Saturday, 12 January
RANGERS (0) 1   ABERDEEN (1) 1
   McLean (51)   Purdie (31)

RANGERS: McCloy, Jardine, Mathieson, Greig, Johnstone, Forsyth, McLean, O'Hara, Parlane, MacDonald, Young (Fyfe)
ABERDEEN: Clark, Boel, Hermiston, Thomson (Williamson), Young, W. Miller, Graham, J. Smith, Taylor, Henry, Purdie

P W D L F A Pts   *Attendance:* 16,000
17 7 8 2 23 14 22   *Referee:* R. H. Davidson

Aberdeen haven't lost at Ibrox now for four years. They were prevented from winning by McLean's back-header from a free kick as Clark came off his line.

No 18 Saturday, 19 January
ABERDEEN (1) 1   CLYDE (0) 1
  Jarvie (41)   McVie (90)
ABERDEEN: Clark, Boel, Hermiston, Thomson, Young, W. Miller (J. Smith), Taylor, Robb, Jarvie, Henry, Purdie
CLYDE: Cairney, Anderson, Swan, McHugh, McVie, Ahern (Boyle), Sullivan, Burns, Miller, McGrain, Beattie
Leading positions

	P	W	D	L	F	A	Pts
1 Celtic	19	16	2	1	54	12	34
2 Hibernian	19	12	4	3	41	22	28
3 Rangers	19	11	4	4	31	16	26
4 Ayr	21	10	5	6	28	22	25
5 ABERDEEN	18	7	9	2	24	15	23

Attendance: 7,000   *Referee:* C. H. Hutton
In the third minute of injury time, McVie headed home from a corner to deny Aberdeen their first double of the season.

No 19 Saturday, 2 February
HIBERNIAN (2) 3   ABERDEEN (1) 1
  O'Rourke 2 (4, 49),   Robb (17)
  Gordon (35)
HIBERNIAN: McArthur, Brownlie, Schaedler, Stanton, Black, Blackley, Edwards, O'Rourke, Gordon, Cropley, Duncan
ABERDEEN: Clark, Williamson, Hermiston, J. Smith, Young, W. Miller, Graham, Robb, Jarvie, Taylor, Purdie (Street)

P	W	D	L	F	A	Pts
19	7	9	3	25	18	23

Attendance: 15,700   *Referee:* R. B. Valentine
Aberdeen have now gone seven league and cup games without a win. It makes you want to weep: Hibs have signed Joe Harper, who sits in the stand to watch his new team demolish his old.

No 20 Saturday, 9 February
ABERDEEN (0) 3   DUMBARTON (0) 0
  Young (50), Robb (86),
  Jarvie (88)
ABERDEEN: Clark, Hermiston, McLelland, J. SMith, Young, W. Miller, Street (Thomson), Robb, Jarvie, Henry, Graham
DUMBARTON: Williams (McIntyre), McKay, Black, Menzies, Cushley, Ruddy, McAdam, Wallace, McCormack, Mathie, Paterson

P	W	D	L	F	A	Pts
20	8	9	3	28	18	25

Attendance: 4,000   *Referee:* B. R. McGinlay
Aberdeen's poor form is reflected in the gate – their lowest for about 16 years. Bobby Street broke his leg after just five minutes on his come-back. Chick McLelland had an uneventful debut.

No 21 Sunday, 24 February
DUNFERMLINE   ABERDEEN (0) 0
ATHLETIC (0) 0
DUNFERMLINE: Karlsen, Brown, Wallace, Thomson, McCallum, Kinninmonth, Cameron, Scott, Mackie, Shaw, Sinclair
ABERDEEN: Clark, Hermiston, McLelland, Thomson, Young, W. Miller, J. Smith (Craig), Robb, Jarvie, Henry, Graham

P	W	D	L	F	A	Pts
21	8	10	3	28	18	26

Attendance: 7,000   *Referee:* A. J. McCririck
Aberdeen's goal held out as if by magic in the dying minutes as relegation-threatened Dunfermline did everything but score.

No 22 Sunday, 3 March
DUNDEE UNITED (0) 0 ABERDEEN (1) 3
                          Robb (18), Smith (63),
                          Narey o.g. (77)
DUNDEE UNITED: Davie, Addison, Kopel, Copland, D. Smith (Narey), W. Smith, Payne, Sheehy (Holt), Cameron, Gardner, Traynor
ABERDEEN: Clark, Hermiston, McLelland, Thomson, Young, W. Miller, J. Smith, Robb, Jarvie, Henry, Graham

P	W	D	L	F	A	Pts
22	9	10	3	31	18	28

Attendance: 6,500   *Referee:* A. F. J. Webster
United contributed to their own downfall in the second half. Joe Smith's flashing cross was turned into his own goal by Addison, under pressure from Jarvie; and when Jarvie's shot banged against a post, Narey ran the ball over the line. Earlier Robb had scored his 100th goal for Aberdeen.

No 23 Saturday, 9 March
ABERDEEN (0) 0   MORTON (0) 0
ABERDEEN: Clark, Hermiston, McLelland, Thomson, Young, W. Miller (Taylor), J. SMith, Robb, Pirie, Jarvie, Graham
MORTON: Baines, Hayes, Ritchie, Anderson (Townsend), Nelson, Rankin, Murray, Reid, McIlmoyle, Hepburn, McCallion

P	W	D	L	F	A	Pts
23	9	11	3	31	18	29

Attendance: 5,000   *Referee:* R. C. Greenlees
Once again Aberdeen have forgotten how to lose goals – and how to score them.

No 24 Saturday, 16 March
ABERDEEN (2) 6   FALKIRK (0) 0
  Young (7), Jarvie
  4 (36, 61, 73, 77),
  Robb (74)
ABERDEEN: Clark, Hermiston, McLelland, Thomson, Young, Hair, J. Smith (Taylor), Robb, Pirie, Jarvie, Graham
FALKIRK: Donaldson, D. Whiteford, Cameron, Markie, Gibson, Wheatley, Hoggan, Fowler (Thomas), Lawson, Smith, Shirra (Harley)

P W D L F A Pts   *Attendance:* 5,500
24 10 11 3 37 18 31   *Referee:* R. D. Henderson

No wonder Falkirk are bottom of the league. Aberdeen parade new signing Billy Pirie and he inspires Jarvie to a four-goal bonanza!

No 25 Saturday, 23 March
HEARTS (0) 0   ABERDEEN (0) 0
HEARTS: Cruickshank, Sneddon, Clunie, Jefferies, Anderson, Brown, Aird, Ford, Busby, Stevenson, Prentice
ABERDEEN: Clark, Hermiston, McLelland, Thomson, Young, Hair, J. Smith, Robb, Pirie, Jarvie, Graham
P W D L F A Pts   *Attendance:* 13,500
25 10 12 3 37 18 32   *Referee:* T. Kellock
Not a game to remember. Three players were booked, including Robb of Aberdeen.

No 26 Saturday, 30 March
ABERDEEN (0) 2   EAST FIFE (0) 0
  Graham (72), Jarvie (77)
ABERDEEN: Clark, Hermiston, McLelland, Thomson, Young, Hair, J. Smith, Robb, Pirie, Jarvie, Graham
EAST FIFE: McGarr, Printy, Gillies, Clarke, Martis, Rae, Miller, Borthwick, Kinnear, O'Connor, Love (McPhee)
P W D L F A Pts   *Attendance:* 5,000
26 11 12 3 39 18 34   *Referee:* A. McKenzie
Are you watching, Willie Ormond? With the World Cup finals only two months away Bobby Clark and Ernie McGarr are the best players on the pitch.

No 27 Saturday, 6 April
AYR UNITED (0) 0   ABERDEEN (0) 0
AYR: A. McLean, Wells, Filippi, McAnespie, Fleming, Tait, Doyle, Graham, Ingram, G. McLean, McCulloch
ABERDEEN: Clark, Hermiston, McClelland, Thomson, Young, W. Miller, J. Smith, Robb, Pirie, Jarvie, Graham
Leading positions

	P	W	D	L	F	A	Pts
1 Celtic	27	20	3	4	70	24	43
2 Rangers	28	17	5	6	54	26	39
3 Hibernian	25	14	7	4	55	34	35
4 ABERDEEN	27	11	13	3	39	18	35
5 Ayr	30	13	7	10	39	36	33

Attendance: 4,500   *Referee:* E. Thomson

Clark's eighth consecutive shut-out. He hasn't been beaten since 2 February. Pirie's header hit a post.

No 28 Monday, 8 April
PARTICK THISTLE (0) 2   ABERDEEN (0) 0
  Craig (65), Glavin (88)

PARTICK: Rough, Houston, Kellachan, Glavin, Campbell, Anderson, Chalmers, McDowell (Gibson), Craig, Rooney, Lawrie
ABERDEEN: Clark, Hermiston, McLelland, Thomson, Young, W. Miller (McCall), J. Smith, Hair, Pirie (Davidson), Jarvie, Graham
P W D L F A Pts   *Attendance:* 4,500
28 11 13 4 39 20 35   *Referee:* R. H. Davidson
For over an hour it looked like Aberdeen would record their ninth game in a row without losing a goal. But then Glavin's shot was only parried by Clark, and Craig swooped.

No 29 Saturday, 13 April
ABERDEEN (1) 2   PARTICK THISTLE (0) 0
  Robb (40), Smith (87)
ABERDEEN: Clark, Hermiston, McLelland, Thomson, Young, W. Miller, J. Smith, Robb, Hair, Jarvie, Graham
PARTICK: Rough, Houston, Kellachan, Glavin, Campbell, Anderson, Chalmers, McDowell (Gibson), Craig, Rooney, Lawrie
P W D L F A Pts   *Attendance:* 6,000
29 12 13 4 41 20 37   *Referee:* W. Anderson
Quick revenge for Aberdeen – but Robb looked offside as he collected McLelland's lob before netting.

No 30 Wednesday, 17 April
ABERDEEN (0) 1   RANGERS (0) 1
  McDougall o.g. (56)   Greig (75)
ABERDEEN: Clark, Hermiston, McLelland, Thomson, Young, W. Miller (McCall), J. Smith, Robb, Pirie, Jarvie, Graham
RANGERS: McCloy, Jardine, Greig, McDougall, Johnstone, Jackson, Young, Scott, Parlane, MacDonald, Fyfe
P W D L F A Pts   *Attendance:* 18,000
30 12 14 4 42 21 38   *Referee:* E. H. Pringle
Aberdeen were grateful to young Ian McDougall for a back-pass which completely nonplussed McCloy. It looked like giving Aberdeen their first home win over Rangers in the league for nine seasons. But then came Greig's raging shot-on-the-run from 25 yards.

No 31 Saturday, 20 April
CELTIC (1) 2   ABERDEEN (0) 0
  Deans (4), Lennox (85)
CELTIC: Connaughan, McGrain, Brogan, Hay, McNeill, McCluskey, Johnstone (Lennox), Murray, Deans (Callaghan), Hood, Dalglish
ABERDEEN: Clark, Hermiston, McLelland, Thomson, Young, W. Miller (Davidson), J. Smith, Hair, Pirie, Jarvie (McCall), Graham
P W D L F A Pts   *Attendance:* 31,000
31 12 14 5 42 23 38   *Referee:* G. B. Smith
Celtic are almost home and dry for their ninth succesive title. They were on their way after just four minutes,

when Johnstone cut the ball in front of Deans. Aberdeen centre-half Willie Young was booked for toppling ex-Don Steve Murray.

No 32 Wednesday, 24 April
ABERDEEN (1) 2   AYR UNITED (0) 1
  Thomson (22),   McLean (64)
  McCall (75)
ABERDEEN: Clark, Hermiston, McLelland, Thomson, Young (Williamson), W. Miller, J. Smith, Hair (Davidson), McCall, Jarvie, Graham
AYR: A. McLean, Wells, Filippi, McAnespie, Fleming, Tait, Doyle, Graham (Docherty), Ingram, G. McLean (Donald), McCulloch

P	W	D	L	F	A	Pts	
32	13	14	5	44	24	40	*Attendance:* 4,000

Referee: n.a.

Ayr's McCulloch was ordered off shortly after Aberdeen's first goal for speaking out of turn. At 1-1 Arthur Graham was also dismissed for hacking down Wells off the ball. When everything had calmed down Walker McCall scored his first senior goal for Aberdeen.

No 33 Saturday, 27 April
ABERDEEN (1) 2   ARBROATH (0) 2
  McLelland (1),   Sellars (74),
  McCall (83)   Cant (80 pen)
ABERDEEN: Clark, Hermiston, McLelland, Thomson, Young, W. Miller, J. Smith, McCall, Pirie (Davidson), Jarvie, Graham
ARBROATH: Marshall, Milne, Buchan, Cargill, Carson, Murray, Sellars, Cant, Fletcher, Rylance, Walker

P	W	D	L	F	A	Pts	
33	13	15	5	46	26	41	*Attendance:* 4,000

Referee: R. H. Davidson

When Willie Young handled the ball in the act of falling, the resultant penalty meant that Aberdeen had conceded two goals at Pittodrie for the first time this season.

No 34 Monday, 29 April
ABERDEEN (0) 0   CELTIC (0) 0
ABERDEEN: Clark, Hermiston, McLelland, Hair, Young, W. Miller, J. Smith, McCall, Pirie (Davidson), Jarvie, Graham
CELTIC: Hunter, McGrain, Quinn, McCluskey, Welsh (Brogan), Dalglish, Hay, Deans (Hood), Davidson, Callaghan

Attendance: 10,500   *Referee:* R. B. Valentine

This was Aberdeen's twelfth goal-less draw of the season. Once Aberdeen had lined up to applaud Celtic's ninth consecutive championship both sides proceeded to miss countless chances.

Aberdeen's complete home and away record:

HOME						AWAY						
P	W	D	L	F	A		W	D	L	F	A	Pts
34	7	9	1	26	9		6	7	4	20	17	42

Scottish League Divison One

	P	W	D	L	F	A	Pts
1 Celtic	34	23	7	4	82	27	53
2 Hibernian	34	20	9	5	75	42	49
3 Rangers	34	21	6	7	67	34	48
4 ABERDEEN	34	13	16	5	46	26	42
5 Dundee	34	16	7	11	67	48	39
6 Hearts	34	14	10	10	54	43	38
7 Ayr United	34	15	8	11	44	40	38
8 Dundee United	34	15	7	12	55	51	37
9 Motherwell	34	14	7	13	45	40	35
10 Dumbarton	34	11	7	16	43	58	29
11 Partick Thistle	34	9	10	15	33	46	28
12 St Johnstone	34	9	10	15	41	60	28
13 Arbroath	34	10	7	17	52	69	27
14 Morton	34	8	10	16	37	49	26
15 Clyde	34	8	9	17	29	65	25
16 Dunfermline Ath.	34	8	8	18	43	65	24
17 East Fife	34	9	6	19	26	51	24
18 Falkirk	34	4	14	16	33	58	22

LEAGUE CUP

Saturday, 11 August
ABERDEEN (1) 3   MOTHERWELL (0) 1
  Hermiston (21 pen)   Lawson (53)
  Smith (54), Graham (61)
ABERDEEN: Clark, Williamson, Hermiston, Thomson, Young, Boel, Graham (R. Miller), Taylor, Jarvie, J. Smith, Purdie
MOTHERWELL: MacRae, John Muir, Wark, Watson, McCallum, Jim Muir, Campbell, Millar, Lawson, McCabe, McClymont

Attendance: 11,000   *Referee:* E. Thomson

Aberdeen's first goal of the new season is a penalty, conceded by McCallum.

Wednesday, 15 August
DUNDEE UNITED (0) 0   ABERDEEN (0) 0
DUNDEE UNITED: McAlpine, Rolland, Kopel, McLeod, D. Smith, W. Smith, K. Cameron (Fleming), Gardner, Payne, Henry, Traynor
ABERDEEN: Clark, Williamson, Hermiston, Thomson, Young, W. Miller, J. Smith, Graham (R. Miller), Taylor, Jarvie, Purdie

Attendance: 6,000   *Referee:* T. Kellock

Representatives of Finn Harps – Aberdeen's UEFA Cup opponents – watch as the Dons knock their heads against a tangerine wall. The wall held firm.

Saturday, 18 August
ABERDEEN (0) 1   EAST FIFE (1) 1
  Williamson (72)   McIvor (31)
ABERDEEN: Clark, Williamson, Hermiston, Thomson, Young, W. Miller, J. Smith, Graham (R. Miller), Taylor, Jarvie, Purdie
EAST FIFE: McGarr, Duncan, Printy, Love, Martis, Clarke, Hegarty, McIvor, Dailey (Walker), Hamilton, McPhee (Noble)

Attendance: 9,000   *Referee:* J. R. P. Gordon

Billy Williamson's face-saving equaliser was a feeble prod over the line after his first effort had been blocked.

Wednesday, 22 August

ABERDEEN (0) 0   DUNDEE UNITED (0) 2
                                         Knox (49),
                                         K. Cameron (74)

ABERDEEN: Clark, Williamson, Hermiston, Thomson, Young (Willoughby), W. Miller, J. Smith, Graham, Taylor, Jarvie, R. Miller

DUNDEE UNITED: McAlpine, Rolland, Kopel, Copland, D. Smith, W. Smith, Knox (Henry), Fleming, K. Cameron, Gardner, McLeod

Attendance: 8,000   *Referee:* R. H. Davidson

Archie Knox is the man who pulls the rug from under Aberdeen, rifling home an angled shot which was deflected past Bobby Clark by Willie Young.

Saturday, 25 August

EAST FIFE (0) 0   ABERDEEN (1) 2
                                       R. Miller (43),
                                       Graham (58)

EAST FIFE: McGarr, Duncan, Printy (Walker), Love, Rutherford, Clarke, Hegarty, McIvor (Noble), Honeyman, McPhee, Ritchie

ABERDEEN: Clark, Williamson, Hermiston, Thomson, Young, W. Miller, J. Smith, Graham, Taylor, Jarvie, R. Miller

Attendance: 4,150   *Referee:* R. D. Henderson

With Aberdeen two up, Willie Miller fouls Hegarty, but Clark is equal to McPhee's penalty.

Wednesday, 29 August

MOTHERWELL (0) 0   ABERDEEN (0) 0

MOTHERWELL: MacRae, John Muir, Wark, Watson, Jim Muir, Goodwin, Campbell, Miller (Goldthorp), Lawson, McCabe, McClymont

ABERDEEN: Clark, Williamson, Hermiston (Willoughby), Thomson, Young, W. Miller, J. Smith, Graham, Taylor, Jarvie, R. Miller

Attendance: 9,800   *Referee:* G. Smith

Aberdeen knew a draw would take them through, unless Dundee United beat East Fife by six clear goals. But the incentive for the group winners is a money-spinning tie with one of the Old Firm, and that produces a titanic struggle at Fir Park. Aberdeen might have won but for MacRae's penalty save from Bertie Miller.

Section 4

	P	W	D	L	F	A	Pts
Motherwell	6	3	1	2	13	6	7
ABERDEEN	6	2	3	1	6	4	7
Dundee United	6	3	1	2	9	10	7
East Fife	6	1	1	4	7	15	3

2nd Round, 1st Leg Wednesday, 12 September

ABERDEEN (1) 3   STIRLING ALBION (0) 0
Graham (24),
Jarvie 2 (71, 80)

ABERDEEN: Clark, Hair, Hermiston, Thomson, Young, W. Miller, J. Smith (Willoughby), Graham, Taylor, Jarvie, R. Miller

STIRLING: Young, Jones, McAlpine, Clark (Christie), McAleer, Carr, McPhee (Downie), Steele, Lawson, McMillan, Murphy

Attendance: 7,000   *Referee:* R. B. Valentine

Such is Aberdeen's historical dominance over Stirling Albion that this is their 21st victory in 26 meetings – and their goals tally is now 95.

2nd Round, 2nd Leg Wednesday, 10 October

STIRLING ALBION (0) 0   ABERDEEN (2) 3
                                     Jarvie 3 (22, 30, 64)

STIRLING: Young, Jones, McAlpine, Duffin, McAleer, Carr, McPhee, Steele, McMillan, Clark (Downie), Lawson

ABERDEEN: Clark, Hair, Hermiston, Thomson, Young, W. Miller, Willoughby, Robb, Taylor, Jarvie, R. Miller

Aberdeen won 6-0 on aggregate

Attendance: 3,000   *Referee:* R. B. Valentine

Two of Jarvie's goals were headers. He's now scored five times against poor Stirling. Have Aberdeen found a new Joe Harper?

Quarter Final 1st Leg Wednesday, 31 October

CELTIC (2) 3   ABERDEEN (1) 2
Dalglish 2 (15, 16),   Jarvie 2 (4, 55)
McCluskey (56)

CELTIC: Hunter, McGrain, Brogan, McCluskey, McNeill, Connelly, Hood, Murray, Deans, Hay, Dalglish

ABERDEEN: Clark, Hair, Hermiston, Thomson, Young, W. Miller, Graham, Robb, Jarvie, J. Smith (Willoughby), Taylor (R. Miller)

Attendance: 28,000   *Referee:* J. W. Paterson

This was Aberdeen's first defeat away from Pittodrie in any competition this season. Graham's knock-down enabled Jarvie to pick his spot. Dalglish poked an equaliser between Clark's legs and within seconds blasted a second. Then, out of nothing, Jarvie directed Robb's shot wide of Hunter, only for Aberdeen to face McCluskey's thunderous drive which went in via the woodwork.

Quarter Final 2nd Leg Wednesday, 21 November

ABERDEEN (0) 0   CELTIC (0) 0

ABERDEEN: Clark, Hair (Williamson), Hermiston, Thomson, Young, W. Miller, J. Miller, Robb, Jarvie, Craig, Graham (R. Miller)

CELTIC: Hunter, McGrain, Brogan, McCluskey, McNeill, Murray, Lennox, Hood, Deans (Johnstone), Callaghan, Dalglish

Celtic won 3-2 on aggregate

Attendance: 16,000   *Referee:* J. W. Paterson

47 free kicks but no goals. That was the sum achievement of this afternoon match. Aberdeen created only one real opening, which fell to Jimmy Miller in the first half. His opening effort was blocked; his follow-up was headed behind by McGrain. Not even the introduction of a third Miller – Bertie – could breathe life into the Dons.

SCOTTISH CUP

3rd Round Sunday, 27 January

ABERDEEN (0) 0   DUNDEE (1) 2
                                 Johnston (32),
                                 Robinson (73)

ABERDEEN: Clark, Williamson (Thomson), Hermiston, Smith, Young, W. Miller (Taylor), Graham, Robb, Jarvie, Henry, Purdie

DUNDEE: Allan, R. Wilson, Johnston, Ford, Phillip, Gemmell, J. Wilson, Robinson, Duncan, J. Scott, Lambie

Attendance: 23,574   *Referee:* G. B. Smith

This is the first time Scottish football has staged official matches on a Sunday. It produces Aberdeen's biggest gate of the season. Dave Robb's first game for the Dons was in a cup-tie at Dens Park six years ago. Dundee's Jimmy Wilson played in that game too – for Aberdeen. This time Dundee win, and win well – although Aberdeen had their moments. Graham's drive came back off a post. Johnston's opener for Dundee took a cruel deflection off Henry. Aberdeen have now failed to win at home since mid-November.

UEFA CUP

1st Round, 1st Leg Wednesday, 19 September

ABERDEEN (3) 4   FINN HARPS (Eire) (0) 1
R. Miller (33),   Harkin (87)
Jarvie 2 (36, 82),
Graham (38)

ABERDEEN: Clark, Hair, Hermiston, Thomson, Young, W. Miller, Willoughby, Graham, Taylor, Jarvie, R. Miller

FINN HARPS: Murray, McGrory, Hutton, McDowell, Sheridan, McDermott, Smith, Nicholl, Bradley, Harkin, Ferry

Attendance: 10,700   *Referee:* E. Axelryd
                                          (Sweden)

How Aberdeen failed to score 20 was a mystery. The luck of the Irish might have had something to do with it: so might Aberdeen's profligate finishing.

1st Round, 2nd Leg Wednesday, 3 October

FINN HARPS (0) 1   ABERDEEN (2) 3
Harkin (66)   Robb (21), Jarvie (28),
                            R. Miller (89)

FINN HARPS: Murray, McDowell, Hutton, O'Doherty, Sheridan, McDermott, Smith, Nicholl, Bradley, Harkin, Ferry (McGrory)

ABERDEEN: Clark, Hair, Hermiston, Thomson (J. Smith), Young, W. Miller, Willoughby, Robb, Graham (Purdie), Jarvie, R. Miller

Aberdeen won 7-2 on aggregate

Attendance: 5,500   *Referee:* F. Geluck
                                          (Belgium)

Finn Park, Ballybofey, proved to be an amenable little vacation for Aberdeen. The appreciative Irish crowd would have welcomed a display of Aberdeen's superior skills – but the Dons couldn't be bothered.

2nd Round, 1st Leg Wednesday, 24 October

ABERDEEN (0) 1   TOTTENHAM
Hermiston (87 pen)   HOTSPUR (England)
                                    (1) 1
                                    Coates (15)

ABERDEEN: Clark, Hair, Hermiston, Thomson (R. Miller), Young, W. Miller, Graham, Robb, Jarvie, J. Smith, Taylor

SPURS: Daines, Evans, Kinnear (Naylor), Pratt, England, Beal, Gilzean, Perryman, McGrath, Peters, Coates (Neighbour)

Attendance: 30,000   *Referee:* S. Patterson
                                          (Belfast)

This is Aberdeen's first competitive home match with an English club. Spurs have won both the Cup-Winners Cup and the UEFA Cup in the past, but are trailing in 15th position in the English first division. Spurs took the lead when Willie Miller tackled McGrath and the ball ran free to Coates, ten yards out. The visitors then fell back, holding out comfortably until Evans brought down Aberdeen sub Bertie Miller from behind. Hermiston's spot-kick kept alive the Dons' chances in London.

2nd Round, 2nd Leg Wednesday, 7 November

TOTTENHAM   ABERDEEN (0) 1
HOTSPUR (2) 4   Jarvie (54)
Peters (13), Neighbour
(36), McGrath 2 (80, 89)

SPURS: Jennings, Evans, Knowles, Pratt, England, Beal, Gilzean, Perryman, Chivers, Peters, Neighbour (McGrath)

ABERDEEN: Clark, Hair, Hermiston, Thomson (Mitchell), Young, W. Miller (R. Miller), Willoughby, Robb, Jarvie, J. Smith, Graham

Spurs won 5-2 on aggregate

Attendance: 21,785   *Referee:* K. Tshenscher
                                          (W. Germany)

Three minutes after Peters had punished Willie Miller's weak clearance Jarvie was pulled down. The referee gave a penalty, then changed his mind after frantic Spurs protests had forced him to consult a linesman. A Thomson miskick allowed Neighbour in for Spurs' second. But Jarvie hooked a goal for Aberdeen, who began to exert pressure until Spurs sub Chris McGrath settled matters.

1973-74 APPEARANCES	League	League Cup	Scottish Cup	UEFA Cup
Clark	34	10	1	4
Young	34	10	1	4
Hermiston	33	10	1	4
Jarvie	32	10	1	4
Thomson	31(+1)	10	−(+1)	4
Graham	31(+1)	9	1	4
W. Miller	31	9	1	4
Joe Smith	23(+2)	8	1	2(+1)
Robb	21	3	1	3
Hair	18	4		4
McLelland	15			
Taylor	14(+3)	9	−(+1)	2
Pirie	9			
Willoughby	8(+3)	1(+4)		3
Boel	7	1		
Purdie	6(+2)	3	1	−(+1)
Henry	6		1	
R. Miller	5(+2)	5(+5)		2(+2)
Craig	4(+4)	1		
McCall	4(+3)			
J. Miller	4(+1)	1		
Williamson	2(+2)	6(+1)	1	
Street	1(+1)			
Mitchell	1			−(+1)
Davidson	−(+5)			
25 players				

GOALS	Total	League	League Cup	Scottish Cup	UEFA Cup
Jarvie	24	13	7		4
Robb	12	11			1
Graham	7	3	3		1
R. Miller	4	1	1		2
Taylor	3	3			
J. Smith	3	2	1		
Hermiston	3	1	1		1
McCall	2	2			
Young	2	2			
Hair	1	1			
McClelland	1	1			
W. Miller	1	1			
Purdie	1	1			
Thomson	1	1			
Williamson	1		1		
own-goals	3	3			
Total	69	46	14		9

Aberdeen have just won the 1976 League Cup and manager Ally McLeod shows his delight. The score Celtic 1, Aberdeen 2, after extra-time.

Season 1974-75

After years of talk and indecision, the complete restructuring of the Scottish League was upon us. As of next season the top ten sides of the old First Division would be reconstituted into a new Premier Division. This prospect made for intense competition during the season in hand. Ordinarily, mid-table sides without hope of fame or shame coast their way through the latter stages of the league programme. Not this time. The battle was on to be a ticket holder for next season's exalted theatre.

Uninvolved in Europe and failing to emerge from their League Cup qualifiers, Aberdeen spent the Autumn months consolidating their league position, rarely having to look over their shoulder at the dog-eat-dog struggle going on behind them. Come the New Year, there were hints of an extended run in the Scottish Cup – fuelled by an intoxicating replay victory at Ibrox in the Third Round. Motherwell, however, had other ideas, and Aberdeen eventually found themselves knocked out in front of their own fans for the second successive season.

As the final weeks of the old league set-up passed away, Aberdeen were unable to improve on 5th position, which yet again was not high enough for admission to next year's UEFA Cup.

For those who could see it, Aberdeen's fortunes in the mid-1970s were imitating those of the late-1950s. After they had won the League Championship in 1954-55, the Dons' points total dropped for five years in a row. Similarly, following the runners-up spot gained under Eddie Turnbull in 1970-71, Aberdeen's points tally had also diminished, gradually but relentlessly, year by year. Next season – with two clubs to be relegated from the new Premier League – might well see Aberdeen embroiled in the throes of relegation.

League:	Fifth
League Cup:	Third in qualifying group
Scottish Cup:	Quarter Final

SCOTTISH LEAGUE DIVISION ONE

No 1 Saturday, 31 August
ABERDEEN (1) 2   HIBERNIAN (1) 3
  Purdie (17), Pirie (77)   Cropley (32, 90),
                           Harper (86)
ABERDEEN: Clark, Hermiston, McLelland, J. Smith, Young, W. Miller, Purdie, Hair, Thomson, Jarvie (Pirie), Graham
HIBERNIAN: McArthur, Bremner, Schaedler, Stanton, Spalding, Blackley (Munro), Cropley, Smith (Edwards), Harper, Gordon, Duncan

P	W	D	L	F	A	Pts
1	0	0	1	2	3	0

Attendance: 13,000
Referee: A. McKenzie

They came in their thousands to witness the painful sight of Joe Harper in a green and white jersey. He sends a free kick screaming past Clark with four minutes remaining – and in injury time has another shot blocked. It fell kindly for Cropley.

No 2 Saturday, 7 September
DUNDEE (0) 0   ABERDEEN (1) 1
                           Purdie (12)
DUNDEE: Allan, R. Wilson, Johnston, Ford (Lambie), Stewart, Gemmell, J. Wilson, Robinson, Hutchison, J. Scott, I. Scott
ABERDEEN: Clark, Hermiston (Williamson), McLelland, J. Smith, Young, W. Miller, Purdie, Hair, Thomson (Jarvie), Pirie, Graham

P	W	D	L	F	A	Pts
2	1	0	1	3	3	2

Attendance: 6,400
Referee: E. H. Pringle

A Bobby Clark clearance was carried on by Hair and Thomson for the unmarked Purdie to out-manoeuvre Allan.

No 3 Saturday, 14 September
ABERDEEN (0) 3   ST JOHNSTONE (0) 1
  Jarvie (68), Hair (70),   Cramond (59)
  Graham (82)
ABERDEEN: Clark, Hermiston, McLelland, J. Smith
(Williamson), Young, W. Miller, Purdie, Hair,
Thomson, Pirie (Jarvie), Graham
ST JOHNSTONE: Nicoll, Smith, Argue, Rennie,
Macdonald, Kinnell, Muir, O'Rourke, McGregor
(Hotson), Cramond, Hall

P W D L F A Pts   *Attendance:* 7,000
3 2 0 1 6 4 4   *Referee:* R. D. Henderson

St Johnstone looked to be maintaining their 100%
league record until Bonthrone made two inspired
substitutions. One of them, Jarvie, immediately sent an
unstoppable header past Nicoll.

No 4 Saturday, 21 September
KILMARNOCK (0) 1   ABERDEEN (0) 0
  McDicken (58)
KILMARNOCK: Stewart, Maxwell, Robertson,
McCulloch, Rodman, McDicken, McSherry, Fleming,
Morrison, Sheed, Smith
ABERDEEN: Clark, Williamson, McLelland, J. Smith,
Young, W. Miller, Purdie (Davidson), Hair, Thomson
(Pirie), Jarvie, Graham

P W D L F A Pts   *Attendance:* 5,000
4 2 0 2 6 5 4   *Referee:* E. Thomson

There is some sort of race going on among Aberdeen
players. Ian Purdie was booked for the fourth time this
season; Willie Miller for the third.

No 5 Saturday, 28 September
ABERDEEN (1) 1   AIRDRIEONIANS (0) 0
  Young (24)
ABERDEEN: Clark, Williamson, McLelland, J. Smith,
Young, W. Miller, Purdie (McCall), Hair, Pirie, Jarvie,
Graham
AIRDRIE: McWilliams, Jonquin, Menzies, Black,
McKinley, Whiteford, Reynolds, Cowan, McCulloch,
Walker, Wilson (McCann)

P W D L F A Pts   *Attendance:* 5,000
5 3 0 2 7 5 6   *Referee:* A. F. J. Webster

Acting skipper Willie Young plays a captain's part and
scores a captain's goal. McWilliams might have saved
the header but for the distraction of Pirie's presence.

No 6 Saturday, 5 October
HEARTS (1) 1   ABERDEEN (3) 4
  Park (45)   Purdie (35), Graham
                         (38), Smith (43),
                         McCall (72)
HEARTS: Garland, Kay, Burrell, Jefferies, Anderson,
Brown, Aird, Ford, Busby, Park, Murray
ABERDEEN: Clark, Williamson, McLelland, J. Smith,
Thomson (Hair), W. Miller, Purdie, Craig, Pirie
(McCall), Jarvie, Graham

P W D L F A Pts   *Attendance:* 8,500
6 4 0 2 11 6 8   *Referee:* B. R. McGinlay

Eddie Thomson was Aberdeen's acting captain on his
old stomping ground. Not a good day for Hearts fans.
After Joe Smith put the Dons three up they were heard
to chant 'Seith must go'. Best of Aberdeen's four was
Arthur Graham's thunderous angled drive.

No 7 Saturday, 12 October
ABERDEEN (2) 3   AYR UNITED (0) 0
  Jarvie (9), Purdie
  (23 pen), McCall (57)
ABERDEEN: Clark, Williamson, McLelland, J. Smith,
Young, W. Miller, Purdie, Craig, McCall, Jarvie,
Graham
AYR: A. McLean, Wells (Ingram), Murphy,
McAnespie, Fleming, Filippi, Doyle, Lannon, Somner
(McCulloch), Dickson, Cameron

P W D L F A Pts   *Attendance:* 6,000
7 5 0 2 14 6 10   *Referee:* K. J. Hope

Ally McLeod's Ayr United are having a tough time.
Jarvie scored once, was brought down for the penalty
and hit the post in the last minute.

No 8 Saturday, 19 October
DUMBARTON (1) 2   ABERDEEN (1) 3
  Wallace (19 pen),   McCall (10), Jarvie
  Cook (70)   (52), Graham (62)
DUMBARTON: Williams, Mullen, Watt, Cushley
(Coleman), Muir, Ruddy, Cook, Wallace, Bourke,
McAdam, Graham
ABERDEEN: Clark, Williamson, McLelland, J. Smith
(Thomson), Young, W. Miller, Purdie, Craig, McCall,
Jarvie, Graham

P W D L F A Pts   *Attendance:* 4,000
8 6 0 2 17 8 12   *Referee:* J. R. P. Gordon

Willie Young nudged Tom McAdam in the air to
concede a penalty. Jarvie and Graham restored
Aberdeen's advantage, but Dumbarton had a goal
disallowed before Cook halved the deficit.

No 9 Saturday, 26 October
ABERDEEN (3) 5   ARBROATH (1) 1
  Williamson 2   Wells (40)
  (16, 70), McCall 2
  (27, 61), Purdie (32)
ABERDEEN: Clark, Williamson, McLelland, J. Smith,
Young, W. Miller, Purdie, Craig, McCall, Jarvie,
Graham
ARBROATH: Marshall, Milne, Rylance, Cargill,
Carson, Murray, Sellars (Reid), Cant (Buchan), Wells,
Fletcher, Yule

Leading positions

	P	W	D	L	F	A	Pts
1 Rangers	9	7	2	0	27	9	16
2 Celtic	8	7	0	1	26	9	14
3 ABERDEEN	9	7	0	2	22	9	14
4 Dundee United	9	4	3	2	19	10	11
5 Hibernian	8	5	1	2	19	12	11

Attendance: 7,000   *Referee:* R. D. Henderson

Five goals in four matches for lanky Walker McCall as Aberdeen extend their winning sequence to five.

No 10 Saturday, 2 November
CELTIC (1) 1   ABERDEEN (0) 0
  Wilson (42)

CELTIC: Hunter, MacDonald, Brogan, Murray, McNeill, McCluskey, Johnstone (Lennox), Dalglish, Deans, Hood, Wilson

ABERDEEN: Clark, Williamson, McLelland, J. Smith, Young, W. Miller, Purdie, Craig, McCall, Jarvie, Graham

P	W	D	L	F	A	Pts	
10	7	0	3	22	10	14	

Attendance: 29,000   *Referee:* G. B. Smith

For the second successive game Ian Purdie fails from the spot. This time it is an expensive miss, after Graham was grabbed by Brogan. The ball hit the post. Aberdeen did not get another chance to cancel out Wilson's earlier goal, the product of a delightful Hood chip to the unmarked Wilson.

No 11 Saturday, 9 November
ABERDEEN (0) 1   PARTICK THISTLE (0) 1
  Purdie (77)   Prudham (68)

ABERDEEN: Clark, Williamson, McLelland, J. Smith, Young, W. Miller, Purdie, Craig, McCall (Davidson), Jarvie, Graham

PARTICK: Rough, J. Hansen, Anderson, Campbell, A. Hansen, Clark, Lawrie, Houston, Glavin, Prudham, Gray

P	W	D	L	F	A	Pts
11	7	1	3	23	11	15

Attendance: 8,000   *Referee:* J. W. Paterson

Two men deny Aberdeen a comfortable victory: Eddie Prudham, on loan to Thistle from Sheffield Wednesday, and goalkeeper Alan Rough.

No 12 Saturday, 16 November
ABERDEEN (0) 3   MORTON (1) 3
  McCall (47), Young   Skovdam (6),
  (85), Graham (87)   Reid (59), Taylor (89)

ABERDEEN: Clark, Williamson, McLelland, J. Smith (Hermiston), Young, W. Miller, Davidson, Craig (Pirie), McCall, Jarvie, Graham

MORTON: Baines, Hayes, Ritchie, Lumsden, Anderson, Rankin, Taylor, Reid, Harley, Skovdam (Murray), McGhee

P	W	D	L	F	A	Pts
12	7	2	3	26	14	16

Attendance: 7,500   *Referee:* W. J. Mullen

Three goals in the last five minutes sends the fans home in a daze. Two headers seemed to have given Aberdeen both points, but Taylor rescued a draw for Morton which they fully deserved.

No 13 Wednesday, 27 November
DUNDEE UNITED (2) 4 ABERDEEN (0) 0
  Fleming 2 (11, 37)
  Narey (65),
  Williamson o.g. (88)

DUNDEE UNITED: McAlpine, Rolland, Kopel, Copland, W. Smith, Houston, Traynor, Narey, Gray, Fleming, McDonald

ABERDEEN: Geoghegan, Williamson, McLelland, J. Smith (Hermiston), Young, W. Miller, Purdie, Craig (Davidson), McCall, Jarvie, Graham

P	W	D	L	F	A	Pts
13	7	2	4	26	28	16

Attendance: 8,000   *Referee:* R. H. Hopkins

A virus kept out Bobby Clark. In stepped Andy Geoghegan, himself not fully fit, to play the worst game of his life – brushing Fleming's cross over his own goal-line to make it 2-0.

No 14 Saturday, 30 November
MOTHERWELL (0) 2   ABERDEEN (1) 1
  McIlwraith (55),   Graham (45)
  Goodwin (80)

MOTHERWELL: Lloyd, W. Watson, Wark (McClymont), R. Watson, McLaren, Goodwin, McIlwraith, Millar, Taylor, Gardiner, Graham (Goldthorp)

ABERDEEN: Clark, Hair, McLelland, Hermiston, Young, W. Miller, Purdie, Davidson, McCall, Jarvie, Graham

P	W	D	L	F	A	Pts
14	7	2	5	27	20	16

Attendance: 3,500   *Referee:* I. M. D. Foote

Jarvie and Miller were booked; Graham gave Aberdeen an interval lead; and still they lost. Scotland manager Willie Ormond was watching them for the first time this season.

No 15 Saturday, 7 December
ABERDEEN (0) 1   RANGERS (1) 2
  Hair (75)   Johnstone (30),
                         McLean (87)

ABERDEEN: Clark, Hair, McLelland, Hermiston, Young, W. Miller, Purdie, Thomson, Jarvie, Street, Graham

RANGERS: Kennedy, Jardine, Greig, Johnstone, Jackson, Forsyth, McKean, McLean, Parlane, MacDonald, Young

P	W	D	L	F	A	Pts
15	7	2	6	28	22	16

Attendance: 25,000   *Referee:* D. Ramsey

Pittodrie is the focus of attention for all the wrong reasons. Before the match could start Rangers fans charged across the pitch towards the Beach End. Rangers bosses Willie Waddell and Jock Wallace had to appeal for order. Once the game was under way Derek Johnstone chested the ball down before firing past Clark. Aberdeen stormed back. Hair nearly burst the net. But then Young was dispossessed by Parlane, who squared for the inrushing McLean.

No 16 Saturday, 14 December
CLYDE (1) 1   ABERDEEN (1) 1
  Boyle (40)   Purdie (34)

CLYDE: Williams, Anderson, Swan, Ahern, McVie, Jim Burns, Sullivan, Ward, Boyle, John Burns, Millar (Ferris)

ABERDEEN: Clark, Hair, McLelland, Hermiston (Williamson), Young, W. Miller, Purdie, Henry, Street, Jarvie, Graham

P	W	D	L	F	A	Pts	*Attendance:* 2,050
16	7	3	6	29	23	17	*Referee:* J. R. Grant

Aberdeen's Ian Hair was sent off in the first half: Clyde's goalscorer, Peter Boyle in the second.

No 17 Saturday, 21 December

ABERDEEN (0) 1   DUNFERMLINE
  Hair (71)   ATHLETIC (1) 1
                                       Forrest (8)

ABERDEEN: Clark, Hair, McLelland, Thomson, Young, W. Miller, Purdie, Henry (Williamson), Street, Jarvie (Davidson), Graham

DUNFERMLINE: Karlsen, Scott, Markey, Thomson, Evans, Kinninmonth, Watson (Sinclair), McNicoll, Forrest, Shaw, Cameron

P	W	D	L	F	A	Pts	*Attendance:* 5,000
17	7	4	6	30	24	18	*Referee:* D. F. Syme

Aberdeen have now gone eight games without a win. If the rot does not stop they will lose a place in next season's ten-team Premier Division.

No 18 Saturday, 28 December

HIBERNIAN (0) 0   ABERDEEN (1) 1
                                       Pirie (18)

HIBERNIAN: McArthur, Brownlie, Schaedler, Stanton, Bremner, Blackley, Edwards, McLeod, Harper, Munro, Duncan

ABERDEEN: Clark, Hair, McLelland, Thomson, Young, W. Miller, Purdie, Henry (Jarvie), Pirie (Davidson), Williamson, Graham

P	W	D	L	F	A	Pts	*Attendance:* 13,200
18	8	4	6	31	24	20	*Referee:* R. Marshall

Five minutes gone and Hibs are given a penalty saved by Clark. Pirie then scores for Aberdeen after Williamson's shot was blocked by McArthur. Throughout the match Harper was harshly treated by ex-collegaue Willie Young. Before the end Aberdeen's Chic McLelland and Hibs' Alec Edwards were sent off.

No 19 Wednesday, 1 January

ABERDEEN (1) 4   DUNDEE (0) 0
  Caldwell o.g. (14)
  Pirie (54), Jarvie (77),
  Hair (79)

ABERDEEN: Clark, Hair, McLelland, Thomson, Young, W. Miller, Purdie, Henry (Davidson), Pirie (Jarvie), Williamson, Graham

DUNDEE: Allan, R. Wilson, Gemmell, Ford, Stewart (Johnston), Phillip, Gordon, Robinson, Wallace (Hutchinson), J. Scott, Caldwell

P	W	D	L	F	A	Pts	*Attendance:* 14,000
19	9	4	6	35	24	22	*Referee:* E. H. Pringle

This was Aberdeen's biggest winning margin in a New Year derby over Dundee for more than 20 years. Drew Jarvie's goal – his first in eleven games – was a peach.

The substitute weaved past two Dundee defenders and whacked the ball past Allan.

No 20 Saturday, 4 January

ST JOHNSTONE (0) 1   ABERDEEN (0) 1
  Macdonald (57)   Davidson (82)

ST JOHNSTONE: Robertson, Smith (Ritchie), Argue, Rennie, Macdonald, Kinnell, Muir, O'Rourke, Hall, Cramond, Lambie (Aitken)

ABERDEEN: Clark, Hair, McLelland, Thomson, Young, W. Miller, Purdie, Henry (Davidson), Pirie (Jarvie), Williamson, Graham

P	W	D	L	F	A	Pts	*Attendance:* 4,500
20	9	5	6	36	25	23	*Referee:* F. A. Phillip

Drama at the death. Jim O'Rourke is pulled down, picks himself up and sees his penalty smartly saved by a limping Bobby Clark. According to the statistics, Aberdeen are the dirtiest team in the First Division.

No 21 Saturday, 11 January

ABERDEEN (2) 4   KILMARNOCK (0) 0
  Jarvie (24), Young (43)
  Pirie (72 pen),
  Graham (89)

ABERDEEN: Clark, Hair, McLelland, Thomson, Young, W. Miller, Purdie, Henry (Pirie), Jarvie, Williamson (Davidson), Graham

KILMARNOCK: A. McCulloch, McLean, Robertson, I. McCulloch (D. Morrison), Rodman, Maxwell, Provan, Smith, E. Morrison (Whyte), Sheed, Fallis

P	W	D	L	F	A	Pts	*Attendance:* 8,500
21	10	5	6	40	25	25	*Referee:* B. R. McGinlay

A bleak day for Kilmarnock, who had two players stretchered off within minutes in the first half.

No 22 Saturday, 1 February

ABERDEEN (2) 2   HEARTS (1) 2
  McClelland (22),   Gibson (15),
  Jarvie (32)   Callachan (70)

ABERDEEN: Clark, Hair, McLelland, Thomson, Young, W. Miller, Purdie, Henry (J. Smith), Jarvie, Williamson, Graham

HEARTS: Cruickshank, Kay, Clunie, Jefferies, Anderson, Brown, Park, Busby, Gibson, T. Murray, Callachan

P	W	D	L	F	A	Pts	*Attendance:* 11,000
22	10	6	6	42	27	26	*Referee:* T. R. Kyle

A fine match. Hearts deserved their early lead, which was cancelled out when McLelland hit the ball on the drop. After Jarvie's low shot put the Dons in front, Callachan levelled with a meteoric shot which went in off the bar.

No 23 Saturday, 8 February

AYR UNITED (0) 2   ABERDEEN (0) 0
  Doyle (71), Graham (79)

AYR: McLean, Taylor, Murphy, McAnespie, Fleming, Fillippi, Doyle, Graham, Ingram, Phillips, McCulloch (Dickson).

ABERDEEN: Clark, Hair, McLelland, Thomson, Young, W Miller, Purdie (Davidson), Henry, Jarvie, Williamson (J. Smith), Graham

P	W	D	L	F	A	Pts		*Attendance:* 5,000
23	10	6	7	42	29	26		*Referee:* D. S. Downie

Smiles for Ayr manager Ally McLeod, but not for Ian Hair, whose attempted header back to Clark fell for Doyle.

No 24 Saturday, 22 February
ABERDEEN (1) 1   DUMBARTON (1) 1
  Graham (9)   Bourke (32)

ABERDEEN: Clark, Hair, McLelland, Thomson (J. Smith), Young, W. Miller, Purdie (Davidson), Henry, Jarvie, Williamson, Graham
DUMBARTON: McGregor, Muir, Watt, C. McAdam, Cushley, Ruddy, Coleman, Bourke, T. McAdam, Graham, Wallace

P	W	D	L	F	A	Pts		*Attendance:* 9,000
24	10	7	7	43	30	27		*Referee:* J. R. P. Gordon

Dumbarton clawed their way back into a match they should have lost by a mile. Arthur Graham scored one and had two more disallowed for offside.

No 25 Saturday, 1 March
ARBROATH (0) 1   ABERDEEN (1) 2
  Cargill (74)   Williamson (11),
                   Graham (49)

ARBROATH: Wilson, Milne, Murray, Cargill, Carson, Smith, Reid, Rylance, Bone, Penman, Fletcher
ABERDEEN: Clark, Hair, McLelland, J. Smith, Young, W. Miller, Purdie (Davidson), Henry, Jarvie, Williamson, Graham

Leading positions

	P	W	D	L	F	A	Pts
1 Rangers	26	20	4	2	72	25	44
2 Celtic	26	18	4	4	69	29	40
3 Hibernian	26	14	7	5	46	29	35
4 Dundee United	25	12	6	7	54	33	30
5 ABERDEEN	25	11	7	7	45	31	29

Attendance: 3,100   *Referee:* J. W. Paterson

Aberdeen coasted through the first half against the basement club, and panicked their way through the second. At 2-1 Fletcher's header thumped against Clark's post and flew into his arms.

No 26 Tuesday, 4 March
AIRDRIEONIANS (1) 2   ABERDEEN (0) 2
  McCann (28),   Graham (61),
  Jonquin (88 pen)   Davidson (77)

AIRDRIE: McWilliams, Jonquin, Cowan, Menzies, Black, Whiteford, McCann, Reynolds, McCulloch (Lapsley), Walker (Anderson), Wilson
ABERDEEN: Clark, Hair, McLelland, J. Smith, Young, W. Miller, Purdie (Davidson), Henry (Cooper), Jarvie, Williamson, Graham

P	W	D	L	F	A	Pts		*Attendance:* 4,000
26	11	8	7	47	33	30		*Referee:* J. Callaghan

Neil Cooper, a former schoolboy international, makes his debut for the Dons. He is denied his win bonus by Young's challenge on Whiteford. Referee Callaghan took an age before deciding that Young's tackle was a penalty.

No 27 Wednesday, 12 March
ABERDEEN (1) 3   CELTIC (0) 2
  Williamson 3 (17, 57   Lynch 2 (53, 62)
  78 pen)

ABERDEEN: Clark, Hair, McLelland, Thomson, Young, W. Miller (McCall), Purdie, J. Smith, Jarvie, Williamson, Graham (Davidson)
CELTIC: Latchford, McGrain, McCluskey, Glavin, McNeill, Connelly, Hood, Wilson, Dalglish, Callaghan, Lynch

P	W	D	L	F	A	Pts		*Attendance:* 15,000
27	12	8	7	50	35	32		*Referee:* G. B. Smith

The men in the news are Jim Hermiston and Billy Williamson. The dropped Don's skipper announces his retirement from the end of the season to join the police force. Williamson's achievement was to bring about Celtic's first league defeat at Pittodrie in nine years. At 2-2 Aberdeen were awarded a penalty. Williamson took responsibility completing his hat-trick off Latchford's post.

No 28 Saturday, 15 March
PARTICK THISTLE (0) 1   ABERDEEN (0) 0
  McQuade (78)

PARTICK: Rough, J. Hansen, Kellachan, Campbell, A. Hansen, Anderson, Houston, Rae, Craig, Somner, McQuade
ABERDEEN: Clark, Hair, Hermiston, Thomson (Davidson), Ward, W. Miller, Purdie, J. Smith, McCall, Williamson, Graham

P	W	D	L	F	A	Pts		*Attendance:* 5,000
28	12	8	8	50	36	32		*Referee:* R. Keggie

Under normal conditions Patrick's mid-table position might see them less than committed. But they are desperate to finish in the top ten for next season's Premier League. There are no easy matches this season. Chic McLelland missed this one through suspension.

No 29 Saturday, 22 March
MORTON (0) 0   ABERDEEN (1) 3
                Robb (17), Williamson
                 (53), Graham (67)

MORTON: Baines, Hayes, Ritchie, Townsend, McNeill, Irvine, Hudson, Lumsden, Hazel, Skovdam, Harley (Taylor)
ABERDEEN: Clark, Hair (Campbell), McLelland, Hermiston, Ward, W. Miller, J. Smith, Robb, McCall, Williamson, Graham

P	W	D	L	F	A	Pts		*Attendance:* 2,500
29	13	8	8	53	36	34		*Referee:* A. McKenzie

Dave Robb celebrated his return after a lengthy absence due to a knee injury with a neat goal from Joe Smith's lob.

No 30 Saturday, 29 March
ABERDEEN (1) 2   DUNDEE UNITED (0) 0
   Williamson (43),
   Hermiston (62 pen)
ABERDEEN: Clark, Hair, McLelland, Hermiston, Young, W. Miller, J. Smith, Robb, Jarvie, Williamson, Graham
DUNDEE UNITED: McAlpine, Rolland, Forsyth (Addison), Copland, Houston, Narey, Sturrock, Hegarty, Gray, W. Smith, Payne (Traynor)

P	W	D	L	F	A	Pts	
30	14	8	8	55	36	36	*Attendance:* 8,000

Referee: R. H. Davidson

Naughty David Narey conceded two penalties for Dundee United. McAlpine saved Robb's, not Hermiston's. Willie Young kept Andy Gray in his pocket all through the game. Both clubs are chasing a UEFA Cup place.

No 31 Saturday, 12 April
RANGERS (0) 3   ABERDEEN (0) 2
   Johnstone (57),   Williamson (55),
   Stein (59),   Hermiston (61 pen)
   Miller (76 pen)
RANGERS: Kennedy, Jardine, Miller, McKean, Jackson, Forsyth, McLean (Fyfe), Stein, Parlane, MacDonald, Johnstone
ABERDEEN: Clark, Hair, McLelland, Hermiston, Young, W. Miller, J. Smith, Robb, Jarvie, Williamson, Graham

P	W	D	L	F	A	Pts	
31	14	8	9	57	39	36	*Attendance:* 40,000

Referee: R. B. Valentine

After 55 minutes it was 0-0. Six minutes later it was 2-2 in this corker of a match. Rangers are already guaranteed the championship: Aberdeen have formally booked their place in next season's Premier League. But the Dons' first league defeat at Ibrox since 1969-70 condemns them to another season out of Europe. Miller conceded Rangers' winning penalty: Williamson was booked for protesting about it.

No 32 Saturday, 19 April
ABERDEEN (3) 4   CLYDE (0) 1
   Hermiston (8 pen)   Harvey (85)
   Jarvie 2 (32, 37),
   W. Miller (83)
ABERDEEN: Clark, Hair, McLelland, Hermiston, Young, W. Miller, J. Smith, Robb, Jarvie, Williamson (McMaster), Graham
CLYDE: Cairney, Anderson, Swan, Ahern, McVie, Boyd (Burns), Sullivan (Hutchison), Millar, Ferris, Harvey, Boyle

P	W	D	L	F	A	Pts	
32	15	8	9	61	40	38	*Attendance:* 3,300

Referee: F. A. Phillips

Playing without tension, Aberdeen perform a demolition job on Clyde – who have no relegation to worry about. Hermiston's penalty was his third in successive games.

No 33 Wednesday, 23 April
ABERDEEN (1) 2   MOTHERWELL (2) 2
   Jarvie (8),   Pettigrew (17),
   Graham (51)   Graham (40)
ABERDEEN: Clark, Hair, McLelland, Hermiston, Young, W. Miller, J. Smith, Robb, Jarvie, Williamson, Graham
MOTHERWELL: Rennie, W. Watson, Wark, R. Watson, McLaren, Millar, Hamilton (Gardner), Pettigrew, Graham, Goodwin, Taylor

P	W	D	L	F	A	Pts	
33	15	9	9	63	42	39	*Attendance:* 8,000

Referee: J. R. P. Gordon

Motherwell love playing at Pittodrie this season. Having won 1-0 in the Scottish Cup, they now need a point to virtually guarantee a place in next season's Premier League. With seconds remaining Robb scored from Graham's centre, but after some hesitation the goal was disallowed by the referee for offside.

No 34 Saturday, 26 April
DUNFERMLINE   ABERDEEN (1) 3
   ATHLETIC (1) 1   Robb 3 (6, 69, 90)
   Shaw (14)
DUNFERMLINE: Karlsen, Scott, Markey (Hamilton), Thomson, Evans, Kinninmonth, Watson, Campbell (Cameron), Smith, Reid, Shaw
ABERDEEN: Clark, Hair, McLelland, Hermiston, Young, W. Miller, J. Smith, Robb, Jarvie, Williamson (McCall), Graham

Attendance: 3,500   *Referee:* A. Paterson

Aberdeen captain Jim Hermiston, plays his last game for the club and comes within inches of an own-goal with a downward header past Clark's post. Willie Miller was booked for the second time in four days.

Aberdeen's complete home and away record:

HOME						AWAY						
P	W	D	L	F	A		W	D	L	F	A	Pts
34	9	6	2	42	20		7	3	7	24	23	41

Scottish League Division One

	P	W	D	L	F	A	Pts
1 Rangers	34	25	6	3	86	33	56
2 Hibernian	34	20	9	5	69	37	49
3 Celtic	34	20	5	9	81	41	45
4 Dundee United	34	19	7	8	72	43	45
5 ABERDEEN	34	16	9	9	66	43	41
6 Dundee	34	16	6	12	48	42	38
7 Ayr United	34	14	8	11	50	61	37
8 Hearts	34	11	13	10	47	52	35
9 St. Johnstone	34	11	12	11	41	44	34
10 Motherwell	34	14	5	15	52	57	33
11 Airdrieonians	34	11	9	14	43	55	31
12 Kilmarnock	34	8	15	11	52	68	31
13 Partick Thistle	34	10	10	14	48	62	30
14 Dumbarton	34	7	10	17	44	55	24
15 Dunfermline	34	7	9	18	46	66	23
16 Clyde	34	6	10	18	40	63	22
17 Morton	34	6	10	18	31	62	22
18 Arbroath	34	5	7	22	34	66	17

LEAGUE CUP

Saturday, 10 August
ABERDEEN (0) 0   HEARTS (0) 1
                         Ford (52)

ABERDEEN: Geoghegan, Hermiston, McLelland, Smith, Hair, Miller, Davidson (McCall), Henry (Purdie), Jarvie, Graham, Campbell
HEARTS: Garland, Sneddon, Jefferies, Cant, Gallacher, Brown, Aird, Ford, Busby, Stevenson, Prentice
Attendance: 11,000   *Referee:* R. B. Valentine
This youthful, makeshift Dons' side was beaten by Donald Ford's wheeling cross-shot.

Wednesday, 14 August
MORTON (2) 3   ABERDEEN (0) 1
  McGhee (23),   Hermiston (86)
  Skovdam (41),
  Hegarty (72)

MORTON: Baines, Hayes, Ritchie, Townsend, Anderson, Rankin, McGhee, Reid, Hazel, Hegarty, Skovdam (Murray)
ABERDEEN: Geoghegan, Hermiston, McLelland, Smith, Hair, Miller, Purdie, Graham, Pirie (Davidson), Jarvie, Campbell
Attendance: 2,000   Referee: J. W. Paterson
Morton adapted themselves to swamp conditions much better than Aberdeen. Morton's opener came when Mark McGhee fended off Willie Miller's challenge to unleash an angled shot from 15 yards.

Saturday, 17 August
DUNFERMLINE   ABERDEEN (1) 1
  ATHLETIC (1) 1   Jarvie (30)
  Sinclair (27)

DUNFERLINE: Karlsen, Thomson, Wallace, R. Campbell, Leishman, Kinninmonth, Watson, I. Campbell, Mackie (Davidson), Shaw, Sinclair
ABERDEEN: Clark, Hermiston, McLelland, Smith (Davidson), Young, Miller, Purdie, Hair, Thomson, Jarvie, Graham
                         Referee: J. R. P. Gordon
Both teams brought on a substitute named Davidson. But all the scoring had already been done.

Wednesday, 21 August
ABERDEEN (1) 4   MORTON (0) 0
  Purdie (24), Thomson
  (53), Jarvie (53),
  Young (75)

ABERDEEN: Clark, Hermiston, McLelland, Smith, Young, Miller, Purdie, Hair, Thomson, Jarvie, Graham
MORTON: Baines, Hayes, Ritchie, Townsend, Nelson, Rankin, McGhee, Reid, Hazel (Hunter), Hegarty, Skovdam
Attendance: 5,000   *Referee:* F. A. Phillips

All things are relative. Morton had lost five goals to Hearts on Saturday. Unlike at Cappielow, McGhee does not get the better of Miller.

Saturday, 24 August
ABERDEEN (0) 3   DUNFERMLINE
  Jarvie (65),   ATHLETIC (0) 0
  Williamson (69),
  Purdie (71)

ABERDEEN: Clark, Hermiston, McLelland, Smith (Pirie), Young, Miller, Purdie, Williamson, Thomson, Jarvie, Graham (McMaster)
DUNFERMLINE: Karlsen, Thomson, Wallace (Evans), Campbell, McNicoll, Kinninmonth, Watson, I. Campbell, Davidson (Scott), Shaw, Sinclair
Attendance: 7,000   Referee: T. Muirhead
For 65 minutes Dunfermline's Norwegian goalkeeper, Geir Karlsen, is the most unpopular man at Pittodrie. Six minutes later all his earlier brilliance was forgiven. Among the Aberdeen substitutes was a youthful John McMaster, who came on for the last few minutes.

Wednesday, 28 August
HEARTS (1) 2   ABERDEEN (0) 1
  Aird 2 (16, 72)   Hermiston (55 pen)

HEARTS: Garland, Sneddon, Jefferies, Cant, Gallacher, Brown, Aird, Ford, Busby, Stevenson, Callachan
ABERDEEN: Clark, Hermiston, McLelland (McMaster), Smith (Pirie), Young, Miller, Purdie, Williamson, Thomson, Jarvie, Graham
Attendance: 14,000   *Referee:* D. F. Syme
This is the first time Hearts have survived the League Cup opening rounds for 14 years. In the event, had Aberdeen won they would have gone through – but they didn't play with any visible sign of urgency. Two crashing Kenny Aird goals beat them. Further cause for concern is Aberdeen's disciplinary record. In six League Cup matches seven cautions have been meted out.

Section 3

	P	W	D	L	F	A	Pts
Hearts	6	4	0	2	13	6	8
Dunfermline	6	2	3	1	8	9	7
ABERDEEN	6	2	1	3	10	7	5
Morton	6	1	2	3	5	14	4

SCOTTISH CUP

3rd Round Saturday, 25 January
ABERDEEN (0) 1   RANGERS (0) 1
  Miller (87)   Scott (67)

ABERDEEN: Clark, Hair, McLelland, Thomson, Young, Miller, Purdie (Davidson), Henry, Jarvie, Williamson, Graham
RANGERS: Kennedy, Jardine, Miller, McDougall, Jackson, Forsyth, McLean, Johnstone (McKean), Parlane, McDonald, Scott
                         Referee: R.H. Davidson

J

An all-ticket match with the league leaders and champions-elect. Purdie's free kick hit the Ranger's post in the first half: Scott hit the Dons' net in the second. Then came a dramatic lob from Willie Miller to earn Aberdeen a second chance.

3rd Round Replay Monday, 10 February
RANGERS (1) 1 *1*   ABERDEEN (1) 1 *2*
  McKean (30)   *(After extra time)*
                          Graham (2),
                          Davidson (112)
RANGERS: Kennedy, Jardine, Miller, Johnstone (O'Hara), Jackson, Forsyth, McKean, McLean, Parlane, MacDonald, Scott (Fyfe)
ABERDEEN: Clark, Hair, McLelland, Thomson, Young, Miller, Purdie, Henry (Smith), Jarvie, Williamson (Davidson), Graham
Attendance: 52,000   *Referee:* R. H. Davidson

Extra time brought Aberdeen's first-ever Scottish Cup victory over Rangers at Ibrox. Perhaps the 'Gers were disconcerted by having to play in all white, for they were quickly a goal down as Graham side-stepped Forsyth to shoot low past Kennedy. McKean's close-range header levelled matters until the second period of extra time. It was Aberdeen's two substitutes who sprung the trap. Joe Smith headed Graham's centre onto a post and Duncan Davidson seized his chance.

4th Round Wednesday, 19 February
DUNDEE UNITED (0) 0   ABERDEEN (1) 1
                          Jarvie (14)
DUNDEE UNITED: McAlpine, Rolland, Kopel, Copland, D. Smith, Houston, Traynor, Narey, Gray, Fleming (Hegarty), McDonald (McLeod)
ABERDEEN: Clark, Hair, McLelland, Thomson, Young, Miller, Purdie, Henry (Smith), Jarvie, Williamson, Graham
Attendance: 22,000   *Referee:* J. W. Paterson

Tragedy for Jim McLean's United as Kopel's backpass was intercepted by Williamson. McAlpine blocked, but Jarvie was following up. In the second half – after Purdie had rattled McAlpine's crossbar – Aberdeen lived on their nerves, with Willie Young neutralising the threat posed by Andy Gray. Five minutes from time Miller was adjudged to have handled. Frank Kopel then made his second blunder of the match, blazing the penalty wide.

Quarter Final Saturday, 8 March
ABERDEEN (0) 0   MOTHERWELL (1) 1
                          Graham (44)
ABERDEEN: Clark, Hair, McLelland, Thomson, Young, Miller (Davidson), Purdie, Henry (Smith), Jarvie, Williamson, Graham
MOTHERWELL: Rennie, W. Watson, Wark, R. Watson, McLaren, Millar, McIlwraithe, Pettigrew, Graham, Gardner, Goldthorp
Attendance: 23,400   *Referee:* I. M. D. Foote

Just before half-time referee Foote awarded Motherwell an indirect free kick just outside the Aberdeen box. Gardner flipped over the ball and Bobby Graham blasted Aberdeen out of the Cup.

1974-75

APPEARANCES	League	League Cup	Scottish Cup
Graham	34	6	4
W. Miller	34	6	4
McLelland	33	6	4
Clark	33	4	4
Young	31	4	4
Jarvie	27(+5)	6	4
Williamson	27(+4)	2	4
Purdie	27	5(+1)	4
Hair	26(+1)	4	4
Joe Smith	23(+3)	6	–(+3)
Thomson	16(+1)	4	4
Hermiston	13(+2)	6	
Henry	11	1	4
McCall	10(+4)	–(+1)	
Craig	8		
Pirie	7(+4)	1(+2)	
Robb	6		
Street	3		
Davidson	2(+14)	1(+2)	–(+3)
Ward	2		
Geoghegan	1	2	
Campbell	–(+1)	2	
Neil Cooper	–(+1)		
McMaster	–(+1)	–(+2)	
24 players			

GOALS	Total	League	League Cup	Scottish Cup
Jarvie	13	9	3	1
Graham	12	11		1
Williamson	10	9	1	
Purdie	9	7	2	
McCall	6	6		
Hermiston	5	3	2	
Hair	4	4		
Pirie	4	4		
Robb	4	4		
Young	4	3	1	
Davidson	3	2		1
Miller	2	1		1
McLelland	1	1		
Smith	1	1		
Thomson	1		1	
own-goals	1	1		
Total	80	66	10	4

Season 1975-76

For some years Aberdeen had been dangerously becalmed, with every indication that ahead lay a storm rather than paradise. But few could have anticipated the waves which rolled over Pittodrie in the Autumn of 1975.

When the players reassembled after their summer break it was to welcome a new internationalist among their ranks – Willie Miller, who had been capped in Romania in June. But the Dons' skipper failed to inspire his side in the League Cup rounds, where they suffered double defeats by Celtic and Hearts.

Aberdeen began their Premier League engagements poorly. During their third match, at home to Dundee United, Willie Young was substituted for the first time in his career. Already in trouble with the SFA over 'incidents' with the Scottish squad in Copenhagen, he now tore off his short, stormed out of the ground, and within days had been transferred to Tottenham.

Further bad results followed. Consecutive defeats by Rangers and Celtic in early October left Aberdeen precariously placed, and Jimmy Bonthrone knew it was time to quit. Some weeks later Ally McLeod was recruited from his post for the last nine years as manager of Ayr United.

McLeod soon had Aberdeen on the move. December victories over both of the Old Firm were just part of a nine-match unbeaten run which had fans thinking ahead to a possible place in the UEFA Cup. By early February everything at Pittodrie was blossoming, especially with a Scottish Cup visit to Ibrox looming.

But something suddenly snapped. The Dons went into an accelerating spiral without a bottom. Rangers crushed Aberdeen's cup hopes without fuss. In the league McLeod watched helplessly as his side won only one of eleven games. As they trotted out for their final fixture, at home to Hibs, Aberdeen already had one foot and a heel over the relegation line. As it turned out they were reprieved – on goal difference. They had flirted with the drop on various occasions since the War, but never with such intensity as in those bleak early months of 1976.

League:	Seventh
League Cup:	Third in qualifying group
Scottish Cup:	Fourth Round

SCOTTISH PREMIER LEAGUE

No 1 Saturday, 30 August

DUNDEE (1) 3　　　　**ABERDEEN (2) 2**
Ford (2), Gemmell　　　Smith (3),
(79 pen), Hoggan (86)　Willamson (37)

DUNDEE: Allan, Wilson, Johnston (Sinclair), Ford, Stewart (Gemmell), Phillip, Hoggan, Martin, Gordon, Anderson, Purdie

ABERDEEN: Clark, Hair, McLelland, Scott, Young, Miller, J. Smith, Robb, McMaster (Jarvie), Williamson, Graham

P	W	D	L	F	A	Pts
1	0	0	1	2	3	0

Attendance: 6,050
Referee: W. Paterson

Aberdeen looked to have the game won. But former Don, Ian Purdie won a fortuitous penalty – scored by Gemmell. Then Purdie fouled Hair but was allowed to cross for Hoggan's winner.

251

No 2 Saturday, 6 September

ABERDEEN (2) 2   MOTHERWELL (1) 2
  Robb (17),   Pettigrew 2 (19, 73)
  Williamson (38)

ABERDEEN: Clark, Hair (Pirie), McLelland, Scott, Young, Miller, J. Smith, Robb, McMaster (Thomson), Williamson, Graham

MOTHERWELL: Rennie, W. Watson, Wark, R. Watson (McLaren), McVie, Stevens, McAdam, Pettigrew, Graham, Davidson, Taylor (Millar)

P	W	D	L	F	A	Pts	
2	0	1	1	4	5	1	*Attendance:* 5,500
							Referee: A. McKenzie

Willie Pettigrew is a name to conjure with. It is he who denies Aberdeen their first league win.

No 3 Saturday, 13 September

ABERDEEN (1) 1   DUNDEE UNITED (2) 3
  Scott (25)   Sturrock (22),
                             Hegarty (45),
                             Copland (67)

ABERDEEN: Geoghegan, Hair, McLelland, Scott, Young (Pirie), Miller, J. Smith, Robb, Jarvie, Williamson, Graham

DUNDEE UNITED: McAlpine, Rolland, Kopel, Copland, W. Smith (Hegarty), Narey (Traynor), Rennie, Payne, Gray, Houston, Sturrock

Bottom positions

	P	W	D	L	F	A	Pts
7 Hearts	3	1	0	2	3	5	2
8 St Johnstone	3	1	0	2	1	3	2
9 Dundee	3	1	0	2	5	9	2
10 ABERDEEN	3	0	1	2	5	8	1

Attendance: 5,500   *Referee:* D. F. Syme

Aberdeen are left propping up the table. Just after half time Joe Smith was sent off for a flash of temper at Hegarty. Later Willie Young is substituted. He tears off his shirt, storms out of the ground and never plays for Aberdeen again.

No 4 Saturday, 20 September

HEARTS (2) 2   ABERDEEN (2) 2
  Gibson (4),   Scott (7),
  Prentice (5)   Williamson (8)

HEARTS: Cruickshank, Clunie, Kay, Brown (Aird), Anderson, Murray, Dark, Busby, Gibson, Callachan, Prentice

ABERDEEN: Geoghegan, Hair, McLelland, Scott, Ward, Miller, J. Smith (Thomson), Robb, Jarvie, Williamson, Graham

P	W	D	L	F	A	Pts	
4	0	2	2	7	10	2	*Attendance:* 9,500
							Referee: R. Davidson

Miller was at fault for Hearts' first goal; Geoghegan for their second. But then Scott beat Cruickshank with a low shot and Williamson's effort trickled through the keeper's legs. 2-2, and only eight minutes played. Robb might have scored near the end but his shot troubled the corner flag, not the goal.

No 5 Saturday, 27 September

ABERDEEN (1) 3   AYR UNITED (0) 1
  Williamson (33),   Graham (75)
  Scott 2 (48, 77)

ABERDEEN: Geoghegan, Hair, McLelland, Scott, Ward, Miller, J. Smith (Hather), Robb, Jarvie, Williamson, Graham

AYR: Sproat, Wells, Murphy, Paton (Cameron), McAnespie, McSherry, Doyle, Graham, Ingram, McCulloch, Dickson (McDonald)

P	W	D	L	F	A	Pts	
5	1	2	2	10	11	4	*Attendance:* 4,500
							Referee: W. J. Mullen

A nostalgic moment for older Aberdeen fans. Jimmy Bonthrone brings on John Hather as a second-half substitute, son of the flying Jack Hather from the 1950s.

No 6 Saturday, 4 October

RANGERS (1) 1   ABERDEEN (0) 0
  McDougall (16)

RANGERS: McCloy, Jardine, Dawson, Greig, Jackson, Miller, McLean, McDougall, Parlane, Johnstone, Young

ABERDEEN: Geoghegan, Hair, McLelland, Scott, Ward, Miller, Thomson, Robb, Jarvie, Williamson (Cooper), Graham

P	W	D	L	F	A	Pts	
6	1	2	3	10	12	4	*Attendance:* 22,000
							Referee: R. H. Davidson

Rangers are top of the Premier League, but it's difficult to see why, based on this dreary affair. As for Aberdeen, they looked aimless and dreadful. McDougall's goal was a messy affair, after McLean's shot had spun off a post.

No 7 Saturday, 11 October

ABERDEEN (0) 1   CELTIC (2) 2
  Scott (59)   Dalglish (15),
                             Deans (43)

ABERDEEN: Clark, Thomson (Williamson), Hair, Ward (Pirie), Miller, Scott, Robb, Jarvie, Henry, Graham

CELTIC: Latchford, McGrain, Lynch, McCluskey, MacDonald, Edvaldsson, Wilson, Dalglish, Deans (Lennox), Callaghan, Hood (Ritchie)

Bottom positions

	P	W	D	L	F	A	Pts
7 Hearts	7	2	2	3	8	11	6
8 Dundee	7	2	2	3	11	15	6
9 ABERDEEN	7	1	2	4	11	14	4
10 St Johnstone	7	2	0	5	9	14	4

Attendance: 18,000   *Referee:* G. B. Smith

Miller's crazy back-pass was snapped up by Dalglish. It put 10-man Celtic ahead – Paul Wilson having been sent off for throwing the ball into Thomson's face. Aberdeen had been playing above themselves, and could never quite get back into contention as Celtic funnelled back in the second half. This was the result that broke the camel's back, and shortly afterwards Jimmy Bonthrone quit.

No 8 Saturday, 18 October
ABERDEEN (0) 2   ST JOHNSTONE (0) 0
    Pirie 2 (55, 63)
ABERDEEN: Clark, Hair, Williamson, J. Smith,
Thomson, Miller, Scott, Robb, Pirie, Jarvie (Rougvie),
Graham
ST JOHNSTONE: Robertson, G. Smith, S. Smith,
Ritchie (Hotson), McDonald, Kinnell, Muir,
O'Rourke, Thomson, Cramond, Lambie

P	W	D	L	F	A	Pts		*Attendance:* 5,100
8	2	2	4	13	14	6		*Referee:* E. Thomson

Managerless Aberdeen see off their rivals for the
wooden spoon – but it wasn't easy. Three cheers for the
forgotten man of Pittodrie – Billy Pirie.

No 9 Saturday, 25 October
HIBERNIAN (1) 3   ABERDEEN (0) 1
    Jarvie o.g. (32)   Robb (47)
    Bremner (48),
    Smith (87)
HIBERNIAN: McArthur, Brownlie, Schaedler,
Stanton, Barry, Blackley, McLeod (Smith), Bremner,
Harper, Munro, Duncan
ABERDEEN: Clark, Hair, Williamson, J. Smith
Thomson, Miller, Scott, Robb, Pirie, Jarvie
(McMaster), Graham

P	W	D	L	F	A	Pts		*Attendance:* 11,100
9	2	2	5	14	17	6		*Referee:* H. Alexander

Eddie Thomson kept Joe Harper quiet throughout.
Until the 87th minute. Then Thomson's 'push' on the
wee man gave Hibs a free kick. It was taken quickly by
Harper, rolling the ball into the path of substitute
Bobby Smith.

No 10 Saturday, 1 November
ABERDEEN (0) 2   DUNDEE (0) 0
    Scott (72),
    Williamson (74 pen)·
ABERDEEN: Clark, Hair, Williamson, J. Smith,
Thomson, Miller, Scott, Robb, Pirie (McMaster),
Jarvie, Graham
DUNDEE: Allan, Wilson, Johnston (Caldwell),
Robinson, Stewart, Ford, Laing, Strachan (Phillip),
Wallace, Gordon, Purdie

P	W	D	L	F	A	Pts		*Attendance:* 6,300
10	3	2	5	16	17	8		*Referee:* A. Ferguson

Dundee's Gordon Strachan looked a nifty little player in
the first half when Dundee were going well. But then
Jocky Scott netted against his old club, and when
goalkeeper Allan pulled down Graham, Ford was
booked for disputing the penalty award.

No 11 Saturday, 8 November
MOTHERWELL (2) 3   ABERDEEN (0) 0
    Taylor (17),
    Graham (39),
    Millar (78 pen)

MOTHERWELL: Rennie, Millar, Wark, R. Watson,
McVie, McLaren, McAdam (Gardner), Pettigrew,
Graham, McIlwraithe, Taylor
ABERDEEN: Clark, Hair, Williamson, J. Smith,
Thomson, Miller, Scott, Robb, Jarvie, Rougvie,
Graham

P	W	D	L	F	A	Pts		*Attendance:* 6,300
11	3	2	6	16	20	8		*Referee:* J. R. P. Gordon

New manager Ally McLeod sees his new team for the
first time, and doesn't like what he sees. He comes
down from the stand to the dug-out for the second half.

No 12 Saturday, 15 November
DUNDEE UNITED (0) 1   ABERDEEN (1) 2
    Hegarty (52)   Williamson (3 pen),
                  Scott (60)
DUNDEE UNITED: McAlpine, Rolland, Fleming
(Traynor), Rennie, Houston, Narey, Holt, Payne,
Hegarty, McAdam, Sturrock
ABERDEEN: Clark, Hair, Williamson, J. Smith,
Thomson, Miller, Scott, Robb, Jarvie, McMaster
(Ward), Graham

P	W	D	L	F	A	Pts		*Attendance:* 4,700
12	4	2	6	18	21	10		*Referee:* R. Marshall

Incidents galore! Down goes Jarvie and Williamson
bangs in the penalty. After Hegarty had headed United
level, Scott restores the Don's advantage – at the second
attempt. Jarvie is then sent off after pole-axing Rennie.
Before the final whistle Hamish McAlpine wrestled
Jocky Scott to the ground 40 yards out of goal – and
was only booked.

No 13 Saturday, 22 November
ABERDEEN (0) 0   HEARTS (0) 0
ABERDEEN: Geoghegan, Hair, Williamson, J. Smith,
Thomson, Miller, Scott, Robb (Pirie), Jarvie,
McMaster, Graham
HEARTS: Cruickshank, Clunie, Jefferies, Brown,
Gallacher, Murray, Park, Busby, Gibson, Callachan,
Prentice (Fraser)

P	W	D	L	F	A	Pts		*Attendance:* 11,400
13	4	3	6	18	21	11		*Referee:* C. H. Hutton

'Come along to see the rejuvenated Dons' was Ally
McLeod's hype. What a joke.

No 14 Saturday, 29 November
AYR UNITED (0) 1   ABERDEEN (0) 0
    Murphy (50)
AYR: Sproat, McDonald, Murphy, McAnespie,
Fleming, McSherry, Doyle, Graham, Ingram, Phillips
(Dickson), McCulloch
ABERDEEN: Geoghegan, Hair, Williamson, J. Smith,
Thomson, Miller, Scott, Robb, Jarvie (McCall),
McMaster (McLelland), Graham

P	W	D	L	F	A	Pts		*Attendance:* 6,000
14	4	3	7	18	22	11		*Referee:* T. R. Kyle

When Ayr full-back John Murphy tossed in an aimless centre, Andy Geoghegan took a swipe – and guess what happened. McLeod's old team look better than his new.

No 15 Saturday, 6 December
ABERDEEN (0) 1   RANGERS (0) 0
  Jarvie (83)
ABERDEEN: Geoghegan, Williamson, McLelland, J. Smith, Thomson, Miller, Scott, Robb, Jarvie, McMaster, Graham
RANGERS: Kennedy, Jardine, Greig, Forsyth, Jackson, MacDonald, McKean, Hamilton, Henderson, McLean, Johnstone
Bottom positions

		P	W	D	L	F	A	Pts
7	Dundee	15	5	4	6	23	29	14
8	ABERDEEN	15	5	3	7	19	22	13
9	Dundee United	15	4	3	8	20	25	11
10	St Johnstone	15	2	0	13	17	35	4

Attendance: 19,600   *Referee:* J. W. Paterson

This was great stuff. Ally McLeod liked to get involved, and he received a stiff finger-wagging from the referee in the second half. He might have called for one of the police dogs, who entertained the crowd before the match and at half-time. They were entertained even more by Jarvie's goal, manufactured by McMaster. This was a good start for Aberdeen's new captain – Willie Miller.

No 16 Saturday, 13 December
CELTIC (0) 0   ABERDEEN (2) 2
                       Jarvie (6),
                       Graham (33)
CELTIC: Latchford, McGrain, Lynch, McCluskey, MacDonald, Edvaldsson, Wilson (Hood), Dalglish, Deans, Callaghan, Lennox
ABERDEEN: Geoghegan, Williamson, McLelland, J. Smith (Hair), Thomson, Miller, Scott (Pirie), Robb, Jarvie, McMaster, Graham

P	W	D	L	F	A	Pts
16	6	3	7	21	22	15

Attendance: 24,000   *Referee:* E. H. Pringle

League leaders Celtic suffer a surprise defeat. Successive wins over both the Old Firm can't be bad – but Eddie Thomson is booked for the third game in a row.

No 17 Saturday, 20 December
ST JOHNSTONE (0) 1   ABERDEEN (0) 1
  O'Rourke (83)   Williamson (80)
ST JOHNSTONE: Robertson, G. Smith, Ritchie, Roberts, MacDonald, Anderson, C. Smith, O'Rourke, Muir, Cramond, Lambie
ABERDEEN: Geoghegan, Williamson, McLelland, J. Smith, Thomson, Miller, Scott (Hair), Robb, Jarvie, McMaster (Pirie), Graham

P	W	D	L	F	A	Pts
17	6	4	7	22	23	16

Attendance: 3,500   *Referee:* W. J. Mullen

St Johnstone were heading for their 11th straight defeat until Lambie's shot came back off the bar and O'Rourke headed it back.

No 18 Saturday, 27 December
ABERDEEN (1) 2   HIBERNIAN (2) 2
  McMaster (18),   Bremner (10),
  Williamson (56)   Duncan (20)
ABERDEEN: Geoghegan, Williamson, McLelland, J. Smith, Thomson, Miller, Scott, Robb, Jarvie, McMaster, Graham
HIBERNIAN: McArthur, Brownlie, Schaedler (Spalding), Stanton, Barry, Blackley, Edwards, Bremner, Harper, Smith, Duncan

P	W	D	L	F	A	Pts
18	6	5	7	24	25	17

Attendance: 17,600   *Referee:* D. F. T. Syme

Pittodrie certainly got its moneys-worth. Billy Williamson wasted a penalty and Hibs' Alec Edwards was later ordered off for clattering Thomson. Earlier the crowd had cheered as Aberdeen twice came from behind.

No 19 Thursday, 1 January
DUNDEE (1) 1   ABERDEEN (2) 3
  Hutchinson (4)   Robb (14), Scott (28),
                         Graham (62)
DUNDEE: Allan, Caldwell, Gemmell (Robinson), Ford, Stewart, Phillip, Laing, Strachan, Wallace, Mackie, Hutchinson (Purdie)
ABERDEEN: Geoghegan, Williamson, McLelland, J. Smith, Thomson, Miller, Scott, Robb, Jarvie, McMaster, Graham

P	W	D	L	F	A	Pts
19	7	5	7	27	26	19

Attendance: 10,000

Sleety snow discouraged spectators turning out. Aberdeen's revival discouraged them even more.

No 20 Saturday, 3 January
ABERDEEN (0) 0   MOTHERWELL (0) 0
ABERDEEN: Geoghegan, Williamson, McLelland, J. Smith (Hair), Thomson, Miller, Scott, Robb (Pirie), Jarvie, McMaster, Graham
MOTHERWELL: Rennie, W. Watson, Wark, R. Watson, McVie, Stevens, McAdam, Pettigrew, Davidson (Taylor), McLaren, Marinello

P	W	D	L	F	A	Pts
20	7	6	7	27	26	20

Attendance: 16,200   *Referee:* H. Alexander

No goals, but a super penalty save by Geoghegan off Willie Watson early on. Before the game an example of McLeod public relations was put into effect. All the players carried placards bearing the words 'Happy New Year', which were tossed to the crowd.

No 21 Saturday, 10 January
ABERDEEN (2) 5   DUNDEE UNITED (0) 3
  Graham 2 (23, 88)   Reid 2 (62, 80 pen)
  Scott 3 (25 pen,   Hegarty (66)
  52 pen, 72)
ABERDEEN: Geoghegan, Williamson, McLelland, J. Smith (Pirie), Thomson, Miller, Scott, Robb (Hair), Jarvie, McMaster, Graham
DUNDEE UNITED: McAlpine, Rolland, Kopel, Rennie (Steele), Smith, Narey, Houston, Fleming, Hegarty, McAdam, Reid

P W D L F A Pts *Attendance:* 9,600
21 8 6 7 32 29 22 *Referee:* B. R. McGinlay

Ally McLeod believes in manager participation. He was to be seen urging his side forward in the second half as United threatened to steal a point in this thriller.

No 22 Saturday, 17 January

HEARTS (1) 3 ABERDEEN (1) 3
  Gibson (26),   McMaster (13),
  Anderson (73), Scott (58),
  Prentice (87)   Pirie (84)

HEARTS: Graham, Clunie, Jefferies, Callachan, Anderson, Kay, Aird, Park (Fraser), Gibson, Shaw (Brown), Prentice

ABERDEEN: Geoghegan, Williamson, McLelland, J. Smith, Garner, Miller, Scott, Robb, Jarvie (Pirie), McMaster (Hair), Graham

P W D L F A Pts *Attendance:* 10,300
22 8 7 7 35 32 23 *Referee:* R. Davidson

Aberdeen's Willie Garner makes his debut in this memorable game. Three times the Dons led, and three times they were pegged back. With Aberdeen 2-1 ahead, Geoghegan managed to keep out Prentice's penalty.

No 23 Saturday, 31 January

ABERDEEN (1) 2 AYR UNITED (0) 1
  Pirie (43),   Graham (79 pen)
  McMaster (61)

ABERDEEN: Geoghegan, Williamson, McLelland, J. Smith, Thomson, Miller, Pirie, Robb, Jarvie, McMaster, Graham

AYR: Sproat, Wells, Murphy, McAnespie, Fleming, McDonald (McCulloch), Doyle, Graham, Ingram, McSherry, Robertson

P W D L F A Pts *Attendance:* 9,900
23 9 7 7 37 33 25 *Referee:* W. Anderson

The McLeod magic seems to be working. Ayr were the last team to beat Aberdeen – nine league games ago. The Dons are now entrenched in 5th position, with Dundee United, who are in the fatal 9th spot, eleven points behind.

No 24 Saturday, 7 February

RANGERS (2) 2 ABERDEEN (0) 1
  Henderson (24), Pirie (77)
  McDonald (45)

RANGERS: McCloy, Miller, Greig, Forsyth, Jackson, MacDonald, McKean, Hamilton (Jardine), Henderson, (Parlane), McLean, Johnstone

ABERDEEN: Geoghegan, Williamson (Pirie), McLelland, J. Smith, Thomson, Miller, Scott, Robb, Jarvie (Fleming), McMaster, Graham

P W D L F A Pts *Attendance:* 20,000
24 9 7 8 38 35 25 *Referee:* E. Thomson

Aberdeen had plenty of chances to score before Pirie did so, but fluffed them all. Biggest culprit was Drew Jarvie. Aberdeen will have to do better than this in next week's Scottish Cup clash.

No 25 Saturday, 21 February

ABERDEEN (0) 0 CELTIC (0) 1
                  Lennox (80)

ABERDEEN: Clark, Hair, McLelland, J. Smith, Garner, Miller, Pirie, Williamson, Jarvie (Robb), McMaster, Graham

CELTIC: Latchford, McGrain, Lynch, McCluskey, Aitken, Edvaldsson, Ritchie (Lennox), Dalglish, Deans, Glavin, Wilson

P W D L F A Pts *Attendance:* 18,200
25 9 7 9 38 36 25 *Referee:* J. W. Paterson

This game took a long time to warm up, and was settled by a goal from Bobby Lennox, the last of the Lisbon Lions still with Celtic. He put the final touch to Dalglish's net-bound lob.

No 26 Saturday, 28 February

ABERDEEN (1) 3 ST JOHNSTONE (0) 0
  Pirie 2 (25, 75),
  Scott (56)

ABERDEEN: Clark, Hair, McLelland, J. Smith, Garner, Miller, McMaster (Scott), Williamson, Pirie (Street), Fleming, Campbell

ST JOHNSTONE: Robertson, G. Smith, Ritchie, Anderson, Hamilton, Kinnell, Muir, O'Rourke, S. Smith, Cramond, Lambie (Thomson)

P W D L F A Pts *Attendance:* 5,900
26 10 7 9 41 36 27 *Referee:* T. R. Kyle

St Johnstone are already doomed to a brief stay in the Premier League. McLeod's new striking partnership of Pirie and Fleming looks promising.

No 27 Saturday, 13 March

ABERDEEN (0) 0 DUNDEE (0) 1
                  Hutchinson (88)

ABERDEEN: Clark, Williamson, McLelland, Docherty, Thomson, Miller, Graham, Scott, Pirie (Jarvie), Fleming, Campbell

DUNDEE: Allan, Wilson, Johnston, Robinson, Phillip, Caldwell, Mackie, Gordon, Wallace, Hutchinson, Laing (Strachan)

P W D L F A Pts *Attendance:* 6,500
27 10 7 10 41 37 27 *Referee:* G. B. Smith

There was never a derby between these two as boring as this – or so unexpected a defeat brought about by Hutchinson's unstoppable header.

No 28 Saturday, 20 March

MOTHERWELL (1) 2 ABERDEEN (0) 1
  Pettigrew (5),   Fleming (72)
  Davidson (88)

MOTHERWELL: Rennie, Millar, Wark, R. Watson, McLaren, Stevens, Gardner (Davidson), Pettigrew, Graham, Taylor, Marinello

ABERDEEN: Clark, Hair, McLelland, J. Smith, Thomson, Miller, Scott, Williamson, Fleming, Pirie (Gibson), Graham

P W D L F A Pts   *Attendance:* 5,900
28 10 7 11 42 39 27   *Referee:* E. Thomson

Aberdeen just can't beat Motherwell of late. Fleming's rising shot looked like saving a point – but once again a late, late goal defeats them.

No 29 Saturday, 27 March
DUNDEE UNITED (0) 1   ABERDEEN (0) 0
G. Fleming (64)

DUNDEE UNITED: McAlpine, Rolland, Kopel, Forsyth, Houston, Narey, Hall, Fleming, Hegarty, McAdam (Steele), Reid

ABERDEEN: Clark, Williamson, McLelland, J. Smith, Thomson, Miller, McMaster, Robb, Scott, Fleming, Graham (Gibson)

P W D L F A Pts   *Attendance:* 4,900
29 10 7 12 42 40 27   *Referee:* W. J. Mullen

When Aberdeen beat Ayr on 31 January all looked rosy in the Pittodrie garden. But a sequence of odd-goal defeats, coupled with Dundee United's extraordinary revival, is pushing Aberdeen to the brink. Hamish McAlpine saved at least three shots with his legs.

No 30 Wednesday, 31 March
HIBERNIAN (1) 3   ABERDEEN (1) 2
Murray (26),   Scott (15),
Muir (48),   Fleming (49)
Blackley (90)

HIBERNIAN: McDonald, Brownlie, Schaedler, Stanton, Spalding, Blackley, Edwards (Muir), Murray, Wilson, Bremner, Duncan

ABERDEEN: Clark, Williamson, McLelland, J. Smith, Thomson, Miller, Hair, Jarvie, Scott, Fleming, Graham

P W D L F A Pts   *Attendance:* 7,200
30 10 7 13 44 43 27   *Referee:* C. H. Hutton

The dark clouds are hovering over Aberdeen after yet another defeat suffered in the closing seconds. Murray's corner kick bobbled about crazily until the ball fell to Blackley's feet six inches from the line.

No 31 Wednesday, 7 April
ABERDEEN (0) 0   HEARTS (2) 3
Gibson 2 (7, 84),
Aird (40)

ABERDEEN: Clark, Williamson, McLelland, J. Smith, Thomson, Miller, Scott, Fleming, Jarvie, Hair (Robb), Graham

HEARTS: Cruickshank, Brown, Jefferies, Callachan, Gallacher, Kay (Fraser), Aird, Busby, Shaw, Gibson, Prentice

P W D L F A Pts   *Attendance:* 6,000
31 10 7 14 44 46 27   *Referee:* C. H. Hutton

Demoralisation has set in after this fifth successive defeat. Hearts eased their own problems,and left the Pittodrie crowd chanting 'Harper, Harper'. Gibson's insulting first goal, hooked over his shoulder, put Aberdeen on the slippery slope.

No 32 Saturday, 10 April
AYR UNITED (0) 1   ABERDEEN (0) 1
Graham (50)   Jarvie (86)

AYR: Sproat, Wells, Murphy, Fleming, Tait, Fillippi, McSherry, Graham, Ingram (Phillips), Cramond, Robertson

ABERDEEN: Clark, Williamson, McLelland, J. Smith (Garner), Thomson, Miller, Robb, Hair, Jarvie, Fleming, Graham (Scott)

P W D L F A Pts   *Attendance:* 5,700
32 10 8 14 45 47 28   *Referee:* D. Syme

At last a late goal for Aberdeen. But the price is high: Williamson was sent off for bringing down Robertson. Aberdeen had only ten men when Jarvie scrambled the ball over the line.

No 33 Wednesday, 14 April
ABERDEEN (0) 0   RANGERS (0) 0

ABERDEEN: Clark, Hair, McLelland, Thomson, Garner, Miller, Robb, Williamson, Jarvie, Fleming, J. Smith

RANGERS: McCloy, Miller, Greig, Forsyth, Jackson, MacDonald, McKean (Parlane), Hamilton, Henderson, McLean (Jardine), Johnstone

P W D L F A Pts   *Attendance:* 17,900
33 10 9 14 45 47 29

Just after half time Robb commits a crazy tackle on Hamilton and is ordered off. Yet Aberdeen continue to fight to a standstill. This time there is a standing ovation for them at the end.

No 34 Saturday, 17 April
CELTIC (1) 1   ABERDEEN (1) 1
Dalglish (25)   Edvaldsson o.g. (40)

CELTIC: Latchford, McGrain, Edvaldsson, Glavin, Aitken, Callaghan, Doyle (Ritchie), Dalglish, Deans, Burns, Lennox (Wilson)

ABERDEEN: Clark, Hair, McLelland, Thomson, Garner, Miller, Robb, Williamson, Jarvie, Fleming, J. Smith

P W D L F A Pts   *Attendance:* 29,000
34 10 10 14 46 48 30   *Referee:* J. R. P. Gordon

Aberdeen skipper Willie Miller makes it a hat-trick – but not one to be proud off. Early in the second half he sent Roy Aitken into orbit and became the third Don to be dismissed in successive games. Edvaldsson's error could be a lifeline to Aberdeen.

No 35 Wednesday, 21 April
ST JOHNSTONE (1) 2   ABERDEEN (0) 0
Hotson (35),
Thomson (62)

ST JOHNSTONE: Robertson, G. Smith, McBain, Anderson, Roberts, Kinnell, Henderson (Muir), O'Rourke, McGregor, Thomson, Hotson

ABERDEEN: Clark, Hair, McLelland, Cooper (Scott), Garner, Miller, Robb, Williamson, Jarvie (McMaster), Fleming, J. Smith

Bottom positions

	P	W	D	L	F	A	Pts
5 ABERDEEN	35	10	10	15	46	50	30
6 Hearts	33	11	8	14	37	45	30
7 Dundee United	33	11	7	15	44	47	29
8 Ayr	33	12	5	16	39	52	29
9 Dundee	34	10	9	15	48	61	29
10 St Johnstone	34	3	4	27	29	78	10

Attendance: 2,500   *Referee:* D. Ramsay

Is this what the proponents of the Premier League had in mind? With one match to play Aberdeen are in the top half of the table, yet are one of five clubs who will accompany St Johnstone out of the trap door. Before today St Johnstone had played 29 league and cup games without the taste of victory. Their deserved win seems set to deprive Aberdeen of the elite status they have held for so long.

No 36 Saturday, 24 April
ABERDEEN (1) 3   HIBERNIAN (0) 0
 Jarvie (30),
 Smith (67),
 Robb (68)
ABERDEEN: Clark, Hair, McLelland, J. Smith, Garner, Miller, Robb, Williamson, Jarvie, Fleming (Scott), W. McCall
HIBERNIAN: McDonald, Smith, Schaedler, Stanton, Spalding, Blackley, Murray, Muir, McGhee, McLeod, Duncan (Paterson)

Attendance: 11,000   *Referee:* W. Anderson

Pity Dave Robb who, with responsibility for a make-or-break first-half penalty, watches it saved by McDonald. His guilt was eased when Jarvie netted from close in and vanished completely when Joe Smith volleyed the goal-of-the-season after half-time. Robb even scored himself a minute later. Aberdeen are safe – for another year.

Aberdeen's complete home and away record:

HOME						AWAY						
P	W	D	L	F	A	W	D	L	F	A		Pts
36	8	5	5	27	19	3	5	10	22	31		32

Scottish League Premier Division

	P	W	D	L	F	A	Pts
1 Rangers	36	23	8	5	59	24	54
2 Celtic	36	21	6	9	71	42	48
3 Hibernian	36	20	7	9	58	40	43
4 Motherwell	36	16	8	12	57	49	40
5 Hearts	36	13	9	14	39	44	35
6 Ayr United	36	14	5	17	46	59	33
7 ABERDEEN	36	11	10	15	49	50	32
8 Dundee United	36	12	8	16	46	48	32
9 Dundee	36	11	10	15	49	62	32
10 St. Johnstone	36	3	5	28	29	79	11

LEAGUE CUP

Saturday, 9 August
CELTIC (1) 1   ABERDEEN (0) 0
 Dalglish (10)

CELTIC: Latchford, McGrain, Lynch, McCluskey, MacDonald, Edvaldsson, Hood (McNamara), Dalglish, Wilson, Glavin, Lennox
ABERDEEN: Clark, Thomson (Williamson), McLelland, Hair, Young, Miller, Smith, Robb, Jarvie, Rougvie, Graham (Campbell)

Attendance: 32,000   *Referee:* J. R. P. Gordon

Celtic may have lost the league title for the first time in nine years but they are the reigning League Cup holders. Dalglish sprung the offside trap after the Dons' defence moved out after clearing a corner. Later Jarvie hoofed the ball over the bar from four yards.

Wednesday, 13 August
ABERDEEN (2) 2   DUMBARTON (0) 0
 Graham (7), Jarvie (37)
ABERDEEN: Clark, Hair, McLelland, Gibson, Young, Miller, Smith, Robb, Jarvie (Williamson), Rougvie (Thomson), Graham
DUMBARTON: Williams, Brown, Watt, Ruddy, Muir, Graham, Cook, McLean, Wallace (Coleman), McKinlay (McAdam), Bourke

Attendance: 6,000   *Referee:* T. Muirhead

All four teams now have two points, with everything to play for. Aberdeen won more comfortably than the scoreline would suggest.

Saturday, 16 August
ABERDEEN (0) 1   HEARTS (0) 2
 Williamson (50)   Ford (72),
                          Hancock (77)
ABERDEEN: Clark, Hair, McLelland, Gibson (Henry), Young, Miller, Smith, Robb, Williamson, Rougvie, Graham
HEARTS: Cruickshank, Kay (Park), Clunie, Callachan, Anderson, Murray, Brown, Busby, Hancock, Ford, Prentice

Attendance: 8,000   *Referee:* R. B. Valentine

Rain had washed away the white lines. Sawdust was sprinkled everywhere. Dave Robb's first-half penalty rebounded from the crossbar. Three Hearts players were booked.

Wednesday, 20 August
DUMBARTON (0) 0   ABERDEEN (0) 1
                          Hair (72)
DUMBARTON: Williams, Brown, Watt, Bennett (Ruddy), Muir, Graham, Cook, McLean, Bourke, McAdam (Coleman), Wallace
ABERDEEN: Clark, Hair, McLelland, Scott, Young, Miller, Smith, Robb, Jarvie, Williamson (Pirie), Campbell

Referee: T. Kellock

Full-back Ian Hair landed the decisive touch in a goalmouth scramble to keep the Dons' chances alive. English scouts take notes on Willie Young.

Saturday, 23 August
HEARTS (1) 1   ABERDEEN (0) 0
  Prentice (2)

HEARTS: Cruickshank, Kay, Clunie, Jefferies, Anderson, Murray, Brown, Busby, Hancock, Ford, Prentice (Callachan)

ABERDEEN: Clark, Hair, McLelland, Scotƚ, Young, Miller, Smith, Robb, Jarvie (Rougvie), Pirie, Graham

Attendance: 11,000   Referee: H. Alexander

Brown's second-minute corner kick was headed out to Prentice. There seemed to be too many bodies between him and goal for him to score. But he did. This ends Aberdeen's chances of heading Section 3.

Wednesday, 27 August
ABERDEEN (0) 0   CELTIC (1) 2
                            Lennox (5), Ritchie (86)

ABERDEEN: Clark, Hair, McLelland, Scott, Young, Miller, Smith (Rougvie), Robb, Pirie, McMaster, Graham

CELTIC: Latchford, McGrain, Lynch, McCluskey (Connelly), MacDonald, Edvaldsson, McNamara, Wilson (Ritchie), Dalglish, Callaghan, Lennox

Attendance: 13,000   *Referee:* E. H. Pringle

Celtic won with style, going ahead after Dalglish squared the ball to Lennox. Substitute Ritchie had only been on the field two minutes before racing through without hindrance for number two.

Section 3

	P	W	D	L	F	A	Pts
Celtic	6	5	0	1	17	4	10
Hearts	6	4	0	2	13	8	8
ABERDEEN	6	2	0	4	4	6	4
Dumbarton	6	1	0	5	5	21	2

SCOTTISH CUP

3rd Round Saturday, 24 January
ALLOA (0) 0   ABERDEEN (2) 4
                            Scott (38), McMaster
                            (42), Miller (64),
                            Robb (72)

ALLOA: A. Thomson, McCann, Wilkinson, McGarry, Stewart, Miller, Low, J. Thomson, Wilson, Campbell, Russell (Morrison)

ABERDEEN: Geoghegan, Williamson, McLelland, Smith, Garner, Miller, Scott, Robb, Jarvie, McMaster, Graham

Attendance: 6,300   *Referee:* A. Paterson

Second Division (i.e. in effect the new third division) Alloa had to suffer the invasion of the Aberdeen thugs. Players were sent to the safety of the dressing rooms for fifteen minutes as spectators sought refuge from the bricks and bottles by spilling onto the pitch.

4th Round Saturday, 14 February
RANGERS (1) 4   ABERDEEN (0) 1
  Johnstone (43),   Smith (68)
  McDonald (46),
  Henderson (75),
  Parlane (86)

RANGERS: McCloy, Miller, Greig, Forsyth (Parlane), Jackson, MacDonald, McKean, Hamilton (Jardine), Henderson, McLean, Johnstone

ABERDEEN: Geoghegan, Williamson, McLelland, Smith, Thomson (Hair), Miller, Scott, Robb, Jarvie, McMaster (Pirie), Graham

Attendance: 53,000   *Referee:* J. R. P. Gordon

Defeats in league and cup at Ibrox on successive Saturdays have brought the Dons down to earth. They were always chasing the improbable in this match — except for the few minutes following Joe Smith's blinding shot in the second half.

1975-76
APPEARANCES

	League	League Cup	Scottish Cup
Miller	36	6	2
Williamson	35(+1)	2(+2)	2
Joe Smith	33	6	2
Graham	31	5	2
Jarvie	30(+2)	4	2
Robb	30(+2)	6	2
McLelland	29(+1)	6	2
Scott	28(+4)	3	2
Thomson	26(+2)	1(+1)	1
Hair	24(+5)	6	−(+1)
Clark	20	6	
McMaster	18(+3)	1	2
Geoghegan	16		2
Fleming	11(+1)		
Pirie	8(+10)	2(+1)	−(+1)
Garner	7(+1)		1
Ward	4(+1)		
Young	3	6	
Campbell	2	1(+1)	
Rougvie	1(+1)	3(+2)	
Neil Cooper	1(+1)		
Henry	1	−(+1)	
Docherty	1		
McCall	1(+1)		
Gibson	−(+2)	2	
Street	−(+1)		
Hather	−(+1)		

27 players

GOALS	Total	League	League Cup	Scottish Cup	GOALS	Total	League	League Cup	Scottish Cup
Scott	15	14		1	Smith	3	2		1
Williamson	9	8	1		Fleming	2	2		
Pirie	7	7			Hair	1		1	
Graham	5	4	1		Miller	1			1
Jarvie	5	4	1		own-goals	1	1		
Robb	5	4		1	Totals	58	49	4	5
McMaster	4	3		1					

1976 League Cup success. (Left) Lord Provost R. L. Lennox holds aloft the trophy, supported by Graham and Harper. (Right) Aberdeen Directors, Chris Anderson and Dick Donald proudly show the Cup.

Season 1976-77

In football, as in life, the line between success and failure is often so thin as to be invisible. Had Aberdeen mustered one fewer point in 1975-76 they would have been relegated and the extraordinary future awaiting Ally McLeod would never have come to pass. Permitted another chance in the Premier Division, McLeod immediately strengthened his side. Full-back Stuart Kennedy was recruited from Falkirk; midfielder Dominic Sullivan from Clyde; and – the shrewdest move of all – Joe Harper swopped the green shirt of Hibs for the red of Aberdeen. King Joey had come home.

The upturn in the Dons' fortunes was nothing less than spectacular. When Aberdeen beat Motherwell in early November, not only did McLeod's team sit proudly on top of the league, but they were looking forward to an appointment at Hampden with Celtic in the League Cup Final.

Again, Lady Luck was determined to have her say. On the balance of play Celtic scarcely deserved to lose – Willie Miller admitted as much – but it was he who held aloft the trophy, and Ally McLeod who would later reap the fruit of his team's fortune.

Possession of the League Cup guaranteed Aberdeen a place in the following season's UEFA Cup. For a while, they were on course for admission to the champions' cup. The Dons continued to lead the pack into January, whereupon Celtic simply stepped on the throttle.

The only disappointment suffered in this memorable season was reserved for the Scottish Cup, where Aberdeen were knocked out in front of their own fans for the third time in four years. But Ally McLeod had already made his mark. When Willie Ormond quit as manager of the national team the telephone rang at Pittodrie.

League:	Third
League Cup:	Winners
Scottish Cup:	Fourth Round

SCOTTISH PREMIER DIVISION

No 1 Saturday, 4 September

ABERDEEN (1) 2   HEARTS (1) 2
Fleming (6), Robb (86)   Busby (1), Park (88)

ABERDEEN: Clark, Hair, McLelland, J. Smith, Garner, Miller, Sullivan (Robb), Williamson, Harper, Fleming, Graham

HEARTS: Cruickshank, Brown, Kay, Jefferies (Shaw), Gallacher, Clunie, Park, Busby, Gibson, Callachan, Prentice

P	W	D	L	F	A	Pts	
1	0	1	0	2	2	1	*Attendance:* 11,100

Referee: K. J. Hope

24 seconds have been played and Busby drills Prentice's cross past Clark. Harper then provides Fleming with a chance he can't miss. Near the end Robb also has a simple goal, but it's cancelled out by Park's grass trimming drive.

No 2 Saturday, 11 September

AYR UNITED (0) 0   ABERDEEN (2) 5
                    Fleming (27),
                    Sullivan 2 (40, 86),
                    Harper 2 (60, 85)

AYR: Sproat, Fillippi, Murphy, Fleming, McDonald, McSherry, Phillips, Graham (Ingram) (Gray), McCulloch, Cramond, Robertson

ABERDEEN: Clark, Kennedy, McLelland, J. Smith, Garner, Miller, Sullivan, Fleming, Harper, Robb, Campbell

P	W	D	L	F	A	Pts	
2	1	1	0	7	2	3	*Attendance:* 4,800

Referee: G. B. Smith

Once Fleming headed over the stranded Sproat, Ayr were always chasing a lost cause.

No 3 Saturday, 18 September
ABERDEEN (0) 2   KILMARNOCK (0) 0
   Jarvie (83), Gibson (88)
ABERDEEN: Clark, Williamson, McLelland, J. Smith,
Garner, Miller, Sullivan, Fleming (Jarvie), Harper,
Robb (Gibson), Graham
KILMARNOCK: Stewart, McLean, Robertson,
Murdoch, Clarke, Welsh, Provan, McCulloch, Fallis,
Sheed, Smith

P W D L F A Pts   *Attendance:* 8,700
3 2 1 0 9 2 5   *Referee:* A. G. McFaull

Graham beat McLean for the umpteenth time and
slipped the ball back for substitute Jarvie to sweep low
past Stewart, at which point Killie defenders besiege the
referee – without avail.

No 4 Saturday, 25 September
HIBERNIAN (0) 0   ABERDEEN (0) 0
HIBERNIAN: McDonald, Brownlie, Smith, Bremner,
Stewart, Blackley, Murray, Muir (Spalding), Scott,
McNamara, Duncan
ABERDEEN: Clark, Thomson, McLelland, J. Smith
(Scott), Garner, Miller, Sullivan, Fleming, Harper,
Robb, Graham

P W D L F A Pts   *Attendance:* 9,300
4 2 2 0 9 2 6   *Referee:* B. R. McGinlay

The most predictable feature of this match is that Joe
Harper was booed every time he touched the ball, as he
returns to the ground he recently left.

No 5 Saturday, 2 October
PARTICK THISTLE (1) 2 ABERDEEN (2) 2
   Somner (23 pen),   Harper (10),
   McQuade (62)   Fleming (43)
PARTICK: Rough, Mackie, Whittaker, A. Hansen,
Campbell, Anderson, Houston, Gibson (Love),
McQuade, Somner, Johnston
ABERDEEN: Clark, Thomson, McLelland, J. Smith,
Garner, Miller, Sullivan, Fleming (Scott), Harper,
Robb, Graham

Leading positions
                  P W D L F A Pts
1 Dundee United   5 5 0 0 11 3 10
2 ABERDEEN   5 2 3 0 11 4 7
3 Rangers   5 1 4 0 8 6 6
4 Celtic   5 1 3 1 9 6 5

Attendance: 6,500   *Referee:* W. J. Mullen

Fleming restored the Dons' lead with a completely
miscued shot that left Rough looking disgusted.
McQuade's far-post header made the Patrick keeper feel
better.

No 6 Saturday, 16 October
RANGERS (0) 1   ABERDEEN (0) 0
   MacDonald (77)
RANGERS: Kennedy, Jardine, Miller, Greig, Jackson,
Denny, McLean, Hamilton (McKean), Parlane,
MacDonald, Johnstone (Henderson)

ABERDEEN: Clark, Kennedy, McLelland, J. Smith,
Garner, Miller, Sullivan, Robb, Thomson (Rougvie),
Fleming, Graham (Campbell)

P W D L F A Pts   *Attendance:* 26,000
6 2 3 1 11 5 7   *Referee:* J. R. P. Gordon

With Harper sidelined through injury, Rangers' Alex
MacDonald was probably the smallest man on the pitch.
Parlane's back-header found him in sweet isolation and
MacDonald headed wide of Clark.

No 7 Saturday, 23 October
ABERDEEN (0) 2   CELTIC (0) 1
   Harper 2 (63, 77 pen)   Dalglish (56 pen)
ABERDEEN: Clark, Kennedy, Williamson, J. Smith,
Garner, Miller, Sullivan (Jarvie), Scott, Harper, Shirra,
Graham
CELTIC: Latchford, McGrain, Lynch, Stanton,
MacDonald, Aitken, Doyle, Glavin, Craig, Dalglish,
Wilson

P W D L F A Pts   *Attendance:* 19,400
7 3 3 1 13 6 9   *Referee:* G. B. Smith

A game of two penalties. Willie Miller tripped Wilson
on the edge of the box for Dalglish to open the scoring.
Then, after Harper had equalised by dribbling the ball
round Latchford, Stanton upended Arthur Graham.

No 8 Saturday, 30 October
ABERDEEN (1) 3   DUNDEE UNITED (1) 2
   Jarvie (22), Harper (46), Sturrock (11),
   Williamson (57)   Wallace (84)
ABERDEEN: Clark, Kennedy, Williamson, Shirra,
Garner, Miller, Sullivan, Scott, Harper, Jarvie, Graham
DUNDEE UNITED: McAlpine, Rolland, Kopel,
Fleming, Forsyth, Narey, Sturrock, Wallace, Hegarty,
McAdam, Payne

P W D L F A Pts   *Attendance:* 18,600
8 4 3 1 16 8 11   *Referee:* D. F. Syme

Aberdeen are already celebrating their place at
Hampden for the League Cup final as they inflict this
defeat on the league leaders. Sturrock's overhead kick
took Clark by surprise, but Jarvie's point-blank header
and a wheeling shot-on-the turn by Harper turned the
tables.

No 9 Tuesday, 2 November
ABERDEEN (0) 3   MOTHERWELL (0) 1
   Jarvie (64), Sullivan (71), O'Rourke (89)
   Harper (85)
ABERDEEN: MacLean, Kennedy, Williamson,
J. Smith, Garner, Miller, Sullivan, Scott, Harper,
Jarvie, Graham
MOTHERWELL: Rennie, McLaren, Wark, Millar,
McVie, Stevens (McAdam), Marinello, Pettigrew
(O'Rourke), Graham, Davidson, Kennedy

Leading positions
                  P W D L F A Pts
1 ABERDEEN   9 5 3 1 19 9 13
2 Dundee United   8 6 0 2 16 12 12
3 Celtic   9 4 3 2 19 9 11

Attendance: 15,200   *Referee:* H. Alexander

Motherwell resisted in the first-half – and were executed, clean and simple, in the second. Both Joe Harper and Aberdeen are top of their respective charts.

No 10 Wednesday, 10 November
HEARTS (1) 2   ABERDEEN (0) 1
  Jefferies 2 (40, 52)   Harper (65)
HEARTS: Wilson, Brown, Kay, Jefferies (Fraser), Gallacher, Clunie, Shaw, Busby, Gibson, Park, Prentice
ABERDEEN: Clark, Kennedy, Williamson, J. Smith, Garner, Miller, Sullivan (Robb), Scott, Harper, Jarvie (Shirra), Graham

P W D L F A Pts   *Attendance:* 12,000
10 5 3 2 20 11 13   *Referee:* A. Ferguson

League Cup holders the Dons may be: invincible they are not. This was Hearts first league win of the season, secured by two identical goals: two pull-backs by Brown; two lethal strikes by Jefferies.

No 11 Saturday, 20 November
KILMARNOCK (1) 1   ABERDEEN (0) 2
  Smith (42 pen)   Scott (55), Kennedy (80)
KILMARNOCK: Stewart, Maxwell, Robertson, Murdoch, Clarke, Welsh, Provan, McLean, Fallis, Sheed, Smith
ABERDEEN: Clark, Kennedy, Williamson, J. Smith, Garner, Miller, Sullivan (Shirra), Scott, Harper, Jarvie, Graham

P W D L F A Pts   *Attendance:* 6,000
11 6 3 2 22 12 15   *Referee:* K. J. Hope

Bobby Clark gives away a rare penalty when diving at Gordon Smith's feet. Stuart Kennedy scores a rare goal – in fact it's his first for Aberdeen.

No 12 Wednesday, 24 November
ABERDEEN (0) 1   AYR UNITED (0) 0
  Harper (71 pen)
ABERDEEN: Clark, Kennedy, Williamson (Sullivan), J. Smith, Garner, Miller, Shirra, Scott, Harper, Jarvie, Graham
AYR: Geoghegan, Wells, Murphy (Kelly), Fleming, Fillippi, McAnespie, McCall, McSherry, Masterton, McCulloch, Cramond

P W D L F A Pts   *Attendance:* 10,600
12 7 3 2 23 12 17   *Referee:* G. B. Smith

Ayr could hardly get the ball out of their penalty area, but the solitary goal which took Aberdeen back to the top of the league was settled by a penalty. It brought about Ayr's 11th consecutive league defeat at Pittodrie.

No 13 Saturday, 27 November
ABERDEEN (1)1   HIBERNIAN (0) 0
  Harper (35)
ABERDEEN: Clark, Kennedy, McLelland, J. Smith (Thomson), Garner, Miller, Sullivan, Scott, Harper, Jarvie, Graham

HIBERNIAN: McDonald, Brownlie, Schaedler, Bremner, Stewart, Spalding, Duncan (Murray), McGhee, Scott, Smith, Fyfe
Leading positions

	P	W	D	L	F	A	Pts
1 ABERDEEN	13	8	3	2	24	12	19
2 Dundee	13	9	1	3	28	19	19
3 Celtic	12	7	3	2	26	13	17
4 Rangers	13	5	5	3	20	13	15

Attendance: 14,800   *Referee:* W. Anderson

What a goal by Joe Harper. He slaloms round three defenders with the ball glued to his toes, and then whacks the ball past McDonald from twenty yards.

No 14 Sunday, 26 December
CELTIC (2) 2   ABERDEEN (2) 2
  Craig 2 (32, 45)   Jarvie 2 (22, 37)
CELTIC: Latchford, McGrain, Burns, Stanton, MacDonald, Aitken, Doyle, Glavin, Craig, Dalglish, Wilson
ABERDEEN: Clark, Kennedy, McLelland, J. Smith, Garner, Miller, Sullivan, Shirra, Harper, Jarvie, Graham

P W D L F A Pts   *Attendance:* 47,000
14 8 4 2 26 14 20   *Referee:* H. Alexander

On a pitch more suitable to ice-hockey, both sets of players gave their all. Man-of-the-match was Drew Jarvie for much else besides two goals. In the second half Celtic's Craig was within a whisker of his hat-trick, but Clark managed to turn his poke against a post.

No 15 Monday, 3 January
ABERDEEN (3) 4   HEARTS (0) 1
  Harper 3 (21, 38, 58),   Callachan (60 pen)
  Jarvie (44)
ABERDEEN: Clark, Kennedy, McLelland, J. Smith, Garner, Miller, Sullivan, Shirra, Harper, Jarvie, Graham (Robb)
HEARTS: Cruickshank, Clunie (Park), Kay, Jefferies, Gallacher, Fraser (Aird), Shaw, Brown, Gibson, Callachan, Prentice

P W D L F A Pts   *Attendance:* 18,800
15 9 4 2 30 15 22   *Referee:* T. R. Kyle

The Hearts hoodoo is burst: Aberdeen last beat the Jam Tarts at Pittodrie in November 1973. This was the occasion when Joe Harper turned professional juggler, insolently flipping the ball away from his marker, Gallacher, for the first two goals.

No 16 Saturday, 8 January
AYR UNITED (0) 0   ABERDEEN (0) 0
AYR: Geoghegan, Wells, Murphy, Fleming, Fillippi, McAnespie, McCall, McSherry, Masterton, McCulloch, Cramond
ABERDEEN: Clark, Kennedy, McLelland, J. Smith, Garner, Miller, Sullivan, Shirra, Harper, Jarvie, Graham

P W D L F A Pts   *Attendance:* 5,600

16 9 5 2 30 15 23   *Referee:* A. Ferguson

Struggling Ayr knock Aberdeen out of their stride. Ex-Don Andy Geoghegan frustrated Aberdeen's few scoring efforts.

No 17 Wednesday, 12 January

ABERDEEN (1) 1   PARTICK THISTLE (0) 1

  Harper (29)   Somner (84)

ABERDEEN: Clark, Kennedy, Williamson, J. Smith (Shirra), Garner, Miller, Sullivan, Scott (Robb), Harper, Jarvie, Graham

PARTICK: Rough, Mackie, Whittaker, J. Hansen, Campbell, A. Hansen, Houston, Somner, Marr (Kelly), Melrose, Craig (Love)

P W D L F A Pts   *Attendance:* 10,000

17 9 6 2 31 16 24   *Referee:* G. B. Smith

Aberdeen needed to win to go back above Celtic to the top of the league. But Love took a Thistle corner, and Somner jumped the highest.

No 18 Wednesday, 19 January

ABERDEEN (1) 3   RANGERS (1) 3

  Jarvie (40), Scott (60),   Miller (44), MacDonald

  Smith (64)   (80), Johnstone (86)

ABERDEEN: Clark, Kennedy, McLelland, J. Smith, Garner, Miller, Sullivan, Scott, Harper, Jarvie, Graham

RANGERS: Kennedy, Jardine, Miller, Forsyth, Jackson, Watson, McLean, O'Hara (MacDonald), Parland (McKean), Greig, Johnstone

Leading positions

	P	W	D	L	F	A	Pts
1 ABERDEEN	18	9	7	2	34	19	25
2 Celtic	16	10	4	2	34	18	24
3 Rangers	19	8	6	4	28	17	22
4 Dundee United	17	9	3	3	30	23	21

Attendance: 21,000   *Referee:* R. B. Valentine

Pittodrie rapturously greeted Joe Smith's thunderbolt to put the Dons 3-1 ahead, but then watched open-mouthed as MacDonald's 20-yarder and Johnstone's header from McLean's corner rescued a point for Rangers.

No 19 Saturday, 22 January

HIBERNIAN (0) 0   ABERDEEN (0) 0

HIBERNIAN: McDonald, Brownlie, Spalding, Bremner, Stewart, Blackley, Edwards, Scott, McGhee, Smith, Duncan

ABERDEEN: Clark, Kennedy, McLelland, J. Smith (Shirra), Garner, Miller, Sullivan (Robb), Scott, Fleming, Jarvie, Graham

P W D L F A Pts   *Attendance:* 11,500.

19 9 8 2 34 19 26   *Referee:* D. F. T. Syme

Four straight draws is not championship form – and Celtic leap-frog over Aberdeen. Without the injured Harper, Aberdeen's firepower is greatly reduced. But at least Easter Road fans can't boo him.

No 20 Saturday, 5 February

PARTICK THISTLE (1) 2   ABERDEEN (0) 1

  Melrose (25), Somner (49)   Jarvie (69)

PARTICK: Rough, Mackie, Whittaker, J. Hansen, Campbell, A. Hansen, Houston, Somner, Love, Melrose (McQuade), Craig

ABERDEEN: Clark, Kennedy, McLelland, J. Smith (Robb), Garner, Miller, Sullivan, Shirra, Harper, Jarvie, Graham

P W D L F A Pts   *Attendance:* 5,000

20 9 8 3 35 21 26   *Referee:* E. Thomson

Aberdeen adopt a 4-4-2 line-up, but still cannot defeat Thistle, who went ahead from a Craig corner.

No 21 Monday 7 February

ABERDEEN (0) 2   KILMARNOCK (0) 0

  McLelland (73),

  Graham (85)

ABERDEEN: Clark, Kennedy, McLelland, J. Smith, Garner, Miller, Sullivan (Scott), Shirra (Robb), Harper, Jarvie, Graham

KILMARNOCK: Stewart, Maxwell, Robertson, Murdoch, Clarke, McDicken, Provan, McCulloch, Fallis, Sheed, McLean

P W D L F A Pts   *Attendance:* 7,700

21 10 8 3 37 21 28   *Referee:* R. B. Valentine

Aberdeen could do everything but score until Chic McLelland tried a hopeful pot-shot from 30 yards – his first goal of the season.

No 22 Saturday, 19 February

RANGERS (0) 1   ABERDEEN (0) 0

  Miller (89 pen)

RANGERS: Kennedy, Jardine, Miller, Greig, Jackson, Watson, McLean (McKean), Hamilton (MCDougall), Parlane, MacDonald, Johnstone

ABERDEEN: Clark, Kennedy, McLelland, J. Smith, Garner, Miller, Sullivan, Scott (Thomson), Harper, Jarvie (Shirra), Graham

Leading positions

	P	W	D	L	F	A	Pts
1 Celtic	21	15	4	2	52	22	34
2 Rangers	23	11	7	5	36	22	29
3 ABERDEEN	22	10	8	4	37	22	28
4 Dundee United	21	12	4	5	42	27	28

Attendance: 14,000   *Referee:* H. Alexander

Aberdeen lose their 2nd position as a result of Willie Miller's late blunder. He fails to control McLelland's pass; Derek Johnstone streaked away, and Miller dragged him down. His namesake – Alex – performed the honours from the spot.

No 23 Saturday, 5 March

ABERDEEN (1) 2   CELTIC (0) 0

  Graham (21), Harper (89)

ABERDEEN: Clark, Kennedy, McLelland, J. Smith, Garner, Miller, Davidson (Sullivan), Fleming (Scott), Harper, Shirra, Graham

CELTIC: Latchford, McGrain, Lynch, Stanton, Edvaldsson, McCluskey (Conn), Doyle, Glavin, Craig, Aitken, Dalglish

P	W	D	L	F	A	Pts	
23	11	8	4	39	22	30	*Attendance:* 21,700

Referee: J. R. P. Gordon

How Aberdeen survived Celtic's second-half onslaught we shall never know. They became so desperate that Lynch nearly tore Graham's jersey off his back. Harper's late goal broke his goal famine. 'Easy, easy' chanted the fans. It was anything but.

No 24 Saturday, 12 March
ABERDEEN (0) 0　　　DUNDEE UNITED (1) 1
　　　　　　　　　　　　Sturrock (14)

ABERDEEN: Clark, Kennedy, McLelland, J. Smith, Garner, Miller, Sullivan (Scott), Davidson, Harper, Shirra (Thomson), Graham

DUNDEE UNITED: McAlpine, Rolland, Williamson, Fleming, Smith, Narey, Sturrock, Houston, Hegarty, McAdam (Kopel), Payne

P	W	D	L	F	A	Pts	
24	11	8	5	39	23	30	*Attendance:* 12,600

Referee: I. M. D. Foote

Aberdeen slip to 4th after this defeat. Is there to be a repeat of the Spring collapse of last season?

No 25 Wednesday, 16 March
DUNDEE UNITED (3) 3　ABERDEEN (1) 2
　Narey (2), Hegarty (6),　　Smith (9), Harper (72)
　McAdam (35)

DUNDEE UNITED: McAlpine, Rolland, Williamson, G. Fleming (Wallace), W. Smith, Narey, Sturrock, Houston, Hegarty, McAdam (Addison), Payne

ABERDEEN: Clark, Kennedy, McLelland, J. Smith, Garner, Miller, Campbell (McMaster), Fleming, Harper, Shirra (Davidson), Graham

P	W	D	L	F	A	Pts	
25	11	8	6	41	26	30	*Attendance:* 7,100

Referee: E. Thomson

A game to savour, even though it brought Aberdeen's second defeat by Jim McLean's men in four days. David Narey outwitted Aberdeen's offside trap for the first goal. It might have ended up 3-3, except that Hamish McAlpine was able to fall on Willie Miller's deflected header on the goal-line.

No 26 Saturday, 19 March
HEARTS (0) 1　　　　ABERDEEN (1) 1
　Park (78)　　　　　　Fleming (5)

HEARTS: Cruickshank, Brown, Kay, Bannon (Shaw), Gallacher, Clunie, Robertson, Busby, Gibson, Park, Prentice

ABERDEEN: Clark, Kennedy, McLelland, J. Smith, Garner, Miller, Campbell (Davidson), Fleming, Harper, Shirra, Graham

P	W	D	L	F	A	Pts	
26	11	9	6	42	27	31	*Attendance:* 8,500

Referee: W. Anderson

Hearts are fighting a losing battle to stay in the Premier League. Fleming scores for Aberdeen after his header returns to him off a post. In the closing stages Park levelled, and then vibrated Clark's crossbar.

No 27 Wednesday, 23 March
ABERDEEN (0) 2　　　MOTHERWELL (1) 1
　Davidson (76),　　　Wark (20)
　Graham (88)

ABERDEEN: Clark, Kennedy, McLelland, J. Smith, Garner, Miller, Campbell (Sullivan), Fleming (Davidson), Harper, Shirra, Graham

MOTHERWELL: Rennie, Watson, Wark, McAdam, McLaren, Stevens, J. Miller, Pettigrew, R. Graham, P. Miller, O'Rourke (Marinello)

P	W	D	L	F	A	Pts	
27	12	9	6	44	28	33	*Attendance:* 7,500

Referee: B. R. McGinlay

Motherwell scored out of the blue in the first half and elected to protect their lead at all costs in the second. Super-sub Duncan Davidson chested down Miller's lob before equalising. Graham claimed the winner in a penalty box as congested as Clapham Junction.

No 28 Saturday, 26 March
ABERDEEN (0) 0　　　AYR UNITED (1) 2
　　　　　　　　　　　McCall (2),
　　　　　　　　　　　Masterton (66)

ABERDEEN: Clark, Kennedy, McLelland (Scott), J. Smith, Garner, Miller, Sullivan (Rougvie), Davidson, Harper, Shirra, Graham

AYR: Sproat, Wells, Brogan, Fleming, Fillippi, McAnespie, McSherry, McCall (Phillips), Masterton, McCulloch, Cramond (Kelly)

P	W	D	L	F	A	Pts	
28	12	9	7	44	30	33	*Attendance:* 6,100

Referee: W. J. Mullen

Aberdeen have booked their place in Europe by virtue of winning the League Cup. They therefore have little to play for in the league. And it shows. Walker McCall, Ayr's first scorer, had just been transferred from Pittodrie.

No 29 Saturday, 2 April
KILMARNOCK (1) 1　　ABERDEEN (1) 2
　McCulloch (10)　　　Graham (44),
　　　　　　　　　　　Davidson (46)

KILMARNOCK: Stewart, Maxwell, Robertson, McCulloch, Clarke, McDicken, Provan, Jardine, Fallis (Sharp), Murdoch, Smith

ABERDEEN: MacLean, Kennedy, Shirra, J. Smith, Garner, Miller, Reilly (Fleming), Davidson, Harper, McMaster (Rougvie), Graham

P	W	D	L	F	A	Pts	
29	13	9	7	46	31	35	*Attendance:* 4,000

Referee: D. A. Murdoch

A reshuffled Dons' side overcame bottom-club Kilmarnock. In the second half Killie's Fallis missed a simple chance to equalise and was promptly substituted.

No 30 Tuesday, 5 April
MOTHERWELL (0) 1　　ABERDEEN (0) 1
　Pettigrew (67)　　　Harper (89)

MOTHERWELL: Hunter, Watson, Wark, P. Millar, McLaren, Stevens, J. Miller, Pettigrew, R. Graham, Davidson, O'Rourke

ABERDEEN: McLean, Kennedy, McLelland, J. Smith, Garner, Miller, Sullivan, Davidson, Harper, Shirra (Fleming), Graham

P	W	D	L	F	A	Pts		Attendance: 4,500
30	13	10	7	47	32	36		Referee: I. M. D. Foote

Aberdeen reserve keeper Ally MacLean kept out Davidson's penalty with his knees, and even got a touch to Pettigrew's goal. But there is no-one better at bagging late goals than Joe Harper.

No 31 Saturday, 9 April
ABERDEEN (0) 0   HIBERNIAN (0) 0
ABERDEEN: MacLean, Kennedy, Shirra, J. Smith, Garner, Miller, Sullivan (Thomson), Fleming (Davidson), Harper, Robb, Graham
HIBERNIAN: McDonald, Brownlie, Shaedler, Bremner, Stewart, Blackley, Brazil, McLeod, Scott, Smith, Duncan

P	W	D	L	F	A	Pts		Attendance: 7,900
31	13	11	7	47	32	37		Referee: K. Stewart

Duncan Davidson earns his second caution of the week. Ally MacLean saves his second penalty of the week – mind you it was he who brought Hibs' McLeod down.

No 32 Wednesday, 13 April
DUNDEE UNITED (2) 2   ABERDEEN (1) 3
  Sturrock (6), Rolland (40)   Scott (5), Rougvie (55),
                                      Smith (65)
DUNDEE UNITED: McAlpine, Rolland, Kopel, Rennie, Smith (Hall), Narey, Sturrock, Houston, Hegarty, McAdam, Payne
ABERDEEN: MacLean, Kennedy, Shirra, J. Smith, Garner, Miller, Sullivan, Scott, Harper, Rougvie, Graham

P	W	D	L	F	A	Pts		Attendance: 4,000
32	14	11	7	50	34	39		

Aberdeen lost at Tannadice by the same score last month. The reason Joe Harper's name is not on the score-sheet is because McAlpine flung himself to save the wee man's late spot-kick.

No 33 Saturday, 16 April
ABERDEEN (0) 0   PARTICK THISTLE (1) 2
                                Deans 2 (36, 51)
ABERDEEN: MacLean, Kennedy, Shirra, J. Smith, Garner, Miller, Sullivan (Fleming), Scott, Harper, Rougvie (Davidson), Graham
PARTICK: Rough, J. Hansen, Whittaker, Campbell, Marr, A. Hansen, Houston, Deans, Gibson, Somner, Craig

P	W	D	L	F	A	Pts		Attendance: 5,800
33	14	11	8	50	36	39		Referee: G. B. Smith

Partick have taken six points out of eight against Aberdeen this season. Ex-Parkhead star Dixie Deans did the damage. Silky Alan Hansen took the eye in defence.

No 34 Wednesday, 20 April
CELTIC (2) 4   ABERDEEN (1) 1
  Conn (19), Glavin (37),   Jarvie (29)
  Craig (61), Dalglish (85)
CELTIC: Latchford, McGrain, Lynch, Stanton, MacDonald, Aitken, Doyle, Glavin, Craig, Dalglish, Conn
ABERDEEN: MacLean, Kennedy, McLelland, J. Smith (Rougvie), Garner, Miller, Sullivan, Davidson, Harper, Jarvie, Graham

P	W	D	L	F	A	Pts		Attendance: 27,000
34	14	11	9	51	40	39		Referee: D. Ramsay

Celtic celebrated the Premier League championship in impressive style, gaining their first victory in five attempts over Aberdeen this season. The Dons courteously applauded Jock Stein's team onto the pitch.

No 35 Saturday, 23 April
MOTHERWELL (1) 1   ABERDEEN (0) 3
  Kennedy (30)   Davidson 2 (79, 85),
                                   Graham (84)
MOTHERWELL: Hunter, Mungall, Wark, McAdam, MacLaren, Stevens, J. Miller, Pettigrew, Kennedy (Graham), Davidson, O'Neill
ABERDEEN: MacLean, Kennedy, McLelland, J. Smith, Garner, Miller, Shirra, Davidson, Harper, Jarvie (Fleming), Graham

P	W	D	L	F	A	Pts		Attendance: 4,200
35	15	11	9	54	41	41		Referee: A. McGunnigle

Lucky, lucky Aberdeen. They had taken a mauling for the first 79 minutes. Joe Harper laid on the last two goals – but by then they should have been dead and buried.

No 36 Saturday, 30 April
ABERDEEN (2) 2   RANGERS (1) 1
  Harper (10 pen),   Johnstone (25)
  Davidson (34)
ABERDEEN: MacLean, Kennedy, McLelland, J. Smith, Garner, Miller, Harper, Davidson (Sullivan), Fleming (Shirra), Jarvie, Graham
RANGERS: Kennedy, Jardine, Greig, Forsyth, Jackson, Watson (Armour), McLean, Hamilton, Parlane, MacDonald, Johnstone

Attendance: 13,500   *Referee:* R. B. Valentine

A contrast to the run-of-the-mill end of season match. Rangers' John Greig was sent off and five other players cautioned. Premier League leading scorer Joe Harper netted from the spot after Hamilton's challenge on Stuart Kennedy. It was Harper's free kick which squirmed out of the Rangers' keeper's hands for Davidson to tap in the winner.

Aberdeen's complete home and away record:

HOME						AWAY					
P	W	D	L	F	A	W	D	L	F	A	Pts
36	11	4	3	30	18	5	7	6	26	24	43

Scottish League Premier Division 1976-77

	P	W	D	L	F	A	Pts
1 Celtic	36	23	9	4	79	39	55
2 Rangers	36	18	10	8	62	37	46
3 ABERDEEN	36	16	11	9	56	42	43
4 Dundee United	36	16	9	11	54	45	41
5 Partick Thistle	36	11	13	12	40	44	35
6 Hibernian	36	8	18	10	34	35	34
7 Motherwell	36	10	12	14	57	60	32
8 Ayr United	36	11	8	17	44	68	30
9 Hearts	36	7	13	16	49	66	27
10 Kilmarnock	36	4	9	23	32	71	17

LEAGUE CUP

Saturday, 14 August
ABERDEEN (2) 2　　　　KILMARNOCK (0) 0
　Harper (4), Graham (27)
ABERDEEN: MacLean, Kennedy, McLelland, Smith, Garner, Cooper, Sullivan, Fleming, Harper, McMaster (Jarvie), Graham
KILMARNOCK: Stewart, McLean, Robertson, Murdoch, Clarke, Welsh, Provan, McCulloch, McDicken (Maxwell), Sheed, Smith
Attendance: 10,850　　　*Referee:* T. Kellock
Joe Harper is appointed captain for the day to anoint his return to Pittodrie. Within minutes his neat header puts him back on the goal trail.

Wednesday, 18 August
ST MIRREN (1) 2　　　　ABERDEEN (2) 3
　Borthwick (24 pen),　　Fleming 2 (14, 44),
　Hislop (61)　　　　　Harper (53)
ST MIRREN: Hunter, Johnstone, Mowatt, Fitzpatrick, Reid (Hislop), Young, Stark, Borthwick, McGarvey, Richardson, McGillivray (Gibson)
ABERDEEN: MacLean, Kennedy, McLelland, Smith, Garner, Cooper, Sullivan, Fleming (Jarvie), Harper, McMaster, Graham
　　　　　　　　Referee: T. Muirhead
Paisley's floodlights are not the brightest in the world. But Fleming peers through the dusk to net twice before limping off. Billy Stark twice came close to an equaliser for the First Division side.

Saturday, 21 August
ABERDEEN (0) 1　　　　AYR UNITED (0) 0
　Harper (63 pen)
ABERDEEN: MacLean, Kennedy, McLelland, Smith, Garner, Cooper, Sullivan, Jarvie (Williamson), Harper, McMaster (Robb), Graham
AYR: Sproat, Fillippi, Murphy, Fleming, Hislop, McDonald, Gray (Ingram), Graham, Phillips, McCulloch, Cramond
Attendance: 9,700　　　*Referee:* I. M. D. Foote
McDonald handles, Harper nets from the spot, and that's good enough for two more points.

Wednesday, 25 August
ABERDEEN (3) 4　　　　ST MIRREN (0) 0
　Harper 2 (4 pen, 41),
　Williamson 2 (39, 66)
ABERDEEN: Clark, Kennedy, McLelland, Smith, Garner, Miller, Sullivan, Williamson, Harper, Scott, Graham
ST MIRREN: Hunter, Johnstone, Mowatt, Fitzpatrick, Reid, Young, Stark (Gibson), Borthwick, McGarvey, Richardson, McGillivray
Attendance: 8,200　　　*Referee:* W. J. Mullen
Aberdeen are all but through to the quarter-finals after this emphatic win over Alex Ferguson's St Mirren. Harper gained a penalty after being tripped by Reid, which he took himself.

Saturday, 28 August
AYR UNITED (1) 1　　　ABERDEEN (0) 1
　Phillips (2)　　　　　Harper (79)
AYR: Sproat, Fillippi, Murphy, Fleming (Gray), McDonald, McSherry, Phillips, Graham, Ingram, McCulloch (Hislop), Robertson
ABERDEEN: Clark, Kennedy, McLelland, Smith, Garner, Miller, Sullivan, Williamson, Harper, Scott (Fleming), Graham
　　　　　　　　Referee: D. F. Syme
Ayr full-back Fillippi missed a cross: Harper, hiding behind him, didn't. Aberdeen might have won but for Harper's late boob in front of a begging goal.

Wednesday, 1 September
KILMARNOCK (1) 2　　ABERDEEN (0) 1
　Smith (40), Welsh (67)　Harper (87)
KILMARNOCK: Stewart, McLean, Robertson, Murdoch, Clarke, Welsh, Provan, McCulloch, Fallis, Sheed (Maxwell), Smith
ABERDEEN: Clark, Kennedy (Thomson), McLelland, Smith, Garner, Miller, Sullivan (Fleming), Williamson, Harper, Scott, Graham
Attendance: 2,700　　　*Referee:* W. Anderson
However badly Aberdeen play, it seems you can't stop Joe Harper scoring. He has netted in every League Cup match so far.

Section 2

	P	W	D	L	F	A	Pts
ABERDEEN	6	4	1	1	12	4	9
Ayr United	6	2	2	2	8	8	6
Kilmarnock	6	2	1	3	6	8	5
St Mirren	6	1	2	3	7	12	4

Quarter Final 1st Leg Wednesday, 22 September
ABERDEEN (0) 1　　　STIRLING ALBION (0) 0
　Harper (65)
ABERDEEN: Clark, Thomson, McLelland, Smith, Garner, Miller, Sullivan, Gibson (Fleming), Harper, Scott (Robb), Graham
STIRLING: Young, Nicol, Steedman, Burns, Kennedy, Carr, McPhee, Clark, Downie (Thomson), Steele, Armstrong

Attendance: 7,000   *Referee:* E. H. Pringle

All Aberdeen could show for their intense pressure against the Second Division side was Harper's goal, when he latched onto Fleming's header into the box.

Quarter Final 2nd Leg Wednesday, 6 October
STIRLING   ABERDEEN (0) 0 *0*
ALBION (0) 1 *1*   *(After Extra Time)*
Gray (50)

STIRLING: Young, Burns, Steedman, Clark, Kennedy, Carr, McPhee, Duffin, Gray (Steele), Thomson, Armstrong

ABERDEEN: Clark, Kennedy, McLelland, Smith, Garner, Miller, Sullivan (Scott), Fleming (Williamson), Harper, Robb, Graham

1-1 on aggregate

Attendance: 3,700   *Referee:* E. H. Pringle

Why Scotland boss Willie Ormond should want to brave a howling rainstorm is a mystery. Aberdeen didn't impress him, being unable to overcome Gray's header from a Duffin free kick. Extra time failed to produce a winner.

Quarter Final Replay (Dens Park) Monday, 18 October
STIRLING ALBION (0) 0   ABERDEEN (2) 2
                       Scott (9),
                       Smith (40)

STIRLING: Young, Burns, Steedman, Clark, Kennedy, Carr, McPhee (Nicol), Duffin, Gray (Steele), Thomson, Armstrong

ABERDEEN: Clark, Kennedy, McLelland, Smith, Garner, Miller, Sullivan (Campbell), Scott, Harper, Thomson (Jarvie), Graham

Attendance: 4,000   Referee: E. H. Pringle

When Scott ran Harper's cross into the net Aberdeen seized the initiative. When Joe Smith's daisy-trimmer passed through a dozen pairs of legs, the Dons were comfortably through.

Semi Final (Hampden) Wednesday, 27 October
RANGERS (1) 1   ABERDEEN (2) 5
McDonald (15)   Scott 3 (2, 14, 73),
                 Harper (64), Jarvie (66)

RANGERS: Kennedy, Jardine, Miller, Greig, Jackson, Watson, McLean, McKean (Hamilton), Parlane, MacDonald, Henderson

ABERDEEN: Clark, Kennedy, Williamson, Smith (Thomson), Garner, Miller, Sullivan, Scott, Harper, Jarvie, Graham

Attendance: 21,000   *Referee:* W. Anderson

Only eleven days earlier Rangers had beaten the Dons 1-0 at Ibrox in the league. Now there was the spectacle of manager Ally McLeod and coach George Murray hugging each other like chimpanzees on the running track as Aberdeen knock the final nails into Rangers' coffin. They were prepared to forget the uncomfortable 50 minutes when Rangers threatened to equalise: instead preferring to celebrate Drew Jarvie's screaming volley from outside the box.

League Cup Final (Hampden) Saturday, 6 November
CELTIC (1) 1 *1*   ABERDEEN (1) 1 *2*
Dalglish (11 pen)   *(After Extra Time)*
                 Jarvie (24), Robb (93)

CELTIC: Latchford, McGrain, Lynch, Edvaldsson, MacDonald, Aitken, Doyle, Glavin, Dalglish, Burns (Lennox), Wilson

ABERDEEN: Clark, Kennedy, Williamson, Smith, Garner, Miller, Sullivan, Scott, Harper, Jarvie (Robb), Graham

Attendance: 69,679   *Referee:* J. W. Paterson

This was Celtic's 13th consecutive appearance in the League Cup Final – Aberdeen's first since 1955. The Dons have the worst possible start, a harsh penalty award against Jarvie's attentions on Dalglish – who scored from the spot and indulged in some niggly exchanges with Harper. But the wee man is all smiles as he heads Graham's centre back across goal for Jarvie to head the equaliser. In the second half Celtic threatened to take control, but Aberdeen forced the game into extra time. Just three minutes of the extra period had been played when up popped substitute Dave Robb for what transpired to be the winning goal. Back in Aberdeen the city went mad, but Willie Miller was prepared to be conciliatory: 'Celtic were desperately unlucky', he admitted.

SCOTTISH CUP

3rd Round Saturday, 29 January
DUNFERMLINE   ABERDEEN (0) 1
ATHLETIC (0) 0   Harper (58)

DUNFERMLINE: Whyte, Thomson, Markey, Scott, Salton, Meakin, Watson, Bowie (McLeod), Georgeson, Evans, Donaldson

ABERDEEN: Clark, Kennedy, McLelland, Smith, Garner, Miller, Sullivan, Scott, Harper, Jarvie, Graham

                 Referee: J. R. P. Gordon

Dunfermline are in mid-table in Division 2. As at Alloa last year the game is marred by hooligan violence. The match was played on an ice rink and was settled by Harper's mis-hit shot which was deflected past Whyte.

4th Round Saturday, 26 February
DUNDEE (0) 0   ABERDEEN (0) 0

DUNDEE: Donaldson, Ford, Johnston, Caldwell, Phillip, McPhail, Hoggan (Sinclair), Strachan, Pirie, Hutchinson (Robinson), Purdie

ABERDEEN: Clark, Kennedy, McLelland, Smith, Garner, Miller, Sullivan (Robb), Davidson, Harper, Shirra, Graham

                 Referee: K. Stewart

The only victor in this match was the tension. Aberdeen had to do a lot of defending against the First Division side.

4th Round Replay Wednesday, 2 March
ABERDEEN (0) 1   DUNDEE (1) 2
  Davidson (52)   Hutchinson 2 (11, 76)

ABERDEEN: Clark, Kennedy, McLelland, Smith, Garner, Miller, Scott (Robb), Davidson, Harper, Shirra, Graham

DUNDEE: Donaldson, Ford, Johnston, Caldwell (Laing), Phillip, McPhail, Robinson, Strachan, Pirie (Sinclair), Hutchinson, Purdie

Attendance: 18,375   *Referee:* K. Stewart

Willie Miller might be emerging as one of the world's great defenders, but he will have nightmares after this. The Dons had fought back from Hutchinson's headed goal for Dundee. Jocky Scott's drive was saved by Donaldson but not held, and Davidson was first on the scene. But then Miller completely fluffed an intended backpass to Clark, and there was no way back for Aberdeen. The crowd did not keep their thoughts about Miller to themselves as Dundee completed their second Scottish Cup victory at Pittodrie in four years.

1976-77

APPEARANCES	League	League Cup	Scottish Cup
Garner	36	11	3
Miller	36	8	3
Graham	35	11	3
Joe Smith	35	11	3
Harper	34	11	3
Kennedy	32	10	3
Sullivan	28(+4)	11	2
Clark	27	8	3
McLelland	25	9	3
Shirra	20(+6)		2
Jarvie	18(+2)	3(+3)	1
Scott	13(+6)	7(+1)	2

1976-77

APPEARANCES	League	League Cup	Scottish Cup
Fleming	13(+4)	3(+3)	
Williamson	9	5(+2)	
MacLean	9	3	
Davidson	8(+5)		2
Robb	6(+7)	1(+3)	–(+2)
Campbell	4(+1)	–(+1)	
Thomson	3(+4)	2(+2)	
Rougvie	2(+4)		
McMaster	1(+1)	3	
Hair	1		
Reilly	1		
Gibson	–(+1)	1	
Neil Cooper		3	
25 players			

GOALS	Total	League	League Cup	Scottish Cup
Harper	28	18	9	1
Jarvie	11	9	2	
Scott	7	3	4	
Davidson	6	5		1
Graham	6	5	1	
Fleming	6	4	2	
Smith	4	3	1	
Sullivan	3	3		
Williamson	3	1	2	
Robb	2	1	1	
Kennedy	1	1		
McLelland	1	1		
Rougvie	1	1		
Gibson	1	1		
Total	80	56	22	2

The Aberdeen squad in 1979. Back row: Ian Scanlon, Doug Considine, Willie Garner, Alex McLeish, Bobby Clark, Steve Archibald, Mark McGhee, Neil Cooper, Doug Rougvie. Front row: Joe Harper, John McMaster, Drew Jarvie, Willie Miller, Gordon Strachan, Dom Sullivan, Duncan Davidson and Stuart Kennedy.

Season 1977-78

Billy McNeill, McLeod's successor, was in every sense a one-club man, hero of Celtic's Lisbon Lions. His first act in the first match of the season was to appear on the pitch wearing Aberdeen red, an unspoken announcement that previous loyalty to the green of Celtic was (temporarily) forgotten.

McNeill had to overcome the loss of another of Aberdeen's home-grown stars, for Arthur Graham had decamped to Leeds. In fairness. Graham's loss was hardly missed as the Dons embarked on an outstanding season marred only by the absence of silverware to show for their efforts.

Aberdeen did not taste defeat in any competition until late September, when the tactically shrewd Belgian side, R W Molenbeek, put paid to the Dons' UEFA Cup dreams at Pittodrie. The League Cup, proudly adorning the Pittodrie boardroom, was now to be defended under new rules. No longer would the competition commence on a league basis, but on European principles, namely the two-leg knock-out. It was in defence of this trophy that Aberdeen suffered their one black mark of the season, a humiliating 6-1 hammer-blow at Ibrox.

So, one domestic trophy had gone, but two more remained to be contested. In the league Aberdeen set off in pursuit of Rangers, an 18-match unbeaten run leaving them narrowly short of Rangers' 55 points.

Having seen both the league and League Cup head for Ibrox, Aberdeen's chances of preventing a Rangers clean sweep rested on the Scottish Cup Final. Alas, Aberdeen froze on the occasion, causing the name of 'Rangers' to hang over Aberdeen's season like a pall. The club that was poised for a famous double was left with nothing.

Before the month of May was through McNeill's mentor, Jock Stein, relinquished the manager's chair at Parkhead in favour of a younger man. When all the haggling was done, that man was Billy McNeill.

League:	Runners Up
League Cup:	Third Round
Scottish Cup:	Runners Up
UEFA Cup	First Round

SCOTTISH PREMIER DIVISION

No 1 Saturday, 13 August

ABERDEEN (1) 3   RANGERS (1) 1
   Jarvie 2 (11, 60),   Russell (31)
   Harper (62)

ABERDEEN: Clark, Kennedy, McLelland, J. Smith (Davidson), Garner, Miller, Jarvie, Shirra, Harper, Fleming, McMaster

RANGERS: McCloy, Jardine, Miller, Forsyth, Jackson, MacDonald, McKay (McKean), Russell, Parlane, Robertson, Cooper

P	W	D	L	F	A	Pts
1	1	0	0	3	1	2

Attendance: 22,000
Referee: T. Muirhead

For an ex-Celtic man this was just the start Billy McNeill wanted. He strolled onto the pitch wearing a red shirt – which brought a rapturous ovation from the Dons' fans.

No 2 Saturday, 20 August

CLYDEBANK (1) 1   ABERDEEN (0) 3
   Larnach (27)   Garner (71),
                    Harper (77),
                    Davidson (78)

CLYDEBANK: Gallacher, Hall (Ronald), Abel, Fallon, McLauchlin, Houston, O'Brien, McColl, Larnach, McCallan, Lumsden

ABERDEEN: Clark, Kennedy, McLelland, Shirra, Garner, Miller, Sullivan, Jarvie, Harper, Fleming, McMaster (Davidson)

P W D L F A Pts   *Attendance:* 7,000
2 2 0 0 6 2 4   *Referee:* D. Downie

Whatever Billy McNeill said to his troops at the interval must have been potent. From being totally outwitted in the first half, Aberdeen administered the KO punch afterwards. Harper's goal was not scored with his foot, but with his stomach

No 3 Saturday, 27 August
ABERDEEN (0) 0   DUNDEE UNITED (0) 0

ABERDEEN: Clark, Kennedy, McLelland, Shirra, Garner, Miller, Sullivan (Davidson), Jarvie, Harper, Fleming, McMaster

DUNDEE UNITED: McAlpine, Rolland, Kopel, Robinson (McAdam), Hegarty, Narey, Sturrock, Wallace, Kirkwood, Addison, Fleming

P W D L F A Pts   *Attendance:* 16,100
3 2 1 0 6 2 5   *Referee:* G. B. Smith

Ally McLeod returns to Pittodrie: this time looking objectively at both sets of players. Both sides kicked off with unbeaten records – and were determined to protect them.

No 4 Saturday, 10 September
AYR UNITED (0) 0   ABERDEEN (0) 1
                       Harper (89)

AYR: Sproat, Rodman, Kelly, Fleming, McCall, Masterton, McCulloch, McAnespie, Brogan (Fillipi), Phillips, Cramond

ABERDEEN: Clark, Kennedy, McLelland, Shirra, Garner, Miller, Jarvie, Robb, Harper, Fleming, McMaster

P W D L F A Pts   *Attendance:* 8,500
4 3 1 0 7 2 7   *Referee:* B. R. McGinlay

Back from the USA, Dave Robb is ineligible for next week's UEFA Cup match in Belgium. The watching spies are relieved, for he was Aberdeen's best performer.

No 5 Saturday, 17 September
ABERDEEN (0) 2   CELTIC (0) 1
Fleming 2 (58, 67)   Garner o.g. (49)

ABERDEEN: Clark, Kennedy, McLelland, Shirra, Garner, Miller, Davidson, Jarvie, Harper, Fleming, McMaster

CELTIC: Latchford, McGrain, Lynch, Edvaldsson, MacDonald, McWilliams, Glavin, McAdam, Craig (Doyle), Aitken, Wilson

P W D L F A Pts   *Attendance:* 25,800
5 4 1 0 9 3 9   *Referee:* J. W. Paterson

If Billy McNeill had mixed feelings about this result he didn't show it. This was Celtic's fourth defeat in five games. They looked like ending that sequence with Willie Garner's spectacular header past Clark. Then Fleming took his turn: his first goal went in off a post; his second, a header, gave Latchford no chance.

No 6 Saturday, 24 September
ABERDEEN (1) 2   PARTICK THISTLE (1) 1
Harper 2 (32 pen, 49)   Houston (7)

ABERDEEN: Clark, Kennedy, McLelland, Shirra, Garner, Miller, Davidson, Jarvie, Harper, Fleming, McMaster

PARTICK: Rough, Mackie, Whittaker, Gibson, Marr, Campbell, Houston, Melrose (McQuade), Love, Somner, Craig

P W D L F A Pts   *Attendance:* 11,900
6 5 1 0 11 4 11   *Referee:* n.a.

Considering Aberdeen's all-round dominance, Thistle escaped ridiculously lightly.

No 7 Saturday, 1 October
MOTHERWELL (0) 1   ABERDEEN (1) 1
O'Neill (53)   McMaster (20)

MOTHERWELL: Rennie, Watson, Wark, Miller, McVie, Stevens, McLaren, O'Neill, McAdam (O'Rourke), Davidson, Purdie (Marinello)

ABERDEEN: Clark, Kennedy, McLelland, Robb (Sullivan), Garner, Miller, Davidson, Jarvie, Harper, Fleming, McMaster

P W D L F A Pts   *Attendance:* 6,500
7 5 2 0 12 5 12   *Referee:* K. Hope

Willie Miller collects his third caution of the season as Aberdeen protect their unbeaten league record. McMaster enjoyed his delicious volley.

No 8 Saturday, 8 October
ST MIRREN (0) 0   ABERDEEN (2) 4
                        Jarvie 3 (24, 41, 83),
                        Fleming (65)

ST MIRREN: Hunter, Beckett (Abercrombie), Young, Fitzpatrick, Reid, Copland, Docherty, Stark, McGarvey, Richardson, Hyslop

ABERDEEN: Clark, Kennedy, McLelland, J. Smith, Garner, Miller, Sullivan, Jarvie, Harper, Fleming, McMaster

Leading positions

	P	W	D	L	F	A	Pts
1 ABERDEEN	8	6	2	0	16	5	14
2 Dundee United	8	5	2	1	12	4	12
3 Rangers	8	5	1	2	18	11	11

Attendance: 12,900   *Referee:* E. Thomson

Alex Ferguson's St Mirren team don't relish entertaining the Dons. His sides last home defeat was over a year ago – in the League Cup – against Aberdeen.

No 9 Saturday, 15 October
ABERDEEN (1)   HIBERNIAN (1) 2
Jarvie (12)   Smith o.g. (22),
                        McLeod (66)

ABERDEEN: Clark, Kennedy, McLelland, J. Smith, Garner, Miller, Sullivan (Davidson), Jarvie (Scott), Harper, Fleming, McMaster

HIBERNIAN: McDonald, Brownlie, Smith, Brazil, Stewart, McNamara, McLeod, Bremner, Henderson, Higgins, Duncan

P	W	D	L	F	A	Pts	*Attendance:* 11,900
9	6	2	1	17	7	14	*Referee:* T. Muirhead

Tragedy for Joe Smith as Aberdeen's unbeaten record goes up in smoke. He sticks out his foot towards Bobby Smith's inswinging corner and prods it past Clark.

There was no argument about Hibs' winner, a raging 30-yarder from McLeod.

No 10 Saturday, 22 October

RANGERS (1) 3   ABERDEEN (1) 1
  Jardine (31 pen),   Harper (37 pen)
  Smith (69)
  MacDonald (72)

RANGERS: Kennedy, Jardine, Greig, Forsyth, Jackson, MacDonald, McLean, Russell, Johnstone, Smith, Cooper

ABERDEEN: Clark, Kennedy, McLelland, J. Smith, Garner, Miller, Jarvie, Shirra, Harper, Fleming, McMaster (Sullivan)

P	W	D	L	F	A	Pts	*Attendance:* 35,000
10	6	2	2	18	10	14	*Referee:* H. Alexander

Rangers leap-frog over Aberdeen to the top of the league after this gruelling battle of Ibrox. Bobby Clark faced two Sandy Jardine penalties, and saved the second one. In between, Harper had netted one himself and Chic McLelland found himself ordered off for his challenge on Davie Cooper.

No 11 Saturday, 29 October

ABERDEEN (0) 1   CLYDEBANK (0) 1
  Harper (52)   McCallan (64)

ABERDEEN: Clark, Kennedy, McLelland, J. Smith, Garner, Miller, Jarvie, Shirra (Davidson), Harper, Fleming, McMaster

CLYDEBANK: Gallacher, Hall, Abel, Fallon, McCormack, Hay, McNaughton (Lumsden), McColl, Larnach, McCallan, Colgan

P	W	D	L	F	A	Pts	*Attendance:* 9,000
11	6	3	2	19	11	15	*Referee:* D. A. Murdoch

Bottom of the table Bankies are there for the taking. But all of a sudden Clark is left clutching at mid-air as a free kick is flighted in, and McCallan accepted the gift.

No 12 Saturday, 5 November

DUNDEE UNITED (0) 0 ABERDEEN (0) 1
                       Fleming (89)

DUNDEE UNITED: McAlpine, Rolland, Kopel, Fleming (Holt), Hegarty, Narey, Addison, Bourke (Wallace), Kirkwood, Wallace, Payne

ABERDEEN: Clark, Kennedy, McLelland, J. Smith, Garner, Miller, Robb, Jarvie (Campbell), Harper, Fleming, Strachan

P	W	D	L	F	A	Pts	*Attendance:* 10,100
12	7	3	2	20	11	17	*Referee:* I. M. D. Foote

The most notable feature of this match was the quick return to Tayside for Aberdeen debutant Gordon Strachan, signed from Dundee. Narey was left cursing his late inattentive pass-back.

No 13 Saturday, 12 November

ABERDEEN (0) 0   AYR UNITED (0) 0

ABERDEEN: Clark, Kennedy, McLelland, J. Smith (Sullivan), Garner, Miller, Robb, Jarvie, Harper, Fleming, Strachan

AYR: Sproat, Redman, Kelly, Fleming, Hyslop, McAnespie, McLaughlin (McAllister), McCall, Masterton, Hannah (Christie), Cramond

P	W	D	L	F	A	Pts	*Attendance:* 9,400
13	7	4	2	20	11	18	*Referee:* G. B. Smith

After sixteen minutes Joe Smith collides with Hyslop, is carried off, and has his career permanently wrecked. Twenty minutes later Ayr's Cramond was sent packing for his foul on Kennedy.

No 14 Saturday, 19 November

CELTIC (1) 3   ABERDEEN (1) 2
  Lynch (32 pen),   Jarvie (15),
  Aitken (48),   Harper (70 pen)
  Edvaldsson (75)

CELTIC: Latchford, Filippi, Lynch, Munro, MacDonald, Aitken, Doyle, Edvaldsson, Craig (Wilson), McAdam, Conn

ABERDEEN: Clark, Kennedy, McLelland, Sullivan, Garner, Miller, Jarvie, Robb, Harper, Fleming (McMaster), Strachan

P	W	D	L	F	A	Pts	*Attendance:* 27,000
14	7	4	3	22	14	18	*Referee:* E. H. Pringle

Whether Celtic would have won without a debatable equalising penalty, we shall never know. Filippi's shot struck Garner and a linesman flagged. Celtic settled the argument with Edvaldsson's winning goal, a swivelling shot which nearly ripped the net off its rigging.

No 15 Saturday, 26 November

PARTICK THISTLE (1) 1 ABERDEEN (0) 0
  Somner (8)

PARTICK: Rough, Mackie, Whittaker, Gibson, Anderson, Marr, Houston, Somner, O'Hara, Melrose, Craig

ABERDEEN: Clark, Kennedy, McLelland, Sullivan, Garner, Miller, Jarvie, Robb, Fleming, McMaster (Grant), Strachan

Leading positions

	P	W	D	L	F	A	Pts
1 Rangers	15	10	3	2	37	18	23
2 Partick Thistle	15	9	2	4	23	20	20
3 Dundee United	15	7	4	4	19	9	18
4 ABERDEEN	15	7	4	4	22	15	18

Attendance: 13,000   *Referee:* W. J. Mullen

Aberdeen's slide continues. Literally. The soggy pitch was virtually unplayable. But after Somner's early header Thistle weren't complaining.

No 16 Saturday, 3 December
ABERDEEN (2) 4			MOTHERWELL (1) 1
　Robb 3 (12, 51, 73)		Pettigrew (32)
　Strachan (16)
ABERDEEN: Clark, Kennedy, McLelland, Strachan, Garner, Miller, Sullivan, Jarvie, Harper (Fleming), Gibson, Robb
MOTHERWELL: Rennie, Watson, Wark, J. Miller, McLaren, Stevens, Marinello, Pettigrew, O'Rourke, Davidson, P. Millar (Purdie)

P　W　D　L　F　A Pts		*Attendance:* 9,500
16　8　4　4　26 16 20		*Referee:* B. R. McGinlay

The chief question on this bitterly cold day was which of Dave Robb's stunning three goals was the best? Each of them was an example of power-house shooting.

No 17 Saturday, 10 December
ABERDEEN (1) 3			ST MIRREN (0) 1
　Robb (7),			Hyslop (84)
　Gibson 2 (47, 53)
ABERDEEN: Clark, Kennedy, Glennie, Strachan (McMaster), Garner, Miller, Sullivan, Jarvie, Fleming, Gibson, Robb
ST MIRREN: Hunter, Beckett (Young), Munro, Fitzpatrick, Reid, Copland, Richardson (Leonard), Stark, McGarvey, Abercrombie, Hyslop

P　W　D　L　F　A Pts		*Attendance:* 10,000
17　9　4　4　29 17 22		*Referee:* E. Thomson

More great goals to savour. Robb's free kick fairly demolished the defensive wall. But then he was upstaged by Gibson.

No 18 Saturday, 17 December
HIBERNIAN (1) 2			ABERDEEN (0) 0
　Murray (33),
　Duncan (54)
HIBERNIAN: McDonald, Brownlie, Smith, McNamara, Stewart, Brazil, Murray, McLeod, Hutchinson, Duncan, McGhee
ABERDEEN: Clark, Kennedy, Glennie, Cooper, Garner, Miller, Sullivan, Jarvie, Harper, Gibson (Fleming), Robb (Davidson)

P　W　D　L　F　A Pts		*Attendance:* 6,600
18　9　4　5　29 19 22		*Referee:* J. R. P. Gordon

Hibernian brought about Aberdeen's first defeat of the season; now they inflict their last. Curiously, Willie Miller was played in midfield.

No 19 Saturday, 24 December
ABERDEEN (2) 4			RANGERS (0) 0
　Gibson (30),
　Robb (40), Harper (76),
　Jarvie (85)
ABERDEEN: Clark, Kennedy, McLelland, McMaster, Garner, Miller, Sullivan, Jarvie, Harper, Gibson, Robb
RANGERS: Kennedy, Jardine, Greig, Forsyth, Jackson, MacDonald, McLean, Russell, Johnstone, Smith (Parlane), Cooper

Leading positions
	P	W	D	L	F	A	Pts
1 Rangers	18	12	3	3	42	23	27
2 ABERDEEN	19	10	4	5	33	19	24
3 Partick	18	10	3	5	29	26	23

Attendance: 21,000		*Referee:* J. W. Paterson

Aberdeen inform Rangers that the championship race is not yet over with this crushing victory. Last season Rangers' John Greig was sent off at Pittodrie, and the crowd roar for similar punishment at each of his crunching tackles. At last he was booked, nothing worse.

No 20 Saturday, 31 December
CLYDEBANK (0) 0			ABERDEEN (1) 1
					McMaster (35)
CLYDEBANK: King, Hall, Colgan, Fallon, McCormick, Houston, O'Brien, McColl, McNaughton, McCallan, Lumsden
ABERDEEN: Clark, Kennedy (Davidson), McLelland, McMaster, Garner, Miller, Sullivan, Jarvie, Harper, Gibson (Fleming), Robb

P　W　D　L　F　A Pts		*Attendance:* 3,000
20　11　4　5　34 19 26		*Referee:* n.a.

A Hogmanay present to John McMaster from Bankies' keeper King, who – wide of his goal – miscues a clearance straight to John McMaster's feet.

No 21 Monday, 2 January
ABERDEEN (0) 1			DUNDEE UNITED (0) 0
　Fleming (80)
ABERDEEN: Clark, Rougvie, McLelland, McMaster, McLeish, Miller, Sullivan, Jarvie, Harper, Gibson (Fleming), Robb
DUNDEE UNITED: McAlpine, Rolland, Kopel, Rennie, Hegarty, Narey, Sturrock, Addison, Dodds (Kirkwood), Fleming, Payne (Wallace)

P　W　D　L　F　A Pts		*Attendance:* 23,000
21　12　4　5　35 19 28

Alex McLeish, not yet 19 makes a surprise debut after Willie Garner and Bobby Glennie are dropped and fined by Billy McNeill.

No 22 Saturday, 7 January
AYR UNITED (0) 1			ABERDEEN (1) 1
　McCall (63)			McMaster (1)
AYR: Sproat, Rodman, Kelly, Fleming, Hyslop, McAnespie, McCall, McSherry, Masterton, McLaughlin, Crammond
ABERDEEN: Clark, Rougvie, McLelland, McMaster (Fleming), Garner, Miller, Sullivan (Watson), Archibald, Harper, Gibson, Jarvie

P　W　D　L　F　A Pts		*Attendance:* 5,900
22　12　5　5　36 20 29		*Referee:* I. M. D. Foote

Two more Dons' baptisms: one for Steve Archibald; the other for substitute Andy Watson. A former Don, Walker McCall deprived them of the perfect result.

No 23 Saturday, 14 January
ABERDEEN (1) 2			CELTIC (0) 1
　Sullivan 2 (31, 71)		MacDonald (75)

ABERDEEN: Clark, Kennedy, McLelland, McMaster, Garner, Miller, Sullivan, Davidson, Gibson, Jarvie, Robb

CELTIC: Latchford, Filippi, Lynch, Aitken, MacDonald, Munro, Glavin, Edvaldsson, McCluskey, McAdam, Wilson (Burns)

P	W	D	L	F	A	Pts	*Attendance: 24,600*
23	13	5	5	38	21	31	*Referee:* W. Mullen

A fourth consecutive defeat plunges Celtic deeper into the relegation mire. They would have snatched a point when Garner handled late in the game, except that Lynch's penalty came back off a post. This was the match when Celtic tried to play two centre forwards. They had two No 9s on the pitch – until the referee noticed and sent McAdam off to change into No 10 shorts.

No 24 Saturday, 4 February
MOTHERWELL (0) 0   ABERDEEN (0) 0
MOTHERWELL: Rennie, Watson, Wark, Millar, McVie, Stevens, Marinello, Pettigrew, O'Rourke, Davidson, Miller (Clinging)

ABERDEEN: Clark, Kennedy, McLelland, McMaster, Garner, Miller, Strachan, Sullivan, Harper, Jarvie, Davidson

P	W	D	L	F	A	Pts	*Attendance: 8,800*
24	13	6	5	38	21	32	

Under Roger Hynd's management Motherwell are having a good run. They were by no means second fiddle in this match.

No 25 Saturday, 25 February
ABERDEEN (1) 3   HIBERNIAN (0) 0
Stewart o.g. (21),
Davidson (49),
Miller (71)

ABERDEEN: Clark, Kennedy, McLelland, McMaster, Garner, Miller, Sullivan, Archibald, Harper, Strachan, Davidson

HIBERNIAN: McDonald, Brownlie, Smith, Bremner, Stewart (Brazil), McNamara, Murray, McLeod, Hutchinson, Duncan, McGhee

Leading positions

	P	W	D	L	F	A	Pts
1 Rangers	25	18	4	3	58	28	40
2 ABERDEEN	25	14	6	5	41	21	34
3 Dundee United	23	10	6	7	27	17	26

Attendance: 11,200   *Referee:* K. J. Hope

The spooky fog which enveloped Pittodrie had a peculiar effect on Hibs' skipper George Stewart, who floated a header over his keeper into the net. His counterpart, Willie Miller, was involved in a four-man move which culminated in his ferocious shot.

No 26 Saturday, 4 March
RANGERS (0) 0   ABERDEEN (2) 3
Archibald 2 (22, 78),
Harper (38)

RANGERS: Kennedy, Miller, Greig, Forsyth, Jackson, MacDonald, McLean, Russell (Dawson), Johnstone, Smith (Parlane), Cooper

ABERDEEN: Clark, Kennedy, McLelland, McMaster, Garner, Miller, Sullivan, Archibald, Harper, Jarvie, Davidson

P	W	D	L	F	A	Pts	*Attendance: 40,000*
26	15	6	5	44	21	36	*Referee:* T. Muirhead

Rangers' lead is cut to four points after this heroic win. Joe Harper scored one and made two more – both netted by Archibald's lethal finishing. The most articulate comment on the way the match went was made by the Ibrox fans, who began to drain away long before the end.

No 27 Saturday, 18 March
DUNDEE UNITED (0) 0   ABERDEEN (0) 0
DUNDEE UNITED: McAlpine, Rennie, Kopel, Fleming, Hegarty, Sturrock, Addison, Wallace, Holt, Payne

ABERDEEN: Clark, Kennedy, McLelland, McMaster, Garner, Miller, Sullivan, Archibald, Fleming (Strachan), Jarvie, Davidson

P	W	D	L	F	A	Pts	*Attendance: 9,700*
27	15	7	5	44	21	37	*Referee:* n.a.

The conditions were perfect, but the game was a flop. Both teams knew each other too intimately to produce surprises.

No 28 Tuesday, 21 March
ABERDEEN (0) 2   CLYDEBANK (0) 0
Davidson (58),
Archibald (67)

ABERDEEN: Clark, Kennedy, Ritchie, McMaster, Garner, Miller, Strachan, Archibald, Gibson (Grant), Jarvie, Davidson

CLYDEBANK: Gallacher, Gourlay, Abel, Fallon, McCormack, Houston, O'Brien, McColl, Millar, Lumsden, Ronalds (Bradbury), Gahagan

P	W	D	L	F	A	Pts	*Attendance: 9,600*
28	16	7	5	46	21	39	

Strachan's inch-perfect pass to Davidson, who outpaced Gallacher, brought the first goal. Davidson's header off the bar fell to Archibald for the second.

No 29 Saturday, 25 March
ABERDEEN (2) 4   AYR UNITED (0) 1
Davidson (17),   Masterton (62)
Archibald (34),
Jarvie 2 (49, 74)

ABERDEEN: Clark, Kennedy, Ritchie, McMaster, Garner, Miller, Strachan (Sullivan), Archibald, Harper, Jarvie, Davidson

AYR: Sproat, Wells, Sim (McLaughlin), Tait, Fleming, Kelly, McCall, McSherry, Masterton, Cramond, McCulloch

Leading positions

	P	W	D	L	F	A	Pts
1 Rangers	28	19	4	5	60	34	42
2 ABERDEEN	29	17	7	5	50	22	41

Attendance: 11,000

Rangers have lost at Celtic and the league is now becoming exciting. As for Ayr, they're heading down.

No 30 Wednesday, 29 March

ST MIRREN (0) 1	ABERDEEN (1) 2
Stark (52)	Davidson (36),
	Archibald (66)

ST MIRREN: McCulloch, Beckett, Munro, Fitzpatrick, Reid, Copland, Abercrombie (Leonard), Stark, Bone, Richardson (Hyslop), McGarvey

ABERDEEN: Clark, Kennedy, Ritchie, McMaster, Garner, Miller, Sullivan, Archibald, Harper, Jarvie, Davidson

P	W	D	L	F	A	Pts	
30	18	7	5	52	23	43	*Attendance:* 5,900
							Referee: J. McGunnigle

Saints are not yet safe from the drop. Paisley's new super-powered floodlights were reflected in the pools of water which had already submerged the pitch by half-time. Billy Stark's top-spin lob set the game up for a furious finish. Archibald's winner took Aberdeen to the top of the league.

No 31 Saturday, 1 April

CELTIC (1) 2	ABERDEEN (0) 2
Glavin (34),	Davidson (57),
Edvaldsson (58)	Sullivan (66)

CELTIC: Latchford, Sneddon, Lynch, Aitken, MacDonald, Dowie, Glavin, Edvaldsson, McAdam, Burns, Doyle (McCluskey)

ABERDEEN: Clark, Kennedy, Ritchie, McMaster, Garner, Miller, Sullivan, Archibald, Harper, Jarvie, Davidson

P	W	D	L	F	A	Pts	
31	18	8	5	54	25	44	*Attendance:* 24,000
							Referee: W. Anderson

Celtic appear to be safe now. Aberdeen earned their point with a stunning goal by Dom Sullivan, who exchanged passes with Harper before letting fly.

No 32 Tuesday, 4 April

ABERDEEN (2) 2	PARTICK THISTLE (1) 1
Harper 2 (13, 16)	Frame (27)

ABERDEEN: Clark, Kennedy, Ritchie, McMaster, Garner, Miller, Sullivan, Archibald (Strachan), Harper, Jarvie, Davidson

PARTICK: Rough, McAdam, Whittaker (Campbell), Marr, Craig (Mackie), Love, Frame, O'Hara, Somner, McQuade

P	W	D	L	F	A	Pts	
32	19	8	5	56	26	46	*Attendance:* 16,000
							Referee: R. B. Valentine

Harper did his stuff in the first half: his defenders did theirs in the second as Thistle always threatened to snatch a point.

No 33 Saturday, 8 April

PARTICK THISTLE (0) 0	ABERDEEN (2) 2
	Harper (17),
	McMaster (22)

PARTICK: Rough, McAdam, Whittaker, Gibson, Campbell, Marr (Mackie), Houston, Frame, Love, Somner, Craig (O'Hara)

ABERDEEN: Clark, Kennedy, Ritchie, McMaster, Garner, Miller, Sullivan, Archibald, Harper, Jarvie, Davidson

Leading positions

	P	W	D	L	F	A	Pts
1 ABERDEEN	33	20	8	5	58	26	48
2 Rangers	31	20	6	5	67	38	46

Attendance: 7,000   *Referee:* E. Thomson

O.K. That's two wins over Partick inside five days. Now for the Jags again in the Scottish Cup semi-final.

No 34 Saturday, 15 April

ABERDEEN (4) 5	MOTHERWELL (0) 0
Jarvie 2 (8, 14),	
Harper (13),	
Davidson 2 (32, 55)	

ABERDEEN: Clark, Kennedy, Ritchie, McMaster, Garner, Miller, Sullivan, Fleming, Harper, Jarvie, Davidson

MOTHERWELL: Rennie, Watson, Wark, Miller, McLaren, Stevens, Marinello (Kennedy), Pettigrew, Clinging (McVie), Davidson, Mungall

P	W	D	L	F	A	Pts	
34	21	8	5	63	26	50	*Attendance:* 16,200
							Referee: D. F. T. Syme

Aberdeen's biggest win of the season gives them a healthy goal-difference advantage over Rangers. The double is on! The standing ovation at the finish was just reward for a devastating display.

No 35 Saturday, 22 April

ABERDEEN (1) 4	ST MIRREN (2) 2
Harper 3 (42, 61, 82),	McGarvey (2),
Miller (49)	Bone (10)

ABERDEEN: Clark, Kennedy, Ritchie, McMaster, Garner, Miller, Sullivan, Fleming, Harper, Jarvie, Davidson

ST MIRREN: McCulloch, Beckett, Munro, Fitzpatrick, Dunlop, Copland, Abercrombie (Young), Stark, Bone, Richardson, McGarvey

P	W	D	L	F	A	Pts	
35	22	8	5	67	28	52	*Attendance:* 17,300
							Referee: T. R. Kyle

What a shock for the Dons as they find themselves 2-0 down to Alex Ferguson's much improved side. But nobody can suppress Joe Harper when he's in this mood. All his goals were netted from close in – where he likes them. A tumultuous reception greets the Dons as they troop off.

No 36 Saturday, 29 April

HIBERNIAN (0) 1	ABERDEEN (0) 1
Duncan (87)	Scanlon (79)

HIBERNIAN: McDonald, Brownlie, Smith, McNamara, Stewart, Bremner, Murray, McLeod, Rae, Duncan, Higgins

ABERDEEN: Clark, Kennedy, Ritchie, McMaster, Garner, Miller, Sullivan, Fleming (Scanlon), Harper, Jarvie, Davidson

Attendance: 11,400　　　*Referee:* I. M. D. Foote

To become champions Aberdeen had to take one point more than Rangers gained at home to Motherwell. Aberdeen's 23rd game without defeat was not enough. Substitute Ian Scanlon, on his debut, took the ball round McDonald to give the Dons new hope, but Arthur Duncan climbed high to nod in the equaliser. Three minutes later Aberdeen learned that Rangers had won 2-0.

Aberdeen's complete home and away record:

HOME						AWAY					
P	W	D	L	F	A	W	D	L	F	A	Pts
36	14	3	1	43	13	8	6	4	25	16	53

Scottish League Premier Division

	P	W	D	L	F	A	Pts
1 Rangers	36	24	7	5	76	39	55
2 ABERDEEN	36	22	9	5	68	29	53
3 Dundee United	36	16	8	12	42	32	40
4 Hibernian	36	15	7	14	51	43	37
5 Celtic	36	15	6	15	63	54	36
6 Motherwell	36	13	7	16	45	52	33
7 Partick Thistle	36	14	5	17	52	64	33
8 St Mirren	36	11	8	17	52	63	30
9 Ayr United	36	9	6	21	36	68	24
10 Clydebank	36	6	7	23	23	64	19

LEAGUE CUP

1st Round, 1st Leg Wednesday, 17 August
ABERDEEN (1) 3　　　AIRDRIEONIANS (0) 1
　Fleming 2 (43, 71),　　　Kerr (77)
　Shirra (78)

ABERDEEN: Clark, Kennedy, McLelland, Smith (Davidson), Garner, Miller, Sullivan, Shirra, Harper, Fleming, Jarvie

AIRDRIE: Brian, Jonquin, Lapsley, Black, Collins, Cowan, McGowan (Wilson), McVeigh, Kerr, McCulloch, Clark

Attendance: 10,400　　　*Referee:* W. J. Mullen

The League Cup has a new format. After being played in group sections for thirty years it is now a straight knock-out, based on two-leg matches up to and including the quarter-finals. This particular game was held up for several minutes in the first half when Airdrie won a corner. None of their playes wanted to take it.

1st Round, 2nd Leg Wednesday, 24 August
AIRDRIEONIANS (0) 0　ABERDEEN (1) 2
　　　　　　　　　McMaster 2 (23, 57)

AIRDRIE: McWilliams, Jonquin, Cowan, Anderson, Collins, McCulloch, Wilson, McVeigh, Kerr, Walker, Lapsley

ABERDEEN: Clark, Kennedy, McLelland, Shirra, Garner, Miller, Sullivan, Jarvie, Harper (Davidson), Fleming, McMaster

Attendance: 3,000　　　Referee: W. J. Mullen

John McMaster came close to registering his first hat-trick in senior football. His late free kick beat McWilliams, but was chalked off for an infringement on the goal-line.

2nd Round, 1st Leg Wednesday 31 August
ABERDEEN (2) 5　　　COWDENBEATH (0) 0
　Harper 3 (1, 43, 81),
　Fleming 2 (83, 84)

ABERDEEN: Clark, Kennedy, McLelland, Smith (Davidson), Garner, Miller, Jarvie, Shirra, Harper, Fleming, McMaster

COWDENBEATH: McGarr, Thomson, Carpenter, Purdie, Aitken, Fair, Harley, Hunter, Graham, Steele, Marshall (Jobson)

Referee: D. Ramsay

Against feeble Second Division opposition Joe Harper breaks Harry Yorston's all-time scoring record for Aberdeen.

2nd Round, 2nd Leg Saturday, 2 September
COWDENBEATH (0) 0　ABERDEEN (3) 5
　　　　　　　　　Davidson (16),
　　　　　　　　　McMaster (20),
　　　　　　　　　Harper 3 (45 pen, 61, 72)

COWDENBEATH: McGarr, Ward, Carpenter, Thomson (Graham), Aitken, Fair, Hunter, Harley, Marshall (Purdie), Steele, Caithness

ABERDEEN: Clark, Kennedy, McLelland, Shirra, Garner, Miller, Jarvie, Davidson, Harper, Fleming, McMaster

Attendance: 1,780　　　*Referee:* D. Ramsay

Joe Harper casually wrapped up his second successive hat-trick against the Fifers. But this time he was a naughty boy and was booked beforehand.

3rd Round, 1st Leg Wednesday, 5 October
RANGERS (4) 6　　　ABERDEEN (0) 1
　Smith 3 (3, 44, 72),　　　Davidson (80)
　Johnstone (30),
　Miller (45 pen),
　MacDonald (85)

RANGERS: Kennedy, Jardine, Miller, Forsyth, Jackson, MacDonald, McLean, Russell, Johnstone, Smith, Cooper

ABERDEEN: Clark, Kennedy, McLelland, Robb, Garner, Miller, Jarvie, Davidson, Harper, Fleming (Sullivan), McMaster

Attendance: 25,000　　　*Referee:* G. B. Smith

Rangers look brilliant – especially Gordon Smith. Billy McNeill describes them as the best Rangers team he has ever seen. Enough said.

3rd Round, 2nd Leg Wednesday, 26 October
ABERDEEN (1) 3   RANGERS (1) 1
  J. Smith (38),   G. Smith (30)
  Jarvie 2 (59, 65)
ABERDEEN: Clark, Kennedy, McLelland, Smith, Garner, Miller, Jarvie, Shirra (Davidson), Harper, Fleming, McMaster
RANGERS: Kennedy, Jardine, Miller (Parlane), Forsyth, Greig, MacDonald, McLean, Russell, Johnston, Smith (McKean), Cooper

Attendance: 15,600   Referee: G. B. Smith

Aberdeen said goodbye to the League Cup in the best possible spirit, storming back after Rangers had gone 7-1 ahead on aggregate. The Don's pride was restored, but the cup was gone.

SCOTTISH CUP

3rd Round, Monday, 6 February
ABERDEEN (1) 2   AYR UNITED (0) 0
  Harper 2 (18 pen, 83)
ABERDEEN: Clark, Kennedy, McLelland, McMaster, Garner, Miller, Davidson, Sullivan, Harper, Strachan, Jarvie
AYR: Sproat, Wells, Murphy, Fleming, Hyslop, Rodman (Sim), McSherry, McLaughlin, Masterton, Hannah, Christie (McLelland)

                    Referee: J. R. P. Gordon

There was never a sniff of a sensation for Ayr in the puddles of Pittodrie once Harper had sent Sproat the wrong way from the spot.

4th Round Monday, 27 February
ABERDEEN (1) 3   ST JOHNSTONE (0) 0
  Davidson (11),
  Harper (75),
  Jarvie (89)
ABERDEEN: Clark, Kennedy, McLelland, McMaster, Garner, Miller, Sullivan, Fleming, Harper, Strachan (Jarvie), Davidson
ST JOHNSTONE: Geoghegan, McKay, Houston, Rutherford, O'Brien, Clunie, Pelosi, Brogan, O'Connor, Thomson, Ross (Lawson)

Attendance: 15,600   *Referee:* R. B. Valentine

Davidson put Aberdeen ahead amid the lashing feet, but then they stood around like wallflowers as St Johnstone rallied. It was that man again who settled the nerves.

Quarter Final Saturday, 11 March
ABERDEEN (1) 2   MORTON (0) 2
  Davidson (31),   Ritchie (87)
  Jarvie (85)   Goldthorp (90)
ABERDEEN: Clark, Kennedy, McLelland, McMaster, Garner, Miller, Strachan, Sullivan, Gibson (Fleming), Jarvie, Davidson
MORTON: Connaghan, Lynch, Holmes, Anderson, Orr, Veitch (Mitchell), McNeil, Brown (Thomas), Evans, Goldthorp, Ritchie

Attendance: 18,000   *Referee:* J. R. P. Gordon

Who would have believed that First Division Morton could pull off an escape act like this? When Jarvie made it 2-0 with five minutes to play it looked like goodbye Morton. But it wasn't, and their delerious fans rushed on to the field to embrace their heroes at the end.

Quarter Final Replay Wednesday, 15 March
MORTON (1) 1   ABERDEEN (2) 2
  McNeil (45)   McMaster (27),
                    Fleming (31)
MORTON: Connaghan, Lynch, Holmes, Anderson, Orr, Veitch (Thomas), McNeil, Brown, Evans, Goldthorp, Ritchie
ABERDEEN: Clark, Kennedy, McLelland, McMaster, Garner, Miller, Strachan, Sullivan, Fleming, Jarvie, Davidson

                    Referee: J. R. P. Gordon

In heavy sleet Aberdeen survived a cliff-hanger. Davidson was felled by Holmes and up stepped McMaster – in Harper's absence – to do the necessary. Fleming increased the lead with an explosive volley. With the last kick of the first half McNeil contrived a dazzling solo goal to keep the fans on tenterhooks till the end.

Semi Final (Hampden) Wednesday, 12 April
PARTICK THISTLE (0) 2   ABERDEEN (2) 4
  Melrose 2 (64, 88)   Fleming 2 (32, 39, 77)
                    Harper (71 pen)
PARTICK: Rough, Anderson, Whittaker, Campbell, Marr, Craig (Melrose), Houston, O'Hara, Somner, Gibson, McQuade
ABERDEEN: Clark, Kennedy, Ritchie (McLelland), McMaster, Garner, Miller, Sullivan, Fleming, Harper, Jarvie, Davidson

Attendance: 12,300   *Referee:* D. Syme

This is Aberdeen's third win over Thistle in nine days. In all of them the Dons started off with a bang, establishing a two-goal advantage, and were then forced to live dangerously. Substitute Melrose's overhead kick to make it 2-1 gave Aberdeen the flutters until Harper calmed things down with a penalty.

Scottish Cup Final (Hampden) Saturday, 6 May
RANGERS (1) 2   ABERDEEN (0) 1
  MacDonald (35),   Ritchie (85)
  Johnstone (57)
RANGERS: McCloy, Jardine, Greig, Forsyth, Jackson, MacDonald, McLean, Russell, Johnstone, Smith, Cooper
ABERDEEN: Clark, Kennedy, Ritchie, McMaster, Garner, Miller, Sullivan, Fleming (Scanlon), Harper, Jarvie, Davidson

Attendance: 61,563   *Referee:* B. R. McGinlay

Even before this match got under way Rangers were threatening to ruin Aberdeen's season completely. It was the 'Gers who wrestled the League Cup off the

Dons and who pipped them for the championship. Were they now going to make a clean sweep at Aberdeen's expense? They did just that. Aberdeen, quite simply, froze. The pulsating football of the past few months was but a hollow memory. MacDonald put Rangers ahead with a header that passed through Clark's hands. Johnstone gave the Dons' keeper no chance with a second, flashing, header. Ritchie's consolation goal for Aberdeen was a joke, a mis-hit effort from six yards that ended up in the net via McCloy's crossbar.

UEFA Cup

1st Round, 1st Leg Wednesday, 14 September
R W MOLENBEEK   ABERDEEN (0) 0
  (Belgium) (0) 0

MOLENBEEK: Ruiter (Leonard), Dumon, Den Haese, Alhinho, Des_nghere, Boskamp, Cordiez, Olsen, Gorez, Wellens, Van Haecke (Wissmann)

ABERDEEN: Clark, Kennedy, McLelland, Shirra, Garner, Miller, Davidson, Jarvie, Harper, Fleming, McMaster

Attendance: 14,000   *Referee:* M. Bjorck
                                        (Sweden)

Molenbeek reached the last four of the UEFA Cup last season, and retired unbeaten on the away-goals rule against Athletico Bilbao. For the Dons, only Clark, Miller, Jarvie and Harper have European experience to fall back on. Nevertheless, Aberdeen played with commendable composure, their worst scare coming six minutes from time when Clark had to hoist the ball off the line with the crowd screaming for a goal.

1st Round, 2nd Leg Wednesday, 28 September
ABERDEEN (0) 1   R W MOLENBEEK (0) 2
  Jarvie (78)   Gorez (46),
                          Wellens (84)

ABERDEEN: Clark, Kennedy, McLelland, Shirra (Sullivan), Garner, Miller, Jarvie, Davidson, Harper, Fleming, McMaster

MOLENBEEK: Ruiter, Dumon, Lafont, Alhinho, Desanghere, Boskamp, Cordiez, Olsen, Gorez, Wellens (Reygaeret), Wissmann

Attendance: 26,000   *Referee:* A. Delmer
                                        (France)

R W Molenbeek won 2-1 on aggregate.

This was Aberdeen's first defeat of the season in any competition. Straight from the resumption Miller failed to connect with a cross and Gorez was unmarked for his header. Aberdeen now needed to score twice under the away-goals rule. Jarvie gave them hope when Ruiter punched a centre to his feet, but Aberdeen then over-committed themselves to attack and paid the price.

1977-78

APPEARANCES	League	League Cup	Scottish Cup	UEFA Cup
Miller	36	6	6	2
Clark	36	6	6	2
Garner	35	6	6	2
Jarvie	35	6	5(+1)	2
Kennedy	34	6	6	2
Harper	31	6	4	2
McMaster	30(+2)	5	6	2
Sullivan	25(+4)	2(+1)	6	–(+1)
McLelland	25	6	4(+1)	2
Fleming	20(+5)	6	4(+1)	2
Davidson	17(+7)	2(+4)	6	2
Robb	13	1		
Strachan	10(+2)		4	
Archibald	10			
Gibson	9		1	
Ritchie	9		2	
Shirra	8	5		2
Joe Smith	7	3		
Glennie	3			
Neil Cooper	1			
McLeish	1			
Rougvie	1			
Grant	–(+2)			
Scott	–(+1)			
Campbell	–(+1)			
Watson	–(+1)			
Scanlon	–(+1)			–(+1)
27 players				

GOALS	Total	League	League Cup	Scottish Cup	UEFA Cup
Harper	27	17	6	4	
Jarvie	17	12	2	2	1
Fleming	13	5	4	4	
Davidson	12	8	2	2	
McMaster	8	4	3	1	
Robb	5	5			
Archibald	5	5			
Gibson	3	3			
Sullivan	3	3			
Miller	2	2			
Strachan	1	1			
Garner	1	1			
Scanlon	1	1			
Shirra	1		1		
Joe Smith	1		1		
Ritchie	1			1	
own-goals	1	1			
Total	102	68	19	14	

Season 1978-79

When Alex Ferguson took over at Pittodrie, filling the gap left by Billy McNeill, he had a tough act to follow. Could the Dons improve upon runners-up spot in both the league and the Scottish Cup? The answer was – No, they couldn't. Ferguson took time to settle. Distracted by the failing health of his father and by the continuing recriminations that followed his acrimonious departure from St Mirren, he was content to find his feet gradually.

Nevertheless, early progress was made in the league and League Cup. In December Aberdeen beat Hibs in the League Cup semi-final, with the final put on ice for another three and a half months. The league was turning into an unexpectedly open contest. There were no outstanding sides in 1978-79, and Aberdeen still held second spot as the season entered March. Then Celtic put on a late burst, coming from nowhere to take the title, leaving Aberdeen to slide down to fourth by the season's end.

By then they had also lost the delayed League Cup Final, 2-1 to Rangers. Aberdeen had as much of the play as their opponents, but the controversial sending-off of Doug Rougvie for an unproven assault on Derek Johnstone caused much lingering bitterness.

Aberdeen's interest in the Scottish Cup terminated in the semi-finals, when Hibs exacted revenge for their defeat at the same stage of the League Cup. In Europe, the Dons had been eligible for the Cup-Winners Cup owing to Rangers' presence in the European Cup. Once again Aberdeen failed to progress beyond the second round, despite giving the Fortuna Düsseldorf defence a fearful pounding at Pittodrie.

The Dons' continuing debt to Joe Harper was incalculable. In his three seasons with Aberdeen since his return he had scored 28, 27, and now 33 goals in official competition.

League:	Fourth
League Cup:	Runners Up
Scottish Cup:	Semi-Final
European Cup-Winners Cup:	Second Round

SCOTTISH PREMIER DIVISION

No 1 Saturday, 12 August

HEARTS (1) 1	ABERDEEN (2) 4
Bannon (4)	Davidson (23),
	Harper (37),
	Archibald 2 (64, 86)

HEARTS: Dunlop, Kidd, Fraser, McNicoll, Jefferies, Liddell, Park, Bannon, Gibson (Prentice), Shaw, Robertson (Tierney)

ABERDEEN: Leighton, Kennedy, McLelland, McMaster, Garner, Miller, Sullivan, Archibald, Harper, Jarvie, Davidson (Scanlon)

P	W	D	L	F	A	Pts	*Attendance:* 11,500
1	1	0	0	4	1	2	

Young goalkeeper Jim Leighton did not wish to lose a goal so early in his senior baptism. But thereafter Aberdeen slowly steam-rolled the opposition. Hearts' Dunlop had a much worse game than Leighton.

No 2 Saturday, 19 August

ABERDEEN (1) 3	MORTON (1) 1
Harper 3 (2, 56, 82)	Ritchie (39)

ABERDEEN: Leighton, Kennedy, McLelland, McMaster, Garner, Miller, Sullivan, Archibald, Harper, Jarvie, Davidson (Scanlon)

MORTON: Connaghan, Hayes, Holmes, Anderson, Orr, Rooney, Russell, Miller, McLean (Rae), Scott, Ritchie

278

P W D L F A Pts   *Attendance:* 14,500
2 2 0 0 7 2 4   *Referee:* I. M. D. Foote

Harper has now passed the 200-goal mark in all matches for Aberdeen. He shows how to take them after just 90 seconds, taking Sullivan's pass on his chest and shooting on the run past Connaghan. Earlier in the week Pat Stanton joined the Dons as Assistant Manager.

No 3 Saturday, 26 August
DUNDEE UNITED (0) 1   ABERDEEN (1) 1
  Hegarty (78)   Harper (20)

DUNDEE UNITED: McAlpine, Stark (Kopel), Stewart, Fleming, Hegarty, Narey, Sturrock, Addison, Frye, Holt, Payne

ABERDEEN: Leighton, Kennedy, McLelland, McMaster, Garner, Miller, Sullivan, Archibald (Fleming), Harper, Jarvie, Davidson (Scanlon)

P W D L F A Pts   *Attendance:* 10,000
3 2 1 0 8 3 5   *Referee:* D. Ramsay

A nasty, heated match which ended with fighting on the pitch and on the terraces.

No 4 Saturday, 9 September
ABERDEEN (1) 4   MOTHERWELL (0) 0
  Harper 2 (39, 50 pen),
  Archibald 2 (67, 72)

ABERDEEN: Leighton, Kennedy, McLelland, McMaster, Garner, Miller, Sullivan (Strachan), Archibald, Harper, Jarvie, Scanlon

MOTHERWELL: Latchford, Miller, Wark, Boyd (McLeod), McVie, Stevens, Marinello, Pettigrew, Larnach, McLaren, Clinging

P W D L F A Pts   *Attendance:* 13,200
4 3 1 0 12 3 7   *Referee:* A. G. McFaull

Joe Harper is a marked man. When two 'Well players send him into orbit both are booked. Harper was almost cautioned for his furious retaliation.

No 5 Saturday, 16 September
RANGERS (1) 1   ABERDEEN (0) 1
  A. Forsyth (39 pen)   Sullivan (90)

RANGERS: McCloy, Jardine, A. Forsyth, T. Forsyth, Jackson, MacDonald, McLean, Russell, Parlane, Johnstone, Smith

ABERDEEN: Leighton, Kennedy, McLelland, McMaster, McLeish, Miller, Sullivan, Archibald (Strachan), Harper, Jarvie, Scanlon (Rougvie)

Leading positions

	P	W	D	L	F	A	Pts
1 Celtic	5	4	0	1	14	4	8
2 ABERDEEN	5	3	2	0	13	4	8
3 Hibernian	5	2	3	0	3	1	7

Attendance: 25,000   *Referee:* W. Anderson

Ibrox is reduced to a bomb-site as reconstruction work begins. The unfamiliar surroundings are having their effects on the Rangers players who have still not won in the league this season. They are on their way when young McLeish concedes a penalty. But deep into injury time Sullivan pops up to meet Strachan's cross.

No 6 Saturday, 23 September
HIBERNIAN (2) 2   ABERDEEN (1) 1
  Rae (9), McLeod (41 pen)   Jarvie (19)

HIBERNIAN: McDonald, Duncan, Smith, Rae, Fleming, McNamara (Stewart), Temperley, McLeod, Hutchinson (O'Brien), Callachan, Higgins

ABERDEEN: Leighton, Kennedy, McLelland, McMaster, McLeish, Miller, Sullivan (Rougvie), Archibald, Harper, Jarvie, Scanlon (Davidson)

P W D L F A Pts   *Attendance:* 12,100
6 3 2 1 14 6 8   *Referee:* J. R. P. Gordon

Both sides scored with headers before Willie Miller upended Smith. The Dons had held their own in the first half, but never looked like saving the game in the second.

No 7 Saturday, 30 September
ABERDEEN (0) 1   PARTICK THISTLE (1) 1
  Archibald (56)   Somner (43 pen)

ABERDEEN: Leighton, Kennedy, McLelland, McMaster, McLeish, Miller, Strachan, Archibald, Harper, Jarvie, Scanlon (Fleming)

PARTICK: Rough, McKinnon, Whittaker, Campbell, Marr, Gibson, Houston, Park (O'Hara), Somner, Melrose (McAdam), Love

P W D L F A Pts   *Attendance:* 11,100
7 3 3 1 15 7 9   *Referee:* G. B. Smith

A game which started as a bore and ended with a roar. Aberdeen were up against it after Leighton grassed Melrose. There followed the 'Alan Rough Show' as Scotland's keeper earned overtime.

No 8 Saturday, 7 October
ABERDEEN (3) 4   CELTIC (1) 1
  Archibald 2 (21, 54),   McAdam (43)
  Harper (23 pen),
  Jarvie (33)

ABERDEEN: Leighton, Kennedy, McLelland, McMaster, McLeish, Miller, Strachan, Archibald, Harper, Jarvie, Sullivan

CELTIC: Latchford, Filippi, Sneddon, Aitken, MacDonald, Edvaldsson (Glavin), Provan, Conroy, McAdam, Burns (Lennox), McCluskey

P W D L F A Pts   *Attendance:* 25,000
8 4 3 1 19 8 11   *Referee:* J. R. P. Gordon

'We're going to win the league.' So sang the Celtic contingent after the final whistle. But not even the belated introduction of the Lisbon Lion – Bobby Lennox – could avert this devastating defeat.

No 9 Saturday, 14 October
ST MIRREN (0) 2   ABERDEEN (0) 1
  Bone (60), McGarvey (66)   Harper (84)

ST MIRREN: Thomson, Young, Munro, Fitzpatrick, Dunlop, Copland, Richardson, Stark, Bone, Abercrombie, McGarvey

ABERDEEN: Leighton, Kennedy, McLelland (Rougvie), McMaster, McLeish, Miller, Strachan (Scanlon), Archibald, Harper, Jarvie, Sullivan

P W D L F A Pts   *Attendance:* 11,000
9 4 3 2 20 10 11   *Referee:* D. F. Syme

Aberdeen would have gone top had they won, but Alex Ferguson's return to Paisley leaves him looking a worried man. St Mirren won, and won well.

No 10 Saturday, 21 October

ABERDEEN (0) 1	HEARTS (1) 2
Harper (59 pen)	O'Connor (1),
	McQuade (78)

ABERDEEN: Leighton, Kennedy (Fleming), McLelland, McMaster (Strachan), McLeish, Miller, Sullivan, Archibald, Harper, Jarvie, Scanlon

HEARTS: Dunlop, Kidd (Brown), Jefferies, McNicoll, Liddell, Fraser, Gibson, Bannon, O'Connor, Busby, Robertson (McQuade)

P W D L F A Pts   *Attendance:* 12,800
10 4 3 3 21 12 11   *Referee:* T. R. Kyle

Perhaps Aberdeen drank poisoned beer in Düsseldorf. They were dreadful. Hearts' sub McQuade had only been on for four minutes when he unleashed the kind of shot from 25 yards that strikers dream about.

No 11 Saturday, 29 October

MORTON (2) 2	ABERDEEN (1) 1
Ritchie (19), Russell (21)	Jarvie (18)

MORTON: Connaghan, Hayes, Holmes, Evans, Orr, Rooney, Russell (Tolmie), Miller, Thomson, Scott, Ritchie

ABERDEEN: Leighton, Rougvie, Ritchie (Fleming), McMaster, McLeish, Miller, Sullivan, Archibald, Harper, Jarvie, Scanlon (J. Smith)

P W D L F A Pts   *Attendance:* 7,000
11 4 3 4 22 14 11   *Referee:* M. Delaney

The Dons are on a losing run. Andy Ritchie is performing wonders for Morton. His equaliser swirled in front of Leighton: his cross two minutes later was pushed in by Russell.

No 12 Saturday, 4 November

ABERDEEN (1) 1	DUNDEE UNITED (0) 0
Harper (7 pen)	

ABERDEEN: Clark, Rougvie, McLelland, Fleming (Scanlon), McLeish, Miller, Strachan, Archibald, Harper, Jarvie (J. Smith), Sullivan

DUNDEE UNITED: McAlpine, Stewart, Kopel, Fleming, Hegarty, Narey, Stark, Sturrock, Payne (Dodds), Kirkwood, Addison (Robinson)

P W D L F A Pts   *Attendance:* 14,900
12 5 3 4 23 14 13   *Referee:* K. J. Hope

Poor, poor United. The better team by far, yet somehow they lost. They trailed to a Harper penalty when the wee man was flattened by Hegarty, then proceeded to fritter away countless chances. Worst of all was Ray Stewart's penalty miss.

No 13 Saturday, 11 November

MOTHERWELL (0) 1	ABERDEEN (0) 1
Wilson (55)	Scanlon (56)

MOTHERWELL: Rennie, Carr, Wark, McLaren, McVie, Stevens, Marinello, Pettigrew, Larnach, Millar (Clinging), Wilson

ABERDEEN: Clark, Kennedy, McLelland, McMaster (Considine), Rougvie, Miller, Strachan, Fleming (Scanlon), Harper, Jarvie, Sullivan

P W D L F A Pts   *Attendance:* 5,400
13 5 4 4 24 15 14   *Referee:* J. Renton

Everything happened in the second half. Willie Miller fluffs a pass back to Clark. Scanlon swivels and hits an instant equaliser. Rougvie is ordered off for an off-the-ball incident – but soon Pettigrew is walking off, too.

No 14 Saturday, 18 November

ABERDEEN (0) 0	RANGERS (0) 0

ABERDEEN: Clark, Kennedy, McLelland, McMaster, Rougvie, Miller, Scanlon, Archibald, Harper, Sullivan, Scanlon (Fleming)

RANGERS: McCloy, Jardine, Dawson, Johnstone, Jackson, MacDonald, McLean, Russell, Parlane, Smith, Watson

P W D L F A Pts   *Attendance:* 26,000
14 5 5 4 24 15 15   *Referee:* G. B. Smith

How on earth did Rangers leave Pittodrie with a point? Harper slid a penalty wide of a post, and Peter McCloy saved thrillingly from Archibald and Fleming.

No 15 Saturday, 25 November

ABERDEEN (2) 4	HIBERNIAN (0) 1
Fleming (19),	Hutchinson (85)
Sullivan (36)	
Harper 2 (69, 80)	

ABERDEEN: Clark, Kennedy, McLelland, McMaster (Jarvie), Rougvie, Miller, Strachan, Fleming, Harper, Sullivan, Davidson (Cooper)

HIBERNIAN: McDonald, Duncan, Smith, Bremner, McNamara, Mathieson, McLeod, Refvik, Callachan, Hutchinson

Leading positions

	P	W	D	L	F	A	Pts
1 Dundee	15	6	6	3	19	14	18
2 ABERDEEN	15	6	5	4	28	16	17
3 Celtic	15	7	3	5	25	19	17
4 Partick	15	7	3	5	16	14	17

Attendance: 14,300   *Referee:* A. McGunnigle

Aberdeen at last got their act together. Their first three goals were scorching drives. Their fourth was a leaping header by – Joe Harper.

No 16 Saturday, 9 December

CELTIC (0) 0	ABERDEEN (0) 0

CELTIC: Baines, Filippi, Lynch, Aitken, MacDonald, Edvaldsson, Provan, McLeod, McAdam (Conn), Burns, Doyle

ABERDEEN: Clark, Kennedy, McLelland, McMaster (Archibald), Rougvie, Miller, Strachan, Fleming, Harper, Jarvie, Sullivan

P W D L F A Pts   *Attendance:* 24,000
16 6 6 4 28 16 18   *Referee:* W. Anderson
Not the best of games. The biggest cheer of the afternoon greeted the news that Rangers were losing at Tannadice.

No 17 Saturday, 16 December
ABERDEEN (0) 1   ST MIRREN (1) 1
  McMaster (55)   Stark (19)
ABERDEEN: Clark, Kennedy, McLelland, McMaster, Rougvie, Miller, Strachan, Archibald, Harper, Sullivan, Scanlon (Fleming)
ST MIRREN: Thomson, Beckett, Munro, Fitzpatrick, Dunlop, Copland, Richardson, Stark, Bone, Abercrombie, McGarvey (Hyslop)
P W D L F A Pts   *Attendance:* 12,700
17 6 7 4 29 17 19   *Referee:* R. R. Cuthill
McMaster saved a point for the Dons with a glancing header that didn't go where he intended – except that it ended up in the net.

No 18 Saturday, 23 December
HEARTS (0) 0   ABERDEEN (0) 0
HEARTS: Dunlop, Kidd, Fraser, McNicoll, Jefferies, Craig, Gibson (McQuade), Bannon, O'Connor, Busby, Robertson
ABERDEEN: Clark, Kennedy, McLelland, McMaster, Rougvie, Cooper, Strachan, Archibald (Fleming), Harper, Sullivan (Considine), Scanlon
P W D L F A Pts   *Attendance:* 9,500
18 6 8 4 29 17 20   *Referee:* I. M. D. Foote
Oh what a festive bore. Harper was so bad that when he aimed a kick at Bannon, he missed. When Hearts' McQuade came on at Pittodrie he burst the net. He had no such opportunities this time.

No 19 Saturday, 30 December
ABERDEEN (0) 1   MORTON (0) 2
  Harper (88)   Ritchie (59),
               McNeill (67)
ABERDEEN: Clark, Kennedy, McLelland, McMaster, Rougvie, Miller, Strachan (Cooper), Archibald, Harper, Sullivan, Scanlon (Fleming)
MORTON: Brcic, Hayes, Anderson, McLaren, Orr, Rooney, McNeill, Hutchinson, Thomson, Scott, Ritchie
P W D L F A Pts   *Attendance:* 8,000
19 6 8 5 30 19 20   *Referee:* A. G. McFaull
Morton took it on the chin for an hour, and then allowed Andy Ritchie to lay Aberdeen out. The languid striker robbed McLelland and squeezed the ball past Clark. Earlier Harper had squandered a penalty. On the pitch and on the terraces everybody froze in the snow.

No 20 Saturday, 20 January
HIBERNIAN (0) 1   ABERDEEN (1) 1
  Duncan (51)   Harper (15)

HIBERNIAN: McArthur, Brazil, Duncan, Bremner, Stewart, McNamara, Refvik (Higgins), McLeod, Hutchinson, Callachan, Lambie
ABERDEEN: Clark, Kennedy, McLelland, Strachan (Archibald), Rougvie, Miller, Sullivan, Scanlon, Harper, Jarvie, Davidson (Cooper)
P W D L F A Pts   *Attendance:* 6,000
20 6 9 5 31 20 21   *Referee:* J. R. S. Renton
Sweet music for Joe Harper as he silences the Hibs boo-boys when scoring from Scanlon's cut back. But when Clark punched out Higgins' header Arthur Duncan hit it sweetly back from over 30 yards.

No 21 Saturday, 24 February
ST MIRREN (0) 2   ABERDEEN (1) 2
  McGarvey (61),   Archibald (23),
  Copland (83)   Strachan (58)
ST MIRREN: Thomson, Young, Munro, Fitzpatrick, Dunlop, Copland, Richardson, Stark, Bone, Torrance, McGarvey
ABERDEEN: Clark, Kennedy, Considine, McMaster, Rougvie, Miller, Sullivan, Archibald, Scanlon, Jarvie (Davidson), Strachan
P W D L F A Pts   *Attendance:* 11,500
21 6 10 5 33 22 22   *Referee:* D. A. Murdoch
There was a sting in the Paisley tail. Two raging volleys put Aberdeen in control. Alex Ferguson was still leaping about celebrating Strachan's goal when McGarvey chipped Clark. Soon Ian Scanlon was sent off, then Willie Miller for seeking revenge on McGarvey. Copland's equaliser was the final blow.

No 22 Wednesday, 28 February
ABERDEEN (0) 2   PARTICK THISTLE (0) 1
  McMaster (73),   Gibson (84)
  Archibald (86)
ABERDEEN: Clark, Kennedy, Considine, McMaster, Rougvie, McLeish, Sullivan, Archibald, Scanlon, Jarvie (Harper), Strachan (McLelland)
PARTICK: Rough, McKinnon, Whittaker, Anderson, McAdam (Gibson), Campbell, Houston, Somner, Marr, O'Hara, Park
P W D L F A Pts   *Attendance:* 12,500
22 7 10 5 35 23 24   *Referee:* W. Anderson
Partick look a negative side, devoid of ideas. Their equaliser, a first-timer by Gibson, looks to have earned them a point, but Archibald stole it back with Rough rooted to his line.

No 23 Saturday, 3 March
CELTIC (0) 1   ABERDEEN (0) 0
  Conn (65)
CELTIC: Latchford, McGrain, Lynch, Aitken, MacDonald, Edvaldsson, Provan, McLeod, Conn, Burns (Filippi), Doyle
ABERDEEN: Clark, Kennedy, McLelland, McMaster, Rougvie, Miller, Sullivan, Archibald, Scanlon, Jarvie (Harper), Strachan (Considine)

K

Leading positions

	P	W	D	L	F	A	Pts
1 St Mirren	22	10	5	7	27	21	25
2 ABERDEEN	23	7	10	6	35	24	24
3 Rangers	21	8	8	5	27	21	24
4 Dundee United	21	8	7	6	26	20	23
5 Partick	21	8	7	6	22	20	23

Attendance: 26,000   *Referee:* J. R. S. Renton

A ragged match, settled by Alfie Conn on his comeback. Aberdeen looked more likely to lose another goal than score one themselves.

No 24 Saturday, 17 March
ABERDEEN (0) 0   DUNDEE UNITED (0) 2
                                              Sturrock (55),
                                              Fleming (71)
ABERDEEN: Clark, Kennedy, McLelland, McMaster (Strachan), Rougvie, Miller, Sullivan, Archibald, Harper (McLeish), Jarvie, Davidson
DUNDEE UNITED: McAlpine, Stewart, Stark, Phillip (Addison), Hegarty, Narey, Holt, Sturrock, Dodds, Fleming, Kirkwood

P	W	D	L	F	A	Pts
24	7	10	7	35	26	24

Attendance: 10,000   *Referee:* I. M. D. Foote

The Dons players could hardly be seen wearing an all-white strip on a snow-covered pitch. Sturrock scored United's first goal, and crossed on to Fleming's head for the second.

No 25 Monday 26 March
ABERDEEN (3) 8   MOTHERWELL (0) 0
  Harper 3 (20, 44, 47),
  McMaster (39), Archibald
  2 (51, 86), Strachan (77),
  Davidson (89)
ABERDEEN: Clark, Kennedy, McLelland, McMaster, Rougvie, Miller, Sullivan (Strachan), Archibald, Harper, Jarvie, Davidson
MOTHERWELL: Rennie, Kennedy, Wark, Kane (Mungall), Dempsey (Somerville), McLeod, Smith, Wilson, Larnach, Clinging, Donnelly

P	W	D	L	F	A	Pts
25	8	10	7	43	26	26

Attendance: 7,000   *Referee:* B. R. McGinlay

When Duncan Davidson led a posse of pursuing defenders to bag No 8 it established a new Premier League scoring record.

No 26 Wednesday, 4 April
MORTON (0) 0   ABERDEEN (1) 1
                                    Cooper (24)
MORTON: Baines, Hayes, Holmes, Anderson, Orr, Thomson, McNeill, Miller, Hutchinson (Russell), Tolmie, Ritchie
ABERDEEN: Gardiner, Kennedy, McLelland, Cooper, McLeish, Miller, McGhee (Hamilton), Watson, Harper, Jarvie (McMaster), Strachan

P	W	D	L	F	A	Pts
26	9	10	7	44	26	28

Attendance: 7,000   *Referee:* E. H. Pringle

New signing Mark McGhee makes a quick return to one of his old clubs, and misses two first-half sitters.

No 27 Saturday, 7 April
ABERDEEN (0) 0   HIBERNIAN (0) 0
ABERDEEN: Gardiner, Kennedy, McLelland, Cooper (Hamilton), McLeish (Rougvie), Miller, McGhee, Watson, Harper, Jarvie, Strachan
HIBERNIAN: McArthur, Brazil, Duncan, Bremner, Stewart, McNamara, Rae, McLeod, Campbell, Callachan, Brown

P	W	D	L	F	A	Pts
27	9	11	7	44	26	29

Attendance: 10,000   *Referee:* D. F. T. Syme

In four days' time these two will meet in the Scottish Cup semi-final. For the first 70 minutes this contest was staged as a sparring session. When Aberdeen woke up, McArthur frustrated them.

No 28 Saturday, 14 April
PARTICK THISTLE (0) 0   ABERDEEN (1) 1
                                                McGhee (4)
PARTICK: Rough, McKinnon, Whittaker, Anderson, Marr, Gibson (O'Hara), Houston, Melrose, Love (Campbell), Somner, Park
ABERDEEN: Clark, Kennedy, Hamilton, McLeish, Rougvie, Miller, McGhee, Archibald, Sullivan (McMaster), Strachan, Scanlon

P	W	D	L	F	A	Pts
28	10	11	7	45	26	31

Attendance: 6,000   Referee: T. Muirhead

Mark McGhee scores his first goal for Aberdeen, picking up Strachan's shrewd pass.

No 29 Wednesday, 18 April
MOTHERWELL (0) 1   ABERDEEN (0) 1
  Stevens (70)   McLeish (77)
MOTHERWELL: Rennie, Hare, Watt, Carberry (Wilson), Mackin, Stevens, Larnach, Pettigrew, Clinging, Irvine, Donnelly
ABERDEEN: Clark, Kennedy, Hamilton, McLeish, Garner, Miller, McGhee, Archibald, Sullivan (Jarvie), Strachan, Scanlon

P	W	D	L	F	A	Pts
29	10	12	7	46	27	32

Attendance: 2,700   *Referee:* A. McGunnigle

With Motherwell already relegated, this was a point lost by Aberdeen. They would have lost both save for McLeish's deliberate 20-yard drive. He followed this with a crass tackle and was booked.

No 30 Saturday, 21 April
ABERDEEN (1) 1   CELTIC (1) 1
  Strachan (24)   Lynch (40 pen)
ABERDEEN: Clark, Kennedy, Hamilton, McLeish, Garner, Miller, McGhee, Archibald, Sullivan, Strachan, Scanlon
CELTIC: Latchford, McGrain, Lynch, Aitken, Edvaldsson, McLeod, Provan, Conroy, Davidson (McAdam), Burns, McCluskey (Doyle)

Leading positions

	P	W	D	L	F	A	Pts
1 Dundee United	33	17	7	9	51	32	41
2 Rangers	28	13	9	6	38	26	35
3 Celtic	28	14	6	8	45	30	34
4 ABERDEEN	30	10	13	7	47	28	33

Attendance: 19,400   *Referee:* E. H. Pringle

This result was no good to either side if they still hoped to lift the title. Aberdeen might have held on to Strachan's conversion of Sullivan's pass but for Willie Miller recklessly dropping Conroy.

No 31 Wednesday, 25 April

ABERDEEN (1) 2   RANGERS (0) 1
  Archibald (5),   Smith (61)
  McGhee (82)

ABERDEEN: Clark, Hamilton, McLelland, McLeish, Garner, Miller, McGhee, Archibald, Sullivan (McMaster), Strachan, Scanlon

RANGERS: McCloy, Miller (Urquhart), Dawson, Jardine, Johnstone, MacDonald, McLean, Russell, Parlane, Smith, Cooper

P	W	D	L	F	A	Pts
31	11	13	7	49	29	35

Attendance: 17,000   *Referee:* T. Kellock

When Gordon Smith teased his way along the bye-line to shoot between Clark and his near post it seemed Aberdeen had blown it. But Mark McGhee frees himself of shackles in the box to drive past McCloy.

No 32 Saturday, 28 April

ABERDEEN (1) 1   ST MIRREN (0) 2
  Archibald (16)   Torrance (67), Stark (69)

ABERDEEN: Clark, Kennedy, Hamilton, McLeish, Garner, Miller, McGhee, Archibald, Sullivan, Strachan, McMaster (Harper)

ST MIRREN: Thomson, Young, Munro (Docherty), Fitzpatrick, Dunlop, Copland, Stark, Weir, McGarvey, Abercrombie, Torrance

P	W	D	L	F	A	Pts
32	11	13	8	50	31	35

Attendance: 13,000   *Referee:* R. B. Valentine

Joe Harper's fourth penalty miss of the season – near the end – not only cost Aberdeen a point, but probably their place in Europe. Saints' Billy Stark continues to score useful goals against the Dons, and Fitzpatrick was sent off for fouling Strachan.

No 33 Wednesday, 2 May

ABERDEEN (2) 5   HEARTS (0) 0
  McGhee 2 (24, 71),
  Strachan (31),
  Scanlon (55),
  Sullivan (79)

ABERDEEN: Clark, Kennedy, Hamilton, Strachan, Garner, Miller, McGhee, Archibald, Sullivan, Jarvie, Scanlon

HEARTS: Allan, Brown, Black, Fraser, Liddell, More, Gibson, Tierney (Jefferies), Stewart, Craig (Scott), McQuade

P	W	D	L	F	A	Pts
33	12	13	8	55	31	37

Attendance: 6,000   *Referee:* H. Alexander

Doomed Hearts had no heart. Mark McGhee scored one with his left, one with his right, and could have had several more.

No 34 Saturday, 5 May

DUNDEE UNITED (1) 2   ABERDEEN (0) 2
  Payne (37), Stewart (68)   Jarvie (58),
                                    Strachan (82 pen)

DUNDEE UNITED: McAlpine, Stewart, Stark, Fleming, Hegarty, Narey, Addison (Kirkwood), Sturrock, Dodds, Holt, Payne

ABERDEEN: Clark, Kennedy, Hamilton, McLeish, Garner, Miller, McGhee, Archibald, Strachan, Jarvie, Scanlon

P	W	D	L	F	A	Pts
34	12	14	8	57	33	38

Attendance: 7,800   *Referee:* C. White

The most unpopular man at Tannadice was referee White for giving Aberdeen a late penalty when Stewart was supposed to have handled.

No 35 Monday, 7 May

RANGERS (0) 2   ABERDEEN (0) 0
  Smith (59), Cooper (62)

RANGERS: McCloy, Jardine, Dawson, Johnstone, Jackson, MacDonald, McLean, Russell, Parlane, Smith, Cooper

ABERDEEN: Clark, Kennedy, Hamilton, McLeish, Garner, Miller, McGhee, Archibald, Sullivan (Jarvie), Strachan, Scanlon (Rougvie)

P	W	D	L	F	A	Pts
35	12	14	9	57	35	38

Attendance: 28,000   *Referee:* D. F. T. Syme

Rangers are on the brink of another championship. Davie Cooper split the defence for the 'Gers' first goal, and then picked up the ball after Miller had driven it against him, for the second.

No 36 Friday, 11 May

PARTICK THISTLE (0) 1   ABERDEEN (1) 2
  O'Hara (76)   Harper (24), Sullivan (89)

PARTICK: Rough, McKinnon (Clark), Whittaker, Marr, McAdam, Doyle, Melrose, Gibson, O'Hara, Somner, Park (Campbell)

ABERDEEN: Clark, Hamilton, Considine, Sullivan, Garner, Miller, McGhee (Cooper), Archibald, Harper, Strachan, Scanlon

Attendance: 4,000   *Referee:* T. Kellock

Joe Harper announces his return to the first team with a typical goal – prodding the ball into the net from six yards. In the last minute Neil Cooper hit the bar and Sullivan, following up, did the rest.

Aberdeen's complete home and away record:

HOME						AWAY						
P	W	D	L	F	A		W	D	L	F	A	Pts
36	9	5	4	39	16		4	9	5	20	20	40

Scottish League Premier Division 1978-79

	P	W	D	L	F	A	Pts
1 Celtic	36	21	6	9	61	37	48
2 Rangers	36	18	9	9	52	35	45
3 Dundee United	36	18	8	10	56	37	44
4 ABERDEEN	36	13	14	9	59	36	40
5 Hibernian	36	12	13	11	44	48	37
6 St Mirren	36	15	6	15	45	41	36
7 Morton	36	12	12	12	52	53	36
8 Partick Thistle	36	13	8	15	42	39	34
9 Hearts	36	8	7	21	39	71	23
10 Motherwell	36	5	7	24	33	86	17

LEAGUE CUP

2nd Round, 1st Leg Wednesday, 30 August

MEADOWBANK	ABERDEEN (3) 5
THISTLE (0) 0	Sullivan (18), Jarvie (26),
	Kennedy (29),
	Archibald (63),
	Fleming (73)

MEADOWBANK: Sinclair, O'Rourke, Fraser, Stewart, Wight, Carr, Leetion, J. Hancock (Johnstone), Adair (Downie), Davidson, S. Hancock

ABERDEEN: Gardiner, Kennedy, McLelland, McMaster, Garner, Miller, Sullivan, Archibald (Fleming), Harper, Jarvie (Strachan), Scanlon

Attendance: 3,500   *Referee:* J. R. Gordon

Meadowbank still haven't a game in the Second Division this season. All they wanted to do was score, never mind how many they let in.

2nd Round, 2nd Leg Saturday, 2 September

ABERDEEN (2) 4	MEADOWBANK
Archibald (16),	THISTLE (0) 0
Harper 2 (44, 50),	
Scanlon (87)	

ABERDEEN: Leighton, Kennedy, McLelland, McMaster, Garner, Miller, Sullivan (Strachan), Archibald, Harper, Jarvie, Scanlon

MEADOWBANK: Sinclair, O'Rourke, Fraser, Stewart (Mooney), Wight, Carr, Leetion, J. Hancock, S. Hancock, Downie, Davidson (Johnston)

Attendance: 6,850   *Referee:* J. R. P. Gordon

All that Meadowbank could manage was to have Wight dismissed for an ugly foul on Leighton.

3rd Round, 1st Leg Wednesday, 4 October

HAMILTON	ABERDEEN (1) 1
ACADEMICALS (0) 0	Scanlon (19)

HAMILTON: Ferguson, Grant, Kellachan, Fairlie, Dempsey, Alexander, Young (McGregor), Graham, Howie, Glavin, Reilly

ABERDEEN: Leighton, Kennedy, McLelland, McMaster (Rougvie), McLeish, Miller, Strachan, Davidson, Fleming, Jarvie, Scanlon

Attendance: 5,500   *Referee:* D. McFaull

A miserable, drizzly evening. A miserable match, apart from Fleming's and Scanlon's exchanges which led to the goal.

3rd Round, 2nd Leg Wednesday, 11 October

ABERDEEN (5) 7	HAMILTON
Rougvie (3), Harper	ACADEMICALS (1) 1
4 (9, 36 pen, 80, 86 pen),	Fairlie (2)
Sullivan (22),	
Kennedy (31)	

ABERDEEN: Leighton, Kennedy, McLelland, Rougvie, McLeish, Miller, Sullivan, Archibald, Harper, Fleming, Scanlon (Strachan)

HAMILTON: Ferguson, Grant, Kellachan, Fairlie, Dempsey, Alexander, Young (McDowell), Graham, Howie, Glavin, Reilly (Wright)

Attendance: 10,000   *Referee:* E. H. Pringle

For 60 seconds Hamilton dreamed of a sensation, as Fairlie ran 20 yards with the ball to level the aggregate scores. It was just what the game needed, for Hamilton were then hung, drawn and quartered.

Quarter Final 1st Leg Wednesday, 8 November

AYR UNITED (1) 3	ABERDEEN (2) 3
Cramond (3), McCall (48),	Sullivan (8),
S. McLelland (60)	Harper 2 (40, 71)

AYR: Sproat, Wells, Connor, McColl, McAllister, McSherry, McCall, McLaughlin, McLelland, Cramond, Christie

ABERDEEN: Clark, Kennedy, McLelland, McMaster (Fleming), McLeish, (Rougvie), Miller, Strachan, Archibald, Harper, Jarvie, Sullivan

Attendance: 6,300   *Referee:* B. R. McGinlay

Plenty of goals: plenty of bookings – including one for Ayr's manager, Ally McLeod, who wouldn't sit still in his dug-out. Ten minutes after the interval Archibald was sent packing for battering Sproat.

Quarter Final 2nd Leg Wednesday, 15 November

ABERDEEN (2) 3	AYR UNITED (1) 1
C. McLelland (25),	McLaughlin (9)
Harper (44),	
Archibald (85)	

ABERDEEN: Gardiner, Kennedy, McLelland, McMaster, Rougvie, Miller, Strachan, Archibald, Fleming (Scanlon), Harper, Sullivan

AYR: Sproat, Wells, Connor, McColl, McAllister, McSherry, McCall, McLaughlin, McLelland, Cramond (Phillips), Christie

Attendance: 13,000   *Referee:* T. Muirhead

Ayr followed Hamilton's example and hit Aberdeen when they were still cold. Ayr were looking forward to their 14th match without defeat until Aberdeen gradually exerted their superiority. Chic McLelland's surging overlap brought the Dons level.

Semi Final (Dens Park) Wednesday, 13 December

HIBERNIAN (0) 0 0	ABERDEEN (0) 1 1
	(After Extra Time)
	Kennedy (106)

HIBERNIAN: McDonald, Duncan, Kilgour, Bremner, Stewart, McNamara, Smith, McLeod, Refvik (Higgins), Callachan, Hutchinson

ABERDEEN: Clark, Kennedy, McLelland, Sullivan, Rougvie, Miller, Strachan, Archibald, Harper, Jarvie (McMaster), Scanlon (Cooper)

Attendance: 21,050   *Referee:* T. Muirhead

The second period of extra time was upon us when full-back Stuart Kennedy flighted an angled lob over McDonald's straining fingers. Earlier, the Hibs keeper had been the main reason for taking the tie into extra time – especially when touching Harper's volley against an upright.

League Cup Final (Hampden) Saturday, 31 March
RANGERS (0) 2   ABERDEEN (0) 1
  MacDonald (77),   Davidson (58)
  Jackson (90)

RANGERS: McCloy, Jardine, Dawson, Johnstone, Jackson, MacDonald, McLean, Russell, Urquhart (Miller), Smith, Cooper (Parlane)
ABERDEEN: Clark, Kennedy, McLelland, McMaster, Rougvie, Miller, Strachan, Archibald, Harper, Jarvie, Davidson (McLeish)

Referee: I. M. D. Foote

So, for the second time in a year Aberdeen come off worse in a cup final with Rangers. But this time Aberdeen did not freeze. They scored first when Davidson's header eluded McCloy's grasp. Unfortunately McMaster deflected MacDonald's shot wide of Bobby Clark. The game was already hard. Six players had been booked, culminating with Doug Rougvie being sent off for allegedly assaulting Johnstone. Colin Jackson's injury-time header was a punishment Aberdeen did not deserve.

SCOTTISH CUP

3rd Round Saturday, 27 January
HAMILTON   ABERDEEN (2) 2
  ACADEMICALS (0) 0   Miller (75), Harper (80)

HAMILTON: Ferguson, Frew, Kellachan, Fairlie, Dempsey, Alexander, Grant, Graham, Howie, McDowell, McManus
ABERDEEN: Clark, Kennedy, Considine, Strachan, Rougvie, Miller, Sullivan, Archibald, Harper, Jarvie (McMaster), Scanlon

Attendance: 8,000   *Referee:* I. M. D. Foote

Gordon Strachan takes the ball towards goal in an attempt to outwit the offside trap. Ferguson can't hold his shot, and Miller's follow-up screams past him.

4th Round Wednesday, 21 February
ABERDEEN (4) 6   AYR UNITED (0) 2
  Archibald 2 (4, 44),   Phillips (67),
  McMaster (12),   McLaughlin (87 pen)
  Scanlon 2 (34, 70),
  Harper (77)

ABERDEEN: Clark, Kennedy, Considine, McMaster, Rougvie, Miller, Sullivan (Harper), Archibald (Cooper), Scanlon, Jarvie, Strachan

AYR: Sproat, Wells, Kelly (Hannah), Fleeting, McAllister, McSherry, Phillips, McLaughlin, Connor, Cramond, Christie (McLelland)

Attendance: 11,500   *Referee:* R. B. Valentine

Aberdeen didn't have it this easy when the teams met in the League Cup in November. Mind you, Ayr had eleven men then. This time Jim McSherry was expelled six minutes from time.

Quarter Final Saturday, 10 March
ABERDEEN (1) 1   CELTIC (1) 1
  Harper (26)   Doyle (25)

ABERDEEN: Clark, Kennedy, McLelland, McMaster, McLeish, Miller, Sullivan, Archibald, Harper, Scanlon (Davidson), Strachan
CELTIC: Latchford, McGrain, Lynch, Aitken, MacDonald, Edvaldsson, Provan, McLeod, Conn, Burns, Doyle

Referee: I. M. D. Foote

Edvaldsson's header fell to Doyle to net from close range. Within seconds Kennedy despatched the ball into Harper's path, and King Joey volleyed an unforgettable goal past the advancing Latchford. Five players were booked.

Quarter Final Replay Wednesday, 14 March
CELTIC (0) 1   ABERDEEN (2) 2
  Lennox (63)   Davidson (2),
          Archibald (13)

CELTIC: Latchford, McGrain, Lynch, Aitken, MacDonald, Edvaldsson, Provan, McLeod, Conn (Lennox), Burns, Doyle
ABERDEEN: Clark, Kennedy, McLelland, McMaster, Rougvie, Miller, Sullivan (McLeish), Archibald, Harper (Scanlon), Jarvie, Davidson

Attendance: 37,000   *Referee:* I. M. D. Foote

Parkhead goes silent in two minutes after Harper had guided the ball into the path of Duncan Davidson – and is comatose as Archibald pops the ball over the stranded Latchford. Lennox was played onside by a ricochet between Rougvie and Miller to pull a goal back. Near the end missiles rained down from the terraces and there was some argy-bargy in the players' tunnel.

Semi Final (Hampden) Wednesday, 11 April
HIBERNIAN (2) 2   ABERDEEN (1) 1
  Rae (37),   Archibald (28)
  McLeod (43 pen)

HIBERNIAN: McArthur, Brazil, Duncan, Bremner, Stewart, McNamara, Rae, McLeod, Campbell, Callaghan, Brown
ABERDEEN: Gardiner, Kennedy, McLelland (Hamilton), Watson (McLeish), Rougvie, Miller, Strachan, Archibald, Harper, Jarvie, Scanlon

Attendance: 9,900   *Referee:* R. B. Valentine

Sweet revenge for Hibs, who lost to Aberdeen at the same stage in the League Cup four months earlier. It was an eerie spectacle: sparsely populated, mist-shrouded stadium. Aberdeen simply could not overcome their Hampden hoodoo. The decisive goal came from the spot after Rougvie made a hash of a tackle on McLeod. In the second half Harper managed to miss from a range of twelve inches.

EUROPEAN CUP-WINNERS CUP

1st Round, 1st Leg Wednesday, 13 September
MAREK DIMITROV   ABERDEEN (1) 2
  (Bulgaria) (0) 3   Jarvie (5), Harper (76)
  V. Petrov 2 (66, 70),
  I. Petrov (90)
MAREK: Stoinov, Sevdin, Kolev, Karakolev, Palev (Vukov), Rainov, Pargov, Tomov, I. Petrov, V. Petrov, Dimitrov
ABERDEEN: Leighton, Kennedy, McLelland, McMaster, Garner (Rougvie), Miller, Sullivan, Archibald, Harper, Jarvie, Scanlon
Attendance: 20,000   *Referee:* J. Van Melkebeke
                                (Belgium)

Although Aberdeen lost the Scottish Cup Final to Rangers, the Ibrox club are engaged in the European champions cup – hence the Dons' appearance in the Cup-Winners Cup. In Bulgaria the Petrov twins caused Aberdeen all kinds of bother. In aquatic conditions Verislav Petrov headed two goals from twin Ivan's crosses. In injury time Leighton was clearly impeded as Ivan the Terrible scrambled a goal for himself. Earlier in the second half Willie Garner had been carried off with a broken leg.

1st Round, 2nd Leg Wednesday, 27 September
ABERDEEN (0) 3   MAREK DIMITROV (0) 0
  Strachan (63), Jarvie (75),
  Harper (81)
ABERDEEN: Leighton, Kennedy, McLelland, McMaster, McLeish, Miller, Sullivan (Strachan), Archibald, Harper, Jarvie, Scanlon
MAREK: Stoinov, Sevdin, Kolev, Karakolev, Palev, Rainov, Pargov (Brankov), Tomov, I. Petrov, V. Petrov, Dimitrov (Vukov)

Aberdeen won 5-3 on aggregate
Attendance: 21,100   *Referee:* J. N. I. Keizer
                                (Holland)

A 1-0 win was all Aberdeen needed, but it took them over an hour to break down a packed Bulgarian defence. Substitute Strachan raced in to meet McMaster's chip. Stoinov almost saved – but not quite.

2nd Round, 1st Leg Wednesday, 18 October
FORTUNA   ABERDEEN (0) 0
  DÜSSELDORF
  (W. Germany) (1) 3
  Gunther 2 (15, 58),
  Zimmermann (81)
FORTUNA: Woyka, Brei, Zewe, Zimmermann, Baltes, Kohnen, Fanz, Lund (Bommer), Gunther (Schmitz), Allofs, Seel

ABERDEEN: Leighton, Kennedy, McLelland, McMaster (Scanlon), McLeish, Miller, Rougvie, Archibald, Harper, Jarvie (Strachan), Sullivan
Attendance: 10,000

The ball skidded off McMaster's head in front of Gunther, who claims the first goal. The Dons' back line statically appealed for offside as the same player burst through for the second. Zimmermann's 25-yard free kick past the Aberdeen wall was touched, but not saved, by Leighton.

2nd Round, 2nd Leg Wednesday, 1 November
ABERDEEN (0) 2   FORTUNA
  McLelland (54),   DÜSSELDORF (0) 0
  Jarvie (57)
ABERDEEN: Clark, Rougvie, McLelland, McMaster (Scanlon), McLeish, Miller, Strachan (Fleming), Archibald, Harper, Jarvie, Sullivan
FORTUNA: Woyka, Brei, Zewe, Zimmermann, Baltes, Kohnen, Weikl, Lund, Gunther, Allofs, Seel (Zimmer)
Attendance: 16,800

Bobby Clark was recalled for his first competitive match of the season after breaking his thumb. But he was largely idle. How Fortuna held out was a mystery, as in the final fifteen minutes the ball flew everywhere but in their net. Jarvie shot against Woyka, then into the side netting. Archibald's header was touched over: Jarvie hooked the ball inches too high, etc., etc.

1978-79

APPEARANCES	League	League Cup	Scottish Cup	Cup Winners Cup
Miller	34	8	5	4
Kennedy	32	8	5	3
Sullivan	32	6	4	4
Archibald	30(+2)	7	5	4
Strachan	26(+5)	5(+3)	4	1(+2)
Harper	25(+3)	7	4(+1)	4
McLelland	25(+1)	8	3	4
Jarvie	24(+3)	6	4	4
McMaster	24(+3)	6(+1)	3(+1)	4
Clark	23	3	4	1
Scanlon	22(+6)	5(+1)	4(+1)	2(+2)
McLeish	18(+1)	3(+1)	1(+2)	3
Rougvie	16(+5)	4(+2)	4	2(+1)
Garner	12	2		1
Leighton	11	3		3
McGhee	11			
Hamilton	9(+2)		–(+1)	
Davidson	7(+2)	2	1(+1)	
Fleming	4(+8)	3(+2)		–(+1)
Neil Cooper	3(+4)	–(+1)	–(+1)	
Considine	3(+3)		2	
Gardiner	2	2	1	
Watson	2		1	
Ritchie	1			
Joe Smith	–(+2)			
25 players				

GOALS	Total	League	League Cup	Scottish Cup	Cup Winners Cup
Harper	33	19	9	3	2
Archibald	20	13	3	4	
Jarvie	8	4	1		3
Sullivan	7	4	3		
Strachan	6	5			1
Scanlon	6	2	2	2	
McGhee	4	4			
McMaster	4	3		1	
Davidson	4	2	1	1	

GOALS	Total	League	League Cup	Scottish Cup	Cup Winners Cup
Kennedy	3		3		
Fleming	2	1	1		
McLelland	2		1		1
Cooper	1	1			
McLeish	1	1			
Rougvie	1		1		
Miller	1			1	
Total	103	59	25	12	7

Aberdeen clinch the Premier League at Easter Road, Edinburgh, on Saturday, 3rd May 1980, defeating Hibs by 5 goals to 0.

Season 1979-80

1979-80 was a peculiar, if ultimately memorable season. It was the year that one trophy seemingly destined for Pittodrie slipped away at the last moment, while another – altogether bigger prize – suddenly ended up in Aberdeen's lap.

The one that got away was the League Cup. In a barnstorming Autumn crusade Aberdeen took on Rangers in the third round, and beat them home and away. They were then paired with Celtic in the quarter finals – and beat them twice too. In the semis Aberdeen thought they deserved better than to be linked with their perennial bogey team and league leaders – Morton. But they survived. Just.

In the Final Ferguson's team faced Jim McLean's Dundee United, who had marched all the way to Hampden by stamping on all the little tiddlers who were thrown up on their path. They enjoyed what was probably the cushiest road to Hampden any Scottish team has ever trod. United's luck with the draw was followed by luck on the day. Aberdeen couldn't deliver the knock-out punch, so the teams tried again four days later at Dens Park. There, in monsoon conditions, Aberdeen learned that you cannot expect a second chance in a cup final. The trophy went over the road to Tannadice.

The weather and their League Cup engagements were playing havoc with Aberdeen's league fixtures. At one stage they were ten points behind Celtic – though with three games in hand. All Aberdeen could do was strike a winning sequence and hope that Celtic stumbled on the run-in. Celtic did more than stumble: they fell flat on their faces. In the space of 19 days in April they lost 5-1 at Dundee and twice at home to Aberdeen. The Dons' second win put their noses in front with just four matches to play – three of them away from home. They refused to panic and the title was theirs. Aberdeen were the Scottish champions for the first time in 25 years. More than that, the traditional fear of the Old Firm had been exorcised. Rangers faced Aberdeen seven times in all competitions. And beat them once. Celtic played the Dons six times. And beat them once. Together with Dundee United's success in the League Cup, there was talk of a 'New Firm' rising to challenge the geographical balance of power in Scottish football.

League:	Champions
League Cup:	Runners-Up
Scottish Cup:	Semi-Final
UEFA Cup:	First Round

SCOTTISH LEAGUE PREMIER DIVISION

No 1 Saturday, 11 August
PARTICK THISTLE (0) 1   ABERDEEN (0) 0
  McAdam (89 pen)
PARTICK: Rough, McKinnon, Whittaker, Gibson, Campbell (Wilson), Anderson, Park, Doyle, McAdam, Melrose, O'Hara
ABERDEEN: Clark, Rougvie, Considine, Cooper (Jarvie), Garner, McLeish, McGhee (Bell), Archibald, Sullivan, McMaster, Davidson

P	W	D	L	F	A	Pts
1	0	0	1	0	1	0

Attendance: 5,500
Referee: H. Robertson

The referee was about to blow for time when Alex McLeish's hand came in contact with the ball. Earlier Rougvie had grabbed Park by the shirt to prevent him bursting clear. Said Alex Ferguson in the *Green Final*, 'Don't laugh, but I've got a scent about the way things are going to turn out this season'.

No 2 Saturday, 18 August
ABERDEEN (1) 3   HIBERNIAN (0) 0
  Archibald (44),
  McMaster 2 (73, 89)
ABERDEEN: Clark, Kennedy, Considine, McLeish,
Garner, Miller, McGhee, Archibald, Strachan,
McMaster, Davidson (Jarvie)
HIBERNIAN: McArthur, Brazil, Duncan, Bremner,
Paterson, McNamara, Callachan, Campbell,
Hutchinson, J. Brown (Rae), Higgins

P	W	D	L	F	A	Pts	
2	1	0	1	3	1	2	

Attendance: 12,000
Referee: M. Delaney

Hibs' gesture of defiance in the first half came when
Campbell's shot hit the junction. 1-0, Archibald's
header. 2-0, McMaster's long-range drive. 3-0,
McMaster dribbles the ball round the keeper.

No 3 Saturday, 25 August
DUNDEE UNITED (0) 1   ABERDEEN (1) 3
  Sturrock (89)   McGhee (24),
                          Harper (59),
                          Archibald (63)
DUNDEE UNITED: Bonetti, Stewart, Kopel, Phillip
(Kirkwood), Stark, Narey, Addison, Sturrock, Dodds
(Ballantyne), Pettigrew, Payne
ABERDEEN: Clark, Kennedy, Considine, McLeish,
Garner, Miller, McGhee, Archibald, Harper
(Davidson), McMaster (Jarvie), Strachan

P	W	D	L	F	A	Pts	
3	2	0	1	6	2	4	

Attendance: 11,000

There is much interest in 37-year old ex-England
goalkeeper Peter Bonetti. He makes a mess of the
second goal, losing an aerial duel to Archibald before
Harper netted.

No 4 Saturday, 8 September
MORTON (1) 3   ABERDEEN (1) 2
  Thomson 2 (20, 64),   Archibald (34),
  Ritchie (60 pen)   McMaster (74)
MORTON: Baines, Hayes, Holmes, Anderson, Orr,
Rooney, McNeil, Hutchison, Thomson (McLaren),
Tolmie (Scott), Ritchie
ABERDEEN: Clark, Kennedy, Considine (Sullivan),
McLeish, Garner, Miller, McGhee (Jarvie), Archibald,
Harper, McMaster, Strachan

P	W	D	L	F	A	Pts	
4	2	0	2	8	5	4	

Attendance: 7,000
Referee: A. McGunnigle

Andy Ritchie destroyed Aberdeen virtually single-
handed – with a little assistance from Thomson, who
was tripped in the box by McLeish for Ritchie's
penalty.

No 5 Saturday, 15 September
ABERDEEN (1) 3   RANGERS (1) 1
  McMaster (19),   Johnstone (35)
  Strachan (75 pen),
  Rougvie (80)
ABERDEEN: Clark, Kennedy, Considine, McLeish,
Garner (Rougvie), Miller, Jarvie (Harper), Archibald,
Strachan, McMaster, Scanlon
RANGERS: McCloy, Jardine, Dawson, Stevens,
Jackson, Watson, Cooper, Russell, Johnstone,
MacDonald, Smith

Leading positions

	P	W	D	L	F	A	Pts
1 Celtic	5	3	2	0	15	7	8
2 ABERDEEN	5	3	0	2	11	6	6
3 Morton	5	3	0	2	13	10	6
4 Partick	5	2	2	1	6	5	6
5 Kilmarnock	5	2	2	1	4	7	6

Attendance: 23,000
Referee: A. G. McFaull

Eintracht Frankfurt spies are given plenty to think
about by this rampaging Dons' performance. There is
gleeful anticipation about the renewed acquaintance of
Derek Johnstone and Doug Rougvie – following
Rougvie's expulsion during last season's League Cup
Final. When he comes on as a second half sub he
immediately sets his Hampden tormentor spinning in
the air.

No 6 Saturday, 22 September
ABERDEEN (1) 1   CELTIC (1) 2
  Strachan (2)   Aitken (40), Doyle (74)
ABERDEEN: Clark, Kennedy, Considine (Rougvie),
McLeish, Garner, Miller, Jarvie (Davidson), Archibald,
Strachan, McMaster, Scanlon
CELTIC: Latchford, Sneddon, McGrain, Aitken,
MacDonald, McAdam, Doyle, Conroy, Lennox,
McLeod, Burns

P	W	D	L	F	A	Pts	
6	3	0	3	12	8	6	

Attendance: 22,000
Referee: T. Muirhead

This was a shameful match, full of hatred, not football.
Strachan streaked through the middle to give Aberdeen
the perfect start, but in the 34th minute was the victim
of a horrendous assault by Tommy Burns – who was
summarily expelled. Kennedy then tripped Lennox.
McLeod's penalty was blocked but Aitken was the first
to react.

No 7 Saturday, 29 September
DUNDEE (0) 0   ABERDEEN (2) 4
                          Jarvie 2 (8, 9),
                          Harper (77),
                          Archibald (80)
DUNDEE: Donaldson, Turnbull, Schaedler, Watson
(Fletcher), Glennie, McGeachie, Murphy, Miller,
Sinclair, McLaren, Shirra
ABERDEEN: Clark, Kennedy, Considine, Bell
(Scanlon), Garner, McLeish, Sullivan, Archibald,
Harper, McMaster, Jarvie

P	W	D	L	F	A	Pts	
7	4	0	3	16	8	8	

Attendance: 11,800
Referee: T. Kellock

Two quick headers from Drew Jarvie's balding head
settled the destiny of this match. Now for Eintracht
Frankfurt.

No 8 Saturday, 6 October
ST MIRREN (1) 2   ABERDEEN (1) 2
  Stark (14), Docherty (89)   Archibald (7),
                              Harper (68)
ST MIRREN: Thomson, Young, Munro, Richardson (Abercrombie), Dunlop, Copland, Bone, Stark, Torrance (Logan), McDougall, Docherty
ABERDEEN: Clark, Kennedy, Considine, McLeish, Garner (Sullivan), Miller, Strachan, Archibald, Harper, McMaster, Scanlon

P W D L F A Pts   *Attendance:* 8,600
8 4 1 3 18 10 9   *Referee:* D. A. Murdoch

Alex Ferguson was just seconds from seeing his new club beat his old for the first time, only to see Docherty fire a dramatic equaliser from a hectic scramble.

No 9 Saturday, 13 October
ABERDEEN (2) 3   KILMARNOCK (1) 1
  Scanlon (34),   Houston (11)
  Strachan (40 pen),
  Jarvie (89)
ABERDEEN: Clark, Kennedy, Considine, McLeish, Garner, Miller, Strachan, Archibald, Harper, McMaster (Sullivan), Scanlon (Jarvie)
KILMARNOCK: McCulloch, McLean, Robertson, Clark, Clarke, McDicken, Gibson, Maxwell, Bourke, Mauchlin (Cairnie), Houston (Street)

P W D L F A Pts   *Attendance:* 12,000
9 5 1 3 21 11 11   *Referee:* K. J. Hope

The Dons threw everything at Killie from the start and left themselves open to the counter-punch. Willie Miller did something unusual: he won a penalty instead of giving one away.

No 10 Saturday, 20 October
ABERDEEN (0) 1   PARTICK THISTLE (1) 1
  Davidson (62)   Doyle (44)
ABERDEEN: Clark, Kennedy, McMaster, McLeish, Garner, Miller, Strachan, Archibald, Harper, Jarvie (Bell), Scanlon (Davidson)
PARTICK: Rough, McKinnon, Whittaker, Campbell, Marr, O'Hara (Doyle), Park, Gibson, McGregor, McAdam, Love

Leading positions
                    P   W   D   L   F   A Pts
1 Celtic   10   6   3   1 23 10 15
2 Morton   10   6   2   2 24 15 14
3 ABERDEEN   10   5   2   3 22 12 12
4 Partick   10   4   4   2 12 10 12

Attendance: 8,000   *Referee:* H. Alexander

Two subs got into the act. Partick's Doyle volleyed McMaster's clearance back past Clark. Jarvie headed across goal to set up Davidson's equaliser. Thereafter Alan Rough took the honours.

No 11 Saturday, 27 October
HIBERNIAN (1) 1   ABERDEEN (0) 1
  Hutchinson (17)   Watson (89)

HIBERNIAN: McArthur, Brazil, J. Brown, S. Brown (Campbell), Paterson, Rae, Callaghan, Ward, Hutchinson, McLeod, Higgins
ABERDEEN: Clark, Kennedy, Considine (Watson), McLeish, Garner, Miller, Strachan, Archibald, Jarvie (Harper), McMaster, Scanlon

P W D L F A Pts   *Attendance:* 6,500
11 5 3 3 23 13 13   *Referee:* J. Renton

Hibs are rooted to the bottom of the Premier League, and rue Andy Watson's lethal shot from ten yards. Strachan set up the goal. Harper's appearance as a substitute didn't go down well with the local fans.

No 12 Saturday, 3 November
ABERDEEN (0) 0   DUNDEE UNITED (2) 3
                          Pettigrew (11),
                          Phillip (13), Bannon (81)
ABERDEEN: Clark, Kennedy, Considine, McLeish, Garner (Jarvie), Miller, Strachan, Archibald, Harper (Davidson), McMaster, Scanlon
DUNDEE UNITED: McAlpine, Stark, Kopel, Phillip, Hegarty, Narey, Bannon, Sturrock, Pettigrew, Fleming, Payne

P W D L F A Pts   *Attendance:* 11,000
12 5 3 4 23 16 13   *Referee:* I. M. D. Foote

Tangerine-scarved United fans were chanting 'Easy, Easy' before the end. And it was. Newcastle's scout came to look at Steve Archibald. He could have saved his train fare.

No 13 Saturday, 10 November
ABERDEEN (1) 1   MORTON (1) 2
  McLeish (4)   Thomson (15),
                          Ritchie (77)
ABERDEEN: Clark, Kennedy, Rougvie, Jarvie, McLeish, Miller, Strachan, Archibald, Watson (Harper), McMaster, Scanlon
MORTON: Baines, Hayes, Holmes, Anderson, McLaughlin, Orr, McNeil, Hutchinson, Thomson, Russell (Tolmie), Ritchie

P W D L F A Pts   *Attendance:* 11,000
13 5 3 5 24 18 13   *Referee:* M. Delaney

Andy Ritchie did his usual. Ambled about, looked lethargic, put the ball right on Thomson's instep, and finally controlled the ball with his left foot and scored with his right. McLeish's early rocket ended up counting for nothing.

No 14 Saturday, 17 November
RANGERS (0) 0   ABERDEEN (0) 1
                          Archibald (87)
RANGERS: McCloy, A. Forsyth, Dawson, Stevens, Jardine, Watson, McLean, Miller (J. MacDonald), Johnstone, A. MacDonald, Smith
ABERDEEN: Clark, Kennedy, Rougvie, McLeish, Garner, Miller, Strachan, Archibald, Harper, McMaster, Scanlon (McGhee)

P W D L F A Pts   *Attendance:* 18,000
14 6 3 5 25 18 15   *Referee:* D. Ramsay

An untidy game on an unhelpful pitch. It was an afternoon better spent indoors in front of the fire. Rangers have won only two of their last nine games and lost this one when Archibald poked the ball past McCloy; then gave it a bit of help when it stuck in the mud on the goal-line.

No 15 Saturday, 15 December
ABERDEEN (0) 2   ST MIRREN (0) 0
  McLeish (65),
  Hamilton (69)

ABERDEEN: Clark, Kennedy, McMaster (Rougvie), McLeish, Garner, Miller, Strachan, Archibald, Hamilton (McGhee), Jarvie, Hewitt

ST MIRREN: Thomson, Young, Abercrombie, Richardson, Fulton, Copland, Bone, Stark, Somner, McDougall, Weir

Leading positions

	P	W	D	L	F	A	Pts
1 Celtic	16	10	3	3	34	15	23
2 Morton	16	10	3	3	34	18	23
3 Rangers	18	8	3	7	26	23	19
4 ABERDEEN	15	7	3	5	27	18	17
5 St Mirren	17	6	5	6	24	29	17

Attendance: 6,000   *Referee:* D. F. Syme

Aberdeen's John Hewitt makes his debut in a match against opponents who include three future Dons – Stark, McDougall and Weir. Billy Thomson has a nightmare match, allowing both goals to slip through his legs.

No 16 Saturday, 5 January
MORTON (0) 1   ABERDEEN (0) 0
  McLaren (80)

MORTON: Baines, Hayes, Holmes, Anderson, McLaughlin, Orr, McLaren, Craig (Tolmie), Hutchinson, Scott, Ritchie

ABERDEEN: Clark, Kennedy, Considine, McLeish, Garner, Rougvie, Strachan, Archibald, Hamilton (McGhee), McMaster, Jarvie

P	W	D	L	F	A	Pts
16	7	3	6	27	19	17

Attendance: 7,000   *Referee:* B. R. McGinlay

The Cappielow pitch was so dreadful that during the interval a workman came on to try to fill in the pot-holes. This was Aberdeen's third league defeat by their bogey team this season, but they will not now lose on their league travels for the remainder of the season.

No 17 Saturday, 12 January
ABERDEEN (1) 3   RANGERS (1) 2
  Strachan (2),   J. McDonald (11),
  Archibald (70),   Jackson (49)
  Hamilton (89)

ABERDEEN: Clark, Kennedy, Considine, McLeish, Garner, Rougvie, Strachan, Archibald, Hamilton, McMaster, Scanlon (Hewitt)

RANGERS: McCloy, Jardine, Dawson (Smith), Forsyth, Jackson, Stevens, McLean, Russell, Parlane, A. MacDonald, J. McDonald

P	W	D	L	F	A	Pts
17	8	3	6	30	21	19

Attendance: 19,500
Referee: R. B. Valentine

Aberdeen capped and tailed an enthralling match with two delicious goals. Strachan opened the way with a 20-yard rocket. After Rangers had gone ahead Derek Hamilton squared for Archibald to level, and then had the joy of bagging that vital winner.

No 18 Saturday, 19 January
ABERDEEN (0) 0   CELTIC (0) 0

ABERDEEN: Clark, Kennedy, Considine, McLeish, Garner, Rougvie, Strachan, Archibald, Hamilton, McMaster, Scanlon (Jarvie)

CELTIC: Latchford, Sneddon, McGrain, Aitken, MacDonald, McAdam, Provan, Sullivan, Lennox, McLeod, Doyle

P	W	D	L	F	A	Pts
18	8	4	6	30	21	20

Attendance: 24.000

A point suits Celtic more than Aberdeen, so the gap remains ten points – though Aberdeen have three games in hand. The match started brightly but soon slumped. In needed a goal to lift it but didn't get one. Dominic Sullivan makes his first visit to Pittodrie since his transfer.

No 19 Saturday, 2 February
DUNDEE (1) 1   ABERDEEN (1) 3
  Redford:(20)   Jarvie 2 (2, 84),
                  Hamilton (71)

DUNDEE: Donaldson, Barr, Schaedler, Millar, Glennie, Shirra, Fletcher, Mackie, Pirie, Redford, Murphy

ABERDEEN: Clark, Kennedy, Rougvie, McLeish, Garner, Miller, Strachan, Jarvie, Hamilton, Bell, Scanlon

P	W	D	L	F	A	Pts
19	9	4	6	33	22	22

Attendance: 7,650   *Referee:* D. Syme

This was the only Premier League match to go ahead in white-capped Scotland. Late headers by Hamilton and Jarvie on the straw-strewn pitch secured both points.

No 20 Saturday, 9 February
ST MIRREN (0) 1   ABERDEEN (0) 1
  Stark (55 pen)   Strachan (47)

ST MIRREN: Thomson, Young, Munro, Richardson, Fulton, Copland, Bone, Stark, Somner, McDougall, Weir

ABERDEEN: Clark, Kennedy, McMaster, McLeish, Garner, Miller, Strachan, Jarvie, Hamilton, Bell (McGhee), Scanlon (Hewitt)

Leading positions

	P	W	D	L	F	A	Pts
1 Celtic	22	12	7	3	41	19	31
2 Morton	23	11	4	8	42	32	26
3 ABERDEEN	20	9	5	6	34	23	23
4 St Mirren	21	8	7	6	31	34	23

Attendance: 9,000   *Referee:* A. F. Harris

Billy Stark's goals against Aberdeen are becoming a nuisance. This time it's a penalty after Garner took the legs from under Peter Weir. Near the end Bobby Clark stuck out a foot to stop Frank McDougall scoring.

No 21 Saturday, 23 February
ABERDEEN (0) 1   KILMARNOCK (2) 2
  Archibald (88)   Street (4),
                             Garner o.g. (42)
ABERDEEN: Leighton, Kennedy, Hamilton, McLeish, Garner (Watson), Miller, Strachan, Archibald, Scanlon, Jarvie, Hewitt (Davidson)
KILMARNOCK: McCulloch, Welsh, McLean, Clark, McDicken, Houston, Mauchlen, Gibson, Cramond, Street

P W D L F A Pts   *Attendance:* 10,500
21 9 5 7 35 25 23   *Referee:* K. J. Hope

The Dons are in total disarray after Jim Leighton pushes Ormond's cross to the feet of Street, and Garner stabs another cross into his own goal.

No 22 Saturday, 1 March
ABERDEEN (1) 1   PARTICK THISTLE (1) 1
  Jarvie (41)   Melrose (28)
ABERDEEN: Clark, Kennedy, McMaster, McLeish, Rougvie, Miller, Strachan (Watson), Archibald, Hamilton, Jarvie, Scanlon
PARTICK: Rough, McKinnon, Whittaker, Campbell, McAdam, O'Hara, Doyle, Gibson, Jardine, Melrose, Wilson (McDonald)

P W D L F A Pts   *Attendance:* 9,000
22 9 6 7 36 26 24   *Referee:* E. H. Pringle

Next week the teams meet again in the Scottish Cup. Partick were encouraged when Melrose headed the ball through Clark's hands. Jarvie equalised after McKinnon had cleared off the line.

No 23 Saturday, 15 March
ABERDEEN (1) 2   DUNDEE UNITED (0) 1
  Jarvie (41), Watson (72)   Kirkwood (56)
ABERDEEN: Clark, Kennedy, Rougvie, Watson (Bell), McLeish, Miller, Strachan, Archibald, Hamilton (McGhee), McMaster, Jarvie
DUNDEE UNITED: McAlpine, Stark, Kopel, Fleming (Addison), Hegarty, Narey, Bannon, Sturrock, Pettigrew, Holt (Milne), Kirkwood

P W D L F A Pts   *Attendance:* 10,000
23 10 6 7 38 27 26   *Referee:* A. McGunnigle

United need a point in their battle against relegation and they seem to have earned one when Kirkwood's long innocuous cross was allowed by a trance-like Clark to swing into the net. Mark McGhee dragged defenders with him to permit Watson to restore the lead.

No 24 Wednesday, 19 March
ABERDEEN (1) 3   DUNDEE (0) 0
  Watson (29), Jarvie (80),
  Miller (87)
ABERDEEN: Clark, Kennedy, Rougvie, Watson, McLeish, Miller, Strachan, Archibald, Hamilton (Scanlon), McMaster, Jarvie

DUNDEE: Donaldson, Barr, Schaedler, McLaren, Glennie, McGeachie, Mackie, Millar, Fleming, Sinclair (Corrigan), Murphy (Ferguson)

P W D L F A Pts   *Attendance:* 7,000
24 11 6 7 41 27 28   *Referee:* B. R. McGinlay

Aberdeen were never going to lose. But they were never sure of winning until John McMaster turned the ball into the path of Drew Jarvie – who has now scored six goals in three matches against Dundee this season.

No 25 Saturday, 22 March
ABERDEEN (0) 1   MORTON (0) 0
  Jarvie (51)
ABERDEEN: Clark, Kennedy, Rougvie, Watson (McGhee), McLeish, Miller, Strachan, Archibald, Jarvie, McMaster, Scanlon
MORTON: Baines, Orr, Holmes, Anderson, McLaughlin, Rooney, Scott, McLaren, Thomson, Hutchinson (Tolmie), Ritchie

Leading positions

	P	W	D	L	F	A	Pts
1 Celtic	26	13	10	3	47	24	36
2 ABERDEEN	25	12	6	7	42	27	30
3 Morton	28	12	5	11	46	39	29
4 St Mirren	26	10	9	7	40	40	29

Attendance: 7,250   *Referee:* C. J. White

Morton's early season bubble has burst, and the Dons gather their first league points from the Cappielow side. Drew Jarvie's fifth goal in successive games came after McGhee's effort had hit the post and Archibald's follow-up was cleared off the line.

No 26 Saturday, 29 March
RANGERS (1) 2   ABERDEEN (1) 2
  Jardine (44 pen),   Archibald (35),
  J. McDonald (60)   Jarvie (84)
RANGERS: McCloy, Jardine, Dawson, Forsyth, Jackson, Stevens, McLean, Russell, Cooper, Smith, J. McDonald
ABERDEEN: Clark, Kennedy, McMaster (Bell), McLeish, Rougvie, Miller, Strachan, Archibald, McGhee, Jarvie, Scanlon

P W D L F A Pts   *Attendance:* 20,000
26 12 7 7 44 29 31   *Referee:* K. J. Hope

This is the sixth meeting of the sides this season in league and League Cup – and Rangers haven't won any of them. McLeish's tackle on Gordon Smith produced Rangers' equaliser. John McDonald steered home Russell's shot, but Drew Jarvie – the Dons man in form – rescued a point.

No 27 Tuesday, 1 April
KILMARNOCK (0) 0   ABERDEEN (1) 4
                             Clarke o.g. (26),
                             Strachan (69),
                             Kennedy (78),
                             McGhee (86)

KILMARNOCK: McCulloch, Welsh, McLean, Maxwell, Clarke, McDicken, Houston, Mauchlen, Doherty, Cramond (Gibson), Street

ABERDEEN: Clark, Kennedy, Rougvie, Watson (Scanlon), McLeish, Miller, Strachan, Archibald, McGhee, McMaster, Bell (Jarvie)

P	W	D	L	F	A	Pts	*Attendance:* 5,000
27	13	7	7	48	29	33	*Referee:* A. Ferguson

Killie's Paul Clarke got in the way of McGhee's effort for goal No 1. Best of the lot was Stuart Kennedy's surging run from his own half outpacing the pursuing defenders. Overall, Aberdeen's most irresistible performance of the season.

No 28 Saturday, 5 April
CELTIC (1) 1   ABERDEEN (1) 2
 Doyle (23)   Jarvie (19), McGhee (56)

CELTIC: Latchford, Sneddon, McGrain, Aitken, MacDonald, McAdam (Lennox), Provan, Doyle, McGarvey, McLeod, Burns

ABERDEEN: Clark, Kennedy, Rougvie, Watson (Bell), McLeish, Miller, Strachan, Archibald, McGhee, Jarvie (McMaster), Scanlon

P	W	D	L	F	A	Pts	*Attendance:* 40,000
28	14	7	7	50	30	35	*Referee:* D. Ramsay

Aberdeen simply had to win. McGhee took the ball round Latchford for Jarvie's opener. Doyle's back-header made it all square. After a Scanlon shot was blocked, McGhee thumped the rebound past Latchford. Then drama. Clark pushed McGarvey. Penalty. Clark dived to save from Lennox and Celtic's unbeaten home record had gone.

No 29 Monday, 7 April
ABERDEEN (0) 2   DUNDEE (1) 1
 Strachan (60 pen),   Fleming (3)
 Jarvie (74)

ABERDEEN: Clark, Kennedy, Rougvie (McMaster), Watson, McLeish, Miller, Strachan, Archibald, McGhee, Jarvie, Scanlon

DUNDEE: Donaldson, Barr, Millar, McLaren, Glennie, McGeachie, Mackie, Sinclair (Corrigan), Fleming, Shirra, Ferguson

Leading positions

	P	W	D	L	F	A	Pts
1 Celtic	29	15	10	4	53	26	40
2 ABERDEEN	29	15	7	7	52	31	37
3 Morton	31	14	6	11	50	40	34
4 St Mirren	29	12	10	7	45	41	34

Attendance: 12,000   *Referee:* K. Stewart

Former Don, Ian Fleming, does Aberdeen no favours with his quick-off-the-mark volley past Clark. But when Mark McGhee landed on his bottom after worming his way through the Dundee defence, Strachan obliged with a penalty.

No 30 Wednesday, 16 April
ABERDEEN (0) 1   HIBERNIAN (0) 1
 Watson (80)   Rae (66)

ABERDEEN: Clark, Kennedy, McMaster, Rougvie, McLeish, Miller, Strachan, Archibald, McGhee (Hamilton), Jarvie, Scanlon (Watson)

HIBERNIAN: McArthur, McNamara, Duncan, Paterson, Stewart, Rae, Callachan, Lambie, Torrance (McLeod), Hutchinson, Best

P	W	D	L	F	A	Pts	*Attendance:* 16,000
30	15	8	7	53	32	38	*Referee:* D. A. Murdoch

Pittodrie is rocked by rumours that Steve Archibald is on the point of signing for Tottenham. If the Dons can't beat sad, dejected Hibs, how can anybody take seriously their claim to the championship? Hibs paraded George Best – who did absolutely nothing, apart from being booked.

No 31 Saturday, 19 April
KILMARNOCK (1) 1   ABERDEEN (3) 3
 Gibson (15 pen)   Strachan (13 pen),
                                     McGhee (24),
                                     Archibald (25)

KILMARNOCK: McCulloch, Welsh, Robertson, Clark, Clarke, McDicken, Gibson, Mauchlen, Bourke, McLean, Street

ABERDEEN: Clark, Kennedy, McMaster, Hamilton, Rougvie, Miller, Strachan, Archibald, McGhee (Scanlon), Jarvie, Watson

P	W	D	L	F	A	Pts	*Attendance:* 7,500
31	16	8	7	56	33	40	*Referee:* I. M. D. Foote

Astonishing news from Dens Park. Celtic have lost 5-1 to Dundee. Aberdeen hero is Willie Miller. After conceding Kilmarnock's equalising penalty, the Dons' skipper takes a heavy knock in the second half. Alex Ferguson calls for him to come off. But Miller refuses.

No 32 Wednesday, 23 April
CELTIC (1) 1   ABERDEEN (2) 3
 McCluskey (11 pen)   Archibald (9),
                                     McGhee (45),
                                     Strachan (65)

CELTIC: Latchford, McGrain, McLeod, Aitken, MacDonald, McAdam, Provan, Conroy (McGarvey), McCluskey, Burns, Doyle

ABERDEEN: Clark, Kennedy, Rougvie, Watson, McLeish, Miller, Strachan, Archibald, McGhee, McMaster, Scanlon

Leading positions

	P	W	D	L	F	A	Pts
1 ABERDEEN	32	17	8	7	59	34	42
2 Celtic	33	16	10	7	57	37	42
3 St Mirren	32	14	11	7	51	44	39

Attendance: 48,000   *Referee:* D. S. Downie

This is Aberdeen's most vital league match of the season. The result is an even more emphatic win at Parkhead than that secured earlier in the month. It provided a contrast in emotions for Gordon Strachan, having a penalty saved by Latchford at 1-1, before side-footing the third and decisive goal when Latchford dropped the ball.

No 33 Saturday, 26 April
ABERDEEN (2) 2   ST MIRREN (0) 0
  Scanlon (25),
  Rougvie (42)
ABERDEEN: Clark, Kennedy, Rougvie, Watson,
McLeish, Miller, Strachan, Archibald, McGhee,
McMaster, Scanlon
ST MIRREN: Thomson, Young, Abercrombie, Munro,
Fulton, Copland, Bone, Stark, Somner, Weir, Logan

P	W	D	L	F	A	Pts	
33	18	8	7	61	34	44	

Attendance: 20,000
Referee: R. B. Valentine

Pittodrie senses the incredible. St Mirren can still win
the championship themselves. McGhee's scintillating
run brought him a corner, headed in by Scanlon. Then
Thomson plunges to parry Archibald's flick, but big
Doug Rougvie is in the right spot. Now Aberdeen have
three away games left.

No 34 Tuesday, 29 April
DUNDEE UNITED (0) 1   ABERDEEN (1) 1
  Holt (49)   Strachan (16)
DUNDEE UNITED: Graham, Kirkwood, Stark,
Phillip, Hegarty, Narey, Bannon, Sturrock, Pettigrew
(Milne), Holt, Dodds
ABERDEEN: Clark, Kennedy, Rougvie, McMaster,
McLeish, Miller, Strachan, Archibald, McGhee
(Hamilton), Jarvie (Watson), Scanlon

P	W	D	L	F	A	Pts
34	18	9	7	62	35	45

Attendance: 12,950
Referee: D. S. Downie

Aberdeen use up their game in hand over Celtic and
move one point clear. Scotland's Player of the Year,
Gordon Strachan, fires in the first goal that United have
conceded in 16 hours of league football. It flew in from
almost 30 yards and would have deserved both points.

No 35 Saturday, 3 May
HIBERNIAN (0) 0   ABERDEEN (2) 5
                         Archibald (26),
                         Watson (28),
                         Scanlon 2 (67, 88),
                         McGhee (84)
HIBERNIAN: Huggins, Brown, Duncan, Paterson,
Stewart, Callachan, Murray, McNamara, Torrance,
Brazil, Cormack
ABERDEEN: Clark, Kennedy, Rougvie, Watson,
McLeish, Miller, Strachan, Archibald, McGhee,
McMaster, Scanlon

P	W	D	L	F	A	Pts
35	19	9	7	67	35	47

Attendance: 12,900
Referee: B. R. McGinlay

'Here we go, here we go.' Aberdeen never had any
problem with bottom-placed Hibs, or with young Dave
Huggins making his home debut in goal. But all the
transistors were turned into Paisley. The Dons would be
champions if Celtic dropped a point. Celtic were
awarded a penalty with ten minutes to play, but after
consulting a linesman the referee changed his mind and
decided the infringement was outside the box. The
match ended goal-less and Aberdeen were the Kings of
Scotland.

No 36 Wednesday, 7 May
PARTICK THISTLE (1) 1   ABERDEEN (1) 1
  Melrose (22)   McKinnon o.g. (23)
PARTICK: McNab, McKinnon, Whittaker, Higgins,
Campbell, Anderson, Park, Melrose, McAdam
(Jardine), O'Hara, McDonald (Gibson)
ABERDEEN: Clark, Kennedy, Rougvie, McMaster,
McLeish, Miller, Jarvie, Archibald, McGhee, Watson,
Scanlon (Bell)

Attendance: 6,500   *Referee:* T. Kellock

Mathematically, Celtic can still win the title if Partick
beat Aberdeen by ten clear goals. All Aberdeen had to
play for was their self-respect: they haven't beaten
Thistle all season in the league.

Aberdeen's complete home and away record:

	HOME						AWAY						
P	W	D	L	F	A		W	D	L	F	A	Pts
36	10	4	4	30	18		9	6	3	38	18	48

Scottish League Premier Division 1979-80

		P	W	D	L	F	A	Pts
1	ABERDEEN	36	19	10	7	68	36	48
2	Celtic	36	18	11	7	61	38	47
3	St Mirren	36	15	12	9	56	49	42
4	Dundee United	36	12	13	11	43	30	37
5	Rangers	36	15	7	14	50	46	37
6	Morton	36	14	8	14	51	46	36
7	Partick Thistle	36	11	14	11	43	47	36
8	Kilmarnock	36	11	11	14	36	52	33
9	Dundee	36	10	6	20	47	73	26
10	Hibernian	36	6	6	24	29	67	18

LEAGUE CUP

1st Round, 1st Leg Wednesday, 15 August
ABERDEEN (3) 4   ARBROATH (0) 0
  McGhee (6),
  Davidson (16),
  McMaster (26),
  Jarvie (62)
ABERDEEN: Clark, Kennedy, Considine, McLeish,
Garner, Rougvie, McGhee, Archibald (Jarvie),
Strachan, McMaster, Davidson
ARBROATH: Lister, McKenzie, Rylance, Cargill,
Carson, Wilson, Stark (Forsyth), Gavine, Mylles, Kidd,
Yule (Copeland)

Attendance: 8,000   *Referee:* W. Waddell

The Dons wore black armbands, and a minute's silence
was observed, in memory of William Gauld, the
Pittodrie groundsman, who died at the weekend.

1st Round, 2nd Leg Wednesday, 22 August
ARBROATH (2) 2   ABERDEEN (1) 1
  Wilson (16), Mylles (33)   Harper (36)
ARBROATH: Lister, Scrimgeour, Rylance, Cargill,
McKenzie, Kydd, Wilson, Gavine, Mylles, Kidd, Yule
(Stark)

ABERDEEN: Clark, Kennedy, Considine, McLeish, Garner, Miller, Strachan (Bell), Archibald, Harper, McMaster, Jarvie

Attendance: 2,200   *Referee:* T. Muirhead

When Mylles headed past Clark to halve Aberdeen's four-goal advantage, the match took on added urgency. Try as they might, the Dons couldn't achieve a face-saving draw.

2nd Round, 1st Leg Wednesday, 29 August

MEADOWBANK   ABERDEEN (1) 5
THISTLE (0) 0   McGhee (26),
                    Strachan (70),
                    McMaster 2 (75, 85),
                    Garner (80)

MEADOWBANK: Johnston, Dunn, Fraser, Brown, Wight, Leetion, Small, Boyd, Jobson, Conroy, Davidson

ABERDEEN: Clark, Kennedy, Considine, McLeish, Garner, Rougvie, McGhee, Archibald, Harper (Davidson), McMaster, Strachan

Attendance: 1,200   *Referee:* K. Stewart

Aberdeen repeated the scoreline achieved at Meadowbank in the League Cup last season. Thistle gave a good account of themselves until their legs gave way.

2nd Round, 2nd Leg Saturday, 1 September

ABERDEEN (0) 2   MEADOWBANK
McMaster (47),   THISTLE (0) 2
Strachan (71 pen)   Jobson 2 (65, 84)

ABERDEEN: Clark, Kennedy, Considine, McLeish (Jarvie), Garner, Rougvie, McGhee (Davidson), Archibald, Harper, McMaster, Strachan

MEADOWBANK: Johnston, Dunn, Fraser, Forte, Brown, Leetion, McKenna, Boyd, Jobson, Conroy, Ross (McGowan)

Referee: A. C. Harris

Meadowbank succeeded in producing a few blushes, if not an upset. Jobson's second equaliser was an insulting free kick bent round the Dons' defensive wall.

3rd Round, 1st Leg Wednesday, 26 September

ABERDEEN (2) 3   RANGERS (0) 1
Garner (27), Harper (35),   Johnstone (73)
McLeish (66)

ABERDEEN: Clark, Kennedy, Considine, McLeish, Garner, Miller, Strachan, Archibald, Harper, McMaster (Rougvie), Scanlon

RANGERS: McCloy, Jardine, Dawson, Stevens, Jackson, Watson, Cooper, Miller, Johnstone, McDonald (McLean), Smith

Attendance: 22,000   *Referee:* R. B. Valentine

Harper headed on to Garner, who headed the Dons in front. Scanlon hit the bar, the rebound hit McCloy, and Harper poked a second. McLeish's 20-yard try flew out of McCloy's hands and over the line. Derek Johnstone's lob sent up an enthralling second leg.

3rd Round, 2nd Leg Wednesday, 10 October

RANGERS (0) 0   ABERDEEN (2) 2
                    Harper (33),
                    Strachan (36)

RANGERS: McCloy, Jardine, Dawson, Stevens, Jackson, Watson (Smith), McLean (Mackay), McDonald, Johnstone, Parlane, Cooper

ABERDEEN: Clark, Kennedy, Considine, McLeish, Garner, Miller, Strachan (Sullivan), Archibald (McMaster), Harper, Jarvie, Scanlon

Attendance: 35,000   *Referee:* E. H. Pringle

Aberdeen tormented Rangers, publicly humiliated them and made partial amends for the controversial defeat in last year's final. Harper's one-two with Archibald ended 'Gers hopes, and Strachan's blistering shot left them without anywhere to hide.

Quarter Final 1st Leg Wednesday, 31 October

ABERDEEN (2) 3   CELTIC (1) 2
Archibald 3 (6, 29, 61)   Edvaldsson (1),
                    Provan (70)

ABERDEEN: Clark, Kennedy, Considine, McLeish, Garner, Miller, Strachan, Archibald, Harper (Jarvie), McMaster, Scanlon (Bell)

CELTIC: Latchford, Sneddon, McGrain, Aitken, MacDonald, McLeod, Provan, Edvaldsson, McAdam, Conroy, Doyle (Lennox)

Attendance: 24,000   *Referee:* G. B. Smith

An all-ticket crowd saw an all-ticket cracker – and the sight of Willie Miller changing his torn shorts in the dug-out. Hat-trick hero Steve Archibald showed the variety of his talents. No 1 was with his left foot, No 2 with his head, and No 3 with his right foot. If he'd scored a 4th, it would have been with his backside.

Quarter Final 2nd Leg Saturday, 24 November

CELTIC (0) 0   ABERDEEN (0) 1
                    McGhee (50)

CELTIC: Latchford, Sneddon, McGrain, Aitken, McAdam, McLeod, Provan, McCluskey (MacDonald), Edvaldsson, Conroy, Lennox

ABERDEEN: Clark, Kennedy, Rougvie, McLeish, Garner, Miller, Strachan, Archibald, Harper (McGhee), McMaster, Scanlon

Referee: B. R. McGinlay

Joe Harper was carried off early, and his replacement – McGhee – relieved the pressure around Clark by being in the right place to collect Garner's knockdown. There were four bookings – Harper, McLeish and Rougvie of Aberdeen.

Semi Final (Hampden) Saturday, 1 December

MORTON (0) 1   ABERDEEN (2) 2
Ritchie (81 pen)   McGhee (14),
                    Strachan (44 pen)

MORTON: Baines, Hayes, Holmes, Anderson, McLaughlin, Orr, McNeil (Tolmie), Millar (Scott), Thomson, Hutchinson, Ritchie

ABERDEEN: Clark, Kennedy, Rougvie, McLeish, Garner, Miller, Strachan, Archibald, McGhee, McMaster, Scanlon

Referee: A. W. Waddell

It looked so easy for Aberdeen in the first half. But in the second, the Premier League leaders were frustrated by Ritchie's prodigious shot which came back off Clark's bar, and by Orr's thunderbolt 'goal' that was disallowed for some reason. The valium dose for Aberdeen by the close was excessive.

League Cup Final (Hampden) Saturday, 8 December
DUNDEE UNITED (0) 0   ABERDEEN (0) 0
(After Extra Time)

DUNDEE UNITED: McAlpine, Stark, Kopel, Phillip (Fleming), Hegarty, Narey, Bannon, Sturrock, Pettigrew, Holt, Payne (Murray)
ABERDEEN: Clark, Kennedy, Rougvie, McLeish, Garner, Miller, Strachan, Archibald, McGhee (Jarvie), McMaster, Scanlon

Attendance: 21,173   *Referee: B. R. McGinlay*

Dundee United have reached Hampden despite not having had to play a single Premier League opponent en route. Aberdeen have had to contend with both of the Old Firm, plus league leaders Morton. Hampden's smallest ever crowd for a League Cup Final sees Aberdeen in undisputed command. But they fritter their chances, especially Willie Garner's header which rolled along the goal-line before stopping in the mud.

League Cup Final Replay (Dens Park) Wednesday, 12 December
DUNDEE UNITED (1) 3   ABERDEEN (0) 0
    Pettigrew 2 (14, 66),
    Sturrock (76)

DUNDEE UNITED: McAlpine, Stark, Kopel, Fleming, Hegarty, Narey, Bannon, Sturrock, Pettigrew, Holt, Kirkwood
ABERDEEN: Clark, Kennedy, Rougvie, McLeish, Garner, Miller, Strachan, Archibald, McGhee (Jarvie), McMaster, Scanlon

Attendance: 30,000   *Referee: B. R. McGinlay*

Pressure by both clubs has the Bell's League Cup Final transferred from Hampden to Dens Park. The pitch was hardly playable, and Aberdeen were well and truly sunk on it. They brought instant unpopularity upon themselves when they took the field and trotted straight to the United 'end'. Dundee United, reprieved on Saturday, won without contradiction. Willie Pettigrew, their £100,000 buy, sprang the leak in the Dons' bows to help United win their first-ever trophy.

SCOTTISH CUP

3rd Round Saturday, 26 January
ARBROATH (1) 1   ABERDEEN (1) 1
    Stark (45)   Archibald (25)

ARBROATH: Lister, McKenzie, Scrimgeour (Durno), Cargill, Wells, Kidd, Stark (Yule), Mylles, Barbour, Gavine, Wilson

ABERDEEN: Clark, Kennedy, Considine (Bell), McLeish, Rougvie, Miller, Strachan (Davidson), Archibald, Hamilton, McMaster, Scanlon

Referee: D. Ramsay

Five months earlier Aberdeen lost 2-1 at Arbroath in the League Cup. Aberdeen are simply too terrible to believe, and will have to try again as a consequence of Considine being caught in possession by Stark. Representatives of English First Division strugglers Bristol City take in Willie Miller's performance.

3rd Round Replay Wednesday, 30 January
ABERDEEN (1) 5   ARBROATH (0) 0
    Hamilton (3),
    Scanlon 3 (50, 66, 86 pen),
    Archibald (62)

ABERDEEN: Clark, Kennedy, McMaster, McLeish, Rougvie, Miller, Strachan (Bell), Archibald (Hewitt), Hamilton, Jarvie, Scanlon

ARBROATH: Lister, McKenzie, Scrimgeour, Cargill, Wells, Kidd, Stark, Mylles, Gavine (Durno), Barbour (Yule), Wilson

Attendance: 10,000   *Referee: D. Ramsay*

Aberdeen's defence are permitted the day off as Arbroath summon all hands to man the barricades. They couldn't prevent Ian Scanlon scoring his first hat-trick for Aberdeen.

4th Round Saturday, 16 February
ABERDEEN (4) 8   AIRDRIEONIANS (0) 0
    Archbald 4 (11, 15, 43, 45),
    Miller (79), Strachan (80),
    McMaster (86)
    Scanlon (90)

ABERDEEN: Leighton, Kennedy, McMaster, Bell, Garner, Miller, Strachan, Archibald, Hamilton (Davidson), Jarvie, Scanlon

AIRDRIE: McGarr, Erwin (McGuire), Lapsley, Walker, March, Anderson, McClymont, Clark, McCulloch, Gordon, McKeown (Hamilton)

Attendance: 11,000   *Referee: R. Valentine*

Airdrie are chasing promotion to the Premier Division. They are now probably having second thoughts. Goal of the match was Willie Miller's airborne scissors-kick. Airdrie were not helped by having McCulloch and March sent off.

Quarter Final Saturday, 8 March
PARTICK THISTLE (0) 1   ABERDEEN (0) 2
    McAdam (88)   Jarvie (62),
                         Archibald (83)

PARTICK: Rough, McKinnon, Whittaker, Campbell, McAdam, Anderson, Doyle, Melrose, O'Hara, Gibson, Wilson (McDonald)

ABERDEEN: Clark, Kennedy, McMaster, McLeish, Rougvie, Miller, Strachan, Archibald, Hamilton, Jarvie, Watson (Bell)

Referee: J. R. S. Renton

For the first 45 minutes Aberdeen operated with a five-man defensive screen – Thistle fashion. Then Jarvie's head connected with Archibald's flick-on. Kennedy and Watson bruised Rough's woodwork before the game produced its late flurry.

Semi Final (Celtic Park) Saturday, 12 April
RANGERS (0) 1   ABERDEEN (0) 0
  Johnstone (75)
RANGERS: McCloy, Jardine, Miller, Forsyth, Jackson, Stevens, Cooper, Russell, Johnstone, Smith, J. McDonald
ABERDEEN: Clark, Kennedy, Rougvie, Watson (McMaster), McLeish, Miller, Strachan, Archibald, McGhee (Bell), Jarvie, Scanlon

Attendance: n.a.   *Referee:* D. S. Downie

Lucky '7' for Rangers as they beat Aberdeen for the first time in seven attempts this season. They needed four players booked to gain this distinction. Derek Johnstone's only contribution to the match was to hook a low shot past Clark from the edge of the box.

UEFA CUP

1st Round, 1st Leg Wednesday, 19 September
ABERDEEN (0) 1   EINTRACHT
  Harper (52)   FRANKFURT (1) 1
                  (West Germany)
                  Cha Bum Kun (13)
ABERDEEN: Clark, Kennedy, Considine, Sullivan, Garner, Miller, Strachan, Archibald, Harper (Jarvie), McMaster (Davidson), Scanlon
EINTRACHT: Funk, Müller, Neuberger, Korbel, Pezzey, Lorant, Holzenbein, Trapp, Lottermann (Karger), Grabowski, Cha Bum Kun

Attendance: 20,000   *Referee:* L. Agnolin (Italy)

Eintracht's great claim to fame was when losing the 1960 European Cup Final 7-3 to Real Madrid at Hampden Park. Their current side includes six internationals, most notable among them being Jurgen Grabowski and Bernd Holzenbein. But it was South Korean international Cha Bum Kun who seized on Holzenbein's misplaced header. 0-1. Harper then chested down Scanlon's cross, fended off two challenges and slid the ball past Funk.

1st Round, 2nd Leg Wednesday, 3 October
EINTRACHT   ABERDEEN (0) 0
  FRANKFURT (0) 1
  Holzenbein (50)
EINTRACHT: Funk, Müller, Neuberger, Korbel, Pezzey, Lorant, Holzenbein, Nachtweih, Karger (Borchers), Grabowski, Cha Bum Kun
ABERDEEN: Clark, Kennedy, Considine (Garner), Jarvie, McLeish, Miller, Strachan, Archibald, Harper, McMaster (Sullivan), Scanlon

Attendance: 20,000   *Referee:* A. L. Castillo (Spain)

In the Wald Stadium it took a goal by 33-year old Holzenbein to put Aberdeen out of European football for another year. Earlier Strachan's effort had struck Funk's body. McMaster's point-blank shot was also kept out. At the close, Cha Bum Kun wobbled the Dons' crossbar.

1979-80

APPEARANCES	League	League Cup	Scottish Cup	UEFA Cup
Clark	35	11	4	2
Kennedy	35	11	5	2
McLeish	35	11	4	1
Archibald	34	11	5	2
Strachan	33	11	5	2
McMaster	32(+2)	10(+1)	4(+1)	2
Miller	31	8	5	2
Scanlon	25(+4)	7	4	2
Jarvie	22(+8)	2(+5)	4	1(+1)
Rougvie	22(+3)	7(+1)	4	
Garner	20	11	1	1(+1)
McGhee	15(+6)	6(+1)	1	
Considine	14	7	1	2
Watson	12(+5)		2	
Hamilton	11(+2)		4	
Harper	8(+3)	7		2
Bell	4(+6)	−(+2)	1(+4)	
Davidson	2(+5)	1(+2)	−(+2)	−(+1)
Sullivan	2(+3)	−(+1)	−(+1)	1(+1)
Hewitt	2(+2)			
Neil Cooper	1			
Leighton	1		1	
22 players				

GOALS	Total	League	League Cup	Scottish Cup	UEFA Cup
Archibald	22	12	3	7	
Strachan	15	10	4	1	
Jarvie	14	12	1	1	
McGhee	10	6	4		
McMaster	9	4	4	1	
Scanlon	8	4		4	
Harper	7	3	3		1
Watson	5	5			
Hamilton	4	3		1	
McLeish	3	2	1		
Rougvie	2	2			
Davidson	1	2	1		
Miller	1	1		1	
Garner	2		2		
Kennedy	1	1			
own-goals	2	2			
Total	108	68	23	16	1

Season 1980-81

1980-81 could really be summed up in one word – Liverpool. Aberdeen's first crack at the European Cup brought them a daunting appointment with the legendary English champions. Both before and afterwards, the shadow of Anfield hung over every match Aberdeen played. The occasion itself was one of humiliation for the Dons: sunk by a goal of genius at Pittodrie; buried under an avalanche at Anfield.

At the time, Aberdeen were perched on top of the league. That in itself was praiseworthy, for key positions were disrupted for one reason or another. Bobby Clark's injured back meant permanent promotion for 20-year old Jim Leighton. Joe Harper's No 9 shirt had finally been seized by Mark McGhee; while leading goalscorer Steve Archibald had signed for Tottenham. Before the end of 1980 both John McMaster and Gordon Strachan received the injuries that would keep them sidelined till the following season.

Even so, the Dons' winning momentum (Liverpool apart) carried them through much of the Autumn. They tumbled from the League Cup just a week before their execution at Anfield, but still they marched ever-onwards in the league. They were unbeaten after 15 league fixtures – as they had been for the concluding 15 matches of the previous season. In going for a record 31st unbeaten game Aberdeen were undone by their bogey-team, Morton.

The plaster finally crumbled in the first weeks of 1981. A string of league defeats enabled Celtic to pass them in the fast lane, while Morton – who else? – trod upon Aberdeen in the Scottish Cup.

One final statistical record deserves mention. On all their travels on league, League Cup and Scottish Cup business in 1980-81, Aberdeen never conceded more than a single goal – which puts Liverpool's achievement in scoring four into better perspective.

League:	Runners-up
League Cup:	Quarter Final
Scottish Cup:	Fourth Round
European Cup:	Second Round

SCOTTISH PREMIER DIVISION

No 1 Saturday, 9 August

ST MIRREN (0) 0   ABERDEEN (1) 1
                 Jarvie (23)

ST MIRREN: Thomson, Young, Beckett, Richardson, Fulton, Copland, Abercrombie, Stark, Somner, Weir, Logan (McDougall)

ABERDEEN: Leighton, Kennedy, McMaster, Watson, McLeish, Miller, Strachan, Hewitt (Cowan), McGhee, Jarvie, Scanlon

P	W	D	L	F	A	Pts	
1	1	0	0	1	0	2	*Attendance:* 7,000

Referee: A. G. McFaull

This was Alex Ferguson's first win at Paisley since his move to Pittodrie. It was the Saints who 'scored' first, but it didn't count. Billy Stark was offside. Bobby Clark's back injury gives Leighton his chance in goal. He takes it.

No 2 Saturday, 16 August

ABERDEEN (1) 1   DUNDEE UNITED (1) 1
Strachan (29 pen)   Hegarty (23)

ABERDEEN: Leighton, Kennedy, McMaster, Watson (Bell), McLeish, Miller, Strachan, Cowan, McGhee, Jarvie (Hewitt), Scanlon

DUNDEE UNITED: McAlpine, Kirkwood, Stark, Phillip, Hegarty, Narey, Milne (Kopel), Sturrock, Payne, Addison, Bannon

P	W	D	L	F	A	Pts	
2	1	1	0	2	1	3	*Attendance:* 12,000

Referee: R. Cuthill

Matches between these two often end in stalemate. Hegarty had nobody within ten yards of him as he headed United in front. Fortunately Eamonn Bannon then chopped down Mark McGhee in full flight. After the match Archie Knox joins the club as assistant manager.

No 3 Saturday, 23 August
AIRDRIEONIANS (0) 0   ABERDEEN (2) 4
                       McGhee (1), Cowan (8),
                       Jarvie (70), Scanlon (74)
AIRDRIE: McGarr, Erwin, Rodger, Walker, March,
Anderson, McKeown, Clark, Russell, Gordon, McGuire
ABERDEEN: Leighton, Kennedy, McMaster, Watson
(Considine), McLeish, Miller, Strachan, Cowan
(Hewitt), McGhee, Jarvie, Scanlon

P W D L F A Pts   *Attendance:* 6,000
3 2 1 0 6 1 5   *Referee:* A. Waddell

23 seconds after kick-off McMaster's threaded pass to
McGhee produces the first goal. Then it was McGhee's
turn to make a goal for Cowan.

No 4 Saturday, 6 September
ABERDEEN (1) 6   MORTON (0) 0
 Miller (14),
 Scanlon 2 (46, 57),
 Hewitt (84), Strachan (86),
 McMaster (87)
ABERDEEN: Leighton, Kennedy, Rougvie, Watson
(Bell), McLeish, Miller, Strachan, McMaster, McGhee,
Jarvie (Hewitt), Scanlon
MORTON: Baines, Wilkie, Holmes, Anderson, Orr,
McLaren, McNeil, Rooney, Thomson, Cochrane,
Ritchie (Tolmie)

P W D L F A Pts   *Attendance:* 10,000
4 3 1 0 12 1 7   *Referee:* D. F. T. Syme

The Premier League championship flag fluttered over
the Paddock end. Miller anoints it by bursting the net
from 25 yards. Then his forwards take over. The
following Wednesday, Strachan scores Scotland's goal
against Sweden in Stockholm.

No 5 Saturday, 13 September
RANGERS (1) 1   ABERDEEN (1) 1
 McAdam (38)   Strachan (29 pen)
RANGERS: McCloy, Jardine, Miller, Forsyth
(Johnstone), Jackson, Bett, Cooper, McLean, McAdam,
Redford, W. Johnston
ABERDEEN: Leighton, Kennedy, Rougvie, Watson,
McLeish, Miller, Strachan, McMaster, McGhee
(Hamilton), Hewitt (Bell), Scanlon

P W D L F A Pts   *Attendance:* 32,000
5 3 2 0 13 2 8   *Referee:* B. R. McGinlay

This top-of-the-table clash produced a penalty for
Aberdeen when Tom Forsyth downed Rougvie, and an
equaliser for Rangers when McAdam's head connected
with Cooper's cross.

No 6 Saturday, 20 September
PARTICK THISTLE (0) 0   ABERDEEN (0) 1
                        McGhee (76)
PARTICK: Rough, Doyle, Whittaker, Campbell,
O'Hara (Scott), Welsh, Park, Gibson, Higgins, Watson,
McDonald

ABERDEEN: Leighton, Kennedy, Rougvie, Bell,
McLeish, Miller, Strachan, McMaster, McGhee, Hewitt
(Hamilton), Scanlon

P W D L F A Pts   *Attendance:* 6,000
6 4 2 0 14 2 10   *Referee:* G. B. Smith

Not the best of matches. Not the best of goals –
poached by Mark McGhee in a goalmouth scramble.

No 7 Saturday, 27 September
ABERDEEN (0) 2   CELTIC (2) 2
 McGhee (72),   Nicholas (7 pen),
 McAdam o.g. (74)   Burns (17)
ABERDEEN: Leighton, Kennedy, Hamilton
(Scanlon), Watson, Rougvie, Miller, Strachan,
McMaster, McGhee, Bell, Hewitt (McCall)
CELTIC: Bonner, Sneddon, McGrain, McAdam,
MacDonald, Conroy, Provan, Sullivan, McGarvey,
Burns (McLeod), Nicholas

P W D L F A Pts   *Attendance:* 23,000
7 4 3 0 16 4 11   *Referee:* R. B. Valentine

Aberdeen were out for the count. Willie Miller sent
Tommy Burns into orbit. Before he re-entered the
atmosphere Charlie Nicholas scored from the spot – his
12th goal in nine games. Burns headed a second with
John Hewitt off the field receiving treatment. But then
came a second-half reprieve. McGhee prodded past
Bonner, and within seconds McAdam sent the ball into
his own net.

No 8 Saturday, 4 October
HEARTS (0) 0   ABERDEEN (0) 1
                   Rougvie (65)
HEARTS: Brough, Jefferies, Shields, Denny, McVie,
Kidd, Bowman, Gibson, O'Connor, Robertson,
MacDonald
ABERDEEN: Leighton, Kennedy, Rougvie, Bell,
Garner (Watson), Miller, Strachan, McCall (Scanlon),
McGhee, Jarvie, McMaster

P W D L F A Pts   *Attendance:* 10,000
8 5 3 0 17 4 13   *Referee:* P. McLeish

Aberdeen are still in Vienna – in mind if not in body.
But they are thankful to big Doug Rougvie, who
cushions a pass on his chest before banging his first goal
of the season.

No 9 Saturday, 11 October
ABERDEEN (0) 2   KILMARNOCK (0) 0
 Scanlon (48), Jarvie (77)
ABERDEEN: De Clerck, Kennedy, Rougvie, Watson,
Cooper (Bell), Miller, Strachan, McMaster, McGhee
(Cowan), Jarvie, Scanlon
KILMARNOCK: Brown, Robertson, Cockburn, Clark,
Clarke, McDicken, Houston, Mauchlen, Gibson,
Cramond, Street

P W D L F A Pts   *Attendance:* 12,000
9 6 3 0 19 4 15   *Referee:* J. R. S. Renton

Kilmarnock are bottom. They were the last team to beat
Aberdeen in the Premier League. That was 24 matches

ago, and Aberdeen now establish a new record with their unbeaten sequence. 16-year old Neale Cooper makes his senior debut.

No 10 Saturday, 18 October

ABERDEEN (1) 3	ST MIRREN (0) 2
McMaster (34),	Copland (62),
McGhee 2 (70, 72)	Miller o.g. (63)

ABERDEEN: Leighton, Kennedy, Rougvie, Watson, McLeish, Miller, Strachan, McMaster, McGhee, Jarvie, Scanlon

ST MIRREN: Thomson, Young, Beckett, Richardson, McCormack, Copland, McDougall, Stark, Somner, Weir, Abercrombie

P	W	D	L	F	A	Pts	Attendance: 8,000
10	7	3	0	22	17	17	Referee: E. H. Pringle

What a turn-around. St Mirren turn a 1-0 deficit into a 2-1 lead as Copland's effort is deflected by Andy Watson and, seconds later, Leighton, Miller and Frank McDougall all collide in a heap of bodies. The ball ends up in the net. But Mark McGhee charges to the rescue.

No 11 Saturday, 25 October

DUNDEE UNITED (1) 1	ABERDEEN (2) 3
Sturrock (4)	Strachan (10),
	McGhee (24), Hewitt (86)

DUNDEE UNITED: McAlpine, Kirkwood, Kopel, Hope, Hegarty, Narey, Pettigrew, Gibson, Payne, Sturrock, Bannon

ABERDEEN: Leighton, Kennedy, Rougvie, Bell, McLeish, Miller, Strachan, Cowan (Hewitt), McGhee, Jarvie, Scanlon

P	W	D	L	F	A	Pts	Attendance: 10,000
11	8	3	0	25	7	19	Referee: J. A. R. Wales

Aberdeen ought to have been demoralised by Liverpool's performance at Pittodrie. But they weren't. They hit back from Sturrock's thumping drive with a Strachan one-two with McGhee, followed by a moment of McGhee magic as he leaves three defenders flapping at mid-air.

No 12 Saturday, 1 November

ABERDEEN (3) 4	AIRDRIEONIANS (0) 1
McCall 3 (5, 27, 48),	Miller o.g. (82)
McGhee (40)	

ABERDEEN: Leighton, Dornan, Rougvie, Watson, McLeish (Cooper), Miller, Strachan, McCall, McGhee (Davidson), Jarvie, Scanlon

AIRDRIE: Martin, Walker, Rodgers, McCluskey, March, N. Anderson, Thompson, Clark, Russell, Gordon, McKeown

P	W	D	L	F	A	Pts	Attendance: 9,000
12	9	3	0	29	8	21	Referee: A. C. Harris

Walker McCall's first full game since returning from Atlanta Chiefs brings him a memorable hat-trick. Airdrie's Jim March clatters him and is expelled.

No 13 Saturday, 8 November

CELTIC (0) 0	ABERDEEN (1) 2
	McCall 2 (31, 56)

CELTIC: Bonner, Sneddon, McGrain, Aitken, McAdam, Conroy (McCluskey), Provan, Sullivan, McGarvey, Burns, Nicholas

ABERDEEN: Leighton, Dornan (Considine), Rougvie, Watson, McLeish, Cooper, Strachan, McCall, McGhee (Hewitt), Bell, Scanlon

P	W	D	L	F	A	Pts	Attendance: 29,000
13	10	3	0	31	8	23	Referee: B. Robertson

This was the famous match in which Mark McGhee twice loaded the gun for Walker McCall to fire two lethal bullets – and which saw Gordon Strachan attacked on the pitch by a lunatic Celtic fan in the second half.

No 14 Saturday, 15 November

ABERDEEN (0) 2	PARTICK THISTLE (0) 1
Bell (61),	O'Hara (58)
Strachan (76 pen)	

ABERDEEN: Leighton, Rougvie, Considine, Watson, McLeish, Miller, Strachan, McCall, McGhee, Bell, Scanlon (Hewitt)

PARTICK: Rough, Doyle, Lapsley, Campbell, Welsh, Whittaker, Park, O'Hara, Clark, Watson, Jardine

P	W	D	L	F	A	Pts	Attendance: 10,000
14	11	3	0	33	9	25	Referee: E. H. Pringle

O'Hara scored for Thistle from 25 yards. Bell equalised for the Dons from one fifth of that distance. Campbell handled McCall's shot for the penalty.

No 15 Saturday, 22 November

KILMARNOCK (1) 1	ABERDEEN (0) 1
Miller o.g. (35)	McLeish (89)

KILMARNOCK: Wilson, McLean, Robertson, Mauchlen, Clarke, McDicken, Houston, Maxwell, McBride, Cramond, Street

ABERDEEN: Leighton, Kennedy, Considine, Watson, McLeish, Miller, Strachan, McCall (Hewitt), McGhee, Jarvie, Scanlon (Hamilton)

Leading positions

	P	W	D	L	F	A	Pts
1 ABERDEEN	15	11	4	0	34	10	26
2 Rangers	15	8	7	0	33	10	23
3 Celtic	15	9	2	4	31	18	20
4 Dundee United	15	5	6	4	19	18	16

Attendance: 3,500　　　　*Referee: A. Waddell*

The writing is on the wall. Willie Miller's fourth own-goal in five weeks almost gave Killie their second win of the season. Alex McLeish's thumping header preserved the Dons' long-standing unbeaten record.

No 16 Saturday, 6 December

MORTON (0) 1	ABERDEEN (0) 0
Rooney (85)	

MORTON: Baines, Hayes, Holmes, Rooney, McLaughlin, Orr, McNeil (Ritchie), Cochrane, Thomson, Tolmie, Busby

ABERDEEN: Leighton, Kennedy, Considine, Watson, McLeish, Miller, Strachan, Hewitt (McCall), McGhee, Jarvie (Angus), Scanlon

P W D L F A Pts   *Attendance: 7,000*
16 11 4 1 34 11 26   *Referee:* H. Alexander

It had to be Morton. It had to be Andy Ritchie. It was the substitute's cross which landed on Jim Rooney's head to bring about Aberdeen's first league defeat in 31 games.

No 17 Saturday, 13 December
ABERDEEN (0) 2   RANGERS (0) 0
   McGhee (67),
   Johnstone o.g. (79)

ABERDEEN: Leighton, Kennedy, Considine, Watson, McLeish, Miller, Strachan, McCall, McGhee, Angus, Scanlon

RANGERS: McCloy, Miller, Dawson, D. Johnstone, Jackson, Redford, McLean, Russell, McAdam, McDonald, W. Johnston

P W D L F A Pts   *Attendance: 20,000*
17 12 4 1 36 11 28   *Referee:* D. S. Downie

Ian Angus plays his first full game as Rangers continue their dismal run at Pittodrie. McCloy has no chance with McGhee's flashing shot or with McCall's chip which Derek Johnstone unwittingly heads into his own net.

No 18 Saturday, 20 December
PARTICK THISTLE (1) 1   ABERDEEN (1) 1
   Watson (8 pen)   McCall (20)

PARTICK: Rough, Doyle, Whittaker, Campbell, Anderson, Watson, Park, Jardine, Torrance, O'Hara, Clark

ABERDEEN: Leighton, Kennedy, Considine, McLeish, Garner (Simpson), Miller, Strachan, McCall, McGhee, Angus, Scanlon (Davidson)

P W D L F A Pts   *Attendance: 4,000*
18 12 5 1 37 12 29   *Referee:* A. Ferguson

Now it's Neil Simpson's turn to be introduced to the first team. He isn't impressed by Premier League refereeing. Both sides are awarded ridiculously soft spot-kicks. Partick's Watson netted his; Aberdeen's Strachan missed.

No 19 Saturday, 27 December
ABERDEEN (2) 4   CELTIC (0) 1
   McLeish (9), Miller (40),   Nicholas (71)
   McCall (47),
   Strachan (69 pen)

ABERDEEN: Leighton, Kennedy, Considine, Watson, McLeish, Miller, Strachan, McCall, McGhee, Bell (Rougvie), Scanlon

CELTIC: Bonner, McGrain, Reid, Aitken, MacDonald, McAdam, Conroy (Provan), Weir, McGarvey, Burns, McCluskey (Nicholas)

Leading positions

	P	W	D	L	F	A	Pts
1 ABERDEEN	19	13	5	1	41	13	31
2 Celtic	20	13	2	5	41	25	28
3 Rangers	18	8	8	2	34	14	24
4 Dundee United	19	7	7	5	27	25	21

Attendance: 24,000   *Referee:* D. Ramsay

This four-pointer is one Celtic cannot afford to lose. On a sanded, frosty pitch it is the defensive duo of Miller and McLeish who put the skids under Celtic.

No 20 Tuesday, 30 December
ABERDEEN (0) 1   DUNDEE UNITED (1) 1
   Scanlon (81 pen)   Dodds (38)

ABERDEEN: Leighton, Kennedy, Considine, Watson, McLeish, Miller, Strachan, McCall (Hewitt), McGhee, Bell (Angus), Scanlon

DUNDEE UNITED: McAlpine, Holt, Kopel, Phillip, Hegarty, Narey, Bannon, Milne, Gibson, Sturrock, Dodds

P W D L F A Pts   *Attendance:* 22,000
20 13 6 1 42 14 32   *Referee:* A. Waddell

Scotland boss Jock Stein assessed a fine competitive match. Dodds' header was only cancelled out by a debatable penalty awarded when McGhee collided with Narey. But Gordon Strachan received an injury that would keep him out for the rest of the season.

No 21 Saturday, 3 January
ST MIRREN (0) 1   ABERDEEN (0) 1
   Bone (55)   Scanlon (69 pen)

ST MIRREN: Thomson, Young, Beckett, McCormack, Fulton, Copland, Bone, Stark, Somner, Richardson, Weir

ABERDEEN: Leighton, Kennedy, Rougvie, Watson, McLeish, Miller, Simpson, McCall (Hewitt), McGhee, Angus, Scanlon

P W D L F A Pts   *Attendance:* 11,000
21 13 7 1 43 15 33   *Referee:* A. McGunnigle

A goal to raise the roof! – unfortunately it was scored by St Mirren's Jimmy Bone, who ran half the pitch before beating Leighton. But then McCormack felled Simpson, and for the second successive game Scanlon rescued the Dons from the spot.

No 22 Saturday, 10 January
HEARTS (0) 0   ABERDEEN (1) 2
               McCall (34),
               McGhee (57)

HEARTS: Brough, Hamilton, Shields, More, Liddell, Masterton (Robinson), Hamill, Gibson, Conn (O'Connor), O'Brien, MacDonald

ABERDEEN: Leighton, Kennedy, Rougvie (Considine), Watson, McLeish, Miller, Simpson, McCall, McGhee (Jarvie), Angus, Scanlon

P W D L F A Pts   *Attendance:* 8,000
22 14 7 1 45 15 35   *Referee:* W. Anderson

Desperate Hearts look doomed. But Aberdeen keep their noses one point ahead of Celtic.

No 23 Saturday, 31 January
RANGERS (0) 1   ABERDEEN (0) 0
   Johnstone (64)

RANGERS: McCloy, Jardine, Dawson, Stevens, Jackson, Bett, W. Johnston, Russell, D. Johnstone, Redford, McDonald

ABERDEEN: Leighton, Hamilton, Rougvie, Watson (Harrow), McLeish, Cooper (Considine), Jarvie, McCall, McGhee, Angus, Scanlon

Leading positions

	P	W	D	L	F	A	Pts
1 Celtic	24	17	2	5	51	27	36
2 ABERDEEN	23	14	7	2	45	16	35
3 Rangers	22	10	10	2	39	16	30

Attendance: 32,500   *Referee:* R. B. Valentine

At long last Aberdeen are kicked off their perch. The Dons' barricade finally cracked when Derek Johnstone outmanoeuvred Rougvie before scoring.

No 24 Saturday, 7 February
ABERDEEN (0) 0   MORTON (0) 1
                                      Busby (73)

ABERDEEN: Leighton, Hamilton, Considine, Simpson, McLeish, Rougvie, Bell (Watson), Harrow (McCall), McGhee, Angus, Scanlon

MORTON: Baines, Hayes, Holmes, Rooney, McLaughlin, Orr, Busby, Marr, Thomson, Tolmie, Ritchie

P	W	D	L	F	A	Pts
24	14	7	3	45	17	35

Attendance: 11,000   *Referee:* I. M. B. Foote

Oh, no! Morton again with a late winner. This time it's Drew Busby to head home Holmes' cross. Scanlon then headed onto the bar.

No 25 Saturday, 21 February
AIRDRIEONIANS (0) 0   ABERDEEN (0) 0

AIRDRIE: Gardiner, Cairney, Rodger, Walker, G. Anderson, McCluskey, Flood, Russell, N. Anderson, Gordon, Clark

ABERDEEN: Leighton, Kennedy, Rougvie, Watson (Angus), McLeish, Miller, Simpson, Harrow, McGhee, Jarvie, Scanlon (Considine)

P	W	D	L	F	A	Pts
25	14	8	3	45	17	36

Attendance: 5,000   *Referee:* H. Alexander

Former Dons goalkeeper John Gardiner hardly had a shot to save as Aberdeen's drought continues. It's now four league and Cup matches without a goal.

No 26 Saturday, 28 February
ABERDEEN (1) 1   ST MIRREN (1) 2
Jarvie (40)   Richardson (6),
                                      McDougall (58)

ABERDEEN: Leighton, Kennedy, Rougvie, Watson, McLeish, Miller, Simpson, Harrow (Angus), McGhee (Hewitt), Jarvie, Scanlon

ST MIRREN: Thomson, Beckett, McCormack, Richardson, Fulton, Copland, McDougall, Stark, Somner, Abercrombie, Weir

P	W	D	L	F	A	Pts
26	14	8	4	46	19	36

Attendance: 8,000   *Referee:* J. J. Timmons

Celtic are pulling themselves clear at the top. Frank McDougall's glancing header is his first goal against Aberdeen. Liverpool scouts eye up Saints' winger Peter Weir.

No 27 Saturday, 7 March
ABERDEEN (2) 4   HEARTS (0) 1
McCall (38),   Hamill (69)
Hamilton (42), Jarvie (53),
Angus (65)

ABERDEEN: Leighton, Kennedy, Hamilton (Rougvie), Angus, McLeish, Miller, Simpson, McCall (Hewitt), McGhee, Jarvie, Scanlon

HEARTS: Brough, Hamilton, Shields, More, F. Liddell, Hamill, Mackay (O'Brien), Gibson, McShane (Bowman), G. Liddell, Kidd

P	W	D	L	F	A	Pts
27	15	8	4	50	20	38

Attendance: 11,000   *Referee:* D. Syme

Ferguson drops Rougvie, Watson and Harrow in an effort to secure Aberdeen's first league win in eight weeks.

No 28 Saturday, 14 March
KILMARNOCK (0) 1   ABERDEEN (0) 0
Doherty (59)

KILMARNOCK: McCulloch, Robin, Cockburn, Clark, Armstrong, McDicken, McBride, McLean, Bourke, Mauchlen, Doherty

ABERDEEN: Leighton, Kennedy, Hamilton (Rougvie), Angus, McLeish, Miller, Simpson, McCall (Watson), McGhee, Jarvie, Scanlon

P	W	D	L	F	A	Pts
28	15	8	5	50	21	38

Attendance: 2,500   *Referee:* C. J. White

Feeble Kilmarnock's third win of the season leaves Aberdeen wondering where it all went wrong. Celtic have one hand on their crown.

No 29 Saturday, 28 March
CELTIC (0) 1   ABERDEEN (1) 1
McCluskey (85)   Harrow (17)

CELTIC: Bonner, McGrain, Reid, Sullivan, McAdam, Aitken, Provan, McLeod, McGarvey, Burns, Nicholas (McCluskey)

ABERDEEN: Leighton, Kennedy, Rougvie, Watson, McLeish, Miller, Simpson, Bell (Jarvie), McGhee, Harrow (McCall), Scanlon

Leading positions

	P	W	D	L	F	A	Pts
1 Celtic	30	22	3	5	71	31	47
2 ABERDEEN	29	15	9	5	51	22	39
3 Dundee United	30	15	8	7	56	32	38

Attendance: 35,000   *Referee:* K. J. Hope

A win at Parkhead would keep Aberdeen's spirits up – but even that tonic was denied them by McCluskey's hook over Leighton's arms. Minutes earlier Leighton had kept out McLeod's penalty as Aberdeen tried to hang on to Andy Harrow's first goal for Aberdeen.

No 30 Wednesday, 1 April
ABERDEEN (1) 3   PARTICK THISTLE (0) 1
  Simpson (2),   K. Watson (58)
  McGhee (64),
  McLeish (75)
ABERDEEN: Leighton, Kennedy, Rougvie (Cooper), Watson, McLeish, Miller, Simpson, Angus, McGhee, Harrow, Scanlon
PARTICK: McNab, McKinnon (Doyle), Whittaker, Welsh, Campbell, Watson (Jardine), Park, McDonald, Higgins, Lapsley, Clark

P	W	D	L	F	A	Pts	*Attendance:* 8,000
30	16	9	5	54	23	41	*Referee:* T. Muirhead

Aberdeen lost their way after Neil Simpson banged back a rebound. A scrambled equaliser forced them to pull themselves together, which they did with two 'Mac' headers.

No 31 Saturday, 4 April
MORTON (0) 1   ABERDEEN (1) 3
  Tolmie (58)   McGhee (21),
                 Rougvie (50),
                 Simpson (89)
MORTON: Baines, Hayes, Holmes, Rooney, McLaughlin, Wilkie, McNeil, Busby, Thomson, Tolmie, Ritchie (McNab)
ABERDEEN: Leighton, Kennedy, Rougvie, Watson, McLeish, Miller, Simpson, Angus, McGhee, Harrow (Jarvie), Scanlon (Duncanson)

P	W	D	L	F	A	Pts	*Attendance:* 5,000
31	17	9	5	57	24	43	*Referee:* B. R. McGinlay

Morton have the cheek to let Aberdeen win this one – having already wrecked their season in both league and cup.

No 32 Saturday, 11 April
ABERDEEN (0) 1   HEARTS (0) 0
  Rougvie (85)
ABERDEEN: Leighton, Kennedy, Rougvie, Watson (Jarvie), Cooper (Hewitt), Miller, Simpson, Angus, McGhee, Harrow, Scanlon
HEARTS: Brough, Denny, Shields, Bowman, F. Liddell, Hamill, Mackay, Gibson, G. Liddell, Robertson, Kidd

P	W	D	L	F	A	Pts	*Attendance:* 6,000
32	18	9	5	58	24	45	*Referee:* W. P. Knowles

Hearts can't save themselves from relegation. Rougvie's glancing header kept up Aberdeen's nominal chances of overtaking Celtic.

No 33 Saturday, 18 April
ABERDEEN (2) 3   AIRDRIEONIANS (0) 0
  McGhee 2 (26, 78),
  McCall (27)
ABERDEEN: Leighton, Kennedy, Rougvie, Bell, McLeish, Miller, Simpson, McCall, McGhee, Angus (Jarvie), Hewitt

AIRDRIE: Martin, Cairney (Thomson), Rodger, Erwin, G. Anderson, McCluskey, Flood, Clark (McCafferty), N. Anderson, McKeown, McGuire

P	W	D	L	F	A	Pts	*Attendance:* 7,000
33	19	9	5	61	24	47	*Referee:* D. S. Downie

Hoping against hope that Rangers beat Celtic, Aberdeen play relaxed, delightful football – none more so than Mark McGhee, whose twinkling footwork steals the show.

No 34 Wednesday, 22 April
ABERDEEN (0) 0   RANGERS (0) 0
ABERDEEN: Leighton, Kennedy, Rougvie, Bell, McLeish, Miller, Simpson (Watson), Scanlon (Harrow), McGhee, Angus, Hewitt
RANGERS: Stewart, Jardine, Miller, Stevens, Forsyth, Bett, McLean, Russell, Johnstone, Redford, McAdam

P	W	D	L	F	A	Pts	*Attendance:* 15,000
34	19	10	5	61	24	48	*Referee:* D. Ramsay

Aberdeen had most of the play but Rangers had more of the shots at goal. It ended up as a stalemate. The title is now formally Celtic's.

No 35 Saturday, 25 April
DUNDEE UNITED (0) 0   ABERDEEN (0) 0
DUNDEE UNITED: McAlpine, Holt, Murray, Kirkwood, Hegarty (Gough), Stark, Bannon, Milne, Pettigrew, Sturrock, Payne (Gibson)
ABERDEEN: Leighton, Kennedy, Rougvie, Bell, McLeish, Miller, Simpson, Scanlon, McGhee, Angus (Jarvie), Hewitt

P	W	D	L	F	A	Pts	*Attendance:* 6,000
35	19	11	5	61	24	49	*Referee:* G. B. Smith

Beset by injuries, the Aberdeen line-up is remodelled at Tannadice. How ironic that despite their wretched Spring Aberdeen have now overtaken last season's title-winning 48 points.

No 36 Saturday, 2 May
ABERDEEN (0) 0   KILMARNOCK (0) 2
                 McDicken (53),
                 McCready (56)
ABERDEEN: Leighton, Kennedy, Rougvie, Watson (Jarvie), McLeish, Miller, Simpson, McGhee, Harper, Angus (Harrow), Hewitt
KILMARNOCK: McCulloch, Robin, Cockburn, Clark, Armstrong, McDicken, McCready, McLean, Bourke, Mauchlen, Eadie

Attendance: 6,000   *Referee:* M. Delaney

An emotional return for Joe Harper in his first and last appearance of the season. Kilmarnock are not impressed.

Aberdeen's complete home and away record:

HOME						AWAY						
P	W	D	L	F	A		W	D	L	F	A	Pts
36	11	4	3	39	16		8	7	3	22	10	49

Premier Division

	P	W	D	L	F	A	Pts
1 Celtic	36	26	4	6	84	37	56
2 ABERDEEN	36	19	11	6	61	26	49
3 Rangers	36	16	12	8	60	32	44
4 St Mirren	36	18	8	10	56	47	44
5 Dundee United	36	17	9	10	66	42	43
6 Partick Thistle	36	10	10	16	32	48	30
7 Airdrieonians	36	10	9	17	36	55	29
8 Morton	36	10	8	18	36	58	28
9 Kilmarnock	36	5	9	22	23	65	19
10 Hearts	36	6	6	24	27	71	18

LEAGUE CUP

2nd Round, 1st Leg Wednesday, 27 August
ABERDEEN (4) 8   BERWICK RANGERS
  McGhee 3 (7, 31, 82),   (0) 1
  Jarvie 2 (11, 19),   Egan (63)
  Watson 2 (46, 86),
  Bell (90)
ABERDEEN: Leighton, Kennedy, McMaster, Watson, McLeish, Miller, Strachan (Bell), Cowan (Rougvie), McGhee, Jarvie, Scanlon
BERWICK: McLaren, McCann, Deakin, McDougall, McDowell, D. Smith, Davidson, Romaines, G. Smith, Tait, Egan
Attendance: 7,500   Referee: R. B. Valentine
Best Berwick player was keeper Ian McLaren. He even stopped a McGhee penalty.

2nd Round, 2nd Leg Saturday, 30 August
BERWICK RANGERS   ABERDEEN (3) 4
  (0) 0   Strachan (3), Hewitt (7),
                   de Clerck (22),
                   Kennedy (89)
BERWICK: Davidson, McCann, Deakin, Gregson, McDowell, Mayes, D. Smith, Romaines, McLeod, Tait, Egan
ABERDEEN: de Clerck, Kennedy, Rougvie, Garner, McLeish (Cowan), Miller, Strachan, Bell, Morrison, Hewitt, Davidson
Aberdeen won 12-1 on aggregate
Attendance: 1,100   *Referee:* M. Delaney
Goal of the century! Aberdeen's Belgian goalkeeper, Mark de Clerck, drop-kicked a clearance. It bounced over Davidson's head and into the Berwick net. It's the first goal ever scored by an Aberdeen goalkeeper in a competitive fixture.

3rd Round, 1st Leg Wednesday, 3 September
RANGERS (1) 1   ABERDEEN (0) 0
  McAdam (1)
RANGERS: McCloy, Jardine, Miller, Forsyth, Jackson, Bett, McLean (Stevens), McDonald (Johnston), McAdam, Redford, Cooper
ABERDEEN: Leighton, Kennedy, Rougvie, Watson, McLeish, Miller, Strachan, McMaster, McGhee, Jarvie (Hewitt), Scanlon (Bell)

Referee: K. J. Hope
Willie Johnston was sent off for the 13th time in his career, only twelve minutes after coming on as a substitute, for a horrendous stamping foul on McMaster. Altogether eight players were booked. The goal, incidentally, was a McAdam header after 45 seconds.

3rd Round, 2nd Leg Wednesday, 24 September
ABERDEEN (2) 3   RANGERS (0) 1
  McMaster (5),   McAdam (47)
  Strachan 2 (29 pen, 90 pen)
ABERDEEN: Leighton, Kennedy, Rougvie, Watson, McLeish, Miller, Strachan, McMaster, McGhee, Bell (Hewitt), Scanlon
RANGERS: McCloy, Jardine, Miller, Forsyth, Jackson, Bett, Cooper (McLean), Johnstone, McAdam, Redford, Johnston (McDonald)
Aberdeen won 3-2 on aggregate
Attendance: 24,000   *Referee:* G. B. Smith
Matches don't come any more thrilling than this. McMaster scored from 25 yards. Strachan put Aberdeen ahead from the spot after Jardine involuntarily handled. McAdam burst through to level the overall scores. Rangers' Jim Bett banged the Dons' bar, and in injury time Hewitt was brought to earth by Colin Jackson. The referee consulted a linesman and Strachan did the rest.

Quarter Final 1st Leg Wednesday, 8 October
DUNDEE (0) 0   ABERDEEN (0) 0
DUNDEE: Geddes, Barr, Williamson, Fraser, Glennie, McLaren, Mackie, McGeachie, Sinclair, Fleming (Murphy), Shirra
ABERDEEN: Leighton, Kennedy, McMaster, Watson, Rougvie, Miller, Strachan, Jarvie (Considine), McGhee, Bell (Cowan), Scanlon
Attendance: 10,300   *Referee:* B. R. McGinlay
The last time Aberdeen played a League Cup match at Dens Park was in the Final ten months earlier. They are probably satisfied with this first-leg result, but not with their finishing.

Quarter Final 2nd Leg Wednesday, 29 October
ABERDEEN (0) 0   DUNDEE (0) 1
                Fraser (85)
ABERDEEN: Leighton, Kennedy (Watson), Rougvie, Bell, McLeish, Miller, Strachan, Cowan, McGhee, Jarvie, Scanlon
DUNDEE: Geddes, Barr, Schaedler, Fraser, Glennie, McLaren, Murphy, McGeachie, Sinclair, Mackie (Fletcher), Williamson
Dundee won 1-0 on aggregate
Attendance: 14,000   *Referee:* T. Muirhead
Dundee's defence remained intact for the sixth time in the competition. Aberdeen are harried into mistakes and Pittodrie is stunned when Cammy Fraser – a newcomer from Hearts – pounces on Rougvie's headed clearance to shoot in off the post.

SCOTTISH CUP

3rd Round Saturday, 24 January
RAITH ROVERS (0) 1   ABERDEEN (1) 2
 Harris (62)   Jarvie 2 (10, 68)
RAITH ROVERS: McDermott, McDonough, Candlish, Ford, Forsyth, Steele, Lawson, Urquhart, Harris, Steen, Mitchell
ABERDEEN: Leighton, Rougvie, Considine, Watson, McLeish, Cooper, Bell, McCall, McGhee, Jarvie, Hewitt (Scanlon)

Attendance: 10,000   *Referee:* R. B. Valentine

Thank goodness for veteran Drew Jarvie. One with his head, another with his foot, eventually sees Aberdeen through.

4th Round Saturday, 14 February
MORTON (1) 1   ABERDEEN (0) 0
 Ritchie (21)
MORTON: Baines, Hayes, Holmes, Rooney, McLaughlin, Orr, Busby, Marr, Thomson, McNeil, Ritchie (Houston)
ABERDEEN: Leighton, Kennedy, Considine, Watson, McLeish, Miller, Bell (Davidson), McCall (Hamilton), McGhee, Harrow, Angus

Attendance: n.a.   *Referee:* H. Alexander

Last week Morton dealt Aberdeen's title hopes a massive jolt. Now they boot the Dons out of the Scottish Cup with a sensational goal from Andy Ritchie, who tied several Aberdeen defenders up in knots before concluding with a deadly finish. We didn't know it then, but it was to be Aberdeen's last defeat in the Scottish Cup until April 1985.

EUROPEAN CUP

1st Round, 1st Leg Wednesday, 17 September
ABERDEEN (1) 1   AUSTRIA MEMPHIS
 McGhee (31)   (Austria) (0) 0
ABERDEEN: Leighton, Kennedy, Rougvie, Watson (Bell), McLeish, Miller, Strachan, McMaster, McGhee, Jarvie, Scanlon (Hewitt)
AUSTRIA: Koncilia, R. Sara, Obermayer, Pospischil, Baumeister, J. Sara, Dihanich, Daxbacher, Furst (Zore), Gasselich, Schachner (Borgan)

Attendance: 20,000   *Referee:* R. Nyhus
                        (Norway)

Willie Miller leads Aberdeen into the European Cup for the first time. By the halfway stage they have a McGhee goal to their credit, but should have been a couple of goals behind. Chief culprit among the star-studded Austrians is Walter Schachner. The visitors forgot about attacking in the second half.

1st Round, 2nd Leg Wednesday, 1 October
AUSTRIA MEMPHIS   ABERDEEN (0) 0
 (0) 0

AUSTRIA: Koncilia, R. Sara, Obermayer, J. Sara, Zore (Borgan), Dihanich, Daxbacher, Furst, Baumeister (Pfeiler), Gasselich, Schachner
ABERDEEN: Leighton, Kennedy, Rougvie, Watson, Garner, Miller, Strachan, McMaster, McGhee, Bell, Scanlon

Aberdeen won 1-0 on aggregate

Attendance: 37,000   *Referee:* E. Azim-Zaide
                        (Russia)

No wonder Alex Ferguson is proud of his players as they draw the sting from their hosts. Mark McGhee might have popped one in near the end.

2nd Round, 1st Leg Wednesday, 22 October
ABERDEEN (0) 0   LIVERPOOL (1) 1
                      McDermott (5)
ABERDEEN: Leighton, Kennedy, Rougvie, Watson, McLeish, Miller, Strachan, McMaster (Bell), McGhee, Jarvie (Hewitt), Scanlon
LIVERPOOL: Clemence, Neal, A. Kennedy, Thompson, R. Kennedy, Hansen, Dalglish, Lee (Case), Johnson, McDermott, Souness

Attendance: 24,000   *Referee:* A. Jarguz (Poland)

McMaster, off the pitch receiving treatment, is unable to prevent Terry McDermott haring into space to chip Johnson's pass over Leighton from an almost impossible angle. When McMaster returned he was scythed down by Ray Kennedy and was put out of the game for a year. The much-anticipated meeting between the Scottish and English champions was like pitching men against boys.

2nd Round, 2nd Leg Wednesday, 5 November
LIVERPOOL (2) 4   ABERDEEN (0) 0
 Miller o.g. (37), Neal (43),
 Dalglish (58), Hansen (70)
LIVERPOOL: Clemence, Neal, A. Kennedy (Cohen), Thompson, R. Kennedy, Hansen, Dalglish, Lee, Johnson, McDermott, Souness
ABERDEEN: Leighton, Dornan, Rougvie (Cooper), Watson, McLeish, Miller, Strachan, Bell (Hewitt), McGhee, Jarvie, Scanlon

Liverpool won 5-0 on aggregate

Attendance: 36,182   *Referee:* A. Prokop
                        (E. Germany)

Out of the League Cup last week, out of the European Cup tonight. This return leg turned on two moments: when Mark McGhee beat two defenders but failed to beat Clemence; and when Willie Miller sliced a corner into his own net. The second half was simply embarrassing for Aberdeen.

1980-81 APPEARANCES

	League	League Cup	Scottish Cup	European Cup
McGhee	36	5	2	4
Leighton	35	5	2	4
Miller	33	6	1	4
Scanlon	32(+2)	5	-(+1)	4
McLeish	32	5	2	3
Kennedy	31	6	1	3
Watson	26(+4)	4(+1)	2	4
Rougvie	25(+3)	5(+1)	1	4
Strachan	20	6		4
Jarvie	16(+7)	4	1	3
Angus	15(+4)		1	
Simpson	15(+1)			
Bell	13(+4)	4(+2)	2	2(+2)
McCall	15(+4)		2	
McMaster	10	4		3
Hewitt	9(+12)	1(+2)	1	-(+3)
Harrow	7(+3)		1	
Considine	8(+4)	-(+1)	2	
Hamilton	5(+3)		-(+1)	
Neale Cooper	4(+2)		1	-(+1)
Cowan	3(+2)	2(+2)		
Dornan	2			1
Garner	2	1		1
Harper	1			
de Clerck	1	1		
Davidson	-(+4)	1		-(+1)
Morrison		1		

27 players

GOALS

	Total	League	League Cup	Scottish Cup	European Cup
McGhee	17	13	3		1
McCall	10	10			
Strachan	9	6	3		
Jarvie	9	5	2	2	
Scanlon	6	6			
McLeish	3	3			
Rougvie	3	3			
Hewitt	3	2	1		
McMaster	3	2	1		
Miller	2	2			
Simpson	2	2			
Bell	2	1	1		
Watson	2			2	
Angus	1	1			
Cowan	1	1			
Harrow	1	1			
de Clerck	1		1		
Kennedy	1		1		
Hamilton	1	1			
own-goals	2	2			
Total	79	61	15	2	1

The Aberdeen squad in season 1981-82. Back row: Simpson, Hamilton, Watson, Angus Harrow. Centre row: Bell, Weir, Clark, McCall, Leighton, Rougvie, Considine, Cooper. Front row: McMaster, Hewitt, Kennedy, McGhee, Miller, Jarvie, Strachan and McLeish.

Season 1981-82

The 1981-82 season ended on the highest possible note with a win in the Scottish Cup Final. But in the months leading up to that famous Saturday at Hampden Aberdeen's season looked once again like leaving them as bridesmaids.

Alex Ferguson seemed to have difficulty in instilling into his players the length of a league season. Aberdeen either had a good Autumn or a good Spring. But not both. Aberdeen concluded 1979-80 (the championship year) and 1981-82 with a bang. In between, in 1980-81, they were a spent force by Christmas.

There were high hopes for success in 1981-82, not least because of the signing of winger Peter Weir from St Mirren, with Ian Scanlon going to Love Street in part-exchange. In the League Cup Aberdeen were scuppered by Dundee United in the semi-final. The Dons even brought back a first-leg lead from Tannadice, but United overhauled it at Pittodrie. In the UEFA Cup Aberdeen skipped past holders Ipswich in a manner to suggest that the traumas of Liverpool had been put to good purpose. Alas, the Dons committed hara-kiri against Hamburg in the Third Round.

When Aberdeen set course for the Scottish Cup in January it was the only trophy left for them to win – for Celtic were out of sight over the horizon in the league. John Hewitt set the ball rolling by banging it into the Motherwell net only 9.6 seconds after kick-off. By the time Aberdeen took the field against Rangers in the Final they had gone 25 League and Cup games with only one defeat, and had finished the League tugging on Celtic's coat-tails. When, early in extra time, Mark McGhee headed Aberdeen in front for the first time he had no idea of the magical consequences that would follow in the months to come.

With a Scottish Cup winners medal under their belts, Jim Leighton, Willie Miller, Alex McLeish and Gordon Strachan set off to do battle in Spain for the World Cup.

League:	Runners up
League Cup:	Semi Final
Scottish Cup:	Winners
UEFA Cup:	Third Round

SCOTTISH PREMIER DIVISION

No 1 Saturday, 29 August
DUNDEE UNITED (3) 4   ABERDEEN (0) 1
  Sturrock (8),   McLeish (49)
  Holt (10),
  Pettigrew (33),
  Bannon (60 pen)

DUNDEE UNITED: McAlpine, Stark, Murray, Holt, Hegarty, Narey, Bannon, Kirkwood, Pettigrew, Sturrock, Dodds

ABERDEEN: Leighton, Kennedy, Rougvie (Watson), Cooper, McLeish, Miller, Strachan, Bell (Jarvie), McGhee, Hewitt, Weir

P	W	D	L	F	A	Pts	
1	0	0	1	1	4	0	

Attendance: 10,600
Referee: D. Ramsey

Jock Stein took in an entertaining match with United on top of their game. Aberdeen's defence simply could not come to grips with Paul Sturrock's trickery.

No 2 Saturday, 5 September
ABERDEEN (1) 1   CELTIC (2) 3
  Strachan (2 pen)   Burns (8),
                 McGarvey 2 (26, 55)

ABERDEEN: Leighton, Kennedy, Cooper, Watson, McLeish, Miller, Strachan, Bell (McMaster), McGhee (Cowan), McCall, Hewitt

CELTIC: Bonner, McGrain, Reid, Aitken, McAdam, McLeod, Provan, Sullivan, McGarvey, Burns, McCluskey

P	W	D	L	F	A	Pts	
2	0	0	2	2	7	0	

Attendance: 18,800
Referee: B. R. McGinlay

307

Penalty for Aberdeen as McAdam crashes into McCall. Strachan nets and is then assaulted by a Celtic fan on the pitch. Police arrived just in time. Thereafter Celtic turn on the style to leave Aberdeen totally flummoxed.

No 3 Saturday, 12 September
PARTICK THISTLE (0) 0   ABERDEEN (0) 2
                         McCall (71)
                         Cowan (88)
PARTICK: Rough, Doyle, Lapsley, Kay, Dunlop, O'Hara, Park, Higgins, Sweeney, McDonald, Clark
ABERDEEN: Leighton, Kennedy, Rougvie, Watson, McLeish, Miller (Simpson), Strachan, Cooper, McCall, McMaster (Cowan), Hewitt

P W D L F A Pts   *Attendance:* 3,600
3 1 0 2 4 7 2   *Referee:* A. W. Waddell

Two teams with no points between them battle for the right to claim bottom spot. Partick win that battle. It was the aerial power of Walker McCall and Steve Cowan that did the trick.

No 4 Saturday, 19 September
ABERDEEN (0) 1   HIBERNIAN (0) 0
Simpson (85)
ABERDEEN: Leighton, Kennedy, Rougvie, Cooper, McLeish, Miller, Strachan, Watson (Simpson), McGhee, Hewitt (McCall), Weir
HIBERNIAN: McArthur, Sneddon, Flavell, McNamara, Paterson, McLaren, Callachan, Rae, McLeod, Duncan, Murray

P W D L F A Pts   *Attendance:* 10,900
4 2 0 2 5 7 4   *Referee:* T. Muirhead

The crowd were growing restive, but they eventually leave contented, thanks to Neil Simpson's crisp goal, which sends Hibs to their first league defeat.

No 5 Saturday, 26 September
AIRDRIEONIANS (0) 0   ABERDEEN (3) 4
                       McLeish (26),
                       Weir 2 (39, 58),
                       Hewitt (41)
AIRDRIE: Martin, Erwin, Rodger, Walker, March, McCluskey, McKeown (Flood), Campbell, McGuire, Gordon, Anderson
ABERDEEN: Leighton, Kennedy, Rougvie, Watson, McLeish, Miller, Strachan, Cooper, McGhee, Hewitt (Cowan), Weir

P W D L F A Pts   *Attendance:* 3,000
5 3 0 2 9 7 6   *Referee:* D. M. Galloway

Torrential rain cannot dampen Aberdeen's spirits as they give Airdrie a good hiding and prepare for the UEFA Cup visit of Ipswich. McLeish's header, Weir's volley, and Hewitt's thunderbolt settled the issue before half-time.

No 6 Saturday, 3 October
ABERDEEN (0) 2   MORTON (0) 0
Watson (69),
Rougvie (77)

ABERDEEN: Leighton, Kennedy, Rougvie, Watson, McLeish (Cooper), Miller, Strachan, Simpson, McCall, Cowan (McGhee), Weir
MORTON: Baines, Hayes, Holmes, Rooney, McLaughlin, Orr, Houston, Cochrane, Busby, Hutchison, McNeil

P W D L F A Pts   *Attendance:* 11,000
6 4 0 2 11 7 8   *Referee:* K. J. Hope

As so often in the past, Morton didn't appear to have any desire to score. The difference was that this time they didn't.

No 7 Saturday, 10 October
RANGERS (0) 0   ABERDEEN (0) 0
RANGERS: Stewart, Jardine, Dawson, Stevens, Forsyth, Bett, Cooper, Russell, McAdam, McDonald, Johnston (Redford)
ABERDEEN: Leighton, Kennedy, Rougvie, Watson, Cooper, Miller, Strachan, Simpson (McMaster), McGhee, Hewitt (Harrow), Weir

P W D L F A Pts   *Attendance:* 28,000
7 4 1 2 11 7 9   *Referee:* J. R. S. Renton

No skill. Only muscle, and five bookings. There should have been more. On the hour Jim Leighton saved a John McDonald penalty conceded by Willie Miller. Leighton has now not conceded a goal in seven league and League Cup matches.

No 8 Saturday, 17 October
ST MIRREN (1) 1   ABERDEEN (1) 2
McAvennie (32)   Watson 2 (17, 57)
ST MIRREN: Thomson, Young, Beckett, McCormack, Fulton (Logan), Copland, McAvennie, Stark, Bone, Abercrombie, Scanlon
ABERDEEN: Leighton, Kennedy, Rougvie, Watson, McLeish, Miller, Strachan, Simpson (McMaster), McGhee, Hewitt, Weir

P W D L F   A Pts   *Attendance:* 6,900
8 5 1 2 13 8 11   *Referee:* A. Ferguson

Andy Watson sets things moving with a long-range shot. A Stark-McAvennie combination brings the equaliser. Substitute John McMaster's slide-rule pass brings the winner.

No 9 Saturday, 24 October
ABERDEEN (2) 2   DUNDEE (0) 1
McCall (40),   Stephen (76)
Rougvie (41)
ABERDEEN: Leighton, Kennedy, Rougvie, Simpson, Cooper, Miller, Strachan, McMaster (Watson), McGhee, McCall, Weir
DUNDEE: Geddes, Barr, Cameron, Kidd (Stephen), Glennie, McDonald, Ferguson, Bell, Mackie, McGeachie, Murphy

P W D L F   A Pts   *Attendance:* 11,500
9 6 1 2 15 9 13   *Referee:* B. Robertson

Dundee may be bottom, but they made Aberdeen sweat after Ray Stephen connected with Murphy's corner. Leaders Celtic lost at Easter Road.

No 10 Saturday, 31 October
ABERDEEN (1) 1   DUNDEE UNITED (0) 1
  Black (9)   Milne (56)
ABERDEEN: Leighton, Kennedy, Rougvie, McMaster, Cooper, Miller, Strachan, Black, McGhee (Watson), Hewitt, Simpson
DUNDEE UNITED: Graham, Holt, Murray, Phillip (Gough), Hegarty, Narey, Bannon, Milne, Kirkwood, Sturrock, Dodds
Leading positions

	P	W	D	L	F	A	Pts
1 Celtic	10	8	1	1	23	9	17
2 ABERDEEN	10	6	2	2	16	10	14
3 St. Mirren	10	5	2	3	15	12	12

Attendance: 11,000   *Referee:* G. B. Smith

Three days previously Jim McLean's men had won 3-0 at Pittodrie to end the Dons' interest in the League Cup. In the league it's a different story. United have won only twice all season. Ferguson produces another youngster, 17-year old Eric Black, who climbs higher than anybody else to meet Strachan's corner.

No 11 Saturday, 7 November
CELTIC (1) 2   ABERDEEN (0) 1
  McGarvey (40),   Strachan (90)
  McCluskey (72)
CELTIC: Bonner, Moyes, Reid, Aitken, McAdam, McLeod, Provan, Sullivan, McGarvey, Burns (Conroy), McCluskey
ABERDEEN: Leighton, Kennedy, Cooper, Watson (Hewitt), McLeish, Miller, Strachan, Simpson, McGhee, Black (McMaster), Weir

P	W	D	L	F	A	Pts
11	6	2	3	17	12	14

Attendance: 29,300   *Referee:* D. Ramsay

Celtic were the last team to beat the Dons in the league – over two months ago. Aberdeen put on a good show. But McGarvey's exquisite lob puts Celtic ahead, and McCluskey's exploitation of a poor Cooper clearance produced a second goal.

No 12 Saturday, 14 November
ABERDEEN (1) 2   PARTICK THISTLE (0) 1
  Harrow (10)   Clark (60)
  Watson (84)
ABERDEEN: Leighton, Kennedy, McMaster, Cooper, McLeish (Watson), Miller, Strachan, Black (McGhee), Harrow, Simpson, Weir
PARTICK: Rough, Murray, Lapsley, Dunlop, Whittaker, Watson, Park, McDonald, Johnstone (O'Hara), Doyle, Clark

P	W	D	L	F	A	Pts
12	7	2	3	19	13	16

Attendance: 11,200   *Referee:* D. M. Galloway

Well done, Andy Watson. The substitute flashes home a header from McGhee's centre after it looks like Aberdeen have thrown away a point.

No 13 Saturday, 21 November
HIBERNIAN (1) 1   ABERDEEN (0) 1
  Callachan (27)   Simpson (63)

HIBERNIAN: McArthur, Sneddon, Schaedler, Brazil, Paterson, Duncan, Callachan, Rae, McLeod (McLaren), Rodier (Murray), Flavell
ABERDEEN: Leighton, Kennedy, McMaster, Watson, Cooper (Cowan), Miller, Strachan, McCall (Harrow), McGhee, Simpson, Weir

P	W	D	L	F	A	Pts
13	7	3	3	20	14	17

Attendance: 7,600   *Referee:* T. Timmons

Several Hamburg spies make notes on their future UEFA Cup opponents. Simpson saved the day in a hectic goalmouth melee.

No 14 Saturday, 28 November
ABERDEEN (0) 0   AIRDRIEONIANS (0) 0
ABERDEEN: Leighton, Kennedy, McMaster, Watson, McLeish, Miller, Bell (Simpson), Cooper, McGhee, Harrow (Black), Weir
AIRDRIE: Martin, Erwin (McKeown), Rodger, Walker, March, McCluskey, McGuire, Clark, Anderson, Gordon, Flood

P	W	D	L	F	A	Pts
14	7	4	3	20	14	18

Attendance: 8,000   *Referee:* C. J. White

Airdrie have the worst defensive record in the Premier League. But that doesn't help Aberdeen who stumble their way through an arid performance. Sandy Clark even hit Leighton's post.

No 15 Saturday, 5 December
MORTON (0) 2   ABERDEEN (0) 1
  McNeil (58),   Hewitt (64)
  Houston (72)
MORTON: Baines, Hayes, Holmes, Rooney, McLaughlin, Orr, McNeil, Docherty, Busby, Hutchison, Houston
ABERDEEN: Leighton, Kennedy, McMaster (Cooper), Watson, McLeish, Miller, Strachan, Black, McGhee (Hewitt), Simpson, Weir
Leading positions

	P	W	D	L	F	A	Pts
1 Celtic	15	11	3	1	34	15	25
2 Dundee United	14	7	4	3	26	12	18
3 St Mirren	15	7	4	4	23	18	18
4 ABERDEEN	15	7	4	4	21	16	18

Attendance: 3,100   *Referee:* D. Syme

Morton are back to their old tricks again. Aberdeen have won on only one of their past six visits to Cappielow. Just after Hewitt equalised Black headed against Morton's crossbar. Then Willie Miller attempted a backpass which fell suicidally short, and Aberdeen had lost.

No 16 Saturday, 30 January
ABERDEEN (1) 1   CELTIC (1) 3
  McMaster (2)   McCluskey (28 pen)
                        McLeod (71)
                        McGarvey (76)
ABERDEEN: Leighton, Kennedy, Rougvie, McMaster, McLeish, Miller, Strachan, Bell, McGhee (Black), Hewitt, Weir

CELTIC: Bonner, McGrain, Reid, Aitken, McAdam, McLeod, Sullivan, McStay, McGarvey, Burns, McCluskey

P	W	D	L	F	A	Pts
16	7	4	5	22	19	18

Attendance: 20,000
Referee: R. B. Valentine

Aberdeen's first league match for nearly two months sees them steam-rollered by Celtic – who have now taken six points out of six against Aberdeen so far this season. The Dons drop to 6th in the league, despite the wonderful start given them by John McMaster's left foot shot.

No 17 Wednesday, 3 February
PARTICK THISTLE (0) 0   ABERDEEN (0) 0
PARTICK: Rough, McKinnon, Whittaker, Anderson, Dunlop (Park), Watson, McDonald, Jardine, Higgins, Doyle, Clark (Johnston)
ABERDEEN: Leighton, Kennedy, Rougvie, McMaster (Watson), McLeish, Miller, Strachan, Bell, Black (Cowan), Hewitt, Weir

P	W	D	L	F	A	Pts
17	7	5	5	22	19	19

Attendance: 3,300
Referee: R. R. Cuthill

The nearest that Aberdeen came to a goal was John Hewitt's header came back off Rough's crossbar. Maurice Johnston later brought a full-length save from Jim Leighton.

No 18 Saturday, 6 February
ABERDEEN (0) 0   MORTON (0) 0
ABERDEEN: Leighton, Kennedy, Rougvie, Watson, McLeish, Miller, Strachan, Bell (McMaster), Black (Harrow), Hewitt, Weir
MORTON: Baines, Hayes, Holmes, Rooney, McLaughlin, Duffy, Houston, Docherty, Hutchison, Slavin, Ritchie

P	W	D	L	F	A	Pts
18	7	6	5	22	19	20

Attendance: 7,200
Referee: E. H. Pringle

Poor form and wretched weather means it is now three months since Aberdeen last won a league match. Morton are not in charitable mood. Are they ever?

No 19 Saturday, 20 February
AIRDRIEONIANS (0) 0   ABERDEEN (0) 3
                      Hewitt (47),
                      McGhee 2 (74, 75)
AIRDRIE: Martin, McCluskey, Rodger, Campbell, G. Anderson, N. Anderson, McKeown, Clark, McDonagh, Gordon, Flood
ABERDEEN: Leighton, Kennedy, Rougvie, McMaster, McLeish, Miller, Strachan, Simpson, McGhee, Hewitt, Weir (Jarvie)

P	W	D	L	F	A	Pts
19	8	6	5	25	19	22

Attendance: 3,500.
Referee: B. Robertson

This, believe it or not, is the first time Mark McGhee has scored in the league all season. This result is Aberdeen's first away win since 17 October.

No 20 Saturday, 27 February
ABERDEEN (0) 0   DUNDEE (0) 0

ABERDEEN: Leighton, Kennedy, McMaster, Bell (Cooper), McLeish, Miller, Strachan, Simpson, McGhee, Jarvie (Cowan), Hewitt
DUNDEE: Geddes, McKimmie, McLelland, Fraser, Smith, Glennie, Ferguson, Kidd, Fleming (Stephen), McGeachie (Cameron), Mackie
Leading positions

	P	W	D	L	F	A	Pts
1 Celtic	21	13	5	3	42	21	31
2 St. Mirren	21	10	7	4	32	22	27
3 Rangers	21	9	8	4	33	25	26
4 ABERDEEN	20	8	7	5	25	19	23

Attendance: 8,950
Referee: A. W. Waddell

Dundee are propping up the league, and travel north with five straight defeats to their name. More frustration for Aberdeen.

No 21 Wednesday, 10 March
ABERDEEN (1) 3   HIBERNIAN (1) 1
  Cooper (1),   Rae (28)
  Strachan (48 pen)
  Jarvie (83)
ABERDEEN: Leighton, Kennedy, Hamilton (Watson), McMaster, McLeish, Miller, Strachan, Cooper, McGhee, Simpson (Jarvie), Hewitt
HIBERNIAN: McArthur, Sneddon, Duncan, McLaren, Paterson, McNamara, Callachan, Murray, McLeod, Rae, Flavell

P	W	D	L	F	A	Pts
21	9	7	5	28	20	25

Attendance: 8,700
Referee: K. J. Hope

Following Neale Cooper's cracking goal inside 35 seconds, Hibs are under such intense pressure for the rest of the first half that they pass the ball back to McArthur no fewer than 14 times.

No 22 Saturday, 13 March
RANGERS (0) 1   ABERDEEN (2) 3
  Johnstone (63)   Cowan (9),
                           Cooper (34),
                           Watson (83)
RANGERS: Stewart, Jardine, Dawson, McAdam, Jackson, Bett, Cooper, Russell, Johnstone, Miller (McDonald), Redford
ABERDEEN: Leighton, Kennedy, Rougvie, McMaster (Watson), McLeish, Miller, Strachan, Cooper, McGhee, Simpson, Cowan (Jarvie)

P	W	D	L	F	A	Pts
22	10	7	5	31	21	27

Attendance: 20,000
Referee: H. Alexander

Man-of-the-match Jim Leighton saved Aberdeen by saving a Jim Bett penalty when the Dons led 1-0. Cowan's volley and Neale Cooper's header put Aberdeen on the victory trail.

No 23 Wednesday, 17 March
DUNDEE (0) 0   ABERDEEN (1) 3
                           Simpson (13).
                           Hewitt (53),
                           Cowan (73)

DUNDEE: Geddes, Cameron, McLelland, Fraser, Smith, Glennie, Mackie, Kidd, Fleming, McGeachie, Murphy (Sinclair)

ABERDEEN: Leighton, Kennedy, Rougvie, Watson, McLeish, Miller (Cowan), Strachan, Simpson, McGhee, McMaster, Hewitt

P	W	D	L	F	A	Pts	Attendance: 6,100
23	11	7	5	34	21	29	Referee: D. F. Syme

It's not often that Willie Miller is unable to continue after injury. But he is led off after a crushing tackle by Bobby Glennie. But by then Aberdeen are coasting.

No 24 Saturday, 20 March
ABERDEEN (1) 2   DUNDEE UNITED (0) 1
 Hewitt (43),   Dodds (47)
 McLeish (74)

ABERDEEN: Leighton, Kennedy, Rougvie, Watson (McMaster), McLeish, Miller, Strachan, Cooper, McGhee, Simpson, Hewitt (Cowan)

DUNDEE UNITED: McAlpine, Holt, Stark, Gough, Hegarty, Narey, Bannon, Gibson, Kirkwood, Sturrock, Dodds

P	W	D	L	F	A	Pts	Attendance: 12,100
24	12	7	5	36	22	31	Referee: K. J. Hope

Stuart Kennedy's marauding run down the right touchline ends in a perfect centre and the perfect header from Alex McLeish.

No 25 Saturday, 27 March
CELTIC (0) 0   ABERDEEN (0) 1
              Kennedy (69)

CELTIC: Bonner, McGrain, Reid (Moyes), Aitken, McAdam, McLeod, Crainie, Sullivan, McGarvey, McCluskey, Burns

ABERDEEN: Leighton, Kennedy, Rougvie (McMaster), Simpson, McLeish, Miller, Strachan, Cooper, McGhee, Hewitt (Cowan), Weir

Leading positions

	P	W	D	L	F	A	Pts
1 Celtic	25	16	5	4	50	24	37
2 ABERDEEN	25	13	7	5	37	22	33
3 Rangers	26	11	10	5	41	31	32
4 St Mirren	25	12	7	6	40	30	31

Attendance: 30,100   *Referee:* D. Ramsay

The Premier League needed this result to keep the championship on ice a little longer. Stuart Kennedy's left-foot lob from the touchline sailed over Pat Bonner's head. Near the end a penalty was given to Celtic for Miller's nudge on McCluskey — who shot wide.

No 26 Saturday, 10 April
HIBERNIAN (0) 0   ABERDEEN (1) 3
              Jarvie (7),
              Strachan (61),
              McGhee (85)

HIBERNIAN: McArthur, Sneddon, Flavell, McNamara (Schaedler), Paterson, Brazil, McLaren, Jamieson, McLeod (Rodier), Rae, Duncan

ABERDEEN: Leighton, Mitchell, Rougvie, McMaster (Simpson), McLeish, Miller, Strachan, Watson, McGhee, Jarvie (Black), Weir

P	W	D	L	F	A	Pts	Attendance: 8,000
26	14	7	5	40	22	35	Referee: W. McLeish

Jarvie's head connected with Weir's flag-kick, 1-0. Strachan collected a return pass from McGhee for a whizz-bang second goal.

No 27 Wednesday, 14 April
ABERDEEN (0) 4   ST MIRREN (0) 1
 Rougvie 2 (62, 85)   Stark (49)
 Strachan (72),
 Simpson (77)

ABERDEEN: Leighton, Rougvie, McMaster, Watson (Cooper), McLeish, Miller, Strachan, Simpson, McGhee, Cowan (Jarvie), Weir

ST MIRREN: Money, Walker, Fulton, Fitzpatrick, Copland, Abercrombie, Stark, Curran (Bone), McEachran, McAvennie, Scanlon (Logan)

P	W	D	L	F	A	Pts	Attendance: 12,100
27	15	7	5	44	23	37	Referee: B. R. McGinlay

It's not often that Doug Rougvie scores – let alone scores two. But it's his big leg that equalised for Aberdeen in a scramble, and his head adds another. Goal of the match was Neil Simpson's thunderbolt.

No 28 Saturday, 17 April
MORTON (1) 2   ABERDEEN (0) 1
 McNeil (4),   McGhee (81)
 Holmes (90)

MORTON: Baines, Hayes, Holmes, Rooney, McLaughlin, Duffy, McNeil, Docherty, Cochrane, Hutchison, Ritchie (Busby)

ABERDEEN: Leighton, Kennedy, Rougvie, Cooper, McLeish, Miller, Jarvie (Simpson), Watson (McMaster), McGhee, Hewitt, Weir

P	W	D	L	F	A	Pts	Attendance: 3,000
28	15	7	6	45	25	37	Referee: B. R. McGinlay

It makes you want to weep. Morton end Aberdeen's long unbeaten run – as they did last season. This time the 90 minutes have been well consumed by the time Holmes fires his cruel winner, after the ball rebounds off the referee.

No 29 Wednesday, 21 April
ABERDEEN (2) 3   RANGERS (0) 1
 McGhee (7),   Johnstone (69)
 Rougvie (34),
 Black (56)

ABERDEEN: Leighton, Kennedy, Rougvie, Cooper (McMaster), McLeish, Miller, Black, Simpson, McGhee (Jarvie), Bell, Weir

RANGERS: Stewart, Dawson, Black, Jardine, McLelland, Bett, Dalziel, Russell, Johnstone, McDonald, Lyall (McAdam)

P	W	D	L	F	A	Pts	Attendance: 8,750
29	16	7	6	48	26	39	Referee: E. H. Pringle

Rangers have not defeated Aberdeen at Pittodrie for 17 games. Goalkeeper Stewart couldn't quite keep out McGhee's opener. He then failed to gather Eric Black's cross for the second, or Black's volley for the third.

No 30 Saturday, 24 April

ABERDEEN (0) 2   AIRDRIEONIANS (0) 0
  McGhee (55),
  Black (73)

ABERDEEN: Leighton, Kennedy, Rougvie, McMaster, McLeish, Miller, Black, Simpson, McGhee (Jarvie), Bell (Watson), Weir
AIRDRIE: Martin, Cairney, Rodger, Anderson, March, Gordon, Walker, Clark, Campbell, Flood, McKeown (Erwin)
Leading positions

	P	W	D	L	F	A	Pts
1 Celtic	32	22	6	4	70	30	50
2 ABERDEEN	30	17	7	6	50	26	41
3 Rangers	32	13	11	8	47	40	37

Attendance: 8,000   Referee: A. W. Waddell

All the talk is that Airdrie striker Sandy Clark is heading for Pittodrie – permanently. He never does transfer to Aberdeen, and his glaring misses in this match are probably responsible.

No 31 Saturday, 1 May

DUNDEE (0) 0   ABERDEEN (2) 5
                         McLeish (21),
                         Harrow (27),
                         Glennie o.g. (48),
                         Bell (51),
                         McCall (59)

DUNDEE: Geddes, Barr, McKimmie, Fraser, Smith, Glennie, Ferguson (Markie), Stephen, Sinclair, Kidd, McGeachie
ABERDEEN: Leighton, Kennedy, Rougvie, McMaster, McLeish, Miller, Black (Watson), Simpson (McCall), Harrow, Bell, Weir

P	W	D	L	F	A	Pts	
31	18	7	6	55	26	43	

Attendance: 6,400   Referee: E. Pringle

Aberdeen's highest score of the season does their relegation-threatened neighbours no favours whatsoever. Dundee goalkeeper Bobby Geddes made a present of the first three goals, all from corners.

No 32 Monday, 3 May

ABERDEEN (2) 3   PARTICK THISTLE (1) 1
  McCall (16),   Doyle (39)
  Watson (31),
  Hewitt (88)

ABERDEEN: Leighton, Kennedy, Rougvie, Watson, McLeish, Miller, Black, Bell, McCall (Cooper), Angus, Weir (Hewitt)
PARTICK: Rough, Murray, Lapsley, Whittaker, Dunlop, Watson, (McDonald), (McDowell), Park, Jardine, Johnston, Doyle, O'Hara

P	W	D	L	F	A	Pts
32	19	7	6	58	27	45

Attendance: 6,000   Referee: D. S. Downie

Thistle now look resigned to the drop. Meanwhile, Celtic were drawing 0-0 at home to St. Mirren and Aberdeen have to win every game to equal Celtic's 53 points.

No 33 Wednesday, 5 May

DUNDEE UNITED (1) 1   ABERDEEN (2) 2
  Hegarty (43)   Hewitt 2 (15, 37)

DUNDEE UNITED: McAlpine, Holt, Stark (Malpas), Gough, Hegarty, Narey, Bannon, Milne, Kirkwood (Reilly), Sturrock, Dodds
ABERDEEN: Leighton, Kennedy, Rougvie, McMaster, McLeish, Miller, Strachan (Cowan), Cooper, McGhee, Simpson (Watson), Hewitt

P	W	D	L	F	A	Pts	
33	20	7	6	60	28	47	

Attendance: 6,600   Referee: E. H. Pringle

Three games in five days, and you'd never believe it was the end of the season as Aberdeen continue to pick up steam.

No 34 Saturday, 8 May

ABERDEEN (3) 5   ST MIRREN (1) 1
  Strachan 2 (6, 24 pen) Spiers (38)
  McGhee 2 (12, 76),
  Cooper (59)

ABERDEEN: Leighton, Kennedy, Rougvie, McMaster, McLeish (Bell), Miller, Strachan, Cooper, McGhee, Simpson, Hewitt
ST MIRREN: Thomson, Stark, Beckett, Fitzpatrick, Fulton, Copland, McDougall (Logan), Richardson (Bone), Somner, McAvennie, Spiers
Leading positions

	P	W	D	L	F	A	Pts
1 Celtic	35	23	7	5	76	33	53
2 ABERDEEN	34	21	7	6	65	29	49

Attendance: 9,000   Referee: J. Duncan

Celtic are not quite home and dry – they lose 3-0 at Tannadice. Aberdeen can only become champions if they secure big wins in their last two matches while Celtic lose at home to St Mirren.

No 35 Wednesday, 12 May

ST MIRREN (0) 0   ABERDEEN (1) 2
                         McLeish (34),
                         Rougvie (61)

ST MIRREN: Thomson, Beckett (Somner), Walker, Fitzpatrick, Fulton, Copland, McEachran (Spiers), Stark, Bone, McAvennie, Richardson
ABERDEEN: Leighton, Kennedy, Rougvie, McMaster (Bell), McLeish, Miller, Strachan (Watson), Cooper, McGhee, Simpson, Hewitt

P	W	D	L	F	A	Pts	
35	22	7	6	67	29	51	

Attendance: 3,950   Referee: M. Delaney

Aberdeen certainly have the Indian sign over St Mirren. Just like Morton have the Indian sign over Aberdeen. The Dons' tall defenders McLeish and Rougvie move upfield to score with a header apiece.

No 36 Saturday, 15 May
ABERDEEN (4) 4   RANGERS (0) 0
  Jackson o.g. (23),
  Hewitt 3 (28, 39, 43)
ABERDEEN: Leighton, Kennedy, Rougvie, Cooper, McMaster, Miller, Strachan (Watson), Simpson, McGhee, Hewitt, Weir (McMaster)
RANGERS: Stewart, Jardine, Dawson, McClelland, Jackson, Bett, Cooper, Miller, Dalziel, Redford, McDonald
Attendance: 18,000   *Referee:* R. B. Valentine
Aberdeen meet Rangers in next week's Scottish Cup Final, and are well served by a John Hewitt hat-trick. Had Celtic lost 0-2 at home to St Mirren, the Dons would have been champions. But Celtic won 3-0.

Aberdeen's complete home and away record:

	HOME					AWAY					
P	W	D	L	F	A	W	D	L	F	A	Pts
36	12	4	2	36	15	11	3	4	35	14	53

Premier Division

	P	W	D	L	F	A	Pts
1 Celtic	36	24	7	5	79	33	55
2 ABERDEEN	36	23	7	6	71	29	53
3 Rangers	36	16	11	9	57	45	43
4 Dundee United	36	15	10	11	61	38	40
5 St Mirren	36	14	9	13	49	52	37
6 Hibernian	36	11	14	11	38	40	36
7 Morton	36	9	12	15	31	54	30
8 Dundee	36	11	4	21	46	72	26
9 Partick Thistle	36	6	10	20	35	59	22
10 Airdrieonians	36	5	8	23	31	76	18

LEAGUE CUP

Saturday, 8 August
ABERDEEN (2) 3   KILMARNOCK (0) 0
  McGhee 2 (4, 27),
  Kennedy (48)
ABERDEEN: Leighton, Kennedy, McMaster, Cooper, McLeish, Miller, Strachan, Harrow, McGhee, Bell, Weir
KILMARNOCK: McCulloch, McLean, Cockburn, Clark, (McBride), Armstrong, McDicken, Gallagher, Mauchlen, Bourke, Bryce, McCready
Referee: D. S. Downie
Only a goalpost prevented a Mark McGhee hat-trick on the opening day of the season.

Wednesday, 12 August
HEARTS (0) 1   ABERDEEN (0) 0
  Robertson (65)
HEARTS: Smith, More, Shields, Byrne, R. MacDonald, McLaren, Bowman, Robertson, G. Liddell, A. MacDonald, Hamill
ABERDEEN: Leighton, Kennedy, McMaster, Cooper, McLeish, Miller, Strachan, Bell, McGhee (Hewitt), Harrow (Jarvie), Weir

Attendance: 10,400   Referee: A. Ferguson
The goal that undermines Aberdeen's chances of qualifying from Section 3 was scored by Chris Robertson, whose wheeling shot-on-the-turn went in off a post.

Saturday, 15 August
ABERDEEN (2) 3   AIRDRIEONIANS (0) 0
  Hewitt (12),
  Weir (37),
  Strachan (89 pen)
ABERDEEN: Leighton, Kennedy, Hamilton, Cooper, McLeish, Miller, Strachan, Bell, McGhee, Hewitt, Weir
AIRDRIE: Martin, Walker, Rodger, McCluskey, March, N. Anderson, Kerr, Clark, Campbell, Gordon, Flood
Attendance: 7,000   *Referee:* G. B. Smith
Headers by John Hewitt and Peter Weir in the first half ended Airdrie's challenge, and set up the crunch return with Hearts.

Wednesday, 19 August
ABERDEEN (1) 3   HEARTS (0) 0
  Bell (35),
  Strachan (62 pen),
  Hewitt (72)
ABERDEEN: Leighton, Kennedy, McMaster (Watson), Cooper, McLeish, Miller, Strachan, Bell (McCall), McGhee, Hewitt, Weir
HEARTS: Smith, More, Shields, Byrne (Kidd), R. MacDonald, McLaren, Bowman (O'Connor), Robertson, McCoy, A. MacDonald, Hamill
Attendance: 8,000   *Referee:* R. B. Valentine
The first-division side couldn't repeat the upset of last week. Dougie Bell's long-range drive was poor reward for Aberdeen's first-half dominance.

Saturday, 22 August
KILMARNOCK (0) 0   ABERDEEN (2) 3
        Strachan 2 (26 pen, 33)
        McGhee (78)
KILMARNOCK: McCulloch, McLean, Cockburn, Clark, Armstrong, McDicken, Gallagher, Mauchlen, Bourke, Cramond (Robertson), McCready
ABERDEEN: Leighton, Kennedy, Rougvie (McMaster), Cooper, McLeish, Miller, Strachan, Bell (Watson), McGhee, Hewitt, Weir
Referee: M. Delaney
Coupled with Hearts' loss to Airdrie, Aberdeen's win takes them through to the knock-out stages. Strachan's third penalty in as many games sets things rolling.

Wednesday, 26 August
AIRDRIEONIANS (0) 0   ABERDEEN (0) 0
AIRDRIE: Martin, Gordon, Rodger, McCluskey, Erwin, Kerr, Flood, Clark, N. Anderson, McGuire, McKeown

L

ABERDEEN: Leighton, Rougvie, Angus, Watson, McLeish, Miller, Harrow (Hewitt), Bell (Jarvie), McCall, McMaster, Weir

Attendance: 3,000   *Referee:* E. H. Pringle

Ipswich manager Bobby Robson assesses his team's future UEFA Cup opponents. But Ferguson left out four first-team players.

Section 3

	P	W	D	L	F	A	Pts
ABERDEEN	6	4	1	1	12	1	9
Kilmarnock	6	2	2	2	5	8	6
Hearts	6	2	1	3	5	9	5
Airdrieonians	6	1	2	3	4	8	4

Quarter Final 1st Leg Wednesday, 2 September
ABERDEEN (4) 5   BERWICK RANGERS
Cooper (27),   (0) 0
Strachan 2 (33, 43 pen)
Bell (40),
McCall (87)

ABERDEEN: Leighton, Kennedy, McMaster, Cooper (Jarvie), McLeish, Miller, Strachan, Bell, McGhee, Hewitt, Weir (McCall)

BERWICK: McDermott, McCann, Black (McGlinchey), McCulloch, Dixon, Muir, Davidson, Moyes, Lawson, Tait (Romaines), Armstrong

Attendance: 6,500   *Referee:* R. B. Valentine

Berwick played the whole of the second half with ten men – and the last ten minutes with nine – following expulsions for McCulloch and Muir.

Quarter Final 2nd Leg Wednesday, 23 September
BERWICK RANGERS   ABERDEEN (2) 3
(0) 0   McMaster (21),
                               McGhee (38),
                               Harrow (87)

BERWICK: Glynn, Moyes, McCann, Marshall, Dixon, Muir, Romaines, Lawson (Krawiec), Armstrong, Tait, Black

ABERDEEN: Leighton, Kennedy, Rougvie, Watson, McLeish, Miller, Simpson, McCall, McGhee (Harrow), McMaster (Jarvie), Weir

Aberdeen won 8-0 on aggregate

Attendance: 1,200   *Referee:* T. Muirhead

All Berwick had to play for was their pride. At 8-0 on aggregate it's doubtful whether they achieved even that objective.

Semi Final 1st Leg Wednesday, 7 October
DUNDEE UNITED (0) 0   ABERDEEN (1) 1
                               Weir (23)

DUNDEE UNITED: McAlpine, Stark (Gough), Kopel, Phillip, Hegarty, Narey, Bannon, Milne, Kirkwood, Sturrock, Dodds.

ABERDEEN: Leighton, Kennedy, Rougvie, Watson, Cooper, Miller, Strachan, Simpson (McMaster), McGhee, Hewitt (Harrow), Weir

Attendance: 15,000   *Referee:* B. R. McGinlay

Dundee United are going for their third successive League Cup. Peter Weir headed the vital goal while United's Davie Dodds was off the field having stitches inserted in a head gash.

Semi Final 2nd Leg Wednesday, 28 October
ABERDEEN (0) 0   DUNDEE UNITED (2) 3
                               Sturrock 2 (7, 83),
                               Milne (38)

ABERDEEN: Leighton, Kennedy, Rougvie, Watson, Cooper, Miller, Strachan, Simpson (Bell), McGhee, Hewitt, Weir (McCall)

DUNDEE UNITED: McAlpine, Holt, Murray, Phillip, Hegarty, Narey, Bannon, Milne, Kirkwood, Sturrock, Dodds.

United won 3-1 on aggregate.

Attendance: 21,000   *Referee:* K. J. Hope

Unlucky 13 for Aberdeen, as their long unbeaten run comes to an end. Mistakes by Willie Miller and Jim Leighton cost Aberdeen the first two goals – and as Aberdeen piled on the pressure Paul Sturrock streaked away for the killer goal.

SCOTTISH CUP

3rd Round, Saturday, 23 January
MOTHERWELL (0) 0   ABERDEEN (1) 1
                               Hewitt (1)

MOTHERWELL: Sproat, McLeod (Coyne), Wark, McLelland, Carson, Forbes, McLaughlin, Rafferty, Irvine, O'Hara, Gahagan

ABERDEEN: Leighton, Kennedy, Rougvie, Cooper, McLeish, Miller, Strachan (McMaster), Bell, McGhee (Black), Hewitt, Weir

Attendance: 12,700   *Referee:* G. Smith

Alex Ferguson has just turned down the chance to manage Wolves. Motherwell are unbeaten in 18 first-division games, but concede the fastest goal in the history of the Scottish Cup. Kennedy's long cross reaches John Hewitt, who picks his spot in 9.6 seconds exactly. In the second half 'Well's Brian McLaughlin was sent off.

4th Round Saturday, 13 February
ABERDEEN (1) 1   CELTIC (0) 0
Hewitt (19)

ABERDEEN: Leighton, Kennedy, Rougvie, McMaster, McLeish, Miller, Strachan, Simpson (Bell), McGhee, Hewitt, Weir

CELTIC: Bonner, McGrain, Reid, Aitken, McAdam, McLeod, Sullivan (Halpin), McStay, McGarvey, Burns, McCluskey

Attendance: 24,000   *Referee:* K. J. Hope

Twice in the league this season Celtic have come from behind to win at Pittodrie. But not this time. John Hewitt follows up his record-breaking goal against Motherwell with an acrobatic flick to beat Bonner. Thereafter chances came and went at both ends.

Quarter Final Saturday, 6 March

ABERDEEN (2) 4   KILMARNOCK (2) 2
McGhee (20),   McGivern (1),
Simpson (35),   Gallagher (36)
Strachan 2 (60 pen, 64 pen)

ABERDEEN: Leighton, Kennedy, Hamilton,
McMaster, McLeish, Miller, Strachan (Watson),
Cooper, McGhee, Simpson, Hewitt
KILMARNOCK: McCulloch, McLean, Robertson,
Clark, Armstrong (McDicken), Clarke, Gallagher,
McLeod (Bryson), Bourke, Mauchlen, McGivern

Attendance: 11,000   *Referee:* R. B. Valentine

First-Division Kilmarnock take a first-minute lead from
a whipped centre. They then hit back after Aberdeen
had gone in front. In the second half McLean retaliated
against Cooper and was sent for an early bath. Then two
penalties, both for fouls on Strachan, both conceded by
Mauchlen.

Semi Final (Celtic Park) Saturday, 3 April

ST MIRREN (0) 1   ABERDEEN (0) 1
McDougall (61)   Strachan (66 pen)

ST MIRREN: Thomson, Beckett, Abercrombie,
Richardson, McCormack, Copland, Bone, Stark,
McDougall, McAvennie, Scanlon
ABERDEEN: Leighton, Kennedy, Rougvie (Bell),
McMaster, McLeish, Miller, Strachan, Cooper,
McGhee, Simpson, Hewitt (Jarvie)

Attendance: 16,782   *Referee:* H. Alexander

Chances are created, and scorned at either end before
Frank McDougall forces a corner and then scores from
it. Within minutes Thomson had pulled down McGhee
and Strachan took the kick. Almost immediately
Abercrombie flattened Strachan and was sent off.

Semi Final Replay (Dens Park) Wednesday, 7 April

ST MIRREN (1) 2   ABERDEEN (2) 3
McAvennie (17),   McGhee (6),
Somner (56)   Simpson (35),
                   Weir (74)

ST MIRREN: Thomson, Beckett, McCormack,
Richardson, Fulton (Fitzpatrick), Copland, McDougall,
Stark (Bone), Somner, McAvennie, Scanlon
ABERDEEN: Leighton, Rougvie, McMaster, Cooper,
McLeish, Miller, Strachan, Simpson, McGhee, Hewitt,
Weir (Watson)

Attendance: 15,670   *Referee:* H. Alexander

Aberdeen enjoy playing Cup semi-finals at Dens Park.
This is their fourth win there since the War. The
submerged pitch threatened to make a lottery of the
result. Poor Billy Thomson in the Saints' goal couldn't
hold McGhee's shot. Nor Simpson's. Aberdeen's
defence was almost as fragile. But at last Weir hit the
winner with a first-time shot.

Scottish Cup Final (Hampden) Saturday, 22 May

RANGERS (1) 1 *1*   ABERDEEN (1) 1 *4*
McDonald (15)   *(After Extra Time)*
                   McLeish (32),
                   McGhee (93),
                   Strachan (103),
                   Cooper (110)

RANGERS: Stewart, Jardine (McAdam), Dawson,
McClelland, Jackson, Bett, Cooper, Russell, Dalziel
(McLean), Miller, McDonald
ABERDEEN: Leighton, Kennedy, Rougvie, McMaster
(Bell), McLeish, Miller, Strachan, Cooper, McGhee,
Simpson, Hewitt (Black)

Attendance: 53,788   *Referee:* B. R. McGinlay

Peter Weir had to be left out, injured. John McDonald
leapt full length to head Dalziel's cross past Jim
Leighton. There followed an exquisite equaliser from
Don's man-of-the-match Alex McLeish. When Hewitt's
corner was cleared out to him, the centre-half curled a
delicious shot inside the far junction. Mark McGhee had
not played impressively as the match went into extra
time, but when Gordon Strachan's searching cross
dropped over his shoulder, McGhee headed past
Stewart on the run. Soon Dougie Bell crashed a shot
against a post. McGhee flicked the ball back and
Strachan scored from a range of six inches. When
Cooper ran onto a rebound from Stewart, Rangers'
humiliation was complete.

UEFA Cup

1st Round, 1st Leg Wednesday, 16 September

IPSWICH TOWN (1) 1   ABERDEEN (0) 1
Thijssen (45)   Hewitt (51)

IPSWICH: Cooper, Mills, McCall, Thijssen, Osman,
Butcher, Wark, Muhren, O'Callaghan, Brazil, Gates
ABERDEEN: Leighton, Kennedy, Rougvie, Watson,
McLeish, Miller, Strachan, Cooper, McGhee, Hewitt,
Weir

                   Referee: G. Menegali (Italy)

Aberdeen have been paired with the defending UEFA
Cup holders. The English press concur after this first-
leg match that Aberdeen turned in a superb show. They
became only the third team to avoid defeat at Portman
Road in 24 European ties. Aberdeen's vital away goal
came when McLeish headed Weir's corner down to
Hewitt.

1st Round, 2nd Leg Wednesday, 30 September

ABERDEEN (1) 3   IPSWICH TOWN (1) 1
Strachan (19 pen),   Wark (33 pen)
Weir 2 (55, 85)

ABERDEEN: Leighton, Kennedy, Rougvie, Watson
(Bell), McLeish, Miller, Strachan, Cooper (Simpson),
McGhee, Hewitt, Weir

IPSWICH: Cooper, Mills, McCall, Thijssen
(O'Callaghan), Osman, Butcher, Wark, Muhren,
Mariner, Brazil, Gates

Aberdeen won 4-2 on aggregate

Attendance: 24,000   *Referee:* M. Vautrot
                                        (France)

Wonderful Aberdeen! Before the match Ipswich boss Bobby Robson said Aberdeen could not play better than they did at Portman Road. He was wrong. Wark felled Strachan: penalty to Aberdeen. Cooper felled Gates: penalty to Ipswich. Then two crackers from Peter Weir, one with either foot. In the last minute Ipswich keeper Paul Cooper saved a second Strachan penalty at the second take.

2nd Round, 1st Leg Wednesday, 21 October
ABERDEEN (3) 3   ARGES PITESTI
    Strachan (11),   (Romania) (0) 0
    Weir (24),
    Hewitt (44)
ABERDEEN: Leighton, Kennedy, Rougvie, Watson, Cooper, Miller, Strachan, McMaster (Angus), McGhee, Hewitt (McCall), Weir
ARGES: Ariciu (Cristian), Zanfir, Barbulescu (Moicieanu), Tulpan, Stancu, Cirstea, Baluta, Kallo, Radu, Ignat, Turcu

Attendance: 22,000   *Referee:* S. I. Thime
                                        (Norway)

At half-time Aberdeen had every reason for celebration. But three quarters of an hour later there were nagging doubts. Why did they miss so many chances? Most remarkable of their three earlier goals was Weir's who somehow netted as the ball was about to go out of play for a goal-kick.

2nd Round, 2nd Leg Wednesday, 4 November
ARGES PITESTI (2) 2   ABERDEEN (0) 2
    Radu (31),   Strachan (55 pen),
    Barbulescu (36)   Hewitt (85)
ARGES: Cristian, Barbulescu, Badea, Eduard, Stancu, Cirstea, Baluta (Nica), Kallo, Radu, Ignat, Turcu (Moicieanu)
ABERDEEN: Leighton, Kennedy, Rougvie (Simpson), Cooper, McLeish, Miller, Strachan, Watson, McGee, McMaster (Hewitt), Weir

Aberdeen won 5-2 on aggregate

                             Referee: J. Redelfs
                                        (W Germany)

Aberdeen progress beyond the first two rounds of a European competition for the first time. For a while those missed chances at Pittodrie looked expensive. Radu's far-post header and Barbulescu's curling free kick left Aberdeen 2-0 down at the break. The Romanians' hopes were killed only when Weir was tripped in the box.

3rd Round, 1st Leg Wednesday, 25 November
ABERDEEN (1) 3   S V HAMBURG
    Black (23),   (W Germany) (0) 2
    Watson (65),   Hrubesch 2 (52, 87)
    Hewitt (81)

ABERDEEN: Leighton, Kennedy, McMaster, Watson, Rougvie (Cooper), Miller, Strachan, Black, McGhee (McCall), Simpson, Hewitt
HAMBURG: Stein, Kaltz, Memering, Groh, Beckenbauer, Hartwig (Hidien), Milewski (Hieronymus), Wehmeyer, Hrubesch, Magath, Bastrup

Attendance: 24,000   *Referee:* R. Schoeters
                                        (Belgium)

Legendary Franz Beckenbauer is just one of countless internationals in the German side. But Aberdeen take all the credit for this stirring match – and all the brickbats. Black soars like a bird to make it 1-0. He then headed against the bar. Tragedy when Leighton and Kennedy play silly beggars on the edge of the box. Kennedy loses possession – fatally. Watson made it 2-1. It could have been 3-1 except that Stein saves Strachan's penalty. Hewitt does make it 3-1. At the death, while Rougvie is off injured. Hrubesch crashes the ball in off Leighton's body to cries of frustration from the Dons' bench.

3rd Round, 2nd Leg Wednesday, 9 December
S V HAMBURG (1) 3   ABERDEEN (0) 1
    Hrubesch (33),   McGhee (79)
    Memering (59 pen),
    Jakobs (67)
HAMBURG: Stein, Wehmeyer, Groh, Jakobs, Beckenbauer, Von Heesen, Milewski, Memering, Hrubesch, Magath, Bastrup
ABERDEEN: Leighton, Kennedy (McGhee), McMaster, Watson, McLeish, Miller, Strachan (Bell), Cooper, Black, Simpson, Hewitt
Hamburg won 5-4 on aggregate

Attendance: 45,000   *Referee:* R. Juschka
                                        (Russia)

Aberdeen lost this tie at Pittodrie, not at the Volksparkstadion. Once the snow had been cleared from the pitch Hamburg proceeded to teach Aberdeen the arts of the game. Hrubesch's header put the Germans ahead on the away-goals rule. Aberdeen were out of it from that moment, despite Mark McGhee scoring his first goal for months.

Bobby Clark, a highly successful keeper with the Dons.

APPEARANCES	League	League Cup	Scottish Cup	UEFA Cup
Leighton	36	10	6	6
Miller	36	10	6	6
Kennedy	34	9	6	6
McLeish	32	8	6	4
Strachan	30	8	6	6
McGhee	29(+2)	9	6	5(+1)
Rougvie	28	5	5	5
Weir	25	10	3	4
Simpson	24(+5)	3	5	2(+2)
Cooper	22(+5)	8	5	5(+1)
Hewitt	22(+3)	6(+2)	6	5(+1)
McMaster	21(+10)	6(+2)	5(+1)	4
Watson	18(+12)	4(+2)	−(+2)	6
Bell	11(+2)	7(+1)	1(+3)	−(+2)
Black	10(+3)		−(+2)	2
McCall	6(+2)	2(+3)		−(+2)
Cowan	3(+10)			
Jarvie	3(+7)	−(+4)	−(+1)	
Harrow	3(+3)	3(+3)		
Angus	1	1		−(+1)
Hamilton	1	1	1	
Mitchell	1			
22 players				

GOALS	Total	League	League Cup	Scottish Cup	UEFA Cup
Strachan	20	7	6	4	3
Hewitt	19	11	2	2	4
McGhee	16	8	4	3	1
Weir	8	2	2	1	3
Watson	7	6			1
Rougvie	6	6			
McLeish	6	5		1	
Simpson	6	4		2	
McCall	5	4	1		
Cooper	5	3	1	1	
Black	4	3			1
Cowan	3	3			
Harrow	3	2	1		
Bell	3	1	2		
Jarvie	2	2			
Kennedy	2	1	1		
McMaster	2	1	1		
own-goals	2	2			
Totals	119	71	21	14	13

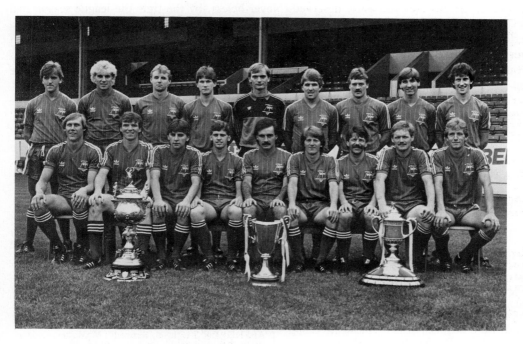

The Aberdeen squad in August 1983, winners of the Scottish Cup and European Cup Winners Cup. Back row: Weir, Cooper, Cowan, Angus, Leighton, McGhee, Bell, Mitchell, Stark. Front row: Rougvie, McLeish, Hewitt, Black, Miller, Strachan, Kennedy, McMaster and Simpson.

Season 1982-83

Everybody involved with Aberdeen F.C. knew that the team had not yet reached its peak and was destined for even greater honours. None of the first-team players moved elsewhere, thereby fostering the team-spirit so important to all great sides.

Aberdeen's first major disappointment in 1982-83 was losing to Dundee United in the League Cup for the third time in four seasons. That was in October, but it was to be many months before the Dons tasted any further disappointment.

As the players awoke on the morning of Wednesday, 16 March they were top of the league; they were through to the semi-finals of the Scottish Cup; and that evening they had an engagement with the mighty Bayern Munich in the quarter-final of the European Cup-Winners Cup. The circumstances of that match would write a chapter in Pittodrie folklore, as the Dons twice came from behind to win through amid scenes of utter pandemonium. In the penultimate hurdle Aberdeen swamped the Belgians of Waterschei to stake a place in their first European final.

At one stage it looked like Aberdeen were heading for a treble of monumental proportions. But faltering league form, which brought three defeats in four matches, eventually cost them the championship they so clearly deserved. Nevertheless, by the time the league season had run its course Aberdeen already had both hands around the Cup-Winners Cup, after a performance against Real Madrid in Gothenberg which stands as the apotheosis of everything that Alex Ferguson has achieved at Pittodrie. Ten days later the Scottish Cup was brought home, too, as the curtain came down on a season to eclipse all others. Never before had an Aberdeen team won two trophies in the same season.

The explanation behind Aberdeen's triumph in 1982-83 was straightforward: they had the meanest of defences, coupled with a potent strike-force which saw no fewer than six players' goal-tallies reach double figures.

League:	Third
League Cup:	Quarter Final
Scottish Cup:	Winners
European Cup Winners Cup:	Winners

SCOTTISH PREMIER DIVISION

No 1 Saturday, 4 September
DUNDEE UNITED (2) 2   ABERDEEN (0) 0
  Malpas (18), Dodds (40)

DUNDEE UNITED: McAlpine, Malpas, Stark (Bannon), Gough, Hegarty, Narey, Britton, Milne, Kirkwood, Sturrock, Dodds

ABERDEEN: Leighton, Kennedy, McMaster, Cooper, McLeish, Miller, Strachan, Simpson, McGhee, Bell (Weir), Black (Hewitt)

P	W	D	L	F	A	Pts	
1	0	0	1	0	2	0	*Attendance:* 11,700
							Referee: A. Ferguson

Aberdeen were almost a goal down in the first minute of the new league season. Dodds' header was net-bound until Leighton turned it onto the bar.

No 2 Saturday, 11 September
ABERDEEN (2) 4   MORTON (1) 1
  Strachan (15 pen),   McNeil (11)
  Black (42), Simpson (55),
  Hewitt (70)

ABERDEEN: Leighton, Kennedy, McMaster, Cooper (Bell), Rougvie, Miller, Strachan, Black (Hewitt), McGhee, Simpson, Weir

MORTON: Baines, Houston, Docherty, Rooney, McLaughlin, Duffy, Gavigan, McNeil (Jackson), Hutchison, Cochrane, McNab

318

P W D L F A Pts   *Attendance:* 8,000
2 1 0 1 4 3 2   *Referee:* C. C. Sinclair

This result is a tonic against the Dons' bugbear – Morton. Morton's cause was handicapped from the 35th minute when Jim Duffy was sent off for a foul on Eric Black.

No 3 Saturday, 18 September
ST MIRREN (0) 1   ABERDEEN (0) 1
  Scanlon (75)   McGhee (64)
ST MIRREN: Thomson, Wilson, McAveety, Fitzpatrick, McCormack, Copland, McAvennie, Stark, McDougall, Richardson, Scanlon (Logan)
ABERDEEN: Leighton, Kennedy, McMaster, Cooper, McLeish, Miller, Strachan, Simpson (Rougvie), Black, Hewitt (McGhee), Weir

P W D L F A Pts   *Attendance:* 4,800
3 1 1 1 5 4 3   *Referee:* B. Robertson

Substitute Mark McGhee scored with his first touch. Former Don, Ian Scanlon, then took the smile off his face.

No 4 Saturday, 25 September
ABERDEEN (0) 1   RANGERS (0) 2
  Strachan (73 pen)   Johnstone (49),
                            Prytz (62)
ABERDEEN: Leighton, Kennedy, Rougvie, Cooper, McLeish, Miller, Strachan, Simpson, McGhee, Bell, Black (Weir)
RANGERS: Stewart, McKinnon, Dawson, McClelland, Paterson, Bett, Cooper, Prytz, Johnstone, Russell, Redford

P W D L F A Pts   *Attendance:* 22,000
4 1 1 2 6 6 3   *Referee:* B. R. McGinlay

A day for Ibrox to celebrate, as Rangers notch their first-ever Premier League victory at Pittodrie. Two headed goals from unmarked Rangers players were enough to fend off Aberdeen's furious riposte.

No 5 Saturday, 2 October
ABERDEEN (0) 2   MOTHERWELL (1) 1
  Cowan (66), Miller (89)   Edvaldsson (25)
ABERDEEN: Leighton, Kennedy, Rougvie (Watson), McMaster, McLeish, Miller, Strachan, Simpson, McGhee, Hewitt (Cowan), Weir
MOTHERWELL: Sproat, McLeod, Forsyth, Carson, Edvaldsson, Rafferty, Clinging, (Coyle), Flavell, McClelland, Conn (Clelland), O'Hara

P W D L F A Pts   *Attendance:* 8,000
5 2 1 2 8 7 5   *Referee:* D. Ramsay

Motherwell come north with only one point to their name. Johann Edvaldsson looked like trebling that tally as he collected O'Hara's free kick. But substitute Cowan nets with his first touch and Willie Miller scores an unforgettable winner with an overhead kick.

No 6 Saturday, 9 October
CELTIC (0) 1   ABERDEEN (0) 3
  Nicholas (68)   Strachan (54 pen),
                            Simpson (58),
                            McGhee (86)
CELTIC: Bonner, McGrain, Reid, Aitken, McAdam, Sinclair, Provan, McStay, McGarvey, McLeod, Nicholas
ABERDEEN: Leighton, Cooper, Rougvie, McMaster, McLeish, Miller, Strachan, Simpson, McGhee, Bell (Watson), Weir

P W D L F A Pts   *Attendance:* 29,700
6 3 1 2 11 8 7   *Referee:* A. W. Waddell

Parkhead is where the action is, as Celtic tumble to their first league defeat. Reid's handling gives Aberdeen a penalty. With the score at 2-1 Danny McGrain removed Weir's legs and was ordered off. When McGhee scored a third, Celtic boss Billy McNeill ran onto the pitch to remonstrate.

No 7 Saturday, 16 October
ABERDEEN (1) 1   DUNDEE (0) 0
  Weir (34)
ABERDEEN: Leighton, Cooper, Rougvie, McMaster, McLeish, Miller, Strachan (Black), Simpson (Watson), McGhee, Bell, Weir
DUNDEE: Kelly, Glennie, McKimmie, Fraser, Smith, McDonald (Scrimgeour), Ferguson, Fleming, Bell (Sinclair), Mackie, Stephen

P W D L F A Pts   *Attendance:* 9,000
7 4 1 2 12 8 9   *Referee:* E. Pringle

Peter Weir teed-up a thumping 20-yard shot to open his account for the season. Jim Leighton preserved both points with a flying save from Fleming.

No 8 Saturday, 23 October
KILMARNOCK (0) 0   ABERDEEN (1) 2
                           Black (2), Hewitt (76)
KILMARNOCK: McCulloch, Robertson, McLeod, Clark, McDicken, Clarke, McGivern, McLean (Bourke), Gallacher, McClure, Bryson
ABERDEEN: Leighton, Cooper, Rougvie, McMaster, McLeish, Miller, Strachan (Hewitt), Simpson, Black, Bell, Weir

P W D L F A Pts   *Attendance:* 3,400
8 5 1 2 14 8 11   *Referee:* R. R. Cuthill

A flawless goal for Aberdeen after just two minutes. Strachan sends Rougvie away down the left and his cross is met by a crushing Black header.

No 9 Saturday, 30 October
HIBERNIAN (0) 1   ABERDEEN (0) 1
  Murray (67)   Weir (90)
HIBERNIAN: McArthur, Sneddon, Duncan, McNamara, Rae, Turnbull, Callaghan (Robertson), Conroy, Irvine, Thomson, Murray
ABERDEEN: Gunn, Cooper, Rougvie, McMaster, McLeish, Miller, Strachan, Simpson (Watson), Black, Bell (Hewitt), Weir

P W D L F A Pts
9 5 2 2 15 9 12

Attendance: 6,000
Referee: H. Alexander

The final seconds were ticking away when Rougvie provides the pass and Peter Weir provides the finish. Bryan Gunn had a useful debut in the Dons' goal.

No 10 Saturday, 6 November

ABERDEEN (3) 5
Cooper (23),
Rougvie 2 (29, 41),
Black (72), Strachan (85)

DUNDEE UNITED (1) 1
Gough (19)

ABERDEEN: Leighton, Kennedy, Rougvie, Cooper, McLeish, Miller, Strachan, Simpson, McGhee, Black, Weir

DUNDEE UNITED: McAlpine, Malpas, Stark, Gough, Hegarty, Narey, Bannon, Milne, Kirkwood, Holt, Dodds

Leading positions

	P	W	D	L	F	A	Pts
1 Celtic	10	8	1	1	26	12	17
2 ABERDEEN	10	6	2	2	20	10	14
3 Dundee United	10	5	4	1	18	8	14
4 Rangers	10	4	5	1	21	11	13

Attendance: 10,000   *Referee:* G. Smith

Dundee United were not only unbeaten; their defence had been pierced only three times in nine matches. There followed a 5-star blitz by the Dons that had the crowd roaring. The only disappointment was that Doug Rougvie did not gain his hat-trick.

No 11 Saturday, 13 November

MORTON (0) 1
McNab (14)

ABERDEEN (0) 1
Simpson (85)

MORTON: Baines, Houston, Holmes, Rooney, Hutchison, Docherty, McNeil, McNab, Gavigan, Cochrane, Higgins

ABERDEEN: Leighton, Kennedy, Rougvie, Cooper, McLeish, Miller, Strachan, Simpson, McGhee (Bell), Black, Weir

P W D L F A Pts
11 6 3 2 21 11 15

Attendance: 3,000
Referee: C. J. White

Roy Baines stood between Aberdeen and their equaliser. But the Morton keeper concedes defeat to Neil Simpson's screamer from a Strachan corner.

No 12 Saturday, 20 November

ABERDEEN (1) 4
Black (39),
Strachan (66 pen),
McGhee (79), Hewitt (90)

ST MIRREN (0) 0

ABERDEEN: Leighton, Kennedy, Rougvie, Cooper, McLeish, Miller, Strachan, Simpson (Hewitt), McGhee, Bell, Black

ST MIRREN: Thomson, Wilson, Clarke, Fitzpatrick, Fulton, Copland, Stark (McDougall), Richardson, Somner, McAvennie, Abercrombie

P W D L F A Pts
12 7 3 2 25 11 17

Attendance: 10,000
Referee: R. B. Valentine

Once they'd taken the measure of St Mirren's muscular resolve, Aberdeen won with ease. Strachan scored from a second-half penalty – but later in the season Billy Thomson would face Gordon Strachan again from the spot.

No 13 Saturday, 27 November

RANGERS (0) 0

ABERDEEN (0) 1
Black (69)

RANGERS: Stewart, McKinnon, Dawson (Mackay), McClelland, McPherson, Bett, Cooper, Prytz, Johnstone (Dalziel), Redford, McDonald

ABERDEEN: Leighton, Kennedy, Rougvie, Cooper (Black), McLeish, Miller, Strachan, Simpson, McGhee, Bell, Weir

P W D L F A Pts
13 8 3 2 26 11 19

Attendance: 24,000
Referee: A. Ferguson

Rangers looked to be taking the ascendancy in the second half until Weir strolled past McKinnon and Eric Black – the substitute – finished off with a mighty header.

No 14 Saturday, 4 December

MOTHERWELL (0) 0

ABERDEEN (0) 2
Strachan (50 pen),
Weir (66)

MOTHERWELL: Sproat, McLeod, Forsyth, Forbes, Edvaldsson, Mauchlen, Gahagan, Flavell, McClelland, Rafferty, O'Hara

ABERDEEN: Leighton, Kennedy, Rougvie, Cooper, McLeish, Miller, Strachan, Simpson, Black (Hewitt) (Watson), Bell, Weir

P W D L F A Pts
14 9 3 2 28 11 21

Attendance: 4,900
Referee: T. Muirhead

This win takes Aberdeen within two points of Celtic at the top. Strachan converts another penalty, this time after Mauchlen leaps to make a goalkeeper's save on the line.

No 15 Saturday, 11 December

ABERDEEN (1) 1
McGhee (18)

CELTIC (1) 2
McLeod (16),
Provan (59)

ABERDEEN: Leighton, Kennedy, Rougvie (Hewitt), Cooper, McLeish, Miller, Strachan, Simpson, McGhee, Bell (Black), Weir

CELTIC: Bonner, McGrain, Sinclair, Aitken, McAdam, McLeod, Provan, McStay, McGarvey, Burns, Nicholas

	P	W	D	L	F	A	Pts
1 Celtic	14	12	1	1	39	16	25
2 Dundee United	14	9	4	1	34	10	22
3 ABERDEEN	15	9	3	3	29	13	21
4 Rangers	14	4	7	3	24	17	15

Attendance: 25,000   *Referee:* K. Hope

Aberdeen were deflated by two wicked deflections that turned harmless shots into unstoppable goals. Miller changed the direction of McLeod's attempt. McLeish's chest altered the angle of Provan's winner.

No 16 Saturday, 18 December
DUNDEE (0) 0   ABERDEEN (1) 2
                     McGhee 2 (28, 54)
DUNDEE: Kelly, Glennie (McGlashan), McKimmie, Fraser, Smith, MacDonald, Murphy, Bell, Sinclair, Mackie, Stephen (McGeachie)
ABERDEEN: Leighton, Kennedy, Rougvie, Cooper, McLeish, Miller, Strachan, Simpson, McGhee, Black, Weir

P	W	D	L	F	A	Pts	*Attendance:* 6,500
16	10	3	3	31	13	23	*Referee:* J. Duncan

An orange ball was called for on the white frosty pitch. Dundee tempers became frosty with McGhee's first goal – when both Simpson and Cooper were yards offside.

No 17 Monday, 27 December
ABERDEEN (1) 2   KILMARNOCK (0) 0
  Weir (4), Miller (87)
ABERDEEN: Leighton, Kennedy, Rougvie, Cooper, McLeish, Miller, Strachan, Simpson, McGhee (McCall), Black, Weir
KILMARNOCK: McCulloch, McLean, Robertson, J. Clark, McDicken, P. Clarke, McGivern, McLeod, Bourke, Cockburn, Gallagher (Bryson)

P	W	D	L	F	A	Pts	*Attendance:* 14,500
17	11	3	3	33	13	25	*Referee:* H. Young

Arctic weather – especially for poor Jim Leighton who was allowed to stand idle from first to last. 14,500 freezing souls paid at the turnstiles – not to see Kilmarnock but to acquire vouchers for the Bayern Munich match.

No 18 Saturday, 1 January
ABERDEEN (2) 2   HIBERNIAN (0) 0
  McGhee 2 (1, 24)
ABERDEEN: Leighton, Kennedy, Rougvie, Bell, McLeish, Miller, Strachan (Watson), Simpson, McGhee, Black (McCall), Weir
HIBERNIAN: Rough, Sneddon, Turnbull, (Thomson), Rae, Jamieson, McNamara, Callachan (Byrne), Conroy, Duncan, Reid, Murray

P	W	D	L	F	A	Pts	*Attendance:* 14,000
18	12	3	3	35	13	27	*Referee:* n.a.

Twenty seconds into the first match of the new year and Mark McGhee side-foots his first goal past a stranded Rough.

No 19 Monday, 3 January
DUNDEE UNITED (0) 0   ABERDEEN (2) 3
                       Simpson (27), Weir (43),
                       McGhee (89)
DUNDEE UNITED: McAlpine, Stark, Malpas (Holt), Gough, Hegarty, Narey, Bannon, Milne, Kirkwood (Reilly), Sturrock, Dodds
ABERDEEN: Leighton, Kennedy, Rougvie, Cooper, McLeish, Miller, Strachan (Black), Simpson (McMaster), McGhee, Bell, Weir

P	W	D	L	F	A	Pts	*Attendance:* 14,000
19	13	3	3	38	13	29	*Referee:* B. R. McGinlay

This is Dundee United's first defeat at Tannadice since May 1982, when their conquerors were – you-know-who. Aberdeen have now scored eight times in three matches this season against United, who have let in only six goals in their other 15 games.

No 20 Saturday, 8 January
ABERDEEN (0) 2   MORTON (0) 0
  Simpson (70),
  McGhee (84)
ABERDEEN: Leighton, Kennedy, Rougvie, Cooper (Watson), McLeish, Miller, Black (McMaster), Simpson, McGhee, Bell, Weir
MORTON: Baines, Houston, Holmes, Rooney, McLaughlin, Duffy, Payne, Gibson, Hutchison, Cochrane, McNab (Slavin)

Leading positions

	P	W	D	L	F	A	Pts
1 Celtic	19	16	2	1	53	20	34
2 ABERDEEN	20	14	3	3	40	13	31
3 Dundee United	19	12	4	3	44	16	28
4 Rangers	19	6	8	5	28	23	20

Attendance: 14,000   *Referee:* M. Delaney

The goalmouths had to be swept of snow. At last the ball broke to Neil Simpson 18 yards out. McGhee added a second when dribbling round the goalkeeper.

No 21 Saturday, 15 January
ST MIRREN (1) 1   ABERDEEN (0) 1
  Scanlon (45)   Black (75)
ST MIRREN: Thomson, Wilson, Clarke, Walker, Fulton, Abercrombie, Stark, Richardson, McDougall, McAvennie, Scanlon
ABERDEEN: Leighton, Kennedy, Rougvie, Watson (Black), McLeish, Miller, Strachan, Simpson (McMaster), McGhee, Bell, Weir

P	W	D	L	F	A	Pts	*Attendance:* 4,500
21	14	4	3	41	14	32	*Referee:* A. W. Waddell

When Ian Scanlon did the dirty on his old team-mates he prevented Aberdeen equalling a Premier League record of six successive shut-outs. Now the players are bound for Spain for a holiday.

No 22 Saturday, 22 January
ABERDEEN (1) 2   RANGERS (0) 0
  Rougvie (34),
  McGhee (77)
ABERDEEN: Leighton, Kennedy, Rougvie, Cooper (McMaster), McLeish, Miller, Strachan (Simpson), Black, McGhee, Bell, Weir
RANGERS: McCloy, McKinnon, Redford, Stevens, McClelland, Bett, Cooper, Prytz, Kennedy, Dawson, Johnstone (McDonald)

P	W	D	L	F	A	Pts	*Attendance:* 22,000
22	15	4	3	43	14	34	*Referee:* K. J. Hope

M

Despite the comparatively close score, this was one of the most one-sided of matches against Rangers in recent years. Unfortunately the fists also flew. Near the end Rangers sub John McDonald butted Dougie Bell and off he went amid unsavoury scenes.

No 23 Tuesday, 8 February
ABERDEEN (2) 5   MOTHERWELL (1) 1
  McLeish (36),   Rafferty (10)
  McMaster (38),
  McGhee (52), Black (67),
  Cooper (71)
ABERDEEN: Leighton, Kennedy, Rougvie, McMaster, McLeish, Miller, Black (Cooper), Simpson, McGhee, Bell, Weir (Watson)
MOTHERWELL: Walker, Flavell, Dornan, Carson, Edvaldsson, Forbes (Coyne), McClair, Rafferty, Harrow, Mauchlen, O'Hara

P	W	D	L	F	A	Pts	*Attendance:* 13,000
23	16	4	3	48	15	36	*Referee:* J. R. S. Renton

The scoreline doesn't tell the story that Motherwell held the lead for 26 minutes, until Alex McLeish did his striker's job. The centre-half netted with his foot, not his head – a rarity.

No 24 Saturday, 12 February
CELTIC (1) 1   ABERDEEN (2) 3
  Nicholas (34)   Black 3 (44, 45, 71)
CELTIC: Bonner, McGrain, Reid, Aitken, McAdam, Sinclair, Provan, McStay, McGarvey, McLeod, Nicholas
ABERDEEN: Leighton, Kennedy, Rougvie, Cooper, McLeish, Miller, Black, Simpson, McGhee, Bell, Weir
Leading positions

	P	W	D	L	F	A	Pts
1 ABERDEEN	24	17	4	3	51	16	38
2 Celtic	23	17	3	3	60	27	37
3 Dundee United	23	14	6	3	53	19	34

Attendance: 42,800   *Referee:* R. B. Valentine
Aberdeen leap over Celtic to the top after teenager Eric Black's glorious hat-trick. He is the first player to score three times against Celtic in memory. Two of his goals were in the dying seconds of the first half, and the watching spies of Bayern Munich are mighty impressed.

No 25 Saturday, 26 February
ABERDEEN (0) 3   DUNDEE (1) 1
  Weir (58), Black (85),   Stephen (6)
  Bell (90)
ABERDEEN: Leighton, Kennedy, Rougvie (Cooper), McMaster, McLeish, Miller, Black, Watson (Simpson), McGhee, Bell, Weir
DUNDEE: Kelly, McGeachie, McKimmie, Fraser, Smith, MacDonald, Ferguson, Scrimgeour, Kidd, Mackie, Stephen

P	W	D	L	F	A	Pts	*Attendance:* 11,400
25	18	4	3	54	17	40	*Referee:* D. Syme

For an hour it seemed as though Dundee were going to gain revenge for their cup elimination of last week. But then Aberdeen put their appointment with Bayern Munich out of their minds. Weir's diving header was followed by Black's sensational overhead kick.

No 26 Saturday, 5 March
KILMARNOCK (0) 1   ABERDEEN (2) 2
  Gallagher (65)   Watson (13),
               McGhee (26)
KILMARNOCK: McCulloch, McClurg, Cockburn, J. Clark, McDicken, R. Clark, McGivern (Muir), McLeod (McLean), Bourke, Simpson, Gallagher
ABERDEEN: Leighton, Kennedy, Rougvie (McMaster), Cooper, McLeish, Miller, Strachan, Simpson, McGhee, Watson, Black

P	W	D	L	F	A	Pts	*Attendance:* 2,400
26	19	4	3	56	18	42	*Referee:* J. Duncan

A first-half picnic turned into a second-half struggle against bottom-of-the-table Killie. An uncharacteristic mix-up between Leighton and McLeish let Kilmarnock back into the match.

No 27 Saturday, 19 March
ABERDEEN (0) 1   DUNDEE UNITED (2) 2
  Strachan (66 pen)   Milne 2 (26, 30)
ABERDEEN: Leighton, Cooper, Rougvie, McMaster, McLeish, Miller, Strachan, Bell (Simpson), McGhee, Hewitt, Weir (Black)
DUNDEE UNITED: McAlpine, Stark, Malpas, Gough, Hegarty, Narey, Bannon, Milne, Kirkwood, Phillip, Dodds
Leading positions

	P	W	D	L	F	A	Pts
1 ABERDEEN	27	19	4	4	57	20	42
2 Dundee United	27	17	7	3	65	25	41
3 Celtic	26	19	3	4	68	29	41

Attendance: 22,800   *Referee:* E. H. Pringle
After the heroics against Bayern Munich, Aberdeen dare not suffer any reaction. They do. The match belonged to United's Ralph Milne, the ball crashing down off the bar for his first goal, and being swept past Leighton for his second. After the interval Milne swung a kick at McLeish, succeeded, and was sent off.

No 28 Saturday, 26 March
MORTON (1) 1   ABERDEEN (0) 2
  Ritchie (30)   Watson (83), Black (90)
MORTON: Kyle, Houston, Holmes, Rooney, McLaughlin, Docherty, McNeil, McNab, Hutchison, Cochrane, Ritchie (Payne)
ABERDEEN: Leighton, Kennedy, McMaster, Cooper (Waton), Rougvie (McLeish), Miller, Strachan, Simpson, McGhee, Black, Weir

P	W	D	L	F	A	Pts	*Attendance:* 4,000
28	20	4	4	59	21	44	

Brinkmanship at its best. Ritchie scores from a free kick, 30 yards out. Near the end sub Watson stabs a close-range equaliser. In injury time Black's left foot steals the second point.

No 29 Saturday, 2 April
ABERDEEN (0) 0   ST MIRREN (0) 1
                                  McEachran (73)
ABERDEEN: Leighton, Kennedy, McMaster
(Rougvie), Cooper (Watson), McLeish, Miller,
Strachan, Simpson, McGhee, Black, Weir
ST MIRREN: Thomson, Wilson, Clarke (McEachran),
McCormack, Fulton, Copland, Logan, Richardson,
Wardrope (McDougall), McAvennie, Abercrombie

P	W	D	L	F	A	Pts	*Attendance:* 12,000
29	20	4	5	59	22	44	*Referee:* R. B. Valentine

Injury-wrecked St Mirren wreck the Dons' title hopes
in driving snow. With the first half into injury time
Strachan's penalty slides wide of a post. Worse was to
come when Saints' second substitute drives a rebound
from McLeish wide of Leighton.

No 30 Saturday, 9 April
RANGERS (1) 2   ABERDEEN (1) 1
Redford (21), Bett (86)   McLeish (15)
RANGERS: McCloy, Dawson, McClelland,
McPherson, Paterson, Bett, Russell (Dalziel),
McKinnon, Clark, Redford, McDonald (Cooper)
ABERDEEN: Leighton, Kennedy, Rougvie
(McMaster), Cooper, McLeish, Miller, Strachan,
Simpson, McGhee, Bell, Weir (Black)
Leading positions

	P	W	D	L	F	A	Pts
1 Celtic	31	22	5	4	77	30	49
2 Dundee	31	19	8	4	73	32	46
3 ABERDEEN	30	20	4	6	60	24	44

Attendance: 19,800   *Referee:* A. W. Waddell

Alex McLeish's 250th appearance for Aberdeen was
marked with a typical thumping header. Unfortunately
Redford swept home a curling cross to level the scores.
With Aberdeen pressing forward continuously, Rangers
broke away for Jim Bett to snatch a cruel winner.

No 31 Saturday, 23 April
ABERDEEN (1) 1   CELTIC (0) 0
McGhee (34)
ABERDEEN: Leighton, Cooper, Rougvie, McMaster,
McLeish, Miller, Strachan, Watson, McGhee
(Falconer), Hewitt, Weir (Simpson)
CELTIC: Bonner, McGrain, Reid (Moyes), Aitken,
McAdam, McLeod, Provan, McStay, Nicholas, Burns
McGarvey

P	W	D	L	F	A	Pts	*Attendance:* 24,500
31	21	4	6	61	24	46	*Referee:* A. Ferguson

With a place booked in the European Cup-Winners Cup
Final and the Scottish Cup Final Aberdeen know they
have to beat Celtic to retain interest in the league.
Under the worried eyes of Alfredo di Stefano of Real
Madrid, the vital goal, a McGhee header, entered the
net via a post and Aitken's foot.

No 32 Wednesdday, 27 April
MOTHERWELL (0) 0   ABERDEEN (1) 3
                                  McGhee (11),
                                  Strachan (58),
                                  Hewitt (74)
MOTHERWELL: Walker, Dornan, McLeod, Wark,
Edvaldsson, Flavell, Gahagan, Rafferty, Harrow
(Cormack), McClair, O'Hara
ABERDEEN: Leighton, Cooper (Angus), Rougvie,
McMaster, McLeish, Miller, Strachan, Simpson,
McGhee (Hamilton), Watson, Hewitt

P	W	D	L	F	A	Pts	*Attendance:* 6,700
32	22	4	6	64	24	48	*Referee:* E. H. Pringle

Not as easy as the score suggests. Two Motherwell goals
were chalked off, and Leighton saved miraculously from
McClair to prevent an equaliser.

No 33 Saturday, 30 April
DUNDEE (0) 0   ABERDEEN (2) 2
                                  Hewitt (3), Strachan (40)
DUNDEE: Kelly, McGeachie (Kidd), McKimmie,
Fraser, Smith, MacDonald, Mackie, Glennie,
Davidson, Scrimgeour, Ferguson
ABERDEEN: Leighton, Cooper (Angus), Rougvie,
McMaster, McLeish, Miller, Strachan, Simpson,
McGhee, Watson (Black), Hewitt

P	W	D	L	F	A	Pts	*Attendance:* 10,100
33	23	4	6	66	24	50	*Referee:* D. Downie

Goal average might well prove decisive in the race for
the title. While Aberdeen netted two, Dundee United
were scoring four, and Celtic five.

No 34 Tuesday, 3 May
HIBERNIAN (0) 0   ABERDEEN (0) 0
HIBERNIAN: Rough, McKee, Sneddon, Brazil,
Welsh, Rice, Callachan, Irvine, Murray (Harvey),
Thomson, Duncan
ABERDEEN: Leighton, Cooper, McMaster, Watson,
McLeish, Miller, Strachan, Hewitt, McGhee, Angus
(Rougvie), Weir (Cowan)
Leading positions

	P	W	D	L	F	A	Pts
1 Dundee United	34	22	8	4	84	34	52
2 Celtic	34	23	5	6	84	34	51
3 ABERDEEN	34	23	5	6	66	24	51

Attendance: 8,000   *Referee:* B. R. McGinlay

Aberdeen needed to win 9-0 to go top on goal
difference. Gordon Strachan's penalty misses look like
costing Aberdeen the championship. This time his kick
is saved by Rough in the 23rd minute.

No 35 Thursday, 5 May
ABERDEEN (2) 5   KILMARNOCK (0) 0
Strachan 2 (30, 58),
McMaster (39),
Angus 2 (46, 85)

ABERDEEN: Leighton, Mitchell, McMaster, Watson (Bell), Rougvie, Miller, Strachan, Porteous (Black), Hewitt, Angus, Weir

KILMARNOCK: McCulloch, Cockburn, R. Clark, J. Clark, McDicken, P. Clarke, McGivern, McLeod, Bryson, Simpson (Mair), Gallacher

P	W	D	L	F	A	Pts
35	24	5	6	71	24	53

Attendance: 12,500   *Referee:* R. B. Valentine

This match was scheduled for Saturday but was brought forward by two days to give the Dons more time to prepare for Gothenburg. This straightforward win enabled Aberdeen to sit on top of the league till the weekend. Goal of the match was No 4, the result of McMaster's 60-yard lobbed pass to the feet of Strachan.

No 36 Saturday, 14 May
ABERDEEN (2) 5   HIBERNIAN (0) 0
    Brazil o.g. (9),
    McGhee (30),
    Strachan (70 pen),
    Cowan (78), Angus (87)

ABERDEEN: Leighton, Rougvie, McMaster, Watson, McLeish (Hamilton), Miller, Strachan, Black (Cowan), McGhee, Angus, Weir

HIBERNIAN: Rough, Conroy (McKee), Sneddon, Brazil, Welsh (Harvey), McNamara, Callachan, Rice, Irvine, Thomson, Duncan

Attendance: 24,000   *Referee:* D. Syme

The Hib's players line up to applaud the Cup-Winners Cup holders onto the pitch. And well they might They were then flattened. But Aberdeen could only lift the title if Dundee United lost and Celtic drew. They both won.

Aberdeen's complete home and away record:

HOME						AWAY					
P	W	D	L	F	A	W	D	L	F	A	Pts
36	14	0	4	46	12	11	5	2	30	12	55

Premier Division

	P	W	D	L	F	A	Pts
1 Dundee United	36	24	8	4	90	35	56
2 Celtic	36	25	5	6	90	36	55
3 ABERDEEN	36	25	5	6	76	24	55
4 Rangers	36	13	12	11	52	41	38
5 St Mirren	36	11	12	13	47	51	34
6 Dundee	36	9	11	16	42	53	29
7 Hibernian	36	7	15	14	35	51	29
8 Motherwell	36	11	5	20	39	73	27
9 Morton	36	6	8	22	30	74	20
10 Kilmarnock	36	3	11	22	28	91	17

LEAGUE CUP

Wednesday, 11 August
MORTON (1) 2   ABERDEEN (1) 2
    Hutchison (21),   Strachan (12),
    Ritchie (85 pen)   McGhee (53)

MORTON: Baines, Houston (Higgins), Holmes, Rooney, McLaughlin, Duffy, McNeil, Docherty, Hutchison, Cochrane, Ritchie

ABERDEEN: Leighton, Kennedy, Rougvie, Cooper, McLeish, Miller, Strachan, Black (Cowan), McGhee, Angus, Weir (Simpson)

Attendance: 3,500   *Referee:* H. Alexander

Willie Miller has just re-signed for the club, but he now costs Aberdeen a point when he handles from Hutchison.

Saturday, 14 August
ABERDEEN (2) 3   DUNDEE (1) 3
    Black 3 (30, 45, 85)   Stephen 2 (43, 80),
                                 Ferguson (59 pen)

ABERDEEN: Leighton, Kennedy, Rougvie, Cooper, McLeish, Miller, Strachan, Black, McGhee (Hamilton), Simpson, Angus (Hewitt)

DUNDEE: Blair, McKimmie, McLelland, Fraser, MacDonald, Glennie, Ferguson, McGeachie, Sinclair, Mackie, Stephen

Attendance: 9,000   *Referee:* B. R. McGinlay

How strange. Aberdeen applied nearly all the pressure, but until Eric Black completed his hat-trick near the end Aberdeen might well have lost.

Saturday, 21 August
ABERDEEN (2) 3   DUMBARTON (0) 0
    McGhee (5),
    Strachan 2 (13, 70)

ABERDEEN: Leighton, Kennedy, McMaster, Simpson, McLeish, Miller, Strachan, Black, McGhee (Hewitt), Bell (Rougvie), Weir

DUMBARTON: Carson, Walker (Stevenson), McGowan, Clougherty, Close, Coyle, Blair (Burnett), Brown, Dunlop, Donnelly, McGrogan

Attendance: 6,500   *Referee:* D. Downie

Dumbarton keeper Tom Carson stands between Aberdeen and an inflated score. For some reason Willie Miller seemed determined to score a goal himself. He failed.

Wednesday, 25 August
ABERDEEN (2) 3   MORTON (0) 0
    Rougvie (19),
    Bell 2 (27, 48)

ABERDEEN: Leighton, Rougvie, McMaster, Cooper, McLeish, Miller, Strachan (Hewitt), Black, McGhee, Bell, Simpson (Angus)

MORTON: Baines, Houston, Holmes, Rooney, McLaughlin, Duffy, McNeil, Docherty, Hutchison, Cochrane, Ritchie (Gavigan)

Attendance: 12,000   *Referee:* R. B. Valentine

Near the end Aberdeen were down to nine men as Black and Hewitt were unable to continue. By then Aberdeen could have been down to three and Morton still wouldn't have won.

European Cup Winners Cup celebrations. Alex Ferguson holds the Cup aloft at Pittodrie after city tour.

Scottish Cup Winners 1983. The Dons show off the trophy to their supporters in Union Street, Aberdeen.

Saturday, 28 August
DUNDEE (0) 1   ABERDEEN (2) 5
Stephen (65)   Strachan 4 (23, 52, 53,
                                63), McGhee (28)

DUNDEE: R. Geddes, McKimmie, McLelland,
Fraser, Glennie, McGeachie, Ferguson, A. Geddes
(Kidd), Sinclair (Davidson), Mackie, Stephen
ABERDEEN: Leighton, Kennedy, McMaster, Cooper,
Rougvie (Black) (Angus), Miller, Strachan, Simpson,
McGhee, Bell, Hewitt

Attendance: 7,000   *Referee:* D. Galloway

Gordon Strachan is still living off his World Cup
memories. He takes Dundee apart virtually single-
handed – including a chip over Geddes from all of 35
yards.

Wednesday, 8 September
DUMBARTON (0) 1   ABERDEEN (0) 2
Donnelly (89 pen)   Bell (76), Hewitt (85)

DUMBARTON: Carson, Brown, McNeil
(M. McGowan), P. McGowan, Close, Coyle, Craig,
Burnett, Dunlop, Donnelly, Stevenson (Blair)
ABERDEEN: Leighton, Mitchell, McMaster, Cooper,
McLeish (Cowan), Miller, Black, Watson, Hewitt,
Simpson (Bell), Weir

Attendance: 3,000

Aberdeen had to lose 5-0 to first-division Dumbarton
to let Morton qualify at their expense. That's never
likely – especially once Doug Bell has scored through a
heap of legs.

Section 2

	P	W	D	L	F	A	Pts
ABERDEEN	6	4	2	0	18	7	10
Morton	6	3	2	1	16	11	8
Dundee	6	2	2	2	14	19	6
Dumbarton	6	0	0	6	7	18	0

Quarter Final 1st Leg Wednesday, 22 September
ABERDEEN (1) 1   DUNDEE UNITED (2) 3
McGhee (14)   Gough (25), Bannon (31),
                            Kirkwood (80)

ABERDEEN: Leighton, Rougvie (Kennedy),
McMaster, Cooper, McLeish, Miller, Strachan, Watson
(Black), McGhee, Hewitt, Weir
DUNDEE UNITED: McAlpine, Phillip (Malpas),
Stark, Gough, Hegarty, Narey, Bannon, Milne,
Kirkwood, Sturrock, Dodds

Attendance: 13,000   *Referee:* H. Alexander

United's Hegarty hesitated to let in McGhee. Gough
was almost on his haunches to head the equaliser.
Bannon fired the next goal off the crossbar. Kirkwood's
header into an unguarded net gave Aberdeen an uphill
climb in the return.

Quarter Final 2nd Leg Wednesday, 6 October
DUNDEE UNITED (0) 1 ABERDEEN (0) 0
Sturrock (72 pen)

DUNDEE UNITED: McAlpine, Phillip, Stark,
Gough, Hegarty, Narey, Malpas, Milne, Kirkwood,
Sturrock, Dodds
ABERDEEN: Leighton, Cooper, Rougvie, McMaster,
McLeish, Miller, Strachan, Simpson, McGhee (Black),
Hewitt, Weir

United won 4-1 on aggregate

Attendance: 11,750   *Referee:* G. B. Smith

Strachan and Weir on the flanks meant that United's
defence was under constant pressure. Aberdeen's
chances died when Simpson was adjudged to have
handled Hegarty's header.

SCOTTISH CUP

3rd Round Saturday, 29 January
HIBERNIAN (0) 1   ABERDEEN (2) 4
Rae (65)   Weir (33), Simpson (35),
                            Watson (83),
                            McGhee (84)

HIBERNIAN: Rough, Sneddon, Schaedler, Rice, Rae,
McNamara, Callachan (Irvine), Conroy (Welsh),
Duncan, Thomson, Murray
ABERDEEN: Leighton, Kennedy, Rougvie, McMaster
(Watson), McLeish, Miller, Black, Simpson, McGhee,
Bell, Weir

Attendance: 20,000   *Referee:* A. Ferguson

Aberdeen hit Hibs with the old one-two. Twice. After
Rae's 20-yarder threatened to spark a Hibs revival, up
popped Andy Watson to run half the length of the soggy
pitch to put the game beyond them.

4th Round Saturday, 19 February
ABERDEEN (0) 1   DUNDEE (0) 0
Simpson (46)

ABERDEEN: Leighton, Kennedy, Rougvie, Cooper,
McLeish, Miller, Black, Simpson, McGhee, Bell, Weir
DUNDEE: Kelly, McGeachie, McKimmie, Fraser,
Smith, McDonald, Ferguson, Bell (Glennie), Sinclair,
Mackie, Stephen

Attendance: 20,000   *Referee:* H. Alexander

Dundee may only have lost by one goal, but they were
beaten by the breadth of the Tay. Simpson ended their
resistance 53 seconds after the start of the second half,
following up when Black's shot was blocked.

Quarter Final Saturday, 12 March
PARTICK THISTLE (0) 1 ABERDEEN (1) 2
McDonald (63)   Cooper (4), Weir (72)

PARTICK: McNab, G. Doyle, Whittaker, Murray,
Jackson, Watson, Park, McDonald, Johnston, J. Doyle,
O'Hara
ABERDEEN: Leighton, Kennedy, Rougvie, Cooper,
McLeish, Miller, Strachan, Simpson, McGhee, Bell
(Black), Weir

Attendance: 12,000

Aberdeen prepare for the visit of Bayern with a patchy performance against first division Partick. After McDonald had blasted Thistle level, Weir curled a free kick – Brazilian style – round wall and keeper.

Semi Final (Hampden) Saturday, 16 April
CELTIC (0) 0   ABERDEEN (0) 1
                           Weir (65)
CELTIC: Bonner, Sinclair, Reid, Aitken, McAdam, McLeod, Provan, McStay, McCluskey (Crainie), Burns, McGarvey
ABERDEEN: Leighton, Kennedy, Rougvie, Cooper (Weir), McLeish, Miller, Strachan, Simpson, McGhee, Bell, Black (Watson)
Attendance: n.a.   *Referee:* A. Ferguson
Neither side had any interest in playing football. There was no sign of a goal at either end when substitute Weir raced in to head Black's cross just inside a post.

Scottish Cup Final (Hampden) Saturday, 21 May
RANGERS (0) 0 *0*   ABERDEEN (0) 0 *1*
                              (After Extra Time)
                              Black (116)
RANGERS: McCloy, Dawson, McClelland, McPherson, Paterson, Bett, Cooper (Davies), McKinnon, Clark, Russell, McDonald (Dalziel)
ABERDEEN: Leighton, Rougvie (Watson), McMaster, Cooper, McLeish, Miller, Strachan, Simpson, McGhee, Black, Weir (Hewitt)
Attendance: 62,970   *Referee:* D. Syme
Aberdeen field the same eleven as won the Cup-Winners Cup. They are overwhelming favourites, but perhaps Rangers saw more of the ball in a lacklustre 90 minutes. There were only four minutes of extra time left when Paterson deflected McGhee's low cross high in the air for Black to nod into an empty net. Alex Ferguson was so disappointed with the quality of his team's performance that he publicly criticised them. He later apologised.

EUROPEAN CUP-WINNERS CUP

Preliminary Round 1st Leg Wednesday, 18 August
ABERDEEN (4) 7   SION (Switzerland) (0) 0
   Black (5), Strachan (21),
   Hewitt (22), Simpson (34),
   Balet o.g. (56),
   McGhee (62), Kennedy (81)
ABERDEEN: Leighton, Kennedy, McMaster, Simpson, McLeish, Miller, Strachan, Black (Weir), McGhee, Bell (Rougvie), Hewitt
SION: Pittier, J. Valentini, P. Valentini, Balet, Richard, Lopez, Bregy, Luisler (Cucinotto), B. Karlen, Cina, Caernicky
Attendance: 13,000   *Referee:* K. T. Tritachler
                                    (W. Germany)
Aberdeen have drawn the short straw and must play a preliminary round with the Swiss Cup-holders for right

of entry to the first round. All the goals are spread around; even a Swiss defender claims one. When was the last time six different players of the same side all scored in one match?

Preliminary Round 2nd Leg Wednesday, 1 September
SION (1) 1   ABERDEEN (1) 4
   Bregy (28)   Hewitt (27), Miller (61),
                           McGhee 2 (65, 72)
SION: Pittier, Valentini, L. Karlen, Moulin, Richard, Lopez, Bregy, Luisler (B. Karlen), Caernicky, Cucinotto, Cina (Tachet)
ABERDEEN: Leighton, Kennedy, McMaster, Simpson, Cooper, Miller, Strachan (Black), Bell (McLeish), McGhee, Hewitt, Weir
Aberdeen won 11-1 on aggregate
Attendance: 2,400   *Referee:* J. Glazar
                                    (Yugoslavia)
Aberdeen take time off from this formality to admire the breathtaking Alpine scenery surrounding the Tourbillon Stadium.

1st Round, 1st Leg Wednesday, 15 September
ABERDEEN (1) 1   DINAMO TIRANE
   Hewitt (29)   (Albania) (0) 0
ABERDEEN: Leighton, Kennedy (Black), McMaster, Bell (Cooper), Rougvie, Miller, Strachan, Simpson, McGhee, Hewitt, Weir
TIRANA: Luarasi, Kugi, Bragu, Targai, Ruci, Xhafa (Dauti), Gega (Musai), Kanai, Zeri, Fagekugi, Demorrail
Attendance: 15,000   *Referee:* L. Delsemme
                                    (Belgium)
Despite controlling the game from the first whistle Aberdeen take just the slenderest lead over to Albania. Fortunately Luarasi couldn't hold Bell's shot. The ball bounced off the keeper's chest and Hewitt was left with a yawning goal.

1st Round, 2nd Leg Wednesday 29 September
DINAMO TIRANE (0) 0   ABERDEEN (0) 0
TIRANE: Luarasi, Kugi, Dauti (Noea), Targai, Gega, Ruci, Delia, Kanai, Zeri, Marko, Demorrail (Agalliu)
ABERDEEN: Leighton, Kennedy, Rougvie, Cooper (McMaster), McLeish, Miller, Strachan, Simpson, McGhee (Hewitt), Bell, Weir
Aberdeen won 1-0 on aggregate
Attendance: 20,000   *Referee:* J. Szaavo
                                    (Hungary)
European football at its worst: professional guarding of a one-goal lead at its best. Dinamo never threatened to score, nor Aberdeen to let them, in sweltering conditions.

2nd Round, 1st Leg Wednesday, 20 October
ABERDEEN (0) 2   LECH POZNAN (Poland)
   McGhee (55), Weir (57)   (0) 0

ABERDEEN: Leighton, Cooper, McMaster, Bell (Kennedy), McLeish, Miller, Strachan, Simpson, McGhee, Black (Hewitt), Weir

LECH POZNAN: Plesnierowicz, Pawlak, Szewczyk, Adamiec, Barczak, Strugarek (Kryzyzanowski), Kupcewicz (Niewiadonski), Oblewski, Malek, Okonski, Bak

Attendance: 17,600   *Referee:* E. Mulder
                                              (Holland)

Two goals to take to Poland, but it should have been so many more. Black struck the bar twice and Strachan a post. McGhee converted the Dons' ninth corner and two minutes later Weir turned in Strachan's cross.

2nd Round, 2nd Leg Wednesday, 3 November
LECH POZNAN (0) 0   ABERDEEN (0) 1
                                             Bell (59)

LECH POZNAN: Plesnierowicz, Pawlak, Szewczyk (Kryzyzanowski), Adamiec, Barczak, Malek, Niewialdonski, Oblewski (Stroinski), Kupcewicz, Okonski, Bak

ABERDEEN: Leighton, Kennedy, Rougvie, McMaster (Cooper), McLeish, Miller, Strachan, Simpson, McGhee, Bell, Weir

Aberdeen won 3-0 on aggregate

Attendance: 30,000   *Referee:* T. Tokat (Turkey)

Aberdeen have reached the quarter-finals of a European tournament for the first time in 15 years of trying. The Dons' goal was under no particular threat before Bell bundled in McGhee's back-header from Weir's corner. That meant Lech needed four goals.

Quarter Final 1st Leg Wednesday, 2 March
BAYERN MUNICH   ABERDEEN (0) 0
  (W. Germany) (0) 0

BAYERN: Müller, Dremmler, Horsmann, Grobe, Augenthaler, Kraus, Nachtweih, Breitner, Hoeness, Del Haye, Rummenigge

ABERDEEN: Leighton, Kennedy, Rougvie, Cooper, McLeish, Miller, Black (Strachan), Simpson, McGhee, Bell, Weir

Attendance: 35,000   *Referee:* E. C. Guruceta
                                              Muro (Spain)

Aberdeen's 45th European match, played in Munich's Olympic Stadium, produced a result which was no more than they deserved. The composure of the Dons against the former European champions, brimming with internationals, astonished those critics who felt that Aberdeen were about to be eaten alive. Bayern's long-range efforts were thrillingly foiled by Leighton, and McGhee and Weir both came close to snatching a breakaway goal.

Quarter Final 2nd Leg Wednesday, 16 March
ABERDEEN (1) 3   BAYERN MUNICH (1) 2
  Simpson (38),   Augenthaler (10),
  McLeish (76), Hewitt (77)   Pflugler (61)

ABERDEEN: Leighton, Kennedy (McMaster), Rougvie, Cooper, McLeish, Miller, Strachan, Simpson (Hewitt), McGhee, Black, Weir

BAYERN: Müller, Dremmler, Horsmann, Grobe, Augenthaler, Kraus, Pflugler (Mathy), Breitner, Hoeness, Del Haye, Rummenigge

Aberdeen won 3-2 on aggregate

Attendance: 24,000   *Referee:* M. Vautrot
                                              (France)

The teams emerged to a tumultuous reception. In ten minutes Augenthaler stunned Pittodrie with a 30-yard shot which Leighton touched but could not save. McLeish headed against the bar before the Dons drew level. Black headed back from beyond the far post and Simpson just beat a defender to force the ball over the line. Bayern went back in front with Pflugler's glorious volley which beat Leighton at the foot of his near post. McMaster came on as sub: then Hewitt too. McLeish jumped higher than Augenthaler to meet Strachan's free kick, and Müller could only push the header into the side of the goal. Within seconds Müller made a leaping save from Black's header. Hewitt launched himself at the loose ball and screwed it between the keeper's legs. Pandemonium. Pittodrie demanded its heroes return for a lap of honour at the end. This was undeniably Aberdeen's finest hour.

Semi Final 1st Leg Wednesday, 6 April
ABERDEEN (2) 5   WATERSCHEI (Belgium)
  Black (2), Simpson (4),   (0) 1
  McGhee 2 (67, 84),   Gudmundsson (74)
  Weir (69)

ABERDEEN: Leighton, Kennedy, Rougvie, Bell (Cooper), McLeish, Miller, Strachan, Simpson, McGhee, Black (Hewitt), Weir

WATERSCHEI: Pudelko, Martos, Bialousz, David, Van Kraay (Conninx), Coenen (Plessers), P. Janssen, Clijsters, Voordeckers, Gudmundsson, R. Jansen

Attendance: 24,000   *Referee:* P. Bergamo (Italy)

Anyone arriving four minutes late would have missed Aberdeen's first two goals as they blitz the Belgians. Bell set off on a slalom and sent the ball to the far post where it was turned in by Black. Then Simpson bulldozed his way through to shoot home off the keeper. After the break Bell made a goal for McGhee. Weir launched himself into a diving header – 4-0. Gudmundsson headed over Leighton and into the net off the bar before McGhee finished the job after the ball had flown about on the Belgian goal-line. The super-Dons look to be in the Final.

Semi Final 2nd Leg Tuesday, 19 April
WATERSCHEI (0) 1   ABERDEEN (0) 0
  Voordeckers (73)

WATERSCHEI: Pudalko, Martos, P. Plessers, David, Van Kraay, I. Plessers, P. Janssen, Clijsters, Voordeckers, Gudmundsson (Massignani), R. Janssen

ABERDEEN: Leighton, Kennedy, Rougvie, McMaster, McLeish, Miller, Hewitt, Simpson (Angus), McGhee (Falconer), Watson, Weir

Aberdeen won 5-2 on aggregate

Attendance: 15,000   *Referee:* A Prokop
(E. Germany)

Unless Aberdeen lose 4-0 they are through to the Final. In the Belgian town of Genk they are comfortably in control. The only disappointment is losing their first match in the competition, after Miller and McLeish had both slipped when trying to thwart Voordeckers. Unfortunately, though he does not know it yet, the knee injury to Stuart Kennedy will end his career. As a pleasant touch, before the match both sets of players were presented with boxes of strawberries. Better than raspberries.

European Cup-Winners Cup Final (Gothenberg)
Wednesday, 11 May
REAL MADRID (Spain)   ABERDEEN (1) 1 2
  (1) 1 *1*   *(After Extra Time)*
Juanito (14 pen)   Black (7), Hewitt (112)
REAL MADRID: Augustin, Juan Hose, Camacho (San Jose), Metgod, Bonet, Gallego, Juanito, Angel, Santillana, Stielike (Salguero), Isidro
ABERDEEN: Leighton, Rougvie, McMaster, Cooper, McLeish, Miller, Strachan, Simpson, McGhee, Black (Hewitt), Weir

Attendance: 17,800   *Referee:* G. Menajali (Italy)

14,000 Aberdeen supporters made the trip to Gothenberg – any way they could. They went to see the Dons take on the most famous name in European football – Real Madrid – six times winners of the European Cup. In torrential rain Black leant into a shoulder-high volley which left the crossbar twanging and Augustin wringing his fingers. In seven minutes McLeish's header was parried by the keeper but the ball fell to the feet of Black who screwed it inside the far post. Tragically McLeish's backpass falls short and Leighton brings down Santillana. In the second half Aberdeen pour forward in waves, without success. In extra time Weir despatched the ball to McGhee down the left. The ball was chipped onto the onrushing Hewitt's head and Augustin, committed to cutting out the cross, was stranded. Thereafter Aberdeen had the chances to make it safe, but lived nervously as a twice-taken free kick by Salguero on the edge of the box flew inches past the far post. As the final whistle blew the city of Aberdeen turned into the site of a carnival.

APPEARANCES	League	League Cup	Scottish Cup	Cup-Winners Cup
Miller	36	8	5	11
Leighton	35	8	5	11
McLeish	33(+1)	7	5	9(+1)
Rougvie	32(+3)	6(+1)	5	8(+1)
Strachan	32	7	3	9(+1)
McGhee	31(+1)	7	5	11
Simpson	29(+4)	6(+1)	5	11
Cooper	29(+2)	7	4	6(+3)
Weir	29(+2)	5	4(+1)	10(+1)
Kennedy	25	4(+1)	4	9(+1)
Black	23(+9)	5(+3)	4(+1)	6(+2)
Bell	20(+3)	3(+1)	4	8
McMaster	19(+6)	6	2	7(+2)
Hewitt	9(+7)	4(+3)	−(+1)	4(+5)
Watson	8(+10)	2	−(+3)	1
Angus	3(+2)	2(+2)		−(+1)
Gunn	1			
Mitchell	1	1		
Porteous	1			
Cowan	−(+3)	−(+2)		
Hamilton	−(+2)	−(+1)		
McCall	−(+2)			
Falconer	−(+1)			−(+1)
23 players				

GOALS	Total	League	League Cup	Scottish Cup	Cup-Winners Cup
McGhee	27	16	4	1	6
Strachan	20	12	7		1
Black	19	12	3	1	3
Weir	12	6		3	2
Hewitt	11	5	1		5
Simpson	10	5		2	3
Bell	5	1	3		1
Rougvie	4	3	1		
Angus	3	3			
McLeish	3	2			1
Watson	3	2		1	
Miller	3	2			1
Cooper	3	2		1	
Cowan	2	2			
McMaster	2	2			
Kennedy	1				1
own-goals	2	1			1
Total	129	76	19	9	25

Season 1983-84

Having watched his side climb the pinnacles of Europe, Alex Ferguson needed to keep his players' feet on the ground while guarding against any complacency. The first-team squad in 1983-84 showed two acquisitions. Billy Stark arrived from St. Mirren in the close season as cover for whenever Gordon Strachan decided to move on. Stewart McKimmie signed in December from Dundee, a replacement full-back for the prematurely retired Stuart Kennedy.

Almost the first thing McKimmie did was help with his new club win the European Super Cup (not a cup, but a plaque) in the annual confrontation between the respective holders of the European Cup and the Cup-Winners Cup. Aberdeen's opponents were SV Hamburg, who had outmanoeuvred the Dons in the UEFA two years previously.

Back in September it has looked like Aberdeen would be under new management. But Ferguson, after days of tense speculation, finally rejected the invitation to succeed John Greig at Rangers and instead committed himself to a five-year contract with Aberdeen.

By early March the Dons were in line for a domestic treble, as well as retention of the Cup-Winners Cup. But Celtic nudged Aberdeen from the League Cup in a tetchy two-leg semi final, and six weeks later – at the same stage – Porto became the first club ever to prevent Aberdeen scoring in both legs of a European encounter. By then Aberdeen were almost home and dry in the league – they had been out in front since September – and the crowning glory to another famous season was reserved for their third successive Scottish Cup Final. Having beaten Rangers twice at Hampden, it was now Celtic's turn to feel Aberdeen's heat in extra time.

League:	Champions
League Cup:	Semi Final
Scottish Cup:	Winners
European Cup-Winners Cup:	Semi Final
European Super Cup:	Winners

SCOTTISH PREMIER DIVISION

No 1 Saturday, 20 August
ABERDEEN (1) 3   DUNDEE (0) 0
  Strachan (40 pen),
  Hewitt (49),
  McGeachie o.g. (83)
ABERDEEN: Leighton, Rougvie, McMaster, Cooper, McLeish, Miller, Strachan (Bell), Stark, Black, Hewitt (Simpson), Weir
DUNDEE: Kelly, McGeachie, McKinlay, Fraser, Smith, Glennie, Mackie, Geddes (Sinclair), Stephen, McKimmie, Kidd

P	W	D	L	F	A	Pts
1	1	0	0	3	0	2

Attendance: 14,300
Referee: A. Waddell

It is now 7½ years since Dundee won a league game at Pittodrie. They fell behind when Strachan was upended by Glennie and took the penalty himself. Dundee's Stewart McKimmie was booked for protesting.

No 2 Saturday, 3 September
ABERDEEN (2) 5   ST JOHNSTONE (0) 0
  Miller (7),
  Black 2 (11, 68)
  McGhee (67),
  Stark (77)
ABERDEEN: Leighton, Rougvie, McMaster, Cooper, McLeish, Miller, Stark, Bell, Black, Hewitt (McGhee), Weir (Simpson)

ST JOHNSTONE: McDonald, Kilgour, McVicar, Beedie (Branigan), Caldwell, Rutherford, Gibson, Brogan, Blair, Morton, Addison

P	W	D	L	F	A	Pts	*Attendance:* 12,400
2	2	0	0	8	0	4	*Referee:* H. Young

In five league and league cup games Aberdeen have now found the net 24 times.

No 3 Saturday, 10 September
MOTHERWELL (0) 1   ABERDEEN (1) 1
  Gahagan (80)   McGhee (33)

MOTHERWELL: Walker, Dornan, Wark, Carson, Edvaldsson, Mauchlen, Gahagan, Rafferty, Gillespie, Ritchie, Forbes (Cormack)

ABERDEEN: Leighton, Rougvie, McMaster, Cooper, McLeish, Miller, Stark (Mitchell), Black (Hewitt), McGhee, Bell, Weir

P	W	D	L	F	A	Pts	*Attendance:* 6,200
3	2	1	0	9	1	5	*Referee:* D. M. Galloway

Andy Ritchie was a thorn in Aberdeen's side when he was at Morton. Now he glides past two defenders and puts his cross onto Gahagan's head. Near the end Leighton booted the ball into the crowd and was booked for time-wasting.

No 4 Saturday, 17 September
RANGERS (0) 0   ABERDEEN (0) 2
                       McGhee 2 (70, 80)

RANGERS: McCloy, Dawson, McClelland, McPherson, Paterson, McKinnon, Prytz, McCoist, Clark, Russell, Cooper

ABERDEEN: Leighton, Rougvie, McMaster, Cooper, McLeish, Miller, Cowan (Hewitt), Simpson, McGhee, Bell, Weir

P	W	D	L	F	A	Pts	*Attendance:* 27,500
4	3	1	0	11	1	7	*Referee:* J. Duncan

Crisis time at Ibrox. Rangers have earned only one point all season. McGhee got both goals, but veteran keeper McCloy should have stopped them both.

No 5 Saturday, 24 September
ABERDEEN (0) 1   DUNDEE UNITED (1) 2
  Strachan (78 pen)   Bannon (36),
                       Kirkwood (52)

ABERDEEN: Leighton, Rougvie, McMaster, Cooper, McLeish, Miller, Cowan (Hewitt), Simpson, McGhee, Bell (Strachan), Weir

DUNDEE UNITED: McAlpine, Kirkwood, Stark, Gough, Hegarty, Narey, Bannon, Milne, Malpas, Holt, Dodds

Leading positions

	P	W	D	L	F	A	Pts
1 Dundee United	5	5	0	0	17	3	10
2 Celtic	5	5	0	0	18	5	10
3 Hearts	5	5	0	0	10	4	10
4 ABERDEEN	5	3	1	1	12	3	7

Attendance: 21,100   *Referee:* H. Alexander

Remarkably three clubs still have 100% records, among them defending champions Dundee United. Eamonn Bannon volleyed them in front. John McMaster blazed a penalty over the bar. Kirkwood made it 2-0 and Ralph Milne was booked for celebrating with the United fans. Then Narey conceded his second penalty of the match and Strachan did better than McMaster.

No 6 Saturday, 1 October
HEARTS (0) 0   ABERDEEN (1) 2
                       Weir 2 (28, 73)

HEARTS: Smith, Kidd, Cowie, Jardine, R. MacDonald, McLaren, Bowman, Robertson, Bone, A. MacDonald, Clark

ABERDEEN: Leighton, Rougvie, McMaster, Cooper, McLeish, Miller, Strachan, Simpson, McGhee, Stark (Falconer), Weir

P	W	D	L	F	A	Pts	*Attendance:* 18,200
6	4	1	1	14	3	9	*Referee:* W. McLeish

A rough-house match, turned Aberdeen's way by a delicious Strachan pass which sets McGhee clear on the right. When the cross came over, Stark missed it but Weir didn't.

No 7 Saturday, 8 October
ABERDEEN (1) 5   ST MIRREN (0) 0
  Stark 2 (30, 47),
  McGhee (56),
  Falconer (60),
  Miller (76)

ABERDEEN: Leighton, McIntyre, McMaster, Cooper, McLeish, Miller, Stark, Simpson, McGhee, Falconer, Weir

ST MIRREN: Thomson, Clarke, Cousar, McCormack, Fulton, Abercrombie, McAvennie, Fitzpatrick, McDougall, Alexander (Sinclair) (Cameron), Scanlon

P	W	D	L	F	A	Pts	*Attendance:* 13,000
7	5	1	1	19	3	11	*Referee:* B. R. McGinlay

St Mirren have a new manager, Alex Miller. He watched his team's destruction through closed fingers. The best goal was the last, Willie Miller's thunderous shot from outside the box. Saint's full-back Clarke was sent off for downing Weir.

No 8 Saturday, 15 October
HIBERNIAN (0) 2   ABERDEEN (1) 1
  Irvine 2 (69, 88)   Rougvie (13)

HIBERNIAN: Rough, Sneddon, Schaedler, Blackley, Jamieson, McNamara, Brazil, Turnbull, Irvine, Thomson, Duncan

ABERDEEN: Leighton, Rougvie, McMaster, Cooper, McLeish, Miller, Stark, Simpson, McGhee, Falconer (Hewitt), Weir

P	W	D	L	F	A	Pts	*Attendance:* 7,000
8	5	1	2	20	5	11	*Referee:* A. Ferguson

Hibs' Willie Irvine went into the referee's book three times. First for his diving headed equaliser. Then for his dramatic winner. And finally a caution for time-wasting.

No 9 Saturday, 22 October

ABERDEEN (1) 3	CELTIC (0) 1
Hewitt (43),	Aitken (88)
McLeish (55),	
Strachan (74 pen)	

ABERDEEN: Leighton, McIntyre, Rougvie, Cooper, McLeish, Miller, Strachan (Simpson), Hewitt, McGhee, Bell, Weir
CELTIC: Bonner, McGrain, Sinclair, Aitken, McAdam, McLeod (Reid), Provan, McStay, McGarvey, Burns, McClair

P	W	D	L	F	A	Pts	*Attendance:* 23,000
9	6	1	2	23	6	13	*Referee:* H. Alexander

Another unpleasant, violent confrontation. What football there was brought the Dons headed goals by Hewitt and McLeish. There followed two Aberdeen penalties in two minutes, conceded by McAdam and McStay in turn. Bonner saved the first, not the second.

No 10 Saturday, 29 October

DUNDEE (1) 1	ABERDEEN (2) 3
Glennie (27)	Strachan (37 pen),
	Weir (44),
	Bell (73)

DUNDEE: R. Geddes, McKimmie, McKinlay, Fraser, Smith, Glennie (McGeachie), Mackie, Stephen, Ferguson, Richardson, A. Geddes
ABERDEEN: Leighton, Rougvie, Angus, Simpson (Porteous), McLeish, Miller, Strachan, Hewitt, McGhee, Bell, Weir

Leading positions

	P	W	D	L	F	A	Pts
1 ABERDEEN	10	7	1	2	26	7	15
2 Dundee United	9	7	1	1	22	8	15
3 Celtic	10	6	2	2	27	13	14
4 Hearts	10	6	2	2	13	8	14

Attendance: 7,800   *Referee:* T. Muirhead

Aberdeen hit the front for the first time, as the bombshell that Rangers want Alex Ferguson as manager rocks the city. Dons fans chant 'Fergie must stay'. Aberdeen climbed back into the match with a mysterious penalty award, after Bobby Glennie's goal-of-the-season from 35 yards, had put Dundee in front.

No 11 Saturday, 5 November

ST JOHNSTONE (0) 0	ABERDEEN (3) 5
	Weir (26),
	Hewitt 3 (32, 33, 64)
	Strachan (82 pen)

ST JOHNSTONE: McDonald, Kilgour, Caldwell (Day), Lyons, Kennedy, Rutherford, Gibson, Brogan, Blair, Morton, Beedie
ABERDEEN: Leighton, McIntyre, Rougvie (Angus), Simpson, McLeish, Miller, Strachan, Hewitt, McGhee (Black), Bell, Weir

P	W	D	L	F	A	Pts	*Attendance:* 6,100
11	8	1	2	31	7	17	*Referee:* H. Williamson

Aberdeen could have had 10. Hewitt's hat-trick was something special: two headers either side of a marauding sole run. Altogether a good way to celebrate Ferguson's announcement that he's staying at Pittodrie.

No 12 Saturday, 12 November

ABERDEEN (2) 3	RANGERS (0) 0
Simpson (5),	
Hewitt (9),	
Porteous (68)	

ABERDEEN: Leighton, Cooper, Rougvie, Simpson, McLeish, Miller, Strachan, Hewitt (Angus), McGhee, Bell, Weir (Porteous)
RANGERS: McCloy, McKinnon, Dawson, McClelland, Paterson, McPherson, McCoist, Nicholl, Mitchell (Kennedy), Redford, Cooper (Russell)

P	W	D	L	F	A	Pts	*Attendance:* 23,000
12	9	1	2	34	7	19	*Referee:* A. Waddell

Rangers didn't get Alex Ferguson. Nor Jim McLean. They turned to former manager Jock Wallace instead. He steps onto the pitch to acknowledge the Rangers supporters, then sits back to watch his new club taken apart. If Neil Simpson's goal was a screamer, substitute Ian Porteous' from 25 yards was simply breathtaking. Earlier in the week Aberdeen had been voted best team in Europe.

No 13 Saturday, 19 November

ABERDEEN (1) 2	HEARTS (0) 0
Rougvie (33),	
Simpson (89)	

ABERDEEN: Leighton, Cooper, Rougvie, Simpson, McLeish, Miller, Strachan, Hewitt (Porteous), McGhee, Bell, Weir
HEARTS: Smith, Kidd, Cowie, Jardine, R. MacDonald, McLaren (Johnstone), Park, Mackay, Bone, A. MacDonald, Robertson

P	W	D	L	F	A	Pts	*Attendance:* 20,000
13	10	1	2	36	7	21	*Referee:* M. Delaney

SFA officials make a pre-match presentation to the Dons in recognition of their double cup trophies last season. Rougvie scored his goal with his chest.

No 14 Saturday, 26 November

DUNDEE UNITED (0) 0	ABERDEEN (1) 2
	Bell (8),
	Strachan (74)

DUNDEE UNITED: McAlpine, Malpas, Murray, Gough, Hegarty, Narey, Bannon, Milne, McGinnis (Sturrock), Holt, Dodds
ABERDEEN: Leighton, Cooper, Rougvie, Simpson, McLeish, Miller, Strachan, Hewitt, McGhee, Bell, Weir

P	W	D	L	F	A	Pts	*Attendance:* 16,900
14	11	1	2	38	7	23	*Referee:* G. Smith

A vital win, highlighted by Gordon Strachan's clinching goal. He received the ball from McGhee, rounded Narey and McAlpine and netted from an angle so acute as to appear impossible. Real Madrid are after his signature. So are Hamburg – and others.

No 15 Saturday, 3 December

ABERDEEN (1) 3   MOTHERWELL (0) 1
McGhee (31),   Gahagan (46)
Strachan (68 pen),
Falconer (77)

ABERDEEN: Leighton, McIntyre, Rougvie, Simpson, McLeish, Miller, Strachan, Falconer, McGhee, Bell (Porteous), Weir

MOTHERWELL: Walker, Dornan, Wark, McLeod, Carson, Mauchlen, Gahagan, McAllister, Alexander (Cormack), Forbes, McFadden

P	W	D	L	F	A	Pts
15	12	1	2	41	8	25

Attendance: 17,800
Referee: R. Cuthill

Gahagan stunned Aberdeen with an out-of-the-blue equaliser. But McFadden foolishly pulled down Gordon Strachan, who got up to restore the lead.

No 16 Saturday, 10 December

CELTIC (0) 0   ABERDEEN (0) 0

CELTIC: Bonner, McGrain, Reid, Aitken, McAdam, McLeod, McClair, P. McStay, McGarvey, Burns, Melrose

ABERDEEN: Leighton, Cooper (Angus), Rougvie, Simpson, McLeish, Miller, Strachan, Hewitt (Falconer), McGhee, Bell, Weir

Leading positions

	P	W	D	L	F	A	Pts
1 ABERDEEN	16	12	2	2	41	8	26
2 Celtic	16	10	3	3	39	18	23
3 Dundee United	16	9	3	4	31	15	21

Attendance: 25,900   *Referee:* A. Ferguson

No goals but another no-holds-barred encounter. In the 71st minute Celtic's Melrose elbowed Rougvie in the face, and off he went.

No 17 Saturday, 17 December

ABERDEEN (1) 2   HIBERNIAN (0) 1
McGhee (1),   Irvine (81)
Blackley o.g. (55)

ABERDEEN: Leighton, McKimmie, Angus, Simpson, McLeish, Rougvie, Strachan (Falconer), Hewitt (Black), McGhee, Bell, Weir

HIBERNIAN: Rough, Sneddon, Brazil, Turnbull, Jamieson, Blackley, Callachan, Harvey, Irvine, Thomson, Duncan

P	W	D	L	F	A	Pts
17	13	2	2	43	9	28

Attendance: 13,000
Referee: I. Cathcart

Stewart McKimmie makes his debut for Aberdeen as Hibs provide two Christmas presents. In the first minute Jamieson completely missed Bell's cross, which fell to McGhee. Then Blackley went one better, ramming Strachan's cross into his own goal.

No 18 Saturday, 24 December

ST MIRREN (0) 0   ABERDEEN (2) 3
                          Bell (4),
                          McLeish (26),
                          McGhee (86)

ST MIRREN: Thomson, Hamilton, Whinnie, Cooper, Fulton, Abercrombie, Fitzpatrick, McAvennie, McDougall, McCormack, Scanlon

ABERDEEN: Leighton, McKimmie, Rougvie, Simpson, McLeish, Miller, Strachan, Black (Hewitt), McGhee, Bell, Weir

P	W	D	L	F	A	Pts
18	14	2	2	46	9	30

Attendance: 6,700
Referee: W. McLeish

Aberdeen never bothered to climb out of second gear. Strachan was booed every time he touched the ball. Saints' Whinnie was sent off in the second half.

No 19 Saturday, 31 December

ABERDEEN (2) 5   DUNDEE (0) 2
McKinlay o.g. (4),   Mackie (85),
Strachan 2 (22, 80 pen), Ferguson (88)
Weir (63),
Hewitt (68)

ABERDEEN: Leighton, McKimmie, McMaster, Angus, Rougvie, Miller (McIntyre), Strachan, Hewitt, Black, Bell, Weir (Porteous)

DUNDEE: R. Geddes, Glennie, McKinlay, Fraser, Smith, McDonald, Mackie, Richardson (Kidd), Ferguson, McCall, A. Geddes (Paterson)

P	W	D	L	F	A	Pts
19	15	2	2	51	11	32

Attendance: 18,300.
Referee: T. Muirhead

For 85 minutes Aberdeen were as irresistible as gravity. For the last 5 they became sloppy – which would eventually wreck their attempt to establish a new defensive record.

No 20 Saturday, 7 January

RANGERS (0) 1   ABERDEEN (0) 1
Cooper (48 pen)   Hewitt (68)

RANGERS: Walker, Fraser, Dawson, McClelland, McAdam, Redford, Russell, Williamson, Clark, McPherson, Cooper

ABERDEEN: Leighton, McKimmie, Rougvie, Simpson (Cooper), McLeish, Miller, Strachan, Black, McGhee, Bell (Hewitt), Weir

Leading positions

	P	W	D	L	F	A	Pts
1 ABERDEEN	20	15	3	2	52	12	33
2 Celtic	20	12	5	3	46	22	29
3 Dundee United	19	11	4	4	36	18	26

Attendance: 37,500   *Referee:* A. Huett

After half an hour Ally Dawson and Eric Black indulge in some argy-bargy, reducing the match to 10-a-side. Rangers did enough to win, and scored first from the spot after Leighton had impeded Williamson. McGhee hit a post before Peter Weir's electrifying run loaded the gun for Hewitt.

No 21 Saturday, 4 February
ABERDEEN (1) 1   CELTIC (0) 0
  Hewitt (19)
ABERDEEN: Leighton, McKimmie, Rougvie, Cooper, McLeish, Miller, Strachan, Simpson (Falconer), McGhee, Hewitt (Bell), Weir
CELTIC: Bonner, McGrain (W. McStay), Reid, Aitken, McAdam, Sinclair, McClair, P. McStay, McGarvey, McLeod, Burns (Melrose)

P	W	D	L	F	A	Pts	*Attendance:* 22,500
21	16	3	2	53	12	35	*Referee:* L. Thow

A month has been lost to the weather. Celtic's defeat puts them six points behind the Dons. Weir's fierce low cross was touched away by Bonner, but only to the feet of Hewitt. Leighton blocked McClair's attempted equaliser with his legs.

No 22 Saturday, 11 February
MOTHERWELL (0) 0   ABERDEEN (1) 4
                       Strachan 2 (37, 51),
                       Black (69),
                       Hewitt (76)
MOTHERWELL: Sproat, Dornan, MacLeod, McAllister, Carson, Mauchlen, Boyd, Rafferty, Harrow, Black, McFadden (McBride)
ABERDEEN: Leighton, McKimmie, Rougvie, McMaster, McLeish, Miller, Strachan, Bell (Black), McGhee, Hewitt, Weir (Mitchell)

P	W	D	L	F	A	Pts	*Attendance:* 6,100
22	17	3	2	57	12	37	*Referee:* A. Waddell

Motherwell are looking for only their second league win of the season – and they are still looking. Aside from the four goals the game produced six bookings and some unsavoury crowd scenes. During the week ex-Don Willie Garner was appointed assistant manager.

No 23 Saturday, 25 February
HIBERNIAN (0) 0   ABERDEEN (1) 2
                      Black (28),
                      McGhee (85)
HIBERNIAN: R. Rae, McKee, Schaedler, G. Rae, Jamieson, Rice, Callachan, Kane, Irvine, Turnbull, Harvey (McGeachie)
ABERDEEN: Leighton, McKimmie, Rougvie, Cooper (McMaster), McLeish, Miller, Mitchell, Black, McGhee, Angus, Hewitt (Porteous)

P	W	D	L	F	A	Pts	*Attendance:* 8,000
23	18	3	2	59	12	39	*Referee:* H. P. Williamson

Eric Black's blistering free kick meant that Aberdeen were forced onto the defensive for the rest of the match. Black headed on to McGhee for the second goal.

No 24 Saturday, 3 March
ABERDEEN (1) 2   ST MIRREN (0) 0
  Strachan (32 pen),
  Hewitt (89)
ABERDEEN: Leighton, McKimmie, Rougvie, Cooper, McLeish, Miller, Strachan (Hewitt), Black, McGhee, Angus, Bell

ST MIRREN: Thomson, Hamilton, Clarke, Cooper, Fulton, McCormack, Fitzpatrick, McAvennie, McDougall, Abercrombie, Scanlon

P	W	D	L	F	A	Pts	*Attendance:* 14,500
24	19	3	2	61	12	41	*Referee:* C. Sinclair

When Mark Fulton toppled Neale Cooper without ceremony it gave Gordon Strachan the chance to score his 100th goal for Aberdeen.

No 25 Saturday, 31 March
CELTIC (1) 1   ABERDEEN (0) 0
  Melrose (35)
CELTIC: Bonner, McGrain, Reid, Aitken, McAdam, W. McStay, McClair, P. McStay (Provan), Melrose, McLeod, Burns
ABERDEEN: Leighton, McKimmie, Rougvie, Cooper, McLeish, Miller, Strachan, Black (Mitchell), McGhee, Angus (Porteous), Hewitt

Leading positions

	P	W	D	L	F	A	Pts
1 ABERDEEN	25	19	3	3	61	12	41
2 Celtic	27	16	5	6	61	32	37
3 Dundee United	24	14	6	4	46	22	34

Attendance: 19,200   *Referee:* D. S. Downie

Celtic simply had to win to keep alive their chances. Melrose scored with a 5 m.p.h. shot. Aberdeen pressed continuously and unavailingly, throughout the second half.

No 26 Monday, 2 April
ABERDEEN (0) 1   HEARTS (0) 1
  Porteous (46)   Robertson (62)
ABERDEEN: Leighton, McKimmie, Rougvie, Cooper, McLeish, Miller, Porteous, Simpson, McGhee, Angus, Hewitt (Wright)
HEARTS: Smith, Kidd, Cowie, Jardine, R. MacDonald, Levein (Park), Bowman, Mackay, Bone, A. MacDonald (Johnston), Robertson

P	W	D	L	F	A	Pts	*Attendance:* 16,200
26	19	4	3	62	14	42	*Referee:* R. B. Valentine

Aberdeen drop their third point inside three days. They dominated everything but taking goal-chances. Porteous scored after a one-two with McGhee, but it was cancelled out when Hearts' John Robertson took on Cooper before unleashing a low shot.

No 27 Saturday, 7 April
ABERDEEN (2) 2   MOTHERWELL (0)
  McGhee (12),   Rafferty (84)
  Strachan (37)
ABERDEEN: Leighton, Mitchell, Rougvie, Cooper, McLeish, Miller, Strachan, Black, McGhee, McKimmie (Porteous), Angus (Hewitt)
MOTHERWELL: Maxwell, McLeod, Black, Forbes, Kennedy, Lyall, McFadden (Alexander), Rafferty, Boyd, McAllister, Harrow (Alexander)

P	W	D	L	F	A	Pts	*Attendance:* 15,500
27	20	4	3	64	15	44	*Referee:* A. Roy

Cologne F.C. officials assess the performance of Gordon Strachan. He was brilliant, coolly slotting the ball past Motherwell's debut keeper Maxwell.

No 28 Wednesday, 18 April

ABERDEEN (3) 5   DUNDEE UNITED (1) 1
  Rougvie 2 (10, 67),   Reilly (34)
  McGhee 2 (27, 37),
  Black (63)

ABERDEEN: Leighton, Mitchell, Rougvie, Simpson, McLeish, Miller, Strachan, Black, McGhee (Stark), Bell, Angus (Weir)

DUNDEE UNITED: McAlpine, Stark, Malpas, Gough (Holt), Hegarty, Narey, Bannon, Kirkwood, Reilly, Coyne (Clark), Dodds

P W D L F A Pts   *Attendance:* 19,600
28 21 4 3 69 16 46   *Referee:* H. Young

Aberdeen were simply irresistable. No wonder Alex Ferguson was purring with pleasure after this. Eric Black ended his personal famine with a thunderous header. Billy Stark and Peter Weir come off the bench after lengthy injuries. But Weir goes off again.

No 29 Saturday, 21 April

ST JOHNSTONE (0) 0   ABERDEEN (0) 2
                      Stark (75),
                      McGhee (78)

ST JOHNSTONE: Baines, Kilgour, Morton, Beedie, Barron, Rutherford, Gibson, Brogan, Scott, Blair, Lyons

ABERDEEN: Leighton, Mitchell, Rougvie, Simpson, McLeish, Miller, Stark, Black (McGhee), Porteous (McIntyre), Bell, Hewitt

P W D L F A Pts   *Attendance:* 6,200
29 22 4 3 71 16 48   *Referee:* K. J. Hope

Celtic's defeat at Ibrox means that the title is virtually secure for Aberdeen. It took the arrival of substitute Mark McGhee to spark the Dons into life.

No 30 Saturday, 28 April

DUNDEE (0) 0   ABERDEEN (0) 1
                      Black (67)

DUNDEE: Geddes, McInally, McKinlay, Shannon, Smith, Glennie, Hendry (Harris), Richardson (Kidd), McCall, McGeachie, Ferguson

ABERDEEN: Leighton, McKimmie, Rougvie, Simpson (Bell), Cooper, Miller, Strachan, Black, McGhee, Stark, Hewitt

Leading positions

	P	W	D	L	F	A	Pts
1 ABERDEEN	30	23	4	3	72	16	50
2 Celtic	34	21	6	7	78	39	48
3 Dundee United	30	17	7	6	59	32	41

Attendance: 6,700   *Referee:* H. Young

Dundee are involved in a frightful scrap with St Johnstone to avoid relegation. They didn't appreciate McKinlay's terrible pass-back which landed at the feet of Eric Black.

No 31 Monday, 30 April

ABERDEEN (0) 1   ST JOHNSTONE (0) 0
  Hewitt (80)

ABERDEEN: Leighton, Mitchell (Stark), Rougvie, McKimmie, McLeish, Miller, Strachan, Bell, McGhee, Hewitt, Weir (Porteous)

ST JOHNSTONE: Baines, Beedie, Morton, Addison, Woods, Barron, Gibson, Brogan, Scott, Blair, Reid

P W D L F A Pts   *Attendance:* 11,500
31 24 4 3 73 16 52   *Referee:* B. R. McGinlay

St Johnstone are staging a stirring rally to avoid the drop. They scarcely deserved to lose to John Hewitt's well-timed finish to McGhee's cross. Only freak results can deprive Aberdeen of the title now.

No 32 Wednesday, 2 May

HEARTS (0) 0   ABERDEEN (0) 1
                      McKimmie (61)

HEARTS: Smith, Kidd, Cowie, Jardine, R. MacDonald, Levein, Bowman, Mackay, Bone, Robertson, Park (Johsnton)

ABERDEEN: Leighton, McKimmie, Rougvie, Cooper, McLeish, Miller, Strachan, Simpson, McGhee, Hewitt (Black), Weir

P W D L F A Pts   *Attendance:* 12,000
32 25 4 3 74 16 54

Willie Miller celebrates his 29th birthday as Stewart McKimmie's first goal for Aberdeen seals the title. Earlier in the day Miller had been voted Scotland's Player of the Year.

No 33 Saturday, 5 May

ABERDEEN (0) 2   HIBERNIAN (2) 2
  Stark (61),   McGeachie (23),
  Porteous (90)   Rice (26)

ABERDEEN: Leighton, Mitchell, McKimmie (McIntyre), Cooper, Rougvie, Miller, Porteous, Black (Hewitt), McGhee, Stark, Weir

HIBERNIAN: Rough, McKee, Schaedler, Sneddon, Rae, Blackley, Callachan, Jamieson, Irvine, Rice, McGeachie

P W D L F A Pts   *Attendance:* 17,000
33 25 5 3 76 18 55   *Referee:* A. Ferguson

This was supposed to be Aberdeen's championship party. But Hibs gate-crashed and would have won except for a generous referee. In injury-time Stark and McGhee fouled Alan Rough, and the ball broke loose to Porteous.

No 34 Monday, 7 May

DUNDEE UNITED (0) 0   ABERDEEN (0) 0

DUNDEE UNITED: McAlpine, Malpas, Munro, Gough, Hegarty, Narey, Bannon, Holt, Coyne, Sturrock, Taylor

ABERDEEN: Leighton, McIntyre (Stark), Rougvie, Cooper, McLeish, Miller, Strachan, McKimmie, Cowan, Hewitt (Falconer), Weir

P W D L F A Pts   *Attendance:* 8,000
34 25 6 3 76 18 56   *Referee:* n.a.

Not for the first time in recent seasons this fixture ends in deadlock. The point gained equals the record total of 56 established for the Premier Division.

No 35 Wednesday, 9 May
ABERDEEN (0) 0   RANGERS (0) 0

ABERDEEN: Leighton, McIntyre, Rougvie, Cooper, McLeish, Miller, Porteous (Hewitt), Stark, McGhee, McKimmie, Cowan
RANGERS: McCloy, Fraser, McClelland, McPherson, Paterson, Redford, Russell, Williamson (Ferguson), Clark, McCoist, Cooper

P W D L F A Pts   *Attendance:* 16,200
35 25 7 3 76 18 57   *Referee:* R. B. Valentine

Not a game to remember, except that it took Aberdeen's points tally to 57, a Premier League record. Before the match Gordon Strachan signed for Manchester United, but he is free to play for Aberdeen in the Scottish Cup Final.

No 36 Saturday, 12 May
ST MIRREN (1) 3   ABERDEEN (1) 2
  McDougall (18),   Money o.g. (23),
  Abercrombie (47),   Stark (87 pen)
  Alexander (83)

ST MIRREN: Money, Clarke, Winnie, Cooper, Fulton, McCormack, Jarvie, McAvennie, McDougall, Abercrombie, Cameron (Alexander)
ABERDEEN: Leighton, Robertson, McMaster, Cooper, Rougvie, McIntyre, Porteous (McKimmie), Falconer, Cowan, Stark, Hewitt (McGhee)

Attendance: 3,500   *Referee:* M. Delaney

Alex Ferguson sends out a team of babes. Aberdeen concede three goals for the one and only time this season. They therefore equal, but don't beat, the Premier League's best defensive record.

Aberdeen's complete home and away record:

	HOME						AWAY														Pts
P W D L F A							W D L F A						
36 14 3 1 46 12							11 4 3 32 9					57

Scottish Premier Division

		P	W	D	L	F	A	Pts
1	ABERDEEN	36	25	7	4	78	21	57
2	Celtic	36	21	8	7	80	41	50
3	Dundee United	36	18	11	7	67	39	47
4	Rangers	36	15	12	9	53	41	42
5	Hearts	36	10	16	10	38	47	36
6	St. Mirren	36	9	14	13	55	59	32
7	Hibernian	36	12	7	17	45	55	31
8	Dundee	36	11	5	20	50	74	27
9	St Johnstone	36	10	3	23	36	81	23
10	Motherwell	36	4	7	25	31	75	15

LEAGUE CUP

2nd Round, 1st Leg Wednesday, 24 August
ABERDEEN (3) 9   RAITH ROVERS (0) 0
  Stark 3 (19, 62, 78),
  Porteous (28),
  Black 4 (44, 51 pen, 65, 69),
  Hewitt (59)

ABERDEEN: Leighton, Rougvie, McMaster, Bell, McLeish, Miller, Porteous, Stark, Black, Hewitt, Weir
RAITH: Graham, Ferguson, Sweeney, Urquhart, More, Thomson, Smith, Kerr, Marshall, Robertson, Hill (Spence)

Attendance: 9,650   *Referee:* H. Alexander

Nine goals – and Aberdeen also hit the wood three times.

2nd Round, 2nd Leg Saturday, 27 August
RAITH ROVERS (0) 0   ABERDEEN (1) 3
                         Hewitt 2 (35, 69),
                         Stark (86)

RAITH: Graham, Ferguson, Sweeney, Urquhart, More, Thomson, Smith, Kerr, Harris, Marshall, Robertson
ABERDEEN: Leighton, Rougvie, McMaster, Bell, McLeish, Miller, Porteous (Falconer), Stark, Black, Hewitt, Weir

Aberdeen won 12-0 on aggregate

Attendance: 3,000   *Referee:* R. B. Valentine

One wonders what was the point of this match. Were Raith looking to score 10?

Wednesday, 31 August (Group Rounds)
ABERDEEN (2) 4   MEADOWBANK
  McGhee 2 (19, 90),   THISTLE (0) 0
  Stark (32),
  Black (55)

ABERDEEN: Leighton, Cooper, McMaster, Bell, McLeish, Miller, Black (Simpson), Stark, McGhee, Hewitt (Porteous), Weir
MEADOWBANK: McQueen, Dunn, Lawson, Godfrey, Stewart, Korotkich, Hendrie, Tomassi, Smith (Stalker), Boyd, Sprott

Attendance: 10,000   *Referee:* G. B. Smith

Aberdeen had all the ball, all the play, but only four goals.

Wednesday, 7 September
ST JOHNSTONE (0) 0   ABERDEEN (1) 1
                         Miller (23)

ST JOHNSTONE: J. McDonald, Kilgour, McVicar, Addison, Caldwell, Rutherford, Gibson, Brogan, Brannigan (Blair), Morton, Beedie
ABERDEEN: Leighton, Rougvie, McMaster, Cooper, McLeish, Miller, Simpson (Stark), Bell, Black (Hewitt), McGhee, Weir

Attendance: 6,000   *Referee:* D. S. Downie

Four days earlier Aberdeen had whacked 5 past St Johnstone in the league at Pittodrie. This time the Dons have to settle for Miller's bundled goal from Weir's corner.

Wednesday, 5 October
ABERDEEN (0) 0   DUNDEE (0) 0
ABERDEEN: Leighton, McIntyre, McMaster, Cooper, McLeish, Miller, Strachan (Stark), Simpson, McGhee, Falconer (Hewitt), Weir
DUNDEE: R. Geddes, McGeachie, McKimmie, A. Geddes, Smith, MacDonald, Ferguson, Stephen, McCall, Fraser, McKinlay
Attendance: 13,200   *Referee:* D. F. T. Syme
Dundee's objective was to keep a clean sheet in order to share top spot in Section 3 with Aberdeen.

Wednesday, 26 October
ABERDEEN (1) 1   ST JOHNSTONE (0) 0
  Simpson (12)
ABERDEEN: Leighton, McIntyre (Angus), Rougvie, Cooper, McLeish, Miller, Strachan, Simpson, Hewitt, Bell, Falconer
ST JOHNSTONE: Baines, Kilgour, McVicar, Barron, Kennedy, Rutherford, Gibson, Lyons, Brannigan (Blair), Morton, Beedie (Brogan)
Attendance: 12,700   *Referee:* A. M. Roy
After Simpson capitalised on a one-two with Hewitt Aberdeen got themselves in a rut.

Wednesday, 9 November
MEADOWBANK   ABERDEEN (0) 3
  THISTLE (0) 1   Porteous (55),
  Sprott (72 pen)   Stewart o.g. (61)
                       Hewitt (67)
MEADOWBANK: McQueen, Dunn, Moyes, Holt, Stewart, Boyd, Hendrie, Lawson, Robertson (Tomassi), Korotkich (Smith), Sprott
ABERDEEN: Leighton, McIntyre, Rougvie, Simpson, McLeish, Cooper, Strachan, Hewitt, McGhee, Bell (Angus), Weir (Porteous)
Attendance: 2,700   *Referee:* B. R. McGinlay
Dons substitute Ian Porteous collected Strachan's knock-down to net, but before then Aberdeen had rarely looked like scoring.

Wednesday, 30 November
DUNDEE (1) 1   ABERDEEN (1) 2
  Fraser (62)   McGhee (18),
                       Bell (46)
DUNDEE: R. Geddes, McKimmie, McKinlay, Fraser, Smith, Glennie (Kidd), Mackie, A. Geddes (McGlashan), Ferguson, McCall, Stephen
ABERDEEN: Leighton, Cooper, Rougvie, Simpson, McLeish, Miller, Strachan (Falconer), Hewitt (McMaster), McGhee, Bell, Weir
Attendance: 11,000   *Referee:* H. Young

Dundee needed to win to qualify for the semi-finals at Aberdeen's expense. It looked a tall order when McGhee scored his 100th goal for Aberdeen with a cross-cum-shot which Geddes might have intercepted. He might also have kept out Bell's optimistic effort.

Section 3

	P	W	D	L	F	A	Pts
ABERDEEN	6	5	1	0	11	2	11
Dundee	6	3	2	1	8	4	8
Meadowbank	6	1	2	3	4	10	4
St Johnstone	6	0	1	5	2	9	1

Semi Final 1st Leg Wednesday, 22 February
ABERDEEN (0) 0   CELTIC (0) 0
ABERDEEN: Leighton, Rougvie, McMaster (Mitchell), Cooper, McLeish, Miller, Strachan, Black, McGhee, Angus, Weir (Hewitt)
CELTIC: Bonner, McGrain, Reid, Aitken, McAdam, Sinclair, McClair, P. McStay, McGarvey, McLeod, Burns
Attendance: 20,074   *Referee:* B. R. McGinlay
It was Aberdeen who wanted the first-leg lead, but Celtic who would have deserved it. The nearest Aberdeen came was a Strachan volley from 25 yards which crashed off the bar in the opening minutes. Thereafter the better chances fell to Celtic.

Semi Final 2nd Leg Saturday, 10 March
CELTIC (0) 1   ABERDEEN (0) 0
  Reid (54 pen)
CELTIC: Bonner, McGrain, Reid, Aitken, McAdam, Sinclair (Provan), McClair, P. McStay, McGarvey, McLeod, Burns
ABERDEEN: Leighton, Cooper, Rougvie, Simpson (Falconer), McLeish, Miller, Strachan, Bell, Black, Angus, Hewitt
Celtic won 1-0 on aggregate
Attendance: 41,169   *Referee:* R. B. Valentine
Six more bookings, ugly crowd violence, and a penalty when Bell and Angus supposedly sandwiched Burns. Aberdeen had been going strongly for four trophies: now they're left chasing three.

SCOTTISH CUP

3rd Round, Monday, 13 February
ABERDEEN (0) 1   KILMARNOCK (0) 1
  Weir (83)   Gallacher (90)
ABERDEEN: Leighton, McKimmie, Rougvie, McMaster (Porteous), McLeish, Miller, Strachan, Black, McGhee, Hewitt (Cooper), Weir
KILMARNOCK: McCulloch, McLean, Robertson, McDicken (McKinna), P. Clarke, R. Clark, McGivern, MacLeod, Gallacher, Simpson, Bryson (Cockburn)
Attendance: 15,000   *Referee:* J. R. S. Renton
Aberdeen bang their heads against Killie's brick wall, until McGhee, Porteous and Strachan set up the chance

for Weir. A replay is the last thing Aberdeen need, but it's what they've got after Gallacher outpaced McLeish at the death.

3rd Round Replay Wednesday, 15 February
KILMARNOCK (0) 1   ABERDEEN (2) 3
  McKinna (63)   Strachan (30),
                             Miller (35),
                             Weir (84)
KILMARNOCK: McCulloch, McLean, Robertson, Cochrane, P. Clarke, R. Clark, McGivern, MacLeod, Gallacher, Simpson, McKinna
ABERDEEN: Leighton, McKimmie, Rougvie (Hewitt), Cooper, McLeish, Miller, Strachan (Porteous), Black, McGhee, Angus, Weir
Attendance: 6,200   *Referee:* J. R. S. Renton
Strachan plays one-twos with Miller, Black and McGhee to score a classic goal. After Miller adds a second goal Kilmarnock rally in a furious second half, climaxed with McKinna's back-header.

4th Round Saturday, 18 February
CLYDE (0) 0   ABERDEEN (1) 2
                             Angus (15),
                             Cooper (56)
CLYDE: Atkins, McFarlane, McQueen, Ahern, Flexney, Evans, Reilly, McVeigh, Masterton, O'Neill (Doherty), Frye
ABERDEEN: Leighton, McKimmie (McMaster), Rougvie, Cooper, McLeish, Miller, Strachan, Black, McGhee (Hewitt), Angus, Weir
Attendance: 10,000   *Referee:* A. Huett
First Division Clyde did their best on a beautiful spring-like afternoon, but were a beaten side following Angus' deflected drive.

Quarter Final Saturday, 17 March
ABERDEEN (0) 0   DUNDEE UNITED (0) 0
ABERDEEN: Leighton, McKimmie, Rougvie, Cooper, McLeish, Miller, Strachan (Hewitt), Black, McGhee, Simpson, Angus
DUNDEE UNITED: McAlpine, Stark, Malpas, Gough, Holt, Narey, Bannon, Kirkwood (Clark), Coyne, Milne, Dodds
Attendance: 22,500   *Referee:* B. R. McGinlay
Without the injured Sturrock and Hegarty, United look to be content with a replay. The woodwork saved them twice.

Quarter Final Replay Wednesday, 28 March
DUNDEE UNITED (0) 0 ABERDEEN (1) 1
                             McGhee (2)
DUNDEE UNITED: McAlpine, Stark (Clark), Malpas, McGinnis (Taylor), Hegarty, Narey, Holt, Kirkwood, Milne, Sturrock, Dodds
ABERDEEN: Leighton, McKimmie, Rougvie (Mitchell), Cooper, McLeish, Miller, Strachan, Simpson, McGhee, Black, Angus

Attendance: 16,000   *Referee:* B. R. McGinlay
McAlpine's weak goal-kick is chested down by Cooper and switched forward to Mark McGhee coming in from the left. And that's that. United were without the unfit Gough and Bannon, and missed them. This is Aberdeen's first win over Dundee United under Alex Ferguson in cup competition.

Semi Final (Tynecastle) Saturday, 14 April
DUNDEE (0) 0   ABERDEEN (1) 2
                             Porteous (28),
                             Strachan (89)
DUNDEE: Geddes, Glennie, McKinlay, Fraser, Smith, MacDonald, Mackie (McGlashan), Richardson (Stephen), Harris, McGeachie, Kidd
ABERDEEN: Leighton, Mitchell, Rougvie, Simpson, McLeish, Miller, Strachan, Black, Porteous (Bell), Angus, Hewitt (Cowan)
Attendance: 17,650   *Referee:* B. R. McGinlay
An untidy semi-final. Dundee had much of the first-half play. Harris jumped above Leighton to head home, but the referee adjudged he'd fouled the keeper. Porteous broke the ice when a Hewitt corner was missed by the entire Dundee defence. Six more bookings.

Scottish Cup Final (Hampden) Saturday, 19 May
CELTIC (0) 1 *1*   ABERDEEN (1) 1 *2*
P. McStay (86)   *(After Extra Time)*
                             Black (23),
                             McGhee (98)
CELTIC: Bonner, McGrain, Reid (Melrose), Aitken, W. McStay, McLeod, Provan, P. McStay, McGarvey, Burns, McClair (Sinclair)
ABERDEEN: Leighton, McKimmie, Rougvie (Stark), Cooper, McLeish, Miller, Strachan, Simpson, McGhee, Black, Weir (Bell)
                           Referee: R. B. Valentine
This was the 99th Scottish Cup Final. Strachan's corner is headed back by McLeish, McGhee clashes with Aitken, and the ball loops over to Black who screws the shoulder-high volley past the advancing Bonner. Five minutes before half-time Aitken races across and almost severs McGhee at the neck. He becomes the first player sent off in a Scottish Cup Final since Rangers' Jock Buchanan in 1929. Celtic raised themselves in the second half and equalised when the ball broke back to Paul McStay. In extra time Bell fires the ball against a post, Strachan flips it back and McGhee – playing his last game for Aberdeen before his transfer to Hamburg – first-timed it inside the near post.

EUROPEAN CUP-WINNERS CUP

1st Round, 1st Leg Wednesday, 14 September
AKRANES (Iceland) (1) 1 ABERDEEN (1) 2
  Halldorsson (28)   McGhee 2 (29, 88)
AKRANES: Sigurdsson, Pordarson, Askelsson, Larusson, Halldorsson, Johannesson (Ingolsson), Hakonarsson, Jonsson, Omarsson, Tryggvason, Sveinsson

ABERDEEN: Leighton, Mitchell, Rougvie, Cooper (McMaster), McLeish, Miller, Stark (Cowan), Simpson, McGhee, Bell, Hewitt.

Attendance: 5,500   *Referee:* R. Daly (Eire)

Joy for Akranes as Halldorsson heads in a corner. The scorer's mistake then lets in McGhee to lob an instant equaliser. In the second half Leighton parries Sveinsson's penalty, before McGhee rose to meet Hewitt's corner.

1st Round, 2nd Leg Wednesday, 28 September
ABERDEEN (0) 1   AKRANES (0) 1
   Strachan (69 pen)   Askelsson (89 pen)

ABERDEEN: Leighton, Cooper, McMaster, Simpson, McLeish, Miller, Strachan, Stark (Porteous), McGhee, Hewitt, Weir (Bell)

AKRANES: Sigurdsson, Pordarson, Askelsson, Larusson, Halldorsson, Johannesson, Hakonarsson, Jonsson, Omarsson, Tryggvason, Sveinsson

Aberdeen won 3-2 on aggregate

Attendance: 12,500   *Referee:* R. Nyhus
                                      (Norway)

The edge to Aberdeen's game was missing. It looked like Strachan's penalty, after McGhee was felled by Halldorsson, would be enouth – until Tryggvason was barged off the ball by Cooper.

2nd Round, 1st Leg Wednesday, 19 October
BEVEREN (Belgium) (0) 0 ABERDEEN (0) 0

BEVEREN: de Wilde, Jaspers, Pfaff, Lambrichts, Baecke, Stalmans (Gortz), Schonberger, Albert, Theunis, Martens, Creve

ABERDEEN: Leighton, Rougvie, McMaster, Cooper, McLeish, Miller, Hewitt, Simpson, McGhee, Bell (Strachan), Weir

Attendance: 21,000   *Referee:* J. Krchnak
                                (Czechoslovakia)

Beveren saw Aberdeen crush their Belgian compatriots Waterschei last season. Aberdeen are becoming so professional in European competition that Beveren had few chances to break through. Aberdeen's tactics were to stifle Beveren's attacking moves in their infancy – well away from Leighton's goal. This succeeded in frustrating the Belgians, who were top of their league after 10 unbeaten games.

2nd Round, 2nd Leg Wednesday, 2 November
ABERDEEN (2) 4   BEVEREN (0) 1
   Strachan 2 (37 pen, 60)   Theunis (83)
   Simpson (45),
   Weir (69)

ABERDEEN: Leighton, Cooper, Rougvie, Simpson (Angus), McLeish, Miller, Strachan, Hewitt, McGhee, Bell, Weir (Black)

BEVEREN: de Wilde, Jaspers, Garot, Lambrichts, Baecke, Pfaff (Creve), Schonberger, Albert, Theunis, Martens, Kusto (Stalmans)

Aberdeen won 4-1 on aggregate

Attendance: 22,500   *Referee:* Lund-Sorensen
                                (Denmark)

Before the kick-off Alex Ferguson announced he was staying at Pittodrie and not joining Rangers. The match turned into a party of celebration. After de Wilde had crashed into Hewitt in the box. Aberdeen simply wiped the floor with Beveren. Man-of-the-match was undoubtedly Peter Weir.

Quarter Final 1st Leg Wednesday, 7 March
UJPEST DOSZA   ABERDEEN (0) 0
   (Hungary) (0) 2

   Kisznyer (50),
   Heredi (82)

UJPEST DOSZA: Szendrei, B. Kovacs, J. Kovacs, Kardas, Toth, Steidl, Heredi, Kisznyer, Kiss, Toriczik, Fekete

ABERDEEN: Leighton, McKimmie, Rougvie, Cooper, McLeish, Miller, Strachan (Simpson), Black (Hewitt), McGhee, Angus, Bell

Attendance: 29,000   *Referee:* T. Tokat (Turkey)

The Megyeri Stadium in Budapest is the setting for Aberdeen's first defeat in 28 competitive matches – and also one of the most extraordinary defeats ever suffered in Europe. The better team by far, Aberdeen fell behind to a free kick and then proceeded to waste glorious chances. Strachan rounded the keeper and shot against a post. When Szendrei dropped the ball at McGhee's feet the Dons striker could only prod it back against the fallen keeper's body from a range of two feet. To add insult to injury Heredi then outpaced Miller to streak away for a second Hungarian goal.

Quarter Final 2nd Leg Wednesday, 21 March
ABERDEEN (1) 2 3   UJPEST DOZSA (0) 0 0
   McGhee 3 (37, 88, 93)   *(After Extra Time)*

ABERDEEN: Leighton, Cooper, McKimmie, Simpson, McLeish, Miller, Strachan, Black, McGhee, Bell (Angus), Hewitt (Falconer)

UJPEST DOZSA: Szendrei, B. Kovacs, J. Kovacs, Toth, Kisznyer, Kardos, Kiss, Steidl, Torocsik, Fekete (Bogdan) (Szebegyinski), Heredi

Aberdeen won 3-2 on aggregate

Attendance: 22,800   *Referee:* A. Ponnet
                                (Belgium)

Another night to enter Pittodrie folklore. The Hungarian goal endures siege conditions. At last McGhee is unmolested to head in Strachan's cross. But with the Dons two minutes from defeat McGhee sidefooted Falconer's cross past Szendrei. Three minutes into extra time Strachan's centre eluded everybody except McGhee, running in at the far post. Shortly afterwards the Hungarian keeper butted McLeish, and off he went.

Semi Final 1st Leg Wednesday, 11 April
PORTO (Portugal) (1) 1   ABERDEEN (0) 0
   Gomes (14)

PORTO: Ze Beto, Joao, Pinto, Inacio, Lima Pereira, Ed Luis, J. Magalhaes, Frasco (Walsh), Sousa, Gomes, J. Pacheco, Costa (Vermelinho)

ABERDEEN: Leighton, McKimmie, Rougvie (Mitchell), Cooper, McLeish, Miller, Strachan, Black, McGhee, Simpson, Bell (Hewitt)

Attendance: 65,000   *Referee:* J. Igna (Romania)

When the draw for the quarter-finals had been made back at Christmas Alex Ferguson said he would fancy Porto. Silly man. Fernando Gomes' header, after a corner had been back-headed to him, was all Porto had to show for their first-half superiority. Aberdeen shut the door in the second half in an atmosphere of seething passion.

Semi Final 2nd Leg Wednesday, 25 April
ABERDEEN (0) 0   PORTO (0) 1
                                        Vermelinho (75)

ABERDEEN: Leighton, McKimmie (Cooper), Rougvie, Simpson, McLeish, Miller, Strachan, Black, McGhee, Bell, Hewitt (Weir)

PORTO: Ze Beto, Pinto, Luis, Pereira, Eurico, Magalhaes (Costa), Frasco (Quinito), Sousa, Gomes, J. Pacheco, Vermelinho

Porto won 2-0 on aggregate

Attendance: 23,000   *Referee:* J. Krchnak (Czechoslovakia)

Magnificent Porto end the Pittodrie dream of a second Cup-Winners Cup. Early on, in a misty stadium, McGhee magically jinked his way round two defenders in the box, but most of the magic belonged to the Portuguese. A semi-fit Peter Weir was pushed on as a desperate substitute, but two minutes later Vermelino broke away to chip the ball over a stranded Leighton.

EUROPEAN SUPER CUP

1st Leg Tuesday, 22 November
S V HAMBURG (0) 0   ABERDEEN (0) 0

HAMBURG: Stein, Schroder, Wehmeyer, Jacobs, Hieronymus, Hartwig (Wuttke), Roff, Groh, Schatzschneider, Magath, Von Heeson

ABERDEEN: Leighton, Cooper, Rougvie, Simpson, McLeish, Miller, Strachan, Hewitt, McGhee, Bell, Weir

Attendance: 15,000   *Referee:* A. Christov (Czechoslovakia)

Two years earlier Hamburg eliminated Aberdeen from the UEFA Cup. The Dons' progress in that time is clearly demonstrated. Again, Aberdeen plan their 'early defence' strategy in their opponents' half, though with only limited success. Instead it was the Dons' back four which had to do all the defending. Aberdeen's best creative moment came when McGhee waltzed around two defenders but shot tamely at Stein.

2nd Leg Tuesday, 20 December
ABERDEEN (0) 2   S V HAMBURG (0) 0
Simpson (47),
McGhee (64)

ABERDEEN: Leighton, McKimmie, McMaster, Simpson, McLeish, Miller, Strachan, Hewitt (Black), McGhee, Bell, Weir

HAMBURG: Stein, Kaltz (Hanson), Wehmeyer, Jacobs, Hieronymus, Hartwig, Schroder, Groh, Schatzschneider (Wuttke), Magath, Roff

Aberdeen won 2-0 on aggregate

Attendance: 22,500   *Referee:* H. Brummeier (Austria)

A subdued first half played in depressing drizzle. Neil Simpson's goal, following a 60-yard Weir dash down the touchline, was slightly against the general run of play. But from that moment Hamburg were overwhelmed. Perhaps both sets of players were confused. It was Hamburg who wore all red, while the Dons sported white shirts with black shorts.

1983-84
APPEARANCES

	League	League Cup	Scottish Cup	Cup-Winners Cup	Super Cup
Leighton	36	10	7	8	2
Rougvie	35	8	7	6	1
Miller	34	9	7	8	2
McLeish	32	10	7	8	2
McGhee	30(+3)	6	6	8	2
Weir	26(+1)	8	4	3(+1)	2
Cooper	25(+1)	8	5(+1)	7(+1)	1
Strachan	24(+1)	6	7	6(+1)	2
Hewitt	22(+11)	7(+3)	2(+3)	6(+2)	2
Bell	21(+3)	8	−(+2)	7(+1)	2
Simpson	21(+3)	6(+1)	4	7(+1)	
McKimmie	17(+1)		6	4	1
Black	14(+4)	6	7	4(+1)	−(+1)
McMaster	11(+1)	6(+1)	1(+1)	2(+1)	1
Stark	11(+3)	3(+2)	−(+1)	2	
Angus	9(+3)	2(+2)	5	1(+2)	
McIntyre	7(+4)	3			
Mitchell	6(+3)	−(+1)	1(+1)	1(+1)	
Porteous	5(+9)	2(+2)	1(+2)	−(+1)	
Cowan	5		−(+1)	−(+1)	
Falconer	4(+5)	2(+3)		−(+1)	
Robertson	1				
Wright	−(+1)				

23 players

GOALS	Totals	League	League Cup	Scottish Cup	Cup-Winners Cup
McGhee	24	13	3	2	5
Strachan	18	13		2	3
Hewitt	16	12	4		
Black	12	6	5	1	
Stark	11	6	5		
Weir	8	5		2	1
Porteous	6	3	2	1	
Simpson	5	2	1		1
Rougvie	4	4			
Bell	4	3	1		

GOALS	Totals	League	League Cup	Scottish Cup	Cup-Winners Cup
Miller	4	2	1	1	
Falconer	2	2			
McLeish	2	2			
McKimmie	1	1			
Angus	1			1	
Cooper	1			1	
own-goals	5	4	1		
Totals	124	78	23	11	10

SUPER CUP: McGhee (1), Simpson (1), Total (2)

Aberdeen win the Premier League at Pittodrie by drawing 1-1 with Celtic on 27th April, 1985. The players are saluted by the fans.

Season 1984-85

Alex Ferguson spent the summer of 1984 trying to pick up the pieces, once three of his key players – Strachan, McGhee and Rougvie – had departed in search of fresh challenges. Each department of his side needed strengthening. Stark filled Strachan's slot, Frank McDougall was signed from St Mirren to fill in for McGhee, while Tommy McQueen was snapped up from Clyde to take over from Rougvie.

This new-look team provided a season that was both outstanding and yet also a grave disappointment. The failings began in the League Cup when Aberdeen's first opponents, unsung Airdrie, dumped them on their famous backsides. The gloom continued in the European Cup – the trophy coveted by Ferguson above all others. Aberdeen had three opportunities to thrust aside Dynamo Berlin. They could have guaranteed their survival in the first leg at Pittodrie; they should have been safe when Ian Angus scored a fine goal in Berlin; Willie Miller then had a penalty kick standing between Aberdeen and the second round. Alas, it was Berlin who went through. Come the Spring it was Dundee United's turn to wield the axe. It fell in a semi-final replay in the 100th Scottish Cup, wrecking Aberdeen's hopes of an unprecedented fourth consecutive Hampden appearance.

But while the Dons were proving strangely vulnerable in the various cup competitions, their league form was simply irresistible. They led from the first day of the season to the last. In retaining the championship Aberdeen established a new record points total for the Premier Division, already held by themselves. This maintained the remarkable record of year-by-year improvement under Fergie. In his first season at Pittodrie in 1978-79 Aberdeen accumulated 40 points. Thereafter the tally was 48, 49, 53, 55, 57 and now 59. As a bonus, the Dons netted 89 league goals, a post-War record for the club and just one short of the Premier League record – held jointly by Celtic and Dundee United.

League:	Champions
League Cup:	Second Round
Scottish Cup:	Semi Final
European Cup:	First Round

SCOTTISH PREMIER DIVISION

No 1 Saturday, 11 August

ABERDEEN (1) 3   DUNDEE (2) 2
Stark (12),   Stephen (29),
Black 2 (56, 82)   Rafferty (30)

ABERDEEN: Leighton, Mitchell, McQueen, Bell, McLeish, Miller, Stark (Porteous), Simpson, Hewitt, Black, Falconer (Cowan)

DUNDEE: Geddes, McGeachie, McKinlay, Rafferty, McCormack, Glennie, Kidd (McWilliams), Stephen (Smith), McCall, Connor, Harris

P	W	D	L	F	A	Pts
1	1	0	0	3	2	2

Attendance: 14,700

What a shock for Aberdeen as Dundee's Stephen scores off a post and within seconds Rafferty fires in from a short free kick. The aerial ability of Eric Black eventually saved the day.

No 2 Saturday, 18 August

ST MIRREN (0) 0   ABERDEEN (2) 2
                                   Stark (5), Falconer (20)

ST MIRREN: Money, Wilson, Hamilton, Rooney, Fulton, Clarke, Fitzpatrick, McAvennie, Gallagher, Abercrombie, Scanlon (Mackie)

ABERDEEN: Leighton, McKimmie, McQueen, Stark, McLeish, Miller, Porteous, Simpson, McDougall (Angus), Bell, Falconer

P W D L F A Pts   *Attendance:* 5,400
2 2 0 0 5 2 4

Set pieces brought both Aberdeen goals – both headers. St Mirren had more attempts at goal than Aberdeen but couldn't find the net. That's the name of the game.

No 3 Saturday, 25 August
DUNDEE UNITED (0) 0   ABERDEEN (1) 2
                       Black 2 (13 pen, 89)
DUNDEE UNITED: Thomson, Kirkwood, Malpas, Gough, Hegarty, Narey, Bannon, Milne (Coyne), Beedie (Holt), Sturrock, Dodds
ABERDEEN: Leighton, McKimmie, McQueen, Stark, McLeish, Miller, Black, Simpson, McDougall, Bell, Falconer
P W D L F A Pts   *Attendance:* 13,000
3 3 0 0 7 2 6   *Referee:* G. Smith
Aberdeen do enjoy playing at Tannadice. This was their 19th Premier League visit, and they have still only lost four times. Ex-St Mirren keeper Thomson brought down ex-St Mirren striker McDougall for Aberdeen's penalty.

No 4 Saturday, 1 September
ABERDEEN (2) 4   HIBERNINAN (0) 1
  McKimmie (39),   Jamieson (70)
  Simpson (42), Black (57),
  McDougall (68)
ABERDEEN: Leighton, McKimmie, McQueen, Stark, McLeish, Miller, Black, Simpson (Angus), McDougall, Bell, Falconer (Hewitt)
HIBERNIAN: Rough, McKee, Schaedler, Sneddon, Rae, McNamara, Harvey (Jamieson), Brazil, Kane, Rice, Thomson (McGeachie)
P W D L F A Pts   *Attendance:* 13,800
4 4 0 0 11 3 8   *Referee:* B. R. McGinlay
Frank McDougall adds the finishing touch to his home debut. Hibs manager Pat Stanton was 'sent off' after naughty words to a linesman.

No 5 Saturday, 8 September
MORTON (0) 0   ABERDEEN (2) 3
             Stark (11), Falconer (15),
             Black (86 pen)
MORTON: McDermott, McClurg, Holmes (Turner), Wilson, Dunlop, Duffy, Robertson, McNab, O'Hara, Docherty, McNeil
ABERDEEN: Leighton, McKimmie, McQueen, Stark, McLeish, Miller, Black, Simpson, McDougall (Hewitt), Bell (Angus), Falconer
Leading positions

	P	W	D	L	F	A	Pts
1 ABERDEEN	5	5	0	0	14	3	10
2 Rangers	5	3	2	0	6	1	8
3 St Mirren	5	3	1	1	7	3	7
4 Celtic	5	1	4	0	7	2	6

Attendance: 5,000   *Referee:* D. Hope

Aberdeen try to lay their Cappielow bogey, with only three wins on that ground in ten visits beforehand. Eric Black was involved in all the goals.

No 6 Saturday, 15 September
ABERDEEN (0) 0   RANGERS (0) 0
ABERDEEN: Leighton, McKimmie, McQueen, Stark, McLeish, Miller, Hewitt (Porteous), Simpson (Angus), McDougall, Cooper, Falconer
RANGERS: Walker, McKinnon, Dawson, McClelland, Paterson, Redford, Russell (McPherson), Fraser, Ferguson (McDonald), McCoist, Cooper
P W D L F A Pts   *Attendance:* 22,500
6 5 1 0 14 3 11   *Referee:* H. Young
This game needed a goal. Frank McDougall drew Walker off his line then shot wide of an empty target.

No 7 Saturday, 22 September
DUMBARTON (0) 0   ABERDEEN (0) 2
                 Miller (77), Falconer (85)
DUMBARTON: Arthur, Kay, M. McGowan, T. Coyle, McNeill, Clougherty, Ashwood, Craig, P. McGowan, Crawley, J. Coyle
ABERDEEN: Leighton, McKimmie, McQueen, Cooper, McLeish, Miller, Black, Simpson, McDougall (Porteous), Bell, Angus (Falconer)
P W D L F A Pts   *Attendance:* 4,500
7 6 1 0 16 3 13   *Referee:* T. Muirhead
Newly-promoted Dumbarton are ruffling some feathers. Willie Miller ruffles theirs with a thunderbolt left-footed shot to teach his forwards how to do it.

No 8 Saturday, 29 September
ABERDEEN (0) 4   HEARTS (0) 0
  McDougall 2 (46, 84),
  Falconer (48), Angus (74)
ABERDEEN: Leighton, McKimmie, McQueen, Cooper, McLeish, Miller, Bell (Stark), Simpson, Black (McDougall), Angus, Falconer
HEARTS: Smith, Kidd, Cowie, Jardine (O'Connor), R. MacDonald, Levein, Park (Whittaker), Robertson, Bone, A. MacDonald, Black
P W D L F A Pts   *Attendance:* 16,300
8 7 1 0 20 3 15   *Referee:* D. Syme
Henry Smith stopped a Black penalty in the first half. Frank McDougall came out for the second and swept home Falconer's cross after just 17 seconds.

No 9 Saturday, 6 October
CELTIC (1) 2   ABERDEEN (0) 1
  McGarvey (29),   McDougall (47)
  Provan (80)
CELTIC: Bonner, McGrain, Reid, Aitken, McAdam, Grant, Colquhoun (Provan), P. McStay, McClair, McLeod, McGarvey
ABERDEEN: Leighton, McKimmie, McQueen, Cooper, McLeish, Miller, Black, Simpson, McDougall, Angus (Hewitt), Stark (Porteous)

P W D L F A Pts
9 7 1 1 21 5 15

Attendance: 31,400
Referee: R. Valentine

It never rains but it pours. After Aberdeen's tragic penalty failures in Berlin, they come up with another at Parkhead. Shortly after McDougall had volleyed Aberdeen level, Billy Stark was the sinner from the spot. To add insult, Provan's 25-yard free kick deserved to win any match.

No 10 Saturday, 13 October

DUNDEE (1) 1   ABERDEEN (2) 2
  Connor (45)   McDougall (24),
                        Stark (27)

DUNDEE: Carson, McGeachie, McKinlay, Rafferty, McCormack, Glennie, Forsyth (McWilliams), Brown, McCall, Connor, Stephen (Kidd)
ABERDEEN: Leighton, McKimmie, McQueen, Cooper, McLeish, Miller, Black, Simpson, McDougall (Porteous), Angus, Stark (Falconer)

Leading positions

	P	W	D	L	F	A	Pts
1 ABERDEEN	10	8	1	1	23	6	17
2 Celtic	10	6	4	0	18	6	16
3 Rangers	10	6	3	1	11	2	15

Attendance: 11,000   *Referee:* A. Roy

Seven players were booked as these two teams set about one another. Connor's goal for Dundee on the stroke of half-time transformed the match. How Aberdeen held out in the second half they will never know.

No 11 Saturday, 20 October

ABERDEEN (2) 4   ST MIRREN (0) 0
  McDougall 2 (13, 69 pen),
  Porteous (39), Stark (86)

ABERDEEN: Leighton, McKimmie, McQueen, Stark, McLeish, Miller, Porteous (Falconer), Simpson, McDougall, Black, Angus
ST MIRREN: Stewart, Wilson, Winnie, Rooney, Cooper, Clarke, Fitzpatrick, McAvennie, McDowell, Abercrombie (Cameron), Mackie

P W D L F A Pts
11 9 1 1 27 6 19

Attendance: 14,100
Referee: D. T. McVicar

St Mirren's task was difficult enough even before Jim Rooney was sent off just before half-time for a fierce challenge on Angus. He had already been booked. It's Frank McDougall's turn to take penalties.

No 12 Tuesday, 6 November

HIBERNIAN (0) 0   ABERDEEN (1) 3
                          McDougall (41),
                          Black (53), Stark (89)

HIBERNIAN: Rough, Sneddon, McKee, Craig, Jamieson, McNamara, Callachan, Durie (Brazil), Irvine, Rice, Kane (Thomson)
ABERDEEN: Leighton, Mitchell, McQueen, Stark, McLeish, Miller, Porteous (Weir), Simpson, McDougall, Black, Angus

P W D L F A Pts

Attendance: 8,000

A tale of two goalkeepers. Jim Leighton comfortably saved Durie's penalty to keep the score 1-0. Then Alan Rough fumbled Black's header into the net.

No 13 Saturday, 10 November

ABERDEEN (2) 3   MORTON (1) 1
  McDougall (32),   Clinging (8)
  Miller (42), Simpson (73)

ABERDEEN: Leighton, McKimmie, McQueen (Porteous), Stark (Mitchell), McLeish, Miller, Black, Simpson, McDougall, Angus, Weir
MORTON: McDermott, Wilson, Holmes, O'Hara, Mackin, Duffy, Robertson, Docherty, Gillespie, Pettigrew (McNeil), Clinging

P W D L F A Pts
13 11 1 1 33 7 23

Attendance: 14,500
Referee: H. F. Williamson

Peter Weir is welcomed back for his first game of the season. Clinging's raging goal for Morton after McQueen's feeble clearance put Aberdeen to the test. They passed.

No 14 Saturday, 17 November

RANGERS (1) 1   ABERDEEN (1) 2
  Mitchell (7)   Stark (19),
                         McDougall (61)

RANGERS: McCloy, McKinnon, Dawson, McPherson, Paterson, Redford, Prytz (McMinn), Fraser, Mitchell, Ferguson (Russell), Cooper
ABERDEEN: Leighton, McKimmie, Angus, Stark, McLeish, Miller, Black (Cowan), Simpson, McDougall, Cooper, Weir

P W D L F A Pts
14 12 1 1 35 8 25

Attendance: 44,000
Referee: H. Alexander

Rangers suffer their first home defeat of the season, despite the deflected goal scored for them by Dave Mitchell – later to play for Australia against Scotland in the World Cup. Frank McDougall won the game with his tenth league goal of the season.

No 15 Saturday, 24 November

ABERDEEN (1) 1   DUMBARTON (0) 0
  McDougall (1)

ABERDEEN: Leighton, McKimmie, Angus (Cowan), Stark, McLeish, Miller, Black, Simpson, McDougall, Cooper (McQueen), Weir
DUMBARTON: Arthur, Kay, M. McGowan, T. Coyle, McCahill, Clougherty, Simpson, Robertson, Bourke (McCaig), Craig, P. McGowan (J. Coyle)

Leading positions

	P	W	D	L	F	A	Pts
1 ABERDEEN	15	13	1	1	36	8	27
2 Celtic	15	10	4	1	36	11	24
3 Rangers	15	7	6	2	17	7	20

Attendance: 13,200   *Referee:* D. M. Galloway

The worst thing to happen in this match was for Frank McDougall to score within 30 seconds – and to find his name on the scoresheet for the eight successive game. Thereafter everything went flat.

No 16 Saturday, 1 December
HEARTS (1) 1   ABERDEEN (1) 2
  A. MacDonald (43)   Cowan (30), Stark 52)
HEARTS: Smith, Kidd, Whittaker, Jardine, Levein, Black, Bowman, Robertson, Clark, MacDonald (Bone), Park (Johnston)
ABERDEEN: Leighton, McKimmie, McQueen, Stark, McLeish, Miller, Cowan, Simpson, McDougall (Hewitt), Angus (Mitchell), Weir

P	W	D	L	F	A	Pts		
16	14	1	1	38	9	29		

Attendance: 10,000
Referee: A. Ferguson

Cowan's cracking volley nearly broke Henry Smith's fingers. Miller and Leighton uncharacteristically made a present of a goal to Alex MacDonald. Billy Stark's header would not take 'No' for an answer.

No 17 Saturday, 8 December
ABERDEEN (2) 4   CELTIC (0) 2
  Black 2 (33, 61),   Johnston (57 pen),
  McKimmie (44),   McGarvey (84)
  McDougall (85)
ABERDEEN: Leighton, McKimmie, McQueen, Stark (Mitchell), McLeish, Miller, Black, Simpson, McDougall, Angus, Weir (Hewitt)
CELTIC: Bonner, McGrain, McLeod, Aitken, McAdam, McClair, Provan, McStay, Johnston, Burns, McGarvey

P	W	D	L	F	A	Pts		
17	15	1	1	42	11	31		

Attendance: 23,000
Referee: H. Young

The match of the season – or any other season. A soaring header by Black and a deflected 30-yarder by McKimmie gave Aberdeen a commanding interval lead. Celtic fought back to score twice after the resumption but on both occasions Aberdeen hit back within minutes.

No 18 Saturday, 15 December
ABERDEEN (0) 0   DUNDEE (0) 0
ABERDEEN: Leighton, McKimmie, McQueen (Cowan), Stark, McLeish (Cooper), Miller, Black, Simpson, McDougall, Angus, Hewitt
DUNDEE: Carson, McGeachie, McKinlay, McCormack, Smith, Glennie, Stephen, Brown, McCall (Richardson), Connor, Rafferty

P	W	D	L	F	A	Pts		
18	15	2	1	42	11	32		

Attendance: 14,000
Referee: J. Duncan

Archie Knox has been in charge of Dundee for one year since leaving the assistant manager's post at Pittodrie. McDougall's header against a post almost deprived lively Dundee of a point they fully deserved.

No 19 Saturday, 22 December
ABERDEEN (0) 0   DUNDEE UNITED (0) 1
                    Gough (48)
ABERDEEN: Leighton, McKimmie, McQueen, Stark, Cooper, W. Miller, Falconer, (J. Miller), Simpson, McDougall, Angus (Mitchell), Weir

DUNDEE UNITED: McAlpine, Malpas, Holt, Gough, Hegarty, Narey, Bannon, Taylor, Coyne, Beedie, Dodds

P	W	D	L	F	A	Pts		
19	15	2	2	42	12	32		

Attendance: 16,400
Referee: K. J. Hope

Forget the score. Dundee United murdered Aberdeen. They were the last team to win at Pittodrie fifteen months ago. McDougall is the lastest penalty-waster, after he had been toppled by Gough. But that was a mere hiccup in the Dundee United show.

No 20 Saturday, 29 December
ST MIRREN (2) 2   ABERDEEN (1) 2
  Gallagher (18),   McDougall 2 (12, 82)
  McAvennie (33)
ST MIRREN: Money, Wilson, Hamilton, Rooney, Fulton, Clark, Fitzpatrick, McAvennie, Gallagher, Abercrombie, Spiers
ABERDEEN: Leighton, McKimmie, McQueen, Stark (Falconer), Cooper, Miller, Black, Bell (Angus), McDougall, Mitchell, Weir

P	W	D	L	F	A	Pts		
20	15	3	2	44	14	33		

Attendance: 6,300
Referee: W. N. Crombie

A splendid match to see out the year. Aberdeen must have thought they'd lost it when Frank McAvennie cut inside to beat Leighton. But McDougall latched onto a long through-ball to spare Aberdeen's blushes.

No 21 Wednesday, 2 January
DUNDEE UNITED (1) 2   ABERDEEN (1) 1
  Dodds (29), Gough (77)   McQueen (24 pen)
DUNDEE UNITED: McAlpine, Malpas, Holt, Gough, Hegarty, Narey, Bannon, Taylor (Clark), Sturrock (Beaumont), Beedie, Dodds
ABERDEEN: Leighton, McKimmie (Stark), McQueen, Mitchell, Cooper, Miller, Falconer (Cowan), Simpson, McDougall, Bell, Weir

Leading positions

	P	W	D	L	F	A	Pts
1 ABERDEEN	21	15	3	3	45	16	33
2 Celtic	21	13	5	3	48	20	31
3 Rangers	21	9	9	3	27	14	27
4 Dundee United	21	11	4	6	38	24	26

Attendance: 21,900   *Referee:* D. S. Downie

Two points from four games has let other teams have a sniff of the title. United were always the better team and won the match – as they had at Pittodrie eleven days earlier – with an unchallenged Gough header.

No 22 Saturday, 5 January
ABERDEEN (1) 2   HIBERNIAN (0) 0
  Weir (26), McKimmie (76)
ABERDEEN: Gunn, Mitchell, McQueen, McKimmie, Cooper, Miller, Falconer (Hewitt), Simpson, McDougall, Bell (Angus), Weir
HIBERNIAN: Rough, Sneddon, Schaedler, Brazil, Rae, McNamara, Weir, Kane, Harris, Jamieson, Rice (Craig)

P W D L F A Pts
22 16 3 3 47 16 35

Attendance: 13,700
Referee: M. Delaney

The only good thing to come out of this game is the result, as Aberdeen continue to flounder. Tommy Craig, once of Aberdeen a long time ago, came on as a Hibs substitute.

No 23 Saturday, 12 January
ABERDEEN (1) 5   MORTON (0) 0
   Weir (27), Cooper (58),
   McDougall (60),
   Mitchell (80), Cowan (88)
ABERDEEN: Leighton, McKimmie, McQueen, Stark (Mitchell), Cooper, Miller, Hewitt, Simpson, McDougall (Cowan), Bell, Weir
MORTON: McDermott, Docherty, Holmes, Fleeting, Welsh, Duffy, Robertson, Sullivan, O'Hara, Doak, Clinging (Wilson)

P W D L F A Pts
23 17 3 3 52 16 37

Attendance: 11,000
Referee: H. Young

The sand on the frozen Pittodrie pitch was presumably to help Aberdeen prepare for their midwinter break to Egypt. Goal of the match was Cowan's chip over McDermott's head.

No 24 Saturday, 19 January
ABERDEEN (2) 5   RANGERS (0) 1
   McDougall 3 (11, 14, 72),   Prytz (75)
   Black (58),
   McQueen (81 pen)
ABERDEEN: Leighton, McKimmie, McQueen, Stark (Mitchell), Cooper, Miller, Black, Simpson, McDougall, Bell (Hewitt), Weir
RANGERS: Walker, McKinnon, Dawson, McPherson, Paterson, Prytz, McCoist, D. Ferguson (Redford), Johnstone, McDonald (McMinn), Cooper

P W D L F A Pts
24 18 3 3 57 17 39

Attendance: 22,000

This result didn't do Rangers boss Jock Wallace's hernia any good at all. Derek Johnstone returned to the Ibrox fold and stood back as Frank McDougall bagged his first hat-trick for the Dons. The game's only black spot was the sending-off of Stewart McKimmie and Ally Dawson in the first half.

No 25 Saturday, 2 February
DUMBARTON (0) 0   ABERDEEN (1) 2
                       Stark (36), Black (66)
DUMBARTON: Arthur, Kay, M. McGowan, McCahill, McNeill, Clougherty, P. McGowan (J. Coyle), Craig, Ashwood (Bourke), T. Coyle, Crawley
ABERDEEN: Leighton, McKimmie, McQueen, Cooper, McLeish, Miller, Black, Simpson, McDougall, Stark, Weir

Leading positions

	P	W	D	L	F	A	Pts
1 ABERDEEN	25	19	3	3	59	17	41
2 Celtic	22	14	5	3	50	20	33
3 Rangers	25	10	10	5	33	23	30
4 Dundee United	23	12	4	7	40	25	28

Attendance: 3,500   *Referee:* A. N. Huett

Dumbarton made life difficult for Aberdeen, but were eventually beaten by two fine headers. Stark suffered a fractured skull for his pains.

No 26 Saturday, 9 February
ABERDEEN (2) 2   HEARTS (0) 2
   Simpson (21), Weir (34)   Watson (65),
                              Robertson (71)
ABERDEEN: Leighton, McKimmie, McQueen, Cooper, McLeish, Miller, Black, Simpson, McDougall (Hewitt), Bell (Angus), Weir
HEARTS: Smith, Kidd, Whittaker, Jardine, MacDonald, Levein, Watson, Mackay, Clark, Robertson, Black

P W D L F A Pts
26 19 4 3 61 19 42

Attendance: 14,700
Referee: T. Muirhead

Never in Alex Ferguson's seven-year reign at Pittodrie has his team lost after being two goals in front. But Hearts came close. McQueen of Aberdeen and Kidd of Hearts gifted goals to their opponents with daft back-passes.

No 27 Saturday, 23 February
CELTIC (0) 2   ABERDEEN (0) 0
   Johnston (66),
   P. McStay (90 pen)
CELTIC: Bonner, W. McStay, McGrain, Aitken, McAdam, O'Leary, Grant (Provan), P. McStay, Johnston, McLeod, McGarvey
ABERDEEN: Leighton, McKimmie, McQueen, Cooper, McLeish, Miller, Black, Simpson (Bell), Cowan (Hewitt), Angus, Weir

P W D L F A Pts
27 19 4 4 61 21 42

Attendance: 48,800
Referee: B. R. McGinlay

Another thoroughly unpleasant match between these two sides, turned Celtic's way by Mo Johnston's hooked goal, after Aitken had nodded on a Provan corner. The result keeps the championship very much an open race.

No 28 Saturday, 2 March
ABERDEEN (1) 3   ST MIRREN (0) 0
   Stark (27), Black (67),
   Cowan (90)
ABERDEEN: Leighton, McKimmie, McQueen, Stark, McLeish, Mitchell, Black, Simpson, Porteous, Angus, Weir (Cowan)
ST MIRREN: Money, Wilson, Winnie, Rooney, Godfrey, Clarke, Fitzpatrick, McAvennie, Gallagher, Abercrombie, Mackie

P W D L F A Pts
28 20 4 4 64 21 44

Attendance: 12,000
Referee: H. Alexander

Magic Aberdeen. This was exhibition stuff for 90 minutes, orchestrated by Stark and Porteous. Celtic draw at Tannadice.

No 29 Saturday, 16 March
DUNDEE (0) 0   ABERDEEN (2) 4
                      Black (42),
                      Stark 2 (43, 48),
                      Simpson (66)
DUNDEE: Geddes, McGeachie, McKinlay, Rafferty, Smith, McCormack (Richardson), Stephen, Brown, Harvey (McCall), Connor, McWilliams
ABERDEEN: Leighton, McKimmie, McQueen, Stark (Bell), McLeish, Miller, Black, Simpson, Hewitt (Mitchell), Angus, Cowan

P	W	D	L	F	A	Pts
29	21	4	4	68	21	46

Attendance: 9,200
Referee: D. D. Hope

The pitch had to be cleared of overnight snow. Two crushing goals just before the interval sank Dundee's spirits. Thereafter Aberdeen turned on the style – then heard that Celtic had lost at home to Hibs.

No 30 Saturday, 23 March
HIBERNIAN (0) 0   ABERDEEN (1) 5
                    Black 3 (13, 70, 89),
                    McQueen (49 pen),
                    Hewitt (71)
HIBERNIAN: Rough, Sneddon, Schaedler, McKee, Rae, Brazil, Callachan, Kane, Irvine, Rice, McBride
ABERDEEN: Leighton, McKimmie, McQueen, Stark, McLeish, Miller, Black, Simpson, Hewitt, Angus (Bell), Cowan

Leading positions

	P	W	D	L	F	A	Pts
1 ABERDEEN	30	22	4	4	73	21	48
2 Celtic	28	17	6	5	63	25	40
3 Dundee United	29	16	6	7	51	26	38

Attendance: 9,000
Referee: A. Ferguson

Having beaten Celtic last week, Hibs are left in no doubt who are the rightful champions. Hibernian's relegation cloud hovers lower. After the Dons' third goal, missiles were thrown onto the pitch to deepen the Easter Road misery. The SFA will take its revenge.

No 31 Saturday, 30 March
ABERDEEN (2) 4   DUNDEE UNITED (0) 2
 Hewitt 2 (35, 43),   Bannon (49 pen),
 Stark (70), Cowan (71)   Reilly (74)
ABERDEEN: Leighton, McKimmie, McQueen (Cooper), Stark, McLeish, Miller, Black, Bell, Hewitt, Angus, Cowan (Falconer)
DUNDEE UNITED: Thomson, Malpas, Kirkwood, Gough, Hegarty, Beaumont, Bannon, Taylor, Beedie (Reilly), Sturrock, Dodds

P	W	D	L	F	A	Pts
31	23	4	4	77	23	50

Attendance: 15,500
Referee: J. Duncan

Sixteen goals in four games as Aberdeen sprint to the finishing line. Best of the day was Hewitt's second, an unstoppable effort which left Billy Thomson motionless.

No 32 Saturday, 6 April
RANGERS (0) 1   ABERDEEN (2) 2
 Prytz (63)   Cowan (26), Black (42)
RANGERS: Walker, Dawson, Munro, McPherson, Johnstone, Redford, Prytz, Fraser, Ferguson, McCoist, Cooper
ABERDEEN: Leighton, McKimmie, Cooper, Stark, McLeish, Miller, Black (Falconer), Bell, Hewitt, Angus (McQueen), Cowan

P	W	D	L	F	A	Pts
32	24	4	4	79	24	52

Attendance: 23,400
Referee: A. W. Waddell

Nicky Walker, the Rangers' keeper could only palm out McKimmie's cross, and Cowan lashed it back past him. Black's tap-in was Aberdeen's 79th league goal of the season – a Premier League record for the club. When Prytz drove in a fine goal for Rangers, Aberdeen simply shut up shop.

No 33 Saturday, 20 April
ABERDEEN (2) 4   DUMBARTON (0) 0
 McLeish (24), Angus (35),
 Kay o.g. (50), Stark (65)
ABERDEEN: Leighton, McKimmie, McQueen, Stark, McLeish, Miller, Black. Simpson (Cowan), Hewitt, Bell, Angus
DUMBARTON: Arthur, Kay, Sinclair, T. Coyle, McCahill, Montgomerie, Ashwood, Robertson, McIver, Crawley, J. Coyle

P	W	D	L	F	A	Pts
33	25	4	4	83	24	54

Attendance: 12,500
Referee: J. R. Renton

Alex McLeish's rocket – his first goal of the season – made Willie Miller jealous. He spent the rest of the match desperately trying to score one himself.

No 34 Saturday, 27 April
ABERDEEN (0) 1   CELTIC (1) 1
 Miller (61)   Aitken (40 pen)
ABERDEEN: Leighton, McKimmie, Miller, Porteous, Simpson, McQueen, Stark, McDougall (Cowan), Bell (Cooper), Hewitt
CELTIC: Bonner, W. McStay, McGrain, Aitken, McAdam, McLeod, Grant (Provan), P. McStay, Johnston, Burns, McGarvey

P	W	D	L	F	A	Pts
34	25	5	4	84	25	55

Attendance: 23,000
Referee: G. B. Smith

Mathematically Aberdeen wanted two points for the title – but even one would leave Celtic without a prayer. Celtic were given a gift of a penalty when Stark nudged Johnston. Willie Miller launched himself at Porteous' free-kick to head the equaliser off the post. A second Celtic goal was disallowed for a debatable push on Leighton. Hewitt missed a sitter for Aberdeen in the final seconds.

No 35 Saturday, 4 May
HEARTS (0) 0   ABERDEEN (3) 3
               McDougall 3 (21, 32, 34)
HEARTS: Smith, Kidd, Murray, Jardine, Cowie (Watson), Levein, Sandison, Robertson, Clark, Mackay (McNaughton), Black

ABERDEEN: Leighton, Mitchell, McQueen, Stark, McLeish, McKimmie, Porteous, Simpson, McDougall, Bell (McMaster), Hewitt (Cowan)

P W D L F A Pts   *Attendance:* 8,300
35 26 5 4 87 25 57   *Referee:* B. R. McGinlay

Frank McDougall's second hat-trick of the season puts the seal of approval on his first year with Aberdeen. His third goal was a delicious volley.

No 36 Saturday, 11 May
MORTON (1) 1   ABERDEEN (0) 2
  Thomson (40)   Stark (59),
                           McDougall (61)
MORTON: McDermott, Docherty, Holmes, Sullivan, Boag, O'Hara, Turner, Alexander, Gillespie, Thomson (Welsh), Clinging
ABERDEEN: Gunn, McKimmie, McQueen, Stark, McLeish (Bell), Miller, Black, Simpson, McDougall, Angus, Porteous (Hewitt)

Attendance: 3,600   *Referee:* D. D. Hope

Aberdeen have two records to go for. One point will break the Premier League record which they broke themselves twelve months ago. Three goals will equal the record of 90 shared by Celtic and Dundee United. They achieve the first milestone – not the second.

Aberdeen's complete home and away record:

HOME						AWAY					
P	W	D	L	F	A	W	D	L	F	A	Pts
36	13	4	1	49	13	14	1	3	40	13	59

Premier Division 1984-85

	P	W	D	L	F	A	Pts
1 ABERDEEN	36	27	5	4	89	26	59
2 Celtic	36	22	8	6	77	30	52
3 Dundee United	36	20	7	9	67	33	47
4 Rangers	36	13	12	11	47	38	38
5 St Mirren	36	17	4	15	51	56	38
6 Dundee	36	15	7	14	48	50	37
7 Hearts	36	13	5	18	47	64	31
8 Hibernian	36	10	7	19	38	61	27
9 Dumbarton	36	6	7	23	29	64	19
10 Morton	36	5	2	29	29	100	12

LEAGUE CUP

2nd Round Wednesday, 22 August
AIRDRIEONIANS (2) 3   ABERDEEN (1) 1
  McCabe (3), Flood (33),   Stark (11)
  Yule (55)
AIRDRIE: Black, Fairlie, Flood, Lawrie, McCabe, Martin, Paterson, Rodger, Steven, Yule, Gillies
ABERDEEN: Leighton, McKimmie, McQueen, Stark, McLeish, W. Miller, Porteous (Grant), Simpson, Cowan, Bell, Falconer (Wright)

Attendance: 5,000   *Referee:* n.a.

Airdrie manager Ally McLeod enjoyed this result. His part-timers crush Aberdeen under foot.

SCOTTISH CUP

3rd Round Wednesday, 30 January
ABERDEEN (1) 5   ALLOA (0) 0
  Hewitt (29),
  Stark 3 (58, 69, 83),
  Simpson (68)
ABERDEEN: Leighton, Mitchell, McQueen, Stark, Cooper, W. Miller, Black, Simpson, Hewitt, Bell (McLeish), Weir
ALLOA: Lowrie, Thompson (Harris), Haggart, Thomson, Dall, Martin, Mackie, Kelly, Sorbie (Murray), Barr, Lloyd

Attendance: 13,500   *Referee:* W. N. Crombie

Alloa are the pace-setters in Division Two. Only in the last half-hour did Aberdeen make their superiority plain. Nearly all the goals were close-in messy affairs.

4th Round Saturday, 16 February
RAITH ROVERS (1) 1   ABERDEEN (2) 2
  Smith (39 pen)   McDougall 2 (30, 43 pen)
RAITH: Blair, Candlish, Sweeney, Urquhart, More, Phillip, Smith, Elvin, Marshall, Robertson, Wright
ABERDEEN: Leighton, Mitchell, McKimmie, Cooper, McLeish, W. Miller, Black, Simpson, McDougall, Angus, Weir

Attendance: 10,140   *Referee:* A. Ferguson

Raith are in the bottom half of Division Two. McDougall nets with a flying overhead kick. Miller handled on the line, conceding a penalty. Weir is then upended by Urquhart for McDougall to restore the lead.

Quarter Final Saturday, 9 March
HEARTS (0) 1   ABERDEEN (0) 1
  Clark (51)   Black (78)
HEARTS: Smith, Kidd, Whittaker, Jardine, R. MacDonald, Berry, Mackay, Watson (A. MacDonald), Clark, Robertson, Black
ABERDEEN: Leighton, McKimmie, McQueen (Bell), Cooper (Porteous), McLeish, W. Miller, Black, Simpson, McDougall, Angus, Stark

Attendance: 19,000   *Referee:* B. R. McGinlay

Until today all Eric Black's goals in the Scottish Cup had been reserved for Finals. The game was all huff and puff. Leighton touched a cross out to Sandy Clark who gratefully netted from eight yards. Up soared Black to equalise and drown Hearts' premature congratulations.

Quarter Final Replay Wednesday, 13 March
ABERDEEN (1) 1   HEARTS (0) 0
  Stark (25)
ABERDEEN: Leighton, Mitchell (Bell), McKimmie, Stark, McLeish, W. Miller, Black, Simpson, Porteous (Cowan), Angus, Hewitt
HEARTS: Smith, Kidd, Whittaker, Jardine, R. MacDonald, Levein, Mackay, Berry (Watson), Clark, Robertson (McNaughton), Black

Attendance: 23,000   *Referee:* B. R. McGinlay

After just 15 minutes Hearts' Roddy MacDonald was sent off for leaving his elbow in Eric Black's face. When Stark, lurking at the far post, headed in Hewitt's free kick Hearts were left with a mountain to climb – one which they never looked like scaling.

Semi Final (Tynecastle) Saturday, 13 April
DUNDEE UNITED (0) 0   ABERDEEN (0) 0

DUNDEE UNITED: McAlpine, Malpas, Holt, Gough, Hegarty (Beedie), Narey, Bannon, Taylor (Clark), Kirkwood, Sturrock, Dodds

ABERDEEN: Leighton, McKimmie, Cooper, Stark, McLeish, W. Miller, Black, Simpson, Hewitt (Angus), Bell, Cowan

Attendance: 18,485   *Referee:* H. Alexander

This was an action replay of the 1980 League Cup Final. Aberdeen had most of the play and most of the chances. But the match ended goal-less and United won the replay. Hewitt missed a gaping goal by inches, and Stark's header flew off the inside of a post into McAlpine's arms. Near the end Cowan drove frivolously over the bar. In a lighter moment Billy Kirkwood and Willie Miller became entangled after a fierce collision, whereupon Kirkwood kissed Miller on the forehead.

Semi Final Replay (Tynecastle) Wednesday, 17 April
DUNDEE UNITED (1) 2   ABERDEEN (0) 1
   Sturrock (5), Beedie (59)   Angus (86)

DUNDEE UNITED: McAlpine, Malpas, Holt, Gough, Beedie, Narey, Bannon, Milne (Beaumont), Kirkwood, Sturrock, Dodds

ABERDEEN: Leighton, McKimmie, Cooper, Stark, McLeish, W. Miller, Black, Simpson, Hewitt (McQueen), Bell (Angus), Cowan

Attendance: 10,771   *Referee:* H. Alexander

Aberdeen's four-year run of 23 undefeated games in the Scottish Cup came to an end in controversial circumstances. Sturrock's close-range header put United in control. Two minutes after Cooper had been expelled for leaving Milne in a mangled heap, Beedie unleashed a volley which almost burst Leighton's net. Next it was Dodds' turn for the lonely walk after molesting Miller on the touchline. Angus' hooked goal gave belated hope to Aberdeen, whereupon Malpas looked to have handled in the box. The referee didn't think so.

EUROPEAN CUP

1st Round, 1st Leg Wednesday, 19 September
ABERDEEN (1) 2   DYNAMO BERLIN
   Black 2 (33, 67)   (E. Germany) (0) 1
                              Schulz (82)

ABERDEEN: Leighton, McKimmie, McQueen, Stark, McLeish, W. Miller, Bell (Simpson), Hewitt (Falconer), Black, Cooper, Angus

DYNAMO: Rudwaleit, Ksienzyk, Trieloff, Backs, Rohde, Trappa, Schulz, Maeck, Pastor (Grether), Ernst (Terletzki), Thom

Attendance: 20,000   *Referee:* M. Van
                                 Langenhove (Belgium)

Frank McDougall was ineligible, banned for four matches when with St mirren for fighting in a match with Feyenoord. For two thirds of the match Aberdeen turned in a high octane performance; two Eric Black headers got the better of a 6'6" goalkeeper. The Germans finished strongly, however, and Schulz was left unattended from a corner to score the game's third headed goal.

1st Round, 2nd Leg Wednesday, 3 October
DYNAMO BERLIN   ABERDEEN (0) 1 *1*
   (0) 2 *2*   (*After Extra Time*)
   Thom (49), Ernst (84)   Angus (67)

DYNAMO: Rudwaleit, Ksienzyk, Trieloff, Backs (Grether), Rohde, Trappa, Schulz, Maeck, Pastor (Terletzki), Ernst, Thom

ABERDEEN: Leighton, McKimmie, McQueen, Cooper, McLeish, W. Miller, Stark, Simpson, Black, Angus (Porteous), Falconer (Hewitt)

3-3 on aggregate. Dynamo Berlin won 5-4 on penalties

Attendance: 20,000   *Referee:* L. Agnolin (Italy)

Agony for Aberdeen as they exit from the European Cup at first hurdle. Thom's flicked goal on the blind side put the East Germans ahead on away goals. Angus' searing drive put Aberdeen back in control. Suicidal inattentiveness allowed Ernst to bundle the ball past Leighton and send the match into extra time, whereupon Willie Miller chipped against the bar. And so to penalties. Porteous, McQueen, Hewitt, and Stark put Aberdeen on the brink of success, as Schulz sends the Germans' third kick against the crossbar. Miller's penalty could make sure, but Rudwaleit leapt to save – and then again from Black' subsequent effort. Trieloff netted the decisive kick.

Alex McLeish gets in a header against Dundee United at Pittodrie in March 1985.

1984-85 APPEARANCES

	League	League Cup	Scottish Cup	European Cup
Leighton	34	1	6	2
W. Miller	34	1	6	2
McKimmie	34	1	5	2
McQueen	33(+2)	1	2(+1)	2
Simpson	33	1	6	1(+1)
Stark	30(+2)	1	5	2
McLeish	30	1	5(+1)	2
McDougall	27(+1)		2	
Black	27		6	2
Angus	21(+7)		3(+2)	2
Bell	18(+4)	1	3(+2)	1
Cooper	17(+3)		5	2
Weir	15(+1)		2	
Hewitt	11(+10)		4	1(+1)
Falconer	10(+6)	1		1(+1)
Mitchell	7(+7)		3	
Porteous	7(+6)	1	1(+1)	−(+1)
Cowan	6(+10)	1	2(+1)	
Gunn	2			
J. Miller	−(+1)			
McMaster	−(+1)			
Grant			−(+1)	
Wright			−(+1)	
23 players				

GOALS

	Total	League	League Cup	Scottish Cup	European Cup
McDougall	24	22		2	
Stark	20	15	1	4	
Black	20	17		1	2
Cowan	5	5			
Simpson	5	4		1	
Falconer	4	4			
Hewitt	4	3		1	
Angus	4	2		1	1
McKimmie	3	3			
McQueen	3	3			
W. Miller	3	3			
Weir	3	3			
Cooper	1	1			
McLeish	1	1			
Mitchell	1	1			
Porteous	1	1			
own-goals	1	1			
Total	103	89	1	10	3

The Aberdeen players celebrate after defeating Hearts 3-0 in the 1986 Scottish Cup Final at Hampden Park.

Season 1985-86

It is a measure of the standards attained at Pittodrie in the 1980s that 1985-86 should be regarded as a partial failure. Yet halfway through the season everything looked smoothly on course for a clear-up of domestic and European honours. By mid-December not only were Aberdeen occupying their accustomed position looking down on the rest of the league, but they had already claimed the season's first trophy – the Skol League Cup. It was the one competition hitherto to have had frustrated Alex Ferguson, and was won with undeniable panache against a Hibernian team who were grateful not to be overrun.

It is often the case that winning a trophy in the Autumn rather than in the Spring produces complacency, and an unconscious feeling that the job's been done already. Whatever the cause, Aberdeen's league form deteriorated – particularly away from home. They actually went five whole months without a win on opponents' soil, and even at home the goals-supply dried up alarmingly.

It was not easy to pinpoint the source of the malaise. Apart from the purchase of Jim Bett from the Belgian club Lokeren, and the departure of Doug Bell to Ibrox, the first-team squad was largely unchanged. Injuries did their best to disrupt continuity, though Aberdeen's ripening youngsters helped cover up any cracks.

Even in the face of the team's stuttering league progress they were still in the race up to mid-April, when Celtic won 1-0 at Pittodrie en route to overhauling Hearts on the last day of the season.

That all was not well with the Dons was made abundantly clear during the visits of two relatively unsung clubs in the European Cup. In the second round the Swiss champions, Servette Geneva, outshone Aberdeen yet somehow lost 1-0. In the quarter finals Gothenberg were transparently superior in every aspect of the game, their last-gasp equaliser denying Aberdeen the narrow lead they had hoped to defend in Sweden.

But how can you criticise a team which wins two cups in one year? Not content with the Skol League Cup, Aberdeen were back at Hampden in May for the Scottish Cup Final. There they succeeded in putting the final holes in Hearts' sinking season. It was Aberdeen's fourth Scottish Cup victory in five years, and the first that did not require extra time.

League:	Fourth
Skol League Cup:	Winners
Scottish Cup:	Winners
European Cup:	Quarter Final

SCOTTISH PREMIER DIVISION

No 1 Saturday, 10 August

ABERDEEN (0) 3   HIBERNIAN (0) 0
Bett (68),
McDougall 2 (79, 89)

ABERDEEN: Leighton, McKimmie, McQueen, Stark, McLeish, Miller, Black (Hewitt), Simpson, McDougall, Bett, Weir

HIBERNIAN: Rough, Sneddon, Munro, Kane, Rae, Hunter, Weir, Collins, Irvine (Durie), Cowan, McBride

P	W	D	L	F	A	Pts
1	1	0	0	3	0	2

Attendance: 15,000
Referee: K. J. Hope

The Premier League Championship flag was unfurled over Pittodrie, whereupon Hibs took it upon themselves to ruin the occasion. They looked the more capable side until debut-boy Jim Bett rifled in a superb goal.

No 2 Saturday, 17 August
DUNDEE UNITED (1) 1   ABERDEEN (1) 1
  Sturrock (41)   McKimmie (36)
DUNDEE UNITED: McAlpine, Beaumont, Malpas, Gough, Hegarty, Narey, Bannon, Beedie, Redford, Sturrock, Dodds
ABERDEEN: Gunn, McKimmie, Cooper, Stark, McLeish, Miller, Black (Hewitt), Simpson, McDougall, Bett, Weir

P	W	D	L	F	A	Pts
2	1	1	0	4	3	3

Attendance: 14,350
Referee: D. S. Downie

Manchester United's chief scout took in this game. High-quality goals at either end would have impressed him, scored by McKimmie's power and Sturrock's guile.

No 3 Saturday, 24 August
ABERDEEN (1) 1   MOTHERWELL (1) 1
  McKimmie (19)   Blair (32)
ABERDEEN: Gunn, McKimmie, McQueen (Cooper), Stark, McLeish, Miller, Hewitt, Simpson, McDougall (Black), Bett, Weir
MOTHERWELL: Gardiner, McLeod, Murray, Kennedy, Forbes, Boyd, Clark, Dornan, Harrow, McStay, Blair

P	W	D	L	F	A	Pts
3	1	2	0	5	2	4

Attendance: 14,100
Referee: B. R. McGinlay

Another spectacular goal from Stewart McKimmie crowns Aberdeen's bright opening. But Miller's mistimed tackle let in Blair and the Dons struggled thereafter.

No 4 Saturday, 31 August
DUNDEE (0) 1   ABERDEEN (0) 3
  R. Black (88)   Simpson (48),
                       Stark 2 (62, 80)
DUNDEE: Geddes, Shannon, Glennie, McCormack, Smith, Duffy, Steven (McWilliams), Brown, Black, Connor, Jack (Waddell)
ABERDEEN: Leighton, McKimmie, Mitchell, Stark, McLeish, Miller, Black, Simpson, McDougall (McIntyre), Bett, Weir (Hewitt)

P	W	D	L	F	A	Pts
4	2	2	0	8	3	6

Attendance: 7,500
Referee: W. Crombie

Dundee held their own for the first half. But then Bett's drive was deflected out to Simpson, and frustration ruined the home team's chances.

No 5 Saturday, 7 September
ABERDEEN (1) 3   HEARTS (0) 0
  Stark (32),
  Wright (75),
  Black (90)
ABERDEEN: Leighton, McKimmie, Mitchell, Stark (Wright), McLeish, Miller, Black, Simpson, McDougall (Cooper), Bett, Hewitt
HEARTS: Smith, Cowie, Whittaker, Jardine, MacDonald, Levein, Colquhoun (Mackay), Watson, McNaughton, Cherry, Black (Sandison)

Leading positions

	P	W	D	L	F	A	Pts
1 Rangers	5	4	1	0	11	3	9
2 ABERDEEN	5	3	2	0	11	3	8
3 Celtic	5	3	2	0	11	3	8
4 Dundee United	5	3	1	1	6	3	7

Attendance: 12,000
Referee: M. Delaney

18-year old substitute Paul Wright peels off his tracksuit and within minutes sends a 25-yard bullet past Smith.

No 6 Saturday, 14 September
CELTIC (1) 2   ABERDEEN (0) 1
  McClair 2 (32, 88)   McDougall (85)
CELTIC: Bonner, McGrain, Burns, Aitken, McGugan, Grant, Provan, McStay, Johnston, McLeod, McClair
ABERDEEN: Leighton, McKimmie, Mitchell, Stark (Cooper), McLeish, Miller, Black, Simpson, McDougall, Bett, Hewitt (Weir)

P	W	D	L	F	A	Pts
6	3	2	1	12	5	8

Attendance: 39,450
Referee: D. Syme

A big crowd pay their respects to Jock Stein with a minute's silence before the match. Three Aberdeen fans laid a wreath behind Pat Bonner's goal. A frightful mix-up in the Celtic defence allows Aberdeen a late equaliser they scarcely deserve but the home team sweep to the other end where McClair powers in a header from Provan's corner.

No 7 Saturday, 21 September
ABERDEEN (0) 1   ST MIRREN (0) 1
  McQueen (46 pen)   Spiers (61 pen)
ABERDEEN: Leighton, McKimmie, McQueen (McDougall), Stark, McLeish, Miller, Black, Cooper, Hewitt (Porteous), Bett, Gray
ST MIRREN: Money, Wilson, Hamilton, Rooney, Godfrey, Clarke, Fitzpatrick, Cooper (McDowell), McGarvey, Gallagher, Spiers (Mackie)

P	W	D	L	F	A	Pts
7	3	3	1	13	6	9

Attendance: 12,600
Referee: J. Duncan

Two unconvincing penalty awards, one to either side. Campbell Money got a hand to McQueen's kick; Leighton dived the wrong way for Spiers – but made up with a leaping save in the final minute.

No 8 Saturday, 28 September
RANGERS (0) 0   ABERDEEN (1) 3
                     McLeish (30),
                     Stark (38),
                     Hewitt (84)
RANGERS: Walker, Burns, Munro, McPherson, Paterson, Durrant (McMinn), McCoist, Russell, Williamson (McKinnon), Bell, Cooper
ABERDEEN: Leighton, McKimmie, Mitchell, Stark (Gray), McLeish, Miller, Black, Simpson, McDougall (Falconer), Cooper, Hewitt

P	W	D	L	F	A	Pts
8	4	3	1	16	6	11

Attendance: 37,600
Referee: G. B. Smith

Drama at Ibrox. Rangers players Hugh Burns and Craig Paterson were sent off in this appalling violent spectacle. No sooner had Burns departed than McLeish headed in the ensuing free kick. Then it was Paterson's turn to walk after body-checking Cooper. In the second half there was even a pitch invasion.

No 9 Saturday, 5 October
ABERDEEN (2) 3   CLYDEBANK (1) 1
  Black (1),   Conroy (7)
  McDougall (9),
  McKimmie (86)
ABERDEEN: Leighton, McKimmie, Mitchell, Stark (Angus), McLeish, Miller, Black (Falconer), Simpson, McDougall, Cooper, Hewitt
CLYDEBANK: Gallacher, Dickson, Given, Treanor, Auld (Smith), Maher, Hughes, Shanks, Larnach, Conroy, Moore

P W D L F A Pts   *Attendance:* 11,400
9 5 3 1 19 7 13   *Referee:* D. S. Downie

Clydebank keeper Gallacher's feeble touch on to Black in the first minute was the prelude to a burst of scoring. But as the match wore on the players went to sleep in the sun.

No 10 Saturday, 12 October
HIBERNIAN (1) 1   ABERDEEN (0) 1
  Cowan (26),   Gray (82)
HIBERNIAN: Rough, Sneddon, Munro, Brazil, Rae, Hunter, Kane, Chisholm, Cowan, Durie, McBride
ABERDEEN: Leighton, McNimmie, Mitchell (Gray), Stark, McLeish, Miller, Angus, Simpson (Wright), McDougall, Cooper, Hewitt

Leading positions
	P	W	D	L	F	A	Pts
1 ABERDEEN	10	5	4	1	20	8	14
2 Celtic	9	6	2	1	17	5	14
3 Rangers	10	6	2	2	16	8	14
4 St Mirren	10	5	1	4	17	15	11

Attendance: 12,000   *Referee:* H. F. Williamson

These two sides meet again in the League Cup Final in a fortnight, so Aberdeen are grateful for the face-saving equaliser which takes them to the top of the table for the first time this season.

No 11 Saturday, 19 October
ABERDEEN (3) 3   DUNDEE UNITED (1) 2
  Hewitt 2 (5, 24)   Sturrock (2)
  McDougall (17)   Redford (51)
ABERDEEN: Leighton, McKimmie, Mitchell, Stark, McLeish, Miller, Gray (Black), Simpson (McIntyre), McDougall, Cooper, Hewitt
DUNDEE UNITED: Thomson, McGinnis, Malpas, Gough, Hegarty, Narey, Bannon, Milne, Kirkwood (Holt), Sturrock, Redford (Clark)

P W D L F A Pts   *Attendance:* 15,150
11 6 4 1 23 10 16   *Referee:* G. B. Smith

If Sturrock's 2nd-minute goal, wheeling onto the ball from fifteen yards was a cracker, then Hewitt's answer –

a magnificent volley – was a candidate for 'goal of the season'. Alex Ferguson was impressed, both as the manager of Aberdeen and of Scotland.

No 12 Wednesday, 30 October
HEARTS (1) 1   ABERDEEN (0) 0
  Levein (15)
HEARTS: Smith, Kidd, Whittaker, A. Jardine, Berry, Levein, Colquhoun, I. Jardine (Black), Clark, Robertson, Mackay
ABERDEEN: Leighton, McKimmie, Angus (Bett), Gray, McLeish, Miller, Weir, Simpson, McDougall (Wright), Cooper, Hewitt

P W D L F A Pts   *Attendance:* 12,450
12 6 4 2 23 11 16   *Referee:* L. Thow

This was Hearts' first league victory over Aberdeen at Tynecastle for seven years as the new League Cup holders are brought down to earth. Levein outjumped Leighton to meet Colquhoun's corner kick. At the death Smith saved splendidly from Simpson.

No 13 Saturday, 2 November
ABERDEEN (1) 4   CELTIC (1) 1
  McDougall 4 (27, 48, 55,   Provan (43)
  64)
ABERDEEN: Leighton, McKimmie, Mitchell, Stark (Bett), McLeish, Miller, Black, Simpson, McDougall, Cooper, Hewitt (Wright)
CELTIC: Bonner, W. McStay, McGrain, Aitken, McAdam (McGugan), Grant, Provan, P. McStay, McClair, Burns, McInally (Chalmers)

P W D L F A Pts   *Attendance:* 22,000
13 7 4 2 27 12 18   *Referee:* B. R. McGinlay

Of late Celtic have been shipping goals like a sieve. Frank McDougall enters the record books as the first Aberdeen player in memory to score four goals against Celtic. Eight players were booked – six in green and white hoops.

No 14 Saturday, 9 November
ABERDEEN (1) 4   DUNDEE (1) 1
  McLeish (21),   Stephen (6)
  McDougall (67),
  Stark 2 (83, 87)
ABERDEEN: Leighton, McKimmie, Mitchell, Stark, McLeish, Miller, Gray, Bett, McDougall, Angus (Falconer), Weir
DUNDEE: Geddes, Shannon, Glennie, McCormack, Smith, Duffy, McWilliams, Brown (Hendry), Stephen, Connor, McKinlay

Leading positions
	P	W	D	L	F	A	Pts
1 ABERDEEN	14	8	4	2	31	13	20
2 Rangers	14	7	3	4	21	12	17
3 Celtic	13	7	2	4	20	16	16
4 Dundee United	13	5	4	4	18	13	14
5 Hearts	14	5	4	5	16	19	14

Attendance: 12,000   *Referee:* I. R. Cathcart

A pre-match flu bug cut down Cooper, Simpson and Hewitt. Then, after taking the lead, Dundee were cut down by Aberdeen. Three headers and a McDougall half-volley was the final tally.

No 15 Saturday, 16 November
MOTHERWELL (1) 1   ABERDEEN (0) 1
  Wright (21 pen)   McDougall (57 pen)
MOTHERWELL: Gardiner, Wishart, Murray, Dornan, Forbes, McCart, Gahagan, MacLeod, Harrow (Reilly), Wright, Blair
ABERDEEN: Leighton, McKimmie, Mitchell (Angus), Stark, McLeish, Miller, Gray (Hewitt), Simpson, McDougall, Bett, Weir

P	W	D	L	F	A	Pts	
15	8	5	2	32	14	21	

Attendance: 4,950
Referee: D. S. Downie

A game disfigured by penalties. McLeish punched away the ball for the first. Then Hewitt fell over and was astonished to find he'd won a penalty. Finally McLeish almost severed Reilly's legs, but the referee incredibly turned a blind eye.

No 16 Saturday, 23 November
ST MIRREN (1) 1   ABERDEEN (0) 0
  Rooney (45)
ST MIRREN: Money, Wilson, Winnie, Rooney, Godfrey, Clarke, Fitzpatrick, Cooper, McGarvey, Gallagher, Spiers
ABERDEEN: Leighton, McKimmie, Mitchell (McQueen), Stark, McLeish, Miller, Hewitt (Angus), Simpson, McDougall, Cooper, Weir

P	W	D	L	F	A	Pts	
16	8	5	3	32	15	21	

Attendance: 3,900
Referee: D. Syme

Just before half-time Neale Cooper left the field with a facial injury. In his absence Jim Rooney leapt to head Spiers' cross past Leighton.

No 17 Tuesday, 10 December
CLYDEBANK (1) 2   ABERDEEN (0) 1
  Larnach (8),   Black (60)
  Dickson (53)
CLYDEBANK: Gallagher, Dickson, Given, Maher, Auld, Treanor, Shanks, Hughes (Moore), Larnach (Ronald), Conroy, McCabe
ABERDEEN: Leighton, McKimmie, Mitchell (Weir), Stark, McLeish, Angus, Black, Simpson, J. Miller, Cooper, Falconer (McDougall)

P	W	D	L	F	A	Pts	
17	8	5	4	33	17	21	

Attendance: 2,100

The crowd at Kilbowie Park can't believe this. Larnach heads in after Hughes' thunderous free kick crashed off the bar. Dickson stabbed in McCabe's drilled cross. The Bankies then resist Aberdeen's furious climax.

No 18 Saturday, 14 December
ABERDEEN (1) 4   HIBERNIAN (0) 0
  Angus (18),
  Weir (78),
  J. Miller (87),
  McLeish (89)
ABERDEEN: Gunn, McKimmie, Mitchell, Stark (Weir), McLeish, Cooper, Black, Simpson, McDougall, Angus, J. Miller
HIBERNIAN: Rough, Sneddon, Milne, Rae, Fulton, Hunter, Kane, Chisholm, Cowan, Durie, Callachan (May)

Leading positions

	P	W	D	L	F	A	Pts
1 ABERDEEN	18	9	5	4	37	17	23
2 Hearts	19	8	6	5	28	22	22
3 Rangers	18	8	6	6	25	19	20
4 Celtic	16	8	4	4	24	18	20
5 Dundee United	16	7	4	4	24	15	19

Attendance: 11,500
Referee: W. P. Knowles

Hibs' Durie was sent packing in the second half after Cooper took a ride on his knee. The whole Hibs team was then sent packing as Aberdeen opened the vaults. Jim Leighton was surprisingly 'rested'.

No 19 Saturday, 21 December
DUNDEE UNITED (2) 2   ABERDEEN (1) 1
  Bannon (9 pen),   Stark (28)
  Sturrock (40)
DUNDEE UNITED: Thomson, Malpas, Holt, Gough, Hegarty, Narey, Bannon, Gallacher, Sturrock, Redford, Dodds
ABERDEEN: Leighton, McKimmie, Mitchell, Stark, McLeish, W. Miller, Black, Angus, McDougall (Weir), Cooper (McQueen), J. Miller

P	W	D	L	F	A	Pts	
19	9	5	5	38	19	23	

Attendance: 10,100.
Referee: A. Ferguson

Leighton restored to the team, whips Hegarty's legs from under him. Penalty. Stark crashes an equaliser from outside the box. Then Dodds sent Sturrock away for the winner. In the second half Alex Ferguson was 'sent off' from the dug-out to the jeers of the home fans. This result knocks Aberdeen off the top spot.

No 20 Wednesday, 1 January
DUNDEE (0) 0   ABERDEEN (0) 0
DUNDEE: Geddes, Glennie, McKinlay, Kidd (Rafferty), Smith, Duffy, Shannon, Brown, Harvey (Hendry), Connor, Stephen
ABERDEEN: Leighton, McKimmie, McQueen, Stark, McLeish, W. Miller, Black, Grey (Angus), Falconer (Wright), Cooper, J. Miller

P	W	D	L	F	A	Pts	
20	9	6	5	38	19	24	

Attendance: 9,100
Referee: J. R. S. Renton

Aberdeen have won their last 12 Premier League games at Dens Park. So it's unlucky 13th. How Aberdeen's defence survived a tortuous first half is a question Archie Knox cannot answer.

No 21 Saturday, 4 January
ABERDEEN (2) 3   ST MIRREN (0) 1
Black 2 (2, 19),   Gallagher (55)
Weir (58)

ABERDEEN: Leighton, Cooper, McQueen, Stark, McLeish, W. Miller, Black, Gray (Falconer), J. Miller, Bett, Weir
ST MIRREN: Money, Wilson, Abercrombie, Rooney, Godfrey, Cooper, Fitzpatrick, Mackie, McGarvey, Gallagher (Spiers), Winnie

P W D L F A Pts   *Attendance:* 11,500
21 10 6 5 41 20 26   *Referee:* T. Muirhead

Eric Black's goal-poaching restores Aberdeen's winning ways. The first goal came after Joe Miller's effort had been blocked; the second when Black snapped up Wilson's stupid back-pass.

No 22 Saturday, 11 January
CELTIC (1) 1   ABERDEEN (1) 1
Grant (19)   J. Miller (14)

CELTIC: Latchford, W. McStay, McGrain, Aitken, O'Leary, Grant, McClair, P. McStay, McGhee, McLeod (Archdeacon), Johnston
ABERDEEN: Leighton, McKimmie, McQueen, Cooper, McLeish, W. Miller, Black, Simpson, J. Miller (McDougall), Bett, Weir (Stark)

P W D L F A Pts   *Attendance:* 31,300
22 10 7 5 42 21 27   *Referee:* J. Duncan

Hailstones the size of marbles littered the pitch beforehand. They'd melted by the time Joe Miller squeezed the ball past Latchford – at the second attempt. Five minutes later Peter Grant began and finished the move which brought Celtic level. It's now three years since Aberdeen won at Parkhead.

No 23 Saturday, 18 January
ABERDEEN (0) 0   HEARTS (0) 1
    Colquhoun (83)

ABERDEEN: Leighton, McKimmie, McQueen (Mitchell), Stark, McLeish, W. Miller, Black, Simpson, McDougall (J. Miller), Bett, Weir
HEARTS: Smith, Kidd, Black, A. Jardine, Berry, Levein, Colquhoun, I. Jardine, Clark, Mackay, Robertson (McAdam)

Leading positions

	P	W	D	L	F	A	Pts
1 Hearts	25	13	7	5	39	25	33
2 Dundee United	22	11	7	4	36	19	29
3 Celtic	23	11	6	6	36	28	28
4 ABERDEEN	23	10	7	6	42	22	27

Attendance: 21,500   *Referee:* J. McCluskey

Hearts' unbeaten run is now 17 games, as they inflict Aberdeen's first home defeat in 13 months. Twice at the close of the first half Hearts were only inches from a goal. Leighton touched Ian Jardine's volley against a post, and Sandy Clark made the miss of the century. Aberdeen appeared to have weathered the storm when Colquhoun raced through to beat Leighton.

No 24 Saturday, 1 February
RANGERS (0) 1   ABERDEEN (1) 1
Burns (52)   J. Miller (3)

RANGERS: Walker, Burns, Dawson, Johnstone, Beattie, Bell, McMinn, McCoist, Williamson, McPherson, Cooper
ABERDEEN: Leighton, McKimmie, McQueen, Stark (Mitchell), McLeish, W. Miller, Black, Simpson, J. Miller, Bett, Weir

P W D L F A Pts   *Attendance:* 29,500
24 10 8 6 43 23 28   *Referee:* R. B. Valentine

With this result Aberdeen complete an unwanted sequence of visiting all the Premier League grounds without winning any. That sequence might have been broken but for McQueen's terrible back-pass, intercepted by Burns.

No 25 Saturday, 8 February
ABERDEEN (2) 4   CLYDEBANK (0) 1
Bett (15 pen),   Conroy (88)
Black 3 (29, 34, 53)

ABERDEEN: Leighton, McKimmie, Angus, Stark (Porteous), McLeish, W. Miller, Black, Simpson (Mitchell), McDougall, Bett, J. Miller
CLYDEBANK: Gallacher, Dickson, Given, Fallon, Auld, McGhie, Moore, Davies, Gibson, Lloyd, McCabe (Conroy)

P W D L F A Pts   *Attendance:* 10,940
25 11 8 6 47 24 30   *Referee:* K. J. Hope

This was Eric Black's match, as he ploughed through the snow. Two textbook headers, with a cracking shot thrown in for good measure.

No 26 Wednesday, 19 February
ABERDEEN (0) 1   RANGERS (0) 0
Angus (67)

ABERDEEN: Leighton, McKimmie, McQueen (Angus), Cooper, McLeish, W. Miller, Black, Simpson, McDougall (Wright), Bett, J. Miller
RANGERS: Walker, Burns, Dawson, Johnstone (Cooper), Paterson, Bell, McMinn, McCoist, Williamson, McPherson, Durrant (Fraser)

Leading positions

	P	W	D	L	F	A	Pts
1 Hearts	27	14	8	5	43	27	36
2 ABERDEEN	26	12	8	6	48	24	32
3 Dundee United	24	12	8	4	41	20	32
4 Celtic	25	12	7	6	40	30	31

Attendance: 18,700   *Referee:* J. Duncan

Super match, played on a treacherous white pitch, highlighted by substitute Ian Angus' lethal strike of the ball which produced the one and only goal. Unfortunately there were seven bookings and Jim Bett and ex-Don Dougie Bell were sent off at the end of the first half after clashing in midfield.

No 27 Saturday, 22 February
HIBERNIAN (0) 0   ABERDEEN (1) 1
    Wright (13)

HIBERNIAN: Rough, Brazil, Munro, Rae, Fulton, Hunter, Kane, May, Cowan, Durie, Tortolano
ABERDEEN: Leighton, McKimmie, Angus, Stark (Mitchell), McLeish, W. Miller, Black, Simpson, Wright, Cooper, J. Miller (Hewitt)

P	W	D	L	F	A	Pts	
27	13	8	6	49	24	34	

Attendance: 9,000
Referee: J. R. S. Renton

This was Aberdeen's first away win in the league for five months. Paul Wright took advantage of Rae's stumble. But Hibs had their moments in the second half.

No 28 Saturday, 15 March
ST MIRREN (1) 1   ABERDEEN (1) 1
Clarke (20)   W. Miller (33)

ST MIRREN: Money, Wilson (Rooney), Abercrombie, Cooper, Godfrey, Clarke, Hamilton, Winnie, McGarvey, Gallagher, Spiers
ABERDEEN: Leighton, McKimmie, McQueen (Stark), Cooper, McLeish, W. Miller, J. Miller (Porteous), Angus, Wright, Bett, Hewitt

P	W	D	L	F	A	Pts
28	13	9	6	50	25	35

Attendance: 4,450
Referee: D. T. McVicar

After Willie Miller's swerving equaliser, St Mirren hit the woodwork three times in a matter of seconds. Reprieved, Aberdeen missed chance after chance to snatch both points.

No 29 Saturday, 22 March
ABERDEEN (0) 0   DUNDEE (0) 0

ABERDEEN: Leighton, McKimmie, Angus, Cooper, McLeish, W. Miller, J. Miller, Stark, Wright (Mitchell), Bett, Hewitt (Falconer)
DUNDEE: Geddes, Shannon, McKinlay, Rafferty, Smith (McCormack), Duffy, Mennie, Brown, Harvey, Connor, Stephen

P	W	D	L	F	A	Pts
29	13	10	6	50	25	36

Attendance: 13,000
Referee: T. Muirhead

Having suffered their cruel cup elimination at Pittodrie three days earlier, Dundee are in no mood to assist Aberdeen's title surge.

No 30 Saturday, 29 March
MOTHERWELL (0) 0   ABERDEEN (1) 1
                        Hewitt (7)

MOTHERWELL: Gardiner, Wishart, Murray, Doyle (Dornan), Forbes, Boyd, Baptie, MacLeod, Reilly, Wright, Walker
ABERDEEN: Gunn, McKimmie, McQueen, Stark, Cooper, W. Miller, J. Miller (Gray), Angus, Hewitt, Bett, McMaster

P	W	D	L	F	A	Pts
30	14	10	6	51	25	38

Attendance: 4,300
Referee: A. Huett

Gothenburg have ended Aberdeen's European dreams, and Motherwell do their best to make Aberdeen forget about the league championship. In the last minute Dornan's header flew off Aberdeen's post.

No 31 Wednesday, 9 April
ABERDEEN (2) 3   MOTHERWELL (1) 2
Bett (2),   Reilly (38),
McDougall (35),   Kennedy (76)
Weir (81)

ABERDEEN: Gunn, McKimmie, McQueen, McMaster (McIntyre), McLeish, W. Miller, Black, Gray, McDougall (J. Miller), Bett, Weir
MOTHERWELL: Gardiner, Wishart, Murray, MacLeod (Baptie), Forbes, Boyd, Dornan (Gahagan), Kennedy, Reilly, Wright, Walker

Leading positions

	P	W	D	L	F	A	Pts
1 Hearts	32	18	9	5	54	30	45
2 Dundee United	31	16	10	5	54	24	42
3 ABERDEEN	31	15	10	6	54	27	40
4 Celtic	31	15	10	6	55	38	40

Attendance: 10,300
Referee: A. Ferguson

What a start for Jim Bett who almost burst the ball, never mind the net, from McMaster's pass. McDougall's miscued header made it 2-0 before Motherwell began their fightback. Aberdeen were rescued by Weir latching onto Black's back-header.

No 32 Saturday, 12 April
ABERDEEN (0) 0   CELTIC (0) 1
                        Johnston (49)

ABERDEEN: Gunn, McKimmie, McQueen (McMaster), Stark, McLeish, W. Miller, Black, Mitchell, J. Miller, Bett, Hewitt
CELTIC: Bonner, McGrain, Whyte, Aitken, O'Leary (Archdeacon), Grant, McClair, McStay, Johnston, McLeod, Burns

P	W	D	L	F	A	Pts
32	15	10	7	54	28	40

Attendance: 22,000
Referee: W. Crombie

A match that both sides desperately needed to win – but neither deserved to. It was an altogether scrappy affair, turned Celtic's way by a fine individual goal by Maurice Johnston, who wriggled past several defenders before producing a deadly finish.

No 33 Wednesday, 16 April
ABERDEEN (0) 0   DUNDEE UNITED (1) 1
                        Gough (26)

ABERDEEN: Gunn, McKimmie, Mitchell, Robertson, McLeish, W. Miller, Black (McMaster), Angus (Porteous), J. Miller, Bett, Weir
DUNDEE UNITED: Thomson, Malpas, Holt, Gough, Hegarty, Narey, Clark (Kirkwood), Gallacher (Bannon), Beedie, Sturrock, Redford

P	W	D	L	F	A	Pts
33	15	10	8	54	29	40

Attendance: 8,500
Referee: D. F. T. Syme

Filthy weather, and a filthy result for Aberdeen, as they relinquish their last hold on the champions cup. Gough pulled down Sturrock's cross to fire past Gunn.

No 34 Sunday, 20 April
HEARTS (0) 1   ABERDEEN (0) 1
Colquhoun (87)   Weir (72 pen)

HEARTS: Smith, Cowie, Whittaker, A. Jardine, Berry, Levein, Colquhoun, K. Black, Clark, Mackay (I. Jardine), Robertson

ABERDEEN: Gunn, McKimmie, McQueen, McMaster, McLeish, W. Miller, Hewitt (Black), Mitchell (Robertson), J. Miller, Bett, Weir

P	W	D	L	F	A	Pts
34	15	11	8	55	30	41

Attendance: 19,600

Referee: R. B. Valentine

Scotland's first-ever live league match on TV. On a Sunday too. With Aberdeen having dropped out of the title chase, the occasion loses some of its intended sparkle. The Dons looked decidedly superior, but required a mysterious penalty to take the lead and threaten Hearts' seven-month unbeaten run. But McQueen makes a hash of a clearance and Colquhoun rams the ball past Gunn.

No 35 Saturday, 26 April

ABERDEEN (0) 1   RANGERS (0) 1
  Hewitt (57)   McMinn (50)

ABERDEEN: Gunn, Mitchell (Porteous), McIntyre (Wright), McMaster, McLeish, W. Miller, Gray, Robertson, J. Miller, Hewitt, Weir

RANGERS: McCloy, Burns, Munro, McKinnon, McPherson, Dawson, D. Ferguson, Durrant, McCoist, McMinn, Cooper

P	W	D	L	F	A	Pts
35	15	12	8	56	31	42

Referee: J. McCluskey

A strange-looking Aberdeen side partook of a match remembered for Ted McMinn's bewildering goal. The lanky Ranger meandered from his own half past several Dons defenders before applying the perfect finish. Aberdeen looked to be heading for a third consecutive home defeat until Hewitt poked in the equaliser from 15 yards.

No 36 Saturday, 3 May

CLYDEBANK (0) 0   ABERDEEN (5) 6
                         Stark (9),
                         McMaster (10),
                         Weir (16),
                         Hewitt (29),
                         McDougall 2 (38, 66)

CLYDEBANK: Gallacher, Dickson, Given, Fallon, Auld, McGhie, Moore, Hughes, Bain (Gibson), Conroy, McCabe

ABERDEEN: Gunn, McKimmie, McQueen, Stark, Irvine, McIntye, Gray (Porteous), Hewitt, McDougall, McMaster (Robertson), Weir

Attendance: 2,380

A few more performances like this earlier in the season, and the Dons would still be champions. Pick of the bunch was Peter Weir's effort, ghosting past three defenders before producing a lethal finish. Elsewhere Hearts lose the title during the last 7 minutes of the season.

Aberdeen's complete home and away record:

HOME						AWAY					
P	W	D	L	F	A		W	D	L	F	A	Pts
36	11	4	3	38	15		5	8	5	24	16	44

Premier Division

	P	W	D	L	F	A	Pts
1 Celtic	36	20	10	6	67	38	50
2 Hearts	36	20	10	6	59	33	50
3 Dundee United	36	18	11	7	59	31	47
4 ABERDEEN	36	16	12	8	62	31	44
5 Rangers	36	13	9	14	53	45	35
6 Dundee	36	14	7	15	45	51	35
7 St Mirren	36	13	5	18	42	63	31
8 Hibernian	36	11	6	19	49	63	28
9 Motherwell	36	7	6	23	33	66	20
10 Clydebank	36	6	8	22	29	77	20

LEAGUE CUP

2nd Round Wednesday, 21 August

ABERDEEN (2) 5   AYR UNITED (0) 0
  Stark 2 (3, 55),
  McQueen (39 pen),
  McDougall 2 (84, 86)

ABERDEEN: Gunn, McKimmie, (Cooper), McQueen, Stark, McLeish, Miller, Hewitt, Simpson (Black), McDougall, Bett, Weir

AYR: Purdie, McCann, Buchanan, Anderson, McAllister, Collins, March, McNiven, McDonald, Irons, Murphy

Attendance: 12,400   *Referee:* R. B. Valentine

Aberdeen showed a welcome ruthlessness, fighting for the ball even when the victory was in their pocket.

3rd Round Wednesday, 28 August

ST JOHNSTONE (0) 0   ABERDEEN (1) 2
                            Hewitt (27),
                            McDougall (86)

ST JOHNSTONE: Balavage, Miller, McGonigie, Barron, Winter, Morton, Gibson, McGurn, Ward (Johnstone), Reid, Williamson (McDaid)

ABERDEEN: Gunn, McKimmie, McQueen (Stark), Gray, McLeish, Miller, Hewitt, Simpson, McDougall, Bett, Weir

Attendance: 5,000   *Referee:* A. Ferguson

Frank McDougall is developing a taste for late goals, once the opposition is on its way to the mortuary.

Quarter Final Wednesday, 4 September

ABERDEEN (1) 1   HEARTS (0) 0
  Black (24)

ABERDEEN: Leighton, McKimmie, Mitchell, Stark, McLeish, Miller, Black, Simpson, McDougall, Bett, Weir

HEARTS: Smith, Kidd, Whittaker, Jardine, MacDonald, Levein, Watson, Mackay (Cherry), Clark, Robertson (Colquhoun), Black

Attendance: 13,050

Jock Stein popped in for a check on his Pittodrie internationals. He watched as Henry Smith and Roddy MacDonald presented a goal to Eric Black. Hearts never looked like equalising.

Semi Final 1st Leg, Wednesday, 25 September
DUNDEE UNITED (0) 0   ABERDEEN (0) 1
                                    Black (63)
DUNDEE UNITED: McAlpine, Malpas, Holt, Gough, Hegarty, Narey, Bannon, Beaumont (Redford), Beedie (Kirkwood), Sturrock, Dodds
ABERDEEN: Leighton, McKimmie, Mitchell, Stark, McLeish, Miller, Black, Simpson (Gray), McDougall (Falconer), Cooper, Hewitt
Attendance: 12,850   *Referee:* M. Delaney
Too many fouls and free kicks to allow free-flowing football. Shortly after Eric Black headed in Hewitt's cross, Richard Gough was ordered off for fouling Hewitt.

Semi Final 2nd Leg Wednesday, 9 October
ABERDEEN (0) 1   DUNDEE UNITED (0) 0
  McDougall (68)
ABERDEEN: Leighton, McKimmie, Mitchell, Stark (Gray), McLeish, Miller, Angus, Simpson, McDougall, Cooper, Hewitt
DUNDEE UNITED: McAlpine (Kirkwood), McGinnis (Redford), Holt, Gough, Hegarty, Narey, Bannon, Milne, Malpas, Sturrock, Dodds
Attendance: 20,000   *Referee:* R. B. Valentine
Three times Dundee United have knocked Aberdeen out of the League Cup in recent years. This was a stirring cup-tie. Chances fell at both ends – most of them to Aberdeen – before Hewitt's low cross was met by Frank McDougall. United keeper Hamish McAlpine had earlier been injured and after the goal he had to leave the field.

SKOL LEAGUE CUP FINAL (Hampden) Sunday, 27 October
HIBERNIAN (0) 0   ABERDEEN (2) 3
                                    Black 2 (9, 62),
                                    Stark (12)
HIBERNIAN: Rough, Sneddon, Munro, Brazil (Harris), Fulton, Hunter, Kane, Chisholm, Cowan, Durie, McBride (Collins)
ABERDEEN: Leighton, McKimmie, Mitchell, Stark, McLeish, Miller, Black (Gray), Simpson, McDougall, Cooper, Hewitt
Attendance: 40,050   *Referee:* R. B. Valentine
Alex Ferguson's side have never won the League Cup under his management. This match became known as the 12-minute final, for that was all it took for Hibs' challenge to be thrown to the wind. Man-of-the-match John Hewitt burrowed into the Hibs defence before landing his cross on Eric Black's head. Three minutes later Hewitt plonks the ball towards Billy Stark, and it's all over. Aberdeen have not conceded a goal in the whole competition, extending over six matches.

SCOTTISH CUP

3rd Round Wednesday, 5 February
ABERDEEN (1) 4   MONTROSE (0) 1
  Stark (27),   Brown (56 pen)
  Miller (47),
  McDougall (74),
  McLeish (81)
ABERDEEN: Leighton, McKimmie, McQueen, Stark, McLeish, W. Miller, Black, Simpson, McDougall, Bett, Weir (Porteous)
MONTROSE: Charles, Barr, McLelland, Brown, Sheran, Forbes, Allan, Bennett, Somner, Wright (Millar), McManus (Duffy)
Attendance: 8,788   *Referee:* R. B. Valentine
A blizzard raged throughout. The Montrose team craftily played in all white so they were totally invisible to their opponents – especially McQueen, who obviously didn't see Barr as he brought him down for a penalty.

4th Round Saturday, 15 February
ARBROATH (0) 0   ABERDEEN (0) 1
                                    J. Miller (47)
ARBROATH: Jackson, Lynch, Hill, Curran, Taylor, Jack, Fotheringham, Mackie, Torrance, McWalker, Brannigan
ABERDEEN: Leighton, Cooper, McQueen, Bett, McLeish, W. Miller, Black, Simpson, McDougall, Angus, J. Miller
Attendance: 6,000   *Referee:* W. Crombie
On a bitterly cold and blustery day Aberdeen's only moment to cheer was Joe Miller's composure in controlling Cooper's cross before beating Jackson. The Second Division side never gave up.

Quarter Final Saturday, 8 March
DUNDEE (1) 2   ABERDEEN (1) 2
  Harvey (26),   Hewitt 2 (23, 74)
  Brown (67)
DUNDEE: Geddes, Forsyth, McKinlay, Shannon, Smith, Duffy, Hendry (Rafferty), Brown, Harvey, Connor, Mennie
ABERDEEN: Leighton, McKimmie, Angus, Cooper, McLeish, W. Miller, Black, Simpson (Stark), Hewitt, Bett, Weir (Wright)
Attendance: 13,000   *Referee:* B. R. McGinlay
A cup-tie to warm the blood. End to end stuff. Nothing between the teams. But Aberdeen could be grateful to Dundee keeper Bobby Geddes for the dreadful blunder – letting Simpson poach the ball off his toes – which led to Hewitt's second headed goal.

Quarter Final Replay Wednesday, 12 March
ABERDEEN (1) 1 2   DUNDEE (1) 1 1
  Black (37),   *(After Extra Time)*
  Weir (101)   Stephen (19)

Frank McDougall in action against Servette of Switzerland in a European Cup match played at Pittodrie on 6th November, 1985, before 19,000 spectators.

ABERDEEN: Leighton, Cooper, McKimmie, Stark (Angus), McLeish, W. Miller, Black (Wright), Simpson, Hewitt, Bett, Weir

DUNDEE: Geddes, Forsyth (Glennie), McKinlay, Shannon, Smith, Duffy, Stephen (Hendry), Brown, Harvey, Connor, Mennie

Attendance: 20,400   *Referee:* B. R. McGinlay

Poor Dundee. They hardly deserved to lose. They grabbed the game by the scruff of the neck in the second half, but couldn't force the winner. They could only stand and admire the genius of Peter Weir who floated the ball over Geddes' head and in off the far post.

Semi Final (Dens Park) Saturday, 5 April
HIBERNIAN (0) 0   ABERDEEN (2) 3
                              Stark (20),
                              Black (35),
                              J. Miller (81)

HIBERNIAN: Rough, Sneddon, Munro, May, Fulton, Rae, Tortolano (McBride), Chisholm, Cowan, Durie (Harris), Collins.

ABERDEEN: Gunn, McKimmie, Angus, Stark, (McMaster), McLeish, W. Miller, Black, Cooper (J. Miller), McDougall, Bett, Hewitt

Attendance: 19,165   *Referee:* K. Hope

This is Aberdeen's seventh Scottish Cup semi-final in eight seasons under Fergie. Hibs showed the early sparkle. Gunn pushed Collins' deflected shot against the bar. But two crosses produced two headed goals by Stark and Black – the same pair who had destroyed Hibs in the League Cup Final. Hewitt also centred for Joe Miller's headed goal.

Scottish Cup Final (Hampden) Saturday, 10 May
HEARTS (0) 0   ABERDEEN (1) 3
                          Hewitt 2 (5, 48),
                          Stark (75)

HEARTS: Smith, Kidd, Whittaker, Jardine, Berry, Levein, Colquhoun, Black, Clark, Mackay, Robertson

ABERDEEN: Leighton, McKimmie, McQueen, McMaster (Stark), McLeish, W. Miller, Hewitt (J. Miller), Cooper, McDougall, Bett, Weir

Attendance: 62,841   *Referee:* H. Alexander

One of the best Scottish Cup Finals of recent years. Eric Black is omitted after it is learned he is to sign for French club Metz. Hearts are out to make amends for being pipped by Celtic in the league, but they are rocked by John Hewitt's break away goal and clinical finish. Hearts' Robertson lobs inches over Aberdeen's bar. The writing was on the wall for the Jam Tarts when McDougall dummied Weir's cross, enabling Hewitt to flash in his second goal. Berry dented Leighton's crossbar. In a punishing climax Billy Stark headed a third, and Hearts captain Walker Kidd was sent off for throwing the ball in Aberdeen players' faces.

EUROPEAN CUP

1st Round, 1st Leg Wednesday, 18 September
AKRANES (Iceland) (1) 1   ABERDEEN (0) 3
   Ingolfsson (36 pen)   Black (56),
                                Hewitt (62),
                                Stark (64)

AKRANES: Kirstinsson, G. Pordarson, Gudmundsson, Larusson, Askelsson, Johannesson, Hakonarson, Ingolfsson, K. Pordarson, O. Pordarson, Sveinsson

ABERDEEN: Leighton, McKimmie, McQueen, Stark (Mitchell), McLeish, W. Miller, Black (Wright), Cooper, Hewitt, Bett, Gray

Attendance: 7,000   *Referee:* T. Ass (Norway)

Aberdeen would be happy with a repeat of the 2-1 victory achieved in the same stadium two years ago in the Cup-Winners Cup. In the event they go one better. But problems loomed when Akranes were awarded a ridiculously soft penalty. Before Black equalised he had hit a post, while Stark twice hit the bar.

1st Round, 2nd Leg Wednesday, 2 October
ABERDEEN (1) 4   AKRANES (1) 1
   Simpson (5),   Johanesson (32)
   Hewitt (63)
   Gray (65),
   Falconer (67)

ABERDEEN: Leighton, McKimmie, Mitchell (Angus), Gray, McLeish, W. Miller, Black, Simpson, Wright (Falconer), Cooper, Hewitt

AKRANES: Kirstinsson, G. Pordarson, Gudmundsson, Larusson, Askelsson, Johannesson (Bardason), Hakonarson, Ingolfsson, K. Pordarson, O. Pordarson, Sveinsson (Rafnsson)

Aberdeen won 7-2 on aggregate

Attendance: 14,700   *Referee:* J. Kinsella (Eire)

Three goals in a four-minute spell gave the fans something to shout about. Until then Akranes were heading for an honourable draw.

2nd Round, 1st Leg Wednesday, 23 October
SERVETTE (Switzerland)   ABERDEEN (0) 0
   (0) 0

SERVETTE: De Choudens, Schnyder, Bianchi, Hasler, Renquin, Decastel (Opoku), Geiger, Ley Ravello, Magnusson, Jaccord (Christiansen), Besnard

ABERDEEN: Leighton, McKimmie, Mitchell, Stark (Angus), McLeish, W. Miller, Weir (Gray), Simpson, McDougall, Cooper, Hewitt

Attendance: 8,000   *Referee:* M. Petrovic
                                      (Yugoslavia)

Aberdeen went about their task in Geneva quietly and unspectacularly and managed to bore the small crowd to death. The Dons might even have won when McLeish headed a Mitchell free kick against the bar.

2nd Round, 2nd Leg Wednesday, 6 November
ABERDEEN (1) 1   SERVETTE (0) 0
   McDougall (23)

Rising star Steve Gray shows his skills in a match against Hibs played at Pittodrie in August, 1986.

ABERDEEN: Leighton, McKimmie, Weir, Stark (Mitchell), McLeish, W. Miller, Bett, Simpson, McDougall, Cooper, Hewitt (Gray)

SERVETTE: De Choudens, Schnyder, Bianchi, Hasler, Renquin, Decastel, Geiger, Ley Ravello, Magnusson, Castella, Kok

Aberdeen won 1-0 on aggregate

Attendance: 19,000   *Referee:* A. L. Castillo
                                        (Spain)

Lucky, lucky Aberdeen. Once Frank McDougall had broken the deadlock by diving to meet Weir's centre, Aberdeen were forced to stand aside as the Swiss turned on their skills. Alex Ferguson described their second-half performance as 'the finest I have seen from a team visiting Pittodrie for a European tie'. Twice Leighton's woodwork was bruised.

Quarter Final 1st Leg Wednesday, 5 March

ABERDEEN (1) 2   **I. F. K. GOTHENBURG**
  W. Miller (16),   **(Sweden) 1 2**
  Hewitt (79)   Tord Holmgren (42),
                               Ekstrom (89)

ABERDEEN: Gunn, Cooper, Angus, Stark, McLeish, W. Miller, Black, Simpson (McKimmie), J. Miller (Hewitt), Bett, Weir

GOTHENBURG: Wernersson, Svensson (Kullberg), Hysen, Larsson, Fredriksson, R. Nilsson, Pettersson (Carlsson), Tord Holmgren, Tommy Holmgren, Ekstrom, T. Nilsson

Attendance: 22,000   *Referee:* D. Pauly
                                        (W Germany)

Gothenburg are Sweden's outstanding club side. They won the UEFA Cup in 1982. Emerging from their mid-winter hibernation they are not regarded as a particular dangers to Aberdeen. After Pittodrie had observed a one-minute silence for the assassinated Swedish Prime Minister, Olaf Palme, Willie Miller marked his 50th European appearance with a raging left-footed shot. Unfortunately, Gothenburg dictated the rest of the match, releasing their abundant skills. Bryan Gunn kept Aberdeen alive till the last minute when Johnny Ekstrom broke free to score with ease.

Quarter Final 2nd Leg Wednesday, 19 March

I. F. K. GOTHENBURG   ABERDEEN (0) 0
  (0) 0

GOTHENBURG: Wernersson, Svensson (Kullberg), Hysen, Larsson, Fredriksson, R. Nilsson, Petterson, Tord Holmgren, Tommy Holmgren (Johansson), Ekstrom, T. Nilsson

ABERDEEN: Leighton, McKimmie, Mitchell (Stark), Cooper, McLeish, W. Miller, Black (McDougall), Angus, Hewitt, Bett, Weir

Aggregate score 2-2. Gothenburg won on away-goals rule

Attendance: 44,400   *Referee:* Woehrer
                                        (Austria)

Gothenburg were quite happy to rest on the goals they scored at Pittodrie. Neither side had a goal-scoring chance worthy of the name. Not only do Aberdeen go out of the European Cup despite being unbeaten, but the gorgeous memories of the Ullevi Stadium, Gothenburg – site of their greatest triumph – are now dimmed with sadness.

1985-86

APPEARANCES	League	League Cup	Scottish Cup	European Cup
McLeish	34	6	6	6
McKimmie	34	6	5	5(+1)
W. Miller	33	6	6	6
Stark	28(+2)	5(+1)	3(+2)	4(+1)
Leighton	26	4	5	5
Black	23(+3)	3(+1)	5	4
McDougall	22(+3)	6	4	2(+1)
Bett	22(+2)	3	6	4
Simpson	22	6	4	4
Cooper	20(+3)	3(+1)	5	6
Hewitt	18(+5)	5	4	5(+1)
Mitchell	18(+5)	4		3(+2)
Weir	17(+4)	3	4	4
J. Miller	17		1(+2)	1
McQueen	15(+2)	2	3	1
Angus	12(+5)	1	3(+1)	2(+2)
Gray	10(+4)	1(+3)		2(+2)
Gunn	10	2	1	1
McMaster	5(+2)		1(+1)	
Wright	3(+7)		–(+2)	1(+1)
Falconer	2(+6)	–(+1)		–(+1)
McIntyre	2(+3)			
Robertson	2(+1)			
Irvine	1			
Porteous	–(+6)		–(+1)	
25 players				

GOALS	Total	League	League Cup	Scottish Cup	European Cup
McDougall	20	14	4	1	1
Stark	15	8	3	3	1
Black	15	8	4	2	1
Hewitt	14	6	1	4	3
Weir	6	5		1	
J. Miller	5	3		2	
McLeish	4	3		1	
McKimmie	3	3			
Bett	3	3			
W. Miller	3	1		1	1
Angus	2	2			
Wright	2	2			
McQueen	2	1	1		
Gray	2	1			1
Simpson	2	1			1
McMaster	1	1			
Falconer	1				1
Total	100	62	13	15	10

Aberdeen Appearances 1946-47 — 1985-86

The list includes only those players who have appeared in 50 or more matches in the Scottish League, League Cup, Scottish Cup, and European competitions. Other first-team matches are excluded.

	League	League Cup	Scottish Cup	Europe
Miller (Willie)	444(+1)	91	57	51
Clark	424(+1)	95	49	23
Hather	264	52	34	
McLeish	247(+2)	51(+1)	37(+3)	38(+1)
Robb	237(+13)	47(+4)	25(+2)	16
Little	234(+2)	45	22(+1)	1
Jarvie	230(+35)	52(+12)	25(+3)	16(+1)
Hogg	226	44	23	
Kennedy (Stuart)	223	54(+1)	29	25(+1)
Shewan	222	46	26	8
Leighton	214	41	32	41
Graham (Arthur)	212(+8)	43(+1)	21(+1)	11
Martin	206	52	33	
Glen	203	42	24	
Yorston	201	47	29	
Harper	200(+7)	57	21(+1)	14
Hermiston	193(+2)	45	15	15
Harris	188	54	31	
Ogston	179	34	17	
Wishart	178	36	22	
Strachan	175(+8)	43(+3)	29	30(+4)
McMillan	172	45	23	8
McMaster	171(+32)	47(+7)	24(+5)	25(+3)
Young	168	30	23	
Hamilton (George)	164	48	27	
Rougvie	162(+19)	38(+7)	26	26(+2)
McGhee	152(+12)	33(+1)	20	30(+1)
McLelland	152(+2)	35	16(+1)	6
Simpson	144(+13)	22(+2)	24	27(+4)
Burns	142	34	16	
Petersen	139(+3)	31	21	7
Smith (Joe)	134(+8)	34	9(+3)	2(+1)
McKenna	134	30	17	
Young (Willie)	133	31	12	11
Caldwell	132	30	16	
Brownlee	132	25	10	
Buchan (Martin)	130(+2)	23	20	11(+1)
Mitchell	129	34	21	
Kinnell	129	23	12	
Forrest	125(+3)	25(+2)	20	11
Cooke	125	26	14	
Thomson	121(+8)	17(+3)	5(+1)	4
Winchester	120(+3)	30	15	
Cooper (Neale)	117(+16)	26(+1)	25(+1)	6(+6)
Allister	117	25	21	
Weir	112(+8)	26	17(+1)	23(+2)
Garner	112(+1)	31	11	5(+1)
Mulhall	110	31	9	
Davidson (Norman)	110	23	14	
Leggat	109	26	16	
Bennett	109	16	12	
Buckley	106	26	20	
Whyte	105	24	20	4
Boel	104(+1)	22	16	6
Baird (Archie)	104	23	17	
Clunie	104	21	16	
Smith (Jim)	103	15	14	8
Murray (Steve)	101	22	10	7
Coutts	99	13	10	
Black	97(+19)	14(+4)	22(+3)	18(+4)
Taylor	96(+13)	26(+2)	6(+3)	9(+2)
Hewitt	93(+40)	23(+10)	17(+4)	23(+13)
Emery	89	25	11	
Morrison	89	13	6	
Bell	87(+22)	23(+6)	11(+11)	20(+5)
Sullivan	87(+11)	19(+2)	12(+1)	5(+2)
Williamson	86(+7)	16(+7)	10	
Murray (George)	86(+3)	20	11	5(+2)
Wilson	86	20	11	4
McKimmie	85(+1)	7	16	12(+1)
Willoughby	84(+20)	23(+4)	6(+3)	9(+1)
Pearson	84	18	14	
Ewen	83	12	13	
Scanlon	79(+13)	17(+1)	8(+3)	8(+2)
Fraser	75	19	7	
Archibald	74(+2)	18	10	6
Johnston	73(+2)	6	15	2
Smith (Billy)	73	19	6	
Anderson	71	19	13	
Waddell	71	20	4	
Stark	69(+7)	9(+3)	8(+3)	8(+1)
Hair	69(+6)	14	4(+1)	4
Johnstone (George)	69	24	10	
Boyd	69	16	4	
Watson (Andy)	66(+32)	10(+3)	5(+5)	11
Williams	66	17	10	
Baird (Hugh)	66	12	8	
Cummings	63	17	7	
Melrose	63	11	11	2
Angus	61(+21)	6(+4)	12(+3)	5(+6)
Taylor (George)	57	11	8	
Allan	53	2	4	
Fleming	52(+19)	12(+5)	4(+1)	2(+1)
Kerrigan	52	5	6	
Shaw	50	17	14	
McDougall	49(+4)	6	6	2(+1)
McQueen	48(+4)	3	5(+1)	3
Scott	41(+11)	10(+1)	4	
Davidson (Duncan)	36(+42)	7(+8)	9(+7)	2(+1)
McCall (Walker)	36(+16)	2(+4)	2	-(+2)

Bracket denotes that the appearance was as a substitute.

Aberdeen Goalscorers 1946-47 — 1985-86

The list includes only those players who have scored 10 or more goals in the Scottish League, League Cup, Scottish Cup, and European competitions. Other first-team matches are excluded.

	Total	League	League Cup	Scottish Cup	Europe
Harper	199	125	51	15	8
Yorston	141	98	22	21	
Hamilton (George)	135	85	33	17	
Jarvie	131	85	29	7	10
Hather	104	78	16	10	
Robb	99	78	9	10	2
Little	99	79	12	8	
McGhee	98	60	18	6	14
Winchester	94	72	12	10	
Buckley	92	58	18	16	
Leggat	92	64	21	7	
Strachan	89	54	20	7	8
Davidson (Norman)	84	55	16	13	
Black	70	46	12	5	7
Hewitt	67	39	9	7	12
Forrest	62	44	8	8	2
Wishart	62	45	10	7	
Cummings	50	34	5	11	
Archibald	47	30	6	11	
Graham (Arthur)	46	34	9	1	2
Stark	46	29	9	7	1
McDougall	44	36	4	3	1
Mulhall	42	30	10	2	
Brownlee	39	28	6	5	
Baird (Archie)	37	26	9	2	
Johnston	37	32		5	
Smith (Jim)	37	21	8	5	3
Weir	36	21	2	7	6
Wilson (Jimmy)	35	25	7	3	
McMaster	33	20	9	4	
Williams (Stan)	31	17	8	6	
Harris	30	18	7	5	
Simpson	30	18	1	5	6
Cooke	29	26	3		
Kerrigan	29	26	1	2	
Taylor	29	23	3	1	2
Davidson (Duncan)	27	18	4	5	
Allister	26	20	2	4	
Boyd	26	21	4	1	
Hay	26	23	3		
Kelly (Archie)	26	21	3	2	
Baird (Hugh)	25	21	2	2	
Emery	25	17	6	2	
Ewen	25	18	6	1	

	Total	League	League Cup	Scottish Cup	Europe
Glen	25	22	3		
Kinnell	25	20	1	4	
Murray (Steve)	25	20	1	1	3
Miller (Willie)	24	15	1	6	2
Fleming	23	12	7	4	
McCall (Walker)	23	22	1		
McLeish	23	19	1	2	1
Williamson	23	18	5		
Scott	22	17	4	1	
Rougvie	21	19	2		
Scanlon	21	13	2	6	
Melrose	18	12	2	3	1
Rodger	17	13		4	
Watson	17	13	2	1	1
Hermiston	16	10	5		1
Pearson	16	10	2	4	
Allan	15	15			
McCall	15	8	5	2	
O'Neil	15	9	2	4	
Willoughby	15	10	3	1	1
Bell	14	6	7		1
Munro	14	8	1		5
Purdie	14	10	3	1	
Young (Willie)	14	10	3	1	
Kiddie	13	11	2		
Millar	13	4	8	1	
Smith (Dave)	13	8	4	1	
Sullivan	13	10	3		
Hume	12	4	6	2	
Ravn	12	9	1	2	
Smith (Joe)	12	8	3	1	
Angus	11	9		1	1
Buchan (Martin)	11	9	1		1
Callaghan	11	8		3	
Cowan	11	11			
Petersen	11	7	1	2	1
Pirie	11	11			
Storrie	11	3	3	1	4
Cooper (Neale)	10	6	2	2	
Craig	10	8	1	1	
Delaney	10	7	2	1	
Miller (Bertie)	10	6	1	1	2
Varga	10	10			
Whyte	10	7	2	1	